November 13–16, 2016
Sanibel Island, FL, USA

Association for Computing Machinery

Advancing Computing as a Science & Profession

GROUP'16

Conference Program

Sponsored by:

ACM SIGCHI

Supported by:

Microsoft Research & National Science Foundation

Association for
Computing Machinery

Advancing Computing as a Science & Profession

The Association for Computing Machinery
2 Penn Plaza, Suite 701
New York, New York 10121-0701

Notice to Past Authors of ACM-Published Articles
ACM intends to create a complete electronic archive of all articles and/or other material previously published by ACM. If you have written a work that has been previously published by ACM in any journal or conference proceedings prior to 1978, or any SIG Newsletter at any time, and you do NOT want this work to appear in the ACM Digital Library, please inform permissions@acm.org, stating the title of the work, the author(s), and where and when published.

ISBN: 978-1-4503-4276-6 (Digital)

ISBN: 978-1-4503-4714-3 (Print)

Additional copies may be ordered prepaid from:

ACM Order Department
PO Box 30777
New York, NY 10087-0777, USA

Phone: 1-800-342-6626 (USA and Canada)
+1-212-626-0500 (Global)
Fax: +1-212-944-1318
E-mail: acmhelp@acm.org
Hours of Operation: 8:30 am – 4:30 pm ET

Printed in the USA

ACM GROUP 2016 - Chairs' Welcome

It is our great pleasure to welcome you to the *19th ACM International Conference on Supporting Group Work - ACM GROUP 2016*. This year's conference continues the series' tradition of being truly international in both participation and organizational structure. The ACM GROUP 2016 program features diverse social, technical and cultural research traditions, as well as scholars from a wide range of disciplines, including Human Computer Interaction, Computer Supported Cooperative Work, Organization Science, Small Group Research, Computational Social Science, Sociotechnical System Design, Critical Design, Educational Technology and Computer Supported Collaborative Learning. Participants in the program will discuss the latest findings within areas such as editing systems; enterprise social networks; local communities; volunteering; adoption, appropriation and domestication of technologies; and mobile computing.

In recent years, ACM GROUP has been experimenting with different ideas to expand the scope of the conference. Working Papers were, for instance, added in 2014 with the idea to help a set of participants develop journal papers through short presentations and active engagement with the conference attendees. This new venue was a success and has been integrated into the conference. This year, the ACM GROUP program chairs introduce three innovations:

1) ACM GROUP 2016 will open with a *Keynote Symposium on Systems Work* to reflect on the current state of the art and science in systems work, as well as on its future;

2) A new track called *Design Fictions: Exploring Future Research Agendas* to explore possible futures for research on the relationships between computers and people; and,

3) A *JCSCW Papers* session, featuring authors of recently published papers from *CSCW, the Journal of Collaborative Computing and Work Practices (Springer).*

Across all venues, we received 159 submissions from 22 countries in North and South America, Europe, India and Asia:

Venue or Track	*Reviewed*	*Accepted*	
Research Papers	111	36	32%
Design Fictions	9	4	44%
Work-in-Progress Papers	6	4	67%
Posters and Demonstrations	12	11	92%
Workshops	5	3	60%
Doctoral Consortium	16	12	75%

These numbers show that ACM GROUP remains vibrant, with an almost equal number of reviewed research papers as in previous years, and record numbers of reviewed submissions for posters and doctoral colloquium. Research papers and design fictions continued the tradition of being completely reviewed by the Program Committee members without external reviewers. As in prior years, reviewing was conducted in two rounds. During the first round all committee members served exclusively as reviewers. In the second round, one reviewer on each paper was assigned the Primary AC role and asked to lead an online discussion of the paper and write a Meta-Review based on the content of the reviews and the discussion. The goal of the discussion and Meta-Review was to generate a proposed accept/reject decision. The program chairs then made their final decisions by considering all of the review scores and comments. Submissions for other venues were reviewed by their respective chairs.

Putting together ACM GROUP 2016 has been a truly collaborative and international effort. Many of our GROUP colleagues have generously contributed their time and effort to send their work, organize the conference, review papers, lead the Doctoral Colloquium, convene workshops, chair venues and sessions, and serve as student volunteers. The conference would not be possible without their efforts. We first thank the authors for providing the content of the program. We would then like to thank Eric Baumer (Cornell University) and Mark Blythe (Northumbria University) for organizing the new venue of design fictions. We are also very grateful to Luigina Ciolfi (Sheffield Hallam University) and Sue Fussell (Cornell University) for chairing the works-in-progress venue; Adriana Vivacqua (Federal University of Rio de Janeiro), Alex Boden (Fraunhofer FIT) and Nassim Jafarinaimi (Georgia Tech) for organizing the poster session; Fabiano Pinatti (University of Siegen), Erika Poole (Healthwise) and Jennifer Marlow (FXPal) for organizing the workshops; and, Wayne Lutters (University of Maryland, Baltimore County) for chairing the doctoral colloquium. We acknowledge the hard work of David Gurzick (Hood College) as our webmaster; Hanna Söderholm (University of Borås), Casey Fiesler (University of Colorado, Boulder) and Hao-Chuan Wang (National Tsing Hua University) as our superstar publicity co-chairs; Alison Murphy (The Pennsylvania State University) and Konstantin Aal (University of Siegen) for recruiting and coordinating the important team of student volunteers; and, Matthieu Tixier (Troyes University of Technology) for his diligent work on putting together the conference proceedings. Special thanks to Stephen Hayne (Colorado State University) for this and many past years of keeping a watchful eye on our finances, and to Sean Goggins (University of Michigan) for taking care of local arrangements.

We would also like to thank Mark Ackermann (University of Michigan), Hilda Tellioglu (Vienna University of Technology), Kori Inkpen (Microsoft Research), Pernille Bjorn (IT University Copenhagen) and Tom Gross (University of Bamberg) for serving on the ACM GROUP Steering Committee and guiding the conference's future.

We appreciate the work of Sheridan Printing Company for assembling our proceedings. We also express our gratitude to the international program committee for providing constructive feedback to all authors.

Finally, we would like to thank our sponsors, ACM SIGCHI and the SIGCHI Student Travel Grant program, National Science Foundation, and Microsoft Research for their continued support of ACM GROUP. *THANK YOU ALL SO VERY MUCH!*

Stephan Lukosch
GROUP'16 General Chair
Delft University of Technology

Aleksandra Sarcevic
GROUP'16 General Chair
Drexel University

Myriam Lewkowicz
GROUP'16 Program Chair
Troyes University of Technology

Michael Muller
GROUP'16 Program Chair
IBM Research

Table of Contents

Session: Posters and Demos

Workshops

Doctoral Consortium

GROUP 2016 Conference Organization

General Chairs:	Stephan Lukosch *(Delft University of Technology, Netherlands)* Aleksandra Sarcevic *(Drexel University, USA)*
Program Chairs:	Myriam Lewkowicz *(Troyes University of Technology, France)* Michael Muller *(IBM Research, USA)*
Design Fiction Chairs:	Eric Baumer *(Cornell University, USA)* Mark Blythe *(Northumbria University, UK)*
Working Papers Chairs:	Luigina Ciolfi *(Sheffield Hallam University, UK)* Sue Fussell *(Cornell University, USA)*
Poster Chairs:	Adriana Vivacqua *(Federal University of Rio de Janeiro, Brazil)* Alexander Boden *(Fraunhofer FIT, Germany)* Nassim Jafarinaimi *(Georgia Tech, USA)*
Workshop Chairs:	Fabiano Pinatti *(University of Siegen, Germany)* Erika Poole *(Healthwise, USA)* Jennifer Marlow *(FXPal, USA)*
Doctoral Consortium Chair:	Wayne Lutters *(UMBC, USA)*
Doctoral Consortium Mentors:	Cecilia Aragon *(University of Washington, USA)* Michael Prilla *(Clausthal University of Technology, Germany)*
Treasurer & Registration Chair:	Stephen Hayne *(Colorado State University, USA)*
Webmaster:	David Gurzick *(Hood College, USA)*
Publicity Chairs:	Hanna Söderholm *(University of Borås, Sweden)* Casey Fiesler *(University of Colorado, USA)* Hao-Chuan Wang *(National Tsing Hua University, Taiwan)*
Proceedings Chairs:	Matthieu Tixier *(Troyes University of Technology, France)*
Local Arrangements Chair:	Sean Goggins *(University of Missouri, USA)*
Student Volunteer Chairs:	Alison Murphy *(Penn State University, USA)* Konstantin Aal *(University of Siegen, Germany)*

Steering Committee: Mark Ackerman *(University of Michigan, USA)*
Hilda Tellioğlu *(Vienna University of Technology, Austria)*
Kori Inkpen *(Microsoft Research, USA)*
Pernille Bjørn *(University of Copenhagen, Denmark)*
Tom Gross *(University of Bamberg, Germany)*

Program Committee: Mark Ackerman, *(University of Michigan)*
Jeffrey Bardzell, *(Indiana University)*
Shaowen Bardzell, *(Indiana University)*
Louise Barkhuus, *(ITU)*
Pernille Bjørn, *(University of Copenhagen)*
Jeanette Blomberg, *(IBM Almaden Research Center)*
Alexander Boden, *(Fraunhofer FIT)*
Marcos Borges, *(Universidade Federal do Rio de Janeiro)*
Luigina Ciolfi, *(Sheffield Hallam University)*
Gregorio Convertino, *(Informatica Corporation)*
Cleidson de Souza, *(Federal University of Pará and Vale Institute of Technology)*
Rogerio DePaula, *(IBM Brazil)*
Tawanna Dillahunt, *(University of Michigan)*
Gunnar Ellingsen, *(UiT - The Arctic University of Norway)*
Tom Erickson, *(IBM T. J. Watson Research Center)*
Shelly Farnham, *(Third Place Technologies)*
Geraldine Fitzpatrick, *(Vienna University of Technology)*
Susan Fussell, *(Cornell University)*
Darren Gergle, *(Northwestern University)*
Sean Goggins, *(University of Missouri)*
Sukeshini Grandhi, *(Eastern Connecticut State University)*
Ning Gu, *(Fudan University)*
David Gurzick, *(Hood College)*
Carl Gutwin, *(University of Saskatchewan)*
Gillian Hayes, *(UC Irvine)*
Stephen Hayne, *(Colorado State University)*
Thomas Herrmann, *(Ruhr-Universität Bochum)*
Morten Hertzum, *(University of Copenhagen)*
Josh Introne, *(Michigan State University)*
Michal Jacovi, *(IBM Research - Haifa)*
Isa Jahnke, *(University of Missouri)*
Ben Kirman, *(University of Lincoln)*
Airi Lampinen, *(Mobile Life Center)*
Silvia Lindtner, *(University of Michigan)*
Jennifer Marlow, *(FXPAL)*
David Martin, *(Xerox Research Centre Europe)*
David McDonald, *(University of Washington)*
Claudia Mueller, *(University of Siegen)*

Program Committee (continued):

Lisa Nathan, *(University of British Columbia)*
Jacki O'Neill, *(Microsoft Research, India)*
Katie Pine, *(Intel/University of Irvine)*
Michael Prilla, *(Clausthal University of Technology)*
Wolfgang Prinz, *(Fraunhofer FIT)*
Dave Randall, *(University of Siegen)*
Madhu Reddy, *(Northwestern University)*
Lionel Robert Jr., *(University of Michigan)*
Scott Robertson, *(University of Hawaii)*
Kjeld Schmidt, *(Copenhagen Business School)*
Stacey Scott, *(University of Waterloo)*
Sadat Shami, *(IBM)*
Carla Simone, *(University di Milano-Bicocca)*
Hanna Söderholm, *(University of Boras)*
Anthony Tang, *(University of Calgary)*
Stephanie Teasley, *(University of Michigan)*
Hilda Tellioğlu, *(Vienna University of Technology)*
Matthieu Tixier, *(Troyes University of Technology)*
Adriana Vivacqua, *(Universidade Federal do Rio de Janeiro)*
Leon Watts, *(University of Bath)*
Susan Winter, *(University of Maryland)*
Volker Wulf, *(University of Siegen)*
Naomi Yamashita, *(NTT)*

Sponsor: SIGCHI

Supporters: Microsoft Research

NSF

Keynote Symposium on Systems Work

Myriam Lewkowicz
ICD, HETIC, Tech-CICO,
Troyes University of Technology, UMR 6281, CNRS
12, rue Marie Curie CS 42060
10004 TROYES CEDEX, France
myriam.lewkowicz@utt.fr

Michael Muller
Cognitive User Experience
IBM Research
75 Binney Street
Cambridge MA USA 02142
michael_muller@us.ibm.com

1. Objective

The opening Keynote of GROUP 2016 is a Symposium of people who work on systems. We chose the word "symposium" because we envision diverse perspectives, short position statements and discussion, but very little of the debate or competition of a panel. The aim is to reflect the diversity and the breadth of perspectives in the GROUP community. We will think together about the current state of the art and science in systems work, and the future of systems work.

Of course, there is no single endeavor called "systems," and there is no single genre for a "systems paper." (The same kind of statement can be made about quantitative work, qualitative work, theory work…) We hope that the Symposium will help all of us – "systems people" and others – to consider the different contributions that systems work has made to GROUP, and the possible future contributions. Moreover, we may find new ways in which our various research streams can interact, and inform one another.

The participants of the Symposium received a list of topics/questions as possible starting points for their position statement.

2. Topics

The Symposium will address five main topics that we have identified as starting point to discuss systems work, and on which the participants and the audience could have different perspectives.

2.1 Why do we build systems?

Here, we want to address the broad range of motivations to do systems work. Some of us build systems as parts of an intervention in order to help a community, to empower marginalized groups, or more generally to make a political change. But systems can also be used as a means to do theory research, the system being a means to pursue an hypothesis on how people would behave in a particular situation, or to do design research, to try out a novel or speculative idea, including an ambiguous or controversial design concept and see what new social phenomena occur around the new design. And sometimes systems work pursues new technology infrastructures that enable new forms of collaboration, or that make new forms of collaboration practical for the first time.

GROUP '16, November 13-16, 2016, Sanibel Island, FL, USA
ACM 978-1-4503-4276-6/16/11.
http://dx.doi.org/10.1145/2957276.2957317

2.2 What is the starting point for the systems work?

With this question, we plan to discuss the issues that we have in mind when we plan our systems work, and in particular how are we going to make decisions about the kinds of systems we are going to build, and how do we plan to include or deal with the users, and more generally the stakeholders of the system. We would also like to discuss about the case of an organizational mandate to build something for a specific purpose, customer, or audience; does it change our methods, our goal, etc?

2.3 What is the ending point?

We would like to talk about the different ways of evaluating systems work, and more precisely interact about how do we discern the value of a system. Are we designing systems in an interdisciplinary way? or a specialist way?

We will discuss how do we build systems, and how do we work with researchers from other disciplines if we involve them in the process, both in terms of method and in terms of interest; how might researchers from other disciplines become interested in the systems we build?

2.4 What does the reader get from a systems paper?

Finally, we will try to state how to deliver value in a systems paper, or, in other words: If a behavioral or social paper might provide "implications for design" or "implications for theory," then what types of "implications" would a systems paper provide?

3. Participants

Carl Gutwin, University of Saskatchewan, Canada. His main research areas are computer-supported cooperative work, interaction techniques, and surface computing.

Kori Inkpen, Microsoft Research, USA. Her main research area is Human Computer Interaction with a focus on Computer Supported Collaboration. Currently her research is focused on video communication for telepresence.

Stephan Lukosch, Delft University of Technology, The Netherlands. His current research focuses on designing engaging environments for participatory systems. Using augmented reality, he researches environments for virtual co-location in which individuals can virtually be at any place in the world and coordinate their activities with others and exchange their experiences.

Anne Weibert, University of Siegen, Germany. Her research areas are computer-based collaborative project work and inherent processes of technology appropriation, intercultural learning, and community-building.

Machine Learning and Grounded Theory Method: Convergence, Divergence, and Combination

Michael Muller[a], Shion Guha[b], Eric P.S. Baumer[c], David Mimno[c], and N. Sadat Shami[d]
[a]IBM Research, [b]Marquette University, [c]Cornell University, [d]IBM
[a]One Rogers Street
Cambridge MA USA 02142
{michael_muller, sadat}@us.ibm.com, shion.guha@marquette.edu,
{ericpsb,dm655}@cornell.edu

ABSTRACT
Grounded Theory Method (GTM) and Machine Learning (ML) are often considered to be quite different. In this note, we explore unexpected convergences between these methods. We propose new research directions that can further clarify the relationships between these methods, and that can use those relationships to strengthen our ability to describe our phenomena and develop stronger hybrid theories.

Keywords
Grounded theory; Axial coding; Coding families; Machine learning; Supervised learning; Unsupervised learning.

1. INTRODUCTION
Researchers in CHI and (E)CSCW often think of qualitative analysis and machine learning as very different domains (e.g., [1, 9, 10, 21]), even though some researchers may use one of these methods as a tool to understand or summarize work done via the other method (e.g., [2, 3, 33, 58]). However, there are multiple convergences between these two research traditions (e.g., [6, 45]). These convergences can lead to interesting hypotheses and potential methods (e.g., [6]). In this note, we continue a conversation begun by [5] about two specific convergences, which we hope will open a discussion of additional convergences and new ways of conducting mixed-methods research.

This note proceeds as follows. In the Background section, we provide brief introductions to machine learning (ML) and grounded theory method (GTM), with a focus on setting up our points of convergence. In the Convergences section, we explicate similarities between these two distinct research traditions. We also consider some differences between the two approaches (Divergences). In the Discussion section, we propose three ways to transform the convergences into new research hypotheses and mixed-methods inquiries.

2. Background
Researchers are increasingly interested in combining quantitative "big data" methods with qualitative "small data" methods [10, 23]. Traditional qualitative scholarship often focuses on in-depth analysis of specific, local phenomena, with the intention of generalizing to other sites and other people. Traditional quantitative scholarship often focuses on generalizable results from more numerous data points, which tend to have less context associated with each observation.

GROUP '16, November 13-16, 2016, Sanibel Island, FL, USA
 ISBN 978-1-4503-4276-6/16/11…$15.00
DOI: http://dx.doi.org/10.1145/2957276.2957280

2.1 Combining Big Data and Small Data
In one example, in an influential series of studies, De Choudhury and colleagues studied linguistic signs of affect [13], and more specifically depression [14], in social media posts – a characteristic quantitative, "big data" study method. Their goal was not to provide detailed analyses of postings or posters, but rather to understand large-scale phenomena. In a second example, Menking and Erickson used grounded theory method to understand aspects of women's experiences in with participation in Wikipedia [40]. Their goal was not to provide a statistical summary of such phenomena, or a large-scale analysis of quantitative patterns among participation data, but rather to develop a theory that described the experiences of individual women. These are two out of many examples that seem to argue that the quantitative domain works differently from the qualitative domain. But is that true? What if we could enjoy the virtues of both ways of inquiring?

Computational social science and digital humanities are beginning to use large-scale computational analysis in conjunction with close analytic reading. Blevins used topic modeling as a way to structure a detailed inquiry into the extensive and idiosyncratic diaries of Martha Ballard, an 18th-19th-century midwife [8]. Jockers used a topic model to study themes in 3000 novels, but only after a laborious, iterative process of document and vocabulary curation [34]. Rhody used similar topic-based methods to identify figurative language in poetic texts [49]. Only with contextual human analysis were the identified word-clusters recognized as the surface form of a repeated metaphor

Within the CHI and CSCW disciplines, Thom-Santelli et al. used "heuristics from grounded theory" in alternation with large-scale data analysis, for iterative guidance on a series of interview samples [56]. In a very recent demo, Arazy et al. similarly proposed using machine-learning to reveal patterns in log data from peer production; they suggested that those patterns could then be studied using grounded theory method [2].

Here, we suggest a deeper convergence. In the next two subsections, we describe two analytic trends in machine learning, and we show that they are closely related to two well-established approaches in grounded theory method.

2.2 Machine Learning: Current Approaches
Machine learning centers around statistical models and algorithms. The models consist of two types of variables: those that are observed in data (*features*) and those that are not observed. The algorithms find values for unobserved variables

that best fit the values of the observed variables. For instance, given a corpus of emails, for each message we can observe a set of words and a label of spam or not-spam. We can then use an algorithm to infer *latent* variables that correspond to the "spamminess" of each word. Most ML algorithms function by iteratively refining a model until it fits the data within some threshold of acceptability.

2.2.1 Types of Machine Learning Methods

We often divide machine learning into two categories: supervised and unsupervised learning [37]. In supervised models, the latent variables define a relationship between two types of observed variables, inputs and outputs. Regression, classification, and confirmatory factor analysis are common examples. In unsupervised models, the latent variables suggest a (hopefully) simpler description of the observed variables. Clustering, principal components analysis, topic modeling, and exploratory factor analysis are common examples.

There is a strong bias towards standard, pre-existing data that is accompanied by well-known quantitative evaluation metrics. This approach obviates the difficult human labor involved in creating such data sets [34]. When new labeled data sets are collected, they are increasingly built using crowdsourced annotation platforms such as Amazon Mechanical Turk [51]. These crowdsourced, human annotated datasets are often referred to as gold standards and have become widely used in HCI/CSCW [13, 50].

There is growing recognition of the important role to be played in ML by in-depth human analysis and interpretation. Wagstaff argues that machine learning research has become dangerously disconnected from the real world, and recommends that domain experts be involved [59]. Some scholars [60] have attempted to answer this call by incorporating focus groups and feedback from doctors to build a system that predicts fetal hypoxia and makes judicious medical interventions. Sen et al. [50] criticize the focus on labeled datasets, saying that the notion of a one -size-fits-all gold standard is risky and inconsistent with existing social science theory. They show that labeling with different cultural groups on the same dataset often creates markedly different labeled datasets – a concept already understood in social sciences [39].

2.3 Grounded Theory Method

Grounded theory method provides a set of rigorous methods for constructing theory directly from data, in a way that "grounds" that theory in data. The founders of grounded theory, Barney Glaser and Anselm Strauss, published four major works [27, 28, 29, 30] before they fell into disagreement and developed major bodies of work and method that contrasted with one another (e.g., [17, 26, 54, 55], and especially [24]). This history of their disagreement has been well-described in the research literature [11, 35, 43], and is beyond the scope of this note. Here, we focus on the potential relationship of each respective author's work to trends in machine learning.

One of several crucial aspects of the intellectual discipline of grounded theory is a rigorous way of coding data [15, 48, 52]. Over several revisions of their account of methods, Corbin and Strauss provided a series of data-driven operations to develop a high-quality description of a domain [17, 54, 55]; grounded theory researchers sometimes refer to these volumes as "the cookbook." Charmaz integrated aspects of the Straussian and Glaserian approaches into a disciplined set of practices that she refers to as "Grounded Theory Method" (GTM) [15]. There is general agreement [11, 35, 43, 44, 52] on the following overview of the method: The researcher begins with *open coding*, in which each description is specific to particular points in the data. Over time, the researcher formalizes and organizes these codes through *axial coding*, which begins to establish relationships among the open codes. Through the use of *constant comparison* of data with data, and of data with emerging theory, the researcher constructs *dimensions*, which are collections of open and axial codes that, collectively, describe major differences across the range of the data. The emergent theory (codes, categories, dimensions) suggests new questions, and the researcher uses that theory to select new sites to study, or new people to interview, to test the emergent theory at its weakest points. This process is generally termed *theoretical sampling*, and is a procedural manifestation of the underlying concept of *abductive logic* [15, 48, 57].

As the codes become more abstract, the researcher can begin to relate the data-grounded theory (i.e., based on the codes) with formal, published theory [15, 17, 28, 55]. The researcher chooses certain of these axial codes (categories and dimensions) as the focus of her/his report, and engages in further *selective coding* around these chosen attributes, deepening the analysis further [15, 17, 24-29, 35, 48, 52, 54, 55].

GTM thus provides a set of agreed core practices (three levels of coding, from open to axial to selective) and core *ways of thinking* about data (constant comparison, theoretical sampling) which are derived from philosophical bases in pragmatism and abduction [11, 15, 16, 43, 44, 48, 54, 55, 57].[1]

2.3.1 Types of Grounded Theory Method Approaches

Among the points of disagreement between Glaser and Strauss (e.g., [24]) was the method and formality of coding – i.e., the influence (or constraint) of prior work on developing new theory from new data [35]. While Strauss made a series of differing proposals about core concepts (i.e., codes) in grounded theory (e.g., [54, 55]), many grounded theory researchers who derive their work from Strauss, tend to ignore these divergent advices, focusing instead on the core notion of the gradual development of open and axial codes into categories and dimensions of analysis, as summarized above (e.g., [15]; see also multiple chapters in [11]). Thus, one of Strauss's (later, Corbin's and Strauss's) contributions to GTM is a rigorous yet relatively unencumbered approach to coding. Through a rigorous process, codes emerge [17, 55] or are constructed [15] de novo, without constraints based on previous coding schemes or reference volumes.

By contrast, Glaser developed a rigorous set of coding families [26]. These families grew incrementally over time, from an initial set of 18 coding families [26] to 40 coding families [16, 25]. Thus, one of Glaser's contributions to grounded theory is a rich set of tested coding families that can serve as a bridge between initial open codes (nascent theory) and more formal theory, and between past and present in GTM.

3. Convergences

Despite the different world-views, there are attributes in common between ML and GTM. Each process makes major claims to be grounded in the data. Each process begins with, and returns to, the data. Each process develops interim components of theory (GTM dimensions or ML features) that describe major differences across

[1] For comparative purposes, we note that a conventional statistical analysis may at first appear to be a simple, executable method, but in fact involves many decisions by the researcher regarding sample size and provenance, data quality issues and possible transformations of variables, selection of appropriate control variables and conditions, moderating factors, and covariates.

the range of the data. Each process is iterative. Neither process is complete when the data are analyzed; rather each process requires interpretation and theory-building after the data are complete. This is to say, while each process is strongly guided by methods, practices, and protocols, each process crucially requires human interpretation and human judgment at each stop of theory-building. We describe two similarities of method in depth here.

3.1 Pattern Discovery / Unsupervised ML / Straussian GTM

Straussian GTM is often recommended as a disciplined way of entering a new field of study, unconstrained by prior theory [11, 15, 17, 28, 44, 52, 54, 55]. Through a series of *constant comparisons* of data with data, and of data with theory, the researcher develops an initial theory, iteratively tests it with new data, and gradually develops a stronger and more interesting theory with better fit to the data. To do this, the researcher must make a series of decisions about which categories or dimensions of the data are important. S/he can then collect more data to confirm or disconfirm those candidate dimensions, and to establish new hypotheses for further qualitative inquiries (new samples or sites for the next iteration of GTM analysis) [15, 17, 28, 43, 44, 54, 55].

Unsupervised learning approaches in ML, such as clustering and topic-modeling, have been characterized in similar ways [22, 32]. Through a series of data-driven clustering and grouping explorations, the researcher develops an initial sense of the possible underlying patterns in the data, iteratively tests clustering parameters, and gradually finds a stronger and more interesting set of parameters with better fit to the data. To do this, the researcher must make a series of decisions about which parameters are important. S/he can then refine those parameters and experiment with higher-order interactions that involve the subset of parameters, thus confirming or disconfirming those candidate parameters.

While these two descriptions are not perfectly matched, they exhibit strong similarities. Both methods are exploratory; both methods are grounded in the data; both methods involve iterative and testable intermediate versions, and both methods require human discernment to refine their models. The researcher's problem is, in part, to find the best data that correspond to the hypothesized structure of the current knowledge.

3.2 Prediction-Validation / Supervised ML / Glaserian GT

A second area of similarity occurs in Glaserian GTM. Glaserian GTM explores a new domain, but with guidance from one or more of Glaser's coding families [16, 25, 26]. Part of the researcher's task is to choose the coding family that has the strongest fit to the data, and the best relationship to formal (preceding) theory. Different coding families may be confirmed or disconfirmed by collecting more data, in new samples or at new sites chosen to make a strong test of the current coding family(ies).

Supervised learning in ML (e.g., regression, decision trees, random forests, and many other predictive methods) operates in somewhat similar ways. In supervised learning, there is a concept of *ground truth* or *gold standard*, in which the nature of the categories in the data is known a priori, and for which the researcher tries to find the best predictors [38, 61]. Different predictive parameters may be tested, en masse or individually, and may be confirmed or disconfirmed through further analysis.

We see similarities between GTM coding families and ML ground truth measures: Both are known a priori; both serve as a kind of bridge between established knowledge and new data; both require human discernment to refine their models. The researcher's problem is, in part, to find the best data that correspond to the hypothesized structure of the current data, based on preceding knowledge.

4. Evaluating the Quality of Results

ML and GTM differ in their approaches to evaluating the quality of results.

4.1 Quality and Fit

A frequent concern in ML is to avoid *overfitting*, which is a model that performs well on training data, but fails to generalize to new data. ML establishes quality using statistical comparisons between a model's predictions and actual data. For example, cross-validation tests the robustness of a solution within a data sample [36]. A computed model may also be applied to a new set of data or to held-out data, or different models compared on the same set of data [19]. In each case, statistical tests for the degree of fit determine quality.

In the case of supervised learning, it is also common to test the accuracy of the computed model from one dataset, through a comparison of correctly vs. incorrectly classified data points in a second dataset (i.e., in a confusion matrix) [53]. Thus, the robustness of a ML analysis *depends crucially on a search for unexpected* data (i.e., disconfirmation of the current version of the model), and is *tested by recourse to more data*.

Formal GTM follows a process that iteratively tests both internal coherence of the emergent theory, and the ability of the theory to describe new data. Some GTM researchers make reference to the logic of *abduction* [15, 48, 57]. While the details are beyond the scope of a note, the core steps of abductive logic include: collecting a small amount of data; constructing an initial theory based on those data; determining the weakest point of the theory; and then collecting a second small amount of data designed to break the theory – i.e., to test it at its weakest point; and iterating this process until there is no new learning (the theory is stable)[2]. This abductive process in GTM is broadly described as *theoretical sampling*, because each iteration of the emerging theory is used to select additional data to test it [15, 48, 52, 57]. The comparisons of data with data, and data with theory, are consistent with the principle of constant comparison mentioned earlier. Similarly to issue of overfitting in ML, the robustness of an emergent theory in grounded theory method *depends crucially on a search for unexpected data* (which signal a need to continue developing the emergent theory), and is *tested by recourse to more data* (see [34, 44] for further details on the necessity of unexpected data to guide theoretical sampling in GTM).

Essentially, the difference is analogous to performance vs. description. ML assesses quality by testing how well a learned model performs on new data. GTM assess quality by asking how well a theory describes data from a novel context.

4.2 Iteration and Human Evaluation

Both ML and GTM follow iterative processes. In GTM, human researcher(s) iteratively analyze data while revising their theories

---

[2] Some ML algorithms, such as perceptron and SVM, focus on those data points where the model fits poorest. These points are tested in a prescribed iterative process, though, rather than strategically selected by the researcher.

about those data. In ML, an algorithm iteratively refines a mathematical model for the data until the model converges and satisfactorily explains the data. Both these iterative processes also occur at multiple, nested levels, drawing attention to two differences.

First, at the lowest level, ML fully automates the iteration. Algorithmic iteration takes place while a model is fitted to data, and requires no human intervention. In grounded theory, iteration through the data is done by the human researchers.

Second, at the higher level, human judgments play a role in both processes. In GTM, following principles of theoretical sampling [15, 52], a human researcher may intentionally seek out data that challenges an existing theory. In ML, a human researcher may use preliminary results to tune aspects of the analysis, such as a stopword list, number of categories, number of iterations, optimization calculation, hyperparameter values, etc. [34].

However, the role of human judgments is reported differently in research results. The human level of iteration is integral to GTM, and is both described in canonical texts and often reported in research results. By contrast, in ML, this higher level creates a dialogic iteration between human researcher and computational algorithm, but it is rarely described as such. Instead, ML is often described as a linear process, from data collection and curation through feature extraction to classifier training and testing, rather than an iterative process of trial and error. This difference draws attention to divergent disciplinary norms, divergences to which future work will need to attend.

5. Research Directions

In related work, Baumer et al. [6] proposed a *Conjecture* about the relationship between GTM and the specific ML technique of topic modeling. This conjecture asserts that any theoretical concept identified via grounded theory or similar analyses should occur in part via linguistic regularities that can be detected by algorithms. Put differently, the two different methods should be capable of generating comparable results. Baumer et al. suggest that future research should investigate the conditions under which this conjecture holds.

In this section, we propose several more integrated combinations of methods, in which conclusions would be based on the weaving-together of methods and outcomes. We consider three "configurations of methods." Each of these configurations is from unpublished research. We provide a sketch of how the analyses might proceed. We hope that other researchers will propose more diverse configurations.

5.1 Comparative Sequential Methods

Our first two configurations propose to use the methods sequentially, with one method structuring a series of smaller research projects using the other method. There are two variations in this approach, differing in terms of primacy.

GTM→ML. In an analysis of group discourse, we might discover different types of contributions. Once we have texts grouped in this way, we could then apply ML methods in a quantitative analysis of the linguistic attributes of each type of contribution.

> **Example GTM→ML:** In a study of social media use within an organizations' Intranet, we have found 30 distinct types of postings. GTM could help us to combine these types into higher-order conceptual classifications, such as texts that *originate* a discussion; vs. texts that *respond* to a previously-originated discussion; vs. texts that *curate* or *evaluate* the contributions to a discussion. We could then apply text analysis and ML to understand the large-scale linguistic phenomena within each type of contribution, such as implicit sentiment [31], linguistic style matching [18], or framing [6, 12].

ML→GTM. The inverse of this strategy could also be adopted. We could begin with a ML classification against a ground-truth outcome measure. Once this formal classification was complete, we could then apply GTM to search for emergent properties within each of the ML classes.

> **Example ML→GTM:** Mitra and Gilbert used ML to classify and predict *successful* vs. *unsuccessful* Kickstarter proposals [42]. In an extension of this work, we could apply GTM to study how the words and tuples that they identified combined conceptually into persuasive strategies and implicit appeals that were made in each class of proposals.

5.2 Hybrid Iterative Methods

Our third configuration puts the two sets of methods in a more integrated, iterative process. Following the examples of [8, 49], and especially [2, 56], we propose an expansion of the GTM concept of theoretical sampling to put these two methods into constructive, iterative dialogue. An initial analysis could perform large-scale pattern analysis, similarly to Azary et al.'s analysis of Wikipedia texts [2]. The revealed patterns would then point to interesting cases, which could be studied via GTM, similarly to Thom-Santelli et al.'s approach to using macro-scale data patterns in order to select sites (persons) for open-ended interviews, which were then analyzed via GTM approaches [56].

We propose that researchers could alternate between developing each iterative step in a series of evolving GTM *theories* of a phenomenon, and each iterative step in a successively refined ML *model* of that phenomenon (i.e., one complete run of a topic-modeling algorithm). Each of these small iteration steps is a form of constant comparison, and would require comparison to each type of data. Each method would inform the other method, with a progressive strengthening of the core representation of each method (i.e., a *theory* composed of *dimensions* in GTM; a *model* composed of *features* in ML). Theoretical sampling would become more complex, and potentially more powerful, because each theory or model would suggest new data to sample in the domain of the other theory or model (i.e., from GTM theory to ML data, and from ML model to GTM data).

> **Example Iterative:** In a study of online forums for patients and informal caregivers, we might want to understand how people are evaluating the option of palliative care. One forum for "Palliative Care" contains 5758 postings organized into 177 human-specified topics, authored by 969 contributors.[3] Postings can be long and complex, and therefore resist classification approaches that place each data item into at most one class.
>
> We might use the more flexible ML method of topic modeling, which assumes that each posting may be drawn from one or more latent topics [8]. We could then select the subset of individuals associated with certain topics, and apply GTM to understand the themes and concerns of the patients and caregivers. So far, this step is an example of the **ML→GTM** configuration discussed above. We could then use the emergent dimensions from the GTM analysis (e.g.,

[3] See, e.g., https://community.breastcancer.org/forum/77. Posts were extracted on 25 November 2015.

complexly interleaved themes of fear and hope) to reconfigure the topic-modeling analysis, and then derive a second iteration of topics. This step looks more like the **GTM→ML** configuration discussed above. The revised topic model would then suggest new sets of postings to be analyzed via GTM.

Overall, this process sketch applies the GTM principle of *constant comparison* of data with theory (in ML and in GTM), and of data with data (in the interplay of GTM and ML). The process also applies the GTM principle of *theoretical sampling*, in which the current state of the analysis (i.e., the emergent theory) is used to select the next site or dataset for the next iteration of the analysis.

6. Conclusion

In writing this paper, we wondered if the similarities between GTM and ML arose from a deeper resonance. We note that the Hybrid idea makes sense because GTM and ML pursue similar core research program ("strategies," as it were), even though they use different methods ("tactics," as it were). It may be that these two methods – and, probably, other methods in HCI and CSCW – reflect common goals of inquiry in knowing and describing our phenomena (e.g., [47]). While clearly beyond the scope of the current paper, we hope other researchers will explore to what extent similarities (or divergences) among different methods may contribute to a deeper convergence of research methods.

7. REFERENCES

[1] Chee Siang Ang, Ania Bobrowicz, Diane J. Schiano, and Bonnie Nardi (2013). Data in the wild: Some reflections. *Interactions 20*(2), 39-43.

[2] Ofer Arazy, Henry Brausen, David Turner, Adam Balila, Eleni Stroulia, and Joel Lanir (2015). coDNA: Visualizing peer production processes. *CSCW 2015 Companion*, 5-8.

[3] Ohad Barzilay, Orit Hazzan, and Amiram Yehudai (2009). Characterizing example embedding as a software activity. *Proc. SUITE 2009*, 5-8.

[4] Eric P.S. Baumer, Elisha Elovic, Ying "Crystal" Qin, Francesca Polletta, and Geri K. Gay (2015). Testing and comparing computational approaches for identifying the language of framing in political news. *Proc NAACL 2015*, 1472–1482.

[5] Eric P. S. Baumer, Shion Guha, Emily Quan, David Mimno, and Geri K. Gay (2015). How social media non-use influences the likelihood of reversion: Perceived addiction, boundary negotiation, subjective mood, and social connections. *Social Media + Society 1*(2),.

[6] Eric P.S. Baumer, David Mimno, Shion Guha, Emily Quan, and Geri Gay (2016). Comparing grounded theory and topic-modeling: Extreme divergence or unlikely convergence? *JASIST*, in revision.

[7] Christopher M Bishop (2006). *Pattern Recognition and Machine Learning*, Springer, NY, NY, USA.

[8] Cameron Blevins (2010). Topic modeling Martha Ballard's diary. *Cameron Blevins* (blog), 1 April 2010, http://www.cameronblevins.org/posts/topic-modeling-martha-ballards-diary/ .

[9] Jeanette Blomberg and Helena Karasti (2013). Reflections on 25 years of ethnography in CSCW. *CSCW 22*(4-6), 373-423.

[10] danah boyd and Kate Crawford (2012). Critical questions for big data. *Info. Comm. & Soc. 15*(5), 662-679.

[11] Anthony Bryant and Kathy Charmaz (2007). *The Sage handbook of grounded theory*. London, UK, Sage.

[12] Dallas Card,Amber E. Boydstun, Justin H. Gross, Philip Resnik, and Noah A. Smith (2015). The media frames corpus: Annotations of frames across issues. *Proc ACL 2015*, 438-444.

[13] Munmun De Choudhury and Scott Counts (2013). Understanding affect in the workplace via social media. *Proc. CSCW 2013*, 303-316.

[14] Munmum De Choudhury, Scott Counts, Eric J. Horvitz, and Aaron Hoff (2014). Characterizing and predicting postpartum depression from shared facebook data. *Proc. CSCW 2014*, 626-638

[15] Kathy Charmaz (2006). *Constructing grounded theory: A practical guide through qualitative analysis*. London, UK, Sage.

[16] Ólavur Christiansen (2008). The rationale for the use of classic GT. *Grounded Theory Review 7*(2), http://groundedtheoryreview.com/2008/06/30/1046/

[17] Juliet Corbin and Anselm L. Strauss (2007). *Basics of quail-tative research: Techniques and procedures for developing grounded theory. 3rd edition*. Newbury Park, CA, USA: Sage.

[18] Cristian Danescu-Niculescu-Mizil, Lilian Lee,, Bo Pang, and Jon Kleinberg, J. (2012). Echoes of power: Language effects and power differences in social interaction. *Proc WWW 2012*, 699-708.

[19] Janez Demšar. (2006). "Statistical comparisons of classifiers over multiple data sets." *The Journal of Machine Learning Research* 7,1-30.

[20] James Dougherty, Ron Kohavi, and Mehran Sahami (1995). Supervised and unsupervised discretization of continuous features. *Proc. 12th Int. Conf. Machine Learning*, 194-202.

[21] Paul Dourish (2014). Reading and interpretation ethno-graphy. In Judith S. Olson and Wendy A. Kellogg (eds.), *Ways of knowing in HCI*. New York, NY, USA, Springer.

[22] Jennifer G. Dy and Carla E. Brodley. (2004). Feature selection for unsupervised learning. *J. Mach. Learn. Res.* 5 (December 2004), 845-889.

[23] Danyel Fisher, Rob DeLine, Mary Czerwinski, and Steven Drucker (2012). Interactions with big data analytics. *Interactions 19*(3), 50-59.

[24] Barney G. Glaser (1992). *Emergences vs. forcing: Basics of grounded theory analysis*. Mill Valley, CA, USA: Sociology Press.

[25] Barney G. Glaser (2005). *The grounded theory perspective III: Theoretical coding*. Mill Valley, CA, USA: Sociology Press.

[26] Barney G. Glaser (1978). *Theoretical sensitivity: Advances in the methodology of grounded theory*. Mill Valley, CA, USA: Sociology Press.

[27] Barney G. Glaser and Anselm L. Strauss (1965a). *Awareness of dying*. Chicago, Aldine.

[28] Barney G. Glaser and Anselm L. Strauss (1967). *The discovery of grounded theory: Strategies for qualitative research*. Chicago, Aldine.

[29] Barney G. Glaser and Anselm L. Strauss (1965b). Discovery of substantive theory: A basic strategy for qualitative analysis. *Am. Beh. Sci. 8*, 5-12.

[30] Barney G. Glaser and Anselm L. Strauss (1968). *Time for dying*. Chicago, Aldine.

[31] Stephan Greene and Philip Resnik (2009). More than words: Syntactic packaging and implicit sentiment. *Proc HLT 2009*, 503–511.

[32] Isabelle Guyon and André Elisseeff. (2003). An introduction to variable and feature selection. *J. Mach. Learn. Res.* 3 (March 2003), 1157-1182

[33] Rashina Hoda (2011). *Self-organizing agile teams: A grounded theory*. PhD thesis, Victoria University of Wellington, 2011.

[34] Matthew Jockers. 2013. *Macroanalysis*. University of Illinois Press: Champaign, IL.

[35] Udo Kelle (2005). "Emergence" vs. "forcing" of empirical data? A crucial problem of "grounded theory" reconsidered. *FQS 6*(2), art. 27.

[36] Ron Kohavi. (1995) "A study of cross-validation and bootstrap for accuracy estimation and model selection." *IJCAI 14*(2).

[37] Ron Kohavi, (1998). Glossary of terms, "Special issue on applications of machine learning and the knowledge discovery process." http://robotics.stanford.edu/~ronnyk/glossary.htm

[38] Scott Krig (2014). *Computer vision metrics: Survey, taxonomy, and analysis*. Apress, Chapter 7.

[39] Karen S. Kurasaki (2000). Intercoder reliability for validating conclusions drawn from open-ended interview data. *Field methods, 12*(3), 179-194.

[40] Amanda Menking and Ingrid Erickson (2015). The heart work of Wikipedia: Gendered, emotional labor in the world's largest online encyclopedia. *Proc. CHI 2015*, 207-210.

[41] Tom Mitchell, 2006, "The discipline of machine learning". URL: http://www-cgi.cs.cmu.edu/~tom/pubs/MachineLearningTR.pdf

[42] Tanushree Mitra and Eric Gilbert (2014). The language that gets people to give: Phrases that predict success on Kickstarter. *Proc. CSCW 2014*, 49-61.

[43] Janice M. Morse, Phyllis Noerager Stern, Juliet Corbin, Barbara Bowers, Adele E. Clarke, and Kathy Charmaz (2009). *Developing grounded theory: The second generation*. Walnut Creek, CA, USA, Left Coast Press.

[44] Michael Muller (2014). Curiosity, creativity, and surprise as analytic tools: Grounded theory method. In Judith S. Olson and Wendy A. Kellogg (eds.), *Ways of knowing in HCI*. New York, NY, USA, Springer.

[45] Michael Muller, Shion Guha, Matthew Davis, Werner Geyer, and Sadat Shami (2015). Developing data-driven theories via grounded theory method and machine learning. Presentation at Human Computer Interaction Consortium, Watsonville, CA, USA, June 2015. Slides available at http://www.slideshare.net/traincroft/hcic-muller-guha-davis-geyer-shami-2015-0629

[46] Wanda J. Orlikowski and Jack J. Baroudi. 1991. Studying Information Technology in Organizations: Research Approaches and Assumptions. *Information Systems Research 2*(1), 1–28. http://doi.org/10.1287/isre.2.1.1

[47] Judith S. Olson and Wendy A. Kellogg (2014) (eds.), *Ways of knowing in HCI*. New York, NY, USA, Springer.

[48] Jo Reichertz (2007). Abduction: The logic of discovery of grounded theory. In Anthony Bryant and Kathy Charmaz (eds.), *The Sage handbook of grounded theory*. Thousand Oaks, CA, USA: Sage.

[49] Lisa Rhody. 2012. Topic modeling and figurative language. *Journal of Digital Humanities 2*, 1.

[50] Shilad Sen, Margaret E. Giesel, Rebecca Gold, Benjamin Hillmann, Matt Lesicko, Samuel Naden, Jesse Russell, Zixiao "Ken" Wang, and Brent Hecht. (2015). Turkers, Scholars, "Arafat" and "Peace": Cultural Communities and Algorithmic Gold Standards. *Proc. CSCW*, 826-838.

[51] Rion Snow, Brendan O'Connor, Daniel Jurafsky, and Andrew Y. Ng (2008). Cheap and fast---but is it good?: evaluating non-expert annotations for natural language tasks. *Proc. Conf. Empir. Meth. Nat. Lang. Proc.*, 254-263.

[52] Susan Leigh Star (2007). Living grounded theory. In Antho-ny Bryant and Kathy Charmaz (eds.), *The Sage handbook of grounded theory*. Thousand Oaks, CA, USA: Sage.

[53] Stephen V Stehman. (1997). "Selecting and interpreting measures of thematic classification accuracy." *Remote sensing of Environment* 62.1,77-89.

[54] Anselm L. Strauss (1987). *Qualitative analysis for social scientists*. Cambridge, UK: Cambridge University Press.

[55] Anselm L. Strauss and Juliet Corbin (1990). *Basics of qualitative research: Grounded theory procedures and techniques*. Newbury Park, CA, USA: Sage.

[56] Jennifer Thom-Santelli, Michael Muller, and David Millen (2008). Social tagging roles: Publishers, evangelists, leaders. *Proc CHI 2008*, 1041-1044.

[57] Stefan Timmermans and Iddo Tavory (2012). Theory construction in qualitative research: From grounded theory to abductive analysis. *Socio. Theor. 30*(3), 167-186.

[58] Christopher Vendome, Mario Linares-Vásquez, Gabriele Bavota, Massimiliano Di Penta, Daniel German, and Denys Poshyvanyk (2015). License usage and changes: A large-scale study of Java projects on GitHub. *Proc. IEEE Int. Conf. Prog. Comp. 2015*, 218-228.

[59] Kiri L. Wagstaff, K. (2012). Machine learning that matters. arXiv preprint arXiv:1206.4656, or http://www.wkiri.com/research/ papers/wagstaff-MLmatters-12.pdf

[60] Philip A. Warrick, Emily F. Hamilton, Robert E. Kearney, and Doina Precup (2012). A machine learning approach to the detection of fetal hypoxia during labor and delivery. *AI Magazine, 33*(2), 79-90.

[61] Janyce M. Wiebe, Rebecca F. Bruce, and Thomas P. O'Hara. 1999. Development and use of a gold-standard data set for subjectivity classifications. In *Proceedings of the 37th annual meeting of the Association for Computational Linguistics on Computational Linguistics* (ACL '99). Association for Computational Linguistics, Stroudsburg, PA, USA, 246-253.

Beyond the Individual: The Dynamic Features of Distributed Affect

Taylor Jackson Scott
University of Washington
428 Sieg Hall
Seattle, WA 98195
omni@uw.edu

Daniel Perry
UC Berkeley
102 South Hall
Berkeley, CA 94720
dperry@berkeley.edu

Alison Williams
Ravensbourne
London SE10 0EW
United Kingdom
alisonwilliams62@gmail.com

Cecilia R. Aragon
University of Washington
428 Sieg Hall
Seattle, WA 98195
aragon@uw.edu

ABSTRACT

Affect has been identified as an important component of the communication practices of distributed teams. Our emerging theory of *distributed affect* moves beyond the individual as the primary unit of analysis, focusing instead on affect as a dynamic group process. Drawing upon a data set of over four years of chat logs from a distributed scientific collaboration relying on text-based communication to coordinate their work, we expand upon the framework of distributed affect and characterize the concept through five features: *transference, resonance, pervasiveness, persistence*, and *representation*. These features provide a set of descriptive components for interactions between people and their environment, their tools, and their present and historical references as part of a dynamical system of affect. We examine specific events in the group's history which highlight the dynamic way affect is operating in this context, and how it influences factors such as creative problem solving. The framework we describe offers a unique analytic lens for the study of computer-supported group work, and a useful tool for framing questions about the continued study of affect in collaborative teams.

Keywords

Distributed affect; distributed groups; computer-mediated communication; collaborative creativity.

1. INTRODUCTION

Affect underlies and informs all human interaction, and is central to group functioning. Acknowledgment and understanding of its role in driving group creativity [6] and productive working [4], particularly under pressure, is often lacking or denied [51] especially in technological and scientific areas [40]. This paper offers a framework for a deeper understanding of affect's impact, focusing on distributed groups that are communicating predominantly through text chat.

Although the mechanisms of distributed cognition [34, 49, 50] have been extensively studied in distributed teams, less work has been done on the operation of affect beyond the individual. To address this gap, we examine how affect is dynamically distributed when people collaborate, specifically through text-based media, drawing on an extensive data set of chat logs derived over four years from the Nearby Supernova Factory (SNfactory), an international astrophysics collaboration between French and American scientists [3]. We build upon two sets of related research on affect in groups using text-based communication: Aragon and Williams' work [6] where the term distributed affect is used without detail; and works by Scott et al. [47] and Brooks et al. [10] identifying and codifying a taxonomy of affect in chat logs. These demonstrations that affective processes are visible in groups' text-based communication in decision-making [42] establish the need to describe in more detail how affect operates within the processes of distributed groups.

GROUP '16, Nov 13 - 16, 2016, Sanibel Island, FL, USA.

ACM 978-1-4503-4276-6/16/11 $15.00
DOI: http://dx.doi.org/10.1145/2957276.2957277

Our research builds upon previous work on cognition, postulating that Hutchins' [34, 49, 50] and Arrow et al.'s [7] respective approaches to group cognitive dynamics apply equally to affect, and that an affective ecosystem of dynamics between group members and their environment can be observed in our chat data set. We describe these interactions in detail in the Results Section below.

The question underlying this research is: "What is distributed affect, and how does it work?" In this paper, we identify five distinct features of distributed affect that, we posit, provide the mechanism for understanding its operation within a group context: *transference, resonance, pervasiveness, persistence,* and *representation.* We describe the five features and provide examples of each based on key affective events in the data set. This effort builds upon previous work in affect and emotion, distributed cognition and dynamical systems to explicate each of the features of distributed affect.

We utilize computer-mediated discourse analysis (CMDA) [32] as our primary means of qualitative analysis to study affective responses to unforeseen events occurring in our data set, mapping affective interactions over the four years of the collaboration. CMDA is a linguistics-based content analysis method specifically formulated for computer-mediated communication (CMC), and its different levels of language can be used to examine expressions of affect as we have operationalized them. The features are then examined in context to demonstrate their usefulness in accounting for the dynamic affective interaction of the group members as they go about their work. Through this analysis, we position our framework as an effective tool for posing and answering research questions about the operation and importance of affect in distributed teams and the unique ways that the communication of affect occurs in text-based media.

1.1 Definitions

We define affect as a state distinct from cognition [45], and as a person's 'capacity to affect and be affected' by other people [5]. Although this is a broad definition, we agree with Brennan [9] and Smith-Lovin [48], who describe it as a "physiological shift accompanying a judgment," while acknowledging that its definition is both more complicated and nuanced. The wide range of affective phenomena that we are accounting for is further informed by Ekkekakis' definition of affect as a "broader concept than mood and emotion" which provides the experiential substrate upon which moods and emotions are woven [17].

The events analyzed from the chat logs are predominantly tackled by the astrophysicists through creativity and problem-solving, searching for an operation to transfer the given (problematical) state of the system to a goal state [18]. We follow Mayer [38] to define creativity as: (1) novel, (2) useful with a valued outcome, and (3) a time-based process.

We use 'distributed' in two senses: for teams who span different time zones, countries, languages and cultures [16]; and for the attributes of those distributed teams, including distributed cognition [34, 49, 50] and distributed affect [6].

2. BACKGROUND AND RELATED WORK

The three main areas of literature pertaining to this paper are: a) the substance of human interactions (affect and emotion, distributed cognition and dynamical systems), b) one particular type of interaction, text-based communication, and c) previous work on distributed affect.

2.1 Affect and Emotion

The study of affect has moved beyond psychology into multiple disciplines, including geography [5], literary studies [46], feminist studies [9], and HCI [39]. Recent thinking posits affect as more than a "non-rational phenomenon" [5] emphasizing the importance of understanding the dynamics of affective life, and affect's physiological aspects. Seeing affect as plural, rather than singular, Anderson suggests that affects are interwoven through all aspects of life, "organized and patterned as part of diverse socio-spatial formations" [5]. Moore and Isen's [39] work on positive and negative affect and Watson et al.'s PANAS (Positive And Negative Affect Schedule) [53] also proposes that people are affected by or affect others, and that the affect is shared. Paralleling this, Hatfield, et al. [30, 31] examine 'emotional contagion': how affect and emotion are transmitted between people. They describe a *multiply determined* family of psychophysiological, behavioral, and social phenomena that is also *multilevel* where "the precipitating stimuli arise from one individual, act upon (i.e. are perceived and interpreted by) one or more other individuals, and yield corresponding or complementary emotions [...] in these individuals" [30, 31]. These concepts of emotional contagion have further been applied within computer-mediated communication by Hancock et al. [29], finding relationships between affect and the production of words, terms, and message rates. However, they did not account for more dynamical relationships over time, which we have found to be a crucial component of our findings. Additionally, both Barsade and George [8, 22] acknowledge that "group emotions" do exist and have an effect on group dynamics but also that the process by which these effects occur is not well understood, a question our research directly addresses. The laboratory studies carried out by Barsade showed strong evidence of emotional contagion in groups, but he specifically calls for future research to focus on a longitudinal study in an ongoing working team, which is precisely what we set out to do.

Gottman et al.'s [25] methodologies for analyzing affect in recorded exchanges by married couples have been applied to organizational domains by Jung and Leifer [36] to understand interaction dynamics and the performance of engineering design teams. These complex readings of affect and emotion inform our extended framework of distributed affect and its dynamical quality as evidenced across the SNfactory data set (details to be provided in the Dynamical Systems subsection below).

2.2 Distributed Cognition

Hutchins' concept of distributed cognition [34], "extends the reach of what is considered *cognitive* beyond the individual to encompass interactions between people and with resources and materials in the environment" [33] and where "interaction [is] a source of novel structure" [35]. Cognitive processes thus extend beyond the individual to other members of a social group, involving coordination between people and their environmental context, and are capable of being distributed temporally so the outcomes of earlier events impact later events [33]. Recent work in the study of cognition acknowledges the importance of distributed cognition, contrasting the 'extended' with the 'brainbound' mind [13], and proposing a "potent, slow, pattern-based learning [enabling us] to learn to deal with highly complex situations in a remarkably nuanced and efficient manner" [13].

Aragon and Williams [6] note that Hutchins does not explicitly call out possible affective states driving the collaborative problem-solving demonstrated by the distributed navigation system he references [34], despite the high levels of stress involved in the operation that might have been thought, inevitably, to have played a part. Furthermore, Clark's discussions of the extended mind [13, 14] focus on cognition but not affect. However, the growing body of literature on affect and emotion previously referenced demonstrates the importance of affective states in group interaction, laying the groundwork for this paper.

2.3 Dynamical Systems

McGrath et al. [37] argue that complexity, adaptation, and dynamic cross-level interaction are essential characteristics of groups, referencing both Abraham's [1] work in dynamical systems theory in the context of psychology, and complexity and chaos theory [43]. A dynamical systems approach has been used in previous research to analyze communication patterns and affect. Arrow et al. [7], studying the dynamics of concocted groups (i.e. built purposively), observe "the coordination network of an operating group connects members, tasks, and tools – both the tangible resources of hardware and money and the intangible resources of knowledge and procedures – into a functional whole." We have observed these principles of dynamical systems at play in distributed group problem-solving and creativity, and this has informed our framing of distributed affect, particularly in relation to groups as "inherently dynamic systems, operating via processes that unfold over time [and] are dependent both on the group's past history and on its anticipated future" [37]; and what Arrow et al. [7] call *affective* and *cognitive integration.*

2.4 Text-Based Communication

Chat is a central computer-based collaborative tool, used by teams for general communication, and extensively for problem-solving when there are events to be dealt with (i.e. things going wrong, or things going right). Events catalyze affect, positive as well as negative, which is expressed in the chat through content (what is said) and expression (how it is said) [6]. In face-to-face communication, affect is frequently communicated through unconscious, spontaneous, non-verbal expressions such as body language, speech rhythm, and intonation. In contrast, text-based communication, with fewer expressly non-verbal channels available, requires more explicit, deliberate expression of affect, although some evidence exists of spontaneous non-verbal cues still playing a role in the interpretation of affect in text-based communication. For example, Gill et al. [21] found that the length of a message had an impact on how well participants agreed on any particular affect being expressed in a blog post, particularly where the affect expressed had low agreement among interpreters.

While the communication of affect was previously believed to occur purely through spontaneous non-verbal cues such as message length, the results of research on text-based chat communication suggest otherwise. Hancock et al. [29] reported that *spontaneous* non-verbal cues (such as message frequency) were not responsible for the spread of emotions between text-based chat partners. Rather, in an earlier study, Hancock, Landrigan and Silver [28] found that the use of intentional verbal and nonverbal cues such as disagreement and punctuation were accurate predictors for how a chat partner could correctly discern their partner's affective state. Similarly, Guillory et al. [26] found that people intentionally use verbal and nonverbal cues to communicate affect in text-based chat, and Walther and D'Addario's [52] study of the intentional use of emoticons found that a smiley face amplified a positive message while a negative message became more strongly interpreted as negative with a frown face.

These studies suggest that the expression of affect in text-based communication may be a more cognitive, deliberate, and explicit act than in face-to-face communication, and as such, represents a rich account of the intentional expression of affective states of the participants where evidence of distributed affect can be empirically observed.

2.5 Distributed Affect

Aragon and Williams [6] propose the concept of distributed affect as part of a dynamical systems theory addressing how affect helps maintain and accelerate creativity across a distributed group through the creation of what they term creative resonance. They propose a distributed dynamical system that describes how "[t]he affect within the system makes the connections between ideas and between people stickier" and how when local dynamics [7] are tuned to develop socio-emotional links with other group members "there is a greater possibility of distributed affect creating the [creative] resonance that drives and grows ideation." They suggest "the information to be transferred must include the two strands of cognition and affect. Thus we have not only distributed cognition but also distributed affect."

3. METHODS

We arrived at the extended framework of distributed affect and a description of its interactions in the context of our data through mixed methods [46], using multiple sources of data and in two distinct phases discussed in the following sections. Although Aragon and Williams name distributed affect and provide evidence for its existence in text-based communication and its contribution to group creativity, the exact nature of distributed affect as a comprehensive theory remains – as they suggested – to be described, hence our first research question:

RQ1: What are the features of distributed affect?

Our underpinning methodology in phase one in the service of RQ1 is constructivist grounded theory whose structure, while requiring a rigorous 'fit' with the data [41], permits initial concepts and findings ('exploratory conceptual and theoretical development') [19] to emerge early in the process and to mature iteratively through the constant comparative method [24] over the course of the study. The grounded approach allows the use of data of 'whatever type' [23] from multiple sources [11]. In the first phase of the research we analyzed data into categories as they were collected and tested findings as they emerged. Our multiple sources of data included the chat logs themselves, as we immersed ourselves deeply in the copious amounts of text, researched and constructed a taxonomy of affect within the logs and scrutinized early work on distributed affect; our continual reflections and discussions, captured in notes and memos; and the pertinent literature and our reading of it in this emerging context, again noted and memo-ed. Constructivist grounded theory [11], in contrast to grounded theory [24], encourages wide reading at all stages of the research. This identification of the features does not in-and-of-itself describe the mechanisms by which DA operates which is addressed in our second research question:

RQ2: How do these proposed features interact with one another and how does this interaction contribute to group dynamics such as the collaborative problem solving that the group displays?

In the second phase of the study we used computer-mediated discourse analysis (CMDA) as a rigorous means of examining the chat logs for evidence of how the features are operationalized and enacted in the data set (RQ2). We employed Weiss and Cropanzano's Affective Events Theory (AET) [54] to identify events where affect levels would likely be high. Where we identified the features in action, we then described them, using the constant comparative method, until we were satisfied that each category (i.e. each feature) was saturated. These methods are discussed in further detail in the following sections.

3.1 Our Data

The dataset analyzed for this paper is a text-based chat log corpus from the SNfactory group with approximately 485,000 messages sent over a period of four years. The group used text chat (AOL Instant Messenger) as their primary means of synchronous communication to jointly make scientific and operational decisions about the telescope they were remotely and collaboratively operating [6]. The group consisted of about 30 core members who were physically located at various sites in the U.S. and France, none of which were at the telescope site on Mauna Kea, Hawaii, U.S. The typical number of people engaging in the chat on any given night is 4-6, although this number varies from 2-10. Given the nightly and cyclical nature of the scientists' work, the chat is organized into 24-hour periods that we refer to as separate "logs" in this paper. The logs were coded for affect using a taxonomy of 42 distinct codes that were arrived at through an adapted grounded theory approach as part of our earlier research in this area [47]. This taxonomy included substantive codes that were not mutually exclusive, as well as valence and intensity labels. Using this technique, nearly 67,000 (approximately 14%) lines of the corpus were manually coded using each chat message as a discrete element, and it is these coded logs that form the central focus of our analysis.

We recognize the necessary interpretive nature inherent in this type of qualitative coding. In this research we remained mindful of Glaser's [1992] principle of distance in conceptualizing the data while at the same time "embrac[ing] and discuss[ing] the idiosyncrasies of unique ethnographic encounters" [44] as reflective researchers. Our goal in applying these codes was to capture the affective expressions that could be empirically observed in the text, rather than any attempt to infer the internal state of the speaker. To assess reliability of the coding, Cohen's kappa was calculated over all messages coded by two or more people [47], achieving an overall kappa value of 0.647, with per-code kappas ranging from about 0.4 to 0.8.

Our previous work coding the data and the writing of digests and field notes described in Section 3.3 formed a substantial part of the first phase of our study, the exploratory conceptual and theoretical development [19] of distributed affect and the emergence of its features.

3.2 Sampling the Corpus

The telescope and its specialized software are the integral shared instruments of the SNfactory and a main focus of their communication. Problems that arise, especially equipment and software failures, can adversely impact crucial data gathering opportunities. Immediate solutions to these problems as they arise are a high priority for the group and these events lead to frequent instances of problem-solving communication in the chat logs. For example, the scientists explicitly focus on debugging the telescope in 59 chat logs, and they collaborated to solve more complex errors in 23 chat logs. The SNfactory's computer infrastructure is also a potential target for hackers. A possible unauthorized access to the SNfactory instruments and collected data required the scientists to assess the problem and repair any possible damage speedily.

For our examination of the emergent properties of distributed affect we adopted a purposive sampling approach, in which we identified events recorded in the logs that held a high possibility of affect, owing to their out-of-the-ordinary nature. Weiss and Cropanzano's Affective Events Theory (AET) highlights the role of workplace events as proximal causes for affective reactions [54], promoting affective cycles among group members. We therefore focused on three kinds of events that produced both negative and positive affective states: discovery of a security threat, shared system bugs, and shared tool failure, selected through an iterative process that identified recurring problem solving events in the dataset involving the interaction of several SNfactory members. We combined keyword and affect code searches over the chat logs to select data to analyze more closely. This method was repeated with different keywords to generate a list of logs containing potential events to analyze further. These three event types reveal the highly-layered and complex role that distributed affect plays in the dynamics of the group as they use collaborative problem solving to resolve these critical issues.

3.3 Writing Digests of the Chat Logs

Charmaz describes memos as an opportunity to become "actively engaged" in the data, grounding your emerging analysis [12]. We abstracted relevant information from the full conversational records in the selected chat logs by writing "digests," drawing on and expanding on the traditional memoing techniques of the constant comparative method.

Treating the chat log as a high-fidelity record of what transpired during any given shift, we "replayed" the events and wrote "field notes" in the form of episodic time stamped summaries taken directly from the logs. We also included reader comments, which are semi-analytic asides that provide the opportunity to note interpretive insights. Based on these field notes, we produced memos of several paragraphs that included causal claims about what is captured in the summary. In contrast to the field notes, these write-ups took an analytical perspective on the phenomena of affect and events. These digests performed two functions: as high-level summaries that enabled us to identify phenomena of interest in the emergent phase, and as entry points into the chat logs as our study moved into its analysis phase. During the course of coding the data and writing the digests, five features of distributed affect emerged: *transference, resonance, pervasiveness, persistence,* and *representation.* We describe these features in further detail in Section 4.

3.4 Computer-Mediated Discourse Analysis

CMDA applies "methods adapted from language-focused disciplines such as linguistics, communication, and rhetoric to the analysis of computer-mediated communication...[and has] at its core the analysis of logs of verbal interaction" [32] and thus takes advantage of the unique qualities of online discourse that occur in our chat logs. Of key importance to our analysis is that CMDA is specifically formulated to apply to the examination of five levels of language in CMC. These levels were particularly relevant in scrutinizing the chat logs for evidence of each of the emergent features of distributed affect. Each of these levels is described below (ranging from smallest to largest unit of analysis) [32] including a brief discussion of how they specifically correspond to our dataset. These levels of language played an integral role in how we went about operationalizing the features of distributed affect in Section 5.1.

1. Structure: Structural phenomena include the use of special typography or orthography, novel word formations, and sentence structure. This level can be found in our own dataset in the use of emoticons, intentionally deformed spellings and punctuation, and in the use of all caps.

2. Meaning: This level includes the meaning of words and utterances. Our data allow for us to make judgments about technical terms, foreign language use, and utterances that are specific to the technical work being carried out which go beyond usages found in normal conversation.

3. Interaction: The interactional level includes turn-taking, topic development, and other means of negotiating interactive exchanges. Turn taking is clearly demonstrated in the ordering of the messages in the log, and topic development is of importance to us in identifying shifts in the tone of a conversation as well as the focus of participants in addressing their work.

4. Social Behavior: The social level includes linguistic expressions of play, conflict, power, and group membership over multiple exchanges. Given the large number of ever-shifting participants in any given log, there are a variety of social dynamics that we examine in our data. It is also at this level that we would expect to have the most salient discussion of the affect codes which have been applied to a message.

5. Participation Patterns: These patterns are measured by frequency and length of messages posted and responses received in threads or other extended discourse samples. Our logs include information about the speaker and the time a message was sent (timestamp). This allowed us to measure the frequency of participation for each participant in a given log and leverage this information as an additional indicator of other levels.

We operationalized each of the features into well-defined concepts that can be directly observed in the logs in accordance with the five levels of language. Using a phenomenon-based sampling technique [32] a qualitative analysis was carried out, informed by relevant discourse phenomena as outlined in the CMDA approach, the previously applied substantive affect codes from the taxonomy, as well as the specific distributed affect features identified in the logs. The details of how these features were operationalized, as well as a presentation of our analysis and discussion of the features in context can be found in Section 5.1.

4. THE FIVE FEATURES

Throughout the first phase of our research, the framework of distributed affect evolved to describe in more detail a dynamical interplay between members of a distributed group. In this section we expand upon the mechanism whereby affect moves from being, in Aragon and Williams' [6] terms, an observation of affective states of individuals in a distributed group, to a dynamical property of that group's interaction with each other and with their context. We define and describe the five features of distributed affect as observed in the data as well as their relationship to existing theories below (RQ1). While the features themselves are a direct result of our examination of the data, this discussion of related literature is referenced to better situate our contribution within the context of other relevant work in this area and is representative of the sources we consulted as we were engaged in the grounded approach [11] we detailed in Section 3.

4.1 Transference

Transference: the passing and sharing of affect between members of the group.

Although transference of affective states is evidenced in work on emotional contagion [26], and we see additional evidence of this sharing and passing of affect in our own data, we focus on how affect is transferred to multiple participants at the same time. We examine this process at the level of the entire group, rather than in dyadic pairs, to account for the sharing of affective states that can become pervasive across the entire group.

Additionally, we posit that this transference of affect is one of the key mechanisms by which the other features are catalyzed and precipitated. We see examples in the data of transference of affect not only between human members of the group, but also transference of affective states to technical and conceptual artifacts which are related to the group's work and social lives.

4.2 Resonance

Resonance: the amplification and damping of affective states via positive and negative feedback loops.

Resonance describes how the affective states can build in positive or negative feedback loops between members of the group. This concept shares similarities with Aragon and Williams' [6] "creative resonance" in which ideas are amplified or damped according to affective and social aspects of group interactions within a system. We extend this understanding to include the production of new and additional affective states (e.g., how the damping or amplifying of one affective state, such as confusion, can precipitate that of another, such as surprise or apprehension).

4.3 Pervasiveness

Pervasiveness: the spread of one or more affective states throughout the group currently engaged in the chat.

Previous research in emotional contagion offers evidence of affect shared and spread among individual members of a group [8]. Pervasiveness, in our framework of distributed affect, is concerned with the dynamics of the group as a whole, including collaborative tools and interfaces.

4.4 Persistence

Persistence: a lasting, non-interruptive temporal duration of affective states in the group.

Persistence of distributed affect stands in contrast to the relatively short-lived and interruptive experiences typically associated with an individual emotion. While persistence as a term has been used in the psychology literature in reference to an emotional state felt or demonstrated over time [42], the unit of analysis has largely been that of the individual, not that of a more complex group system. Similarly, in text-based analysis of chat data, researchers have used persistence to refer to the likelihood that users might switch between emotional states as determined by a mean score of individual users [20]. Aragon and Williams [6] note the importance of temporal context in understanding creative resonance within the larger unit of analysis of a dynamic group.

4.5 Representation

Representation: Affect stored in a representational form within shared tools, events, memories, cultural artifacts, and historical artifacts.

This feature is similar to concepts of representational media in Hutchins' theory of distributed cognition [34]. For example, when scientists refer to "telescope stuck," this phrase holds context-dependent pre-existing negative affect among the group members who know the difficulty of having the telescope in this state.

5. ANALYSIS

We now build upon our presentation of the features to address RQ2, fleshing out the framework of distributed affect to address relevant factors, how and why they are related, and in which contexts the features apply. In order to empirically identify these features and highlight their interactions in the data, we utilized the previously discussed levels of language highlighted by the CMDA method (structure, meaning, interaction, social behavior, and participation patterns) as a means of operationalizing the features of distributed affect defined and described in the previous section. The levels of language served as a guide for surfacing and structuring the key elements that would best account for the unique ways that the features manifest themselves in this unique text-based medium [32]. The specifics of this step in the CMDA process are highlighted here to provide additional context for how these features were analyzed within the event-driven examples from our data.

Transference is operationalized when:

a) A speaker absorbs and reflects back a newly introduced expression of affect. For instance, transference can be observed as a change in the initial affective expression of a participant (e.g. substance, valence, intensity), as a result of exposure to the affective expression of another participant.

b) An artifact (which may be digital, cultural, or ideational) is imbued with an affective state by a member of the group.

Resonance is operationalized through:

a) Fluctuating intensity (increasing or decreasing) of the lexis including words, punctuation, capitalization, lengthening of vowel sounds, and emoticons; for example: "frustration…frustration!!!... FRUSTRAAATION!?!?".

b) Repetition of affective content and expressions occurring between participants over a given window of time, often resulting in amplification or damping of the other participants' affective expressions.

Pervasiveness is operationalized when:

a) A majority of the participating members of the group are expressing the same affect within a given window of time.

b) A new participant is exposed to the affective state of the group and also begins to express similar affect.

Persistence is operationalized through:

a) The sustained, repeated and pervasive expression of similar affect (e.g. substance, valence, intensity) by one or more members of the group over a given window of time.

Representation is operationalized when:

a) An ideational representation is invoked to express or produce an affective response in the group (e.g. saying "here we go again" when the telescope is stuck).

5.1 Interactions and Context of the Features

In this section we look at the five features in the context of the previously identified affect-laden event types based on AET as described in Section 3.2.: discovery of a security threat ("Hacked?"), shared system bugs ("No vacation from bugs!"), and shared tool failure ("Stuck again"). Each of these acute events calls forward distributed cognition in how the team members respond intellectually to the situation; here we examine how the group's *affect* is distributed. Through the examination of distributed affect's operationalized features, we demonstrate how they map to real-world interactions between members of the group in the chat logs (for the sake of privacy, pseudonyms have been used below). At times the features display an ordering, as transference and resonance can often occur as processes that precede and influence the pervasiveness and persistence of affect as expressed in the group. These features can also occur in overlapping ways with feedback loops, with one or more features building on each other as dynamical systems. In this section we examine how these features emerge and are interacting in the system, and are also contributing to some goal of the group, in three individual event types. Examining the behavior of the affect features and mapping their patterns over periods of time longer than a single event is part of future work on the corpus.

5.1.1 "Hacked?"

In this example of a highly affective event, we observe the features of transference, persistence, pervasiveness, and resonance at play.

The SNfactory scientists implicitly rely on their software and systems to aid them in their highly technical work, and any possible compromise of their integrity or reliability is seen as a potentially major threat to overcome and prevent. Because the SNfactory system is a high-profile operation, it is a prime target for compromise. The scientists had obvious concerns over this eventuality, and therefore we purposely sampled this type of event, observing a varied series of affective responses in the group as they worked towards a solution.

In the chat log prior to the evidence of the hacker arising, the affective state of the four members of the group currently participating in the chat is *pervasive*: everyone is focused on their work, making simple inquiries about ongoing tasks, and many of the preceding messages (~50) are coded as 'no affect'. We note that the majority of participants are expressing the same types of affect, specifically 'agreement' or 'no affect,' and that when a new member (Will) joins, he also begins to express similar affect; thus the pervasive mood in the group spreads to the new member. We have observed this pervasiveness of affect in the chat logs, and it also serves to set the stage for the oncoming event.

Phil first notices something may be awry when he notes "very funny history in account ccd" (3:58:28 am) meaning that he has found some unusual activity in one of the logs he is checking which indicates that there was a potentially unauthorized access to an adult website by an outside party that should not have occurred. This information triggers a flurry of questions and information-seeking activity as the group members work to understand the situation. The other three scientists meet this news with surprise and confusion, and we see a display of this affect when Roger replies with "whaaaaaaaaa" (4:00:13 am). The *transference* of this negative affect then occurs between all of the other participants in the chat except for one. Although a *pervasive* and *persistent* state of negative affect sets in for the others, Simon actually tries to combat this by damping the building of negative affect (*resonance*) by injecting humor into the situation. He inquires "what site ;p" (4:00:35 am), with the emoticon representing a winking face with the tongue sticking out indicating a light-hearted joke that he is curious which site was accessed. Although this joke is met initially with laughter (e.g. "hahahahaha") from one of the other scientists, the damping effect of this humor is short lived as the discussion quickly returns to a long series of technical and logistical back-and-forth attempting to get to the bottom of the issue.

Time	Name	Message	Affect
03:58:28AM	Phil:	very funny history in account ccd	amusement
03:59:03AM	Simon:	I find it empty	confusion
03:59:15AM	Phil:	which shell do you use?	interest
03:59:16AM	Will:	me too	agreement
03:59:20AM		csh	no affect
03:59:23AM	Phil:	ahhh	surprise
03:59:39AM		bash history had some curls to a porn site	surprise
04:00:00AM	Will:	bad!	disgust, surprise, anger
04:00:08AM	Simon:	hacked?	interest
04:00:13AM	Roger:	whaaaaaaaaaaaa	surprise, confusion
04:00:17AM	Phil:	I hope not	apprehension
04:00:22AM	Will:	how old?	interest
04:00:29AM	Phil:	impossible to tell	no affect
04:00:35AM	Simon:	what site ;p	amusement
04:00:37AM	Phil:	it was before I logged in	no affect
04:00:45AM	Simon:	they all say that Phil	amusement
04:00:46AM	Phil:	hahahahaha	amusement

Table 1. Excerpt of chat log containing the SNfactory participants discovering possible evidence of a hack, as well as the corresponding affect codes.

We then enter a long stretch of dialogue that is coded with persistently negative valence affect codes (apprehension, confusion, annoyance), and these affective states are *pervasive* across the entire group attempting to solve the problem. Simon intermittently continues to try and damp this negative affect by making further humorous comments and lighthearted jokes that are often accompanied by an appropriate emoticon. Eventually it is indicated by Phil that "it may not be an intruder, just someone with a misguided cut-and paste" (4:23:53 am). This comment is followed up with several more jokes from Simon, and these seem to achieve their desired damping effect and finally break the *persistent* and *pervasive* negative mood of the group. We then see a shift towards all of the members of the group sending messages that were coded with 'amusement' and other positive valence affect codes, signaling a transition to a new state of positive *pervasiveness* which alleviates all of the tension from the preceding half an hour of chat, along with the sense of a resolution to their problem. At this point, Simon suggests that they return to finishing their current telescope scan before conditions for viewing are no longer suitable. The rest of the group agrees that the potential hacker situation will need to be returned to later if it is deemed to be an actual threat, and thanks to Simon's continued damping of the negative affect resonating throughout the group, they are able to return to progress on their primary goal, thus resolving their immediate problem.

This example shows several of the features operating at once, feeding into one another (transference and resonance leading to a pervasive and persistent affective state) or serving to mitigate the effects of one or more features (Simon's humor working to defuse the situation and bring levity back to the group). At no point is any one person specifically setting the overall affective tone for the group, but rather the combined affective contributions and responses of all of the members trigger the group's global dynamic and problem solving. Through this dynamic the affective properties of the entire group assume a level of importance that moves beyond individual interactions highlighting the significance of the distributed nature of the mechanisms we see at the heart of the framework we develop.

5.1.2 *"No vacation from bugs!"*

This instance from the chat logs exhibits the features of resonance and its damping, and representation at play across the group as they work to solve a problem with a software bug.

Fixing software bugs absorbs SNfactory scientists' time and energy as they impact the group's ability to collect data and effectively monitor the telescope. In this particular event, Roger, one of the core contributors of software code in the group, gets increasingly frustrated and upset as he realizes that no one contacted him the previous evening regarding a system bug. When he is first introduced to the chat he asks playfully "any buggies?" to which one of the participants replies "big one" to which Roger replies two seconds later with "shit". Here we see how a bug in the software acts as a *representational* object, having developed negative affective attributes based on previous shared group experiences in finding and fixing them. There is no need to explain why a bug might be bad for their workflow, as the implications of a "big one" are pre-existing in the group. Roger's negative affect increases and starts to resonate as he goes from confusion about the bug throughout the next hour of the event to increased annoyance and frustration at having not been contacted earlier as he gains more information about it. We see the resonance of this negative affect exemplified by the use of elongated speech patterns such as "Baaaaaaaaaaaaaad" (5:07:36), and within one single minute period the use of four frowning faces to indicate his state of displeasure. Roger's negative affect starts to resonate in other participants: Paul, for example, immediately after this strong resonance in Roger, expresses the same type of frowning face, and then in other participants who use these same elongated speech patterns as they work on their continued efforts at debugging "Grrrrrrrrrrrrrrrrrrrrrrrrrrrrrrrrrrr" (6:01:14 pm).

Time	Name	Message	Affect
4:14:16 PM	Roger:	any buggies?	interest
4:14:20 PM	Rita:	big one	apprehension frustration
4:14:22 PM	Roger:	shit	apprehension frustration anger
4:18:42 PM	Rita:	this append twice on standard ...with more than 1 finding chart (first guess)	no affect
4:21:30 PM	Roger:	I am utterly confused	confusion annoyance
-		-	-
5:06:56 PM	Roger:	Someone not looking at image reconstructions?	interest annoyance
5:07:23 PM	Patrick	yes Rita ...saw them ...but didn't react ...	apprehension
5:07:36 PM	Roger:	Baaaaaaaaaaaaaaaad Rita	annoyance anger
5:07:56 PM		Now life is much harder for online guys ... :(	annoyance frustration apprehension
5:08:02 PM		We have to try to debug in vacuum	annoyance frustration
5:08:14 PM		:(:(:(	sadness frustration
5:08:27 PM	Paul:	:(	sadness frustration
5:10:28 PM	Roger:	this is so annoying	frustration annoyance

Table 2. Excerpt of chat log containing the SNfactory participants working together to debug their software, as well as the corresponding affect codes.

Once Roger finds the source of the bug ("SHIT there it is") the negative affect is damped, and this damping is reinforced by Patrick, a French scientist, who initiates the shift to positive affect saying "relax ... we got a standard today" to which Roger agrees "Yes, relazed (sic) now, because i know the bug!" (6:12:02 pm). Positive affect can now be seen resonating in the system as the members see the solution to their problem. We see the expressions of affect change with the expression of positive smiley emoticons among several group members showing persistence of this new affect state.

5.1.3 *"Stuck again."*

Here we observe the features of representation, transference and pervasiveness in the chat logs.

The most common of the type of events we sampled from our dataset is the telescope getting stuck. When this happens the scientists are no longer able to do their work, and face losing important and valuable opportunities for observation; so there is significant pressure to get the telescope working again. Because the scientists operating the telescope are doing so remotely and therefore do not have direct physical access to the telescope, if they are unable to resolve the problem themselves they have to contact another party physically located near the telescope to resolve the problem.

This particular telescope stuck event begins when Roger notes "hmmm...telescope is sticky" (2:43:29 am). This news is met with responses that are coded with annoyance, frustration, confusion, and even anger (all negative valence and high intensity) by the three primary participants in the chat at the time, and by a fourth member who joins later in the log as well. In this case, we see the negative affect not only being transferred between the group, but also being transferred to the telescope itself as a shared artifact which is becoming the focus of this negative affect. As well as transference, we see further evidence of the previously noted frequent occurrence of the telescope being invoked as a representation of negative affect specifically when it is stuck. Throughout this portion of the chat log, there are numerous examples of a reference made to the stuck telescope being followed by utterances coded for negative affect. For instance, after an initial attempt to use the available software-based resources to try and unstick the telescope, Will says "stuck again" (2:59:43 am) and Roger, Will, and Morris all respond with messages that are coded as negative affect which is directed at the telescope.

Time	Name	Message	Affect
2:53:30 AM	Roger:	tele_unstick failed	no affect
2:53:36 AM		trying again	no affect
2:54:21 AM		looks like gonna fail again	anticipation
2:55:14 AM	Will:	I guess try sending it the other way?	supportive
2:55:39 AM	Roger:	gonna see if I can zslew back - - it tried the "one way then the other"	no affect
2:55:45 AM		but that failed	no affect
2:57:52 AM	Will:	what was the other instrument when you started?	interest
2:58:05 AM		maybe they changed instruments and didn't get the balance right	interest, supportive
2:58:56 AM	Roger:	didn't notice	no affect
2:59:10 AM		but I called summit and Ed was there when it was time for flats	no affect
2:59:15 AM		I see if he is still there...	no affect
2:59:33 AM		calling	no affect
2:59:43 PM	Will:	stuck again	annoyance
3:00:04 PM	Roger:	yes	agreement

Table 3. Excerpt of chat log containing the SNfactory participants coping with the telescope being stuck, as well as the corresponding affect codes.

Of particular interest in this example are also simultaneous occurrences of messages that were coded as positive, supportive affective expressions that immediately follow these small initial build-ups of negative affect. These bursts of supportive, positively coded messages are, we suggest, acting as negative feedback loops which serve to damp the resonance of the negative affect that pervades the group whenever the telescope being stuck is mentioned and as they work to solve this problem. This dynamic group process is, we posit, a way to maintain affective equilibrium during this highly stressful time, and thus prevent the situation from sliding into an unchecked stream of negativity and counter-productivity. This dynamical loop occurs repeatedly throughout this log as members join or leave the chat.

6. DISCUSSION

We have presented three narratives, from the many in the logs, that show the dynamic interplay of the five features of distributed affect evidenced in the corpus. These examples were identified based on the sampling techniques noted above, but are by no means exhaustive. Given the size of the corpus, and the guidelines of the CMDA process, we sampled by phenomenon once we had identified a suitable candidate log. This allowed us to show the features at work in several different contexts that are highly relevant to the group, as well as providing specific instances of how the features interact with one another.

Russ [45] has suggested that moderate amounts of negative affect can facilitate problem solving, whereas negative affect levels that are too high may stifle creativity, resulting in a curvilinear relationship. The features of our distributed affect model provide a means to describe these dynamic relationships as affect is spread or damped among members and tools in the group.

The analysis of the above examples shows how group members and representational artifacts act as agents providing affect feedback loops that can support problem solving across the entire group. These feedback processes mirror similar feedback loops researched by Arrow et al. [7] in a complex systems approach to understanding small group organizations. In the 'hacked' example above, Simon's playful quips are eventually able to damp the pervasive negative affect that grows during the discovery of the hack, and push the group back towards a state of equilibrium to continue telescope scans. In the 'bug' example, negative affect resonates at a growing frequency as group members work to find the source of a bug, yet the tension is released quickly when the bug is fixed and the problem is solved. In this case the software bug itself is acting as the representational agent that instigates and damps the pervasiveness of the affective state. Similarly, in the example of the telescope being stuck, the negative affect is damped by negative feedback loops as group members share supportive messages.

As can be seen from these illustrative examples, the global affective state of the group as it is described through the interactions of the five features frequently plays a critical role in maintaining and progressing the problem solving displayed by the group. Observed patterns in the logs further suggest that while the transference and resonance of affect may exist in bursty cycles based on the impact of outside contextual dynamics (e.g., the discovery of a bug or telescope failure), feedback loops of affect states including humor and support occur in more regular and persistent intervals to help the group more quickly return to a state of equilibrium when problem solving.

These examples also show how affective state is stored and propagated not only in the group members themselves, but also as stored representations and references in artifacts (e.g., the stuck telescope) based on past experiences of the group. There is strong evidence to suggest that not only must the unit of analysis shift beyond the individual when considering affect in this type of distributed, collaborative setting, but also that multiple features, interacting with one another in a dynamic system, must be accounted for. While our framework is formulated to capture this dynamic interplay, additional research is needed to provide a more thorough account of how artifacts are employed in this context, and the unique properties that distinguish them from the human actors in the system.

The kind of computer supported cooperative work we have examined here is increasingly taking place between distributed groups who have to rely on tools, such as online chat, that do not allow for the rich, multimodal forms of communication which accompany face-to-face interactions. As we have noted, while affect has been studied in research on computer-based collaborative systems, the focus is usually on the cognitive properties of the group [27, 50]. Our analysis demonstrates the importance of considering affect from a dynamical systems approach that operates at the level of the group rather than solely as a property of the individual, the crucial role that distributed affect plays in how these groups carry out their work, and how that affect is conveyed and propagated in the text-based medium. Our framework of distributed affect can serve as a theoretical lens to provide scaffolding and guidance for researchers wishing to examine the role of affect in their own similar data. At the core of this contribution are the five features and how we have defined and operationalized them within the specific textual phenomena that are of primary importance when analyzing the expression of affect in this context. These features, and subsequent examples from our data, we hope provide a helpful tool for researchers wishing to be able to articulate questions about affect and emotion in their own investigations into collaborative groups in a much more robust and dynamic way than might otherwise be possible. We have provided a means for related research to move beyond the analysis of affect as a phenomenon that is necessarily tied to the individual, and instead have put forward a framework that can highlight the affective properties and dynamics at the group level.

7. LIMITATIONS AND FUTURE WORK

For this initial inquiry we chose to focus on salient events that act as catalysts for the communication of affect; our goal was to better describe these features of distributed affect and their interactions through an examination of relevant examples from the corpus of chat logs. There is undoubtedly still work to be done to continue to develop and fully describe the specific properties and interplay of the features in order to clarify their operation and identification as unique but interrelated aspects of the same overall framework, and to better situate them within the larger context of potential states of the group. As referenced earlier, it would be useful to examine the role that affect plays during "down" times as well. There may be equally important normative and meaningful instances of distributed affect, for example the important element of trust-building, which are taking place on a less dramatic level during times not accounted for through our method of sampling. Additionally, our research accounts for only a single chat data set. We intend to extend our study to other text data sets to further test the emerging theory of distributed affect and to examine our formulation against examples from other settings. While we posit that our current framework is well suited to collaborative chat, due to the unique properties of this form of communication, there may be additional features of distributed affect yet to be identified. We intend to expand our analysis to look for such mechanisms that may account for the distribution of affect in other forms of communication beyond text.

While we have focused on selected event types in this qualitative analysis described in Section 5.1, the five features also provide a means to examine longitudinal group patterns in future work and could be applied in a more quantitative manner to also examine patterns occurring over longer time scales than a single event. Additionally, we also propose a more discrete examination of creative outcomes related to the five features of DA. While previous work has argued for a more complex understanding of affect and creativity that moves beyond simply binning positive and negative affect [15] we would like to further address how the cyclical states of affect as captured by the features relate to specific areas of creativity such as the fluency, originality, and flexibility of ideas over time.

8. CONCLUSION

Our expanded framework of distributed affect has potential implications for distributed collaborations that utilize CMC and the design of the interfaces that enable it; furthermore, the distributed affect framework, as a theoretical lens, can provide scaffolding and guidance for researchers examining the role of affect in their own data. We believe that a rich account of the role that distributed affect plays in collaborative, distributed groups will provide valuable insights into addressing the socio-technical gap that has been identified as a key issue in research on computer-based collaborative systems [2].

The major contribution that our framework of distributed affect makes, however, is a means for examining affect as a dynamic and ongoing distributed phenomenon, existing – as distributed cognition does – beyond the unit of any one individual person. We posit that this dynamical socio-technical system describes the affective interactions between people and their environment, their tools, and their present and historical references. We offer the five features and how their interactions contributed to group dynamics in this paper as a first step in outlining the components and mechanisms of a theory of distributed affect.

9. REFERENCES

[1] Abraham, F. D. 1990. *A Visual Introduction to Dynamical Systems Theory for Psychology*. Aerial Press, Santa Cruz, CA.

[2] Ackerman, M. S. 2000. The intellectual challenge of CSCW: the gap between social requirements and technical feasibility. *Hum.-Comput. Interact.* 15, 2 (September 2000), 179-203.

[3] Aldering, G., et al. 2002. Overview of the Nearby Supernova Factory. In *Proceedings of the SPIE*, 61-72.

[4] Amabile, T. M. & Kramer, S. J. 2011. The power of small wins. *Harvard Business Review*, 89 (5), 70-80.

[5] Anderson, B. 2014. *Encountering Affect: Capabilities, Apparatuses, Conditions.* Ashgate, Farnham UK.

[6] Aragon, C. R. and Williams, A. 2011. Collaborative Creativity: a Complex Systems Model with Distributed Affect. In *Proc. CHI 2011*. ACM, 1875-1884.

[7] Arrow, H., McGrath, J. and Berdahl, J. L. 2000. *Small Groups as Complex Systems.* Sage, CA.

[8] Barsade, S. G. 2002. The Ripple Effect: Emotional Contagion and its Influence on Group Behavior. *Administrative Science Quarterly. 47*, 4, 2002, 644-676.

[9] Brennan, T. 2004. *The Transmission of Affect.* Ithaca: Cornell University Press.

[10] Brooks, M., Kuksenok, K., Torkildson, M.K., Perry, D., Robinson, J.J., Scott, T.J., Anicello, O., Zukowski, A., Harris, P., and Aragon, C.R. 2013. Statistical Affect Detection in Collaborative Chat. In *Proc. CSCW 2013*, ACM, 317-328.

[11] Charmaz, K. 2000. Grounded Theory: Objectivist and Constructivist Methods. In *Handbook of Qualitative Research*: 2nd Edition. N. K. Denzin & Y. S. Lincoln (Eds) London: Sage.

[12] Charmaz, K. 2006. *Constructing grounded theory: A practical guide through qualitative analysis.* Sage Publications.

[13] Clark, A. 2011. *Supersizing the Mind.* Oxford University Press, Oxford UK.

[14] Clark, A. 1997. *Being There.* MIT Press, Cambridge.

[15] De Dreu, C.K., Baas, M. & Nijstad, B. A. 2008. Hedonic tone and activation level in the mood-creativity link: Toward a dual pathway to creativity model. *Journal of Personality and Social Psychology*, Vol. 94(5), May 2008, pp. 739-756.

[16] Edwards, H., et al. 2008. Global Software Development: Project Decomposition and Task Allocation. *Int'l Conference on Business and Information* (2008).

[17] Ekkekakis, P. 2013. *The measurement of affect, mood, and emotion: A guide for health-behavioral research.* Cambridge University Press.

[18] Fischer, A. Greiff, S. and Funke, J. 2012. The Process of Solving Complex Problems. In *The Journal of Problem Solving* Vol. 4, no. 1.

[19] Furniss, D., Blandford, A. and Curzon, P. 2011. Confessions from a Grounded Theory PhD: Experiences and Lessons Learnt. In *Proc. CHI 2011* pp. 113-122.

[20] Garas, A., Garcia, D., Skowron, M. and Schweitzer, F. 2012. Emotional persistence in online chatting communities. *Scientific Reports, 2.* Article 402 CyberEmotions.

[21] Gill A., Gergle, D., French, R. and Oberlander, J. 2008. Emotion Rating from Short Blog Texts. In *Proc. CSCW 2008.*

[22] George, J. M. 1990. Personality, affect, and behavior in groups. *J. of applied psychology* 75, no. 2: 107.

[23] Glaser, B. G. 1992. *Basics of Grounded Theory Analysis: Emergence Vs. Forcing.* Mill Valley, CA: Sociology Press.

[24] Glaser, B. G. 1978. *Theoretical Sensitivity: Advances in the Methodology of Grounded Theory.* Mill Valley, CA: Sociology Press.

[25] Gottman, J. M. 2014. *What predicts divorce?: The relationship between marital processes and marital outcomes.* Psychology Press.

[26] Guillory, J., Spiegel, J., Drislane, M., Weiss, B., Donner, W. and Hancock, J. 2011. Upset Now? Emotion Contagion in Distributed Groups. In *Proceedings of the 2011 Annual Conference on Human Factors in Computing Systems* (Vancouver, BC, Canada). ACM, 745-748.

[27] Halverson, C. A. 2002. Activity Theory and Distributed Cognition: Or What Does CSCW Need to DO with Theories? *Comput. Supported Coop. Work* 11, 1-2 (April 2002), 243-267.

[28] Hancock, J. T., Landrigan, C., and Silver, C. 2007. Expressing emotion in text-based communication. In *Proceedings of SIGCHI' 07: ACM Conference on Human factors in computing systems,* 929-932.

[29] Hancock, J. T., Gee, K., Ciaccio, K., and Lin, J. M. H. 2008. I'm sad you're sad: Emotional contagion in CMC. In *Proceedings of CSCW '08: ACM Conference on Computer Supported Cooperative Work,* 295-298.

[30] Hatfield, E., Cacioppo, J. T., and Rapson, R. 1993. Emotional Contagion. In *Current Directions in Psychological Science, 2, 3,* 96-99.

[31] Hatfield, E., Cacioppo, J. T. and Rapson, R. 1994. Emotional Contagion. In *Studies in Emotion and Social Interaction.* Cambridge University Press, Cambridge.

[32] Herring, S. C. 2004. Computer-Mediated Discourse Analysis: An Approach to Researching Online Behavior. In Barab, S. A., Kling, R., & Gray, J. H. (Eds.). *Designing for Virtual Communities in the Service of Learning* (pp. 338-376). Cambridge University Press, New York.

[33] Hollan, J., Hutchins, E., and Kirsh, D. 2000. Distributed Cognition: Toward a New Foundation for Human-Computer Interaction Research. In *ACM Trans. on Computer-Human Interaction,* 7(2), 174-196.

[34] Hutchins, E. 1995. *Cognition in the wild.* MIT Press, Cambridge, Mass.

[35] Hutchins, E. 2000. Distributed Cognition. In Ed. J.D. Wright *Int'l Encyclopedia of Social and Behavioral Sciences.* Univ. of California, San Diego.

[36] Jung, M. F. and Leifer, L. J. 2011. A method to study affective dynamics and performance in engineering design teams. In *Proc. of the 18th Int'l Conference on Engineering Design (ICED 11) Lyngby/Copenhagen, Denmark, 15-19.08.*

[37] McGrath, J. E., Arrow, H. and Berdahl, J. L. 2000. The Study of Groups: Past, Present, and Future. *Personality and Social Psychology Review.* Vol. 4, No. 1, 95–105.

[38] Mayer, R. E. 1999. Fifty Years of Creativity Research. In ed. Sternberg, R. J. *Handbook of Creativity.* Cambridge University Press, New York.

[39] Moore, B. S. and Isen, A. M. 1990. *Affect and social behavior.* Cambridge University Press, Cambridge.

[40] Osbeck, L., Nersessian, N. J., Malone, K. &. Newstetter W. 2011. *Science as Psychology: Sense-making and Identity in Science Practice.* New York, NY: Cambridge University Press

[41] Pidgeon, N. and Henwood, K. 1996. Grounded Theory: Practical Implementation. In . Richardson, J. T. E. (Ed.). *Handbook of Qualitative Research and Methods for Psychology and the Social Sciences.* Oxford: Wiley.

[42] Plutchik, R. 1990. *The Emotions.* University Press of America, New York.

[43] Prigogine I. and Stengers, I. 1984. *Order out of Chaos.* Bantam, London.

[44] Rode, J. A. 2011. Reflexivity in digital anthropology. In *Proceedings of the SIGCHI Conference on Human Factors in Computing Systems* (CHI '11). ACM, New York, NY, USA, 123-132.

[45] Russ, S. W. 1993. *Affect and Creativity: the Role of Affect and Play in the Creative Process.* L. Erlbaum Associates, Hillsdale, N.J.

[46] Sandelowski, M. 2008. Tables or Tableaux? The Challenges of Writing and Reading Mixed Methods Studies. In *The Mixed Methods Reader* V. L. Plano Clark and J. W. Creswell (Eds.). London: Sage.

[47] Scott, T. J., Kuksenok, K., Perry, D., Brooks, M., Anicello O., and Aragon, C. R. 2012. Adapting Grounded Theory to Construct a Taxonomy of Affect in Collaborative Online Chat. *Proc. SIGDOC 2012*, (pp. 197-204). ACM.

[48] Smith-Lovin, L. 1995. The Sociology of Affect and Emotion. In *Sociological Perspectives on Social Psychology*, eds. Karen Cook, Gary Alan Fine, and James S. House. Boston: Allyn and Bacon.

[49] Stahl, G. 2011. Theories of cognition in CSCW. In *Proc. ECSCW 2011: 24-28 September 2011, Aarhus Denmark.* Springer, London.

[50] Stahl, G. 2006. *Group Cognition: Computer Support for Building Collaborative Knowledge.* MIT Press, Cambridge, Mass.

[51] Urch Druskat, V., Sala, F., and Mount, J. 2006. Introduction: Emotional Intelligence and Work Performance. *Linking Emotional Intelligence and Performance at Work: Current Research Evidence with Individuals and Groups.* New Jersey: Lawrence Erlbaum Associates.

[52] Walther, J., and D'Addario, K. 2001. The Impacts of Emoticons on Message Interpretation in Computer Mediated Communication. *Social Science Computer Review. 19*, 324-347.

[53] Watson, D., Clark, L. A., and Tellegen, A. 1988. Development and validation of brief measures of positive and negative affect: the PANAS scales. *J. Personality and Social Psychology* 54.6: 1063.

[54] Weiss, H. M., and Cropanzano, R. 1996. Affective Events Theory: A Theoretical Discussion of the Structure, Causes and Consequences of Affective Experiences at Work. in (Eds.), Staw B. M. and Cummings L. L., *Research in Organizational Behavior*, Vol. 18 (pp. 1-74). Greenwich, CT: JAI Press.

Chess as a Conversation: Artefact-Based Communication in Online Competitive Board Games

Gregor McEwan and Carl Gutwin
Computer Science Department, University of Saskatchewan
110 Science Place, Saskatoon, Saskatchewan
gregor.mcewan@usask.ca; gutwin@cs.usask.ca

ABSTRACT
Online board-game sites are popular settings for group activity. However, unlike many kinds of group interaction, previous research has found that there is often little verbal conversation during games, which seems strange in a social situation. One reason that has been suggested for the lack of talk is that actions in the game are themselves communicative acts that can replace verbal utterances. There is little known, however, about how games can substitute for verbal conversation. In this paper we carry out a study exploring meaning and shared understanding through the moves of a board game. Participants played a board game and then retrospectively analysed the communicative meaning of each move; we analysed their responses as indicative of "joint actions" in four layers of interaction. Our study shows that game moves can provide a great deal of communication, and that there are both similarities and differences to verbal conversations at each level. The *physical* layer, containing the board, is a foundation similar to that of people speaking the same language. The *syntactic* layer, consisting of the game rules, allows demonstration of expertise but is not noticed by players except in unusual circumstances. The *strategic* layer, consisting of competitive use of the syntactic rules, diverges considerably from a verbal conversation in terms of shared understanding, because players are actively attempting to avoid revealing their meaning. The *personality* layer allows players to make inferences about the other player as a person, just as in verbal communication. Our analysis provides new evidence that even simple turn-based games contain a great deal of interaction richness and subtlety, and that the different levels of communication should be considered by designers as a real and legitimate vehicle for social interaction.

CCS Concepts
• **Human-centered computing → Computer supported cooperative work**

Keywords
Online board games; Artefact-based conversation; Chess

1. INTRODUCTION
Online game sites – where people can play traditional board and card games – are popular places for shared activity. Many of these sites are very successful: for example, the site PlayOK.com has more than five million registered users, and has been operating for more than eleven years. Although online game sites clearly provide a setting for group activity (since there are multiple people concurrently engaged in playing the game), these spaces do not conform to typical definitions of community [8]. In particular, studies have shown that online board games often progress without any verbal communication [8], which seems strange in a supposedly social setting. Earlier work has suggested that the game moves themselves may be a mechanism for social interaction, taking over the role that is normally played by conversation: that is, the shared actions of a game can be a legitimate non-verbal way to engage in Simmel's concept of 'sociability' [13], or Brown and Bell's idea of 'performing a friendship' [1]. However, previous work does not make clear what kind of social interaction a game really is, and how game actions are similar to or different from verbal utterances.

GROUP '16, November 13 - 16, 2016, Sanibel Island, FL, USA

ACM 978-1-4503-4276-6/16/11…$15.00
DOI: http://dx.doi.org/10.1145/2957276.2957314

If we accept that a game can be seen as a conversation, we must then consider the question of what kind of conversation a game is. There are several ways in which we might analyse game-based interaction in more detail, based on previous work in CSCW. First, we could use work on artefact-based coordination [11,12], which focuses on the coordinative power of artefacts in loosely-coupled collaborative work (e.g., such as the role of blueprints and CAD drawings in an architectural project). This artefact-centred stance is to some degree a response to the predisposition in CSCW to focus on discursive and conversational communication.

Second, we could use the concept of feedthrough [3], in which manipulations that change an artefact can provide valuable awareness information to other people. The concept of feedthrough also implies communication – Dix and colleagues indicate that feedthrough provides an artefact-based communication channel that may replace verbal interaction. However, feedthrough also implies indirectness – that is, that the information provided to others in the group is implicit rather than explicit communication. This is true in some contexts of a board game, since the main intent of a player's move is to change the state of the board and advance the game. However, game moves can be interpreted on multiple levels, and in some cases a player's move can be seen as a very explicit communicative act (e.g., moving a chess piece clearly states "I have moved; it's now your turn" in addition to changing the state of the board).

Third, we could use the theoretical framework of communication proposed by Clark [2], in which actions and artefact manipulations can be seen in strongly communicative terms – to the point that they can take the explicit role of utterances in a conversation. The main elements of Clark's theory are:

- Actions in the world can be explicit communicative acts (Clark calls these *manifesting actions* and *verbal evidence*) – for example moving a chess piece "says" something explicit and concrete to another person (e.g. "it's your move");

- The idea of *joint actions*, in which the communicative acts consist of sending meaning through signals to an audience that is monitored for understanding, with the goal of jointly achieving *shared understanding*;
- The idea of *layers of communication*, suggesting that a single utterance or action can have different meanings at different contexts; this is similar to the idea of 'double level language' in CSCW [10];
- The idea of *common ground* – shared knowledge that allows people to interpret each other's communicative acts, and to simplify their communication because they know how the other person is likely to interpret their contribution.

In this paper we employ both Clark's framework and the idea of feedthrough, because these best encompass the characteristics of the game-based interactions that we have observed, and because the temporal, turn-based, and back-and-forth nature of board games does seem to suggest the idea of a conversation of sorts being carried out by the participants.

To investigate games as conversations, we conducted an observational study where we asked participants to play a game of chess, checkers, or backgammon online; we then we asked them to discuss their interpretations of each move in the game. By comparing interview responses from both opponents we gained insight into the information flow and shared understanding that was present during the games. We use Clark's layers of interaction to understand the game communication, and consider four layers: the *physical layer* – the physical pieces and board; the *syntactic layer* – the rules which constrain the physical; the *strategic layer* – the players' use of the rules; and the *personality layer* – the expression of personal characteristics through strategy.

Games make interesting 'conversations' because although they are competitive, they are also based on cooperative activity at other layers. For example, communication at the syntactic layer is a cooperative activity concerned with making progress in the game. Players cooperate to make this level work by taking a place at the table, making a move during their turn, and so forth. In most on-line game sites, however, the basic rules are managed by the interface so that players do not have to explicitly negotiate conflicts. This means that the "conversation" at this layer typically proceeds without any misunderstandings or need for repair.

At the strategic layer, however, we found that game actions are much more equivocal and open to interpretation. Most of the time, expert players agreed about the meaning of game moves and what the move showed about the other person's intentions. However, there were many more misunderstandings than what typically occurs in verbal conversation – at the strategic level, individual turns are underspecified compared to verbal utterances. This is partly because people do not actually want to maintain shared understanding, and so strategies like conversational repair that are part of the semantic level of a verbal conversation are missing from a game; it is often to a player's advantage if their opponent does not understand their strategy. The underspecified nature of game moves was highlighted in a few instances where people deliberately attempted to deceive the other player. Finally, players gathered knowledge of their opponent's playing style and personality to adjust their own approach to the games. This knowledge came from both previous experiences with the opponent and interpretation of moves during the game.

These observations show that games can be a rich form of action-based interaction, and can be as subtle and diverse as many verbal conversations. This kind of analysis of games is important because games have not been thought of as vehicles for social interaction, but also because there are many design decisions that can affect communication in online game interfaces – particularly at the physical layer, where augmentations could enrich communication, and at the strategic layer, where the under-specified nature of the 'language of a game' is an important part of the gameplay that should not be artificially constrained.

2. RELATED WORK

Our investigation of games as conversations is based upon previous CSCW work on social interaction in online game sites, communication through artefacts, and Clark's [2] ideas about language and joint action.

2.1 Game-Based Conversation in Game Sites

Various studies of online games have noted that social interaction happens without explicit verbal utterances. For example, studies of Massively Multiplayer Online Games [4,9] have observed complex interaction between players with little verbal interaction. Similarly, McEwan et al. investigated the PlayOK game site [8] and, while finding a great deal of game activity, also found a very small amount of chat. They suggested that the moves within the game could be considered as communicative acts and that the resulting game conversations served as a replacement social interaction for the missing verbal exchanges.

This idea of actions as meaningful social interaction was also explored by Brown and colleagues in their study of the virtual environment *There* [1]. This study emphasised the importance of being able to "do things with others" and "perform" a friendship. In *There*, a core component of performing friendships was interacting around objects, and referring to those objects. The combination of these two ideas – actions replacing verbal utterances, and building relationships through action – led directly to this work.

2.2 Communication and Coordination Around and Through Artefacts

Much CSCW research has emphasised the importance of communication through artefacts. For example, workplace studies such Heath and Luff's study of a London Underground control room [6] showed how important it is for individuals to make their actions on artefacts visible to their colleagues. Public visibility resulted in strong mutual awareness of actions which enabled tightly interwoven actions. Heath and Luff's work also describes how individuals purposefully make actions visible on their own artefacts so that others can see them – essentially using an implicit communication channel for explicit communication purposes.

Studies of workplace interactions such as the London Underground show the importance of how people orient their bodies and their speech around workplace artefacts, but in a board game site, there is a clear and obvious shared artefact that everyone focuses on. This leads us to the concept of *feedthrough*, which describes how artefacts themselves can be a channel for communication [3]. When artefacts are manipulated, the feedback information that they produce can be received by everyone who can observe that information – and what is feedback to the person carrying out the manipulation is feedthrough to others. As Dix and colleagues state:

The presence of feedthrough effectively creates an additional channel of communication through the artefacts themselves. In real life, cooperating over physical objects, this communication through the artefact is often more important than direct communication. For example, imagine you are moving a large piano. You may say things to each other – 'move your end up a bit', 'careful of the step' – but in fact the most important thing is the feel of the other person's movements through the movements of the piano. This sort of communication is effective partly because it is tied so intimately to the work itself, and partly because it is implicit, unconsciously noticed and acted upon. ([3], p. 207)

As with the bodily orientation described above, feedthrough is primarily an implicit communication channel, but can be exploited for explicit communication as well. That is, once I know that another person is maintaining awareness of changes to artefacts, I can intentionally manipulate an object to send a signal without any verbal communication. This behaviour has been observed by several researchers, such as Norman's study of airline pilots: "When the captain reaches across the cockpit over to the first officer's side and lowers the landing-gear lever, the motion [...] not only controls the landing gear, but just as important, it acts as a natural communication between the two pilots, letting both know that the action has been done" ([14], p. 142).

In games, feedthrough is often used to coordinate actions such as turn-taking. However, feedthrough implies a level of indirection. In the piano example above, the movers are responding to changes in the piano, which happens to be connected to another person. In games, while the players are responding to changes in a shared artefact again, the board is the vehicle through which the players express themselves. Rather than the participants acting around the artefact, they use it as a medium for communication.

2.3 Language and Joint Action

Clark and colleagues (e.g., [2,15]) analyse real-world conversation using a framework of *Joint Actions* to describe successful communication. A successful communication act results in both parties having sufficient common understanding for the interaction to proceed. Joint actions are so named because building shared understanding through conversation is a joint project between sender and audience. The sender sends a *signal* with an intended meaning, and the audience attempts to understand it. Signals can take any form that sends meaning, such as verbal utterances, gestures, semaphores, or movement of objects. The sender must also be convinced that the audience is participating in the joint action, and must see that they understand the signal as intended. This is achieved as the sender observes the receiver for signals that they are cooperating in the joint action.

Clark indicates two particular types of joint action that communicate meaning without verbal interaction. First, *manifesting actions* are physical acts that completely replace verbal utterances. For example, Clark gives the example of placing groceries onto a checkout counter – this action is essentially the same as the utterance "I wish to purchase these items" ([3], p. 169). Second, *visual evidence* is a physical action that provides evidence to another person that they have been understood. Clark's example involves one person getting another to centre a candlestick on a table, and says "Okay, now push it farther – farther – a little more – right there. Good." ([3], p. 326). Each movement of the candlestick provides visual evidence that the instructions have been understood, and replace a repeated verbal utterance "is this the correct position?".

A critical foundation for all types of joint action is that the sender and audience start with some shared knowledge, or *common ground* [15]. Common ground is the mutual knowledge that people take advantage of to increase their communicative efficiency: for manifesting actions and visual evidence to work, for example, the sender has to understand what the receiver can see. In addition, the principle of least collaborative effort suggests that people expend only the minimum effort in composing an utterance that they believe is necessary for their message to get across to the hearer [15]. If they can exploit common ground, they can reduce the work that goes into communication.

Clark also develops the concept of *layers* in interaction. He explains layers through an example of children playing a Wild West make-believe game. The children's activities simultaneously happen on two layers: the first is the real world where they are in a suburban backyard, while the second is in the fantasy world that they have created. So digging in a pile of dirt (real world layer) corresponds to mining for gold (fantasy world layer). Each action exists in all layers but has different meanings. Robinson's idea of *double-level language* [10] is a similar concept as applied to group interaction, and suggests that successful groupware requires capabilities for at least formal and cultural channels of communication.

In our study, we make use of Clark's terminology and structure but our focus is on communication through game moves in online board games. This differs from Clark's everyday conversational settings because games have specific formal rules and because some aspects of the interaction are competitive. These elements can result in very different structure than cooperative conversation.

3. Study Methodology

The goal of our study was to explore the communicative power of moves in online board games, and the degree of shared understanding that is developed between players of these games even when there is no verbal interaction. We wanted to gain insight into the building of shared understanding, both about the game and opponent, as the game progressed. To achieve this, we asked people to play a game online and then participate in individual retrospective interviews where they discussed the meanings that they intended in each of their moves, and the meanings that they interpreted from each move by their opponent.

3.1 Participants

Participants responded to recruitment emails asking for expert players of Chess, Backgammon, or Checkers. We asked for expert players so that there would be interesting strategic play, and to produce insightful commentary on opponent strategy. The participants who responded to our request varied somewhat in experience, though all were able to play the games without clarification on rules.

Table 1: Study pairs by game type and expertise.

	Chess	Checkers	Backgammon
Beginner	1	1	
Intermediate	2	1	
Expert	2		2

Nine pairs participated in the study. shows the distribution of game types and expertise. Expertise levels were assigned by investigators based on both the players' own comments in the pre-questionnaire and the insight of their interview responses. All pairs were of approximately equal ability and fell within the same level of expertise.

We had three types of relationship between pairs: strangers who had not met before coming to the study session; friends who had not played together or had only played a few games; and friends who had played together a substantial amount.

3.2 Procedure

Participants first filled out a short questionnaire about their experience, relationship to their opponent, and how often they had played against that person. They then played a game of their choosing against each other online using the PlayOK.com site (see Figure 1). They were separated physically so that they could not converse verbally while playing. The game interface did provide a text chat and each group was told that they could use it if they wanted, but none of the pairs did. The games were twenty-minute timed games, meaning that each player had a maximum of ten minutes to make all of their moves.

After the game, each participant was interviewed separately for 30 minutes about the game they just played. The investigator set up a real world board and replayed each move. After each move the investigator asked open-ended questions about the meaning of each move (both the player's and their opponent's), such as "What did this move mean?", "Why did you make this move?", or "Why did your opponent make this move?" After each question, the interviewer often asked clarifying follow-up questions.

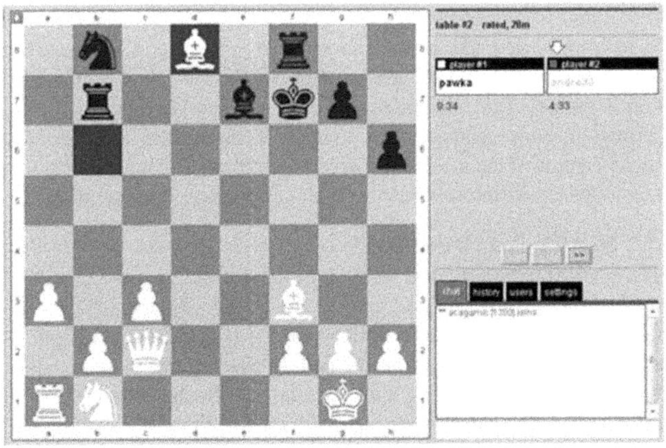

Figure 1: PlayOK game interface

3.3 Analysis of Shared Understanding in a Game as Conversation

One investigator watched videos of the interviews and summarised people's comments. We were interested in whether players were able to interpret information from their opponent's moves, and whether the game moves would lead to shared understanding at the different layers. We compared our summaries from both players and coded the interpretation of each move. Initially, we were just interested in whether both players agreed on what the move meant. However we quickly discovered that there were different reasons for disagreement that were worth teasing apart – sometimes players contradicted each other, sometimes they misunderstood, and sometimes they did not know what a move meant in terms of their opponent's strategy. Finally, we discovered some cases of deliberate deception. Our final coding categories for tracking shared understanding were:

1. *Agreement*: players agreed on the meaning of the move.
2. *Diverging interpretation*: players commented on different aspects of the meaning of a move.
3. *Misunderstanding*: a player misunderstood the intent of their opponent's move.
4. *Unknown*: a player did not know why a move was made.
5. *Contradiction*: players directly contradicted each other.
6. *Deception*: a player explicitly wished to deceive their opponent.

Moves often received multiple tags to reflect that multiple comments were made about each move, and that a single comment could fit multiple categories.

4. Observations: Four Layers of the Game-As-Conversation

We used Clark's concept of interaction layers to help understand the different types of communication that were occurring in the games. We used four layers:

1. *Physical*: the board and pieces used for the game
2. *Syntactic*: the rules of the game
3. *Strategic*: the dynamic and intentional progression through static states
4. *Personality*: the interpretation of the opponent through their use of strategy

4.1 Communication at the Physical Layer

The physical layer consists of the board and pieces (although it does not have to be physical – for example, it could be displayed on a screen as in the first part of our study, or on a real world board as in the second part). Players in general did not comment on the physical layer in the interviews, and seemed to take this layer almost entirely for granted – the only comment we received about this layer was from one player who expressed how different the real board looked and felt compared to the online game interface. There was such a strong shared understanding at this layer that players did not think about it, suggesting that people come to a board game with a substantial amount of common ground about what board games are and how they work. If the physical layer can be compared to a language (i.e., the "language of board games"), then all participants in our study were fluent speakers, and there were no episodes of miscommunication during the study. This is similar to verbal conversations in which native speakers do not consciously notice the mechanical production of sounds in the language.

The player's comment on the difference in appearance and feel of the real and online boards, however, hints at an interesting deeper issue that is relevant for online board game sites. In the online version of the games, player embodiments are extremely limited – when a player makes a move, their opponent sees nothing in the interface until the move is complete, and then sees their opponent's piece move. Importantly, there is no information available about the timing of the move – the opponent might be agonizing over several options, with expressions of indecision crossing their face, and their pointer hovering over different pieces; or, perhaps they simply paused to take a drink of coffee. It could be of great interest to see the differences in information gathered about an opponent's personality with different degrees of information provided at this level of the 'conversation'. We speculate that there is often a 'poker face' effect in more serious settings such as tournaments, in which players attempt to reduce their outward expression to hide their internal thoughts from their opponents. Even though players do not often consciously think about this layer, information can 'bubble up' to be used to make inferences at higher layers.

4.2 Communication at the Syntactic Layer

This layer specifies the basic rules of the game and is built on the foundation of the physical layer. For the game to be played it is not sufficient to have just the physical board and pieces – the game also needs rules specifying the starting state, the way that players take turns, the way that pieces can be moved, and the termination conditions for winning the game. Board pieces are moved according to strict rules; in checkers, for example, a piece can only move one space diagonally to an empty square (unless it jumps). The syntactic level of interaction is highly constrained, and so the "statements" made in this layer are well known to most players. If this layer is a language, it is "the language of chess" (or whatever game is being played).

Participants also made very little mention of this layer during our interviews. All of our participants were experienced enough to know the rules of the game (i.e., they were "fluent" in that language) and so these rules were accepted as common ground. Players also assumed that the interviewers shared this common ground, and so saw no need to discuss this layer. For example, participants assumed that we (the investigators) knew a knight could move to a particular place, and that we were more interested in *why* they moved it there than the mere fact that they had done so. The few comments that we heard during interviews were only from explicit prompting, and were often dismissive; for example, when an interviewer asked about a chess move that was forced, the participants replied *"That was the only move he had an option to do, so... [trails off]"*.

In only one case, a participant did make a comment that discussed the syntactic layer. He mentioned an obscure rule in chess ("en passant," a special kind of pawn capture), knowledge of which was often a good indicator of an experienced player. His comment indicated that there could be complexity in communication at the syntactic layer. This is similar to spoken conversation in which people make assumptions about a person's sophistication or level of learning based on their vocabulary. There is a wider range of expression in spoken language than in a board game, however; whereas people can be at many different levels of expertise in a language, there are only a few different levels of experience in the language of a particular game.

4.2.1 Signalling and Layers

At the syntactic layer, competitive games are more easily conceptualised as a cooperative activity. The players are engaging in a joint action to successfully complete the game. Both players work toward a common goal of a completed game. The work that they perform is making a legal action when it is their turn.

Using Clark's concept of *action ladders* [2], the signals of this communication are piece movements. This has to be true as piece movements are the only transmission of information between the players. The current player (A) moves a piece for her opponent (B) to perceive. The move is a signal that forms the basis for A to tell B that she has moved and it is now B's turn to move so that the game can progress. This signalling process with regard to turn taking is broken down in the action ladder in Table 2.

Table 2: Action ladder for game move.

Level	A	B
4	A proposes that it is B's turn to move	B considers the proposal that it is his turn to move
3	A signals that she has moved and asks B to move	B recognises that A is asking B to move
2	A presents movement of X as a signal.	B identifies A's movement of X as a signal
1	A moves piece X	B perceives that A has moved piece X

There is considerably more than signalling a change in turn that can be conveyed in moving a piece, however. Moves also communicate information about the state of the game such as new positions, captures, or even winning.

4.3 Communication at the Strategic Layer

The strategic layer is the competitive layer where players strive to gain advantage over their opponent and eventually win the game. Movements take on strategic and tactical meanings. For example, moving a bishop in chess may have several meanings, such as threatening the king if another piece in the way moves later (called a "revealed check"), placing pressure on a center pawn with other pieces, or starting a short tactical sequence that may result in a stronger position. While these meanings all make use of the rules of the game of chess (i.e., the syntactic layer), and are built upon those rules, they are not about making simple movements to jointly complete a game. They also involve something more than just the state of the board.

At the strategic layer, the meaning of a game action is much less clear than at the syntactic layer – whereas at the lower level a move is unequivocal (assuming both players are fluent in the rules of the game), strategic-layer meanings are much harder to determine. If we compare this layer to verbal interaction, interactions are structured like arguments – where interaction is to a degree antagonistic and where the true meaning and intention of a statement is not always obvious. In conversational arguments, people make statements that are opposed to the views of the other person, but do so in a way that there is a shared understanding of the content of the argument. As Jackson and Jacobs [7] state, the syntactic and strategic layers can be separated for both chess and argumentation:

Just as the rules of chess are independent of the planning processes that allow people play the game, so the rules of argument are independent of the comprehension processes that allow persons to see the relevance of data to [a] claim. ([7], p. 18).

We can draw the analogy further if we consider each move as a claim in an argument. When moving, a player puts forward a proposal that they should have influence over an area, threaten a piece, or some other part of strategy. The response is firstly another proposal or support for a previous claim, and secondly a rejection or counter to the opponent's move. This exchange continues until the disagreement is resolved and the game is won.

Another framework that can help to guide understanding of the strategic and syntactic layers is Grice's Maxims of Conversation [5]. Verbal conversations, even arguments, generally follow a set of conventions that allow the interaction to proceed to a mutually agreed-upon goal – namely, the resolution of the question under discussion. For the conversation to progress, participants have to contribute, and the maxims describe the properties of contributions.

Grice's framework consists of four categories of maxims, summarised in Table 3. At the syntactic layer, an online game is perfectly Gricean: each move contains just the right amount of information for a player to understand what has happened and what is expected as a reply. In an online system it is generally impossible to violate the game rules, and so the truth quality of each move is guaranteed. A move is always relevant to the progression of the game as it always means that the turn is over and the next turn should begin. Finally, the manner of a move is syntactically clear, unambiguous, brief, and orderly. At the strategic layer, however, game interaction often encapsulates these principles but also frequently bends or breaks the principles, as shown below.

Table 3: Grice's Maxims of Conversation.

Quantity	Make your contribution as informative as required Do not make your contribution more informative than required
Quality	Do not say what you believe to be false Do not say that for which you lack sufficient evidence
Relation	Be relevant
Manner	Avoid obscurity of expression; Avoid ambiguity Be brief; Be orderly

Before investigating each of the categories of shared understanding in players' interpretation of game moves (i.e., agreement, diverging interpretation, misunderstanding, contradiction, or deception), we compared the counts of each category for the different skill levels of our participants, and for the different game types. Figure 2 and Figure 3 show the total counts in each category. The figures suggest some potentially interesting differences between game types and skill levels: anecdotally, we found that there was less room for expressive communication in the simpler rules of checkers; backgammon seemed largely about risk management; and the complex interrelationships of chess pieces gave the most material for discussion. However, we have insufficient data in the current study to explore these issues with any certainty. Consequently, we consider data from all the games together for the remainder of our discussion.

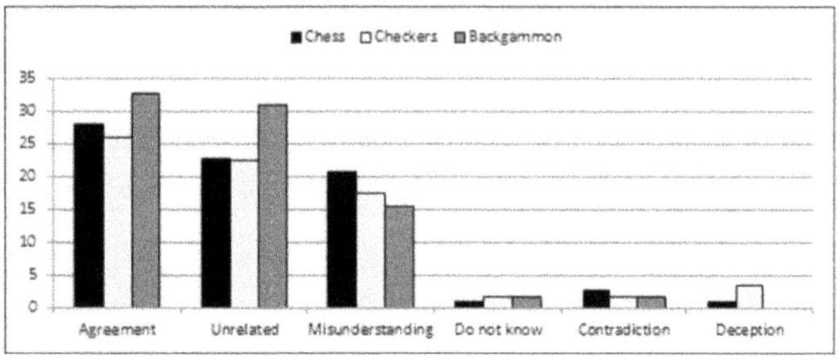

Figure 2: Total event counts for all games in each category of agreement, by game type.

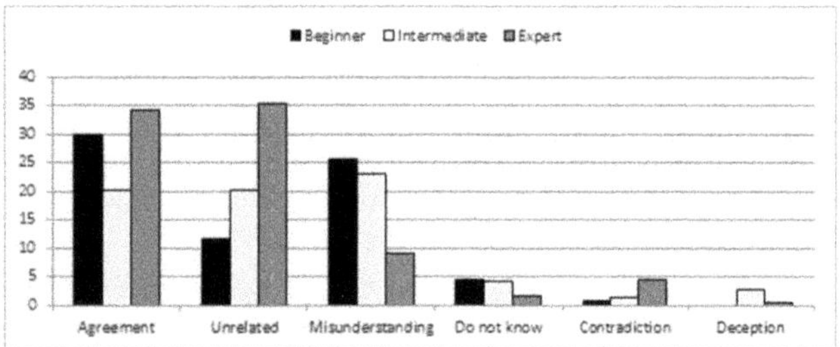

Figure 3: Total event counts for all games in each category of agreement, by player experience.

4.3.1 Agreement about the meaning of game moves

We coded agreements when players made equivalent comments about a move. It is important to note that they did not have to agree on the value of the move, just on the reasoning for it.

In Table 4 (a) the players agree about both the attacking and the positional benefits of a move in chess. Even in the very brief comments that they each made about this move, they both identified the same elements as important. This suggests that the communicative aspects of the move were clear at the strategic layer, and that the players had a shared understanding (even though shared understanding is not the goal). The example in Table 4 (b) shows a much more complex example of agreement. Despite the complexity of the situation and the reasoning behind the move, both players are in complete agreement about its meaning. In this case, the move was a reasonable replacement for the statement "I am protecting my pawn."

Approximately 25-30% of the time players were in agreement with each other. This is the category where they definitely achieved shared understanding in the sense of conversational argument. They may not have agreed on the value of the move, but they agreed on the meaning of the signal at the strategy layer.

4.3.2 Diverging interpretation

The results of our coding also showed a large number of moves where the two players discussed different aspects of the meaning of the move. Players were interviewed separately and the interviewer did not prompt specific topics, so this occurred often.

Table 4: Examples of agreement.

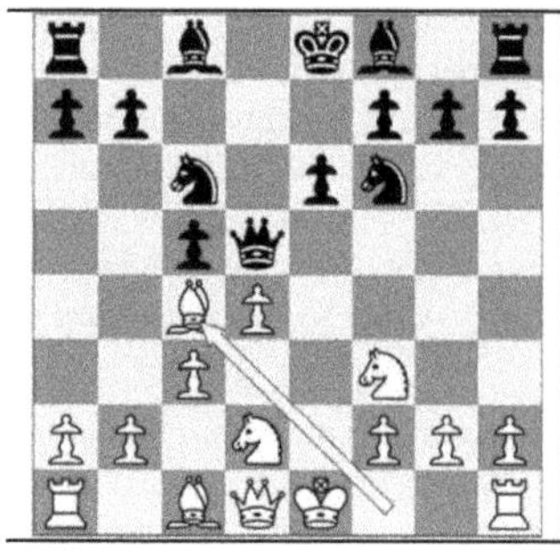	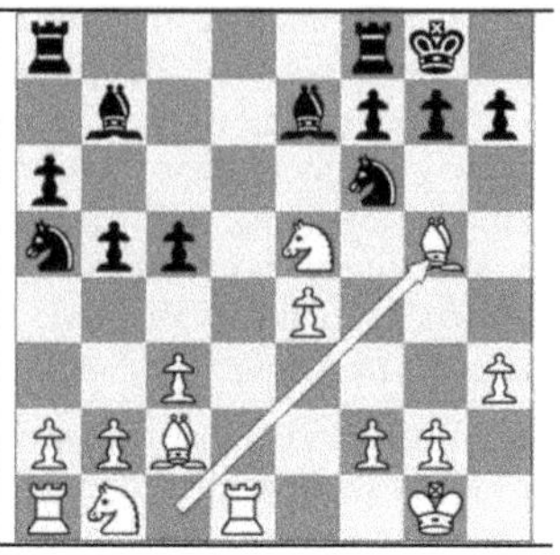
White's Comments	**White's Comments**
It accomplishes two things. So it lets me castle next turn if I feel like it. It also puts his queen under threat.	He's attacking this pawn [on e4] twice and I'm only defending it once. But the problem is if he ... takes the pawn with the bishop and then I take back with the bishop and he takes with the knight... his bishop on e7 is left hanging because of [my bishop on g5]. So he can't take the pawn now, it's protected.
Black's Comments	**Black's Comments**
It gave him an opportunity both to attack my queen and to castle on the next move.	I have two pieces attacking the pawn and he has one defending, if I use [my knight] to attack it, he can just take my bishop so it's essentially a defence against that.
(a)	(b)

Table 5 (a) shows an example of comments that were coded as diverging. The main reason for the divergence is the underspecified nature of individual moves, especially at the start of a game – that is, a move could mean many different things at the strategy level, and the overall meaning cannot be determined without more information (i.e., further moves). Although this seems different from most conversations (where the syntactic meaning of a statement often closely corresponds to its strategic meaning), there are situations where statements are similarly underspecified. For example, when an orator begins a speech with a personal anecdote, it is difficult to determine the importance of the story to the overall argument, even though the meaning of each sentence is clear.

In our interviews, players speculated on the directions that the game could take from the point of the move in question. However, the space of options is often so large that they were easily able to talk about different topics. In the example of Table 5 (a), both players were experts and the situation was simple enough that we as investigators were reasonably sure that they knew and would agree on the topics that the other was discussing. An interesting point made by White is that early moves are "all in some book somewhere and we know exactly what's happening" – this is similar to structured conversations such as formal speeches, where the early stages of the speech have a pattern that is well known but that does not provide much information about the overall meaning of the argument.

Table 5 (b) demonstrates another source of diverging interpretation. One player chose to discuss the possible outcomes of the move, while the other player chose to comment directly on the quality of the move. This exchange also helps to explain the one main anomaly of Figure 2, where experts had many more instances of diverging interpretation. More experienced players gathered so much information from the state of play that when the interviewer asked them to comment they chose from a wide range of topics. Given so many options, it is hardly surprising that they often chose differently. In contrast, beginners only saw the immediately obvious aspects and so talked about the same things, either agreeing or disagreeing more clearly on the meaning of a move.

Table 5: Examples of diverging interpretation.

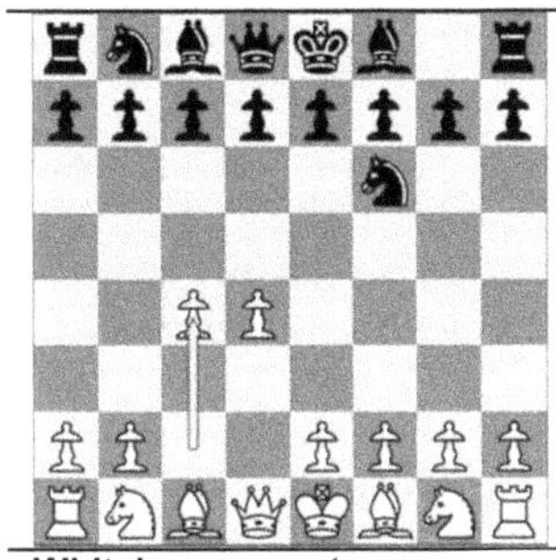	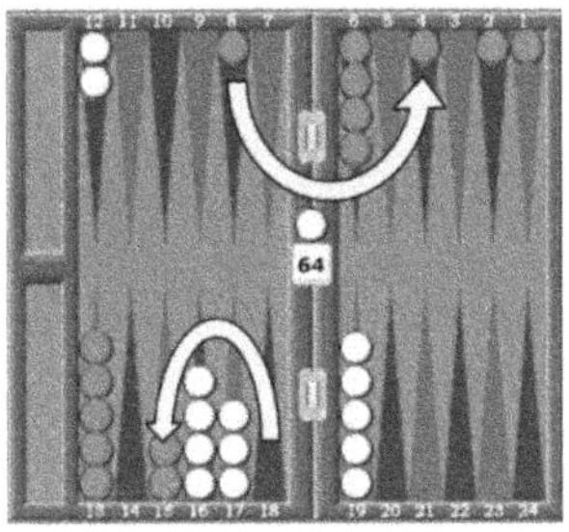
White's comments	**White's comments**
White: Typical continuation of a d4 opening. [...] and his next move he has to choose which opening he wants to play. Interviewer: So his options are still pretty open? W: I would say so yeah. I mean if he defends like this [pawn to g6] to stay really open, [pawn to e6] he could go into a queen's gambit or something else. Or he could play the Benko which is [pawn to c5]. I: Do you think he has a good impression of what you're trying to do at this point? W: Oh yeah, he knows exactly what I'm trying to do ... we're just playing theory for the first 10 to 15 moves. This is all in some book somewhere and we know exactly what's happening	[18 to 15] makes sense that he wants to save the lonely piece here. And again he was obsessed to hunt down the lonely piece of mine but it's a very dangerous play. See I could get any one, two, or four and he would start over, it would cost him a lot to again move a lonely piece all around again to here.
Black comments	**Red's Comments**
I've got a few choices here, such as [pawn to f6] allows the bishop to come out [to b4] then [his] knight comes out [to c3]. I didn't feel like playing that ... I could have played this [pawn to e6], then this [pawn to f5] or that [pawn to d6]. I didn't feel like playing that. I played [pawn to c5] and this leads to an Indian opening system. It's not as popular as it used to be but I'm familiar with it and it leads to interesting positions.	You know that's actually not a bad move. It's slightly risky No actually it was a bad move. Well, if you calculate the odds it would probably be pretty close but looking back I probably should have saved one of these guys. That's a much better choice. Bad move from me.
(a)	(b)

4.3.3 Misunderstanding about game moves: failure of shared understanding

There were several instances where players misunderstood the meaning of their opponent's move, did not know the meaning, or came to the opposite conclusion than their opponent. For example, the example in Table 6 shows Black believing a move to be weak, while White has fairly strong motivations for it. It is likely that both (expert) players agreed on the strategy represented by the move, the strategic layer also involves judgements of the value of the strategy.

Experts had fewer cases of misunderstanding than other players, which makes sense as experts have more practice in understanding strategies and intentions in the game. That there are many instances of this category, however, is an example of how game interactions differ from verbal conversations. Misunderstandings do occur in verbal conversation, but people monitor their audience for understanding and are generally quick to make repairs. It is interesting to note that game moves are underspecified compared to verbal utterances, but in situations where verbal statements become more equivocal and more open to interpretation (e.g., in situations such as negotiations or discussions about relationships), misunderstandings can occur more frequently.

Part of the structure of games is that players do not want their opponent to know their strategy, and so misunderstanding is a desirable part of the game's design, as it leads to greater uncertainty in the outcome. As a result, game moves frequently do not fulfil the Gricean maxims, particularly in terms of making contributions informative and avoiding obscurity. In general, the strategy-layer meaning of moves is strongly underspecified, which is an important part of the game.

Table 6: Example of Misunderstanding.

White's Comments
Protecting my knight. Another reason for the ... Benko [strategy] on the queen side is that a lot of the time these pawns will become queens ... I am a pawn up after all ... so it's possible that I could crash through him on the queen side and gain a queen.
Black's Comments
I guess it's OK. I didn't expect it to tell you the truth. I was expecting him to do something [in the centre] because that would be in keeping with ... he's trying to bust me open to get to my king ... I didn't think it was the best move but I guess it wasn't horrible.

4.3.4 Unknown meaning

In a few cases, a player explicitly stated that they did not know the reason for their opponent's move, as illustrated in Table 7. There were very few times when players were unable to interpret a move – possibly because players always had a perspective of the game and so fit their opponent's moves into that constructed narrative.

Table 7: Example of Unknown.

Black's Comments
I'm not sure. That one, I'm really not sure.

4.3.5 Deception

There were an extremely small numbers of explicit deceptions. Players assumed that their opponent knew what they were doing, at least in the larger strategy sense. Expert players were well justified in that opinion, while intermediate and beginner players were unaware of divergence.

Table 8: Example of deception.

Black comments
I was hoping that he wouldn't see what I had intended in the next few moves ... I thought he would think it's a weak move ... he would get to exchange this fairly strong bishop for his knight and also weaken my pawn structure. So I'm assuming it would be too good to be true for him. Almost. Almost too good to be true.
B: He did go for it. He did take it. And so what he was expecting of course was [pawn takes the knight] otherwise he wouldn't have done that. But what I can do now is because this knight's no longer protected by ... this knight I can bring my rook down and capture that knight. So that's a fair exchange, but now his knight's being threatened and his bishop's being threatened. [H]e can still understand my overall strategy [but] it's the little shorter strategies – tactics I guess – that are tougher to see.
White Comments
I didn't even think, I just thought if I take the bishop right now we just take another pair of pieces off the board ... I just did it automatically, I took the bishop. But the problem with that, of course, is that if I take the bishop he doesn't have to take back with the pawn, he can take with the rook down here [rook to d2] because [the knight] no longer has any defence and now he's attacking both my undefended bishop here and my knight up here and so I end up losing a piece. [As] soon as I took the bishop I saw that ... I had blundered, but it was too late.

The example in Table 8 shows one of the rare cases of deliberate deception. There are two comments here that demonstrate that, for most of the time, each player is very aware of what their opponent is doing. First, Black comments that while White knows his overall strategy, it is still possible to use small deceiving tactics. Second, Black says that "as soon as I [moved] I saw that I had blundered" giving a good indication of exactly how long he was deceived.

Deception was rare, but is interesting as it shows players deliberately breaking the Gricean maxims. Common strategies were: to make the move ambiguous in the hope that the opponent picked an incorrect interpretation (as in Table 9); playing less informative moves first in an attack; and not over-playing the situation with too many moves. All of these strategies make use of the underspecified nature of moves at the strategy level.

4.4 Communication at the Personality Layer

As might be expected, the existing relationship of the pairs – strangers, friends who did not play, and friends who played often - made a substantial difference at the personality layer.

Strangers were interesting in terms of how they formed opinions during the game. Unsurprisingly, they started with very general assumptions about other players. For example, one player said, *"People are usually a bit more reluctant to take first blood I find"* when explaining why he thought his opponent would not engage in a piece swap in chess. They refined their opinions based on how the opponent played. For example:

"I start to gauge people when they capture pieces [and] based on which pieces they're willing to sacrifice. So I look at what they're willing to risk rather than position."

"[That the opponent did not swap pieces] tells me that he's a little more defensive and not as aggressive as a player – not as willing to take risks."

More interestingly, they also made use of the limited information in the online interface, for example:

"He doesn't make any unnecessary moves, he doesn't do anything stupid, he sees that there are different opportunities there. You can see that from the reaction time, he doesn't consider doing something stupid up here or something like that."

There were many different impressions formed about opponents:

"So he likes to attack, he doesn't want to defend."

"he is playing fun. Like, I play a little more like, more cautious, more taking precaution"

"it's just ... a posturing, getting prepared to do something maybe two to three moves ahead."

"[he's] kind of tricky over the chessboard"

With friends that had not played before, we also saw some evidence that knowledge of personality could be used to interpret game moves. For example, one player explained an opponent's move by saying "*because she's a very tentative person*". We did not see many examples of this, however.

Friends that had played each other many times before often referred to their opponent's playing style. There was a particular congruity between expert chess players in this relationship category, especially at the start of games as they played set sequences based on established theory ("from book" as they referred to it). They recognised the sequences and knew the favourite sequences of their opponent, commenting *"this is our usual opening"* or *"we always play this opening"*.

At this layer, players make use of information from all the other layers to form impressions of opponents. This is analogous to drawing conclusions about someone during verbal conversation based on language and accent (physical layer), dialect and word choice (syntactic layer), and topics of conversation and kinds of rhetorical structures (strategy layer). In general, just as in verbal contexts, people will use whatever information is available to them from the game to make inferences about the person they are interacting with – and it was clear that the moves of the game provided ample information about personality.

The common ground established at this level is primarily in establishing membership of a cultural group. The game conversations are analogous to Simmel's sociable verbal conversations [13], where people are participating because they enjoy the interaction. Each utterance establishes or extends a link to some piece of common ground to further the conversation. For example, in a chess game, each move can reference simpler techniques (e.g. revealed check, forking, pinning) to more complex strategies about establishing control of territory and managing threats. The extreme example of this shared understanding is when the experts played "from book", where they recognised established opening sequences to games. Using and recognising these components of gameplay both establishes the player as part of the in-group (and helps to determine where they are in the group) and establishes a level of common ground between the players.

5. Implications for Design

Our main contribution is the exploration of the idea of game moves as communicative acts, and a more detailed understanding of games as rich and subtle vehicles for shared social interaction. However, we believe that the details of the study are of interest to designers and other researchers, and some specific lessons can be taken from the work. First, we reinforce the earlier conclusions from Brown and Bell's [1] and McEwan et al.'s work [8] about games being legitimate forms of social interaction, even without verbal conversation. Our analysis shows that action-based interaction is rich and diverse, and is worth considering during the design of game sites and game interfaces.

Second, the current paucity of information provided by the physical layer in online games is worth commenting on. Current designs only make available the minimum amount of information needed to play the games. Any additional information provided at this level would potentially provide a richer communicative experience. For example, providing a telepointer in the game interface could provide additional information at the physical layer (e.g., how confidently a player makes a move) that could add complexity to a "language" that is currently taken almost entirely for granted.

Third, the strategy layer provides some interesting possibilities and questions for computational environments. There are many possibilities for enhancing strategy-layer aspects in an online game with features such as trying out moves, heat maps of what other players have done, analysis of the opponent's moves, and so on. Such augmentations could make it easier for players to interpret each other's moves, but could also ruin the beauty of the very under-specified "strategy language" of the game. Making it easier for people to understand each other at the strategy layer may not be a good thing – this is a topic we plan to explore in future work.

Finally, we consider our general methodological approach to be a contribution and believe it would be interesting to apply it in a variety of other situations involving artefact-based communication. We were able to gain considerable insight into the communication by participants performing a full interaction followed by in-situ, semi-formal interviews and analysing the communication using a layered language model. In some situations, these methods would be difficult to repeat, such as activities that are much less constrained than a board game. However, the idea is worthwhile and, for example, it would be interesting to see what this kind of analysis would reveal in a workflow-oriented setting.

Combining these points shows the how our work here can contribute to design of collaborative systems. By using Clark's framework and our analysis techniques, likely modified for a new situation, researchers can build a more complete picture of communication that includes actions. Our discussion here highlights how the different layers of communication need to be treated differently – allowing more explicit communication at the physical layer or restricting the rules at the syntactic layer does not necessarily mean removing rich, ambiguous expression at the strategic or personality layers.

In some cases, more restriction at the lower layers leads to more creativity and expression at the higher. For example, memes involve simple composition of well-known images (and sometimes text), and players of the game Minecraft™ have built some amazingly complex structures in a very simple environment. Engaging in these activities establishes people in a group and makes them part of an action-based conversation.

6. Conclusion

Many board game sites, despite being highly socially active, do not have much verbal conversation. To try and account for this anomaly, previous research has suggested that games can be substitutes for verbal conversations. To explore this idea we explored board game interactions according to Clark's theories of language use [2]. By analysing in-situ interviews from board game players through four Clarkian layers – physical, syntactic, strategic, and personality – we found that the physical and syntactic layer interactions are cooperative, and form the foundation for the competitive strategic layer. While the interaction resembles a verbal conversation in many ways, there is more misunderstanding than in many verbal conversations – the strategic layer differs substantially from a verbal conversation in terms of its goals and structures, with shared understanding no longer the primary goal of the interaction. Finally, we found that the personality layer is typically under-specified but players are still able to make judgements about their opponents' styles and personalities.

Our study shows that even simple and highly-constrained games like chess and checkers can be rich and detailed 'conversations' between players. Action-based interaction has been to some degree overlooked by CSCW, compared with research into verbal interaction. Building on foundational work by several researchers, we have provided new understanding of how artefact-based communication and interaction works – and that it is detailed, complex, and important. We also contribute a method for investigating action-based interaction that could be applied to other settings, and suggest ways in which our analysis can inform designers' work in supporting different layers of communication through a game's interface.

Acknowledgments

Our thanks to the expert players who participated in the study, and to NSERC and the GRAND NCE for supporting the research.

7. References

[1] Brown, B., & Bell, M. (2006). Play and Sociability in There: Some Lessons from Online Games for Collaborative Virtual Environments. In R. Schroeder & A.-S. Axelsson (Eds.), *Avatars at Work and Play* (Vol. 34, pp. 227–245). Berlin/Heidelberg: Springer-Verlag.

[2] Clark, H. H. (1996). *Using language*. New York: Cambridge University Press.

[3] Dix, A. (1997). Challenges for cooperative work on the web: An analytical approach. *Computer Supported Cooperative Work (CSCW)*, 6(2), 135–156.

[4] Ducheneaut, N., Yee, N., Nickell, E., & Moore, R. J. (2006). "Alone together?": exploring the social dynamics of massively multiplayer online games. In *Proc. CHI'06* (pp. 407–416). New York, NY, USA: ACM. doi:10.1145/1124772.1124834

[5] Grice, H. P. (1975). Logic and conversation. *Syntax and Semantics*, 3, 41–58.

[6] Heath, C., & Luff, P. (1991). Collaborative activity and technological design: task coordination in London underground control rooms. In *Proc.ECSCW'91* (pp. 65–80). Norwell, MA, USA: Kluwer Academic Publishers.

[7] Jackson, S., & Jacobs, S. (1980). Structure of conversational argument: Pragmatic bases for the enthymeme. *Quarterly Journal of Speech*, 66(3), 251–265. doi:10.1080/00335638009383524

[8] McEwan, G., Gutwin, C., Mandryk, R. L., & Nacke, L. (2012). "I'm just here to play games": social dynamics and sociality in an online game site. In *Proc. CSCW'12* (pp. 549–558). New York, NY, USA: ACM. doi:10.1145/2145204.2145289

[9] Nardi, B., & Harris, J. (2006). Strangers and friends: collaborative play in world of warcraft. In *Proc. CSCW'06* (pp. 149–158), New York, NY, USA: ACM. doi:10.1145/1180875.1180898

[10] Robinson, M. (1991). 'Double-level languages and co-operative working.' *AI & society*, 5(1), 34–60.

[11] Schmidt, K., & Wagner, I. (2004). Ordering systems: Coordinative practices and artifacts in architectural design and planning. *Computer Supported Cooperative Work (CSCW)*, 13(5), 349–408.

[12] Schmidt, Kjeld, & Simonee, C. (1996). Coordination mechanisms: Towards a conceptual foundation of CSCW systems design. *Computer Supported Cooperative Work (CSCW)*, 5(2-3), 155–200. doi:10.1007/BF00133655

[13] Simmel, G. (1949). The sociology of sociability. (E. C. Hughes, Trans.) *The American Journal of Sociology*, 55(3), 254–261.

[14] Norman, D. *Things that make us smart: defending human attributes in the age of the machine*. Basic Books, 1993.

[15] Clark, H., and Brennan, S., Grounding in Communication, in *Readings in Groupware and Computer Supported Cooperative Work*, R. M. Baecker ed., 1991, 222-233.

Habits of the Heart(rate): Social Interpretation of Biosignals in Two Interaction Contexts

Nick Merrill
BioSENSE Lab, School of Information
University of California, Berkeley
Berkeley, CA, USA
nick@ischool.berkeley.edu

Coye Cheshire
BioSENSE Lab, School of Information
University of California, Berkeley
Berkeley, CA, USA
coye@ischool.berkeley.edu

ABSTRACT
We investigate interpretations of a biosignal (heartrate) in uncertain social interactions. We describe the quantitative and qualitative results of a randomized vignette experiment in which subjects were asked to make assessments about an acquaintance based on an imagined scenario that included shared heartrate information. We compare the results of this experiment in adversarial and non-adversarial contexts of interaction. We find that elevated heartrate transmits cues about mood in both contexts, but that these cues do not appear to impact assessments of trustworthiness, reliability and dependability. Counter to our expectations, we find that normal (rather than elevated) heartrate leads to negative trust-related assessments, but only in an adversarial context. Our qualitative analysis points to the role of social expectations in shaping contextual interpretations of heartrate, and reveals individual differences in the way interpretations are constructed. We unpack some of the ways that social meanings can arise from biosensor data, and discuss considerations for those designing interactions with wearables.

CCS Concepts
H.5.3. Group and Organization Interfaces.

Keywords
Computer-mediated communication; biosignals; heartrate; trust; cooperation

1. INTRODUCTION
What could your heartrate possibly tell another person about you? Past work has cited intimacy as a grounds for heartrate sharing [1,16,21,26]. However, it is not clear that these applications capture the full expressive capacity of heartrate as a computer-mediated cue. Does sharing a heartrate always "enhance" intimacy and trust? What is the social interpretation of an elevated heartrate in different contexts of interaction?

As biosensors become smaller and cheaper, more consumer devices are presenting users and application designers with opportunities to share their physiological data with others [18,22,23].

GROUP'16, November 13–16, 2016, Sanibel Island, FL, USA.

ACM 978-1-4503-4276-6/16/11…$15.00.
http://dx.doi.org/10.1145/2957276.2957313

In fact, designers are already beginning to play with the notion that social and contextual interpretation may color people's interpretations of biosignals. The advertising copy for Cardiogr.am, one smartwatch app, reads,

Your heart beats 102,000 times per day, and it reacts to everything that happens in your life—what you're eating, how you exercise, a stressful moment, or a happy memory. What's your heart telling you?

This application, along with many others, capitalizes on the idea that people project contextual interpretations onto heartrates, making them potentially interesting to share socially. However, few empirical studies examine how context shapes the interpretation of another person's heartrate [25], or how these interpretations might affect attributions of mood or emotion, or fundamental social attitudes such as trust.

In this paper, we investigate how individuals make social interpretations about a rudimentary biosignal (heartrate) in conditions of uncertainty, focusing on dyadic interactions between acquaintances. Dyadic relations, which are present in all groups, function as a fundamental starting point for understanding interpersonal collaboration and group interactions [4].

We describe the quantitative and qualitative results of a randomized vignette experiment in which subjects make assessments about an acquaintance based on an imagined scenario that included shared heartrate information. We examine two contexts in this study: an uncertain, non-adversarial context and an uncertain, adversarial context. These two contexts, differing only by a few words, ask participants to imagine they are meeting someone "for a movie" (non-adversarial) or "to discuss a legal dispute" (adversarial).

We find that a high heartrate transmits negative cues about mood in both contexts of interaction, but that these cues do not appear to impact assessments of trustworthiness, reliability or dependability. Counter to our initial predictions, we find that *normal* (rather than elevated) heartrate leads to negative trust-related assessments, but only in the adversarial context. In qualitative assessments of subjects' attitudes and beliefs, we find that normal heartrate in the adversarial condition conflicts with expectations about how the participant believes the acquaintance should feel, signaling a lack of concern or seriousness, which appears to lead individuals to view the acquaintance as less trustworthy. In contrast, subjects in the non-adversarial context relate elevated heartrate to empathy and identification rather than trustworthiness. We also find a small number of subjects read different social interpretations onto the heartrate signal, including a very small minority who did not infer any relationship between the heartrate and the social situation.

Where past work establishes that heartrate has contextual meanings, this study aims to establish the relative effect of the *elevated* (versus *normal*) signal on social attitudes regarding trust, reliability and dependability. Understanding these effects could shed light on why people agree or refuse to disclose biosignals in interpersonal relationships and groups, and what individuals risk by making such disclosures. As we better understand the social interpretations of biosignals, we can inform the design of technologies that facilitate biosignal sharing in groups.

2. SOCIAL INTERPRETATIONS FROM PHYSIOLOGICAL SIGNALS

To date, most work on the contextual interpretation of sensor data has focused on individual interpretation of individual data (c.f. quantified self). In contrast, our work attempts to move toward an understanding of how biosignals are interpreted in interpersonal interactions – the quantified *social* self. This shift is motivated, in part, by an increasing number of consumer applications that support sharing biosignals such as heartrate. Especially pertinent to our study, it is not well understood what heartrate actually *signals* to another person in a social interaction. How might the contextual, social interpretation of another person's biosignals affect social interpretations of mood (e.g., anxiety, calmness), or attitudes about trustworthiness and dependability?

Goffman [12:56] makes an important distinction between the cues that we intend to give to others, and those that are "given off" unintentionally through our numerous non-verbal actions and behaviors. We view physiological signals such as heartrate as a form of non-verbal signaling that can "give off" more information to others than the sender may desire [15]. This type of personal data revealed through discreet sensors paired with mobile communication technologies has, until recently, been unavailable in most forms of social interaction.

As Donath (2007) argues, when we use communication technologies for interpersonal and group interactions, we do so as a way to keep track of our evolving relationships with other people and, critically, to know whom to trust [10]. Crucially, we rely on signals such as verbal communication, facial expressions, gestures, and other patterns of activity to help us fill the gap between what someone is doing and why they are doing it [11]. So, when new forms of biosensory information, like heartrate, are suddenly available in social interaction, significant questions arise surrounding the inferences that we might draw from these signals, how the context in which they are presented may shape our interpretations, and how this information may affect our subsequent beliefs and behaviors towards others.

2.1 Contextual interpretations of sensor data

Prior work interrogates the contextual interpretation of personal data from certain kinds of sensors [6,7], but physiological data has received less attention, despite two crucial differences from sensors that capture information such as location (e.g., GPS). First, biosensor data are intrinsically ambiguous: whereas a GPS coordinate refers to one specific place, heartrates do not have one-to-one mappings to physical activities or emotions. Second, physiological phenomena vary from person to person; 60bpm could be high or low depending on whose heartrate it is.

A relatively large body of work has looked at how the transmission of physiological data might play a role in computer-mediated communication. One class of application has attempted to explicitly encourage or discourage certain behavioral outcomes, making some biosignals apparent such that the transmission of the data acts as a social cue [2,19]. Another class of prototypes explores how signals might affect feelings of intimacy, particularly between romantic partners [1], and several applications focus on the transmission of heartrate as a means to achieve this effect [16,25,26].

Despite a number of applications that transmit biosignals socially, there remains little work on how people *interpret* the biosignals they see from others. Past studies on heartrate sharing indicate that people do read social emotional cues in the heartrates of other people [20,25]. However, it is still not well-understood what social meanings these signals take on in different social contexts and, in contrast to the findings of previous studies, it is not clear that the social consequences of transmitting physiological data will always be positive (e.g., increased intimacy).

In this study, we are particularly interested in trust, due its centrality to the study of group behavior, and to the claims of prior research on heartrate sharing [16]. We apply the encapsulated interest view of trust [14], in which one person's interest is intrinsically connected with the interests of another person [5]. Since trust between individuals is only salient in the presence of risk and uncertainty [8], we test our hypotheses about the effects of heartrate information on evaluations of trust in social contexts with different degrees of risk and uncertainty.

2.2 The social meaning of a heartrate

Compared to social interpretations of physiological signals, interpretations of one's own signals are slightly better-understood from empirical research. Individuals' interpretations of their own heartrate have received particular attention (see [24] for a review). Studies have generally revealed that, when individuals believe that their heartrate is elevated, they sometimes believe their mood and emotions to be more negative [27].

If lay interpretations of one's own heartrate can yield negative self-interpretations, sharing heartrate information could also yield negative effects on mood and trustworthiness, particularly during uncertain interactions where something is at stake (such as time, money, or other valued resources). To investigate, we use a mixed-methods approach combining quantitative and qualitative analyses of a survey-based vignette experiment.

3. INTERPRETING BIOSIGNALS IN UNCERTAIN SOCIAL INTERACTIONS

Based on aforementioned studies of individual's negative emotional interpretation of their own heartrate, we believe that this negative valence will be mirrored in people's interpretations of the heartrates of others in uncertain situations. Our investigation begins with two key predictions about negative assessments of one's partner in an uncertain social situation. We test both hypotheses in two different contexts of interaction (adversarial and non-adversarial) to understand how the context of risk and uncertainty affects social interpretations of heartrate.

3.1.1 Heartrate and Mood

Past work indicates that people tend to make negative inferences about mood and emotion from elevated heartrates [9,13,27]. As such, our first hypothesis predicts that participants will adjust their attitudes about the mood of their partner when their partner's heartrate is elevated, as opposed to normal:

Hypothesis 1: When individuals believe that their partner has an elevated heartrate in an uncertain social interaction, they will report their partner as being (1a), less calm (1b), more emotional (1c), and more easily upset (1d), compared to those who believe that their partner has a normal heartrate.

3.1.2 *Heartrate and Trustworthiness*

Where Hypothesis 1 predicts that individuals will make negative assessments about an acquaintance's mood based on elevated heartrate, our second hypothesis predicts that individuals will make negative assessments about dispositions to *behave* in a reliable, dependable and trustworthy manner. Thus, both hypotheses stem from the same base assumption that, all things being equal, elevated heartrate has a primarily negative connotation with attitudes and behaviors of another person.

Hypothesis 2: When individuals believe that their partner has an elevated heartrate in an uncertain social interaction, they will make negative assessments about the partner's trustworthiness (2a), reliability (2b), and dependability (2c), compared to those who believe that their partner has a normal heartrate.

4. A SURVEY-BASED EXPERIMENT

To test our hypotheses, we conducted a survey-based vignette experiment. Vignette studies involve short descriptions of a scenario, designed to elucidate opinions, attitudes, and beliefs about that particular situation [17].

In this vignette study, we compare two different contexts of interaction. We do not create separate hypotheses for the two different contexts; rather, we are interested in comparing and contrasting the two different contexts to see how they might interact with social interpretations of heartrate. We provide our participants with either an adversarial or a non-adversarial social context. In the adversarial scenario, the participant is waiting to meet an acquaintance about a legal dispute. In the non-adversarial scenario, the participant is waiting at a movie theater for an acquaintance so that they can see a film together.

In all scenarios, the acquaintance sends a message via smartphone indicating that he or she is running late due to slow traffic. The person who is waiting does not know if the acquaintance will make it on time or not, or whether the acquaintance is being honest about their tardiness. Within each context, we manipulate a small piece of information about the heartrate of the acquaintance: We tell the participant that the heartrate of the acquaintance has been shared by the acquaintances' smartphone and it is either elevated or normal.

4.1 Sample

Our sample was undergraduate students recruited from the population of a large, public university on the West Coast of the U.S. Potential participants were asked to participate in a short online survey, and they did not know the nature of the questions or the topic of the study in advance. All participants were paid a $5 Amazon gift card. One hundred and three participants (103) completed the experiment survey instrument. The pool was weighted toward women; in our sample, 65% were women and 34% are male, and 2% (2 subjects) did not identify with either gender. With random assignment, the same overall gender split was maintained across conditions. The mean age of participants was 23.

4.2 Vignettes

Each participant in the study saw only one of the four possible vignettes. After the vignette, the survey included free response questions about subjects' reactions to and interpretations of the situation described in the vignette, as well as 7-point Likert scale questions (Strongly Agree to Strongly Disagree) in which subjects evaluated the other person's disposition ("This person is emotional", "This person is anxious", "This person is easily upset", and "This person is calm"). In addition, we asked participants to indicate whether the other person was "trustworthy," "reliable," and "dependable" using the same 7-point agreement scale.

There are two contexts of interaction (adversarial and non-adversarial) and two heartrate conditions (normal and elevated), creating four distinct vignettes based on social context and heartrate (HR): adversarial elevated HR, adversarial normal HR, non-adversarial elevated HR, and non-adversarial normal HR. Participants were randomly assigned into one of the four conditions. We manipulated these heartrate conditions by making a key wording change as indicated in the two context vignettes below.

Non-Adversarial:

You planned to meet your acquaintance for a movie at seven. It's 7:15, and you're standing alone in front of the theater. Your phone buzzes, and you see a message from this person that says, "I'm running late, traffic was really slow." Through your smartphone, you are able to see this person's heartrate, which the app designates as [normal / elevated]. *It is currently 75 degrees and sunny. Your movie starts at 7:20.*

Adversarial:

You planned to meet your acquaintance at seven to discuss a difficult legal dispute between the two of you. It's 7:15, and you're standing alone in front of the meeting spot. Your phone buzzes, and you see a message from this person that says, "I'm running late, traffic was really slow." Through your smartphone, you are able to see this person's heartrate, which the app designates as [normal / elevated]. *It is currently 75 degrees and sunny.*

5. QUANTITATIVE RESULTS

We apply both quantitative and qualitative analyses to investigate our research questions and hypotheses. The study is based around an experimental design, but we also place significant emphasis on open-ended responses to better understand participants' thought processes, beliefs, and rationale for their choices in the vignettes.

Our first hypothesis predicts that individuals will make negative attributions about the mood of the acquaintance in this uncertain situation when they believe that the acquaintance has an elevated heartrate (compared to normal heartrate). Given our four separate measures of mood, we conducted a multivariate analysis of variance (MANOVA) to test the hypothesis that there are one or more mean differences between the normal/elevated heartrate conditions, and/or between the two contexts of interaction (non-adversarial and adversarial).

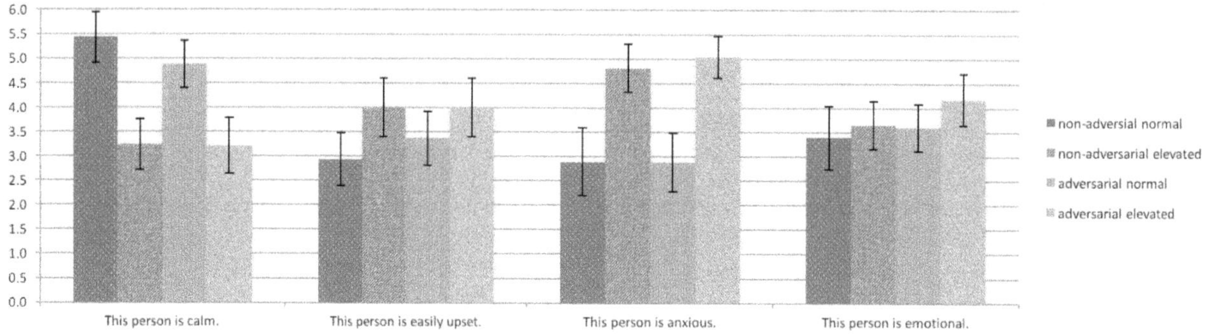

Figure 1. Mood-related evaluation means by condition (bars represent standard deviation).

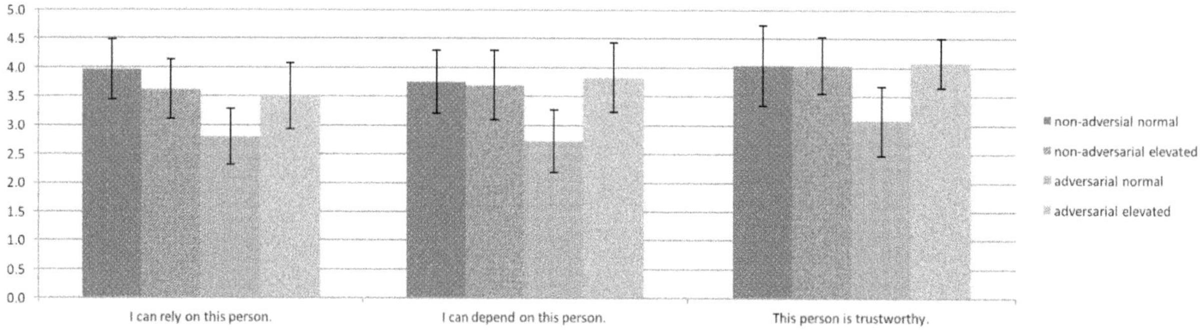

Figure 2. Trust-related evaluation means by condition (bars represent standard deviation).

We found a strong, statistically significant effect and a medium practical association between emotional attributions and heartrate condition, F (4, 96) = 32.89, $p < .001$; partial eta squared = .58. Turning to the individual outcomes, we find that subjects' perceptions of the acquaintance in the vignette's anxiety, his/her tendency to be easily upset, his/her tendency to be emotional, and his/her lack of calmness were all significantly higher in the elevated heartrate conditions when compared to the normal heartrate conditions (see Figure 1). We found no significant effect for the two contexts of interaction, F (4, 96) = 1.072, p = .38, and no significant effect for the context x heartrate condition interaction, F (4, 96) = 1.65, p = .17. In sum, individuals significantly rate acquaintances with elevated heartrate as more anxious, easily upset, and less calm than those with normal heartrates. In the non-adversarial context, individuals did not rate the acquaintances as significantly more emotional in the elevated condition compared to normal, but this difference was statistically significant in the adversarial context.

The context of interaction (non-adversarial, adversarial) does not have any effect on mood ratings. With clear statistical and practical significance for the overall effect of mood attributions by heartrate condition in both contexts of interaction, Hypothesis 1 is supported.

Our second hypothesis predicts that individuals will make negative assessments about how certain they are regarding the acquaintances' trustworthiness characteristics when the individual has an elevated versus a normal heartrate. We find a statistically and practically significant effect for the heartrate conditions, F (3, 97) = 4.19, $p < .01$; partial eta squared = .12. However, we also find statistically significant effects for both the context of interaction, F (3, 97) = 2.82, $p < .05$, and the context x heartrate condition interaction, F (3, 97) = 2.75, $p < .05$.

A closer inspection of the individual mean differences reveals that the means for all three outcomes (reliability, dependability and trustworthiness) are all *lower* in the normal condition compared to the elevated condition in the adversarial context (see Figure 2). This result is the opposite of what Hypothesis 2 predicts.

In the non-adversarial context, we find no statistically significant differences in trust-related evaluations between heartrate conditions. Thus, it is the interaction between the context and the heartrate condition that explains the results: individuals rate acquaintances with normal heartrates significantly *lower* in terms of trustworthiness, dependability and reliability than those with higher heartrates—*but only in the adversarial condition.* Individuals do not rate acquaintances any differently on these three outcomes between the heartrate conditions within the non-adversarial context. In fact, the means for these outcomes are very similar across all conditions and contexts, with the sole exception of the adversarial, normal condition. The mean differences for the trust-related outcomes between the normal and the elevated conditions within the adversarial context are all highly statistically significant ($p < .01$) and highly practically significant: Cohen's d = 1.1 (trustworthiness); 1.07 (dependability); 0.68 (reliability).

Hypothesis 2 is therefore not supported. However, the strong findings (statistically and practically significant) in the opposite direction from our prediction warrant further exploration in the qualitative results and discussion below.

6. QUALITATIVE RESULTS

Directly after the vignette, participants were asked four free-response questions about their reactions to the situation described in the vignette: 1) How do you react to this message, 2) What makes you react this way, 3) What is the ideal outcome of this situation, and 4) What is the worst possible outcome of this situation? The open-field responses were coded into two broad, non-overlapping categories: those that mentioned a negative emotional reaction to the scenario, and those that included a mention of what the other person in the situation might be thinking or feeling. Responses in the latter category were further sub-divided by experimental condition for analysis.

6.1 Adversarial Context

This section reports on the qualitative analysis of free responses given by subjects in the adversarial (legal dispute) context.

6.1.1 Normal heartrate

In the adversarial (legal dispute) context, many subjects who saw a normal heartrate directly indicated that they were negatively adjusting their appraisal of the other person, either in their sympathy toward the other person, or in their judgment of that person's trustworthiness. We find that normal heartrate in the adversarial condition appears to be in conflict with the subjects' expectations about how the acquaintance should feel..

I will feel less sympathetic to this person because their heart rate doesn't show that they are stressed or upset.

I feel annoyed because a higher heart rate would indicate that the person cares about the meeting

The normal heartrate implies that my acquaintance isn't taking this meeting seriously. However, it is difficult to say that my acquaintance does not care or is lying. For example, I have no knowledge of the traffic to determine if my acquaintance is lying.

Here, participants read a lack of care or concern into the acquaintance's normal heartrate, but did not feel the biosignal provided definitive evidence as to whether or not the acquaintance was being truthful. For some participants, however, normal heartrate indicated deception:

I would think this person is lying. If they were in a rush, their heartrate would be faster.

I feel like he is lying and is taking his time I say "hurry up please I can't wait any longer. You are lying to me" It makes me angry to see that his heartrate is normal through all of this. Mine is spiking out of control.

These responses could help to explain the surprising quantitative results of Hypothesis 2 in the adversarial context: the intersection of the adversarial context with normal heartrate led many participants to view the acquaintance as unsympathetic and, in some cases, disingenuous. As we see below, these negative reactions stand in stark contrast to the interpretations in the elevated heartrate condition.

6.1.2 Elevated heartrate

In general, participants in the adversarial context viewed elevated heartrate as a signal that the acquaintance cared about being late.

Since it shows that the person is trying their best to come, as shown by the elevated heartrate, I would still feel ok.

I would believe my acquaintance. An elevated heartrate tells me she is probably rushing/hurrying over. I have data from the phone to validate what she is saying to a certain extent.

In these quotes, participants used the elevated heartrate to validate their acquaintance's claim, thus positively assessing their honesty. A few subjects spoke to the power of data in creating what appeared to be objective facts about the other person.

I won't be angry because seeing this person's heart rate being elevated, it must mean they're in a hurry. Seeing metrics make it easier to believe someone.

I feel like I'm in a position of power. With the capacity to check someone's heart rate, I can instantly tell how they are feeling. In a way, it is almost like a lie detector.

In both of these quotes, we see attitudes about the presumed authority or "neutrality" of data *interacting with beliefs about the body* (namely, the relationship between heartrate and emotion, or truthfulness), creating a context in which wearables data can be used to construct social judgments or assessments. How these assessments play out will vary in different social situations, with different sensors, and in different contexts of use. Such variations should be explored much more deeply in future work.

6.2 Non-Adversarial Context

This section reports on the qualitative analysis of subjects in the non-adversarial context (meeting for a movie),

6.2.1 Normal heartrate

In the non-adversarial context, many participants reported that normal heartrate conveyed a lack of appropriate social concern:

"At first I believe that maybe my acquaintance is running late; however, when I discover that their heart rate is normal I wonder why it isn't higher..."

"It seems like they are too nonchalant about it"

"I feel frustrated because it seems like the person isn't concerned about making me wait."

In these cases, interpretations focused on what the other person was thinking or feeling. As we saw in the adversarial context, normal heartrate seems to be in conflict with expectations. However, unlike in the adversarial context, we did not find evidence that subjects were re-appraising their trust toward the other person. Interestingly, two participants read the normal heartrate positively, as a sign that the other person was telling the truth.

"If his heartrate is normal, then he is probably not lying. I would still be slightly annoyed at this."

"it's OK. her heartbeat was normal, so no lies"

These subjects seemed to feel annoyed by the partner's normal heartrate. However, in contrast to the adversarial context, no subjects explicitly stated that the other person seemed less trustworthy, honest or reliable as a result.

6.2.2 Elevated heartrate

The majority of respondents in the non-adversarial indicated that the elevated heartrate was a token of the other person's regret for being late to the movie. Many participants in this condition indicated that they would have a more sympathetic reaction to the text message as a result of seeing an elevated heartrate.

Elevated heart rate tells me that the acquaintance at least cares that he/she is late and there's no point in getting mad.

I would text her back "No problem! I'll grab the tickets and will wait for you out front." It seems obvious she's in a hurry to get there, and is late because of traffic.

I will feel apologetic because I can see that this person's heartrate is elevated and I do no want him/her to feel worried/ stressed about making a movie.

I would feel anxiety about being late for the movie and pity because they seem anxious. I don't like being rushed and get anxious when I am rushed

In these responses, heartrate generally seemed to signal that the acquaintance was stressed. While stress is generally assumed to be negative, in this case it seems to engender identification and empathy with the acquaintance. This example gestures toward the highly contextual nature of heartrate's social meaning, and why more work should examine the consequences of these different interpretations.

6.3 Other interpretations of heartrate: Relevancy, validity, creepiness

In addition to the major themes noted above, we also found a few other important interpretations. A small handful of participants (12 total) mentioned aspects other than the immediate social interaction in relation to the shared heartrate display. The points that surfaced surrounded concerns about privacy, doubts about the accuracy of the sensing device, and doubts about the relevance of heartrate to the particular context.

6.3.1 Privacy and disclosure concerns

Only three subjects in the entire experiment pool (n=103) commented on the potential for invasiveness or over-disclosure in heartrate sharing.

(non-adversarial + normal heartrate) I feel like I'm violating my acquaintance's private information by knowing their heart beat.

(adversarial + normal heartrate) I do suspect the person is lying since his heart rate is normal. I think the extra info of the heart rate is the reason I have a neg. suggestion towards the person. I think the reported heart rate is a bad idea.

Given that heartrate sharing is not (yet) widely deployed in consumer devices, it is somewhat surprising that only a few subjects commented on privacy concerns. This could be partially explained by the fact that the scenario was imagined, rather that simulated, and because subjects might have anticipated our interest in their reactions to the interface.

6.3.2 Validity of the device's data

Four subjects mentioned the possibility that the device, or the intuitive inferences drawn from it, may be inaccurate.

(adversarial + elevated heartrate) Heart rate could be elevated for many reasons, and just like studies with lie detectors, it may possibly indicate lying, but also could indicate other things. It's just a number, not a definite answer of lying or not. And even then, you've got to forgive people.

(adversarial + normal heartrate) The normal heartrate implies that my acquaintance isn't taking this meeting seriously. However, it is difficult to say that my acquaintance does not care or is lying. For example, I have no knowledge of the traffic to determine if my acquaintance is lying. Additionally, my smartphone can be wrong; I don't know how accurate this technology is, especially since it is a very new piece of technology.

Our study did not reference any existing device, so it is possible that the fallibility of particular devices was not on subjects' minds. However, the trust that people place in sensing devices, and the presumed authority of their data, should be explored thoroughly in future work.

6.3.3 Relevance of heartrate to the social situation

Only two subjects in the entire study who mentioned heartrate felt that the data was not necessarily related to the specific social situation described in the vignette:

(non-adversarial / elevated heartrate) My initial reaction would probably be to ask them if everything is okay. Their heart rate should probably not be elevated since they are only driving and weather conditions are not abnormal.

(adversarial / normal heartrate) There may be reasons why his/her heartrate is normal and why he/she may be late in the first place, so I'm not concerned about that."

Across all conditions, the fact that the vast majority of participants inferred a causal relationship between the heartrate information and the particular social situation highlights the relatively reliable effect of context in priming subjects to draw such inferences. Our results indicate that simply making the heartrate salient, in the absence of other cues, invites people to project a causal narrative on the mood, intentions, and behavior of others.

7. DISCUSSION

We began this investigation by asking how individuals might interpret heartrate information in uncertain social interactions. Our hypotheses are both based on the simple rationalization that the kinds of negative attributions that people tend to make about their own heartrate will be echoed in their social interpretations of others' heartrates in uncertain contexts. We found, however, a much more complex story about the social interpretation of biosignals and the context of interaction.

Our first hypothesis predicts that an elevated heartrate will be negatively associated with assessments about mood and dispositions in uncertain social interactions, both adversarial and non-adversarial. We found strong support for this hypothesis in both contexts, across our outcome attributions, in line with prior works' findings regarding interpretation of one's own heartrate [24]. Our second hypothesis predicts that an elevated heartrate will lead to negative assessments about the partners' trustworthiness, dependability and reliability. As with our first hypothesis, we expected that pre-existing negative connotations with heartrate might translate into negative expectations of trust-related behavior.

We rejected the second hypothesis in both contexts of interaction. In the non-adversarial context, we found no difference in assessments of trustworthiness, dependability or reliability in the elevated and normal heartrate conditions. Furthermore, we found that the average assessments on these three outcomes were nearly identical between the elevated condition in the adversarial context and the elevated and normal conditions in the non-adversarial context.

Most surprisingly, we find a decrease in trustworthiness, dependability, and reliability in the *normal* heartrate condition, but only in the adversarial context. As noted in the quantitative results, the differences between the elevated and normal conditions in the adversarial context were highly statistically significant: each of the trust-related measures saw an average decrease of one full point (on a 7-point scale) in the normal condition compared to the elevated condition.

To help explain these results, we turn to our qualitative analyses of the adversarial (legal dispute) context. Subjects in the adversarial context seemed to have *expected* their partner to have an elevated heartrate. When the partner had a normal heartrate, participants viewed it as evidence that s/he is not bothered enough, not taking the situation seriously, or perhaps even lying. Indeed, many participants explicitly stated in the open text responses that they trusted the partner less because his or her heartrate was normal.

Why do we not see the same effect in the non-adversarial context? Turning again to the qualitative data, we find that participants took elevated heartrate as a token of their acquaintances' genuine desire to arrive on time. It seems that elevated heartrate led many participants in the non-adversarial context to increase their empathy, identification, and understanding of the partners' situation. Thus, even though individuals in the non-adversarial condition associate elevated heartrate with anxiety, lack of calmness, and being easily upset, the negative emotional interpretations do not seem to translate to evaluations of one's trustworthiness, dependability or reliability.

Taken together, we see that heartrate does not inherently (or consistently) affect trust-related outcomes. Instead, social expectations shape interpretations of the heartrate biosignal to create highly contextual, socially-specific meanings. CMC researchers have long noted that, when cues are omitted from technology-mediated interaction, people tend to fill in the gaps [3,10]. However, individuals may interpret new types of interpersonal data in ways we do not yet understand. Our work provides some evidence that such interpretations might have real social consequences. The fact that heartrate alone can significantly alter one's perception of trustworthiness in an adversarial context is an important step towards the larger goal of unpacking social interpretations (and their effects) in technology-supported social interaction. (For one thing, the mostly positive social interpretations of heartrate observed in past work are likely highly dependent on the social context in which they were observed).

Finally, we note a diversity of opinions and interpretations within conditions. For example, a few subjects took normal heartrate as proof of honesty, the opposite view from the majority of subjects. A few subjects did not feel there was necessarily any relationship between heartrate and the social situation at hand. A small minority (three subjects) mentioned concerns around privacy or disclosure. The wide range of views, sometimes contradictory, highlights the complexity intrinsic to interfaces that collect and share biosignals, and warrants future studies into social and contextual interpretation of data from wearable devices.

8. LIMITATIONS

Our vignette experiment examined a single type of scenario in two different contexts, using text-based answers. We still have a limited picture of the range of theoretically important contexts in which individuals may observe and interpret biosignals about others, and a limited understanding of how the rich cues present in realistic interaction contexts might bare on our findings. Our study focused on a first-time interaction with an imagined heartrate sharing interface. We do not know how our findings would hold over time, and it is very likely that social meanings of any biosignal could become more consistent over time. The vignette scenario was contrived from believable, but currently non-existent smartphone technology. Either due to participants' suspension of their disbelief or due to their actual attitudes about the heartrate sharing, few participants raised questions regarding privacy implications of these scenarios.

Since the vignette study took place online, we could have missed the sorts of rich contextual cues that might be captured by live interviews or other in-person methods. Furthermore, the internet presents a wide array of distractions to survey-takers, and our survey was not able to detect the participants' attention on the task (e.g.., we could not detect whether the subject was switching between tabs in their web browser, or taking breaks during the survey), nor did we monitor how long subjects spent filling out the survey.

9. FUTURE WORK

Our experiments provide evidence that interpretations of biosignals from sensors (such as wearables) can affect social attributions and behaviors towards others. Nevertheless, many questions persist. Future work should approach similar topics with controlled, lab-based experimental methods. Controlled, behavioral experiments could help us ask more specific questions about how elevated heartrate affects perceptions of risk in uncertain interactions, e.g. when money is at stake. Such studies could lead to a more robust understanding of how the transmission of biosignals might affect social behavior. Future work should also investigate the degree to which our findings are unique to heartrate. Other biosignals (e.g., galvanic skin response, electroencephalography or EEG), could offer different affordances for sense-making. It is unclear from our work how the social interpretation of the signals from these devices could affect social behaviors such as dyadic and group trust.

Future work should also investigate the mechanisms by which contextual interpretations of heartrate arise. Specifically, future work should study the effect of the signal's representation on the attributions made by participants. In this study, subjects saw a normative interpretation of heartrate ("elevated" versus "normal"); however, it is unclear how a more more or less ambiguous, or more or less numerical interface might have affected our results. Meanwhile, the meaning of a given biosignal is certainly mediated by a number of factors, including culture and lived experiences. Much work remains in determining how biosignals give rise to any interpretations, and to what extent these interpretations are influenced by both beliefs about a given signal and the way interfaces represent this signal.

Finally, future work should more closely examine the relationship between people's social interpretations of biosensor data, and their assessment of the risk associated with disclosing these signals. As biosensing devices become more pervasive, people will more often be faced with decisions to disclose these data to others, either socially, or for services (e.g., health care, insurance) [23]. Consumers' willingness to (or refusal) to disclose their signals will certainly stem from their intuitive interpretation of what these signals might say about them, at least in part. As such, processes of consent in disclosing wearables data present a clear priority for future work.

10. CONCLUSION

We find that sharing heartrate can negatively influence trusting attitudes. However, heartrate alone does not communicate trust. Instead, individual's social expectations interact with the heartrate data to produce context-specific meanings. Complicating matters further, our qualitative data reveal a diversity of interpretations regarding the relevance and meaning of a heartrate in context, and the privacy implications of biosensing technologies. Our findings advance and complicate our understanding of the role that biosignal sharing can play in social, computer-mediated contexts, and motivate more detailed study into the mechanisms by which social interpretations arise from basic physiological signals.

11. ACKNOWLEDGMENTS

This work was supported by funding from the National Science Foundation (ACI-VOSS 1322270). Thanks to Noura Howell for her comments on earlier versions of this paper.

12. REFERENCES

1. Genevieve Bell, Tim Brooke, Elizabeth Churchill, and Eric Paulos. 2003. Intimate Ubiquitous Computing. *In: Proceedings of Ubicomp 2003, ACM,* Press, 3–6.
2. Tony Bergstrom and Karrie Karahalios. 2012. Distorting Social Feedback in Visualizations of Conversation. IEEE, 533–542. http://doi.org/10.1109/HICSS.2012.222
3. Kirsten Boehner, Rogério DePaula, Paul Dourish, and Phoebe Sengers. 2007. How emotion is made and measured. *International Journal of Human-Computer Studies* 65, 4: 275–291.
4. Coye Cheshire, Alexandra Gerbasi, and Karen S. Cook. 2010. Trust and Transitions in Modes of Exchange. *Social Psychology Quarterly.* http://doi.org/10.1177/0190272509359615
5. Coye Cheshire. 2009. *eTrust: Forming Relationships in the Online World: Forming Relationships in the Online World.* Russell Sage Foundation.
6. Eun Kyoung Choe, Sunny Consolvo, Jaeyeon Jung, Beverly Harrison, and Julie A. Kientz. 2011. Living in a glass house: a survey of private moments in the home. ACM Press, 41. http://doi.org/10.1145/2030112.2030118
7. Sunny Consolvo, Ian E. Smith, Tara Matthews, Anthony LaMarca, Jason Tabert, and Pauline Powledge. 2005. Location disclosure to social relations: why, when, & what people want to share. ACM Press, 81. http://doi.org/10.1145/1054972.1054985
8. K. S. Cook, T. Yamagishi, C. Cheshire, R. Cooper, M. Matsuda, and R. Mashima. 2005. Trust Building via Risk Taking: A Cross-Societal Experiment. *Social Psychology Quarterly* 68, 2: 121–142. http://doi.org/10.1177/019027250506800202
9. Michael D. Decaria, Stewart Proctor, and Thomas E. Malloy. 1974. The effect of false heart rate feedback on self-reports of anxiety and on actual heart rate. *Behaviour Research and Therapy* 12, 3: 251–253. http://doi.org/10.1016/0005-7967(74)90122-3
10. Judith Donath. 2007. Signals in social supernets. *Journal of Computer-Mediated Communication* 13, 1: 231–251.
11. Judith S Donath and others. 1999. Identity and deception in the virtual community. *Communities in cyberspace* 1996: 29–59.
12. Erving Goffman and others. 1978. *The presentation of self in everyday life.* Harmondsworth.
13. Jun Gu, Chen-Bo Zhong, and Elizabeth Page-Gould. 2013. Listen to your heart: When false somatic feedback shapes moral behavior. *Journal of Experimental Psychology: General* 142, 2: 307–312. http://doi.org/10.1037/a0029549
14. Russell Hardin. 2002. *Trust and trustworthiness.* Russell Sage Foundation.
15. Noura Howell, Laura Devendorf, Rundong Kevin Tian, et al. 2016. Biosignals as Social Cues: Ambiguity and Emotional Interpretation in Social Displays of Skin Conductance. *DIS '16 Proceedings of the Designing Interactive Systems Conference*, ACM.
16. Joris H. Janssen, Jeremy N. Bailenson, Wijnand A. IJsselsteijn, and Joyce H.D.M. Westerink. 2010. Intimate Heartbeats: Opportunities for Affective Communication Technology. *IEEE Transactions on Affective Computing* 1, 2: 72–80. http://doi.org/10.1109/T-AFFC.2010.13
17. N. Jenkins, M. Bloor, J. Fischer, L. Berney, and J. Neale. 2010. Putting it in context: the use of vignettes in qualitative interviewing. *Qualitative Research* 10, 2: 175–198. http://doi.org/10.1177/1468794109356737
18. Jacob Kastrenakes. 2014. Apple Watch uses four sensors to detect your pulse. *The Verge*. Retrieved from http://www.theverge.com/2014/9/9/6126991/apple-watch-four-back-sensors-detect-activity
19. Taemie Kim, Agnes Chang, Lindsey Holland, and Alex Sandy Pentland. 2008. Meeting mediator: enhancing group collaboration with sociometric feedback. *CHI '08 Extended Abstracts on Human Factors in Computing Systems*, ACM, 3183–3188.
20. Gilad Lotan and Christian Croft. 2007. imPulse. ACM Press, 1983. http://doi.org/10.1145/1240866.1240936
21. Hyeryung Christine Min and Tek-Jin Nam. 2014. Biosignal sharing for affective connectedness. ACM Press, 2191–2196. http://doi.org/10.1145/2559206.2581345
22. Mike Murphy. 2015. Nikon made a camera that lets dogs take photos of things they like. *Quartz*. Retrieved from http://qz.com/407959/nikon-made-a-camera-that-lets-dogs-take-photos-of-things-they-like/
23. Jose Pagliery. 2015. Would you wear a tracker to get an insurance discount? *CNN Money*. Retrieved from http://money.cnn.com/2015/04/08/technology/security/insurance-data-tracking/
24. Brian Parkinson. 1985. Emotional effects of false automatic feedback. *Psychological Bulletin* 98, 3: 471–494. http://doi.org/10.1037/0033-2909.98.3.471
25. Petr Slovák, Joris Janssen, and Geraldine Fitzpatrick. 2012. Understanding heart rate sharing: towards unpacking physiosocial space. ACM Press, 859. http://doi.org/10.1145/2207676.2208526
26. Julia Werner, Reto Wettach, and Eva Hornecker. 2008. United-pulse: feeling your partner's pulse. ACM Press, 535. http://doi.org/10.1145/1409240.1409338
27. David Young, Richard Hirschman, and Michael Clark. 1982. Nonveridical heart rate feedback and emotional attribution. *Bulletin of the Psychonomic Society* 20, 6: 301–304. http://doi.org/10.3758/BF03330108

Near Real-Time Peer-to-Peer Shared Editing on Extensible Data Types

Petru Nicolaescu
RWTH Aachen University
Lehrstuhl Informatik 5
Ahornstr. 55
52074 Aachen, Germany
nicolaescu@dbis.rwth-aachen.de

Kevin Jahns
RWTH Aachen University
Lehrstuhl Informatik 5
Ahornstr. 55
52074 Aachen, Germany
jahns@dbis.rwth-aachen.de

Michael Derntl
Eberhard Karls Universität
Tübingen eScience-Center
Wilhelmstr. 32
72074 Tübingen, Germany
michael.derntl@uni-tuebingen.de

Ralf Klamma
RWTH Aachen University
Lehrstuhl Informatik 5
Ahornstr. 55
52074 Aachen, Germany
klamma@dbis.rwth-aachen.de

ABSTRACT

Near real-time collaboration using Web browsers is becoming rapidly more and more popular for many applications such as text editing, coding, sketching and others. These applications require reliable algorithms to ensure consistency among the participating Web clients. Operational Transformation (OT) and more recently Commutative Replicated Data Types (CRDT) have become widely adopted solutions for this kind of problem. However, most existing approaches are non-trivial and require trade-offs between expressiveness, suitable infrastructure, performance and simplicity. The ever growing number of potential use cases, the new possibilities of cutting-edge messaging protocols that shaped the near real-time Web, and the use of N-way communication between clients (e.g. WebRTC), create a need for peer-to-peer algorithms that perform well and are not restricted to only a few supported data types. In this paper, we present YATA, an approach for peer-to-peer shared editing applications that ensures convergence, preserves user intentions, allows offline editing and can be utilized for arbitrary data types in the Web browser. Using Yjs, its open-source JavaScript library implementation, we have evaluated the performance and multiple usage of YATA in Web and mobile browsers, both on test and real-world data. The promising evaluation results as well as the uptake by many commercial vendors and open-source projects indicate a wide applicability of YATA.

GROUP '16, November 13-16, 2016, Sanibel Island, FL, USA

DOI: http://dx.doi.org/10.1145/2957276.2957310

CCS Concepts

•Human-centered computing → Collaborative and social computing; Computer supported cooperative work; Collaborative and social computing systems and tools; Synchronous editors; *Collaborative interaction; Open source software;* **•Computing methodologies → Concurrent algorithms;**

Keywords

Near real-time collaborative editing; commutative replicated data types; operational transformation; peer-to-peer information systems

1. INTRODUCTION

Near real-time (NRT) collaboration techniques have been intensively studied by the CSCW community during the past three decades [6, 30, 26, 29]. Mostly directed towards shared editing, highly relevant works include OT [6] algorithms and systems for enabling concurrent editing on the Web. These approaches leverage optimistic and reliable concurrency control mechanisms that lead to widely adopted OT-based systems such as Google Docs. A major advantage is that these systems do not require any locking mechanisms to ensure consistency of the shared data [10]. In a NRT setting, the user agents apply edits immediately to their local copy, while concurrently sending notifications of those changes via communication protocols to the remote user agents. All copies have to eventually have the same content, regardless of the order of the received operations or problems that might occur during the message propagation, such as temporary connection loss.

Recent advances on the Web allowed the development of fast and reliable communication protocols, such as WebRTC, Websockets, XMPP over Websockets, Server-Sent Events, which were also quickly adopted by Web communities, industry and academia. Besides enabling the message propagation technology stack required for shared editing systems, such protocols can leverage the use of peer-to-peer (P2P) shared editing algorithms and offer a fast and reliable communication infrastructure for their implementations. Thus, P2P approaches became a viable alternative to the more traditional client-server approaches [3]. This is due to the fact that each collaborator receives the updates in a N-way communication and applies them locally, without the need to wait for acknowledgment data, orders or transformed operations from a central server. In consequence, existing NRT collaboration algorithms need to adapt to new performance requirements, which is not a trivial task, especially in the case of massive collaboration, with a scaling number of users and changes [20].

With few exceptions, available OT algorithms are designed for client-server architectures. Algorithms that do support N-way P2P message propagation still rely on propagating a state vector (e.g., COT [29]) with each message. Moreover, algorithms that need preprocessing on the server side cannot be used in such P2P settings. In the past decade, CRDT algorithms [20, 2, 21, 23] emerged in the distributed systems specialization area and were also used in collaborative editing [1]. These have a small document update size and do not rely on vector clocks (e.g., the WooT approach [20]), and can therefore suit the new communication protocols and practices on the Web. A short comparison of the different algorithms is given in Section 2.

Regardless of being P2P or a client-server approach, the available NRT collaboration tools (e.g. OT-based) mostly support linear data or other specific ones (e.g. tree-like [11]) for ensuring the above described properties. Applications based on complex models must therefore map the underlying data to the data structure that is supported by the used collaboration framework. However, this process is time consuming, application-specific, and often hard to achieve. Moreover, there are few open-source implementations that work directly in Web browsers, can be used P2P and offer a developer-friendly, easy and intuitive way for rapidly enabling NRT collaboration on custom data types.

To overcome these shortages of existing algorithms, we present a new approach called YATA (Yet Another Transformation Approach) for enabling NRT collaboration on extendable data types and Yjs, its open-source implementation. We have developed an efficient algorithm that ensures the convergence and intention preservation for collaboration on shared data types. By design YATA inherently leads to fewer conflicts, exposes a favorable run time complexity, supports offline editing (i.e. given a peer that is joining the collaboration session with unsynchronized changes) and collaboration on various data types. The algorithm uses an internal linked list representation, similar to the CDRT approaches WooT [20] and WooTH [1]. However, as it has been proven that keeping deleted operations leads to a loss of performance, YATA solves this disadvantage by introducing a garbage collector for avoiding a drastic increase of unnecessary operations.

For exploiting YATA in Web applications, the algorithm was implemented as an open-source framework called Yjs[1] [19], which can be used with multiple communication protocols, including P2P, federated or client-server. By means of Yjs, which is already garnering interest from the open-source community, we have observed YATA's performance and consider it to be very promising for leveraging lightweight applications, where collaboration logic can be easily engineered on the client side. Finally, besides the usage in real-world open-source products, Yjs has been thoroughly evaluated in a simulated distributed environment for performance, testing the conflict resolution and its scalability, with very good results.

The rest of this paper is organized as follows. First, in Section 2 we give a short introduction to consistency maintenance algorithms, their development within the CSCW community and describe their most relevant features. Section 3 describes the YATA approach, offers a formal proof that it converges regardless of the number of peers involved in collaboration and presents a time and space complexity analysis. Furthermore, we offer the details for extending the approach to other data types in Section 4. Section 5 shortly describes the Yjs framework. The consistency tests performed for our approach and the usage of the framework in real applications are presented in Section 6. Finally, Section 7 summarizes the main contributions and provides an outlook for this work.

[1]http://y-js.org

2. RELATED WORK

Previous studies present various techniques for solving conflicts in collaborative editing settings. Coined during late 1980s, concurrency control [6, 27] includes locking (pessimistic, mutually exclusive mechanism), transactions, single active participation (token-based participation), dependency detection (timestamps for conflict detection), differential synchronization (client-server asynchronous approach) [7] and three-way merge (classic versioning systems).

The most prominent mechanisms for optimistic concurrency control are OT [6, 26, 27, 28] and CRDT [20, 21, 31, 23]. OT algorithms distinguish between a *control algorithm* and a *transformation function* [28]. The former determine the concurrent operations to be transformed against other operations according to concurrency/context relations. The latter determine how to transform a pair of operations according to their type, position and other parameters. The responsibilities of these two components are defined by a set of transformation properties and conditions. An overview of OT control algorithms, their verification and available state of the art systems are given in [28, 32, 17, 13]. In contrast, CRDT algorithms offer optimistic concurrency control by defining commutative operations that do not conflict with each other [24]. In the following, we provide a brief selection of relevant OT and CRDT algorithms.

The *Google OT* approach for Google Wave/Google Docs [32] is based on the *Jupiter* approach [18]. In both cases the server has to preprocess operations before one is executed and propagated to all clients. There is no direct communication between clients. Similarly, the client also preprocesses received operations before it executes them. Since the client has its own history buffer, it can use the same preprocessing algorithm as the server. *Generalized OT* (GOT) [27], *GOT Optimized* (GOTO) [26] and *AnyUndo* [25] are algorithms that do not depend on a server that preprocesses operations. The AnyUndo OT algorithm extends GOTO with undo capabilities, while reusing its transformation algorithm. The space complexity of this algorithm is nearly as good as the Jupiter approach, but its time complexity can be quadratic. Moreover, it has been shown that the GOTO and AnyUndo approaches work if there are transformation functions that fulfill CP1 [22] and CP2 properties [22]. Sun et al. [28] describe these transformation properties—correctness criteria used in OT literature, needed to achieve convergence (CP1, CP2). Violations of these properties result in inconsistent replicas of a shared document. Similar to GOTO/AnyUndo, the *Context-based OT* (COT) [30] algorithm does not need server-side preprocessing. Furthermore, the algorithm enables direct communication between the clients. The idea behind COT is to save every received operation "as is" in a document state and preprocess it afterwards given the operation context. COT has a simplified design, as only one transformation function must be defined. The downside of this approach is that a state vector must be transmitted with every operation, where the size of the state vector is proportional to the number of users in a collaborative session. The *Time Interval Based Operational Transformation* (TIBOT) approach sends operations to all other clients in an N-way communication model. However, each client is only allowed to send the operations at a certain time interval [16]. This significantly reduces complexity, for the price that updates may take longer to be processed. Similarly, the successor approach TIBOT2 maintains a distributed total ordering schema on the execution sequence of operations, allowing N-way communication between clients. Moreover, it avoids both CP1 and CP2 [32] via a more efficient remote processing approach.

All in all, OT approaches still have several drawbacks, such as scaling problems in peer-to-peer and cloud networks with dynamic (join/leave) user behavior [1] and a high complexity in solving convergence. This is a reason why most OT implementations [13] are restricted to linear data structures or specific ones, such as tree-like [9, 4, 11, 12]. Moreover, the complexity was a reason for slowing down the spread of collaborative applications on the Web, which flourished with the uprise of Google and cloud-based systems.

On the other side, CRDT systems are designed for peer-to-peer environments and to perform and achieve consistency for a big number of users. They can be state-based or operation-based [24]. *Without OT* (WooT) [20] is an approach built for consistency preservation in P2P systems. It uses a monotonic linearization function to ensure convergence as a solution to topological sort. According to [20], WooT supports linear structures, lists, block of texts and ordered trees. It generates partial orders for operations, which are represented as elements and assigned a unique identifier. Moreover, it makes use of an unique identifier for each collaborating site and one for each operation, a value for the effect of an operation and the identifiers of previous and next operations for each given "character value" of an insert operation. WooT uses tombstones (i.e. no elements are deleted, they are only marked for deletion), which means that operations are not deleted. Each site maintains besides the identifier a logical clock, a sequence for character values and a structure for pending operations. Similar to YATA, WooT was designed to work in a P2P architecture and it is independent from the order of reception of operations. WooTO and WooTH [1] improve the WooT algorithm in terms of performance [1], via a linked list and a hash table for optimizing retrieval, update and insertion of operations. They were inspired by the replicated growing array (RGA) approach [23, 1], which introduced update operations in addition to the classic insertions and deletions. Lagoot [31] provides a totally-ordered set of elements and was developed for linear data, extended with an undo mechanism based on a PN-Counter [31, 24]. It does not require tombstones, which makes the algorithm more efficient compared to similar mechanisms such as WooT.

3. THE YATA APPROACH

The YATA approach is created to provide a scalable solution for P2P optimistic concurrency control on the Web. The main goals are to allow the P2P collaborative editing of Web pages (DOM elements), graphs, lists, objects and arbitrary types in the Web browser, using cutting-edge protocols for message propagation. Therefore, the algorithm proposes a basic structure using a linked list, which can be extended to achieve collaboration on new shareable data types. YATA's linked list internal representation and a collection of predefined rules limit the number of possible conflicts and ensure intention preservation and convergence. The core idea is enforcing a total order on the shared data types. YATA also supports offline editing, being meant to cope with requirements coming from both Web and mobile clients, such as small operation updates for low bandwidth, on and off connections, random message order at receive time, etc.

YATA currently supports collaboration on linear data, trees, associative arrays and graphs. Using those types, it is possible to create more complex data types.

In the following we formalize our approach and exemplify YATA'S behavior on text (linear data). After giving the assumptions, definitions and describing how convergence is achieved, we extend the linear representation to more data types and explain how those are further realized using YATA.

3.1 Requirements

Unique identifiers. Each user is represented by an unique identifier (*userid*). Additionally, each user gets an *operation counter* which gets incremented every time a user creates an operation. Upon its creation, the operation thus gets assigned a unique identifier which is composed of the *userid* and the current *operation counter*.

Operations. YATA represents linear data (e.g. text) as a doubly linked list. We define only two types of changes on this representation: *insert* and *delete*. As it is shown in Figure 1, every element in the linked list is represented by an insert operation (also named *insertion*). When an insertion is deleted, it is just marked as such and not removed from the list (i.e. tombstone approach). Therefore, delete operations do not have an effect on our insert algorithm. In Section 3.5 we define a garbage collection mechanism that, in combination with our insert algorithm 3.4, can remove deleted insertions.

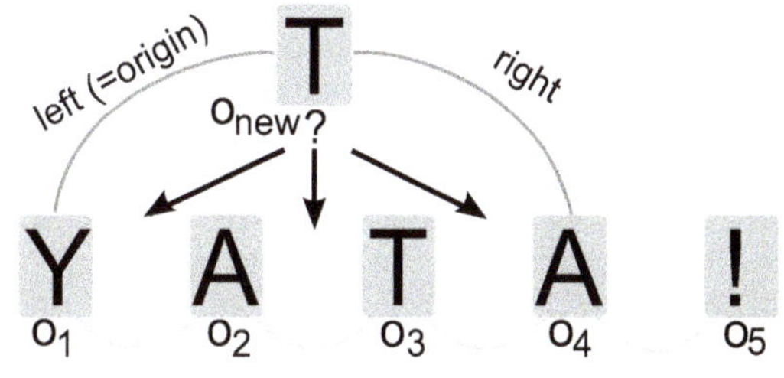

Figure 1: Integration example on text (linear) type.

We denote an insert operation as $o_k(id_k, origin_k, left_k, right_k, isDeleted_k, content_k)$, where id_k is o_k's unique identifier, $content_k$ is the content (e.g. a character), $isDeleted_k$ is a flag that marks an insertion as deleted, and $origin_k$, $left_k$, $right_k$ are references to other already existing insertions. We represent linear data as a doubly linked list S of insertions. Therefore, $left_k$, and $right_k$ reference to the previous node, respectively next node in the list. $origin_k$ denotes the direct predecessor at creation time (i.e., the node after which it was originally integrated to).

We define $<$ as the natural predecessor relation on S.

$$o_1 < o_2 \Leftrightarrow o_1 \text{ is a predecessor of } o_2 \quad (1)$$

$$o_1 \leq o_2 \Leftrightarrow o_1 < o_2 \vee o_1 \equiv o_2 \quad (2)$$

Example. When a user creates a new insertion at a local site, this is integrated between two insertions o_i, and o_j. The newly created insertion is therefore defined as: $o_{new}(id_k, o_i, o_i, o_j, false, content_{new})$. Note that $left_{new}$, and $right_{new}$ are defined when an insertion has been applied to the list and may change when new insertions are integrated into S, but $origin_{new}$, defined at insertion creation time is never modified. After the user integrates a new insertion at his local site he sends it (via broadcast), as is, to all users.

A special case occurs when an insertion is performed at the beginning or at the end of S, because there is no insertion to refer to as $left_*$, respectively $right_*$. This can be fixed by using special *delimiters*, which denote the beginning and the end of S, respectively. Therefore, we assume without loss of generality that an insertion always defines $origin_k$, $left_k$, and $right_k$.

3.2 YATA

The example in Figure 1 shows how a received operation o_{new} is integrated in S. Here, the red connections reference the intention of the insertion, which is defined through $left_{new}$ and $right_{new}$ - i.e. insert the letter between these two letters. When the insertion is integrated, YATA assures that it will be placed somewhere between these letters. Convergence is therefore ensured, unless one or more remote operations were already inserted between $left_{new}$ and $right_{new}$, which then leads to a conflict that needs to be solved.

Definition: ***Intention Preservation***.

The intention of an insertion o_i is preserved if and only if the insertion is integrated somewhere between $left_i$ and $right_i$. This notion of intention preservation conforms to the natural perception for the intention of text insertions and it is similar to other definitions found in the literature. In [2], the intention preservation is defined when each character inserted by a user between two other characters in a document keeps its relative position between its neighbors during the editing process.

The concurrent insertion problem.

In the example in Figure 1, the intention of the insertion of "T" is that should be inserted between the characters "Y" and the "A" - e.g., at creation time, "T" sees only "YA". However, a letter sequence "AT" has been already inserted between these two letters. In the example, o_2, and o_3 conflict with o_{new}.

Definition: ***Conflicting insertions***.

Keeping the above notations, assuming $S = left_{new} \cdot c_1 \cdot c_2 \cdot .. \cdot c_n \cdot right_{new}$, then we say that o_{new} conflicts with $c_1..c_n$.

In the following we define a function $<_c$ that specifies a position for o_{new} in the set of conflicting insertions $(c_1..c_n)$. As such o_{new} is integrated between c_i, and c_{i+1} when $c_i <_c o_{new} <_c c_{i+1}$. Furthermore, we show that every site converges when integrating with $<_c$ (i.e., we prove that $<_c$ is a strict total order function).

In the following we will frequently refer to the graphical representation of insertions as it is shown in Figure 1. The insertion o_{new} has three references/connections. On the left hand site of o_{new} there is a $origin_{new}$ connection, and a $left_{new}$ connection to o_1. On the right hand site of o_{new} there is a $right_{new}$ connection to o_4. While $left_{new}$, and $right_{new}$ define the usual predecessor/successor relation in a linked list. The $origin_{new}$ connection will never change and is employed to find the strict total order function $<_c$.

We compose the following three rules in order to find a strict total order $<_c$ on conflicting operations.

Rule 1 We forbid crossing of *origin* connections (red lines in the graphical representation) between conflicting insertions. This rule is easily explained using the graphical representation of insertions in the linked list. As we stated before, every insertion has an origin connection to an insertion to the left (to a predecessor). Only when two operations are concurrently inserted after the same insertion, they will have the same origin.

Figure 2: No line crossing.

Figure 2 illustrates the two cases that are allowed when line crossing is forbidden. Either, one operation is between the other operation and its origin, or the origin of the one operation is a successor of the other operation. Therefore, the following formula must hold for conflicting insertions o_1 and o_2:

$$o_1 <_{rule1} o_2 \Leftrightarrow o_1 < origin_2 \vee origin_2 \leq origin_1 \quad (3)$$

Rule 2 Specifies transitivity on $<_c$. Let $o_1 <_c o_2$. Then following rule ensures, that there is no o that is greater than o_2, but smaller than o_1, with respect to $<_c$

$$o_1 <_{rule2} o_2 \Leftrightarrow \forall o : o_2 <_c o \rightarrow o_1 \leq o \Leftrightarrow \nexists o : o_2 <_c o < o_1 \quad (4)$$

Rule 3 When two conflicting insertions have the same origin, the insertion with the smaller creator id is to the left. We borrow this rule from the OT approach. But in OT this rule is applied when the position parameters are equal.

$$o_1 <_{rule3} o_2 \Leftrightarrow origin_1 \equiv origin_2 \rightarrow creator_1 < creator_2 \quad (5)$$

We get retrieve the total order function $<_c$ by enforcing all three rules:

$$\begin{aligned} o_1 <_c o_2 &\Longleftrightarrow o_1 <_{rule1} o_2 \wedge o_1 <_{rule2} o_2 \wedge o_1 <_{rule3} o_2 \\ &\Leftrightarrow o_1 < origin_2 \vee origin_2 \leq origin_1 \\ &\wedge \nexists o : o_2 <_c o < o_1 \\ &\wedge origin_1 \equiv origin_2 \rightarrow creator_1 < creator_2 \\ o_1 \leq_c o_2 &\Leftrightarrow o_1 <_c o_2 \vee o_1 \equiv o_2 \end{aligned} \quad (6)$$

3.3 Correctness

$<_c$ only depends on the $origin_*$ connection, and we specified above, that $origin_*$ never changes. We can conclude that whenever two sites compare conflicting insertions, they will find the same order for insertions. Furthermore, this implies that all sites will eventually converge. Finally, we prove that $<_c$ is a strict total order function, i.e. $\leq_c$ is a total order on conflicting operations. Therefore, we have to show that for all conflicting insertions o_1, o_2, and o_3 the ordering function $\leq_c$ is *antisymmetric*, *transitive*, and *total*.

$$
\begin{aligned}
o_1 \leq_c o_2 \land o_2 \leq_c o_1 &\;\Rightarrow\; o_1 \equiv o_2 \text{ (antisymmetry)} && (7)\\
o_1 \leq_c o_2 \land o_2 \leq_c o_3 &\;\Rightarrow\; o_1 \leq_c o_3 \text{ (transitivity)} && (8)\\
o_1 \leq_c o_2 &\;\lor\; o_2 \leq_c o_1 \text{ (totality)} && (9)
\end{aligned}
$$

PROOF ANTISYMMETRY. Let o_1, and o_2 be insertions, with $o_1 \leq_c o_2 \land o_2 \leq_c o_1$.
Case 1: $(origin_1 \equiv origin_2)$:

$$
\begin{aligned}
& o_1 \leq_c o_2 \land o_2 \leq_c o_1\\
\overset{6}{\Rightarrow}\;& (o_1 <_c o_2 \land o_2 <_c o_1) \lor o_1 \equiv o_2\\
\overset{\text{Rule 3}}{\Rightarrow}\;& (creator_1 < creator_2 \land creator_2 < creator_1) \lor o_1 \equiv o_2\\
\Leftrightarrow\;& o_1 \equiv o_2
\end{aligned}
$$

The reasoning here is that the user id has a total ordering.
Case 2: $(origin_1 < origin_2)$:

$$
\begin{aligned}
& o_1 \leq_c o_2 \land o_2 \leq_c o_1\\
\Leftrightarrow\;& (o_1 \leq o_2 \land o_2 \leq o_1) \land (o_1 \leq_c o_2 \land o_2 \leq_c o_1)\\
\Leftrightarrow\;& (o_1 \leq o_2 \land o_2 \leq o_1) \land (o_1 \equiv o_2 \lor (o_1 <_c o_2 \land o_2 <_c o_1))\\
\overset{\text{Rule 1}}{\Rightarrow}\;& o_1 \leq o_2 \land o_2 \leq o_1\\
\land\;& o_1 \equiv o_2 \lor ((o_1 < origin_2 \lor \underbrace{origin_2 \leq origin_1}_{false})\\
& \land(o_2 < origin_1 \lor \underbrace{origin_1 \leq origin_2}_{true}))\\
\Rightarrow\;& o_1 \leq o_2 \land o_2 \leq o_1 \land (o_1 \equiv o_2 \lor o_1 < origin_2)\\
\Rightarrow\;& (o_1 \leq o_2 \land o_2 \leq o_1 < origin_2) \lor o_1 \equiv o_2\\
\overset{origin_2 \overset{!}{<} o_2}{\Rightarrow}\;& o_1 \equiv o_2
\end{aligned}
$$

Case 3: $(origin_2 < origin_1)$: Similar to Case 2.

PROOF TRANSITIVITY. Let o_1, o_2, and o_3 be insertions, with $o_1 \leq_c o_2 \land o_2 \leq_c o_3$, o_3 conflicts with o_1, and w.l.o.g. $o_1 \neq o_2 \neq o_3$.

$$
\begin{aligned}
& o_1 <_c o_2 \land o_2 <_c o_3\\
\overset{\text{Rule 2}}{\Rightarrow}\;& (\forall o : o_2 <_c o \rightarrow o_1 \leq o) \land (o_2 <_c o_3)\\
\Rightarrow\;& (o_2 <_c o_3 \rightarrow o_1 \leq o_3) \land (o_2 <_c o_3)\\
\Rightarrow\;& o_1 < o_3\\
\Leftrightarrow\;& o_1 <_c o_3
\end{aligned}
$$

PROOF TOTALITY. Let o_1, o_2 be insertions, with $o_1 \neq o_2$. Totality is fulfilled if the following statement holds:

$$
\begin{aligned}
o_1 <_c o_2 \lor o_2 <_c o_1 &\;\Leftarrow\; true\\
&\text{if and only if}\\
\neg(o_1 <_c o_2 \lor o_2 <_c o_1) &\;\Rightarrow\; false
\end{aligned}
$$

When we apply the ordering relation (6) we get the formula in Figure 3 and show for each case that totality is fulfilled.
Case 1 ($origin_1 \equiv origin_2$ and $creator_1 < creator_2$):

$$
\begin{aligned}
& \text{First steps are depicted in Figure 3}\\
\Rightarrow\;& \exists o_2 < o < o_1\\
\Rightarrow\;& o_2 < o_1\\
\overset{\text{Rule 3}}{\Rightarrow}\;& false
\end{aligned}
$$

Case 2 ($origin_1 \equiv origin_2$ and $creator_2 > creator_1$): Similar to case 1.
Case 3 $(origin_1 < origin_2)$:

$$
\begin{aligned}
& \text{Figure 3}\\
\Rightarrow\;& (\neg(o_1 < origin_2) \lor (\exists o : o_2 < o < o_1))\\
& \land(\exists o : o_1 < o < o_2)\\
\Leftrightarrow\;& (\neg(o_1 < origin_2) \land (\exists o : o_1 < o < o_2))\\
& \lor(\exists o : o_2 < o < o_1 \land \exists o : o_1 < o < o_2)\\
\Rightarrow\;& (\neg(o_1 < origin_2) \land (\exists o : o_1 < o < o_2))\\
& \lor(o_2 < o_1 \land o_1 < o_2)\\
\overset{\text{antisymmetry}}{\Rightarrow}\;& \neg(o_1 < origin_2) \land (\exists o : o_1 < o < o_2)\\
\Rightarrow\;& origin_2 \leq o_1 \land o_1 < o_2\\
\overset{\text{assumption}}{\Rightarrow}\;& origin_1 < origin_2 \leq o_1 \land o_1 < o_2\\
\Rightarrow\;& origin_1 < origin_2 \leq o_1 < o_2\\
\overset{o_1 \text{ and } o_2 \text{ conflict}}{\Leftrightarrow}\;& origin_1 < origin_2 < o_1 < o_2\\
\overset{\text{Rule 1}}{\Rightarrow}\;& false
\end{aligned}
$$

Case 4 $(origin_2 < origin_1)$: Similar to Case 3.

$$
\begin{aligned}
& \neg(o_1 <_c o_2) \land \neg(o_2 <_c o_1)\\
\Leftrightarrow\;& \neg((o_1 < origin_2 \lor origin_2 \leq origin_1) \land (\nexists o : o_2 <_c o < o_1) \land (origin_1 \equiv origin_2 \rightarrow creator_1 < creator_2))\\
\land\;& \neg((o_2 < origin_1 \lor origin_1 \leq origin_2) \land (\nexists o : o_1 <_c o < o_2) \land (origin_2 \equiv origin_1 \rightarrow creator_2 < creator_1))\\
\Leftrightarrow\;& (\neg(o_1 < origin_2) \land \neg(origin_2 \leq origin_1)) \lor (\exists o_2 <_c o < o_1) \lor (origin_1 \equiv origin_2 \land \neg(creator_1 < creator_2))\\
\land\;& (\neg(o_2 < origin_1) \land \neg(origin_1 \leq origin_2)) \lor (\exists o_1 <_c o < o_2) \lor (origin_2 \equiv origin_1 \land \neg(creator_2 < creator_1))\\
\Leftrightarrow\;& (\neg(o_1 < origin_2) \land \neg(origin_2 \leq origin_1)) \lor (\exists o_2 < o < o_1) \lor (origin_1 \equiv origin_2 \land \neg(creator_1 < creator_2))\\
\land\;& (\neg(o_2 < origin_1) \land \neg(origin_1 \leq origin_2)) \lor (\exists o_1 < o < o_2) \lor (origin_2 \equiv origin_1 \land \neg(creator_2 < creator_1))
\end{aligned}
$$

Figure 3: Derivation of totality on (6).

3.4 Insert Algorithm

Previously, we proved that there exists a total order relation on conflicting insertions. In this section we show how we can compute the new position for an insertion, when we already have an ordered list of insertions.

Listing 3.4 shows how the conflicting insertion can be solved algorithmically. The algorithm exploits property (3) (no line crossing) as a breaking condition. Therefore, we stop computing when origin connections definitely will cross.

The worst case time complexity of the algorithm is $O(|C|^2)$ where $|C|$ is the number of conflicting operations. In the case that the breaking condition is reached in the first iteration, no positions are compared. This is why the best case time complexity is $O(1)$. A complexity analysis is presented in Section 3.7.

```
// Insert 'i' in a list of
// conflicting operations 'ops'.
insert(i, ops){
  i.position = ops[0].position
  for o in ops do
    // Rule 2:
    // Search for the last operation
    // that is to the left of i.
    if (o < i.origin
        OR i.origin <= o.origin)
      AND (o.origin != i.origin
        OR o.creator < i.creator) do
      // rule 1 and 3:
      // If this formula is fulfilled,
      //   i is a successor of o.
      i.position = o.position + 1
    else do
      if i.origin > o.origin do
        // Breaking condition,
        // Rule 1 is no longer satisfied
        // since otherwise origin
        // connections would cross.
        break
}
```

3.5 Garbage Collection

In the literature, garbage collection has been also proposed in [21] where "cold" areas of a document are identified or in Logoot [31], which uses a graveyard for removed operations. Conceptually, an insertion marked for deletion can be garbage collected when all sites received the remove operation and have in their internal representation the operation that is to be garbage collected. However, it is hard to determine if all collaborators know simultaneously that a content was deleted. Ideally, using classic methods such as state vectors, a mechanism where YATA ensures that all sites have applied a removal can be a candidate solution. As a downside, such a mechanism would require more network resources and leads to a decrease in performance, especially in P2P settings. An optimal solution to this issue is still being considered.

In the current approach, the problem is simplified by assuming that all users retrieved a certain remove operation after a fixed time period t which can be set according to the expected protocol and network characteristics (e.g., 30 s). In practice, YATA uses two buffers for garbage collection, to ensure that list elements are not directly removed. As such, once o_k can be garbage collected, it will be moved into the first buffer. If nothing changes, after t seconds it will be copied into the second array and from here will be removed by the garbage collector (i.e., can be safely removed from the list and the buffer). From our practical experiences and the use in production, such a delay is sufficient to ensure that content will be removed safely, without any losses that may lead to inconsistencies. This is in line with experiments performed for assessing the NRT criteria and measuring the time in which operations are being applied. These experiments (cf. Figure 9, Section 6) show that the average time for receiving and applying a remove operation using text (with a length under 10^3 characters) at a remote site is approx. 12 ms. Under the same conditions, receiving and applying a single remove operation with a length of 10^5 characters at a remote site is done within an average time of 39.3 ms (SD 2.45 ms), from a pool of ten measurements.

As a consequence of YATA's rules, in some cases it is not possible to remove insert operations. The reason is that for an operation that is inserted between two undeleted insert-type operations, this could lead to a deleted predecessor or successor (cf. Figure 4).

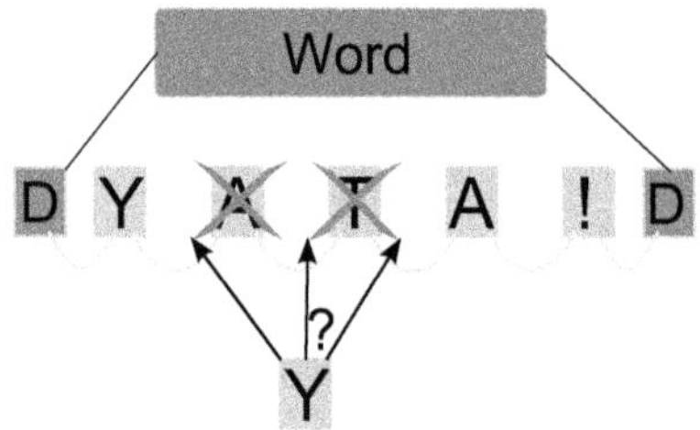

Figure 4: Insertion between deleted characters.

In order to ensure consistency, YATA demands that a new insertion is always inserted between the most left non-deleted character and its direct successor. Only then, the garbage collector can remove all operations that are to the right of the first deleted insertion.

Furthermore, due to its design, the garbage collector in YATA may break late join mechanisms. This is because when a user is offline for a period longer than t seconds, it will still hold references to deleted operations, while online users who already performed certain removals do not. Therefore, YATA does not support garbage collection for a site while it is offline.

3.6 Offline Editing Support

YATA supports offline editing using the internal data representation which is maintained at each client. Once clients are online, YATA performs a check for diverged states of the shared data and synchronizes it.

Every site holds a state vector. It saves the next expected operation id per user. As an example, consider *user1* with *userid* 1 is in a session with *user2* with *userid* 2. Both users created two operations. As we explained above, the operation id is defined as a tuple of *userid* and *operationcounter*. Therefore, the state vector is expressed as:
$[(1, 2), (2, 2)]$ (assuming we start counting with 0).

For synchronization, the state vector is not sent with each operation, but it is sent only once to all clients. A user that receives a state vector compares it with the local state vector and sends all remaining operations to the synchronizing client. In order to make operations integrable on the remote instances, operations are sent in the order and the form in which they were created. Our YATA's implementation can transform integrated operations to their original form.

3.7 Complexity Analysis

The complexity of YATA depends on the retrieval efficiency of insertions. As such, the retrieval of a specific operation can be efficiently implemented using a balanced tree, which exposes time complexities of $O(log(H))$ for insertion and retrieval. Here, H denotes the number of all applied operations in the balanced tree implementation. The best case time complexity for applying an operation is $O(log(H))$ - i.e. there are no conflicting operations. The worst case time complexity is $O(log(H) + C^2)$ and only depends on the amount of conflicting operations (C). A comparison with other CRDTs performance, adapted from [1] is depicted in Table 1. In this comparison, H the total number of operations that affect a shared document.

CRDT	LOCAL		REMOTE	
	INS	DEL	INS	DEL
WooT	$O(H^3)$	$O(H)$	$O(H^3)$	$O(H)$
WooTO	$O(H^2)$	$O(H)$	$O(H^2)$	$O(H)$
Logoot	$O(H)$	$O(1)$	$O(H \cdot log(H))$	$O(H \cdot log(H))$
RGA	$O(H)$	$O(H)$	$O(H)$	$O(log(H))$
YATA	$O(log(H))$	$O(log(H))$	$O(H^2)$	$O(log(H))$

Table 1: Worst case time complexity analysis, adapted from [1].

Discussion As it can be observed, compared to classical CRDT tombstone approaches (such as WooT or WooTO), YATA has a better time complexity. As expected, non-tombstone approaches (such as Logoot of RGA) output a better time complexity for some operation types. Regardless of the complexity, YATA offers an approach for client-side conflict resolution, which is not common among existing CRDTs. It proposes a simple data type that can be used to compose more complex ones (cf. Section 4). In Section 6, we show that YATA's implementation fulfills NRT scenarios and give an overview on its usage performance.

A downside of the YATA approach is that when each character is represented as an operation, the space complexity is $O(|D|)$, where $|D|$ is the size of the shared document. In OT for example, it is possible to have an empty history buffer, when garbage collection is enabled.

However, YATA outputs the following advantages over OT approaches:

- Time-complexity: YATA reduces time to synchronize, when late join is supported.
- The size of propagated messages is small: there are no state vectors that need to be propagated with each operation. OT approaches for handling tree-like data require the user to send a path-vector with each operation. This usually has the length of the depth of the changed element, which is not necessary in YATA.
- It is possible to define many data types.

4. EXTENDABLE TYPES

This section describes some of the basic operation types and the general data structures which YATA supports. Building on top of the data structures, one can implement certain abstract data types and thus enable collaboration on common data formats such as JSON and XML. The supported types currently include linear data types (e.g., arrays, linked lists, sorted arrays, bitmaps), trees, graphs and associative arrays.

4.1 List Manager Operation

A List Manager (cf. Figure 5) is an abstract operation type that manages insert operations. It basically handles two delimiters that denote the beginning and the end of the list, as exemplified in the algorithm's description. Hence, new insertions are placed somewhere between these delimiters according to YATA's rules.

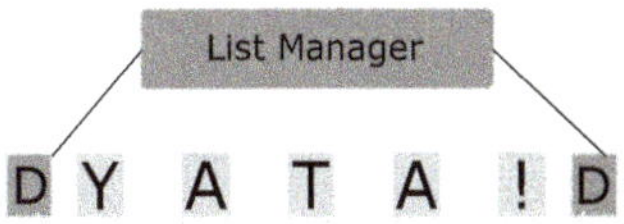

Figure 5: Illustration of the List operation type.

The List Manager operation also handles how to address the elements in the associative list and how to transform it to a certain data type (e.g. String). It represents linear data structures such as lists and arrays, but it can also be used in order to represent tree-like data structures. In this case, the trees are achieved by allowing the content of insertions to contain in their turn List Managers.

4.2 Replace Manager Operation

YATA supports only insert and delete operations. However, when dealing with more complex types, update operations are also required in order to ease the development. As such, YATA supports updates of existing content by offering a dedicated type which enables content replacement. A Replace Manager (cf. Figure6 handles the replace functionality. As a basic example, consider the case where two users (with user ids 1 and 2) concurrently replace the number 0 in a text with their respective user id. In order to keep consistency, each site should reflect the replace operation and reach the same content, i.e. either 1 or 2 will replace the old number 0. YATA solves this problem by transforming it into an already solved problem, using data types which ensure consistency.

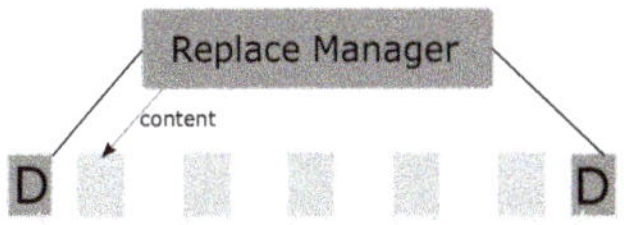

Figure 6: Illustration of the Replace Manager operation type.

The Replace Manager inherits its functionality from the List Manager. Using this data representation, the first insertion (which must not be a Delimiter) of a Replace Manager denotes the actual content. In consequence, in order to replace this content once a user performs a new insertion, the new content will be added as the first insertion of the Replace Manager. In Figure 6 the red line references the current content of the Replace Manager. Since YATA ensures that all sites will have the same content in the end, all sites eventually reference the same insertion as the content of the Replace Manager. Moreover, in order to free up memory all other insertions can be implicitly deleted.

4.3 Map Manager Operation

A map is also known as a dictionary, or an associative array. It is an abstract data type that maps *keys* to *values*.

Figure 7 depicts YATA's representation of a Map Manager operation. In order to support concurrent actions on a shared map, we assign each *key* to a Replace Manager. Therefore, the values addressed by keys will converge upon concurrent changes performed by multiple users i.e., users collaboratively edit the content addressed by a specific key. We can use any map data structure to map *keys* to Replace Managers. The values can contain primitive data types or YATA own types. This construct is suitable for easily enabling collaboration on name/value pairs (e.g., objects, dictionaries, etc.). The current *value* of a *key* is replaced and retrieved by accessing the respective Replace Manager.

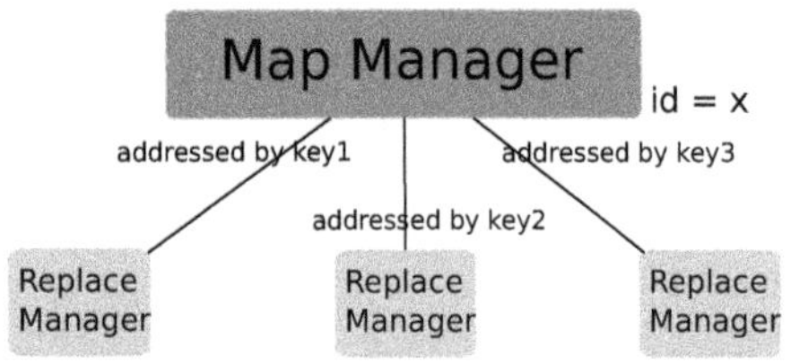

Figure 7: Illustration of the Map Manager operation type.

4.4 Representation of Specific Data Formats

Using YATA, by combining the simple types explained above, data formats such as JSON or XML can be realized as shared data types.

The JSON data format is built on collections of name/-value pairs and ordered lists of values. Hence, with YATA JSON can be easily created by using a Map Manager, in combination with other data types which can be used for the attributes, such as further Map Manager operations or List operations (for attributes implementing strings or arrays).

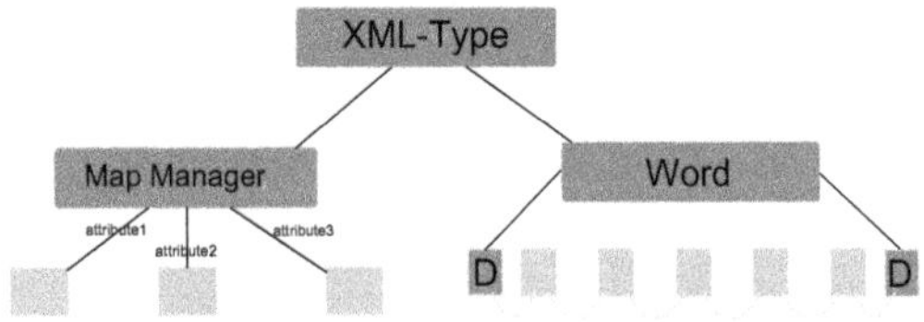

Figure 8: Illustration of XML as an operation type.

YATA can also enable NRT collaboration on XML (cf. Figure 8). An XML DOM Element[2] has XML attributes and an ordered list of children (XML elements or XML text). Therefore, we compose an XML-Type in YATA as a Map Manager (which handles the XML attributes) and a List Manager (which handles the children). However, since the List Manager and the Map Manager support to insert any value, we have to put some restrictions to the structure of the XML-Type:

- The Map Manager, which handles the XML attributes, must only map from a non-empty string to a non-empty string
- The List Manager, which handles the children, must only contain other XML types, or strings which represent XML text elements

5. YJS: THE P2P SHARED EDITING FRAMEWORK

As already introduced, Yjs [19] is the open-source implementation of the YATA approach. In contrast to similar OT, CRDT and shared editing implementations that support only a very limited number of document structures or represent them differently, the Yjs framework encourages developers to build custom data types. A custom type can use existing implemented types (as previously explained) in order to give meaning to the actions on the data and to fire custom events. At the time of writing this paper, Yjs has implemented support for *list*, *associative arrays*, *XML*,*text*, and *rich text* types. Yjs works on modern Web browsers, including mobile (on Android devices) and offers a quick and easy way to embed collaboration in Web applications.

In order to maintain modularity and to be able to employ Yjs in various Web engineering settings, the communication protocols and the shared data type formats support are implemented as dedicated interchangeable modules. This greatly simplifies the process of integrating the framework into an existing project, since such projects typically use diverse communication protocols (e.g., WebRTC, Web Sockets, XMPP), and collaborate on various data types and data formats (e.g., XML, JSON, graphs). The support for the different communication protocols is implemented in connector modules. The collection of connector modules and type modules are available as open-source JavaScript libraries on GitHub[3]. Currently, connectors are implemented for WebRTC, Web Sockets and XMPP.

6. EVALUATION

6.1 Performance

Apart from the correctness reasoning explained above, we have evaluated the approach and the Yjs library in terms of responsiveness - how quickly an operation is integrated into each user's local structure and scalability - what is the impact of the number of users in this setting [19].

In order to evaluate the speed and correctness of YATA we performed multiple automatic tests simulating many users working exhaustively on a single shared document. The simulation introduced certain constraints: generation of random operations, different arrival orders of operations at different sites and network delay with operations which were

[2]http://www.w3.org/TR/REC-xml/
[3]https://github.com/y-js

not ready to be applied because they were dependent on other pending operations. As our implementation is meant for client-side applications and runs on the Web, we could not use existing benchmarking tools described in the literature [1]. Moreover, using collaboration logs from online text editing systems such as Wikipedia would have lead to very few conflicts on the shared document. Instead, we chose an alternative approach with the goal to measure the fulfillment of the NRT scenario in distributed settings. We first used the testing environment with a test connector to measure the scaling capability with the number of operations by measuring how many concurrent operations YATA can apply locally. Second, we measured the time performance for applying insert and delete operations between two Yjs instances, including the network delay using the Web Sockets connector. Similar to [1], we consider that the framework performs in NRT if the response time for the insert operation is in average under 50ms.

The testing environment can be configured with respect to number of users and number of actions that are created. Furthermore, it is possible to configure the test environment in such a way that the collaboration is restricted to a specific data type (e.g. text only or text and JSON with primitive data types). The users are collaborating concurrently with each other, whereby each simulated user can perform one of the following actions: *wait* for a time period, *retrieve an operation* from a random collaborator, *go offline* (all operations that are currently sent to the users get lost. After going offline, the user is allowed to create more operations, simulating late join), *go online* (user reconnects to all users, retrieves all missing operations, and sends all offline generated operations). For text, a user can perform insert and delete actions. For JSON, the user can perform randomly the following actions: find a random child, create a new property, replace an existing property or delete a property.

When a configured amount of actions are executed, the simulated users stop generating additional actions and wait for all incoming operations to be executed. When the data types of every simulated instance converge, we consider that the test framework succeeds.

We used our test framework with the creation and execution of 10000 actions on Text and JSON with a specified number of users, ranging from one to ten. The test ran on one CPU only (Intel i7 - 3.40 GHz). All mentioned constraints were considered. We ran the test 15 times in order to get good average times. The time to create 10000 random actions and apply them to all collaborators was measured and divided by the number of users times the number of created actions: operation per millisecond $= \frac{time}{10000 \times |users|}$ The time for transforming operations did not thwart the performance noticeably. For a setting with 7 and 8 users, the test framework registered 250 operations executed in one ms, whereas for 9 and 10 users the average time was approx. 230 operations per ms. This did not even change when we restricted the test framework to work on text only, where even more conflicts should happen.

The time performance was measured using two Yjs instances using one Chrome browser on a laptop (Intel i7 - 2.8 GHz) with a wireless Eduroam connection. Using Web Sockets connector, we measured the time difference (in ms) between applying an insert or delete operation on the first instance and applying the same operation on the second instance.

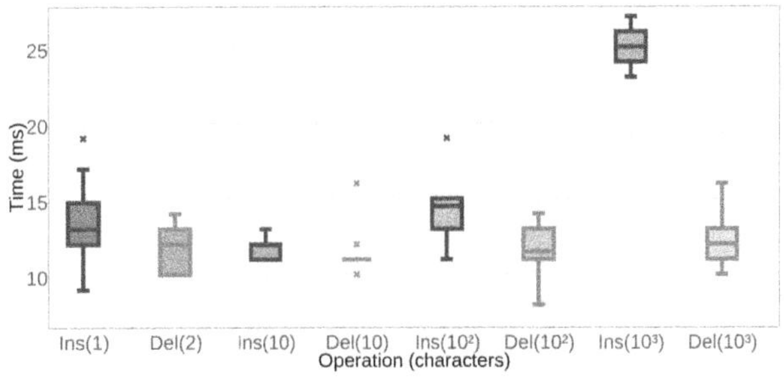

Figure 9: NRT performance for applying one remote operation with different content sizes

This shows the delay between creating an operation on a site and seeing the effects of that change at the second site, including the delay created from the message propagation across the communication channel (i.e., Web Sockets).

The experiment (cf. Figure 9) was performed with a single insert or delete operation using a text editor. Each operation was executed ten times in order to obtain a reliable estimation. We also increased the content of each operation (in characters), ranging from 1 to 10^3 characters. The results for the insert operations are represented in gray and for the delete operations in blue. As it can be observed, the average time for all operations is smaller than 25 ms. We also used the same environment to write a text of 1000 characters. Here, we obtained an average execution time for an operation of 12 ms, which is consistent with the results presented in the figure for inserting and deleting one character.

Overall, the test results fulfill our expectations for the framework's performance in NRT settings.

6.2 Applications

Overall, the Yjs library with its various connectors and types was well received by the open-source developer community. The library's Website and repository analytics show that the Website gathered over one year more than 11600 page views from over 4500 users and the library over 800 downloads.

Yjs was used to enable shared editing with the popular Quill rich text editor, which is very similar to Google Docs. The richtext component is already used by two companies in production, for NRT shared text editing on the Web, embedded in WebRTC video meeting tools.

As shown in Figure 10, Yjs is currently used for synchronizing 3D objects movement across multiple users in the Web browser[4].

Here, the Map Manager is used in order to synchronize the position properties of a Javascript 3D object. This is possible by observing changes in the x3dom 3D object representation and ensuring that the object's coordinate values are converging across all sites. The synchronization performance and accuracy is currently being evaluated with students of the Faculty of Medicine from RWTH Aachen University, in an Exploratory Teaching Spaces project that aims to support formal and informal learning through NRT collaboration.

Furthermore, Yjs was used to create a tool for achieving

[4]http://eiche.informatik.rwth-aachen.de/3dnrt

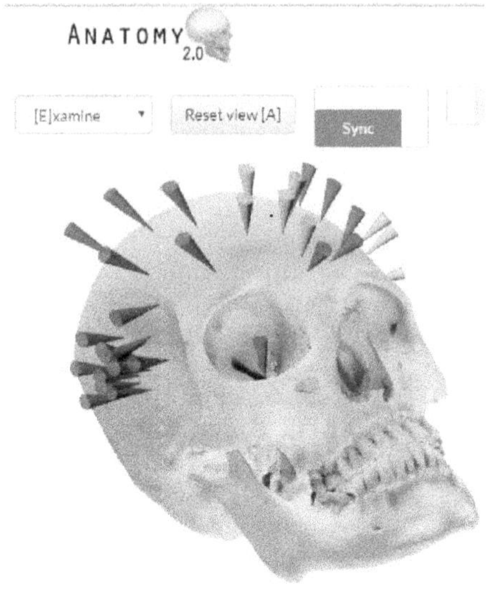

Figure 10: Illustration of the 3D objects synchronization with Yjs.

liquid Web applications [8], by providing a seamless user experience in using different Polymer Web components distributed across various devices. The evaluation of a Yjs-based collaborative drawing tool on Web videos [14] (performed using the WebRTC connector) showed that during concurrent drawings the framework proved to be reliable while keeping the NRT behavior, for all participating peers. Several other examples for manipulating text, HTML5 elements, JSON objects and additional usages in various projects are provided on the Yjs Website.

Moreover, Yjs is currently being integrated into SyncMeta [5] (cf. Figure 11), a framework for enabling NRT collaborative (meta) modeling on the Web.

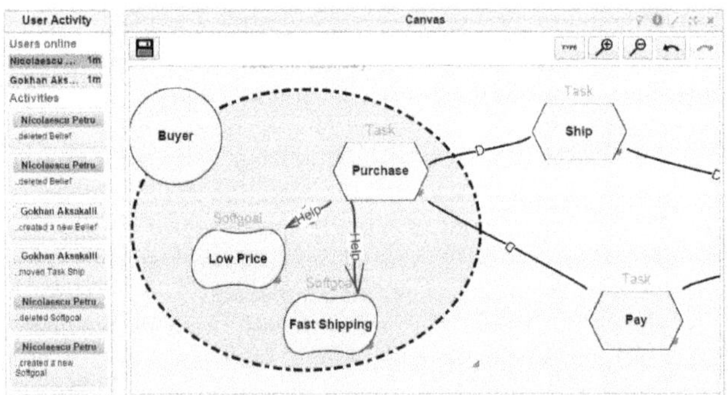

Figure 11: Illustration of graph editing with Yjs.

SyncMeta is using an OT solution for enabling shared editing on text and ensuring that the created nodes and edges are converging during the modeling process at all sites. However, this solution uses timestamps for ensuring the consistency in a P2P manner, which does not scale well with an increasing number of users. However, by synchronizing the underlying JSON model representation using YATA, Yjs is a perfect candidate for achieving scalable optimistic NRT collaborative modeling. The Yjs implementation benefits from the advantages of YATA over OT algorithms. Thus, it guarantees a faster synchronization of the graph elements and their respective properties with an increasing number of users and operation content size in P2P settings. Moreover, Yjs SyncMeta reduces the network traffic through the smaller size of messages, while keeping the reliability and hence the convergence of the shared models across collaborators.

7. CONCLUSION AND FUTURE WORK

In this work, we have described YATA, a new scalable P2P approach for maintaining consistency of shared arbitrary data types, designed for NRT settings on the Web. We proved that it ensures convergence and that it has several advantages compared to other existing algorithms for shared editing. The contributions of YATA rely on its flexibility for various shared data types, as well as in its performance regarding the necessary number of exchanged updates between collaboration sites, time to convergence and its support for offline editing (enabled by YATA's late join mechanism). Its' open-source implementation, Yjs, supports multiple NRT communication protocols and can be easily used into existing and new applications for facilitating NRT collaboration and shared editing.

In the future, we plan to change the available garbage collection mechanism in order to support operation removal while working offline. Moreover, we want to improve the Yjs framework implementation with new supported data types and persistence mechanisms for increasing the performance. Concerning persistence we are exploring efficient methods for the storage of shared data in the P2P network that can be included into the framework.

As the main motivation for developing YATA and Yjs was to enable easy NRT collaboration for online communities, we plan to use Yjs for the collaborative engineering of Web applications and synchronizing the application content and state across multiple devices [15].

8. ACKNOWLEDGMENTS

This research was funded in part by the European Commission in the projects "Layers" (FP7-318209) and "Metis" (531262-LLP-2012-ES-KA3-KA3MP).

9. REFERENCES

[1] M. Ahmed-Nacer, C.-L. Ignat, G. Oster, H.-G. Roh, and P. Urso. Evaluating CRDTs for Real-time Document Editing. In *Proceedings of the 11th ACM symposium on Document engineering*, pages 103–112. ACM New York, 2011.

[2] L. Andre, S. Martin, G. Oster, and C.-L. Ignat. Supporting Adaptable Granularity of Changes for Massive-scale Collaborative Editing. In *Collaboratecom 2013*. IEEE, 2013.

[3] S. Androutsellis-Theotokis and D. Spinellis. A Survey of Peer-to-peer Content Distribution Technologies. *ACM Computing Surveys*, 36(4):335–371, 2004.

[4] A. H. Davis, C. Sun, and J. Lu. Generalizing Operational Transformation to the Standard General Markup Language. In *CSCW '02*, pages 58–67. ACM, 2002.

[5] M. Derntl, P. Nicolaescu, S. Erdtmann, R. Klamma, and M. Jarke. Near Real-Time Collaborative

Conceptual Modeling on the Web. In *ER'15*, volume 9381, pages 344–357. Springer International Publishing, 2015.

[6] C. A. Ellis and S. J. Gibbs. Concurrency Control in Groupware Systems. In *ACM SIGMOD '89*, volume 18, pages 399–407. ACM, 1989.

[7] N. Fraser. Differential synchronization. In *Proceedings of the 2009 ACM Symposium on Document Engineering*, pages 13–20. ACM, 2009.

[8] A. Gallidabino and C. Pautasso. The Liquid.js Framework for Migrating and Cloning Stateful Web Components across Multiple Devices. In *WWW'16 Companion*, pages 183–186, 2016.

[9] A. R. S. Gerlicher. A Framework for Real-time Collaborative Engineering in the Automotive Industries. In *CDVE'06*, pages 164–173. Springer-Verlag, 2006.

[10] J. Grudin. Computer-Supported Cooperative Work: History and Focus. *Computer*, 27(5):19–26, 1994.

[11] C. Ignat and M. C. Norrie. Tree-based Model Algorithm for Maintaining Consistency in Real-Time Collaborative Editing Systems. In *CSCW '02*. ACM, 2002.

[12] C.-L. Ignat and M. C. Norrie. Multi-level Editing of Hierarchical Documents. *Computer Supported Cooperative Work*, 17(5-6):423–468, 2008.

[13] I. Koren, A. Guth, and R. Klamma. Shared Editing on the Web: A Classification of Developer Support Libraries. Collaboratecom 2013, pages 468–477. IEEE, 2013.

[14] I. Koren, P. Nicolaescu, and R. Klamma. Collaborative Drawing Annotations on Web Videos. In *ICWE'15*, volume 9114. Springer, 2015.

[15] D. Kovachev, D. Renzel, P. Nicolaescu, I. Koren, and R. Klamma. DireWolf: A Framework for Widget-based Distributed User Interfaces. *Journal of Web Engineering*, 13(3&4):203–222, 2014.

[16] R. Li, Du Li, and C. Sun. A Time Interval Based Consistency Control Algorithm for Interactive Groupware Applications. In *ICPADS '04*, pages 429–436. IEEE Computer Society, 2004.

[17] Y. Liu, Y. Xu, S. J. Zhang, and C. Sun. Formal Verification of Operational Transformation. In *FM 2014: Formal Methods*, volume 8442, pages 432–448. Springer International Publishing, 2014.

[18] D. A. Nichols, P. Curtis, M. Dixon, and J. Lamping. High-latency, Low-bandwidth Windowing in the Jupiter Collaboration System. In *UIST '95*, pages 111–120. ACM, 1995.

[19] P. Nicolaescu, K. Jahns, M. Derntl, and R. Klamma. Yjs: A Framework for Near Real-Time P2P Shared Editing on Arbitrary Data Types. In *ICWE'15*, volume 9114, pages 675–678. Springer, 2015.

[20] G. Oster, P. Urso, P. Molli, and A. Imine. Data Consistency for P2P Collaborative Editing. In *CSCW '06*, pages 259–268. ACM Press.

[21] N. Preguiça, J. M. Marques, M. Shapiro, and M. Letia. A Commutative Replicated Data Type for Cooperative Editing. In *29th IEEE International Conference on Distributed Computing Systems, 2009*, pages 395–403. IEEE, 2009.

[22] M. Ressel, D. Nitsche-Ruhland, and R. Gunzenhäuser. An Integrating, Transformation-oriented Approach to Concurrency Control and Undo in Group Editors. In *CSCW '96*, pages 288–297. ACM, 1996.

[23] H.-G. Roh, M. Jeon, J.-S. Kim, and J. Lee. Replicated Abstract Data Types: Building Blocks for Collaborative Applications. *Journal of Parallel and Distributed Computing*, 71(3):354–368, 2011.

[24] M. Shapiro, N. Preguiça, C. Baquero, and M. Zawirski. A comprehensive study of Convergent and Commutative Replicated Data Types, 2011.

[25] C. Sun. Undo As Concurrent Inverse in Group Editors. *ACM Transactions on Computer-Human Interaction*, 9(4):309–361, 2002.

[26] C. Sun and C. Ellis. Operational Transformation in Real-time Group Editors: Issues, Algorithms, and Achievements. In *CSCW '98*, pages 59–68.

[27] C. Sun, X. Jia, Y. Zhang, Y. Yang, and D. Chen. Achieving Convergence, Causality Preservation, and Intention Preservation in Real-time Cooperative Editing Systems. *ACM Transactions on Computer-Human Interaction*, 5(1):63–108, 1998.

[28] C. Sun, Y. Xu, and A. Agustina. Exhaustive Search of Puzzles in Operational Transformation. In *CSCW '14*, pages 519–529. ACM, 2014.

[29] D. Sun and Chengzheng Sun. Context-Based Operational Transformation in Distributed Collaborative Editing Systems. *IEEE Transactions on Parallel and Distributed Systems*, 20(10):1454–1470, 2009.

[30] D. Sun and C. Sun. Operation Context and Context-based Operational Transformation. In *CSCW '06*, pages 279–288. ACM Press, 2006.

[31] S. Weiss, P. Urso, and P. Molli. Logoot-Undo: Distributed Collaborative Editing System on P2P Networks. *IEEE Transactions on Parallel and Distributed Systems*, 21(8):1162–1174, 2010.

[32] Y. Xu, C. Sun, and M. Li. Achieving Convergence in Operational Transformation: Conditions, Mechanisms and Systems. In *CSCW '14*, pages 505–518. ACM, 2014.

High Responsiveness for Group Editing CRDTs

Loïck Briot
Université de Lorraine
Nancy, France
loick.briot@mines-nancy.org

Pascal Urso
Université de Lorraine
Loria & Inria
Nancy, France
pascal.urso@loria.fr

Marc Shapiro
Sorbonne Universités
UPMC-LIP6 & Inria
Paris, France
marc.shapiro@acm.org

ABSTRACT

Group editing is a crucial feature for many end-user applications. It requires high responsiveness, which can be provided only by optimistic replication algorithms, which come in two classes: classical Operational Transformation (OT), or more recent Conflict-Free Replicated Data Types (CRDTs).

Typically, CRDTs perform better on *downstream* operations, i.e., when merging concurrent operations than OT, because the former have logarithmic complexity and the latter quadratic. However, CRDTs are often less responsive, because their *upstream* complexity is linear. To improve this, this paper proposes to interpose an auxiliary data structure, called the *identifier data structure* in front of the base CRDT. The identifier structure ensures logarithmic complexity and does not require replication or synchronization. Combined with a block-wise storage approach, this approach improves upstream execution time by several orders of magnitude, with negligeable impact on memory occupation, network bandwidth, and downstream execution performance.

Keywords

CRDT; linear data structure; tombstones management

1. INTRODUCTION

Mass remote collaboration tools are increasingly used. Massive group editing appears in many end-user applications such as Wikipedia, Google Docs, Office, Evernote, Dropbox, or VCSs such as git or svn. Group editing aims to allow a large number of users to edit the same document at the same time and from different places. Centralized platforms such as Google Docs offer world wide group editing service to millions of users but limit the number of participants to a document [3]. An alternative to centralized platforms is to take advantage of availability and scalability of decentralized peer-to-peer networks.

In group editing, high responsiveness is crucial [22]. Every user device hosts a replica of the document that she/he modify at will. The user observes the effect of her/his modification immediately, without any locking mechanism – or even network latency – perturbing his interaction. This behavior is called *optimistic replication* [19]. Also, the modification must be propagated to other users' devices and applied there with the same effect. Group editing systems distinguish *upstream* and *downstream operation execution.* A user's modification is applied immediately to some first, so-called *upstream* replica, and then sent to other replicas *(downstream).* Delivering a downstream operation merges its effects with concurrent modifications. Merging arbitrary modifications is a difficult and error-prone task, and thus many mechanisms have been proposed.

Operational Transformation (OT) is an established mechanism for group editing applications [14, 17, 23] because this class of algorithms promises very high responsiveness for upstream operations execution. However, in a decentralized context, downstream execution of OT algorithms is complex and expensive because each replica must reorder its history and transform concurrent operations, implying a $O(N^2k)$ complexity with N the number of operations and k the number of replica.

To avoid this issue, Conflict-Free Replicated Data Types (CRDTs) have been proposed [13, 15, 25]. This class of algorithms uses operations whose downstream execution is commutative; this enables to keep the consistency of the collaborative document easily, without using transformations. Ahmed-Nacer et al. [6] show in particular that downstream execution of CRDT algorithms is more efficient by a factor between 25 to 1000 compared to representative OT algorithms.

However, upstream execution – and thus responsiveness – of CRDT algorithms often performs poorly. These algorithms associate a unique identifier with each element in the document. Unique identifiers allow a quicker and easier downstream execution, but must be generated and retrieved during upstream execution. A first improvement is to coarsen the granularity to identify large blocks rather than single characters [26]. Indeed, collaborative documents are often written block by block – copy/paste or batch operations for instance. The fewer elements in the document, the less computation is needed to apply and merge modifications. Moreover, each element contains metadata (including unique identifiers), so the fewer elements there are, the less memory overhead. Nevertheless, an algorithm with, say, linear complexity, remains linear using blocks. Furthermore, blocks slow down upstream execution, since elements are of different sizes, and retrieving element identifiers affected by user modifications requires to traverse the document. Fi-

GROUP '16, November 13-16, 2016, Sanibel Island, FL, USA

 ISBN 978-1-4503-4276-6/16/11... $15.00
DOI: http://dx.doi.org/10.1145/2957276.2957300

nally, block-based algorithms remain relatively inefficient in execution complexity.

In this paper we propose a solution, easily adaptable to most algorithms, and that improves responsiveness considerably. The idea is to have an efficient auxiliary data structure – called the *identifier structure* – dedicated to CRDT identifiers. This data structure has no consistency requirements between replicas; and each peer can modify its own structure independently and efficiently; thus, there are no issues due to concurrency. More specifically, we implement this insight for element-based and block-based CRDT algorithms. Our solution is easy to implement; it decreases upstream complexity, without significantly degrading downstream complexity. Its memory and bandwidth usage is similar to the original algorithm.

The remainder of this paper proceeds as follows. Section 2 introduces the state of the art of the current knowledge in group editing OT and CRDT algorithms, as well as some definitions useful in the following sections. Section 3 presents our identifier structure for improving upstream complexity of CRDT algorithms and proposes its application on two different CRDT. Section 4 demonstrates how to combine our approach with block management. Section 5 evaluates our implementations with several and various experiments. Section 6 concludes.

2. BACKGROUND, STATE OF THE ART AND RELATED WORK

2.1 Definitions

To clarify and unify the presentation of the existing approaches we introduce the following definitions [9].

- **replica**: Several peers can edit a document from different places. Each peer hosts its own *replica* of the collaborative document. The replica contains elements visible to the end user as well as metadata required to manage eventual consistency.
- **operation**: When a peer apply user modification, it modifies its replica and generates *operations*. These operations are sent by the peer to the other peers. These operations contain the necessary data and metadata to ensure consistency when executed on the other peers.
- **upstream**: The process of applying user modification and generating corresponding operation(s) is called *upstream update*.
- **downstream** The process of executing remote operation coming from another peer and modifying the receiving replica is called *downstream update*.

2.2 Operational Transformation

Operational Transformation (OT) [17] is an optimistic replication mechanism [19]. It was the first approach used in the real-time group editing field and has been studied in the literature [14, 22].

In the OT approach, downstream operations are transformed before their integration in order to handle concurrency. The transformations should preserve the "intentions" of the user [22]. To ensure consistency, a received downstream operation is transformed against every concurrent update operation in a specific order.

The two main issues of OT algorithms in a decentralized context are consistency and scalability. Consistency issues are due to difficulties to define correct transformation functions. For linear documents, the only known transformation functions that are correct in a peer-to-peer context are the Tombstones Transformation Functions (TTF) [14]. However, tombstones impact responsiveness negatively since the upstream procedure must count them for every modification. Scalability issues are due to history ordering and downstream transformations. History ordering has a $O(N^2k)$ complexity[1] and requires vector clocks [12] whose impact negatively memory and bandwidth usage and limit the scalability of the approach.

2.3 Conflict-free Replicated Data Types

An alternative approach, called Conflict-free Replicated Data Type (CRDT), has been proposed [11]. The insight behind CRDT is to design a set of commutative update operations. Thus, no transformation and no history ordering is necessary. Commutative operations can be applied in any order, and are guaranteed to converge. The literature proposes several CRDT algorithms, but in what follows we mention only the most representative ones in the context of group editing.

2.3.1 WOOT

WOOT [13] was the first CDRT algorithm proposed for group editing. It is based on the principle that in a text document, an element is inserted between two others. In the WOOT approach, each element is identified by a unique identifier and linked to the two elements between which its was inserted. WOOT identifiers are composed of the identifier of the upstream peer and the value of local clock of this peer time. A deterministic algorithm orders the elements inserted in the same region, which is quite complex and is more less efficient than more recent CRDTs. Moreover, since each element position is relative to its neighbors, elements cannot be completely removed from the document, but are turned into invisible "tombstones". As TTF, these tombstones must be counted and impact upstream execution complexity. Optimized versions of this algorithm have been proposed [24], but only improve downstream complexity [6].

2.3.2 TreeDoc

TreeDoc [15] is a CRDT based on a binary unbalanced tree of elements. An element's a unique identifier is its path in the tree. This approach supports dichotomic search, but is expensive when the tree is unbalanced, for instance when many inserts occurs at the end of the document. It is impossible to balance the tree without synchronizing all nodes, because the tree must be the same at all peers in order to generate consistent operations. TreeDoc uses tombstones but they can be purged in some conditions. For example once a deleted node does not have any visible children, it can be safely removed.

2.3.3 Logoot

Logoot [25] is a CRDT that uses a lexicographic order to totally order the document elements. A Logoot identifier is a list of triples of integers. The first integer of the triple is a priority, the second is the upstream peer ID and the third is the upstream logical clock. When an insertion happens, the new element's ID ensures that it will be placed at the

[1] N is the number of operations and k is the number of replicas.

wanted position. Element identifiers are stored into an array. Upstream insertion consists of directly accessing elements n and $n+1$, generating an identifier between them, and shifting the table to place the new element. Shifting a whole document is costly.

Another issue of Logoot is that the size of identifiers grows and becomes costly in terms of memory and performance. Identifiers grow faster when there are several insertions in the same part of the document. Let's say a peer p' (with clock $'i'$) decides to insert an element between two successive identifiers $[\langle p, i, n\rangle]$ and $[\langle p, i, n+1\rangle]$. The new identifier will be $[\langle p, i, n\rangle\langle p', i', n'\rangle]$.

2.3.4 LogootSplit

LogootSplit [7] is a block version of Logoot. Blocks are of different sizes and created trough copy-paste or buffering as a whole single Logoot identifier, reducing memory usage. Block algorithms must be able to split blocks in order to remove a part or to insert an element within the block. An offset number is present in the LoogotSplit identifiers to identify block's parts in a unique manner.

Three different versions of LogootSplit have been proposed, the most efficient being the one using an AVL tree to organize the nodes.

2.3.5 RGA

The Replicated Growable Array (RGA) algorithm [18] uses the fact that every element is included immediately after another one in a text document. RGA data structure is essentially a linked-list, in which a node has a content, an identifier, a flag to say if the node is a tombstone, and the identifier of the next node in the list. A RGA identifier is composed of the upstream peer ID (sid) and of the sum of the upstream vector clock value during insertion (sum). Identifier i_1 is said to "precede" i_2 ($i_1 \prec i_2$) if $sum_1 < sum_2$ or $sum_1 = sum_2 \wedge sid_1 < sid_2$.

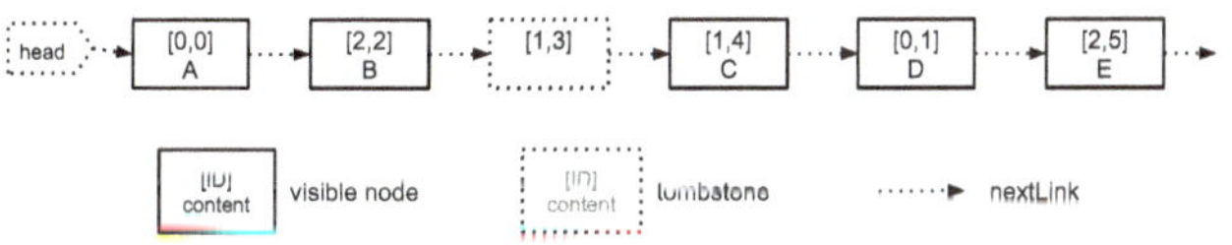

Figure 1: Example of a RGA list

An insertion operation contains the identifiers of both the new node and the node that it follows (called *reference node*). Insertion consists in placing the new node to the right of the reference node and at the left of the first node whose identifier **precedes** the new identifier. This simple and efficient procedure orders concurrent inserts. Moreover, to retrieve reference nodes, RGA uses a hash map, keyed by node identifier, mapped to the node itself.

In the common cases, the new node is inserted just after its reference node, but other computations are required if there are concurrent insert. Suppose three peers work on a collaborative document. We note o_x the operation that inserts the node N_x whose identifier is i_x. The initial state of the document is n_1n_5 with $i_1 = [0,2]$ and $i_5 = [2,1]$. The three peers concurrently insert a node just after N_1. Peer 0 inserts n_4, whose identifier is $i_4 = [0,3]$, Peer 1 inserts n_3 with $i_3 = [1,4]$, and Peer 2 n_2 with $i_2 = [2,5]$. Therefore, $i_5 \prec i_4 \prec i_3 \prec i_2$. The result below shows for each peer a different execution order, which nonetheless reach a convergent state.

$$Peer0 : n_1n_5 \rightarrow_{o_4} n_1n_4n_5 \rightarrow_{o_2} n_1n_2n_4n_5 \rightarrow_{o_3} n_1n_2n_3n_4n_5$$

$$Peer1 : n_1n_5 \rightarrow_{o_3} n_1n_3n_5 \rightarrow_{o_2} n_1n_2n_3n_5 \rightarrow_{o_4} n_1n_2n_3n_4n_5$$

$$Peer2 : n_1n_5 \rightarrow_{o_2} n_1n_2n_5 \rightarrow_{o_3} n_1n_2n_3n_5 \rightarrow_{o_4} n_1n_2n_3n_4n_5$$

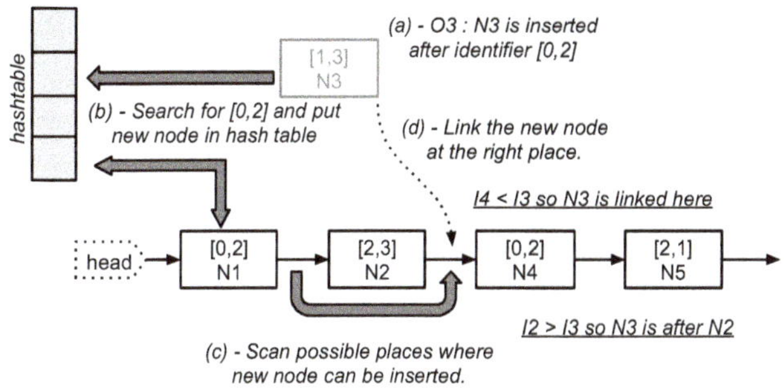

Figure 2: Execution of operation o_3 at Peer 0

2.4 Summary

If we consider a high degree of responsiveness as a – at most – logarithmic complexity for upstream execution, then none of the existing algorithms present such performance. Indeed, each one has a flaw that affect upstream execution :

- OT needs to count TTF tombstones
- RGA and WOOT also needs to count tombstones.
- Logoot needs to shift its array and, as LogootSplit, needs to manage growing identifiers.
- Treedoc needs to traverse an unbalanced tree.
- Block approaches need to count block sizes.

We consider upstream efficiency as the most noticeable by the user [20]. However, downstream efficiency is also important, and RGA score best by this metric [6].

3. THE IDENTIFIER DATA STRUCTURE

The basic idea of our solution is to build an identifier data structure local to each peer. This is easily adaptable to the most CRDT algorithms, and improve upstream complexity. This structure must not augment remote complexity of algorithms, and must not use excessive memory compared to the base algorithm. Our approach really on the classic CRDT algorithm, and update the identifier structure on the side.

Figure 3 illustrate our solution. It shows the different steps in which our identifier structure is used. The step 1 is the user action. The steps 2 correspond to the steps where we use our structure to retrieve the node(s) corresponding to the user's action. The steps 3-5 are the base replication algorithm unmodified. The step 6-7 updates the identifier structure according to remote operations.

The critical steps are to retrieve efficiently identifiers from a user position (step 2) and conversely to update the identifier structure during downstream (step 6). To achieve this, we first observe that all the base CRDT algorithms manage a structure composed of nodes identified by a unique identifier. Our identifier structure will contain a set of organized nodes, called idNode. A idNode has a reference to an

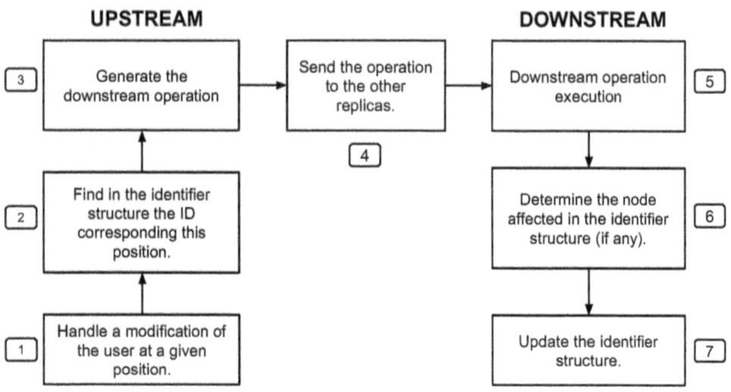

Figure 3: Steps to generate and execute an operation with our identifier structure

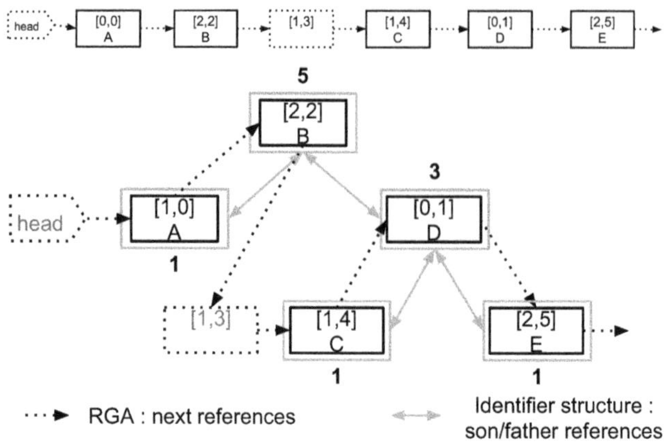

Figure 4: Example of a base and identifier structure for RGA

base CRDT node, as well as references to other idNodes to enable efficient traversal. Symmetrically, each node of the base data structure contains a reference to the corresponding idNode.

3.1 Retrieving CRDT identifiers

Retrieving a CRDT identifier is straightforward in algorithms such as Logoot that have no tombstones and single identifier per element. It is more complex for algorithms using tombstones and/or blocks. The naive solution used in RGA, WOOT, or LogootSplit consists in counting visible elements, starting from the head of the document, until the appropriate position is reached. Such procedures have a linear complexity, i.e. $O(N)$ with N the number of element ever inserted in the document, including tombstones.

The identifier data structure allows to map efficiently position of user modification to CRDT identifier. This data structure can be a skip list [16] when CRDT identifiers are totally ordered – e.g. Treedoc or Logoot identifiers – or a weighted binary tree for other CRDT.

A weighted tree contains a set of idNodes, one of them being the root of the tree. A idNode contains a *left child*, a *right child*, and a *parent* references to idNodes, a *weight* which is the total size of the sub-tree, and a reference to an base CRDT node. We add to the base CRDT node a reference to the corresponding idNode.

In the case of RGA, for instance, an base node contains a unique identifier, a content, a next reference, and a tombstone flag. We add to this RGA node, a reference to an idNode, whose reference is unset when the node becomes a tombstone.

Figure 4 illustrates the structure described above. The base RGA structure is drawn with dotted lines, whereas the new identifier structure is drawn with plain lines. Notice that identifier and base structures are decoupled – each structure has its own way to traverse the nodes – but both are linked. Only the non-tombstone nodes belongs to the identifier structure. Tombstones such as one identified by [1,3] are not present in the identifier structure, limiting memory overhead.

The weight of a node is the size of the subtree. The algorithm to find the node corresponding to a given position is the following:[2]

```
function FINDPOSINIDENTIFIERTREE(pos)
    if pos == 0 then
        return head.identifier
    else
        node = root                          ▷ Begins from the tree's root
        while pos ≠ node.leftWeight() + 1 do
            if pos < node.leftWeight() + 1 then
                node = node.leftChild()          ▷ Goes left
            else
                pos = pos − (node.leftWeight() + 1)
                node = node.rightChild()         ▷ Goes right
        return node.identifier
```

The procedure traverses only the height of the tree. Let's suppose the user wants to insert element "X" after the third position in the RGA structure described in Figure 4. The FINDPOSINIDENTIFIERTREE procedure,

1. with $pos = 3 \geq 2$, goes to the right of $\{[2,2], B\}$
2. with $pos = 1 < 2$, goes to the left of $\{[0,1], D\}$
3. with $pos = 1$, returns $\{[1,4], C\}$.

Then, the new element "X" is inserted as the right-most child of the left sub-tree of $\{[1,4], C\}$ – here, directly to left of $\{[1,4], C\}$. The weights of the ancestors of the new node are updated as shown in red in Figure 5. The generated insertion operation (step 3) will contain the new node $\{[3,5], X\}$ and its *reference* $[1,4]$.

Such an identifier structure can be easily adapted to similar tombstone-based algorithms such as WOOT, but also to block-based algorithm including the size of the nodes content in weights (see Section 3). It is also beneficial in a no-tombstone and no-block algorithm such as Logoot (see Section 3.3). With a balanced tree or a periodically balanced tree (see Section 5), the complexity of upstream execution is $O(log(n))$ with n the number of visible elements.

3.2 Updating identifier structure during downstream

As described above, we rely of the base CRDT algorithm to apply downstream operation. In RGA, for instance, an insertion consists of following the RGA list (presented with

[2]The method $leftWeight()$ returns the weight of the left child of a node (0 if their is no left child).

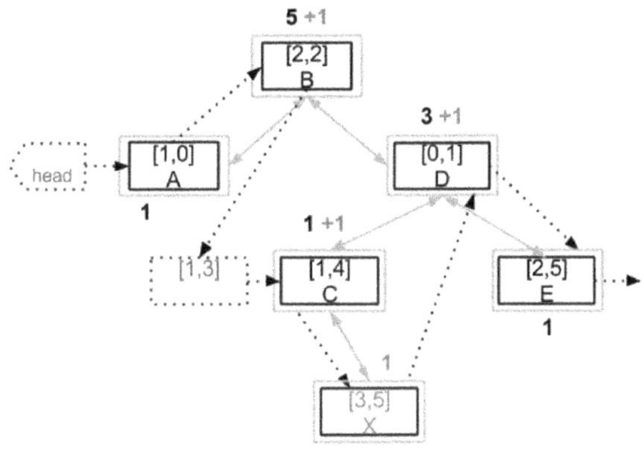

Figure 5: Upstream insertion

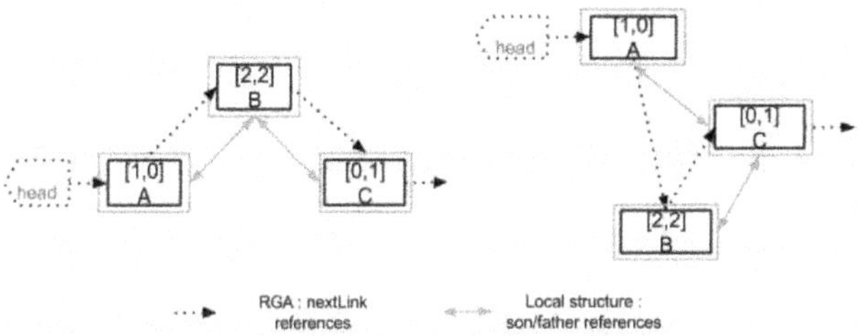

Figure 6: Two possible identifier tree states for the same RGA base state

dotted lines in Figure 4), starting from the reference node until it finds a node with a lesser identifier (*target node*).[3]

After the target node has been identified by the base algorithm we update the identifier structure. However, the target node might be a tombstone, and thus not belonging to the identifier structure. If the downstream operation is also a deletion we don't need to do anything. If the operation is an insertion, we continue to follow the base RGA linked-list chaining until the first non-tombstone node and we insert the new idNode at the left of this node.

```
function INSERTDOWNSTREAM(target, newNode)
    while target.nextLink ≠ null ∧ ¬target.visible do
        target = target.nextLink
    if ¬target.visible then              ▷ insertion at the end
        INSERTRIGHT(root, newNode)
    else
        INSERTBEFORE(target, newNode)
```

INSERTRIGHT inserts a node at the right-most position in the tree. INSERTBEFORE inserts a node at the right-most node of the left child of a substree. Both procedures update the corresponding weights.

Considering algorithms such as Logoot (or Treedoc), the problem is a bit different since there is no linked link. However, in these cases, since the identifier structure are totally ordered, the identifier structure is a binary search tree. So, we can simply traverse the tree to update it.

Last but not least, each peer can use an arbitrary identifier structure, including different shapes for it. This means that identifier structure can be different for each peer even if they base structure is the same. For instance, in Figure 6, we show two peers that have the same base RGA state but two different identifier data structures. This enable a peer to balance its identifier tree locally without synchronizing with the other peers.

3.3 Logoot with identifier structure

Our approach can be applied beneficially to the other single-element CRDT algorithms. For instance, we can apply it to Logoot [25]. The base Logoot algorithm uses an array to store identifiers and does not use tombstones. It retrieves identifiers for generating operations in constant time, but upstream complexity is affected by the shifting of the array to insert (or remove) an element. In essence, the complexity of the shift is $O(n)$.

We can replace this array by a skip list or the same weighted tree than above. The gain obtained by removing the shift exceeds the overhead due to the structure traversal which is only in $O(log(n))$.[4]

Considering downstream execution, the base Logoot uses a binary search to retrieve the targeted identifier. Since Logoot identifiers are totally ordered, the identifier tree structure is a binary search tree. Thus, the search of the target element for downstream execution will use the identifier structure with the same algorithmic cost. Furthermore, once the targeted element is found, updating the structure is done in constant time $O(1)$ in contrast to shifting the array in $O(n)$.

4. RGATREESPLIT: A BLOCK-WISE RGA WITH IDENTIFIER STRUCTURE

Since RGA is the most efficient algorithm for downstream execution, and since block-wise algorithm improve efficiency of both upstream and downstream execution [26], we propose a new algorithm called RGATreeSplit that combine these concepts.

To be able to handle blocks in a RGA algorithm, some changes are required on the base structure. These changes will be described in the next section. In the late section, we apply our identifier structure concept on this block-wise algorithm.

4.1 Block-wise RGA

A block-wise RGA node contains the information usual to RGA with some additional metadata. This algorithm uses the notions of split and offset introduced by Yu [26]. A block identifier is composed of a CRDT identifier plus an offset. When a node is first inserted, its offset is 0. Splitting a node whose offset is x at position pos produces to two nodes: a first one with offset x, and a second one with offset $x+pos$. In this way, each node is always uniquely identified. There is an additional reference to nodes, called splitLink. This reference enables quick access to all the nodes of the resulting from the split of a node by linking the two resulting nodes directly. This reference is set when a node is split in two parts.

In summary, a block-wise RGA node contains the following attributes:

[3]RGA uses an hash table to start directly from the reference node.

[4]Assuming a balanced, or periodically re-balanced tree.

content : a block of elements. The content can be freed when the node becomes a tombstone in order to minimize memory consumption.

identifier : the RGA unique identifier of the node.

nextLink : the base RGA linked-list reference.

offset : the offset of the node within the node originally inserted by the user.

splitLink : next part of the block in case of a split.

length : the length of the content of the node. When a node becomes a tombstone, the content is freed but the length of the node is saved. This enables to split tombstones and to handle concurrent operations correctly.

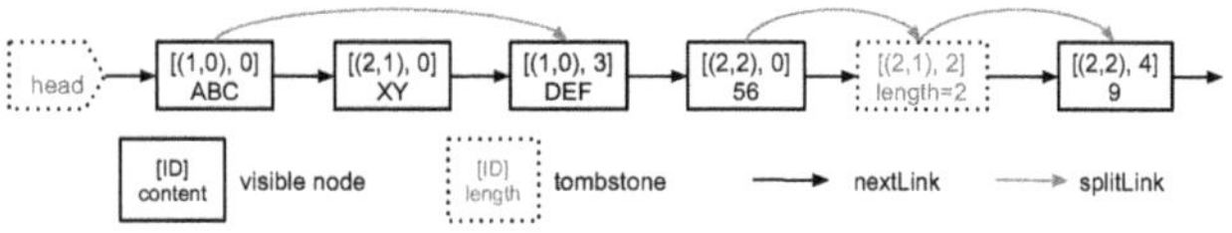

Figure 7: Example of a block-wise RGA structure

Figure 7 shows an example of a block-wise structure for RGA. The state of the structure results from the following modifications, starting from an empty document.

1. A user inserts "ABCDEF" in replica 1, the identifier is $[[1,0],0]$.
2. After receiving "ABCDEF", a user inserts "XY" at position 3 in replica 2. The identifier is $[[2,1],0]$. The block "ABCDEF" is split into "ABC" with identifier $[[1,0],0]$ and "DEF" with identifier $[[1,0],3]$.
3. A user inserts "56789" at the end in replica 2, the identifier is $[[2,2],0]$.
4. A user deletes "78". Block "56789" is split into "56" with identifier $[[2,2],0]$, a tombstone with identifier $[[2,2],2]$, and the "9" with identifier $[[2,2],4]$.

The function FINDOFFSET returns the node corresponding to the operation's offset. The inputs are the identifier of the node sought and the offset. We start from the base hash table reference and we follow the splitLink chaining. For instance, in the above example, an operation targeting identifier $[[1,0],4]$ has an effect on the block "DEF" with identifier $[[1,0],3]$ and length 3.

---

function FINDOFFSET(identifer, offset)
  $node = hashtable.get(identifier)$
  while $node.offset + node.length < offset$ **do**
    $node = node.splitLink$
  return $node$

The splitLink chaining allows good performance but is not mandatory, especially in tombstone-based approaches. Indeed, following the RGA nextLink chaining is still possible. Also, an alternative to a physical splitting of the block, is to keep them intact and to reference the parts of the blocks in the RGA structure. A precise performance analysis should be conduct to determine the optimal solution, especially in term of memory usage, but the whole complexity is equivalent for all alternatives.

4.2 Identifier data structure of RGATreeSplit

We now discuss the addition of the identifier structure to RGASplit. It is similar to the one described in Section 3. However, some generalization is need. First, we need to take block length into account in the FINDPOSINIDENTIFIERTREE function, generalized as follow.[5]

---

function FINDPOSINIDENTIFIERTREE(pos)
  if $pos == 0$ **then**
    return $head.identifier$
  $node = root$ ▷ Begins from the tree's root
  while $\neg(pos > node.leftWeight() + node.length \wedge pos \leq node.leftWeight() + node.length)$ **do**
    if $pos \leq node.leftWeight() + node.length$ **then**
      $node = node.leftChild()$ ▷ Goes left
    else
      $pos = pos - (node.leftWeight() + node.length)$
      $node = node.rightChild()$ ▷ Goes right
  return $[node.identifier, pos + node.offset - node.leftWeight]$

Second, when the target node is found, it can be necessary to split it. Indeed, a user insertion applied within a block, will create three new blocks (the two split parts and the new one). A simple solution is first to replace the original block by the new node, to INSERTBEFORE the left part of the split block and to INSERTAFTER the right part. Figure 8 illustrates this procedure. The block "XYZ" is inserted at position 5 in the string "ABCDEFGHIJ". The block "XYZ" replaces and splits the block "DEFG". The two parts "DE" and "FG" are respectively inserted before and after the new block "XYZ".

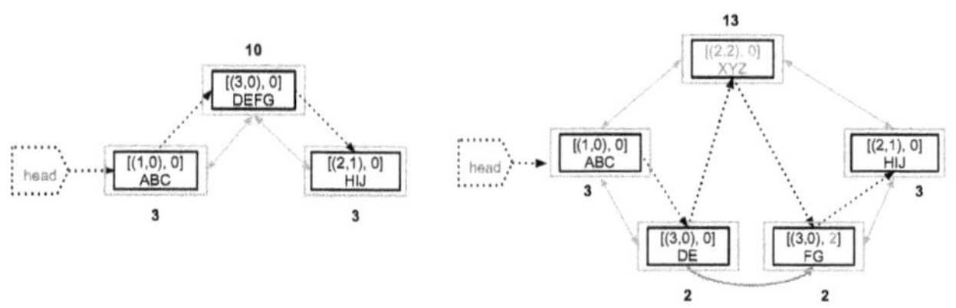

Figure 8: Before and after split

5. EVALUATION AND EXPERIMENTS

In this section, we evaluate our approach, by comparing implementations of the solutions presented above, to existing implementations of the best comparable replication algorithms.

To conduct this experimentation, we use a Java benchmarking framework [6, 7], in which the original authors of TreeDoc, RGA, and Logootsplit implemented their algorithms. Within this framework, we implement four new algorithms: RGA with an identifier structure, Logoot with an identifier structure, RGA with blocks, and RGATreeSplit.

5.1 Implementations

The binary weighted tree identifier structure as presented in Section 3 can be implemented in two ways: always balanced or unbalanced with periodic re-balancing. Furthermore, there exist several algorithms for each. For simplicity, we re-use existing implementations and/or naive algorithms.

[5]With blocks of length 1 and null offsets, this function correspond with its definition in the single element approach.

For the RGA and Logoot identifier structure, we use Apache's TreeList [1]. This Java collection implements a list as a balanced tree. Positions in the list are retrieved using weights similarly to what we have presented above.[6] We add references in both direction between visible CRDT nodes and TreeList nodes. To further simplify the downstream execution implementation, we traverse the height of the tree to find the position of a TreeList node, and we use the base add or remove methods of the TreeList to update the tree. All operations, whether upstream or downstream, executes in $O(log(n))$.

For the RGATreeSplit algorithm, we implement a simple weighted and unbalanced binary tree for our identifier structure. To keep good performance during long-term execution, we periodically re-balance the tree by brute-force copying the visible nodes into a new balanced tree. Each replica is re-balanced independently when the number of operations since the last re-balancing reaches $k\frac{n}{ln(n)}$, with n the number of nodes, and k and arbitrary constant factor.[7]

The re-balancing procedure execution time is taken into account in the experimental results presented below. For shake of implementation simplicity, we call it during downstream execution. However, to ensure real-time responsiveness, the system should call it when idle, and can interrupt it as soon as an upstream or downstream operation is received.

Our implementations, especially the RGATreeSplit could be improved by using a balanced (n-ary-)tree, or a smarter re-balancing algorithm [21], and finer studies to detect when to re-balance the tree. However, the goal of the experiments is only to demonstrate that our approach greatly improves upstream execution performance even using a naive implementation and preserves good downstream performance.

All the implementations and the benchmark platform are publicly available at
https://github.com/score-team/replication-benchmarker/.

5.2 Experiments

The following experiments were executed on the Grid5000 experimental facility [8]. The nodes are powered by Intel Xeon X3440 processors (2.53GHz) with 16GB of RAM and run a Wheezy-x64-big-1.0 operating systems which based on Debian. Moreover the benchmark is not multi-threaded, therefore each algorithm uses only one core.

We randomly generated different types of traces to evaluate the performance of our algorithms. A trace is a sequence of user modifications on a text document on which we apply on all studied algorithms. Thus, all algorithm execute the same set of modifications.

We conduct two series of experiments: the first concerns modifications that only affect one element, the second contains block modifications. In the block series, 20% of the modifications are block modifications and the average length of a block is 20 elements (Gaussian normal distribution with standard deviation $\sigma = 2$).

The other parameters the same for both series. Each series contains six experiments traces containing respectively 5000, 10000, 15000, 20000, 30000 and 40000 modifications. As results may sightly depend on the content of the traces, we generated, three different traces for each experiment. Each trace simulates 10 peers that work on the same text document. Each modification is concurrent to 2 other modifications ($\sigma = 1$). 80% of modifications are insertions, and 20% are deletions following to an existing study in group editing performance [6]. We keep the number of peers fixed since previous experiments [5] have demonstrated that this parameter does not influence the CRDTs performance, contrary to the number of operations.

For each experiment we measured the average upstream execution time, the average downstream execution time, the bandwidth consumed – i.e., the total size of data transmitted between peers – and memory occupation (as the average of memory occupation during the last 100 operations). Time is measured using the Java System.nanotime() method, and the bandwidth and memory occupation are measured by means of a library from the EMMA coverage tool [2]. The algorithms evaluated are the original RGA, Logoot, LogootSplitAVL, TreeDoc, and the four new CRDT described above: RGA with a TreeList identifier structure (called RGATreeList), Logoot with a TreeList identifier structure (called LogootTreeList), RGA with blocks (called RGASplit) and RGATreeSplit.

5.3 Single element series

In this series, each modification affects only one text element. The average execution time for upstream and downstream is presented in Figure 9, and memory occupation is presented in Figure 10.

We observe that RGA and RGASplit achieve roughly the same performance, and the same for RGATreeList and RGATreeSplit. This was expected. The main result here, is that identifier structure drastically improves the upstream performance. RGATreeList, RGATreeSplit and LogootTree are superior to RGA, RGASplit and Logoot respectively. These three algorithms have the best observed performance and are not affected by the length of the experiment. Downstream performance of RGA approaches is sightly degraded, due to identifier structure updating but remains better than non-RGA approaches.

As expected, LogootTree has better performance than Logoot in downstream, but more surprisingly, also has better performance than LogootSplitAVL, even though the latter also uses a balanced binary search tree.

Bandwidth is not affected by the use of the identifier structure, since only base RGA or Logoot operations are sent between peers.[8] Memory occupation is only slightly affected due to the identifier structure. TreeDoc has the lowest memory footprint thanks to the absence of auxiliary structure and fewer tombstones than RGA, but has high bandwidth usage, due to its identifier length.

5.4 Block modification series

In this series, 20% of user modifications are block modifications (average length 20, $\sigma = 2$). The average execution time for upstream and downstream is presented in Figure 11, and memory occupation and bandwidth are presented in Figure 12.

Observe first, in such case, all the block-wise algorithms improve both upstream and downstream performance compared to non-block versions: LogootSplitAVL, RGASplit and RGATreeSplit versus Logoot, RGA, and RGATreeList

[6]In Apache's TreeList, weights (called relative positions) are the size of the left subtree.

[7]We empirically identified $k = 5$ as a adequate factor.

[8]RGATreeList has slightly better bandwidth usage than RGATreeSplit since block operations contains offsets.

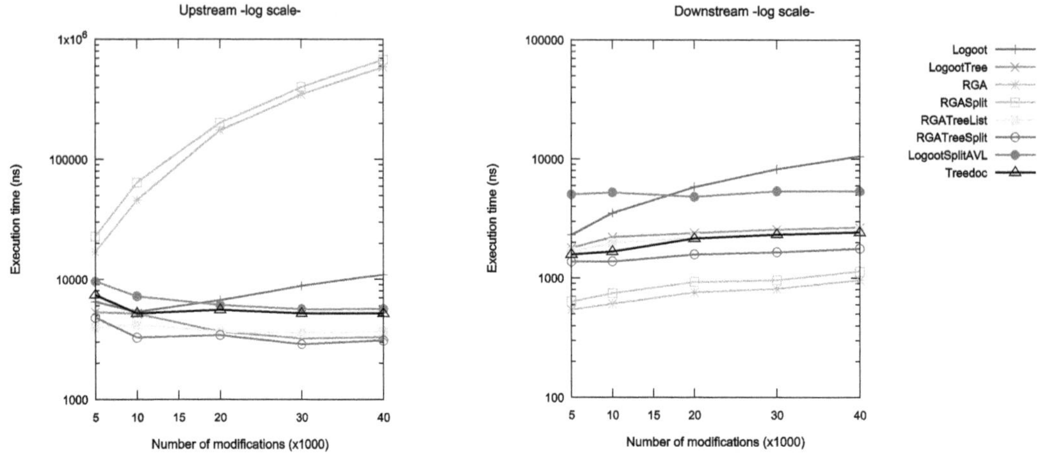

Figure 9: Execution time – single element series

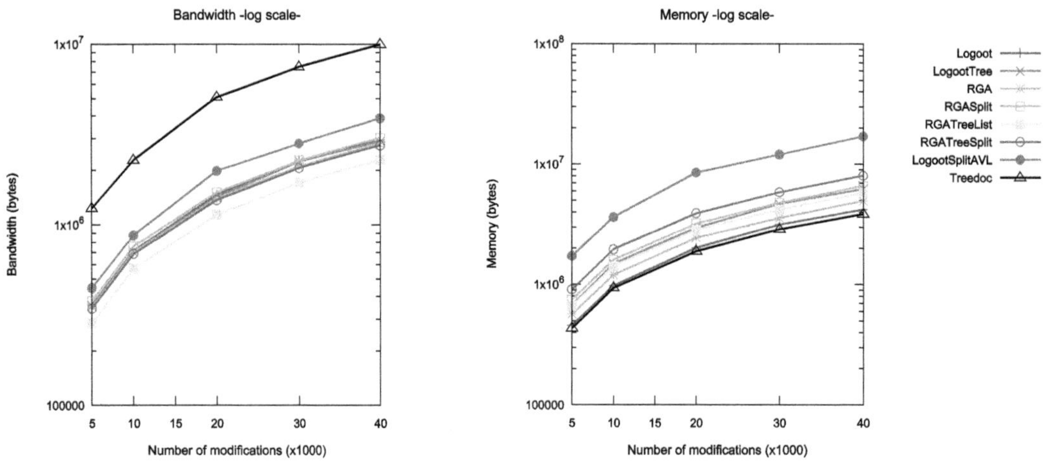

Figure 10: Memory occupation – single element series

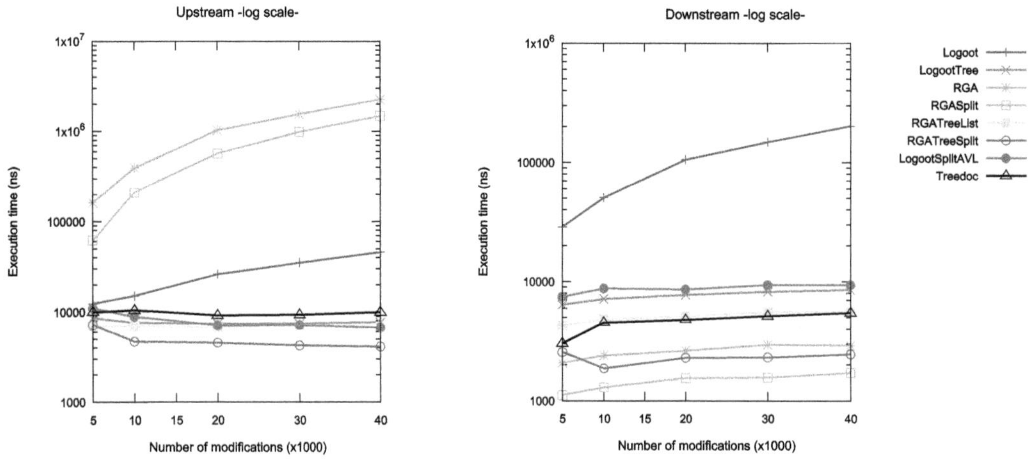

Figure 11: Execution time – block series

respectively. However, block management is not enough to guaranty high responsiveness. Indeed, RGASplit performs quite poorly and deteriorates over time. Furthermore, LogootSplitAVL and TreeDoc have worse downstream performance than the original RGA algorithm while RGATreeSplit has the best overall performance.

LogootTree performs worse than RGATreeSplit, but surprisingly again, it performs similarly to LogootSplitAVL, even without block management.

Concerning memory, block-based approaches improve both bandwidth and memory usage. RGATreeSplit and RGASplit have the best results. We note that TreeDoc obtains better bandwidth performance than in the single element series due to a kind of compression of operations engendered by block modifications.

Concerning ease of implementation, we note that RGATreeSplit and LogootTree obtain better performance than LogootSplitAVL while having a simpler code (respectively 747 and 391 versus 1,255 non-commenting source statement measured using JavaNCSS [4]). Indeed, our approach allows to use an existing or simple data structure contrary to LogootSplitAVL that requires its own and specific data structure.

6. CONCLUSION

In this paper, we present an approach to improve responsiveness of CRDT algorithms. This approach is based on an additional identifier structure that can be adapted to the CRDT algorithms, including block-wise algorithms, to achieve logarithmic complexity. Experiments demonstrate that we reach the best overall performance among existing CRDT algorithms. Even though our implementation is quite naive and can be improved.

More particularly, we significantly improve performance of incorporating users' modifications. This aspect is important since users can directly observe it, and may otherwise lead to user un-satisfaction [10].

We suggest that a similar approach may be applicable to other CRDT data types such as sets or structured documents and also to operational transformations, in order to improve the responsiveness of the TTF solution, and possibly to improve the downstream execution by identifying the operations to transform more efficiently.

Acknowledgment

This research is supported in part by European FP7 project 609 551 SyncFree (2013–2016).

http://syncfree.lip6.fr/ .

References

[1] Apache TreeList. https://commons.apache.org/proper/commons-collections/apidocs/org/apache/commons/collections4/list/TreeList.html.

[2] Emma code coverage tool. http://emma.sourceforge.net/.

[3] Google. drive help: Limits on sharing. retrieved 19 february 2016. URL https://support.google.com/drive/answer/2494827.

[4] JavaNCSS. http://www.kclee.de/clemens/java/javancss/.

[5] M. Ahmed-Nacer. *Evaluation methodology for replicated data types*. Theses, Université de Lorraine, May 2015. URL https://tel.archives-ouvertes.fr/tel-01252234.

[6] M. Ahmed-Nacer, C.-L. Ignat, G. Oster, H.-G. Roh, and P. Urso. Evaluating CRDTs for real-time document editing. In ACM, editor, *ACM Symposium on Document Engineering*, page 10 pages, San Francisco, CA, USA, september 2011.

[7] L. André, S. Martin, G. Oster, and C.-L. Ignat. Supporting adaptable granularity of changes for massive-scale collaborative editing. In *International Conference on Collaborative Computing: Networking, Applications and Worksharing (Collaboratecom)*, pages 50–59, Austin, TX, USA, Oct 2013. .

[8] D. Balouek, A. Carpen Amarie, G. Charrier, F. Desprez, E. Jeannot, E. Jeanvoine, A. Lèbre, D. Margery, N. Niclausse, L. Nussbaum, O. Richard, C. Pérez, F. Quesnel, C. Rohr, and L. Sarzyniec. Adding virtualization capabilities to the Grid'5000 testbed. In I. Ivanov, M. Sinderen, F. Leymann, and T. Shan, editors, *Cloud Computing and Services Science*, volume 367 of *Communications in Computer and Information Science*, pages 3–20. Springer International Publishing, 2013. ISBN 978-3-319-04518-4. .

[9] P. A. Bernstein and S. Das. Rethinking eventual consistency. In *Proceedings of the 2013 ACM SIGMOD International Conference on Management of Data*, pages 923–928, New York, NY, USA, 2013. ACM.

[10] C. Jay, M. Glencross, and R. Hubbold. Modeling the effects of delayed haptic and visual feedback in a collaborative virtual environment. *ACM Transactions on Computer-Human Interaction*, 14(2), August 2007. ISSN 1073-0516. . URL http://doi.acm.org/10.1145/1275511.1275514.

[11] M. Leţia, N. Preguiça, and M. Shapiro. CRDTs: Consistency without concurrency control. In *SOSP W. on Large Scale Distributed Systems and Middleware (LADIS)*, pages 29–34, Big Sky, MT, USA, October 2009. ACM SIGOPS.

[12] F. Mattern. Virtual time and global states of distributed systems. In *International Workshop on Parallel and Distributed Algorithms*, pages 215–226, Château de Bonas, France, October 1989. Elsevier Science Publishers.

[13] G. Oster, P. Urso, P. Molli, and A. Imine. Data Consistency for P2P Collaborative Editing. In *Conference on Computer-Supported Cooperative Work (CSCW)*, pages 259–267, Banff, Alberta, Canada, nov 2006. ACM Press.

[14] G. Oster, P. Urso, P. Molli, and A. Imine. Tombstone transformation functions for ensuring consistency in collaborative editing systems. In *International Conference on Collaborative Computing: Networking, Applications and Worksharing (CollaborateCom 2006)*, Atlanta, Georgia, USA, November 2006. IEEE Press.

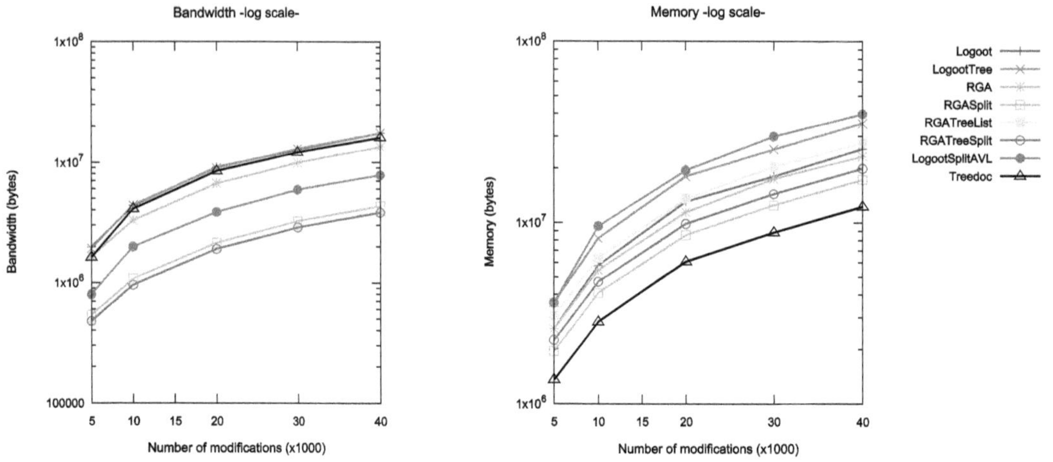

Figure 12: Memory occupation – block series

[15] N. M. Preguiça, J. M. Marquès, M. Shapiro, and M. Leţia. A commutative replicated data type for cooperative editing. In *International Conference on Distributed Computing Systems (ICDCS)*, pages 395–403, Montréal, QC, Canada, 2009. IEEE Computer Society.

[16] W. Pugh. Skip lists: a probabilistic alternative to balanced trees. *Communications of the ACM*, 33(6):668–676, 1990.

[17] M. Ressel, D. Nitsche-Ruhland, and R. Gunzenhäuser. An integrating, transformation-oriented approach to concurrency control and undo in group editors. In *Conference on Computer supported cooperative work (CSCW)*, pages 288–297, Boston, MA, USA, 1996.

[18] H.-G. Roh, M. Jeon, J.-S. Kim, and J. Lee. Replicated abstract data types: Building blocks for collaborative applications. *Journal of Parallel and Distributed Computing*, 71(3):354 – 368, 2011. ISSN 0743-7315.

[19] Y. Saito and M. Shapiro. Optimistic replication. *ACM Computing Surveys*, 37(1):42–81, 2005. ISSN 0360-0300.

[20] B. Shneiderman. Response Time and Display Rate in Human Performance with Computers. *ACM Computing Surveys*, 16(3):265–285, September 1984. ISSN 0360-0300. . URL http://doi.acm.org/10.1145/2514.2517.

[21] Q. F. Stout and B. L. Warren. Tree rebalancing in optimal time and space. *Commun. ACM*, 29(9):902–908, September 1986. ISSN 0001-0782. . URL http://doi.acm.org/10.1145/6592.6599.

[22] C. Sun, X. Jia, Y. Zhang, Y. Yang, and D. Chen. Achieving convergence, causality preservation, and intention preservation in real-time cooperative editing systems. *ACM Transactions on Computer-Human Interaction (TOCHI)*, 5(1):63–108, March 1998. ISSN 1073-0516.

[23] N. Vidot, M. Cart, J. Ferrié, and M. Suleiman. Copies convergence in a distributed real-time collaborative environment. In *Conference on Computer supported cooperative work (CSCW)*, pages 171–180, Philadelphia, PN, United States, 2000. ACM. ISBN 1-58113-222-0.

[24] S. Weiss, P. Urso, and P. Molli. Wooki: a P2P Wiki-based Collaborative Writing Tool. In *International Conference on Web Information Systems Engineering (WISE)*, pages 503–512, Nancy, France, December 2007. Springer.

[25] S. Weiss, P. Urso, and P. Molli. Logoot: A scalable optimistic replication algorithm for collaborative editing on P2P networks. In *29th IEEE International Conference on Distributed Computing Systems (ICDCS 2009)*, pages 404 –412, Montréal, QC, Canada, jun. 2009. IEEE Computer Society.

[26] W. Yu. A string-wise CRDT for group editing. In *Proceedings of the 17th ACM International Conference on Supporting Group Work*, GROUP '12, pages 141–144, New York, NY, USA, 2012. ACM. ISBN 978-1-4503-1486-2. . URL http://doi.acm.org/10.1145/2389176.2389198.

Operational Transformation for Real-time Synchronization of Shared Workspace in Cloud Storage

Agustina Ng and Chengzheng Sun
School of Computer Science and Engineering
Nanyang Technological University
{Agustina, CZSun}@ntu.edu.sg

ABSTRACT

Cloud storage is widely used to share and collaborate on files over the Internet; consistency maintenance of replicated files in the face of concurrency is a major challenge. In this paper, we present a novel *CSOT* (*Cloud Storage Operational Transformation*) solution to support real-time file synchronization in front-end cloud storage and achieve consistent and desirable concurrent operation combined-effects that cannot be fully achieved by any existing cloud storage systems. We have formally verified algorithmic correctness of CSOT, built a proof-of-concept implementation, and experimentally compared results produced by CSOT and three industrial cloud storage systems, Microsoft OneDrive, Google Drive, and Dropbox, under the same collection of concurrent operation testing cases. CSOT is the first to extend OT consistency maintenance capability to shared workspaces in cloud storage and contributes to advancement of cloud-based collaboration technologies.

CCS Concepts

• Human-centered computing~Collaborative and social computing systems and tools • Human-centered computing~Computer supported cooperative work

Keywords

Cloud Storage; Consistency; Synchronization, Operational Transformation; Real-time Collaboration.

1. INTRODUCTION

Cloud storage is emerging as one of the main cloud computing applications for data sharing and collaboration [6],[15],[27]. Cloud storage systems, such as Dropbox[1], Google Drive[2] (GDrive), and Microsoft OneDrive[3], allow users not only to store and share files on the provider's data centers, but also to replicate them on mutiple personal devices. With such systems, users can access and modify replicated files in the same way as accessing native file systems on their personal computing devices; modifications to those files will be automatically synchronized to the provider's storage and among multiple replicas on the users' devices. Real-time synchronization and consistency maintenance of replicated files is a challenging issue in cloud storage.

Existing cloud storage systems have been using proprietary synchronization techniques (e.g. [28]) to achieve a variety of results in the face of concurrency, but none of them has ever explicitly specified what consistency requirements are provided to end-users. There were some prior research on consistency maintenance of *back-end* cloud storage replicas maintained by cloud storage service providers for fault tolerance, availability, recovery, fast access, etc [3],[11],[15],[18]. Consistency of back-end storage replicas is different from and complementary to that of *front-end* cloud storage replicas, i.e. replicated files on end-users' computers. One major difference is: back-end storage replicas are transparent to end-users, wheras front-end storage replicas are visible to and directly manipulated by end-users. This work focuses on file synchronization and consistency maintenance of *front-end* cloud storage.

Operational Transformation (*OT*) [7],[23],[29] is an established consistency maintenance technique for collaborative editing systems, particularly suitable for collaborative applications running over long-latency communication networks like the Internet [7],[10],[19]. OT has been widely used in both academia (e.g. [1],[25],[26]) and industries (e.g. Google Docs[4], and CodoxWord[5]) for supporting conflict resolution and consistency maintenance of shared documents in distributed collaborative text editors, word processors, 2D spreadsheets, 3D design systems, etc. In this work, we extend OT from consistency maintenance within individual documents/files to across a collection of documents/files in a shared workspace in cloud storage. This work is inspired by the following observation: collaborative manipulation of a collection of replicated files in cloud storage can be modeled as collaborative editing of a shared workspace consisting of those replicated files; user-generated file manipulation operations can be modeled as editing operations over this shared workspace; and file synchronization in cloud storage can be mapped into consistency maintenance of the shared workspace, which OT is naturally suitable to support.

Despite the similarities between file synchronization in a workspace and collaborative editing of an individual document, there exist important differences between them. One difference is

[1] https://www.dropbox.com/
[2] https://drive.google.com/
[3] http://onedrive.live.com/
[4] https://docs.google.com
[5] http://www.codoxware.com

GROUP '16, November 13-16, 2016, Sanibel Island, FL, USA.
© 2016 ACM. ISBN 978-1-4503-4276-6/16/11…$15.00
DOI: http://dx.doi.org/10.1145/2957276.2957278

in data and operation granularity: operations in cloud storage are targeting coarse-grained objects like files or folders in a shared workspace, whereas operations in ordinary editors are targeting fine-grained objects, such as characters, words, or graphics in an ordinary text or graphics document. Furthermore, data models (i.e. general structures of shared workspaces or documents) and operation models (primitive operations that users may generate to manipulate the workspaces or documents) are all different from each other. These differences have major impacts on consistency requirements and conflict resolution strategies, which necessitates the design of different OT solutions.

File synchronization can be in *real-time* or *non-real-time*. By real-time, we mean user-generated file manipulation operations are executed at the local replica immediately and propagated to other replicas (if online) as soon as possible. Non-real-time file synchronization means workspace replicas may not be online at the same time and file synchronization (e.g. file manipulation operation propagation and remote execution) may not occur immediately. For example, some computer devices hosting replicas may be offline and file synchronization among them may be delayed until they are reconnected to the network. It is well-known that OT techniques can be used to support both real-time and non-real-time collaboration [9],[21]. In this paper, we focus on *real-time* synchronization of replicated files in the shared workspace, and will extend the OT techniques presented in this paper to non-real-time file synchronization in future work.

The rest of this paper is organized as follows. First, we present a motivating example for operation conflict and consistency issues in cloud storage. Next, we define the basic data and operation models in cloud storage. Then, we discuss and define conflict and compatible relations for basic operations, and their desired combined-effects. Next, we present CSOT algorithms, its formal verification and prototype implementation. Afterwards, we discuss the main discoveries from concurrency benchmark study of the CSOT prototype, Dropbox, OneDrive, and GDrive. Then, we compare our work with prior work. Finally, we conclude this work and discuss future work.

2. A MOTIVATING EXAMPLE SCENARIO

It is well-known that multi-user concurrent manipulation of replicated files on different devices may conflict and result in inconsistent effects [23]. To illustrate, consider the scenario shown in Figure 1 (a), where three users U_1, U_2, and U_3 are sharing a tree of files/folders, hosted on a cloud storage central server and replicated on local disks of different computers owned by those users. Three operations are simultaneously generated: O_1 = *RN*("*A*", "*D*") to *rename* a folder from "*A*" to "*D*"; O_2 = *UP*("*A*/*B*") to *update* (by saving) the contents of a file with the pathname "*A*/*B*"; and O_3 = *DL*("*A*/*C*") to *delete* the file with the pathname "*A*/*C*". Although these three operations are targeting at different folders/files, they potentially *conflict* because they may produce inconsistent results when executed in different orders at different user sites [1], as shown in Figure 1 (b):

1. At U_1 site, O_1 is first executed to change the folder name "*A*" to "*D*"; but O_2 and O_3 will fail due to non-existence of pathnames of "*A*/*B*" (referred by O_2) and "*A*/*C*" (referred by O_3), respectively, after the execution of O_1.
2. At U_2 site, O_2 is first executed to update the file "*A*/*B*"; O_1 is then executed to change the folder name "*A*" to "*D*"; but O_3 will fail due to the prior execution of O_1.
3. At U_3 site, O_3 is first executed to delete the file "*A*/*C*"; O_2 is then executed to update the file "*A*/*B*"; and O_1 is finally executed to change the folder name "*A*" to "*D*".
4. At the cloud storage center, O_2 is first executed to update the file "*A*/*B*"; O_3 is executed to delete the file "*A*/*C*"; and O_1 is finally executed to change the folder name "*A*" to "*D*". The final result is the same as at U_3 site.

In this example, O_1 is conflicting with both O_2 and O_3; but O_2 and O_3 are *compatible* as they produce the same results when executed in different orders.

A basic consistency requirement is to ensure all replicated files are convergent after executing the same group of concurrent

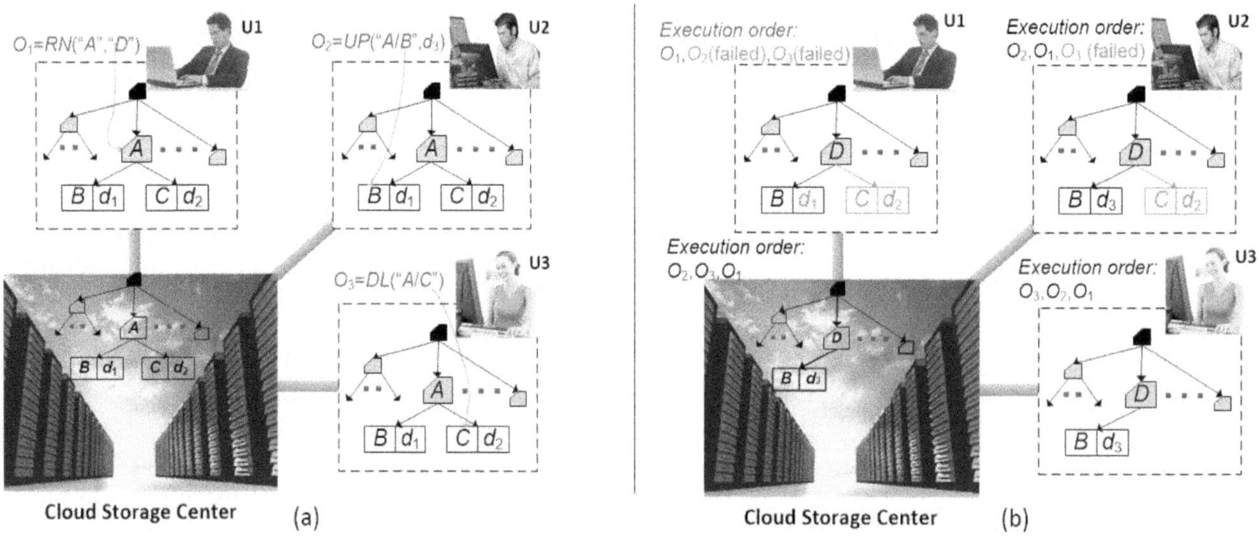

is the root of the cloud storage. A is a folder named *A*. B d1 a file named *B* and contains data d_1.
→ is a parent/child relation from a folder to another file/folder.

Figure 1. (a) Three users are sharing a tree of files/folders in a cloud storage and concurrently manipulate the shared tree. (b) Inconsistent states are created after executing concurrent operations in different orders at different sites.

operations, regardless whether they are compatible or conflicting. Achieving convergent results is, however, an insufficient consistency requirement for many applications [1],[24]. Another important requirement is for concurrent operations to achieve meaningful and desirable *combined-effects* – integrated effects of concurrent operations, independent of their execution orders.

When two concurrent operations conflict, one possible combined-effect is to preserve the effect of only one operation, e.g. by serializing operations [7]. This combined-effect meets the convergence requirement at the price of losing some users' work. For the example in Figure 1 (b), if the serialization order is to execute O_1 followed by O_2 and O_3, then only the effect of O_1 can be preserved (i.e. the folder is renamed), but O_2 and O_3 will fail (as shown at U_1 site) and non-trivial work encapsulated in O_2 will be lost. A more desirable combined-effect is to preserve the effects of all operations in the face of conflicts, i.e. "*A/B*" is updated, "*A/C*" is deleted, and "*A*" is renamed to "*D*" at all sites. Explicit description of combined-effects is important for *end-users* to understand the behavior of a collaborative application, and for *system-builders* to devise techniques to support the required effects in the face of concurrency.

3. DATA AND OPERATION MODELS

To devise an OT solution to a new application domain like cloud storage, it is necessary to first define precisely the replicated file data model of the shared workspace and the basic file manipulation operation model in cloud storage.

3.1 Data Model

A replicated workspace in cloud storage can be modeled as a hierarchical tree structure as follows.

Definition 1. Replicated Workspace. A replicated workspace in a cloud storage is described as a tree of connected nodes, denoted by $T = (N, A)$:

1. $N = \{n_0, n_1, n_2, ..., n_r\}$ is a set of nodes, where each node represents a file or a folder; and n_0 represents the root folder of the tree T; and
2. $A = \{a_1, a_2, ..., a_s\}$ is a set of arrows, where each arrow $a_k = (n_i, n_j)$, $1 \leq k \leq s$, $0 \leq i \neq j \leq r$, represents a *parent-child* relation from a folder n_i to another folder or a file n_j in T; and a node can only have one parent.

In real cloud storage systems, a replicated workspace can be the full tree of files under one user's account if the user maps the complete cloud storage under his/her account to multiple personal computing devices; file manipulation operations within this tree, by any collaborators, will be synchronized to maintain consistency. A replicated workspace can also be a subtree of a user's cloud storage if the user shares this subtree among collaborators; file synchronization will be confined within the shared subtree.

By Definition 1, a file cannot have a child, but a folder can have both files and folders as its children. A file node n has a *data* attribute, denoted by *n.data*, which represents the contents (e.g. a word document) of this file. Every node n has a *name*, denoted by *n.name*, which is a string of characters. For conciseness, we simply use single capital character strings "*A*", "*B*", "*C*", ..., to denote node names, and assume two children of the same parent cannot have the same name, but children under different parents can have the same name. In real systems, however, files or folders may be named under different constraints (e.g. case-sensitive vs. case-insensitive strings) imposed by operating systems, but the OT solution presented in this paper is independent of specific naming schemes.

The pathname of a node, i.e. the sequence of node names from the root to this node, is unique due to the naming restriction, and used to address the node in a replicated workspace. Since all pathnames in the same tree have the same root, the root name is omitted in a pathname. We use "/" to separate the node names in a pathname.

Definition 2. Pathname Relations. Two pathnames p_1 and p_2 under the same tree may have the following relations:

1. $p_1 = p_2$ if they are equal;
2. $p_1 \sqsubset p_2$ if p_1 is included in but not equal to p_2, i.e. the node referred to by p_1 is an upstream node of (or between the root node and) the node referred to by p_2;
3. $p_2 \sqsubset p_1$ if p_2 is included in but not equal to p_1, i.e. the node referred to by p_2 is an upstream node of the node referred to by p_1; or
4. $p_1 \boxtimes p_2$ if $p_1 \neq p_2$, $p_1 \not\sqsubset p_2$, and $p_2 \not\sqsubset p_1$, i.e. they refer to nodes on different streams.

If $p_1 \boxtimes p_2$, we say that p_1 and p_2 refer to two *independent* nodes; otherwise, they refer to two *dependent* nodes.

In Figure 1 we have "*A*" $\sqsubset$ "*A/B*" and "*A*" $\sqsubset$ "*A/C*", which are dependent node references; "*A/B*" $\boxtimes$ "*A/C*", which is an independent node reference. For conciseness, we use $p_1 \sqsubseteq p_2$ to denote $p_1 = p_2$ or $p_1 \sqsubset p_2$. We introduce the following notations to map pathnames and nodes, and to refer to aspects of a pathname in the tree T:

1. *pathname*(n) refers to the pathname of a node n;
2. *node*(p) refers to the node with a pathname p;
3. T_p = *subtree*(p) refers to the subtree with *node*(p) as root;
4. *root*(T) refers to the root node of the tree T;
5. p = *parentpath*(p) + "/" + *nodename*(p), where *nodename*(p) refers to the last node name in p; *parentpath*(p) refers to the pathname of the parent node of *node*(p);
6. *parentnode*(p) = *node*(*parentpath*(p)), refers to the node with a pathname *parentpath*(p);
7. *isValid*(p) checks whether p is a valid pathname.

3.2 Operation Model

There are four basic operations that users can perform to modify a replicated workspace in cloud storage:

1. *CR*(p, T_p): to create a subtree T_p with a pathname p. A T_p can be reduced to a single file or folder node.
2. *DL*(p): to delete *subtree*(p) with *node*(p) as its root.
3. *RN*(p, q): to change *nodename*(p) to q.
4. *UP*(p, d): to set the content of a file *node*(p) to data d.

For each operation to be successfully generated and executed, it must satisfy certain *preconditions*. After executing an operation on a replicated workspace, its effects can be described as *postconditions* of this operation. In the absence of concurrency, preconditions of an operation can always be met at remote sites if it can be generated and executed successfully at the local site. However, in the presence of concurrency, preconditions met at the local site may be violated at a remote site due to the execution effects of other concurrent operations. Violation of preconditions may cause execution failures and result in inconsistency [1]. For example, an update operation may be generated and executed successfully at the local site, but fail at a remote site if the pathname to this file has been changed by another concurrent operation. We give specifications of the basic operations, including *preconditions* and *postconditions*, in Definition 3.

Definition 3. Single Operation Effects in a Replicated Workspace. Let O be an operation defined on a tree $T = (N, A)$. Preconditions and postconditions of O, denoted by *Pre-O* and *Post-O*, respectively, are specified as follows:

1. $O = CR(p, T_p)$: Create a subtree $T_p = (N_p, A_p)$ with a pathname p:
   - *Pre-CR*: *parentpath*(p) refers to an existing folder node, and there exists no node with the pathname p, i.e. $isValid(parentpath(p)) \wedge !isValid(p)$.
   - *Post-CR*: the subtree T_p is created and an arrow from the *parentnode*(p) to *root*(T_p) is added, i.e. $T' = (N', A')$, where $N' = N \cup N_p$ and $A' = A \cup A_p \cup \{(parentnode(p), root(T_p))\}$.
2. $O = DL(p)$: Delete $T_p = subtree(p)$ with *node*(p) as its root:
   - *Pre-DL*: *node*(p) exists, i.e. *isValid*(p).
   - *Post-DL*: the arrow from the *parentnode*(p) to *node*(p) is deleted, and the subtree T_p is deleted, i.e. $T' = (N', A')$, where $N' = N \setminus N_p$ and $A' = A \setminus A_p \setminus \{(parentnode(p), node(p))\}$.
3. $O = RN(p, q)$: Change *nodename*(p) to q.
   - *Pre-RN*: *node*(p) exists; $node(parentpath(p) + \text{"/"} + q)$ does not exist, i.e. $isValid(p) \wedge !isValid(parentpath(p) + \text{"/"} + q)$.
   - *Post-RN*: the *name* attribute of *node*(p) is set to q, i.e. $T' = (N', A')$, where $N' = \{n \mid (n \in N) \wedge (pathname(n) = p \rightarrow n.name = q)\}$, and $A' = A$.
4. $O = UP(p, d)$: Set the content of a *node*(p) to data d.
   - *Pre-UP*: the node referred to by p is an existing file, i.e. *isValid*(p).
   - *Post-UP*: the *data* attribute of the file with the pathname p is set to d, i.e. $T = (N', A')$ where $N' = \{n \mid (n \in N) \wedge (pathname(n) = p \rightarrow n.data = d)\}$ and $A' = A$.

In addition to the above four operations, cloud storage may provide other operations for users to manipulate their files, such as *move* that moves a $subtree(p_1) = T_{p1}$ to a new root node with a pathname p_2. A *move* operation can be achieved by a $DL(p_1)$ followed by a $CR(p_2, T_{p1})$. Readers are referred to [30] for how to use OT to support a *move* operation represented by a *DL* and *CR*.

4. OPERATION RELATIONS

4.1 Causal and Concurrent Relations

File manipulation operations generated by users may have causal or concurrent relations. Following Lamport [14], relations among operations are defined as follows.

Definition 4. Causal Relation "$\rightarrow$". Given two operations O_1 and O_2, generated at sites i and j, respectively, O_1 is causally before O_2, denoted by $O_1 \rightarrow O_2$, iff: (1) $i = j$ and the generation of O_1 happened before the generation of O_2; (2) $i \neq j$ and the execution of O_1 at site j happened before the generation of O_2; or (3) there exists an operation O_x such that $O_1 \rightarrow O_x$ and $O_x \rightarrow O_2$.

Definition 5. Concurrent Relation "$\|$". Given two operations O_1 and O_2, O_1 and O_2 are concurrent, denoted by $O_1 \parallel O_2$, iff neither $O_1 \rightarrow O_2$ nor $O_2 \rightarrow O_1$.

In cloud storage, user-generated file manipulation operations are executed immediately at the local replica to give fast response to the local user, and then synchronized with remote replicas for consistency maintenance. Concurrent operations may be executed in different orders.

4.2 Conflict and Compatible Relations

Concurrent operations may have conflict or compatible relations, depending on whether they produce inconsistent tree states when executed in different orders, as defined in Definition 6 and Definition 7, respectively.

Definition 6. Conflict "$\otimes$". Given two operations O_1 and O_2, they have a conflict relation, denoted by $O_1 \otimes O_2$, iff: (1) $O_1 \parallel O_2$; and (2) different execution orders of O_1 and O_2 result in inconsistent tree states.

Definition 7. Compatible "$\odot$". Given two operations O_1 and O_2, they have a compatible relation, denoted by $O_1 \odot O_2$, iff they do not have a conflict relation, i.e. $\neg(O_1 \otimes O_2)$.

One necessary condition for two concurrent operations to have a conflict relation is that their target pathnames have a *dependency* relation (i.e. $p_1 \sqsubset p_2$ or $p_2 \sqsubset p_1$). This is because if their target pathnames do not have such a relation, their effects must be confined to different subtrees of the workspace, and different orders of executions must result in the same state.

Guided by this condition and Definitions 1, 2, 5, and 6, we conducted comprehensive analysis on the effects achieved by executing every pair of operations (with all possible target relations) in different orders; and we found conflicts may occur only among six pairs of operations: *CR-CR*, *CR-RN*, *DL-RN*, *RN-RN*, *RN-UP*, and *UP-UP*, under specific target pathname relations as summarized in Table 1. Two concrete examples of such conflicts, *RN-UP* and *DL-RN* conflicts, can be found in Figure 1.We have also conducted theoretical verification on conflict/

Table 1. Conflict and compatible relations.

	$CR(p_2, T_{p2})$	$DL(p_2)$	$RN(p_2, q_2)$	$UP(p_2, d_2)$
$CR(p_1, T_{p1})$	$\otimes \leftrightarrow (p_1 = p_2)$	$\odot$	$\otimes \leftrightarrow (p_2 \sqsubset p_1) \vee ((parentpath(p_1) = parentpath(p_2)) \wedge (nodename(p_1) = q_2))$	$\odot$
$DL(p_1)$		$\odot$	$\otimes \leftrightarrow (p_2 \sqsubseteq p_1)$	$\odot$
$RN(p_1, q_1)$			$\otimes \leftrightarrow (p_1 \sqsubseteq p_2) \vee (p_2 \sqsubset p_1) \vee ((parentpath(p_1) = parentpath(p_2)) \wedge (q_1 = q_2))$	$\otimes \leftrightarrow (p_1 \sqsubseteq p_2)$
$UP(p_1, d_1)$				$\otimes \leftrightarrow (p_1 = p_2)$

compatible relations among all pairs of basic operations in Table 1. For every pair of operations, the verification follows the same steps: (1) derive all possible dependency relations among the targets of two operations (without violating *Pre-O* in Definition 3); (2) if no dependency relation is possible, then the two operations are always compatible; (3) otherwise, for every possible dependency relation, derive the workspace states by executing operations in different orders (according to *Post-O* in Definition 3); and (4) if replicated workspace states are inconsistent under any dependency relation, the two operations conflict; otherwise, they are compatible under those relations. The proof of one theorem for *RN-DL* is provided in Appendix.

5. COMBINED-EFFECTS

5.1 Consistency Requirements

From general consistency requirements for collaborative editing systems [1],[24], we derive the following consistency requirements for replicated workspaces in cloud storage:

1. *Causality preservation*: operations with causal relationships must be executed in their causal orders.
2. *Convergence*: after executing the same group of operations at all sites, the replicated workspace states must be identical.
3. *Intention-confined effect*: changes to the workspace must be confined to those produced by user-generated operations.
4. *Aggressive effect preservation*: effects of compatible operations should be preserved fully; effects of conflicting operations should be preserved as much as possible.

5.2 Combined-Effects

Guided by the general consistency requirements above, basic single operation effects in Definition 3, and conflict and compatible relations in Table 1, we define combined-effects for each pair of operations in Definition 8.

Definition 8. Combined-Effects (CE) of Concurrent Operations. Given two basic operations O_1 and O_2 defined on the same tree state, their combined-effect is as follows:

$CE_{DL\odot!DL}$. In case $O_1 \odot O_2$, where $O_1 = DL(p_1)$, O_2 is a non-*DL* operation (i.e. *CR*, *RN*, and *UP*) with a target p_2, and $p_1 \sqsubset p_2$ if O_1 is a *CR* or *RN* and $p_1 \sqsubseteq p_2$ if O_1 is an *UP*, the combined-effect is: (1) all nodes and arrows within $subtree(p_1)$, except those on the path from $node(p_1)$ to $node(p_2)$ or within $subtree(p_2)$, are deleted; and (2) the full effect of O_2.

$CE_{O1\odot O2}$. In case $O_1 \odot O_2$, where O_1 and O_2 are any pair of operations with target relations that are not covered by $CE_{DL\odot!DL}$, the combined-effect is whatever effect achieved by executing them in any order without transformation.

$CE_{CR\otimes CR}$. In case $O_1 = CR(p_1, T_{p1})$, $O_2 = CR(p_2, T_{p2})$, and $O_1 \otimes O_2$, where it must be $p_1 = p_2$, then both T_{p1} and T_{p2} are created with unique names for their roots.

$CE_{CR\otimes RN}$. When $O_1 = CR(p_1, T_{p1})$, $O_2 = RN(p_2, q_2)$, and $O_1 \otimes O_2$:

a. If $(parentpath(p_1) = parentpath(p_2)) \wedge (nodename(p_1) = q_2)$, then (1) the new subtree T_{p1} is created with a unique root name; and (2) $nodename(p_2)$ is changed to a unique name.
b. If $p_2 \sqsubset p_1$, then (1) $nodename(p_2)$ is changed to q_2; and (2) T_{p1} is created under $subtree(parentpath(p_2) + \text{"/"} + q_2)$.

$CE_{DL\otimes RN}$. When $O_1 = DL(p_1)$, $O_2 = RN(p_2, q_2)$, and $O_1 \otimes O_2$:

a. If $p_1 = p_2$, then $subtree(p_1)$ is not deleted but $nodename(p_1)$ is changed to q_2.
b. If $p_2 \sqsubset p_1$, then: (1) $subtree(p_1)$ is deleted; and (2) $nodename(p_2)$ is changed to q_2.

$CE_{RN\otimes RN}$. When $O_1 = RN(p_1, q_1)$, $O_2 = RN(p_2, q_2)$, and $O_1 \otimes O_2$:

a. If $p_1 = p_2$, then $nodename(p_1)$ is changed to either q_1 or q_2, depending on the priority of O_1 and O_2.
b. If $(parentpath(p_1) = parentpath(p_2)) \wedge (q_1 = q_2)$, then $nodename(p_1)$ and $nodename(p_2)$ are changed to unique names.
c. If $p_1 \sqsubset p_2 \vee p_2 \sqsubset p_1$, then: (1) $nodename(p_1)$ is changed to q_1; and (2) $nodename(p_2)$ is changed to q_2.

$CE_{RN\otimes UP}$. When $O_1 = RN(p_1, q_1)$, $O_2 = UP(p_2, d_2)$, and $O_1 \otimes O_2$, it must be $p_1 \sqsubseteq p_2$, so: (1) the content of $node(p_2)$ is set to d_2; and (2) $nodename(p_1)$ is changed to q_1.

$CE_{UP\otimes UP}$. When $O_1 = UP(p_1, d_1)$, $O_2 = UP(p_2, d_2)$, and $O_1 \otimes O_2$, it must be $p_1 = p_2$, so: (1) a new file with a unique name is created under $parentnode(p_1)$ and its content is set to d_1; and (2) the content of $node(p_2)$ is set d_2.

The rationale behind all above combined-effect definitions is the general consistency requirement *aggressive effect preservation* as elaborated in the previous section. It can be checked that the effects of both O_1 and O_2 are preserved in all cases, except for the following three cases: (a) $CE_{DL\odot!DL}$ preserves the full effect of *!DL* but partial effect of *DL*; (b) $CE_{DL\otimes RN}$, where $p_1 = p_2$, only preserves the effect of *RN;* and (c) $CE_{RN\otimes RN}$, where $p_1 = p_2$, only preserves the effect of one *RN*. Concrete examples and alternative combined-effects are provided in the benchmark study section.

6. DESIGN OF CSOT

6.1 Basic Ideas

The basic idea of OT is to transform an operation defined on one state into another operation on a new state, so that the transformed operation can be correctly executed on the new state and achieve document consistency in the face of concurrent operations [24]. To illustrate how OT may work for cloud storage, consider the two concurrent operations $O_1 = RN(\text{"A"}, \text{"D"})$ and $O_3 = DL(\text{"A/C"})$ in Figure 1 (a). Based on Definition 8, the combined-effect for such a pair of *DL* and *RN* is defined by $CE_{DL\otimes RN}$-(b): the file $node(\text{"A/C"})$ is deleted and $nodename(\text{"A"})$ is changed to "D". When O_3 is executed after O_1, the execution of O_3 will fail because the pathname "A/C" no longer exists due to the prior execution of O_1 has changed the pathname of the node targeted by O_3 to "D/C". With OT, however, O_3 can be transformed against O_1 to become $DL(\text{"D/C"})$, which uses the updated pathname for the target. The execution of $DL(\text{"D/C"})$ will delete $subtree(\text{"D/C"})$ and achieves the consistent $CE_{DL\otimes RN}$-(b).

6.2 CSOT Transformation Functions

An OT system consists of control algorithms [24],[26],[31] and transformation functions [1],[24],[29],[30]. Control algorithms are generic and determine the order and conditions for operation transformation and execution, while transformation functions are application-specific and perform the actual transformation between a pair of operations according to their types and parameters. Control algorithms are generally required to meet a set of well-defined context-based conditions, e.g., to ensure two operations involved in a transformation be defined on the same document state or context [26]. The correctness of transformation functions are related to two convergence properties: one is

Convergence Property 1 (*CP1*) [23], which ensures the same document is produced by executing two concurrent and mutually transformed operations in different orders; the other is *Convergence Property 2* (*CP2*) [23], which ensures the same operation is produced in transforming one operation against two concurrent operations in different orders. Past research has found that it is relatively easy for transformation functions to preserve CP1 but difficult to preserve CP2. A number of control algorithms that can avoid requiring transformation functions to preserve CP2 have been invented [26],[31].

To reduce the complexity of transformation functions for cloud storage, we have adopted the existing COT control algorithm [26] in the CSOT system. One main reason for choosing COT is its capability of avoiding CP2, so we only need to design CSOT transformation functions capable of preserving a CP1 and well-defined combined effects.

For each pair of operation types x and y, we have defined a specific transformation function *Txy*. Due to space limitation, we elaborate only one representative function *Tcrcr* below, and provide the full list of CSOT functions in Appendix.

Tcrcr ($CR(p_1, T_{p1})$, $CR(p_2, T_{p2})$):

```
if p1 = p2 then        // CE_{CR⊗CR}
    p1' = p1 + CreateUniqueString(uid1, sid1, oid1);
    q2' = nodename(p2) + CreateUniqueString(uid2, sid2, oid2);
    return [RN(p2, q2'), CR(p1', Tp1)];
else return [CR(p1, Tp1)];        // CE_{O1⊙O2}
```

Tcrcr transforms $CR(p_1, T_{p1})$ against $CR(p_2, T_{p2})$, which is assumed to have been executed before $CR(p_1, T_{p1})$. If p_1 and p_2 are the same, the two operations are conflicting; their combined-effects should be: *two new subtrees T_{p1} and T_{p2} are created with different root node names*, as specified by $CE_{CR \otimes CR}$ in Definition 8. To achieve this effect, two different node names $nodename(p_1')$ and q_2' are generated, and $CR(p_1, T_{p1})$ is transformed into a list of two operations $[RN(p_2, q_2'), CR(p_1', T_{p1})]$, where $RN(p_2, q_2')$ renames the subtree already created by $CR(p_2, T_{p2})$ from $nodename(p_2)$ to q_2'; and $CR(p_1', T_{p1})$ creates a new subtree under the pathname p_1'. If p_1 and p_2 are different, the two operations are compatible; *Tcrcr* simply returns the original $CR(p_1, T_{p1})$, which will achieve $CE_{O1 \odot O2}$ as specified in Definition 8.

In *Tcrcr*, a subroutine *CreateUniqueString*(*uid*, *sid*, *oid*) is used, which generates a unique string based on the user identifier (*uid*), session identifier (*sid*), and operation identifier (*oid*). The unique string must be the same at all collaborating sites for the same operation. It is necessary to use *sid* as part of the string to ensure that it is unique across different sessions.

6.3 Theoretical Verification

According to OT theories [23],[24],[26] and due to the integration with CP2-avoidance OT control algorithms [31], CSOT transformation functions are only required to meet the following *CP1-CE* property:

1. *Convergence Property 1* (*CP1*): given O_1 and O_2 defined on the same tree state T, if $O_1' = Transform(O_1, O_2)$, and $O_2' = Transform(O_2, O_1)$, then applying O_1 followed by O_2' must result in the same state as applying O_2 followed by O_1', i.e. $T \circ O_1 \circ O_2' = T \circ O_2 \circ O_1'$; and
2. *Combined-Effect* (*CE*): the resulting state must meet the combined-effect defined in Definition 8, i.e. $T \circ O_1 \circ O_2' = T \circ O_2 \circ O_1' = CE$. *CP1* is a general requirement of OT systems, while *CE* is a domain-specific requirement.

We have verified all CSOT transformation functions according to the *CP1-CE* property. The basic verification strategy is as follows: for each possible target relations of two operations, we derive (based on *Post-O* in Definition 3) two replicated workspace states by applying the two operations (one is transformed) to the same initial state in different orders; and then check whether the two resulting states are the same (the general *CP1* requirement) and meet the specific *CE* requirements in Definition 8. Verification for one pair of operations (*DL-RN*) is provided in Appendix.

7. PROTOTYPING AND BENCHMARKING

We have built a proof-of-concept implementation of CSOT to provide a vehicle for experimental study of cloud storage file synchronization techniques. In parallel with the design and prototype implementation of CSOT, we have developed a suite of benchmark testing cases, called *concurrency benchmark*, for deriving what combined-effects can be achieved by a cloud storage system in executing concurrent operation, independent of file synchronization techniques used. We have applied the same concurrency benchmark to the CSOT prototype and three industrial systems: Dropbox, Microsoft OneDrive, and Google Drive (GDrive), to evaluate the combined-effects they produce.

7.1 Benchmark Case Derivation

To achieve a comprehensive coverage of testing cases in the concurrency benchmark, we consider all possible combinations of pair-wise operations along multiple dimensions of variation: *operation types* (*CR, DL, RN, UP*), *number of targets* in each operation (one for *CR, DL, UP*; two for *RN*), *target pathname relations* ($p_1 = p_2$, $p_1 \sqsubset p_2$, $p_2 \sqsubset p_1$, and $p_1 \boxtimes p_2$), and *target types* (*file* or *folder*), which could have impacts on the combined-effects of two operations. By combining all possible variations in these dimensions, and eliminating redundant and impossible cases, we have derived a total of 61 distinctive testing cases for pair-wise concurrent operations from the same state (listed in Table 1 in Appendix), which are the basis for creating concrete testing cases. Every concurrency testing case is made of operations that could actually be generated by users and results produced by these operations are visible to them and have impacts on their work.

It is worth pointing out that these concurrency testing cases are independent of the notion of *conflicting/compatible* operations, defined in this paper. This concurrency benchmark is applicable to cloud storage which may not use any conflict concept to solve the file synchronization problem and achieve certain combined-effects of pair-wise concurrent operations, regardless whether the system designers were aware of this or not.

7.2 Benchmark Execution

We create two independently executable programs to simulate two end-users who issue the two *original* operations involved in each case. These two programs are executed on two Internet-connected computers (with MS Windows), each of which has a shared and replicated folder on OneDrive, GDrive, and Dropbox, respectively. First, the synchronization of the tested cloud storage is disabled (to ensure operation concurrency) and two operations are executed on the same initial replicated states on two computers independently; then, the synchronization is enabled to let the cloud storage system synchronize the replicas (using their proprietary techniques) on the two computers; finally, combined effects produced for each case are collected and examined. The process for testing CSOT is different: each computer executes two operations on the same state in different orders: one operation is *original* and another is *transformed* by CSOT, which will produce two combined-effects on two computers for comparison. We developed a software tool to automate the execution steps for all benchmarking cases and help derive the final results.

7.3 Operations Targeting Independent Nodes

This is a broad category of benchmark cases, in which the two concurrent operations O_1 and O_2 are targeting at *independent* nodes in the shared workspace. More precisely, O_1 = $CR/DL/RN/UP$ and $O_2 = CR/DL/RN/UP$, and $p_1 \boxtimes p_2$, where p_1 and p_2 are target pathnames of O_1 and O_2, respectively. Under all such cases, CSOT and the three industrial systems uniformly produce convergent final results on different computers and achieve the same combined-effect, denoted as $\boldsymbol{CE}_{O1\boxtimes O2}$ and sketched below:

$\boldsymbol{CE}_{O1\boxtimes O2}$ — *union effects of* O_1 *and* O_2, *i.e. effects of both operations are fully preserved in the final result.*

Result Analysis: $CE_{O1\boxtimes O2}$ is covered by $CE_{O1\odot O2}$ in Definition 8, which preserves the effects of all operations as if O_1 and O_2 were executed individually in any order. Such combined-effect is ideal to users. It is good but not suprising to see that the three systems could produce the same results as CSOT under all these cases.

7.4 Operations Targeting Dependent Nodes

The outcomes are quite different in another broad and complementary category of benchmark cases, in which pathnames p_1 and p_2 of two concurrent operations refer to *dependent* nodes, i.e. $p_1 = p_2$, $p_1 \sqsubset p_2$, or $p_2 \sqsubset p_1$. In this category, only CSOT can produce the results as specified in Definition 8 under all cases; three industrial systems produce the same result in only one case of *DL vs DL*[6], but different results under other cases. Some of those different results are undesirable to users, or even inconsistent. Two representative cases are described below.

7.4.1 RN vs UP

Case Description: $O_1 = RN(p_1, q_1)$, $O_2 = UP(p_2, d_2)$, $p_1 = p_2$ (if p_1 refers to a file) or $p_1 \sqsubset p_2$ (if p_1 refers to a folder), and p_2 may refer to a file only. In this case, $node(p_1)$ is the same as $parentnode(p_2)$, or between the root and $parentnode(p_2)$.

Benchmark Results:

1. CSOT and GDrive (when p_1 refers to either a file or a folder), OneDrive (if p_1 refers to a folder) achieve the same combined-effect $\boldsymbol{CE}_{RN\sqsubseteq UP}$, as sketched below:

   $\boldsymbol{CE}_{RN\sqsubseteq UP}$ — *nodename*(p_1) *is changed to* q_1*; and the updated node*(p_2) *is preserved under a new pathname* p_2'*, which is obtained by replacing nodename*(p_1) *in* p_2 *with* q_1*, i.e.* $p_2' = parentpath(p_1) + \text{"/"} + q_1 + \text{"/"} + (p_1 - p_2)$[7].

2. OneDrive (if p_1 refers to a file) and Dropbox (if p_1 refers to a file/folder) achieve an *Alternative Combined-Effect*, denoted as $\boldsymbol{ACE}_{RN\sqsubseteq UP}$ and sketched below:

   $\boldsymbol{ACE}_{RN\sqsubseteq UP}$ — *nodename*(p_1) *is changed to* q_1*; and a new path is created, which includes duplications of all nodes from node*(p_1) *to parentnode*(p_2)*, plus a duplication of file node*(p_2) *with the updated content* d_2.

For instance, let $O_1 = RN(A, F)$ and $O_2 = UP(A/B/C/D, d_2)$, generated from the same workspace T_1. Their alternative combined-effects are given in Figure 2.

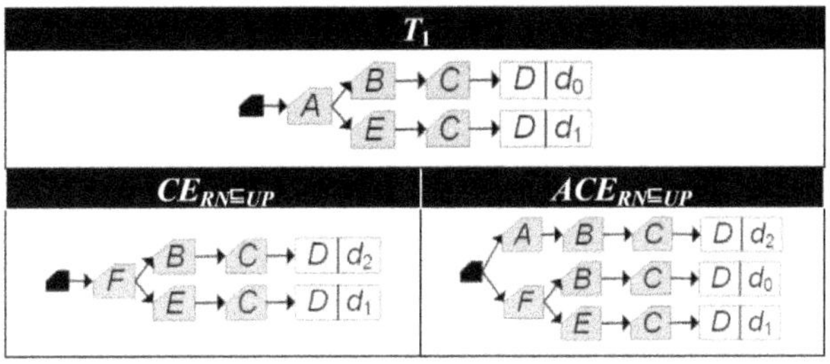

Figure 2. Illustration of $\boldsymbol{CE}_{RN\sqsubseteq UP}$ and $\boldsymbol{ACE}_{RN\sqsubseteq UP}$.

Result Analysis: $CE_{RN\sqsubseteq UP}$ represents the same combined-effect as specified by $CE_{RN\otimes UP}$ in Definition 8, which achieves the effects of both operations with a change of the name of the updated file (but preserves its updated contents), which is simple for the user to manage and for the system designer to implement.

$ACE_{RN\sqsubseteq UP}$ creates a new path and duplicates the original file *node*(p_2), which is costly (in space), unnecessary as effects of both operations can be preserved without this new path and duplication, and could be confusing to users as creating this new path is not the intention of any operation involved [24]. It is worth pointing out that such undesirable result is not an isolated case as similar results are also produced under other cases, including:

1. $O_1 = CR(p_1, T_{p1})$ *vs* $O_2 = RN(p_2, q_2)$, where $p_2 \sqsubset p_1$, p_2 may refer to a folder only, and p_1 may refer to a file or folder.
2. $O_1 = RN(p_1, q_1)$ *vs* $RN(p_2, q_2)$, where $p_1 \sqsubset p_2$, p_1 may refer to a folder only, and p_2 may refer to a file or folder.

7.4.2 CR vs CR

Case Description: $O_1 = CR(p_1, T_{p1})$, $O_2 = CR(p_2, T_{p2})$, $p_1 = p_2$, p_1 and p_2 may refer to files or folders. In this case, *node*(p_1) is the same as *node*(p_2).

Benchmark Results:

1. CSOT (when p_1 and p_2 refer to folders or files), OneDrive and Dropbox (if p_1 and p_2 refer to files only), achieve the combined-effect $\boldsymbol{CE}_{CR=CR}$, as sketched below:

   $\boldsymbol{CE}_{CR=CR}$ — *two new subtrees* T_{p1} *and* T_{p2} *are created with different root node names.*

2. OneDrive and Dropbox, if p_1 and p_2 refer to folders, achieve an alternative combined-effect $\boldsymbol{ACE}_{CR=CR}$, as sketched below:

   $\boldsymbol{ACE}_{CR=CR}$ — *two subtrees* T_{p1} *and* T_{p2} *are recursively merged into a single subtree under the same pathname* p_1.

3. GDrive, if p_1 and p_2 refer to either files or folders, achieves an *Inconsistent Alternative Combined-Effect*: $\boldsymbol{IACE}_{CR=CR}$, as sketched below:

   $\boldsymbol{IACE}_{CR=CR}$ — *the same pathname* p_1 *is used as the pathname of both the newly created subtree* T_{p1} *and* T_{p2} *at the replica on the cloud storage server; but* p_1 *is mapped into inconsistent pathnames at replicas on different users' computing devices.*

---

[6] *Case Description:* $O_1 = DL(p_1)$ vs $O_2 = DL(p_2)$, where $p_1 \sqsubseteq p_2$, p_1 may only refer to a folder, and p_2 may refer to a folder or file. Under this case, all three industrial systems and CSOT produce the same combined-effect $CE_{DL\sqsubseteq DL}$: *everything under subtree*(p_1)*, including subtree*(p_2)*, is deleted,* which is covered by $CE_{O1\odot O2}$ in Definition 1.Definition 8.

[7] $(p_1 - p_2)$ represents a substring of p_1, obtained by subtracting the prefix p_2 from p_1, where $p_2 \sqsubset p_1$.

For instance, let $O_1 = CR(A/D, D\rightarrow E\rightarrow F(d_1))$ and $O_2 = CR(A/D, D\rightarrow E\rightarrow F(d_2))$, generated from the same workspace T_2. Their combined-effects are in Figure 3.

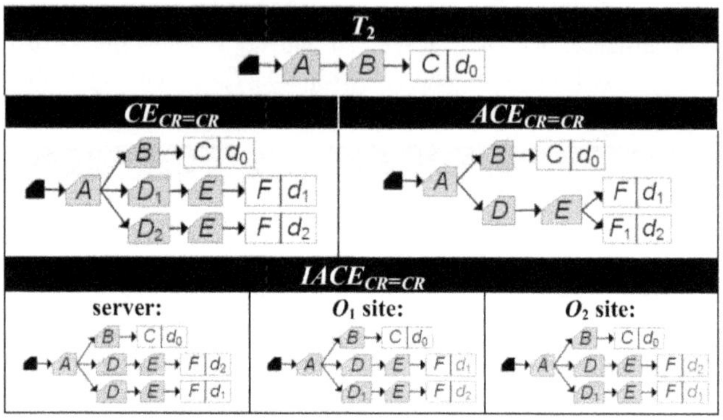

Figure 3. Illustration of $CE_{CR=CR}$, $ACE_{CR=CR}$ and $IACE_{CR=CR}$.

Result Analysis: Among these three combined-effects, $\boldsymbol{CE_{CR=CR}}$ is the same as $\boldsymbol{CE_{CR\otimes CR}}$ in Definition 8; this result is able to preserve the effects of both *CR* operations with only minor change of one file or folder name, which is simple to manage by end-users, and from our experience of prototyping CSOT, it is also simple to implement.

$ACE_{CR=CR}$ merges two independently created subtrees into a single subtree. We consider this merge unnecessary and confusing to users because: (1) the merging is not the intention of any operation involved [24]; (2) files and folders under T_{p1} and T_{p2} may have conflicting names and require recursive resolution, which is difficult for users to understand and complex to implement by the underlying system; and (3) it may create a non-trivial burden to users who need to unmerge the merged subtrees.

$IACE_{CR=CR}$ creates two different subtrees under the *same* pathname at the replica on the GDrive server; such *name-sharing* is allowed as files or folders in GDrive are distinguished by internal unique identifiers (rather than by names). However, a *name-mismatching* inconsistency will occur when these different files or folders with the same pathnames are replicated on conventional file systems (e.g. Windows) that do not permit the same pathname for different files/folders (as shown in Figure 3): on the user-side replica where $CR(p_1, T_{p1})$ is locally generated and executed before $CR(p_2, T_{p2})$, the root of T_{p1} will keep the original pathname p_1, and the root of T_{p2} will be changed to the new pathname p_1 + "(1)"; on the other user-side replica where $CR(p_2, T_{p2})$ is locally generated and executed before $CR(p_1, T_{p1})$, the root of T_{p2} will keep the pathname p_1, and the root of T_{p1} will be changed to the new pathname p_1 + "(1)", which means the same pathname refers to different files or folders on different replicated workspaces. Such inconsistent results are undoubtedly problematic to users.

Similar undesirable and inconsistent results are also found under other benchmark cases, including:

1. $O_1 = RN(p_1, q_1)$ vs $RN(p_2, q_2)$, where $p_1 = p_2$, p_1 and p_2 may refer to files or folders.
2. $O_1 = RN(p_1, q_1)$ vs $O_2 = RN(p_2, q_2)$, where $(parentpath(p_1) = parentpath(p_2)) \wedge (q_1 = q_2)$, p_1 and p_2 may refer to files and folders.

Overall, the concurrency benchmark developed from this work has been quite effective in revealing a range of problems hidden in the results produced by real-world cloud storage systems. With this benchmark, we have experimentally confirmed that the CSOT prototype can achieve the combined-effects as specified in Definition 8 and preserve the convergence property, but none of three industrial systems is able to achieve such results under all cases. Moreover, we also found the three industrial systems can collectively produce the full set of results specified in Definition 8, i.e. each combined-effect specified in Definition 8 is delivered by at least one of these systems (as illustrated in all benchmark cases elaborated in this section), which we regard as a real-world validation of the combined-effects proposed in this work.

8. COMPARISON TO RELATED WORK

8.1 Prior OT Work for Hierarchical Models

There have been multiple prior OT approaches to support co-editing individual documents with tree-like or hierarchical data and operation models, including HTML/XML documents [5], Dependency Graphs (DGs) [1], and word processor documents [25]. These prior OT systems have data and operation models, hence corresponding transformation functions, that are quite different from each other and from CSOT.

The first tree-based OT in [5] and CSOT seem to support three similar operations: *create* (or *insert* in [5]), *delete*, and *update* (or *change* in [5]), but these operations are actually quite different in terms of their granularity and addressing schemes (which are fundamental to OT function design): a tree node in [5] has the granularity of character or element in a shared HTML/XML document and is addressed by a vector of positional references, which are sequentially ordered and may be shifted by the execution of other concurrent operations; in CSOT, however, a tree node has the granularity of file/folder in a shared workspace of cloud storage, and is addressed by a unique pathname that does not shift (but may change) due to the execution of other concurrent operations. Those fundamental differences have led us to devising special CSOT transformation strategies that have never been seen in prior OT solutions based on (linear or hierarchical) positional reference data models like that in [5],[25]: operation conflicts have to be detected by exhaustive analysis of pathname dependency relations and operation pre-/post-conditions, instead of simply comparing *left-equal-right* positional relations between operations in [5],[25]; one operation may be transformed into two different operations, e.g. a *CR* is transformed into an *RN* and a *CR* in *Tcrcr*; and an operation type may be changed in transformation, e.g. an *UP* is transformed into a *CR* in *Tupdl* in Appendix. Moreover, CSOT supports one additional *rename* operation, which has added significant complexities in conflict detection and resolution in cloud storage: most operation conflicts (see Table 1) and inconsistent or undesirable results (see Section 7) occur in scenarios involving one or two *rename* operations.

For the OT solution in [1], a DG consists of graphic data nodes that can be *created* or *deleted* in insolation, and dynamically *connected* and *disconnected* with each other; attribute values of a node can be *updated* and the updated value propagates among connected nodes (from up-stream to low-stream nodes), which may cause *dependency-conflict* in the face of concurrency, and resolving this conflict is the focus of [1]. Operation models in [1] and CSOT have seemingly the same three operations *create*, *update*, and *delete*, but they are very different in nature: a file or folder is always created under an existing folder or root in cloud storage, rather than in isolation as in [1] (that's why there is no *connect* or *disconnect* operations in CSOT); an *update* to a file in CSOT never propagates the value among connected nodes as in [1], etc. These and other differences have led to a whole set of different issues addressed by CSOT, which cannot be adapted from the OT solution in [1].

A prior OT-based file synchronizer was proposed in [17], which is not for supporting cloud storage systems, but similar to CSOT in designing transformation functions for file system operations. A total of three operations are supported in [17]: (1) *mkfile* to create a file; (2) *mkdir* to create a folder; and (3) *mv* to move a file or folder to a new position. For three different operations, there should have been $9 = 3 \times 3$ transformation functions, but only three functions (for *mkfile-mkfile, mkfile-mv,* and *mv-mkfile)* are defined; the missing ones, e.g. *mv-mkdir* and *mv-mv,* actually involves challenging technical issues. The defined transformation functions, such as *mkfile-mv* and *mv-mkfile,* have limited capabilities, e.g. they dealt with conflicts caused by *identical* operation targets (i.e. $p_1 = p_2$) only, but did not and could not cope with conflicts caused by *dependent* operation targets (i.e. $p_1 \sqsubset p_2$), which are common in hierarchical tree-like systems. Last but not least, the design of transformation functions in [17] was concerned with preserving convergence (CP1), without concern or verification on the combined-effects of concurrent operations.

There was another alternative OT approach proposed for tree-based hierarchical documents in [13], which is based on designing tree-aware OT control algorithms, rather than transformation functions for handling tree-structures as done in this CSOT work and other work [1],[5],[17],[25],[30].

8.2 Prior non-OT Synchronization Techniques

There exist a rich body of publications on non-OT synchronization and consistency maintenance techniques for distributed file systems, and document management and version control systems, including Coda [18], SVN [4], etc. Like CSOT, Coda is also operation-based: it propagates a log of operations for synchronization. But unlike CSOT, Coda locks the system during the entire synchronization time and is not able to automatically resolve all detected conflicts, e.g. $CR \otimes CR$, $RN \otimes RN$ (when $(parentpath(p_1) = parentpath(p_2)) \wedge (q_1 = q_2)$), $DL \otimes UP$, and $UP \otimes UP$ conflicts. Those conflicting files will be marked as conflicts and become inaccessible by Coda users until they are manually resolved by users.

Conventional version control systems like SVN[8] and Git[9] are state-based: they propagate document or workspace states and use *diff* algorithms [12] to detect file conflicts; users are responsible for resolving detected conflicts. In contrast, OT solutions are operation-based: they execute, propagate and transform operations; conflicts are detected and resolved automatically. Among the four basic operations supported by CSOT, only $CR(p, T_p)$ and $UP(p, d)$ may carry a parameter of potentially large sizes, e.g. T_p for a subtree of file/folders, and d for contents of a file, which may cost communication bandwidth; but such costs cannot be avoided by other file synchronization techniques as well. In general, operation-based consistency solutions are more efficient and suitable to real-time collaborations, than state-based solutions [20]. One future work is to conduct detailed performance study on the CSOT solution, in terms of communication (for data propagation and notification), computation (for conflict resolution and synchronization), and storage (for state and data replication and buffering) overhead, and compare the CSOT performance with file synchronization techniques in other cloud storage systems. For comparison with other non-OT techniques, readers are referred to [7],[10],[17],[20],[24].

[8] https://subversion.apache.org/

[9] http://git-scm.com/

8.3 Prior Concurrency Benchmarking Work

In the fields of software testing and parallel/distributed computing, concurrency benchmarking is commonly used to debug and/or measure performance of concurrent programs or algorithms [2],[8],[16],[22]. Such benchmarks are often made of low-level tests created to explore various execution patterns, paths, or data structures of concurrent programs or algorithms for debugging and/or performance evaluation purposes. In contrast, the concurrency benchmark developed from this work is made of high-level actions performed by users (not programs) to derive user-visible results and detect inconsistency problems in cloud storage systems, independent of internal synchronization algorithms used by underlying systems. The concurrency benchmark in this work addresses correctness issues of underlying systems (from the end-user point of views), but does not address performance issues.

9. CONCLUSIONS AND FUTURE WORK

In this paper, we have contributed a novel *Operational Transformation* (*OT*) solution, named *CSOT* (*Cloud Storage OT*), to real-time synchronization of replicated files in front-end cloud storage. This work is the first to extend OT to shared workspaces in cloud storage. We have formally verified algorithmic correctness of CSOT, built a proof-of-concept implementation, and experimentally compared results produced by CSOT and three industrial cloud storage systems (Dropbox, MS OneDrive, and Google Drive) under the same concurrency benchmark. Our benchmark study has confirmed that CSOT can achieve the combined-effects as defined in this work under all cases.

From the benchmark study, we have discovered that the three major cloud storage systems can produce consistent and desirable combined-effects when concurrent operations are targeting independent data objects in cloud storage, but may produce results different from each other, some of which are undesirable, confusing to users or even inconsistent, when concurrent operations are targeting dependent data objects. These discoveries contribute to the general knowledge on what inconsistency problems exist in existing cloud storage systems. Such knowledge can help users to better understand and use cloud storage for their collaborative work, and cloud storage service providers to improve their techniques to achieve better consistency.

Cloud storage provides excellent infrastructures for supporting a wide range of collaborative applications, as well as great opportunities for collaborative technology research. There are lots of exciting future work. One ongoing work in our group is to devise OT techniques to achieve seamless integration of two distinctive levels of real-time collaboration in cloud storage: (1) real-time file manipulation and synchronization of a shared workspace in cloud storage, which can be supported by *CSOT* as presented in this paper; and (2) real-time collaborative editing of individual documents hosted on cloud storage, using OT-supported tools like CodoxWord.

10. ACKNOWLEDGEMENTS

This research is partially supported by an Academic Research Fund Tier 2 (MOE2015-T2-1-087) and Tier 1 (2012-T1-001-091) Grants from Ministry of Education Singapore. The authors wish to thank anonymous reviewers for their insightful and constructive comments and suggestions.

11. REFERENCES

[1] Agustina, C. Sun, and D. Xu. Operational transformation for dependency conflict resolution in real-time collaborative 3D design systems. In *Proc. ACM CSCW 2012*, 1401-1410.

[2] J.S. Bradbury, et al. Using combinatorial benchmark construction to improve the assessment of concurrency bug detection tools. In *Proc. 2012 Workshop on Parallel and Distributed Systems: Testing, Analysis, and Debugging*, 25-35.

[3] B. Calder, et al. Windows azure storage: a highly available cloud storage service with strong consistency. In *Proc. ACM SOSP 2011*, 143-157.

[4] B. Collins-Sussman. The subversion project: building a better CVS. *Linux Journal 2002*, 94(3).

[5] A. Davis, C. Sun and J. Lu. Generalizing operational transformation to the standard general markup language. In *Proc. ACM CSCW 2002,* 58-67.

[6] I. Drago, et al. Inside dropbox: understanding personal cloud storage services. In *Proc. ACM IMC 2012*, 481-494.

[7] C.A. Ellis and S.J. Gibbs. Concurrency control in groupware systems. In *Proc. ACM SIGMOD 1989*, 399-407.

[8] Y. Eytani, et al. Towards a framework and a benchmark for testing tools for multi-threaded programs. Special Issue: Parallel and Distributed Systems: Testing and Debugging. *Concurrency and Computation: Practice and Experience*, 19 (3), 2007, 267-279.

[9] H. Fan, C. Sun, and H. Shen. ATCoPE: any-time collaborative programming environment for seamless integration of real-time and non-real-time teamwork in software development. In *Proc. ACM GROUP 2012*, 107-116.

[10] S. Greenberg and D. Marwood. Real time groupware as distributed system: concurrency control and its effect on the interface. In *Proc. ACM CSCW 1994*, 207-217

[11] S. Gilbert, and N. Lynch. Brewer's conjecture and the feasibility of consistent, available, partition-tolerant web services. *ACM SIGACT News*, 33(2), 2002, 51-59.

[12] J.W. Hunt and M.D. McIlroy. An algorithm for differential file comparison. *Computing Science Technical Report*, 1976, 41.

[13] C. Ignat, and M.C. Norrie. Customizable collaborative editor relying on treeOPT algorithm. In *Proc. ECSCW 2003*, 315-334.

[14] L. Lamport. Time, clocks, and the ordering of events in a distributed system. *CACM*, 21(7), 1978, 558-565.

[15] W. Lloyd, et al. Don't settle for eventual: scalable causal consistency for wide-area storage with cops. In *Proc. ACM SOSP 2011*, 401-416.

[16] N. Jalbert, C. Pereira, G. Pokam, and K.S. Radbench. A concurrency bug benchmark suite. *USENIX HotPar 2011.*

[17] P. Molli, G. Oster, H. Skaf-Molli, and A. Imine. Using the transformational approach to build a safe and generic data synchronizer. In *Proc. ACM GROUP 2003*, 212-220.

[18] M. Satyanarayanan, J.J. Kistler, P. Kumar, M.E. Okasaki, E.H. Siegel, & D.C. Steere. Coda: A highly available file system for a distributed workstation environment. *IEEE Transactions* on *Computers*, 39(4), 1990, 447-459.

[19] B. Shao, D. Li, and N. Gu. A sequence transformation algorithm for supporting cooperative work on mobile devices. In *Proc. ACM CSCW 2010*, 159-168.

[20] H.F. Shen and C. Sun. Flexible merging for asynchronous collaborative systems. In *Proc. of Tenth International Conf. on Cooperative Info. Systems*, Lecture Notes in Computer Science 2519, 2002, 304-321.

[21] H.F. Shen and C. Sun. Flexible notification for collaborative systems. In *Proc. ACM CSCW 2002*, 77-86.

[22] L.A. Smith, J.M. Bull, J. Obdrizalek. A Parallel java grande benchmark suite. In *Proc. ACM/IEEE Conf. on Supercomputing 2001*, 6.

[23] C. Sun and C. Ellis. Operational transformation in real-time group editors: issues, algorithms, and achievements. In *Proc. ACM CSCW 1998*, 59-68.

[24] C. Sun, X. Jia, Y. Zhang, Y. Yang, and D. Chen. Achieving convergence, causality preservation, and intention preservation in real-time cooperative editing systems. *ACM TOCHI*, 5(1), 1998, 63-108.

[25] C. Sun, et al. Transparent adaptation of single-user applications for multi-user real-time collaboration. *ACM TOCHI*, 13(4), 2006, 531-582.

[26] D. Sun and C. Sun. Operation context and context-based operational transformation. In *Proc. ACM CSCW 2006*, 279-288.

[27] J.C. Tang, et al. What do you see in the cloud? Understanding the cloud-based user experience through practices. *HCI–INTERACT 2013*, 678-695.

[28] A. Tridgell. Efficient algorithms for sorting and synchronization. Canberra: Australian National University, 1999.

[29] D. Wang, A. Mah, and S. Lassen. Google wave operational transformation. Whitepaper. Retrieved Mar. 18, 2015 from http://www.waveprotocol.org/whitepapers/operational-transform.

[30] S. Xia, D. Sun, C. Sun, and D. Chen. Collaborative object grouping in graphics editing systems. In *Proc. IEEE Collaborative Computing: Networking, Applications and Worksharing*, 2005, 10.

[31] Y. Xu, C. Sun, and M. Li. Achieving convergence in operational transformation: conditions, mechanisms and systems. In *Proc. ACM CSCW 2014*, 505-518.

APPENDIX of this paper can be found at: http://www.ntu.edu.sg/home/czsun/group2016_114_Appendix.pdf

Designing for Inclusion: Supporting Gender Diversity in Independent Innovation Teams

Julie S. Hui
Northwestern University
Evanston, IL
juliehui@u.northwestern.edu

Shelly D. Farnham
Third Place Technologies
Seattle, WA
shelly@thirdplacetechnologies.com

ABSTRACT
We study how independent innovation teams develop an environment of inclusion to support gender diversity. Through a mixed-methods study involving surveys and interviews with people involved in independent innovation, we sought to better understand the mechanisms by which their teams fostered a sense of inclusion to support gender diversity via interpersonal practices and communication and collaboration technology usage. By understanding how inclusion supports gender diversity, we discuss design implications to help more diverse independent innovation teams form and function.

Author Keywords
Diversity; Gender diversity; Teamwork; Socio-technical tools; Collaboration; Community

ACM Classification Keywords
H.5.3. [Information Interfaces and Presentation (e.g. HCI)]: Computer-supported cooperative work

INTRODUCTION
Innovation activity drives the growth of our economy by introducing new products and services that change the way we live and interact. With advancements in communication and collaboration tools, it is easier than ever to form and work together in *independent innovation teams*—teams assembled outside the context of an enterprise that aim to create new artifacts, products, or services. For example, an independent innovation team could be a startup developing a new mobile application, a group of hobbyists designing a new Arduino device, or a collaboration between artists and technologists to create an interactive community art installation.

However, self-formed teams tend to be less diverse than those created under managerial leadership [8]. Having less diverse teams limits innovation because diversity positively influences team performance in problem-solving capabilities and creativity [4,56,63,80]. Unfortunately, simply assembling diverse teams does not necessarily lead to positive outcomes. Successful diverse teams need inclusive work environments that limit friction, yet bring out the positive benefits of having different people work together [19,60]. Feeling included is associated with greater team loyalty and work ethic [1], which are important factors in helping diverse teams thrive [82]. We define *inclusion* in the workplace as being given equal opportunities, the ability to influence decision-making processes, and opportunities to establish personal connections with others [2,60]. We ask, *how do independent innovation teams foster inclusive work environments,* and, *what is the role of the surrounding socio-technical environment in supporting inclusion during diverse team formation and ongoing work?*

GROUP '16, November 13-16, 2016, Sanibel Island, FL, USA

DOI: http://dx.doi.org/10.1145/2957276.2957290

Because independent innovation teams have no overarching corporate structure, it is imperative to understand how these teams develop inclusion and how aspects of the socio-technical environment, including surrounding creative communities and technologies used, influence the psychological experience of working together. While many sociocultural factors determine *what* information is shared, communication and collaboration technologies affect *how* people communicate and whether or not individuals appear as capable or trustworthy [22,54]. Informed by our empirical findings, we contribute design implications to better foster inclusive work practices in independent innovation teams.

Given the scope of this study, we limit our focus to gender diversity as gender minorities face unique barriers to opportunities in many innovation settings [85]. For instance, as the number of new male entrepreneurs continues to increase, the number of new female entrepreneurs is decreasing [29]. Designing gender inclusive technologies is a key direction in the future of HCI work [16]. However, few have studied opportunities for better gender diversity and inclusivity from the lens of communication and collaboration technologies for teams. Motivated to reduce the gaps in innovation activity between genders and to build on existing HCI work on gender inclusive technologies, we use an empirical study to understand how socio-technical systems can better support gender diverse team formation and ongoing work.

We adopted a mixed-methods approach by first surveying 132 people involved in independent innovation teams to understand the relationship between gender diversity, technology usage, and perceptions of inclusion. To gain a richer understanding of what factors affect feelings of inclusion in the team, we then performed follow-up interviews with 20 people who have been or are involved in independent innovation teams of varying gender diversity. We conclude with a discussion and design implications for how communication and collaboration technologies could support diversity by fostering more inclusive work environments.

RELATED WORK

In order to understand how to support gender diverse independent innovation teams, we must also study the surrounding socio-technical environment—technologies being used and communities from which they form.

Supporting Gender Diversity Through HCI

The success of gender-diverse teams is influenced by how members feel in work environments [60,67]. This may explain the conflicting findings on the effects of diversity because simply creating diverse teams does not inherently produce positive outcomes. Some find evidence that gender diversity supports higher levels of team innovation [63], problem solving ability [39][26], and healthier work climates [27], while others find that it interferes with team innovation [40,77] and causes greater interpersonal friction, such as increased misunderstandings and conflicts over power and responsibilities [82].

Creating an inclusive work environment has been shown to mediate the relationship between diversity and conflict in teams [60]. A climate of inclusion is fostered by providing equal opportunities in the workplace, the ability to inform decisions, and opportunities to get to know each other and be accepted for oneself [2,60]. Many of these tenants are parallel to the central commitments of feminism—agency, fulfillment, identity, equity, empowerment, diversity, and social justice [7]. Bardzell argues that by designing interactive systems with these commitments in mind, we can foster more socially aware and higher quality interactions. In this study, we seek to understand how social practices and technologies are adopted and used to support values of inclusion in the context of independent innovation teams.

Theories of socio-technical systems have described how the history of male-dominated technology development has limited the design of communication and collaboration tools [7]. While many have focused on creating tools to increase team productivity [31,35,62], few have focused on how these tools support gender inclusive team work environments [38]. Previous work on gender inclusive technologies have primarily focused on how men and women use software differently. This work finds that women tend to have lower self-efficacy when using software, which means they are less likely to explore and use new features that could improve their work practice [9–11,15,17].

Others described how technologies influence inclusion in distributed teams [38]. Some find more personal communication tool usage, like phone or video calling, allows people to more easily find common ground [79] and express themselves in delicate social situations. Furthermore, collaboration tools that foster greater transparency, such as seeing each others' profiles and project work, help form impressions about someone's personality and skills [22,54].

We build on this research to understand how communication and collaboration tools support inclusive practices in the formation and ongoing work of independent innovation teams. However, we acknowledge that communication and collaboration technologies are used in a greater societal context, and that simply changing a team's technology usage will not necessarily change interpersonal behavior. Comparatively, technology is not just the messenger, but a way to support relationship building based on its designed affordances [7], providing a possible avenue for affecting how diverse teams form and function.

Communities and Cultures of Innovation

A team's environment is also often a reflection of the communities in which it belongs. Because independent innovation teams tend to be less diverse than those created in the context of managerial leadership [8], we explore whether non-enterprise communities take the place of companies in providing norms that shape team culture. We see evidence that creative communities, such as hackerspaces [6,32,51], co-working spaces, art groups, craft groups [75], and DIY communities [47,65], provide resources, social expectations, and interpersonal support needed for team formation.

Creating an environment where people can safely test ideas and connect with others is crucial for creating a healthy work environment, especially for marginalized individuals who may feel judged on their differences. Research on persistence among underrepresented populations describes the importance of interacting with role models and demographically similar peers to support feeling included [52,83]. In addition, limited resources and not feeling like one belongs are major factors in why minorities often leave new environments [37,82]. Creative communities not only connect people with similar interests [81], but also provide a place where people have the resources and social support to produce new innovations in a safe environment [7,32].

In order to support gender diverse teams that form from these communities, we must understand how people interact in these community environments. Previous HCI researchers have studied the pros and cons of community communication channels [84] and have built web platforms to support community decision making [25,50]. For instance Zhang et al. highlight how mailing lists, one type of community communication tool, support "serendipitous discoveries" of content, but limit further discussion [84]. We contribute to this related work by understanding how these technologies support or hinder gender diverse independent innovation team forming from community environments.

PART 1: SURVEY

We first performed a survey study of 132 people involved in independent innovation teams to understand how team technology usage and gender diversity interact to influence perceptions of inclusion and innovation.

Methods

Procedure

Participants were required to be involved in teams of three or more people formed within the past five years with a goal to create a new artifact, product, or service. We recruited participants through 15 email lists for maker groups (e.g. Dorkbot), co-working spaces (e.g. Impact Hub), and art and tech communities (e.g. Burning Man). We also recruited from female-based project groups (e.g. Geek Girl Carrots) to sample for a representative number of women. Furthermore, we recruited through Craigslist and advertisements placed in city newspapers to reduce bias towards those involved in existing communities.

During recruitment, participants were told that the study was about understanding how independent innovation teams formed and worked, and how new technologies could be designed to support this process. Participants were not made aware that the study was primarily on team diversity in order to limit self-selection towards individuals who were more open to diversity practices. The majority of the survey asked questions about team formation, community involvement, and basic demographics. Each participant completed the 20-minute survey and were gifted a $10 Amazon gift card as well as given the opportunity to sign up for a one hour follow-up interview for an extra $50. Survey data was analyzed while interviews were being performed, which allowed semi-structured interview questions to be updated over the course of the study.

Survey

The survey asked questions about personal demographics, technology use, feelings of inclusion, and perception of team innovation. We also asked similar questions about being involved in a greater community as previous work describes the importance of community culture on team environment [81]. The following variables were collected:

Individual Variables

Demographics. Participant gender, race, and age.

Team and Community Perception Variables

Demographics. Participants reported the team type(s) (technological, art, maker, entrepreneurial) and number of people involved.

Gender Diversity. Gender diversity at the team level was calculated using the Blau diversity index [12], which gives the probability of picking two people of the same type (with replacement). Team level gender were self-reported by participants. Participants estimated community level demographics by giving the percentage of each gender.

Technology Use. Technology use was measured by asking on a scale of 1 to 7 how important 18 types of communication and collaboration tools [30] were for interacting with one's teammates and community members (1=Not at all, 7=Very much so).

Inclusion. Personal feelings of inclusion were measured using five items adapted from a standardized measure of inclusion and exclusion in workplace environments [58]. For team perceptions, items included, *'I feel part of informal discussions in this collaboration'* and *'I am able to influence collaboration decisions.'* For community perceptions, items included, *'I feel part of informal discussion in this community,' 'I am able to influence community decisions,'* and *'I feel isolated in this community'* (1=Not at all, 7=Very much so).

Innovation. Perceptions of innovation were measured using five items adapted from Anderson and West's standardized measure of work group innovation [3]. For team perceptions, items included, *'This collaboration is always moving toward the development of new answers,'* and *'This collaboration is open and responsive to change.'* For community perceptions, items included, *'This community is always moving toward the development of new answers,' 'This community is open and responsive to change,'* and *'Assistance in developing new ideas is readily available in this community'* (1=Not at all, 7=Very much so).

We emphasize that these are individual perceptions of the team and community. We collected individual perceptions because it is their perceptions that influence how they feel and act within the team, which determines whether they stay in the team and future decisions to participate in independent innovation teams. Furthermore, we feel that perceptions of team diversity are fairly accurate as most teams had less than ten people, making it easy for participants to recall team members' gender.

Participants

We initially received 197 responses within a three-month period. We excluded 3 under the age of 18, 50 from outside the United States, and 12 for filling out less than half of the survey. We focused on people in the United States in order to minimize confounding factors related to differences in work practices between countries. Of the remaining 132 participants, 40.2% were female. One participant identified their gender as non-binary. Ages ranged from 20 to 61. 76.5% identified as Caucasian, 1.5% Black or African American, 7.6% Asian, 3.8% Hispanic or Latino, and 4.5% Native American. Of these participants, 5.3% were of mixed race.

Survey Results

Teams were on average 41% female. For male respondents, 65% of their teams were reported to be a majority male (33% all male). For female respondents, 50% were a majority female (7.5% all female). The measure of team gender

Socio-technical Tools	Collaboration Mean	Collaboration SD	Community Mean	Community SD
Email (one-to-one)	6.0	1.34	5.8	1.64
Online file sharing	5.0	1.99	4.6	2.11
Real-time doc editing	5.0	1.89	4.9	1.94
Phone calling	5.0	1.87	4.9	1.95
Email lists	4.9	2.19	5.8	1.48
Mobile text messaging	4.7	1.95	4.9	1.91
Calendar sharing systems	4.6	1.95	4.8	1.99
Social networking sites	4.2	2.11	5.3	1.80
Video calling	4.2	2.29	4.6	2.07
Online chat	4.1	2.23	4.5	2.16
Website or blog	4.0	2.27	4.7	1.99
Code sharing systems	3.8	2.44	3.8	2.27
Online discussion boards	3.7	2.33	4.9	2.06
Project management	3.7	2.36	4.2	2.20
Video sharing sites	3.6	2.14	4.2	2.10
Photo sharing sites	3.5	2.32	4.1	2.13
Online member directory	3.3	2.36	4.3	2.27
Other mobile messaging	3.1	2.40	3.8	2.34

Table 1. Mean importance of socio-technical tools for communicating and sharing, in either collaboration or community contexts, where 1 = not at all and 7 = extremely so.

diversity ranged from 0 to .5 with a mean of .35 (*SD* = .19). This meant that on average, if one were to choose two random people from a team, there would be a 35% chance of choosing two people of the same gender. The majority of the teams were ten people or less, with 38.6% 3-4 person teams, 23.5% 5-10, and 25.8% 11 or more. Teamwork was performed collocated (*M* = 5.17, *SD* = 1.63) and distributed (*M* = 5.2, *SD* = 1.69) (1=Very rarely, and 7=Very much so).

Communities were on average 44% female with gender diversity of .40 (*SD* = .18). Participants for the most part reported that their independent innovation team belonged to a larger community context (*M* = 5.9, *SD* = 1.47), and that they themselves were involved in this community (*M* = 5.7, *SD* = 1.42) (1=Not at all and 7=Very much so). These community contexts included co-working spaces, makerspaces, startup groups, and arts communities.

Technology Usage

Participants were asked how important various communication and collaboration technologies were for interacting with team and community members. Between *team* members, email was rated as most important, followed by online file sharing, real-time document editing, and phone calling. Between *community* members, email and mailing lists were reported as most important. See Table 1.

In order to identify the key factors in technology usage, we performed a factor analysis (with varimax rotation) on the ratings for these tools. At both the team and community levels, three factors emerged with factor loadings over 0.6 and an eigenvalue over 1: **1) group communication** referred to tools that typically supported one to many communication, such as online discussion boards, social networking sites, mailing lists, and online member directories; **2) personal communication** referred to tools that typically supported one-to-one or richer communication, such as personal emails, phone calling, and video calling, and **3) project collaboration** referred to tools that typically supported work sharing and collaboration, such as online file sharing tools, code sharing systems, real-time document editing tools, and project management systems.

Team:	Inclusion	Innovation
Participant Variables		
Female	.15	**.33**
Team Perception Variables		
Gender Diversity	-.03	.11
Project Collaboration Tools	-.10	**.26**
Group Communication Tools	**-.55**	.05
Personal Communication Tools	.17	**.32**
Community Perception Variables		
Extent team is in community	.12	**.47**
Gender Diversity	.11	**.21**
Inclusion	**.39**	**.28**

Table 2. Pearson's correlations between diversity, importance of socio-technical tools, collaboration inclusion, and innovation, at both the collaboration and the community level. Bolded items are significant at the p< .05 level.

Environment for Inclusion and Innovation

We first examined the relationship between diversity, inclusion, and innovation through Pearson correlations. As can be seen from Table 2, women tended to rate their collaborations as more innovative than did men. The team's gender diversity did not overall correlate with perceptions of team inclusion or innovation. However, participants in teams that more often used group communication tools were less likely to rate their team as inclusive.

To understand the role of community, we performed Pearson correlations and found that feelings of inclusion in the community were positively correlated with team inclusion. We also found that community membership, community gender diversity, and feelings of inclusion were positively correlated with perceptions of team innovation. See Table 2. Perception of community level of gender diversity was also significally correlated with team gender diversity ($r(130) = .62, p < .01$). We refrain from making bold claims as these variables are individual perceptions of the team and community. However, we find it useful to see how individual perceptions about one's team are highly related to one's perceptions of their community.

To test the relationship between gender status, technology usage, and inclusion, we performed a regression analyses for

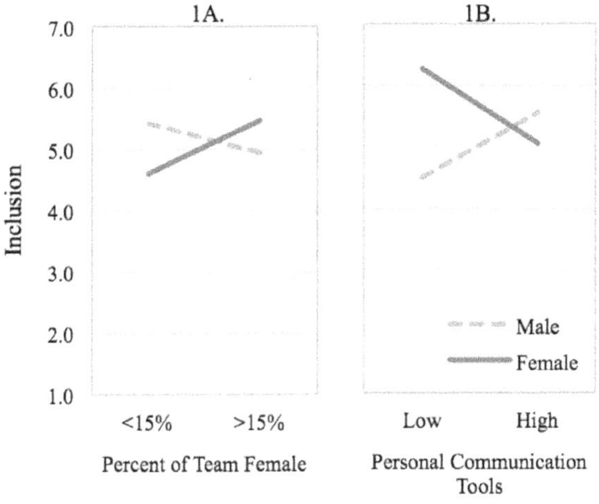

Figure 1: Women feel more included the more women there are in the team while men feel less included (1A). Women feel less included the more the team uses personal communication tools, while men feel more included (1B).

male-dominated technology-based teams to test for main and interaction effects. Teams were classified as male-dominated if they were 85% or more male based on the minority effect—negative effects of minority membership become particularly pronounced in groups that have only a small percentage (one or two people in small teams) of the minority group [41]. We found a marginally significant interaction effect where in male-dominated, tech-focused teams, females felt less included, and men felt more included ($F(1,54) = 3.15$, $p < .08$, 2-tailed, $\Delta r^2 = .05$). See Figure 1A. We also found that women in male-dominant, tech-focused teams felt *less* included in teams that used personal communication tools more, whereas men in male-dominant, tech-focused teams felt more included ($F(1, 42) = 6.16$, $p < .05$, 2-tailed, $\Delta r^2 = .10$) See Figure 1B.

PART 2: INTERVIEWS

We sought further information with interview data to understand *how* independent innovation teams foster inclusive work environments, and the role of the surrounding socio-technical environment (e.g. technology, community) in this process. We performed follow-up interviews with people involved in both high and low gender diverse independent innovation teams.

Methods

Participants

We follow with a nested study design [68] by recruiting 20 interview participants from the initial survey population. This allowed us to reinforce and further explain the source of the survey results. In order to better understand perspectives in high and low gender diverse teams, we performed a theoretical sampling [34] by recruiting participants who worked on teams representing a range of gender diversity. We interviewed 20 participants (13 females), including 2 African-American, 2 Hispanic/Latino, 3 Asian, 2 of Native American/Caucasian mixed race, and 11 Caucasian participants.

Procedure

Interview participants were selected by contacting every survey participant who expressed interest in being interviewed, following up more with female participants in order to get a gender balanced interview sample. However, only a fraction of these interested participants were actually able to participate in the interview given the time commitment of meeting at a quiet location with access to a white board. Interviews were on average 1-hour, took place in person both during the weekday and weekend, and were both audio and video recorded. Participants were also gifted $50 or a comparable amount in company products for their participation. We followed a semi-structured interview protocol where we asked questions about collaboration environment, diversity of people involved, role of a greater creative community, and participant's experience as a gender minority in their team if relevant.

To better understand the role of technology, we asked what communication and collaboration technologies were adopted or dropped, in what situations were certain technologies used, who preferred which technologies, and how they felt when communicating with team members through these different mediums. We initially found that participants were uncomfortable answering questions like, "How do you think technologies supported gender diversity in your team?" Rather, participants responded much more openly to questions of whether or not they felt included in their team and what roles technology and social practices played in supporting positive or negative interpersonal experiences. Stepping back and asking these broader questions about inclusion made it easier for participants to share stories in the context of technology use. Participants were able to reflect on why they used certain tools and how they felt using them with others, which allowed us to collect data on which tool features fostered inclusive work practices.

Throughout the interviews, participants were also asked to visualize their experiences in a *mapping activity*, similar to [64], in which they sketched how they became involved in the team, major events and times of transition, and what technologies were used and when (e.g. Figures 2, 3, and 4). This helped participants to not only reflect on their experiences, but also helped us identify unique areas to inquire further [74]. For instance, if participants described being friends with their teammates in a maker community before forming a project team, we could inquire about how they first became friends in the community environment and the socio-technical supports provided by the community to form a team. Or if a participant drew that their team heavily relied on text messaging towards the end of the project, we could further inquire about this behavior and how they felt when participating in this practice. Interviews were transcribed immediately following the interview using an online transcription service.

Analysis

We took a qualitative analysis approach [57] by performing two coding cycles where we carefully read and re-read transcripts focusing on issues of technology usage, community, and psychological experiences related to inclusion. We also referred back to printed out photographs of the mapping activity to identify patterns of tool use. We first identified 54 initial codes around technology usage (e.g. "texting for idea sharing"), offline practices (e.g. "encouraging others to participate"), and psychological experiences related to inclusion (e.g. "excitement"; "feeling left out"). These 54 codes were then grouped into 19 higher-level codes by combining those describing psychological experiences with related tool usage or offline practices. For example, "opportunity to fail safely" and "shared document editing tools" were grouped together when an excerpt described a participant feeling more comfortable voicing tenuous ideas in a platform that supported cooperative text editing.

Codes were then further grouped into the three themes around how inclusive teams are formed and continue to function over time based on a theoretical framework of building group inclusion [1]. Levine et al.'s model describes how group inclusion is achieved through processes of evaluation, commitment, and role transition. *Investigation* involves efforts by the newcomer and existing group members to determine the newcomer's involvement will lead to his or her satisfaction and contribution to the group's goals. *Socialization* involves efforts to maintain relationships by attempting to fulfill mutual expectations and expressing positive affect between group members. *Maintenance* involves efforts to meaningfully participate in the group.

These stages of building inclusion informed our final three themes for how independent innovation teams build inclusion in gender diverse teams. For example, the theme, "Communities as Catalyst" describes how creative communities provide opportunities for team members to evaluate each other during early stages of team formation; whereas the theme, "Participation Safety and Socialization" describes how in order to establish positive affect between group members in gender diverse teams, the minority gender needed to have a sense of participation safety. Thirdly, the theme "Regular Opportunities for Participation," describes how participants used collaboration tools to become involved in the project through opportunities to inform the work and decision making processes. We discuss within each theme how technology affordances within these contexts support inclusive practices.

Interview Results

The interview findings describe how members of independent innovation teams develop a team environment for inclusion. We describe how communities act as a catalyst to inclusive team formation, and how teams leverage technologies to encourage opportunities for participation and participation safety—key factors in inclusive environments [2,60].

PID	Age	Gender	Team Size	# Female
1	35	F	4	1
2	31	F	6	2
3	53	M	4	0
4	30	F	6	5
5	35	F	12	4
6	42	F	12	9
7	54	F	6	2
8	56	M	5	0
9	46	F	14	10
10	44	M	8	0
11	31	M	3	1
12	43	M	4	1
13	31	F	15	12
14	49	F	4	3
15	31	F	3	3
16	34	M	3	1
17	56	F	11	5
18	38	M	3	0
19	37	F	6	4
20	33	F	6	4

Table 3: Table of interview participants.

Communities as Catalyst

In alignment with the survey results, participants in inclusive gender diverse teams often reported meeting teammates within a diverse community environment in which they also felt included. However, even though community leaders encouraged people to make connections, the promoted socialization tools often did not support these actions well. For example, certain group communication tools like listservs supported awareness between people with similar interests (P2, P5, P9, P14, P16, P17), but did not necessarily provide the functionality to easily develop stronger connections needed for team formation.

P2 who was a gender minority in her team, described finding project teammates through a discussion on the community listserv. She pitched her project idea to the community-wide email thread, identified many people were interested in the topic, but found it difficult to get the team started in the same online environment:

> *"And of course, as things start to spike, [the community leaders] were like could you stop spamming the listserv with your contact information."* (P2)

After moving the conversation elsewhere, she expressed not knowing who to include in the project formation going forward, concerned that she was excluding people who may have been interested in the project and had only been observing passively until that point.

While technologies facilitated more community-wide communication, many participants preferred meeting others in-person to build trusting professional connections. For instance, P5 described first meeting two male community members in the kitchen of a co-working space. She would later form a startup with them to develop an app that connects local farmers to consumers:

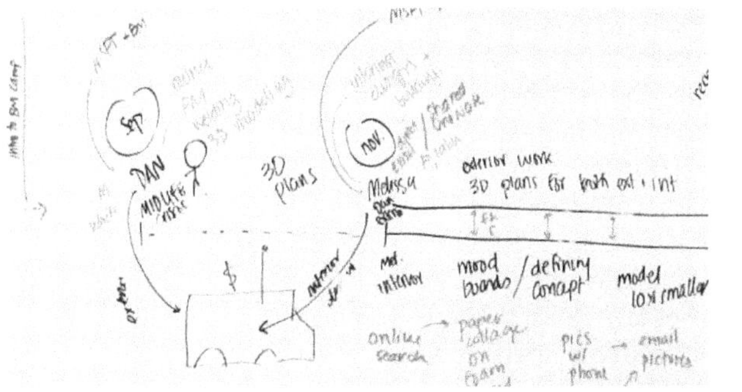

Figure 2: Example from a P1's mapping activity showing how she became involved in her ad-hoc innovation (black) team through a previous community (blue).

"You know, it's those casual meetings that you forget...I jumped out there to get a coffee and we chatted...It was very brief, five minutes, just chatting, made within six sentences a connection...I think I had that level of in-person connection that laid the groundwork for me to feel more comfortable." (P5)

Shared community spaces that encourage socialization sparked interactions between demographically different individuals, which then often led to future collaborations. Other ways participants identified teammates included introductions through existing inter-personal connections (e.g. friend of a friend), and public postings (e.g. Craigslist).

Community involvement also provides a way for people to form bonds over shared values and interests, interpersonal factors that eventually outweigh initial effects of demographic homophily (e.g. same gender) [44,70,71]. For example, one participant who was the only woman and person of color on her team described forming an immediate connection with a team member when she realized they were part of the same art community:

"You get this edge when you realize someone is from [X community]. It's like you know a lot more about them as soon as you find out because you know they're arty, and they do hard work." (P1)

In a way, shared community membership provided a vetting process that helped new team members evaluate each other more positively, an initial step to building a foundation for inclusive teams. In Figure 2, P1 drew how she became involved in the independent innovation team (black) by meeting the person at a community event (blue).

One co-working space displayed how they valued their diverse membership through a wall showing individual pictures of all of its members with their name and project interests below. Even though this community had an online directory that provided the same functionality, members found that the physical wall to be more useful when introducing and describing the community to new members because it provided a more visually accessible way to evaluate the community's values and diversity.

In addition to belonging to diverse communities, female participants in particular described the benefits of participating in female-focused communities or communities with role models, such as coding groups for women, to build confidence and persevere in environments where they are perceived as different. Three participants (P11, P17, P10) found these communities to be so important that they went on to start their own groups for others:

"I have a Muslim female group on LinkedIn, so I share a lot of information about coding for women, and I share it in my community for women who may be interested in coding." (P17)

We find that the socio-technical features of communities serve a key role in the formation of gender diverse independent innovation teams by fostering initial communication both online and offline, and highlighting meaningful similarities that may not be initially salient.

Participation Safety and Socialization

While more personal avenues of communication (e.g. phone, video calls, shared spaces) were seen as useful for impression formation, participants who were gender minorities on their team described how these channels sometimes highlighted patterns of social dominance. For instance, P7 who was working in a male-dominant tech start-up described how communicating with the three men on her team through video and phone calls brought to light sexualized topics:

"We pick up a bit of sexism that they're not even aware of...Sort of like flirty jokes. They got on the phone...and they were talking about him putting lotion on his bald head...It was just a vibe. I can't remember exactly. I tend to like freeze and tune it out." (P7)

While describing her experience, P7 drew out a possible a conference-calling interface that would allow her to more easily communicate through written comments and PowerPoint slides (Figure 3) rather than a live discussion, suggesting that she preferred non-verbal forms of communication in particularly uncomfortable situations where she felt her colleagues were acting aggressive or dominant.

These interview findings correlate with our survey data, which revealed how female participants in male-dominated tech projects felt less included the more they used personal communication tools. We highlight that this finding was only apparent in male-dominated tech projects. Women working with men in other areas, such as art and design, did not report feeling particularly excluded, suggesting that certain professional fields may be less supportive of inclusion than others, or more susceptible to stereotype threat.

In contrast, Caucasian male participants who were part of male-dominant tech teams (P3, P8, P12) did not mention being uncomfortable using more personalized communication mediums, but rather preferred it. P8 described that he saw communication technologies as useful for starting a conversation, but preferred in-person meetings *to "read with the*

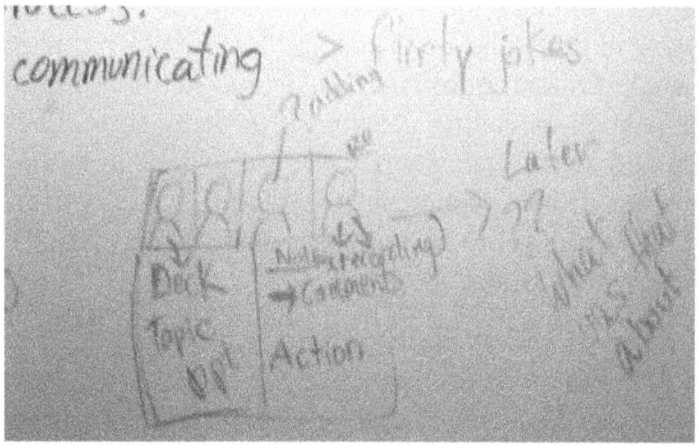

Figure 3: P7 prototypes out a video calling system that allows people on the call to communicate through written comments and shared PowerPoint slides.

body language" because *"if you don't have that, the phone calls are really worthless."* The reliance on body language is beneficial for building trust between people who look and act similar, but may be less supportive of building connections between diverse people who often look different and have different patterns of speaking.

One Caucasian male community leader hoping to increase gender diversity described how he asked some of the female office workers to hang out in the hackerspace to make it more inviting to female newcomers. But, he found that the male participants' conversation topics, like guns, still created a less than inviting atmosphere (P3). Another participant expressed similar frustration when trying to network at a start-up community event:

> *"There's a lot of unconscious self selection out by groups that don't feel welcome...These guys were like, 'Well, we just hired whoever the best person is for the job.' And I'm like, 'You don't realize that your whole like bro thing makes a lot of people not want to work for you or makes them sort of hide themselves personally, which means they're also hiding some of their professional capacity from you because you've created a work environment where they don't feel comfortable.'" (P2)*

Conversely, participants who were part of teams that strived to develop more inclusive environments described using certain communication practices to encourage people to participate in group conversations. For example, P5 described how her team adopted phrases like "Yes, and," which have been shown to encourage group camaraderie and collaborative creativity [33]. Similarly, one participant described how her Japanese colleague had to explain to the team that the other Asian participants did not feel comfortable arguing during team meetings on the phone and in person (P13). In response, one person was designated as meeting facilitator to make sure all voices were heard. Rather than relying on a human resources facilitator or moving employees to a different team during times of conflict, members of independent innovation teams had to self-identify the challenges that hindered diversity and identify new solutions themselves.

Regular Opportunities for Participation

To encourage a continued sense of inclusion beyond team formation, we found tools that supported shared document editing and immediate low-fidelity communication (e.g. texting), made it easier for gender diverse teams to make collaborative decisions and maintain mutual awareness. Rather than creating hierarchies between team members, various participants described how their teams avoided designating power and chose to divide responsibilities based on skillsets. For example, participants explained that *"there wasn't a leader that was designated by an organization"* (P4) and that their collaborations were more *"fluid"* and *"organic"* (P1, P6), suggesting that people involved in independent innovation teams tend to adopt different work mindsets compared to those who work in enterprise teams where there are clear power structures.

This aversion to hierarchy was also reflected in the types of communication and collaboration tools they preferred to use. One female participant who was a project manager described how real-time document editing tools allowed her to communicate more easily with male engineers on her team:

> *"Somehow tracks changes was a fight...It's like this is what I want to say, no this is what I want to say, which is not a conversation, right? Like we can't test things...Whereas with Google Docs, you can just be looking at something and start talking and writing things down and look at it together." (P2)*

Consistent with established work on inclusion [2], participants described how they felt more committed to the team when they had equal opportunities to contribute to project work and decisions.

P6, who was working on a crowdsourced art installation described how her team relied heavily on shared documents to allow all members to co-develop instruction for building their final product. In the mapping activity (Figure 4), she listed using 2-3 different technologies at each stage of the project that allowed all team members to communicate with

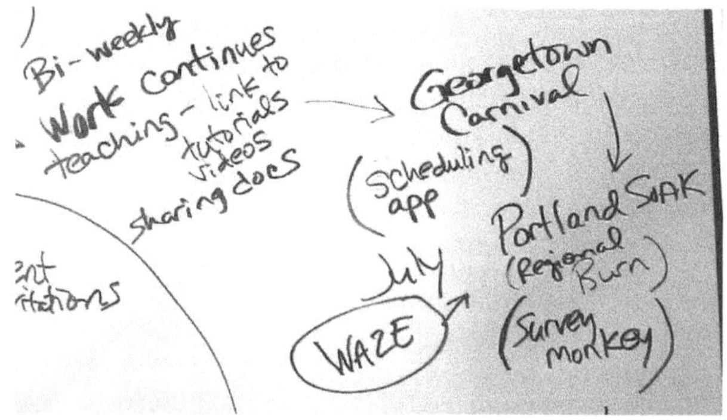

Figure 4: P6 describes how her team used multiple types of communication technologies to keep members of the team aware of what was happening.

each other openly and at any time of day.

Figure 5: Mechanisms and challenges to establishing and sustaining inclusion in independent innovation teams inspired by Levine et al.'s model of developing group inclusion [49].

P11 emphasized that when adopting new collaboration tools, his team found it necessary to establish expectations allowing for equal rather than hierarchical participation:

> *"[One team member] just started assigning us stuff and with no context. And then all of a sudden people were getting more work, so that was bad...It's definitely necessary to create some norms to say, 'Hey, you can't just start assigning people to stuff. You need to have a conversation first.'" (P11)*

While various existing project management tools allow people to assign tasks to team members, participants were wary of using these features fearing that it may cause tension. Tools that supported greater opportunities for participation among all members helped participants feel like they were kept in the loop, reducing team friction.

Overall, we find that creative communities provide an avenue for diverse people to connect over shared project interests, while participation safety and opportunities to participate early on promotes team socialization and maintenance, features needed for group inclusion (See Figure 5) [49].

LIMITATIONS

Before discussing research contributions, we acknowledge limitations to our study. First, survey data on team and community variables was based on self-report. While we cannot make accurate statements about actual team innovation or inclusion, we do not see this as a major problem as it is the individual's perceptions that drive how they feel and act within the team. Furthermore, because teams tended to be less than 10 people, we believed participants could accurately report the gender distribution of teammates. Because only one survey participant reported their gender as non-binary, our findings may not represent the experiences of LGBTQIA people who are also minorities in many innovation settings. We hope that our findings, which mainly describe self-identified female experiences as gender minorities, might still provide useful design implications for forming teams of all genders. Thirdly, interview participants were recruited primarily from one major metropolitan area so that interviews could be in person. Our results may describe a unique innovation culture. However, many of our themes were supported by related work on inclusion and group work practices, suggesting that our findings have implications for independent innovation teams in general. In addition, we also only interview people who have successfully become involved in independent innovation teams. While this biases our sample towards those particularly motivated or supported, our data show that they are still obstacles in managing diversity. We saw the follow-up interviews as a way to identify opportunities for helping those in less supportive environments.

DISCUSSION AND DESIGN IMPLICATIONS

Designing for diversity is difficult due to the sensitive nature of the topic [66]. When dealing with topics that are uncomfortable or psychologically threatening, such as how one's implicit biases affect gender diversity, people are often less receptive to design suggestions that address the problem overtly [14,42,43]. Creating communication and collaboration technologies "to support minorities" is problematic in that it can trigger stereotype threat and a defensive reaction in the dominant population.

Through our survey and interviews, we find that certain team and community practices, in addition to the technologies they use, affect how gender minorities feel when joining and working in male-dominated independent innovation teams. For instance, our quantitative and qualitative findings show that the more a male-dominant team uses "richer" mediums, such as synchronous audio and visual communication channels, there is a higher risk that gender minority participants feel less included. These findings conflict with original work on media richness theory, in which Daft and Lengel argue that "managers will turn to rich media when they deal with the difficult, changing, unpredictable human dimensions of organizations" [23].

Our data show that while richer media allow for greater feedback and social cues, which are typically more useful during interpersonal communication, they also highlight certain microaggressions that often happen to marginalized people [72]. These encounters play a large part in the psychological experience of being part of a team and have been a major reason for why women drop out of male-dominant careers at a higher rate than men [72]. These findings are supported by previous work by Kiesler et al. in which they describe how the affordances of social technologies can mask typically salient features (e.g. gender), making it easier for demographically diverse people to bond over intellectual interests rather than more superficial factors [44,70,71].

However, initially hiding certain traits online, such as gender, between team members only masks the underlying problem rather than addressing it. Motivated by related work on offline interventions to support diversity, tool designers could develop tools that encourage greater awareness of implicit biases in computer-mediated environments. Recent work by Burnett et al. describe a systematic inspection method to evaluate the gender inclusivity of software by prompting the software designers to reflect on how women and men with different technology backgrounds and confidence levels might react to usability issues [17].

Furthermore, various systems have been developed to provide communication-based feedback during group meetings to identify how often teams agreed or disagreed with their colleagues [48] or how dominant certain people are in meetings [45]. Others have created tools to encourage listening in group communication [46]. Encouraging more equal communication between team members can help change engrained communication patterns reflecting social dominance. One could imagine similar systems that would identify how frequently team members respond to or agree with other team members to identify underlying gender-based patterns of attention. Future tools could monitor speaking patterns between minority and majority populations in order to highlight instances where balanced discussions are lacking. For instance, if the tool highlighted that men were significantly more likely to respond positively to comments made by other men, it could signal to them to watch how they encourage others to share their thoughts. Research on speaking time show that men are perceived as more dominant the more they speak, while this effect is significantly less pronounced for women [55]. People who speak more also do not realize the extent to which they are perceived as dominant [55], suggesting that a dominance awareness tool might be useful.

However, such "diversity targeted" tools may not produce the desired affect because people are less likely to respond to overt messages due to the sensitive nature of the topic [42,43]. Furthermore, because there is no overarching company structure to enforce the use of diversity awareness tools, independent innovation teams that elect to start using these tools are more likely already making efforts to support greater gender diversity. Rather, we examine how do we design for gender diversity in teams and communities that are not particularly supportive already.

In their work on designing games for social activism, Kaufman et al. suggest a model of "embedded design" as a way to develop games with a social activism goal (e.g. highlighting implicit biases) without making the game overtly about social activism [42,43]. They suggest three "embedding" strategies: 1) Intermixing- balancing "on-message" and "off-message" content to make the former less threatening, 2) Obfuscating- highlighting a certain genre or purpose to hide the actual intent, and 3) Distancing- using fiction and metaphor to distance players' identities with the game's characters. While these strategies are designed for games, we could apply parts of these principles to the design of communication and collaboration technologies to better support the formation and ongoing work of gender diverse teams.

Designing for Inclusion

In this study, we suggest an "obfuscating" approach by *designing for inclusion* with the underlying primary goal to develop team environments and technologies that support gender diversity. Our goal of designing for inclusion is motivated by previous work and our study findings, which has shown that gender diverse teams are more likely to succeed if they foster inclusive work environments [60]. In addition, related work in HCI on designing gender-inclusive technologies has found that inclusive technologies benefit all users by promoting more user-friendly interfaces and user self-efficacy [15,17].

Compared to previous work on gender-inclusive technologies in HCI [9–11,15,17], we focus less on people's relationship with software, and more on how software's designed affordances influence people's relationship with each other. Therefore, while previous work on gender inclusive technology suggests features that support self-efficacy for using the software itself, like editing program bugs [15], we suggest design implications that support communication self-efficacy, such as promoting confidence to speak up and express one's opinions online. For instance, women with low communication self-efficacy could opt-in for scaffolds on how to communicate more assertively or regularly with teammates. Recently, such communication tools have become adopted among women in email settings, such as a Chrome plug-in that highlights when an email includes the words "sorry," "just," and "I think" [21]. Similarly, if someone wanted to disagree or share an idea during a meeting, but did not know how to affectively interject, such a tool could provide phrases and volume alerts to signal how to appear more assertive.

While women could adopt tools to support their work practice, our study participants primarily called for team-wide tools that could better support equal opportunities for participation in project work. Tools that support co-ownership of documents and projects have been praised for their ability to promote better collaboration through shared awareness [54]. However, participants described the importance of establishing norms when working with these tools, considering that the same tool can be used in multiple different ways by different users [59]. By applying previous work arguing that non-hierarchical organizations still need structure to be productive and coherent [25], we argue that teams must establish norms when using communication and collaboration technologies to support inclusive work practices. In the future, existing tools could provide tutorials that describe different ways teams could use their tools to promote more balanced communication practices. For instance, P11 described how his team members preferred having a conversation together verbally before putting a task on the project management tool to-do list. Such practices could be suggested in tool tutorials to better support a more open and inclusive work environment among all members.

Communication and collaboration tools could also help teams onboard new members in online discussions. Our findings show that the affordances of various group communication tools, like listserves, make it difficult for new members to become active members if they have low participation self-efficacy. Future group communication tools could notify established members to introduce new members or invite them to participate in a discussion thread. These suggested designs support work on opinion diversity which describes the importance of including minority opinions in innovation work [24].

Similar to previous work on communities of practice [81] and third spaces [61], we find that community culture influences team formation and individual identity. Our interview data show that while group communication tools enable discovery of demographically diverse people with similar interests, they do not make it easy to create more personalized groups that could lead to team formation. Participants asked for easier ways to form and visualize sub-groups that would make it easier for project teams to form in a community discussion environment.

As previously argued by Hinds and Bailey [38], while it is possible to create a separate email thread, these conversations are often difficult to manage because people forget to include certain interested members who then do not have access to previous conversation topics. Similarly, while it is possible to create a separate email list, this often leads to being emailed the same thing multiple times and information overload. Creating community communication tools that make it easier to visualize and organize conversation subgroups could encourage more deep conversations between diverse community members that lead to team formation. This work adds to research on transitioning between levels of cooperative work [5] and recent work on re-designing group communication systems [84].

Participants also found that meeting community members in person better encouraged the socialization opportunities needed to foster team formation. While previous literature describe the benefits of co-located work [13,73] and having shared common spaces [61], our findings suggest that further programming is often needed to motivate connection between people. Tools that help members organize ad-hoc socialization opportunities in shared spaces could distribute planning efforts among community members, thus taking the load off of overworked community managers. Similar to [20], a tool that coordinates on-demand events, a similar tool could signal ad-hoc socialization opportunities by sending out notifications when someone wants to foster an ad-hoc break in a community common area.

While designing for inclusion might be more effective at promoting adoption of diversity-friendly practices, there is still value in interventions that overtly focus on diversity and inclusion. For instance, research on supporting gender and racial minorities in large organizations describe the concept of "counter-spaces" and "safe spaces" as places where groups of minorities come together to provide each other with emotional and professional support [53,69]. Similar to tools coordinating group discussions in MOOCS [18], community-based tools could scaffold conversations and relationship building between gender minorities in innovation work environments by providing regular topics of discussion both online and offline.

HCI researchers have long focused on designing tools that support behaviors like team creativity [33,36,76] and productivity [28,78]. We argue that designing for inclusion to support gender diversity and gender minority experiences will consequently inspire more successful interactions between diverse team members. Based on our quantitative and qualitative data, we suggest five possible avenues in HCI for supporting gender diversity via inclusion at the team and community level: 1) support ad-hoc socialization in community spaces, 2) make it easier to create and manage sub groups that developed from community-wide discussions, 3) scaffold the creation and practice of minority support groups, 4) provide examples of inclusive work practices in online collaboration environments, and 5) track and flag behavior that may lead to less inclusive communication practices.

CONCLUSION

HCI researchers are increasingly interested in developing technologies that support diversity as well as positive experiences of minority and marginalized populations. We contribute to this growing body of work by studying how independent innovation teams create an environment of inclusion with the underlying goal of supporting gender diversity. Through a survey, we found a relationship between technology usage and how people perceived their team as inclusive. Further investigation through interviews describes how a sense of inclusion is developed during diverse team formation and ongoing work, as well as how collaboration tools can both support and hinder inclusive team practices.

ACKNOWLEDGEMENTS

We thank all the participants for sharing their stories and being part of this study. This work was performed through Microsoft Research.

REFERENCES

1. Dominic Abrams, Michael A. Hogg, and José M. Marques. 2004. *Social psychology of inclusion and exclusion*. Psychology Press.
2. Gordon Willard Allport. 1979. *The Nature of Prejudice*. Basic books.
3. Neal R. Anderson and Michael A. West. 1998. Measuring Climate for Work Group Innovation: Development and Validation of the Team Climate Inventory. *Journal of Organizational Behavior* 19, 3: 235–258.
4. Karen A. Bantel and Susan E. Jackson. 1989. Top Management and Innovations in Banking: Does the Composition of the Top Team Make a Difference? *Strategic Management Journal* 10, S1: 107–124.
5. Jakob Bardram. 1998. Designing for the dynamics of cooperative work activities. *Proc. of the Conference on Computer Supported Cooperative Work*, ACM, 89–98.
6. Jeffrey Bardzell, Shaowen Bardzell, and Austin Toombs. 2014. Now That's Definitely a Proper Hack: Self-Made Tools in Hackerspaces. *Proc. of the Conference on Human Factors in Computing Systems*, ACM, 473–476.
7. Shaowen Bardzell. 2010. Feminist HCI: Taking Stock and Outlining an Agenda for Design. *Proc. of the ACM Conference on Human Factors in Computing Systems*, ACM, 1301–1310.
8. Dan Baugher, Andrew Varanelli Jr, and Ellen Weisbord. 2000. Gender and Culture Diversity Occurring in Self-formed Work Groups. *Journal of Managerial Issues*: 391–407.
9. Laura Beckwith, Margaret Burnett, Susan Wiedenbeck, Curtis Cook, Shraddha Sorte, and Michelle Hastings. 2005. Effectiveness of end-user debugging software features: Are there gender issues? *Proc. of the Conference on Human Factors in Computing Systems*, ACM, 869–878.
10. Laura Beckwith, Derek Inman, Kyle Rector, and Margaret Burnett. 2007. On to the real world: Gender and self-efficacy in Excel. *IEEE Symposium on Visual Languages and Human-Centric Computing*, IEEE, 119–126.
11. Laura Beckwith, Cory Kissinger, Margaret Burnett, et al. 2006. Tinkering and gender in end-user programmers' debugging. *Proceedings of the Conference on Human Factors in computing systems*, ACM, 231–240.
12. Peter Michael Blau. 1977. *Inequality and Heterogeneity: A Primitive Theory of Social Structure*. Free Press New York.
13. Nathan Bos, N. Sadat Shami, Judith S. Olson, Arik Cheshin, and Ning Nan. 2004. In-group/Out-group Effects in Distributed Teams: An Experimental Simulation. *Proc. of the Conference on Computer Supported Cooperative Work*, ACM, 429–436.
14. Jack W. Brehm. 1966. A theory of psychological reactance.
15. Margaret Burnett, Scott D. Fleming, Shamsi Iqbal, et al. 2010. Gender differences and programming environments: across programming populations. *Proceedings of the Symposium on empirical software engineering and measurement*, ACM, 28.
16. Margaret M. Burnett, Elizabeth F. Churchill, and Michael J. Lee. 2015. SIG: Gender-Inclusive Software: What We Know About Building It. *Proc. of the Conference on Human Factors in Computing Systems Extended Abstracts*, ACM, 857–860.
17. Margaret Burnett, Anicia Peters, Charles Hill, and Noha Elarief. 2016. Finding Gender-Inclusiveness Software Issues with GenderMag: A Field Investigation. *Proc. of the Conference on Human Factors in Computing Systems*.
18. Julia Cambre, Chinmay Kulkarni, Michael S. Bernstein, and Scott R. Klemmer. 2014. Talkabout: small-group discussions in massive global classes. *Proc. of the Conference on Learning@Scale*, ACM, 161–162.
19. Jennifer A. Chatman, Jeffrey T. Polzer, Sigal G. Barsade, and Margaret A. Neale. 1998. Being Different Yet Feeling Similar: The Influence of Demographic Composition and Organizational Culture on Work Processes and Outcomes. *Administrative Science Quarterly*: 749–780.
20. Justin Cheng and Michael Bernstein. 2014. Catalyst: Triggering Collective Action with Thresholds. *Proc. of the Conference on Computer Supported Cooperative Work & Social Computing*, ACM, 1211–1221.
21. Cyrus Innovation. Just Not Sorry - The Gmail Plug-in. Retrieved from https://chrome.google.com/webstore/detail/just-not-sorry-the-gmail/fmegmibednnlgojepmidhlhpjbppmlci?hl=en-US
22. Laura Dabbish, Colleen Stuart, Jason Tsay, and Jim Herbsleb. 2012. Social Coding in GitHub: Transparency and Collaboration in an Open Software Repository. *Proc. of the Conference on Computer Supported Cooperative Work and Social Computing*, ACM, 1277–1286.
23. Richard L. Daft and Robert H. Lengel. 1983. *Information Richness: A New Approach to Managerial Behavior and Organizational Design*. Texas A&M University.
24. Carsten KW De Dreu and Michael A. West. 2001. Minority Dissent and Team Innovation: The Importance of Participation in Decision Making. *Journal of applied Psychology* 86, 6: 1191.
25. Charles Frederick DeTar. 2013. *InterTwinkles: Online Tools for Non-hierarchical, Consensus-oriented Decision Making*. Ph.D Dissertation. Massachusetts Institute of Technology, Cambridge, MA.
26. Cristina Díaz-García, Angela González-Moreno, and Francisco Jose Sáez-Martínez. 2013. Gender Diversity Within R&D Teams: Its Impact on Radicalness of Innovation. *Innovation: Management, Policy & Practice* 15, 2: 149–160.

27. Martin Dufwenberg and Astri Muren. 2006. Gender Composition in Teams. *Journal of Economic Behavior & Organization* 61, 1: 50–54.
28. Kate Ehrlich and Marcelo Cataldo. 2014. The Communication Patterns of Technical Leaders: Impact on Product Development Team Performance. *Proc. of the Conference on Computer Supported Cooperative Work & Social Computing*, ACM, 733–744.
29. Robert W. Fairlie, Arnobio Morelix, E.J. Reedy, and Joshua Russell. 2015. *The Kauffman Index: Startup Activity - National Trends*. Ewing Marion Kauffman Foundation.
30. Shelly Farnham, David Keyes, Vicky Yuki, and Chris Tugwell. 2012. Puget sound off: fostering youth civic engagement through citizen journalism. *Proc. of the Conference on Computer Supported Cooperative Work & Social Computing*, ACM, 285–294.
31. Thomas A. Finholt and Gary M. Olson. 1997. From Laboratories to Collaboratories: A New Organizational Form for Scientific Collaboration. *Psychological Science* 8, 1: 28–36.
32. Sarah Fox, Rachel Rose Ulgado, and Daniela K. Rosner. 2015. Hacking Culture, Not Devices: Access and Recognition in Feminist Hackerspaces. *Proc. of the ACM Conference on Computer Supported Cooperative Work and Social Computing*.
33. E. Gerber. 2009. Using Improvisation to Enhance the Effectiveness of Brainstorming. *Proc. of the Conference on Human Factors in Computing Systems*, ACM.
34. Barney G. Glaser and Anselm Strauss. 2009. *The Discovery of Grounded Theory: Strategies for Qualitative Research*. Aldine, New York.
35. Anja Guzzi, Alberto Bacchelli, Yann Riche, and Arie van Deursen. 2015. Supporting Developers' Coordination in the IDE. *Proc. of the Conference on Computer Supported Cooperative Work & Social Computing*, ACM, 518–532.
36. Julia Katherine Haines. 2013. Cultivating Creativity in Diverse Teams. *Proc. of the Conference on Creativity & Cognition*, ACM, 32–41.
37. Leslie RM Hausmann, Janet Ward Schofield, and Rochelle L. Woods. 2007. Sense of Belonging as a Predictor of Intentions to Persist Among African American and White First-year College Students. *Research in Higher Education* 48, 7: 803–839.
38. Pamela J. Hinds and Diane E. Bailey. 2003. Out of sight, out of sync: Understanding conflict in distributed teams. *Organization science* 14, 6: 615–632.
39. Lionel R. Hoffman and Norman R. F. Maier. 1961. Sex Differences, Sex Composition, and Group Problem Solving. *The Journal of Abnormal and Social Psychology* 63, 2: 453.
40. Ute R. Hülsheger, Neil Anderson, and Jesus F. Salgado. 2009. Team-level Predictors of Innovation at Work: A Comprehensive Meta-analysis Spanning Three Decades of Research. *Journal of Applied Psychology* 94, 5: 1128.
41. Charles B. Hutchison. 2009. *What happens when students are in the minority: Experiences and behaviors that impact human performance*. R&L Education.
42. Geoff Kaufman and Mary Flanagan. 2015. A psychologically "embedded" approach to designing games for prosocial causes. *Cyberpsychology* 9, 3.
43. Geoff Kaufman, Mary Flanagan, and Max Seidman. 2015. Creating stealth game interventions for attitude and behavior change: An "Embedded Design" model. *Proc. of the Digital Games Research Association (DiGRA) Conference*.
44. Sara Kiesler, Jane Siegel, and Timothy W. McGuire. 1984. Social psychological aspects of computer-mediated communication. *American psychologist* 39, 10: 1123.
45. Taemie Kim, Agnes Chang, Lindsey Holland, and Alex Sandy Pentland. 2008. Meeting Mediator: Enhancing Group Collaboration Using Sociometric Feedback. *Proc. of the Conference on Computer Supported Cooperative Work*, ACM, 457–466.
46. Travis Kriplean, Michael Toomim, Jonathan Morgan, Alan Borning, and Andrew Ko. 2012. Is This What You Meant?: Promoting Listening on the Web with Reflect. *Proc. of the Conference on Human Factors in Computing Systems*, ACM, 1559–1568.
47. Stacey Kuznetsov and Eric Paulos. 2010. Rise of the Expert Amateur: DIY Projects, Communities, and Cultures. *Proc. of NordiCHI*, ACM.
48. Gilly Leshed, Diego Perez, Jeffrey T. Hancock, et al. 2009. Visualizing Real-time Language based Feedback on Teamwork Behavior in Computer-mediated Groups. *Proc. of the Conference on Human Factors in Computing Systems*, ACM, 537–546.
49. John M. Levine, Richard L. Moreland, and Leslie R. M. Hausmann. 2005. Managing Group Composition: Inclusive and Exclusive Role Transitions. In *The Social Psychology of Inclusion and Exclusion*, Dominic Abrams, Michael A. Hogg and José M. Marques (eds.). Taylor & Francis, New York, NY, 137–160.
50. Myriam Lewkowicz and Manuel Zacklad. 2002. A structured groupware for a collective decision-making aid. *European Journal of Operational Research* 136, 2: 333–339.
51. Silvia Lindtner, Garnet D. Hertz, and Paul Dourish. 2014. Emerging Sites of HCI Innovation: Hackerspaces, Hardware Startups & Incubators. *Proc. of the Conference on Human Factors in Computing Systems*, ACM, 439–448.
52. Penelope Lockwood, Christian H. Jordan, and Ziva Kunda. 2002. Motivation by Positive or Negative Role Models: Regulatory Focus Determines Who Will Best Inspire Us. *Journal of Personality and Social Psychology* 83, 4: 854.
53. Jane Margolis and Allan Fisher. 2003. *Unlocking the clubhouse: Women in computing*. MIT press.

54. Jennifer Marlow, Laura Dabbish, and Jim Herbsleb. 2013. Impression Formation in Online Peer Production: Activity Traces and Personal Profiles in Github. *Proc. of the Conference on Computer Supported Cooperative Work & Social Computing*, ACM, 117–128.
55. Marianne Schmid Mast. 2002. Dominance as Expressed and Inferred Through Speaking Time. *Human Communication Research* 28, 3: 420–450.
56. Poppy Lauretta McLeod and Sharon Alisa Lobel. 1992. The Effects of Ethnic Diversity on Idea Generation in Small Groups. *Academy of Management Journal*, 227–231.
57. Matthew B. Miles and Michael Huberman. 1994. *Qualitative Data Analysis*. Sage Publications, Thousand Oaks, CA.
58. Michal E. Mor-Barak and David A. Cherin. 1998. A tool to expand organizational understanding of workforce diversity: Exploring a measure of inclusion-exclusion. *Administration in Social Work* 22, 1: 47–64.
59. Michael Muller, Kate Ehrlich, Tara Matthews, Adam Perer, Inbal Ronen, and Ido Guy. 2012. Diversity among enterprise online communities: collaborating, teaming, and innovating through social media. *Proc. of the Conference on Human Factors in Computing Systems*, ACM, 2815–2824.
60. Lisa Nishii. 2013. The Benefits of Climate for Inclusion for Gender Diverse Groups. *Academy of Management Journal* 56, 6: 1754–1774.
61. Ray Oldenburg. 1999. *The Great Good Place: Cafes, Coffee Shops, Bookstores, Cars, Hair Salons, and Other Hangouts at the Heart of a Community*. Marlowe, New York.
62. Gary M. Olson and Judy S. Olson. 2000. Distance Matters. *Human-Computer Interaction* 15, 2: 139–178.
63. Christian R. Østergaard, Bram Timmermans, and Kari Kristinsson. 2011. Does a Different View Create Something New? The Effect of Employee Diversity on Innovation. *Research Policy* 40, 3: 500–509.
64. Fatih Kursat Ozenc and Shelly D. Farnham. 2011. Life Modes in Social Media. *Proc. of the Conference on Human Factors in Computing Systems*, ACM, 561–570.
65. Daniela K. Rosner, Silvia Lindtner, Ingrid Erickson, Laura Forlano, Steven J. Jackson, and Beth Kolko. 2014. Making Cultures: Building Things & Building Communities. *Proc. of the Conference on Computer Supported Cooperative Work & Social Computing*, ACM, 113–116.
66. Max Seidman, Mary Flanagan, and Geoff Kaufman. 2015. Failed Games: Lessons Learned from Promising but Problematic Game Prototypes in Designing for Diversity. *Proc. of Diversity of play: Games -- Cultures -- Identities*. Retrieved February 16, 2016 from http://www.digra.org/wp-content/uploads/digital-library/100_Flanagan_etal_Failed-Games.compressed.pdf
67. Rajesh Sethi, Daniel C. Smith, and C. Whan Park. 2001. Cross-functional Product Development Teams, Creativity, and the Innovativeness of New Consumer Products. *Journal of Marketing Research* 38, 1: 73–85.
68. Mario Luis Small. 2011. How to Conduct a Mixed Methods Study: Recent Trends in a Rapidly Growing Literature. *Annual Review of Sociology* 37, 1: 57–86.
69. Daniel Solorzano, Miguel Ceja, and Tara Yosso. 2000. Critical Race Theory, Racial Microaggressions, and Campus Racial Climate: The Experiences of African American College Students. *Journal of Negro Education*: 60–73.
70. Lee Sproull and Sara Kiesler. 1986. Reducing social context cues: Electronic mail in organizational communication. *Management science* 32, 11: 1492–1512.
71. Lee Sproull and Sara Kiesler. 1991. Computers, networks and work. *Scientific American* 265, 3: 116–123.
72. Derald Wing Sue. 2010. *Microaggressions in everyday life: Race, gender, and sexual orientation*. John Wiley & Sons.
73. Stephanie Teasley, Lisa Covi, Mayuram S. Krishnan, and Judith S. Olson. 2000. How Does Radical Collocation Help a Team Succeed? *Proc. of the Conference on Computer supported Cooperative Work*, ACM, 339–346.
74. Maryam Tohidi, William Buxton, Ronald Baecker, and Abigail Sellen. 2006. User sketches: a quick, inexpensive, and effective way to elicit more reflective user feedback. *Proc. of the Nordic Conference on Human-computer interaction: changing roles*, ACM, 105–114.
75. Cristen Torrey, Elizabeth F. Churchill, and David W. McDonald. 2009. Learning How: The Search for Craft Knowledge on the Internet. *Proc. of the Conference on Human Factors in Computing Systems*, ACM, 1371–1380.
76. Priyamvada Tripathi and Winslow Burleson. 2012. Predicting Creativity in the Wild: Experience Sample and Sociometric Modeling of Teams. *Proc. of the Conference on Computer Supported Cooperative Work*, ACM, 1203–1212.
77. Gerben S. Van der Vegt and Onne Janssen. 2003. Joint Impact of Interdependence and Group Diversity on Innovation. *Journal of Management* 29, 5: 729–751.
78. Bogdan Vasilescu, Daryl Posnett, Baishakhi Ray, et al. 2015. Gender and Tenure Diversity in GitHub Teams. *Proc. of the Conference on Human Factors in Computing Systems*, ACM.
79. Elizabeth S. Veinott, Judith Olson, Gary M. Olson, and Xiaolan Fu. 1999. Video helps remote work: Speakers who need to negotiate common ground benefit from seeing each other. *Proc. of the Conference on Human Factors in Computing Systems*, ACM, 302–309. Retrieved May 13, 2016 from http://dl.acm.org/citation.cfm?id=303067
80. Hao-Chuan Wang, Susan Fussell, and Dan Cosley. 2011. From Diversity to Creativity: Stimulating Group

Brainstorming with Cultural Differences and Conversationally-Retrieved Pictures. *Proc. of the Conference on Computer Supported Cooperative Work*, ACM.

81. Etienne Wenger. 1999. *Communities of Practice: Learning, Meaning, and Identity*. Cambridge university press.
82. Katherine Y. Williams and Charles A. O'Reilly. 1998. Demography and Diversity in Organizations: A Review of 40 Years of Research. *Research in Organizational Behavior* 20: 77–140.
83. Donghee Yvette Wohn, Nicole B. Ellison, M. Laeeq Khan, Ryan Fewins-Bliss, and Rebecca Gray. 2013. The Role of Social Media in Shaping First-generation High School Students' College Aspirations: A Social Capital Lens. *Computers & Education* 63: 424–436.
84. Amy X. Zhang, Mark S. Ackerman, and David R. Karger. 2015. Mailing Lists: Why Are They Still Here, What's Wrong With Them, and How Can We Fix Them? *Proc. of the Conference on Human Factors in Computing Systems*, ACM, 4009–4018.
85. 2015. *Women Entrepreneurs are Key to Accelerating Growth*. Kauffman Foundation.

Curating an Infinite Basement: Understanding How People Manage Collections of Sentimental Artifacts

Jasmine Jones
School of Information
University of Michigan, Ann Arbor
Ann Arbor, MI USA
jazzij@umich.edu

Mark S. Ackerman
School of Information and Dept. of EECS
University of Michigan, Ann Arbor
Ann Arbor, MI USA
ackerm@umich.edu

ABSTRACT
Valuable memories are increasingly captured and stored as digital artifacts. However, as people amass these digital mementos, their collections are rarely curated, due to the volume of content, the effort involved, and a general lack of motivation, which can result in important artifacts being obscured and forgotten in an accumulation of content over time. Our study aims to better understand the challenges and goals of people dealing with large collections, and to provide insight into how people select and pay attention to large collections of digital mementos. We conducted an interpretivist analysis of forum data from UnclutterNow.com, where participants discussed issues they face in curating the sentimental artifacts in their homes. We uncovered a number of social, temporal, and spatial affordances and concerns that influence the ways that people curate their memories, and discuss how curation is closely tied to how people use storage and display in their home. In our study, we drew out and unpack "curation regimes" as patterns that people enact to focus the attention they are able to pay to the artifacts in their collections. We close with a discussion of the design opportunities for memory artifacts, which support and facilitate the curatorial processes of users managing digital mementos in everyday life.

Keywords
family memory; memory artifacts; sentimental artifacts; memorabilia; digital memento; curation; collection management; digital curation; ubicomp; pervasive computing

1. INTRODUCTION
As homes increasingly become pervasive environments, possibilities open up for creating new kinds of digital family memories. In these environments, there will be an enormous increase in the amount of personal and family data that can be captured and generated for a memorial purpose. Some of this has already been seen as digital photography and social media vastly increased the amount of personal data people create.

However, Marshall and others have found that currently many, if not most, users find themselves in a state of overload due to a lack of curation [19]. The "benign neglect" users fall back on with respect to their personal digital content allows it to accumulate at a rate and scale that makes it difficult for them to effectively manage their digital artifacts, when management is even a thought at all.

GROUP '16, November 13-16, 2016, Sanibel Island, FL, USA
 ISBN 978-1-4503-4276-6/16/11...$15.00
DOI: http://dx.doi.org/10.1145/2957276.2957316

Digital memorabilia are even more difficult to handle than other digital content because of their idiosyncratic and highly personal nature. While there are efforts to create automated and semi-automated content management systems (e.g. [9]), many activities in selecting and categorizing content, maintaining that content over the long term, and considering what to display – the core of what is called "curation" [26] – remain human-driven tasks. Our work provides a way forward for systems designed to help users effectively manage digital content with sentimental value. Helping users with curation of their digital content would be clearly beneficial.

Little is known about the everyday processes of users involved in creating and maintaining collections of sentimental artifacts. While our goal is to understand what happens when people have too much digital content and essentially infinite storage, we wanted to understand what people do now to manage their current sentimental objects and memorabilia. To this end, we conducted a study investigating the everyday work carried out by users overloaded by collections of physical sentimental artifacts. The limitations of physical objects allowed us to consider the potential help we might offer users with digital collections, especially those of memorabilia, by addressing an important question:

- When faced with an over-abundance of sentimental artifacts, how do people decide what to keep, what to pay attention to, and what to cull?

The Infinite Basement. In large physical collections, the limitations of space usually motivate people to engage with and manage their collections at some level to avoid an unchecked accumulation of things. The digital world, on the other hand, has comparatively unlimited storage, which leads people to regard it as a space needing no active management. In this "infinite basement," the problematic allure of virtually unlimited space means nothing ever has to be culled or gotten rid of due to limited space. However, we find that there may be other concerns that motivate people to curate their possessions.

Thus, in our analysis we turn to the value-oriented motivations that people have to curate and maintain their collections, as these motivations can inform our understanding of how people relate to and interact with burgeoning digital sentimental artifacts. Through an interpretivist analysis of 2405 posts about "sentimental clutter," we were able to uncover the unseen and taken-for-granted processes by which users select, organize, and arrange the items in their collections of memory. Below, we will lay out "curation regimes" or patterns of curatorial preferences that people enact when arranging their sentimental collections, and discuss the social, spatial, and temporal dynamics that positively and negatively influence people's curation of their sentimental collections. In our discussion, we will consider how digital content — with much larger amounts of content and with essentially infinite storage — might be different than what people do with physical artifacts. We will also examine the role memory artifacts might play in facilitating curation as they are integrated into the memory practices that people engage in during the course of their everyday lives. First, however, we discuss the previous literature.

2. RELATED WORK

Using sentimental artifacts, or memorabilia, that carry memory for users is tightly bound up with the activities of creating and maintaining those artifacts. In this section, we briefly examine the HIC/CSCW literature for both of these concerns.

Our work started with Peesapati et al.'s [24] arguments that memory should be conceptualized as an activity integrated into the lives of people, and that digital "memory triggers" should be embedded into everyday life. However, integrating digital memory triggers is not trivial. Golsteijn et al. [8] found that while personal digital artifacts had unique affordances beneficial for memory, they were less likely to be considered cherished possessions. They were not treated with the same regard and value as their physical counterparts. Relatedly, Petrelli et al. [27] note that a key problem for the design of digital mementos is that digital artifacts are not easily integrated into the spatial "topography" of the home along with other physical memory objects.

To integrate the digital more fully into the home, researchers have proposed creating devices that merge some of the interactivity of physical objects with digital mementos. These prototype systems do appear to make digital content more accessible and interactive for their owners, from augmenting physical objects with digital contextual narrative (e.g. Memory Box [2]), to lending tangibility to digital content to allow for more natural interactions (e.g. FM Radio [26]). Additionally Odom and colleagues in recent work (e.g., [21]) have explored how to more carefully use the material affordances of the physical to more skillfully tie digital materials into a combined world. However, physical devices with embedded memories, while promising, rest on the assumption that there is readily available content upon which they can draw that has been preselected to contain meaningful and valuable memory triggers. That is, they assume that curation has already occurred.

The practices and processes of selecting, organizing, maintaining, and displaying a collection of material is broadly considered as curation. Curation, while it has a general meaning, has been extensively studied in institutional archives and library science, as well as applied to data and digital curation. Yakel defines digital curation as "[t]he activity of managing and promoting the use of data from its point of creation, to ensure it is fit for contemporary purpose, and available for discovery and re-use" [30].

Everyday users in their homes are not trained in curation nor given time to do the work, as is the case with professional archivists. Several researchers studying how people manage large collections of digital content have found that in practice, curation of digital content rarely occurs. In research done by Marshall and coauthors (e.g.,[17,18]) on individuals' personal stores of digital content, they summarize that, "Despite the acknowledged importance of digital personal information, it is difficult to convince many people of the urgency of this [curation] problem" ([18], p. 3). The urgency of the problem may not be apparent because users primarily access their archives in short-term retrieval contexts.

In a study of professional photographer's preservation strategies for their "born-digital" images, Buchey [4] found that, while photographers non-selectively dumped all the images from their photo shoots into digital storage, they perceived it to be non-problematic because they primarily only used recently stored photos which they could rely on their memory to retrieve. This finding was echoed by a claim from Whittaker et al. [29] drawn from a meta-review of lifelogging studies, that everyday access to digital content tended to be limited to items recently added to the archive. The predominance of short-term engagement with digital content is quite problematic for digital memory artifacts. Researchers in personal digital archiving refer to efforts to shift digital collection management practices towards long-term considerations as "future-proofing" digital archives (e.g. [7,11,29]).

A key motivation for long-term curation practices in personal digital archives, Marshall [18] argued, is that the over-accumulation of digital material can obscure those items that have long-term value. Further, van House and Churchill [10] stress that "passive preservation," simply leaving a artifact to be rediscovered later, is not enough for ensuring that the artifact is available, findable, retrievable and accessible in the future. Since maintaining long-term value is the principle concern of memory artifacts, addressing the seemingly shortsighted lack of curation that characterizes how people currently manage personal digital stores is of paramount importance. Our study focuses on people managing long-lived collections of items important to themselves and their families, often with artifacts spanning generations, to gain insight into user's motivations for curation over time and how those might translate into a digital world.

Computing researchers have attempted to address the lack of curation. One strand of work focuses on automating curation, such as using content metadata and user's preferences from other sources (e.g. [15,20]) to infer what might be more valuable to users to keep. Others have proposed semi-automated ways to engage and assist users in curating their own content [9]. Our work informs those efforts by revealing patterns in the ways that people approach their collections and how these influence people's preferred curation behavior.

In short, existing research has shown that digital mementos can be useful and important to people. However, with today's abundance of digital content, a lack of curation obscures truly valuable artifacts and makes it difficult for existing systems designed for reminiscing and reflection with memory to present meaningful content. To better understand people's motivations and strategies for curation, and what might inhibit it in the digital realm, we examined curation of long-lived collections in the physical world as a useful analogue for how people deal with large collections of sentimental artifacts.

3. DATA COLLECTION AND ANALYSIS

We examined 2,405 posts on two subforums of a public website devoted to "uncluttering" one's life, that is, getting rid of excess belongings and other objects. On this site, UnClutterNow.com[1], some people aim to be minimalists, some people seem to be recovering borderline hoarders, and many people just have accumulated too many things in their lives. Based on their accounts and descriptions, participants were primarily from three

[1] The names of the site and participants have been anonymized.

geo-cultural regions, North America, Western Europe and Australia. All posts were in English.

We largely focused on posts in the subforum "Sentimental Clutter" where participants discussed issues regarding things that had been important to themselves or other family members, and which formed the basis of personal and family memories. The posts were primarily about problems with objects that invoked remembrances, often with an emotional attachment—what we call sentimental artifacts, memorabilia, or memory objects.

On the Sentimental Clutter subforum, users discussed what constituted sentimental objects, how to rid themselves of excess memory objects, what to keep and store, and what issues they were experiencing in the curation of their memorabilia. Many of the comments were personal stories and advice to others on the forum based on each participant's personal experiences. The subforum postings were almost entirely preoccupied by physical objects, so we supplemented these with posts from the Technology subforum, which included discussions of digital objects, to better understand what was general to sentimental artifacts and what was specific to physical objects. All the posts on the site were from 2010-2013, shortly after the site began, up to when the forum collapsed due to a software change (in the explanation of the forum administrators).

In our qualitative analysis of the forum, we drew out descriptions of participants' memory keeping practices, views of curation, issues around materiality, and design insights. The two authors independently coded the posts, and then together iteratively discussed the codes and organized the codes into themes, following the methods of Charmaz [5] and Clarke [6], updated versions of grounded theory.

We have edited some quotes slightly when necessary for clarity.

4. FINDINGS

Participants in the forum were brought together by a shared experience of at some point feeling *"overwhelmed with our stuff."* The term "*clutter*" signaled for them that they needed to go through some level of curation, to decide what to keep and what to cull from their stores of memorabilia.

Things of sentimental value were designated as clutter by the participants when they interfered with their everyday life and activities and when their artifacts became difficult to engage with because of the sheer quantity. These points are illustrated in a post by LukeMatthew requesting advice on how to "*declutter*" a large paper collection:

...I have accumulated literally thousands (maybe tens of thousands, I'm afraid to count) of pages of documents that contain information I feel is too valuable to just throw away. ... I don't want to lose all this information, but I simply can't have it around anymore in the form it's been in for the past decade. (LukeMatthew)

LukeMatthew's collection was interfering with his way of living by the sheer volume of it in his limited house space. Yet, he valued the documents, and could not simply discard the collection en masse. Others on the forum had similar (if not as dire) problems with their collections of memorabilia. They struggled with too many books, photos, china, Christmas ornaments, records, clothing, love letters, journals, and the like that encroached on their lives, and in some cases the lives of other members of their household, but were nonetheless "*too valuable*" to handle casually.

In the following sections, we outline the challenges participants faced in curating their sentimental collections, including the emotional and resource burdens, and their strategies for effectively handling large amounts of personally significant content.

4.1 The Burden of Curation

While all clutter could "*take over your space*," unchecked accumulations of artifacts with personal significance and associations to memories created an additional emotional and social burden for participants. A particularly poignant set of threads illustrating this problem came from participants seeking advice and support when trying to deal with sentimental collections related to a loved one after they had passed away. Glasscat6 wrote to the forum as one "*aspiring to be a minimalist*," meaning that she wanted to keep only a bare minimum of objects of any kind in her home. Yet, after the death of her brother, she felt unable to continue with the same curation practices she had previously held. She described the internal turmoil she felt at dealing with mementos she had of him.

My own clutter problem was pretty much under control and I am aspiring to be a minimalist. *Until 4 weeks ago. On November 30 my brother was killed in an auto accident. Now I am just awash in conflicting emotions. (Glasscat6)*

Glasscat6 goes on to give an introspective account of her conflict—while she wanted to *"be ruthless"* as a minimalist in paring down her material possessions, she was now faced with the reality that some of these artifacts were the only tangible things she had left of her brother. This had both present implications for her life at home, and also caused concern for how she would pass on memories of her brother in the future.

...I don't want to regret either missing the opportunity to allow my grown children to have a memento from their only uncle, but I don't want to open up a hornet's nest in my own home of items that would be full of painful memories. (Glasscat6)

Participants like Glasscat6 grappled with conflicting desires to hold on to things that represented their loved ones, both for their own memory and for future progeny, while simultaneously desiring to minimize their collections. They also faced the possibility that the continued presence of the memory triggers in their home would serve as *"a weight and a reminder of the pain."* The emotional toll in dealing with this conflict could be intense and there were no easy answers for those seeking advice. Many participants facing this difficult prospect chose to defer it for a later time, like SimplyJamie, who wanted to declutter after losing a spouse, but confessed in a post, *"I don't dare do it YET."*

The emotional burden of dealing with sentimental clutter was not related only to loss. For some participants, artifacts were not only memory triggers, they were symbolic links to an important part of their lives. UnstuffedLife wrote of his great distress after attempting to discard an old collection of music records.

I have kept those records since my teens. ...I felt like someone had punched me in the stomach. I cannot seem to let it go and then tonight I realized why. That music saved my life... I was depressed in my teenage years and music pulled me through. (UnstuffedLife)

Trying to let go of the records was so emotionally taxing for UnstuffedLife that he could not bring himself to completely cull the collection. Participants responded to his distress by recommending that he digitize the music, thereby saving the collection in some form while reducing the space it took. Although digitizing analog media could be quite time-consuming, participants would often recommend this format translation as a way of relieving the physical burden of having too much stuff, but deferring the emotional tax that accompanied curation decisions. We discuss more about translating sentimental artifacts into different forms in later sections.

While many participants struggled with their sentimental objects due to their personal significance, others felt burdened because of the social relationships the artifacts embodied. For example, Scout wanted to donate some of her old clothing, but struggled with the decision because of the time and effort her mother had put into making the clothes for her.

My mom is a talented seamstress and she's made me clothing since I was a baby. ...I have a hard time donating them even if they don't fit my lifestyle anymore. I mean, she slaved over a sewing machine making custom clothing just for me! Sigh.(Scout)

In addition to the time and resources consumed, participants struggling to curate their collections of sentimental artifacts, faced an emotional burden of dealing with the memories and associations linked to the artifacts. Not all participants had this issue, with some easily discarding highly significant artifacts. But those who did could struggle for months and even years to reach their goals to be *"clutter-free"*. Though curation was difficult, participants felt that it was important.

4.1.1 Attending to Attention

As participants described their curation issues and their reactions, an underlying theme emerged from their discussions: a need for providing attention to their artifacts. An important issue for participants, indeed the crux of designating sentimental artifacts as clutter at all, was being able to attend to and interact with the artifacts they had in their possession. They often decried keeping collections hidden away and inaccessible over the long-term: *"it seems a shame to leave things of any sort boxed up, unused." (Cloud)* For them, simply having an artifact was seldom sufficient for the mnemonic purposes that sentimental artifacts served, they had to be interact-able, as articulated by one participant:

Sentimental objects have to be in sight and touched every once in a while. They must be thought about so they don't lose their relevance. (Lenora)

Many participants felt that artifacts tucked away in storage, out of sight and in a space where they would not interfere with everyday life, would eventually have their significance forgotten. This was not acceptable for these participants, and they sought ways to better attend to their collections. Participants enacted many different curation practices to organize and manage their artifacts. Through these practices, participants leveraged the spatial-material layout of their homes and artifacts to maximize the attention they were able to pay to items in their collections.

4.2 Curation Regimes

In her work analyzing individual's practices with personal digital archives, Marshall noted that people tend to non-selectively keep everything when putting digital artifacts into storage [19]. Some participants in our data had similar behavior with their physical artifacts, but we also found a range of strategic patterns of practices that participants enacted as a means of curating their collections. We refer to these management patterns as "curation regimes." In the forum, participants discussed how they enacted these curation regimes to address the tensions they felt in trying to effectively manage their collections, while also accounting for the effort required by these management activities. We discuss the regimes in three parts, based on what people focus on as they enact the regime: *storage, attention,* and *display.* Though our analysis frames these as distinct aspects of curation, we note that participants talked about engaging in several at the same time, in combination or under different circumstances, in their everyday practices. However, we found them to be useful analytical distinctions to further both analysis and design.

4.2.1 Storage Regimes

Two complementary patterns, "Keep It All" and "Deal With It Later," demonstrated participants' attitudes toward storage.

Keep It All. The "Keep It All" regime was often referred to pejoratively in the forum as *"hoarding,"* due to an underlying belief that quantity diminished quality. When dealing with large collections, saving everything, even when all the items had some value, made it difficult for participants to treat the truly special items differentially. Yet participants had a hard time getting rid of things, especially in choosing among all their valuable items. As an example, Kally wrote about her struggle as a *"pack rat"* fitting a large collection of heirlooms into a new, smaller home. For Kally, the social link provided by her heirlooms made it difficult for her to cull items, even when her space was limited.

I admit to being the family historian/pack rat. However, as we move to a much smaller house, I am in a battle with myself as to what to keep and what to abandon. Is rejecting my grandmothers china like disregarding her hopes for me? Will she call me on it when we meet again in the great beyond?! How on earth can I possibly get rid of the china hutch that was my great-grandmothers and my daughters[sic] namesake? (Kally)

For participants like Kally, though their collection was problematically large, they could not in conscience part with anything and opted to keep it all. As we noted earlier, digitization in this regime allowed people to keep some version of the artifacts in their collection, whether by taking a photograph of an object or scanning a 2D document or photo. This "Keep It All" regime, we note, is one seen and decried most often in critiques from personal digital archiving.

Deal With It Later. Relatedly, when managing a particular collection was too difficult participants would instead opt to "Deal With It Later." This regime appears similar to the "Keep It All" regime, with the slight exception that participants put away the collection with the express intention that they would return to it when they were ready. Claymouse elaborated on this regime in her response to the disquiet expressed by another forum participant, Ren, at the prospect of getting rid of a collection of children's dresses hand-embroidered by her mother.

Ren, it doesn't sound like you are ready to part with them [handmade dresses]. Get some archival boxes and packing, and pack them away until you decide what to do with them. If you feel so strongly about them, you shouldn't do anything just yet. (Claymouse)

Claymouse recommended that Ren keep everything, but only temporarily. Packing away her dresses in storage would give her time to figure out what she wanted to do. In this example, Ren followed the advice, and in a post a year later, she decided she was ready to let go of the dresses. However, we noticed that in the cases where participants chose to digitize their item as a means of dealing with it later, action could be postponed indefinitely.

The use of digitization in avoidance of curation was, for our participants, a distinct move from purposefully digitizing content. Participant Ess, for example, recounted that *"digitizing was just procrastination"* when he reflected on how he handled his collection of 20-year-old journals. Digitization-as-procrastination was primarily focused on translating valuable content to a less burdensome form, so participants could hold on to as much as possible.

Procrastination was not necessarily detrimental to participants. Having a temporary space was necessary for some participants as an *"intermediate stage"* between keeping and discarding that allowed them time to process through and decide which items had value to them. A participant commented that taking digital photos to preserve important pages of family Bibles, before getting rid of them, was more "*sensitive*" to the struggle of many on the forum than advice to simply disregard one's emotions in the process.

I especially love the suggestion of taking photos of the pieces you treasure e.g. the bible pages such beautiful sensitive advice for someone having a hard time rather than the old "suck it up" routine lots of other people might do! (E.K.)

Another participant, Jossie, recounted her experience digitizing her collection of photos, and using the time put into it to reflect on what was important to her:

So I spent all this time digitizing. And now I realize that at least half of them I am not really interested in saving even in digital form (I probably will save them, since digital space is cheap, but you get what I mean). I think sometimes you need an intermediate stage to allow yourself to let go. (Jossie)

For participants like Ess, Jossie, and E.K., digitization was a means to defer the active management of their collections to another time, but a time when they were ready to deal with it.

However, digital "Deal With It Later" could become problematic when curation is deferred indefinitely. As in Jossie's case, her digital intermediate stage became a de facto permanent storage for her entire collection, whether she thought each item worth keeping or not. Because the focus at the beginning was on saving things to avoid dealing with them, participants might not take the same care in organizing and annotating the content they were saving as they might do for a more permanent arrangement. This can have ramifications later on, as the digital content that is not actively preserved may become more and more difficult to find, access, and revisit the longer it stays in storage [3,10].

4.2.2 Selection Regimes

In addition to their attitudes toward storage, participants' curation decisions hinged on their relationships with artifacts in their collections. People either cherished individual objects that made up a collection, or valued the collection as a whole. When objects were individually valuable, participants evaluated them each on their own merits. However, when objects were valued as part of a larger collection, participants selected artifacts based on relative value in two ways: an artifact's representational ability and its quality.

Keep Some Representative Examples. Participants less concerned about specific objects, and more interested in maintaining a general memory or sentiment decided to keep a representative sample of a sentimental collection. In this case, the value of the collection was driven by a particular project, outcome, or general association, rather than the particular value of any one of the artifacts. An iconic example of this was children's artwork, which parents in the forum discussed at length to try to find alternatives to keeping drawings, paintings, and school projects en masse. In one thread sharing advice on this issue, a parent suggested to *"find a way to create a keepsake product that showcases the kids' art – without the art itself being the keepsake because there really is too much of it. And, because you have a plan in mind, it makes it a lot easier to decide what and how you process all that amazing, oh-so- special art." (rockabilly)*

The collection was important for this parent, but any piece of it was sufficient to stand for the significance of the whole. By creating a product to incorporate some of the art, she created a way to keep some smaller sample that still fit her purposes.

This regime was also used by people who inherited collections from parents or grandparents that they wanted to keep in some way, but did not have room for. Participants would, for example, keep articles of clothing or a few plates:

I've been hanging onto my grandmother's beautiful china for over 20 years. It has a classic design that still looks good today. I've used it maybe once or twice. It takes up so much cupboard space, I've been considering letting it go. I have begun to think I will keep the small plates as special dessert plates and donate the rest. (MsMonica)

When participants chose to keep representative examples, they might select artifacts that were, in their mind, truly representative of a loved one or important time in their life. Others simply selected items that were good enough for their purposes – whether utilitarian or project-specific.

Keep Only the Best. For many participants, the reduction of a collection to *"only those I'm passionate about"(belle)* was a goal they diligently worked towards. This was very common for the forum participants. *"Weeding out"* those artifacts that might be less valuable, participants would *"ruthlessly pare down"* a collection of artifacts to only a few best or favorites, based on their own personal criteria, often repeatedly evaluating and re-evaluating the worth of an item to them until they could confidently say that it was certainly more precious to them than others, or as Terry put it "*I only keep the stuff that makes me really, really smile." (Terry)*.

Participants might also place artificial constraints on their collections to force themselves to carefully consider the value of the items. *"I chose a box and what didn't fit in the box, didn't stay." (Koala)* The most simple and pervasive forcing solution was to limit themselves to one small box of content, filled with only the best.

4.2.3 Display Regimes

Thirdly, participants curated their collections in order to arrange them for display. As we noted earlier, keeping things in storage was not ideal, and in response, participants were selective about what things they kept. But even when a collection had been honed down, at times it was too large to engage with all at once. In this case, participants used several strategies to gradually allow themselves to interact with their whole collection.

Rotate Through Items on Display. For participants with large collections and sufficient storage space, another strategy was to keep only a few items in active use at a time, periodically rotating through them. For Jasper24 who wanted to keep the objects on display in his home *"to a minimum,"* when he wanted to display a new artifact, either he could discard something else or he could display it among a continual parade of things.

I want to keep the decor in my den to a minimum... Now, if I get a knickknack I do like, something else will have to go or I can simply display one item for a while, then take that down and display another. Ideally, I would like to just have one or two simple pieces in the room. (Jasper24)

In this case, artifacts not currently on display were removed from notice, put in some out-of-the-way storage area such as a closet or basement. This allowed him to keep all his artifacts in his possession and enjoy each of them a few at a time while maintaining his preferences for space.

Maintain a Special Collection. In a more specialized curation regime, participants created subcollections. Similar to rotating through artifacts in a collection, in this regime, entire collections were brought in and out of use. Some collections were localized to place in the house or a special container, such as an album, china nook, or a fireplace mantel. Others were local to a particular time, brought out only during particular occasions. This typically included holidays like Christmas where participants had dedicated material set aside to be interacted with only during that time period (as in [25]). Participant MessHero described a special collection of sentimental greeting cards that were only brought out once a year after Christmas:

... the one thing we have done is create a box for special cards. It's stored with our Christmas ornaments in a plastic tote in the crawl space. We take it out every year and on the day we take down our tree, we go through all the cards – mostly Christmas cards, but also special birthday and anniversary ones as well. It's a tradition... (MessHero)

Creating specialized collections preserved the specialness of artifacts, as they would be accessed only on special occasions. As MessHero described, specialized collections might also acquire some ritual or tradition as participants further marked the specialness of the interaction with this distinct set of things.

In their study of family rituals, Petrelli et al. [25] noted that putting up and taking down specialized Christmas decorations marked the beginning and end of the "performance" of a family's Christmas rituals. Putting decorations back into storage was a phase that transitioned families back into their everyday, "mundane life." Just as interacting with special collections enabled families to set apart a particular period for special activities, we see that the ritual likewise served as a purpose and time for our participants to arrange and attend to certain of their sentimental artifacts.

In summary, curation regimes are, as we stated above, patterns of curation practices and everyday work for our participants. The regimes help explain how people choose to store, select, and display their sentimental artifacts. Again we note that these regimes were often combined. Nonetheless, we believe curation regimes may serve as a useful direction for tools that augment and support curation in everyday life.

While we have described these regimes as participant's own curatorial preferences, there were several important additional factors that influenced how and why people curated their content: materiality, social context, and temporal changes.

4.3 The Importance of Materiality

4.3.1 Focusing Interaction

Physical items appeared to have two important characteristics that helped people place and attend to their memories. First, physical objects have materialities that enable interactions important for people's reminiscing. Second, physical objects serve to focus one's attention on specific times, places, and people. In the following excerpt, Marge describes interacting with a box of her deceased grandfather's old clothes:

...my grandfather passed away a couple years ago. I have a box of his clothes that I cannot bear to part with because when I open the box, it smells like him. (Marge)

The box of clothes did not contain a particular memory for Marge, but drew her into the remembered presence of her grandfather. In keeping the box of clothes, she was not holding onto the clothing per se, but the sensory experience that could only be evoked when coming in contact with the clothes. She goes on to explain that she kept the clothes in a very specific manner in order to maintain the evocative smell and to shape her encounters with it:

I don't go looking for the box, and when it is out of sight it is out of mind. However, when I do come across it, I always open it.... In fact, I've kept them boxed up all this time so that they wouldn't lose his scent. I know it might sound strange, but it is comforting to me. (Marge)

The sensory experience of going through the clothes, as well as the locality of the box containing, and at times, obscuring the collection all came together to create a unique memory for her.

Having a physical item can bring back additional memories and facets of those memories, as opposed to relying solely on recollection. In addition to being more evocative, the physical nature of memory artifacts can serve to focus one's attention on specific places, times, and people, as MadeleineM pointed out:

There are a few other things that I've kept that remind me of him strangely (like the car emergency kit he gave me when I turned 18). (MadeleineM)

Participants found foci in a variety of their material artifacts, from dishes that reminded them of their mother, to baby books and infant boxes from their children. Some people had general memory boxes, which stored a variety of memorabilia. Still others had specific collections, like Christmas boxes that contained family mementos such as old Christmas cards and ornaments.

The visibility and locality of a physical object drew attention to memories that those participants wished to foster, reminisce about, or honor. Placing memory artifacts, therefore, is part of the curation process for these participants.

4.3.2 Repurposing the Material

As well, sentimental artifacts with an additional purpose were more likely to find a place in participant's homes and lives. When participants appreciated an artifact and wished to keep it despite its lack of purpose, they would often transform it, either in whole or part to give it a renewed purpose. The process was an attempt to reshape artifacts that were un-keepable in their current state, to fit them into the material environment of a home and into the life of the owner.

For example, Wendi shared how her partner's mother melted down some sentimental jewelry into new pieces that she and her daughter could wear and be reminded of her grandmother often.

My partner's mother had some inherited jewelry that was unwearably old-fashioned but had a lot of sentimental value, so she took it to a jeweler and had it all melted down and refashioned. The best stones went into bangles for her and her daughter...[We] wear the new jewelry regularly. It reminds her and her daughter of the grandmothers they loved. (Wendi)

For this family, being able (and willing) to use the jewelry in their everyday lives was more important than maintaining its current form. They prioritized the sentimental value attached to the jewelry and decided to use the material to create a new set of items that they could share and wear often. In this case, they created items with a similar purpose to the original by creating more fashionable jewelry. Another participant trying to reduce a large collection of souvenir t-shirts amassed from all her life experiences and travels decided to reuse the cloth material of the t-shirt to create completely different objects:

I have 3 strategies 1) get fewer souvenir t-shirts 2) make shopping bags from the old t-shirt and 3) I am currently making a Gee's Bend/modern style quilt with my old college t-shirts. (greenGal)

Creating new artifacts out of old ones was a popular strategy that craftier participants employed to make a collection more manageable. Many appropriated long-standing re-use traditions, such as quilting, to guide their renovation efforts. In addition, having a concrete goal of creating a keepsake helped participants distill their collections by providing a set context of use.

Repurposing an artifact or collection was a distinct and deliberate alternative to digitization when participants needed to compress large and unwieldy collections. While both changed the form of a memento, digitization kept only the trace of an artifact's existence, retaining a shadow of its physical form and none of the physicality that made it useful. On the other hand, in repurposing, artifacts were re-envisioned as a useful item or set of items, intimately linked to the original memory through a shared material base.

4.4 Social Norms and Arrangements

In addition to their personal values and situated needs, people were deeply affected by their social arrangements. In addition to their own emotions and introspection, participants often had to consider their familial context when making curation decisions. As Kirk and Sellen [13] noted, many different family members might have an emotional attachment to the same artifacts. When that sentiment differed among individuals, the handling of the sentimental artifact could cause family tensions and disagreements. Participants described curation as a process influenced by social pressure, subject to social expectation, or dependent on others to fully carry out. We explicate these social tensions through three kinds of situations: dealing with artifacts that symbolize important social relationships, managing artifacts under shared control, and handling artifacts that are distributed socially.

Artifacts that symbolized important social relationships were often a contentious topic for participants. A perceived lack of regard for the artifact and what it symbolized could cause tension. For example, Scout recounted her difficulty in curating a collection of mix tapes her husband had given her while dating. For Scout, the mix tapes had lost their original sentimental value. She had preserved the content, which was important to her, but she no longer wanted to keep them in physical form:

...I have a bunch of mix tapes he made for me in high school. It was a sweet gesture, and I appreciated it, but it's time for them to go. All my music is digital now, these are duplicated, and we longer have a tape player anyway. They serve no use. You'd think I was shooting him through the heart by mentioning this. He says things like "Doesn't our past mean anything to you?"(Scout)

For Scout, her husband still assigned meaning to the physical objects, and culling them seemed to him like a disregard for the past of their relationship. When interacting with a collection that holds shared sentimental value, Scout could not make curation decisions based on her sole preferences. She had to account for how her husband would perceive and react to her handling of the mixtapes. That left her feeling that her husband *"is holding me back from decluttering."*

For some participants, the sentimental artifacts might ostensibly belong to themselves solely, but nonetheless, they could feel pressured by family to give account for their curation actions. Ctr2004 recounted having to explain her rationale for discarding her collection of childhood mementos to her mother:

I know my mother had some trouble when I donated or trashed some childhood items. In turn showed her all the things I did chose [sic] to keep and explained why those items meant something to me. (ctr2004)

While some participants could pre-empt their family members, like ctr2004, and explain their actions after the artifact had already been handled, many other participants did not want to risk the ire or disappointment of their family members that the loss of a treasured artifact might cause.

An especially pervasive example of this tension in values and curation were negotiations around handling heirlooms or what parents wanted children to perceive as heirlooms. One generation would attach value and significance to an object, and part of their curation process was to hand down or gift a set of artifacts to others in their family.

VickiC recounted the history and burden of a cherished heirloom rocking chair that had been passed down from her grandmother, to her mother, and now to her. Her mother had downsized her home into a smaller apartment and had finally given her the chair:

I have a rocking chair that my grandmother rocked my mother in when she was a baby. My mother gave it to me...after they moved into an apartment. ...I couldn't say no. Even as a little girl, she talked about giving it to me when I had my own home. (VickiC)

VickiC's mother cherished the rocking chair and expected it to be similarly valued by her daughter and handled with special care. From the giver's perspective, it might appear to be an act of generosity to *"bless"* other family members with their excess or unwanted artifacts. However, the inheritors might not share a sense of the value of the artifact or agree with how it was to be handled in their care, if it were to be kept at all. VickiC continued her story, sharing that she only planned to keep the chair until her parents died and were no longer around to care what she did with it.

I resent that chair. ...I wish I could have sold it ... but I was too afraid she'd want to see the chair again. (VickiC)

Tensions arose as people in a shared curatorial relationship, by choice or not, disagreed on how a sentimental artifact was to be handled. In some cases, the artifact featured in several people's memories and each of them had opinions on how it should be preserved as a token reminder. In other cases, the artifact was considered a symbol of a relationship or continuity within a family, but held particular significance only to one member and not to others.

A third social situation arose when multiple people had parts of the same collection. In her post, K described giving away some of her antique items kept from her grandparents to some of her family members:

Much of what I have is antiques and they really are lovely but I just have too many dishes, figurines, etc. I do know there are other family members who don't have any tangible memories of our grandparents and so sharing these items not only reduces my load but blesses them as well. (K)

For K, giving away some of her heirlooms to other family members allowed her to reduce some of the burden of keeping a large collection, while not actually having to discard the item. In some cases, this strategy worked out fine. Yet in others, as we see in the examples above, the coordinated care of this distributed sentimental collection comes with its own, primarily social, costs and challenges. Participant Sulim summed up the tensions in navigating this shared handling of a distributed collection of sentimental artifacts, saying "*The fault doesn't really lie with the objects or even with the question of keeping them, but with the uncomfortable family dynamics that get brought up when one person is designated keeper by the other people who 'want' the stuff but don't want to be inconvenienced by dealing with it.*" *(Sulim)*

In summary, curation is often socially contextualized, and potential services to facilitate curation must take into account the social context of these types of decisions in order to be effective. Curation can be an individual and personal process, but it can also be bound up in social norms and familial expectations, becoming a negotiated process.

4.5 Curation Changes Over Time

Participants' personal valuations of their memory artifacts were not constant. They changed over time, and this in turn changed their view of how these artifacts should be handled. The dynamics of shifting identities and the evolving meaning of sentimental artifacts was most salient in the forum when participants described rediscovered artifacts they had kept from their psychologically earlier selves. Participants continuously re-assessed the value of their memorabilia against their changing life history, current identity, social contexts, and activities.

4.5.1 Changing Emotional Valence

Curation might shift because of the changing emotional valence of an artifact, for example negatively with photographs containing people who had harmed them or with shared sentimental objects after a divorce. Alternatively, some participants reported growing closer to memorabilia after deaths in the family.

Change was very common for participants. To refer to our earlier findings, many participants enacting a "Deal With It Later" regime demonstrated this shift. When they were unable to deal with emotionally charged artifacts, usually negatively valenced, they would wait for some time until the intensity of the emotion calmed or the valence shifted into a more positive memory.

4.5.2 Reflecting Past and Current Identity

Participants' current identity was also an important consideration in their curation, as participants juxtaposed their current self-identity against the memorabilia of their earlier lives. In a particularly illuminative set of posts about how to deal with old diaries and journals, participants discussed their tensions with keeping things of sentimental value that they felt no longer represented their personality.

Some discussants preferred to purge their sentimental artifacts of anything that was not currently representative of their identity. For example, participant Alten found 20-year old diaries that had been stored away, and felt immediately obliged to destroy the contents, since his younger perspective was different than his current way of thinking:

I recently rediscovered 10 years worth of paper diaries I had kept through the 90s, and was filled with horror realising I still had them. A brief glance through the pages caused me to cringe at my former perspective, and I immediately wanted to shred them. (Alten)

The thoughts of Alten's younger self were an unwelcome stowaway in his home. Participants like Alten were uncomfortable with contradicting their current identities and worried that others would misinterpret these anachronisms. Alten continued:

I keep thinking how I'd hate to die and have these diaries left behind as a record of my thoughts – and that's because thoughts evolve and old diaries are no longer an accurate reflection of my thoughts and feelings. (Alten)

Those who preferred to purge felt that their "old history" was no longer an accurate representation of their current personality and state of mind. They preferred to keep only those artifacts that were an accurate reflection of their contemporary identity.

Not all participants reacted negatively to encountering their past identity. Some, like Zigzag, thought it was important to keep the journals of her youth, as they served as a record of her past:

Oh, I could never get rid of my own journals!...It's a fascinating document of my late teens through university. Some of it just makes me cringe mightily, but I could never throw them away. (Zigzag)

Although the juxtaposition of her past and present was uncomfortable, the value of Zigzag's journals did not change. Whether choosing to purge or to keep a record of their past identity, participants considered the audience that would be privy to what they left behind.

4.6 Summary

In summary, in our analysis of the major themes and insights into curation behaviors that characterize how people react and respond when they have "*too much stuff*," we found that curation of sentimental content is effortful, not only because of the time, but also because of the emotional burden of curating memory. Nevertheless, participants felt it was an important process to continually engage in, even when they were not overwhelmed by excess, because the purpose of sentimental artifacts could only be fulfilled when they were given the proper attention.

To curate their collections for an appropriate level of attention, participants enacted curation regimes based on their attitudes about storage, relationship to individual artifacts and the collection as a whole, as well as the intended display and use for their artifacts in their homes and lives. When unwieldy collections that participants wanted to keep did not fit into their current home, they might also repurpose the artifacts in ways that integrated it more naturally into their lives. The material nature of the artifact was often used to facilitate re-purposing.

Interwoven throughout participants' deliberations were decisions about how to deal with the changing sentiment associated with their collections over time, as their identity and circumstances changed, as well as how to account for other social and interpersonal influences that directed their actions.

In the following section, we discuss curation as a set of attention-directing processes and provide implications for designers of next-generation digital memory artifacts and curation support systems.

5. DISCUSSION: CURATING ATTENTION

In our findings we discuss a number of reasons and ways that people select, arrange and adapt their collections of sentimental artifacts. We note that with an "infinite basement" of digital storage, curation decisions need no longer be based on limited space, but instead are based on the need for attention. As Simon [28] pointed out, when space is unlimited, it is attention that becomes the scarce resource. Participants put their effort into maximizing the attention they were able to pay to the artifacts in their sentimental collections. Attention was the focus, whether they were strategically leveraging their storage spaces to hide or put away things that were not appropriate or needed, or carefully selecting artifacts to hone down a large collection, or crafting meaningful ways to display and interact with their collections in their homes.

5.1 Leveraging the Infinite Basement

For physical objects, storage and attention are often intertwined. Objects that can be attended to must also have storage, and deciding about limited storage is based on what is worthy of attention. For digital objects and with an infinite basement, this is no longer true.

One way to reconsider the relationship between storage and attention, is to consider that for some participants, storage served as a background staging area, allowing them to bring things in and out of attention. When some participants needed time to process the emotional significance of an artifact, storage was intentionally short-term and served as an intermediate place where they could defer dealing with highly charged artifacts. For others, storage was a temporary but indefinite holding area as participants struggled to find an appropriate means and timing to discard artifacts they did not want to display or keep. Yet others, with enough storage and large enough collections, rotated important artifacts in and out of storage, bringing those selected artifacts into display.

Artifacts intentionally kept in storage were not simply "*boxed up*" and unused. This is hopeful for addressing the problems of digital storage found by Marshall [19]. We see that storage can be a useful waypoint for enabling and encouraging curation. For designers, a challenge then is to conceptualize digital storage both in design models and in users' mental models as more than a convenient dumping heap (which it might be for some collections), but also as an active and dynamic repository of artifacts destined for display and interaction.

5.2 Placing and Arrangement

Other researchers have noted that the arrangement of sentimental artifacts in people's homes symbolizes participant's personal and familial identity and their relation to others [13,27]. We call out this notion of arrangement, and propose that it is not simply an aesthetic or symbolic practice but also one fundamental to how people order and manage of the artifacts themselves.

The ways participants were able to place, arrange and re-purpose artifacts in their collection stemmed largely from the materiality of the artifacts they worked with. We believe this finding opens a promising new design space for digital curation systems. In previous research on creating "*cherishable*" digital artifacts [8] and technology heirlooms [1], physicality was shown to be beneficial for artifacts for reflection and reminiscing. However, the value beyond the simple evocativeness of embodying collections of digital mementos has yet to be explored.

Translating "born digital" traces into a physical form can enable people to better engage with their large sentimental collections to curate more meaningful memory artifacts by taking advantage of users multi-modal and multi-sensory abilities, lending corporeality to digital traces, and providing a platform that merges into the material environment of their homes. It is quite possible that learning how to "place" digital memories will be a necessary step in understanding how to deal with the onslaught of digital capture and the expansion of digital storage in constructing usable memory artifacts.

5.3 Navigating Shared Ownership

While arranging artifacts around their homes was a way for participants to enact their own identities and relationships, it could cause tensions when their perspectives were not aligned with others. In her study of grandparents, Lindley [16] noted that people with heirlooms and other memory artifacts in their possession considered themselves as stewards and caretakers of certain sentimental artifacts, and thought that the family shared ownership of these items rather than any individual.

In many contexts, a person in possession of a physical artifact is accorded the most privileges and an assumption of final authority. However, we saw that participants could be heavily influenced in how they handled their collection by the opinions and desires of others, even against their own preferences. A person's curation behavior regarding a family's shared artifacts could be markedly different than how they treat other, more personal artifacts.

Dealing with physical artifacts in situations of stewardship and shared ownership, where no one person can lay exclusive claim to a particular artifact, has necessitated extensive social practices to establish ways of dealing with conflict in the material world. Explicit permissions are rarely defined, although as we saw in our data, implicit expectations can be articulated. Tools to help people with the curation of digital artifacts will have to consider how to translate this stewardship model suitably.

For example, an interactive memory box prototype built by Kirk et al. [12] demonstrated that curating digital memorabilia in a collaborative family content can be a contentious activity. It was assumed that giving all family members the ability to add and organize content would be beneficial, but instead even members of the same household experienced stress and contention in the shared curation experience. The existence and ongoing negotiation of these tensions was taken as status quo for Kirk et al.'s participants, but it is not well accounted for in design. In our future work, we will further explore the tensions in shared and collective memory as it is mediated through in representative artifacts, in an endeavor to develop a design approach sensitive to conflicting values inherent in shared ownership.

5.4 Responding to Changing Sentiment

Participants repeatedly emphasized the dynamic nature of curation. Though they might arrange the artifacts in their home and navigate social dynamics in a certain way at present, their curation strategies were not static, but shifted and evolved as they and their social worlds changed over time.

Memory researchers in HCI and CSCW have begun to adopt the perspective that memory is a dynamic process, an ongoing productive accomplishment as people by themselves and in groups reinterpret the past in light of present circumstances and identities [16,23]. This perspective allows us to account for the dynamics of memory and emotion in curating large collections of sentimental artifacts, especially in considering how and why the sentiment of artifacts changes over time.

A key challenge in incorporating change into the design space is that sentiment does not change for every person in the same way. People may have different impressions of a shared past experience [31], and our data show how these impressions may also evolve differently based on each individual's changing context and personality. A shift in sentiment may also signal a shift in the valence of the memory itself, and can be dramatic – for instance a happy memory might suddenly become quite painful after a loss – and this shift in sentiment may not be shared among all the people who share a particular memory. Systems that facilitate communal recollecting from traces of the past will need to consider tailoring experiences for people with mixed and at times conflicting preferences.

As designers work to create technologies active in an emotional design context such as memory, they must take into account not only differences in sentiment, but also how sentiment changes over time and for different people. Systems designed to create and enhance shared digital memory must be able to address diverging perspectives, both internal to an individual and among different users, to adequately support and mediate these complex contexts.

In all these issues, we emphasize the need for designers to focus more on *integrating* new artifacts and systems into people's environments. Integration requires attention beyond aesthetics to consider the processes by which people include memory artifacts.

6. CONCLUSION

In this paper, we addressed the question of how people deal with an overabundance of sentimental artifacts. We examined physical "sentimental clutter" as a way to understand the means and motivations by which people curate large collections of memorabilia. We unpack how people select and organize content, maintain that content, and consider what to display and use in order to extrapolate how they might interact with large collections of digital mementos. Through an analysis of a forum featuring conversations about issues with sentimental artifacts, we uncovered social, temporal, and spatial concerns that influence the ways that people curate their memories. We drew out curation regimes as patterns of curation practices that people enact in relation to their preferences for storage and selection, as well as to manage the attention they wish to pay to their memorabilia and sentimental artifacts. Based on these findings, we also presented design suggestions about how memory artifacts might be created to fit in and support the curatorial processes of users in everyday life.

An area for further investigation is to take into account families from different sociocultural and economic backgrounds and living situations than the participants featured in our study. Although there appeared to be a wide range of attitudes and preferences represented among our participants, we know from our prior pilot studies that there are significant differences across cultures and living situations in how people create and maintain family memory and the role of objects in those practices. Future work might compare people living in different material cultures, perhaps in different geographic locations, for commonalities and differences to provide a more holistic view of curation in the digital age.

7. ACKNOWLEDGMENTS

We thank the members of the SocialWorlds Research Group and the Michigan Interactive and Social Computing Group, as well as the participants in the Personal Information Management workshop at CHI'16 for their generous feedback. We especially thank David Merritt and Cathy Marshall. This work was supported by an NSF Graduate Fellowship and the School of Information.

8. REFERENCES

[1] Banks, R., Kirk, D., and Sellen, A. A Design Perspective on Three Technology Heirlooms. *Human-Computer Interaction 27*, 1-2 (2012), 63–91.

[2] Barthel, R., Leder Mackley, K., Hudson-Smith, A., Karpovich, A., Jode, M., and Speed, C. An internet of old things as an augmented memory system. *Personal and Ubiquitous Computing 17*, 2 (2011), 321–333.

[3] Bentley, F.R., Kaye, J. "Jofish," Shamma, D.A., and Guerra-Gomez, J.A. The 32 Days of Christmas: Understanding Temporal Intent in Image Search Queries. *Proceedings of the 2016 CHI Conference on Human Factors in Computing Systems*, (2016), 5710–5714.

[4] Bushey, J. He shoots, he stores: New photographic practice in the digital age. *Archivaria 65*, 1 (2008), 125–149.

[5] Charmaz, K. Charmaz Grounded Theory in the 21st Century. In N. Denzin and Y.S. Lincoln, eds., *The SAGE Handbook of Qualitative Research.* Sage, 2005, 507–536.

[6] Clarke, A. Situational Analysis: Grounded Theory After the Postmodern Turn. *Symbolic Interaction 4*, 4 (2005), 83–144.

[7] Findlay, C. Future proof: ensuring the long-term accessibility of technology-dependent records. *Records Management Journal 12*, 3 (2002), 87–93.

[8] Golsteijn, C., van den Hoven, E., Frohlich, D., and Sellen, A. Towards a More Cherishable Digital Object. *Proceedings of the 2012 Conference on Designing Interactive Systems - DIS '12*, ACM Press (2012), 655–664.

[9] Gulotta, R., Sciuto, A., Kelliher, A., and Forlizzi, J. Curatorial Agents: How Systems Shape Our Understanding of Personal and Familial Digital Information. *Proceedings of the 2015 CHI Conference on Human Factors in Computing Systems 1*, (2015), 3453–3462.

[10] Van House, N. and Churchill, E.F. Technologies of memory: Key issues and critical perspectives. *Memory Studies 1*, 3 (2008), 295–310.

[11] Janssen, B. Panel: Papers and prints: out of the file cabinet, scrapbooking, and scanning. *Conference on Personal Digital Archiving*, (2010).

[12] Kirk, D.S., Izadi, S., Sellen, A., Taylor, S., Banks, R., and Hilliges, O. Opening up the family archive. *Proceedings of the 2010 ACM conference on Computer supported cooperative work - CSCW '10*, ACM Press (2010), 261.

[13] Kirk, D.S. and Sellen, A. On human remains. *ACM Transactions on Computer-Human Interaction 17*, 3 (2010), 1–43.

[14] Lee, H.-C., Tsai, W.-C., Wang, P.-H., Liang, R.-H., and Hsu, J. The reflexive printer. *Proceedings of the 2014 Conference on Designing interactive systems - DIS Companion '14*, ACM Press (2014), 97–100.

[15] Li, J., Lim, J.H., and Tian, Q. Automatic summarization for personal digital photos. *Proceedings of the 2003 Joint Conference of the 4th International Conference on Information, Communications and Signal Processing and 4th Pacific-Rim Conference on Multimedia- ICICS-PCM 2003*, (2003), 1536–1540.

[16] Lindley, S.E. Before I Forget : From Personal Memory to Family History. *Human–Computer Interaction*, (2012), 37–41.

[17] Marshall, C.C., Bly, S., and Brun-Cottan, F. The long term fate of our digital belongings: Toward a service model for personal archives. *Archiving Conference*, (2006), 25–30.

[18] Marshall, C.C. How people manage personal information over a lifetime. *Personal Information Management*, (2007), 57–75.

[19] Marshall, C.C. Rethinking personal digital archiving, part 1: Four challenges from the field. *D-Lib Magazine 14*, 2008.

[20] Obrador, P., Oliveira, R. De, and Oliver, N. Supporting Personal Photo Storytelling for Social Albums. *Human Factors*, (2010), 561–570.

[21] Odom, W.T., Sellen, A.J., Banks, R., et al. Designing for slowness, anticipation and re-visitation. *Proceedings of the 2014 ACM SIGCHI Conference on Human Factors in Computing Systems - CHI '14*, ACM Press (2014), 1961–1970.

[22] Oleksik, G. and Brown, L.M. Sonic gems: exploring the potential of audio recording as a form of sentimental memory capture. *BCS-HCI '08*, British Computer Society (2008), 163–172.

[23] Olick, J.K. 'Collective memory': A memoir and prospect. *Memory Studies 1*, 1 (2008), 23–29.

[24] Peesapati, S.T., Schwanda, V., Schultz, J., Lepage, M., Jeong, S., and Cosley, D. Pensieve : Supporting Everyday Reminiscence. *Proceedings of the 2010 ACM SIGCHI conference on Human factors in Computing Systems - CHI '10*, (2010), 2027–2036.

[25] Petrelli, D. and Light, A. Family rituals and the potential for interaction design : a study of Christmas. *ACM Transactions on Computer-Human Interaction 21*, 3 (2014), 1–29.

[26] Petrelli, D., Villar, N., Kalnikaite, V., Dib, L., and Whittaker, S. FM radio: family interplay with sonic mementos. *Proceedings of the 28th international conference on Human factors in computing systems*, 2010, 2371–2380.

[27] Petrelli, D., Whittaker, S., and Brockmeier, J. AutoTopography: What can Physical Mementos tell us about Digital Memories. *Proceeding of the twenty-sixth annual CHI conference on Human factors in computing systems - CHI '08*, ACM Press (2008), 53.

[28] Simon, H. a. Designing organizations for an information-rich world. In *Computers, communications, and the public interest.* 1971, 37.

[29] Whittaker, S., Kalnikaitė, V., Petrelli, D., et al. Socio-technical lifelogging: Deriving design principles for a future proof digital past. *Human–Computer Interaction 27*, 1-2 (2012), 37–62.

[30] Yakel, E. Digital curation. *OCLC Systems & Services 23*, 4 (2007), 335–340.

[31] Zhao, X., Schwanda Sosik, V., and Cosley, D. It's complicated: how romantic partners use facebook. *Proceedings of the 2012 ACM SIGCHI Conference on Human Factors in Computing Systems - CHI '12*, (2012), 771–780.

Help Me Help You: Shared Reflection for Personal Data

Lisa Graham[1], Anthony Tang[2], and Carman Neustaedter[3]

[1]Schulich School of Engineering
[2]Department of Computer Science
University of Calgary
{ lmgraham, tonyt }@ucalgary.ca

[3]School of Interactive Arts and Technology
Simon Fraser University
carman@sfu.ca

ABSTRACT

Dramatic advances in sensor and computing miniaturization for personal data collection are making Personal Informatics (PI) tools a reality. Yet, advances in data collection have not been matched with similar advances in tools to promote, support, and facilitate reflection on this data. This gap leaves people with large swaths of data, but very little understanding of how to make sense of the data or to derive actionable insights. In this work, we explore a process called shared reflection, where individuals are paired with other data collectors, and asked (through prompts) to reflect on one another's data. Based on a six-week study where 15 participants collected different kinds of personal data and engaged in a shared reflection process, we show that participants gained transformative insights from others' reflections on their data. While this was promising, we discuss practical challenges in deploying this idea into real world personal informatics tools. In particular, while shared reflection can be appropriated to effectively bootstrap reflection on one's data, this needs to be balanced against privacy and control concerns.

CCS Concepts

Human-centered computing → Human computer interaction (HCI) → Empirical studies in HCI

Keywords

Shared reflection; personal informatics; personal data analytics; reflection.

1. INTRODUCTION

Personal informatics is the process of collecting personal data, and analyzing this data to facilitate decision-making in one's life [32]. Dramatic increases in computing power (e.g. smartphones) along with increasingly powerful sensing technologies (e.g. [26][51]) have made collecting this data very easy. We are increasingly seeing the use of this tracking technology to improve people's health and well-being (e.g. [3]). This shift is a natural consequence not only of the power of the data tracking and collection technologies, but also the increasingly popular notion of self-directed care (e.g. [6]).

Yet, the presence of data is insufficient to generate actionable insight; rather, Li et al. [32] argue that this can only result from reflecting on one's data to understand what is happening. Like Baumer et al [4], we see the value of reflection in both the possibility of actionable outcomes, and in and of itself as a meaningful self-discovery process (i.e. learning). We take an educational perspective of personal informatics (and therefore reflection)—in this way, people making use of personal informatics tools are learners, and the data gathering efforts are in support of this learning. As with Moon [42], we consider reflection as having a critical role in this learning process. Here, already known information is combined with new information (as a mental reprocessing of knowledge) to produce new knowledge or insight. Thus, reflection represents a form of deeper learning that goes beyond the data itself. In this work, we introduce a strategy called shared reflection that relies on a community of like-minded learners to engage in reciprocal reflection of personal data to help bootstrap one's self-discovery and learning process.

We began with the "learning by teaching" framework, which argues that learners can gain valuable insight into a subject matter by teaching it to others [23]. A simple variation of this idea that has gained popularity in classrooms is peer review of work (e.g. essays, presentations, etc. [52]). Our basic idea with shared reflection was to have learners perform "peer review" of one another's data, providing feedback and analysis of the data—a process we call shared reflection. We expected that this process would result in several benefits: (1) learners receiving direct feedback (and new ideas) about his/her data and collection strategy; (2) a learner gaining experience thinking about data by studying another person's data collection and strategies, and finally (3) the learner being able to take these experiences and reapply the ideas back to his/her own data.

To explore the benefits, challenges, and nuances of shared reflection, we designed and conducted a 6-week study with 15 participants. These participants used the shared reflection strategy as their primary method of reflecting on their data. Based on our analysis of the data, we found that learners benefited substantially from the feedback they would receive, as this provided new perspectives on their data, helping them to derive new insight. Furthermore, being able to see the data collection practices of others was useful. On the other hand, we did not see evidence that learners gained meaningfully from the practice of reflecting on others' data itself. Our study also raised questions about how to properly motivate learners, whether learners need to be collecting the same kinds of data, and how to make the process, which is highly dependent on others, less brittle.

We make two contributions in this paper: first, we articulate shared reflection as a new way to support reflection for personal data; second, we present the results of a formative evaluation of the strategy through a study of 15 participants. We begin by outlining literature that led us to the shared reflection strategy. We then describe several considerations in employing the strategy, and outline the variation we selected for our study. We follow this with the study we conducted, and the findings from this study.

GROUP '16, November 13-16, 2016, Sanibel Island, FL, USA

DOI: http://dx.doi.org/10.1145/2957276.2957293.

Finally, we distill lessons from this study, and outline directions for future work.

2. RELATED WORK

As argued by Baumer [2], reflection is increasingly becoming a popular notion within the Human-Computer Interaction domain. This reflects a level of maturity in the field, but also a recognition of the power of reflection as a cognitive process for deeper learning and understanding. Reflection in this sense is a well-known process within the learning community [2][42][48][52][53]. Several researchers have explored this concept in the workplace to support learning (e.g. [44][28][16])—much of this reflects the *in situ* nature of learning in these context, and the idea is to support reflection-on-action [48] through the experiences of others (e.g. [13]). Prilla & Renner [43] for instance, explore the use of TalkReflection as a method to allow employees of public organizations to reflect on and improve in their job functions. This application allowed employees to post "reflections" (short essays) on experiences in the workplace, which then acted as prompts for others to respond. They found that this collaborative reflection supported learning by allowing more experienced members of teams pass on their knowledge and experiences in response to those with less experience.

The utility of reflection as a process motivates our work here. Our specific interest is in how we can use it as a process to support personal informatics—a wholly different domain compared to prior work exploring collaborative reflection. As we will see, the varying approaches to data collection, as well as the type of data that is collected make it unclear whether experience can be passed on in as straightforward a fashion as in a workplace. To set the stage for our work, we describe two areas of work that have inspired and motivated us. First, we outline work in the personal informatics space that explores how we can support reflection of personal data. Second, we describe social learning, and how researchers have leveraged these ideas for technology designs. We then synthesize these lessons as a set of considerations for our work.

2.1 Reflection in Personal Informatics Tools

Personal Informatics (PI) tools are designed and used to give its users data upon which actionable insight can be developed and applied [32]. Li et al. [32] outline a five-stage PI process whereby a person: (1) finds motivation to examine some aspect of his/her life; (2) collects information about that part of his/her life; (3) integrates that data into a meaningful form; (4) reflects on the data resulting in an increase in self-knowledge, and finally (5) takes action by (perhaps) changing his/her behaviour as a consequence of that self-knowledge. While there exists a considerable body of PI work, very little has focused specifically on how to support self-reflection beyond implicit "by glancing" reflection [2] cf. [20].

Prescriptive Reflection. A large body of early work could be described as persuasive technology, where a designer uses the design to persuade the user to behave in a certain way [21]. For instance, Fish'n'Steps [34], UbiFit [14], UbiGreen [27], present interfaces that visualize data where desirable behaviours (e.g. physical activity, "green" modes of transportation) are rewarded with pleasant visualizations and negative behaviours (e.g. lack of exercise) result in unpleasant visualizations: for example, in Fish'n'Steps, the fish look sad, and the UbiFit garden becomes bare without flowers. Similarly, many tools rely on competitive (or at least comparative) social tactics, whereby users could compare their behaviours with others (e.g. [9][17]) or an arbitrary threshold, such as a step count. In these situations, reflection is reduced to a simple question: did I do enough? Finally, we have also seen efforts to present this information in ways that are familiar to the user in the form of natural language (e.g. [6]). In all of these cases, the approach tends to be prescriptive—rather than allowing the user to come to ideas or decisions on his/her own, the tool dictates the "correct choice" for the user to follow. Such an approach may not be appropriate in situations where "correct behavior" is unclear; furthermore, it may be undesirable as it obviates autonomy and self-discovery, which characterise deep learning/reflection [8].

Informational Visualizations for Reflection. Other tools attempt to facilitate discovery through rich visual representation without necessarily imposing a particular interpretation of the data. These efforts have come in the form of visualizations that illustrate highs, lows, and hopefully trends (e.g. [12]). These explorations have touched on many different domains (beyond our scope here), but include things like sleep [11], music listening histories [5], residential water usage [17], to mobility and social interactions [15], and even activity [20]. Importantly, these kinds of visualizations rely on the viewer to interpret the visualization, to make sense of it, and understand it within his or her context [24]. In effect, they support self-discovery.

This "self-discovery" support perspective resonates with us in that it is a *personal interpretation* of one's *own data*, and one arrives at it from one's *own perspective*. Depending on personal circumstances, people may need to interpret data in very different ways. For instance, MacLeod et al. [36] report on a participant who will consume alcohol even though it may cause a him a seizure, because it was acceptable to him in certain social situations.

Deliberate Engagement for Reflection. Very recent efforts by Baumer and colleagues' work can be seen as a reaction to these, where rather than relying on users to reflect of their own accord, the design deliberately engages people with their data and the reflective process (e.g. [3][4][30]). For instance, Baumer [3] noticed that people began reinterpreting photos of what was healthful, rather than adhering to what might be prescriptive norms. Similarly, Khovanskaya et al. [30] explore reflection on the infrastructure of data collection by provoking it deliberately through a design that reflects either a brokenness, or a creepiness, etc. Thudt et al. [51] explore the design of playful, interactive visualizations as a way to engage the reflective process through search. Finally, Baumer [2] focuses on the concept of reflection by articulating several different perspectives from which we can consider reflection (philosophical, cognitive, critical, learning), and articulating new axes upon which we can engage reflective process (breakdowns, inquiry, critique).

Our work here builds on the ideas outlined by Baumer [2]—specifically, we are interested in "bootstrapping" reflection as a learning process. Like Isaacs et al [29], we explicitly engage learners in the process of reflection: both on their own data, and on others' data. In so doing, we are interested in engaging the cognitive process of reflection by having people considering the challenges of others (i.e. thereby making it a social task).

2.2 Social Learning for Personal Informatics

The Quantified Self (QS) movement is an open membership organization that promotes self-learning through data collection. In their exploration of how Quantified Selfers learn from their data, Choe et al. [12] discuss the important role of Quantified Self Meetups (gatherings or meetings). Here, members share and articulate what they have learned, asking and answering questions from other Quantified Selfers about their process. Presenting members consequently need to make their learnings coherent through a storytelling process; furthermore, attendees benefit from being able to engage in active inquiry (i.e. question asking). Learning theorists from the constructivist tradition place strong value on such social processes in learning [53]. This perspective suggests that learning comes from a type of active inquiry—asking questions. The dialogue from storytelling and explanation also reveals underlying assumptions, etc. that can prompt conversation (and therefore additional learning). This type of "deeper learning" matches with adult learners' motivations—specifically, that they are interested in developing new knowledge based on their existing knowledge, and being critical of what is being taught [8].

Asking Questions. Many researchers have explored how people use online systems to support asking questions in a variety of contexts (e.g. technical questions [38], health [13], etc.). One challenge with this approach, however, is that it depends on people being able to frame their query in terms of an explicit question. An interesting approach to this problem has been to consider non-explicit queries, where the question is implicit based on users' (learners') interactions with a system. Bateman et al. [1] provide users with search terms/results that colleagues have used, and do so in-context while users are typing in their own search queries. Chilana et al. [10] explore a similar approach, providing users with tooltip web search queries for features that a user is exploring. Here, the queries are mined from the web rather than gathered from a known expert. These approaches are unique because rather than presupposing a correct answer, the central premise is to gather information on behalf the user, and allow the user to choose to make use of it.

Getting Feedback. Prompting this active inquiry and learning without dictating the outcome of the learning is challenging, particularly when the learners are novices. Luther et al.'s efforts are instructive: here, novices on a crowdsourcing platform are asked to provide critiques of visual/interaction designs [35]. The authors noted that by providing these novices with some scaffolding (by way of a rubric), they were able to generate critiques that were meaningfully usable by designers afterward. Similarly, Tinapple et al. [52] study how peer-based critique can be supported in a classroom using a tool call Critviz. In both cases, there was some evidence that the people providing the critiques were themselves learning how to produce more effectively.

In the personal informatics domain, we are interested in this type of feedback, because rather than knowing a priori what kind of feedback is appropriate and necessary, how to interpret the data is unclear. Here, the meaning is ambiguous, depends on the person reading the data, and it is a rich diversity of feedback that is valued. Sadler [47] provides a framework suggesting good feedback allows learners to understand what is intended (conceptual), to compare themselves to that standard (specific), and provides direction to take steps towards that standard (actionable). In the personal informatics domain, such a framework may not be applicable. Thus, the core idea is then to gather the feedback, present it to the learner, and allow him/her to interpret it.

3. SHARED REFLECTION

To address the challenge of supporting reflection in personal informatics, we formulated a set of basic ideas around the idea of learners providing reciprocal feedback as a way to deliberately engage with reflection. These were grounded in prior literature on the use of critique and feedback [35][52]. Here, we outline some considerations on this idea, describe the process that we chose as a way of instantiating those considerations, and describe the benefits that we expected from this process. Later, in our study, we evaluate and expand on these considerations to form a more nuanced understanding of shared reflection.

3.1 Considerations

Learning through active (prompted) engagement with data. Rather than relying on people to simply think about their data on their own, we feel that shared reflection should rely on active participation in a reflective process. Here, we specifically are interested in ways of prompting people to take time to actively think about the data rather than relying on them to find time to do it at their leisure. Like Baumer [2], we feel that engagement needs to go beyond looking at tables of numbers.

Verbalizing reflection as prose / narrative makes it concrete. We have seen that many people from the QS movement benefit from QS meetups, where they discuss their experiences of collecting and making sense of their data [12]. This type of storytelling (and indeed, preparing for the storytelling) likely supports reflection, transforming it from disconnected abstract thoughts to something much more concrete. This verbalizing (whether oral or written) makes it a more definite narrative, and we believe this will encourage people to gain more meaningful insight. For instance, if one were making an assertion about another person's data as feedback, one would likely work to ensure that the assertion was appropriately supported by the data (or, at the least, to explain one's thinking process).

Other people do things differently than us. Leverage this as a source of surprise and inspiration. This consideration is at the heart of our thinking about shared reflection. Seeing other people's data and reflecting on it is easier than trying to derive new insight (or questions) of one's own data, because others collect different kinds of data, perform the collection differently, or have different goals than us. We thus have perspectives that are different from others, and might be worth sharing. By the same token, seeing what others have to say about one's own data can cause reflection because it may prompt a breakdown or surprise (i.e. "Oh, I never thought of it that way."). This kind of breakdown is important in prompting transformative changes in how people think [2].

3.2 Process, Alternatives and Drawbacks

Initially, we imagined a four-part process for shared reflection. For example, we assume two data collectors, Alice and Bob, have collected data about themselves.

1. **Trade data.** Alice sends her data to Bob; Bob sends his data to Alice.
2. **Reflect on someone else's data.** Alice reflects on Bob's data, and writes him feedback based on her perspective; Bob does the same for Alice's data.
3. **Trade feedback.** Alice sends her feedback to Bob; Bob does the same.
4. **Reflect on feedback.** Alice reflects on her data and the feedback she received from Bob by writing a paragraph. Bob does the same.
5. **Repeat.** The process repeats with additional data collection.

Each step of the process demands active engagement from learners. The first step requires packaging up one's data in a way that is interpretable to others, potentially along with information about how to understand the data that is being collected and why. The second step reveals how others are doing collection, and asks collectors to reflect on that practice and what is in front of them in an active way, preparing a verbal narrative as feedback to the other learner. The third step provides the learner with someone else's feedback. In the fourth step, the learner is now asked to explicitly reflect on that feedback (along with the original data) by preparing a written statement. Throughout this, the learner can revisit his data collection strategy or goals as a consequence of what has been learned.

In our study, we used a variation of this process. Since there were many people in the network, we simply gave each participant someone else's data to study and provide feedback on (i.e. rather than necessarily swapping within a pair). We settled on this process after considering several variations on the above-listed basic process. Our final approach to this process was mainly due to pragmatic considerations of conducting the study, but raises several open questions:

Dialogue. *Should Bob see Alice's response to Bob's feedback once Alice has written it? And, should Bob be given another chance to respond?* To make it clear what we expected of participants (and partly to protect their identities from one another), we did not provide participants with a mechanism to communicate with one another directly. Instead, all communication went through the first author via email.

Homogenous data collection. *Do Alice and Bob need to be collecting similar kinds of data?* We considered allowing feedback only from participants collecting similar kinds of data (as they would be more familiar with the domain), but also the opposite of that scenario, where participants would only give feedback to those collecting different kinds of data (as they would be more apt to provide a unique perspective). In our study, we opened it up to any kind of data collection—participants did not need to be collecting the same kind of data. This was a pragmatic choice: we were interested more in the notion that participants would benefit from getting a variety of perspectives on their data collection, rather than in feedback strictly from people familiar with the domain.

Anonymous feedback. *Should Alice and Bob remain anonymous? Would it be more likely in a real-world scenario that family members would be providing feedback?* To protect participants' anonymity, we opted for anonymous feedback in our study.

Making it "public." *Should all data, feedback, and reflections be open to all participants?* Other systems such as Critviz [52] provide all data and feedback in an open forum. This has the benefit of allowing people to "dive deep" into all the content and ideas that have been generated by others—regardless of whether the feedback is about one's own work. It thus gives learners access to a wide range of ideas right away, and potentially right at the point where they are interested in thinking more about new possibilities. We chose not to do this in this study. While there is great learning potential in this approach, we were interested in whether the feedback *on its own* would induce meaningful reflection, and keeping a simple model of feedback would allow us to trace the source of inspiration.

Stratification based on experience. *Should novices be getting feedback from other novices?* We considered pairing novice data collectors with more experienced ones, but realized that the metric for expertise was not only highly subjective but that expertise might actually be a domain-specific. Thus, for the purpose of our study, we did not use this strategy.

Drawbacks. One drawback of the process as outlined above is that it is time and labour intensive. It takes time on the part of learners and does not come without effort. Another drawback is that even though we have taken steps to maintain the anonymity of participants by not sharing their names or contact information with one another, they are still sharing personal data about themselves. While it turned out not to be the case in our study, some types of personal data can be used to identify someone (e.g. GPS/location data). If a learner wants his data to remain private, this may be problematic with shared reflection due to the explicit demand to share the data with someone else.

4. Study

We designed and conducted a study to understand the strengths and weaknesses of our shared reflection process and to learn how we could improve it. As outlined earlier, the shared reflection process asks people to analyze and reflect on others' data, to receive others' feedback on one's own data, and to explicitly reflect on one's data. Our interest here was to understand how these additional tasks of analyzing others' data (and getting others' feedback) would influence our participants' understanding of their own data. Thus, we focused on two research questions in this study:

1. How does receiving feedback from another person assist/change one's own reflection process?

2. How does reflecting on another person's data support change in one's own reflection process?

4.1 Participants

A total of 15 participants (9 females) were recruited for the main study with ages ranging from 20-74 (median 38). Participants were located across Canada and the United States. Four additional participants were recruited for a pilot study, two of whom were ultimately rolled into the main study. Participants were recruited via public advertising spaces, email lists, Meetup groups, presentations, and in-person. Advertisements asked for people who were interested in personal data collection (whether they currently collected data or not) and in learning more about themselves. Participants were remunerated with up to $20 for participating in the study and entered into a draw for $100 on completion of the study.

4.2 Design

We designed a six-week field study with three phases:

Phase 1: Pre-Study Questionnaire. The online pre-study questionnaire collected demographics, experience and current practices in data collection (if any), and responses to a set of structured questions to help participants identify personal goals for the study (i.e. what data would they collect and to what end). For instance: Whether or not you currently collect data, what data are you interested in collecting? Why are you interested in collecting this data? What are you expecting to learn from this study?

Phase 2: Data Collection and Reflection (6-weeks). For six weeks, participants collected data. Participants were asked to collect data in an activity log. Participants were free to choose the type of data that was to be collected, and how it was to be recorded (a sample log was provided if needed). At the end of each week, participants submitted their data collection logs.

Starting at week two, participants were given a week's worth of data from another participant in the study and asked to provide some feedback about it. This feedback was submitted to the researchers and then returned to the original owner anonymously. The original owner would then be asked to study and think about this feedback before writing a response. This response was then submitted to the researchers. Each week, participants were given the data of a different participant if possible. These activities were repeated each week until the end of week six.

Phase 3: Post-Study Questionnaire. After the last week of data collection, participants completed a post-study questionnaire which asked them to reflect on what they had done and learned over the last six weeks. For instance: Has your understanding of your data collection changed? What have you learned from this study? Were you able to fulfill your objectives?

Participants were free to choose their goals and the type(s) of data they wanted to collect for the duration of the study. In addition, they were allowed to choose the way in which they collected the data (i.e. using activity trackers, using mobile applications, by hand, etc.).

4.2.1 Pilot Study

Our resulting field-study approach was informed by a pilot study where we compared the shared reflection approach to a control condition (e.g. no externally supported reflection). The controls in this pilot test did not report any meaningful change in their understanding of themselves or their data. In contrast, the two pilot participants who were in the shared reflection condition had already started to demonstrate that they were learning from working with one another through their shared reflection process. These participants expressed very high levels of motivation in comparison to the other participants. As a consequence, we began the main study, adding these two participants into the main study (i.e. without changing their protocol).

4.3 Data and Analysis

We collected three sources of data: pre-study questionnaires, submitted content from participants during the study, and the post-study questionnaires. The submitted content included the following for each participant: their submitted data, the feedback they received from other participants on their data, and their reflections on that feedback. The pre-study and post-study questionnaires allowed us to see the difference between what they thought they understood from their data to what they had at the outset, and the submitted content allowed us to track this change through their process.

We conducted a thematic analysis of the data, iteratively identifying and exploring patterns that we observed within the data. We focused on the types of ideas being expressed by participants in their feedback and the responses that participants generated to that feedback. Each idea was thematically coded using an open coding process, allowing us to see when and how ideas were introduced to participants and how they appropriated these ideas into their own reflective processes.

Coding process. Each piece of submitted feedback or response were divided into phrases. Most phrases were complete sentences, though some sentences contained multiple phrases. Each phrase was evaluated and assigned a code. This process was repeated for all phrases in all weeks for each participant, where we added codes to the master list as needed. Once the initial coding was done, a second person reviewed the codes for consistency and validation.

For example, when coding a phrase from a participant ("The amount of data collected is sustainable, but if other sorts of data could also be collected, it may help narrow down causal variables."), this phrase would be coded with two different codes. The first part of the phrase ("The amount of data collected is sustainable") would be coded as an *Observation*. The second part of the phrase ("if other sorts of data could also be collected, it may help narrow down causal variables.") would be coded as a *Suggestion*.

4.4 Data Collected

Table 1 summarizes the types of data that participants tracked. Participants were free to record the data in whatever way they wanted (some used paper diaries, others used Excel, and so forth). Although many participants chose to track one type of data, some participants experimented with multiple types, either dropping some as they discovered they were not interesting after a few weeks, or completely changing what they were collecting. Participants were aware that their data would be shared with other participants, but none expressed that this sharing affected their choice of what data they would track.

Over the course of the study, one third of participants changed the data they were collecting in some way. Some people found that the data they initially chose to collect was not getting them the information they were hoping for, so they completely changed their goals and data type. Of the participants who changed the data they were collecting, most of them (60%) made their modifications in Week 3 (i.e. after one round of feedback). It is interesting to note that all of these participants were also collecting multiple types of data. One participant showed a clear refinement of their initial goal as they learned the benefits and drawbacks of what they initially chose to collect.

When the data was passed between participants (i.e. from the collector to the person providing feedback), it was done so in raw form. In many cases, these would be simple tables of data—usually with columns like date, description, amount—however, this varied widely depending on the kind of data that was being collected. There was no common visualization tool provided.

Participant	Data Collected
P1	Physical activity (6 weeks)
P2	Food (5 weeks), time (6 weeks)
P3	Teaching effectiveness (6 weeks)
P4	Physical activity (2 weeks), mileage (4 weeks)
P5	Physical activity (6 weeks)
P6	Physical activity (6 weeks)
P7	Screen time (6 weeks)
P8	Physical activity (6 weeks)
P9	Music practice time (6 weeks)
P10	Wearing aligners (3 weeks), physical activity (3 weeks), physical ailments (6 weeks)
P11	Physical activity (2 weeks), study time (6 weeks)
P12	Weather (6 weeks)
P13	Food (6 weeks), physical activity (4 weeks)
P14	Physical activity (6 weeks)
P15	Mileage (6 weeks)

Table 1. Summary of the data collected by main study participants.

4.5 Exemplars

We begin by providing commentary on three participants, where their experiences accord with three clusters of participants. These general clusters generally reflected participants' experience prior experience with data collection (none, some, a lot): within each of the three clusters, participants' reactions to shared reflection were relatively similar. We describe these as personal stories, as the concreteness of each participant's experiences explain the role of shared reflection in their learning. We chose three participants: one with no experience collecting data, one with a limited amount of experience collecting, and finally one with considerable data collection experience to demonstrate how the shared reflection process affected their practices. As illustrated by Table 1, these participants were not necessarily representative of a cluster in terms of the data that was collected; rather, we focus here primarily on their experience of shared reflection. These exemplars were chosen because their responses to the feedback were descriptively rich.

4.5.1 Sarah: No Data Collection Experience

Sarah had not previously collected data. Initially, Sarah collected three types of data: information about her teeth aligner usage to ensure she was using them the recommended 20-22 hours per day, ear aches to determine what factors might instigate them, and pushups to strengthen her arms. As the study progressed, she dropped all but the earache data. She refined her earache tracking to determining which foods worsened the symptoms. Sarah's experience represents three participants in the study.

As the study progressed, she figured out what types of data were most interesting and relevant to her while removing unnecessary data. Many changes to Sarah's process was prompted by others: for instance, from week 4, Sarah modified her pain scale from 1-10 to 1-5—this allowed her to not worry so much about the granularity of the pain, but record quickly a rough sense of the magnitude. Sarah also regularly shared resources (links to articles, etc.) to others, and received such links from another participant (i.e. via the feedback that she wrote to others, or via the feedback that she received). Her responses indicate that she had read through these links and had found them interesting and useful.

In the post-study survey, Sarah expressed that she felt as though she learned a lot from the study. In particular, she identified that learning the right kind of data to collect was very important—something that is reflected in the evolution of her data collection over the six weeks. Although Sarah did not fulfill her objectives from the pre-study survey, she also acknowledged her goals had changed, and that she did meet her goals in some other areas. This is a common occurrence for people new to data collection [32], and is often prompted by reflection. Of note, Sarah pointed out that there were the benefits of seeing what other people were doing in their personal data collection practices, as they helped her to make changes to her own process.

4.5.2 Esther: Limited Data Collection Experience

Esther collects and reviews data, but does not know how to use the data. For the duration of the study, Esther collected music practice data with the goal of improving musical performance. Esther, in her experience and focus, represents nine participants in the study.

Esther's logs included time/date of practice, duration, a description of what was practiced, and then a set of annotated notes. These notes were useful to the reviewers, as they found a way of cutting through the raw data to understand what Esther was trying to do, or reasons for shorter practice sessions. In addition, Esther provided other kinds of data on various weeks: sound clips of musical passages that she had difficulty with, or had finally perfected.

Esther took the feedback very seriously, reflecting on the comments and changing her process as suggested. For instance, in Week 5, a commenter suggested:

> I think that the notes section of these data files would benefit from a bit more direction and focus. If the goal is to play through songs without any mistakes, perhaps by recording trouble sections, areas where you'd like to improve on, etc, it could help pinpoint exactly where you most need to improve. – Week 5 commenter

> "More direction and focus" is exactly what my practice needs, plus clear insights into "trouble" sections of various songs -- certain areas where I repeatedly find myself stumbling and making the same mistakes over and over again... I will try to record more, since my digital piano has that capability, so I can be more aware of when and where my mistakes are most likely to occur, in order to work on those sections. I will also try to be more "mindful" of my physical and mental responses, so I can correlate them with the likelihood of fumbling, as well as whether my pain levels affect my playing ability, or whether I'm able to "play through" them. – Esther's response

This vignette illustrates how shared reflection worked for Esther. First, the commenter identifies and articulates the central issue for Esther in a way that she finds exciting. Second, the commenter provides a bit of direction as to how to execute on addressing the issue. Then, Esther takes that idea and pushes it in a direction that resonates and makes sense for her. This means that Esther not only changes the process through which she collects and makes sense of data, but that the way in which she is thinking about her goals has evolved.

In one case for Esther, the commenter misinterpreted her comments about pain in her hands (from practices) as being something that needed to be overcome (not Esther's intention). Based on this though, Esther realizes that an underlying issue for her has been carpal tunnel, and ends up finding a potential solution to the problem:

> The part about ***things usually get better*** (above) didn't exactly materialize that way, in my case, as far as my practicing the [ukulele] went... I did a little online research and found out that CTS is common among musicians, and that they benefit from doing stretching exercises before practicing, like athletes do before they work out. I did some of the exercises suggested in a couple of online articles before I practiced the piano today (1/2 hour) to see if that helped. – Esther's response to week 4 feedback (emphasis was hers, quoting the feedback)

In this case, the stretching did not help, but in some ways, it is immaterial. The point is that the feedback comment, even if it was a bit offside, was clearly a different perspective on Esther's situation. It sent her down a path of self-discovery to actions that she had never considered.

Esther took the feedback and reflection very seriously. Her responses were thoughtful and nuanced. Though she responded more deeply to the comments she received than most participants, she represents our participants in this cluster in the sense that they would consider the suggestions and sometimes end up taking them on in their practice.

In the post-study survey, Esther mentioned that seeing other participant's data logs were helpful to her in terms of seeing what other people collected. She felt that she learned a lot about herself throughout the study including what factors affected her practices. Another point Esther made was that she was more motivated to continue practicing regularly due to keeping regular logs. She was also interested in finding out what other people in the study had learned, which hints at an interest in some sort of interaction with others.

This exemplar illustrates one way in which someone with minimal knowledge of data collection can explore personal goals and refine activities to align with personal values and objectives. In Esther's case, there is clear evidence of exploring different types

Code (count)	Description	Example
Observation (74)	Re-iterating the data	I'm not sure I got everything, but what I got was related to aligners being in or out, pushups, what foods were affecting tinnitus.
Extrapolation (45)	Interpreting the data	I assume it's a teenager or young adult.
Suggestion (99)	Ideas to make changes to data collection or interpret data	I may suggest changing the ringing scale to 5, with 5 being worst and 0 being non-existent.
Sharing (57)	Providing resources such as books, articles, etc or referencing personal experiences	I did similar food tracking...and it helped a lot
Support (113)	Providing words of encouragement	This is a great data sample.
Clarification (40)	Asking questions to better understand the data or person collecting the data	How long has this person been collecting data?
Shout Out (1)	Request for information from others	Anyone know any exercises to relieve the symptoms ... in my thumb, especially?

Table 2: Codes for participants' feedback on others' data.

of data collection, refining goals, and reacting to other people's feedback by both accepting and rejecting suggestions.

4.5.3 Larry: Significant Data Collection Experience

Larry collects data, and saw this as an opportunity to push his understanding of his data. Larry's goal was to track physical metrics, activities, and diet to lose fat and gain muscle. Of note, Larry makes use of graphs to analyze his data. This case represents three participants in the study.

Larry did not make use of the provided template in his data collection. Starting in Week 1, it was apparent he was familiar with the area in which he was collecting data. His goal was fairly well defined and the justification of his methods and processes were extremely precise. An interesting part of Larry's data is that he used cumulative data collection and included cumulative graphs in his weekly submissions.

In responding to comments, Larry mentioned that some of the comments he received from others did not provide enough constructive criticism on his methods. Thus, he was somewhat disappointed in what shared reflection was able to provide him. Many of his concerns were centred around extrapolating meaningful information from his data, which he wanted more thoughts on. Starting in Week 4, Larry's comments become much shorter and he spent minimal time extrapolating his data. At this point, he mentioned that he believed he had extracted most of the interesting information from the data in previous weeks and didn't feel the need to re-iterate what had already been learned. Thus, at this point in the study, the shared reflection method was providing limited benefit despite the extra efforts he needed to leave comments for others and read theirs on his data.

Larry illustrates how an experienced data collector may not stay motivated/engaged with a shared reflection process for a long period of time. It seemed as though Larry's engagement declined once he no longer saw personal gains in the process.

4.6 Findings

Our findings suggest that participants gained valuable insight from the shared reflection process. Mainly, these insights came directly from feedback received from others, where participants would indicate that they made changes based on this feedback. In a limited number of cases (as with Sarah and Esther, above), participants indicated that the act of reviewing others' data was useful in helping them to understand new possibilities (e.g. data collection strategies). Furthermore, as in Larry case (above), some participants seemed to reach a "ceiling effect," where others' feedback no longer helped them in their reflection.

Overall Learning. When asked what they learned in the study, participants answered the question in a variety of ways. Some focused on what they learned from their data (5/15) while others focused on what strategies and techniques they learned (10/15). A few of the participants (3/15) highlighted interactions with other participants in some way in their responses. These people found it interesting to see what other people were doing and also felt more motivated to keep up with their data collection when they knew they would be held accountable.

To understand the nature, role, and impact of the feedback that participants receive, we frame the reminder of our findings in three sections: first, we describe the nature of the feedback that participants sent to others; second, we discuss participants' reactions to this feedback, and finally, we articulate several salient challenges that became apparent in our study.

4.6.1 Feedback on Others' Data

We coded both the feedback participants generated for others and that which they supplied in their self-reflections. Table 2 illustrates the final codes that our process produced, along with the number of phrases that were coded with those categories.

Support. The most popular code was support, where the feedback was mainly intended as social support (akin to [49]). For instance:

> "It takes a lot of motivation to make it out every day, especially in the winter, so good to see training sessions for 3 consecutive days." - from P1's analysis of P4's data (code: support)

> "I can tell you are trying really hard" - from P2's analysis of P6's data (code: support)

Such comments were rarely actionably useful for the participant receiving the feedback, though from prior work, we know that such words of encouragement have two effects on participants: (1) it can make them feel accountable to others, and (2) it can help encourage them to continue in their practice.

Observations and suggestions. Participants seemed eager to help others out as much as possible and often tried to make sense of the data by writing out their observations as a way of framing advice or suggestions.

> "It looks as though there are 2 weeks of data from a runner/jogger keeping track of distances run, both with a partner and alone, in order to increase endurance & cardiovascular performance, with the goal of working up to 50 km (31.0686 miles), "even ONCE A DAY!"." - from P9's analysis of P4's data (code: observation)

Based on their observations, they frequently offered suggestions to improve data collection practices. The nature of these suggestions were far ranging. Some would suggest simple data presentation practices for legibility/interpretability:

Code (count)	Description	Example
Response (123)	Addressing comments provided by another participant	Thanks for the comments, which, obviously, someone put a great deal of thought into before expressed.
Observation (51)	Re-iterating the data	The main data I'm concerned with is distance and speed
Extrapolation (82)	Interpreting the data	While the scale doesn't show much improvement, I believe my energy level and overall health and well-being has improved
Re-evaluation (30)	Revising data collection or evaluation methods	The first...offered some time management advice, where the second...offered a method of improving my training tracing through the addition of including comments. I am hoping to put both into practice.
Speculation (30)	Guessing what could happen in the future	I had hoped that adding exercise, without changing my diet, would result in more weight loss
Sharing (89)	Providing resources such as books, articles, etc or referencing personal experience	The following study, which I just completed, inspired an engrossing piano practice session afterward

Table 3: Codes for participants' responses to others' feedback

"... I would suggest putting sub-totals for each category." - from P6's analysis of P2's data (code: suggestion)

Others would go a bit deeper, offering suggestions for alternate ways to collect, or alternate measures to collect in order to help the original participant achieve his/her goals:

"... one thing I would suggest is trying to use other sensors, such as heart rate monitors etc. to find an approximate calorie deficit created by the exercise" - from P11's analysis of P14's data (code: suggestion)

Some suggestions offered alternate ways for participants to think about their data:

"It would be interesting to learn more about your experiences and see additional data collected alongside it. What was your mood like? Was the exercise too much? Too little? Did you feel pushed?" - from P2's analysis of P1's data (code: clarification and suggestion)

"I would be interested to see the total number of contributions vs the number of different students that spoke." - from P1's analysis of P3's data (code: suggestion)

These kinds of suggestions are far richer, and potentially provocative. Here, the participants offer opportunities for the original participant to engage in reflection on breakdowns (i.e. changes in how they considered the data), and potentially transforming how they now can think about the data [2]. In the next section, we discuss how these suggestions affected participants' practice.

Sharing as suggestions. By chance, some participants were paired with others who had similar goals in the past. In these cases, the feedback took on a reflective tone: participants shared knowledge and resources from their own past to their partner as a way of supporting or providing suggestion. We observed instances where participants would share personal experiences, to suggesting books or articles that they thought would be useful.

"... I did some research on practicing habits and such when I was starting out and I found this helpful article on making the most of practice time, it is attached, maybe it will help this participant as well." - from P1's analysis of P9's data (code: sharing)

4.6.2 Responding to Others' Feedback

We also coded participants' reflections on the feedback they received (Table 3). When reflecting on their own data, participants tended to spend a lot of time acknowledging and responding to the comments provided by other participants. Overall, this is encouraging, as it means that the feedback acted as a new anchor upon which to think about their data. Here, we see P12 simply responding to questions that P15 had posted about her data:

"Thank-you for the nice comment on my data. I just use it for year to year comparisons of the date and what the weather was like the previous year..." - from P12's reflection on P15's feedback (codes: response and response)

A lot of participants' follow-up comments seemed in direct response to the feedback they received. Although it was clear the participants would not see these responses to feedback, it seemed natural for participants to write their responses in this way.

New observations. There were some instances of participants making observations about their data based on the feedback they had received. In many cases, such reflections now seemed liked revelations based on what the feedback writer had written (say as a benchmark)—a "breakdown" in Baumer's terms [2]:

"My weight fluctuates a lot" - from P5's reflection on P10's feedback (code: observation)

"The gas part of the study is fluctuating" - from P15's reflection on P1's feedback (code: observation)

"I see I stayed up with a screen often" - from P7's reflection on P14's feedback (code: observation)

Rationalizing choices. Other comments made by participants included re-evaluating their methods based on other participant's comments or their own extrapolations and speculations on what may happen in the future if they were to perform certain actions. Again, these are examples of transformative reflection (Baumer [2]), as they are fundamentally changing how the participant thinks about the problem at hand—beyond simply how one needs to think about analysis, and even how the data is to be collected.

Here, P2 has suggested that P8 consider collecting additional information to help P8 to achieve his goal of losing weight, including caloric intake, hunger pangs, and mood. P8's response indicates that he has given it some thought, but has chosen not to follow through:

"This would be something I would consider making a diary of to incorporate it with my lifestyle after I am in the routine. I think if I was to make recording to much information at this point would perhaps work in reverse for me as I don't want to make this a "make work" activity." - from P8's reflection on P2's feedback (codes: re-evaluation and speculation)

In providing comments on P10's data, P5 made a suggestion for the scale P10 was using:

"As a note on the ringing scale. The values go from 3 to 7 to 8. I may suggest changing the ringing scale to 5, with 5 being worst and 0 being non-existent. I made this suggestion simply because the variable cannot be measured, and a smaller scale may help reduce ambiguities in the intensity between close values." - from P5's analysis of P10's data (code: suggestion)

Although P10 did not explicitly address this in their reflection, the data log they submitted the following week showed a change in their scale from 1-10 to 1-5.

Transforming reflection. Based on feedback they received, some participants acted on a question and actively re-interpreted their data. Here, we see P7 re-evaluating his data to determine trends. This is a transformative reflection [2], as it shows that P7 is actively reconsidering the way he thinks about his data:

> "Through week three, I learned I wake-up later if I spend less time with backlit screens at night: r=-0.78 (r^2=0.6)." - from P7's reflection on P9's feedback (code: extrapolation)

In the following reflection, P9 references both P4's comments and P1's resource in enhancing their practice sessions:

> "I will keep those above comments about my diaries, along with those of the person who sent the article on how to practice, by my piano for handy reference." - from P9's reflection on P4's feedback (code: response)

4.6.3 Challenges

We noted several challenges participants encountered in our study. These challenges included issues with our concrete instantiation of shared reflection, and also perhaps limits with the approach itself.

Clarification required/desired. Many participants found it frustrating that they were writing in a one-way fashion. When writing feedback, they could not be certain they were interpreting the data or the original participant's goals properly. Some found it exciting to have a "kindred spirit" who was performing the same kind of data collection; however, it was frustrating that queries could not be responded to.

Some of the participants attempted to extrapolate the data and make sense of what was going on in others' data. In these cases, they often wished to clarify their understanding with more background information on why the data was being collected and the history of the collector. It is unclear exactly what the purpose of these kinds of comments were, as participants were not actually engaged in a (repeated) dialogue with one another; however, it seems clear that in some cases, an ongoing dialogue would have been preferred over the "one and done" approach our protocol mandated. Here, P6 seems to be trying to make sure that s/he is understanding what is being collected (i.e. articulating his/her assumptions of the data):

> "Screen time, I am guessing might include watching tv/movies, computer work/email/Internet, and gaming." - from P6's analysis of P7's data (code: extrapolation)

In another instance, P9 seems to ask a question of P4 (for P9's sake) within the context of responding to and thinking about P4's data. But, P9's query here, even though it was a real cry for attention, would not get a response in our instantiation of shared reflection:

> "Anyone know any exercises to relieve the symptoms (numbness, tingling, pain) in my thumb, especially?" - from P9's analysis of P4's data (code: shout out)

Similarly, participants were sometimes prompted by an interesting idea or insight. Here, a participant seems very excited about the possibility of interacting with the "owner" of the data, but is stymied by our instantiation, which does not allow for direct contact:

> "I'd also be curious to know what the person's reaction was to seeing the comment that I sent them about their own data. I want some sort of anonymous discussion with the person." - from P2's reflection on P8's feedback (code: response)

Ceiling effect. As in Larry's case, we observed a sort of "ceiling effect," where he does not seem to be learning anything new from the ongoing feedback cycle. It is hard to know exactly what to make of this—whether there really is no more to be discovered in the data, or that Larry's fellow participants were simply not generating new insight for him. Nevertheless, it seemed clear that for a small minority of participants (3), they reached a stage of saturation before the entire six weeks was up. While these participants stayed on until the end, the richness of their reflections tailed off over time. This might be a fundamental limitation of the shared reflection approach.

5. DISCUSSION

Our study suggests that shared reflection as an idea shows potential in terms of helping people to engage with their data, and the reflection process. Specifically, we saw that people clearly benefited from getting feedback from others, and this helped them to reframe their understanding of either their data or collection strategy/process. Furthermore, by viewing others' data and trying to understand their data collection practices, participants found the process helpful. On the other hand, we did not uncover concrete evidence that participants benefited from *writing feedback* for others. To be clear: we expected participants to learn by writing feedback for others; however, our suspicion is that we simply did not have a good way of assessing whether this kind of learning actually took place. We outline a number of practical challenges that need to be overcome for shared reflection to work in the real world:

Dialogue, anonymity, and "making it public." Our approach of having people write feedback, and respond to it when received from others made the interaction between participants very hollow. In effect, we asked people to care, at least for a while, about one another in their pursuit of their goals. Yet, we did not provide any means for them to follow up on the progress of others. Although this suited the purpose of our study, it seems that facilitating further interaction (while not forcing it) might allow for the supportive aspects of such health sharing sites to surface (e.g. [3][49]). Others have seen that the support can meaningfully impact not only motivation, but a sense of community, belonging, and adherence to activities that support one's goals [19]. The down side of supporting this type of dialogue is that people providing feedback might feel frustrated if their feedback/comments are not taken into account in subsequent data collection cycles. This could discourage further engagement and participation, which would be undesirable.

If supporting dialogue is an approach to be taken, then strict anonymity may prevent real bonds from forming. From an ethical perspective, we chose to protect participants' identity, but this goal would be obviated if participants were voluntarily joining up on a site for the express purpose of helping one another out. This is not to say that real identities need to be used; rather that the source of contributions (be they data, or feedback, or just comments) should be identifiable (i.e. with pseudonyms).

Finally, we saw that participants enjoyed seeing what others had already collected in terms of their process and data. Being able to see this information, if it were public, would provide a source of inspiration for people that are early in their personal informatics journey. Furthermore, it could also be used as a template (e.g. if someone else has similar goals, and has already successfully collected data to that effect).

Homogeneity of data and expertise. As discussed at length earlier, we did not, in this study, address the issue of homogeneity of data collection, or the expertise issue. While we chose not to do so here for practical reasons, it does seem likely that people who are familiar with a collection domain (and have expertise) will be able to offer meaningful input and suggestions to novices. In some ways, the system here parallels Q&A sites that connect experts with novices (e.g. StackOverflow, Quora). It may be instructive to explore how these sites maintain a user base and address motivation.

Reflecting on reflection: Social learning in shared reflection. The shared reflection process we outline in this paper is similar to, but distinct from the collaborative reflection that we have seen in the past [44]: beyond focusing on a distinct domain (i.e. personal informatics data rather than work experiences), the shared reflection here emphasizes the shared task or responsibility of reflecting on the data at hand rather than simply asking for others for their experiences. In our study design, we made this reflection demand explicit by asking participants to reflect on the feedback as a separate, distinct part of the process. In so doing, we saw definite progress and change on the part of participants based on the feedback (e.g. Sarah, Esther)—that is, they developed new knowledge that was actionable [8]. We thus mimicked the kinds of learnings that we might expect from the Quantified Self Meetups as described by Choe et al. [12], and saw that the feedback was understandable in a practical way [47].

Yet the design of our shared reflection was imperfect in relation to the learning theories outlined at the outset. As described earlier, many participants would have liked to have had a more open "back and forth" with the people providing them with feedback. The limited one-directional flow of feedback meant that participants could not engage in the question asking and dialogue that underpins much of social learning [8][53]. Thus, our approach could most certainly be improved, again, by providing a mechanism to engage in dialogue with those providing feedback.

Challenge: Shared reflection is onerous. In our instantiation of the process, the weekly commitment seemed too much for some participants. Some did not reply promptly and needed to be reminded to provide feedback both to others and for their own data. In some ways, it is like learning in an elementary school—when learners are engaged, learning is an effective, efficient process. Yet here, it plays a secondary role in people's lives and is easily put aside if the work seems too much. As in Larry's case, since he felt he had reached his "ceiling" early, he might not be particularly motivated to engage deeply in the process. Sadly, it is people like Larry (i.e. with considerable experience) who would make a community richer by providing his insight to others.

The dependencies that shared reflection imposes make it very brittle. In our study, participants who did not write feedback would subsequently delay participants (who were to receive that feedback) downstream. Practical implementation needs to deal with this and the motivation issue as described above. This is not to say that it needs to engage people for a long term. It may well be the case that users could use a shared reflection for a short period of time—just enough to help them bootstrap their own reflection processes, and this would be enough.

Challenge: Privacy. The shared reflection process necessarily raises questions about data privacy, and about the circle of participants that one would feel comfortable working with. Unfortunately, we do not have clear answers here. The participants we worked with came into the study knowing that their personal data would be shared with strangers. Thus, it is possible that they may have chosen data sources that were not overly revealing, tailored their data in such a way to present their ideal selves, or self-selected in ways that we would not see this issue crop up. A related issue is how to practically implement this system with a circle of participants—does it work better or worse if the other participants are known to oneself? This remains unclear and warrants further study.

6. CONCLUSIONS

We have seen that shared reflection can work. People benefit by seeing their data from others' perspectives, and this can affect not only their collection practice, but also how they view their data, and themselves. Rather than relying on reflection to just "happen," shared reflection makes the process explicit, and demands engagement. This type of engagement is onerous though—for some experienced data collectors, the value is not evident if others cannot provide a new and meaningful perspective. But, for the vast majority of the participants in our study, they clearly benefited from the strategy. Deploying this strategy in a commercial project introduces many other challenges, and we look forward to exploring the motivation issue in future work.

ACKNOWLEDGMENTS

Thank you to our participants, and NSERC and QEII for funding this study.

REFERENCES

[1] Bateman et al. (2013).Social navigation for loosely-coupled information seeking in tightly-knit groups using webwear. CSCW 2013, 955-966

[2] Baumer, E.P. (2015). Reflective informatics: conceptual dimensions for designing technologies of reflection. CHI 2015, 585-594.

[3] Baumer, E.P. et al. (2012). Prescriptive persuasion and open-ended social awareness: Expanding the design space of mobile health. CSCW 2012, 475-484.

[4] Baumer, E.P.S., et al. (2014). Reviewing reflection: on the use of reflection in interactive system design. DIS 2014, 93-102.

[5] Baur, D. et al. (2010). The streems of our lives: visualizing listening histories in context. IEEE TVCG 16 (6), 1119-1128.

[6] Bentley et al. (2013). Health mashups: presenting statistical patterns between wellbeing data and context in natural language to promote behavior change. ACM ToCHI 20 (5), 1-27.

[7] Bodenheimer, T. et al. (2002). Patient self-management of chronic disease in primary care. Journal of the American Medical Association 288 (19), 2469–2475.

[8] Cercone, K. (2008). Characteristics of adult learners with implications for online learning design. Association for the Advancement of Computing in Education Journal 16 (2), 137-159.

[9] Chen, Y. and Pu, P. (2014). HealthyTogether: exploring social incentives for mobile fitness applications. ChineseCHI 2014, 25-34.

[10] Chilana, P. et al. (2012) LemonAid: selection-based crowdsourced contextual help for web applications. CHI 2012, 1549-1558

[11] Choe, E.K. et al. (2014). Understanding quantified-selfers' practices in collecting and exploring personal data. CHI 2014, 1143-1152.

[12] Choe, E.K. et al. (2015). Characterizing visualization insights from quantified selfers' personal data presentations. IEEE CG&A 35 (4), 28-37.

[13] Civan, A. et al. (2009). Locating patient expertise in everyday life. GROUP 2009, 291-300.

[14] Consolvo, S. et al. (2008). Flowers or a robot army?: encouraging awareness & activity with personal, mobile displays. Ubicomp 2008, 54–63.
[15] Cuttone, A. et al. (2013). A mobile personal informatics system with interactive visualizations of mobility and social interactions. In *Proceedings of the 1st ACM International Workshop on Personal Data Meets Distributed Multimedia.* PDM '13, 27-30.
[16] De Groot, E. et al. (2014). Critically reflective dialogues in learning communities of professionals. *Studies in Continuing Education 36* (1), 15-37.
[17] Erickson, T. et al. (2012). The dubuque water portal: evaluation of the uptake, use and impact of residential water consumption feedback. CHI 2012, 675–684.
[18] Epstein, D. et al. (2014). Taming data complexity in lifelogs: exploring visual cuts of personal informatics data. DIS 2014, 667-676.
[19] Epstein, D.A. et al. (2015). From "nobody cares" to "way to go!": a design framework for social sharing in personal informatics. CSCW 2015, 1622-1636.
[20] Fan, C. et al. (2012). A spark of activity: exploring informative art as visualization for physical activity. UbiComp '12, 81-84.
[21] Fogg, B.J. (2003). *Persuasive Technology: Using Computers to Change What We Think and Do*. Morgan Kaufmann, San Francisco, CA.
[22] Frost, J. and Smith, B.K. (2003). Visualizing health: imagery in diabetes education. DUX '03, 1-14.
[23] Grzega, J. and Schoener, M. (2008). The didactic model ldl (lernen durch lehren) as a way of preparing students for communication in a knowledge society. *Journal of Education for Teaching* 34 (3), 167-175.
[24] Huang, D. et al. (2015). Personal visualization and personal visual analytics. IEEE CG&A 21 (3), 420-433.
[25] Froehlich, J. et al. (2009). UbiGreen: investigating a mobile tool for tracking and supporting green transportation habits. CHI 2009, 1043–1052
[26] Froehlich, J. et al. (2012). The design and evaluation of prototype eco-feedback displays for fixture-level water usage data. CHI 2012, 2367-2376
[27] Froehlich, J. (2008). The design of eco-feedback technology. CHI 2010, 1999-2008
[28] Hoyrup, S. (2004). Reflection as a core process in organizational learning. *Journal of Workplace Learning 16*, (8), 442-454.
[29] Isaacs, E. et al. (2013). Echoes from the past: how technology mediated reflection improves well-being. CHI 2013, 1071-1080.
[30] Khovanskaya, V. et al. (2013). "Everybody knows what you're doing": a critical design approach to personal informatics. CHI 2013, 3403-3412.
[31] Lee, M.L. and Dey, A.K. (2011). Reflecting on pills and phone use: supporting awareness of functional abilities for older adults. CHI 2011, 2095-2104.
[32] Li, I. et al. (2010). A stage-based model of personal informatics systems. CHI 2010, 557-566.
[33] Li, I., et al. (2011). Understanding my data, myself: supporting self-reflection with ubicomp technologies. UbiComp '11, 405-414.
[34] Lin, J. J. et al. (2006). Fish'n'Steps: encouraging physical activity with an interactive computer game. UbiComp 2006, 261-278.
[35] Luther, K. et al. (2015). Structuring, aggregating, and evaluating crowdsourced design critique. CSCW 2015, 473-485
[36] MacLeod, H. et al. (2013). Personal informatics in chronic illness management. GI '13, 149-156.
[37] Maitland, J. and Chalmers, M (2011). Designing for peer involvement in weight management. CHI 11, 315-324.
[38] Mamykina, L. et al. (2011). Design lessons from the fastest q&a site in the west. CHI 2011, 2857-2866.
[39] Mamykina, L. et al. (2008). MAHI: investigation of social scaffolding for reflective thinking in diabetes management. CHI 2008, 477–486.
[40] Mattila, E. et al. (2010). Empowering citizens for well-being and chronic disease management with wellness diary. IEEE Information Technology in Biomedicine 14 (2), 456–463.
[41] Marcu, G. et al. (2014). Designing for collaborative reflection. PervasiveHealth '14, 9-16.
[42] Moon, J. (1999). Reflection in learning and professional development. Abingdon, Oxon: RoutledgeFalmer.
[43] Prilla, M., and Renner, B. (2014). Supporting collaborative reflection at work: a comparative case analysis. GROUP 2014, 182-193.
[44] Prilla, M. et al. (2012). Collaborative reflection at work: supporting informal learning at a healthcare workplace. GROUP 2012, 55-64.
[45] Rivera-Pelayo, V. et al. (2012). Applying quantified self approaches to support reflective learning. LAK '12, 111-114.
[46] Rooksby, J. et al. (2014). Personal tracking as lived informatics. CHI 2014, 1163-1172.
[47] Sadler, D. R. (1989). Formative assessment and the design of instructional systems. Instr. Sci. 18, (2), 119–144
[48] Schön, D. A. (1983). *The Reflective Practioner*. Basic Books: New York.
[49] Skeels, M. M. et al. (2010). Catalyzing social support for breast cancer patients. CHI 2010, 173-182
[50] Thieme, A., et al. (2012). "We've bin watching you": designing for reflection and social persuasion to promote sustainable lifestyles. CHI 2012, 2337-2346.
[51] Thudt, A. et al. (2012). The bohemian bookshelf: supporting serendipitous book discoveries through information visualization. CHI 2012, 1461-1470.
[52] Tinapple, D. et al. (2013). Critviz: Web-based software supporting peer critique in large creative classrooms. Bulletin of the IEEE Technical Committee on Learning Technology 15, 1.
[53] Vygotsky, L. (1978). Mind in Society. London: Harvard University Press.
[54] Yu, H., et al. (2011). A simple curious agent to help people be curious. AAMAS '11, 1159-1160.

Raising your Eminence inside the Enterprise Social Network

Shiri Kremer-Davidson, Inbal Ronen, Lior Leiba, Avi Kaplan, Maya Barnea
IBM Research - Haifa
Haifa, Israel
{shiri, inbal, leiba, avika, mayab}@il.ibm.com

ABSTRACT

Companies are motivating their employees to become socially engaged in enterprise social networks as a means to raise employee engagement. This is also beneficial for employees as it provides an opportunity for them to get a voice and raise their eminence. Unfortunately, not all employees are born 'social butterflies' and many have difficulties in becoming more socially active. Failing to engage in an effective manner creates frustration which over time decreases their activity and lowers their chance to become socially eminent. This paper is a first of a kind study that reveals insights on social behavioral patterns of socially eminent employees. We extracted a comprehensive set of tips and recommendations to help employees become more socially eminent and investigate if and how eminent employees engage differently than others. We conducted interviews with top socially eminent employees and a quantitative inspection of bloggers behavioral patterns. Furthermore, we show that indeed best practices stated by socially eminent employees are fulfilled by eminent bloggers and less by others. We also found differences in how socially eminent employees engage compared to less eminent employees.

Keywords

Social Media; Enterprise; Workplace; Collaboration; Social Analytics; Engagement Analytics; Eminence; Best Practices.

1. INTRODUCTION

More and more companies are realizing the importance of having their workforce engaged. Many research studies have shown a correlation between employee engagement and company success in areas such as quality of service and product development, sales increase, employee retention, profit and total shareholder returns [23,14,15,31]. For example, it was shown that highly engaged organizations have a double rate of success compared to lower engaged organizations and have lower absenteeism and turnover [3]. Employee engagement is a strong predictor of positive organizational performance and the more engaged employees are, the more likely their employers are to exceed the industry average in revenue growth [26].

When trying to articulate the characteristics of an engaged employee Markos and Sridevi [26] found that engaged employees are emotionally attached to their organization and highly involved in their job with a great enthusiasm for the success of their employer. On the other hand, employees who are not engaged may be satisfied, but are not emotionally connected to their workplaces and are less likely to put in discretionary effort. Moreover, employees who are actively disengaged are emotionally disconnected from their work and workplace and might jeopardize their teams' performance [38].

One factor of an engaged workforce, is a collaborative workforce. When examining the power of collaboration, a Google initiated a cross industry survey [12] found that most respondents agreed that their organization would be more successful if employees were able to work in more flexible and collaborative ways. They saw that in the majority of companies that foster a culture of knowledge-sharing and collaboration employee morale and job satisfaction are high. In particular, they found that the third most mentioned serious threat to organizations in terms of people management is a disengaged workforce. They emphasize the importance of choosing the right collaboration tools for the organization.

One way of fostering collaboration in an enterprise is through the use of social media tools within the organization [8, 13, 24, 28, 32]. For instance one of the latest Gartner reports [9] emphasizes the importance of boosting employee engagement with social technologies in the digital workplace. They report that social technologies can assist in many of the factors that contribute to having engaged employees. For example, social technologies can open additional bidirectional communication channels between employees and their managers allowing managers to better see and impact progress and get a real understanding of their employee's role and contribution. Likewise, employees can gain peer recognition to their contributions. In general, employees who are using social networking tools effectively can benefit by getting a voice and reputation in their enterprise.

The Merriam Webster dictionary defines an eminent person as "successful, well-known and respected" [27]. Similarly, we refer to 'socially eminent' as being *socially* successful, well known and respected in the social networking sphere. But, do all employees who decide to socially engage in enterprise social networking sites become socially eminent and gain reputation? The answer is unfortunately not. Social eminence is established by being socially active *effectively* and thus drawing a crowd to one's contributions, having many followers, etc. This can, for example, be measured by how many people and in what manner interact with a person's content through reading, commenting or liking [20].

In the extreme, employees can contribute content that does not draw any attention or they can spam which might impede their peers' respect. One's content needs to reach an audience, to be noticed and to generate reaction. Even more so, employees need to draw people to *follow* them as an expression of interest in their future content.

GROUP '16, November 13-16, 2016, Sanibel Island, FL, USA
© 2016 ACM. ISBN 978-1-4503-4276-6/16/11…$15.00
DOI: http://dx.doi.org/10.1145/2957276.2957281

This way the content creator will become known and eminent in the social networking sphere of the organization. Being actively followed differentiates socially eminent employees from social spammers or social trolls [29]. For example, social trolls' contents generate reaction but not in a positive, leading way. Thus being socially engaged does not suffice to become socially eminent. Being social eminence can then contribute to general eminence which increases positive reputation and leads to influence, promotion and rewards [17].

In this paper we ask the following questions: do socially eminent employees engage differently than other employees using the enterprise social network? Are there best practices and tips that can assist not eminent employees become more socially eminent inside their organization? Are the best practices stated by the eminent employees indeed fulfilled by a socially eminent employee population?

To answer these questions we used both qualitative and quantitative research approaches. Through interviews with top socially eminent employees we learned on their engagement patterns and collected best practices and tips on what they did in order to become eminent and make people aware of their content and expertise within the enterprise social network. We also investigated what they do to maintain their role and why. We then analyzed the behavioral patterns of all bloggers in the enterprise and compared those patterns of eminent with less eminent bloggers in order to investigate whether the best practices stated by the eminent interviewees were indeed fulfilled by this similar population.

The paper is organized as follows. Section 2 provides related work; Section 3 describes the research setting of the interviews and blogger analysis; Section 4 includes results and sections 5 and 6 provide a discussion and conclusions respectively.

2. RELATED WORK

In this paper we identify behavioral patterns of socially eminent employees in an enterprise social networking environment. Holzblatt et al. [16] evaluated the uses and benefits of an enterprise social media platform. They found that the level of value users experienced in using the social platform is related to patterns of users' activity. Active contributors in all areas experienced greater value than both, moderate contributors and readers. In general, readers did not find the social platform beneficial for them, but those of them who accessed the system more, found it more valuable. As they found, not all employees use an enterprise social platform in similar capacity and not all do become socially eminent. They divided employees based on their level of contribution and usage of the enterprise social network and found active contributors are 5% of the population, moderate contributors are 14%, and most 81% are readers. Thus, although companies are realizing the importance of social media in the enterprise, they still have difficulties in onboarding the majority of their employees to become contributors. Some companies try to encourage adoption using different gamification techniques such as points and badges [2, 28, 30, 37]. Interestingly enough, it has even been shown that removing such incentives after they have been used by employees can reduce overall contribution within the social networking system [35].

We refer to social eminence as being socially active in an effective manner that draws a crowd to one's contributions, generates reactions and results in many followers, etc. Literature includes similar related definitions such as being socially reputable, or having social impact [1, 6, 34]. Jacovi et.al [20] examined various definitions of social reputation in particular trustworthiness, influence, expertise, and impact,. They found that impact has the highest overlap with reputation.

In order to be able to draw people to become more socially engaged we tried to understand what motivates employees to become socially eminent. Ehrlich et al. [11] investigated what motivated employees to contribute to enterprise social networks, in particular communities. They found that employees want to help others (but limit their participation to the community directly related to their daily work) and often encourage and draw others to contribute to the community as a way of generating new valued information. Interestingly though, they did not find evidence of contribution in order to enhance online reputation. Chin et al. [7] found self-interest (i.e., enjoyment of helping others and reputation enhancement), knowledge, self-efficacy and time commitment as motivators.

Although many socially engage, only a minority becomes socially eminent. Some studies attempted to investigate interaction patterns with socially reputable employees. Mark et al. [25] found that such employees' network size was the strongest (negative) predictor of employees' ratings by their colleagues, whereas number of followers was the strongest positive predictor [25]. Jacovi et al. [20] similarly found that the number of followers is the strongest indicator to most reputation types and that the network size is the weakest indicator to all types of reputation. For impact, along with number of followers, getting highest levels of responses on blogs and forums are strongest indicators. From this we conclude that eminent employees are likely to have many followers, get high level of reaction to their blogs and forum topics but do not invest time to maintain a network.

But can all employees contribute content that can generate high reactions and become socially eminent? Probably not. We did not find literature that checks this in the enterprise setting but found a few sites that provide tips on how to contribute in enterprise social applications [4] and many more in public social networks [5, 22,3]. We have seen studies describing how people use blogging within and outside the enterprise [10, 4, 17, 19]. In the context of eminence, Singh et al. [32] examined how to attract more readers to blogs in the enterprise.

3. RESEARCH SETTING AND STUDY

This research was conducted using both qualitative and quantitative research methods. The qualitative part included a set of interviews with top socially eminent employees within the company. The quantitative part consisted of an in-depth investigation of the company's bloggers social behavioral patterns.

3.1 IBM Connections

This research was performed over a dataset of an internal deployment of IBM Connections (Connections) [18] within our company. Connections is an enterprise social networking platform which includes several collaboration applications. The Microblogging application enables writing microblogs (status updates) on your own or someone else's wall. Wikis enable co-editing of web pages, Forums allow discussions of topics and Blogs enable posting of blog posts. The Files application supports uploading and sharing of files. Each application enables commenting and liking of its entries as a means to engage over them. People can be directly addressed by using @mention in the text, which results in an email notification of the mentioned people. Content items, especially microblogs can include hashtags to indicate the topics discussed in the post. Communities enable the inclusion of all above applications in the context of a topic or project. Connections enables inviting other employees into one's network. It also supports following people or content items. Employees are updated through their activity stream or via an email digest on activities of and on their followed people and items. People and content items can be tagged.

The analyses of this paper were performed over a graph populated with all social activities performed within our enterprise in Connections. The data was collected using an API which provides information such as for each item who created it, the people involved, dates and content. During the year preceding this research 453,250 employees performed at least one activity in Connections. Table 1 details the activity across the different applications.

Table 1. Number of Entities and People active last year

Entry Type	Entities created	People active
Blog Posts	449,222	83,491
Forum Topics	283,301	59,043
Wiki Pages	1,018,093	71,400
Microblog Posts	757,049	105,120
Files	3,328,380	153,021

3.2 Interviews

In order to collect tips and best practices on how to become socially eminent through social networks in an enterprise, we conducted a set of interviews. We selected 16 employees who are known to be top socially eminent within our enterprise. Some of them are social evangelists advancing the social platform within the work environment. The interviewees originated from a variety of organizations and geographies.

Out of this set 12 employees agreed to be interviewed. They included 8 males and 4 females from 6 different organizations inside the company. On average they have been working in IBM for 14 years (spanning from 2-25). 5 have customer facing roles, 8 have management roles and the other 4 are regular employees. 5 of the interviewees have started using the enterprise social network in the past 5 years, whereas the others were early adopters and have been socially active inside the enterprise for more than 5 years.

The interviews were conducted face to face or over the phone and lasted 45-60 minutes. An interview consisted of 4 parts. The first included general questions about the employees and their role. The second part focused on their social activity starting point. In particular - when and how they started using the enterprise social network and when they started placing more opinionated content for getting a voice inside the enterprise. The third part focused on their ongoing social behavior meaning how they currently used the rich variety of social applications inside Connections, did they use any special styling to their content? Did they promote their contributions and how? What application generated most reactions to them? The fourth part focused on extracting tips they may have for people that want to get more eminent and on outlining bad practices they have encountered

3.3 Bloggers

In order to quantitatively verify the responses of the interviewees we inspected the set of 41,632 employees who contributed at least one blog entry in the past year into the Connection's Blogs application. This set included employees from 85 countries and all organizations of the company. We decided to focus on bloggers since successful blogging is linked to being reputable [17] or socially eminent.

We divided the bloggers into three groups based on the number of blog entries they posted and the number of comments those received in the past year. This division enabled us to separate between socially eminent bloggers who have gained reputational status from blogging [17] to bloggers that post in similar quantity but whose blogs draw smaller engagement through commenting. As such, we defined the 'eminent' group (EMI) as employees who posted more than 10 blog entries a year that overall received more than 50 comments from others (805). We defined the 'top' group (TOP) as employees who posted more than 10 blog entries a year but got less than 50 comments (3,934). The third group, which we defined as the 'others' group (OTH), included employees who contributed less than 10 blog entries in the past year (36,893).

We extracted a rich set of indicators on these employees' social behavior patterns such as: number of content items they contributed on the variety of social applications, number of comments they replied to, number of @mention they used, etc.

Out of our interviewees 7 classified as EMI, 3 as TOP and 2 do not blog internally.

4. RESULTS

In the following we describe the results of both parts of the study.

4.1 INTERVIEWS

This section includes a qualitative summary of the interviews.

4.1.1 Starting point

When examining what made the interviewees become active in the enterprise social network, we found that all were intrigued by public social networks (e.g., Facebook, Twitter) and also understood the benefit and value a social network can provide them inside the enterprise in terms of the engagement and increased efficiency of their daily work. One interviewee pointed out that he "wanted to enjoy its power inside the enterprise and do social in a professional way". Another who works mainly from home said that he "wanted to use it to better connect to people that were not in the same physical location" as him. They also stated that they enjoyed the feedback they were getting from their readers. This motivated them to increase their activity.

The social applications the interviewees started with were very diverse where the usage of Wikis and Blogs slightly preceded Microblogs, Files and Forums. Some started their social journey inside the enterprise social network directly with 'opinioned' applications such as Blogs and Microblogs. They were already blogging and active in public social networks and found Connections a useful platform for raising and discussing ideas internally with their colleagues. Interestingly, 2/3 of the interviewees specified that they had an internal role model in these early stages which appears to be a good way to start one's social engagement journey.

4.1.2 Ongoing

We wanted to understand how the interviewees use Connections in their day to day work in order to identify various usage patterns that can be further recommended and applied to other employees.

Regarding the usage of applications at the time of the interview compared to when they started, we found out that the usage of the 'opinionated' applications, increased significantly as well as Files, while the use of Wikis dropped. Interviewees specified that most reactions they received originated from three applications: Blogs, Microblogs and Forums. As one person explained, they can "place provocative statements or offer something or ask for help which all generate reactions".

A content item's impact stems from its reach. Hence we investigated how the interviewees overcame one of the main challenges in social networking - attracting readers to their content. We started by checking their use of 'styling' techniques. As can be seen in Figure 1, they specified mostly hashtags, images and @mention. Hashtags related to ease of searching and organizing one's thoughts, images as a way of grabbing the reader's eye or attention and helping one better relate to the content, and @mention for promoting the content to specific people (and their followers).

Other promotion techniques included posting a microblog with a link to the content at relevant locations (such as a community, blog or on one's wall) and tagging the content for easy finding.

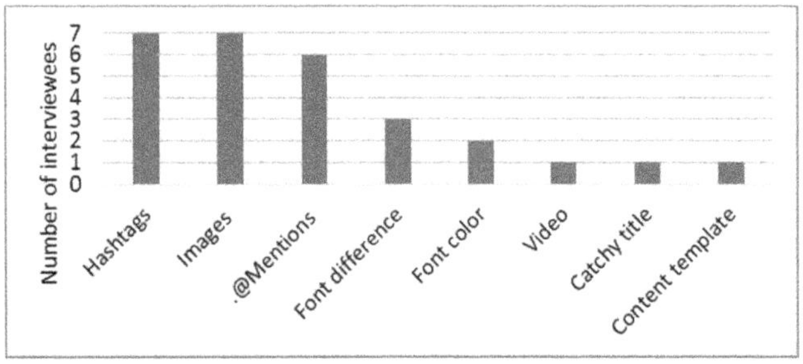

Figure 1. Content 'Styling' techniques

For further eliciting the interviewees' best practices, we asked them to rate the importance of a set of statements in relation to raising their social eminence on a 1-5 Likert scale. The averaged results are presented in Figure 2. From the figure (and also observing the rate distribution) we can conclude the following *recommended* patterns: to be a good social 'citizen' in the enterprise (by responding to comments and liking other's content), to produce quality content and to ensure that it is distributed (through the quality of one's network and mentioning others). Aspects like the time of day or actively promoting one's content got low importance rates. Regarding the latter, most of the interviewees initially claimed they did not promote their content but when they elaborated on how they drew a wider crowd to their content they mentioned various 'promotion' techniques.

4.1.3 *Tips and Recommendations*

In this section we asked for explicit tips and recommendations for raising one's eminence in the enterprise. Each interviewee was asked to provide 5-6 tips which resulted in a variety of responses. We categorized the tips such that each category includes the essence of the recommendations with some details on the most popular tips.

Get a voice. Most of the interviewees specified that contributing meaningful and unique content is crucial for getting a voice. They stressed the importance of first identifying one's 'social identity' by answering questions such as: who you are, what you want to be known for, what you want to say and how you want to position yourself. Only then to start contributing content that fits that identity. In this stage one should experiment with what topics and styles generate more reaction than others. The interviewees emphasized the need to write naturally and be consistent and positive about the way one exposes oneself.

Interestingly, in this context some interviewees stated that where to start contributing content was not so important (e.g., which application or which community). Moreover, the main message was that employees should stop worrying and thinking everything through but should simply "do it!". Recommended methods varied from starting a community, asking questions on other's or one's own wall, writing microblogs and more. Some mentioned that shifting from email to Connections was a good step of becoming more social. They stressed the importance of having an up to date user profile as there is no second chance for a good first impression.

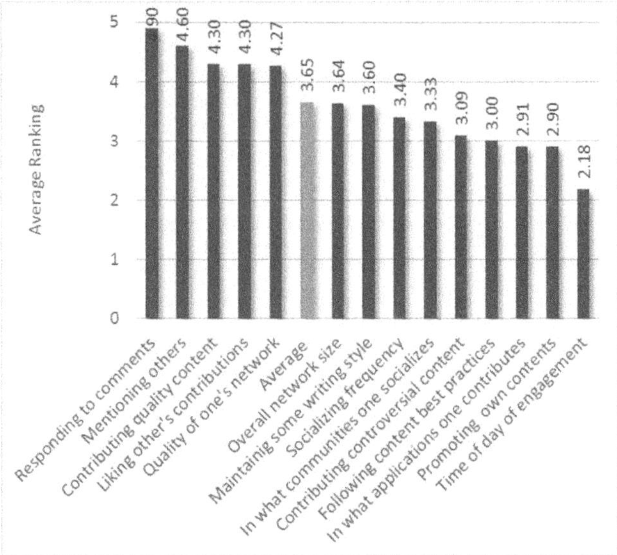

Figure 2. Average rating of importance for raising Social Eminence

Start engaging. In this section two recommendations outran the others. The first was to start by observing and learning other's contributions and responses until gaining confidence and finding one's own writing style. The second was to start the actual engagement with 'passive' methods like liking and sharing other people's content. Interviewees recommended not to be shy and to share information that could interest others while maintaining good quality standards. Some recommended to look at various learning materials such as video snippets and content templates on effective social media usage available online in the company's portal.

Get noticed. Interviewees recommended to search in forums for unanswered questions in one's field of expertise or look for content to contribute that can demonstrate it. Another similar recommendation was to try and identify communities that are of interest in which one can contribute. Others suggested to build a personal landing page (community) to be associated with and contribute one's content to for easier finding. As one person stated "I use blogs to have one point of interaction with my network so they can find my insights easily".

Build and increase your network. About half of the interviewees specified the importance of following interesting people who generate interesting content. Such people could promote oneself in the long run. Other similar tips included adding all co-workers or people with shared interests (e.g., experts on topics one is interested in, leaders in one's field, etc.), to ignore organizational structure and generally use the social applications to interact with anyone one would like. As relationships are built by interacting with people, the more one socializes and responds to other's contributions, the more it increases chances of widening one's network. The importance of monitoring people's feeds for reaching out to a broader network was also suggested. One person stated that "first build a network that you think can help you - overtime you will find yourself helping that network".

Engage with others. Interviewees specified the importance of responding to commenters on one's content as well as "making it a point that you want to hear from others and draw people in by mentioning them and asking questions, and not to socialize for your selfish needs". One interviewee recommended to: "say thank you after getting answers or assistance". Others suggested to use 'like' as an act of appreciation for interesting or useful content and on comments others wrote on one's own contributions.

In addition to general tips for raising one's social eminence we also asked interviewees to provide tips on how to mature from certain limiting socializing patterns.

No readers to one's blog. About half of the interviewees recommended to try to promote one's blog entries by posting links to those on other people's walls and asking for their opinion on the content. Others recommended to take the time and find the right channel to publish (e.g., finding a relevant community). Many interviewees also specified the importance of promoting one's content to relevant people using @mention from within a blog as a way of drawing their (and their followers) attention to it. They recommended mentioning, only when applicable, relevant experts/influencers or people with whom one has shared interests or could be interested in the content. As a rule of thumb "If you cannot find anyone you want to mention rethink if your content is valuable ". Part of the interviewees recommended to take the time to investigate the reasons for not attracting readers to one's content by consulting others or finding the differences to similar blogs. They also suggested to promote the blog by placing a comment pointing to it in other relevant blogs.

Don't know what to say. This situation is common for people who are in their initial socializing attempts. They might either feel they cannot contribute any valuable insight or are shy to do so. Interviewees recommended to look for topics that may be valuable for other people. They suggested identifying such topics by answering question such as: what do you do or are working on, what do you know, what have you discovered, what questions come to you often (e.g. from your team). Some suggested to also look what similar people are contributing to get ideas. Others suggested to start by sharing content in Connections one would otherwise have sent in email. One person suggested not to "start with a long and thoughtful provoking blog" but rather with microblogs and then progress to something bigger.

Using the social network for file storage only. This situation is not optimal as without using other social applications employees are missing the opportunity to draw more employees to their content. Interviewees recommended to promote files contributed via microblogs that include a reference to the file. To those who find this difficult they recommended to use templates like "This file is about ... You may want to read it as it ..."). Such microblogs have high chance of starting a conversation. Others recommended that instead of sharing a file (with a link) via email to contribute the same descriptive content in Connections as a microblog or comment. Another recommended to write a blog entry that mentions the content of the file and spice it up with more details such as the work that lead to it.

4.1.4 Bad Practices

We tried to identify bad practices or habits the interviewees encountered to understand what behavioral patterns to avoid as they might reduce ones social eminence. The top bad practice mentioned by half of the interviewees was spamming. One person said "don't spam, over-engage or post for the sake of posting" as this behavior can withdraw people from reading and engaging with employees thus lowering their eminence in the long run. The second most specified bad practice was being unprofessional with people one socializes with. This includes using abusive/aggressive tone in comments, not respecting other's content, and contributing angry or complaining posts. Many interviewees also complained about situations where people responded off-topic, shifting the discussion from its main route. Other bad practices included: mentioning too many people, telling people to like one's blog, not responding to feedback or @mention, and writing flattery comments to executives.

4.2 Bloggers' Behavioral Patterns

We set out to validate the results of the interviews through analysis of the behavioral patterns of different blogger populations (as described in section 3.3). This was done by extracting different data sets on their social behavior patterns and investigating the differences between the groups using various statistical methods. Significance tests between the groups were performed through one way Anova with post hoc comparisons using the Games-Howell.

4.2.1 Application usage.

We first checked which social applications are most or least used by the bloggers population. We quantified the bloggers' textual contributions in each social application by accumulating of the number of content items and comments they created in the last year. 53% of the bloggers used all social applications at least once, 73% used Files and Wikis while Microblogging was used by only about 54% of the bloggers. Figure 3 shows application usage for the three groups we defined. EMI's lowest is Wikis with 74% and the highest (apart of Blogs) is Microblogs with 89%. When comparing EMI to TOP, more EMI use Microblogs (89% vs 72%). Similar levels exist for Forums and Wikis. The opposite can be seen in Files where more TOP use the Files application than the other groups. Thus we conclude that eminent employees use mostly (along with Blogs) Microblogs, Files and then Forum, and less Wikis. This is aligned with the interview findings.

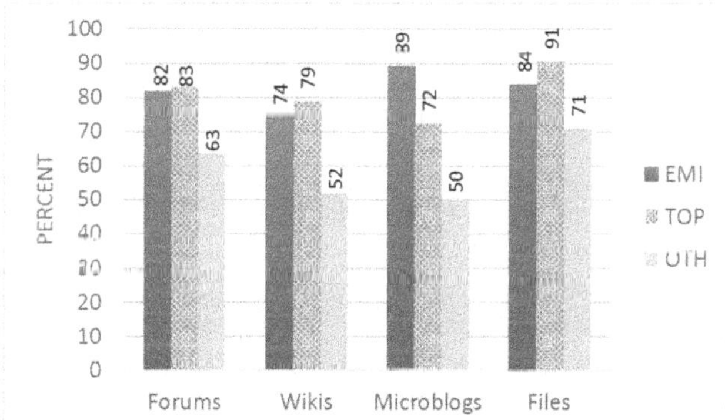

Figure 3. Social Application Usage Percentage

For the entire blogger population all applications are used above average by about 20% thus 80% use them below the average level. Figure 4 shows the percentage of users who used each application above its average usage for the three groups. When comparing EMI to TOP both have similar usage levels of Blogs (above 95%) and Forums (above 41%). The largest difference is in Microblogs where 62% of EMI and only 38% of TOP use it above average. This result strengthens the difference between eminent and less eminent employees as they also microblog more. Only 43% of EMI use Files above average. We assume this is because they feel more comfortable to share their knowledge through blogging.

When examining the significance of the quantity of activities in each social application we found in relation to Microblogs and Blogs applications a significant effect between all groups with p

<.001. For the other applications we found a significance p<0.001 only between EMI to OTH and TOP to OTH but not between EMI to TOP who behave similarly in those applications. The F values are reported in Table 2.

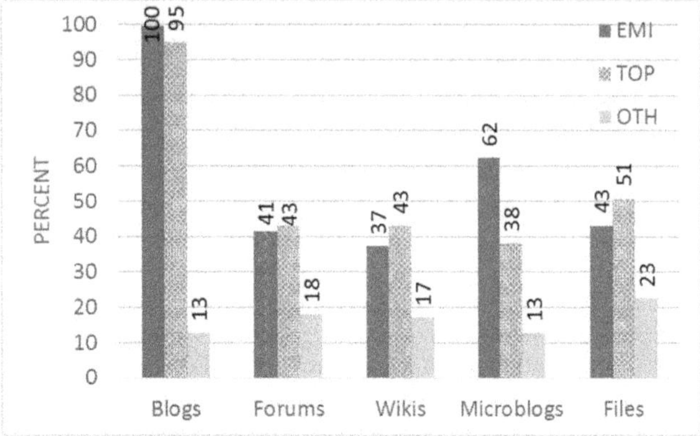

Figure 4. Percentage of Above Average Application Usage

We then analyzed which social applications generate most reaction for the bloggers by summing up the number of likes and comments to their contributions in the different applications and selecting the one with the highest count. Figure 5 shows the percentage of employees that had most reactions per application. As expected from eminent bloggers 90% of EMI got most reactions from their blogs. Only 4% of them got most reactions from Microblogs and 6% from Forums. When comparing this to TOP we see that 58% of them got most reactions from Blogs whereas 24% got most reactions from Forums and 10% from Microblogs.

Table 2. F values of Average Application Usage

	F(2, 41626)
Blogs	10704.01
Forums	331.56
Wikis	390.86
Micro-blogs	338.7
Files	571.61

4.2.2 Behavioral patterns

In the interviews we asked interviewees' opinion on the importance of various behavioral patterns for raising one's eminence inside the enterprise. Following their ordering of the items raised we checked whether eminent employees indeed follow these behavioral patterns and whether others follow them in similar magnitude.

A. Responding to comments

In order to check if eminent bloggers follow the recommendation to respond to comments we first compared the percentage of the bloggers who received comments on their blog entries and responded to those. As can be seen in Table 7 87% of EMI responded to at least one comment on their own blogs. We were surprised to see that only 65% of TOP did so and only 35% of OTH. We expected TOP to have a similar percentage as EMI as they wrote similar amount of blog entries and we would expect them to interact with their audience as well. This emphasizes that 35% of TOP are missing opportunities to engage with people who took time and responded to their contributions. This is one of the most important behaviors eminent employees highlighted in the interviews.

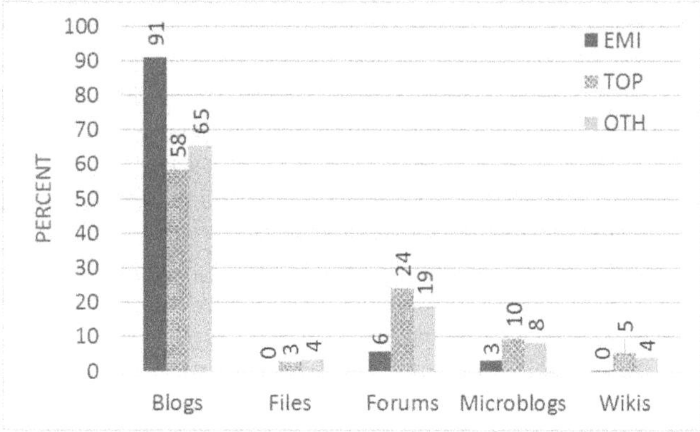

Figure 5. Social Application with Top Reaction Percentage

Table 3. Percentage of Responding to Comments

	EMI	TOP	OTH
Responded to comments	87	65	35

In order to further inspect the difference between the groups we measured the ratio between the numbers of comments employees received to the number of comments they placed on their blog entries. We examined this only for those who responded at least once. We found a significant effect p <.001 F(2, 7509)=104.54 between EMI to TOP and EMI to OTH with high variance explained as partial Eta squared 0.536. Interestingly, there was no significant effect between TOP and OTH as p=0.94.

A2. Liking other's comments

We also inspected if and how bloggers use 'like' as a way of acknowledging people who commented on their blogs. We computed the percentage of employees from each group that gave at least one 'like' on blog comments others placed on their blog. As can be seen in Table 4, 76% of EMI have 'liked' comments that others placed on their blogs whereas only 39% of TOP did so.

Table 4. Percentage of 'Liking' Other's Comments

	EMI	TOP	OTH
'liked' a response	76	39	24

We then measured the ratio between the numbers of 'likes' employees gave to comments others placed on their blog entries to the number of blog comments their blogs received. We included only employees that 'liked' at least one response. We found a significant effect p <.001, F(2, 5049)=387.3 between all groups with a high variance explained via partial Eta squared 0.636.

B. Mentioning others

In order to check how employees use @mention we compared the three groups in two manners: the number of times each employee used it and the average number of @mention employees did per microblog they wrote. As can be seen in Table 5, overall 71% of EMI used @mention at least once compared to only 41% of TOP and 19% of OTH. For the amount of @mention, 58% of EMI did more than average amount of @mention which drops to 26% for TOP and 9% for OTH. Interestingly enough EMI did on average 67 @mention a year while TOP did 15 and OTH only 4. We examined the significance between the groups and saw a significant effect between all groups with p <.001 F(2, 9103)= 231.5.

Table 5. Percentage of @mention

	EMI	TOP	OTH
Used @mention	71	41	19
Used @mention more than average	58	26	9

To inspect this further, we looked at how many employees use @mention more than the average number of @mention per microblog. Results can be seen in Table 6. We found similar behavior indicating that EMI use @mention per microblog much more than the other groups.

Table 6. More than Average @mention Usage per Entry

	EMI	TOP	OTH
@mention usage per microblog above average	46	20	11

C. Network

Our interviewees stressed many times the importance of having a quality network and following the right set of people. To better understand if EMI invest in building a network we compared the groups' network indicators.

Figure 6 shows the means of three indicators of the employee networks: overall network size, number of followers, and number of followed people. It strongly highlights that on average EMI have a much larger network, they follow many more people and indeed have many more followers than employees from the other groups. Moreover, on average they have 6.25 times more followers than TOP employees. This emphasizes their eminent role in the company.

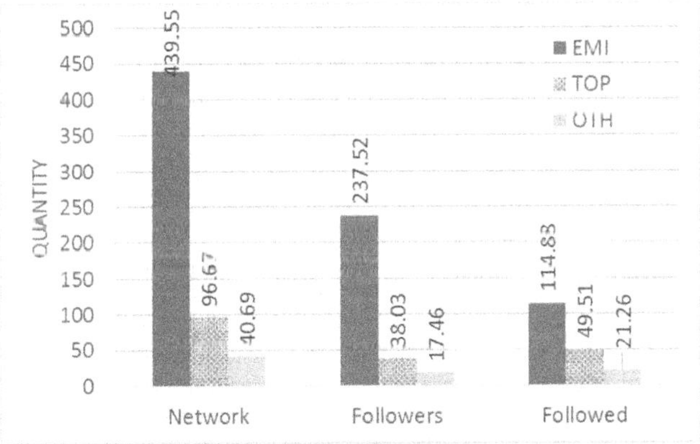

Figure 6. Network Size

We examined the significance of the three indicators between the groups and found significant effect p<.001 between all groups for all and that large part of the variance explained. For network F(2, 41629)= 931.675 and partial eta squared 0.211. For followers F(2, 41629)=3508.723 and partial eta squared 0.217. For followed people F(2, 41629)=931.675 and partial eta squared of 0.11.

D. Time of day of the engagement

One of the items interviewees mentioned as not important for raising one's eminence was the time and day they engage. We found this interesting as some studies showed that in public social networks it is important to engage at certain time periods [21].

To examine this we inspected two things: engagement level per week day and throughout the day. When looking at the average engagement level throughout the week we saw similar results across the groups as can be seen in Figure 7. Monday seems most active for all with an average of over 24% of social activity. The other working days have about 14% activity, while the least is about 2% on Saturday. Monday and Sunday have most variance between the groups. EMI are more active on Sundays than the others (16% vs 12%) whereas they are less active on Mondays (24% vs 28%).

We found significance < 0.01 between all groups for Sunday and Monday. On Tuesday and Wednesday there was significance<0.01 between TOP and OTH only. On the rest of the days there was no significant difference between the groups

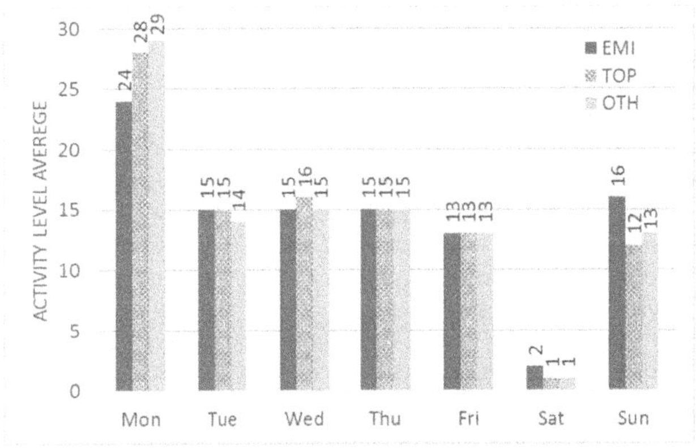

Figure 7. Activity Level by Day of Week

To investigate engagement throughout the day we divided the day into 8 three hour segments. Figure 8 shows the average activity level per time segment. There are slight differences between the groups among all periods. We examined the significance and saw p <0.003 between EMI and TOP, and EMI and OTH between 0-3AM and 3-6AM. We saw p <0.001 between EMI and TOP between 6-9AM. Between 6-9PM we found p <0.037 between all. There was no significance in the rest of the periods.

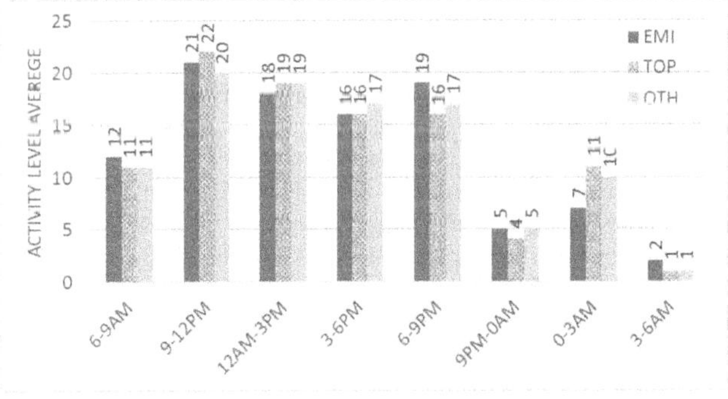

Figure 8. Activity Level by Hour of Day

5. DISCUSSION

In this paper we investigated the behavior of top socially eminent employees in an enterprise internal social network system in order to extract tips and best practices that can help other employees raise their social eminence. This is important both from the employee's and from the enterprise's perspective as being more socially eminent can raise employees' engagement levels.

In the interviews we investigated how socially eminent employees got to their role and what they did to maintain it. When inspecting how they started to be social in the enterprise it was clear that they understood the benefit and value it can give them inside the enterprise and thus decided to invest time in it. The feedback they were getting from their readers motivated them to increase their activity over time. In their early socializing days, they used a rich set of social applications but over time they narrowed the set to mainly more 'opinionated' applications such as Blogs and Microblogs, along with Files. When we inspected what applications eminent bloggers (EMI) use most we also found that they mostly use Blogs, Microblogs, Files and less Forums and Wikis. We saw that EMI use the 'opinionated' applications significantly more than the other groups but for the other applications there is no significance between EMI and TOP. Not surprisingly, our interviewees stated only Blogs, Microblogs and Files (where Blogs was highest) as social applications that generated most reaction to them which was also verified for EMI. Thus we conclude that in order to be eminent one should start by gaining confidence and contributing more opinionated content. We found it interesting that 2/3 of the interviewees had a role model in their early socializing stage from which they learned or fine-tuned how to become more socially eminent.

When discussing their ongoing social behavior, we learned that socially eminent employees have adopted different 'styling' techniques such as using hashtags, images and @mention. They recommended employees to identify their 'social identity' which includes, among others, testing what styles generate more reaction for them. They also stated that @mention was a useful content promotion technique that can draw people to their content.

In one of the questions we aimed to get the socially eminent interviewees' opinion on the importance of various behavioral patterns for raising one's eminence inside the company. The most recommended patterns were: to produce quality content, to ensure that it is distributed widely, to invest time in building a quality network and to be reciprocal and most importantly to be responsive by responding to comments and liking other's content. To verify their input we set out to check whether EMI employees indeed follow the highly ranked patterns and whether less eminent employees use it less. We first checked if EMI respond to comments others wrote on their content. We found that 87% of EMI responded to at least one comment but only 65% of TOP and 35% of OTH. For the ratio between the number of comments they received to the number of responses they placed we found a significant difference (with high variance explained) between EMI to TOP and also to OTH. Interestingly, there was no significance between TOP and OTH. For the usage of 'like' over other's contributions on one's content, we likewise found that most EMI have 'liked' comments that others placed on their blogs whereas less than half of TOP did so. We measured the ratio between the number of 'likes' they did on other's comments on their blogs to the number of comments others placed. We found a significant effect between all groups with high variance explained. Thus we conclude that eminent employees understand the importance of reacting to contributions over their content and thus dedicate the time to react- if through a comment response or a gratitude 'like'- and that indeed less eminent employees do not follow this recommendation enough.

In our investigation, we also examined if EMI indeed mention others in their content. We found that most EMI use @mention but more than half of TOP and one fifth of the OTH population do not. Moreover, EMI do much more mentions per entry on average than TOP employees. Our analysis showed significant effect between all groups. These results emphasize that socially eminent employees indeed use @mention more than the others as recommended.

Interviewees stressed the importance of having a quality network and following the right set of people. In order to check whether socially eminent employees indeed invest in building a network, we compared the means of the networks and saw that on average EMI have a much larger network, they follow many more people and indeed have many more followers than employees from the other groups. In particular, they have on average 6.25 times more followers than TOP employees. This verifies their eminent role in the company. Not surprisingly, when examining the significance of the three indicators between the groups we found a significant effect between all and high portion of the variance explained. It is important to point out that interviewees emphasized that the quality of the network is more important that its size.

The least important pattern, according to the interviewees, was the time of day in which they use the social applications. When looking at the activity levels during different week days we found that EMI are more active on Sundays than others whereas they are less active on Mondays. We assume this is because EMI are more devoted to social activity and thus do so also on weekends and then have less to 'catch-up' on Mondays. We continued this investigation when inspecting the level of engagement throughout the day. We saw that between 6-9PM EMI are a bit more active than the rest. We found significance between EMI and TOP between 6-9AM and between all groups at 6-9PM. There was no significance in the rest of the periods. From this we conclude that there may be minor differences between the groups where socially eminent employees do more social activity over part of the weekend and perhaps stretch a bit more the social activity at the start and end of the working day.

Another topic we found interesting in the interviews was that the pattern "promoting your content" got a relatively low score from the interviewees although such techniques were mentioned by many when they were asked to provide tips. We suspect that the words "self-promotion" may have caused some negative vibes that make it harder for people to relate to it, or that they don't consider the things they mentioned as self-promotion but rather socializing over their content and exposing it to more people.

In the tips section we got many interesting recommendations which we organized under the following categories: get a voice, start engaging, get noticed, building and increasing the network, and engaging with others. Interestingly enough, although we did not define any specific category of recommendations and we asked for 5-6 top recommendations, we saw many repetitions, some by more than half of the interviewees. Few examples include, contributing meaningful and unique content, finding your social identity, not to be shy and to share information that could interest others while maintaining good quality standards. We also collected a set of bad practices where the most mentioned ones were spamming or being unprofessional with people one socializes with.

Throughout our bloggers analysis we found the comparison between the behavioral patterns of the EMI to TOP and TOP to OTH groups insightful. TOP are employees who contribute similar amounts of content to EMI but have a difference in the amount of engagement they get over their contributions. In interviews we saw that socially eminent employees emphasize the importance of reacting and interacting with people and engaging over their content. This was emphasized in the analysis where we saw that EMI indeed engage more with their audience via responding to comments, liking other's contributions, mentioning, etc. Moreover, for responding to comments there was no significant difference between TOP and OTH. Thus we conclude that to be eminent and maintain your eminent role you need to dedicate time to engage back with your content readers. We believe that the recommendations given by the socially eminent employees can be of great value for TOP-like employees as they have already overcome the content contribution obstacle.

In this paper we did not inspect additional collaboration platforms that exist in the enterprise, such as email, software development tools, and more. These platforms also generate social traces and they contribute to eminence as well. This is open for future work.

Some employees in the enterprise are expected to extensively use the internal social network as part of their role description. These employees can be perceived as socially eminent although sometimes their social activity stems mainly from their job requirements. Our interviews included employees whose job role did not require them to be socially active by definition. Interestingly, as they got aware of the social networks' benefits they decided to adopt it and even spread the word to their peers.

6. CONCLUSIONS AND FUTURE WORK

In this study we answered our research questions through a set of interviews with top socially eminent employees in our enterprise social network and a quantitative inspection of different blogger sets behavioral patterns.

This study provides several contributions. First, it is a first of a kind research that reveals insights into a spectrum of social behavioral patterns of socially eminent employees. We learned that socially eminent employees follow various social behavioral patterns that help them better engage with their audience. They build and maintain their social identity by using different styling techniques, they contribute and get most reactions in more 'opinionated' applications such as Blogs and Microblogs, and they understand the value and thus take the time to interact with their content readers and maintain a large network. They enjoy getting feedback from their readers which in turn motivates them to increase their activity. Many had a social role model in their early socializing stages.

Secondly the study shows that socially eminent employees indeed engage differently from other less eminent employees. We show this by inspecting a set of behavioral patterns that interviewees stated as important for raising ones social eminence and comparing eminent and less socially eminent employees some of which have similar activity volumes but are less successful in gaining their eminent role.

Third this research provides a rich set of tips and best practices that if followed can help interested employees increase their social eminence inside the enterprise. The set was built from tips and best practices that were mentioned several times by different interviewees. The latter is very important for both the employees and the enterprise. On the one hand, it can help employees who want to raise their voice inside the enterprise do so with less frustrations and higher success. On the other hand, as they become more socially eminent their engagement increases which is of interest to the company as it can help drive its success.

While our research is limited to a single company using a single social network system, we believe our findings are of importance to other research, social application developers and of course for employees who want to raise their social eminence.

In the future we plan to widen this research by interviewing additional socially eminent experts from other companies who use the same and/or different enterprise social applications to understand if and which of these results are company or system specific. We would also like to compare these results to studies on how socially eminent employees engage in public social networks.

We plan to build, based on the extracted tips and best practices, an innovative personal recommendation system to help employees become more socially eminent in the enterprise.

7. REFERENCES

[1] Agichtein, E., Castillo, C., Donato, D., Gionis, A., & Mishne, G. 2008. Finding high-quality content in social media. In *Proceedings of the 2008 International Conference on Web Search and Data Mining* (pp. 183-194). ACM.

[2] Balakrishna, V., Browning, S., Gordon, J and Trevor, S. 2014. Aligning Social Collaboration with Business Objectives. Whitepaper. Intel Corp. http://www.intel.com/content/dam/www/public/us/en/documents/white-papers/aligning-social-collaboration-with-business-objectives-paper.pdf

[3] Baldoni, J. 2013. Employee Engagement Does More than Boost Productivity. *Harvard Business Review* (Jul. 2013).

[4] Banford, B. and Dobbertin, K. in Blogging 2.0 – How Blogs Increase Collaboration. Xerox. February 2012. https://enterprisematters.blogs.xerox.com/2012/02/23/blogging-2-0-how-blogs-increase-collaboration/#.VpeVs0aBRpE

[5] BloggingTips.com site. http://www.bloggingtips.com/

[6] Chen, B.C., Guo J., Tseng, B., & Yang, J. 2011. User reputation in a comment rating environment. Proc. KDD'11, 159-167.

[7] Chin, C. P. Y., Evans, N., Choo, R. K. K., & Tan, F. B. 2015. What Influences Employees to Use Enterprise Social Networks? A Socio-Technical Perspective.

[8] De Choudhury, M., & Counts, S. 2013. Understanding affect in the workplace via social media. In *Proceedings of the 2013 conference on Computer supported cooperative work* (pp. 303-316). ACM.

[9] Drakos, N., and Gotta, M. Gartner report: Boost Employee Engagement With Social Technologies in the Digital Workplace. 2015. https://www.gartner.com/doc/3024425/boost-employee-engagement-social-technologies

[10] Ehrlich, K., & Shami, N. S. 2010. Microblogging Inside and Outside the Workplace. In *ICWSM 2010*.

[11] Ehrlich, K., Muller, M., Matthews, T., Guy, I., & Ronen, I. 2014. What motivates members to contribute to enterprise online communities?. In *Proceedings of the companion publication of the 17th ACM conference on Computer supported cooperative work & social computing* (pp. 149-152). ACM.

[12] Google. Working better together, June 2015. https://lp.google-mkto.com/rs/248-TPC-286/images/Google_WorkingBetterTogether_June-15.PDF

[13] Gou, L., Zhou, M. X., & Yang, H. 2014. Knowme and shareme: Understanding automatically discovered personality traits from social media and user sharing preferences. In *Proceedings of the SIGCHI Conference on Human Factors in Computing Systems* (pp. 955-964). ACM.

[14] Harter, J. K., Schmidt, F. L., & Hayes, T. L. 2002. Business-unit-level relationship between employee satisfaction, employee engagement, and business outcomes: a meta-analysis. *Journal of applied psychology*, *87*(2), 268.

[15] Harter, J. K., Schmidt, F. L., & Keyes, C. L. 2003. Well-being in the workplace and its relationship to business

outcomes: A review of the Gallup studies. *Flourishing: Positive psychology and the life well-lived*, 2, 205-224.

[16] Holtzblatt, L., Drury, J. L., Weiss, D., Damianos, L. E., & Cuomo, D. 2013. Evaluating the uses and benefits of an enterprise social media platform. *Journal of Social Media for Organizations*, *1*(1), 1

[17] Huang, Y., Singh, P. V., & Ghose, A. 2015. A structural model of employee behavioral dynamics in enterprise social media. *Management Science*, *61*(12), 2825-2844.

[18] IBM Connections: http://www-03.ibm.com/software/products/en/conn

[19] Jackson, A., Yates, J., & Orlikowski, W. 2007. Corporate Blogging: Building community through persistent digital talk. In *System Sciences, 2007. HICSS 2007. 40th Annual Hawaii International Conference on* (pp. 80-80). IEEE.

[20] Jacovi, M., Guy, I., Kremer-Davidson, S., Porat, S., & Aizenbud-Reshef, N. 2014. The perception of others: inferring reputation from social media in the enterprise. In *Proceedings of the 17th ACM conference on Computer supported cooperative work & social computing* (pp. 756-766). ACM.

[21] Kevan, L. 2015. The Biggest Social Science Study: What 4.8 Million Tweets Say About the Best Time to Tweet. In buffersocial blog. https://blog.bufferapp.com/best-time-to-tweet-research

[22] King, C. In SocialMedia Examiner site. 39 Blogging Tips From the Pros. March 2014. http://www.socialmediaexaminer.com/39-blogging-tips/

[23] Kruse, K. 2012. Employee Engagement Research (Master List of 32 Findings). *KEVIN KRUSE* (Sep. 2012).

[24] Mark, G., Iqbal, S. T., Czerwinski, M., & Johns, P. 2014. Bored mondays and focused afternoons: The rhythm of attention and online activity in the workplace. In *Proceedings of the SIGCHI Conference on Human Factors in Computing Systems* (pp. 3025-3034). ACM.

[25] Mark, G., Guy, I., Kremer-Davidson, S., & Jacovi, M. 2014. Most liked, fewest friends: Patterns of enterprise social media use. In *Proceedings of the 17th ACM conference on Computer supported cooperative work & social computing* (pp. 393-404). ACM.

[26] Markos, S., & Sridevi, M. S. 2010. Employee engagement: The key to improving performance. *International Journal of Business and Management*, *5*(12), 89.

[27] Merriam-Webster Dictionary. http://www.merriam-webster.com/dictionary/eminent

[28] Neeli, B. K. 2012. A method to engage employees using gamification in BPO industry. In *Services in Emerging Markets (ICSEM), 2012 Third International Conference on* (pp. 142-146). IEEE.

[29] Ortega, F. J., Troyano, J. A., Cruz, F. L., Vallejo, C. G., & Enríquez, F. (2012). Propagation of trust and distrust for the detection of trolls in a social network. Computer Networks, 56(12), 2884-2895

[30] Pothineni, D., Mishra, P., Rasheed, A., & Sundararajan, D. 2014. Incentive design to mould online behavior: a game mechanics perspective. In *Proceedings of the First International Workshop on Gamification for Information Retrieval* (pp. 27-32). ACM.

[31] Saks, A. M. 2006. Antecedents and consequences of employee engagement. *Journal of managerial psychology*, *21*(7), 600-619.

[32] Shami, N. S., Yang, J., Panc, L., Dugan, C., Ratchford, T., Rasmussen, J. C., & Geyer, W. 2014. Understanding employee social media chatter with enterprise social pulse. In *Proceedings of the 17th ACM conference on Computer supported cooperative work & social computing* (pp. 379-392). ACM.

[33] Singh, P. V., Sahoo, N., & Mukhopadhyay, T. 2014. How to Attract and Retain Readers in Enterprise Blogging?. *Information Systems Research*, *25*(1), 35-52.

[34] Sun, J. & Tang, J. A survey of models and algorithms for social influence analysis. 2011. Charu C. Aggarwal, editor, Social Network Data Analytics, chapter 7, 2011, 177-214.

[35] Thom, J., Millen, D., & DiMicco, J. 2012. Removing gamification from an enterprise SNS. In *Proceedings of the ACM 2012 conference on Computer Supported Cooperative Work* (pp. 1067-1070). ACM.

[36] Tips on how to Be A successful Blogger. https://www.wattpad.com/32822018-tips-on-how-to-be-a-successful-blogger

[37] Trees, L. 2015. Encouraging millennials to collaborate and learn on the job. *Strategic HR Review*, *14*(4), 118-123.

[38] Yu, D., and Harter, J. 2013. In US, Engaged Employees Exercise More, Eat Healthier. (2013).

Exploring Trust and Cooperation Development with Agent-Based Simulation in A Pseudo Scale-free Network

Yi Wang*
IBM Almaden Research Center
San Jose, CA, USA
wangyi@us.ibm.com

David Redmiles
Department of Informatics
University of California, Irvine, CA, USA
redmiles@ics.uci.edu

ABSTRACT

Globally distributed collaboration requires cooperation and trust among team members. Current research suggests that informal, non-work related communication plays a positive role in developing cooperation and trust. However, the way in which teams connect, i.e. via a social network, greatly influences cooperation and trust development. The study described in this paper employs agent-based modeling and simulation to investigate the cooperation and trust development with the presence of informal, non-work-related communication in networked teams. Leveraging game theory, we present a model of how an individual makes strategic decisions when interacting with her social network neighbors. The results of simulation on a pseudo scale-free network reveal the conditions under which informal communication has an impact, how different network degree distributions affect efficient trust and cooperation development, and how it is possible to "seed" trust and cooperation development amongst individuals in specific network positions. This study is the first to use agent-based modeling and simulation to examine the relationships between scale-free networks' topological features (degree distribution), cooperation and trust development, and informal communication.

CCS Concepts

•**Human-centered computing → Computer supported cooperative work;** *Social networks;*

Keywords

Cheap talk; cooperation; trust; distributed collaboration; pseudo scale-free network; agent-based modeling and simulation; game theory

1. INTRODUCTION

Understanding cooperation and trust development in distributed working environments is a central pursuit for CSCW researchers (e.g., [1, 30, 31, 39, 59]). Amongst many factors, informal, non-work related communications play a role in facilitating cooperation and trust development. Indeed, the literature on this theme has provided rich evidence and explanation for advocating informal communication's use in globally distributed collaboration [14, 28, 38, 54]. Our prior work has begun to view informal, non-work related communications as a strategic interaction behavior [51, 52, 53], borrowing the Economic literature concept "cheap talk" [18] to conceptualize it. We continue to use this notion in this paper. Compared with the previous work mentioned above [51, 52, 53], this paper is particularly focusing on the role of "cheap talk" in the context of networks with specific topological attributes.

Cooperation and trust develop in the context of a social network. However, researchers often do not pay sufficient, explicit attention to social networks' impacts on people's behavioral adaptation in distributed collaboration [6, 7, 28]. Social network analysis researchers tend to focus more on extracting structural features of empirical networks, such as online communities (e.g., [56]) or social media networks (e.g., [33]), and adapting them to network models. Although CSCW researchers widely acknowledge digital social networks' power to spread behavioral adaptations, they rarely investigate how specific networks differently affect individuals' behavior [2]. Consequently, how informal communication and network features together shape cooperation and trust development remains unclear. Therefore, it is necessary to examine, in a unified framework, the relationships amongst a network's topological features, cooperation and trust development, and informal communication (cheap talk).

We aim to develop theoretical insights into network features' role in cooperation and trust development with the presence of cheap talk. More specifically, we focus on a scale-free network[1] [4], which is perhaps the most widely reported real world network structure [10, 48] and also allows the emergence of trust and cooperation. To our knowledge, no other study investigates scale-free network cooperation and trust development, particularly accounting for the effects of cheap talk. Leveraging game theory, we developed a decision model to describe agents' strategic choices, and then simulated their strategic decision-making dynamics. In the simulation experiment, we controlled the scale-free network degree exponential in order to establish the relationship between a scale-free network's degree distribution, and cooperation and trust development with cheap talk. This is the first attempt to link degree distribution with dynamic cooperation and trust development processes. Literature has shown that "seeding" (i.e., initiating behavioral changes) amongst a small fraction of individuals at hub positions may trigger behavioral change cascades (e.g., [3]). Ex-

*The work was done while the author was at Department of Informatics in University of California, Irvine.

[1]In this study, we actually focus on "pseudo scale-free network," the detailed explanation is in 4.1.2.

GROUP '16, November 13-16, 2016, Sanibel Island, FL, USA
© 2016 ACM. ISBN 978-1-4503-4276-6/16/11... $15.00
DOI: http://dx.doi.org/10.1145/2957276.2957305

amining our simulation data would help us identify whether any specific seeding strategy promotes scale-free network cooperation and trust development.

Since cheap talk proves to be a useful way to promote cooperation and trust development in general cases [52], our first research question follows:

RQ1: Does cheap talk positively impact a scale-free network's cooperation and trust development?

If cheap talk's positive role could be confirmed, we would then want to examine two specific aspects of network impacts: degree distribution and seeding strategy. Hence, we express the second research question as the following two sub-questions:

RQ2-1: Given the presence of cheap talk, how do scale-free networks' degree distributions influence cooperation and trust development?

RQ2-2: Given the presence of cheap talk, what are the different seeding strategies' impacts on cooperation and trust development?

Three main results emerge from our modeling and simulations. First, we find that cheap talk has positive impacts on cooperation and trust development. Although there are simulation instances that fail to achieve cooperation, group cooperation was established in the majority of simulation instances (72.62%). Second, scale-free networks of different degree distributions yield differing effectiveness and efficiency when it comes to cooperation and trust development. Third, hub position seeding leads to improved cooperation and trust development effectiveness and efficiency. This effect's significance increases when degree distribution is more uneven (i.e. a few individuals have many friends, while the majority have one friend).

Summarizing our contributions, our study represents the attempt of employing agent-based modeling and simulation to link two research streams: cooperation and trust development with cheap talk, and network analysis. Understanding network features' cooperation and trust development role, with the presence of cheap talk, provides both theoretical and practical implications. Theoretically, it helps develop both micro- and macro-level understandings of distributed collaboration when there are multiple social factors. Practically, it provides guidelines for designing and engineering an organizational network that facilitates cooperation and trust development with limited resources. For example, our results indicate "seeding" a cooperative strategy in specific hub positions would help to quicken the establishment of group-wide cooperation norms. Policymakers looking for low-cost efficiency and effectiveness improvement could leverage this knowledge by identifying key individuals for initial cooperation and trust development.

2. BACKGROUND

In this section, we briefly review related literature focusing on two streams: first, cheap talk's role in cooperation and trust development, which provides rich empirical evidence and insights for individual decision-making and behavior; and second, social network analysis, which suggests that structural network features may influence distributed collaboration. Although information communication's role and social networks have been intensively studied, each has developed as a distinct research stream. The literature review leads us to believe that linking these two streams will help understand how cheap talk in networked organizations impacts cooperation and trust development.

2.1 Cooperation and Trust Development with Cheap Talk

The concept of cheap talk emerged from Economics literature [18]. It refers the ordinary, informal, non-work-related talks. While cheap talk does not incur any cost, it also does not directly affect the participants' payoff. There are many instances of cheap talk in CSCW, for example, sharing a funny picture via Facebook messenger with a friend in another country. Although the formal concept of *cheap talk* was just recently introduced to CSCW research communities in [51], a great amount of non-work social workplace interaction literature exists in CSCW. These social interactions are usually conceptualized using terms such as "socialization" [13], "small talk" [8, 46], and "water cooler" [24], and their importance has been noted in [14]. In their qualitative study of a Danish/Indian global software team, Dittrich and Giuffrida [13] identified socialization as one of four IM usage dimensions. They found that a few of the *Skype* chats were purely social, and argued that informal communications provide a trust and social relationship building channel. Similar results were also reported by Cramton and Hinds [11], who argued that casual interactions smoothed cooperation among individuals from three different cultures. In literature such as [58], the authors also show that informal communication helps maintain a sense of connectedness.

These studies established our understanding of informal interaction's importance in maintaining social collaboration relationships, which under-emphasizes work-related information exchange [38]. Recently, researchers began to take another perspective, viewing "informal communication" as a kind of strategic behavior [51]. Compared with traditional social relationship-focused research, the strategic view enables the description, reasoning, and prediction of individual behavior adaptation. For example, [51] presents a game theory model to explain and predict how cheap talk facilitates cooperation and trust development, as well as the conditions ensuring cheap talk's positive impact.

2.2 Network Analysis of Collaboration

Social networks are vital precisely because "no man is an island." Social networks support various distributed collaboration activities, such as information sharing, identifying potential collaborators, and team coordination. There are many studies in CSCW applying social network analysis to the study of different distributed collaborations. For example, Farcooq et al. [17] suggested that displaying network diagrams of researchers who use similar queries in Citeseer helps identify potential collaborators and research communities. Another example applied structural social network metrics to "breaking-news" Wikipedia article revisions, characterizing article editorial pattern [29]. These studies greatly improve our understanding of distributed collaborations. For a more comprehensive review, please refer to [22]. There are also a few studies using controlled experiments to study how cooperation develops given certain specific network structural features [20]. Similar to our work, Suri et al. [49] focused on cooperation and trust development dynamics. They reported a series of web-based experiment in which subjects repetitively played public goods game[2]. They showed that seeding cooperation did not significantly improve cooperation development, which challenges long-held research beliefs. However, their study was limited to a relatively small network (24 nodes) as well as the use of public goods game. Public goods game is an N-person prisoner's dilemma that disallows spontaneous cooperation emergence [5]. We contend that it is necessary to re-examine the results with different networks as well as different game structures.

[2]http://en.wikipedia.org/wiki/Public_goods_game

2.3 Linking Two Research Streams

Although there exists rich literature on both aspects, the combination of these two research streams has not received enough attention. For example, [51, 52] built a solid reasoning on the role of cheap talk, but implicitly assumed all individuals are fully connected, which is almost impossible in the real world. There might be two reasons for this lack of attention to the combined research streams. First of all, it is difficult to observe and infer behavioral changes from empirical social network data, such as identifying whether a person becomes "more cooperative" or "less cooperative" from the traces of her activities. In the few research studies on this topic, the analysis uses a static snapshot of individuals' behaviors rather than allowing people to dynamically adapt their behaviors (e.g., [57]). Secondly, researchers in the two streams prefer different research methods. Small sample experiments, observational study, interviews, and surveys dominate the first stream (e.g., [19]), whereas the second stream often relies on large-scale network empirical data. In spite of these difficulties, it would be valuable to link these two streams to further develop an understanding of cheap talk's role in social network cooperation and trust development. We determined agent-based modeling and simulation would adequately suit this research combination and we will introduce how we built the agent-based model and simulation in the following sections.

3. RESEARCH APPROACH

3.1 Agent Based Modeling and Simulation

In this study, we employed agent-based modeling and simulation to explore cooperation and trust development in a special class of networks (scale-free networks). Leveraging evolutionary game theory, the model expresses strategic behavioral learning and adaptation at both individual and team levels. By simulating an individual's behavior, we capture from the ground-up a complex dynamic systems' behaviors and properties [43]. Agent-based modeling and simulation has been increasingly applied in HCI and CSCW to develop theoretical knowledge and practical design implications [42].

Computer-modeled agent-based simulation is a particularly useful tool for developing new theoretical insights and linking well-defined yet separated research streams [16]. As mentioned in the literature review above, there are well-established theories about cooperation and trust in distributed collaboration, as well as social network analysis on various collaboration systems. Traditionally, though, these theories tend to only consider a single perspective. For instance, social interaction theories suggest informal communication may help to reduce social distance and ease cooperation [11]. Studies such as [49] demonstrate that strategy decisions are greatly influenced by social network members who are closely related to the decision maker, yet these studies do not investigate the decisions' dynamics. Combining them in an agent-based model is feasible and may bring about better understanding. Moreover, the dynamic, adaptive processes at the core of agent-based models make them particularly suitable for analyzing longitudinal, chronically reproduced processes such as behavioral changes and social norm development [16], such as cooperation and trust development.

From an epistemological perspective, modeling and simulation is a generative knowledge development approach that suitably answers "what-if" questions. Agent-based simulation is similarly appropriate for investigating social phenomena that are influenced by complex and interrelated factors. These factors are difficult, if not impossible, to directly observe and assess in real-world settings, and existing theories about them are often too abstract for use in mechanism design. Thus, agent-based modeling and simulation integrate and concretize abstract theory in a virtual experiment environment, which enables researchers to identify places where theories agree, disagree, or are independent of each other, and to pin down factors that organization policymakers could manipulate to produce desirable outcomes [42].

Moreover, using agent-based modeling and simulation as the research method does not mean we exclude or ignore empiricism. In [47], the author argued that abstract modeling and simulation are not abstractions from, or simplifications of, the real world. They represent the counterfactual worlds constructed by the researcher. Of course, there are some gaps between the model world and the real world, but these gaps can be filled by inductive inference. Models describe how the world could, and can, be linked to the real world through implicit inductive reasoning. If we can see the relevant models as instances of some category, some of whose instances actually exist in the real world, we could achieve some degree of empiricism.

3.2 Applying the Research Method

To use agent-based modeling and simulation, we followed the 7-step guidelines in [42]. The key step in this process is building a conceptual model. The main difficulty in developing conceptual model is specifying how agents make behavioral decisions under the influence of their social network position. Based on the game theory model described in [51], we developed a decision model in which an agent's direct neighbors influence his or her behavioral decisions [32]. This model allows individual agents to form and adapt their strategies according to their social network positions, and also considers the restriction of individuals' "bounded rationality" [27]. We translated the conceptual model to computational representations, and implemented it. In this step, since most current scale-free network generators are based on stochastic models that cannot provide precise degree distribution control, we generated our own networks. In the next two sections, we will further introduce how we built the model's conceptual framework, implementation, and virtual experiment design.

4. CONCEPTUAL FRAMEWORK

4.1 Network and Game

4.1.1 Scale-free Network

Consider a finite set of agents $N = \{1, 2, ..., i, ..., n\}$. The relationship between each individual determines a social network. Let $\Gamma \equiv (N, L)$ denotes the social network where $L \subseteq N \times N$ is the set of dyadic interactions among the individuals. Γ is undirected, i.e., $(i, j) \in L$ indicates $(j, i) \in L$. Besides, links to oneself are not allowed, i.e., $(i, i) \notin L$. We further define N_i as the set of individuals who have direct links with i. Formally, $N_i = \{j \in N, such\ that (i, j) \in L\}$, while $k_i \equiv |N_i|$ is the number of neighbors of i, often referred as his or her degree.

A network is characterized by its degree distribution. By convention, we use $P(k)$ to denote the fraction of the nodes with degree $k \geq 1$. Obviously, $k = 0$ indicates a node has no link with others. We assume no isolated individuals exist, hence $P(0) = 0$. There are different types of networks such as *homogeneous* network (all nodes have same degree), *exponential* network (degree follows exponential distribution), and *scale-free* network. In this article, we are particularly interested in *scale-free* network, which exhibits a power-law degree distribution. Formally,

$$P(k) \propto k^{-\lambda}, \lambda \in [2, 3] \quad (1)$$

For a *scale-free* network, the degree variance can be very large, making it a powerful descriptor of real-world social relationships. Empirical evidence has shown that many paradigmatic examples of social networks are characterized by scale-free connectivity distributions [48]. In particular, geographically-distributed teams often use some key members and clusters of co-located team members as cross-site communication hubs, which are two major features of a scale-free network. In general, scale-free networks provide a relatively good abstraction for distributed collaboration. The λ in 1 is the degree exponential. λ is neither directly related to the average degree nor to the number of total edges. However, it does reflect the degree distribution of a scale-free network. In general, the smaller it is, the more even its degree distribution. Intuitively, if λ is smaller, there would be more nodes with more than one link (i.e., more people have more than one "friends" in a network).

4.1.2 Pseudo Scale-free Network

Scale-free networks usually require a relatively large number of nodes ($\geq 10^6$) to avoid the random noise of the small network. However, no real world software engineering team would be that large. Most software project teams have, on average, no more than 150 project members. In a study using ISBSG industry dataset which includes 1238 projects [25], the authors found that the largest team in the ISBSG dataset has 468 members, and most projects have less than 100 members [40]. In this study, we define "pseudo" scale-free network to denote the network whose size is small, while the degree distribution still fits power law [41].

4.1.3 Game Structure

We adopted the payoff structure defined in [51, 52] (see figure 1), in which the classical stag hunt game was modified to describe cheap talk strategies in globally distributed collaboration. There are three strategies an agent may use. To set up a *cheap talk* over the Internet, the proposer must pay a small management cost (e.g., spend extra time to talk about something irrelevant to work). The game structure assumes that the cost is small compared to the benefits from the cooperation ($e << R$). It may not be constant, but it is likely that the fluctuations do not span different orders of magnitude. Furthermore, the game assumes that players' preferences remain consistent (i.e., there is no execution noise). If a player decided to start *cheap talk*, she would use the "*cooperate*" strategy in the following interaction. Therefore, we add a new strategy called "*C-C*" and make the new game contain three strategies $\{C\text{-}C, C, D\}$.

	C-C	C	D		C-C	C	D
C-C	R-e/2	R-e	S-e+g	C-C	1.9	1.8	1.3
C	R	R	S	C	2	2	0.5
D	T-g	T	P	D	0.5	1.5	1

e=0.2, g=1

Figure 1: The payoff structure and a numeric example of different strategies.

If two agents both chose *C-C* in their interaction, they would share the cost of *cheap talk*, and thereby could each receive *R-e/2* payoff. Note that even in cases in which only one agent pays the cost, the **average** payoff of playing (*C-C, C-C*) remains *R-e/2* in the long run. If one plays *C-C* while the other agent plays *C*, the first will pay the cost all by herself. Her payoff is (*R-e, R*). If a player of *C-C* meets another player of *D*, the second player may be punished for refusing to cooperate.[3] We assume that the punishment equals *g* and the *C-C* player receives compensation (the same amount as the punishment), and thus the payoff of this interaction is *(S+g-e, T-g)*. Retaining this part of the payoff structure as it is in the classic form,[4] Fig. 1 illustrates a modified Stag-hunt game with *cheap talk* and a numerical example. In the rest of the paper, we use $u(i, j)$ to denote an agent's payoff when she plays strategy i and the other agent plays j.

[3]Punishment may take many forms, e.g., reputation loss.

The game, with this adapted payoff structure, allows us to describe the interrelated process of cooperation and trust development, whereby trust can be viewed as "expectations of other's cooperative behavior" [1]. If people trust others, they are willing to take risks in order to cooperate, while also expecting others to behave cooperatively [45]. In fact, in many behavioral experiments, researchers generally view cooperation as the establishment of trust [44].

4.2 Individual-level Strategy Change

During each period, one agent will be selected to interact with her neighbors in the network. Before the interaction, she needs to review her strategy and decide whether or not to switch to a new strategy. For example, she might be a defector, but she wants to review whether she needs to be more cooperative to maximize her interaction benefits. She checks all of her neighbors' strategies, and myopically selects a strategy to maximize her expected benefit in the next interaction. The adaptation of her strategy is probabilistic (log-linear discrete choice model [50]), and related to the expected payoff of playing strategy *s* (i.e. $U_i(s)$ at time t according her neighbors' strategies at time $t-1$). Formally, the probability of her strategy choice *s* in strategy space S will satisfy the following conditions:

$$\frac{e^{\beta U_i(s)}}{\sum^{S} e^{\beta U_i(s)}}, \quad \beta \geq 0 \qquad (2)$$

In 2, β refers to the sensitivity towards payoff change: the larger β is, the more likely it is that she chooses the best reply according to his neighbors' actions. Figure 2 presents an example of how people in a network apply this decision rule when $\beta \to +\infty$ (deterministic best-response). In this scenario, A is connected with three individuals: two (red dots) are cooperators and the other (blue dot) uses *C-C*. Her last strategy is *C-C*. When reviewing her strategy, she simply uses equation (2) to determine which strategy is the best reply to her neighbors' strategies. According to the numeric payoff structure in figure 1, if she plays *C*, the expected payoff is: $1 \times \frac{2}{3} + 1 \times \frac{1}{3} = 1$, which is more beneficial than playing *C-C* ($0.9 \times \frac{2}{3} + 0.95 \times \frac{1}{3} = 0.916$). Consequently, she would change her strategy from *C-C* to *C* after reviewing her strategy. The game structure has her exclusively consider her direct neighbor's strategy during the review process because prior empirical and experimental studies such as [49] have reported that individuals' decisions are overwhelmingly influenced by their direct neighbors.

To introduce stochasticity to the dynamic system and reflect agents' "bounded rationality" in decision-making, we allowed agents to make mistakes in strategy formation. In our simulation, we include a small mistake probability in which agents randomly select, instead of carefully calculate, a strategy. This increases the model's real-world applicability, given that people may not form the best reply due to practical restrictions, such as the lack of information about their neighbors, or limited information-processing ability.

[4]It is reasonable to assume that in the classic game the player who plays *defect* would not be punished, since there is no reason for her to give up a risk-dominated strategy without any hint to predict her opponent's action.

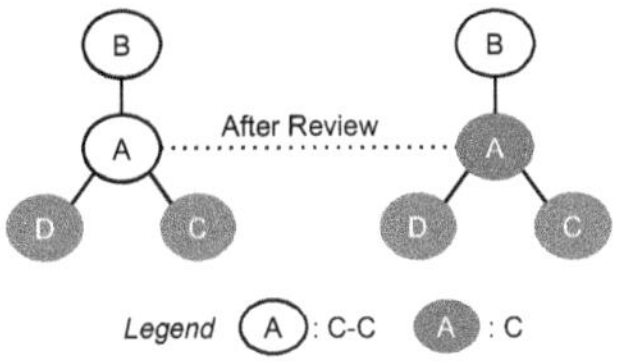

Figure 2: An example of applying the decision model to make decision ($\beta \rightarrow +\infty$). In this example, A changes her strategy after the reviewing process.

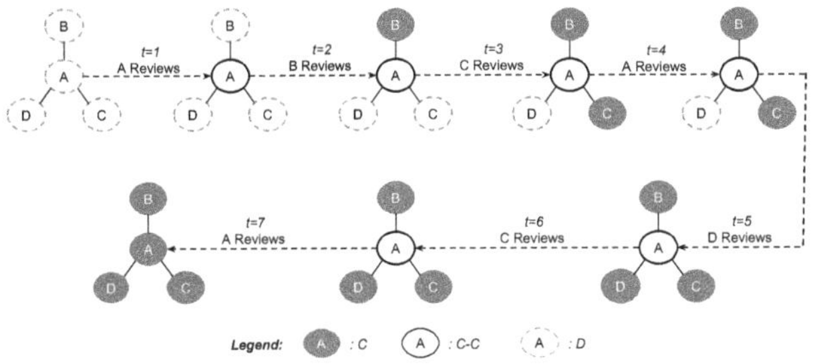

Figure 3: A simple example of individual-level strategy changes that lead to the whole group achieving a homogenous "all-cooperative" state (all agents using same strategy) when $\beta \rightarrow +\infty$. The real simulated process may be much more complex than this example. In addition, it is also possible that the group fails to achieve the "all-cooperate" state.

4.3 Group-level Strategy Dynamics

Individual-level strategy changes may eventually lead to one specific strategy becoming a group-wide norm. As an example, Figure 3 demonstrates one possibility for how individual-level strategy can lead to the adoption of group-wide cooperation. In the example, there are four agents connected with three links. At the beginning, all individuals defect (we use "all-defect" to denote this state). Next, individual A begins to review her strategy and finds she will receive improved results if she changes to *C-C*. In the next round, B is selected for review. Since agent B only connects to agent A, her best reply is *C* when agent A uses *C-C*. The same situation applies to agent C and D. Continuing this process, the system becomes stable when all agents use *C* (we use "all-cooperate" to refer this state). In real-world cases, this process may be much more complex; indeed, the whole process may take thousands of behavioral change instances. However, this example illustrates the main idea behind our simulation. If a simulation does reach "all-cooperate" state, we assume cooperation and trust have been successfully developed among group members. In determining who will be the next individual to review his or her strategy, we incorporate a basic social learning [12] mechanism. That is, if A has changed her strategy in time t, one of her neighbors will be selected to review in time $t+1$; otherwise, the selection of players in time $t+1$ is random. This reflects social reality well, since if your neighbor changes their behavior, you might want to observe it and decide whether or not you need to adapt to those changes.

5. MODEL IMPLEMENTATION AND VIRTUAL EXPERIMENT DESIGN

5.1 Model Implementation

The integration of social network and behavioral decision-making is unique, therefore it is difficult to customize existing simulation platforms such as Vensim DSS or NetLogo to implement our model. Consequently, we used `Python` and `NetworkX`[5] to build the simulation and generate the scale-free networks. To generate a pseudo scale-free network, we first generated a sequence of degrees that follows power distribution with special degree exponential, and then used the configuration model [9, 37] to stochastically generate the network instance which has an exactly prescribed degree sequence[6]. This ensures the degree exponential approximately equals the desired value [10]. The decision model essentially comprises a discrete-time model of difference equations, which can be implemented and run with any language, even on a spreadsheet. We chose `Python` for convenience because `NetworkX` is a `Python` package and also easily to be extended to incorporate additional factors in future research.

5.2 Virtual Experiment Design

To answer the research questions proposed in section 1, we designed a virtual simulation experiment. Table 1 summarizes the experiment's conditions and parameters. RQ1 does not require direct manipulation to the experiment conditions. Since we are primarily interested in evaluating degree distribution's impact (RQ2-1), the main condition is *degree exponential*, which ranges from 2.0 to 3.0. We set the interval as 0.2, thereby generating 6 conditions: $\lambda = 2.0, \lambda = 2.2, \lambda = 2.4, \lambda = 2.6, \lambda = 2.8, \lambda = 3.0$. This interval is not arbitrarily determined. Since the degree sequence generator in NetworkX cannot provide a sequence that fits special degree exponential precisely (in fact, it is not possible for any random sequence generator), there are usually ± 0.1 approximate errors. Consequently, we set the interval as 0.2 to avoid these errors as well as to ensure the generated sequence's exponential of a smaller condition is actually smaller than that of a larger condition.

For each condition, 10 scale-free network instances were generated. For each instance, the model was independently run 100 times, each with 10% node as unique seeding point to start the "trust" strategy. Therefore, we have $6 \times 10 \times 100 = 6000$ simulation trials in total. At the beginning of each simulation, every individuals' default strategy is "*D*". As we mentioned before, agents' rationality is bounded, and they naturally will make mistakes. We set the mistake probability as 0.1, meaning that 1 out of 10 decisions will be a random mistake. For this parameter, sensitivity analyses suggest the main results remain robust when this probability varies between 0 to 0.20%. The same payoff structures were used as the numeric examples in figure 1, enabling us to compare the results in [52]. We also performed sensitivity analyses to the payoff parameters and found general support for robustness. The payoff structure also satisfies the conditions specified in [51, 52], making the results comparable. The team size was set at 100: a typical number for mid-scale distributed collaboration according to prior empirical study [1, 40], and a large enough sample to provide rich dynamics.

6. RESULTS AND FINDINGS

In this section, we report the results of running virtual simulation experiments. We used R3.0.2 for Mac to perform all statistical analyses reported in this section. All diagrams and charts are generated with ggplot2. The analyses yield five propositions, which provide answers to the three main research questions. Table 2 summarized the correspondence between research questions and propositions. The remainder of this section provides more detail.

[5]NetworkX: https://networkx.github.io/
[6]Code avaliable at: https://goo.gl/vpHOaA

Parameter	Definition	Value	Related to Theory Development
N	Population Size	100	N
Payoff	Benefits of using different strategies	See figure 2.	N
λ	Degree Exponential	2.0-3.0, with 0.2 interval	Y (main experiment conditions)
M	Probability of mistake in decision making	0.1	N

Table 1: Summary of model conditions and parameters.

RQs	Proposition	Key Points
RQ1	PROPOSITION I	Cheap talk is positive.
RQ2-1	PROPOSITION II & III	More even degree distribution is usually better.
RQ2-2	PROPOSITION IV & V	Seeding at hubs is better.

Table 2: Summary of findings and corresponding research questions.

6.1 RQ1: Cheap Talk's Positive Impact

First, we wanted to know whether or not cheap talk positively impacts cooperation and trust development. According to [51], without cheap talk the "all-defect" state (all individuals are defectors) remains stable and almost impossible to transfer to the "all-cooperate" state. Figure 4 depicts the percentage of simulation runs that successfully reached the "all-cooperate" state in condition.

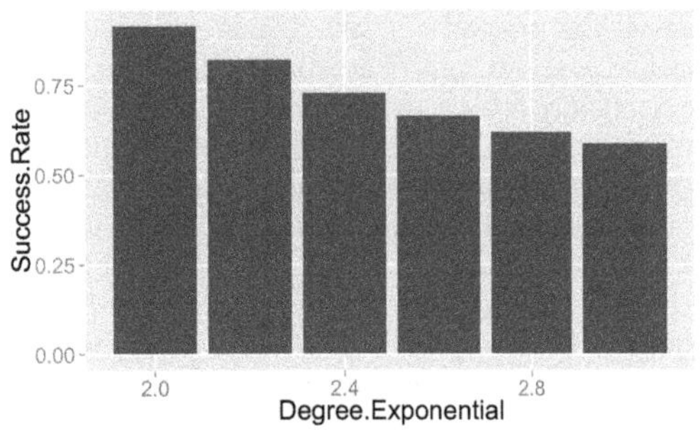

Figure 4: The relationship between degree exponential (x-axis) and success rate (y-axis).

For all 6 conditions, the majority of independent simulation runs successfully reached the stable "cooperation" state. In all 6000 runs, 4357 runs (72.62%) successfully developed cooperation. In all 6 conditions, even the least successful one achieved over 60% success rate. The results at least partially support the claim that cheap talk promotes cooperation and trust when group members form a pseudo scale-free network. In all the successful simulation runs, the "all-cooperate" state actually indicates the disappearance of "cheap talk," which confirms the role of "cheap talk" as a "catalyst." Hence, we have following proposition:

PROPOSITION I: *If individuals' relationships form a pseudo scale-free network, cheap talk with proper punishment to defectors remains an effective way to promote cooperation and trust development. In this process, it still largely functions as catalyst.*

6.2 RQ2-1: Impacts of Degree Distribution

The impacts of degree distribution are evaluated from two perspectives: effectiveness and efficiency. *Effectiveness* is measured by the success rate of reaching the "all-cooperate" state in each condition. *Efficiency* refers to how quickly the "all-cooperate" state is achieved, and therefore it can be measured by the number of total strategy reviews that occurred before reaching the final state.

6.2.1 *Effectiveness*

Figure 4 provides intuitive effectiveness illustration. An obvious pattern emerges whereby the success rate decreases with the degree exponential increase. As mentioned in section 3, the larger the degree exponential, the more individuals who have only one connection. Therefore, cooperation and trust development more easily succeeds when "average" people have more friends. This observation leads to:

PROPOSITION II: *Cheap talk's positive impact o is more significant when the degrees are more evenly distributed. Intuitively, if more people have more than one "friend" in the network, cooperation and trust are more likely to develop.*

6.2.2 *Efficiency*

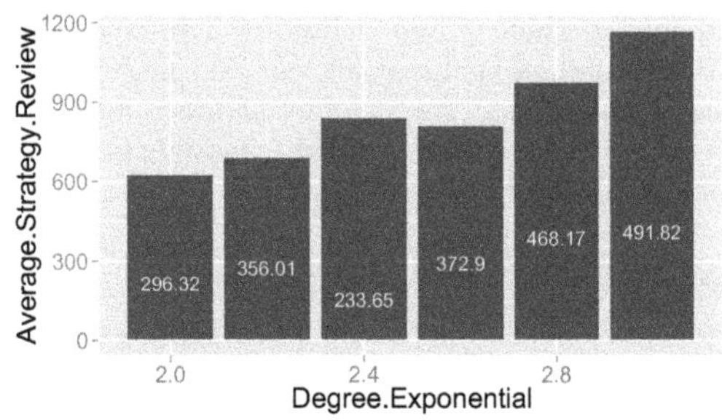

Figure 5: The relationship between degree exponential (x-axis) and average number of strategy reviews (y-axis) before reaching "all-cooperate" state.

We considered whether or not different degree distributions yield different efficiencies in achieving a homogeneous "cooperation" state. Figure 5 shows the average number of strategy reviews that occur before reaching stable cooperation state. We only consider the 4357 cases that successfully reached group-level cooperation. The number displayed on each bar is the standard deviation. Obviously, with the increase of degree exponential, it usually takes more steps to achieve the final state. A one-way ANOVA test was performed to identify whether significant differences exist across different conditions, yielding significant results (*p-value* < 0.001, $F(5, 4351) = 963.9$). We then performed *pairwise t-test* to determine the differences between any two groups. The results show all differences significant at 0.01 level except for two groups: "$\lambda = 2.4$" and "$\lambda = 2.6$." However, the *p-value* is 0.015, which is still significant at the 0.05 level. Hence, our third proposition follows:

PROPOSITION III: *If the degrees are more evenly distributed, cooperation and trust's development will be more efficient. Intuitively, if more people have more than one "friend" in the network, it will take less time to develop cooperation and trust.*

6.3 RQ2-2: Impacts of Seeding Strategies

A network position is considered a "hub" when it satisfies both of the following two heuristic conditions: (1) its degree centrality[7]

[7]Here, to determine the hubs we used simple degree centrality

is in top 10% of all nodes; (2) it has at least three direct links: if a node has only two links, it is more likely a connector than a hub.

Whether or not seeding from hub positions promotes cooperation and trust development is a hot topic in networked collaboration research[49], and there are some contradictory results (see section 2.2). We used our simulation-generated data to examine the specific settings (pseudo scale-free network, stag hunt game with cheap talk, and best-reply decision model). We first identified and separated the simulations that begin from hubs. Then, we compared their results with the whole sample to test the existence of significant differences. In the remainder of this subsection, we present the comparisons of effectiveness and efficiency.

6.3.1 *Effectiveness*

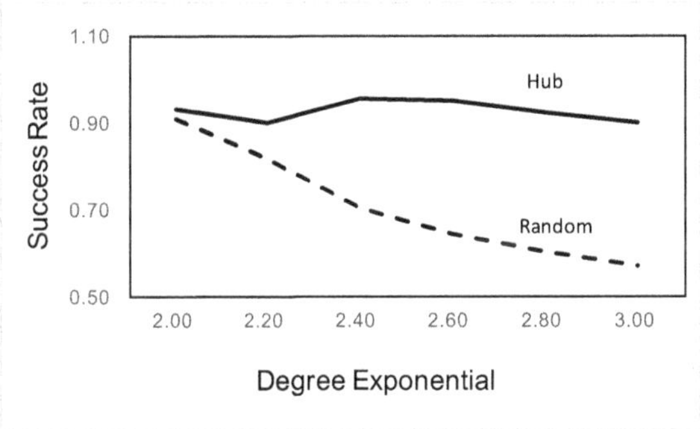

Figure 6: The differences between two seeding strategies (Hub seeding vs. Random seeding) on success rate.

Figure 6 shows the seeding strategies' influence on the effective development of cooperation and trust. When the degree exponential is small, the differences are not very apparent. However, the difference becomes significant when the degree exponential approaches 3.0. For example, the success rate of hub seeding remains around 90% at a 3.0 level, whereas random seeding's success rate barely exceeds 50%. A possible explanation for why the seeding position becomes sensitive with a larger degree exponential is that the group relies more on several key hubs to establish the "cooperation" and transmit "cooperation" to the rest of the group. Since these nodes only account for a small proportion of the whole group, it is possible that some barriers restrict them from becoming co operators. Hence, the whole group may not successfully develop cooperation and trust. Therefore, we can claim:

PROPOSITION IV: *Seeding cooperation and trust in the hubs during the early stages will increase the possibility for the whole group to build cooperation and trust, especially when there are many individuals with only one connection.*

6.3.2 *Efficiency*

From figure 7, it is easy to conclude that seeding from the hubs will greatly improve the efficiency of cooperation and trust development. In general, hub seeding generates 60% in efficiency improvements at least. Although the differences are rather straightforward and intuitive from figure 7, we still performed *t-test* to statistically examine the differences. As expected, all differences are significant at 0.001 level for all 6 conditions[8].

rather than betweenness centrality because the betweenness centrality distributions are alike for nearly all scale-free network [21].

[8]We performed 6 independent *t-tests*. In each test, we performed *t-test* for the number of average strategy reviews in two groups (Hub Seeding & Random Seeding) at a given degree exponential.

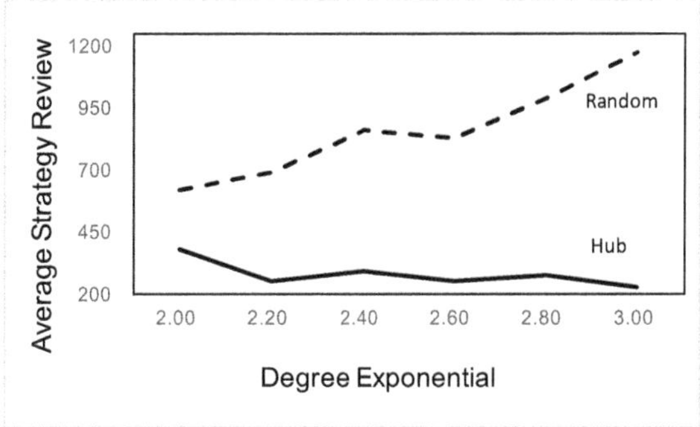

Figure 7: The difference in influence on the average number of strategy reviews occurring before reaching an "all-cooperation" state between two seeding strategies.

This improvement is more apparent with a larger degree exponential, which is unsurprising given its similar effectiveness. When the degree exponential is small, there are fewer differences between hubs and other nodes. However, when degree exponential is large, it is more likely to form a structure in which one big hub links to many nodes with no other connections (similar to the relationship between node A and nodes {B, C, D}. In this situation, the central hub's behavioral changes will immediately influence his or her satellites' behavior. If behavior changes occur in common nodes first, it requires extra time for the hub to be influenced, and then for the hub to "dispatch" to other nodes. Therefore, the seeding strategy is more efficient when most individuals only have one connection. Based on the above discussion, we have:

PROPOSITION V: *Seeding cooperation and trust in the hubs in early stages will shorten (quicken) the process of cooperation and trust development, especially when there are many individuals with only one connection.*

6.4 Sensitivity Analysis

In this section, we present a sensitivity analysis [23] to evaluate the results' robustness. In this experiment, the main threat to robustness is the payoff structure. It is necessary to test whether the results are associated with the specific numeric payoff structure we used in the simulation experiment. In the game's payoff structure, the key feature ensuring the emerge of cooperation is the punishment (g) and cost of online cheap talk (e) [52]. Thus, we parametrized them in the sensitivity analysis. Here, we reuse the network structures generated in the experiment. To simplify the discussion, we only take two conditions of degree exponential (λ), which are 2.0 and 2.6.

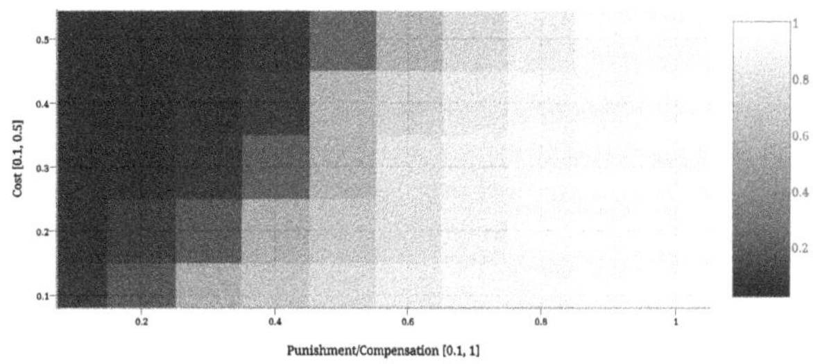

Figure 8: Frequency of achieving all-cooperate as a function of cost (e) and punishment to defector (g), $\lambda = 2.0$.

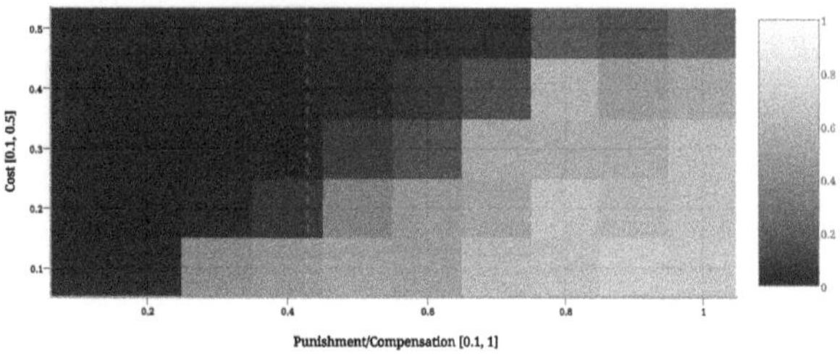

Figure 9: Frequency of achieving all-cooperate as a function of cost (e) and punishment to defector (g), $\lambda = 2.6$.

Figure 8 and 9 plots the sensitivity analysis results. When punishment/compensation is comparable to cost, cheap talk can encourage the majority of individual simulation processes to reach homogeneous cooperation state. This shows the robustness of PROPOSITION I. It is obvious that the PROPOSITION II holds for most situations. For nearly all combinations of (e, g), more individual simulation processes reach "all-cooperate" states in the condition of $\lambda = 2$ than the condition of $\lambda = 2.6$. By employing the similar method, we also tested the sensitivity of PROPOSITION III through PROPOSITION V. The results provide general support for robustness. To keep this paper concise, we omit the details in this section.

The social learning coefficient β is another factor influencing the process. If it is too small, the process may be very slow, because the probability of switching from a low to high payoff strategy may be very low. Given that people may make mistakes at a specific rate (5% in this study), it is even possible that they cannot escape from the low payoff strategy's basin of attraction [15], which may ultimately lead to the failure of trust and cooperation development.

7. DISCUSSION

7.1 Implications to Research

This work has implications for future distributed collaboration and trust research. First, the results summarized in PROPOSITION I expand the findings in [52] by incorporating the influence of social networks. We find that cheap talk not only positively impacts cooperation and trust development when individual agents are fully connected, but also helps to promote cooperation and trust development when agents form a pseudo scale-free network. Moreover, we found that cheap talk functions like a "catalyst" even in the new settings. Second, PROPOSITION II & III characterize the impact of a pseudo scale-free network's degree distribution on cooperation and trust development. Compared to prior social network analysis work in CSCW, ours is the first study relating degree distribution to cooperation and trust development, whereas prior research often focuses on a network's micro-level local features, such as whether or not an individual is located in a specific position [35, 55]. Our study thus helps develop knowledge about how network features influence collaboration. Thirdly, we tested different seeding strategies' impacts on cooperation and trust development (PROPOSITION IV & V). Although there is rich literature on seeding strategies in marketing and information diffusion [48], our study focuses on a less investigated area: seeding strategy's influence on cooperation and trust. Furthermore, we explored the specific conditions in which seeding at the hubs becomes more effective and efficient. "Seeding" for behavior change also extends the traditional application of "seeding" for technology adoption in CSCW literature [34]. In developing our model, we viewed cooperation and trust development as a dynamic, adaptive process, whereas existing CSCW literature usually views "cooperation" as a one-shot behavior when studying it in a social network setting [19].

Our main research method was agent-based modeling and simulation; we demonstrated its powerful research potential when combined with theoretical knowledge crossing different domains, and used to investigate complex distributed collaboration systems. For example, the agent-based model focused on the heavily-researched CSCW research topic of distributed collaboration. The development of the model applied game theory from Economics, and network neighbors' influences from Network Science. To reiterate, we believe the agent-based modeling and simulation will help researchers develop theories that link traditionally less-related research streams, especially when the research targets are complex and dynamic social and technical systems. The modeling and simulation approach performs well with empirical approaches, hence, can be combined to form a full research cycle [42]

7.2 Implications to Distributed Collaboration Practice

Some findings, especially our seeding strategy insights, can be directly applied to distributed collaboration practices. Policymakers may identify team hubs and invest more resources to help them adopt cooperation first. They can also encourage individuals in hub positions to be more open to the changes of those who are not in hubs. In this way, the common nodes' cooperative behavior may be better transmitted to the public by the hubs.

Another possible implication lies in the design of organizational communication networks, considering that our findings indicate that a network with the smaller degree exponential may be more effective and efficient in cooperation and trust development. Policymakers may intentionally manipulate the relationship-building process among group members, for example by creating more opportunities for "common" members to develop relationships. Thus, the degree could be more evenly distributed, and the cooperation and trust development would rely less on those in key positions. The demonstrated positive impact of cheap talk in networked organization settings justifies its practice in cooperation and trust-building. Although we have not explicitly examined the impact of social learning factor (β), it is important to remove the social learning barriers within the team. If learning is slow, the overall results may be unfavorable, for example, it may take more time to reach the cooperation. It is necessary to take some measures to improve social learning among the team members. Those measures may be some incentives that promote some specific behavioral changes.

7.3 Limitations and Future Opportunities

There are several limitations to this study. First, we only considered degree distribution, which is one of many social network features. Even for networks with the same degree distribution, their actual topologies may vary a great deal. We plan to utilize the simulation-generated data to perform more fine-grained analysis, e.g., to study how local network features influence cooperation and trust development. We plan to employ more techniques (see [26] for reference) to provide further analyses, and we expect more refined findings to emerge . In fact, it is possible that some distributed collaboration networks are not pseudo scale-free networks, and therefore we will try to replicate the virtual experiment in other network models. Additionally, this paper focuses on the overall simulation results and does not consider certain details about how individual simulations reach the final state. Studying these detailed simulation records may lead to useful insights and provide further explanation for the results, e.g., how *C-C* strategy is replaced by C strategy; why seeding strategies are more efficient when λ is large; and whether or not there is any dynamic pattern of behavioral change.

The game theory-based decision model is an abstraction of real world decision processes. Other factors may influence people's decisions. For example, conformity may make an individual hesitate to change, even if new behavior yields a better payoff. Incrementally including these social factors may further enhance our understanding of social networks' impact on cooperation development. In addition, people's decisions may also be influenced by those not directly connected to them. The simulation implementation is highly reusable, hence provides an infrastructure to apply more complex decision models. The results can also be viewed as a benchmark for assessing other decision models.

To improve this work's relevance to practice, a possible direction is to replace the artificially generated network with an empirical, observational network. We can also introduce the individual characteristics into the agent model and run simulations to study the system's dynamics. Our own work [53] follows this direction to investigate how individual characteristics, especially baseline trust, influence the trust and cooperation development process.

8. CONCLUSIONS

We introduced an agent-based modeling and simulation study of pseudo scale-free network cooperation and trust development with cheap talk. We applied game theory to develop a decision model that describes how people change their strategies through social learning. Then, we simulated how agents using the decision model form and adapt their behaviors in a pseudo scale-free network to explore the dynamics of cooperation and trust development. Our results confirmed the positive effect of cheap talk in cooperation and trust development. We identified degree distribution's influence on cooperation and trust development in both effectiveness and efficiency. We then compared two seeding strategies using simulation-generated data and found seeding from hubs is generally more effective and efficient. This work establishes links among informal communication (cheap talk), network features, and cooperation and trust development. It suggests rich opportunities for future work, and for designing and improving distributed collaboration systems. Moreover, our study demonstrates the feasibility of using agent-based modeling and simulation to link traditionally separated research streams related to distributed collaboration. The study has potential to evolve into a multi-perspective "testbed" for future research, a type of investigation that CSCW practices could benefit from. For instance, practitioners can leverage this method to evaluate the mechanisms they want to introduce into distributed, collaborative groups, and hence may avoid costly yet common "trial and error." Finally, theoretical knowledge embedded in our model can be paired with creative design to generate effective mechanisms in promoting cooperation and trust, for instance, manipulating the network topology through well-defined incentive mechnisims. The decision and interaction model presented here was primarily based on game theory. Social science (including economics) literature offers a wide range of theoretical results explaining individual and group decision-making. These results could be integrated into our model in the future. For example, we may extend our model by incorporating the homophily [36] among agents and its influence on non-directly linked agents' decisions.

9. REFERENCES

[1] B. Al-Ani, M. J. Bietz, Y. Wang, E. Trainer, B. Koehne, S. Marczak, D. F. Redmiles, and R. Prikladnicki. Globally distributed system developers: their trust expectations and processes. In *Proc. CSCW*, pages 563–574, 2013.

[2] S. Aral. Poked to vote. *Nature*, 489:212–214, 2012.

[3] S. Aral, L. Muchnik, and A. Sundararajan. Engineering social contagions: Optimal network seeding in the presence of homophily. *Network Science*, 1:125–153, 8 2013.

[4] A. Barabási, E. Ravasz, and T. Vicsek. Deterministic scale-free networks. *Physica A: Statistical Mechanics and its Applications*, 299:559–564, 2001.

[5] P. Barclay. Trustworthiness and competitive altruism can also solve the ?tragedy of the commons? *Evolution and Human Behavior*, 25(4):209 – 220, 2004.

[6] R. S. Burt. The network structure of social capital. *Research in organizational behavior*, 22:345–423, 2000.

[7] R. S. Burt. *Neighbor networks: Competitive advantage local and personal*. OUP Oxford, 2010.

[8] J. Cassell and T. Bickmore. Negotiated collusion: Modeling social language and its relationship effects in intelligent agents. *User Modeling and User-Adapted Interaction*, 13(1-2):89–132, 2003.

[9] F. Chung and L. Lu. The average distance in a random graph with given expected degrees. *Internet Mathematics*, 1(1):91–113, 2004.

[10] A. Clauset, C. R. Shalizi, and M. E. Newman. Power-law distributions in empirical data. *SIAM review*, 51(4):661–703, 2009.

[11] C. D. Cramton and P. J. Hinds. Intercultural interaction in distributed teams: Salience of and adaptations to cultural differences. In *Proc. AOM*, pages 1 – 6, 2007.

[12] P. DiMaggio and F. Garip. Network effects and social inequality. *Annual Review of Sociology*, 38:93–118, 2012.

[13] Y. Dittrich and R. Giuffrida. Exploring the role of instant messaging in a global software development project. In *Proc. ICGSE*, pages 103–112, 2011.

[14] N. Ducheneaut. Socialization in an open source software community: A socio-technical analysis. *Computer Supported Cooperative Work (CSCW)*, 14(4):323–368, 2005.

[15] G. Ellison. Basins of attraction, long-run stochastic stability, and the speed of step-by-step evolution. *The Review of Economic Studies*, 67(1):17–45, 2000.

[16] D. Etzion. Diffusion as classification. *Organization Science*, 25(2):420–437, 2014.

[17] U. Farooq, C. Ganoe, J. Carroll, and C. Giles. Supporting distributed scientific collaboration: Implications for designing the citeseer collaboratory. In *Proc. HICSS*, 2007.

[18] J. Farrell and M. Rabin. Cheap talk. *The Journal of Economic Perspectives*, 10(3):103–118, 1996.

[19] G. Gao, P. Hinds, and C. Zhao. Closure vs. structural holes: How social network information and culture affect choice of collaborators. In *Proc. CSCW*, pages 5–18, 2013.

[20] S. Goggins, C. Mascaro, and S. Mascaro. Relief work after the 2010 haiti earthquake: Leadership in an online resource coordination network. In *Proc. CSCW*, pages 57–66, 2012.

[21] K.-I. Goh, E. Oh, H. Jeong, B. Kahng, and D. Kim. Classification of scale-free networks. *Proceedings of the National Academy of Sciences*, 99(20):12583–12588, 2002.

[22] D. Hansen and M. Smith. Social network analysis in hci. In J. S. Olson and W. A. Kellogg, editors, *Ways of Knowing in HCI*, pages 421–447. Springer New York, 2014.

[23] J. R. Harrison, Z. Lin, G. R. Carroll, and K. M. Carley. Simulation modeling in organizational and management

research. *Academy of Management Review*, 32(4):1229–1245, 2007.

[24] J. D. Herbsleb, D. L. Atkins, D. G. Boyer, M. Handel, and T. A. Finholt. Introducing instant messaging and chat in the workplace. In *Proc. CHI*, pages 171–178, 2002.

[25] ISBSG. Isbsg project repository (release 7). http://www.isbsg.org/, 2003.

[26] M. Jackson. *Social and Economic Network*. Princeton University Press, 2010.

[27] D. Kahneman. Maps of bounded rationality: Psychology for behavioral economics. *American Economic Review*, 93(5):1449–1475, 2003.

[28] B. Keegan, D. Gergle, and N. Contractor. Do editors or articles drive collaboration?: Multilevel statistical network analysis of wikipedia coauthorship. In *Proc. CSCW*, pages 427–436, 2012.

[29] B. Keegan, D. Gergle, and N. Contractor. Staying in the loop: Structure and dynamics of wikipedia's breaking news collaborations. In *Proc. WikiSym*, pages 1:1–1:10, 2012.

[30] A. Khawaji, F. Chen, N. Marcus, and J. Zhou. Trust and cooperation in text-based computer-mediated communication. In *Proc. OzCHI*, pages 37–40, 2013.

[31] T. Kim, P. Hinds, and A. Pentland. Awareness as an antidote to distance: Making distributed groups cooperative and consistent. In *Proc. CSCW*, pages 1237–1246, 2012.

[32] J. Kleinberg. Cascading behavior in networks: Algorithmic and economic issues. *Algorithmic game theory*, 24:613–632, 2007.

[33] J. Leskovec, D. Huttenlocher, and J. Kleinberg. Signed networks in social media. In *Proc. CHI*, pages 1361–1370, 2010.

[34] G. Mark and S. Poltrock. Diffusion of a collaborative technology cross distance. In *Proc. Group*, pages 232–241, 2001.

[35] D. W. McDonald. Recommending collaboration with social networks: A comparative evaluation. In *Proc. CHI*, pages 593–600, 2003.

[36] M. McPherson, L. Smith-Lovin, and J. M. Cook. Birds of a feather: Homophily in social networks. *Annual review of sociology*, pages 415–444, 2001.

[37] M. Molloy and B. Reed. A critical point for random graphs with a given degree sequence. *Random structures & algorithms*, 6(2-3):161–180, 1995.

[38] B. A. Nardi, S. Whittaker, and E. Bradner. Interaction and outeraction: Instant messaging in action. In *Proc. CSCW*, pages 79–88, 2000.

[39] G. M. Olson and J. S. Olson. Distance matters. *Hum.-Comput. Interact.*, 15(2):139–178, Sept. 2000.

[40] P. C. Pendharkar and J. A. Rodger. The relationship between software development team size and software development cost. *Commun. ACM*, 52(1):141–144, Jan. 2009.

[41] F. L. Pinheiro, M. D. Santos, F. C. Santos, and J. M. Pacheco. Origin of peer influence in social networks. *Physical review letters*, 112(9):098702, 2014.

[42] Y. Ren and R. Kraut. Agent based modeling to inform the design of multiuser systems. In J. S. Olson and W. A. Kellogg, editors, *Ways of Knowing in HCI*, pages 395–419. Springer New York, 2014.

[43] Y. Ren and R. E. Kraut. Agent-Based Modeling to Inform Online Community Design: Impact of Topical Breadth, Message Volume, and Discussion Moderation on Member Commitment and Contribution. *Human-Computer Interaction*, 29(4):351–389, 2014.

[44] J. Riegelsberger, M. Sasse, and J. D. McCarthy. The researcher's dilemma: evaluating trust in computer-mediated communication. *Intl. Journal of Human-Computer Studies*, 58(6):759 – 781, 2003.

[45] B. Skyrms. Trust, risk, and the social contract. *Synthese*, 160(1):21–25, 2008.

[46] A. Steed, M. Spante, I. Heldal, A.-S. Axelsson, and R. Schroeder. Strangers and friends in caves: an exploratory study of collaboration in networked ipt systems for extended periods of time. In *Proc. I3D*, pages 51–54. ACM, 2003.

[47] R. Sugden. Credible worlds: the status of theoretical models in economics. *J. Econ. Met.*, 7(1):1–31, 2000.

[48] A. Sundararajan, F. Provost, G. Oestreicher-singer, and S. Aral. Information in Digital , Economic , and Social Networks. *Inform. Syst. Res.*, 24(4):883–905, 2013.

[49] S. Suri and D. J. Watts. Cooperation and contagion in web-based, networked public goods experiments. *PloS one*, 6(3):e16836, Jan. 2011.

[50] K. E. Train. *Discrete choice methods with simulation*. Cambridge university press, 2009.

[51] Y. Wang and D. Redmiles. Understanding cheap talk and the emergence of trust in global software engineering: An evolutionary game theory perspective. In *Proc. CHASE*, pages 149–152, 2013.

[52] Y. Wang and D. Redmiles. Cheap talk, cooperation, and trust in global software engineering: An evolutionary game theory model with empirical support. *Empirical Software Engineering*, 2015.

[53] Y. Wang and D. Redmiles. The diffusion of trust and cooperation in teams with individuals' variations on baseline trust. In *Proc. CSCW*, pages 303–318, 2016.

[54] A. Wu, J. M. DiMicco, and D. R. Millen. Detecting professional versus personal closeness using an enterprise social network site. In *Proc. CHI*, pages 1955–1964, 2010.

[55] Z. Xiao and A. S. Tsui. When brokers may not work: The cultural contingency of social capital in chinese high-tech firms. *Administrative Science Quarterly*, 52(1):1–31, 2007.

[56] J. Yang, L. A. Adamic, and M. S. Ackerman. Competing to share expertise: The taskcn knowledge sharing community. In *Proc. ICWSM*, 2008.

[57] J. Yang, Z. Wen, L. A. Adamic, M. S. Ackerman, and C.-Y. Lin. Collaborating globally: Culture and organizational computer-mediated communications. In *Proc. ICIS*, 2011.

[58] D. Zhao and M. B. Rosson. How and why people twitter: The role that micro-blogging plays in informal communication at work. In *Proc. Group*, pages 243–252, 2009.

[59] J. Zheng, E. Veinott, N. Bos, J. S. Olson, and G. M. Olson. Trust without touch: Jumpstarting long-distance trust with initial social activities. In *Proc. CHI*, pages 141–146, 2002.

Influences of Peers, Friends, and Managers on Employee Engagement

Michael Muller[a], N. Sadat Shami[b], Shion Guha[c], Mikhil Masli[b], Werner Geyer[a], Alan Wild[b]
[a]IBM Research, [b]IBM, [c]Marquette University
[a]One Rogers Street, Cambridge MA USA 02142
{michael_muller, sadat, mnmasli, werner.geyer, awild}@us.ibm.com,
shion.guha@marquette.edu

ABSTRACT

Employee engagement is a reflection of an employee's experience of work. Previous research has analyzed each employee's experience in terms of individual factors. We provide the first report of the influence on engagement of peers (who report to the same manager) and friends (who share social ties in an internal social network), using linear regression to model employee engagement in a sample of more than 44,000 employees. We show that an employee's engagement is associated with the engagement of her/his peers, friends, and manager. Our results contribute to analyses of social factors at work, and argue for revisions to existing theories of employee engagement.

Keywords

Employee engagement; Social ties; Social network; Organization; Organization structure.

1. INTRODUCTION

The experience of work has been a core aspect of research in GROUP and CSCW [4, 40, 41]. One measure of the experience of work is the concept of employee engagement [1, 3, 6, 8, 15, 18, 36, 37, 39]. Employee engagement is also an important topic in management studies [1, 36, 47], including its positive association with employee well-being, employee helpful behaviors [15] and performance [32, 33], business success [21] and advice to managers [11, 25] and executives [50, 52], as well as more theoretical discussions in organizational studies [6, 8, 12, 15, 37, 43], and has recently gained attention in CHI, CSCW, and related research as a summary metric of employees' experiences at work and in organizations [39, 44, 45, 46].

Most accounts of employee engagement emphasize the roles of executives [50, 52, 53] and managers [11, 25] in shaping and enhancing engagement of their direct reports – a model that we refer to as the "vertical stack" (Figure 1A). By contrast, Avery et al. reported that "satisfaction with coworkers" is associated with higher engagement [3]. Guha et al. opened a discussion of the importance of employees' social network position (centrality) as a contributing factor of engagement [16]. In this note, we go further, to show mutual influences on employee engagement from the employee's peers (who report to the same manager) and the employee's friends (in an Intranet social network), as well as the employee's manager. Our approach brings together the literature on employee engagement with the literature on social ties in organizations, and argues for a more social view of employee engagement (Figure 1B), and of the theories and measurements in the study of employee engagement.

GROUP '16, November 13-16, 2016, Sanibel Island, FL, USA
© 2016 ACM. ISBN 978-1-4503-4276-6/16/11…$15.00
DOI: http://dx.doi.org/10.1145/2957276.2957292

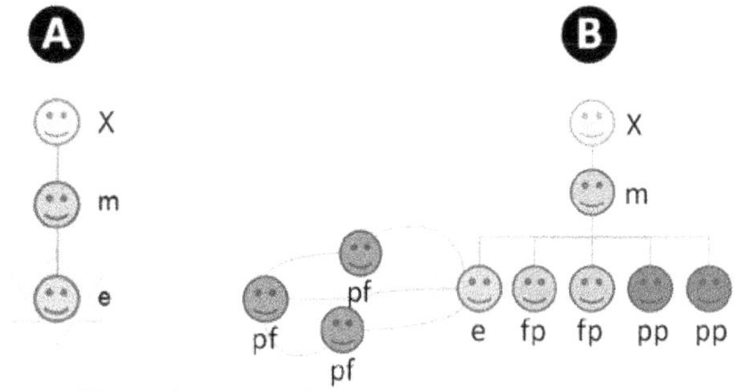

Figure 1. Approaches to employee engagement. A. Vertical stack model, emphasizing the role of Executive, *X*, and Manager, *m*, on the engagement of the employee, *e*. B. Proposed social model, including additional influences by friends, *pf*, and peers, *pp*, and hybrid friends-peers, *fp*.

In the remainder of this note, we provide background, introduce the datasets, and show that influences on engagement by peers and social-network friends are stronger than the influence of managers. We conclude with implications for engagement theory and organizations.

2. Background

While the definition of employee engagement may seem intuitively obvious, there are multiple ways to measure engagement, and each has its own theory behind it. Space does not permit an exploration of these concepts – we recommend [1, 6, 8, 37, 38] and especially [42] for a broader discussion. In general, all definitions involve a positive attitude toward work and the workplace, and many measure of engagement have been associated with practical value to organizations [1, 11, 15, 17, 32, 33, 36]. We hope that recent interest among CHI and CSCW researchers [10, 16, 26, 44, 45] will add to the precision, conceptual richness, and empirical evidence regarding employee engagement.

In this note, we attempt to relate measurements of employee engagement (as summarized above) with the literature on the importance of social ties in organizations [2, 5, 9, 19, 22, 27, 28, 30, 35, 48, 54, 56]. The Utrecht Work Engagement Scale is based on resistance to burnout at work, and consists of three factors: vigor, dedication, and absorption [39]. The Job Engagement Scale includes three different factors: physical, cognitive, and emotional

Table 1. Sources of data, and descriptive statistics, for employees in the datasets.

Data Source	Measurement	N in original dataset	Data Attribute	Range in Sample
Survey	EngagementMean	190,469	Score, 1.0-5.0	1-5
Organization Chart	Manager Peer	130,727 188,906	Count of people Count of people	1 1-453
SNS	Friendship	122,405	Count of people	2-5,488

engagement [18, 33]. Neither of these influential measurement approaches involves social concepts.

Among commercial measures, the Kenexa High Performance Engagement Model considers pride, satisfaction, advocacy (recommendation of the workplace to job-seekers), and retention [53]. Again, social factors are absent. The Gallup "G12" survey includes a single question (among 12) about having a friend at work [18]. These commercial surveys reflect the trend in the business, management, and organizational literatures to emphasize the importance of executive strategies [50, 52], managerial influences [11, 25], and workplace conditions that are under the control of executives and managers [8, 44, 50].

We wanted to know if social factors were also predictive of engagement, as suggested by the research literature on the importance of social ties at work [2, 5, 9, 19 22, 27, 28, 30, 35, 48, 54, 56]. We collected datasets (described below) that consisted of hierarchical ties (derived from an organizational chart) and social ties (derived from an Intranet social network service). Our first research hypothesis was simply:

> **RH1.** Employee engagement is influenced by people to whom the employee has ties.

Our dataset allowed us to consider several types of social ties (Figure 1B). The research literature has emphasized the importance of management in influencing employee engagement [11, 25] – i.e., the vertical stack of Figure 1A. Therefore, we might predict:

> **RH2a.** Employee engagement is influenced more by ties with managers than by other ties.

However, peers may also impact an employee's experience at work [29]. Therefore, we also consider:

> **RH2b.** Employee engagement is influenced more by ties with peers than by other ties.

There is a large research literature that has shown the importance of friendship social ties in the workplace [2, 5, 9, 19, 22, 34, 35, 54, 56]. Therefore, we also might find that:

> **RH2c.** Employee engagement is influenced more by ties with friends than by other ties.

Finally, it is possible that an employee might be friends with a peer co-worker [31, 38]. The category of hybrid friends-peers may represent stronger links, because employees are connected via two types of social ties (peer-ties and friend-ties). Earlier research, using faceted social identity theory, has found stronger results for pairs of people who shared multiple identity facets ([27]; however, see [23, 35] for potential limitations). Therefore, we examine:

> **RH2d.** Employee engagement is influenced most by ties with hybrid friends-peers.

3. Datasets and Method

The study took place in IBM, a large multinational corporation that focuses on technology and services in many countries. IBM has a conventional, hierarchical organization structure. IBM also encourages active use of internal social media similar to [7, 20, 22, 23, 54, 55]. We draw upon data from these two organizational (network) structures for the year 2015.

IBM conducts an annual, voluntary employee engagement survey, using a modified form of the engagement items in the Kenexa High Performance Engagement Model [53]. This survey uses three Likert-style questions (range 1-5, with 5 as highest score), and focuses on pride in working at IBM, the work experience in IBM, and recommendation of IBM as a good place to work. For this note, our data were drawn from the November 2015 survey.

3.1 Sources of Data

For these analyses, we combined anonymized data from the following sources:

- ***Employee engagement survey.*** We examined the mean score from the survey, which we called **EngagementMean**. The mean had a range of 1-5, with 5 as the highest engagement.
- ***Hierarchical organization chart.*** We reduced the hierarchical organization chart into a set of links between managers and their direct reports (employees). From these we derived a manager-link for each employee, and also peer-links, which we defined as employees who report to the same manager.
- ***Friendship social ties.*** Finally, we collected the set of friendship ties ("friending" relationships) from IBM Connections Profiles (the IBM internal social network service). Friending relationships begin when one employee initiates a "friend" request to a second employee through the social network service, and are completed when the second employee accepts the request.[1]

3.2 Data Preparation: Refinement

It was possible for an employee to be linked to another employee through both a *peer* link and a *friend* link (Figure 1B). To maintain independence among our predictors, we separated each employee's links into four categories: the employee's manager (for **RH2a**); the employee's peers (peers who were not also friends, for **RH2b**); the employee's friends (friends who were not also peers, for **RH2c**); and the employee's hybrid "friends-peers" (who were both friends and peers, for **RH2d**). (Throughout this note, we use the word "peer" to mean "peer who is not a friend,"

[1] We thank an anonymous reviewer for pointing out that a "friendship" relationship in a corporate Intranet social network may, not be equivalent to a "friendship" relationship in an Internet social network – or to the conventional offline social definition of friendship.

Table 2. Pearson correlations of influence factors with employee engagement (EngagementMean).

Influence	Correlation	df
Pure peers	.335***	182,147
Pure friends	.241***	116,876
Friends-peers	.280***	61,213
Manager	.175***	129,348

*** p<.001

and we use the word "friend" to mean "friend who is not also a peer." No employee is double-counted in the three relationship types, peer, friend, or friend-peer.)

3.3 Data Preparation: Aggregation

For each type of relationship for each employee, we computed the mean of engagement scores for all of the people who had the specified relationship with the employee. For the manager relationship, this was trivial, because each employee has only one manager. For the pure peers, we computed the mean of the engagement scores for all of the peers of the employee. We performed similar computations for the pure friends, and also for the friends-peers.

4. Results

Not all employees took the survey, and not all employees participated in the SNS. The dataset of employees who had records in all three source systems (Table 1) contained composite records for 81,538 people.

RH1 asked if ties of any type appeared to influence each employee's engagement. We first examined this question via simple Pearson correlations. Table 2 shows that those correlations were significant for all types of ties. **RH1** was confirmed.

The set of hypotheses under **RH2** compared the relative strength of relationships across managers, pure peers, and pure friends.[2] We evaluated these hypotheses via a linear regression fitted to Model 1 (n=44,375):

[1] $$E = \alpha + \beta_{pp}(\text{purepeers}) + \beta_{pf}(\text{purefriends}) + \beta_{m}(\text{manager}) + \beta_{fp}(\text{friendspeers}) + \varepsilon$$

However, 130,778 employees had no hybrid friends-peers. Because they had missing data for friends-peers, their records dropped out of the analysis for Model 1. Therefore, we also tested a simpler Model 2 that omitted any tie that was both peer and friend (n=81,538):

[2] $$E = \alpha + \beta_{pp}(\text{purepeers}) + \beta_{pf}(\text{purefriends}) + \beta_{m}(\text{manager}) + \varepsilon$$

Table 3 summarizes the results of the regressions for both models. All of the influence factors were significant and positive (further confirmation of **RH1**). Because the range of values of the influence factors was the same (1-5), we could directly compare the size of the coefficients within each of the four analyses. Figure 2 shows the confidence limits for each. We note that the relative sizes of the coefficients are consistent between Model 1 and Model 2, and are broadly consistent with the correlation coefficients in Table 2 (with the exception of hybrid friends-peers). Each coefficient is significantly different from all other coefficients within its analysis – again with the exception of a slight overlap between purefriends and friends-peers in Model 1.

[2] We also considered models that included the mutual influence of subordinates upon a manager. However, those models excluded any employee who had no direct reports, thus harshly decreasing the sample size to fewer than 3000 managers. For this note, we omit the "subordinates" term in order to expand the sample sizes as reported for Models 1 and 2, respectively.

Table 3. Regression coefficients for Model 1 and Model 2.

	Model 1 (*including* friends-peers)	Model 2 (*excluding* friends-peers)
Influence	Regression Coefficient (β)	Regression Coefficient (β)
Adjusted R-Square	.158***	.140***
n	44,375	81,538
Pure peers	+.365***	+.429***
Pure friends	+.199***	+.244***
Friendspeers	+.175***	-
Manager	+.045***	+.061***

*** p<.001

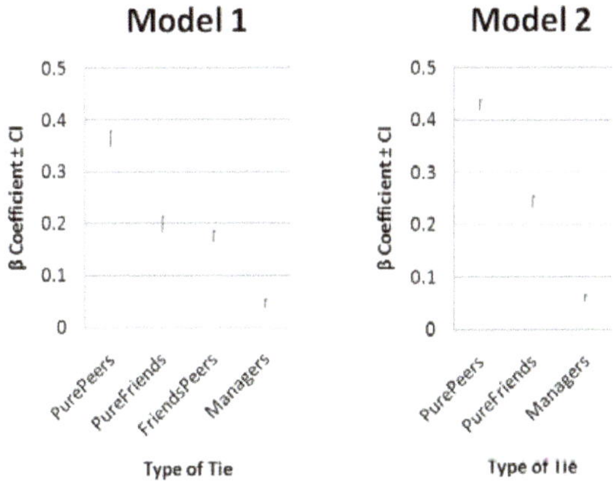

Figure 2. 95% Confidence intervals for regression coefficients in Model 1 and Model 2.

These relationships allow us to confirm **RH2c** (pure peers are most influential), followed by a weaker version of **RH2b** (pure friends). The supports for **RH2a** (manager) and **RH2d** (friends-peers), while significant in each case, are weakest.

Based on [27], we had hypothesized the impact of friend-relation + peer-relation to be additive. In these data, it may be that this hybrid category was more of a confused combination of two different influences, rather than a fusion of two influences into a single omnibus influence. The noisiness of the combination of influences may have reduced the predictive power for the hybrid friends-peers factor.

5. Discussion

Because our datasets had only partial overlap, we tested our more detailed research hypotheses three different ways:

- ***Correlations*** (Table 2), whose *pairwise* restrictions included the largest amount of the data
- ***Exhaustive regression*** (Table 3, Model 1), whose restrictions excluded any employee who had no friends-peers ties

- ***Relaxed regression*** (Table 3, Model 2), which included the larger set of employees with at least survey, manager, peer, and friend data.

The pattern of results across the three analyses is consistent in many aspects. Pure peers have the strongest relationship to Engagement. Pure friends have the next strongest relationship, but are significantly weaker than pure peers. Managers have the weakest relationship. The only exception to these general agreements was in the hybrid category of Friends Peers, which may have been a higher-variance combination of multiple types of relationships. All relationships are highly significant. Thus, the question is not to choose which relationship to measure, but rather how to measure their different, independent contributions to employee engagement.

5.1 Implications for Engagement Theory

Our results provide evidence that social factors may influence employee engagement (**RH1**), and that co-workers (peers) and Intranet friends are the more important of those factors (**RH2b** and **RH2c**, respectively), and are – notably – more important than managers (**RH2a**). This note provides an initial indication that theories and metrics of employee engagement [8, 18, 33, 39, 53] should be re-examined. The conventional vertical stack model of Figure 1A does not include the horizontal relationships with peers and friends (Figure 1B). Our analyses suggest that these relationships are also important factors in employee engagement. More broadly, our results suggest that executives and managers, while important, are not the only contributing factors to employees' engagement. Engagement depends not only on management, but also on peers and friends matter, who may in fact matter *more* than managers.

Nonetheless, managers must exercise some influence on engagement. First, as we reported for **RH2a**, managers do have a weaker but significant influence. Second, managers set the tone for a group of collaborating workers – i.e., for each employee and her/his peers. In this way, the strength of the peer influence or **RH2b** may be an indirect indicator of the workplace tone set by the manager.

5.2 Implications for Theories of Social Ties

These results help to link analysis of social ties (based in part on social media) to employees' experiences of work [4, 40, 41], through an important business metric (see also [2, 9, 19, 21, 28, 56]). In a convergent study, Guha et al. showed that an employee's position in an employee social network may also be predictive of engagement [16]. It will be interesting to compare this note's simple models of social influence, with more complex models that weight the social influence according to network position or homophily, or with other aspects of friendship [18] or affiliation [3].

While different types of homophily facets or social ties may operate similarly [27], these different types of ties may not be equally effective or informative [14, 51]. Our results are consistent with these findings, showing differential effectiveness (**RH2a-d**). In future work, we hope to explore the strength of additional types of ties, such as reply-to links in online discussion groups, or co-membership in online communities. It may be useful to theorize the relative strengths of these different types of workplace ties.

5.3 Implications for Organizations

The use of engagement measures in organizations is becoming an important measure of organizational "health" [1, 11, 17, 18, 21, 32, 52]. Our results have shown that social network factors may influence this type of measure, including online friendships that span geographic boundaries among co-workers in multinational corporations. Organizations may wish to explore whether support for peer- and friend- networking may improve employees' experience of work and the organization (e.g., [3]), and may provide means for sensing changes in employee engagement and perhaps additional channels for increasing engagement through social, mutual support.

Results of an engagement measurement survey may be used to guide actions to improve engagement among employee segments with low engagement scores. Traditionally, such action planning has been conducted with managers as the focal point [11, 25]. Our research suggests that the vertical stack model with the hierarchical top down approach to employee engagement may not be the only way to focus on improving engagement [16]. A more social model shifts the responsibility for improving engagement from the manager alone to all employees. In the long run, the social model may have a higher probability of success in improving engagement than relying on the manager alone. Future research will investigate how effective efforts of improving engagement through peer and friend relationships are.

There is a saying that people join companies but leave managers. Social support from peers and friends may alleviate the effect of poor managers. In organizations following the vertical stack model, engagement is only as strong as the weakest manager. For organizations struggling with retaining key talent because of poor management leadership, social support from peers and friends may impact whether an employee decides to stay or leave. More work is needed to determine the efficacy of peer and friend relationships in improving retention in situations where a manager may be providing poor leadership in the eyes of his or her employees.

5.4 Limitations

We reported on a large-scale hybrid network in IBM, a company that strongly supports doing work through internal social media. Further research is needed to see if these results replicate in other organizations, and/or in organizations that place less emphasis on internal social media.

We note that a majority of the IBM employees lacked survey data or friendship data, and thus limited the sample size. As organizations mature in their use of enterprise social networks, we expect that the coverage of this kind of analysis will increase.

While we have presented our results in terms of influence on an employee by her/his social ties, the relationship is of course bi-directional. The survey data were collected simultaneously. Therefore, although we have written in the language of causal models (e.g., "influence"), a more complete description may need to speak of "mutual influence" and "associations" in place of causal models.

We also note that the formal and observable social ties in our analysis may not correspond to individual employees' views of their own personal social worlds. Asking this number of employees to list their social ties would have disrupted the work of a substantial proportion of the organization. Therefore, we used the formal and observable ties as an approximation of people's experienced social ties.

Finally we acknowledge that there are many definitions and metrics of employee engagement [8, 18, 33, 39, 53]. More research will be needed to determine if these other measures and metrics show the same patterns of social influences.

6. REFERENCES

[1] Simon L. Albrecht (2010). Handbook of employee engagement: Perspectives, issues, research and practice. Edward Elgar, Cheltenham, UK.

[2] Hossam Ali-Hassan, Dorit Nevo, and Michael Wade (2015). Linking dimensions of social media use to job performance. *J. Strat. Info. Sys. 24*(2), 65-89.

[3] Derek R. Avery, Patrick F. McKay, and David C. Wilson (2007). Engaging the aging workforce: The relationship between perceived age similarity, satisfaction with coworkers, and employee engagement. *J. App. Psych. 92*(6), 1542-1556.

[4] Jeanette Blomberg and Helena Karasti (2013). Reflections on 25 years of ethnography in CSCW. *CSCW Journal 22*(4), 373-423.

[5] Stephen P. Borgatti and Pacey C. Foster. (2003). The network paradigm in organizational research: A review and typology. *J. Mgmt 29*(6), 991-1013.

[6] Kimberley Breevaart, Arnold B. Bakker, Evangelia Demerouti, and Jörn Hetland (2012). The measure of state work engagement: A multilevel factor analytic study. *Eur. J. Psych. Assess. 28*(4), 305-312.

[7] Michael J. Brzozowski (2009). Watercooler: Exploring an organization through enterprise social media. *Proc. GROUP 2009*, 219-228.

[8] Eean R. Crawford, Jeffrey A. LePine, and Bruce Louis Rich (2010). Linking job demands and resources to employee engagement and burnout: A theoretical extension and meta-analytic test. *J. App. Psych. 95*(5), 834-848.

[9] Rob Cross, Stephen P. Boratti, and Andrew Parker (2002). Making invisible work visible: Using social network analysis to support strategic collaboration. *California Management Review 57*(4), 25-46.

[10] Munmun De Chouldhery and Scott Counts (2013). Understanding affect in the workplace via social media. *Proc. CSCW 2013*, 303-316.

[11] Emma Donaldson-Feilder and Rachel Lewis (2015). Positive manager behaviour for engagement and wellbeing. In Ronald J. Burke, Kathryn M. Page, and Cary L. Cooper (eds.), *Flourishing in life, work and careers: Individual wellbeing and career experiences*. Cheltenham UK: Edward Elgar.

[12] Mayuri Duggirala, Sameep Mehta, Nanda Kambhatla, and Pooja Arya (2002). Employee engagement: Conceptual model and computational framework. *Proc. Serv. Res. Innov. Inst. Glob. Conf. 2012*, 850-858.

[13] Shelly D. Farnham and Elizabeth F. Churchill (2011). Faceted identity, faceted lives: Social and technical issues with being yourself online. *Proc. CSCW 2011*, 359-368.

[14] Eric Gilbert and Karrie Karahalios (2014). Computing and building around tie strength in social media. *Found. Trends in HCI 7*(3), 237-349.

[15] Matthias HJ Gouthier and Miriam Rhein (2011). Organizational pride and its positive effects on employee behavior. *J. Serv. Mgmt. 22*(5), 633-649.

[16] Shion Guha, Michael Muller, N Sadat Shami, Mikhil Masli and Werner Geyer. 2016. Using Organizational Social Networks to Predict Employee Engagement *Proc. ICWSM* 2016, 571-574.

[17] James K. Harter, Frank L. Schmidt, and Theodore L. Hayes (2002). Business-unit-level relationship between employee satisfaction, employee engagement, and business outcomes: A meta-analysis. *J. App. Psych.87*(2), 268-279.

[18] James K. Harter, Frank L. Schmidt, and Corey L.M. Keyes (2003). Well-being in the workplace and its relationship to business outcomes: A review of the Gallup studies. In Corey L.M. Keyes and Jonathan Haidt (eds.), *Flourishing: The positive person and the good life*, Washington DC US: APA.

[19] Nik R. Hassan (2009). Using social network analysis to measure IT-enabled business process performance. *Info. Sys. Mgmt. 26*(1), 61-76.

[20] Lester J. Holtzblatt and Laurie E. Damianos (2011). Measuring the success of on-line communities in an enterprise networking tool. *Proc. OCSC 2011*, 188-196.

[21] Fatma Jaupi and Shyqyri Llaci (2014). Employee engagement and its relation with key economic indicators. *J. IT Econ Dev. 5*(2), 112-122.

[22] Yoon A. Kim, Jae Yun Moon, and Ji Hye Park (2015). Reconceptualization of SNS use in organizations. *Proc. ICEC 2015*, Article no. 28.

[23] Alina Krischkowsky, Verena Fuchsberger, and Manfred Tscheligi (2014). Revisiting corporate social media: Challenges and implications from a long-term study. *Proc. GROUP 2014*, 157-166.

[24] Victor Lipman (2013). Surprising, disturbing facts from the mother of all employee engagement surveys. *Forbes Leadership*, 23 September 2013. http://www. forbes.com/sites/victorlipman/2013/09/23/surprising-disturbing-facts-from-the-mother-of-all-employee-engagement-surveys/ (accessed 10 October 2015).

[25] Fred Luthans and Suzanne J. Peterson (2002). Employee engagement and manager self-efficacy. *J. Mgmt. Dev. 21*(5), 376-387.

[26] Gloria Mark, Shamsi T. Iqbal, Mary Czerwinski, and Paul Johns (2014). Bored Mondays and focused afternoons: The rhythm of attention and online activity in the workplace. *Proc. CHI 2014*, 3025-3034.

[27] Michael Muller, Werner Geyer, Todd Soule, and John Wafer (2014). Geographical and organizational distances in enterprise crowdfunding. *Proc. CSCW 2014*, 778-789,

[28] Janine Nahapiet,, and Sumantra Ghoshal. (1998). Social capital, intellectual capital, and the organizational advantage. *Acad. Mgmt. Rev. 23*(2). 242-266.

[29] Bonnie A. Nardi (2005). Beyond bandwidth: Dimensions of connection in interpersonal communication. *JCSCW 14*(2), 91-130.

[30] Bonnie A. Nardi, Steve Whittaker, and Heinrich Schwarz (2000). It's not what you know, it's who you know. *First Monday 5*(5).

[31] Bonnie A. Nardi, Steve Whittaker, and Heinrich Schwarz (2002). NetWORKers and their activity in intensionalNetworks. *JCSCW 11*(1-2), 205-242.

[32] P.C. Panigrahi and Sarmistha Mishra (2014). Employee engagement: A strategic tool for performance. *Int. J. Meas. Res. IV*(1), 22-36.

[33] Bruce Louis Rich, Jeffrey A. Lepine, and Eean R. Crawford (2010). Job engagement: Antecedents and effects on job performance. *Acad. Mgmt J. 53*(3), 617-635.

[34] Inbal Ronen, Elad Shahar, Sigalit Ur, Erel Uziel, Sivan Yogev, Naama Zwerdling, David Carmel, Ido Guy, Nadav Har'el, and Shila Ofek-Koifman (2009). Social networks and discovery in the enterprise. *Proc. SIGIR 2009*, 836-836.

[35] John Rooksby and Ian Somerville (2012). The management and use of social network sites in a government department. *JCSCW 21*(4-5), 397-415.

[36] Alan M. Saks (2006). Antecedents and consequences of employee engagement. *J. Mgmt. Psych. 71*(7), 600-619.

[37] Alan M. Saks (2008). The meaning and bleeding of employee engagement: How muddy is the water? *Ind. Org. Psych. 1*(1), 40-43.

[38] Mónica Sara Santos and Jeremy Pitt (2013). Emotions and norms in shared spaces. *Proc. COIN 2013*, 157-176.

[39] Wilmar B. Schaufeli and Arnold B. Bakker (2010). Defining and measuring work engagement: A review. In Arnold B. Bakker and Michael P. Leiter (eds.), *Work engagement: A handbook of essential theory and research*. New York NY USA: Psychology Press.

[40] Kjeld Schmidt and Liam Bannon (2013). Constructing CSCW: The first quarter century. *CSCW Journal 22*(4), 345-372.

[41] Kjeld Schmidt and Liam Bannon (1992). Taking CSCW seriously: Supporting articulation work. *CSCW Journal 1*(1), 7-40.

[42] Piia Seppälä (2013). *Work engagement: Psychometri-cal, psychosocial, and psychophysiological approach*. PhD thesis, Jyväskylän Yliopisto, Finland. Jyväskylä studies in education, psychology, and social research 475.

[43] Piia Seppälä, Saijo Mauno, Taru Feldt, Jari Hakanen, Ulla Kinnunen, Asko Tolvanen, and William Schaufeli (2008). The construct validity of the Utrecht work engagement scale: Multisample and longitudinal evidence. *J. Happ. Stud. 10*, 459-481.

[44] N. Sadat Shami, Michael Muller, Aditya Pal, Mikhil Masli, and Werner Geyer (2015). Inferring employee engagement from social media. *Proc. CHI 2015*, 3999-4008.

[45] N. Sadat Shami, Jiang Yang, Laura Panc, Casey Dugan, Tristan Ratchford, Jamie C. Rasmussen, Yannick M. Assogba, Tal Steier, Todd Soule, Stela Lupashor, Werner Geyer, Ido Guy, and Jonathan Ferrer (2014). Understanding employee social media chatter with enterprise social pulse. *Proc. CSCW 2014*, 379-392.

[46] David Sharek and Eric Wiebe (2015). Investigating real-time predictors of engagement: Implications for adaptive videogames and online training. *Int. J. Gaming & Comp-Med. Sim. 7*(1), 20-37.

[47] Sabine Sonnentag, Christian Dormann, and Evangelia Demerouti (2010). Not all days are created equal: The concept of state work engagement. In Arnold B. Bakker and Michael P. Leiter (Eds.), Work engagement: *A handbook of essential theory and research*. Hove: Psychology Press, 2010.

[48] Charles Steinfield, Joan M. DiMicco, Nicole B. Ellison, and Cliff Lampe (2009). Bowling online: social networking and social capital within the organization. *Proc. C&T 2009*, 245-254.

[49] Tolman & Wiker (n.d.). Why employee engagement has a direct impact on your business bottom line. http://tolmanandwiker.com/employee-engagement-direct-impact-business-bottom-line/

[50] A. Narasima Venkatesh (2015). Employee engagement through leadership. *Am. Int. J. Res. Hum. Arts, Soc. Sci. 9*(4), 333-336.

[51] Jason Wiese, Jun-Ki Min, Jason I. Hong, and John Zimmerman (2015). "You never call, you never write": Call and SMS logs do not always indicate tie strength. *Proc. CSCW 2015*, 765-774.

[52] Jack W. Wiley (2010a). The impact of effective leadership on employee engagement. *Empl. Rel. Today 37*(2), 47-52.

[53] Jack W. Wiley, Ann E. Herman, and Brenda J. Kowske (2010b). Developing and validating a global model of employee engagement. In Simon L. Albrecht (ed.), *Handbook of employee engagement: Perspectives, issues, research and practice*. Edward Elgar, Cheltenham, UK.

[54] Anna Wu, Joan M. DiMicco, and David R. Millen (2010). Detecting professional versus personal closeness using an enterprise social network site. *Proc. CHI 2010*, 1955-1964.

[55] Jiawei Zhang, Yuanhua Lv, and Philip Yu (2015). Enterprise social link recommendation. *Proc. CIKM 2015*, 841-850.

[56] Xiaojun Zhang and Viswanath Venkatesh (2013). Explaining employee job performance: The role of online and offline workplace communication networks. *MIS Quart. 37*(3), 695-722.

[57] Lijun Zhu, Alvin Chin, Ke Zhang, Wenchang Xu, Hao Wang, and Li Zhang (2010). Managing workplace resources in office environments through ephemeral social networks. *Proc. UIC 2010*, 665-679.

Lifecycles of Computer Clubs: Rhythms and Patterns of Collaboration and Learning in an Intercultural Setting

Anne Weibert, Mary-Ann Sprenger, Dave Randall & Volker Wulf
Institute for Information Systems and New Media
University of Siegen
Siegen, Germany
[anne.weibert;mary-ann.sprenger;dave.randall;volker.wulf]@uni-siegen.de

ABSTRACT

This long-term study analyzes the structure of a technology-mediated local initiative fostering cross-cultural understanding and respect: come_IN intercultural computer clubs provide open yet guided access to modern information and computer technology and offer a space for computer-related collaborative practices of children and adults in intercultural German neighborhoods. Our study addresses problems associated with 'cultural integration' and attempts to solve them through this provision. It reveals rhythms, lifecycles and breakdown situations which, transferred to a general level, form the basic structure for a sustainable implementation of a technology-related local initiative fostering cross-cultural understanding and respect. The study is based on field notes taken in three of these clubs.

CCS Concepts

H5.m. Information interfaces and presentation (e.g., HCI): Miscellaneous.

Keywords

Children; Collaboration; Computer Club; Intercultural; Lifecycles.

1. INTRODUCTION

With increasing numbers of people seeking for access and then societal participation, migration is a major issue affecting societies around the world. This entails the question how cross-cultural understanding and respect can be fostered. Managing change in a way as to produce sustainable integration is a non-trivial matter, depending on agreement about specific policy implementation. Here, we present the results of a project founded on a clear implementation policy and reflect on practical consequences. How to achieve cross-cultural understanding and respect is a question that has been approached from diverse ends [16, 24, 27]. *Integration takes place locally.* This slogan sums up recent insights regarding political and economic policy in Germany. Cultural and economic integration is regarded as a 'bottom up' process whereby local initiative eventually translates into structural change, such that core values, common rules and mutual knowledge of and respect for social or cultural differences will become embedded in German society [2, 3, 26]. Initiatives that address these aspects are numerous, encompassing various parts of life. In 2007 these have been systematized in a National Integration Plan, providing overview on integration success in measurable steps [32]. Central areas include language, education and work, community, sports, media, culture and arts. Of course, such policy statements and their implementations do not necessarily translate into *successful* practice and there is a clear need to evaluate practices to see 'what works', what does not and – equally importantly – why.

A special focus of German policy lies in projects addressing the unequal access of migrant communities and mainstream society to computer infrastructure. That is, a central assumption is that the 'digital divide' remains [e.g. 20, 35, 38]: equal access to computer technology and modern media (and skilled handling thereof) are expected to be pre-requisites for access to many parts of modern work life and education; also, technology mediated interactions can widen the space for the creation of a mutual knowledge base, shared understanding of cultural differences and common ground among immigrant communities and mainstream society. Having said that, it is important to understand what the dimensions of this unequal access might be. Highly generalized appeals to 'culture' may overlook gender, age and other differences which impact on the divide. Some parts of our effort, therefore, are concerned with recognizing how these more specific factors manifest.

As part of this effort to understand how 'integration' might be better achieved and how to structure good practice, we have conducted a research project over the last ten years centering on the question of how the digital divide can be bridged. For this, we have founded a network of six intercultural come_IN computer clubs in socially and culturally diverse neighborhoods. They provide open yet guided access to information and computer technology. Also, they offer a space for computer-related collaborative practices of children and adults, thus supporting the development of community structures and language skills.

Our study addresses the issue of how to generate a sustainable implementation of a local, technology-related integration initiative. We structure our analysis and argument as follows. We first give a brief overview on the theoretical discourse around the use of ICTs for integrative purposes. We then describe the background to the development of the come_IN computer clubs in Germany. The subsequent in-depth analysis of these clubs and their activities, we will argue, reveals a number of strengths and weaknesses. This evaluation provides a basis. From there, we derive the general structure of a concept that may serve as a blueprint for others who are aiming to sustainably implement a technology-related local integration initiative. The contribution of this paper is the development of a set of guidelines for how the interplay of social interactions and their technological support can work in an intercultural and intergenerational local context.

GROUP '16, November 13-16, 2016, Sanibel Island, FL, USA
 ISBN 978-1-4503-4276-6/16/11…$15.00
DOI: http://dx.doi.org/10.1145/2957276.2957306

2. RELATED WORKS

The concept of the come_IN intercultural computer clubs was mainly inspired by the US concept of computer clubhouses [22]. Since 1993, when the first club was opened in Boston, the US model has explicitly addressed inner city youth with educationally and socially deprived backgrounds. Relying on principles of situated, collaborative learning and constructionist thinking, the clubhouse's main focus lies on the development and strengthening of individual skills, confidence and creativity. The computer clubhouses open up opportunities for disadvantaged local communities in the cities and their success is well documented in research [e.g. 11, 22, 23].

With the establishment of the come_IN clubs in Germany, the US model of computer clubhouses has been developed further to support foster cross-cultural understanding and respect at the local level, and support intercultural and intergenerational learning. The main incentive is the establishment and strengthening of local relations between different ethnic groups [25, 28], thus promoting a positive impact on identity formation processes [37].

The background to such initiatives lies in a public discourse on integration in Germany, dominated by two larger themes, both of which have been subject of intensive and often emotional debate [9]. Firstly, the so-called "digital divide" describes the discourse on unequal access by migrant communities to computer infrastructure compared to mainstream society [20, 35, 38]. Secondly, there is a discourse on so-called "Parallelgesellschaften", which we may translate as "parallel societies", and which describes processes of ghetto-ization such that migrant communities live with little or no contact with host culture. This is tied up with issues of multiculturalism [13] and debates about the complex relationship between host and immigrant culture [e.g. 14].

We are specifically interested in two dimensions of integration. The first – the structural dimension – is concerned with equal access to all aspects of societal life, such as justice, governmental institutions, education, labor, standard of living, and social security. The second – the cultural dimension – deals with a common basis for living that is based on common language, shared core values, common rules and mutual respect for and knowledge of social and cultural differences. We adopt Charles Taylor's perspective, such that integration at the cultural level is seen as the dialogic or interactional process which constructs identity [31]. Immigration as the starting point of an integration process [e.g. 2, 3] is seen to be followed by different forms of adaptation: integration, accommodation, separation, and marginalization. Important factors for the integration progress are identified in attitudes towards one's own identity as well as the intensity of one's relation to other societal groups. However, what is arguably missing from the discourse (and would be implied in Taylor's view) is recognition of two facts. The first is that 'culture' is an abstraction and called into play by participants much less often than 'community', 'family' and 'neighbourhood' as sources of identity construction and maintenance. As we shall see, such allegiances are central to the task of making activities relevant to participants. The second is that these processes are not smooth. The rhythms of interaction; the longer-term lifecycles we observe, and the occurrence of breakdowns, all mediate the integration process.

This notion of rhythm and recurring patterns has been thoroughly looked into in research in the health-care sector, covering clinical [e.g. 21, 29, 40] as well as non-clinical settings [e.g. 17], and the interdependence of both [e.g. 1, 5]. It has helped to understand what Reddy and Dourish call "orienting features" [21, p. 344] in complex environments, and what Jackson et al. [8] identified to have four central forms – organizational, infrastructural, biographical, and phenomenal – in collaborative scientific work settings.

Following Taylor's view [31] and the argument above, we see progress in integration processes be dependent on the interplay of a number of factors from various parts of life. For example, progress on the job market cannot be looked at without regarding the development of intercultural equality in education, and education matters cannot be judged upon without taking into account the local community structures. Typical studies in the field however, rarely bring together these different perspectives and interactions of different societal actors, instead focusing on single aspects or actors (e.g. on the role of the media [36], or on education [39]). With regard to the impact of technological interventions on integration processes, researchers only recently started to discuss various perspectives together, focusing on their value and effect for a sustainable diversity [9]. In Germany, this has culminated in a National Integration Plan [32] that encompasses aspects of language, education and work, as well as local community structures, sports, media, culture and arts.

So, the necessity of a holistic approach has been recognized in principle. As yet, however, it has been less well evaluated, especially through close empirical study. The long-term analysis of the development of come_IN clubs that we offer here, then, provides an assessment of these ambitious proposals at a local level. Our case study contributes to a better understanding of the constituents necessary for the sustainably lasting implementation of a local, technology-related integration initiative. It reveals practical problems, identifies possible solutions and describes useful practices for the successful implementation of this holistic approach. The focus of our analysis is the interplay of social interactions taking into account the factors mentioned, and their technological support in an intercultural, intergenerational context.

3. INTERCULTURAL COMPUTER CLUBS

Come_IN clubs offer a place for shared practice in a non-directive environment by children and adults. Mostly located in schools in intercultural neighborhoods, they bring together people of different migration background and age to work on joint projects or individual enterprises, study or play. By focusing their collaborative project work on 'community', 'family' and 'neighbourhood' as sources of identity construction, the computer clubs are designed to make a contribution to the development of a new understanding of the neighborhood and one's individual role in it – a prerequisite to the fostering of cross-cultural understanding and respect on the local level. Three principles are important: a) the support of individual and communal creativity, b) joint project work with computers and other modern media, c) a close link between project work, local neighborhood issues and ideas generated by participating children and adults [25, 28, 37].

The neighborhood has a large impact on computer club project topics, e.g. when magazines about the neighborhood are created, an animated film about friendship is made, or a board game is created by means of MIT's programming environment, Scratch [15]. These computer-based projects help to establish and strengthen relationships in the neighborhoods and provide interactional resources which – in some cases – children and adults might not have (gender issues, e.g., along with language barriers, restrict opportunities for some women to engage with the host culture).

This approach of the come_IN computer clubs ties in to the national striving for integration on two levels. For one, participation in the computer club encompasses the opportunity to gain in eloquence with regard to speech and the confident development and negotiation of opinions and perspectives across ages and cultures. And secondly, it also enables technology appropriation and use, thus helping not only the bridging of the "digital divide", but also fostering the chance for equal participation in the various parts of public life, most prominent among them the work sector. With this, the computer clubs assess central elements that have been identified in the National Integration Plan at a local neighborhood level: acquisition and broadening of language skills, education and work, as well as the strengthening of (neighborhood) community ties.

The first come_IN computer club was opened in a medium-sized city in the Rhineland in 2004. The transferability of the concept was tested with the opening of the second computer club in a mid-size town in the Siegerland in 2006. Here, experiences from the first club have been used to enhance social and technical aspects of the concept through participative means. Discussions with club members about previous and proposed activities took place, a more flexible way of playing and working in the club was agreed, and new equipment which better allowed for mobility (i.e. laptops) purchased. Also, the club's file repository got a new structure with personalized logins. The foundation of subsequent clubs followed in 2009. Two are located at a school-center in a mid-size city in the Rhineland, where older children were explicitly targeted. In a small city in the Siegerland, senior citizens adopted the concept in a joint initiative with teenagers in a youth center. A neighborhood initiative founded another club in a primary school in a large city in the Ruhr area.

General structures, rules and practices derived from the pilot club were introduced in all other clubs as they have proven to be successful in practice. Central to this is the voluntary nature of participation: originally, both children and parents were required to join the weekly club meetings to work, learn and play together but this rule was relaxed after a while, and children who could not participate together with a parent (e.g. because the latter had to work during club time), were encouraged to join come_IN together with another family member or friend.

In general, club work is guided by a school teacher and tutors from our research team. The course of each of the one and a half hour long club sessions follows a tripartite structure: 1) the official club meetings start with an initial discussion round about work in progress and/or new projects, 2) the main working period and 3) the closing discussion round about problems, highlights of the day's club session and an outlook on upcoming activity. A 15-minute time slot is provided before the club meeting starts, where children can play and adults have time to commute.

3.1 Technical Support for Common Club Practices

On a material level, special attention is being paid to support the sharing and development of ideas and creative work among participants in the clubs and beyond. Some clubs keep a "treasure box of ideas", a wooden box where children and adults write project plans and ideas for activities on paper cards to make them accessible for later times (Figure 1). This support structure was also implemented to ease the integration of newcomers into the computer club community, as it provides them with a set of ideas.

Figure 1. Some clubs keep project sketches and open questions in a "treasure box of ideas".

Also, an online community platform called come_NET has been introduced to the clubs in order to support their emerging network and to promote the communication among club participants and shared practice over distance by providing various communication features (Figure 2). It uses metaphors, such as 1) a virtual blackboard for entries that are written and read only by participants of the same club and 2) a common, but user-group oriented, mail function. Furthermore, participants can set up a profile, create a photo album, add friends or search for club projects. The platform with all its features has been built up and evaluated to meet the needs of participants in the clubs with regard to age and technological fluency.

Figure 2. The community platform promotes shared practice.

4. METHOD AND DATA

As an evaluative study we are specifically aiming at an understanding of the relationship between stated policy and practical outcomes: the focus of this paper is the description and analysis of lifecycles and breakdown situations in a computer club. It uses qualitative methods, and relies on field notes and transcripts collected as part of a participatory action research [12] perspective. This means that members of the research team are active participants in the computer clubs and routinely act as tutors (and indeed have done so since their inception). Jottings have been taken by tutors during the weekly club sessions and were then completed to full field notes. Their focus in very general terms has been the observable collaborations and interactions of children and adult club participants, their appropriation of media and computer technology, and associated processes of learning and social integration. For our study, field notes constituted the main resource, collected over the period mentioned below.

With this situated participatory action research setup and long-term perspective, our evaluative study falls in line with works from the fields of HCI, computer-supported collaborative work and learning, taking a situated approach to the evaluation of (socio-)technical interventions in complex social settings. Neale et al. [19] have laid out the scope of complexity: "Individual cognitive factors must be considered, as well as cooperative and collaborative factors, usability issues for individuals and groups (ease of use, effectiveness, efficiency, satisfaction), the social and organizational impact, and the larger context that situates the other factors." [19, p. 113]. In their study of computer networking to teach writing, Bruce and Peyton have aimed evaluation at an understanding of "the process whereby realizations of an innovation are generated and to provide insight to practitioners attempting to implement innovative approaches" [4, p. 171]. Like Twidale et al. [34], Bruce and Peyton emphasize a need "to include a 'situated' component, which seeks to understand how that innovation looks in each of its different contexts of use" [4, p. 190].

4.1 Data Collection and Analysis

Central to the study presented here are those three clubs from the computer club network that are located in primary schools. The material we present is taken from a total of eight years of field notes in the case of club A, five years of material in club B, and two years in club C. Participation typically consists of eight children and two mothers in *club A*, eight children and four to five adults in *club B*, and *club C* sees seven to ten children and five to seven adults every week.

It is important to note, that participation in the computer clubs is voluntary and free for everyone in the neighborhood. Participating children and adults are informed about the accompanying research project aiming to equalize access to modern information and computer technology, as well as to support the building of local communities across age, social, cultural and migration differences. Participants are assured that no identifying information is revealed about them. As part of the participatory action research approach, all participants are regularly invited to give feedback on the computer club structure, on completed projects and activities, and thus participate in shaping the overall club structure and course of action.

Coding of material [14, 30] was guided by our focus on the interplay of social interactions and technological support in an intercultural, intergenerational context.

In a first step, we read through the data to identify recurring patterns in the observable collaborations and interactions and their technological support in the computer club. These in hand, we comprehensively coded for the following areas: *Group Experiences, School Year, Project Work, Club Sessions, Completion of Tasks, Individual Involvement* and *Material Matters.*

4.2 The field

Even though similar in their socially and culturally diverse nature, each of the clubs and neighborhoods in focus has its own characteristics. As they are central to the study presented here, we give an overview on each one in the following sections.

4.2.1 City A

The foundation of the computer club in a primary school in city A was made possible above all by the engagement of the primary school's headmistress and a number of parents from the school that educates around 200 children. As there was no IT equipment readily available for the club in the school, it had to find local sponsors for their desk top PCs. Right from the start, the club had a lively awareness of the surrounding neighborhood and conducted several projects with a strong link to it, namely the creation of little brochures called "Neighborhood Stories" about nice as well as disliked places in the quarter, or a soccer tournament with a neighboring Turkish soccer club that resulted in numerous photo and video artifacts. As there were especially mothers accompanying their children, a women's group was active within the club over a period of time, e.g. creating a film about their migration experiences, meeting to cook and eat together, and learning the language.

With regard to cultural background participation in the club is mirroring the general neighborhood structure, Turkish and German children making up for the largest share of computer club participants. 27.8 % of the population in this neighborhood of city A does have a migration background (compared to the city as a whole with 22.4% migrant population), the largest share of which is of Turkish descent, many of them originating from the same region, even the same town, in Turkey. Within that context, the school knows about its significance as a central meeting place. On the school's website it says: "As especially families with migration backgrounds often times live together in very confined space, our school with its outside terrain is an important meeting place for mothers and their children." Participation in the club varied greatly over the years, roughly speaking consisting of an average of eight children and two mothers, but with peaks of up to 30 participants.

4.2.2 City B

The computer club in city B is the second-oldest club in the come_IN network. It was founded in summer 2006. Its foundation was part of a research project regarding the transferability of the come_IN approach. In search of a school as a project partner various primary schools in city B were visited. Diversity of the surrounding neighborhood, number of students with migration background and commitment of the school were some of the decisive criteria. This neighborhood of city B is a multicultural and diverse neighborhood with approximately 3.200 inhabitants; about 25% of whom has a migratory background. The neighborhood's primary school committed itself to the participation in come_IN with great engagement and therefore was chosen as a project partner. During the first months a series of workshops and meetings with teachers, students, their parents and neighbors were conducted to best match the structure of the prospective club to the local needs.

With regard to IT equipment, the computer club in city B had to start from scratch as no equipment was available for it to work with. For almost a school year the computer club sessions were held in normal class rooms using borrowed hardware from the university. During this time a room on the top floor of this small school's (approx. 110 students) historic building was newly furnished and equipped with IT to turn it into a combined computer club room and school library. With regard to cultural background, participation in the club resembles the surrounding neighborhood structure, with the largest share of people being of Turkish descent, followed by people from former Yugoslavia, Italy, Spain, Poland and Russia. More than half of the students have an immigrant background. An average of eight children and four to five adults participate in the club in city B. Approximately half of the participants form a kind of a core group that impels projects and the development of the computer club itself. Early on, many of the conducted projects were related to the neighborhood, e.g. wall calendars with neighborhood pictures have been created and an animated film about the friendship of a girl and a boy living in the neighborhood was produced.

4.2.3 City C

The introduction of the computer club in a neighborhood in the northern part of city C prompted immediate and lively discussion concerning the interests and individual needs of neighborhood inhabitants when the idea of the computer club was first introduced in local discussion rounds and neighborhood initiatives in summer 2009. Computer literacy was seen as important prerequisite for access to, and participation in, various parts of public life. The proposed computer club was expected to provide good help with regard to that matter for children and adults alike. Neighborhood inhabitants, a local non-profit organization and neighborhood managers worked together to bring the club to life in a primary school in the center of the neighborhood that does stand out in the city not only because of its high population density, large number of families, and comparatively young age structure, but also because of its rich diversity of nationalities, cultures and religions (57.7% of the neighborhood population does have a migration background), high unemployment rate, low incomes and restricted access to higher education. Almost every one of the 270 children in school knows two languages; one of the 20 teachers gives native-language lessons in Turkish; also the school offers Islamic and Alevi studies for the children, and provides a number of activities for parents and especially mothers – such as language classes, a "parent's café" and bicycle trainings. In this context, the computer club developed as a stable group of regular participants right from the start. Curiosity for the new opportunity and the demand for participation was high, so that the club established a waiting list and has kept it ever since. The club sees seven to ten children and five to seven adults every week. The migration backgrounds of participants reflect the diversity of the surrounding neighborhood, with children and adults from Turkey, Albania, Macedonia, Tunisia and Morocco.

5. RESULTS

In the following, we present the empirical work which demonstrates rhythms, lifecycles and breakdowns which affect processes designed to be integrative. We argue, in the context of the clubs, that these take specific forms.

5.1 Group experiences

The first thing to note is that the clubs orient to a two-year cycle, because they are geared to the age policies of state schools. The come_IN clubs generally host children from 2nd to 4th grade, when they change to secondary school. Consequences are two-fold: 1) the club finds itself in need to promote itself in order to remain sizeable, and 2) social as well as technological expertise is endangered with certain persons leaving the club. Our study found all clubs to be well aware of the first aspect, and in all cases, the promotion of the computer club was a matter of personal advocacy – of children, adults and teachers. *"Tell your friends! Ask them, if they want to join!"*, the teacher in club B is heard to say regularly, as she encourages children and adults to actively promote the computer club. This can be done formally as well, as with club C, which established a waiting list of children who want to participate. *"Let's see, who we have there who might want to join"*, as the teacher put it when there places became available. Club A and club B also advertised the club at classes and parent teacher meetings.

The second feature is less well recognized, and is usually prompted by the recognition that a particular individual will no longer participate. As a teacher from club C said, *"We'll see how things will be, when she won't attend any more – she really holds things together"*, about a Turkish mother. The mother, the teacher reported, had developed *"the right touch in caring for a good atmosphere"*, e.g. by bringing tea or looking after children who had problems completing homework before joining the general club activity. And a tutor, who had to leave the club for work reasons, left a number of artifacts as visible proof of his expertise: under his guidance some rather tangible projects were made – e.g. the club had built loudspeakers from computer's hard drives, or tore a computer apart to learn about its functionalities before putting it back together.

5.2 The school year

Club activity takes place weekly. Participants gather to pursue their joint projects. This rhythm seems to match the children's abilities to keep track of their work's progress. When this pattern is interrupted, the consequences become evident. The questions that clubs routinely have to deal in these circumstances have the flavor of, What did I do last week? What was my plan to do next, when I was interrupted at the session's close? Where did I save my project?

These interruptions are largely a function of the school year, principally holidays. The most significant is the six week summer break. For the clubs these holidays form a caesura: after that, it is a new school year, with new subjects, new class mates, new rooms. Thus, club activity tends to fit with the breaks. Projects have to be designed to come to a 'natural' conclusion before the break, material and other resources have to be managed in respect of this flow, and 'presentational' activities tend to be organized with an eye on this. A film made in club C is a good example insofar as all of the above factors influenced its production, culminating in its showing at the school's end-of-term celebration, with participating children explaining to the school assembly how it was created.

5.3 Project work

Projects themselves have a significant effect on the rhythm of the clubs, given the focus in the clubs on collaborative activity. They range in length from a couple of sessions to several months. The completion of one project and the start of a new one does, however, mark a hiatus. The club's joint discussion rounds are used for the presentation of completed club projects as well as the negotiation and planning of new project activity. Furthermore, we see club participants regularly gather for a "museum round" in club C, where each of the participants presents his or her share in the project to the others. Participants in club B jointly looked at their completed project work via projector. *"Can you explain to the others, how you did this?"*, asks the teacher encouraging children to present their skills and their share of the work to the others in the club. Club A addressed an even larger audience by distributing their written stories of the neighborhood as booklets in print, selling these "neighborhood stories" for a little money at school events or in public places like the library.

Nevertheless, friction can occur in the time in between a project's formal beginning and end. Children show varying ability to concentrate over a longer period of time – e.g. during an animation film project in the club in club C. *"But we made heaps of pictures already – aren't we done yet?"*, a 9-year old boy asks. Creating hundreds of still images, the children experience learning by doing, how much effort is needed to complete just one minute of moving film. Interruptions are also caused by unexpectedly complex tasks to complete. For the handling of these frictions, our study finds all three clubs placing emphasis on joint opening and closing sessions as a place to solve problems and share expertise. A field note protocol reports the teacher in club C asking: 'Does everyone know, what there is to do today?' Another protocol describes the teacher from club B encouraging the sharing of expertise among the participants: *"Who knows how to do this?"*

5.4 Club sessions

The weekly club meetings are the basic components of each club's life. Here, project work is completed and – encircling this – social structures among the children and adult participants evolve. In general, club sessions are divided into a section of free time for individual play and work at the computer, and a part for the joint project work. Our notes from the very first sessions of club C see this division quickly established. Children and adults make use of the very first session to get to know each other, and then – triggered by the tutors' question *"Do you know what to do with the computer?"* – jointly discuss ideas what they might want to do and explore in their computer club *("Play games." – "You can also use a computer to call home via the internet – my grandma does so!" – "Make a movie." – "Write something.")*. The next session is devoted to familiarization with the group, the room and the computer. Here, a first division of play-time and work-time is made, when the teacher ensures that children don't use the club session solely for playing games. After a couple of sessions, this division has settled: *"Can we start the computer?" – "May I play?"*, boys and girls would ask when entering the computer room for the club session in club C, moving straightaway to "their" computer in the room, before later joining the common project work in the club. Field notes also report on children who had so fully internalized the division of play and work time that they would ask for permission to "skip playtime" and resume last session's project work right away, when they were fond of a project. There is, not surprisingly, a disjuncture between adult and child in attitude. Adults are more likely to place a focus on outcomes and learning progress and sometimes rigidly emphasize the division of play and work: *"Now close that window, sit still and listen, will ya!"* one was heard to say.

In club A, some children and adult participants rejected the discussion rounds for being too time-consuming. They felt that they knew what to do next when working on a long-term project and did not want to lose time talking. As a consequence, the club dropped the initial discussion round for a while. But the rounds were soon resumed, when it became apparent that participants lost structure and motivation for their work. One field note protocol reports a vivid argument in the closing discussion round: unaccomplished goals that had been defined at the beginning of the club session became apparent when participants could not report on further progress because they spent club time entertaining themselves with game play or interest in other's activities. The respective session's field notes also record arguments over who had actually completed tasks as one participant 'recreated' someone else's project, prompting the following exchange: *"He stole my idea!" – "No, I improved it!"*

In all computer clubs, we see tutors, teachers and parents be well aware of the significance of a cooperative atmosphere, where club participants are willing to share expertise and help others. Field notes record how one of the Turkish mothers in the club in club C would engage in supporting a boy in the completion of his homework before he was allowed to join in the general club activity of the day. In turn, that boy was seen to share his word processing skills when helping another design a questionnaire for a school class activity, or passing on acquired knowledge in the use of the programming environment Scratch [15], and explain e.g. how to create a loop. Field note protocols from club B repeatedly report how teachers use the joint discussion rounds to facilitate collaboration by asking questions such as: *"Ok – who can help?"* And regularity in the club's session schedule even helped club alumni to keep in touch with their club long after they had left school. Ever since its foundation, club C has kept the day and time of its sessions stable – so, every now and then, club alumni would join, whenever their new school's schedule permits them to do so (*"I knew that you are here today – so I thought, I'd join."*).

5.5 Completion of tasks

The effective completion of a club project is comprised of several discrete efforts, some more successful than others, and all of which require some degree of coordination. Our data sees each of these situations divide club participants into experts and learners with certain skill levels. In club A there are participants who have already left primary for secondary school, but still participate in the computer club. They tend to have detailed knowledge of certain computer applications, such as Scratch or Gimp and are often introduced to new participants as, "our expert for...". On this very basic level, we find the key to the successful or failed completion of tasks in the openly structured club session. Help rather than instruction, encouragement rather than criticism are fostered among all participants. An example from club A indicates this:

> G: *"I lost my essay. Where's it gone?"*
>
> T: *"Did you save it?"*
>
> G: *"Nooo ....."*
>
> T: *"You do it like this."* (demonstrates)
>
> Girl produces short essay and again forgets to save it.
>
> T: *"Doesn't matter ... I'll show you what to do."*
>
> Minutes later. G: *"Look, I saved it by myself!"* In the following closing discussion she excitedly reported: *"First I didn't feel like writing again, but then I did."*

The open structure, where teacher and tutors can respond to children and adults individually, helps situations where traditional roles are reversed in front of the computer, and parents find themselves in a position as learner with their children teaching them. The club context can exacerbate this at times, putting some parents in a position where they do not only lack technological fluency but are also dependent on their child with regard to language.

On an underlying level, the completion of tasks divides participants into those who are taken up with organization activity and those who are more passively engaged in project work. Our study sees all three clubs struggle to find a balance here, especially in long-term projects where small individual projects are condensed to one common group project (e.g. a game board that consists of several smaller games). Participants face situations where they feel over-challenged by complex tasks. Here, we see parents take over tasks, such as merging smaller games to one large game board or typesetting of a booklet that children would not be able to accomplish on their own. These issues are mainly dealt with in opening and closing discussion rounds.

5.6 Individual involvement

A further complication lies in the fact that individuals – children, parents and teachers – move on, especially where the person in question has a central role. Expertise, knowledge and moral authority can be lost in such circumstances. In club A, the founding teacher retired. As principal, she knew "her" school and its children and parents, and was known for her efforts in personally motivating people to participate in the club. Children and adults relied on her engagement with regard to the development of project ideas, planning of project activity and acquiring of resources. So, her retirement resulted in a decline in participation. It took time and effort for the club participants to reinvigorate the club using methods such as making use of questionnaires distributed among parents to establish interest in the club and lines of engagement, and holding meetings where ideas were 'brainstormed'. This could also be seen in club A when a highly motivated Turkish mother left the club. She had coordinated organizational tasks, and encouraged other Turkish parents in the neighborhood to participate. Due to her migration background, it was easy for her to address other Turkish families and convince them to accompany their kids and join the computer club. Thus, her leaving affected the attendance of some Turkish parents and they left: For them, maintenance of strong community links was less possible after a key figure ceased to participate.

Similar individual difficulties arise over matters of 'discipline'. This was the case in club C when a boy was told by the teacher not to come to the club any longer, because he refused to take part in any joint project work and perceived club sessions as only entailing access to computer play time. Children in the club perceived this decision to be unfair and joint resolution became necessary, with the boy being conditionally allowed back.

Even in environments which are explicitly designed to be collaborative and informal, certain individuals have disproportionate importance for various reasons. These include knowledge and expertise; role in the wider community, and moral authority. It is interesting to note that even in these informal settings, teachers retain some of that moral authority and it influences the behaviour of children. We noted how the teacher in club A could not attend several club sessions in a row because he was involved in a musical course at the time, and this resulted in a rather unstructured mix of play and work activity. Children exploited the absence of the teacher, and some careful emphasis on intergenerational work from thereon had to be generated.

5.7 Material matters

Material matters occasionally produce breakdown situations that interrupt the larger lifecycles of club activity. Our analysis finds these occurrences to be a hindrance, making the continuation of project work difficult and even impossible at times. Most of these frictions concern the storage of the computer clubs project files, such as video, pictures, text documents, and Scratch files. Club A and club C did not have separate, secured storage space on the school's server at first, so they could never be sure that none of the other people in school accessed their data, transformed or deleted it, be it on purpose or by accident. Both clubs first helped themselves by storing and securing files on a USB stick that either the teacher or a tutor would bring to each of the club sessions.

In club A the problem was then solved by storing all data on a central shared hard drive in the local network. Since group and individual project work varies, participants store their data under the group project's name or in their personal folder. Club C benefited from the moving of the school into a new building: a computer room was setup and equipped with a new IT structure. Now, the club had a central shared hard drive, and club participants got personalized logins. Oddly, material problems could also have unexpected benefits. Absence of internet facilities in club B, for instance, tended to result in focused activity since there were fewer distractions available.

6. Analysis

We began by laying out the broad objectives of the computer clubs we are engaged with. These consisted in the main of fostering integration through educationally supportive activities and providing an educational environment that fostered collaborative, community-based activity. However, such objectives cannot be guaranteed. They require constant and active work in order for progress to be made. Further, they require attention to the rhythms, lifecycles and breakdowns that occur in order that policy can be developed which minimizes their effect. We have identified above some patterns that inform us about the interplay of social interactions and their technological support in an intercultural, intergenerational context.

As we suggested, integration is very much an interactional matter, produced out of a complex set of dynamic relationships which we can conceive of as involving a degree of circularity. Grouping these on a timeline unveils a multi-level structure (Figure 3). Our analysis sees intercultural computer clubs develop in very regular movements, ranging from large-scale to more localized situations. On the topmost level, there is the major change affecting the group experience after two years, when 4th graders change school. Six weeks of summer holidays at the end of the school year mark a break in computer club activity. Within that level, the project life-span with the completion of one project and the start of a new one marking a notable step in the club structure. Again, we find a subjacent division into the weekly club sessions as an elementary rhythmic component of each club's life. Finally, we saw the completion of tasks as marking the most basic pattern level, defined by successful or failed completion of individual as well as collaborative tasks. Individual involvement and material matters can prompt irregular and unforeseen incidents, but also can affect all levels.

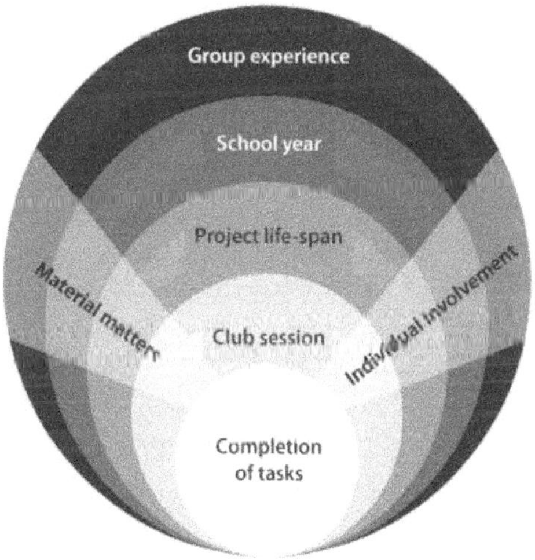

Figure 3. Computer clubs develop in circular movements.

In the following, we will show the circular nature of the above mentioned patterns by exemplifying two of the detected lifecycles: the project life-span being central with regards to club activity, and the club session representing the weekly, basic structure for this activity to unfold. We conclude our analysis with a discussion of implications for design that can be deduced from our findings, and structural connecting points for the online platform, come_NET, fostering and supporting the groupwork and collaboration in the clubs.

Lifecycle	Incident	Approach
Group experience	Every two years 4th graders leave for secondary school.	Clubs make: a) a waiting list (of children who want to participate) and/or b) advertisement among children and parents at classes and parent-teacher meeting.
School year	How to keep track of work in progress with regard to school-related recurring interruption (e.g. holidays).	a) Present project work in classes, parent-teacher conferences and at the school's end-of-term celebration. b) Use a "treasure box of ideas" to not start from scratch into the new school year. c) Advertise the club to parents via letter and at parent-teacher meeting.
Project life-span	Not stringently planned long term projects.	a) Using opening and closing rounds as a place to solve problems and share expertise. b) Encourage the sharing of expertise among the participants themselves.
Club session	Children are eager to play and escape from project activities. Not accomplishing goals. Where can I find help for my problem?	a) Define goals in the initial round. b) Foster a cooperative atmosphere by paying attention to work in progress. c) Discuss next steps and problems in the closing round.
Completion of tasks	Participants can be divided in experts and learners.	a) Respond to children and adults individually. b) Let experts and learners work on common projects to share expertise.
Individual involvement	Expertise and atmosphere getting lost with someone leaving the club.	Sharing expertise beforehand. Personal motivation.
Material matters	Loss of data.	Secure storage of data. Personalized logins.

Table 1. Overview on computer club lifecycles.

6.1 Project life-span

The life-span of club projects ranges from a couple of sessions to several months. Analysis sees their development follow a repetitive structure, consisting of: 1) collection of ideas for and planning of a project, 2) project work, and 3) its completion, punctuated by breakdown or interruption.

In all clubs we saw a close relation of the phases 1) and 3), such that successful planning in the main provided successful results. This was facilitated by established principles of joint discussion, clearly demarcated and where all were encouraged to participate. The joint discussion rounds serve as reliable club structure as it institutionalizes an audience for results and a forum for discussion. Nevertheless, during phases of club project work, our study saw interruptions be frequently caused by participants losing track of their work, by distraction or lack of concentration. Planned structures were mediated by contingency, but such contingencies were themselves mitigated by structures. There was, to use the classic language, a circularity of 'plans and situated actions'. Opening and closing rounds, in this instance, prove to be a dependable support structure.

6.2 Club session

Our study saw a tripartite structure emerge on the level of the weekly club session. Its components: 1) the initial discussion round, where goals for the day's club session are defined and work is distributed among participants; 2) the main working period, where teacher, tutors and parents foster a cooperative atmosphere by paying attention to work in progress and the distribution of relevant expertise to foster success. Opening and closing discussion rounds emerged over time, when the clubs had to develop a means to cope with technical and social problems and frictions that would typically emerge. On the social level, we saw the division of play time and project work cause tension when children would try to escape from group work for a while to play or kid around. We saw especially adult participants, in turn, focused on output and learning progress. On the technical level the clubs needed a place to decide upon and plan the general course of project activity, and to repeatedly come back to that plan ensuring that it was clear to all participants in the club. Our study saw friction occur when children lacked an overview of what to do next and how their individual task was needed for and would fit into the larger common project. Also, participants frequently did not have an overview on expertise and help at hand when encountering problems during their activities in the club. Our data sees these incidents occur over and over again – and finds all three clubs use the discussion rounds as a reliable place to resolve them.

6.3 Exploring Rhythms and Patterns

This exemplary analysis of the two lifecycles shows: each lifecycle is dependent on a balanced interplay of social action and technological intervention. It most importantly involves the development of a stable social structure that is capable of absorbing recurring lifecycles, patterns and breakdown situations, e.g. loss of specific knowledge, expertise and moral authority when a participant leaves. Researchers have shown rhythm to be an orienting feature in multi-faceted environments to be significant in, for instance, the medical context [e.g. 21, 39]. Our study presented here reaffirms this insight in the educational context of computer clubs in intercultural neighborhoods.

We see this insight carried forward on the level of the other lifecycles as well – it even counts for individual involvement and material matters, which otherwise follow a rather irregular and unpredictable structure. We provide an overview in tabular form

(Table 1). The analysis of the two lifecycles – as well as the tabular overview provided below – also shows: the course of each lifecycle is influenced by the interplay of careful planning and situated action. Participants in the clubs act and interact within planned structures, and every now and then have to react to incidents (like loss of data, lack of overview on data storage etc.) interrupting the smooth course of club activity. There is learning involved in this circularity of actions. Interruptions result in the establishment of computer club structures aimed at the prevention of repetition of the interruption: e.g. opening and closing discussions are set up as a place to plan activities and share expertise; a "treasure box of ideas" helps project plans not to get lost; experts and learners team up to secure that no one is left behind in common club project work.

Children take up a special role in all of this: Firstly, they are involved in design issues such as the development of the club's supporting online platform come_NET, thus taking up a position that has been researched by Druin [7] and others [e.g. 6]. Further, children are – just like adults – equally involved in the design process of club structure and project work. Not only do they act as co-designers of club technology, but also have an influence on club and project structures.

6.4 Exploring the Design Space

Our case study finds clearly designed social structures to be most apt to meet local needs and maximize connecting factors, a finding that supports the results from Toombs et al [33] studying community maintenance labor in a hackerspace, extending it to a diverse local neighborhood setting. The open-door policy of our computer clubs maximizes connecting points to new participants, since there are no formal barriers to participation. The explicit local orientation makes for a strong link to everyday needs and interests of the diverse young and adult participants. Discussion rounds secure different opinions, so all are equally heard and empowered to determine the course of events in the club. Division of club sessions in play and project work time secures the seriousness of the initiative. This aspect of empowerment carries forward on the technology level.

Following principles laid out by Druin [7] the newly designed online community platform come_NET is built from a user-centered and user-driven point of view, taking into account specific needs and capabilities of the young and adult computer club participants. On the individual level, technical fluency, reading capabilities and the low attention span of children are considered (e.g. easy readable and short text, iconic and metaphoric representations to alleviate the problems emerging from language barriers, simple and fast two-step registration).

This especially attends to the lifecycle of the *club session*, where our study identified a need for reliable structures supporting a great variation of technological fluency and focus. On the community and collaborative project work level of the *project life-span* lifecycle, come_NET supports club activities by means of functions for communication and shared practice such as a club 'internal blackboard' supporting the collaborative project workflow: here, each club can announce and keep track of the sequence of project actions. Due to the fact, that the storage of data often causes frictions with negative effects on ongoing project work, come_NET can provide a central storage location – thus mainly attending to the lifecycle of *material matters*. Data loss is prevented and an opportunity to extend project work beyond the regular weekly club sessions provided. Also, come_NET browses the computer club files to provide a search facility: participants can search for similar documents to become inspired or use it for an idea of their own.

By providing functions to list, share and store project ideas, aforementioned problems caused by *school year* related recurring interruptions (e.g. holidays) are eased. To follow social integration between club members and the neighborhood, easy to use communication functions (e.g. virtual black boards, discussion forums, chat) are provided. With this, the platform speaks to the *individual involvement* lifecycle as it distributes responsibilities among many and raises awareness among participants for their activities.

7. CONCLUSION AND OUTLOOK

Our study shows that the ambitions for an intercultural, collaborative educational experience designed to facilitate integration are worthwhile and ultimately realizable. However, this necessitates close attention to the rhythms and breakdowns that form part of the larger lifecycle. Our study investigated the constituents for the sustainable implementation of a local, technology-related integration initiative. The close relation of social interaction and technology matters is key, come_IN offering the chance to gain in technological fluency – not for the sake of learning alone, but also to be culturally embedded in local matters. There is a crucial social dimension to this: by means of conducting joint projects of local relevance, children and adults learn to voice opinions, too – they develop skills of listening to the perspectives of others, to value their opinions and to compromise.

Over time this implies an enhanced view of the neighborhood and one's own share in it, as well as advancing language skills to elaborate on this – both prerequisites for integration. This is an effect that is not straightforwardly measurable but is, we believe, qualitatively evident. The openness of the concept which puts people of very diverse backgrounds with regard to origin, cultural background, age and IT knowledge in an equal position as learners maximizes connecting factors.

Generalizing from this setting, we see challenges unfold on several nested lifecycles. The sustainable implementation of a technology-related local integration initiative involves the development of a stable social structure: capable of absorbing the loss of specific knowledge, expertise and moral authority when an engaged participant leaves. This insight reaffirms Reddy and Dourish's notion [21] of rhythm as an orienting feature in complex environments that they among others [e.g. 40] have studied in health care, extending it to the educational setting of computer clubs in intercultural neighborhoods.

We extend Druin's [7] work further by involving participants as co-designers of social club structures as well as project outcomes. Time is the connective factor to the lifecycles – relating, in our case, to the time span of a school year, and the time needed to conduct a club project. Sustainably implementing a technology-related integration initiative involves the development of an eye for, and reaction to, the main recurring interruptions that the respective setting brings about. It involves careful planning of activities in order to involve all participants, reflecting their motivations and abilities, and fostering a cooperative atmosphere among them. Here the next lifecycle is linked in, encompassing the weekly order of activities, structuring them in a way that leaves no one behind: providing ways to share expertise, keeping project tasks challenging yet not over-complex. The sum of local contingencies which engender relative failure or success in turn engender lifecycles which determine the lasting implementation of a technology-related integration initiative on a most basic level. Tangible matters, e.g. of mal-functioning materials, affect this in contingent ways. But they do not determine outcomes once the mobilizing of group experiences through the social structures which have evolved and become planned for, mitigate their effects.

The computer club initiative has existed for more than ten years now, and the network grows. With the current political situation with rising numbers of refugees and migrants especially from Middle Eastern and African countries seeking for access and then participation in society, the initiative's societal concern prevails.

Our evaluative study indicates that a future key to the support of lively computer club activity can also be of virtual nature: come_NET enlarges the possibility of integrating different cultures in the clubs by overcoming cultural and geographical distance. Its utilization fosters a) communication and maintenance of club relations and thereby its participants and b) exchange of ideas, knowledge and material, and with regard to common project work within the clubs, even online cooperative work.

8. ACKNOWLEDGMENTS

We thank all participants from the neighborhoods who are helping us to implement our research approach. The German Ministry of Education and Research (BMBF) provided funding for part of this research (Fkz: ZBWULF08).

9. REFERENCES

[1] Aarhus, R., Ballegard, S. A., and Hansen, T.R. 2009. The eDiary: Bridging home and hospital through healthcare technology. In: *Proc. of ECSCW*, 63-83.

[2] Berry, J.W. 1984. Cultural relations in plural societies. In: Brewer, N.M.M.: *Groups in Contact*, Academic Press, 32-49

[3] Berry, J.W. 1992. Acculturation and adaptation in a new society. In: *International Migration*, 1992, 69-85

[4] Bruce, B., and Peyton, J.K. 1990. A New Writing Environment and an Old Culture: A Situated Evaluation of Computer Networking to Teach Writing. In: *Interactive Learning Environments*, 1:3, 171-191.

[5] Chen, Y. 2011. Health information use in chronic care cycles. In: *Proc. of CSCW*, 485-488, ACM.

[6] Chiasson, S., and Gutwin, C. 2005. Design principles for children's technology. In: *interfaces*, 7, 28.

[7] Druin, A. 1999. *The design of children's technology*. Morgan Kaufmann Publishers.

[8] Jackson, S. J., et al. 2011. Collaborative rhythm: temporal dissonance and alignment in collaborative scientific work. In: *Proc. of CSCW*, 245-254, ACM.

[9] Janssens, M., Bechtold, M., Prarolo, G., and Stenius, V., eds., 2010. *The Sustainability of Cultural Diversity. Nations, Cities and Organizations*. Edward Elgar Publishing.

[10] Jung, M., et al. 2000. *Ausländer und Migranten im Spiegel der Presse. Ein diskurshistorisches Wörterbuch zur Einwanderung seit 1945*. Westdeutscher Verlag.

[11] Kafai, Y. B., Peppler, K. A., and Chapman, R. N., eds., 2009. *The Computer Clubhouse. Constructionism and Creativity in Youth Communities*. Teachers College Press.

[12] Kemmis, S., and McTaggart, R. 1988. *The action research planner*. Deakin University Press.

[13] Klopp, B. 2002. *German Multiculturalism: Immigrant Integration and the Transformation of Citizenship*. Praeger Publishing.

[14] Lofland, J., and Lofland, L.H. 1995. *Analyzing Social Settings: A Guide to Qualitative Observation and Analysis*. Wadsworth Publishing.

[15] Maloney, J., et al. 2010. The Scratch programming language and environment. In: *ACM Transactions on Computing Education (TOCE)*, 10(4), 16.

[16] Miles, R., and Thränhardt, D. 1995. *Migration and European Integration: the Dynamics of Inclusion and Exclusion*. Fairleigh Dickinson University Press.

[17] Moen A., and Brennan P. F. 2005. Health@Home: The Work of Health Information Management in the Household (HIMH): Implications for Consumer Health Informatics (CHI) Innovations. In: *JAMIA*, 648-656.

[18] Mute 2011. *Dis-Integrating Multiculturalism*. Vol. 2 No. 2, Openmute Press.

[19] Neale, D.C., Carroll, J. M., and Rosson, M. B. 2004. Evaluating Computer-Supported Cooperative Work: Models and Frameworks. In: *Proc. of CSCW*, 112-121, ACM.

[20] Norris, P. 2001. *Digital Divide*. Cambridge University Press.

[21] Reddy, M., and Dourish, P. 2002. A Finger on the Pulse: Temporal Rhythms and Information Seeking in Medical Work. In: *Proc. of CSCW*, 344-353, ACM.

[22] Resnick, M., Rusk, N. 1996. The Computer Clubhouse: Preparing for Life in a Digital World. In: *IBM Systems Journal*, vol. 35, no. 3-4, 431-440.

[23] Resnick, M., Rusk, N., and Cooke, S. 1998. The Computer Clubhouse: Technological Fluency in the Inner City. In: Schon, D., Sanyal, B., and Mitchell, W. (eds.), *High Technology and Low-Income Communities*. MIT Press, 1-17.

[24] Schiller, N. G., Basch, L., and Blanc, C. S. 1995. From immigrant to transmigrant: Theorizing transnational migration. In: *Anthropological Quarterly*, 48-63.

[25] Schubert, K., Weibert, A., and Wulf, V. 2011. Locating computer clubs in multicultural neighborhoods: How collaborative project work fosters integration processes. *International Journal of Human-Computer Studies*, *69*(10), 669-678.

[26] Schuck, P. H., and Münz, R., eds. 1998. *Paths to inclusion: the integration of migrants in the United States and Germany*, Berghahn Books.

[27] Snel, E., Engbersen, G., and Leerkes, A. 2006. Transnational involvement and social integration. In: *Global Networks*, 6(3), 285-308.

[28] Stevens, G., Veith, M., and Wulf, V. 2005. Bridging among ethnic communities by cross-cultural communities of practice. In *Communities and Technologies 2005,* 377-396. Springer Netherlands.

[29] Strauss, A. L. 1985. *Social Organization of Medical Work*. University of Chicago Press.

[30] Strauss, A. L., and Corbin, J. 2004. Open Coding. In: Seale, C., *Social Research Methods*: A Reader. Routledge, 303-306.

[31] Taylor, C. 1994. *Multiculturalism: Examining the Politics of Recognition*. Princeton University Press.

[32] The Federal Government 2007. *National Integration Plan. New paths – new opportunities*. Berlin: Presse- und Informationsamt der Bundesregierung.

[33] Toombs, A.L., Bardzell, S., and Bardzell, J. 2015. The Proper Care and Feeding of Hackerspaces: Care Ethics and Cultures of Making. In: *Proc. of CHI*, 629-638, ACM.

[34] Twidale, M., Randall, D., and Bentley, R. 1994. Situated Evaluation for Cooperative Systems. In: *Proc. of CSCW*, 441-452, ACM.

[35] Wagner, G., Pischner, R., and Haisken-Denew, J. 2002. The Changing Digital Divide in Germany. In: *The Internet in Everyday Life*, Blackwell, 164-185.

[36] Weber-Menges, S. 2005. Die Entwicklung ethnischer Medienkulturen – Ein Vorschlag zur Periodisierung. In: Geissler, R., and Poetter, H., *Massenmedien und die Integration ethnischer Minderheiten in Deutschland.* transcript, 241-324.

[37] Weibert, A., and Wulf, V. 2010. All of a sudden we had this dialogue...: intercultural computer clubs' contribution to sustainable integration. In *Proc. of the 3rd Int. Conf. on Intercultural Collaboration,* 93-102, ACM.

[38] Whitte, J., and Mannon, S. 2010. *The Internet and Social Inequality*. Routledge.

[39] Woellert, F. et al. 2009. *Ungenutzte Potentiale. Zur Lage der Integration in Deutschland.* Berlin-Institut für Bevölkerung und Entwicklung.

[40] Zerubavel, E. 1985. *Hidden Rhythms: Schedules and Calendars in Social Life*. University of California Press.

Popup Networks: Creating Decentralized Social Media on Top of Commodity Wireless Routers

Chaya Hiruncharoenvate, Wesley Smith, W. Keith Edwards, Eric Gilbert
School of Interactive Computing & GVU Center
Georgia Institute of Technology
{chaya, wersmith}@gatech.edu, {keith, gilbert}@cc.gatech.edu

ABSTRACT

Recent news has made social media notorious for both abusing user data and allowing governments to scrutinize personal information. Nevertheless, people still enjoy connecting with friends and families through social media but fail to use it to connect to local communities where we live our daily lives. In this paper, we present *Popup Networks*, a new platform for building hyper-local social computing applications, running on home wireless routers via an underlying mesh network. Summative interviews illustrate interests in using Popup Networks to create new local ties and as a backup in the case of Internet disruption. By utilizing locality to ward off external risks, Popup Networks provide alternative privacy, visibility, and economic models compared to traditional social media. While deploying Popup Networks would be an ideal evaluation, we argue that the technical tests and user interviews we conducted are suitable for socially complex systems such as Popup Networks—advocating an agenda moving forward for social computing systems research.

CCS Concepts

•**Human-centered computing** → *Social networking sites;*

Keywords

social computing; mesh networks; internet censorship; social capital

1. INTRODUCTION

Modern social computing systems play an important role in keeping friends and families connected—often over great geographical distances. Beyond simply being fun and engaging, social media use can have important benefits for the people and communities that use it. For example, social media use is associated with having a larger and more diverse network of relations [31], which can in turn be important for job searches and other activities [26]. Sharing photos and reading/posting comments on Facebook help build social capital in geographically-distributed social networks [15], but a larger Facebook audience may not find the post about new neighborhood police patrols very relevant [12]. In short, social media enriches our social networks and makes social ties more accessible than in the past [45]. It's important to note, however, that social media gives little design priviledge to local communities—the places where *local* social capital is generated and *local* ties are created [44].

However, current social media architectures exhibit a number of profound issues. First, the recent outcries of governments' surveillance over social media [29] and questionable practices surrounding user data by social network site operators [33] raise significant questions about privacy via these systems. Second, beyond the U.S., citizens in some countries live under the watchful eye of repressive governments who limit access to the Internet based on what the lawmakers deem appropriate. Part of this problem is the centralization in the Internet's client-server model [13], where control of a few centralized servers is easier than controlling multiple decentralized nodes [21].

We argue that properties around scale, privacy, and economics in today's centralized social media architectures remove users from their local communities, leave services vulnerable to disruption (such as in times of natural disasters), and expose user data to governments and marketers. While decentralized social systems such as Diaspora adopt federated infrastructure to mitigate the problem of a single failure point, they require users to purchase and set up expensive, always-on servers, creating a technical barrier for everyday users. Yet, most households now own and operate a powerful always-on, always-connected servers—*their wireless routers*—within their homes and under their control.

In this paper, we present a novel technical platform called *Popup Networks* intended to address part of this problem. We designed the system around goals that emphasize sustainability, repurposing of existing infrastructure, distributed identity, trust, ownership, and privacy—an approach we call *hyper-local social media.* Our system runs on top of common, consumer-grade wireless routers that are linked via an underlying wireless mesh network, thereby separating the network from the global Internet. A Social API embedded in the system allows developers to easily build applications to support social interactions in the network. Popup Networks use a socially distributed trust protocol called *vouching* to protect privacy and security of user data. Since everything *lives on* and *runs on* the routers, this system is perfect for neighborhood communication where the hyper-local scope communication is not suitable for the global scale of social media. Furthermore, we believe activists and disaster relief efforts can also quickly deploy this system in their local areas where the Internet is no longer a suitable venue, or not available.

To evaluate the system, we conducted two lab tests to understand the technical capabilities of home wireless routers and mesh networks. We also interviewed 13 people to gauge initial impressions for Popup Networks. Participants saw the system as a way to increase social capital among neighbors by acting as an ice breaker

GROUP '16, November 13 - 16, 2016, Sanibel Island, FL, USA

ISBN 978-1-4503-4276-6/16/11...$15.00

DOI: http://dx.doi.org/10.1145/2957276.2957285

to reduce social barriers in meeting new neighbors—primarily ones who share interests. Also, Popup Networks would be a viable communication platform during times of Internet disruption, according to our interviews.

This paper is organized as follows. First, we review the social capital theories and empirical studies that underpin this work. Next, we introduce the design principles that frame Popup Networks. Finally, after describing how theories and architecture drove the Popup Networks design, we present our interview participants' reactions to the system. In summary, this paper's contributions are threefold:

1. A novel social computing technology that provides alternate *privacy, visibility*, and *economic* models relative to traditional social media;

2. An evaluation of this system, incorporating technical tests and user interviews, finding Popup Networks are both feasible and useful;

3. A brief argument for why these methods are appropriate for new social computing technologies, suggesting an agenda moving forward for social computing systems research.

2. LITERATURE REVIEW

In this section, we review three bodies of literature. First, we relate the rich social science literature surrounding social capital to the design goals of Popup Networks. Next, we present current work on distributed social network platforms and the use of wireless mesh network and distinguish how Popup Networks build from them. Finally, we conclude this section by visiting recent events of Internet disruption and censorship caused by political governments and natural disasters, along with the means that researchers and activists presented to get around them.

2.1 Social Capital and the Importance of Local Ties

We know that social communities are strong communities. Through simple, informal activities, communities build social capital [43]. Based on the work of Coleman [17], Bourdieu [14], and Lin [39], social capital is most commonly conceptualized as the sum of the resources embedded in social structure, or the ability to access resources in social networks for some purposeful action; social capital is a resource that plays a pivotal role when communities face challenges requiring collective action, through the means that increase community attachment [47] and empowerment [24], and reduce crime rate [48] and fear and mistrust [46].

While most Americans have few strong ties at the neighborhood level [52], local ties are still important. Neighborhood ties are the source of very specific types of individual support, such as help with child-care, emergency aid, and home improvements [53]. At the community level, social capital available through weak social ties may be more valuable than a network of close, densely-knit cliques of strong ties as weakly bound neighborhood connections are necessary for successful collective action [27].

There is a growing body of research on exactly how and why social media translates into social capital [15, 25]. In this line of research, studies look for the specific features that create social capital. For example, in Facebook certain affordances matter more than others, such as wall posts accounting for more accumulated social capital than simple status updates [15]. However, a gap exists where social network sites often do not provide functionality to discover new local connections—an important factor in building new ties.

While these studies focus on social capital created at a distance over Internet-based social media, the idea that online communities can help local communities is not new. A number of studies from the field of community informatics and others have attempted to design and evaluate Internet interventions for social capital at the neighborhood level [30]. Due to this need to facilitate new tie creation at the local level, new online communities such as Nextdoor[1] and iNeighbors[2] have flourished. However, previous research showed that audience scope and scale can be a problem in community-oriented social media [20, 41].

Despite largely encouraging results of these interventions and the recent boom in social media use, national studies have found that only 4% of Americans use the Internet for neighborhood-level interaction [32]. Together, these findings indicate an opportunity for new approaches to social media, focused on the local level. We believe *Popup Networks can lead to new tie formation and increased bridging capital in local communities*.

2.2 Distributed Social Network Platforms and Mesh Networks

Popup Networks are distributed social network platforms because of how data is separately stored in different nodes. In many cases, distributed social network platforms have arisen in response to the privacy and security concerns inherent to centralized social network sites [20, 55]. Platforms such as Diaspora[3], Friendica[4], and OneSocialWeb[5] are examples of such systems. Some, such as Safebook [19], leverage real-life trust relationships in order to establish privacy in the online system, while others, such as DECENT [35], employ advanced cryptography to preserve the privacy and security of user content and relationships. Virtually all of these decentralized social network platforms use a federated architecture, in which users' data is spread across multiple servers that work together in cooperation via the Internet. From our perspective, these Internet-based platforms rely on a single point of failure—*the Internet*. Additionally, the Internet still leaves these systems vulnerable to malicious acts from hackers and surveillance by ISPs and government.

Perhaps the most important idea of an Internet-free network is the near-ubiquitous presence of residential Wi-Fi. Recent data suggests that over two thirds of U.S. households have broadband connections, with over half of these having a home network [34]. Importantly, in high- and medium-density areas (in other words, both urban environments and many suburban ones), the density of networks means that at any given point multiple Wi-Fi networks are visible and allowing for the creation of *wireless mesh networks*.

The idea of neighborhood and metropolitan wireless mesh networks is not new. Researchers have started to demonstrate the technical feasibility of neighborhood mesh networks in the 2000s [4, 7]. In practice, the Athens Wireless Metropolitan Network (AWMN) began in 2002 when Athenians were fed up with poor Internet service provided by telecommunication companies. Currently, AWMN has more than 1,000 users in the network, serving the connection speed up to 30 times faster than the Internet connection provided by ISP [37]. Researchers have also set up several testbeds such as MIT Roofnet [10] and SMesh [3] to explore and improve on several issues with wireless mesh network. However, most of them utilize

[1]https://nextdoor.com/
[2]https://www.i-neighbors.org/
[3]https://diasporafoundation.org
[4]http://friendica.com
[5]http://onesocialweb.org

specialized equipment, making them inflexible and hard to replicate for general household users [42].

Mesh networks have a fundamentally different structure from traditional wireless networks (as well as wired local area networks). In contrast to traditional network topology, each node in mesh networks must not only deal with its own data, but also potentially serve as a relay for the data of other nodes in the network [56]. This topology means that wireless mesh networks are self-organizing, self-healing, and self-configuring, as nodes automatically connect to each other and determine how to route data as the topology evolves [1]. The unique property that separates Popup Networks from other mesh networks is *Popup Networks repurpose existing home wireless routers as the network infrastructure instead of asking users to install rooftop antenna or other expensive equipment.*

2.3 Internet Freedom and Communication Disruption

Recently, Internet privacy has been jeopardized by increasing surveillance of Internet communication from governments, telecommunication providers, and website providers. The National Security Agency (NSA) has reportedly obtained personal Internet communication data such as email and social networking details from communication providers such as Verizon and AT&T and website operators and communication hubs such as Google and Apple [29]. Furthermore, citizens in several countries also experience Internet censorship where only content deemed appropriate by the governing body is available. Several researchers have explored content censorship in countries such as China and Iran and found that most social network sites that are popular in the western world such as Facebook and Twitter are not fully accessible from those countries [5, 6, 49]. Rather, localized versions are popularized to allow governments to maintain censorship control over "inappropriate" content.

While the First Amendment of the US constitution prohibits Internet censorship by all levels of the government, private entities can allow or deny services as they wish. Amazon removed Wikileaks from its hosting service when political pressure arose in 2010 [40]. The issue of freedom of communication was also brought up when the Bay Area Rapid Transit (BART) decided to shut down cell phone services on August 11, 2011 to prevent protests coordinated via mobile devices at some of its stations [18]. Under repressive governments, it is especially easy for the leaders to disconnect their citizens from the global Internet [21]. Several projects have attempted to use mesh network as an alternate channel for the Internet. In 2011, in the wake of the Stop Online Piracy Act (SOPA), Reddit users spawned a new subgroup to discuss the possibility of a city-wide mesh network to provide a version of the Internet that would not be subjected to government control [28]. Similarly, a group in Oakland, CA is testing a mesh network, called People's Open Network, to reduce the technological gap in the city by providing free Internet through volunteer mesh nodes [51].

Not only do wireless mesh networks provide citizens an advantage in limiting government censorship, but these networks are also useful in the aftermath of natural disasters. The Red Hook Initiative provided Internet connection to Superstorm Sandy survivors during the days that Internet and cell phone connections were not fully restored [36]. In 2013, the Boston mobile networks were highly congested due to chaos surrounding a bombing. Open Garden[6] were shone spotlight because it allows computer and Wi-Fi devices, including cell phones, to share Internet connection using wireless mesh network [2]. While these systems and applications offer similar functionality to Popup Networks, *Popup Networks accelerate the set up process during time intensive disasters by not relying on current communication infrastructure and not requiring extra equipment to be purchased by users or volunteers.*

[6]https://opengarden.com/

3. POPUP NETWORKS DESIGN

Drawing from the literature, we define four high-level design goals for Popup Networks that distinguish it from other social media and mesh network platforms.

Goal 1. Repurpose existing infrastructure. One of the oft-cited downfalls of federated social systems is that they require non-technical users to administer their own, always-on servers. A key insight underlying Popup Networks is that people all over the world already have relatively powerful servers always connected in their homes: their routers. By sitting on top of this infrastructure, we limit the technical burden of federated services on everyday users.

Goal 2. Sustainability and adaptability. Popup Networks is designed to operate independently of other infrastructure. The self-organizing, self-healing, and self-configuring properties of mesh networks do the work of maintaining paths within the network. The decentralization nature of Popup Networks will both allow the system to be independent from communication infrastructure and resistant to service disruption and government censorship.

Goal 3. Locality-based privacy. By default, Popup Networks function at much a smaller scale as our natural, proximity-based scoping mechanism providing different *visibility* by limiting communication exclusively to nearby nodes. Popup Networks application data is forwarded hop-by-hop via neighboring nodes in the network. Applications can specify the limits on information propagation, including the set of nodes that can receive it. To provide different *privacy* than current social media, each router houses all of its own application data locally, which others can request access if or when they choose, strengthening the idea that users do not have to worry that a global or unauthorized audience may see the information they share.

Goal 4. Distributed identity, trust, & ownership. Without a central arbiter handing out accounts and verifying identities (as Facebook or Twitter would), Popup Networks use a decentralized model of identity. Popup Networks use a *vouching* mechanism to indicate trust between users, similar to the vouching system used by the site Couchsurfing. Since Popup Networks offer a different *economic* model in which each user distributively owns and controls her own technical infrastructure and personal data, vouching information allows users to make judgment whether to share their information. Because data is stored locally on each user's node, copies of data are no longer available for mining once a user decides to delete it.

4. POPUP NETWORKS

To achieve the design goals, Popup Networks comprise three major subsystems running on top of residential routers:

1. A **customized router firmware** distribution with mesh networking, web servers, and databases all running on top of the router hardware.

2. A social **API on the router**, implemented via HTTP endpoints, enabling developers to build hyper-local social applications quickly and easily.

3. A socially **distributed model of trust** called *vouching*, permitting users to vouch for others and infer trust signals at the social level.

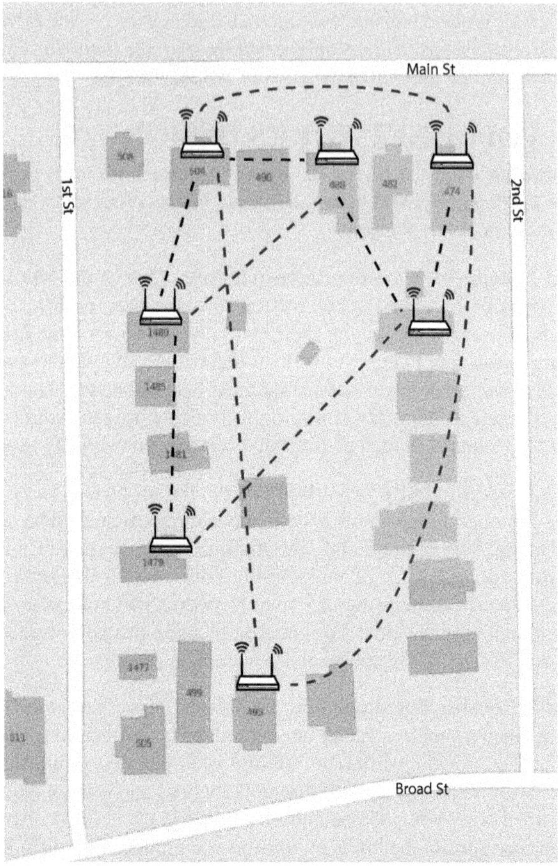

Figure 1: An example residential Popup Networks mesh network. Dotted lines represent wireless mesh network connections between routers; black for direct connections, blue for multi-hop connections. Note that the graph is not fully connected, just as there are missing links in social networks. Nodes adaptively find paths to other nodes with whom they wish to exchange information.

4.1 Implementation

Popup Networks run a customized build of OpenWRT-compatible router. OpenWRT[7] is an open-source Linux distribution for embedded devices, primarily home routers, and enjoys an active support community. For low-level mesh networking, Popup Networks use the Optimized Link State Routing (OLSR) protocol [16]. OLSR is an IP routing protocol optimized for mobile ad hoc networks, which allows nodes to discover and disseminate link state information through the network. The protocol allows Popup Networks to proactively discover routes to all reachable nodes visible in the network. We chose OLSR over other protocols because of its extensive community and its history of production use. (A full discussion of the network performance characteristics of OLSR is beyond the scope of this paper, but see [50] for more detail.) The software has been successfully deployed, for example, on community networks with thousands of nodes, such as the Athens Wireless Metropolitan Network.

On top of OLSR, Popup Networks run a customized LAMP (**L**inux, **A**pache, **M**ySQL, **P**HP) software stack, a common web application server environment. Optimizing for our router's embedded platform, we selected lighttpd, a small memory footprint web server[8] instead of Apache because of its efficiency; our platform also uses the FastCGI interface of PHP for performance reasons.

Our hardware platform leverages multi-radio access points, which are increasingly commonplace in the consumer market. Generally, the multiple radios in these devices are used to provide separate networks on different frequencies (2.4 GHz and 5GHz). Popup Networks repurpose the 5GHz radio solely for communication among other nearby routers running Popup Networks using ad hoc connections. We choose to use the ad hoc mode rather than alternatives (such as Bridge or Wireless Distribution System modes) because ad hoc connections do not require a fixed hierarchy of nodes in the network. OLSR creates a mesh routing layer atop these ad hoc wireless networks, providing a self-organizing and self-healing topology. The 2.4GHz radio is used for its original purpose, allowing clients to connect through it to access the Internet or the mesh. This approach provides a transparent mechanism to create a local neighborhood mesh network at high speed, while also maintaining constant connectivity of other devices inside the home to the Internet. Due to the performance of modern wireless standards, homes can potentially communicate with each other *much* faster than they can with Internet-hosted services; 802.11n networks, for example, have a theoretical maximum speed of 600Mbps, compared to common home Internet speeds in the U.S. of 1.5-12Mbps.

Specifically, we implemented Popup Networks on the D-Link DIR-825 wireless router, using a USB flash drive for extra storage, the software stack, and the database.

4.2 Social API

Popup Networks implement a core social API that allows developers to create hyper-local social media applications quickly and easily. For example, a developer might bring together these API endpoints to recreate Twitter as a hyper-local Popup Networks application. Popup Networks' social API provides basic social application primitives, such as following and vouching (i.e., trust), as well as data storage, communication, identity management, and discovery. It also transparently handles communication with the underlying mesh substrate.

The API follows the REST API model[9], a common design pattern familiar to modern web developers that uses the HTTP verbs (e.g., GET and POST) to wrap API calls. Popup Networks categorize its social API endpoints into six groups based on their purpose and functionality:

Applications API provides a mechanism to determine which applications are installed on a given node, allowing applications to find peer nodes in the network with which they can communicate (applications communicate with other instances of the same application). Not all nodes are assumed to have the same applications installed.

Users API provides information about the human users of the system, a key element in social applications. This API allows applications to both query and update profile information about users, both at the local and remote routers.

Message API supports basic messaging functionality among application instances. Applications can optionally specify a fixed set of authorized recipients of the message, or can allow messages to be public—meaning that they can be seen by all nodes. This API hides the low-level details of the mesh, such as routing and message delivery.

Relationship API provides functionality for establishing the social relationships that exist within the network. Popup Networks use

[7] http://www.openwrt.org

[8] http://www.lighttpd.net

[9] http://en.wikipedia.org/wiki/Representational_state_transfer

"following" relationship to connote a one-way social relationship between users. These are *application-specific*, and applications can use these relationships to manage increased levels of trust and sharing among users. If the application design relies upon bi-directional social connection, the API provides mechanisms to establish both following and followers relationships.

Database API provides a way for applications to store persistent data. Each application has access to a unique, sandboxed data storage area. The API provides a NoSQL-style database rather than a relational database to allow application authors to easily persist custom data structures expressed using JSON or XML. All data resides locally on the router itself; a common Popup Networks design pattern has routers querying the mesh network for data held locally at each node.

Vouching API endpoints allow users to assert that a given Popup Networks person/node pair is trusted, a process we call *vouching*. The API allows users to vouch for each other, and for applications to query whether a user is vouched for (and by whom). Note that this is distinct from following relationships; following relationships exist at the application level, whereas vouching is *global* and transcends particular applications. We design vouching and following relationships to be separated because different applications might have different meanings for following, and vouching is unique and universal throughout the Popup Networks system.

4.3 Vouching

4.3.1 Security Model

Popup Networks implicitly link routers to identities at the social level. However, this presents a core problem: How can I be sure you are who your router says you are? Adopting a worst-case scenario lens, we have to worry about "van attacks" where a villain joins the Popup Networks mesh network and spoofs an identity—either a new or existing one. While clearly an edge case, it may not be as farfetched as it first appears[10].

Leveraging existing relationships, we have re-appropriated the idea of "vouching" from the site Couchsurfing[11]. Couchsurfing is a travel network where participants stay on one another's couches while traveling and host travelers of their own. Vouching is essentially a distributed reputation model where participants put their own reputations on the line to assert that a user is trustworthy. Despite the inherent risks Couchsurfing clearly presents, it is remarkably safe [38]. Analogously, Popup Networks provide high-level APIs that allow users to vouch that the router on the network truly belongs to the person presented at the application layer.

4.3.2 Privacy Model

To preserve privacy of users and their data, privacy in Popup Networks is protected by multiple layers of technical and social infrastructures, fundamental to Popup Networks platform.

The technical infrastructure of Popup Networks helps ensure privacy in two ways. First, the local scope of connections through the wireless mesh network makes snooping harder because the packets are transferred between nodes directly without the need of a hub or switch. Second, encryption protocol can be put in place to prevent eavesdropping. Although encryption is not currently implemented in this version, Popup Networks can be easily extended through the API. We leave the extension of encryption in Popup Networks as future work.

The social infrastructure of Popup Networks also adds an additional layer of privacy protection. When a new or susceptible user joins the network and requests access for personal data, the vouching mechanism can provide social information about the trustworthiness of the questionable user. For example, Bob sees that Alice has vouched for Charlie. Since he trusts Alice, he uses his own judgment to decide that Charlie is trustworthy and allow Charlie to access his information. However, if Bob did not trust Alice, her vouch for Charlie would be meaningless to him. The vouching mechanism acts as another layer of privacy protection on top of the layers from technical infrastructure mentioned earlier.

[10]cf. http://en.wikipedia.org/wiki/Wardriving

[11]https://www.couchsurfing.org/

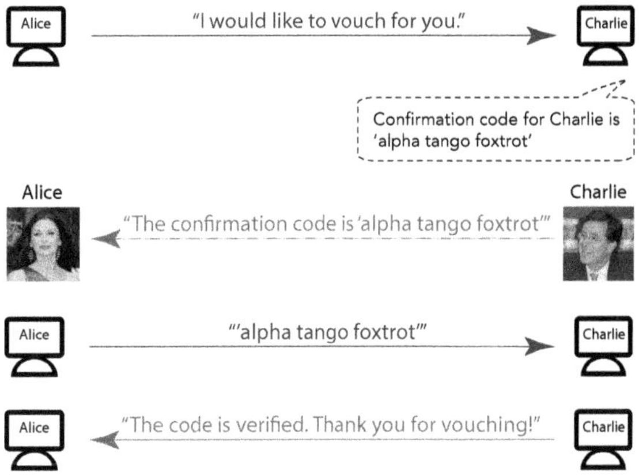

Figure 2: Popup Networks reference vouching implementation. Solid lines represent communication through Popup Networks' mesh network; dotted lines represents *out-of-band* communication, presumably over the phone or in-person.

4.3.3 Example Protocol

Popup Networks ship with a reference implementation of vouching that we consider to be one best practice. Developers can create new vouching mechanisms to suit their specification. At a high level, we have implemented a vouching protocol that forces Popup Networks users to verify one another's identities socially out-of-band. Figure 2 outlines the protocol, which we also describe in detail next.[12]

Alice, Bob, and Charlie are three Popup Networks users. Alice would like to vouch for Charlie who is new to the network. Popup Networks ask them to follow this protocol:

1. Alice visits Charlie's profile page and clicks a button to indicate that she wants to vouch for Charlie. Alice's vouching state for Charlie now changes from **notvouch** to **waiting**, an indication that Alice is waiting for a confirmation from Charlie.

2. Charlie's own router now notify him that Alice would like to vouch for him and generates a random string of words, such as "alpha tango foxtrot." Charlie now needs to give this string to Alice through another channel (e.g., face-to-face, email, phone) where she can verify his identity.

3. Alice receives the string from Charlie and enter to string to Charlie's profile page to confirm his identity. Alice's router checks it against Charlie's router database and changes her vouching state for Charlie to **vouched**.

[12]All images of persons used in this paper are photographs of celebrities from http://www.flickr.com/photos/shankbone/sets/72157623925606177, available under a Creative Commons license.

Figure 3: Messages main page. Messages permits one-to-one messaging between Popup Networks users.

Now, any time someone pings the Popup Networks network for who vouches for Charlie, Alice's router will respond affirmatively, while Bob's router will not. In this way, vouching information is distributed across the entire Popup Networks network; no single point holds it all. While not impossible to fake, Popup Networks' vouching signal carries a significant cost; this tends to make signals valuable in social systems [22].

4.4 Popup Networks Application

Popup Networks are designed to be an open platform[13] that developers can leverage to build hyper-local social computing applications. Developers can use the core APIs to send messages around the network, manage data and caches, as well as to manage social constructs like following (application-specific) and vouching (global-scope). Per-application data-bases on individual routers allow applications to keep their data accessible, yet sandboxed from other applications.

To illustrate the capabilities of Popup Networks, we present *Messages*, a replica of the most popular social application—email—rewritten as a hyper-local version using Popup Networks' social API. We present this application to emphasize the design goals presented earlier in this paper and illustrate how Popup Networks provide full support for common social media features.

Messages is a hyper-local clone of email. Like email, it allows point-to-point text messages between users, but in this case without ever leaving the Popup Networks network. Users simply enter the name of the recipient (a plugin progressively prompts nearby nodes for available users), in the "To:" field.

Messages manages its own tablespace through the database API. Conforming to the typical email standard, Messages stores the email it sends at the database of the recipient. When Alice sends an email to Bob, Alice's router contacts Bob's router via the database API and asks Bob's router to store the message for him. (OLSR guarantees that the nodes visited in transit cannot compromise the messages, so only Bob can read it.) Via the database API, Messages stores information such as the sender's name, sender's IP address, recipient's name, recipient's IP address, email subject, email body, and sent date, using JSON encoded objects. In the prototype version of the application we developed, we did not employ encryption on the message, but developers could extend Messages to include encryption at the application level.

[13]Our code is also open source, and made available under a BSD license. For anonymity reasons during blind review, however, we do not link to it here.

Up\Down	x.4	x.5	x.6	x.7	x.8
x.4		7.56	8.91	5.55	26.81
x.5	12.18		4.13	18.51	20.82
x.6	8.69	5.30		4.05	13.74
x.7	6.24	24.11	3.03		8.42
x.8	25.97	14.91	13.23	8.01	

Table 1: Upload/Download speed test result (Mbps). White indicates direct connection. Blue indicates weak direct connection. Yellow indicates 2-hop connection. Green indicates 3-hop connection.

5. TECHNICAL EVALUATION

We evaluated whether the mesh-based framework and the processing power of consumer-grade wireless routers would sustain the computational and network communication requirement of Popup Networks. As a proof of concept, we conducted two tests in lab settings to evaluate the performance of the consumer-grade wireless routers and the connections over mesh networks.

The first test to evaluate the performance of our routers. We performed 10,000 rounds of a basic PHP function that inserts and deletes a row to a MySQL table on the DIR-825 wireless router with Popup Networks software stack. Our benchmarks indicated that the router completes said operations in 360 seconds. For comparison, an Amazon AWS EC2 instance with a similar software stack took 225 seconds to complete the same task.

The second test evaluated connections over a wireless mesh network. Five DIR-825 wireless routers connected through Popup Networks were placed in different locations across 2 floors of a building. Each router was placed close enough to have a direct link to at least one other router (about 20-30 meters apart, in our test) and far from at least one other router to force multiple-hop connections. Out of 10 possible pairs of connections, our test mesh network topology had 1 pair of weak direct connection, 3 pairs of 2-hop connections, and 2 pairs of 3-hop connections. A speed test was conducted for a transfer of a 2 MB file between every router pair. We measured the average of the download speed in megabit per second (Mbps) over 10 rounds of such transfers.

Table 1 shows the results of the average speed over 10 transfers of 2 MB files for every pair of connections. Note that since all transfers are ultimately between two nodes, the downstream speed of one node is the upstream speed of the other node. In general, 3-hop connections are slower than 2-hop connections, which are slower than direct connections. Weak direct connections are also significantly slower than regular (strong) direct connections. However, multiple-hop and weak connections still provide downstream speed close to the 4 Mbps and upstream speed over the 1 Mbps "broadband connection" defined by the FCC [23].

The two performance tests proved that consumer-grade routers and mesh-based framework can provide resources to sustain a hyper-local social media platform. Although the first test showed that our wireless routers performed with much lower efficiency than a traditional web server, the local scope of Popup Networks will not require as much computational power as social network sites on the Internet, where thousands of users are online at the same time. Our wireless mesh network speed test proved that users will not notice much different in the connection speed between Popup Networks and broadband Internet connections.

6. INITIAL USER IMPRESSIONS

We conducted semi-structured interviews with 13 participants (7 female, age 18-52) to gather initial reactions from potential Popup Networks users. Participants were recruited from campus mailing lists and the neighborhood-centric social network site, Nextdoor. Each interview was approximately 30-45 minutes and was conducted either in person, over telephone, or Internet voice call, and each participant was compensated with $30.

We first asked participants about their use of social media to connect with neighbors and local communities. 10 of our participants reported that in addition to face-to-face contacts, phone calls, and texting, they also used some sort of social media (mailing list, Facebook, Nextdoor) to connect with their neighbors. This large proportion bias is due to the platform (Nextdoor) from where the participants were recruited. Two of our participants expressed that they might have different experiences due to Internet censorship and blocking against social media in their home countries. Then, we showed participants the concept of Popup Networks and the mesh network (Figure 1) and asked about the potential uses of Popup Networks and their privacy and security concerns. Finally, we asked participants about their opinions regarding Popup Networks serving as an alternative solution for Internet connection during service disruption and government censorship.

6.1 Local Communication

Participants see profile information that other people would share as an ice breaker to get to know new neighbors, especially ones who share interests or common characteristics.

> *If I have a neighbor who also goes to [the same school] then probably it's easier to kind of communicate saying "ok my school is here" that might be a good start. (P4)*

> *I think I'd be interested to see [which of] their kids are my kids age or can babysit, and also which schools they go to, which temple, so I could see who's got more in common with me. ... I would look for like-minded people or people with the same kind of things that I have. (P10)*

Regardless of making new connections, participants believe that profiles of their neighbors could act as the "Facebook" of the neighborhood.

> *It would provide, while we have social gatherings, it's kind of nice to be able to have a picture and name because obviously when you are walking around the neighborhood, you don't really know if the person lives in the neighborhood or is just walking around the neighborhood and so this would be a way to put a name and a face together and high level detail around them, as much as they gave out. (P5)*

6.2 Privacy and Security

Participants have similar privacy concerns with Popup Networks as other social network sites. In general, they are willing to share information which might be useful to their neighbors and often compare what information they are willing to share on Popup Networks with what they already put on Facebook or Nextdoor. However, participants who live in an apartment complex have no problems with sharing their apartment number through Popup Networks because their neighbors usually already know which room they reside in.

> *Maybe one piece of additional information would be apartment number because it would just be in your apartment so there would not be a problem with security with the apartment number. (P4)*

> *[I would share to my trusted neighbors] my particular room number. These people will be the ones I know well enough to tell them where I am. A potential use is neighbors borrow stuff from each other so people could do that kind of stuff with this info. (P8)*

However, some participants are concerned that since Popup Networks operate at a hyper-local scope, it is easier for other users to pinpoint their real identity.

> *I won't post [some pictures I post on Facebook] on Popup Networks because sometimes I guess my audience cannot identify me easily on other social media, but in Popup Networks, I'm more identifiable. Maybe, I won't post some things like personal photos or more personal information on Popup Networks. (P11)*

> *I feel a little bit more concerned with [privacy on] Popup Networks because the fact that people are so near to me, and the fact that people stalk me or follow me, but for Facebook, the likelihood of this kind of thing can happen is not as much because people might not be in close proximity. (P13)*

Even for the neighbors that they know, the relationship and trust structure is complex. Our participants do not want a one-size-fit-all privacy policy when coming to sharing personal information.

> *The privacy setting [would be] a great [addition]. Maybe I can show certain posts to certain people. Like Google+ has circles, maybe I can create circles. (P1)*

Participants wish Popup Networks had a more transparent privacy model than traditional social network sites.

> *If each individual has a better control of their privacy and they can choose who to have access to the [information], and make it be upfront unlike Facebook where you have to go in and opt out, where they suddenly make everything open and you have to go back in and make it more private. I think it's better to be private up front and you have a better feature of choosing who to share in the network. (P7)*

6.3 Communication Disruption

While participants see Popup Networks as a promising platform to get around Internet censorship, the limited scope of Popup Networks also limits the variety of content available.

> *[I think Popup Networks can help alleviate the limited connection during censorship], but I think the scope will be limited to the local community not the global community because the issue I have experienced was the global censorship. ... I don't know how Popup Networks can extend the network to other network beyond the neighborhood network. If it could do that, that would be a great thing because we don't even need to connect to the Internet so we don't have any censorship. (P11)*

Popup Networks could also become an infrastructure where people who have access to blocked content can share the content with the network.

> *[M]aybe Popup Networks users could get the content from other social media, other sources which are censored or blocked and put them on Popup Networks and share them with the neighbors who are not well connected to the other social media. Most of people may have limited access to the information resources. Other people who also have the connections to other social media can put useful information in Popup Networks. ... I [also] would share [VPN and proxies] with someone that I know [over Popup Networks], could be my neighbors or relative who may not be my neighbors but live in the same town. (P11)*

Participants also view Popup Networks as an appropriate platform for a quick restoration of communication infrastructure during the time of disasters when traditional communication infrastructures are destroyed.

> *If Popup Networks [are] available during the Internet blockage, I think it would be important in the circumstance of emergency like if there's flood or hurricane, then it would be good. One time, the fire alarm went off and people didn't know what to do and someone need to come out so this kind of thing might be good. (P13)*

7. TOWARDS AN EVALUATION AGENDA FOR SOCIAL SYSTEMS RESEARCH

We did not deploy Popup Networks. This raises the vexing problem of evaluating social computing systems [8]. In this context, a successful evaluation of Popup Networks might resemble seeing it used by the Red Cross after they move into a disaster area, or a small group of neighbors who want to share their Internet connections among one another, or protesters either in the U.S. or abroad. While we would certainly welcome such a use case—and have promoted it or are working to promote—we argue that such standards (common to the UIST community, for example) no longer make sense for social computing research.

It is no accident that the majority of innovation happening around social computing systems takes place in industry (via the startup community and incumbents such as Facebook, primarily), or within the small group of academics working in crowdsourcing. Regarding the former, while we have seen wonderful systems emerge from startups, we would argue that ceding innovation solely to industry would be a path towards irrelevance for social computing. Regarding the latter, we look up to crowdsourcing work such as Soylent [9] and VizWiz [11]; yet, at the same time, it is evidently more straightforward to evaluate those systems because you can plug the software into online micro-labor markets such as Amazon Mechanical Turk.

Where does that leave us with *more social* social computing research systems? We cannot compel people to "be social" the way a typical "systems-style" evaluation might (by compensating participants for their participation). Nor can we plug into a willing and able group of participants as crowdsourcing researchers might with a crowd. Instead, we advocate for a third approach, exemplified by the work we have just presented. As social computing researchers, we think the field should strive for both technical innovation and human-centered relevance. The methods we have employed in this paper reflect that belief, and we hope that this work may serve as a guidepost for future evaluations of innovative social computing systems.

8. LIMITATIONS

The front-line hurdle that can prevent adoption of Popup Networks is the complications in setting up the software architecture of the system. While the Popup Networks software can be deployed as a simple one-step installation package, those who want to install Popup Networks onto their own routers must own wireless routers that are compatible with the custom firmware OpenWRT, and install the firmware on their routers. However, users with moderate to advanced technical skills can easily accomplish this task with the help from the extensive OpenWRT online documentation and support groups.

Regarding Popup Networks' infrastructure, the main technical limitation of using a mesh network to provide underlying communication infrastructure of Popup Networks is the limited reach of the network, as pointed out by participants from our interviews. However, if the network contains a large number of nodes, it can span a large area, as the Athens Wireless Metropolitan Network spans the city of Athens and nearby municipalities[14].

While mesh network systems like Popup Networks can help quickly restore communication infrastructure during disasters, electricity is still needed to power equipment, wireless routers in our case, to facilitate construction of the network. Thus, if there is no electricity, such systems cannot be useful for the affected population. However, wireless routers usually consume little power and can be run off of power generators. Furthermore, further research can utilize the advanced capabilities of smartphones in such a way that smartphones can become nodes in Popup Networks, eliminating the needs of electricity since smartphones can run off of battery power.

We did not conduct a large-scale deployment of Popup Networks. As argued in the previous section, a successful evaluation of Popup Networks relies on specific circumstances that, while possible, do not occur on a daily basis. We believe that the evaluations we performed and the argument we presented justify the novelty of Popup Networks and its contribution of the HCI community.

9. FUTURE WORK

As discussed in the Implementation section, security in Popup Networks can be enhanced with encryption. However, given the significant usability problems known to plague these systems [54], this may present an entire research undertaking on its own. We plan to start by extending the vouching protocol with a distributed public-key infrastructure and propagate this infrastructure throughout the system. Not only this infrastructure will help secure communications, but will also emphasize the concept of distributed identity, trust, and ownership in Popup Networks.

10. CONCLUSION

We presented Popup Networks, a platform for building hyper-local social computing application using home wireless routers. Popup Networks are built on top of a residential mesh network, leveraging their physical proximity; thus, it removes the need for data transfer to the Internet. Popup Networks provide different privacy and security, and a different economic model than traditional social computing platforms.

Popup Networks are composed of three major subsystems: a social API that allows developers to quickly implement applications to extend Popup Networks, a distributed trust model—*vouching*—that facilitates users' trust-making process, and a customized OpenWRT with mesh networking and software stack running on top of a consumer-grade router's firmware. Our performance evaluation proved that Popup Networks' infrastructure has abundant resources to provide high bandwidth connections between nodes. We presented an application—Messages—using Popup Networks' social APIs as a demonstration of its capabilities.

Our interview participants suggested that Popup Networks are a feasible communication platform during the time of Internet disruption such as government censorship and disasters. Furthermore, they showed interests in using Popup Networks to connect with their local ties and meet new neighbors. Exploiting locality allows Popup Networks to achieve its goals to provide a sustainable infrastructure for social computing applications that facilitate communications in hyper-local context.

Finally, we argue that while a deployment would be a perfect evaluation of Popup Networks, the nature of this system presents a great challenge in deploying into suitable communities and cir-

[14]https://wind.awmn.net/?page=nodes

cumstances. Instead, we present this work as an example of how to evaluate innovative social computing systems.

11. REFERENCES

[1] I. F. Akyildiz, X. Wang, and W. Wang. Wireless mesh networks: a survey. *Computer networks*, 47(4):445–487, 2005.

[2] A. Al-Akkad, L. Ramirez, S. Denef, A. Boden, L. Wood, M. BÃijscher, and A. Zimmermann. Reconstructing Normality: The use of infrastructure leftovers in crisis situations as inspiration for the design of resilient technology. In *Proc. OzCHI*, pages 457–466. ACM, 2013.

[3] Y. Amir, C. Danilov, M. Hilsdale, R. Musaloiu-Elefteri, and N. Rivera. Fast handoff for seamless wireless mesh networks. In *Proceedings of the 4th international conference on Mobile systems, applications and services - MobiSys 2006*, page 83, New York, New York, USA, 2006. ACM Press.

[4] P. Antoniadis, B. Grand, A. Satsiou, L. Tassiulas, R. Aguiar, J. Barraca, and S. Sargento. Community Building over Neighborhood Wireless Mesh Networks. *IEEE Technology and Society Magazine*, 27(1):48–56, jan 2008.

[5] S. Aryan, H. Aryan, and J. A. Halderman. Internet censorship in iran: A first look. In *Proc. of the 3rd USENIX Workshop on Free and Open Communications on the Internet*, 2013.

[6] D. Bamman, B. O'Connor, and N. Smith. Censorship and deletion practices in chinese social media. *First Monday*, 17(3), Mar. 2012.

[7] J. P. Barraca, P. Fernandes, S. Sargento, and R. Rocha. An architecture for community mesh networking. In *IEEE International Symposium on Personal, Indoor and Mobile Radio Communications, PIMRC*, 2008.

[8] M. S. Bernstein, M. S. Ackerman, E. H. Chi, and R. C. Miller. The trouble with social computing systems research. In *Proc CHI EA*, pages 389–398. ACM, 2011.

[9] M. S. Bernstein, G. Little, R. C. Miller, B. Hartmann, M. S. Ackerman, D. R. Karger, D. Crowell, and K. Panovich. Soylent: a word processor with a crowd inside. In *Proc. UIST*, pages 313–322. ACM, 2010.

[10] J. Bicket, S. Biswas, D. Aguayo, and R. Morris. Architecture and Evaluation of the MIT Roofnet Mesh Network.

[11] J. P. Bigham, C. Jayant, H. Ji, G. Little, A. Miller, R. C. Miller, R. Miller, A. Tatarowicz, B. White, S. White, et al. Vizwiz: nearly real-time answers to visual questions. In *Proc. UIST*, pages 333–342. ACM, 2010.

[12] J. Binder, A. Howes, and A. Sutcliffe. The problem of conflicting social spheres: effects of network structure on experienced tension in social network sites. In *Proc. CHI*, pages 965–974. ACM, 2009.

[13] M. S. Blumenthal and D. D. Clark. Rethinking the design of the internet: the end-to-end arguments vs. the brave new world. *ACM Transactions on Internet Technology (TOIT)*, 1(1):70–109, 2001.

[14] P. Bourdieu. The forms of social capital. In *Handbook of Theory and Research for the Sociology of Education*, pages 241–258. Greenwood Publishing Group, New York, 1986.

[15] M. Burke, R. Kraut, and C. Marlow. Social capital on facebook: Differentiating uses and users. In *Proc. CHI*, pages 571–580. ACM, 2011.

[16] T. Clausen, P. Jacquet, C. Adjih, A. Laouiti, P. Minet, P. Muhlethaler, A. Qayyum, and L. Viennot. Optimized link state routing protocol (OLSR). *The Internet Society*, 2003.

[17] J. S. Coleman. Social capital in the creation of human capital. *American journal of sociology*, pages S95–S120, 1988.

[18] T. Collins. BART cell phone shutdown: Safety issue or free speech violation?, Aug. 2011.

[19] L. Cutillo, R. Molva, and T. Strufe. Safebook: A privacy-preserving online social network leveraging on real-life trust. *IEEE Communications Magazine*, 47(12):94–101, 2009.

[20] A. Datta, S. Buchegger, L.-H. Vu, T. Strufe, and K. Rzadca. Decentralized Online Social Networks. In *Handbook of Social Network Technologies and Applications*, pages 349–378. Springer US, Boston, MA, 2010.

[21] J. Dibbell. The shadow web. *Scientific American*, 306(3):60–65, Mar. 2012.

[22] J. S. Donath. Identity and deception in the virtual community. *Communities in cyberspace*, 1996:29–59, 1999.

[23] FCC. Sixth broadband deployment report. Technical report, July 2010.

[24] K. J. Geis and C. E. Ross. A new look at urban alienation: The effect of neighborhood disorder on perceived powerlessness. *Social Psychology Quarterly*, pages 232–246, 1998.

[25] E. Gilbert and K. Karahalios. Predicting tie strength with social media. In *Proc. CHI*, pages 211–220. ACM, 2009.

[26] M. Granovetter. *Getting a job: A study of contacts and careers*. University of Chicago Press, 1995.

[27] M. S. Granovetter. The strength of weak ties. *American Journal of Sociology*, 78(6):1360–1380, May 1973.

[28] A. Greenberg. Wary of SOPA, reddit users aim to build a new, censorship-free internet, Nov. 2011.

[29] G. Greenwald and E. MacAskill. NSA prism program taps in to user data of apple, google and others. *The Guardian*, June 2013.

[30] K. Hampton and B. Wellman. Neighboring in netville: How the internet supports community and social capital in a wired suburb. *City & Community*, 2(4):277–311, 2003.

[31] K. N. Hampton, L. S. Goulet, H. Rainie, and K. Purcell. *Social networking sites and our lives: How people's trust, personal relationships, and civic and political involvement are connected to their use of social networking sites and other technologies*. Pew Internet & American Life Project, 2011.

[32] K. N. Hampton, L. F. Sessions, E. J. Her, and L. Rainie. Social isolation and new technology. *Pew Internet & American Life Project*, 2009.

[33] A. Hern. OKCupid: we experiment on users. everyone does. *The Guardian*, July 2014.

[34] J. Horrigan. Home broadband adoption 2009. *Pew Internet & American Life Project*, 2009.

[35] S. Jahid, S. Nilizadeh, P. Mittal, N. Borisov, and A. Kapadia. DECENT: A decentralized architecture for enforcing privacy in online social networks. In *2012 IEEE International Conference on Pervasive Computing and Communications Workshops*, pages 326–332. IEEE, mar 2012.

[36] B. Kazansky. In red hook, mesh network connects sandy survivors still without power, Nov. 2012.

[37] J. Kloc. Greek community creates an off-the-grid internet, Aug. 2013.

[38] D. Lauterbach, H. Truong, T. Shah, and L. Adamic. Surfing a web of trust: Reputation and reciprocity on couchsurfing. com. In *Computational Science and Engineering. International Conference on*, volume 4, pages 346–353. IEEE, 2009.

[39] N. Lin. Building a network theory of social capital. *Connections*, 22(1):28–51, 1999.

[40] E. MacAskill. WikiLeaks website pulled by amazon after US political pressure | media | the guardian, Dec. 2010.

[41] C. A. Masden, C. Grevet, R. E. Grinter, E. Gilbert, and W. K. Edwards. Tensions in scaling-up community social media: A multi-neighborhood study of nextdoor. In *Proc. CHI*, pages 3239–3248. ACM, 2014.

[42] P. H. Pathak and R. Dutta. A Survey of Network Design Problems and Joint Design Approaches in Wireless Mesh Networks. *IEEE Communications Surveys & Tutorials*, 13(3):396–428, 2011.

[43] R. D. Putnam. Bowling alone: America's declining social capital. *Journal of democracy*, 6(1):65–78, 1995.

[44] R. D. Putnam. *Bowling alone: The collapse and revival of American community*. Simon and Schuster, 2000.

[45] H. Rainie, L. Rainie, and B. Wellman. *Networked: The new social operating system*. The MIT Press, 2012.

[46] C. E. Ross. Neighborhood disadvantage and adult depression. *Journal of Health and Social Behavior*, pages 177–187, 2000.

[47] R. J. Sampson. Local friendship ties and community attachment in mass society: A multilevel systemic model. *American Sociological Review*, pages 766–779, 1988.

[48] R. J. Sampson and W. B. Groves. Community structure and crime: Testing social-disorganization theory. *American journal of sociology*, pages 774–802, 1989.

[49] I. Shklovski and N. Kotamraju. Online contribution practices in countries that engage in internet blocking and censorship. In *Proc. CHI*, pages 1109–1118. ACM, 2011.

[50] A. Tonnesen. *Impementing and extending the optimized link state routing protocol*. University of Oslo, Department of Informatics, 2004.

[51] B. Valentine. Oakland's sudo mesh looks to counter censorship and digital divide with a mesh network, July 2014.

[52] B. Wellman. The community question: The intimate networks of east yorkers. *American journal of Sociology*, pages 1201–1231, 1979.

[53] B. Wellman and S. Wortley. Different strokes from different folks: Community ties and social support. *American journal of Sociology*, pages 558–588, 1990.

[54] A. Whitten and J. D. Tygar. Why johnny can't encrypt: A usability evaluation of PGP 5.0. In *Proc. of the 8th USENIX Security Symposium*, volume 99, 1999.

[55] C.-m. A. Yeung, I. Liccardi, K. Lu, O. Seneviratne, and T. Berners-lee. Decentralization : The Future of Online Social Networking. *Artificial Intelligence*, 2:2–7, 2006.

[56] Y. Zhang, J. Luo, and H. Hu. *Wireless mesh networking: architectures, protocols and standards*. CRC Press, 2006.

Improvising Harmony: Opportunities for Technologies to Support Crowd Orchestration

Q. Vera Liao[1, 2]
[1]University of Illinois at Urbana-Champaign
201 North Goodwin Avenue
Urbana, IL 61801
liao28@illinois.edu

Victoria Bellotti[2, 3]
[2]Palo Alto Research Center
3333 Coyote Hill Road
Palo Alto, CA 94304
bellotti@parc.com
Michael.Youngblood@parc.com

Michael Youngblood[2]
[3]Jack Basin School of Engineering
University of California-Santa Cruz
1156 High Street
Santa Cruz, CA 95064

ABSTRACT

This paper details the work of a seldom studied but growing population of members of grassroots, offline-project based groups. We aim to understand how these groups self-organize to enable a large number of volunteers to gather and "get things done," and identify design opportunities for technologies to support such work. By studying the work structure, we identified two types of members, *regular* and *episodic* participants, who differ in structural role, motivation, and type of work they do. We studied two key tasks: 1) project management, which is mostly done collaboratively by the regular participants; and 2) organization of work events—the project implementation, which involve many episodic participants. For both tasks, we report on common practices and tools that are currently used. We then discuss design implications and user requirements for developing specialized tools to support these tasks.

Keywords

Crowd orchestration; volunteer; project collaboration; social computing; peer production.

1. INTRODUCTION

Modern technologies are making it ever easier for groups to self-organize in an ad hoc manner, bootstrapping from chaos into productive, coordinated work [44]. Scholars [3][49] contend that such effort offers an alternative to, and competes with the "traditional institutional forms of getting things done." While the HCI and CSCW communities have a long history of studying technologies to support group work [20][41], and have given ample attention to online peer production groups [31][44][50], we know far less about opportunities for technologies to support grassroots, self-organizing groups that gather many people to "work on the ground" (e.g., organizing events, building community gardens, putting on art performance, and so forth).

We call this growing form of tangible, ad-hoc, and near-term goal-oriented (i.e., small project-based) group endeavor *crowd orchestration* (CO). It poses a number of unique challenges: first, even though they are not traditional volunteer organizations, CO groups depend entirely on *volunteers*. This means they cannot financially reward participants, but must inspire other types of motivation and tailor their practices to cater for the diverse needs of the crowd. Second, grassroots groups usually lack established organizational structures and full-time staff that most formal organizations, like The Red Cross, have. Little is known about how work is divided among large numbers of unpaid participants. Third, as they work on tangible outcomes in the physical world, they often require many people to work at the same time, in the same location, where significant challenges can emerge in collaboration and coordination.

To understand how these groups operate and to identify design opportunities for technologies to support them, we conducted an interview study with 26 individuals in the USA and UK who have participated in CO-like groups. A key finding of our work is the co-existence of *regular participants*, who dedicate a significant amount of time and effort to the group, and *episodic participants*, who only participate occasionally and may not be committed to continuity. Regular and episodic participants tend to take different roles and engage in different types of work.

We started by studying what motivates people to participate in CO groups, and how it varies for the regular and episodic participants, and further, how the varied motivations may inform designs of technologies that support the different types of work that regular and episodic participants do. Specifically, we focused on studying two common tasks of CO groups: 1) *project management*, which is mainly handled by regular participants, and 2) organization of *work events* (i.e., the implementation of project), which often involves large proportion of episodic participants. We examined the common practices and tools that are currently used by CO groups to identify key user requirements for new technologies to support these tasks.

2. RELATED WORK

We ground our study in two genres of scholarship: social science literature on volunteerism, and literature on technologies that support peer production, mainly from the HCI and CSCW communities.

Social science research on volunteerism has covered many topics [56]. Among them, a long lasting interest is what motivates volunteering. Early research mostly studied "traditional" charity-based volunteer organizations, focusing on benevolence and altruism [8][39]. Later, especially as the volunteering scene broadened, scholars recognized a diversity of motivations [9][22]. For example, some volunteer for self-serving reasons such as skills or career development. *Self-Determination Theory* (SDT) [13][46] has been usefully applied to volunteering motivations [18][21][22]. As an expansion of Herzberg's two-factor theory

GROUP '16, November 13-16, 2016, Sanibel Island, FL, USA
© 2016 ACM. ISBN 978-1-4503-4276-6/16/11···$15.00
DOI: http://dx.doi.org/10.1145/2957276.2957303

[25], which contrasts *intrinsic* (for its own sake) with *extrinsic* (from external rewards or punishments) motivation, SDT puts human motivations on a continuum of increasing internalization and proposes the following control mechanisms:

- *External regulation* is based on demands or pressure to attain contingent rewards or avoid punishments.
- *Introjected regulation* is a partly internalized motivation driven by norms or ego-involvement.
- *Identified regulation* comes from understanding the importance or effectiveness of an activity for achieving a desirable end.
- *Integrated regulation* means engaging in an activity because of its assimilation with personal value.
- *Intrinsic regulation* refers to engagement in an activity solely because it is enjoyable.

SDT has been used to explain the varying behaviors of volunteers (e.g., retention and turnover rate [22]) and their work preferences (e.g., task significance and required level of skill [37]). Consistent with this theory, autonomy orientation (i.e., more internalized motivation) and autonomy support (i.e., supporting the internalization of motivation) [17] were found to positively correlate with volunteer productivity and satisfaction [22].

Recent research has also focused on the evolution of volunteering, from the wholly *collective style* by emphasizing affiliation with institutions and long-term commitment, to the inclusion of a more *reflexive style* of volunteering that prioritizes individual interest and needs [24]. One outcome is a rise in episodic volunteering—individuals performing a one-time, or occasional service. Prior work [24] also suggests that ad hoc, project-based arrangements attract people seeking episodic volunteering opportunities, since assignments can be completed in a finite timespan and can be tailored to one's workload preference. In fact, previous literature has linked the rising trend of episodic volunteering to the "expanding field of informal, self-organized initiatives with no center of authority and project-oriented objectives" [24]—a rather accurate description of CO groups.

In the HCI and CSCW community, there has been a growing interest in studying and developing ICTs to support volunteer work. While some believe that ICSs can helpfully improve many aspects of volunteer groups' work, from recruitment, public relation, to project management [36], studies that examine the current practices of ICT use in volunteer groups repeatedly reported underutilization of digital tools, often constrained by the limited financial resource and IT personnel [23][55]. Several recent studies attempted to introduce new technologies for volunteer activities. For example, [35] used participatory design to create database software for non-profit volunteer organizations. [27] developed a mobile tool that supports data collection for volunteer campaigns. [54] explored design opportunities for infrastructure to support everyday, ubiquitous forms of volunteering.

To inform the design of technologies that support large group of volunteer to work together, we can also draw a parallel between research into online peer production and our study of CO groups. The most widely studied peer production systems are Wikipedia [5][28][32][42] and open source software (OSS) development [16]. Recently, researchers have studied digital volunteerism as a new type of peer-production. Examples include social media users self-organizing to assist in disaster response [10][50], and participants of online citizen science projects [27][44].

A main focus of research on peer production has been to understand the work structure of this new form of collaboration. Quantitative analysis of Wikipedia edits revealed a power law distribution of contribution with a small portion of "experts" doing the majority of the work [28]. Drawn from legitimate peripheral participation theory [33], Bryant et al. [5] suggest that some Wikipedia editors progress from peripheral activities to ones that are more and more central to the functioning of the community (e.g., meta-level tasks such as mediating disputes, establishing policies). A similar pattern was reported for open source software development [16]. Studies of disaster relief volunteers on social media also found that the work is organized around a core group of "trusted volunteers," with "occasional and spontaneous" volunteers at the periphery, who mostly join during the intensive post-disaster work period, and contribute mainly in simple unskilled tasks. Some of them may move towards the center of the community [10][50].

Drawing inspiration from social science theories, researchers have studied ways to motivate contribution to peer production. Among others, Karau and William's collective effort model [26] is often cited. It predicts that contributions can be increased by two ways—reducing the contribution costs, and increasing the perceived value of outcomes. Based on it, prior work illustrated that contributions can be effectively increased by technologies that ease the participation (e.g., an automatic task-routing system [12]), and designs that highlight the uniqueness and value of contributions [33][42], provide positive feedback and appreciation [32], and accomplishment of goals [59].

Informed by the above literature, we see design opportunities for technologies that support CO group work in similar ways to support online peer production groups, as they are both project-based, self-organized effort. But they may also differ. For example, CO groups are obviously more constrained by time and location, and involve more face-to-face interactions. To understand how CO groups "get things done," we follow the literature on peer production by studying their work structure and identifying effective strategies that motivate members to contribute to projects. We describe our interview-based research methods in the next section.

3. METHOD

3.1 Recruitment Criteria

We used the following criteria to identify groups we wanted to recruit interviewees from: 1) "self-organizing," i.e., not managed by paid, professional staff. 2) grassroots organizing for tangible objectives. Therefore, "club" types of groups focused on socializing only, or groups targeting social movements such as activism, are not included; 3) work is mainly done in the physical world instead of online. In the interview, in addition to self-reported motivation and experience, we also attempted to inquire general descriptions of the group, if possible, to obtain a rich picture of participating practices.

3.2 Participants

We recruited 26 participants (11 male) from 21 diverse CO groups by posting on social media and mailing lists, directly contacting members via group websites, and snowball recruiting. During analysis, we classified 16 of them to be regular members and 10 to be episodic members. We list brief descriptions of the groups in Table 1.

3.3 Data Collection and Analysis

We conducted semi-structured interviews using a protocol designed to focus on the following areas of interest:

- *Motivation for participation*, including what attracted members to join and to continue contributing, if they do; otherwise, what deterred them.
- *Coordination of work*, where we start by inquiring about work routines and procedures, and focus on understanding how members divide the work, what roles they adopt, and how they work together.
- *Tools used by participants*, including both information and communication technology (ICT) and non-ICT types, their usage, benefits and limitations.

Interviews lasted around 50 minutes and were conducted remotely, via telephone or video conferencing software, and were recorded and then transcribed. Analysis was informed by the grounded theory approach following an iterative open coding process [52]. For each transcript, relevant quotes were selected and copied to a spreadsheet to be analyzed both individually and collectively across transcripts. We first open-coded each quote and used the codes to identify categories based on clustered concepts. Categories were then grouped into broader themes.

During analysis, a prominent theme we identified was the existence of two types of participant – *regular* participants who contribute on a regular basis, and *episodic* participants who perform only occasional or one-time service (details discussed in the next section). We therefore performed a secondary coding to identify descriptions that specifically applied to regular or episodic members. Such descriptions can be either self-referential (e.g., when an interviewee identified to be regular/episodic talked about him or herself), or other-referential with explicit indication of category (e.g., when referring someone else as "core member," or "who only showed up for a couple of hours at the show").

4. RESULTS

4.1 Work Structure of CO Groups

To situate discussion of the work structure of CO groups, we note that while groups that we sampled from work on different projects (see Table 1), two common elements of their work are *work events* and *project management*. For example, G13 is a group working on urban farming project. It has a "planting day" every few weeks when participants will gather to work in the farm. G10 is a group building community housing, and it organizes many "construction days" that people can sign up for to participate in the construction work. G1 is a group working on annual event, and the event itself *is* the work event for the volunteer members. Outside these work events, work is continuously required for project management, which often involves planning, organizing and coordinating the work events, as well as managing the personnel, finance and other resources. In most groups, this is accomplished through holding regular *planning meetings*. Aside from the meetings individuals coordinate via ICTs such as email, phone, social media, etc.

4.1.1 Regular and Episodic Participants

Consistent with literature on volunteerism and peer production [6][16][24][27][50], we identified regular and episodic participants in all the CO groups we sampled. We should mention that this distinction is not dichotomous. Rather, consistent with [24], there is a continuum of regularity of participation. Further, a small portion of episodic participants may become regulars as their engagement deepens [5][50]. We distinguish *regular* and *episodic* participants to highlight a disparity of involvement and contribution levels among members and elucidate differences in roles, motivation and practices.

Table 1: Description of interviewees' groups. Episodic members are labeled with letter E. Project description is on tasks that the volunteer crowds do, not including administrative work.

Group	Subject ID	Group Project Description
G1	P2	Annual neighborhood event with market, performance, etc. Volunteers work on the event day for various tasks
G2	P22 (E)	Donation events to help children in the Middle East. Volunteers take shifts to work at the donation site.
G3	P24 (E)	Accept donated books and giving out to children in the neighborhood. Volunteers take shifts to work at the donation site.
G4	P25 (E)	Organize neighborhood art performance. Volunteers work on the event day.
G5	P3	Breast cancer walk for public awareness. Volunteers work on the event day.
G6	P4, P6	Neighborhood gaming events. Volunteers work on the event day to set things up.
G7	P18 (E)	Yoga practicing events. Volunteers participate at the event day and also work together to set things up.
G8	P20	Group outdoor adventure. Volunteers get together for the scheduled day, both as participants and set up the events.
G9	P1	Building community solar power system. Volunteers sign up for multiple "building days" to build the power system.
G10	P8	Building community shared housing. Volunteers sign up for multiple "building days" to work on the housing construction.
G11	P12 (E), P13, P14	Building community housing for low-income families. Volunteers sign up for multiple "building days".
G12	P5, P11 (E)	Urban farming project for shared food. Volunteers sign up for multiple "planting days" during the farming circle.
G13	P10	Urban farming project for shared food. Volunteers sign up for "planting days".
G14	P19 (E)	Community gardening. Volunteers are assigned individual garden and participate in "work days" for various maintenance tasks.
G15	P23 (E)	Community gardening. Volunteers sign up for gardens and participate in "work days".
G16	P7, P21	Burning Man project. Volunteers build artwork and participate in the event.
G17	P15	Community theater performance. Volunteers take various roles in performance, practice and set up for the performance.
G18	P26 (E)	Performance art show. Volunteers sign up for art show events, work on the stage and various set-up tasks.
G19	P16	Helping local older adults. Volunteers sign up for volunteering slots.
G20	P17	Helping local older adults. Volunteers sign up for volunteering slots.
G21	P9 (E)	Organizing mycological education trip. Volunteers help out during the trip.

We found that episodic participants prefer to participate in events where they can show up for a day of work without long-term commitment. They rarely engage in project management, planning or other organizational activities—even if they are open to them. This echoes previous research [7][24] suggesting that episodic volunteers prefer, and also are most suited for project-based assignments.

Project management work mainly falls to the regular participants, often the most devoted, who contribute significant time and take greater responsibility. Size of the group of regular members range from 3 to about a dozen in the sample of groups we studied. In many ways, their roles resemble those of paid professional staff in formal NPOs. For example, they may adopt the role of *human resources staffer* to recruit new members, *marketing staffer* to promote the group and seek funding, *coordinator* to manage group members, *site manager* to lead work on the ground, *accountant* to handle financial tasks, and so on.

4.1.2 Emergent Hierarchical Structure

Prior work suggests that grassroots groups may not build a hierarchical structure as formal organizations do, due to a lack of clear authority [58]. But almost all the groups we encountered reported a hierarchy—not maintained by power and authority, but *emerging* from different levels of involvement and different roles people adopt. By taking part in organizational work, regular members are seen as the group's "core" and episodic members as the "periphery"—a structure that is reflected in many studies of peer production groups [5][16][27][50]. For example, P2 is in a group organizing annual neighborhood social events. It has a *"planning committee"* of 8 members who meet monthly, and recruit and lead a large number of members who only work on the event days. P10 described the structure of a community farming group as having an "*inner core*" of "*7 or 8 people who are acting to get things done*," an "*outer core*" of "*about 20 people who help lead work parties,*" and episodic volunteers, "*anywhere from 60 to a 120 people show up for 4 or 5 hour work parties.*" (P10)

CO group hierarchies tend to have "distributed leadership," with regular members encouraged to take "local leader" roles for work events or subparts of a project, often leading a group of episodic participants. Local leadership is commonly attained through either repeatedly doing a task—so developing the ability to train and lead others—or through actively volunteering oneself for a role—often to suggest new additions to the project. Local leaders may have complete autonomy in terms of planning and execution, and this allows CO groups to keep administrative costs low.

While hierarchy is often explicitly acknowledged in some way (e.g., by talking about a "core group" or "planning committee"), it is emergent in that there is often no formal admittance to the "core group" but rather it is earned through increasing participation and voluntary accountability. For example, in several groups we studied, planning meetings scaffold such a structure via self-selection: these meetings are open to all, but attendees tend to be those interested in more involvement. Only those who show up on a regular basis are seen as core members, taking on more responsibilities and accountability to the group.

"Interviewer: How did you decide they are the core group? Interviewee: They just kept showing up... kept coming to meetings and then stepping up more and more. Do we decide on it? No, and I don't... it's not even spoken too much, but I realize we can count on each other." (P10)

Table 2. Relevant frequency of code occurrence for each of the motivations from Self Determination Theory

Regulatory styles		Example	Regulars	Episodics
External regulation	Instrumental	Share outcomes; get discounts or other perks	3%	30%
	Social	Enjoy socializing and/or ongoing relationship	25%	16%
Introjected Regulation		Self-improvement; fulfill obligations; follow norms	0%	28%
Identified Regulation		Support the group goals and value the the results	13%	14%
Integrated Regulation		Consist with personal values and beliefs	25%	2%
Intrinsic Regulation		Enjoyment of work	34%	9%

4.2 Motivations of CO Group Members

We were interested in what motivates people to participate in CO groups. Following previous research [21][22][37], we coded CO participants' motivation under the framework of self-determination theory (SDT) [13][18]. By using participant category (Regular or Episodic) as a code we were able to map participant motivations along the SDT spectrum, as shown in Table 2. It shows a different distribution of motivation type between the two categories. Here we discuss each type of motivation and the key findings.

External regulation, means being motivated by extrinsic rewards (or the avoidance of punishments) and following Nov et al. [37], we further divide this into "instrumental rewards" and "social interaction" for volunteering context.

Instrumental rewards: the possibility of sharing the co-produced outcome is often used as an instrumental motivator for participants. Many CO groups also offer rewards such as *"attend the event for free"* (P22). Instrumental rewards were primarily described as motivators by episodic participants. So, given the limited tangible rewards CO groups can afford, people who are primarily motivated by instrumental value may not want to contribute continuously.

Social interaction: the nature of CO work—that it happens in the local community and involves physically gathering—provides ample opportunities for socializing. We found that this motivates both regular and episodic members. Regulars, especially, value social relationships formed through interactions, seeing the "core group" as a *"relationship-based group." (P08)*

Introjected regulation refers to pursing ego-enhancement or filling obligations. We saw it primarily in episodic or early-stage participation, where people are attracted because, for example, they are able to *"learn about operating machines" (P26)*, or *"it gives me a sense of function" (P24)*. Filling social obligations was also reported. For example, a group of company employees might sign up for a work event. However, they were found to be *"not as easy to recruit again as those sign up on their own." (P14)*

Identified regulation, in the context of CO groups, may result from perceiving the value or effectiveness of the group's work, be it creating useful or influential products, helping others in need, etc. This motivation was frequently reported by both episodic and regular participants.

Integrated regulation is primarily seen in regular

participants, who are often motivated by idealistic belief in the group mission. For instance, *"I think that we are definitely strong supporters of the mission, as opposed to just anybody who signs up for a one-time thing" (P14).* Participants are especially likely to join the core when group values match their own. For example, P05 is an active member of a community gardening project because *"I teach this stuff, you know, if I teach sustainability…it's putting into practice what I preach." (P05)*

Intrinsic motivation is characterized as enjoying the activity purely for its own sake. Many regular participants reported this. For example, *"A lot of people who are involved [in the board] love to do theater." (P15).* Meanwhile, not feeling intrinsically motivated (e.g. *"did not like the construction work"* (P13)) was mentioned as a de-motivator that led episodic participants to drop out.

Table 2 highlights differences between regular and episodic members. It suggests that those with more autonomous motivation—intrinsically motivated by enjoyment of the work and its idealistic value—are more likely to be regular members taking core responsibilities. In contrast, those drawn to more extrinsic rewards tend to remain episodic members.

In the rest of the paper, we focus on two key tasks of CO groups: collaborative project management and organization of work events. Given the divergence of participants involved in them—the former mainly done by regular members and the latter by crowds with a large portion of episodic participants—we recognize different needs reflected in the work practices that align with their motivational differences. Specifically, we identify *autonomy support* in regular participants' project management work, and *motivation support* in mobilizing and coordinating crowds.

4.3 Collaborative Project Management

As discussed earlier, we regard the organizational work to put on work events as collaborative project management. This is often divided among core group members, each taking specific *roles*, and collaborating closely, typically by having regular planning meetings to divide work, discuss issues, and report on progress.

4.3.1 Autonomy Support

According to SDT, supporting autonomy fosters more internalized motivation, increasing work satisfaction and productivity [17][18]. For core members, a primary way to support autonomy is to encourage *self-initiative*—choice over what one wants to do. This is reflected in the largely bottom-up process for role assignment: a common tactic is to leave it up to the members to identify what needs doing, decide what they are capable of and interested in doing, and volunteer for the roles. It is viewed as *empowering* for regular members, and many groups explicitly avoid top-down assignment that could undermine autonomous motivations. This is illustrated in the following quote, describing how a new member of a "planning committee" self-assigned his role: *"He just came into the group and you know we do not really define what he is going to be doing… after being at a couple of meetings, he is going to find things that he thinks he would be best at doing within the group." (P02)*

Regular meetings, especially the practice of "reporting and discussing together," seem to support self-initiative by creating *transparency*—through shared awareness of different parts of a project and promptly communicated needs [15]. Regular members reflected on the importance of *"visibility"* and *"asking for help"* to show accountability and facilitate work redistribution: *"The more visible you can make what you are doing the better because for two reasons. People can see that you're trustworthy… they can also see that you need help. They can think to themselves, oh I really know about email systems, or my friend knows, I should connect them." (P04)*

Autonomy support also extends to *competence* and *relatedness*. Competence support is achieved through positive reinforcement and feedback. It means expressing support and trust for regular members, while minimizing intervention and overhead. It is reflected by the "distributed leadership" work structure we discussed earlier, which affords the regulars autonomy to accomplish their goals. Relatedness support is seen in the idea of *"shared ownership."* CO groups as co-production groups cultivate a sense of ownership in their essential value. It is especially important for regular members who invest heavily in group products, and *"have their specific roles and they take ownership over it." (P03).* In particular, co-ownership is reflected in the democratic decision-making among the core members that frequently involves voting, debate and conflict resolution.

4.3.2 Fluidity, Adaptability and the Challenges

In contrast with formal organizations, the bottom-up role assignment of CO groups leads to more fluid, ill-defined roles, where core members may frequently vary responsibilities or switch roles altogether. This is also partly due to the fact that many CO groups are newly emergent grassroots efforts, lacking experience or precedents to copy. As P07, who is a core member for an art project group, pointed out, *"nobody really knows exactly how to do this…so we have to try and figure out like whose idea is the best, who is best at doing what."* P04 also described it as a *"trial and error process"* to redistribute and optimize assignments.

The fluidity also springs from the need to be *adaptive* given the high turnover rate, which is a fundamental characteristic of volunteer groups [37]. One's availability may often be constrained by other life commitments, such as work or travel, so members often temporarily take over others' roles or delegate their own. Interviewees valued accommodating and flexible team mates that they could rely on—*"having people to pick up the slack is very important…where you're not getting paid, and it's all volunteer time, it really helps to have access to that… It's that we have kind of a circulating group of people that someone else could step in and fill the void when someone wants a break." (P11)*

Bottom-up, fluid role self-assignment leads to a few challenges for collaborative project management: 1) uneven, non-optimized work distribution. 5 interviewees who have been in the selected leader position reported high workload, having to take multiple roles, often the unclaimed roles that no one else selected to do. We recognize that relying on discussions at monthly or less frequent meetings may not provide enough transparency and facilitation of work distribution. 2) A lack of clear definition of roles. It leads to overlaps, neglect, or even conflicts between members. This is exacerbated by the fact that the job assigning is often spontaneous and sometimes implicit. For example, one may start "helping out" in a different role when it seems necessary, which is likely to happen when CO group members work in the same physical space.

4.3.3 Tools Supporting Collaborative Project Management

Collaborative project management work spans from co-located physical meetings to remote communications. In particular, we identified a range of tools for *collaborative task management.* 4 interviewees reported having a shared to-do list, either *"a piece of paper passing around"* or bulletin board at the meeting site, updated regularly. A quote from P10 details a common scene at planning meetings and the use of such a shared list in supporting collaborative task identification, assignment, and coordination: *"We have a meeting once a week, and we'll say what needs to get done and how are we going to do it then we make a list on the chalkboard. Sometimes we break into groups and brainstorm... So then, as you have all these tasks up on the list and we start prioritizing it, and we say, 'Okay, who wants to be the leader of that?' then we've got these leaders and we write down, 'what materials do you need and how many people do you think?'" (P10)* As this quote illustrates, the use of these tools aligns closely with the self-initiated role assigning process of the core group, fostering transparency and shared awareness.

4 groups maintain an electronic "shared chalkboard." Two reported using Google Docs and two others created a wiki page for everyone to contribute ideas and action items, track assignments and schedule, etc. These tools provide additional benefits - not only allowing remote and asynchronous project management, but also serving as a repository of reusable information for the future: *"We have Google Docs which helps coordinating like, who is arriving when and what are they bringing... we had one page on there to go—for current schedule to make sure that it is in need of attention...then we have a lot of that are sort of the repository of information that's been accumulated (P07)"*

Other groups simply rely on personal communication applications to do task management work. Consistent with prior research, project management heavily depends on email [1][57]. Most groups reported having a mailing list dedicated to discussion about coordination and logistics, which is indispensable to project management between meetings. While it is a natural extension of group communication, there are well-documented challenges in using email for task management [1][57]. We heard similar problems including overloaded and cluttered messages, lack of timely responses, and disruption of collaboration, for example, *"I try to do zero inbox, that's how I manage it... that's a disaster, hectic," (P06)* and *"people don't check their emails and you don't get a response for days and you just wait." (P02)*

In addition to email, 4 groups reported using forum style discussion tools such as Yahoo or Facebook Groups, often to discuss specific issues in a short timeframe. We heard of groups switching between multiple communication tools for project management. A reason for this is the varying needs for backchannel communications. For example, P07's art project group use Google Docs for structured task management, and a mailing list for group wide communication (e.g., meeting minutes and information requests). When a specific issue comes up, they may switch to a Facebook Group to engage in discussion threads—one benefit she mentioned is that it gives individuals a choice to opt in or out of a particular discussion.

4.4 Design Implications for Supporting Collaborative Project Management

Based on the above analysis, a collaborative project management (PM) tool such as Basecamp or Asana may offer one place for CO groups to do all their work without breakdowns, including task management, one-to-one and group communication, decision-making and archiving. However, no group in our study used such a tool. While we believe technical and financial constraints may play a role, we note that existing tools are developed primarily for managing for-profit projects enacted by paid participants with defined roles and responsibilities (such as regular reporting) that cannot be shirked. So they may fail to anticipate certain needs of CO groups. Here we highlight two points to consider when designing PM tools for CO groups, which are expected to be used both synchronously (i.e., during group meetings) and asynchronously (i.e., outside group meetings) by a group ranging from a couple to a dozen of members.

4.4.1 Supporting Bottom-up Work Assignment

Our analysis revealed that assignment of CO organization work is highly bottom-up, relying on regulars to collectively identify—sometimes to "pool"—tasks that need doing, and to self-assign from the pool. Currently these activities are often supported by rudimentary tool such as chalkboard or shared document. For a specialized PM tool, we recommend a key feature to be an intuitive, fully shared view of a collaboratively created and maintained to-do list, perhaps using the chalkboard metaphor, which allows everyone to add, edit, delete, annotate and self-assign items, as easily as drag-and-drop. Actions should be transparent and easy to track. While some PM tools already provide a shared "project view" for team activities, we emphasize the need for support of collaborative work distribution and redistribution for CO groups—this is often not explicitly supported (e.g., in Basecamp and Asana, one is expected to create one's own task, or assign tasks to someone else, not put tasks up for anyone to commandeer). A CO tool should enable a collaborative process that fosters autonomous motivation. For example, everyone could tag tasks in common pool as time-sensitive, requiring certain skills, etc. to assist the self-selective process. To initiate redistribution, one could "request help" by flagging challenging tasks they are currently taking. "Social reference," by enabling members to recommend tasks to others, could also help optimize the process.

To enhance social transparency and provide a clearer definition of roles, we also recommend a "people view" visualizing each individual's responsibilities and status, etc., as well as ongoing collaboration with and dependency on other group members. This view could also allow users to start backchannel communication for clarification and negotiation of boundaries (e.g., by pointing to specific tasks). P02 mentioned that, as echoed in previous work [42], people often feel uncomfortable doing so in a collaborative context. Lightweight social interaction such as a "help" button to express willingness to support or takeover a task could be used to facilitate the negotiation.

4.4.2 Lightweight, Flexible and Supporting Fluidity

One interviewee mentioned considering Basecamp but concluded that it is too *"heavy weight"* (P06) for a volunteer group, requiring substantial investment from everyone to maintain. This highlights a key shortcoming of existing PM tools: lack of flexibility to accommodate groups with varied levels of involvement and dynamic usage patterns. Current tools often impose procedural controls, such as check-in/check-out, reporting, and tracking individual progress. However, for CO groups, regular members' high autonomy would render these control mechanisms as redundant functional clutter, and their use could be detrimental to intrinsic motivation. Our analysis suggests that tools for regular members should favor unobtrusive visibility, and thus accountability, over supervision and control. So CO support solutions should avoid mandatory actions, rather offering choices, and encouraging members to be visible to others, for example, with a "group news feed," where members can announce their progress and comment on that of others'.

A more critical challenge, as suggested by our analysis, is to support the high fluidity of member responsibilities and dynamic patterns of use. For example, it should allow users to easily indicate temporary leave, role switching or delegation and avoid complex user authorization for such changes. Beyond that, technology should consider how to support knowledge transition for frequent role switching. For example, each task node could be linked to an archiving page that lists all the activities of people who previously worked on a task, as well as resources used and learning materials.

4.5 Organizing Work Events

While the activities of work events vary widely among CO groups, we sought commonalities in procedures that enable a large crowd to perform collective action at a focused time and location. We solicited descriptions from both episodic members who are participants of work events and core members who have acted as *event coordinators*. Unlike role assignment among core members, we identified significantly more centralized *planning* and top-down *assignment* in coordinating work events involving episodic members.

Planning: before work events, the coordinator or a group of regulars plans the goals, procedures and resources required. An important part of this step is the task *breakdown*—to divide work into smaller parts. Consistent with Benkler's suggestion on enabling peer production [4], the parts should be highly modular—independently doable to reduce complexity and coordination costs, and low in granularity—the time and effort required should be minimal in order to draw enough participants, especially those with low motivation.

Assignment: this is often a top-down process to allocate tasks to the working crowd. In some groups, a coordinator makes an announcement about available tasks so participants can choose. In other groups, the coordinator assigns tasks by *profile matching*, based on pre-collected information such as preferences, skills, and availability. We found that groups that are larger, more mature, or engage in more routine activities (as compared to more creative activities such as art project) are more likely to perform top-down assignment.

4.5.1 Motivating Episodic Participants

Since CO groups depend on a large portion of episodic participants who cannot be held accountable for commitments and may have limited motivation, efforts are made to entice contribution and to nurture potential long-term engagement. Drawn from economic and social science theories, contribution to collective effort could be encouraged by adopting two strategies: reducing costs of participation, and increasing perceived value of outcomes [26][31].

We found coordinators invested significant effort in lowering participation cost, to *"make it really easy for people" (P06)*. This means reducing the perceived difficulty and complexity of the work. For instance, by having a coordinator perform all the task breakdown and matching work, one *"only needs to sign up for an event and fill out a short form" (P13)*. In our interviews with episodic members, we noted a *non-transparency* of work planning. Episodic members were mostly unaware of the planning and articulation work (i.e, work division and re-integration) [51], but focused only on the small chunks that were available or assigned to them. They seemed to welcome the simplicity of this approach. They also welcomed explicit coordination [29], where clear instructions were communicated (e.g., overview, procedure and expected time commitment). This helps with *expectation setting*, which minimizes aversion to unknown costs: *"the biggest barriers are fear from the people about whether it's going to work and [how much] time needed...In the email we say the only time that we actually need you to volunteer is like those three or four hours." (P04)*

To emphasize the value of contributions [32][33], some groups publicly acknowledge each individual, or reward those who made substantial contributions. Some coordinators send out personalized thank-you notes. Participants valued the acknowledgement and gratitude they received and recognized the positive effect of an appreciative group leader or coordinator—*"enough for me to think, I am valued" (P22)*. Some coordinators expressed frustration that they could not accurately identify people that should be acknowledged, which is a challenge with large crowds. To be consistent with the norm of "welcoming any level of contribution," and to avoid additional work, most CO groups do not ask participants to log or self-report contributions. Of course this makes it even harder to target individuals for acknowledgement and further engagement.

4.5.2 Challenges for Work Event Coordinators

Our analysis revealed the unique position of and significant challenges for coordinators of CO work events. On the one hand, they act as group leaders at the top of the hierarchy, directing others. On the other hand, they lack authority and must often prioritize serving the satisfaction of others. P03 described her coordinator job as *"customer service"* —attending to individual needs to ensure a positive participation experience. Several other interviewees also mentioned that they would frequently *"check in with everybody"(P06)* and *"make sure people are having fun, not burning out"(P08)*, and sometimes they had to compromise work outcomes for the sake of participants' enjoyment. Some also reported a tension between maintaining formal structures (e.g., standard procedures that reduce individual input) and ensuring individual needs, which piles on extra work for the coordinators.

Another prominent challenge is *dealing with unpredictability*. To retain volunteers and lower participating barriers, CO groups often allow any level of contribution and flexibility to join and leave at any time. Also, many groups adopt a radically inclusive recruiting strategy and the outcome is a large number of loosely associated, potentially "lurking," episodic members. On the one hand, it makes it hard to predict how many people will attend, and what kind of skillset will be available for each event. For example, P10 mentioned there are around 1000 people in the mailing list they use for work event announcement, but there would be only 60-120 attending. On the other hand, lack of accountability (e.g., non-response, absence, dropout) is almost inevitable with crowds, but is amiably tolerated as group norms. Interviewees described various strategies to cope with unpredictability. Some emphasize timely communication. Some rely on having flexible and resilient plans, such as by identifying and prioritizing critical tasks, or substituting with paid workers. Some study attrition rate and its predictors (e.g., weather, volunteering experience) in order to adjust recruitment effort.

4.5.3 Tools Supporting Organizing Work Events

As seen in peer production literature [10][50], over time, organizing procedures get more formalized, which helps to reduce participation cost. We learned that the formalization of coordination procedures is supported by a variety of standard artifacts (e.g., standard lists, forms and brochures), which streamline and reduce variation in procedures. For example, the goal of planning and work breakdown is to create a *job list*. Given that work events are often repetitive in nature, such a list then can be reused, maintained and formalized overtime. In 3 groups, this list was expanded into a brochure with job descriptions sent out to members before work events to facilitate work assignment and *expectation setting*. P09, an episodic participant described such a brochure: *"I received a list of things like cleaning up, bringing wood... we also receive a package, all the documentation about things that we need to bring, like flashlight, and useful information about the agenda." (P09)*

In groups where coordinators perform top-down assignment, a commonly used tool is a form to collect individual information such as work preferences, skillsets and availability. In some groups this is paper-based, handed out when participants sign up, while others use a web-based form such as Google Forms. The forms must be simple and require minimum effort for participants to fill: *"I added a Google form which streamlined the process tremendously... I try to be really specific. So there is like five different things they can volunteer for and I also try to think through like before the event, during the event, little chunks. So they would feel it's really easy to participate." (P06)*

The content of these forms may be entered into a database. Similar as in [53], coordinators often use Microsoft Office™ tools like Excel or Outlook, or create a paper-based "database." The coordinator can then go through the database to match individuals to different tasks. But challenges may arise from trying to satisfy both individual preference and project optimization. For instance, *"part of the challenge is matching people based on not just what they love, but matching them based on skill level" (P20)*.

Communication with crowds takes a major portion of a coordinator's work routines and is supported by various ICT tools. We heard a mix of, and frequent switching between one-to-many mass communication and one-to-one personal communication. Periodically, or prior to work events, coordinators send mass emails *to mobilize* the crowd. These are typically announcements about events, polling for interest and availability. Most use a group-wide mailing list, often on a monthly basis so *"people don't feel overwhelmed" (P10)*. Some groups also cross-post announcements on social media accounts like Facebook, Twitter, Nextdoor, etc. to reach a wider audience. After that, mass communication at a smaller scale happens by gathering contact information of those who responded to a call. More detailed information about the event is sent out, often including job descriptions and other logistics. Some groups also send task assignments at this point. To cope with dropouts, as the event approaches, many coordinators send out a reminder email to confirm availability. In response to mass emails, some participants initiate individual communication threads with the coordinator. These exchanges are usually to communicate availability, to ask specific questions, or to negotiate about tasks.

The communication described above can be highly taxing for coordinators, and is constrained by the event timeline. Several groups thus develop or appropriate existing tools for event-related communication. One example is the use of event organizing websites like Meetup.com, reported by 2 interviewees. Such tools can accommodate the basic event-related communication well, including announcement making, RSVP, group and personal messaging, etc. An additional benefit is the social aspect. Several interviewees sought awareness of other event participants (e.g. *"you can see each other's profiles, and mutual friends you have in common."(P20))*, and communicate with other participants. For example, the commenting section can be appropriated for social Q&A to help collaboratively address individual—especially new—participants' questions.

Existing event organizing tools, however, are mostly developed for social, instead of work events and may fail to support work-related needs, especially for task assignment, like providing task descriptions, requesting specific skills, collecting preferences, sending targeted instructions, taking ownership, etc. Two groups reported developing their own specialized "*event portal*," both featuring a calendar view where members can sign up for different days, indicate preferred tasks and review logistics and instructions. They also allow participants to communicate with coordinators and give timely notice for plan changes (e.g., by cancelling registration). P14 also valued such a tool as a database for keeping records of individuals' contact, profile, work records and also feedback collected.

4.6 Design Implications for Supporting Work Events Organization

Our analysis suggests that a specialized CO work event organization tool that integrates coordination (i.e., task planning and assignment) and communication could facilitate organization of work events. We note that task assignment could seamlessly fit into the communication process—for example, task matching could be performed immediately after an RSVP, and participants could then be grouped for task-specific information and communicate within their group. An integrated tool could also accommodate individual flexibility by enabling self-selection and changes—for example, choosing from a task list, or making changes to an assignment, and the coordinators might only need to be notified or asked for approval, greatly reducing their workload. We emphasize that the tool should aim to improve the experience of both sides: the coordinator, and the participating crowd. Next, we will discuss three key points that we believe can add value to such a tool.

4.6.1 Computation Supported Coordination

At the present time, task assignment is onerous but particularly tractable to computation. A system could easily replace much of the coordinator's work by performing automatic task-matching based on multiple criteria such as self-reported preference, profile and participation history, and the result is likely to be more optimal. A similar idea has already been explored in developing automatic task routing technologies for peer production systems (e.g., Wikipedia) [12]. To satisfy individual preference, the result could be a task recommender system for participants, with default "best match" and other options ranked by selected criteria. Hearing that interviewees repeatedly mentioned that the success of work events is defined in terms of two factors: attainment of project goal, and providing an enjoyable experience, we recommend the matching system to also include individual enjoyment as a key criterion. For example, post-event surveys could be administered to collected individual experiences with different tasks for future reference.

Computational technology could also assist coordinators in coping with unpredictability. To support recruitment planning, it would be valuable to provide suggestions about the number of participants needed, based on the workload and predicted dropout rate, which could be learned from previous records. It could also continuously monitor the RSVP and automatically decide to send additional mobilizing email targeting certain participant groups. Another promising technology for coordinator is one that supports work partitioning, possibly similar to that used for crowdsourcing complex tasks [30]. This would be especially useful for newly formed groups where no job list has yet been created. Given that work event is often constrained by the available skillset, an advanced version of such technology could create customized job lists based on the skills and preferences of those who sign up for a particular working event.

Lastly, specific to the work nature of CO groups, we note a high demand for continuous coordination on the work site, where the coordinators have to keep going around to check in with everyone and deliver necessary resources and instructions. We see opportunities for mobile technology to tremendously ease the on-site coordination, and it could be a natural extension of a work event organization tool. For example, a user could easily report the completion of a task he or she signed up for, thus the tool could monitor the progress of the work event and recommend action items to the coordinator. By creating a full awareness of the work site, it could also help the coordinator identify exceptional individuals and deliver acknowledgement right on time.

4.6.2 Supporting Episodic Use

"One challenge we have is some people are emailed, some people are phoned, some people don't have a phone, some people do Facebook, some people do texts. A really cool tool would be... preset a preference, and that one portal could communicate to your preferred method...." (P08)

The above quote illustrates that one challenge coordinators face is the variety of communication and other tools used by the crowd. We attribute this to lack of motivation for episodic participants to adopt and learn new tools for infrequent use, a problem reported in previous research into episodic volunteering [27]. A work-event organizing tool should thus minimize entry cost (e.g., by providing integration with applications that people already use). For example, an event page could be embedded in email or a Facebook post, and one could opt in to a preferred communication channel. Ideally, a coordinator could make one single announcement and the system would "translate" it into messages sent to each participant's preferred channel.

4.6.3 Supporting Diverse Motivations

"Volunteers usually come for a reason and you have to figure out what the reasons are... some may want to learn skills. Usually it's for people who first come, so I try and take time to teach those people. People also come for the glory, part of this awesome thing. So for them it's very nice there'll be a list on the website and their name next to the work they did. Some think it's rewarding for the community of the group... And just make sure they feel included in that, for example, we usually do toast show barbecue." (P14)

From our analysis, we identified large variation in the CO group members' participating motivation. The above quote illustrates the importance of understanding different motivations and tailoring engaging strategies accordingly, as previous research suggests that a mismatch between motivation and type of reward one receives could reduce satisfaction and productivity [14]. Future work should explore tailoring reward mechanism for individual's motivation, which requires studying how to assess a user's position on the SDT spectrum, hopefully from early on. One potential approach is to explore computational methods for user profiling, for example, by mining behavioral data or texts, which we may learn from previous work on profiling users based on personal value system [11].

5. General Discussion

We present a study of proliferating grassroots, self-organizing volunteer groups that engage in project based work in the physical world. Our work contributes to the volunteerism literature by providing a nuanced analysis of the work practices of this distinct type of group, one of the so-called "modern" volunteering efforts . In particular, we focused on identifying areas of relevance to the HCI community, where computation and communication technologies can be brought to help these groups better collaborate and accomplish their goals. While admittedly there is still a long way to go for developing specialized technologies, we want to draw attention to this growing form of peer production. It is especially pertinent timing given the fast growing trend of "peer economy" and "collaborative consumption" [2][48], which embraces grassroots effort, collaborative ownership and sustainability. Crowd orchestration may be a distinct wave in the tide of collaborative consumption that brings contribution and exchange from the individual to the group level.

By adopting the stance of considering CO groups as a form of "peer production in the physical world," we are able to draw many similarities between them and online peer production groups. In particular, we found they share the disparity of contribution and involvement among individuals, and the evolved job division between regular and episodic participants [5][10][16][27][50]. We also found that they share common strategies to motivate participation and facilitate long-term engagement [10], [32][33][43][59]. Therefore, when developing technologies to support CO groups, we can possibly borrow design guidelines from the current practices of, as well as a rich body of literature on online peer production systems [5][10][16][27][29][32][59].

Despite commonalities, CO groups do certainly have their own characteristic and distinct needs and constraints. While online peer production such as Wikipedia and OOS is often characterized as a distributed model in contrast with the centralized model with managerial hierarchies as in the enterprise, we consider the CO group as a more in-between model. While there are many distributed bottom-up, self-organizing processes to push forward a project, its implementation—i.e., the time-sensitive work event—involves concerted, centralized planning and top-down coordination, which are driven by the specific time, duration and location, against a more distributed model. Meanwhile, we note that episodic participants of CO groups, while on the lower levels of the hierarchy of the work structure, may play a more critical role for the CO group than those in an online peer production group. Previous research into the latter often reports that "occasional contributors" work on peripheral tasks, such as proofreading Wikipedia articles [5], reporting software bug [16]. In contrast, episodic participants often act as the major labor force for the CO group work. This leads to more critical needs for CO group to strive to recruit, motivate and retain episodic members, and to some extent, placing regular members in an accommodating or even 'crowd-pleasing' position.

Moreover, unlike online peer production groups, CO groups do not use information and communication technologies as an integral part of their work, but rather, ICTs are often haphazard exigencies, chosen to satisfy many idiosyncratic and possibly temporary needs. Integrated tools are lacking, and to develop one will require careful consideration of varied work processes and divergent user requirements. So we offer this work as an initial guide to what is currently required to support this growing prospective user base.

6. ACKNOWLEDGMENTS

We thank the 26 anonymous participants. This work was supported by Xerox Corporation

7. REFERENCES

[1] Victoria Bellotti, Nicolas Ducheneaut, Mark Howard, and Ian Smith. 2003. Taking email to task: the design and

evaluation of a task management centered email tool. *In Proc. CHI 2003*, 345-352.

[2] Victoria Bellotti , Alexander Ambard, Daniel Turner, Christina Gossmann, Kamila Demkova, and John M. Carroll. 2015. A Muddle of Models of Motivation for Using Peer-to-Peer Economy Systems. *In Proc. CHI 2015,* 1085-1094.

[3] Yochai Benkler. The Penguin and the Leviathan: How Cooperation Triumphs over Self-Interest. *Crown Business*; 1st Edition (2011).

[4] Yochai Benkler and Helen Nissenbaum. 2006. Commons-based Peer Production and Virtue. *Journal of Political Philosophy*, *14*(4), 394-419.

[5] Susan L. Bryant, Andrea Forte, and Amy Bruckman. 2005. Becoming Wikipedian: transformation of participation in a collaborative online encyclopedia. *In Proc. GROUP 2005*, 1-10.

[6] Marcelo Cataldo and James D. Herbsleb. 2008. Communication networks in geographically distributed software development. *In Proc. CSCW 2008*, 579-588

[7] Ram A. Cnaan and Femida Handy. 2005. Towards understanding episodic volunteering. *Vrijwillige Inzet Onderzocht*, 2(1), 29-35

[8] Gil E. Clary and Mark Snyder. 1991. A functional analysis of altruism and prosocial behavior: The case of volunteerism. *Prosocial behavior. Review of Personality and Social Psychology*, Vol. 12. (pp. 119-148).

[9] Gil E. Clary and Mark Snyder. 1999. The motivations to volunteer theoretical and practical considerations. *Current Directions in Psychological Science*, 8(5), 156-159.

[10] Camille Cobb, Ted McCarthy, Annuska Perkins, Ankitha Bharadwaj, Jared Comis, Brian Do, and Kate Starbird. 2014. Designing for the deluge: understanding & supporting the distributed, collaborative work of crisis volunteers. *In Proc. CSCW 2014*, 888-899.

[11] Jilin Chen, Gary Hsieh, Jalal Mahmud, and Jeff Nichols. 2014. Understanding individuals' personal values from social media word use. In *Proc. CSCW 2014,* 405-414.

[12] Dan Cosley, Dan Frankowski, Loren Terveen, and John Riedl. 2007. SuggestBot: using intelligent task routing to help people find work in wikipedia. *In Proc. IUI 2007,* 32-41.

[13] Edward L. Deci and Richard M. Ryan. 1985. Intrinsic motivation and self-determination in human behavior. New York: Plenum.

[14] Edward L. Deci, Richard Koestner, and Richard M. Ryan. 1999. A meta-analytic review of experiments examining the effects of extrinsic rewards on intrinsic motivation. *Psychological bulletin*, *125*(6), 627.

[15] Paul Dourish and Victoria Bellotti. 1992. Awareness and coordination in shared workspaces. *In Proc. CSCW 1992*, 107-114.

[16] Nicolas Ducheneaut. 2005. Socialization in an open source software community: A socio-technical analysis. *Computer Supported Cooperative Work (CSCW)*,14(4), 323-368.

[17] Marylene Gagné. 2003. The role of autonomy support and autonomy orientation in prosocial behavior engagement. *Motivation and Emotion*, 27, 3, 199-223.

[18] Marylene Gagné. and Edward L. Deci. 2005. Self-determination theory and work motivation. *Journal of Organizational Behavior.,* 26, 331–362.

[19] Maura Galletta, Igor Portoghese, and Adalgisa Battistelli. 2011. Intrinsic motivation, job autonomy and turnover intention in the Italian healthcare: the mediating role of affective commitment. *Journal of Management Research*, 3(2).

[20] Carl Gutwin and Saul Greenberg. 2002. A descriptive framework of workspace awareness for real-time groupware. *Computer Supported Cooperative Work (CSCW)*, 11(3-4), 411-446.

[21] Simona Haivas, Joeri Hofmans, and Roland Pepermans. 2012. Self-determination theory as a framework for exploring volunteer motivation: A study of Romanian volunteers. *Nonprofit and Voluntary Sector Quarterly*, 41,6, 1195-1214.

[22] David A. Harrison. 1995. Volunteer motivation and attendance decisions: Competitive theory testing in multiple samples from a homeless shelter. *Journal of Applied Psychology*, 80(3), 371.

[23] Christopher A. Le Dantec and W. Keith Edwards. 2008. The view from the trenches: Organization, power, and technology at two nonprofit homeless outreach centers. In *Proceedings of the 2008 ACM conference on Computer supported cooperative work* (pp. 589-598). ACM.

[24] Lesley Hustinx and Frans Lammertyn. 2003. Collective and reflexive styles of volunteering: A sociological modernization perspective. Voluntas: *International Journal of Voluntary and Nonprofit Organizations*, 14(2), 167-187.

[25] Frederick I. Herzberg. 1966. Work and the nature of man.

[26] Steven J. Karau and Kipling D. Williams. 1993. Social loafing: A meta-analytic review and theoretical integration. *Journal of Personality and Social Psychology*, 65(4), 681.

[27] Sunyoung Kim, Jennifer Mankoff, and Eric Paulos. 2015. Exploring Barriers to the Adoption of Mobile Technologies for Volunteer Data Collection Campaigns. *In Proc. CHI 2015, 3117-3226.*

[28] Aniket Kittur, Ed Chi, Bryan A. Pendleton, Bongwon Suh, and Todd Mytkowicz. 2007. Power of the few vs. wisdom of the crowd: Wikipedia and the rise of the bourgeoisie. *World Wide Web*, 1(2), 19.

[29] Aniket Kittur and Robert E. Kraut. 2008. Harnessing the wisdom of crowds in wikipedia: quality through coordination. In *Proc. CSCW 2008*, 37-46.

[30] Aniket Kittur, Boris Smus, Susheel Khamkar, and Robert E. Kraut. 2011. Crowdforge: Crowdsourcing complex work. *In Proc. UIST 2011*, 43-52.

[31] Peter Kollock. 1999. The economies of online cooperation. Communities in Cyberspace, 220.

[32] Travis Kriplean, Ivan Beschastnikh, and David W. McDonald. 2008. Articulations of wikiwork: uncovering valued work in wikipedia through barnstars. *In Proc. CSCW 2008*, 47-56.

[33] Jean Lave, and Etienne Wenger. 1991. Situated learning: Legitimate peripheral participation. Cambridge university press.

[34] Kimberly Ling, Gerard Beenen, Pamela Ludford, Xiaoqing Wang, Klarissa Chang, Xin Li, Dan Cosley. 2005. Using social psychology to motivate contributions to online communities. *Journal of Computer Mediated Communication*, 10(4).

[35] Brenda McPhail, Terry Costantino, David Bruckmann, Ross Barclay and Andrew Clement. 1998. CAVEAT exemplar: Participatory design in a non-profit volunteer organisation. *Computer Supported Cooperative Work (CSCW)*, *7*(3-4), 223-241.

[36] Cecelia Merkel, Umer Farooq, Lu Xiao, Craig Ganoe, Mary Beth Rosson, and John M. Carroll. 2007. Managing technology use and learning in nonprofit community organizations: methodological challenges and opportunities. In *Proceedings of the 2007 symposium on Computer human interaction for the management of information technology*, 8.

[37] Valérie Millette, and Marylene Gagné. 2008. Designing volunteers' tasks to maximize motivation, satisfaction and performance: The impact of job characteristics on volunteer engagement. *Motivation and Emotion*, 32,1,11–22.

[38] Oded Nov, David Anderson, and Ofer Arazy. 2010. Volunteer computing: a model of the factors determining contribution to community-based scientific research. *In Proc. WWW 2010*, 741-750.

[39] Allen M. Omoto and Mark Snyder. 1995. Sustained helping without obligation: motivation, longevity of service, and perceived attitude change among AIDS volunteers. *Journal of Personality and Social Psychology*, 68(4), 671.

[40] Jeannette Oostlander, Stefan T. Güntert, Susan van Schie, and Theo Wehner. 2013. Leadership and volunteer motivation: A study using self-determination theory. *Nonprofit and Voluntary Sector Quarterly* 25.

[41] Wanda J. Orlikowski. 1992. Learning from notes: Organizational issues in groupware implementation. *In Proc. CSCW 1992*, 362-369.

[42] Emily Rader. 2009. Yours, mine and (not) ours: social influences on group information repositories. *In Proc. CHI 2009*, 2095-2098.

[43] Al M. Rashid, Kimberly Ling, Regina D. Tassone, Paul Resnick, Robert Kraut, and John Riedl. 2006. Motivating participation by displaying the value of contribution *Proc. CHI 2007,* 955-958.

[44] Howard Rheingold. Smart Mobs: The Next Social Revolution. Basic Books (2003).

[45] Dana Rotman, Jenny Preece, Jen Hammock, Kezee Procita, Derek Hansen, Cynthia Parr, Darcy Lewis, and David Jacobs. 2012. Dynamic changes in motivation in collaborative citizen-science projects. *In Proc. CSCW 2012*, 217-226.

[46] Richard M. Ryan, and Edward L. Deci. 2000. Self-determination theory and the facilitation of intrinsic motivation, social development and well-being. *American Psychologist*, 55,1, 68-78.

[47] Andrea G. Skogland. 2006. Do not forget about your volunteers: A qualitative analysis of factors influencing volunteer turnover. *Health & Social Work*, 31,3, 217-220.

[48] Patrick C. Shih, Victoria Bellotti, Kyungsik Han, and John M. Carroll. 2015. Unequal Time for Unequal Value: Implications of Differing Motivations for Participation in Timebanking. *In Proc. CHI 2015*, 1075-1084.

[49] Clay Shirky. Here Comes Everybody The Power of Organizing Without Organizations. Penguin Books (2009).

[50] Kate Starbird and Leysia Palen. 2013. Working and sustaining the virtual Disaster Desk. *In Proc. CSCW 2013,* 491-502.

[51] Anselm Strauss. 1988. The articulation of project work: An organizational process.*Sociological Quarterly*, 163-178.

[52] Anselm Strauss and Juliet. M. Corbin. 1990. Basics of qualitative research: Grounded theory procedures and techniques. Sage Publications, Inc.

[53] Amos Tversky and Daniel Kahneman, 1973. Availability: A heuristic for judging frequency and probability. *Cognitive Psychology* . 5(2): 207–232.

[54] Amy Voida, Zheng Yao, and Matthias Korn. 2015. (Infra) structures of Volunteering. In *Proc. CSCW 2015*.1704-1716.

[55] Amy Voida, Ellie Harmon, and Ban Al-Ani. 2011. Homebrew databases: Complexities of everyday information management in nonprofit organizations. In Proc. *CSCW 2011*, 915-924.

[56] John Wilson. 2000. Volunteering. Annual review of sociology, 215-240.

[57] Steve Whittaker and Candace Sidner. 1996. Email overload: exploring personal information management of email. *In Proc. CHI 1996,* 276-283.

[58] Wuthnow Robert. Loose Connections: Joining Together in America's Fragmented Communities. (2002).

[59] Haiyi Zhu, Robert Kraut and Aniket Kittur. 2012. Organizing without formal organization: group identification, goal setting and social modeling in directing online production. *In Proc. CSCW 2012,* 935-944.

"Guess what! You're the First to See this Event": Increasing Contribution to Online Production Communities

Corey Jackson, Kevin Crowston, Gabriel Mugar, Carsten Østerlund
School of Information Studies
Syracuse University
Syracuse, New York, USA 13210
{cjacks04,crowston,gmugar,costerlu}@syr.edu

ABSTRACT

In this paper, we describe the results of an online field experiment examining the impacts of messaging about task novelty on the volume of volunteers' contributions to an online citizen science project. Encouraging volunteers to provide a little more content as they work is an attractive strategy to increase the community's output. Prior research found that an important motivation for participation in online citizen science is the wonder of being the first person to observe a particular image. To appeal to this motivation, a pop-up message was added to an online citizen science project that alerted volunteers when they were the first to annotate a particular image. Our analysis reveals that new volunteers who saw these messages increased the volume of annotations they contributed. The results of our study suggest an additional strategy to increase the amount of work volunteers contribute to online communities and citizen science projects specifically.

CCS Concepts

• **Human-centered computing** → *Empirical studies in collaborative and social computing;*

Keywords

citizen science; online communities; experiment; motivation; intention to treat; novelty

1. INTRODUCTION

Ciampaglia et al. [3] note that online voluntary production communities have two options to increase the amount of content generated: increasing the number of new volunteers or increasing the participation and retention of existing volunteers. The research presented here is an exercise in the latter: increasing the contribution of existing volunteers. To increase contributions, online voluntary community managers can make motivational aspects of volunteers' participation more salient and thus increase the likelihood of volunteers' contribution. Motivation in online communities has attracted a significant amount of attention in communities like Wikipedia and free/libre open source software (FLOSS) projects. Studies on Wikipedia, for example, have noted the complex web of motivations for volunteers ranging from recognition of contributions by peers [5] to altruism [14].

As well, it is well known that contribution to online communities follows a long-tail distribution (i.e., power law, 80/20 rule) where a handful of volunteers contribute the majority of the content. For instance, in Wikipedia 1% of the editors contribute 55% of the edits[7]. And on the other end of distribution, most volunteers contribute in only one or two sessions and then never return. Because of the large number of such volunteers, encouraging new volunteers to contribute a little more during their "trial period" could be particularly productive for a project.

In this paper, we present the results of an online experiment testing an approach to motivating contribution. Prior research found that citizen science project volunteers described the wonder of being the first person to observe a particular image as a reason for participation in the project. We therefore hypothesized that emphasizing this novelty would increase motivation and thus increase contributions. We implemented a pop-up message that informed volunteers when they were viewing data no other volunteer had seen previously and examined the impact of these messages on the volunteer's level of contribution. The research question guiding this experiment is: How does novelty messaging impact volunteers' contributions to citizen science projects? Though our analysis, we make two important contributions to the literature on motivation in online production communities:

- We show how novelty messaging can be used as a viable solution to increasing contributions to online communities.
- We describe the implementation of an analysis method for experiment research called *intention-to-treat*, an approach commonly used in medical research, but less seen in Group research.

1.1 Citizen Science

Our study is set in the context of an online citizen science project. Citizen science describes projects in which amateur volunteers collect or analyze data to contribute to scientific research. For example, in The Birdhouse Network (TBN), volunteers place nest boxes in their yards and generate and report data they collected from the boxes. Others projects

GROUP '16, November 13-16, 2016, Sanibel Island, FL, USA

DOI: http://dx.doi.org/10.1145/2957276.2957284

work on data (e.g., images, sound files) collected by scientists. In these projects, volunteers perform tasks such as filtering or transcribing data objects. The resulting data is then returned to the scientists to support their investigations. Galaxy Zoo is an example of the latter type of project. Scientists asked volunteers to identify characteristics of galaxies in images collected by the Sloan Digital Sky Survey telescope to support research on galaxy morphology. The success of Galaxy Zoo led its developers to create the Zooniverse [28], a citizen science platform that currently hosts more than forty collaborative projects. The collaboration between professionals and amateurs is technologically mediated through the project website. As with other online voluntary production communities, Zooniverse projects rely on a steady stream of volunteers to complete project tasks.

2. MOTIVATION TO CONTRIBUTE USER-GENERATED CONTENT

How to motivate contributions to online voluntary production communities has received substantial attention from researchers. The link between motivation and contribution is clear: volunteers in the community are motivated; a positive impact on content production is observed. Thus, increasing the motivational affordances of a volunteer's participation is expected to increase the volume of content generated by that volunteer.

The literature on motivation in online communities is quite diverse. Theories such as social loafing, goal-setting, social awareness, social-identity, uses and gratifications, or collective effort have frequently been operationalized in the design of online communities. A major stream of research draws on psychological research on motivation. For example, studies have found that giving volunteers the opportunity to set goals resulted in an increase in contributions to projects [10, 33, 1]. Social motives have also been explored. For example, [30] experimented with making workers in Amazon's Mechanical Turk aware of the presence (social awareness) of other Turkers to increase volunteers' feelings of attachment (bond based and identity based) to the group and found that when Turkers are assigned to work groups and communication between volunteers within work groups is supported, Turkers show more loyalty to the requester and MTurk.

Studies have examined a range of motives in particular settings. For example, in a survey of open-source programmers, Hars and Ou [8] distinguished between external rewards (e.g., peer recognition) and internal rewards (e.g., self-determination) that are the result of participation in OSS environments. Lakhani and Wolf [15] found that one of the strongest motivators for OSS developers is how creative they feel when working on a project, in addition to the intellectual stimulation they get and the utilitarian motivation of improving programming skills. Oreg and Nov [19] found that building reputation and learning were important motives for contribution to FLOSS. Research has identified somewhat different motivations for contribution to the online encyclopedia Wikipedia. Yang et al. [31] discovered that self-concept motivation was the main factor influencing Wikipedians' knowledge-sharing behaviors. Nov [18] found eight different motivations explaining editing behaviors in Wikipedia, including fun, ideology, enhancement, understanding, career, values, protective, and social.

Kraut et al. [13] synthesized the research literature to provide a set of design claims that highlight motivational aspects of volunteers' participation to encourage contribution in online communities. These are grouped in five categories: (1) selection, sorting, highlighting, (2) framing, (3) feedback and rewards, (4) content, task, and activities, and (5) community structure. For example, related to feedback and rewards is the design claim that receiving sincere feedback about performance increases motivation. There is an opportunity then to encourage volunteers to contribute by exploring how social science theories and design claims can be incorporated into the design of online communities.

2.1 Motivation in Citizen Science

Turning to citizen science projects more specifically, researchers have identified a variety of reasons volunteers contribute. In a survey of citizen science volunteers to the Galaxy Zoo project, [21] analyzed more than eighty statements about why volunteers participate in the project. Twelve categories of motivation emerged, including an interest in astronomy (the topic of many of the projects), wanting to help scientists, contributing to science, enjoying beauty, and learning. Reed et al. [23] surveyed 199 users of Zooniverse and identified three factors explaining why volunteers contribute: social engagement with other volunteers, interaction with the site, and helping (or volunteering). The literature on motivation in citizen science projects has also resulted in descriptions of the dynamic nature of motivation suggesting that motivations shift throughout a volunteer's engagement with a project [27, 26].

Many of these motivations are similar to other online production communities like Wikipedia and FLOSS. However, citizen science communities are unique in that volunteers annotate images that few people have seen previously. For example, the Planet Five shows volunteers images that have not yet been seen by anyone outside professional astronomy communities. Indeed, in many projects, images are automatically collected, so they may not have been viewed by anyone. Along with advertising citizen science as a participatory project, many projects note the possibility of viewing such novel images.

Research suggests that many volunteers are drawn to projects for this reason. For example, among familiar motives such as interest in astronomy, contribution to science, the beauty of galaxy images, and learning about galaxies, Raddick et al. [21] found volunteers were also motivated by discovery (specifically, "I can look at galaxies that few people have seen before"). Reiss [24] listed sixteen different motives leading to intrinsic feelings. Included in the list was curiosity, described as a desire for knowledge which has the potential to lead to wonder. Jackson et al. [11] found that some volunteers reported being motivated by the possibility to discover new data or find anomalies that others had not previously identified, which is related to novelty.

These motives have support in research that identifies motives for action such as novelty seeking (neophilia), sensation seeking, and curiosity. Addressing consumerism and the desire for novel products, Campbell [2] writes "There are those neophiliacs whose craving for the new takes the form of a preference for the novel, the strange or even the bizarre. These are the volunteers who appear to place a high value on the stimulus which is provided by the unfamiliar while perceiving the known as boring." Raymond [22] introduced the idea of neophilia to describe this trait of hackers: that they are excited and pleased by novelty. Sensation seeking has been researched within the context of internet and technology use. For example, [17] surveyed mobile phone users and found volunteers who scored high on sensation seeking used the phone to make calls more often and tended to use more phone features.

Another possibility is that being first is motivating because it leads to the possibility of discovery, another motivating factor identified in surveys. One of the most well-known cases is the discovery in GalaxyZoo of a novel astrophysical object by a Dutch school teacher, which led to the phenomena being named after her: Hanny's Voorwerp [12]. In another Zooniverse project, Seafloor Explorer, volunteers coalesced around a "stripey tube-dwelling creature" after volunteers asked, "what are the tube shape and the stripey creature?" It was discovered that the images displayed a new species, named convict worm[1] by the citizen scientists. In the Stardust @Home project, when a user discovers a dust grain, he or she is listed as a co-author on the article announcing the discovery and is also given the privilege of naming the dust grain.

There have been efforts to stimulate curiosity as a way to motivate work. In Mechanical Turk, Law et al. [16] showed users obscured (i.e., blacked out) visuals that were only revealed when a worker completed parts of the task. Their research showed the intervention improved worker retention, presumably because they were curious to see the image.

However, to our knowledge, there has been no research on motivation that manipulates perceived novelty as a way to influence volunteer participation. Based on the prior literature on motivation in citizen science and our past research examining motivation in Zooniverse projects, we believe that highlighting the novelty of participation can lead to increased motivation resulting in increased work. We hypothesized that mentioning that a data object has not been viewed by other citizen scientists would appeal to a volunteer's desire for discovery, to be first, or to experience novel occurrences. We therefore offer two hypotheses:

H1: Messaging users about the novelty of their experience increases the number of annotations they contribute.

H2: Newcomers contribute more in their first session when shown novelty messaging than newcomers contributing in their first session not shown a novelty message.

3. SETTING: ZOONIVERSE

The context for this experiment is the online citizen science platform Zooniverse (http://www.zooniverse.org), a web-based system that hosts more than forty science projects. Each project is based around a large collection of data objects (e.g., images, sound/video recordings, text) that require some annotation to support further scientific research. For example, determining the shape of galaxies supports research on galaxy morphology; transcribing information from World War I ship logs supports climate and historical research. Some collections can include hundreds of thousand or even millions of objects to be analyzed, much more than a small science team can handle.

The Zooniverse projects recruit volunteers to do the required annotation. Before analyzing the data objects, volunteers are asked to complete tutorials that explain how to identify relevant characteristics of the data objects, though in most cases, the tutorials are short and can be skipped altogether. Each image is analyzed by multiple volunteers and the individual annotations are compared to determine a consensus answer. At the time of the study, the order of presentation of data objects to volunteers was essentially random, though a few project were experimenting with algorithms for matching data objects to volunteers. In addition to annotating data objects, many volunteers contribute to other aspects of the community, e.g., visiting blogs or posting comments to fora; but these activities are not examined in this study.

[1]http://blog.seafloorexplorer.org/tag/convict-worm/

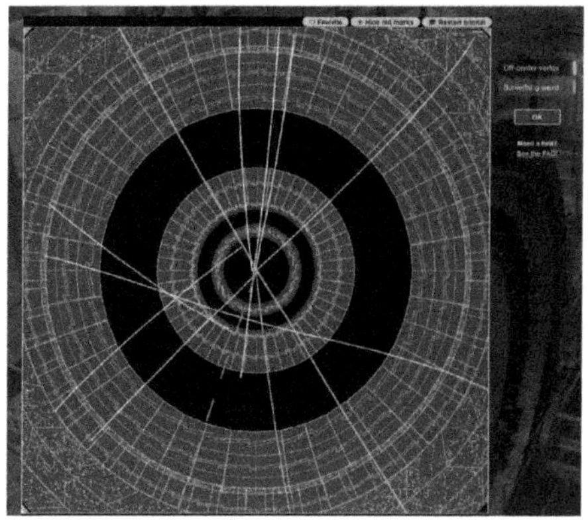

Figure 1: Annotation interface for the Higgs Hunters projects.

3.1 Project: Higgs Hunters

Our study focuses on the Higgs Hunters project. In this project, volunteers annotate images from the Large Hadron Collider (LHC), a particle collider built to search for the Higgs boson particle. The data objects in this project are images of two beams of particles colliding and creating a shower of new particles, possibly including previously unknown particles, such as the Higgs. Charged particles leave a trace in the image; uncharged particles are invisible. The task for the volunteers is to annotate the images for decay anomalies or appearances of off-center vertexes, which are indications that a new uncharged particle was created but then decayed into other charged particles (e.g., the Higgs decays only 10^{22} seconds after it is created). Not all images have off-center vertexes from particles, so seeing a new particle is akin to finding a needle in a haystack.

The annotation interface is shown in Figure 1. To record a find, volunteers click on "Off-centre vertex" on the right-hand side of the window, then mark the location of the vertex and how many tracks appeared. Volunteers are not given any feedback about whether their annotations are correct or if the image is useful for science, because at the time of annotation, neither of those are known. As well, annotations are done independently for the purpose of preventing one volunteer's decisions about an image to influence the annotations done by others.

4. METHODS

4.1 Experiment Design

To manipulate motivation by appealing to volunteers' interest in novelty, beginning in October 2014, the Zooniverse introduced a system that alerted volunteers when they viewed an image that no previous volunteer had seen, specifically, a pop-up message that read "Guess what! You're the first to see this event." The messages were truthful, appearing only for images that had not been previously annotated by any volunteer, so only the one volunteer who was the first to annotate the image saw the message for that image. At the time, the Zooniverse platform did not support random assignment of volunteers to different treatments, so this intervention was added for all volunteers.

Because of this limitation, we studied the impact of the messages using a quasi-experimental design. Project scientists periodically inject new images into the project, resulting in periods where many volunteers see the pop-up message. We used work done during such periods to create the treatment group. However, eventually every image has been viewed at least once, and so the pop-up message is not shown for an extended time as additional annotations are added to the existing images. We used the work done in such periods to create a control group. However, rather than comparing work done by volunteers randomly assigned to treatment or control (a true experiment) we are comparing work done at different times with and without the treatment (a quasi-experiment).

4.2 Data Collection

We collected data from the log files on Zooniverse servers in October 2015. The dataset contained all the annotations done by volunteers up to that time, including a timestamp for each annotation and whether the volunteer was shown the pop-up message (i.e., if they were the first person to see that image). We did not include annotations done by volunteers who were not logged into the system.

The total dataset includes 683,970 annotations contributed by 6,354 volunteers, though not all of these data were used in the analysis. Analysis was done at the session level. Annotations were grouped by volunteer and then into sessions, a series of annotations done by a single volunteer that are separated by a gap of less than 30 minutes. The intuition is that a volunteer generally does some number of annotations in a single sitting (possibly with a short break between annotations) and then takes a longer break, e.g., until the next day. We used a session as the unit of analysis to test the hypothesis that a message might increase interest and so lead to the volunteer's extending the time spent and work done while on the system, resulting in a longer session. There were a total of 17,353 sessions, ranging in length from 1 to 1,504 annotations, with an average of 39 and median of 16 annotations.

For each session, we recorded how many pop-up messages were shown. A total of 28,577 messages were displayed in 3,096 sessions to 1,867 volunteers (i.e., about 18% of sessions had a message and about 29% of volunteers saw a message). Figure 2 shows the number of sessions done per day over time; sessions with at least one message are in blue and sessions with no messages in orange. From the blue areas in the figure it is easy to identify the dates on which new images were added to the system. Immediately after new images are added, a volunteer may see many new objects in a single session: the maximum number of messages in a single session was 419. At other times though, all images will have have had at least one annotation, and a session will have no messages. Note also the very large spike in work done in the first few weeks of the project and the decline in activity over time.

4.3 Within-subjects analysis

We carried out two different analyses on the sessions. Our first analysis was within-subjects, comparing for the same volunteer, the length of sessions that had or did not have a pop-up message. A simple t-test for the difference in session length would be confounded by the large differences in contributions from different volunteers. It might be the case that volunteers who contribute more, e.g., because of higher interest, also see messages more often. We therefore controlled for the individual volunteer by carrying out a repeated measures analysis. Comparing sessions within a subject helped control for the very high variability of contribution to the project, but only partly. Thus, we chose to analyze the data using mixed models since they are more are more sensitive to within-subject variance [4], which is a characteristic of our data. Data were analyzed using the R Statistical package nlme [20]. Since obtaining p-values for mixed models isn't straightforward, our approach relied on comparison of the mixed models using likelihood ratio test which is the probability of seeing the data we collected given a model [?]. We compare a null model (i.e, a model disregarding the fixed effect of treatment) and a "full model" with treatment as a fixed effect. To compare the models we use an ANOVA, which yields a chi-squared value, degrees of freedom, and the p-value. With this, we can conclude that the fixed effect of treatment is significant if the difference between the likelihood of these two models is also significant. The advantage of the within-subject design is that it uses more of the data. A possible confound to this design is that at certain points in the project, seeing a pop-up message becomes a matter of chance, as a part but not all of the images are new. As a result, during those periods, rather than messages causing sessions to be longer (our primary hypothesis), a longer sessions increase the chance of novelty messages being shown.

4.4 Between-subjects analysis

To avoid the confound noted above, we also carried out a between-subjects analysis on a subset of the data using a quasi-experimental design. To form the treatment group (sessions with at least one pop-up message), we identified a two-week period during which new images were available (the middle light blue bar in the inset in Figure 2). We chose a period later in the life of the project when the number of sessions done per day was beginning to plateau, meaning that the sample is not from early joiners whose behavior may differ from other volunteers, and the plateau could not be attributed to non-project events such as holidays. To eliminate possible influences from prior experiences on the system, we only used sessions from volunteers who had their first session during the period, meaning this analysis is restricted to the impact on newcomers. For this analysis, we included all sessions done by those volunteers in the two weeks after their first session (i.e., the group includes some sessions beyond the treatment period for volunteers who joined late in the period). Note though that not all sessions during this period had a pop-up message (as shown by the orange part of the graph), an issue we discuss below.

The control group (sessions with no pop-up message) was formed in a similar fashion. However, because the number

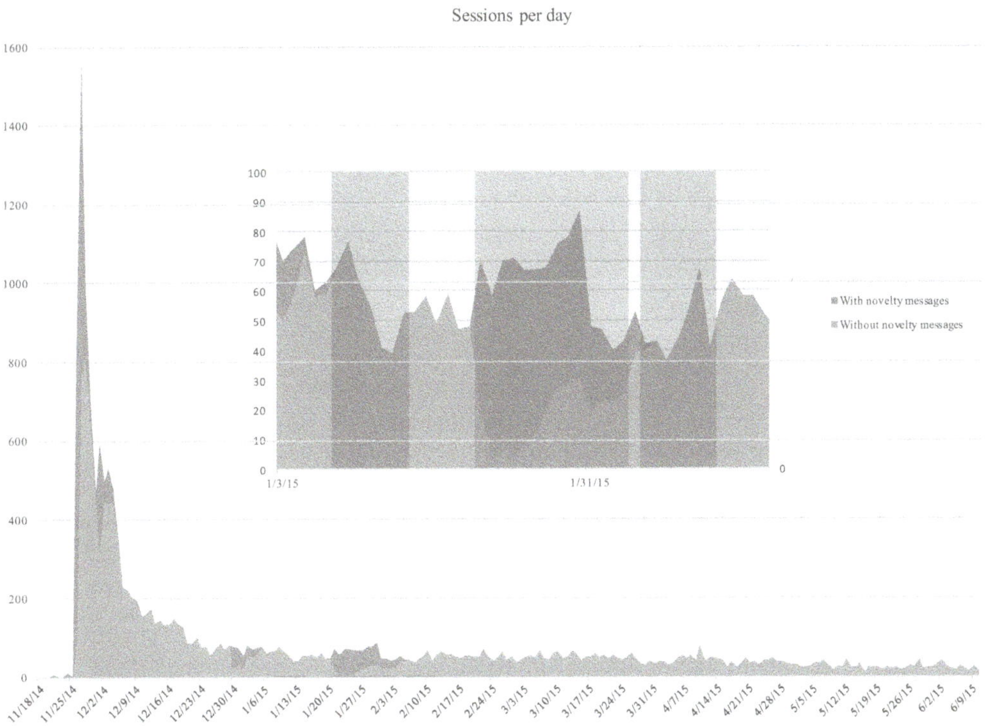

Figure 2: The graph shows the number of sessions per day over time. Sessions with at least one pop-up message are in blue; those without, in orange. The inset shows the periods selected as the treatment period (blue bar) and the two periods selected for the control periods (two purple bars).

of sessions per day was steadily declining over the life of the project, we controlled for maturation by selecting one week just before and one week just after the treatment period. The purple bar in the inset in Figure 2 indicates the first control period, and the last bar, the second control period. Because we followed volunteers for two weeks after their first session, we left a week's gap between the first control period and the treatment period. Even so, we had to drop two sessions from the control group that edged into the treatment period and included a pop-up message. Both control and treatment periods were multiples of 7 days to include all days of the week equally.

5. RESULTS

The contributions of volunteers in online citizen science projects typically follow a long-tail distribution: many volunteers contribute little content, e.g., only a single session, while a dedicated handful of volunteers contribute the majority of content. Higgs Hunters volunteers are no different: most volunteers (71%) contribute in only one session. A handful of dedicated volunteers (eight) contributed more than 11,000 annotations each—a stark contrast in behavior. The average number of sessions by volunteers is 2.73. We computed a 1 percent trimmed mean to illustrate how little work most volunteers contribute. In the trimmed distribution, the average number of sessions dropped to 1.32 (SD=11.52) and the average number of annotations dropped substantially, from 107.65 annotations to 30.47 (SD=699.36). Again pointing to the extremes in volunteers' contribution patterns.

5.1 H1:Pop-ups Increase Contribution

5.1.1 Within-subjects analysis

We analyzed the effects of a message on the number of annotations submitted during sessions. Since the within-subjects comparison relies on a minimum of two observations, we created a subset of cases where a volunteer had at least one session where they saw a message and one session where they did not receive a novelty message. This resulted in 365 unique volunteers and 6,973 volunteer sessions. Novelty messages were shown during 1,355 (19%) sessions. The results revealed that in sessions where messages were shown, volunteers contributed more annotations (see Figure 3). The sessions in which messages were shown had an average of 77.5 (SD=107.6) annotations and a 5% trimmed mean of 55.4 annotations while sessions with no messages shown included on average 41.6 annotations (SD=77.8) and had a 5% trimmed mean of 25.5 - an increase in 35.9 annotations during treatment sessions.

To address the skew in the distribution of session lengths, we log transformed the dependent variable - annotations. Since our data is a repeated measures, we used a linear mixed effects model to compare the number of annotations submitted during sessions of individuals in which they receive a novelty message to those when they failed to receive a message.

To test the significance of this difference, we compared two models: a full model (with the fixed effect treatment) against a reduced model without the fixed effect. As mentioned in the methods, these models can be evaluated using

Experiment Group	Start-End Date (No. days)	No. Volunteers	No. Sessions	Average No. Annotations
Control Prior (CPrG)	1/8/15-1/14/15 (7 days)	107	144	18.1 (SD=26.1)
Control Post (CPG)	2/5/15-2/11/15 (7 days)	76	141	36.8 (SD=53.6)
Pooled Control (PCG)	**14 days**	**183**	**285**	**27.3 (SD=43)**
Treatment (TG)	**1/21/15-2/3/15 (14 days)**	**217**	**356**	**46.4 (SD= 74.7)**

Table 1: Descriptive statistics of treatment and control groups.

Experiment Group		No. Sessions	Average No. Annotations
Treatment (T)	Treated (TT)	223 (62.6%)*	64.7 (SD=84.6)*
	Not treated (T-NT)	133 (37.4%)*	15.7 (SD =37.9)*
Pooled Control (PC)	Hypothetically treated (C-T)	179 (62.6% of 285)**	34.4 (SD =44.4)**
	Hypothetically Not treated (C-NT)	106 (37.4% of 285)**	15.7 (SD =37.9) ***

Table 2: Descriptive statistics for treatment and hypothetically derived control groups. In the table * indicates observed values from population, ** indicates computed values based on observed PC and assumed PC-NT, and * assumed to be same as T-NT.**

Experiment Group		No. Sessions	Average No. Annotations
Treatment Newcomer (TN)	Treated (TTN-Newcomer)	135	51.9 (SD=69.3)
	Not-treated (T-NT-Newcomer)	82	7.1 (SD=10.9)
Pooled Control (PC-Newcomer)	Hypothesized - Treated (HPC-T-Newcomer)	114	24.9 (SD=34.4)
	Hypothesized - Not treated (HPC-NT-Newcomer)	69	7.1 (SD=10.9)

Table 3: Newcomer experiment groups with outcome variable annotations. In the table * indicates observed values from population, ** indicates computed values based on hypothesized control group, and * assumed to be same as T-NT.**

the likelihood ratio test through a chi-squared comparison to determine whether the fixed effect had an impact on the independent variable (i.e., annotations). The results of the comparison revealed that the treatment fixed effect was significant $\chi^2(2)=171.9$, $p<0.0001$.

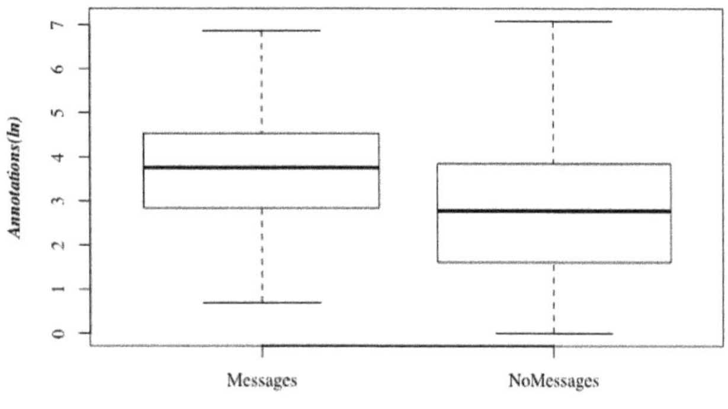

Figure 3: Graph depicting the group differences in the number of annotations in sessions where participants received the treatment and the control.

5.1.2 *Between-subjects analysis*

In the between-subject analysis, we compared the length of sessions done by those who joined during the treatment period with many pop-up messages (the blue bar in Figure 2 to those who joined during a control period without such messages (the purple bars). During the treatment period, 217 new volunteers joined and contributed across 356 sessions (TG). During the first control period, 107 new volunteers joined the project and contributed annotations in 144 sessions, and in the second period, 76 new volunteers joined and contributed in 141 sessions, for a combined total of 183 new volunteers contributing in 285 sessions during the pooled control periods (PCG). The average number of annotations done in those sessions is shown in the final column of Table 1. A t-test shows that the difference between the average session's length in the TG (46.4) and PCG (27.3) is statistically significant ($t(639)=3.83$, $p < .001$), suggesting that the pop-up messages do increase the length of a session.

The estimate above is conservative, since as noted above, not all sessions in the treatment group actually experienced the treatment. Specifically, of the 356 sessions in TG, only 223 had a pop-up message (62.6%); the remaining 133 (37.4%) did not. As a result, our estimate of the impact of the treatment is diluted by the sessions in which the treatment was not seen. The 223 sessions in the subset of sessions that were treated (TT) had 64.7 (SD=84.6) annotations on average, while volunteers' sessions in the treatment but not treated (T-NT) subset contributed only an average of 15.7 (SD=37.94) annotations.

To get a better estimate of the impact of a pop-up message, we apply an intention to treat analysis. Figure 4 shows how the subjects in the analysis are divided into control and treatment group and how the treatment group is further divided into treated and untreated groups. We can observe the average length of a treated session (T-T, 64.7 annotations), so the problem is to find a suitable comparison group of untreated sessions. We cannot simply compare T-T to T-NT

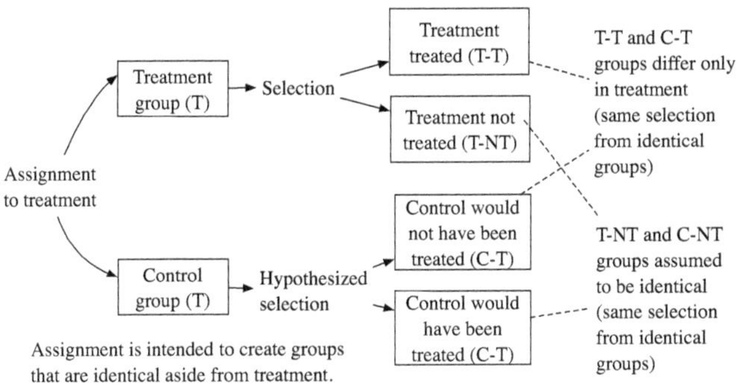

Figure 4: Logic of intention to treat analysis. Regular font indicates observed groups; italics indicate hypothesized groups.

or the entire control group (PCG) because of the confound noted above: at some times seeing a pop-up message is a matter of chance, so a longer session (i.e., from a more interested volunteer) is more likely to have a pop-up. As a result, volunteership in the T-T group is not random, but is related to the outcome variable, meaning the difference between T-T and the other groups could be due to selection rather than the treatment (as shown in Figure 3).

To create a comparison group for T-T we need to select a comparable subset of the control group. Fortunately, it is not necessary to actually carry out the selection; instead, we can do it hypothetically and compute the results. We assume that the control and treatment groups are identical aside from the treatment. Such comparability is the goal of experimental design and is an assumption of a quasi-experimental design. Therefore, had the control group been treated, it would have split in the same proportion as T into a subset that would have received the treatment (C-T, e.g., sessions from more interested control group volunteers) and a subset that would not have received the treatment (C-NT, e.g., sessions from less interested volunteers). As the volunteers of the C-T subgroup are selected in the same way as the T-T subgroup, they should be comparable to the T-T-subgroup, aside from the treatment; and similarly for the C-NT and T-NT subgroups.

We can compute the properties of the C-T subgroup indirectly. Since they are identically selected subsets of assumed-to-be identical groups, T-NT and C-NT are assumed to have identical properties: the same mean number of annotations (15.7) and same standard deviation (37.9). Given the observed properties of C as a whole and the assumed properties of the C-NT subset (the same as T-NT), we can compute the properties of the C-T subgroup to compare to T-T. The results are shown in Table 2. A t-test comparing the mean number of annotations in T-T (64.7, SD= 84.7) to the hypothesized number in C-T (34.3, SD= 44.4) shows a statistically significant difference, $t(400)=4.35$, $p < .001$. As expected, this difference is larger than the difference between the means for the entire control and treatment groups.

Note that these two analyses answer slightly different research questions. The comparison of the whole treatment and control groups shows the impact of implementing the intervention on the expected average length of a session, diluted because not all sessions are treated. The second shows the expected impact of the treatment on a session that actually receives it.

5.2 H2: Intention to Treat - Newcomers

We carried out the same intention to treat analysis examining just the volunteers' first sessions. This was done to examine whether our experimental manipulation had an impact on a population who was unlikely to contribute in future sessions. Such a comparison is interesting because as noted earlier, many volunteers contribute to only one session, so increasing the length of this session may have a big impact on the project. This comparison included 135 sessions in the treatment treated subset (TTN-Newcomer), 82 in the treatment not-treated (T-NT-Newcomer), 114 in the hypothesized pooled control who would have been treated (HPC-T-Newcomer), and 69 in the hypothesized pooled control which would not have been treated (HPC-NT-Newcomer). The descriptive statistics for the population of initial sessions are shown in Table 3. Treated newcomers (TTN-Newcomers) contributed 51.9 annotations (SD=69.3) while those in the hypothesized control (those who would have been treated, HPC-T-Newcomer) contributed only 24.9 (SD=34.4) annotations, a statistically significant difference of 27 annotations, $t(247)=3.8$, $p<.001$.

6. DISCUSSION

Our analysis confirmed both of our hypotheses. First, we found that novelty messaging increases contributions. We showed that message pop-ups alerting volunteers to the fact that they had seen images that had not been viewed by other volunteers almost doubled the number of annotations submitted in a session: from 34.4 to 64.7. We also showed that the messages led to lengthier sessions for the same volunteers (within-subjects): in sessions where volunteers saw a message, they contributed significantly more annotations (77.5 vs. 41.6). Second, we showed that the population most likely to leave the project—namely newcomers in their first session—can be motivated to contribute more prior to their departure. In volunteers' first sessions our experimental manipulation increased the number of annotations from 24.9 to 51.9, again doubling the number of annotations contributed.

Prior surveys and interviews had suggested that volunteers are motivated by seeing images that have not been seen before. However, this paper makes an important contribution by rigorously testing whether making novel experiences known to users works as a method to increase motivation and contribution[2].

6.1 Novelty as a Motivator

Given that very little research in online communities has investigated novelty, we wondered what makes novelty a salient motivator in this context. In Zooniverse it is assumed the citizen scientists are attracted to projects because of the underlying science which supports discovery. Research in psychology offers some explanation. Generally, it is assumed that among other responses, novelty acts as a stimuli to increase interaction and attention of subjects. In a study on child development, Smock and Holt [?] supported a hypothesis which showed that novel objects resulted in significantly more responses (i.e., interaction) than non-novel

[2]As Mark Twain put it, "Supposing is good. Finding out is better."

objects. Berlyne [?] proposed a theory of curiosity motivation which posits that novel stimuli induces longer visual exploration of the stimuli since individuals are curious about the new stimuli. While not frequently cited in the literature on online communities, the introduction of novel data objects (new images in our context) invokes increased attention and curiosity for individuals engaged in the activity. We suspect other communities might benefit from novelty cues to increase individuals' attention and curiosity.

6.2 Implications for Design

The literature on motivation in online production communities like the ones researched in this paper point to a variety of strategies to motivate volunteers to contribute to projects. Our results have clear implications for system designers, specifically that they might want to: a) include such a message if possible and b) spread novel experiences across users and sessions to maximize their impact, rather than having one lucky user see many of them. The most apparent uses of our pop-up might be in citizen science where the goal of the system supports motivation through novel data objects. In the system we studied, there were a total of 28,577 pop-ups (i.e., novel data objects) and only 17,353 user sessions, so there are enough data that each user could see something novel every time they contribute (though implementing such an change might delay processing the data).

We can also imagine how novelty might appear in other communities such as Wikipedia, open source software projects, Q&A communities or blogging sites. In Q& A communities, being the first to respond to a post holds the promise of increased attention to one's comment, i.e., that others after the initial poster will see their responses. The first mover also sets the topic of conversation or is perhaps the first individual to point out a novel feature. For example, in a study of Answerbag, a Q&A site, Gazan et al. [6] found the first submitted answers accumulate 17 percent more rating points than subsequent responses. Gazan et al. [6] also noted: "If there is a first-mover advantage in a social Q&A environment, there must be a measurable benefit to having the equivalent of a dominant market position, regarding some desirable limited good." In online communities where answers are valued highly, being the first to post might make a comment more prominent to readers; in communities where social voting is a feature, it might increase the number of up-votes.

System managers could draw on this motivation in different ways. For example, in open source software communities, designers of projects might highlight novel coding challenges and encourage potential contributors to be the first to solve a particular problem. Wordpress pages encourage authors to publish posts that include a "Be the first to comment" script at the end, in order to encourage readers to start a conversation.

6.3 Encouragement Designs for Similar Experiments

A methodological contribution of this research was the use of an intention to treat approach to analyzing the data (see [9] for more details). The approach was necessary because not all of the sessions selected for the treatment group actually received the treatment. We believe that other interventions in the working of online communities may face the same limitation, meaning that this approach to analyzing the data may be generally useful.

7. LIMITATIONS

There are four limitations we wish to alert the reader to. First, is the experimental design itself: a quasi-experiment. Given the wholesale introduction of the treatment to the population, this design was the only feasible way to analyze the data from the system. A true randomized controlled experiment would have been preferred, but the system was not able to support randomized assignment.

Second, there is the possibility that the effects of the treatment last longer than the single session we analyzed. For example, the effects of a message seen during a volunteer's first session might prompt the volunteer to return for a second session or have continuing impacts in that session. Third, and relatedly, we did not examine whether seeing multiple messages in a session increases the impact of the treatment or if they instead become annoying and a distraction. Future work can explore the temporal dimensions of the effect.

Fourth, while an experiment provides strong evidence for a causal relationship between a treatment and an outcome, there is a trade-off for the richness of data. For example, our analysis does not include possible differences in volunteers that are not captured by the system (e.g., demographics or education). Nor does it provide the kind of rich data needed to illuminate the mechanism of the effect, that is, why volunteers found novelty to be motivating. Prior research found that volunteers report being so motivated, but understanding in more detail exactly why is a question for further in-depth investigation. More research is needed to conclude specifically what drives the observed phenomenon: novelty seeking, discovery, curiosity, sensation seeking, neophilia, some other term or maybe some combination of existing drivers.

8. ACKNOWLEDGEMENTS

Without the Zooniverse volunteers working on the projects and taking the time to answer our questions there would be no paper. Many thanks to the Zooniverse team implementing the experiment. This material is based upon work supported by the National Science Foundation under Grant No. 12-11071.

9. REFERENCES

[1] M. Burke and B. Settles. Plugged in to the community: social motivators in online goal-setting groups. In *Proceedings of the 5th International Conference on Communities and Technologies*, New York, New York, USA, 2011. ACM Press.

[2] C. Campbell. The Desire for the New. In D. Miller, editor, *Consumption Theory and issues in the study of consumption*, page 452. Taylor & Francis, Jan. 2001.

[3] G. L. Ciampaglia and D. Taraborelli. MoodBar. In *CSCW '15: Proceedings of the ACM 2015 conference on Computer Supported Cooperative Work*, pages 734–742, New York, New York, USA, 2015. ACM Press.

[4] A. P. Field, J. Miles, and Z. Field. *Discovering statistics using R*. London ; Thousand Oaks, Calif. : Sage, 2012.

[5] A. Forte and A. S. Bruckman. *From Wikipedia to the classroom: exploring online publication and learning.* International Society of the Learning Sciences, June 2006.

[6] R. Gazan. First-Mover Advantage in a Social Q&A Community. In *2015 48th Hawaii International Conference on System Sciences (HICSS)*, pages 1616–1623. IEEE, Dec. 2014.

[7] R. S. Geiger and A. Halfaker. Using edit sessions to measure participation in wikipedia. In *CSCW '13: Proceedings of the 2013 conference on Computer supported cooperative work*, page 861, New York, New York, USA, Feb. 2013. ACM Request Permissions.

[8] A. Hars and S. Ou. Working for Free? Motivations for Participating in Open-Source Projects. *International Journal of Electronic Commerce*, 6(3), Apr. 2002.

[9] S. Hollis and F. Campbell. What is meant by intention to treat analysis? Survey of published randomised controlled trials. *BMJ*, 319(7211):670–674, 1999.

[10] C. Jackson, K. Crowston, G. Mugar, and C. Østerlund. Encouraging Work in Citizen Science: Experiments in Goal Setting and Anchoring. In *CSCW Companion'16*, San Francisco, 2015.

[11] C. B. Jackson, C. Østerlund, G. Mugar, K. D. Hassman, and K. Crowston. Motivations for Sustained Participation in Crowdsourcing: Case Studies of Citizen Science on the Role of Talk. In *2015 48th Hawaii International Conference on System Sciences (HICSS)*, pages 1624–1634. IEEE, Dec. 2014.

[12] W. C. Keel, C. J. Lintott, K. Schawinski, V. N. Bennert, D. Thomas, A. Manning, S. D. Chojnowski, H. van Arkel, and S. Lynn. The History and Environment of a Faded Quasar: Hubble Space Telescope observations of Hanny's Voorwerp and IC 2497. *The Astronomical Journal*, 144(2):66–39, July 2012.

[13] R. E. Kraut, P. Resnick, S. Kiesler, Y. Ren, Y. Chen, M. Burke, N. Kittur, J. Riedl, and J. Konstan. *Building Successful Online Communities: Evidence-Based Social Design.* The MIT Press, 2012.

[14] S. Kuznetsov. Motivations of contributors to Wikipedia. *ACM SIGCAS computers and society*, 2006.

[15] K. Lakhani and B. J. Wolf. Why hackers do what they do: understanding motivation and effort in free/open source software projects. In J. Feller, B. Fitzgerald, S. Hissam, and K. R. Lakhani, editors, *Perspectives on Free and Open Source Software.* 2005.

[16] E. Law, M. Yin, K. J. Goh, M. Terry, and K. Z. Gajos. Curiosity Killed the Cat, but Makes Crowdwork Better. In *CHI '16: Proceedings of the SIGCHI conference on Human Factors in Computing Systems*, 2016.

[17] L. Leung. Leisure boredom, sensation seeking, self-esteem, and addiction. *Mediated interpersonal communication*, 2008.

[18] O. Nov. What Motivates Wikipedians? *Communications of the ACM*, 50(11):60–64, 2007.

[19] S. Oreg and O. Nov. Exploring motivations for contributing to open source initiatives: The roles of contribution context and personal values. *Computers in Human Behavior*, 24(5):2055–2073, 2008.

[20] J. Pinheiro, D. Bates, S. DebRoy, D. Sarkar, and R Core Team. *nlme: Linear and Nonlinear Mixed Effects Models*, 2016. R package version 3.1-124.

[21] J. Raddick, G. Bracey, P. L. Gay, C. J. Lintott, P. Murray, K. Schawinski, A. S. Szalay, and J. Vandenberg. Galaxy Zoo: Exploring the Motivations of Citizen Science Volunteers. *Astronomy Education Review*, 9(1):1–18, Dec. 2010.

[22] E. S. Raymond. *The New Hacker's Dictionary.* MIT Press, 1996.

[23] J. Reed, J. Raddick, A. Lardner, and K. Carney. An Exploratory Factor Analysis of Motivations for Participating in Zooniverse, a Collection of Virtual Citizen Science Projects. In *2013 46th Hawaii International Conference on System Sciences (HICSS)*, pages 610–619. IEEE, Dec. 2012.

[24] S. Reiss. Multifaceted Nature of Intrinsic Motivation: The Theory of 16 Basic Desires. *Review of General Psychology*, 8(3):179–193, 2004.

[25] C. Rhodes and A. Pullen. Editorial: Neophilia and organization. *Culture and Organization*, 16(1):1–6, Mar. 2010.

[26] D. Rotman, J. Hammock, J. Preece, C. L. Boston, D. L. Hansen, A. Bowser, and Y. He. Does motivation in citizen science change with time and culture? In *CSCW Companion '14*, pages 229–232, New York, New York, USA, 2014. ACM Press.

[27] D. Rotman, J. Preece, J. Hammock, K. Procita, D. Hansen, C. Parr, D. Lewis, and D. Jacobs. Dynamic changes in motivation in collaborative citizen-science projects. In *Proceedings of the ACM 2012 conference on Computer Supported Cooperative Work*, pages 217–226. ACM, 2012.

[28] R. Simpson, K. R. Page, and D. De Roure. Zooniverse: observing the world's largest citizen science platform. In *WWW '14: Proceeding of the 23rd international conference on World Wide Web*, pages 1049–1054, New York, New York, USA, Apr. 2014. ACM.

[29] J. Surowiecki and M. P. Silverman. The Wisdom of Crowds. *American Journal of Physics*, 75(2):190, 2007.

[30] Y. R. Tausczik, L. A. Dabbish, and R. E. Kraut. Building loyalty to online communities through bond and identity-based attachment to sub-groups. In *CSCW '14: Proceedings of the ACM 2014 conference on Computer Supported Cooperative Work*, pages 146–157, New York, New York, USA, 2014. ACM Press.

[31] H.-L. Yang and C.-Y. Lai. Motivations of Wikipedia content contributors. *Computers in Human Behavior*, 26(6):1377–1383, Nov. 2010.

[32] F. Zhang, N. J. Yuan, D. Lian, and X. Xie. Mining novelty-seeking trait across heterogeneous domains. In *WWW '14: Proceeding of the 23rd international conference on World Wide Web*, pages 373–384, New York, New York, USA, 2014. ACM Press.

[33] H. Zhu, R. E. Kraut, and A. Kittur. Organizing without formal organization: group identification, goal setting and social modeling in directing online production. In *CSCW '12: Proceedings of the ACM 2012 conference on Computer Supported Cooperative Work*, New York, New York, USA, 2012.

Motivating Invisible Contributions: Framing Volunteer Classification Design in a Fanfiction Repository

Julia Bullard
University of Texas at Austin
Austin, USA
julia.a.bullard@gmail.com

ABSTRACT

Contributions from the crowd are not just content–sustainable systems require ongoing behind-the-scenes infrastructural work. In this paper, I explore potential strategies for motivating volunteer contributions to large-scale collaborative projects when volunteer contributions are procedural in nature and largely invisible in the published project. I use a user-driven classification system for a large, established, and growing fanfiction collection as an example of a successful project of this type. I compare the challenges and possibilities to those established in the study of open source, wiki, and citizen science projects, which share with classification design a need for distributed human contributions to procedural tasks. Textual analysis of recruiting and training documents, informed by prolonged engagement in the community, reveals strategies that diverge from other HCI research on motivation, such as a focus on work rather than fun and insider rather than public recognition.

Author Keywords

classification systems; user contributions; motivating volunteers; Harry Potter spoiler; invisible work

ACM Classification Keywords

H.3.1 Information Storage and Retrieval: Content Analysis and Indexing

INTRODUCTION

Within the world of scholarly communication, we are familiar with the need for both content and infrastructure: the rapidly growing PubMed collection would hardly be as powerful as it is without the organizing system of the Medical Subject Headings (MeSH) that make these documents findable. As the collection grows in quantity and scope, so must the organizing system expand and develop. User-generated content, from wikis to review sites to fiction and art, benefits from organizing systems that improve findability and accessibility. Organizing systems link items to each other and items to users through descriptive categories and attributes embedded in the collection. Site administrators, content creators, and voracious readers and users benefit when some fraction of the creativity and dedication given to creating content is given to the creation and maintenance of the organizing schema behind them.

Devoted participants in a variety of domains demonstrate a willingness to contribute to the administrative and organizing efforts supporting their activities [17,32]. However, these efforts are largely "invisible" work, obscured by the content of the very systems they enable [48]. Harnessing user interest and expertise to reach the critical mass of volunteers required to create and maintain functioning organizing systems poses a challenge to administrators: how can we motivate committed participation when contributions are less visible and more procedurally determined than the core activity itself? In online, large-scale collaborative systems, an additional challenge is added: how can we motivate volunteers at a distance, without the personal attention and recognition vital to community participation [56]?

I explore this question through the lens of user-driven classification design, or the creation and maintenance by volunteers of a terminology system to support the organization and retrieval of a large and growing set of documents. Unlike folksonomies, which are composed of the aggregate result of many users supplying their own terminology to a set of documents in the system [36], user-driven classification design here refers to the systematic and intentional design of a full classification system with individual tasks distributed among volunteers. Specifically, I examine a long-running, volunteer-driven classification project that organizes and facilitates retrieval for a large and growing set of fanfiction works. Fanfiction is a lauded example of a gift economy [19,20,47] while infrastructural tasks remain underexamined and underacknowledged elements of the exchange [18,54].

User-driven classification design for fanfiction collections illustrates an exemplar of infrastructural work that is invisible both in terms of ideal function and in how it obfuscates the individual human labor behind it. Like many other crowd work platforms and projects, user-driven classification design succeeds only when sufficient numbers of skilled users are motivated to provide appropriate and

GROUP '16, November 13 - 16, 2016, Sanibel Island, FL, USA

ACM 978-1-4503-4276-6/16/11…$15.00
DOI: http://dx.doi.org/10.1145/2957276.2957295

sustained contributions to the system. My analysis of recruiting and training documents reveals how a successful project's volunteers define and motivate their efforts.

The contributions of this study to CSCW and HCI are new ways to address potential and new volunteers in large-scale systems, particularly those in which user contributions are invisible and procedural. The findings regarding how one successful volunteer community understands and motivates procedural tasks are applicable to how organizers can frame other large-scale distributed projects, from open source to citizen science. The presentation or framing of user contributions, rather than the design of the tasks themselves, can have a major impact on the success of a system [33]. Here, I extend our understanding of framing to an extreme of invisibility, one in which contributions are intended to go unnoticed, especially in comparison to the central and celebrated contributions of fiction and feedback. Textual analysis reveals how motivated volunteers believe their tasks are best described to new members and reveals strategies that may have arisen organically and through consensus over time rather than intentional design.

FANFICTION AND VOLUNTEER LABOR

Fanfiction communities are typically studied as a gift economy [19,20,47]. Frameworks that focus on individual and intrinsic motivators, as in serious leisure [49], are less commonly used to explain labor in these communities. Fanfiction scholars have used and adapted the anthropological concept of the gift economy—a system of production, sharing, and exchange of valued goods not based on immediate or definite rewards [35]—to explain the sustainability of members' voluntary labor, explore the values of the community [20], and account for the role of technology [38]. The most visible and the most recognized gifts are fics (works of fiction), artwork, or vids (fan-edited videos) themselves. From a commercial and legal standpoint, it matters that they are gifts; the creation and distribution fics and vids as an ongoing exchange of gifts rather than commodities supports the community's fair use claims [11,47]. However, fics and vids are not the only gifts or labor exchanged in these spaces. In comparison to the highly circulated and highly visible fics and vids, infrastructural work such as user-driven classification design is invisible work [48].

Infrastructural work such as maintaining archives, forums, and wikis [20]; providing episode transcripts [47]; or reblogging fics and vids [54] are also gifts but are underacknowledged as such [54]. The impact of these acts is disproportionate to the little visibility they typically have in their communities or the scholarly literature. For example, administrators of a long-lived fanfiction archive may spark an unresolvable rift within the community by changing submission procedures [18]. Like other forms of infrastructure, these systems are by design less visible than the content they present, but they instantiate particular values [13,60] and become visible when these come into conflict with those of the community [34].

The exchange of fanfiction occurs through a technological infrastructure that requires design, maintenance, and labor. The history of this type of community contribution predates contemporary platforms [18] but the scale of user-generated content platforms drives new requirements and forms of work. A large, diverse set of fanfiction documents is less valuable to its writers and readers when these works cannot be browsed, searched, and found. The system must not only facilitate retrieval but be consistent with community values such as creative freedom and inclusivity. Relevant to this study, it must also sustain volunteer contributions to the growth and maintenance of the system despite having few resources and despite this effort lacking the visibility of the fic content. Notably, The Fanwork Repository[1] succeeds in doing this and without giving public credit or prestige to the volunteers. To explore the possible frameworks for understanding the sustainability of motivation in such an environment, I turn to more established domains of voluntary labor in collaborative systems.

USER LABOR IN LARGE-SCALE SYSTEMS

User-driven classification design is one in a constellation of crowd-based and computer-supported means to support large-scale projects. In the types of projects described in this section, the inputs of a large, distributed group of individuals with varied backgrounds are used to achieve outcomes not possible through traditional work practices or automated inputs alone [40]. Contrasted to paid crowd work, contributors in many of these projects are volunteers and do not receive monetary compensation. From each body of research, I identify motivation strategies that might be appropriate to user-driven classification design and others that contrast sharply with its constraints.

Open Source

Within HCI, open source or FLOSS projects are perhaps the most examined and understood with regards to motivations and outputs. Open source is an exemplar of disruption to established design, labor, and distribution models [41], characteristics it shares with the fanfiction community's relationship to traditional publishing and intellectual property holders [20,47]. Lakhani and Wolf [31] suggest that intrinsic motivation, such as enjoying and receiving intellectual stimulation from the tasks, and extrinsic motivations, such as improving programming skills, are key motivators for open source developers, more important than the more tangible rewards of better pay and career advancement. While these findings align open source more closely to what we would expect to find in the fanfiction community, they do link motivation to the challenge of the work itself. If user-driven classification design is motivated in the same way, we would expect to see these tasks

[1] A pseudonym

presented as challenging, stimulating, and engaging the individual's creativity [31]. Such a presentation would be in sharp contrast to the presentation of professional design, which emphasizes procedurality.

Wikis

One of the most salient characteristics of user-driven classification design is the contrast between the labor of creating and maintaining an organizing infrastructure and the labor of creating the content that rests upon it. Where open source demonstrates a wide range of types and degrees of participation [9], wikis illustrate more clearly a divide between the contribution of content and the contribution of infrastructural work [61]. Wiki activity is usually framed as content contributions, even when the user's participation is measured in hours spent and not articles written or edits made [37]. Exceptions include research into the organizing elements of Wikipedia articles, such as the development of the Category system [52].

An ongoing question in wiki scholarship is how infrastructural or "shaping" contributions differ from content contributions [61]. Yates and Wagner note that while there are some overlaps in motivations for these contributions, such as positive impacts on the individual's reputation, theories that accurately predict one type of contribution are not likely to fit the other [61]. Similarly, there may be a difference in how interventions from senior editors impact these two behaviors, as recent research has shown proportional coverage of notable men and women while organizing behaviors such as out-linking strongly favor articles about men [55]. The development of Wikidata [28] invites similar comparisons between contributions to the data source and to articles. Furthermore, wikis are a popular collaborative platform among fanfiction readers and writers [20,47,54], suggesting that the types of motivation that enable wikis to thrive overlap with those that sustain the gift economies of fanfiction communities.

Citizen Science

Citizen science shares with user-driven classification design the characteristic that the core work is procedural and not credited to individual contributors. Citizen science describes a wide range of projects which use civilian participation to perform scientific research, whether in data collection [45], coding [8,25], or more advanced analysis [27]. The participants in these projects may have training and credentials comparable to the scientists who organize the projects [7] or may lack such credentials or official positions [42]. A common assumption is that—regardless of scientific background—volunteers share an interest in the subject or goals of the project [59].

As with open source software development [31], scholars define citizen science by open participation and open access to project outputs and a contrast against paid crowd work and traditional, Mertonian science [15]—or traditional, corporate software development [41]. The theme of motivation is ubiquitous in literature on citizen science and builds on knowledge gained from wikis and open source.

Citizen science scholars have tested the association between motivations and the purpose of the project or the nature of participant tasks and stages of participant engagement [7,40]. Different types of motivation might negatively interact, deterring some desired populations of participants [29,40], and some types of interactions between scientists and volunteers might discourage ongoing contributions [42]. Motivation is an important topic not only because these projects require a critical mass of participant outputs; there are also ongoing questions of how different tactics for motivation might impact data quality [40,59].

Contributions from this domain include the development of motivation typologies [58], relating motivational frameworks to data quality outputs, and exploring the conflicting motivations of scientists and volunteers [15,46]. The complete set of possible motivations can be simplified as interest, altruism, and, entertainment [40] or personal interests, attribution, and acknowledgement [42]. Common findings include possible associations between participant interests and the topic of the project, participant pride and the scientific and practical outcomes of the project, and the possibility of enjoyment or fun in tasks themselves.

Classification as Procedure

The comparison of large-scale classification projects and citizen science projects is not made solely on the basis of the centrality of the socio computational system or reliance on a volunteer workforce. Just as citizen science is contrasted to Mertonian science [15], open source is to proprietary software development [41], and wikis are to top-down publishing formats, classification is traditionally accomplished through highly regulated processes by authorities with specialized, professional certifications. User-driven classification design asks community members to contribute to organizing tasks usually the province of librarians or small teams within private organizations [43,61]. Traditionally, classification theory has emphasized the scientific, objective, and reproducible nature of classification decisions, starting from an Aristotelian assumption that the world is naturally organized into categories, through arguments that the best classifications approach scientific consensus on relationships of knowledge [5], to contemporary arguments against the inevitability of subjectivity in classification systems [50].

As in the scientific method and scholarly communication, there are advantages to the stance that emphasizes procedurality, such as promoting interoperability between systems created in different institutions [51], improving the efficiency of the construction process [23], and avoiding the appearance of context-specific bias [14]. However, emphasizing the procedural nature of classification construction also means presenting classification systems as ideally correct and classificationists as arguably interchangeable actors performing the set methods of the discipline. This has implications for the recruiting of new classification designers, as each stance offers a distinct version of the ideal skills, attitude, and recognition appropriate to their workers.

USER-DRIVEN CLASSIFICATION DESIGN

Classification systems are deployed to support the organization and retrieval of a collection and arguably (see [10] for an opposing position) should work seamlessly with that collection such that its proper function goes unnoticed. Given the perception of classification design as a procedural discipline, classification systems as ideally independent of any particular classification worker, and ideal classification systems as invisible in operation, how can large-scale collaborative projects motivate volunteers to contribute to the creation and maintenance of these systems?

For the purposes of this study, several common findings from motivation in volunteer-driven collaborative projects are important. Two sets of findings motivate us to discover new explanations, as they predict success for tasks that are credited to individuals and inherently interesting or challenging. First, that intrinsic and extrinsic motivations can and do coexist, intrinsic motivations are the strongest drivers, and inherently interesting or challenging tasks are in themselves motivating for skilled volunteers [31]. Second, that motivations for infrastructural work differ from some motivations for content contributions but overlap in terms of gains to reputation [61].

Two findings suggest avenues of inquiry for analysis of the user-driven classification project. First, Rotman et al. state that the prestige, expertise, and power imbalance between scientists and volunteers can negatively motivate participation [42]. In the reverse of this phenomenon, rigorous training is interpreted by some volunteers as recognition of their value, initiation into a scientific community, and therefore a motivator for commitment to a project [42]. Relatedly, studies of communication among contributors to successful open source projects have found evidence of "we-intention" [3,56], or the use of collective or inclusive forms of address to establish intimacy among team members. This highlights the possibility that the framing of relationships among volunteers and between volunteers and organizers can have meaningful impacts on motivation and performance.

Findings suggest that how contribution tasks are presented is at least as important to motivation as the experience of participation [33], so that projects perceived as "fun" are more likely to succeed [40]. These findings suggest that descriptions of volunteer tasks can either positively frame participation in a motivating way or send a message that volunteer contributions are tedious or unvalued.

This study examines how volunteer contributions are presented in the constrained context of user-generated classification design. While there are an abundance of relevant design implications for motivation from open source, wiki, and citizen science research on task design and rewards, is it possible to frame volunteer efforts in motivating ways when these other choices are constrained and tasks must remain procedural and invisible?

METHODS

Research Site: The Fanwork Repository

This study focuses on the language in recruitment and training documents written by the staff of a large-scale collaborative classification project directed at potential and new volunteers. This study is part of prolonged ethnographic study into the work practices of volunteer classificationists. The data collection, analysis, and discussion in this study are informed by prolonged engagement in fieldwork. Participant ethnography has provided not only access to worker-only communication channels, such as those examined in detail in this study, but also insight into the language of this group, the nuances of its practices, the challenges faced as a group and as individuals, and the changes it has undergone over three years. I have spent three years as participant observer and known researcher in The Fanwork Repository taking part in training exercises, contributing to the classification system each week, reading the active mailing list, reviewing guidelines and procedures in the organization's wiki, participating in group discussions both in the mailing list and in the group's persistent chatroom, and interviewing other volunteers.

The focus in this study is on how the community collectively defines its efforts to itself and to new members. Contextual knowledge about the organization gained through participant observation and interviews informed analysis in clarifying the meaning of concepts, the timing of how volunteers encounter the documents, and the pervasiveness of this rhetoric. Recruitment and training documents represent a relatively stable, codified, and official version of the rhetoric that circulates in this community and that is reinforced in peer interactions. These documents are powerful, valid examples of this community's rhetoric because they are the agreed-upon summary of the volunteer position and its tasks and therefore represent a community's beliefs about itself and because they serve in organizational and temporal terms as the primary (though likely oversimplified and ideal) representation for the purpose of socialization.

This site is chosen as an example of a successful large-scale user-driven classification design project because of its stability over years of use, the functionality in regards to browsing and searching for works in the resulting system, and the continuing interest of volunteers in contributing to the system. Currently, The Fanwork Repository includes over 2 million works and has monthly traffic of 7 million visitors. Users add tens of thousands of new works every month, each with a handful of tags attached.

The classification system created in this site is a "curated folksonomy" [6] in which classificationists manage a large set of user-generated terms to create a navigable thesaurus that combines equivalent terms and creates hierarchical relationships among related terms. Unregulated folksonomies allow users freedom and ease in creating new tags at the cost of retrieval since users can use variant phrasing or misspellings when referring to the same concept [53]. In a curated folksonomy, this is addressed by making links of equivalencies or relationships between tags. Classification workers monitor new tags entered in the system, designate "preferred tags" that receive increased visibility in the browsing interface and in autocomplete fields, and link tags to preferred tags as synonyms. Classification workers sometimes create hierarchies of preferred terms to link broader and narrower concepts, improving recall when users choose the general term and improving precision when users choose the specific term.

Whereas traditional classification designers are expected to impose a particular—even "correct"—paradigm on the collection [21,22], this curated folksonomy model keeps user-submitted tags intact while classification workers seek out equivalencies and explicit relationships among these tags. While the wording and spelling of author's tags remained unchanged, linked tags are treated as a single term in retrieval. The resulting system gives authors flexibility and control in adding tags to their works while supporting findability through search and browse.

Figure 1 outlines a typical sequence of author, classification, and reader interactions with the system. Because classificationists make links without altering the submitted tags, when working correctly, the organizing system provides an unobtrusive background for the collected works themselves. The author is able to enter a tag in his or her own wording, though the system will attempt to suggest similar tags already designated as preferred through autocomplete. The author may choose to enter a new term because the suggestions do not match his or her intended meaning or because he or she favors another phrasing. The reader will see this author's work listed alongside those the classification worker has grouped under a preferred tag—regardless of whether he or she chooses the author's variant, the preferred tag phrasing, or another phrasing in the interface. The author and the reader can access the tag hierarchy page that diagrams the connections between these tags, though the work creation and browsing interfaces do not require that the author or reader ever see these connections. These user experiences are enabled by the classification worker linking the author's idiosyncratic wording as a synonym to a preferred term, which will appear in the autocomplete field for future authors.

The Volunteer Process

Volunteers are the classification workers in this project. The organization recruits volunteers in "recruitment drives," conducted twice a year or according to the volume of unattended or understaffed domains. In these periods, 30 to 100 volunteers join (or re-join) the classification project. Once a year, organizers require volunteers to indicate whether they intend to continue volunteering in the following year and retire individuals as appropriate, though volunteers also reduce their commitments or leave the organization throughout the year. During my time with this organization, the number of classification volunteers has varied between 200 and 240 individuals.

During "recruitment drives," organizers post calls for volunteers on the project's website and request that the message be spread by members across social media. Only during recruitment drives are volunteers eligible to apply to the organization. Organizers often indicate which domains are in immediate need of volunteer effort to attract volunteers with interest and familiarity in those source materials and their fandoms. Interested volunteers fill out an online application. The organization does not disclose how many volunteer applications—if any—are rejected. Designated senior volunteers notify new volunteers of their acceptance, assist them in setting up accounts on various platforms used for distributed work, and instruct them to begin following the training materials within the organization's private wiki.

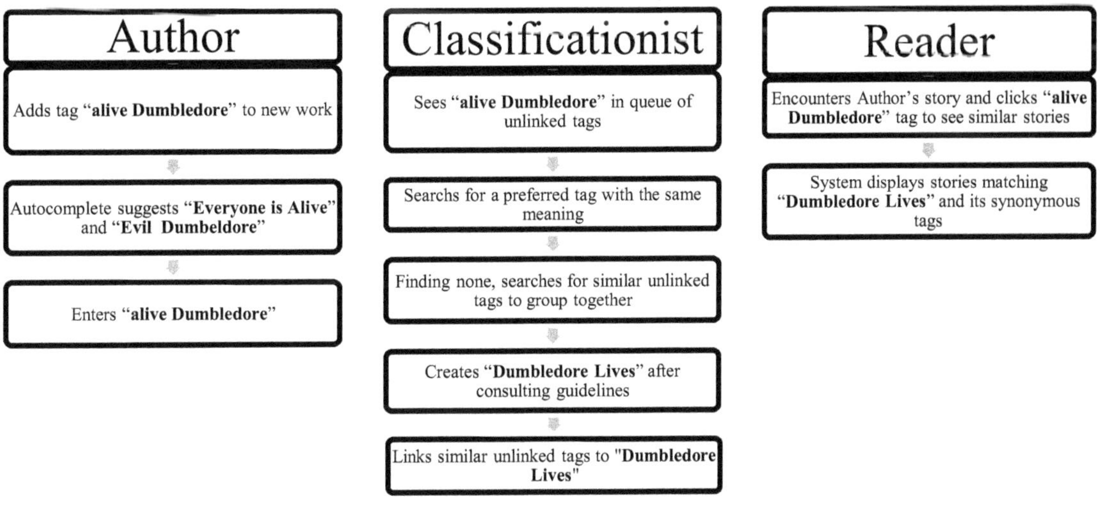

Figure 1. Typical sequences of interaction in the tag system. Authors and readers see a simplified version of the tagging and retrieval system facilitated by the classificationist's work.

Training materials are written collaboratively by the classification volunteers and are subject to regular revision by the group. Minor changes to the documents are prompted by volunteers for clarification or correction while more substantial changes are developed through open discussion among all volunteers. The documents represent the consensus of the volunteer group on best practices and what they believe is most important for new volunteers to know before interacting with the live system. In particular, these documents represent the opinions of the experienced, engaged volunteers who contribute to revisions.

Data Collection

Data collection included the entirety of recruitment and training materials that comprise the required readings for new volunteers. Outward-facing recruiting documents were retrieved from the organization's public site. Inward-facing training documents were retrieved through the author's member account on the organization's wiki. The original document set was collected in March, 2014. The final analysis of this set included revisions made through September 2015. Most changes in the set occurred in training documents and included wiki revisions to add detail to processes, illustrate particular tasks or features with examples, provide updates on known bugs that impact the classification system, and provide instruction to track, address, or workaround known bugs.

Outward-facing recruiting documents included calls for volunteers, information on volunteer positions within the organization, and information on classification positions in the organization in particular. Five such documents addressed to potential volunteers were found and included in analysis. The average word count of these documents was 1410. Two of these documents had an FAQ structure and one resembled a job posting.

Inward-facing training documents included general information for volunteers such as a policy document and an introduction to the classification position, as well as required exercises and assessments for new volunteers. While the internal wiki includes training documents for intermediate and advanced classification tasks intended for experienced volunteers, only the basic exercises and assessments were included for analysis. These exercises are required before volunteers make contributions to the systems, and include guides to the technical features of the site as well to the types of decisions made by classificationists. There were fourteen inward-facing documents in total, eight of which are the required exercises for new volunteers. The average word count of all inward-facing documents was 2155. Each of the eight documents with exercises were primarily ordered steps, interspersed with introductions to different concepts, sidebars for notes on exceptions or important cases, review questions, and images or figures demonstrating platform interfaces or concepts. Two of the remaining documents were similar in structure, but did not include exercises. One document functioned as a landing page for the other documents, as a Category page within a wiki. One document had an FAQ structure. One document was a fillable google form.

Textual Analysis

I analyzed the documents within the qualitative software Atlas.TI. The aim was not to determine volunteer's tasks but how the documents describe these tasks and the position itself. Textual analysis surfaces the values and persuasive elements communicated in documents [1,4,16,26]. I focused on repeated rhetorical styles and word choices. In my analysis, I asked the following questions: What names do they give this position and its tasks? How do they relate these tasks to the project as a whole? How do they characterize these tasks and the type of person that does or should do them?

Iterative close readings of the collected documents revealed repeated topics, patterns of address, and tropes. Those repeated elements that speak to the motivation and retention of volunteers, particularly the distance in status between organizers and volunteers, the characterization of the position and tasks, and the benefits to the volunteer were analyzed in more detail. This form of analysis assumes that word choice—such as the choice to call an activity "work" —is meaningful, even if that choice is made without strategic intent. Especially when certain words, themes, and forms of address are repeated throughout a body of documents, they suggest a particular perspective on the subject matter. Given that the core activity of the fanfiction community is textual, that these volunteers chiefly communicate through text (mailing lists, chatrooms, system documentation, and wikis), and these documents are written by the volunteers themselves, we would have an even greater expectation that the language in these documents is representative of the community's discourse (see [1,18] for similar approaches). Furthermore, the role of these documents in attracting volunteers, defining the position, and detailing tasks and policies grants them a privileged status in the socialization of classification workers. Textual analysis of this data source necessarily privileges the volunteers' own understanding of their work and not an objective, outside truth.

The emergent themes found in this project's recruitment and training documents are explored in the sections below. To protect the anonymity of the research site, illustrative quotations are chosen from among the inward-facing documents alone. Quotations from documents are identified by the notation D#, indicating the document in which they were found.

FINDINGS & DISCUSSION

Four themes present throughout the documents are relevant to the concerns of recruiting and retaining volunteers in large-scale collaborative projects. The first theme is the manner in which the documents address the reader (the potential or new volunteer), which speaks to minimizing the perceived distance between organizers and volunteers. Two themes arise from the language used to describe classification tasks—as a "behind-the-scenes" effort and as a "job." The remaining theme describes the developing message across the documents that training is a substantial commitment for both volunteers and organizers.

Also relevant to the existing research in this area is what we did not find: suggestions of extrinsic rewards to volunteers, such as payment, recognition, or advancement of skills; encouragement to discuss one's tasks in public or an explanation of how to receive or take credit in the community; or assurances of "fun" tasks. I discuss this departure from established wisdom throughout the findings.

"We," "You," and "They" Language

The recruitment and training documents vary in perspective and style of address. Potential and new volunteers are alternatively part of a collective "we" along with the writer, a "you" directly addressed by the writer, or outside of the description of a third-person "they." The changing of perspective across and even within documents could be a product of the collaborative, iterative process through which these documents are written. Regardless, the volunteer experiences them as an intentional, finished product. The use of pronouns can have a substantial impact on the way a document is read and the implied relationship between writer and reader. For example, first person pronouns like "I" and "we" characterize more involved, intimate genres of communication [18, p. 185]. Previous studies of open source communities have observed collective pronoun use in support of an influential "we-intention" in user working groups [3,56].

The collective pronoun "we" is the least common style across the recruitment and training documents. It appears in the form of instructions that describe "our job" and introduce tools that exist "so that we can make sure" to avoid particular mistakes. This language is found only in the inward-facing documents introducing volunteers to the principles and processes of classification work in this venue. In the introduction to the concepts of the classification project it is the dominant mode of address: "We work hard to not oversyn [equate] tags about human identities" (D4). Throughout the exercise-oriented documents, it is used in asides or parenthetical remarks on how "we" usually do things or in offering strategies for completing particular tasks: "While [classification workers] often work on their fandoms alone, you're also part of a team, and it's important for *us* to communicate respectfully with each other" (D17, emphasis added).

The use of "we" language communicates that volunteers are brought into the training process as members of a collective, enjoying a shared status with senior volunteers and staffers who write the instructions. While this type of language continues only sparingly across later training documents, its position in the first of the introductory documents serves to narrow the gap between volunteers and staff. At this point in the process, volunteers have applied and been approved by staffers; giving them insider status this early conveys the staff's decision as weighty and indicates faith in those chosen to undergo training.

Third-person, "they" language is also used in early training documents. It is not the dominant form of address in any single document but is used in subsections of each training document. Of the outward-facing documents, only the document in the genre of a job posting uses a third-person style of address. Where third-person language is used, volunteers are described but not associated with either the reader or the writer. Instead, classification work is conducted by an abstract group who follow particular procedures according to the organization's principles. Tasks are described as the actions of the classification worker, neither the writer nor the reader, as in "[they] control the states of tags in order to organize and connect them" (D3). When discussed in the third-person, volunteers are addressed in the same manner as the non-human elements (tags), having agency but no personal identity. This is the most impersonal form of address, but has the advantage of portraying classification design itself as impersonal: objective, standardized, and broader than the experience or perspective of a given volunteer, resembling scientific discourse. Describing the work in the third-person also has the advantage of presenting the existing tools and processes as inevitable or beyond question; this is just the way things are, rather than the way we have made them or you are likely to treat them. Abstract address elevates established protocols to the levels of scientific fact.

The most common form of address is the second-person "you" and is used across recruitment and training documents. It is the dominant form of address in 4 out of the 5 outward-facing documents. In recruitment documents, this takes the form of the appeal to the potential volunteer, inviting them directly to contribute to the project's goals. It is used in each training document, especially in the introduction and transition sections where the reader is oriented to the purpose of and the estimated time to complete the exercise. In training documents, second-person language is used to direct and project the volunteer's activity: you can contact us in the event of this error; you will learn how to use the following tools; you will follow this procedure when addressing this type of issue. This form of address is used throughout the later training documents, as these are constructed as walkthroughs of various classification decisions and tools—volunteers are directly addressed as they are guided through practice exercises that combine the training documents with the classification interface itself.

Though this mode of training lacks the immediacy of face-to-face interaction, second-person language reintroduces a personal, intimate touch. Second-person language is heavily used in the inset "Notes" interspersed among training documents, as these interjections are primarily used to directly address volunteers about atypical cases and exemptions: "You don't have to change tags at user request if you don't think they should be changed, but you do need to tell Support why so they can explain to the user" (D5). While third-person language characterizes classification tasks as rule-based and procedural, the direct address of "you" functions as a more intimate aside in which the more messy details are imparted.

Two forms of address dominate recruiting and training documents—"we" language in the earliest documents defining the scope and nature of classification work and "you" language across recruitment information and training exercises. Though third-person language is occasionally used and reinforces the objective distance characteristic of the scientific enterprise, it is the exception rather than the rule in the portrayal of classification work. At the cost of downplaying the cultural capital of scientific work, these documents reinforce the social connections between staff and volunteers and among all the project's classification workers, minimizing the perceived distance known to demotivate participation in such projects [42].

Behind the Scenes

When describing the relationship between volunteer tasks and primary activity of the site—the posting and retrieval of user-generated content—the documents refer to the volunteer's work as "behind the scenes" (D2, D3, D17). The large-scale nature of citizen science may mean that any one volunteer's contribution is effectively anonymous; in classification design, the goal is for the entire system to play an unobtrusive background to the collected works themselves. In defining the scope of classification volunteer's work, recruitment documents place the work "behind the scenes" of the day-to-day functioning of the website. This is both in the broader sense that the organization and retrieval system serves the collection and in the specific sense of a curated folksonomy, in which classificationist intervention augments the functionality of existing user tags. The documents repeatedly remind volunteers that management of descriptive metadata is limited by what users have already submitted and cannot exceed that boundary by altering these tags or requesting that users tag differently: "We don't contact individual users directly about their tags—our job is to make links behind the scenes" (D17).

This type of classification work is distinguished from more invasive or top-down classification design through the related rhetoric of "making links" (D17) or "making connections" (D3). Volunteers are instructed to make links and find connections in "the back end" (D3) of the system to augment or improve the functionality of user tags.

This emphasis on the "behind the scenes" or "back end" nature of volunteer participation may risk discouraging participation. Reminding volunteers that their contributions will not be as visible as those of content-creators cuts off types of motivation based on status and recognition in the broader community. However, this language simultaneously stresses the exclusive, insider world to which participation provides access. Volunteers are privy to the inner workings of the collection in a way that typical users—even those whose usernames are published throughout the site—are not. While the broader community of users may not know the details of volunteers' contributions or even appreciate the nature of those contributions, volunteers belong to a more select community mutually aware of their expertise and effort.

A Job

Maintaining the curated folksonomy is characterized as a "job" or "work" by recruitment and training documents: "the work you'll need to do" (D9), "keep your workload manageable" (D10), "Our job is to" (D3, D4, D6, D17), "Your primary job as" (D5), "like all jobs" (D3). The term "work" is used frequently to describe volunteer effort despite the term also being used to refer to the objects of the site's collection, "fan works." Any confusion or unnecessary repetition could be avoided by using a verb like "classify" or "organize" throughout these documents, but "work" is consistently used from the volunteer's FAQ page to the communication policy document: "prioritize work that impacts other [classificationists]" (D19).

While some citizen science projects have benefited from characterizing contribution tasks as "fun" [6,25], volunteers here are not told that classification work will be fun. The strategy here emphasizes the labor and obligation volunteers take on through their contributions. By repeatedly referring to contributions as "work," volunteers as classification "workers," and the volunteer position as a "job," these documents indicate a respect for volunteer's efforts. This language also emphasizes the expectation that volunteers will follow-through on their offer of assistance; participation is not a matter of self-directed "fun" but a commitment and an obligation. This message is reinforced by reminders of the expected or required speed of changes and responses as well as instructions on temporarily leaving the position if circumstances interrupt this level of activity.

The "work" of classification in this system is primarily managing new tags by making links of equivalencies or relationships to existing tags. However, the language of obligation in training documents also emphasizes the information work of documenting these decisions and keeping informed on the topics of discussion across volunteer-specific communication channels: "It's not compulsory to take part in discussions, but you should at least be aware of what's being discussed" (D17). Recruitment documents focus on the central task—making classification decisions to maintain the functionality of the system—while training documents fill out the broader context of these tasks, including maintaining institutional knowledge by explaining decisions for future volunteers and by integrating new strategies and policies developed by peers. Participation in this community extends beyond the immediate queue of tasks into the future of the community; volunteers are in a position to passively shape the perspective of fellow and future volunteers by sharing their decision-making process.

In a single instance, a recruitment document suggests that some potential volunteers might find classification tasks "fun." However, the documents much more consistently refer to obligation, work, and the job. This is a departure from the strategy employed in other user-driven projects. This choice is particularly appropriate for this project because of the considerable training required before volunteers are able to complete tasks; emphasizing the job-like characteristics of the position sets an appropriate expectation regarding the tenure of a volunteer's involvement in the project. Emphasizing fun, on the other hand, might suggest briefer engagements with the project or set the expectation that the volunteers' activity fluctuates with their own interest, rather than the regular monitoring and maintenance requested of these volunteers.

Training Load

Recruitment and training documents continually remind volunteers of the considerable training commitment that precedes contribution to the system. Each training document begins with a comment on the expected time (e.g. "30-45 minutes") it will take to read through and complete any associated exercises. The landing page for required training documents labels each with this time investment information, as well as the deadline by which the volunteer should complete each section. In the six weeks following recruitment into the group, each volunteer is responsible for completing between 4 and 7 hours of training.

Early training documents foreshadow the breadth of topics to be covered in introductory materials as well as the advanced topics to be explored further in the volunteer's career. A recurrent focus on the extent of the training load serves to manage volunteers' expectations, avoiding early burnout or frustration with the training process. According to the suggestions of Rotman et al. [26], it may also serve to remind volunteers of the faith that organizers have in their capacity for specialized knowledge and the benefits of learning. Training in classification principles, the specific goals of the fanfiction project, and the communication policies established among the volunteers are both a means of rendering the volunteer more capable of completing tasks and introducing the volunteer to the mindset of the working classificationist.

The extent of the training load is also invoked in recruitment in terms of the burden this places on organizers. The need to train new volunteers is cited as the primary reason that volunteer recruitment is limited and conducted in scheduled batches or drives. Guiding new classification workers through early technical and conceptual procedures takes such time and effort that, despite the constant and growing need for more hands at the wheel, the process must be limited to avoid overtaking classification tasks. The impact of recruitment on other volunteers is also suggested by the frequent invitations to contact particular organizing bodies in the event of technical issues with accounts, unclear or incomplete instructions, or trouble managing the volunteer workload. Prompts to contact organizers with contact details occur at least once in each training document, highlighting for volunteers the availability of further help as well as reinforcing the image of a committed staff expecting to serve the numerous administrative requests of new volunteers. This impression of the service of organizers and experienced volunteers to new members is reinforced outside of these training documents. In periods following recruitment, organizers routinely use the mailing list to welcome new volunteers and experienced volunteers promote scheduled events in the chatroom to work alongside new recruits and answer their questions.

Just as with the characterization of the volunteer position as a "job," the pervasive reminder of the reciprocal burden of training is appropriate to a project that expects candidates to self-select for those willing to respect the need to act consistent with guidelines. As a trade-off to motivating a broader set of participants, this appeals to potential volunteers more likely to offer high-quality contributions. In some user-driven projects, data quality is ensured by the system, such as in cases where the volunteer's work is automatically checked against a given format or aggregated across the input of many volunteers. The classification work in this project does not offer the same opportunities for system-enforced consistency. Instead, volunteers are trained extensively—to the extent that self-managed exercises and assessments can allow—and constantly reminded of the scope and gravity of the training enterprise.

IMPLICATIONS

Textual analysis has revealed that this project uses some tactics consistent with core HCI findings on motivation, such as a "we-intention", and others that diverge, such as a focus on obligation and behind-the-scenes contributions.

Recruitment and training documents are an opportunity to define the volunteer effort in an attractive way, even when project constraints prevent more active interventions such as gamified volunteer tasks or individual, public recognition of effort. Even in projects that have considerable latitude in the design of tasks, the approach found in The Fanwork Repository may be used, especially as the perceived distance between organizers and volunteers is a perennial challenge [42]. In addition, the language of "job" or obligation rather than personal, hedonistic fulfillment might be more appropriate for projects struggling to establish reliably high-quality contributions from volunteers.

In large-scale collaborative systems, training lacks the personal touch and interpersonal ties that might occur in smaller volunteer-organizer settings. Strategies such as inclusive forms of address and underlining the shared training burden between volunteers and organizers serve to minimize a perceived power imbalance that can deter participation [42]. Particularly in projects in which individual volunteers' contributions are not explicitly and publicly acknowledged, as in the case of many citizen science projects, or in which an indicator of quality is the invisibility of the completed project, as in classification systems, an emphasis on interpersonal obligations and ties is an important component of motivation.

Though gains to status or reputation are common tactics for motivating contributions [30,39,57], this analysis instead suggests that invisibility of volunteer contributions—whether due the anonymity of the masses or the nature of the published project—can be framed as a positive motivation. By characterizing volunteer contributions as "behind the scenes," organizers can shift the source of valued recognition from the broader community to the select insider community of volunteers. The framing devices detailed here provide groundwork for interpersonal motivation by presenting the idea of an insider, "behind-the-scenes" camaraderie. These suggested ties must then be fostered and developed in the course of the volunteer's involvement with the project.

Access to "behind-the-scenes" tasks may also motivate participation by giving volunteers influence over the shaping of their community. One of the possible though less visible (and less discussed) motivations for providing gifts in a gift economy is as "a tool for implementing change or evolution within the group" [38]. This motivation allows for anonymity but requires that the volunteer's effort will in some way change how the community operates. In this analysis, references to "behind-the-scenes" tasks suggest not only exclusivity, but power. For communities that recognize the impact that design choices in infrastructure can have on the functioning of their community, as has been established in the fanfiction community [12,18,19,24,34], such opportunities may be particularly desirable. However, such motivations must be tempered against the desire of individual users to redirect the project to their own values, as is a persistent issue in Wikipedia [2].

The current study opens up the possibility of future work examining framing devices used in similar large-scale volunteer-driven projects, or those that differ in one or more facets. For example, some projects may have developed gamified tasks but can or will not offer public recognition of volunteer efforts. Does the language of their recruitment and training documents stress interpersonal ties and mutual respect among peer volunteers? Studying similar projects is also necessary to determine to what extent this project's success is due to self-selection in this community for those that find organizing tasks intrinsically rewarding or for those that feel obligated to return effort to a community they enjoy. By virtue of this project occurring within the established gift economy of the fanfiction community, the latter is likely at least partially true [20,54].

This study also suggests the need for future work that assesses the relative impact choosing to emphasize insider access or public recognition, obligation or enjoyment. Such findings can shape new approaches to framing a variety of volunteer contributions, from citizen science to user-driven classification design. Experimental designs, for example, could complement the current study by testing for small differences in interest to participate from differing recruitment language [as in 28]. Studies of existing projects, such as this study, inform such experiments by highlighting naturalistic approaches proven through implementation and practice in live and long-running systems.

This line of research can support the recruitment and retention of volunteers for large-scale collaborative projects, though the focus here is on those projects in which the volunteer's contribution is rendered invisible in the finished system. Motivating despite this invisibility is a common challenge for very large projects [4], but in the case of citizen science, user-driven classification design—and to a lesser extent, wikis and open source development—this invisibility is also produced by the paradigms of their parent disciplines, which base claims to validity on the characterization of the individual worker as an interchangeable cog in the machine.

CONCLUSION

The mobilization of large groups of interested, committed, and skilled volunteers is increasingly necessary to provide the infrastructure underneath large collections of user-generated work. Unfortunately, classification work—the manipulation of terminology and term relationships—does not receive the same kind of public attention and glamour as other large-scale collaborative projects. A sustainable classification system is unlikely to engender the same excitement as new scientific findings driven by the Foldit protein game [27], for example. Science and classification projects share in common a tendency to present results as inevitable, the labor behind them as purely procedural, and the workers themselves as interchangeable. While public interest in scientific practice benefits from the status and charm of public spokespeople such as Neil de Grasse Tyson (or Tony Stark), classification as yet remains a type of work without a charismatic public image. It is therefore all the more notable that projects such as that detailed in this study attract the critical mass of volunteers necessary to maintain their organizing systems.

User-driven classification design is one powerful solution to the problem of organizing and making findable and accessible the wealth of user-generated content online, but it does carry the challenge of requiring workers committed to completing largely procedural tasks without recognition. By examining a case in which the textual framing of the project and volunteer's role promotes a feeling of insider inclusivity and job-like obligation, this study offers examples of motivating strategies beyond system design. Such strategies will power projects that connect the large public of content creators with their eager audiences.

ACKNOWLEDGMENTS

I thank my writing group at the School of Information for their help. I also thank the reviewers for their helpful feedback and suggestions.

REFERENCES

1. Ban Al-Ani, Gloria Mark, and Bryan Semaan.

2010. Blogging in a region of conflict. *Proceedings of the 28th international conference on Human factors in computing systems - CHI '10*, ACM Press, 1069. http://doi.org/10.1145/1753326.1753485

2. Judd Antin. 2011. My kind of people? *Proceedings of the 2011 annual conference on Human factors in computing systems - CHI '11*, ACM Press, 3411. http://doi.org/10.1145/1978942.1979451

3. Richard P. Bagozzi and Utpal M Dholakia. 2006. Open Source Software User Communities: A Study of Participation in Linux User Groups. *Management Science* 52, 7: 1099–1115. http://doi.org/10.1287/mnsc.1060.0545

4. Jeffrey Bardzell, S Bardzell, and Austin Toombs. 2014. now that's definitely a proper hack: self-made tools in hackerspaces. *Proceedings of the 32nd annual ACM ...*, 473–476.

5. Henry Evelyn Bliss. 1929. *The Organization of Knowledge and the System of the Sciences*. Holt & Co., New York, NY.

6. Julia Bullard. 2014. Values and negotiation in classification work. *Proceedings of the companion publication of the 17th ACM conference on Computer supported cooperative work & social computing - CSCW Companion '14*: 45–48. http://doi.org/10.1145/2556420.2556820

7. Jeffrey P. Cohn. 2008. Citizen science: Can volunteers do real research? *BioScience* 58, 3: 192–197.

8. Mark Cottman-Fields, Margot Brereton, and Paul Roe. 2013. Virtual birding. *Proceedings of the SIGCHI Conference on Human Factors in Computing Systems - CHI '13*, ACM Press, 2029. http://doi.org/10.1145/2470654.2466268

9. Kevin Crowston and James Howison. 2006. Core and Periphery in Free/Libre and Open Source Software Team Communications. *Proceedings of the 39th Annual Hawaii International Conference on System Sciences (HICSS'06)*, IEEE, 118a–118a. http://doi.org/10.1109/HICSS.2006.101

10. Melanie Feinberg, Daniel Carter, and Julia Bullard. 2014. Always somewhere, never there: using critical design to understand database interactions. *Proceedings of the SIGCHI Conference on Human Factors in Computing Systems*, 1941–1950.

11. Casey Fiesler and Amy S. Bruckman. 2014. Remixers' understandings of fair use online. *Proceedings of the 17th ACM conference on Computer supported cooperative work & social computing - CSCW '14*, ACM Press, 1023–1032. http://doi.org/10.1145/2531602.2531695

12. Casey Fiesler and Amy Bruckman. 2014. Copyright terms in online creative communities. *Proceedings of CHI 2014*, 2551–2556. http://doi.org/10.1145/2559206.2581294

13. Casey Fiesler, Shannon Morrison, and Amy S Bruckman. 2016. An Archive of Their Own: A Case Study of Feminist HCI and Values in Design. *CHI '16 Proceedings of the ACM Conference on Human Factors in Computing Systems*. http://doi.org/10.1145/2858036.2858409

14. MJ Fox and Austin Reece. 2012. Which ethics? Whose morality?: An analysis of ethical standards for information organization. *Knowledge Organization* 39, 5: 377–383.

15. Chiara Franzoni and Henry Sauermann. 2014. Crowd science: The organization of scientific research in open collaborative projects. *Research Policy* 43, 1: 1–20. http://doi.org/10.1016/j.respol.2013.07.005

16. Erin Friess. 2012. Personas and decision making in the design process. *Proceedings of the 2012 ACM annual conference on Human Factors in Computing Systems - CHI '12*, ACM Press, 1209. http://doi.org/10.1145/2207676.2208572

17. Crystal Fulton. 2009. Quid pro quo: Information sharing in leisure activities. *Library Trends* 57, 4: 753–768.

18. Leora Hadas. 2009. The web planet: How the changing Internet divided Doctor Who fan fiction writers. *Transformative Works and Cultures* 3, 3. http://doi.org/10.3983/twc.2009.0129

19. Karen Hellekson and Kristina Busse. 2006. *Fan fiction and fan communities in the age of the internet*. McFarland.

20. Karen Hellekson. 2009. A Fannish Field of Value: Online Fan Gift Culture. *Cinema Journal* 48, 4: 113–118. http://doi.org/10.1353/cj.0.0140

21. Birger Hjørland and Hanne Albrechtsen. 1995. Toward a New Horizon in Information Science: Domain-Analysis. *Journal of the American Society for Information Science* 46, 6: 400–425.

22. Birger Hjørland. 2002. Domain analysis in information science: Eleven approaches – traditional as well as innovative. *Journal of Documentation* 58, 4: 422–462. http://doi.org/10.1108/00220410210431136

23. Gretchen L Hoffman. 2009. Meeting users' needs in cataloging: What is the right thing to do? *Cataloging & Classification quarterly* 47, 7: 631–641. http://doi.org/10.1080/01639370903111999

24. Shannon Fay Johnson. 2014. Fan fiction metadata creation and utilization within fan fiction archives: Three primary models. *Transformative Works and Cultures* 17, 17.

25. Ece Kamar, Severin Hacker, and Eric Horvitz. 2012. Combining human and machine intelligence in large-scale crowdsourcing. *AAMAS '12 Proceedings of the 11th International Conference on Autonomous Agents and Multiagent Systems - Volume 1*, International Foundation for Autonomous Agents and Multiagent Systems, 467–474.

26. Gopinaath Kannabiran, Jeffrey Bardzell, and Shaowen Bardzell. 2011. How HCI talks about sexuality. *Proceedings of the 2011 annual conference on Human factors in computing systems - CHI '11*, ACM Press, 695. http://doi.org/10.1145/1978942.1979043

27. Firas Khatib, Frank DiMaio, Seth Cooper, et al. 2011. Crystal structure of a monomeric retroviral protease solved by protein folding game players. *Nature Structural & Molecular Biology*, September: 8–10. http://doi.org/10.1038/nsmb.2119

28. Daniel Kinzler and Lydia Pintscher. 2014. Wikidata. *Proceedings of The International Symposium on Open Collaboration - OpenSym '14*, ACM Press, 1–1. http://doi.org/10.1145/2641580.2641583

29. Masatomo Kobayashi, Shoma Arita, Toshinari Itoko, Shin Saito, and Hironobu Takagi. 2015. Motivating Multi-Generational Crowd Workers in Social-Purpose Work. *Proceedings of the 18th ACM Conference on Computer Supported Cooperative Work & Social Computing - CSCW '15*, ACM Press, 1813–1824. http://doi.org/10.1145/2675133.2675255

30. Peter Kollock. 1999. The economies of online cooperation: Gifts and public goods in cyberspace. In *Communities in cyberspace*. 220–242.

31. Karim Lakhani and Robert G Wolf. 2003. Why Hackers Do What They Do: Understanding Motivation and Effort in Free/Open Source Software Projects. *Social Science Research Network* 49, September: 1–27. http://doi.org/10.2139/ssrn.443040

32. Charlotte P Lee and Ciaran B Trace. 2009. The role of information in a community of hobbyist collectors. *Journal of the American Society for Information Science* 60, 3: 621–637. http://doi.org/10.1002/asi

33. Kimberly Ling, Gerard Beenen, Pamela Ludford, et al. 2005. Using Social Psychology to Motivate Contributions to Online Communities. *Journal of Computer-Mediated Communication* 10, 4: 00–00. http://doi.org/10.1111/j.1083-6101.2005.tb00273.x

34. Alexis Lothian. 2012. Archival anarchies: Online fandom, subcultural conservation, and the transformative work of digital ephemera. *International Journal of Cultural Studies* 16, 6: 541–556. http://doi.org/10.1177/1367877912459132

35. Marcel Mauss. The Gift : The Form and Reason for Exchange in Archaic Societies.

36. T Bisgaard Munk and Kristian Mørk. 2007. Folksonomy, the power law & the significance of the least effort. *Knowledge organization* 34, 1: 16–33.

37. Oded Nov. 2007. What motivates Wikipedians? *Communications of the ACM* 50, 11: 60–64. http://doi.org/10.1145/1297797.1297798

38. Erika Pearson. 2007. Digital gifts: Participation and gift exchange in Livejournal communities. *First Monday* 12, 5.

39. Jennifer Preece and Ben Shneiderman. 2009. The reader-to-leader framework: Motivating technology-mediated social participation. *AIS Transactions on Human-Computer Interaction* 1, 1: 13–32.

40. Nathan R. Prestopnik and Kevin Crowston. 2011. Gaming for (citizen) science: Exploring motivation and data quality in the context of crowdsourced science through the design and evaluation of a social-computational system. *2011 IEEE Seventh International Conference on e-Science Workshops*: 28–33. http://doi.org/10.1109/eScienceW.2011.14

41. Eric Raymond. 1999. The cathedral and the bazaar. *Knowledge, Technology & Policy* 12, 3: 23–49. http://doi.org/10.1007/s12130-999-1026-0

42. Dana Rotman, Jenny Preece, Jen Hammock, et al. 2012. Dynamic changes in motivation in collaborative citizen-science projects. *Proceedings of the ACM 2012 conference on Computer Supported Cooperative Work - CSCW '12*: 217. http://doi.org/10.1145/2145204.2145238

43. Kjeld Schmidt and I Wagner. 2004. Ordering systems: Coordinative practices and artifacts in architectural design and planning. *Computer Supported Cooperative Work (CSCW)* 13: 349–408.

44. Deboarh Schriffin, Deborah Tannen, and Heidi E. Hamilton (eds.). 2008. *The Handbook of Discourse Analysis*. Blackwell.

45. S. Andrew Sheppard, Andrea Wiggins, and Loren Terveen. 2014. Capturing quality. *Proceedings of the 17th ACM conference on Computer supported cooperative work & social computing - CSCW '14*,

ACM Press, 1234–1245. http://doi.org/10.1145/2531602.2531689

46. Jennifer Shirk, Heidi Ballard, Candie Wilderman, et al. 2012. Public participation in scientific research: A framework for deliberate design. *Ecology & Society* 17, 2.

47. Mel Stanfill and Megan Condis. 2014. Fandom and/as labor. *Transformative Works and Cultures* 15.

48. Susan Leigh Star and Anselm Strauss. 1999. Layers of silence, arenas of voice: The ecology of visible and invisible work. *Computer supported cooperative work (CSCW)*, 1995: 9–30.

49. Robert A Stebbins. 1982. Serious leisure: A conceptual statement. *Pacific Sociological Review* 25, 2: 251–272.

50. Rick Szostak. 2008. Classification, interdisciplinarity, and the study of science. *Journal of Documentation* 64, 3: 319–332. http://doi.org/10.1108/00220410810867551

51. Sarah Theimer. 2012. A cataloger's resolution to become more creative: How and why. *Cataloging & Classification Quarterly* 50, 8: 894–902. http://doi.org/10.1080/01639374.2012.711440

52. Katherine Thornton and DW McDonald. 2012. Tagging Wikipedia: collaboratively creating a category system. *Proceedings of the 2012 ACM Conference on Supporting Group Work*, 219–227.

53. Jennifer Trant. 2009. Studying social tagging and folksonomy: A review and framework. *Journal of Digital Information* 10, 1.

54. Tisha Turk. 2014. Fan work: Labor, worth, and participation in fandom's gift economy. *Transformative Works and Cultures* 15. http://doi.org/10.3983/twc.2014.0518

55. Claudia Wagner, David Garcia, Mohsen Jadidi, and Markus Strohmaier. 2015. It's a Man's Wikipedia? Assessing Gender Inequality in an Online Encyclopedia. *The International AAAI Conference on Web and Social Media (ICWSM2015), Oxford, May 2015.*

56. Kangning Wei, Kevin Crowston, NL Li, and B Heckman. 2014. Understanding group maintenance behavior in free/libre open source software projects: The case of Fire and Gaim. *Information & Management* 51, 3: 297–309. http://doi.org/10.1016/j.im.2014.02.001

57. Andrea Wiggins and Kevin Crowston. 2011. From Conservation to Crowdsourcing: A Typology of Citizen Science. *2011 44th Hawaii International Conference on System Sciences*: 1–10. http://doi.org/10.1109/HICSS.2011.207

58. Andrea Wiggins and Kevin Crowston. 2012. Goals and tasks: Two typologies of citizen science projects. *2012 45th Hawaii International Conference on System Sciences*: 3426–3435. http://doi.org/10.1109/HICSS.2012.295

59. Andrea Wiggins. 2013. Free as in puppies: Compensating for ict constraints in citizen science. *Proceedings of the 2013 conference on Computer supported cooperative work - CSCW '13*: 1469–1480.

60. Langdon Winner. 1980. Do artifacts have politics? *Daedalus* 109, 1: 121–136.

61. Dave Yates and Christian Wagner. 2010. Factors affecting shapers of organizational wikis. *Journal of the American Society for Information Science* 61, 3: 543–554. http://doi.org/10.1002/asi.21266

Barriers to Using, Customizing, and Printing 3D Designs on Thingiverse

Celena Alcock
University of Waterloo
200 University Ave. W
Waterloo, ON, N2L 3G1
calcock@uwaterloo.ca

Nathaniel Hudson
University of Waterloo
200 University Ave. W
Waterloo, ON, N2L 3G1
nathaniel.hudson@uwaterloo.ca

Parmit K. Chilana
University of Waterloo
200 University Ave. W
Waterloo, ON, N2L 3G1
pchilana@uwaterloo.ca

ABSTRACT

Thingiverse is the largest 3D design-sharing online community with millions of users. Thingiverse provides a low-barrier-to-entry for exploring 3D printing as users can quickly download premade 3D designs and ask design-specific questions. In this paper, we investigate users' activities on Thingiverse and their conversations by using quantitative and qualitative analyses. Our findings shed light on various barriers in using, customizing, and printing premade 3D designs. The results suggest that although Thingiverse plays a key role in helping users get started with basic 3D printing, there are many opportunities to streamline the design-download-customize-print workflows. In particular, opportunities exist for designers to provide richer metadata, clarifications, and expert tips to help users succeed in printing objects and customizing existing 3D designs.

Keywords

3D communities; Design discussions; Thingiverse; 3D printing;

1. INTRODUCTION

Digital Fabrication has evolved dramatically over the last few years, with an increasing interest in 3D printing among untrained and nontechnical users [3,7,9]. These users face significant difficulties in learning 3D modeling and developing expertise in complex 3D printing workflows. For example, they rarely research the appropriate software to model their design, do very little planning for their design, and have difficulty thinking in 3 dimensions [5]. As an alternative to learning 3D modelling, users often turn to online communities such as *Thingiverse.com* [2] to download and print premade 3D design files. Thingiverse is the largest online 3D modeling community [13] and allows users to share, download, customize and print 3D designs. Thingiverse contains over 1 million 3D designs, has over 2 million active monthly users, and sees 1.7 million downloads per month [13].

Although Thingiverse facilitates the process of sharing 3D designs, both novice and expert users often have a number of questions related to the printability, functionality, or assembly of the resulting 3D objects [6]. One problem is that designers who post 3D designs do not always share details about whether their design will print on a specific 3D printer, what materials would work, or what the machine settings should be [8]. In addition, designers may be new to 3D modelling and may not be actual users of the objects that they design (e.g., in the assistive technology domain [1]). Furthermore, designers rarely document changes to their design files, and if they do, it is usually through a comment which can be overlooked and difficult to decontextualize [11]. Since Thingiverse is largely community-driven, there is currently no formal provision for screening 3D designs to check for potential issues before the designs are shared on the site.

GROUP '16, November 13-16, 2016, Sanibel Island, FL, USA
© 2016 ACM. ISBN 978-1-4503-4276-6/16/11…$15.00

To help users cope with design-specific issues, Thingiverse provides an embedded social platform for users to post comments and questions on individual 3D designs. In fact, a quick inspection of popular designs on Thingiverse shows that some designs have drawn over 200 comments within a span of a few days of being shared. However, despite the growing active user community on Thingiverse, we know little about how users actually make use of this social platform in tackling 3D design and printing tasks. Knowing the content of design-specific comments and questions can help us better understand the kinds of challenges that may exist for end users and how community participation could be improved on platforms like Thingiverse.

In this paper, we investigate users' conversations on Thingiverse to understand their experiences in using, customizing, and printing premade 3D designs. We carried out quantitative and qualitative analyses to systematically explore user activities on Thingiverse and the content of users' questions, comments, and responses. Our main findings reveal 4 key barriers that users faced in understanding: 1) how a given 3D object would be used or assembled in real life; 2) how a design could be customized or remixed; 3) how a 3D object would print on a given 3D printer; and 4) how a 3D design was actually created. Our findings show that although Thingiverse plays an instrumental role in helping users get started with basic 3D printing, there are many opportunities for designers to provide richer metadata, clarifications, and expert tips to help users succeed in printing objects and customizing existing 3D designs. Our primary contribution is in establishing an understanding of the barriers in using, customizing, and printing premade 3D models based on users' conversations on Thingiverse.

2. AN ANALYSIS OF THINGIVERSE

2.1 Research Approach and Data Collection

To understand users' conversations on Thingiverse, we carried out our study in two parts, as described below.

2.1.1 User Activities on Thingiverse

To get a snapshot of various user activities on Thingiverse, we used their API to download metadata for a sample of 23285 designs, design-specific comments (n=22952) and user profiles (n=21893) of the designers and commenters. We randomly selected this sample from public Thingiverse designs in September 2015 and only considered designs that had been available for at least 4 weeks to ensure that users would have had some time to explore the designs. We looked into the different categories of designs that were uploaded on Thingiverse (Table 1), how actively designers and users were commenting on individual designs, the different file types being shared, and to what extent designs were being customized.

2.1.2 Discussions on Thingiverse

Next, we carried out a qualitative analysis to understand the content of users' design-specific conversations in more detail. We used a uniform random sample of 500 designs and the corresponding comments (n=2202) as our dataset, restricting it to Thingiverse uploads that were designed for 3D printing (i.e., excluding designs for laser-cutting) and had at least one comment. To carry out the qualitative analysis, we wrote our own custom web application that displayed comments to be coded in context of the conversation and the 3D printable design, making it easier for us to understand the (often obscure or complex) designs.

2.2 Data Analysis & Classification Scheme

To systematically classify the content of conversations on Thingiverse, we first created a separate random sample of 120 designs with 460 comments. Three of our researchers conducted an open coding analysis [10] to look for frequently occurring topics. While studying design-specific Q&A, we discovered a wide range of posts, from praising the designer for his/her work to requesting links to similar designs, to understanding how to purchase materials needed for printing the design. Furthermore, users contributed a lot of miscellaneous information on extraneous topics, such as comparing printers (unrelated to the design), jokes, and questions about items that were not a part of the design. Using these observations, we iteratively developed our coding scheme until the researchers settled on a list of 8 codes (shown in Table 2).

To assess the reliability of our coding scheme, we extracted a new random sample of 100 Thingiverse designs with 350 comments, and two researchers individually coded each of the comments. To find the overall agreement between coders we computed the Cohen's Kappa score and found strong agreement in the coding of the Thingiverse discussions (κ=0.82).

We applied our final coding scheme to the 2202 comments in our sample (in most cases, we assigned only one code to a comment, with the exception of a few longer comments).

Before presenting our main findings on the barriers that users faced in using, customizing, and printing premade 3D designs, we provide a brief overview of user activities on Thingiverse.

3. USER ACTIVITIES ON THINGIVERSE

3.1 Design Categories Selected by Users

The Thingiverse community is made up of many different types of designs. When designers upload their models to Thingiverse they are required to choose a category that best represents their design, such as art, household, gadgets, 3D printer parts, and tools. In our larger random sample of 23285 designs, we found that the largest number of designs (20.0%) were in the household category, followed by art (14.5%), 3D printing (14.4%), and fashion (9.9%). Table 1 shows all of these categories and commonly shared designs within each category (except the 8.6% of 3D designs that were uploaded to the "Other" category).

Table 1: Top 8 Categories of Designs on Thingiverse

Category	% of sample	Example
Household	20.0%	Toothpaste tube squeezer
Art	14.5%	Vases, replicas of statues
3D Printing	14.4%	Printable 3D printer parts
Fashion	9.9%	Bracelets, keychains, charms
Hobby	8.3%	Parts for RC vehicles
Gadgets	7.2%	Virtual reality headsets
Toys/Games	5.6%	Printable catapult
Models	5.1%	Figurines of characters
Tools	4.8%	Screwdriver handles
Learning	1.7%	Models of human bones

3.2 Types of Files Shared by Users

Thingiverse users have several options for uploading their 3D design files. Although the majority (84.0%) of files in our sample were 3D models in the STL[1] format, we observed 197 different file types in our sample, including source code files, 2D graphics, and spreadsheet files. STL files are only capable of representing 3D triangle meshes and contain no editor metadata, making them very difficult to modify for an inexperienced user compared to a 3D software package's original source files [5]. The next most common file types were dramatically less common: *OpenSCAD* .SCAD files (3.7%), *SketchUp* .SKP (2.0%), and *Solidworks* .SLDPRT files (1.2%). This fragmentation puts users who want to customize a 3D model in a difficult place—even if the 3D design's source file is available, it may be in a format for software that the user is not familiar with or cannot easily access.

3.3 Likes and Comments on Designs

Similar to many social platforms, Thingiverse allows users to "like" designs so that they can build up a collection of favorite designs. Overall, a given 3D design attracted an average of 14.8 likes and 1.0 comment (0.3 comments by the designer who uploaded the design file). Objects in the Models and Toys & Games categories attracted the most likes, with 37.8 and 27.6 likes per design on average, while Fashion-related designs attracted the fewest (6.7 on average). Comment length, which averaged 30.4 words per comment, also varied across categories. Users in the 3D Printing category, for example, wrote longer comments averaging 37.7 words per comment, while users commenting on Art designs wrote the shortest comments (16.5 words on average).

3.4 Remixing and Customizable Designs

One phenomenon of particular interest on Thingiverse is remixing, where a new variation on a design can be created to meet a different set of needs or constraints [8]. For example, an uploaded phone case might be remixed to include a sports team's logo, or an uploaded tripod can be remixed to use metric screws instead of imperial. Remixes may be roughly grouped into two categories: parametric and freeform. Parametric changes consist simply of altering the object's existing parameters, such as changing the diameter or width of the wheels on a car [12]. Conversely, freeform changes involve the addition of entirely new elements to the design, such as changing the wheels on the car to tank treads.

While remixes can be created manually by importing a 3D model into a typical 3D modelling application, Thingiverse also offers the *MakerBot Customizer* tool (Customizer, for short), a built-in web application that allows for limited 3D design remixing. This tool allows objects that have been modeled in a specific manner using *OpenSCAD.org* to be altered in parametric ways, such as changing the diameter of a ring, or the text on a nametag [14]. These changes can only be parametric, not freeform, and must be explicitly specified by the designer of the customizable design in the SCAD file. After the designer has uploaded this customizable design, other

[1] The STL file format is commonly used for 3D printing, and describes a 3D surface built up of triangles. STL files are typically not used natively by 3D software, but are generated to be shared online or processed by the 3D printer [4].

Table 2. Classification of Design-specific Comments

Code	% of sample	Example	Top Category
Understanding Object Functionality	26.78	*"What makes the watch sit up in the cradle?..."*	3D Printing
Understanding Design Customizability	23.94	*"Any chance you can post the .scad file so I can modify it?..."*	Hobby
Praises/ Positive Reports on Designs	17.13	*"it's beautiful"*	Models
Understanding Design Printability	14.50	*"Would you suggest adding exterior, full, or no support?"*	Learning & Models
Miscellaneous Q/A	7.28	*"Nothing to do with your part, but I need to vent!..."*	Fashion
Understanding Design Creation	6.48	*"This is too cool. What did you use to make this?"*	Toys and Games
Discussion on License Choices	3.43	*"You could make the license include no derivatives, but that is not what you selected."*	Gadgets
Insults/ Negative Reports on Design	0.48	*"Man, this part is full of mistakes"*	Toys and Games

users can alter these parameters using a simple web interface to generate 3D printable STL files.

We found that the Customizer tool was popular among users: close to half of all designs (n=10613, 45.6%) in our dataset had been generated using this tool. However, we also found that all of these customized designs were derived from a small number of 1298 unique parent designs. Furthermore, our dataset included only 236 designs (1.0%) that could actually be customized using the Customizer tool. This suggests that only a small number of designers were creating Customizer-compatible designs, but, if they did make such designs available, users were likely to generate a large number of derivatives. These customizable designs also received about 6 times more likes (89.4 likes/object) compared to 14.1 likes/object across the whole repository.

3.5 User Participation in Discussions

Our analysis of individual users who commented on designs revealed that they were highly active on the site, with 89.9% having liked at least one design, and 64.4% having liked 10 or more designs. More surprising, however, was that 84.0% of these commenters had at least one design uploaded to their profile. This suggests that users who participated in design-specific discussions tended to be more experienced with Thingiverse (in fact, 43.8% of commenters had uploaded at least 10 designs).

Based on our qualitative analysis of the 2202 design-specific comments, we have listed the most frequent to least frequent discussion topics within these comments (Table 2). As with activities on other online forums, we observed that people also used the Thingiverse social platform to post miscellaneous comments, insults, and praises. However, we will focus the next part of our results on conversations that were specific to barriers in using premade 3D designs.

4. BARRIERS TO USING PREMADE 3D DESIGNS ON THINGIVERSE

Prior work shows that there are many stages and barriers around creating and printing 3D designs from scratch [2,5] and non-professional users turn to Thingiverse in hopes of getting easy access to premade designs. However, our results show that this path can also present a number of challenges. Below, we highlight 4 key barriers based on users' questions, comments, and requests posted on individual Thingiverse designs. We also discuss the barriers in relation to the categories (Table 1) that users selected to classify their designs on Thingiverse.

4.1 Understanding Object Functionality

Before users download a design from Thingiverse to print, they need to understand what the design is, how it functions, and in some cases, how it would be assembled after printing. In fact, we observed that understanding the functionality and assembly of the object being designed was the most frequently occurring code in our classification (26.8%). For example, a common question asked by users was simply: *"I don't get it. It looks cool but what is it?..."* Other users had more specific questions about the assembly: *"I have not built a core xy printer yet so i am no expert but i have to ask about the belt tension. Don't you need a way to tension each belt [separately] to ensure that they have the same tension?"*.

Although questions about object functionality occurred frequently among all of the categories on Thingiverse, it was the most common type of question in the 3D printing category. Users asked questions such as, *"if I understand how this works shouldn't there be some sort of feedback to the firmware to adjust the bed during print?"*. As might be expected, fewer questions about object functionality were seen within the Art and Models categories, which featured more ornamental and less mechanical designs.

4.2 Understanding Design Customizability

When users were not satisfied with an existing premade 3D design on Thingiverse, they often asked for a remix or customization (i.e., a change in the design file). In fact, questions about customizing or remixing designs were the second most common theme (23.9%) in our sample. For example, users asked for clarification or made specific requests: *"It looks very nice. Can you please release a version that's just one subcube? I think it would be a lot more workable."* Such requests varied from resizing object parts, adding parts onto designs, or modifying functionality of objects. The hobby and household categories had the largest number of such customization requests.

We also observed that a large number (86%) of customization-related comments were about improving or changing the design's functionality and a small number of comments (14%) were about improving the design's printability. These types of discussions involved comments such as *"Nice improvement on my design! Less print time and less plastic!"* and *"It's too tall for a replicator [printer] so it'd have to be split in 2 parts"*.

Our analysis further revealed that discussions around parametric changes such as changing an object's thickness, length, and adding text to the design accounted for 36% of the comments in remixing for custom needs. These types of requests included comments such as, *"[My] Wife has [a] miniature owl collection - I'd like to print a couple half sized ones. Can you provide scaled down versions[?]"* Surprisingly, ,freeform changes (which are not possible through Customizer) accounted for 64% of the remixing comments. Even if designers were to publish Customizer designs, many of the freeform user needs would still be unmet.

Overall, we found that users only received the customizations they asked for about one third of the time (32%) due to several reasons. For example, sometimes users requested designs that were not practical or would not function as well as the original design: *"I just don't know if it will be stable / wobble free and if I have enough clearance for it to rotate."* Other times designers simply did not have time to follow-up to the request: *"It's not hard necessarily, just tough to make it look nice...I just need to find the spare time to make it."* In other instances, designers simply did not respond to requests or users did not follow up to questions about dimensions or other desired features.

4.3 Understanding Design Printability

Another common barrier revealed in the Thingiverse conversations was trouble with understanding how to properly print the 3D design (14.5%). Users often did not know the correct print settings and it was difficult to receive help since different printer models and setups often required different settings. Common printer settings that were asked about included support structures (used to prevent the design from drooping or falling over during printing), infill (the percentage of the model that should be filled in with material when printed), wall thickness, scale, and printer fan speed. For example, one user posted, *"I [am] new to 3d printing and I really like this file. I am still confused on what supporting is and how to do it so that I can successfully print this blade..."* In addition to diagnosing problems and troubleshooting, users asked the designer about what printer they used, what filament was used, and how long it took to slice and print: *"every time I try to print this it starts spitting filament out in the air when it gets past the handle. could somebody tell me what settings they printed this with?"*

Designs within the model category received the most questions on printability, and many of them were on support structures. Surprisingly, the 3D printing category overall had the fewest questions on basic printability.

4.4 Understanding Design Creation

Although users often turn to Thingiverse to download premade models so that they can bypass the complex 3D modelling tasks [5], our analysis showed that many conversations (6.5%) on Thingiverse were actually about learning 3D design. For example, users were often interested in knowing what software was used for the 3D design (*"...how do you make one of these?"*) and some asked for the actual source files for the design (*"Hey, do you happen to still have the model file lying around?"*). Some users described more advanced usage, such as how to extract 3D models from video games, or how to import models into new pieces of software: *"Any tips on how to explode this file in the latest version of Sketchup?"*

As discussed earlier, users upload design files in hundreds of different formats to Thingiverse. Our analysis further showed that users often do not know the difference between file formats: *"I'm just curious as to why some of the files are "stl" and some ".obj", or more specifically, why not all files in one format or the other?"* Other comments revealed users' frustration in attempting to modify STL files: *"I don't understand how one is supposed to convert this into a stl (or other 3d printable file). I've tried inkscape, openscad, and a number of others. Anyone with knowledge, please help!!"* These comments were particularly common in the toys and games category.

5. DISCUSSION

In this paper, we have presented results from our quantitative and qualitative analyses of user activities and their design-specific conversations on Thingiverse. Among our key findings, we found that commenters on Thingiverse were not just consumers of premade 3D models—in fact, a large majority of them (84%) had uploaded at least one design. But, even these more experienced users tended to face a number of barriers in understanding how a design object actually functions, how it will print, how it can be customized, and how it can be designed from scratch.

Our study shows that although Thingiverse has over a million active users, simply making premade models available to download is not enough. For successful 3D design sharing, we see two opportunities for improvement: 1) designers need to provide additional metadata, clarifications, and expert tips to help users succeed in printing objects; and, 2) users need a better understanding of how and when customization is possible (or not possible) with 3D designs so that they can get better access to desired objects.

5.1 Augmenting Premade Designs

Our analysis showed that many users had to resort to asking the designer how the design functioned, what the recommended print settings were, which type of printer was used by the designer, and what software was used to create the design. Other works have also documented these difficulties in terms of understanding print settings [8] and understanding changes to the design [11]. Our findings suggest that there is opportunity to augment premade designs with printability and software-related information. For example, 3D modelling software could provide context on how a given feature may appear when printed. STL files (that are most widely used on Thingiverse) currently lack context on their own—it could be useful for users to access details such as assembly and print instructions through text and pictures. Future research may investigate interchange file types or better sharing systems that also communicate their designs' context within the 3D printing workflow by including details such as how the design is assembled and what print settings have been used for different 3D printers.

5.2 Helping Users with Customization

In spirit, Thingiverse encourages tinkering and all users to create, remix, and share 3D designs. In fact, the Customizer tool was added with the intention that even non-professional users could create customizable objects [13]. As we discussed in our results, about half of our designs had been generated using the Customizer. However, we have also shown several issues with this tool that emerged in our study. For example, users frequently requested remixes that were freeform in nature and not possible through the Customizer tool. However, designers appeared to be stymied by the difficulty of creating for the Customizer platform and shared only a small number of Customizer-ready designs. We observed that Customizer activity was largely driven by a small number of designers who were able to overcome those difficulties.

One potential avenue for research is investigating alternatives to *OpenSCAD's* scripting paradigm that could allow users to create parametric, customizable models through more user-friendly GUI interfaces. This would particularly be useful for non-professional designers who get frequent requests to generate customizable versions of their 3D models but are not well-versed with complex scripting languages. More generally, there is merit in also exploring how users could more clearly see the level of difficulty involved in creating different customizations for a given design.

In conclusion, our analyses of activities and conversations on Thingiverse have shed light on various challenges associated with using premade 3D designs and we have highlighted research opportunities that can help tackle these challenges.

6. ACKNOWLEDGEMENTS

We thank Nehal Gupta, Johnson Kan and Shaun Kane. This work was funded in part by NSERC (Natural Sciences and Engineering Council of Canada).

7. REFERENCES

[1] Erin Buehler, Stacy Branham, Abdullah Ali, Jeremy J. Chang, Megan Kelly Hofmann, Amy Hurst and Shaun K. Kane. 2015. Sharing is Caring: Assistive Technology Designs on Thingiverse. *Proceedings of the 33rd Annual ACM Conference on Human Factors in Computing Systems*, ACM, 525–534.

[2] Erin Buehler, Shaun K. Kane, and Amy Hurst. 2014. ABC and 3D: Opportunities and Obstacles to 3D Printing in Special Education Environments. *Proceedings of the 16th International ACM SIGACCESS Conference on Computers & Accessibility*, ACM, 107–114.

[3] Juan L. Chulilla. 2011. The cambrian explosion of popular 3D printing. *International Journal of Interactive Multimedia and Artificial Intelligence,* 1 (4).

[4] Todd Grimm. 2004. *User's Guide to Rapid Prototyping.* Society of Manufacturing Engineers, Dearborn, MI.

[5] Nathaniel Hudson, Celena Alcock, and Parmit K. Chilana. Understanding Newcomers to 3D Printing: Motivations, Workflows, and Barriers of Casual Makers. *Proceedings of the SIGCHI Conference on Human Factors in Computing Systems*. ACM, 384-396.

[6] Thomas Ludwig, Oliver Stickel, Alexander Boden, and Volkmar Pipek. 2014. Towards Sociable Technologies: An Empirical Study on Designing Appropriation Infrastructures for 3D Printing. *Proceedings of the 2014 Conference on Designing Interactive Systems*, ACM, 835–844.

[7] Catarina Mota. 2011. The Rise of Personal Fabrication. *Proceedings of the 8th ACM Conference on Creativity and Cognition*, ACM, 279–288.

[8] Lora Oehlberg, Wesley Willett, and Wendy E. Mackay. 2015. Patterns of Physical Design Remixing in Online Maker Communities. *Proceedings of the 33rd Annual ACM Conference on Human Factors in Computing Systems*, ACM, 639–648.

[9] Oliver Stickel, Dominik Hornung, Konstantin Aal, Markus Rohde, and Volker Wulf. 2015. 3D Printing with Marginalized Children—An Exploration in a Palestinian Refugee Camp. In *ECSCW 2015: Proceedings of the 14th European Conference on Computer Supported Cooperative Work,* Springer International Publishing, 19-23.

[10] Anselm L. Strauss and Juliet M. Corbin. 1990. *Basics of qualitative research.* Sage, Newbury Park, CA.

[11] Tiffany Tseng and Mitchel Resnick. 2014. Product Versus Process: Representing and Appropriating DIY Projects Online. *Proceedings of the 2014 Conference on Designing Interactive Systems*, ACM, 425–428.

[12] Robert Woodbury. 2010. *Elements of Parametric Design.* Routledge, New York, NY.

[13] Business Wire. 2015. MakerBot Thingiverse Reaches Landmark 1 Million Uploads and 200 Million Downloads. Retrieved February 17, 2016 from http://www.businesswire.com/news/home/20151029005877/en

[14] MakerBot Customizer Developer Documentation. Retrieved February 16, 2016 from http://customizer.makerbot.com/docs

Building Mood, Building Community: Usage Patterns of an Interactive Art Installation

Leah M. Scolere[1], Eric P. S. Baumer[1,2], Lindsay Reynolds[1], Geri Gay[1,2]
[1]Communication Department [2]Information Science Department
Cornell University
498 Mann Library Building
lms43@cornell.edu

ABSTRACT

To examine the processes by which appropriation happens around an interactive art installation in an organizational context, this paper presents a qualitative, longitudinal study of an interactive art installation called *mood.cloud*. While designed to collect and to visually display building occupants' collective emotion, the installation was not necessarily used or interpreted in this way. Instead, building occupants saw the sensory experience of mood.cloud and the ability to change the display as a way to influence their own feelings, the feelings of others, and the overall workplace ambience. We found that interaction with mood.cloud fostered reflection about the relationship between the *individual* and the *larger collective* that the person is a part of. This relationship, between appropriation for individual benefit and appropriation for the benefit of others, afforded participants the opportunity to become more aware of their own contribution as part of a larger community. These findings suggest an opportunity to design systems around the interplay between appropriation for the individual and appropriation for the community.

Keywords

Interactive art installation; interactive computing technology; workplace; mood.cloud; appropriation; mood; individual; community; design

1. INTRODUCTION

Prior work has investigated technology appropriation of everyday devices and artifacts around task work in organizational contexts [e.g., 16,36] as well as creative appropriation of interactive art in museum settings [e.g., 13,24,31]. Less explored is the appropriation and engagement with interactive installations or what Bødker [4] terms the "big, visible artifact" in organizational contexts. Interactive art installations have the potential to foster greater social awareness and connectedness within workplace settings.

In order to explore social awareness around interactive art installations in organizational contexts, an artist and interdisciplinary team created mood.cloud—a color changing LED light installation designed to display the emotion of building occupants. The designers sought to explore two dimensions of interaction around mood: 1) build community by encouraging participants to input their own mood so that it could be displayed to illuminate collective mood and 2) promote a greater sense of emotional awareness of others and their moods. In order to explore these goals around building community and awareness, mood.cloud was deployed in the atrium entry space of Gates Hall, a multi-story building housing computer science and information science at Cornell University. The atrium, where mood.cloud was installed, is a visible public space housing a coffee shop that is open not only to building occupants but also to the greater public.

In this paper we present a qualitative, longitudinal study of the mood.cloud installation. This study asks: how does engagement with mood.cloud build a sense of awareness of oneself and others in a community?

We examine the multifaceted ways that mood.cloud was used and appropriated by participants. We found that interaction with mood.cloud fostered reflection about the relationship between the *individual* and the *larger collective* of which that the person is a part. We examine this interplay between the individual and the collective along three dimensions: 1) interaction processes 2) awareness of and connection with others, and 3) design implications.

Mood was taken up in a variety of way in which participants reflected on their own mood and how mood was interpreted and communicated by others. Alternately, some participants felt empowered to appropriate mood.cloud to claim space and contribute to something larger. Finally, interaction with mood.cloud fostered reflection about the spatial context and design speculation about new ideas for the installation.

These findings suggest an opportunity to design systems for this interplay between the individual and larger community.

2. RELATED WORK

This study seeks to bring together appropriation literature with interactive installation literature to understand the implications of deploying interactive art installations in organizational contexts on building social awareness and community.

2.1 Appropriation & Interactive Installations

With the increase of ubiquitous technologies, physical spaces are becoming more interactive and designers are experimenting with technologically-driven interactive environments [12]. While these interactive environments span various lifestyle areas from work to leisure, to cultural experiences, *interactive art installations* are a specific type of design which focuses on "providing an experience that is outside of an everyday experience" instead of focusing on function and utility ([32], p.509).

We are interested in the unique focus on "pleasure over function," ([32], p.509) of interactive art installations when they are situated in organizational contexts. While previous work has focused on how playful technology interventions have positively impacted workplace interaction and social cohesiveness [19], our study

GROUP '16, November 13 - 16, 2016, Sanibel Island, FL, USA

ACM 978-1-4503-4276-6/16/11...$15.00
DOI: http://dx.doi.org/10.1145/2957276.2957291

focuses specifically on an interactive art installation. mood.cloud combines interactive computing technology with art to bring experiential interactivity to a workplace setting.

Appropriation is commonly understood as the process by which people adapt technologies for unintended purposes [16] or the ways that users adapt and "integrate technology into their everyday practices" [9]. Similar to Dourish's [16] notion of thinking about appropriation as creation and communication of meaning, we take the position that appropriation is not only about using a tool for an unintended *function* but also the tool or artifact taking on *meanings* that the designer didn't anticipate.

Given that appropriation affords users a sense of control and ownership, changes environment dynamics, and allows for situatedness, it can be beneficial to *design for appropriation* [15]. The designers of mood.cloud leveraged principles of openness such as allowing for interpretation, providing visibility, exposing intentions, and encouraging sharing and learning to make it more likely that users will appropriate the design intervention [15]. For example, the role of the designer in appropriation can be to create a "seamful design" that seeks to expose the opportunities in the design for alternate uses [10]. Similarly, *ambiguity* in the design can encourage the user to make meaning out of the design and interpret how to use it [20,39]. We are inspired by the potential new ways that technologies are taken up by users because we view these new meanings and functions as a form of *creativity* [36] which may influence the design of new innovations or *design from appropriation* [9].

Figure 1. mood.cloud interactive art installation.

Appropriation studies have examined task-oriented technologies and artifacts in terms of phases of appropriation [9], user experience phases over time [28], and dynamic artifact ecologies [5]. While these studies provide a strong foundation for understanding appropriation of common, familiar artifacts, we draw on user engagement studies around interactive installations in order to better understand appropriation of big, visible artifacts such as interactive art installations. Interactive art installations are a unique type of technology intervention because of both their spatiality and materiality which engages a variety of senses and provides an immersive and configurable experience for participants [26, 27].Mathew, Rogers, & Lloyd [31] categorize user engagement with public installations in three high-level phases: *perception*, *interaction*, and *engagement*. Jacucci et al., [26] identified three phases of exploration with interactive art installation: 1) *circumspection* which describes how a new user observes and then decides how to begin interacting, 2) *testing* which describes the how the user explores the installation and 3) *play* where the participant begins to creatively interact and provoke the installation after figuring out the "working principle" of the interactive piece (p. 70). The phases that Jacucci et al., [26] put forth for interacting with art installations are micro-phases of interaction within a compressed time frame of three days rather than more long-term observations. mood.cloud offers an opportunity to understand interaction and appropriation over a longer period of time— in a more longitudinal way.

2.2 Participation

Studies of interactive installations in museum settings have pointed to interactive group participation [24] and the ways people collectively participate in configuring space for each other through their participation [41]. More recently the focus has shifted to interaction that is both individual as well as collective [5,18] where participants created various types of unintended meaning through their participation and appropriation ranging from forms of artistic expression to social media-type posts around user-generated content.

Rather than focusing on individual or group interaction, this study seeks to understand interrelated motivations to participate and appropriate for the benefit of one's self (individual) and for the benefit of the community. While motivation to participate for one's own benefit ("me-regarding") and for the benefit of others ("thee-regarding") motivations have been discussed in relation to online communities and sharing economies [29], we apply that thinking about online communities to offline user motivations to understand appropriation in the context of interactive installations.

mood.cloud is a type of installation which invites users to contribute to the display by inputting their mood. Studies about interactive installations that rely on user-generated content give us insight into user engagement and motivation to participate. Unlike the traditional museum exhibits that consider engagement around an installation in a more finite way, interaction design in more public settings outside of the museum aims for "extended and repeated engagement" ([25] p. 135). Hornecker & Stifter [25] suggest that designing for "creative, communicative, and personal" interaction in interactive art installations will increase engagement. Others such as Morrison, Viller, and Mitchell [32] suggest the importance of designing in opportunities for "free play" in open-ended interactive art installations that give participants the opportunity to actively construct their own meaning (p. 2335). Mathew, Rogers & Lloyd [32] argue that these "social constructions of user-generated and collaborative content" are a kind of "public creativity" (p. 61). Interactive visualization interventions also play a role in fostering social awareness of others [13].

3. MOOD.CLOUD INSTALLATION

mood.cloud is an *interactive data as art installation* (Figure 1) in the atrium entry space of a multi-story college campus building housing computer science and information science. The installation was designed as a collaboration by a media artists and information scientists to explore collective mood in public spaces. More specifically, mood.cloud was designed to explore the impact of a large interactive art display on emotional awareness and feelings of connectedness among people who work in the same physical space. In other words, the designers sought to explore two dimensions of interaction: 1) build community by encouraging participants to input mood so that it could be displayed to illuminate collective mood and 2) promote a greater sense of emotional awareness of others and their moods. How does a visual indicator of collective mood affect the sense of connectedness and emotional awareness of others in an organizational context?

The mood.cloud installation is made up of two key components: 1) *the light cloud sculpture* suspended in space 2) the *interface*-composed of iPad touchscreen mounted on a kiosk directly in front of mood.cloud (Figure 1).

The art installation itself is composed of twenty-four strands composed of 4,320 LED lights twisted in a mobius-like form, and shaped through custom laser-cut, clear acrylic guide pieces, suggesting the image of a cloud. The installation is suspended 5.5 feet off the ground via a supporting beam. The strands of LED lights are encased in clear, flexible PVC tubing wrapped with translucent mesh cable wrap for added texture. The iPad touchscreen shows a collection of images that correspond to emotions. The user selects an image that best captures his or her mood and an algorithm translates it into a color, one of sixteen possible colors, which briefly flashes over the entire sculpture. After the brief flash of color, that same color is displayed on the lowest individual LED light strand of the suspended sculpture.

Up to twenty-four people can enter an image, capturing the collective emotions across an array of 16 colors reflected in mood.cloud (Figure 2). As subsequent users select an image, the bottom LED strand refreshes with the most current color selection and moves up as more users participate, capturing and reflecting collective input from the users (Figure 4).

Figure 2. Participant interacting with PAM interface.

3.1 Software and Input Interface

3.1.1 Software Processing

The LED lights are controlled via Processing[1], run on a mini computer located in a clear acrylic box located directly beneath mood.cloud. When someone selects an image using PAM (described below), that selection is sent to a database, which is fed into Processing and represented as color. The output from Processing is sent to a Teensy Board, which then controls the color and animation of the lights.

3.1.2 Mood.cloud Interface: Photographic Affect Meter (PAM)

The mood.cloud leverages the Photographic Affect Meter (PAM) as the input interface. Designed for mobile devices, PAM is a tool that measures affect through users' selection of photos based on their mood [35]. The photos that are the basis of this tool are validated to represent emotions where each individual emotion is consistently represented in the same location. However, each individual emotion can be represented by three to four photos. More specifically, the photos are mapped in a 4 x 4 grid based on arousal and valence, from low arousal and negative valence in the bottom left corner, to high arousal and positive valence in the upper right corner [35]. When a person selects an image, the screen refreshes, and the photo that displays for that emotion is randomly selected. PAM has also been used in Mood Rhythm (moodrhythm.com), a smart phone app that helps bipolar patients track their daily fluctuations in mood. When people approach the mood.cloud iPad touchscreen, the PAM interfaces asks them to "touch the photo that best captures how you feel right now" and users can select from several screens of photos that range from cuddly puppy photos to a serene landscape photo or an image of a lightning storm (Figure 3).

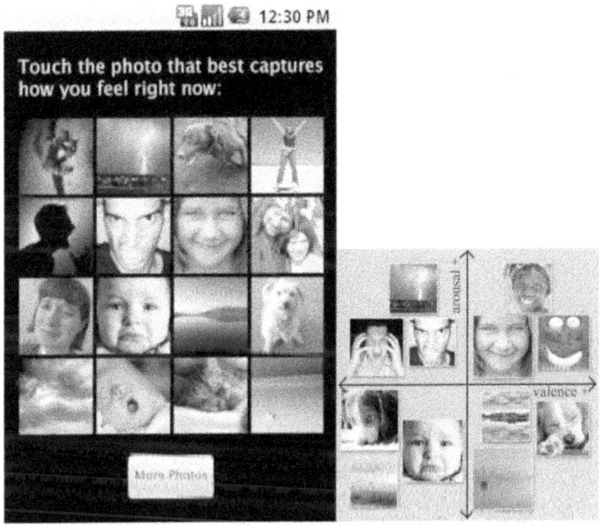

Figure 3. PAM Interface as mobile app

4. METHOD

In order to study the way people understand the mood.cloud installation, we used an interpretivist and naturalistic framework [30]. This framework allows us to gain insight into how users understand and interpret their own interaction with the mood.cloud installation. Additionally, this framework gives us the opportunity to examine more broadly users' assumptions, understandings, and spatial experiences related to their mood.cloud interaction.

4.1 Recruitment

We were concerned with understanding how people interacted with mood.cloud over time so we conducted two phases of interviews: 1) *early phase* of *intercept interviews* within a couple months of the

[1] For more information refer to https://processing.org/

mood.cloud being installed and 2) *later phase* of *in-depth interviews* that took place between seven to eight months after mood.cloud was installed. The intercept interviews were conducted as people finished interacting with mood.cloud. We employed multiple recruitment strategies for the in-depth interviewees. Undergraduate and graduate students who interacted with mood.cloud were recruited from an on campus web-based recruitment system. In addition to students, we recruited the baristas who worked in the coffee shop adjacent to mood.cloud installation as well as university staff and faculty who interacted with mood.cloud through a snowball sample. While understanding how and why individuals do not interact with technology represents an important research area [37,1], the scope of this study focuses specifically on those who interacted directly with mood.cloud rather than randomly sampling from building occupants at large.

4.2 Data Collection & Analysis

After mood.cloud was installed in September of 2014, we conducted a total of 57 interviews. We conducted 32 *intercept interviews* during the fall of 2014 between October and December of 2014. The brief intercept interviews focused primarily on general impressions of the installation and having the user describe their process of interacting with the display—frequency of use, motivations for how and why they chose images, visual of the display, their interpretations of the relationship between the color they chose and the colors already present in the display, the relationship between the images and emotions, and any problem areas with their interaction.

Figure 4. Each LED strand represents an emotion entered by a participant.

Then between March and April of 2015, we conducted 25 semi-structured *in-depth interviews*. The in-depth interviews were intended to supplement the initial impressions and quick descriptions that were collected through the early intercept interviews. The participants included 4 staff members (2F, 2M—2 coffee baristas and 2 university staff members), 5 faculty members (1F, 4M) and 16 students (10F, 6M). The majority of the interviewed students are in communication and information science with the remaining sample representing computer science, design, nutrition, and interdisciplinary studies. The interviews ranged from approximately 30 to 45 minutes and were conducted in person. The interviews were audio recorded and transcribed to ensure accuracy. Participants are referred to either by pseudonym or by participant number throughout the paper. This study was granted IRB permission by the authors' institutional review board.

The interview questions for the in-depth interviews incorporated the process and motivation questions from the intercept interviews and expanded the interview guide in order to allow for the participants to reflect more deeply about not only their experiences with mood.cloud but also to think about the spatial context and representation of their interactions with the installation. Overall, we structured the questions and the overall interview as "open ended process reflection questions" ([11] p. 679) that would encourage the participants to reflect on their own usage and interaction.

The interviews focused on three areas: *impressions, expectations, and description* and included questions about their first interaction with mood.cloud, motivations for use, expectations about the interaction, description of mood.cloud to someone who was unfamiliar with it, and to speculate about how the users might name or title the installation based on their own interaction with it. *Interaction Process* questions focused on the process of interacting with mood.cloud and the users' reflection on that process (how they made decisions, their interpretations of those decisions). *Awareness of others and Connectedness with others* questions focused on the users' thoughts about how their experience with the installation related to other users. *Context, Representation, and Sense of Place* questions focused on how the users thought about the spatial context of the installation in the building, the fit with the building, and speculation about how they might think about the installation differently if it were installed in a different building or context on campus. The last part of the interview gave participants an opportunity to bring up any additional items related to their interaction with mood.cloud and experiences that may not have come up explicitly through our interview questions.

Drawing on grounded theory [22] we approached data collection and analysis as an iterative process, moving continuously back and forth between collecting data and analyzing the data using a "constant comparative method" (p.102). Our ongoing analysis of the initial interview transcripts allowed us to follow up on emerging themes in subsequent interviews, so as to continue to refine the categories and emerging themes during the data collection process. We used a visual mapping technique called *"affinity diagramming"* [3] where initial findings were put onto post-it notes as a physical tool to identify the emerging clusters and groupings of information from the interviews based on the original interview categories. The original broad affinities about participants' reported mood.cloud interaction included: how and when they interacted with the mood.cloud (context), expectations, impressions and why (motivations, intentions), spatial understandings, and their perceptions, speculations and reflections (meanings). We continued interviewing, analyzing transcripts and consulting the literature. From this process, we identified initial emerging themes including awareness of others through participation, publicness of participation, temporality and representation of data, and frequency of change and novelty.

5. FINDINGS

While mood.cloud was designed to explore *collective* mood, this study finds that interaction with mood.cloud prompted participants to reflect on the relationship between the *individual* and the *collective*. Users expressed an awareness of this interplay between self and the larger community: 1) Individual- *How did mood.cloud influence me?* and 2) Collective- *How does my use of mood.cloud influence others? How do others interpret my use of mood.cloud?* Rather than explicitly talking about collective mood, many participants expressed greater awareness of a larger community through individual participation in the interactive art installation.

We examine the multifaceted ways that mood was interpreted and deployed by a community of participants in an organizational context. We found that interaction with mood.cloud fostered reflection about of the relationship between the *individual* and the *larger collective* that the person is a part of. This interplay between the individual and the collective can be examined in three dimensions of use: 1) interaction processes 2) awareness of others & connectedness with others, and 3) design implications.

First, we present an overview of how users interacted with, interpreted, and appropriated mood.cloud. Then, we examine the ways users' interaction with mood.cloud fostered an awareness of oneself and others within the community. Finally, we illustrate the ways participants reflected on the spatial context and imagined new design ideas for mood.cloud.

5.1 Interaction Processes

Participants interacted with, interpreted, and appropriated mood.cloud in multi-faceted ways that help us to understand how people make sense of and orient themselves toward each other around an interactive installation in an organizational context.

5.1.1 Discovering mood.cloud

The first impression for twenty-three people who interacted with mood.cloud was that it was a mix between art, humans, and technology with it being referred to as "an art piece," "sculpture," "someone's art," "weird art thing," as well as a "brain." Several people discussed the way that the installation combined art and intelligence because it communicated information and was not just purely aesthetic.

> It is an interesting art piece. It combines two things. It's a display piece but it tells you something. It's not just there to make the space look nice. It's also there to tell you information, which is not what most art pieces do. (James, undergraduate student)

Others saw mood.cloud as an invitation to interact and explore. One participant described how the form of mood.cloud encouraged exploration.

> I like the shape. It has this very lively feeling similar to when you think of a butterfly. It has that feeling. The shape makes me want to interact with it. (Terry, Female, undergraduate student)

Jacucci & Wagner [27] describe the importance of materiality to engage the senses. Similarly, the sculptural form combined with the tactile quality of the strings of color-changing lights created a dynamic feature at the entry of Gates Hall.

The mood.cloud installation was perceived as embodying, and catalyzing conversations about, the work being done in the building. A coffee barista observed how mood.cloud had become a "conversation piece" for building occupants. Similarly, one faculty member described how mood.cloud "creates lots of conversation." We observed a number of students, faculty, and staff referring to mood cloud as a way to communicate their collective identity as part of the computer science and information science disciplines and the work being done in the building. For many, mood.cloud became a spatial representation of how to communicate their disciplinary identity to others. For example, one faculty member described how mood.cloud has become a "reflection of a value system, something we all value and who we are in the building."

Similarly, visitors to the building or students who took an occasional class in the building (as opposed to those who regularly occupied the building) talked about mood.cloud in a way that helped them make sense out of the identity of those who regularly occupied the building—a kind of spatial shorthand for the identity of those in the building.

5.1.1.1 Use Over Time

The observations and interviews that took place over the course of eight months give us the opportunity to understand engagement with the interactive installation in a more longitudinal way. The very name of the interactive art installation, the way the piece was discussed by the Dean, and the instructions on the display all communicated explicitly to users that they should select images based on how they were feeling and that mood.cloud was designed to *display* collective mood. Based on the early intercept interviews completed within a few months of mood.cloud being installed, 20 of the 32 people interviewed reported that they selected images based on how they were feeling. Eight of those participants described initially selecting images as instructed. Informants reported that they later experimented with mood.cloud, selecting images by finding their "favorite image," "trying something novel," and "trying to get a change to occur." These interactions of experimenting with mood.cloud can be understood in terms of Jacucci et al.'s [26] experimental stage wherein users strive to figure out the "working principle"(p.70) of the interactive piece. With mood.cloud, that working principle entails how the images related more specifically to color change and the way that users understood where their corresponding color selection showed up in the display.

Over time, participants began to select images based on things *other than mood or emotion*. In fact, six months later only 8 of twenty-five in-depth interviewees reported interacting with mood.cloud around their own mood. The majority of participants moved beyond the intended interaction and began creatively to play with and to provoke the installation. For example, one faculty member expressed the sentiment that when he interacted with the installation that he "just pushed buttons to see what would happen and thought it was cool." He described how he "didn't really think about emotions" and "didn't associate mood cloud with emotions as much as thinking about it as an art piece." Another participant described how achieving color change was the most compelling aspect of the installation.

> I like seeing many colors so I think selecting based on how I feel would be less enjoyable than seeing a changing kaleidoscope. (Intercept Interview, Undergraduate)

While mood.cloud was originally designed to collect and visually display the collective emotions of building occupants, for many participants, their interaction with mood.cloud evolved over time with the materiality and sensory experience of the installation becoming most engaging.. Several participants saw their interaction with mood.cloud as a way to influence their own mood—how they *would like* to feel. One undergraduate discussed how she interacted with mood.cloud based on how she "wants to feel" instead of how she actually feels in the moment. Another undergraduate, Sarah, expressed a similar sentiment about how she goes to mood.cloud "to cheer up, not to express the mood that I'm actually feeling." For Sarah, it is about personal play with mood.cloud to boost her own mood. Finally, a faculty member described how "the changing colors make me feel happier." In this way, the sensory experience of color change took precedence over the ostensible focus on mood.

The most recent interviews and observation suggest that, for participants who were in the building on a daily basis, mood.cloud increasingly began to "blend in." When asked what he had noticed over time, a barista noted that mood.cloud has "become a little background for people." A number of participants described how more and more they observed campus visitors and campus tour groups being the primary users of the mood.cloud. One faculty member described how "people in the building show it to guests" and how he "started watching others using it" in lieu of using it himself.

5.1.2 Interpreting Others' Use

Users perceived, and took advantage of, the openness of mood.cloud. This came through in the way that sixteen of the twenty-five interviewees felt empowered to interact with mood.cloud in ways unintended by the designers. In fact, even those who took very seriously the idea of trying to evaluate accurately and input their own mood tended to assume, through their own interaction and observation of mood.cloud, that others were *not selecting images based on mood*. For example, one barista described his observations of how people interact with mood.cloud.

> I'm not sure a lot of people pick the emotion that they feel. Some people pick the picture they like (Male, Barista).

An undergraduate, James, expressed how he carefully considers his mood and "wants to do good by trying to put the right mood in." Yet, at the same time he expressed frustration with the openness of the system.

> The idea that people can just keep pushing buttons kind of defeats the purpose but you don't want to restrict people to only once. (James, Male, Undergraduate)

James tried to follow the instructions and enter mood but ultimately didn't understand the purpose of entering mood or how that might impact others. The sentiment that James expressed illustrates the tension between how designers intended mood.cloud to be used, how participants actually used it, how their use is interpreted by others, and how that interpretation influences future use and meaning making. Other participants expressed more explicitly the openness that they perceived was built into mood.cloud.

> I think this display is exploratory. People are like "oh I wonder what this picture will do." It isn't regulated. I would think the person is experimenting with it. If you had to pick exactly how you feel then that would be different (Nicole, Female, Graduate Student).

The perceived interpretive flexibility and ambiguity of mood.cloud encouraged creative use and active meaning making. However, at the same time this same ambiguity and openness led to uncertainty about how to make sense about others' interactions and use, especially when it came to how to interpret the emotions, feelings, and well-being of others. Fourteen of the twenty-five in-depth interview participants discussed how they wanted less interpretive flexibility. Specifically, seven participants mentioned how they wanted more clarity around trends and patterns to understand how others were feeling.

> I want to be able to see how many people are feeling happy. (Female, Undergraduate)

> I want more of an awareness of trends. Perhaps a poll of the day to show collective mood. (Sam, Male, Graduate Student)

> I would like a key or a legend—for example, yellow means happiness and a lot of people are happy because the sun is out. (Megan, Female, Undergraduate)

These comments indicate how some participants wanted more prescription and less interpretive flexibility. When asked to reflect on future interaction and re-engaging with the installation, users talked about how their individual participation could benefit others' emotions. Three participants discussed how they would more actively contribute if they knew the installation could *improve the mood of others* or "boost people's interaction with each other." A graduate student described how knowing more about the installation, would make him more likely to contribute to influence the mood of others"

> If I knew what a color represented, then if I were to see a blue or sad color, then I would actively contribute to make it not as sad. (Terry, Male, Graduate Student)

> I would interact with it more if I knew it was helping research or helping others or if I knew that the mood.cloud could make you happier. I don't know if that has been determined? (Rachel, Female, Graduate Student)

Similarly, one undergraduate student, Terry, described how, if she knew a certain color would make people happier, then she would try to change the color to make people feel happier.

> T: Does orange mean everyone is happy? If I can tell how to change the color, then I would try to boost the collective mood. If I know that making it more orange is happier, then I would try to do it. If I were to see a sad color, then I would actively contribute to make it not as sad. (Terry)
>
> Interviewer: Why would you want to do that?
>
> Terry: It's human nature. You don't want to see everyone around you sad.

For this participant and others, knowing how their contributions could benefit others would make them more motivated to engage continuously with mood.cloud over time. While the ambiguity afforded participants the ability to construct their own meaning around their interaction and others' interactions with mood.cloud, it left a number of participants wanting more clarity around how their interaction might influence the mood of others. Ultimately, the idea that one could potentially *influence mood* by interacting with technology was very intriguing to a number of participants. Building occupants had high expectations around mood.cloud and wanted, as Brianna stated, to be able to "boost mood."

5.1.3 Appropriating mood.cloud

Within HCI/CSCW literature, appropriation is a process by which people adapt technologies for purposes that were not originally intended by the designer [9,15,16,36]. Appropriation is not only about using a tool for an unintended function but also the tool or artifact taking on a meaning that the designer did not anticipate. As such, appropriation is not a singularly defined process. Participants were simultaneously motivated to appropriate mood.cloud for their own individual benefit as well as for the benefit of others—the larger community.

For many participants, their interaction with mood.cloud evolved over time with the materiality and spatiality of the installation becoming most engaging—the ability to manipulate, experiment, and play with the color of mood.cloud in space.

> The in-person effect is more significant. You are standing right there and the colors shine in on your face. The whole atmosphere is different. There is something more special about it being in front of you and you seeing the colors change. (Nicole, Female, Undergraduate)

Rather than solely using mood.cloud to input emotion, a number of users saw their interaction with the mood.cloud as an outlet to exert influence and leave one's mark within the building. These individuals viewed the installation as an opportunity to exert control or a form of personal expression.

Some of the participants described their interaction with mood.cloud as a way to exert control on the physical environment—a type of *claiming space*. Greg, a graduate student, described how he interacted with mood.cloud in order to *"prove to myself that I still have control over things."* Participants, such as Greg, saw contribution as a way to exert control and help construct the space through changing the color of mood.cloud. In this way, it is both about changing the way the environment looks and feels as well as interaction being a way to adapt and shape the environment.

Similarly, a faculty member described how he likes to use mood.cloud to exert influence.

> I like the dynamics of the colors. I wanted to see how I could influence them. It makes me so happy when I can see the different colors flow through after interacting with mood.cloud (Male, Faculty)

For this participant, the affordance of color manipulation and feedback of seeing one's own strand turn color provides an outlet for influence and personal expression. This perception of control is key to the processes of appropriation and the way that these appropriations contribute to the shaping of space [2].

Similarly, several of the participants discussed how they liked to interact with mood.cloud in order to influence the *color of the surrounding space* by manipulating the color of mood.cloud installation, especially at night in the all glass building.

> At night, the colors of the mood.cloud change the color in the floor. It becomes more powerful and has a greater presence in the space around it. (Greg, Male, Graduate Student)

For this participant, the installation became a way to creatively manipulate the physical environment through light and color on the various architectural surfaces of the interior of the building. The installation was appropriated for a kind of individual *"free play"* [32] with the building surfaces of glass, concrete, and blank walls acting as a canvas for this *public creativity* [31]

Another user mentioned the power of changing the display at the beginning of the day. The baristas who work at the adjacent coffee shop expressed a shared a sense of ownership over mood.cloud and the atrium space. One barista, Molly, described her routine for interacting with the mood.cloud each morning.

> Interviewer: Have you interacted with it?
>
> Molly: Yes, we usually do every time we come in the building early in the morning. We open at 7:15 and the building is usually empty when we open. I like to push the buttons and my goal is to see it all yellow.
>
> Interviewer: Why do you do it? How do you think about that?
>
> Molly: It seems like a fun way to start the day when I first come into the building. Also, knowing that there is nobody else here— So, I wonder, am I the first person of the day to use it?

For Molly, there is a sense of control that comes from changing the ambience of the space. For both Molly and Greg, this sort of presence [21] through the interactive technology of mood.cloud suggests that their interaction with mood.cloud increased their awareness of others within the building. In other words, their appropriation is an interplay between their individual use and their simultaneous awareness of the larger community of participants.

Like Molly, another building occupant, Daria, expressed her motivation in interacting with mood.cloud to change the color of the entire display when no one else in around or when a specific, intended audience is around.

In each of these examples, the participants describe the personal value they get from changing the space through the mood.cloud installation for their benefit and the benefit of others. People's perception of control is key to appropriation and "tailoring culture"([2], p.65). For these participants, mood.cloud became a way of exerting control and shaping space. The designers of mood.cloud intended the installation to bring people together around collective mood. Instead, participants had an increased awareness of the relationship between themselves as individuals and the larger community through participation in mood.cloud around meaning and usage outside of emotion.

5.2 Awareness and Connection

Rather than explicitly discussing feelings of collective emotion, many participants became more aware of their community through individual contribution to mood.cloud.

5.2.1 Awareness of Self, Awareness of Others

The intersection of *personal* interaction within a *public* space afforded by the installation fostered self-reflection and an awareness of others. Several faculty members expressed the ways in which they thought of mood.cloud as an "outlet" and "a place for expression."

> I used it like a diary. I keep a diary and this was another way to reflect on my own personal feelings. For me, it was a very private thing. (Male, Faculty)

This faculty member used the interactive art piece as a kind of *personal reflection tool* about his own thoughts and emotions and created a routine around this use. Yet at the same time, he described an awareness of the others through his interaction with mood.cloud.

> I see an awareness of others or the people in the display where you add your emotions and it snakes through the lights. It is connected to the emotions of others in an interesting way (Male, Faculty)
>
> It is very individual at first and then when you step back from it you start to see how all the colors interact and you have this appreciation of all the people who came together to create the final impression (Kate, Female, Undergraduate)

For these participants, interaction with mood.cloud was both *personal and public*. Interaction with the mood.cloud provided a powerful visual reminder of the relationship between one's own participation and the other members of the community who helped to co-create the visualization. Significantly, since color change happened frequently, the three-dimensional visualization fostered reflection about the presence of others—traces of others who had just interacted with mood.cloud.

5.2.1.1 Awareness & Publicness of Emotions

A small subset of the in-depth interview participants, who reported using mood.cloud to input their own emotions, reflected on how self conscious they were about entering their personal emotions in a public and highly visible space.

> Participant: If there was no one in the building, I would play with it more.
>
> Interviewer: Is it more comfortable at night or with no one around for you to linker around with it?
>
> Participant: Yes, currently there is the coffee crowd and the main entrance path. There are so many people and so much activity around. The question is how public should it be? I want to interact with something that I know is public and I want to feel better but do I want everyone to know the change of color is reflecting *my* mood? (Greg, Male, Graduate Student).

Another graduate student, Kurt, discussed how he preferred the second iPad interface location that was temporarily placed in the coffee shop, a slight distance away from the installation because then people didn't immediately associate the input of emotion and subsequent color change with the person in front of the display.

> People used to interact with it in groups. So I was scared because people were actually looking at me while I was interacting with the mood cloud. I didn't want to pick a bad mood. I was self- conscious. I liked the other interface location that was in the coffee shop. It is more personal and people don't know what I am doing or what emotion I am choosing. People aren't looking at me and judging me. (Kurt, Male, Graduate Student)

In addition to the more general "evaluation apprehension" of being judged while interacting with a public installation [34,8], these participants have a concern about the personal nature of the specific type of content that they are revealing in their interaction. This suggests that the act of sharing emotion, perceived as personal and private in an organizational context, made some participants more aware of the relationship between their own emotions and the way they were perceived and interpreted by the larger community of which they are a part.

5.2.2 Connectedness Through Contribution

A number of the users saw the act of interacting with mood.cloud as a form of participation where their contributions made them feel like they were part of the larger community. Rachel mentioned how she felt "good to see you contributed to this campus collective mood. You feel like you are a part of it, part of Cornell." Similarly, Roger described both the individual and collective aspects of contributing.

> I really like the part where people are coming here and making a contribution. People make it a pretty thing and unique and I like that perspective. (Roger, Male, Graduate Student)

For these participants, contributing made them more *aware* of the larger community that they were a part of—whether that be their colleagues within the building or the university. Several others described how contributing made them feel a part of a larger imagined creative community.

> I think it is the idea of having something that is individual and collective. All these things are their own separate entities and people can affect them separately but it is overall masterpiece that has the impact when you are looking at this weird art sculpture thing. (Kate, Female Undergraduate Student)

> It is the feeling like you added to the display, not like an artist but as a participant toward the artist's work. (Megan, Female, graduate student).

These participants pointed to the way that the physical form of mood.cloud and the visualization of mood communicated this relationship of between the individual and the larger collective. Instead of seeing mood.cloud as being about the display of mood, Megan viewed her interaction with mood.cloud as a way to creatively contribute to the art piece. Megan's interaction is about seeing herself as a participant in an ongoing creative installation by an artist, similar to Mathew, Rogers & Lloyd's [31] notion of "public creativity" around user-generated content.

Several users pointed to their *connection* to others through their individual interaction with mood.cloud. When asked what the display represents, users described the connection they perceived through their interaction with the display.

> I would almost call it a *mood web* or like a *mood quilt* even because I feel like it is a quilt or a web in that it is a connection of fibers that are all working together for one common purpose but have their own little independent flair. (Kate, Female, Undergraduate)

> It is about connectedness. It's like a lot of little balls on a string. You impact one with color and then all of us is part of the community and each one of us contributes. A tap on the display means a change in light. That sense of community is strong in the display and how you are a part of it by little actions. It is this idea that you are in it together and that sense of community and being a team is inherent in this interaction. (Greg, Male Graduate Student)

These participants see their actions as oriented around a highly visible artifact that strengthened their perceived sense of community. For these users, the aspects of both individual participation and collective participation were communicated in the three-dimensional visual representation of the display and fostered a sense of connection with the larger imagined community.

5.3 Design Implications and Speculations

Williams, Kabisch & Dourish [41] argue that "people configure space for each other" and make certain artifacts and activities "seeable" (p.7). Through their interaction with mood.cloud users made the spatial field and building architecture more *"seeable."* Users reflected on the role of mood.cloud within the spatial context and its impact on the mood of the space. Additionally, some users imagined and generated new ideas for mood.cloud.

5.3.1 Reflection on Spatial Context & Mood of Space

The interaction with mood.cloud resulted in the development of new meaning making about the *mood of the space*. While users didn't always think about *their own* feelings and mood related to the installation, through their interaction with mood.cloud participants began to notice *how the space feels*—the mood, atmosphere, and ambience of the physical environment in Gates Hall.

Overall participants described the building architecture as "innovative and modern" and used descriptive terms such as "technology, novel, imaginative, interactive, futuristic, high techy design, smooth, clean lines, and the most technologically advanced building on campus" to describe Gates Hall. Roger, a graduate student, noted how "Gates Hall gives you the feeling of technology and innovation." In many ways, users perceived the form and materiality of mood.cloud as fitting with this high tech vocabulary of the building architecture.

However, the modern and high tech statement of the building architecture was experienced very differently on the scale of the everyday user of the interior spaces. Some users described a spatial contrast that they saw between the spaces of the building and the installation.

> Gates Hall is futuristic and the outside is razory so the warmer colors like yellow and orange of the display make it warm. The design of the display is more circular instead of sharp. I like that contrast of the display with the building (Nicole, Female, Undergraduate Student).

A small number of the undergraduate and graduate student participants described the feeling of the workspace as "not that comfortable", "for work only," "nothing that is warm or inviting," "empty," "kind of scary," and "stressful." One participant noted that "there could be more excitement within the building" and that it "doesn't have much color—all white with glass doors" and that the "furniture is really rough edged." Overall, a majority of the participants saw mood.cloud as making a spatial contribution by adding color, warmth, visual contrast, and liveliness. One faculty member noted how mood.cloud "changed the dynamics of the space and the building." Nicole explained the perceived impact of mood.cloud on the building atmosphere.

> Gates Hall looks so futuristic and modern and not that comfortable. The warmer colors of the display give the building a more appealing feel because the building is grey and all the furniture is really rough edged. It is kind of scary because I am used to buildings like Olin, which is from so long ago. The display made Gates Hall more appealing to me (Nicole, Female, Undergraduate Student)

For this user, the contrast of mood.cloud's form and color enhances the experience of the building architecture. Similarly, another user described her attachment to mood.cloud as an integrated part of what she considers the space.

> Rachel: I don't want mood.cloud to ever leave Gates Hall. I think there could be more excitement within the building and I think the mood.cloud provides some of this aesthetic.

> I: Could you describe a little more about what you mean by "this aesthetic?"

Rachel: I'm talking about the set up. There isn't enough space in there for people to do work and chat. The lab gets so overwhelming and annoying because everyone is always in there. There aren't enough social spaces. (Rachel, Female, Graduate Student)

Similarly, another undergraduate student expressed how the installation contributed to making the building "more socially relaxing." The presence and collective interaction with mood.cloud installation contributed to *making space* more social in contrast to the predominantly *experienced place for work*. In many ways interaction with the installation and its spatial presence brought aspects of the feeling of the space and architecture to the forefront for some of the users.

5.3.2 Imagining Design Ideas

Several participants engaged in imagining the spatial potential of the installation to interact both with the building architecture and with the building occupants. Interaction with the installation spurred on creative idea generation about the installation. These ideas had to do with further integrating the mood.cloud experience with the building architecture and creatively expanding the scope of the installation for amplifying the spatial ambience, developing connectedness between users and their spaces, and signaling or projecting visually outward.

For example, Kate described a way to creatively expand the scope of the installation to amplify the spatial ambience through the imaginative idea of a ceiling design element that works with the existing mood.cloud installation.

K: I was thinking it would be cool if the ceiling could change different hues above it based on the installation. The idea is that when colors flood into mood.cloud that they then leave and go up to the ceiling and then the ceiling takes on a color that is representative of mood.cloud that day. So the display is changing but the ceiling is this more constant, opaque idea.

I: Cool. How do you see ceiling space versus the current mood.cloud display?

K: Ceilings are really interesting. Heat rises and so this idea of generating this heat which is from moving, thinking, interacting bodies through this display that then rises up to create an atmosphere that is then accumulated at the top in this representative color of the thoughts and idea and everything over time.

Kate's new design idea is speculative in how it re-imagines the ways that individual changing interactions could be collected and create a more continuous "atmosphere" that reflects not only mood but interactions, movements, and feeling of space—a display of spatial ambience that is larger than just the display and is more integrated to the building interior by taking over the ceiling space.

Similarly, Kurt, graduate student, expressed how he wanted to expand the scope of collecting mood and awareness of mood by being able to understand how people are feeling in relation to their specific areas of the building—to "locally set mood" to increase the connectedness among building occupants and their workspaces.

A third participant imagined how the activity and interaction on the interior of the building could be projected outward to others outside of the building.

The building is a living entity and there are people inside which really make it a living entity. The building can speak out. So you could have the display on the inside and also subtle ways of reflecting elements of this on the exterior of the building. (Greg, Male, Graduate student)

Each of these participants' ideas is about connecting the building architecture (ceiling, individual spaces, and exterior) with the experiences of the people working within the building such that the architecture on a larger scale begins to communicate more about the shifting feelings, perspectives, and energy of the workplace. In this way, the interactions with mood.cloud were generative in the sense that they encouraged some users to speculate and imagine ways in which the design could contribute more to space-making. The interactive technology combined with the materiality of mood.cloud made the elements of the space—ceiling, façade, interior architecture—more legible as part of the canvas for making space and a way to expand the scope of their collective influence from the atrium space to greater building.

6. DISCUSSION

While designers deployed mood.cloud in order to explore building community and awareness through interaction around mood, our findings show that participants engaged with, interpreted, and appropriated mood.cloud in unanticipated ways.

While the visual indicator or representation of collective emotion in mood.cloud didn't necessarily influence the mood of others, building occupants saw the sensory experience of mood.cloud and the ability to change the color of the display as way to influence their own feelings, to potentially impact the feelings of others and the overall ambience of the workplace.

We found that interaction with mood.cloud fostered reflection about the relationship between the *individual* and the *larger collective* that the person is a part of.

The juxtaposition of the personal, individual interaction with a highly visible and attention garnering response in a public workplace setting fostered a great amount of awareness of oneself and others. This resulted in building various dimensions of social awareness within a workplace setting: fostering a sense of connectedness through contribution, empowering participants to appropriate mood.cloud to influence the feeling of the physical environment, and encouraging reflection about other's use, feelings, and motivations.

Sengers et al., [38] argue that "*affect* can be formally *'designed in'* to a system" *or* we can "*design for"* experiences where users are likely to reflect about or encounter affect in new ways (p.357). This study finds that *designing in* and *designing for* affect are not mutually exclusive. So while affect was 'designed in' or formally built into the design of mood.cloud's representation, technology, and even communication, affect was also *designed for* through mood.cloud's easily manipulated sensory materials of light and color, combined with a certain degree of open-endedness and ambiguity. By "designing in" *and* "designing for" affect, participants felt empowered to appropriate the technology of mood.cloud in ways that fostered reflection on and new experiences of the emotions of others and of the larger building.

6.1.1 Designing for Modes of Appropriation

The materiality of mood.cloud— the way the light and color engaged the user became very experiential. This sensory material experience combined with a certain open-ended design and ambiguity [15,32] was perceived by participants as being "exploratory" and "unregulated," encouraging experimentation and appropriation in ways that were less about mood and more about leaving one's mark and personal expression.

This study identifies two different types of motivation to understand the process of appropriation. We find that it is this interplay between appropriation for individual benefit and appropriation for the benefit of others that affords the opportunity to have participants become more aware of their own contribution as part of a larger community. This suggests that designing for the interplay between different modes of appropriation could be a means for encouraging a community of users to become more aware of others' and their emotions and foster a sense of connectedness between people. While collaborative task based systems have examined presencing or awareness of others, interactive art installations provide an opportunity to foster an awareness of others and their emotions in a more ludic way that could be particularly useful within an organizational context.

In addition to designing common social spaces as part of workplace and academic buildings to encourage interaction, this study points to the potential for interactive art installations to act as "social signifiers" [33] that signal a certain type of atmosphere or ambience apart from the "serious" workplace- a cue that social connectedness is valued, that there are moments that offer respite from the office or the lab, and that playfulness and creativity are encouraged. In this way, interactive art installations can serve to "loosen up" [17] or prompt reflection on [23] the dominant norms of the building. In this study we found that the sense of place for Gates Hall was firmly defined for student participants in the lived experience of the building as a place for *doing work* for computer science and information science students, faculty, and staff. In other words, the types of activities that happen in the building were *perceived* and *experienced* as predominantly work-based activities of research, coursework, labs, etc. The introduction of the interactive installation, mood.cloud served to disrupt this sense of place for many of the building occupants and visitors. mood.cloud acted as a small signifier of sociality and informality within a workplace. Our study points to the potential of interactive art installations to contribute to spatial well-being within the workplace in the way that they can both *signal* a space for sociality as well as *offer* building occupants opportunities to feel as though they are creatively contributing to a larger community. While mood.cloud was a single stand along installation, there is the potential to incorporate multiple interactive art installations within a building in order to create a series of experiential moments throughout the workspaces as way to potentially impact spatial well-being [cf. 7]

In addition to the ways that interactive installations can introduce play and serve to "lighten up the workplace" [19], this study finds that interactive art installations, through their spatiality and sensory engagement, give building occupants an opportunity to engage with shaping space. Sihvonen and Cnossen [40] point to the importance of continual "re-imagining of space while working in it" (p.050) as part of fostering creative work. Although unintended, interaction with mood.cloud fostered reflection, speculation, and imagination about the spatiality of Gates Hall. This suggests that interactive art installations in the workplace could be designed to *invite appropriation of space,* giving building occupants ways to actively and engage with and shape the feeling of their work environment.

6.1.2 Designing for Continued Engagement

Both the spatiality and materiality of mood.cloud invited building occupants to explore and appropriate mood.cloud. In the short term, the abstract notion of contributing to a larger community motivated engagement with mood.cloud. Importantly, our data offer a series of snapshots at specific points in time. Further work would be required to understand in more detail how use and appropriation evolved over time. Regardless, a sense emerged that, when it came to the idea of influencing mood, participants felt that they needed to know what they were contributing towards in a more concrete way in order to sustain and continue to engage with mood.cloud.

Although a number of participants discussed how they felt they were making a contribution to something larger by engaging with mood.cloud, others wanted less ambiguity around what their contribution meant and more importantly how their contribution could benefit the larger community. In other words, participants were motivated to continue participating if they knew how their contributions could help others—influencing the way others felt or influencing the way the space felt. While mood.cloud was compelling as a dynamic and colorful light sculpture, participants wanted more "information" about what the data meant and to be able to see trends and patterns over time as a means of sense-making.

Even though ambiguity can foster creativity in how an artifact or installation is appropriated, in this case participants described wanting less ambiguity in how their interactions with mood.cloud could potentially help others. They wanted to know for example which colors could boost the mood of others and even suggested that getting a notification reminder about contributing to mood.clood to help change the mood of the space or help others would be helpful. It is unclear whether a more prescriptive design would have appeased or exacerbated participants' desire to boost the building's collective mood. With more prescriptive design and feedback, would a desirable result be sought more ardently? An interactive installation like mood.cloud in an organizational context blurs boundaries between art and task-based ubicomp systems, between prescription and interpretation. This positioning can lead to higher expectations for the installation to communicate intended purpose, i.e., to provide potentially less interpretive flexibility, to participants than an interactive art installation located in a gallery setting, but meeting those expectations may also reduce the degree or types of appropriation in which users engage.

7. CONCLUSION

We investigated the way a new technological artifact mediated the interactivity of the surrounding space. The in-the wild deployment of mood.cloud in an organizational context of a university empowered participants to move beyond the mood tracking input function of the installation.

This study makes several important contributions to CSCW and HCI studies. First, by exploring how participants engage with an interactive art installation over a significant time period, we introduce two intertwined modes of appropriation that reveal different types of motivation for participating. In doing so, we show that in addition to looking at phases of appropriation, researchers can also examine the processual aspects of appropriation related to interactive installations. In this study, participants saw the technology of mood.cloud as a means to contribute to something larger, fostering feelings of connectedness. These findings suggest that an opportunity to design systems for this interplay between appropriation for the individual and appropriation for the imagined community.

Our study reveals that interacting through a big, visible artifact such as mood.cloud mediates the interactivity in the surrounding space. mood.cloud encouraged participants to orient toward each other around use, interpretation, and appropriation. While this study offers a particular snapshot in time of user engagement and perceptions of use by participants at that time, it points to the potential of longitudinally studying interactive art installations in organizational contexts to better understand phases of engagement. Future research should continue to explore how a series of linked interactive art installations throughout a building can impact spatial well-being and impact the atmosphere and feeling of the workplace. Future research might examine the spatiality of interactive technologies in enabling building occupants to develop a sense of authorship and ownership of their workplace.

Introduced as a new technological artifact, mood.cloud was appropriated in ways that revealed new spatialities between the installation and building architecture, heightened awareness of the mood of space and the mood of the larger community, and inspired new meaning making.

8. ACKNOWLEDGMENTS

Special thanks to Younghui Kim, visiting artist and the designer of mood.cloud. The installation of mood.cloud was a collaborative effort involving a team of Cornell computer scientists, programmers, and social scientists. In particular we thank Jung-Ho Son, Jacqueline Chien, Hyuns Hong, Leo Kang and all those in the Communication and Information Science Departments at Cornell University who collaborated on the planning and implementation of mood.cloud.

We are very grateful to the group of undergraduate students who helped conduct the intercept interviews. In particular, we would like to acknowledge Rachel Goldman who assisted with the intercept interviews. We would like to acknowledge undergraduate Danielle Grinberg for her assistance in coding, transcribing, and interviewing as a part of this qualitative research project. Special thanks to Lee Humphreys for her advice and feedback on the in-depth interview guide.

We thank Intel Corporation for partial funding of the mood.cloud installation as well as the CIS Dean's Office at Cornell University for their support.

9. REFERENCES

[1] Baumer, E. P. S., Burrell, J., Ames, M. G., Brubaker, J. R., & Dourish, P. (2015). On the Importance and Implications of Studying Technology Non-use. *Interactions*, 22(2), 52–56.

[2] Benyon, D. (2014). Spaces of interaction, places for experience. *Synthesis Lectures on Human-Centered Information*, *7*(2), 1-129.

[3] Beyer, H., & Holtzblatt, K. (1997). Contextual design: defining customer-centered systems. Elsevier.

[4] Bødker, S. (2015). Third-wave HCI, 10 years later---participation and sharing. *interactions*, *22*(5), 24-31.

[5] Bødker, S., Klokmose, C. N., Korn, M., & Polli, A. M. (2014, October). Participatory IT in semi-public spaces. In *Proceedings of the 8th Nordic Conference on Human-Computer Interaction: Fun, Fast, Foundational* (pp. 765-774). ACM.

[6] Bødker, S., & Polli, A. M. (2014, January). Between initial familiarity and future use: A case of collocated collaborative writing. In *COOP 2014-Proceedings of the 11th International Conference on the Design of Cooperative Systems, 27-30 May 2014, Nice (France)* (pp. 137-154). Springer International Publishing.

[7] Brewer, J., Williams, A., & Dourish, P. (2007). A handle on what's going on. In *The 1st International Conference on Tangible and Embedded Interaction* (TEI) (pp. 3–10). Baton Rouge. doi:10.1145/1226969.1226971

[8] Brignull, H., & Rogers, Y. (2003). Enticing people to interact with large public displays in public spaces. In *Proceedings of INTERACT* (Vol. 3, pp. 17-24).

[9] Carroll, J., Howard, S., Vetere, F., Peck, J., & Murphy, J. (2002, January). Just what do the youth of today want? Technology appropriation by young people. In *System Sciences, 2002. HICSS. Proceedings of the 35th Annual Hawaii International Conference on* (pp. 1777-1785). IEEE.

[10] Chalmers, M., & Galani, A. (2004, August). Seamful interweaving: heterogeneity in the theory and design of interactive systems. In *Proceedings of the 5th conference on Designing interactive systems: processes, practices, methods, and techniques* (pp. 243-252). ACM.

[11] Charmaz, K. (2002). Qualitative interviewing and grounded theory analysis. In J. F. Gubrium & J. A. Holstein (Eds.), *Handbook of interview research: context & method* (pp. 675-694). Thousand Oaks, CA: Sage Publications.

[12] Ciolfi, L., & Bannon, L. J. (2005). Space, place and the design of technologically-enhanced physical environments. In *Spaces, spatiality and technology* (pp. 217-232). Springer Netherlands.

[13] Cosley, D., Lewenstein, J., Herman, A., Holloway, J., Baxter, J., Nomura, S., & Gay, G. (2008, April). ArtLinks: fostering social awareness and reflection in museums. In *Proceedings of the SIGCHI Conference on Human Factors in Computing Systems* (pp. 403-412). ACM.

[14] Dalsgaard, P., & Hansen, L. K. (2008). Performing perception—staging aesthetics of interaction. *ACM Transactions on Computer-Human Interaction (TOCHI)*, *15*(3), 13.

[15] Dix, A. (2007, September). Designing for appropriation. In Proceedings of the 21st British HCI Group Annual Conference on People and Computers: HCI... but not as we know it-Volume 2 (pp. 27-30). British Computer Society.

[16] Dourish, P. (2003). The appropriation of interactive technologies: Some lessons from placeless documents. *Computer Supported Cooperative Work (CSCW)*, *12*(4), 465-490.

[17] Franck, K., & Stevens, Q. (Eds.). (2013). *Loose space: possibility and diversity in urban life*. Routledge.

[18] Fritsch, J., Pold, S. B., Vestergaard, L. S., & Lucas, M. (2014). Ink: designing for performative literary interactions. *Personal and Ubiquitous Computing*, *18*(7), 1551-1565.

[19] Gallacher, S., O'Connor, J., Bird, J., Rogers, Y., Capra, L., Harrison, D., & Marshall, P. (2015, February). Mood squeezer: Lightening up the workplace through playful and lightweight interactions. In *Proceedings of the 18th ACM Conference on Computer Supported Cooperative Work & Social Computing* (pp. 891-902). ACM.

[20] Gaver, W. W., Beaver, J., & Benford, S. (2003, April). Ambiguity as a resource for design. In *Proceedings of the SIGCHI conference on Human factors in computing systems* (pp. 233-240). ACM.

[21] Gay, G. (2009). Context-aware mobile computing: affordances of space, social awareness, and social influence. *Synthesis Lectures on human-centered informatics*, *2*(1), 1-62.

[22] Glaser, B. G., & Strauss, A. L. (1967). The discovery of grounded theory: Strategies for qualitative research. Chicago: Aldine Pub. Co

[23] Hallnäs, L., & Redström, J. (2001). Slow Technology – Designing for Reflection. Personal and Ubiquitous Computing, 5(3), 201–212.

[24] Hindmarsh, J., Heath, C., vom Lehn, D., & Cleverly, J. (2002). Creating assemblies: aboard the Ghost Ship. In Proc

CSCW (pp. 156–165). New Orleans, LA: ACM Press. http://dl.acm.org/citation.cfm?id=587101

[25] Hornecker, E., & Stifter, M. (2006, November). Learning from interactive museum installations about interaction design for public settings. In *Proceedings of the 18th Australia conference on Computer-Human Interaction: Design: Activities, Artefacts and Environments* (pp. 135-142). ACM.

[26] Jacucci, G., Spagnolli, A., Chalambalakis, A., Morrison, A., Liikkanen, L., Roveda, S., & Bertoncini, M. (2009). Bodily explorations in space: Social experience of a multimodal art installation. In *Human-Computer Interaction–INTERACT 2009* (pp. 62-75). Springer Berlin Heidelberg.

[27] Jacucci, G., & Wagner, I. (2007, June). Performative roles of materiality for collective creativity. In *Proceedings of the 6th ACM SIGCHI conference on Creativity & cognition* (pp. 73-82). ACM.

[28] Karapanos, E. (2013). User experience over time. In *Modeling Users' Experiences with Interactive Systems* (pp. 57-83). Springer Berlin Heidelberg.

[29] Lessig, L. (2008). Remix: Making art and commerce thrive in the hybrid economy. Penguin.

[30] Lofland, J., Snow, D., Anderson, L., & Lofland, L. H. (2006). *Analyzing social settings: A guide to qualitative observation and analysis* (4th ed.). Belmont, CA: Wadsworth Publishing.

[31] Mathew, A., Rogers, Y., & Lloyd, P. (2011, November). Post-it note art: evaluating public creativity at a user generated art installation. In *Proceedings of the 8th ACM conference on Creativity and cognition* (pp. 61-70). ACM.

[32] Morrison, A. J., Mitchell, P., & Brereton, M. (2007, September). The lens of ludic engagement: evaluating participation in interactive art installations. In *Proceedings of the 15th international conference on Multimedia* (pp. 509-512). ACM.

[33] Norman, D. A. (2008). The way I see it. Signifiers, not affordances.*Interactions*, *15*(6), 18-19

[34] O'Hara, K., Glancy, M., & Robertshaw, S. (2008, November). Understanding collective play in an urban screen game. In *Proceedings of the 2008 ACM conference on Computer supported cooperative work* (pp. 67-76). ACM.

[35] Pollak, J. P., Adams, P., & Gay, G. (2011, May). PAM: a photographic affect meter for frequent, in situ measurement of affect. In *Proceedings of the SIGCHI conference on Human factors in computing systems* (pp. 725-734). ACM.

[36] Salovaara, A., Höök, K., Cheverst, K., Twidale, M., Chalmers, M., & Sas, C. (2011, May). Appropriation and creative use: linking user studies and design. In *CHI'11 Extended Abstracts on Human Factors in Computing Systems* (pp. 37-40). ACM.

[37] Satchell, C., & Dourish, P. (2009). Beyond the user: use and non-use in HCI. In Proc OZCHI (pp. 9–16). Melbourne, Australia: ACM.

[38] Sengers, P., Boehner, K., Mateas, M., & Gay, G. (2008). The disenchantment of affect. *Personal and Ubiquitous Computing*, *12*(5), 347-358.

[39] Sengers, P., & Gaver, B. (2006, June). Staying open to interpretation: engaging multiple meanings in design and evaluation. In *Proceedings of the 6th conference on Designing Interactive systems* (pp. 99-108). ACM.

[40] Sihvonen, T., & Cnossen, B. (2015). Not only a workplace. Reshaping creative work and urban space. *Observatorio (OBS*)*, (SPE1), 47-69.

[41] Williams, A., Kabisch, E., & Dourish, P. (2005). From Interaction to Participation: Configuring Space through Embodied Interaction. In Proc Ubimomp. Tokyo, Japan. http://link.springer.com/chapter/10.1007%2F11551201_17

"Hey, I know what this is!": Cultural Affinities and Early-Stage Appropriation of the Emerging Bitcoin Technology

Yong Ming Kow
City University of Hong Kong
18 Tat Hong Avenue,
Kowloon Tong, Hong Kong SAR
yongmkow@cityu.edu.hk

Xianghua Ding
Shanghai Key Laboratory of Data Science
Fudan University
Shanghai 201203, China
xianghua.ding@gmail.com

ABSTRACT
User appropriation can be immensely helpful to bootstrap emerging technologies; but how do new and lesser known technologies attract these earliest adopters? This paper investigates user appropriation of emerging computing technologies, by focusing on Bitcoin, a digital monetary system supported by a peer-to-peer network of computing devices. We conducted in-depth interviews with sixteen Bitcoin community participants in Hong Kong, Singapore, and Baltimore. We describe user appropriation in this case of Bitcoin as a sociocultural journey—from encounter, research and learning, to socialization. We contribute the concept of *cultural affinities*, including conceptual, contextual and social dimensions, as important mediators leading to early-stage user appropriation.

Keywords
Appropriation; bitcoin; sociocultural.

1. INTRODUCTION
User appropriation of innovation by communities can help bootstrap emerging technologies [16]. However, emerging technologies are by definition promising but yet to be proven; so why would some users choose to contribute their time and effort supporting their development? In HCI, the appropriation literature has largely focused on examining personalization and reuse of matured technologies (e.g., mobile apps and web tools) [3,6,13,27,29,33], but not emerging tools. Likewise, the technology adoption and online community literature has only examined cognitive and relational factors motivating user contributions [7,16,28,31]. Importantly, we lack studies that examine *why people would choose to appropriate a relatively unknown and obscure technology in the first place.*

In this paper, we examine a particular instance of user appropriation in an emerging technology, Bitcoin—a digital monetary system first developed in 2009 by one or several pseudonymous creator(s) [25]. In many ways, a significant portion of early Bitcoin users represented a distinct group of appropriators who were motivated by narratives of techno-utopian vision [18,20,37]. But since 2013, financial technologists have begun to take interest in the technology underlying Bitcoin's digital currency—an open ledger system, known as the "block chain," which enables the exchange of digital tokens securely, with a potential to override the need to involve a counterparty (e.g., a broker and clearing house) in the trade settlement process. This promise of block chain technology to simplify the process of global financial trading is accompanied by recent involvement of new actors in the community, such as bankers, entrepreneurs, and financial institutions. The inclusion of these corporate actors is enriching and expanding a dynamic social environment, which just two years ago had consisted primarily of libertarians resisting technological institutions [18,20,37]. However, what is still unclear is the perspective of end users—how they got involved and became users and contributors.

This paper presents a study exploring end users' perspectives, to understand how they have become involved with Bitcoin and contributed to its development. We performed open-ended interviews of early Bitcoin participants between September 2013 and February 2015. These interviews took place as part of an ethnographic study of Bitcoin communities in Hong Kong, Singapore, and Baltimore. We interviewed a total of 16 participants, most of whom were recruited from open Meetup groups (see Meetup.com). We asked questions related to how they got to know about Bitcoin and their personal opinions at the time of the interviews. All interviews were audio-recorded, transcribed, and analyzed for recurring themes.

We found that while our informants got to learn about Bitcoin in a variety of ways, they shared a common trajectory in the process of becoming active participants, though each individual's own background knowledge in related interests may have led to different degrees of enthusiasm about the technology. With that understanding, we argue that appropriation needs to be explained beyond simple accounts of personalization and reuse, and rather as a continually developing enterprise. In this case of Bitcoin, a user may decide to develop an application or a business on the platform, expanding its sociotechnical infrastructure, thus blurring the line between a user and developer. We address this issue by adding an additional sociocultural frame to the appropriation concept—cultural affinities (consisting of contextual, conceptual, and social dimensions)—to highlight how user participation in appropriating innovations is mediated not by their predesignated roles (i.e., being called a user or a developer), but by their ability to harness sociocultural resources which vary from person to person.

GROUP '16, November 13 - 16, 2016, Sanibel Island, FL, USA

ACM 978-1-4503-4276-6/16/11...$15.00
DOI: http://dx.doi.org/10.1145/2957276.2957279

2. RELATED WORK

Below, we will review related work on user appropriation and user participation, and examine the research gap in the literature.

2.1 User Appropriation

User appropriation is the practice of users performing novel customization, or identifying new uses for technologies [8]. User appropriation is important to product design, for the practice enables customization of a product to users' individual needs [8]. In the case of devising new uses for a technology, user appropriation is also a social practice of transforming an instrumental tool into a status symbol and cultural standard of interaction [2,6], which may include collective appropriation and modification of community technologies for collaborative purposes [2].

The literature currently lacks research work examining *early-stage appropriation*, particularly of emerging technologies requiring significant shepherding in order to becoming useful to people and communities. Importantly, the user appropriation literature in HCI has generally focused on *post-development* practices of user appropriation [6,13,27,29,33]. These include developing technological practices [6,33], providing online help [13], information sharing [27], and leading the appropriation process [29]. In order to successfully examine these post-development practices, previous researchers have studied technologies that were well established; these included the iphone [6], MythTV [13], a social networking site [27], a multimedia messaging service (MMS) [33], and a commercial learning management systems (LMS) [29]. Thus, a study of the Bitcoin context will help to fill a research gap on the topic of appropriation of emerging technologies.

2.2 User Participation in Citizen Science, Online Communities, and Adoption Theories

March, Jacobs, and Salvador [19] highlighted the importance of examining early-stage appropriation practices—to improve our understanding of designing for user involvement and engagement right at the beginning of the technology development. More recently, studies in online communities and citizen science have found community participants to be more willing to contribute information in areas they are familiar with [28,31]. For example, *Galaxy Zoo* is a citizen science project that invited the public to participate in astronomical classification of galaxies using web-based tools [17]. A subsequent survey found that most of Galaxy Zoo's participants already had an interest in astronomy, and thus were considered self-selected to contribute to the project [30]. Eyewire, another citizen science project examining protein folding tasks, shared similar findings regarding participants' previous engagements [14].

In studies of online communities, an issue that inhibits technology adoption is the degree that the technology is sensitive to network externalities, or critical mass issues [31]. That is, the rise in value a user can derive from using the technology depends on the increase in number of people using it (e.g., a network technology like Bitcoin) [9,12,31]. Consequently, the technology would have little value when its network is small. For example, the credit card took decades to become mainstream because it required a critical mass of merchants in order to attract more customers—while in order to attract more merchants, attracting more customers is in turn necessary [9]. In this instance, understanding why early adopters would bootstrap a sparsely used digital network is essential to designing it for successful appropriation.

Other factors that encourage technology adoption include the presence of social influencers (e.g., workplace supervisors and trusted friends) [16,26,38]. However, the availability of social influencers often also depends on the degree to which the technology is already accepted by a large number of social circles. Also, our agency to appropriate early-stage technologies may be unevenly linked to our social positioning (e.g., education, income, and social status) [22]. Thus, Straub [34] argues that it is important for adoption studies to also examine the socio-cultural dimensions beyond social influences, that is, "at the intersection of the cognitive, affective, and contextual factors."

In sum, appropriation studies have been focusing on examining contexts in which the technologies are matured and well accepted by users. We lacked studies examining contexts in which the technologies are new—which begets our research question of under what socio-cultural circumstances the early appropriators would emerge around such technologies. In the next section, we examine the Bitcoin context—particularly its distinctive features, early controversies, and recent development, factors that set the stage for user appropriation.

3. BITCOIN

Bitcoin was published in 2009 by a pseudonymous persona known as Satoshi Nakamoto [25]. While the real identity of Bitcoin's original developer is unknown, its software codes are open sourced, thus ensuring that any developers can examine them. Bitcoin is an interesting emerging technology, as it combines two old propositions regarding design of *money* (the artifact) in a way never seen before. The first proposition is that a bitcoin (note the use of a small letter *b* to refer to the digital tokens, not the technical system) is embodied digitally, and may be sent over informational networks such as the Internet at negligible cost. This feature can also be found in virtual currencies (e.g., *Beenz*, *Flooz*, and *Linden Dollars* of the virtual world *Second Life*). The second proposition is that each bitcoin is issued by a decentralized software system, with its transactions stored in a peer-to-peer database known as the *block chain*; the block chain is not controlled by any institutional issuer. This second feature has never been seen before in other digital monies, due to cryptographers' previous inability to resolve the technical difficulty of maintaining a distributed account of who owns how much money in a decentralized monetary network; this challenge was resolved for the first time through Bitcoin [25].

As a form of digital money—a medium of exchange for goods and services—the bitcoin has not yet encountered sustainable uses; although many startup companies are being tasked to explore markets involving low-cost transmission of monetary value, or requiring open ledger technologies [10]. Due to its many controversies, bitcoin as digital money has received limited support from institutions to support its development. One contentious feature is that bitcoins are generated periodically within a peer-to-peer network, dictated by computer algorithms, in a process not logically controlled by any government entities. This unusual process of monetary production distances itself from government intervention and has led some observers to believe that bitcoins are objects of scams. Perhaps more damaging to Bitcoin's reputation was its early adoption by notorious online black markets, such as the Silk Road, which caused bitcoin use to be associated with illicit activities. These views pose significant cultural barriers to Bitcoin's widespread adoption [15,23].

On the other hand, the block chain has recently captured the interest of financial institutions due to its ability to mediate financial transactions among institutions without the need to involve counterparties such as clearing houses and brokers. In addition, the block chain could also store public data (e.g., smart contracts, accounting ledgers, and intellectual property rights) in a decentralized database, thus leaving an audit trail for regulators to assess a company's financial health or contractual commitments [24,36].

Based on these two different propositions of Bitcoin, the technology has undergone two different stages of appropriation—first as a peer-to-peer digital form of money, and second as an institutionalizable block chain technology. In the first stage, between 2009 and 2012, Bitcoin was largely a peculiar tool used and supported by libertarians, and very contentiously appropriated by online black markets like the *Silk Road.* These early participants networked online through the Bitcoin Forum (bitcointalk.org), IRC channels, and other social media.

The second stage of development, more current and central to our case, is *the emergence of moderate actors—the bankers, entrepreneurs, and technology hobbyists—toward the end of 2012.* From this time, a large number of Meetup and Facebook groups were set up globally across most major global cities. On April 7, 2015, a total of 594 Bitcoin-related Meetup groups could be found across 71 countries. While Bitcoin is particularly appealing to libertarians, who developed beliefs in minimizing roles of the government on many issues including that of money [18,20,21], these new actors are more willing to work with regulators and local businesses. This stance requires a more open attitude towards eventual institutionalization of the technology—what perhaps can be considered as a significant departure from its earlier libertarian framing.

4. METHOD

The Bitcoin communities that are formed through Meetup groups are often localized to one city; that is, they are specific to geographically based Bitcoin communities. Participatory practices within these communities tend to center around networking and identifying collaborators, and subsequently developing shared practices to support local Bitcoin development. When these Meetup groups were initially formed, many of these meetings were only casually held in bars and restaurants, and functioned solely as contexts in which bankers, technologists and hobbyists, entrepreneurs, incubators, and journalists could socialize with each other. Some of these actors have a long-term agenda regarding the Bitcoin technology—for example, an incubator is looking for potential businesses to support, whereas a hobbyist may be interested in identifying Bitcoin-related job opportunities.

Over time, these long-term agendas have been reified into shared purposes which seeded the formation of formal organizations. For example, the Hong Kong Meetup meetings have existed since July 2012, and in June 2014, the most engaged participants also founded the Bitcoin Association of Hong Kong (bitcoinhk.org), which focuses on organizing formal workshops, handles enquiries from the press, and engages with local legislators regarding regulatory policies. The core members in Hong Kong also set up their own private instant messaging groups in which they discuss specific issues such as public opinion, local media coverage, and event organization. We were invited to participate in these private discussion groups.

There were at least three advantages of using the Meetup meetings as a research site: (1) these social events offered an accessible pool of participants whom we could interview; (2) these participants were likely to have previous experience with Bitcoin; and (3) these settings acted as a context where we could observe emerging collaboration across segments of users (e.g., bankers and technologists). The key disadvantage of examining the Meetup meetings was that inexperienced users (who had encountered the technology but remained uninterested) were less likely to attend these meetings which require significant time commitment.

Table 1. List of informants with their backgrounds, when they encountered Bitcoin, and the extent of their participation.

Informant	Background knowledge			Year Encounter Bitcoin	Research and learning	Socializing	Social action
	Libertarianism	Finance and money	Software				
1		✓	✓	2013	✓	✓	
2			✓	2012	✓	✓	
3	✓	✓	✓	2012	✓	✓	✓
4	✓		✓	2011	✓	✓	✓
5			✓	2013	✓		
6	✓	✓	✓	2011	✓	✓	✓
7			✓	2012	✓	✓	
8				2014	✓		
9			✓	2012	✓	✓	(✓)
10		✓	✓	2011	✓	✓	✓
11			✓	2011	✓	✓	
12		✓	✓	2011	✓	✓	(✓)
13		✓	✓	2013	✓	✓	(✓)
14	✓		✓	2011	✓	✓	✓
15		✓		2013	✓	✓	(✓)
16		✓		2013	✓		

(✓) indicates actors who owned Bitcoin startups when they took social actions (i.e., potential conflict of interest)

From September 2013 to February 2015, we conducted in-depth interviews with Bitcoin participants as part of our participant observation work. We primarily participated in local Meetup sessions in Singapore and Hong Kong in order to perform firsthand observation of these meetings. These meetings included casual interactions at bars, public talks and seminars, and even a junk boat trip among core participants in Hong Kong. Each Meetup session was attended by anywhere from five to 50 attendees, and lasted about two hours. As mentioned in the previous section, these attendees were mostly entrepreneurs, bankers, and hobbyists, but also included Bitcoin participants from foreign countries. While some participants were active (i.e., organizing events or developing tools), others joined one of these groups just to find out more.

In June 2014 and January 2015, we attended two 2-day conferences, one in Hong Kong and the other in Singapore, with more than 40 international speakers and hundreds of attendees discussing Bitcoin issues. During our participant observation work, the first author spent about two months, from September to November 2013, reading nearly two hundred online articles, including technical papers, newspaper reports, blogs, and online forum posts, in order to become familiar with technicalities, language, and other practices associated with Bitcoin. Through informal discussions with participants, it became clear that the local discourse primarily revolved around a few key subjects: emerging businesses, technicalities (including security and functionalities), media coverage and public opinion, investment opportunities, and regulatory policies. In particular, a few Bitcoin associations were launched around the middle of 2014 to handle public opinion as well as to engage with local regulatory bodies, although these are relatively recent developments and were not the key concerns of this study.

From these contexts, we invited 16 participants for in-depth interviews. Seven interviewees were residents of Hong Kong, five of Singapore, and four of the US. Among the interviewees from the US, two were from the Meetup group in Baltimore, one when he participated at a conference in Hong Kong, and the other through personal referral. All of our informants were male, with only one (#8) being female. Initially, we asked general questions such as: How did you come across Bitcoin? What do you think about Bitcoin? Are you working on anything related to Bitcoin? What are your future plans? We took field notes during meetings, whereas in-depth interviews were audio-recorded, and transcribed. All the interviews lasted between 30 minutes and an hour.

4.1 Data Analysis

We performed memoing and theoretical sampling during and after each interview [35]. Part of the current theme emerged during the first interview, when the interviewee voluntarily revealed how he learned about Bitcoin through his past participation. We followed this lead to also investigate the other interviewees' past participation before encountering Bitcoin. We utilized the grounded-theory method of axial coding to identify social interactions at different points of the interviewees' encounters [35]. Through axial coding, we identified conditions, actions, and effects of their experiences. Finally, we reduced these codes to those presented in this paper.

As shown in Table 1, seven of our informants had encountered Bitcoin in 2011, but only two of them engaged actively, such as volunteering for open source coding or event organization. The rest learned about Bitcoin primarily through Internet media, and kept this interest as a private activity until the development of local meetings and startup scenes. Of the four informants who learned about Bitcoin in 2012, they mostly heard about it from friends who had encountered Bitcoin earlier. Six informants were relatively recent actors who learned about Bitcoin in 2013, due to the surge of mainstream media reports and public interest in the technology. Of the five informants who took "social action" (i.e., voluntary, nonbusiness efforts to organize events and activities in the local scenes), all of them had heard about Bitcoin much earlier, before 2013. To the best of our knowledge, all nine actors who have taken social actions are still participating in the community as of the writing of this paper. All names mentioned in this paper are pseudonyms.

5. FINDINGS

In this section, we present findings of how our informants came across Bitcoin, deliberated on the technology, and decided to participate along appropriation trajectories. We also highlight that, along with this appropriation trajectory—from encounter, research and learning, to socialization—different forms of *cultural affinities* (elements that bring the actors closer to the sites of the innovation) mediate the journey of users negotiating meanings with the innovation. *Contextual affinity* provides a cultural context (e.g., family environment, work setting, or civic event) in which a user may be exposed to the technology; *conceptual affinity* refers to her use of preconceived ideologies, concepts, and literacy to infer meanings of technological artifacts; *social affinity* describes the degree to which an appropriator can identify others to encourage and advise her in her endeavor. Although conceptually separated, these affinities interacted and worked concurrently in providing incentives for appropriation. And some affinities may be more important during certain stages of the journey.

5.1 Contextual x Social Affinities: Encountering the Technology through Adjacent Community

A social context (e.g., a community setting) offers opportunities for potential appropriators to encounter others who are aware of emerging technologies. After Bitcoin software was published in January 2009, for more than one year it remained a mere technical curiosity. There were very few appropriators apart from a handful of cryptographers and libertarians. Aside from people who belonged to these social groups, few others could have heard of Bitcoin. It was thus not surprising that all of our informants had only come across Bitcoin much later. Yoshi (#6) from Baltimore, who had come into contact with Bitcoin in May 2011, was among our earliest appropriators.

Yoshi first heard about Bitcoin in a tweet posted by an online comic writer:

> There's an online comic I follow. It's written by somebody who's an objectivist, is self-described as, I guess. But his comics are more about just life, but he mentioned it in a Twitter, and while following him, he basically mentioned [Bitcoin].

Yoshi had encountered Bitcoin through a non-Bitcoin community. Other users like Yoshi encountered Bitcoin through a community with minor overlap of interest with early Bitcoin users. These are opportunities where information about an emerging technology can bridge across closely aligned social networks.

The Bitcoin community, particularly after 2012, has also shared significant adjacency with professional interest groups. David (#1), an incubator who is located in East Asia, had invested in eight companies in the US, Germany, Mexico, and Hong Kong. David knew about Bitcoin in September 2011 through a good friend in France. His friend was a financial software engineer, who in turn knew about Bitcoin while following Occupy Wall Street, which took place after the financial crisis in 2008 to protest against the financial institutions in the US:

> I know Bitcoin through a friend who is French... who is an engineer—software engineer, worked in many banks and even for central banks. He mentioned that a lot of people picked up on Bitcoin during the Wall Street

Occupy movement. In Occupy Wall Street I think people started putting up signs or mentioning Bitcoin at that time as an alternative currency.

While Bitcoin is a technical artifact, it was rhetorically framed under rubrics of liberal ideals, such as the idea of a stateless society [20]. The use of Bitcoin could also represent a form of protest against the financial establishment. When viewed as a libertarian artifact, one use of Bitcoin is the ability to pseudonymously buy drugs in online black markets. This was how Zach (#4), from Baltimore, first learned about the technology:

> I was living in San Francisco, and, you know, just wanted to get some weed. Since then I've stopped smoking weed, and I bought through Mt. Gox as well, which was really hard to use ... that's what got me in the door.

Traditional media, like local newspapers, are also possible outlets to learn about Bitcoin. But Bitcoin was not reported by the Hong Kong or Singapore media until early 2013. Tang, a college student from Hong Kong, was among those who only learned about Bitcoin through the media, as he had no access to earlier information sources. "The newspaper was talking about Bitcoin," Tang told us—"that's when I started to do research about Bitcoin."

While knowing that Bitcoin existed was important, all of our informants invariably mentioned that the next thing they did was to enter a phase of research into Bitcoin, and to learn what it was.

5.2 Contextual x Conceptual Affinities: Using What We Know in Research and Learning

By previously performing a relevant role within a community (e.g., being a banker in a financial sector), potential appropriators could embody concepts which can guide their formation of new understandings about emerging technologies. Bitcoin could be understood in many ways. It has been seen as a technical novelty with innovative algorithms. Some others see it as an investment instrument—a way to get rich. Yet others perceive it as a technology that promotes freer trades, a financial law enforcement nightmare, or "magic" Internet money! The truth is that many appropriators have to decide for themselves what Bitcoin is.

In its least contentious form, Bitcoin could be understood purely as a technical novelty. Vincent (#7) is an enterprise resource planning consultant in Singapore. From his perspective, Bitcoin is a technical artifact, and he was looking for a technical description of it. "Then I finally found what is [a] block chain, what is [the] difficulty [in] all this," Vincent said. In the course of his research, he came to a Bitcoin trading site, an IRC channel, but its participants did not answer his questions. Undaunted, Vincent carried on with his research by reading articles on the Internet, and he uncovered a wealth of technical information. But he also found that he had difficulties shepherding his friends through the same process:

> I [have] a programmer background, I understand why. Because, when some new concepts [emerge], we will tend to explore. [And] it's a very tedious [process], and people will say, "Forget it. If it doesn't affect me, then better not touch it."
>
> So, this is what happened to a lot of my friends. ... I can say this is more like intrinsic motivation. ... These are the things that, like the knowledge and know-how, they aren't interested [in}. [But] when they see money [in Bitcoin]... they will start to be interested, but they still don't know how it worked.

Vincent had an interest in programming and, unlike his friends, was able to sustain an interest through a long period of Internet research. In our interviews, we found a variety of initial reactions toward Bitcoin. When asked, many of our informants used their previous experiences and knowledge to explain their reactions.

While Vincent had a technical curiosity, and was clear how Bitcoin worked, he still had questions about where Bitcoin would go from there. "A lot of people still don't know why, even myself, I don't know why bitcoin [price] will shoot up," Vincent told us.

We encountered other informants who quite easily fostered confidence toward Bitcoin. For example, Yoshi told us that he had needed little research, and he immediately "got it" about Bitcoin's utility: "I looked into it, read about it, and all of a sudden, I'm like, 'Hey, I know what this is and what this potential has.'" What is the difference between these two groups of users?

Yoshi was quickly convinced, he explained, due to his personal experience with another virtual currency, *Linden Dollars*:

> Since about 2003, since I started in Beta even, I was involved in *Second Life*... In Second Life, all of that [which happened in Bitcoin] happened too, where the first year, people would make their own stuff and sell it. Then they would set up businesses. By then, it was all casinos, entertainment.
>
> That fascinated me because all of a sudden, it was, as I said, a fast-forward developing of the real-world economy, where eventually, it got to where they actually had financial services right in the game. They had their own banks and stock markets and stuff.
>
> The reason I'm bringing this up with Second Life is that it was just on the brink of developing a really good virtual economy. It was moving into the financial services. Some of us were even considering using Linden Dollars for virtual currency transactions internationally, but once the government stepped in and closed [the use of Linden Dollars for international transactions], it created a domino effect which killed all the financial services in the game.

Not only had Yoshi tried setting up a business in *Second Life*, he witnessed how global financial services may be mediated by a virtual currency. In addition, he is a libertarian, has a degree in finance, and taught himself programming. This mix of relevant literacies gave him a lot of leverage in conceiving uses for the new technology. Zach is another informant who had come to understand Bitcoin from a libertarian angle. Zach mentioned the specific sites he had frequently visited in our interview: "The Bitcoin subreddit, Anarchy or CryptoAnarchy subreddit, the Anarcho-Capitalism subreddits. Do you know Freeman Radio?" And Zach was able to develop trust in the technology through this perspective.

David, who was an Internet entrepreneur himself in the '90s, was able to look at Bitcoin from a business perspective. When he was running his startup, he developed a business model in which clients who advertised at his site would pay him using credit cards. However, David was denied a credit card payment account by his bank, which was tremendously disconcerting, as he recalled:

What's going on? Why these guys in the bank would say no to a young guy trying to start up a business?

For most Internet businesses, credit card is the main medium of payment. To be denied access to this payment option could mean a death knell for these companies. And David explained that banks today have remained highly selective about whom they do business with:

> It's exactly the problem as I had and I guess, many entrepreneurs back in the '90s with Internet. The banks not only are not helping, they are actually preventing you from opening your business because if out of 140 banks, 135 say no, then imagine the tens of hundreds of entrepreneurs who just try 10 banks, and then 10 banks said no, or 20 banks, and then 20 banks say no. What do they do? They don't do it. Right?

From David's perspective, Bitcoin could be an enabler for businesses that, for various reasons, are unable to accept credit card payment.

Even before using Internet searches to research Bitcoin, many of its participants were formerly exposed to libertarianism, finance and money (including virtual currencies), and software. Table 1 shows that 13 of our informants had knowledge of software engineering (sufficient enough to understand concepts behind basic cryptography), while all five of our active volunteers had, in addition, knowledge of at least one other domain (i.e., libertarianism, or finance and money). This pre-acquired knowledge had allowed them to imagine probable use scenarios, and see meanings in Bitcoin's technicalities. The flip side is that those who lack such pre-acquired skills may not even begin researching the technology, as David said of those who kept an arm's length with Bitcoin: "They don't see what it can become. They only see what is going on at that time."

5.3 Conceptual x Social Affinities: Reifying Participation Through Socialization

By developing deeper understanding, and having conceptualized meaningful uses, of emerging technologies, potential appropriators could reach out to and communicate productively with members of new communities, and identify new collaborators. Among our informants, some would progress beyond the research phase and begin to seek social support. Informants like David who had learned about Bitcoin through a close friend had no issue finding a discussant. But most of our informants were only able to reach out to like-minded participants through social media platforms. While personal ties are helpful to promote technological adoption, we found very few informants who had old trusted friends sharing enthusiasm in Bitcoin. Thus, a vast majority of informants have maintained or nurtured their interests by interacting with strangers.

Vincent was among those who were unable to find any close friends who would support his interest in Bitcoin:

> You know, I told my friends about it [but] none of them ... even bother[ed] [to discuss with] me at all. [F]ed up, I just go [on] Facebook, create a group, invite everybody.

Vincent started a Bitcoin Facebook group for Singapore that attracted 904 "likes" from Facebook users.

There is a Bitcoin Meetup group in almost every major city around the world; these groups are critical social infrastructure especially for emerging startups working on Bitcoin-related projects. By June 17, 2014, there were 546 members who had subscribed to the Meetup group based in Hong Kong, 404 in Singapore, and 89 in Baltimore. As few people know about Bitcoin, these meetings provide needed venues for participants to share information or to collaborate with people who are more knowledgeable about the technology. David shared with us his experience working with global startups:

> [T]he Meetups, which are a face-to-face form of meeting, is quite important in Bitcoin. Yeah, I think as a social dimension is critical. There, as you can see, there are values that are shared among Bitcoin, in the Bitcoin community. For example, for now, it's very collaborative... People are quite open to discuss, quite open to help themselves.

Even though close friends are good sources of support for adopters, they could also dissuade their friends from participating. Tang (#5), who first encountered Bitcoin in the local newspaper, started researching it in the following months. Tang often confided to his friends and colleagues about his emerging interest:

> Yeah, I started my research in September. Around that time I had introduced Bitcoin to my friends. Many of them still don't understand what it is. They just think it's very high-risk and maybe it's just like a share... How do you say it? Hoax. My [university] lecturers still gave me the signal that it's not advisable to speculate in Bitcoin.

Tang chose to remain a Bitcoin skeptic after hearing the opinions of his friends. He contemplated working on a university project developing a service robot that could accept Bitcoin, but he soon gave up on the idea. Tang smirked when he told us that he would probably be more convinced, if "at least some international trading companies like Amazon… can use bitcoins to [make purchases]."

Through social supports, many of our other informants have taken social actions, whether investing, using, or developing a related product. From the time our informants heard about Bitcoin until they started taking social actions, this period spanned between several months and more than one year. Yoshi, who had taken the least amount of time considering his earlier exposure to a virtual currency and trading, was our only exception.

6. DISCUSSION

In this study, we explored the question of how end users got involved in early-stage appropriation of an emerging technology, Bitcoin. By focusing on an emerging technology, we were able to uncover a process of appropriation predominantly mediated by sociocultural resources at the users' disposal—who they were, where they worked, whom they knew, and what they knew—that goes beyond the limited consideration of customization and reuse that the literature has focused on.

Importantly, we identified several forms of cultural affinities that mediated the participants' journey of appropriation. We used the term *culture* as defined by Boden et al. [5]:

> a shared web of meanings that shapes roles and interpretations, and is dynamically (re)negotiated by the actors in the course of their daily work... [materialized] in the form of artifacts, practices and routines.

While here we can see cultural elements—artifacts, practices, and routines—as being historically construed, the process of appropriation is emergent.

Throughout the participants' appropriation trajectory—from encounter, research and learning, to participation—all forms of *cultural affinities* (elements that bring the actors closer to the sites of the innovation) mediated the process as users negotiated meanings with the innovation. These affinities interacted with each other to provide motivation for appropriation, even though some affinities may be more important during the early or later stages of the journey. For example, *context* may be more valuable at the beginning of the journey, but as the user begins to *conceptualize* the technology in his mind more regularly, the original context becomes less important than the ideas that now encapsulate his interest. Mediated by these affinities, the appropriation process spirals forward, with participants progressively conceiving new meanings through research and experimentation, while also navigating the sociotechnical labyrinth that challenges attempts to reify the technology in real-world contexts.

6.1 Cultural Affinities: Reasons for Participation

6.1.1 Contextual Affinity

Here, the term *context* is viewed at the level of social settings (e.g., a place or a site), which provide opportunities for our participants to interact with people or media surrounding technological artifacts. Our participants' access to a context is afforded by their social positioning and earlier participation in professional and interest-driven social groups (i.e., through legitimate peripheral participation) (see also [39]).

Contextual affinity provides a cultural context (e.g., family environment, work setting, and civil event) in which a user may be exposed to the technology. For example, in 2011, a community sharing contextual affinity to Bitcoin was the *Silk Road* community. And in late 2011 and early 2012, appropriators like our informant David began to develop access to Bitcoin indirectly through the Occupy Wall Street movement. Between 2011 and 2014, Bitcoin's periphery expanded as its community enlarged, leading to more potential users coming across the technology through overlapping contexts.

Here, we would like to introduce a related concept of *adjacent communities*, which are contexts that are related (i.e., "adjacent") to one another due to overlapping memberships. For example, the Bitcoin communities we examined have overlapping memberships with video game clubs and civil movements. Adjacent communities facilitate movement of actors from one participatory context to another. For example, an actor like David could not have gained knowledge about the inner working of the banking sector without years of experience participating in the startup community. Every actor, depending on their past participation, thus benefits from contextual affinity afforded by their hard-earned social positions, and their associated daily interactions. In other words, a community's contextual affinity does not open endless pathways, but only those leading to where its members have been cross-pollinating artifacts and practices.

6.1.2 Conceptual Affinity

A concept refers to an actor's accumulated knowledge and representations about his social environment. And *conceptual affinity* refers to her use of these concepts to infer meanings of technological artifacts. Conceptual affinity is also cumulative—the more we know, the more we can learn, and the more we will come to know.

Our interviewee data revealed that while any users can learn on their own on the Internet, this is an insufficient condition for developing trust in a technology. If we take literacy to refer to a person's ability to engage with, analyze, and critique new content through the use of her accumulated cognitive operations and representations [11], then most of our successful appropriators, before they encountered Bitcoin, were already pre-equipped with relevant "literacies" through past work, school, or personal hobbies. These literacies are mental toolkits allowing users to imagine Bitcoin interacting in real-world contexts and thus to develop *personal* visions of its potential uses.

The use of conceptual affinity is seen most clearly in the case of Yoshi, who had firsthand experience with virtual trading in *Second Life* using the Linden Dollar. He witnessed how virtual derivatives and virtual exchange could evolve out of virtual currencies; and he could see Bitcoin offering similar utility. "I know what it is," he said when he encountered Bitcoin. Apart from virtual trading experiences, which were rare among our informants, other relevant literacies include finance and money (to imagine Bitcoin being used in marketplaces), software engineering (to understand its technical soundness), and libertarianism (to envision its relevance to a spirited discursive field). Most of our informants had at least one intellectual or technical interest (i.e., libertarianism, finance and money, or software), and most of them were also male (15 out of 16) (see also [1,4,34]). Our informants' conceptions, borrowed from their previous experiences, still may have contained gaps; specifically, they had not yet resolved major and ongoing contradictions between Bitcoin and the wider legal and financial complexes. The point is that these technical backgrounds motivated the informants toward appropriation regardless whether their visions may miss aspects of social realities.

As a technical tool, Bitcoin is unambiguous; but as a social artifact, it could be an investment product, a political statement, or a medium of exchange. Thus, these conceptual tools assist appropriators in their social process of finding potential meanings in technologies.

6.1.3 Social Affinity

Social affinity describes the degree to which an appropriator can identify social supports, while taking time to resolve social stigmas and contradictions surrounding an innovation. Social affinity differs from contextual affinity in that a context may contain many social groups; being in the right context may not guarantee that the user would encounter the right people. Also, technology encounter, and research and learning, can be entirely personal; a user need not discuss these experiences with others. But at times, when he does bring up his new-found ideas with others, he may find welcoming support which encourages him to further his interest. Or he could also find his way into an adjacent community, where he can establish new, supportive relationships.

The truth is that innovations at a very early stage of development often lack public understanding and empathy, making it difficult for early-stage appropriators to leverage social affinity. Among our informants, only a few like David had access to close friends with whom they could discuss Bitcoin. This is a reason some of our informants sought out online communities to identify discussants. But online communities are not always welcoming to learners; for instance, Vincent found that the Bitcoin IRC was unwelcoming to beginners asking basic questions. Instead, he fell back to reading articles on the Internet, and seeking new local ties on Facebook. Unlike online forums, Facebook (also Meetup) communities aggregate and hybridize virtual and local interactions, with social groups conducting the same discourses but oscillating between online and offline formats.

In a community, meanings are conceived through an extended period of social interactions between members [39]. And the Bitcoin meetups provide a cultural blank slate in which members can negotiate new meanings without being overly burdened by social stigmas. This fresh start is important because the technology's current design has inherent contradictions with legal and financial structures, which also vary between countries and localities. Members of local communities (e.g., entrepreneurs), especially those intent on reifying Bitcoin into concrete products, have to resolve these contradictions with law enforcement agencies, local legislatures, finance actors, and the public.

7. CONCLUSIONS AND IMPLICATIONS

In this study, we contributed the notion of *cultural affinities*, filling a research gap within the appropriation literature, which had focused on personalization and reuse of matured technologies. By investigating user appropriation of Bitcoin, an emerging technology, we were able to identify sociocultural factors influencing early-stage appropriation—a phenomenon that is rarely observed among users of matured technologies. We found that during early-stage appropriation, the innovator's key task is not just to provide technical support to users, but to engage them—encouraging them to muster their contextual, conceptual, and social resources—to build a cultural enterprise (e.g., meaningful-use cases and practices that build on techno-utopian narratives). The period of time from users' first encounter to when they were ready to invest their time in the community ranged from months to more than one year among our informants. Importantly, we have pointed out that user-appropriators were in fact already interested in real-world possibilities of the technology (as was reported in previous studies [14,30,32]) through which they could remix meanings. Thus, technological appropriation is not simply a use proposition, but a cultural proposition; the innovators are attempting to engage users to establish a technology that extends existing and notable cultural framings (e.g., Bitcoin as a libertarian tool, or as a financial technology).

A design implication is that, to encourage appropriation, innovators need to identify and develop relationships with these pre-existing and culturally rich communities. Innovators may identify communities (i.e., contexts) that have members who are pre-exposed to the technology (i.e., social affinity), and also the ideologies that motivate their interests (i.e., concepts). Innovators may then invite potential users to codevelop the technology in ways these users perceive to be meaningful. While innovators may claim ownership of the technology's blueprint, its future uses often lie in the hands of its early appropriators. In the case of a radical innovation like Bitcoin, innovators may even consider inviting users to form a whole new community (e.g., through financial and technical support) to develop a newly reified set of meanings and purposes conducive to the innovation. Importantly, cultural affinities provide ways of discovering and identifying user-appropriators who will play important roles fostering their own personal agendas, meanings, ethos, and narratives into emerging technologies.

8. ACKNOWLEDGMENTS

We thank the anonymous reviewers who had provided many relevant angles and perspectives which contributed to the writing of this paper. The work described in this paper was partially supported by grants from City University of Hong Kong (Project No. 7004297), and the National Science Foundation of China (NSFC) under the awards No.61300201.

9. REFERENCES

[1] Serkan Akinci, Safak Aksoy, and Eda Atilgan. 2004. Adoption of Internet banking among sophisticated consumer segments in an advanced developing country. *International Journal of Bank Marketing* 22, MAY 2004: 212–232. http://doi.org/10.1108/02652320410530322

[2] Alex Leavitt. 2016. Collaborative Appropriation: The Emergence of Breaking News Collaborations on reddit.com. *Proceedings of the 30th European Conference on Computer-supported Cooperative Work 2016 Extended Abstract*, ACM Press.

[3] Amaury Belin and Yannick Prié. 2012. DIAM: Towards a model for describing appropriation processes through the evolution of digital artifacts. *Dis 2012*: 645–654. http://doi.org/10.1145/2317956.2318053

[4] Nancy Jo Black, Andy Lockett, Heidi Winklhofer, and Christine Ennew. 2001. The adoption of Internet financial services: a qualitative study. *International Journal of Retail & Distribution Management* 29, 8: 390–398. http://doi.org/10.1108/09590550110397033

[5] Alexander Boden, Gabriela Avram, Liam Bannon, and Volker Wulf. 2012. Knowledge sharing practices and the impact of cultural factors: Reflections on two case studies of offshoring in SME. *Journal of software: Evolution and Process*, 139–152. http://doi.org/10.1002/smr.473

[6] Susanne Bødker and Ellen Christiansen. 2012. Poetry in motion. *Proceedings of the 30th European Conference on Cognitive Ergonomics - ECCE '12*, ACM Press, 78. http://doi.org/10.1145/2448136.2448152

[7] John M. Carroll, Mary Beth Rosson, Umer Farooq, and Jamika D. Burge. 2009. Community collective efficacy. In *Handbook of Research on Socio-Technical Design and Social Networking Systems*. 607–618. Retrieved from http://jcarroll.ist.psu.edu/files/cce2009.pdf

[8] Paul Dourish. 2003. The appropriation of interactive technologies: Some lessons from placeless documents. *Computer Supported Cooperative Work: CSCW: An International Journal* 12, 4: 465–490. http://doi.org/10.1023/A:1026149119426

[9] David S Evans and Richard Schmalensee. 2005. *Paying with plastic: The digital revolution in buying and borrowing*. Retrieved from http://search.proquest.com/docview/38224406?accountid=9630\nhttp://zw4gk5cr3l.search.serialssolutions.com/?ctx_ver=Z39.88-2004&ctx_enc=info:ofi/enc:UTF-8&rfr_id=info:sid/ProQ:ibssshell&rft_val_fmt=info:ofi/fmt:kev:mtx:journal&rft.genre=unknown&rft.jtitle=

[10] Florian Graillot. 2015. Bitcoin Might Be The Next Big Thing In The Remittance Market. *Techcrunch*. Retrieved from http://techcrunch.com/2015/05/25/bitcoin-might-be-the-next-big-thing-in-the-remittance-market/

[11] James Paul Gee. 1989. What is literacy. *Journal of Education* 71, 1: 18–25.

[12] G. Gowrisankaran and J Stavins. 2004. Network externalities and technology adoption: Lessons from electronic payments. *RAND Journal of Economics* 35, 2: 260–276. http://doi.org/10.2307/1593691

[13] Jina Huh, Mark W Newman, and Mark S Ackerman. 2011. Supporting Collaborative Help for Individualized Use.

Proceedings of the SIGCHI Conference on Human Factors in Computing Systems: 3141–3150. http://doi.org/10.1145/1978942.1979408
[14] Ioanna Iacovides, Charlene Jennett, Cassandra Cornish-Trestrail, and Anna L Cox. 2013. Do games attract or sustain engagement in citizen science? A study of volunteer motivations. *CHI '13 Extended Abstracts on Human Factors in Computing Systems*, 1101–1106. http://doi.org/10.1145/2468356.2468553
[15] Jordan Maglich. 2014. Texas Man Arrested For $4.5 Million Bitcoin Ponzi Scheme. *Forbes*. Retrieved from http://www.forbes.com/sites/jordanmaglich/2014/11/06/texas-man-arrested-for-4-5-million-bitcoin-ponzi-scheme/#53ffb18ce1d3
[16] Robert E. Kraut and Paul Resnick. 2012. Building Successful Online Communities: Evidence-Based Social Design. *The MIT Press*: 328. http://doi.org/10.1002/pssb.201300062
[17] Chris J. Lintott, Kevin Schawinski, An??e Slosar, et al. 2008. Galaxy Zoo: Morphologies derived from visual inspection of galaxies from the Sloan Digital Sky Survey. *Monthly Notices of the Royal Astronomical Society* 389, 3: 1179–1189. http://doi.org/10.1111/j.1365-2966.2008.13689.x
[18] Caitlin Lustig and Bonnie Nardi. 2015. Algorithmic Authority: The Case of Bitcoin. http://doi.org/10.1109/HICSS.2015.95
[19] Wendy March, Margot Jacobs, and Tony Salvador. 2005. Designing technology for community appropriation. *CHI 05*, 2126 – 2127. http://doi.org/10.1145/1056808.1057120
[20] Bill Maurer, Taylor C. Nelms, and Lana Swartz. 2013. "When perhaps the real problem is money itself!": the practical materiality of Bitcoin. *Social Semiotics* 23, 2: 261–277. http://doi.org/10.1080/10350330.2013.777594
[21] Timothy May. 1994. Crypto Anarchy and Virtual Communities. In *Crypto Anarchy Cyberstates and Pirate Utopias*. 65–79. Retrieved from http://www.textfiles.com/internet/anarchy
[22] Sally McKechnie, Heidi Winklhofer, and Christine Ennew. 2006. Applying the Technology Acceptance Model to the Online Retailing of Financial Services. *International Journal of Retail & Distribution Management* 34, 4/5: 388–410. http://doi.org/10.1108/09590550610660297
[23] Michelle Price and Lizzie Ko. 2015. Hong Kong lawmakers urge ban on bitcoin as scam victims turn to police. *Reuters*. Retrieved from http://www.reuters.com/article/us-fraud-bitcoin-hongkong-idUSKBN0LF0WS20150211
[24] Mike Orcutt. 2015. Why Bitcoin Could Be Much More Than a Currency. *MIT Technology Review*. Retrieved from https://www.technologyreview.com/s/537246/why-bitcoin-could-be-much-more-than-a-currency/
[25] Satoshi Nakamoto. 2008. Bitcoin: A Peer-to-Peer Electronic Cash System. *www.bitcoin.org*, 9. http://doi.org/10.1007/s10838-008-9062-0
[26] WJ Orlikowski, JA Yates, Orlikowski, Yates, Okamura, and Fujimoto. 1995. Shaping Electronic Communication: The Metastructuring of Technology in the Context of Use. *Organization Science* 6, 4: 423–444. http://doi.org/10.1287/orsc.6.4.423
[27] Bernd Ploderer and Peter Thomas. 2008. Being Online, Living Offline: The Influence of Social Ties over the Appropriation of Social Network Sites. *Information Systems Journal*: 333–342. http://doi.org/10.1145/1460563.1460618
[28] Reid Priedhorsky, Mikhil Masli, and Loren Terveen. 2010. Eliciting and Focusing Geographic Volunteer Work. *2010 Acm Conference on Computer Supported Cooperative Work*: 61–70. http://doi.org/10.1145/1718918.1718931
[29] Pablo-Alejandro Quinones. 2014. Cultivating practice & shepherding technology use. *Proceedings of the 17th ACM conference on Computer supported cooperative work & social computing - CSCW '14*, FEBRUARY 2015: 305–318. http://doi.org/10.1145/2531602.2531698
[30] M. Jordan Raddick, Georgia Bracey, Pamela L. Gay, et al. 2010. Galaxy Zoo: Exploring the Motivations of Citizen Science Volunteers. *Astronomy Education Review* 9, 1: 010103. http://doi.org/10.3847/AER2009036
[31] Paul Resnick, Joseph Konstan, Yan Chen, and Robert E. Kraut. 2011. Starting New Online Communities. In *Evidencebased Social Design Mining the Social Sciences to Build Online Communities*. 231–281.
[32] Joel Ross, Andrew Zaldivar, Lilly Irani, and Bill Tomlinson. 2010. Who are the Turkers? Worker Demographics in Amazon Mechanical Turk. *Chi Ea 2010*: 2863–2872. http://doi.org/10.1145/1753846.1753873
[33] Antti Salovaara. 2007. Appropriation of a MMS-Based Comic Creator : From System Functionalities to Resources for Action. *CHI 2007 Proceedings*: 1117–1126. http://doi.org/10.1145/1240624.1240794
[34] E. T. Straub. 2009. Understanding Technology Adoption: Theory and Future Directions for Informal Learning. *Review of Educational Research* 79, 2: 625–649. http://doi.org/10.3102/0034654308325896
[35] Anselm Strauss and Juliet Corbin. 1990. Basics of Qualitative Research. In *Basics of. Qualitatice Research 2nd edition*. 3–14. http://doi.org/10.4135/9781452230153
[36] Nick Szabo. 1997. Formalizing and securing relationships on public networks. *First Monday* 2, 9. http://doi.org/10.5210/fm.v2i9.548
[37] Joshua Tanenbaum, Karen Tanenbaum, and Ron Wakkary. 2012. Steampunk as Design Fiction. *Chi*, May 5: 1583–1592. http://doi.org/10.1145/2207676.2208279
[38] Viswanath Venkatesh, Michael G Morris, Gordon B Davis, and Fred D Davis. 2003. User acceptance of information technology: Toward a unified view. *MIS Quarterly* 27, 3: 425–478. http://doi.org/10.2307/30036540
[39] E Wenger. 1998. Communities of Practice : Learning as a social system. *Systems thinker* 9, 5: 2–3. http://doi.org/10.2277/0521663636

"It is Not Because You Have Tools that You Must use Them" - The Difficult Domestication of a Telemedicine Toolkit to Manage Emergencies in Nursing Homes

Gérald Gaglio, Myriam Lewkowicz, Matthieu Tixier
ICD, HETIC, Tech-CICO, Troyes University of Technology, UMR 6281, CNRS
12, rue Marie Curie CS 42060
10004 TROYES CEDEX, France
firstname.lastname@utt.fr

ABSTRACT
We conducted a retrospective study on the experimental deployment of a telemedicine toolkit in ten nursing homes. The purpose of the experiment was to see whether the use of these toolkits could allow for better cooperation between nursing homes and the local emergency medical dispatch center to avoid sending costly vehicles and having elderly people unnecessarily discharged at the hospital. We investigated the domestication process of these toolkits by nurses and orderlies from the nursing homes. Our findings show different levels of domestication: for some of the nursing homes, the lack of practical relevance of the toolkit in emergencies and the difficulty to borrow artifacts from doctors prevented complete adoption. For three nursing homes, domestication occurred in an unexpected way in the sense that the objective of the domestication changed. These findings led us to provide recommendations for projects aimed at improving inter-organizational cooperation through artifacts.

Keywords
Telemedicine; domestication; nursing homes; boundary negotiating artifacts

1. INTRODUCTION
A growing number of elderly people end up more or less medicated in nursing homes. These are institutions that regularly deal with complex situations and are faced with deciding whether an emergency requires that a patient should be sent to the hospital - as opposed to situations where people can be treated in the nursing home itself.

Studies have been conducted that showed that people in nursing homes are more likely to be sent to an Emergency Department (ED) than those living in their home [9]. This represents an unfavorable discontinuity of care for frail elderly people [8, 48], and up to 40% of the discharges are considered potentially avoidable [17]. This is an important issue for several reasons. First, this has a negative impact on the short- and mid-term quality of life of the elderly people [36]; second, it has a financial impact on the community [16, 30]. Studies have been conducted to determine how these unnecessary discharges to the ED could be avoided. A recent synthesis of this work can be found in [29]. Among the ten key factors that have been identified in the literature, the following hold our attention: that the nursing home staff should be trained to address emergency situations, that nursing homes should be equipped with diagnostic devices, that the nursing home staff should be educated on acronyms used in these situations to better communicate with doctors, that ED and nursing home staff should better communicate about the patient data, and finally that the decision-making process should be made more transparent by emergency staff to allow for more cooperation with the nursing home staff.

Indeed, we had the opportunity to be involved in a telemedicine experiment involving ten nursing homes around the city of Troyes (France) and the local emergency response service. In France, the emergency medical dispatch center (EMDC) of a region is responsible for providing an adequate response to urgent medical problems that are submitted via a telephone line exclusively for medical emergencies (15 in France, 112 in Europe). The treatment of these phone calls is called regulation of emergencies. The purpose is to evaluate the criticality of the emergency and to determine if the need is a simple emergency support on the phone, a consignment of heavy mobile equipment (mobile intensive care unit), an ambulance being sent, or a consultation with a general practitioner. Each call is managed first by an assistant of medical regulation, who registers the request of urgent medical aid and evaluates, in a few questions, the degree of urgency to pass the caller to the regulating doctor. The regulating doctor decides whether it is a vital emergency (heart problems, breathing difficulties, comas, serious injury from an accident, etc.). Sending out a vehicle is very costly for the community, and the local emergency service cited in the present case study only has three ambulances at its disposal.

The purpose of the studied experiment was to determine whether offering a telemedicine toolkit to the nursing homes could allow for better cooperation between the nursing homes and the emergency medical dispatch center to avoid sending costly vehicles and having elderly people discharged at the hospital unnecessarily. In fact, in France, there is little medical presence in nursing homes to take care of the residents. Most of them do not employ a doctor, but nurses and orderlies among which the labor is very precisely divided. The work is also tightly scheduled and there is a clear paradox: hospitals are hoping that nursing homes can manage the situations of their residents in an independent way, but it is doubtful that nursing homes actually have the means to achieve this autonomy. This is the reason why the regulating doctors in EMDC are concerned, because this lack of medical presence is a potential dis-organization factor.

The telemedicine toolkit is a suitcase that includes devices with which the nursing home staff can perform an electrocardiograph,

GROUP '16, November 13 - 16, 2016, Sanibel Island, FL, USA

ACM 978-1-4503-4276-6/16/11..$15.00
DOI: http://dx.doi.org/10.1145/2957276.2957288.

measure blood pressure and determine how much oxygen people have in their blood; it uses a Tablet PC with an integrated webcam to transmit the data gathered using these instruments to the emergency medical dispatch center so that the nursing home staff can discuss the situation with the medical regulators (Figure 1).

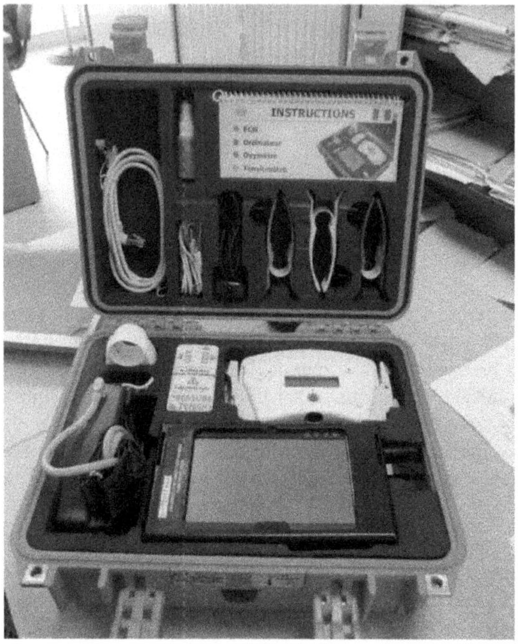

Figure 1: The telemedicine toolkit (in the form of a suitcase)

Having observed the deployment of this telemedicine toolkit in ten nursing homes, we interpret this story by conducting a socio-material analysis of the project from its inception using the domestication framework [38]. By so doing, we aim to adopt a perspective in which the success or failure of an instrumentation project is a socio-material accomplishment performed in and by heterogeneous project actors, and this success or failure is inherently indeterminate [6].

The present study is part of a general research endeavor aiming at looking if telemedicine tools are conducive to cooperation between different organizations in situations described as emergencies.

More precisely, our research questions here are:

1) Have nursing homes engaged in processes seeking to ensure the domestication of these telemedicine tools?

2) What implications can we draw for future telemedicine projects?

In the remaining sections of this paper, we first present existing work related to studying the cooperation between different healthcare organizations and potential conceptual frameworks to analyze the case we have observed. Then, we present the origin of the case and the case itself, following the domestication framework. We then analyze the causes of success and failure and conclude with insights for future projects in this domain.

2. RELATED WORK

2.1 Studies of Cooperation in Healthcare Organizations

Several studies have documented the interweaving of the work of different health professionals (doctors, consultants, clerks, nurses, and orderlies) with the support of numerous tools, documents, charts and processes [2, 5, 20, 43]. These practices distributed on a dense web of artifacts appear to be effortfully choreographed [33] for the sake of patient care [3].

The material side of the support of cooperative practices in healthcare should not hide the dynamic human work required to produce, structure and use these tools [4, 45]. It has been particularly emphasized in investigations of the deployment of EHR (Electronic Health Records) that have shown how professionals work around or adapt Information and Communication Technologies (ICT) to their collaborative work practices [7, 27, 31, 35, 44, 49]. A good example of this adaptation is the one presented by [31] in which the doctors carry personal notes to deal with the lack of availability of patients' EHR at the bedside (contrary to the paper chart solution that existed before). Overlooking the networked and continuous adaptation activity of the nurses to organize the care plan was also presented as an explanation for the failure of a project aimed at deploying a computer-based system in a University Hospital [26].

Moreover, coordinative practices are also attached to the complex network of status and acquaintances in health organizations [43]. These authors highlighted that, even if, in the studied hospital, the process of obtaining radiological examination and data is formally defined and tied to the filling out of a request form, doctors and external medical consultants are found justified by administrative staff and radiologist (being doctors too) in partially following the procedures. Such bypassing and workaround are accepted due to the primary goal, which is caring for patients (against completing administrative processes).

A full understanding of cooperation within and among health organizations is far from being achieved but the previous studies that we listed highlight that: (1) to coordinate themselves, health professionals use and work around a dense web of artifacts; (2) these tools are parts of the professionals' wider coordinative practices, which can evolve to integrate, adapt or reject new artifacts that seem relevant for practical or organizational issues; and (3) statuses and values (such as patients' health) are not neutral in the implementation and use of coordinative artifacts.

Our study of the experimental deployment of a telemedicine toolkit in nursing homes to ease the cooperation between the nursing homes and the local emergency medical dispatch center (EMDC) draws on these on-going research issues but develops them at an inter-organizational level. In fact, to understand the reason why some systems are adopted or not, and the key related factors, it is important to follow deployment processes, to look at them from a user's perspective, and to determine how these users are able, or not, to appropriate the systems.

2.2 Appropriation

Technology use in practice is often quite different than designers anticipate. We often notice unexpected uses and transformations to achieve goals that were never imagined by the designers. Therefore, appropriation, or the way users are integrating technologies into their actions, has been a topic of investigation for researchers in the field, as we can see in the Computer Supported Cooperative Work (CSCW) domain, which has a long tradition of fine-grained observational studies of particular settings in which artifacts are deployed [23].

The appropriation of technologies refers to the installation of new tools and their customization or tailorization, but moreover the organizational learning and the transformation of work practices induced by the introduction of the technology [13]. While tailoring focuses on the technical customizations of artifacts, appropriation also considers the social-technical process of interpreting artifacts in daily work practice. "Appropriation is the way in which technologies are adopted, adapted and incorporated into working practice" [11, p. 467].

We are particularly interested in this approach in which appropriation simultaneously tackles redesigning some aspects of the technology, reconfiguring organizational relations, and reconfiguring aspects of the physical environment [1]. Therefore, the work that we are presenting in this paper focuses on how people make the technologies work within a particular social and material context. Here, we perform a retrospective analysis of the introduction of a telemedicine toolkit to clarify and elaborate the general lessons learned. For conducting this analysis, we decided to use the domestication framework.

2.3 Domestication

The domestication framework addresses the ways in which people in social situations (homes, communities, and families) adopt and use ICTs [18]. The idea is that, when people take up an ICT, they undergo a process by which these ICTs are appropriated, and this process changes both the situation and the meaning of it. The focus of domestication is on the mechanisms by which an ICT is customized and how routine practices are adapted to accept the new ICT [21, 37]. The assumption is that neither the technology nor the social aspect are determinants to understand ICT use, but both aspects co-determine each other. This theory proposes four steps of domestication: appropriation, objectification, incorporation and conversion. In the appropriation phase, the acquisition of the ICT is the main activity; ICT is beginning its new role as a domestic object. Objectification captures how values are expressed through the display of the new ICT and emphasizes where and how the ICT is arranged and displayed. The incorporation phase focuses on how the ICT is used over time by the user. Finally, the conversion phase mediates relations between the households' internal affairs and the public domain or outside world.

The process of domestication offers an account of the innovation process of a media and information technology in all its uncertainty and indeterminacy. Although it has mainly been used to analyze the use of technologies in domestic settings, it was clear from the beginning that it should not be seen as something that only occurs in the home [37]. For instance, [32] or [19] have illustrated "professional domestication," whereby the potential for new ICTs to be fitted into or to fail to find a place within existing work arrangements is observed.

3. ABOUT THE CASE

The experiment ran from February, 2012 to December, 2014 and funding was received from the Regional Healthcare Agency, a public sector organization operating in all of France's 22 regions since the country enacted its 2009 *Hôpital, Santé et Territoires* law. The agency assembles, at a regional level, state and public-health resources to maximize collective efficiency and sustain the National Health Service in the future. To understand what was expected from this experiment, it is worth discussing the ideas motivating its three drivers.

The first is Dr. Van Petegem[1], formerly Head Doctor at the local EMDC and who was still working both as triage doctor in the EMDC and in the ED of the local hospital. Dr. Van Petegem was concerned about the ever-increasing tide of very old people coming to emergency units, notably after calls made by nursing homes to the EMDC team. He was also very critical of his fellow triage doctors' "conditioned reflex" of systematically sending vehicles out for very old people whom the doctors viewed as "bedridden invalids suffering from dementia". Dr. Van Petegem had the occasion to see the telemedicine "suitcases" presented at a conference: *"I was at a conference when I first heard about suitcases being used to transmit data. The idea was that it mainly helped first responders transmit ECG* [electrocardiograph] *readings from their ambulances. I started wondering whether we could use the same idea to decrease the number of old persons being brought to ED… This ultimately became my main goal, with a second one being to bring the medical and medical-social worlds a little closer together. At this latter level I was in luck after meeting Mrs. Parinello at the Doctors Council where I first spoke about my idea. She was very open to it."*

Mrs. Parinello, who runs two old-age nursing homes and is also a local public figure (having been elected a substitute city councilor), agreed to this experiment based on two observations. First, she found that the ED was an hostile environment for nursing home residents who would sometimes have to wait for hours on trolleys in cold corridors before returning to their nursing homes in worse shape than they had left - undermining the idea that people are always supposed to get better when they are treated in hospital [41]. It was also hard for them returning to the nursing home. As much as possible, residents are supposed to be left in the "cocoon" of their "final home" [24]. Mrs. Parinello also described the rocky cooperation between triage doctors and healthcare staff working in nursing homes, especially orderlies who tended to be women without any nursing diplomas. According to her, *"they* [triage doctors] *don't always react very well to us"; "We get told off a lot"*. In other words, there was good reason to doubt the nursing homes' professionalism and the reasons why they were calling the EMDC. This being the case, the suitcase could be viewed as a way of improving the status quo by avoiding people always sending out ambulances and by helping residents to stay in the nursing homes when appropriate. After all, patients complaining about chest pains would normally be reassured when they saw an electrocardiogram machine. The promise was that if fewer nursing home residents were sent to the ED, savings could be achieved.

The third main player in this equation is Maciste Technologies, the small company that has built and is selling the telemedicine "suitcase". The primary contact here was the company's Sales Director. He was very enthusiastic about an experiment that he expected to bring about €120,000 (€12,000 per suitcase) to his financially struggling company. He also hoped a greater familiarization with the world of nursing homes would facilitate entry into this potentially lucrative new market. It is worth noting here that this suitcase solution was not originally defined for this cooperation context. The idea came in 1996 after a meeting between a doctor working in the merchant marine and the founder of Maciste Technologies. They had the idea of simplifying the equipment to make electrocardiographs, and then equipping French merchant marine ships with electrocardiograms for use in case somebody had a heart attack. This led to the portable electrocardiograph being turned little by little into a "suitcase" containing other instruments. These suitcases first took off in the late 2000s when they were being used by a large French airliner trying to avoid costly unplanned stops for passengers who had fallen ill. This initial market breakthrough fell short, however, after

[1] Names have been changed

the stewards union argued that its members were not authorized to carry out electrocardiographs (ECGs).

All of which explains why suitcases would ultimately be brought back to another professional environment - nursing homes in contact with the EMDC.

4. METHODOLOGY

The first author of this paper (sociologist) was involved in the field work and collected a variety of empirical materials from January to June, 2014, in line with the precepts of "combinatory ethnography" [10]. This period has been selected because sufficient time has elapsed since the start of the experiment (at the beginning of 2012). Besides, the first author has maintained regular interactions with the main protagonists of the experiment after June 2014, so that we were able to stay informed of the recent developments of the project.

The aim of this 6 months period of field work was to establish "ethnographic jurisprudence", i.e., a series of case studies or relevant situations "revealing forms of activity" that are original or at least noteworthy [10, p. 51]. The methodological approach adopted here was also inspired by multi-sited ethnography that essentially involves "following people, connections, associations, and relationships across space (because they are substantially continuous but spatially non-contiguous) [25]. The research design proceeds by a series of juxtapositions in which the global is collapsed into and made an integral part of parallel, related local situations, rather than something monolithic or external to them. In terms of the method, multi-sited ethnography involves a spatially dispersed field through which the ethnographer moves – actually, via sojourns in two or more places, or conceptually, by means of techniques of juxtaposition of data" [14, p. 3].

The first data category is semi-directive interviews. The purpose of the interviews was to get a variety of opinions regarding the experiment and to garner information from professional circles into which the suitcases had been launched. This was meant to enhance understanding of the kinds of actions required when an emergency occurred, both before and after the parties in question came into possession of this composite technical object. For so doing, it was important to start meeting relevant representatives from all professional groups with some relationship to the suitcases.

This led to interviewing seven nursing home directors (including one operating in a rural setting who did not have the suitcase but wanted one), three head nurses working in these establishments (who did little care work but managed teams), four front-line nurses with no other hierarchical responsibilities, two coordinating doctors who were generally on-site two afternoons a week and operated at the behest of the residents' treatment doctors (working out of their surgeries), Dr. Van Petegem, two orderlies, the sales director of Maciste Technologies, two relevant members of the Regional Healthcare Agency (the public organization funding the experiment) and one IT specialist responsible for several of the nursing homes participating in the experiment. In total, there were 24 interviews, each lasting approximately 90 minutes, with eight men and sixteen women aged between 23 and 65. They were entirely transcribed and analyzed following the content analysis method [28].

To disprove, confirm or complement any information collected during the interviews, in situ observations were carried out in locations where suitcases could be used. These observations also helped to make empirical descriptions of the ecologies of action, noting off-the-cuff quotes and reconstructing interactional sequences. Unfortunately, it was impossible to observe how the object was being used in emergency situations given the dearth thereof. On the other hand, because researchers are supposed to adapt to the impromptu nature characterizing innovation processes, while improvising responses to what they see, what was observed were planned uses of the apparatus (so-called baseline ECG, see below) – uses for which no plans had been made at first. In addition, we attended a training session in which the equipment was being used, and two days and two nights were spent in nursing homes, as well as two nights at the EMDC.

Third, a series of documents were gathered, with a number of photos also being taking during the observation phases. Written texts involved, for instance, nursing homes' internal memos trying to reassure employees of what would occur if suitcases were used; an angry mail exchange between a care team in a nursing home and the ED unit accusing the former of sending residents "for the tiniest little problem"; and a descriptive questionnaire meant to inform calls to the EMDC from orderlies (called "Esperanto" and described in section 5). Photos were taken whenever deemed necessary; however, not all of the photos were kept. The goal of taking pictures was to communicate the atmosphere on-site, the ecologies of action, the look of objects, etc.

The sum total of these efforts contributed to an indicative logic based on an administration of proof; photos could serve as markers of processes at work, attesting to a greater or lesser attempt at appropriation; an exchange of letters or internal retirement memos could sometimes signal an attempt to solve an argument, etc. All of these methodological processes supplemented an inductive logic as it is usually applied in grounded theory [15], the latter also being relevant to the present exercise.

5. THE DOMESTICATION OF THE TELEMEDICINE TOOLKIT

To present how suitcases were received in the nursing homes (irrespective of the EMDC), the previously mentioned domestication theoretical framework [38] was applied. This framework had originally been conceived for private sphere activities. In this sense, the particularity of a nursing home is that it is both a place where people live and one where they receive care. It is worth stating that the use of suitcases was relatively rare and only occurred in three out of the ten nursing homes involved in the experiment. Nevertheless, a respectable number of 25 remote transmissions of ECG to the EMDC were stated. This total means relatively little, however, given how long the experiment lasted (about three years) and above all given the total number of nursing homes that took part (ten).

5.1 Appropriation

Regarding the acquisition of the technology – something that the domestication model refers to as "appropriation" [38] - what the investigation demonstrated is that the suitcases suffered from an original setback. For instance, two nursing homes were given free suitcases by Maciste Technologies in early 2012 after meeting the sales director, Dr. Van Petegem and Mrs. Parinello. One young nursing home director in Troyes also tried to acquire the equipment when Mrs. Parinello told her that Maciste Technologies was ready to hand out free samples to two establishments (hers and another). Toward the end of 2012, Mrs. Parinello arm-wrestled a Regional Healthcare Agency subsidy for other nursing home members. This is how, in early 2013, suitcases were "suddenly... parachuted" - in one skeptical nurse's words - to establishments where nobody was particularly looking forward to getting them. Mrs. Parinello thought she was doing something good but encountered a great deal of hostility. Despite all her dynamism and experience, most nursing home managers saw things differently. They felt that staff members did not need technically superior equipment because they could simply manage emergency situations by calling the EMDC. This initial differentiation in people's outlook may or may not constitute an example of organizational sensemaking [47].

5.2 Objectification

Across the ten nursing homes participating in the experiment, there was less adoption than might otherwise have been expected. One way of understanding this is by noting that suitcases encountered technical difficulties that appeared over the course of the experiment. Some of the challenges here played out at a spatial level and/or in terms of the fit between material and physical environments - all of which are indicative of the domestication model's "objectification" phase [38]. The main hurdle was related to the Internet connections enabling the remote transmission of data (ECG readings, blood pressure, and saturation) using electronic messaging on the suitcase's Tablet PC. The nursing homes needed to cover as much of their premises as possible so they would be prepared wherever a medical incident occurred. In merchant marine ships, where suitcases had first been used, they were simply equipped with SIM cards, GSM and low bandwidth GPRS connections. This technical solution was not enough for nursing homes because some of their rooms were not covered by the GSM network. Tests undertaken at the beginning of the experiment showed that Tablet PC messages to the EMDC would only arrive if sent from certain locations within the buildings.

Depending on the configuration (number of floors, buildings, area, age, etc.) and other factors such as the thickness of the walls or the number of sockets, two solutions were possible. First, RJ45 sockets could be used to connect the Tablet PC to a wall socket.

Second, participants had the option to use wireless connections, but nursing homes that were already equipped with RJ45 sockets in all resident rooms tended to prefer this solution over Wi-Fi because it did not require spending any more money.

Mrs. Parinello opted for Wi-Fi because her institution lacked a network of RJ45 sockets. Other nursing homes postponed this investment or were happy to use whatever RJ45 socket they already had in their nurses' office. The key here was that suitcases were not products that could be used off-the-shelf. This means that they had to be "objectified" [38] and that they imposed certain "technical requirements", in the words of a technical expert met at the Regional Healthcare Agency.

Another series of obstacles related to legal arguments about liability were raised. A technical expert at the Regional Healthcare Agency, who was opposed to funding the experiment, was quick to suggest that, because medical data is strictly confidential in France, it should not be communicated via unencrypted emails. This explains why the new version of the suitcase (expected for September, 2016) is supposed to use a secure cloud. Note that this is a type of equipment that uses its own weaknesses (and detractors' criticisms) as a means of evolving. In the present case, the suitcase actually transformed over the course of the experiment, as if it were simultaneously ready to be used but also open to redesign, something at odds with the diffusionist schema [34].

5.3 Incorporation

Looking at the incorporation of the suitcase in the work practices of the employees of the nursing homes, the domestication process did, however, follow a number of trajectories that the nursing homes had not predicted, especially the three that were using it at first.

First, - and much like the previously mentioned airline stewards - orderlies in the different participating nursing homes felt a sense of foreboding. This fell into the domain of (professional) values, which is consistent with what is emphasized at this step of the domestication model [38]. It exemplifies doubt (or rather the expression of certainty) that these professionals - often women – were not authorized to carry out ECGs on residents, even in emergency situations. Registered nurses had been trained to do this kind of testing and were experienced in analyzing electrocardiograph results at a basic level. Even more importantly, they had often been given the responsibility of administering ECGs in hospitals, working under a doctor's supervision. Orderlies, on the other hand, had never had any formal ECG training. The argument that broke out at this level went much further, however, than a question of legalities and the interpretation thereof. There was a real fear of being given responsibility for acts that had not been specified in the regulations describing the orderlies' duties, despite this being a professional milieu where tasks were often undertaken by parties other than the ones for whom they had originally been conceived. For instance, orderlies were not authorized to take people's blood pressure but often did this with permission from nurses, their hierarchical superiors. In the present case, however, with suitcases having just arrived in the nursing homes, the orderlies began anticipating a number of risks, even if this was not fully verbalized. All of which created more than a little confusion during the investigation, with discussions sometimes relating to the act itself and, on other occasions, to the validity of the measurements, patients' condition or how ECGs should be interpreted. The way in which this can be analyzed across all of the participating nursing homes is that these various fears caused many orderlies "not to do anything", i.e., not to engage in a process of technological domestication.

The second issue faced when trying to incorporate the suitcase into the existing work practices was the lack of proper definition of "emergencies". In fact, the emergency situations faced by healthcare professionals in these nursing homes did not involve using the suitcases, or certainly not all of the items contained therein. This led to a differentiation between situations that were considered by the professionals to be "real" emergencies that they called: "pure emergencies", "life-threatening emergencies", "distress", or "the resident is dying". Here, the nurses would refer to respiratory distress accompanied by a pulmonary edema, malaises where people lost consciousness, heart attacks, acute vomiting with fever, falls where there was concern that the person had broken their leg, sudden (and violent) dementia, or hemorrhaging. These situations were compared with less critical ones such as a cut after somebody fell or chest pain unaccompanied by any worrisome clinical signs. Actors' reflexivity, which translated in this case by their asking practical questions - such as "Should I use the suitcase?" - drastically reduced the prospect of the suitcase being used in the way that had been expected for an "emergency". The domestication model [38] teaches that elimination is one of the key (mainly temporal) challenges faced during an incorporation phase. The head nurse in the nursing home managed by Mrs. Parinello expressed this as follows:

"*At first it is true that managers presented it to us like... Well at first it was supposed to be used more for problems that happen at night since we don't have as many nurses on the night shift. This was the real aim at first. Management used to say, in fact it still says, that it's "for an emergency". And I always thought "No, I won't use it in an emergency". If somebody is having problems breathing and then they say to us ... Well no, I wouldn't think of using the suitcase because it takes so long to get it ready... I mean just turning on a computer takes so long... So as a nurse I don't think so ... [...] I mean, a 70-year-old resident who can't breathe, I'm going to call EMDC because he has to go to the hospital right away ... So you know, a real emergency ... Maybe later on, it's never happened here, but somebody who has a nasty fall and is bleeding badly, am I going to take out my telemedicine equipment or first stop the bleeding? After all, I'm a nurse working in an emergency situation, trying to help residents. And this may mean starting by giving them oxygen because that provides some relief ... You know when you're choking it's not very nice ... You really expect me to take the time to get out my telemedicine equipment? While the person is choking? You see what I mean?*"

The point here is that in these "real emergency" situations, the health professionals felt the need to act and help people, for instance by immediately ringing the EMDC. Suitcases were extraneous to their expected behavior or actions during these incidents. It takes quite a while to get a suitcase started up and ready to administer an ECG (around eight minutes). This also competed with other medical or care acts (as indicated above) - with several nurses or orderlies insisting on the need to be close to the person in distress, reassuring them by taking their hand, etc. The idea here is that spending time on the suitcase "adds to patients' stress", in the words of a coordinating doctor working in one nursing home.

Therefore, the need to invent other uses for the suitcase, outside of the emergency situations that nursing home professionals described, arose.

Here, "incorporation" [38] took a positive form. The uses created in this way might be called "residential" because they were primarily geared toward nursing home residents and less so toward the idea of saving money by not sending patients to the ED. These uses then became appropriate for a particular site, the "residence", in this case a nursing home. In short, the new uses started being merged into daily work routines and realities of the nursing homes, much in the same way that the staffs were always on the lookout for patients suffering from bedsores. The end result was that the uses observed in the three institutions that had purchased the equipment can be categorized in two ways. The first is surveillance (and in opposition to the "life-threatening emergencies" discussed above), and this is apparent in the following discussion with one of the nurses:

I think that the first time [I was doing an ECG] was a morning when I was all alone. There was an old lady who was complaining about chest pains and the feeling she couldn't breathe. I wasn't sure what to do - it was about 8:30 or 9 AM and I was all alone with some orderly colleagues. I did an ECG and sent it [via email] to EMDC right away [...] After that I rang them to say "I've just sent you an ECG for an old lady" and told them about her symptoms and why I did it. They responded immediately, "It could be serious, she needs to come in right away, we're sending you an ambulance".

The other "residential" use consisted of administering an ECG when things were "normal" in order to provide a baseline for comparison. The idea here was to be able to compare the ECG of an older person when this person is not feeling well to the ECG of the older person when the situation was normal. Dr. Van Petegem had initiated this procedure, ostensibly in response to the confusion and difficulties witnessed when suitcases were used during emergency situations. He visited the nursing homes to talk about the initiative. Several expressed interest in his idea, but only three carried it out systematically.

Finally, during the first year that the experiment ran, the project tended to intensify cooperation between the different nursing homes and the EMDC, but in a way that had little to do with the suitcase. This was a response to the technical difficulties encountered when using the suitcase and to the rare emergency situations that the use of the suitcase helped to tackle. The starting point of this new way of cooperation was a knock against orderlies: doctors from the EMDC were annoyed that orderlies do not use the same language as them:

"When you have orderlies who call medical emergency, the question of the doctor is "could you describe how is Mrs So-and-so?" They often answer, "Not fine". For the doctor receiving the call, "Not fine" doesn't mean anything to him. Conversely, orderlies could say "she is an old woman, but usually she's fine". But for us, in the nursing home, it means that she still has her head even if we have to help with toileting, even if she is incontinent. They don't have the same references in the hospital sector "(interview with Mrs. Collibrini, nursing home director).

As a result, an informal workgroup was created, formed by Dr. Van Petegem, the coordinating doctor working in the nursing home run by Mrs. Parinello, and the head of the sector hospital's geriatrics department. This group put together a descriptive questionnaire, that they named "esperanto" (Figure 2), to help orderlies from nursing homes use a more medically oriented language when interacting with the EMDC. The goal was to support these orderlies and serve as a guide for them. In reality, the document paved the way for a kind of categorization. It included elements pertaining to parties' "initial observations" and taking of life-threatening readings. It then went on to cover typical events (neurologic disorders, chest pain, falls, breathing problems, etc.), providing both precisions and asking questions.

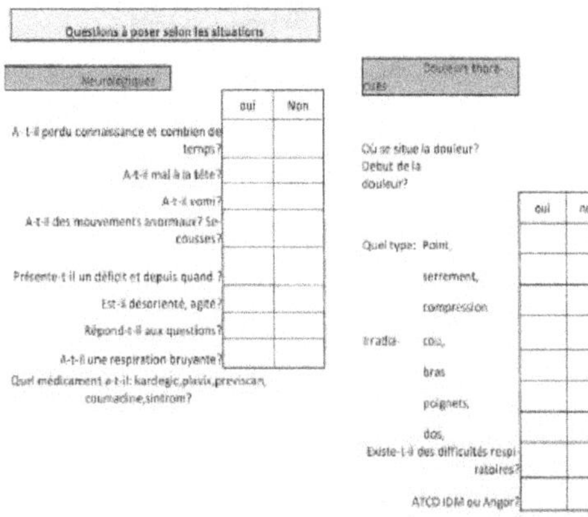

Figure 2: an excerpt of the "esperanto" questionnaire (in French)

In practical terms, the status of these questions was fairly uncertain, and it was unclear whether orderlies were supposed to ask them before calling the EMDC; ask the patient/resident; respond in writing; or prepare for the moment when they would have a triage doctor on the phone. In all probability, each of these options were possible.

5.4 Conversion

The "esperanto" questionnaire approach was highly appreciated by the promoters of the experiment, who must have felt that the suitcases were less important than the prospects they created. This was a bridge to the "conversion" phase of the domestication model [38] in which the use and the incorporation into work practices lead to an evolution of the relationships between the nursing homes and its wider public and organizational context. Since this questionnaire was designed, public communications around the experiment focused on the suitcase's secondary benefits. This attested to an organizational reflexivity driven by managers in the nursing homes pioneering the experiment and by certain other parties. Maciste Technologies also got involved with an approach based on turning the questionnaire into a "prerequisite" for using their equipment. In some nursing homes, the "esperanto" and the suitcase were even seen as an indivisible whole (Figure 3).

This irritated Mrs. Parinello, who stated that, "They [Maciste Technologies] are exploiting us". After all, the questionnaire did have some value. Notably, it drew the fund provider's attention toward the overall ambition of enhancing the extent to which nursing homes might take responsibility for emergencies without any further financial commitments having to be made. In this case, suitcases could no longer be considered central to a network that was itself declining. The questionnaire revealed a growing cooperation between the medical-social sector and hospitals (the "healthcare" sphere). It also revealed an ongoing bridging process (promoters of the suitcase talked about breaking down silos) as well as different parties' attempts to understand one another better, to familiarize themselves with each other, and thereby to improve their mutual effectiveness.

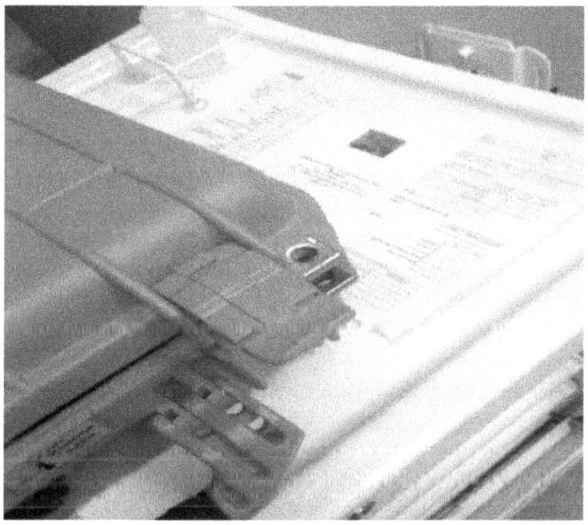

Figure 3: the suitcase and the esperanto as an indivisible whole

Above and beyond the aim of avoiding the unnecessary hospitalization of nursing home residents, the suitcase experiment ended up being part of an attempt to design greater cooperation between social worlds experiencing de facto interaction but whose level of cooperation could, in the eyes of relevant actors, be improved. This explains why the experiment's initiators began talking about "esperanto" and "shared language" when describing what they considered an undeniable success (the questionnaire).

Any discussion here about secondary benefits and "conversion" [38] should also mention the Wi-Fi infrastructure that coincided with the suitcase's arrival. Such connections could then be used for other purposes and would often lead to organizations reflecting upon the link between their residents and the outside world - and specifically whether they should wire up each room over time so that residents could all communicate with the outside world.

A final element is that the three nursing homes where the domestication occurred went even further than expected with their baseline ECGs by systematically doing an ECG for each new resident. Families would be made aware of this when they first came to speak with the nursing home director about moving in their elderly parent. The suitcase, or more specifically the ECG data contained therein, would be used, to some extent, by the nursing home as a way of presenting itself, i.e., communicating a serious image of itself to families.

6. DISCUSSION

As we have just shown, of the ten nursing homes included for the experimental deployment of the suitcase, only three have gone through the four stages of domestication, while the others are locked at one or another step shorter after acquisition. In what follows, we highlight the barriers that we think have hampered domestication as well as disqualified the use of the suitcase for cooperation during emergency situations. Then, we discuss the unexpected impact the suitcase integration had on the three nursing homes that have adopted it.

6.1 Different Levels of Domestication

How can we explain the contrasting situations among the ten nursing homes?

It turns out that two of the three nursing homes that have domesticated the suitcase were pioneers in the project. They were followed by a nursing home led by the daughter of Mrs. Parinello. This nursing home was a pioneer in the unexpected use of the suitcase that we described above for baseline ECG. Therefore, we suggest that the involvement of the top management of the nursing homes is a key factor to achieving all of the steps of the domestication of the toolkit. In fact, introducing the suitcase is a process that has to be managed and organized; the suitcase does not work by itself.

Another important factor that we noticed is the establishment of a common observation as the starting point of rolling-out the suitcases: "we have a problem with the EMDC". This common observation was clearly a motivation to try to improve the cooperation between nursing homes and the EMDC, and the suitcase (or even the "esperanto") was a good candidate to support this improvement. In most of the nursing homes that tried out the suitcase, this starting point (acknowledging the cooperation and communication issues with the EMDC) was not entirely clear, so the need to use a new tool was not obvious; therefore, they did not make the effort to include the suitcase in their work practices.

Finally, the existing technical infrastructure (Wi-Fi, RJ45) and/or the timing of the arrival of the suitcase affected its trajectory. This was particularly the case when the suitcase arrived at the same time as a new integrated information system that deeply impacts professional practices, as we have seen in three of the participating nursing homes. In this context, the suitcase was never prioritized by the management or the care team.

6.2 The Lack of Practical Relevance of the Toolkit in Emergencies

The weak success of the experiment and domestication of the suitcase can also be explained by the weak relevance of the use of ECG in response to "real" emergencies as reported by several of the interviewees from both sides (nursing homes and EMDC members). The informants have detailed practical constraints on their situated action [42] in case of emergency; as we illustrated earlier, if a resident is encountering heart distress, is hardly breathing and is requiring urgent care, nurses and orderlies have no time to perform an ECG, especially if they are not used to it. They are also dependent on doctors to interpret and make sense of the results.

Moreover, from the EMDC triage doctors' point of view, an ECG is only one piece of evidence among others in identifying a critical situation that requires carrying the resident to the hospital. Other measures more easily performed by orderlies (like blood pressure, pulse, and screening patient's eyes) as well as a description of symptoms can support triage doctors in their decision to send an emergency vehicle. Precisely diagnosing heart problems from an ECG for an elderly person is particularly challenging for doctors because most elderly people tend to have non pathological but irregular cardiac measures. The medical interpretation of an ECG takes time and implies a good knowledge of the patient's history that is far from being the case in an emergency situation.

Therefore, in fact, on the occasion of a "real" emergency situation that requires a timely response, ECGs appeared to be of limited use for making the decision to send the patient to the hospital.

6.3 The Difficulty to Borrow Artifacts

As we described in the origin of the case study, the two project leaders (the head of the EMDC and the head of two nursing homes) shared the aim of improving cooperation between the EMDC and the employees of the nursing homes. Their initial idea was to provide suitcases in nursing homes so that orderlies could perform ECGs. As we also described above, they decided later on to offer the orderlies a questionnaire and associated vocabulary (the "esperanto") to help them communicate information about patients to EMDC staff. Using this approach, artifacts (the ECG and the esperanto) were then borrowed from the EMDC with the expectation that this will help orderlies to ensure better cooperation with the EMDC by providing more accurate data to decide whether the resident is in an emergency situation and should be sent to the ED.

Our observation of the deployment of the suitcase and the esperanto (illustrated in the domestication of the toolkit, section 5), as well as the study of existing research on cooperation in healthcare settings, show how much this schematic borrowing strategy needs amendments.

The strategy of borrowing an artifact from one community of practice has been described in the Boundary Negotiating Artefact (BNA) analysis framework [22]. BNA is a useful concept to understand a not well used or controversial artifact that does not succeed as a boundary object [40] at the border of several groups. Regarding the difference of the consensual view of flexibly reusable boundary objects serving coordination and cooperation, BNA shows a more complex and conflicting landscape where groups are pushing their interests and views through artifacts.

In the case we studied, the EMDC cuts down early the attempt from nursing homes to borrow ECG and emergency care language by opposing a strict protocol for using the suitcase: the ECG should be performed only in response to EMDC request during the emergency call, as clearly mentioned by Maciste Technologies during a training session in a nursing home:

You, in any case, you do not decide if you should use the suitcase. OK? Because, this is also the big issue: This is thinking, I have a telemedicine toolkit, I do everything, I send to EMDC, I tell them, now, help yourself. No, this is not how things are going on. There is an existing procedure, that you already know, which is: you call EMDC, this is what you do. It does not change anything; ***this is not because you have tools that you must use them****. The goal is that these tools should be used on the orders of EMDC. Ok?*

The asymmetry of positions and valued expertise between triage doctors in the EMDC and nursing home employees (mainly orderlies and nurses) appear to be at stake, as seen in other medical contexts [43]. For nurses and orderlies, performing an ECG without the explicit order from a doctor would have no organizational rationale or even could be seen as malpractice. Indeed, this has clearly discouraged the use of the suitcase and the initiative of practicing ECG by nursing home employees.

The failure to position the suitcase and the Esperanto as a support for improving cooperation between the EMDC and nursing homes is consistent with existing cooperative work analyses on a "could have been" boundary object [22, 26]. As Star reminds us [39], boundary objects should be thought of both in their material dimension, the artifact, and their process dimension, the practices associated with their production and use. In the case we have presented here, the process dimension was clearly neglected. In other words, a negotiation on how (practically) the suitcase could be used to ensure better cooperation between the EMDC and nursing homes did not occur and was missing. We join Munkvold, Ellingsen, and Monteiro [26] in their analysis that work practices, such as planning or defining an emergency situation in our case, have to be addressed before even specifying the artifact that would allow for better cooperation. This learning appears to us as still neglected in many projects aimed at supporting an evolution of inter-organizational cooperation, or at least cooperation.

6.4 A Domestication in an Unexpected Way

As we described above, facing the rebuttal from the EMDC to change their cooperation practices, three nursing homes have incorporated the suitcases in their work practices in unexpected ways.

Among these three nursing homes, two are headed by Mrs. Parinello and the other by a well-known colleague of hers. They were thus especially involved and interested in trying out the potential of using the suitcase. Then, based on the rationale that orderlies have to be familiar with the suitcase and the ECG exam to be able to perform one in an emergency situation, they started asking the orderlies to perform ECGs for residents outside of emergency situations. This led to these three nursing homes incorporating the suitcase in their work practices and overcoming the restrictive protocol imposed by the EMDC on its use, straying from its initial cooperation purpose.

As we have seen, two unexpected uses were then developed in nursing homes. The first one is the idea of performing an ECG for each resident when the situation is "normal" to get a baseline ECG. This use offers the doctors the opportunity to compare the ECG of a resident in abnormal conditions with a previous measure at a time she or he felt ok. The other unexpected use is to perform surveillance ECGs when residents start complaining about breathing or heart problems, before the situation worsens and eventually becomes an emergency situation.

Thus, the suitcases are no longer presented and used as a support for inter-organizational cooperation in emergency situations. The transformational power of tools when incorporated into work practices is well established in social sciences and CSCW [12]. For the three nursing homes that developed these unexpected uses, the domestication of the suitcase eventually appeared to be an opportunity for organizational learning [46] through the development of practicing baseline and surveillance ECGs.

The incorporation of the suitcase in the existing work practices of the nursing homes has led to reflexivity and redefinition of the very notion of an emergency from the nursing homes point of view. As the suitcases were lacking their initial cooperation purpose, they have been repurposed by nursing home management and staff to fit the particular issues at stake in their context [13], and especially to provide quality care to the residents. In fact, the conversion phase of the domestication of the suitcase, which led to performing baseline ECGs, has contributed to the development of a message from the top-management of the nursing homes to patients and their family. When requesting their consent for ECG, they are also promoting this new practice as a benefit for the good care of the residents. This new practice and its benefit are also emphasized when communicating with the general public and funding agencies. For nursing homes that are early adopters of telemedicine solutions, it shows a clear impact on their identity.

6.5 Limitations and Implications for Future Projects

This case study of course has some limitations. First, we did not have the opportunity to cover the entire experimentation process that lasted two years. We only had the chance to investigate the case during six months. Another limit is that the only emergency situations that we observed did not involve the use of the toolkit. Furthermore, in the three nursing homes that have domesticated the telemedicine toolkit, the new work practices that were implemented are just starting. Indeed, the introduction of the new practices that we described above (baseline and surveillance ECGs) in the nursing homes is far from being unproblematic.

In fact, these "baseline" ECGs were not unanimously welcomed by the head nurses in the nursing homes. They wondered whether an ECG that had been carried out but not read by a doctor could make the institution liable if a resident died from a problem that no one had noticed but could have been detected on the ECG. The worry here was that families might sue the nursing homes, or indeed sue the nurses or orderlies who had carried out an ECG without any medical demand for this. Otherwise, although Maciste Technologies' sales director did not contest the legitimacy of this line of questioning, they did argue that, based on current law, an ECG becomes a medical act once it has been interpreted, but not before. Here, the legal question was whether entering the results of an ECG in an in-house database transformed it into a medical act. Lacking any real clarity, one of the coordinating doctors of a nursing home said that he had refused to interpret ECGs when his manager asked him to do so. A number of doctors treating nursing home residents had also refused, apparently because they had not been trained recently in reading these examinations. This reveals a controversy inside of the experiment that impeded the appropriation of the technology in all of the different nursing homes that were supposed to take part in the project.

It is also important to notice that the regional health authorities did not decide yet about the legality of this particular point. Moreover, we have to mention that, because this experiment is one of the first in France, we were not able to refer to any defined policy on the use of telemedicine in nursing homes.

Despite these limitations, our analysis of the domestication successes and failures in the different nursing homes allows us to provide recommendations for projects aimed at improving inter-organizational cooperation by the use of a toolkit:

- A prerequisite is that all of the concerned organizations acknowledge that they have an issue in terms of cooperation.
- The important and often neglected step is to define the different concrete situations in which this cooperation should occur and how. These descriptions should lead to the choice of the most appropriate socio-material intervention (device, application, protocol, training …).
- A key factor is the involvement of the top-management of the organizations that plan to improve their cooperation with a socio-material intervention.
- The socio-technical infrastructure should be ready before the system is rolled-out: network availability, form and timing of the training sessions, and integration into the existing information system.

7. CONCLUSION

In this paper, we investigated the experimental deployment of a telemedicine toolkit. The aim of this experiment was to try out the pertinence of using this kind of artifact to improve the cooperation between the triage doctors of the EMDC and the nurses and orderlies of nursing homes in a city in France. The goal was to avoid unnecessary discharge of the nursing home residents to the Emergency Department of the local hospital both for quality of life and economic reasons.

We specifically focused on the domestication process that occurred in the ten nursing homes that took part in the experiment. Our study reveals that only three nursing homes fully domesticated the telemedicine toolkit, but in an unexpected way: by finally incorporating their use in their internal work practices and, in this way, making them evolve instead of using the toolkit to cooperate with the EMDC.

Our contribution can be seen at different levels. First, we provide a detailed description of one of the first telemedicine experiments intended to improve cooperation in emergency settings in France, which is part of a large-scale project aimed at developing telemedicine practices to face the shortage of medical resources. Our description and analysis uncover the potential pitfalls and suggest recommendations for future projects. Then, our study adds a new case to the literature on domestication in which this framework was successfully used in a professional setting. It also further develops the BNA framework by providing an instance of the idea of borrowing artifacts.

8. ACKNOWLEDGMENT

This paper has benefited from the ISOTECA project (A2101-02) founded by region Champagne Ardenne (France). We also thank the Regional Health Agency of Champagne Ardenne and all people who have been interviewed during the inquiry.

9. REFERENCES

[1] Balka, E. and Wagner, I. 2006. Making things work: dimensions of configurability as appropriation work. In *Proceedings of the 2006 20th anniversary conference on Computer supported cooperative work* (CSCW '06). ACM, New York, NY, USA, 229-238. DOI=http://dx.doi.org/10.1145/1180875.1180912

[2] Berg, M. 1996. Practices of reading and writing: the constitutive role of the patient record in medical work. *Sociology of health & illness*, 18, 4, 499-524. DOI= http://dx. doi.org/10.1111/1467-9566.ep10939100

[3] Bjørn, P. and Rødje, K. 2008. Triage Drift: A Workplace Study in a Pediatric Emergency Department. *Computer*

Supported Cooperative Work, 17, 4 (August 2008), 395-419. DOI= http://dx.doi.org/10.1007/s10606-008-9079-2

[4] Bjørn, P., & Balka, E. (2007). Health care categories have politics too: Unpacking the managerial agendas of electronic triage systems. In *Proceedings of the 10th European Conference on Computer-Supported Cooperative Work* (Limerick, Ireland, 24-28 September 2007). ECSCW 2007. Springer London, 371-390. DOI= http://dx.doi.org/ 10.1007/978-1-84800-031-5_20

[5] Bossen, C. 2002. The parameters of common information spaces: the heterogeneity of cooperative work at a hospital ward. In *Proceedings of the 2002 ACM conference on Computer supported cooperative work* (CSCW '02). ACM, New York, NY, USA, 176-185. DOI=http://dx.doi.org/10.1145/587078.587104

[6] Cecez-Kecmanovic, D., Kautz, K. and Abrahall, R. 2014. Reframing Success and Failure of Information Systems: A Performative Perspective. *Mis Quarterly*, 38, 2, 561-588.

[7] Collins, S. A., Fred, M., Wilcox, L. and Vawdrey D. 2012. Workarounds used by nurses to overcome design constraints of electronic health records. In *Proceedings of the 11th International Congress on Nursing Informatics*. American Medical Informatics Association.

[8] Creditor, M. C. 1993. Hazards of hospitalization of the elderly. *Ann Intern Med*, 118, 3 (February 1993), 219–23. DOI= http://dx.doi.org/10.7326/0003-4819-118-3-199302010-00011

[9] Crilly, J., Chaboyer, W., Wallis, M., Thalib, L. and Polit, D. 2011. An outcomes evaluation of an Australian Hospital in the Nursing Home admission avoidance programme. *Journal of clinical nursing*, 20, 7-8 (April 2011), 1178-1187. DOI= http://dx.doi.org/10.1111/j.1365-2702.2010.03371.x

[10] Dodier, N. and Baszanger, I. 1997. Totalisation et altérité dans l'enquête ethnographique. *Revue Française de Sociologie*, 38, 1, 37-66.

[11] Dourish, P. 2003. The appropriation of interactive technologies: Some lessons from placeless documents. *Computer Supported Cooperative Work*, 12, 4, 465-490. DOI= http://dx.doi.org/10.1023/A:1026149119426

[12] Dourish, P. and Button, G. 1998. On "technomethodology": Foundational relationships between ethnomethodology and system design. *Human-computer interaction*, 13, 4, 395-432.DOI= http://dx.doi.org/10.1207/s15327051hci1304_2

[13] Draxler, S., Stevens, G., Stein, M., Boden, A., & Randall, D. 2012. Supporting the social context of technology appropriation: on a synthesis of sharing tools and tool knowledge. In *Proceedings of the SIGCHI Conference on Human Factors in Computing Systems* (CHI '12). ACM, New York, NY, USA, 2835-2844. DOI=http://dx.doi.org/10.1145/2207676.2208687

[14] Falzon, M. A. 2009. *Multi-sited ethnography. Theory, praxis and locality in contemporary research*. Ashgate Publishing Compagny, Burlington.

[15] Glaser, B. and Strauss, A. 1967. T*he Discovery of Grounded Theory: Strategies for Qualitative Research*. Aldine, Chicago.

[16] Grabowski, D. C., O'Malley, A. J. and Barhydt, N. R. (2007). The costs and potential savings associated with nursing home hospitalizations. *Health Affairs*, 26, 6 (November 2007), 1753-1761. DOI= http://dx.doi.org/ 10.1377/hlthaff.26.6.1753

[17] Graverholt, B., Riise, T., Jamtvedt, G., Ranhoff, A. H., Krüger, K. and Nortvedt, M. W. 2011. Acute hospital admissions among nursing home residents: a population-based observational study. *BMC health services research*, 11, 1 (May 2011), 1-8. DOI= http://dx.doi.org/10.1186/1472-6963-11-126

[18] Haddon, L. and Silverstone, R. 1992. *Information and Communication Technologies in the Home: The Case of Teleworking*. University of Sussex, PICT.

[19] Harwood, S. A. 2011. The domestication of online technologies by smaller businesses and the 'busy day'. *Information and Organization*, 21, 2 (April 2011), 84-106. DOI= http://dx.doi.org/10.1016/j.infoandorg.2011.03.002

[20] Heath, C. and Luff, P. 1996. Documents and professional practice: "bad" organisational reasons for "good" clinical records. In *Proceedings of the 1996 ACM conference on Computer supported cooperative work* (CSCW '96), Mark S. Ackerman (Ed.). ACM, New York, NY, USA, 354-363. DOI=http://dx.doi.org/10.1145/240080.240342

[21] Hynes, D. and Richardson, H. 2009. What use is domestication theory to information systems research. In *Handbook of research on contemporary theoretical models in information systems*. IGI Global, 482-494 DOI= 10.4018/978-1-60566-659-4.ch027

[22] Lee, C. P. 2007. Boundary negotiating artifacts: Unbinding the routine of boundary objects and embracing chaos in collaborative work. *Computer Supported Cooperative Work*, 16, 3, 307-339. DOI= http://dx.doi.org/10.1007/s10606-007-9044-5

[23] Lindtner, S., Anderson, K. and Dourish, P. 2012. Cultural appropriation: information technologies as sites of transnational imagination. In *Proceedings of the ACM 2012 conference on Computer Supported Cooperative Work* (CSCW '12). ACM, New York, NY, USA, 77-86. DOI=http://dx.doi.org/10.1145/2145204.2145220

[24] Mallon I. 2004. *Vivre en maison de retraite, le dernier chez soi*. Presses Universitaires de Rennes, Rennes, France.

[25] Marcus, G. 1995. Ethnography in/of the World System: The Emergence of Multi-sited Ethnography. *Annual Review of Anthropology*, 24, 95-117.

[26] Munkvold, G., Ellingsen, G. and Eric Monteiro. 2007. From plans to planning: the case of nursing plans. In *Proceedings of the 2007 international ACM conference on Supporting group work* (GROUP '07). ACM, New York, NY, USA, 21-30. DOI=http://dx.doi.org/10.1145/1316624.1316628

[27] Murphy, Alison R. and Reddy, M. C. 2014. Identification and Management of Information Problems by Emergency Department Staff. In *AMIA Annual Symposium Proceedings*. American Medical Informatics Association, 1845-1854.

[28] Neuendorf, K. 2002. *The content analysis guidebook*. Sage, London.

[29] O'Connell, B., Hawkins, M., Considine, J., and Au, C. 2013. Referrals to hospital emergency departments from residential aged care facilities: stuck in a time warp. *Contemporary nurse*, 45, 2, 228-233. DOI= http://dx.doi.org/ 10.5172/conu.2013.45.2.228

[30] Ouslander, J. G., Lamb, G., Perloe, M., Givens, J. H., Kluge, L., Rutland, T., Atherly A. and Saliba, D. (2010). Potentially avoidable hospitalizations of nursing home residents: frequency, causes, and costs. *Journal of the American Geriatrics Society*, 58, 4 (April 2010), 627-635. DOI= http://dx.doi.org/10.1111/j.1532-5415.2010.02768.x

[31] Park, S. Y. and Chen, Y. 2012. Adaptation as Design: Learning from an EMR Deployment Study. In *Proceedings of the SIGCHI Conference on Human Factors in Computing Systems* (CHI '12). ACM, New York, NY, USA, 2097-2106. DOI= http://dx.doi.org/10.1145/2207676.2208361

[32] Pierson, J. 2005. Domestication at work in small businesses. In T. Berker, M. Hartmann, Y. Punie & K. Ward (eds.) *Domestication of media and technologies*. Open University Press, Maidenhead, 205-226.

[33] Pine K. 2012. Fragmentation and choreography: caring for a patient and a chart during childbirth. In *Proceedings of the ACM 2012 conference on Computer Supported Cooperative Work* (CSCW '12). ACM, New York, NY, USA, 887-896. DOI= http://dx.doi.org/10.1145/2145204.2145336

[34] Rogers, E. M. 2003. *Diffusion of Innovations* (5th ed.). Free Press, New York

[35] Saleem, J. J., Russ, A. L., Neddo, A., Blades, P. T., Doebbeling, B. N. and Foresman, B. H. 2011. Paper persistence, workarounds, and communication breakdowns in computerized consultation management. *International journal of medical informatics*, 80, 7, 466-479.

[36] Salvi, F., Morichi, V., Grilli, A., Giorgi, R., De Tommaso, G. and Dessi-Fulgheri, P. 2007. The elderly in the emergency department: a critical review of problems and solutions. *Internal and Emergency Medicine*, 2, 4 (November 2007), 292-301. DOI= http://dx.doi.org/10.1007/s11739-007-0081-3

[37] Silverstone, R. and Haddon, L. 1996. Design and the domestication of information and communication technologies: technical change and everyday life. In Mansell, R. and Silverstone, R., (eds.) Communication by Design. *The Politics of Information and Communication Technologies*. Oxford University Press, Oxford, UK, 44-74.

[38] Silverstone, R. and Hirsch, E. 1992. *Consuming technologies: Media and information in domestic spaces*. Routledge, London.

[39] Star, S. L. 2010. This is not a boundary object: Reflections on the origin of a concept. *Science, Technology & Human Values*, 35, 5, 601-617. DOI= http://dx.doi.org/10.1177/0162243910377624

[40] Star, S. L. and Griesemer, J. 1989. Institutional ecology, 'Translations', and Boundary objects: Amateurs and professionals on Berkeley's museum of vertebrate zoology. *Social Studies of Science*, 19, 3 (August 1989), 387-420. DOI= http://dx.doi.org/10.1177/030631289019003001

[41] Strauss, A., Bucher, R., Ehrlich, D., Schatzman, L. and Sabshin, M. 1963. The hospital and its negotiated order. In Freidson E. (ed.) *The Hospital in Modern Society*. Free Press, New York, 1963, 147-169.

[42] Suchman, L. A. 1987. *Plans and Situated Actions: the Problem of Human-Machine Communication*. Cambridge University Press.

[43] Symon, G., Long, K., and Ellis, J. 1996. The coordination of work activities: cooperation and conflict in a hospital context. *Computer Supported Cooperative Work*, 5, 1 (March 1996), 1-31. DOI= http://dx.doi.org/10.1007/BF00141934

[44] Tang, C., Chen, Y., Semaan, B. C. and Roberson, J. A. 2015. Restructuring Human Infrastructure: The Impact of EHR Deployment in a Volunteer-Dependent Clinic. In *Proceedings of the 18th ACM Conference on Computer Supported Cooperative Work & Social Computing* (CSCW '15). ACM, New York, NY, USA, 649-661. DOI= http://dx.doi.org/10.1145/2675133.2675277

[45] Tellioğlu, H. and Wagner, I. 2001. Work practices surrounding PACS: the politics of space in hospitals. *Computer Supported Cooperative Work*, 10, 2, 163-188. DOI= http://dx.doi.org/10.1023/A:1011298824442

[46] Virkkunen, J. and Kuutti, K. 2000. Understanding organizational learning by focusing on "activity systems". *Accting., Mgmt. & Info. Tech.*, 10, 4 (October, 2000)? 291–319. DOI= http://dx.doi.org/10.1016/S09596-8022(00)00005-9

[47] Weick, K. E., Sutcliffe, K. M. and Obstfeld, D. 2005. Organizing and the process of sensemaking. *Organization Science*, 16, 4 (August 2005), 409-421. DOI= http://dx.doi.org/10.1287/orsc.1050.0133

[48] Wilson, R. S., Hebert, L. E., Scherr, P. A., Dong, X., Leurgens, S. E. and Evans, D. A. 2012. Cognitive decline after hospitalization in a community population of older persons. *Neurology*, 78, 13 (March 2012), 950-956. DOI= http://dx.doi.org/10.1212/WNL.0b013e31824d5894

[49] Zhou X., Ackerman M. and Zheng K. 2011. CPOE workarounds, boundary objects, and assemblages. In *Proceedings of the SIGCHI Conference on Human Factors in Computing Systems* (CHI '11). ACM, New York, NY, USA, 3353-3362. DOI=http://dx.doi.org/10.1145/1978942.1979439

Caring About Sharing: Couples' Practices in Single User Device Access

Maia Jacobs
College of Computing*
Georgia Institute of Technology, GA
mjacobs30@gatech.edu

Henriette Cramer
Spotify*
San Francisco, CA
henriette@spotify.com

Louise Barkhuus
Cornell Tech
New York, NY
barkhuus@cornell.edu

ABSTRACT

Most devices today are developed adhering to a one-user paradigm. Yet within households, couples are often sharing devices and accounts. In this paper we take an in-depth look at sharing practices and preferences of cohabiting couples, and discuss the nuances of existing practices surrounding accounts and devices. We present a qualitative interview and diary study with ten couples, consisting of 20 individual interviews, and individual 8-day diaries. Dichotomous access models do not reflect the sharing practices of our couples; in which intent, access, and utilization all characterized sharing behaviors. We present a detailed description of the intentional and unintentional sharing practices our participants used in their day to day interactions and discuss the different challenges that particularly one type of content pose in terms of issues of privacy. We discuss implications for accounts and devices based on the ways in which content was shared and hidden among collocated couples. We provide a structured account of these sharing practices to inform the design of multi-user settings within future technologies.

Keywords
Groupware; social software; sharing of devices; mobile computing practices.

1. INTRODUCTION

In recent years, personal devices have become more and more sophisticated and essentially contain similar content to a desktop computer or laptop, including personal communication, online social networking and the ability to search the broader Internet. In essence we have reached the stage predicted by Mark Weiser in which tabs, pads and displays are available to most people in the developed world. But one part of Weiser's prediction has yet to come true: the readily sharing of pad sized devices between for example colleagues and family members. In 1991 Weiser envisioned: "Pads are intended to be "scrap computers" (analogous to scrap paper) that can be grabbed and used anywhere; they have no individualized identity and importance." [[29] p. 99] Yet, the majority of personal devices today are developed according to a one-user paradigm. Even most tablets (e.g. iPads) have adopted the phone's user interface and access model where, after initial opening, every single app is readily available (with some exceptions due to type of app and personal settings). However, today many personal devices *are* shared, if not explicitly (i.e. two people only have one phone), then at least ad hoc [20]. From the early mobile phones to iPads and smartphones, particularly close ties and cohabiting couples are using each other's devices and content through shared passwords on a regularly basis [2], [16]. A spectrum exists between the fully personal and fully shared, and we know that even for devices that are usually seen as 'personal' such as smartphones, ownership and access are not limited to the individual [2], [16]. Some services offer different profiles, such as Netflix, in order to support multiple individuals in a household, others are explicitly minded towards no sharing. However, not all account models reflect the intricacies of people's social context, nor the shared tasks that people have to fulfill together [17]. People do not use access models the way in which they were designed, nor should they have to [16].

In this paper we address the sharing of computing technology, particularly elements of personal devices and content that is normally perceived private, either through password protection or broader social context. We look particularly at sharing between cohabiting couples because they represent one of the closest, yet equal dyad of relationships (as opposed to for example child-parent relationships that include a set of socially and biologically construed power dynamics). The dynamics of cohabitating couples is relevant because couples spend considerable amounts of time together, have common household goals to achieve, and potentially purchase and use technology together. Couples navigate both the promotion of intimacy through sharing of private information, as well as the maintenance of individual personal boundaries. As a couple, individuals also create shared boundaries on access to and disclosure of personal information to others outside of the two partners [6].

We distinguish our work by examining how the pervasiveness of mobile and interoperable technologies is reflected in the daily technology uses and habits of co-habiting couples. We aim to expand the design space for shared devices by focusing on why and how couples share single devices and applications. We provide a framework of different types of sharing of devices and content. While "sharing" can be a convoluted term, we specifically use it in this research as a notion to describe how couples provided and received access to personal devices and content through physical sharing, password sharing or other processes. More detailed insight into these practices can provide implications for designing better personal technologies focused on individuals' unique habits, goals, and values. We also discuss how this work leads to implications for

*The majority of this work was performed while at Yahoo.

GROUP '16, November 13-16, 2016, Sanibel Island, FL, USA
© 2016 ACM. ISBN 978-1-4503-4276-6/16/11...$15.00
DOI: http://dx.doi.org/10.1145/2957276.2957296

the design of accounts based on these classes of practices as well as content type. Through a qualitative study of 10 cohabiting couples, our work provides the following contributions:

- We examine how couples share and receive access to each other's personal devices and their content. Our findings reveal that sharing practices were characterized not only by having or not having access, but also by intent and utilization. We structure these practices into four categories: intentional sharing, explicitly not sharing, unintentional access and unintentionally inhibiting access, providing examples in which these activities occur.
- We define three types of shared content, and assess how these content types can be appropriate and sensitive to share. This helps to highlight personal and shared values that ought to be considered in future technology designs.

2. RELATED WORK

2.1 Couples' closeness and boundaries

Couples present an interesting group to study as aspects of collocation and closeness influence daily behaviors and routines. The dynamics in couples are complex, and partners in a couple influence each others' affect and behavior in both mundane and profound ways [10]. They are both an identifiable unit, as well as two individuals with their own preferences. By definition, they share physical spaces, and reach intimacy by sharing their experiences. When apart, couples appear to miss being able to share presence, mood, environment, daily events and activities, in lightweight, playful, pleasant ways [19]. Couples' closeness means they may be more open to certain types of sharing. For example, perceived closeness was found to be the main predictor for willingness to share location [30]. At the same time, they have to manage the dialectic of both closeness and personal space, through simultaneously sharing and maintaining boundaries [6]. Preferences for interpersonal communication are not necessarily stable, and depend on the perceived state of the relationship. For example, research has found that couples distance themselves from each other in conflict situations through technology [9, 20].

Through a better understanding of these behaviors, research has helped to expand the design space for communication and coordination technologies, as couples can require a unique set of design requirements beyond those for individuals or other, less intimate groups. For example, Branham et al.'s work has examined unique ways in which technology can support couples, specifically examining the use of diary sharing to support intimacy [3]. Research within the CHI and CSCW communities have provided new ways to allow long-distance couples to feel closer and share more aspects of their distant lives [1], [19], [23].

In this paper, we focus on cohabiting couples, and extend earlier work on for example in-home technology. Grinter et al. explored the impact of increased technology in the home, and how designers could better align designs to couples' needs [11]. This work revealed that technologies such as recommendation systems, which are designed for individual use, led to new tensions among couples. A recent Pew study also found that technologies can cause issues between couples, mainly due to partners being distracted by their phone (25%) or spending too much time with technology or on the internet (8%). Additionally, 4% of couples reported being upset at something their partner had done online [18]. Helsper and Whitty point out that there is little research on everyday, low-level surveillance on a significant other's online activities in non-abusive relationships [12]. In a large-scale UK-representative survey they were surprised to find that a third of the survey respondents reported actually checking up on a partner's online activity without their partner knowing. Monitoring activities included reading their emails, SMS, instant messaging logs, checking browser history, using monitoring software or even pretending to be another person. Rather than focusing on 'checking up' and potentially problematic online behaviors, we here more qualitatively explore how couples together managed access to devices in the household and each other's accounts.

We extend prior research by examining sharing of devices between collocated couples. By understanding existing access behaviors, we may be able to better align designs of personal devices with user preferences, thus avoiding conflicts instigated by technology access models. As the ubiquity of personal computing has increased, we aim to explore sharing behaviors of these new technologies, and specifically examine the discrepancies between sharing behaviors. Our work expands on this existing knowledge by demonstrating how understanding sharing through couples' intent and utilization of shared access can help future technologies better support the unique needs of collocated couples.

2.2 Sharing, Accounts and Information

A wider body of existing research on shared devices, and shared systems or artifacts, such as calendars [27], exists. Providing partners with access to online accounts appears a relatively widespread behavior. In 2006, Bryant and Campbell found that students were most likely to share passwords with spouses or parents with 13.79% reporting that they do so [5]. Beyond students, a US-representative Pew study found that most couples have separate emails and social media accounts, and that while only a small number share accounts and calendars, a majority of 67% of internet users in a committed relationship had shared passwords to online accounts with their partner [17]. In another survey with 162 participants, one third of the participants reported sharing email account passwords and a quarter shared Facebook passwords with others, again primarily with close friends and romantic partners [15]. Regarding their partners, respondents reported sharing passwords to personal email accounts (17.3%), Facebook (15.4%), cellphones (12.3%), computers (11.7%), and Amazon (11.7%). Some participants also suggested partners would know them well enough to be able to guess their passwords anyway, something we return to in our data.

A pertinent example of the practicalities that necessitate shared access to accounts, or at least the information contained therein, is provided by Lampinen [16], studying multi-person households who host visitors in their shared home through couchsurfing.org. Couchsurfing accounts however, are not designed with multiple people in mind. Lampinen found difficulties with presenting multiple people in a profile designed for one person, managing shared and individual reputations as couch surfer hosts and guests in others' households. They also found intricate coordination to negotiate access to the shared domestic space. One person may for example be in charge of communicating with potential visitors via the Couchsurfing account, but information about the visitors has to be shared with other household members to make a communal decision and coordinate their potential visit. While this Couchsurfing context may appear a case of small business rather than familial coordination, it illustrates the importance of consideration of others' presence beyond just the couples and 'traditional familial unit'.

Sharing access to accounts and devices can fulfill both practical and social goals [16], [24]. Understanding these behaviors, and their motivations, can help provide greater insight into users' needs which in turn feeds into technology design. While past research has shown an overall willingness for couples to share access with one another, we wanted to understand what motivates this willingness, and why couples may choose not to provide access to devices and accounts, and how this manifests in potentially varied practices. When personal information is disclosed to a partner, the sense of ownership over this accessible information shifts from the originating individual to the collective [6]. This involves negotiating how to fulfill such a shared responsibility. It is unclear to which extent this ownership shift also occurs in sharing access to a device and other types of content. We thus also wish to gain insight into the complexities of personal boundaries as they related to shared access practices and technology ownership.

2.3 Access to technologies in the home

Prior studies have noted that access models oftentimes do not appear to take into account the intricacies of existing social practices. Stevens and Wulf emphasize that purely technical mechanisms, focused on either rejection or acceptance of access based on a preconfigured mechanism, do not properly take into account the social practices surrounding access control [26]. In 2007, Brush and Inkpen conducted a study of household technology sharing [4]. They found that generally, household technologies employed a profile model to manage access. While the use of individual profiles afforded customization and privacy, this organization hindered convenience and sharing. Thus, families needed to select between using individual profiles, or sharing a single profile and forgoing personalization. Karlson et al. also note in the context of mobile phones that all-or-nothing access models do not support the range of user needs that they observed [15]. As Bell found in her study of cellphone use and ownership in Asia in the 2000's, technology can maintain individual identities, but is shaped by social roles that make ownership a murky concept [2]. Bell for example describes instances of how parents gave children cellphones as they wanted to ensure their safety and could access the phone to activate the phone's location tracking feature. While parent-child relationships are significantly different from adult couples, this example the complexities of device ownership within households.

Research has aimed to bridge the gap between user needs and the available access models. Egelman et al. suggested a new model for home computers that allowed a "compromise between sharing and personalization [9]." In their model, documents and settings are shared by default, and a person can manually make certain items private through a personal profile. Mazurek et al. find that users themselves create access-control mechanisms. They indicate dimensions that appeared to influence these mechanisms, including 1) Distinguishing read from write access, 2) people's (physical or remote) presence, 3) location, e.g. at home or in public. We return and reflect on these points in relation to our data in the discussion.

In this paper we further explore dimensions that influence device and content sharing practices. We derive design implications from the framework presented to help future technologies better meet the needs of collocated couples.

3. METHOD

Our aim for this study was to understand how collocated couples share devices, accounts, and digital content with one another in their daily lives. We utilized participant interviews focusing on couples' sharing practices and technology preferences. A follow up diary study was then used to gather specific examples of how participants communicated on a daily basis. The diary study helped to provide context to the interviews by providing actual examples of recent sharing behaviors among couples.

These interviews and diaries collected data for two studies, another one focusing on why couples pick particular communication and messaging services to contact each other while apart [8]. In this paper, we focus on the device and account sharing practices in the household.

We used both communication and coordination use cases in this study. While many communication studies between couples exist within the HCI and CSCW community, these usually focus on communication over a distance. We choose to focus on the communication and collaboration while collocated couples are both together and apart in everyday situations.

3.1 Participants

We recruited 10 couples (20 participants) to participate in this study through Craigslist and social media. An initial recruiting survey was used to ensure couples met the requirements of being over 18 years old and living together. The ten participating couples included seven male-female including one transgender participant, two male-male and one female-female. Participants' ages ranged from 19-60 years old and represented a diverse set of careers including students, a professor (outside of a computer science field), a spiritual coach, stay at home parents, a designer, a manager of a small firm, a programmer, and an architect. While all couples lived around the San Francisco Bay area, couples' homes spanned an area of approximately 40 square miles.

The way in which participants had officiated their relationship with their partners varied. Four couples were married, two couples were in a domestic partnership, and four were not married but cohabitating with a significant other. The length of the relationships also ranged, with three being together for less than one year, three together for 1-5 years, one together for 5-10 years, and three together for more than 10 years. Their living situations varied as well. Six of the couples lived by themselves without children or housemates. Two families with children participated. The first family had one child; the other family had two children and a family member living with them. One younger student couple traveled in between a house shared with multiple roommates during the week to their parents on the weekends. One couple lived with another couple as housemates.

As in many qualitative studies, this sample is not meant to be representative of the population, but rather meant to gain insight into a diversity of practices.

3.2 Participant Interviews

We conducted 20 semi-structured interviews to gain an initial understanding of their technology sharing behaviors and motivations for communicating throughout the day. Interviews lasted 1.5-2 hours, and took place at participants' homes or at the researchers' office. The couples were paid $75 per couple as compensation for their time. Interviews resulted in roughly ~1500 minutes of transcribed data to be analyzed; excluded were rapport-building or chats less relevant to our research or sections where interviewees, for example, during home visits had to tend to tasks or children.

The interviews consisted of three sections. First, for interviews that took place in participants' homes, we used a home tour to get an inventory of the technology owned by participants, and to see where the technology was kept. For office interviews, participants were asked to sketch their homes, indicating where they kept technology they owned. This included listing the communication and Internet-connected devices, and identifying who, from their perspective, owned each device. This initial sketching exercise proved useful as both an icebreaker and allowing us to learn about participants' home environments.

For the second part of the interview, participants were provided with two blank daily calendars. Participants were asked to talk aloud as they filled out one of the calendars with a description of a typical workday, and one with a description of a typical non-work day. For this activity we specifically asked participants to discuss when they used technology and when they communicated with their partner. This activity allowed us to understand how participants use technology outside of the home, and how couples communicate with one another.

The final part component of the interview consisted of a semi-structured interview guided by the information that participants shared in the previous activities. Questions focused on personal technology uses, technology sharing behaviors, information sharing, and privacy preferences.

All participants were interviewed individually so that we could gain insight into their personal technology and privacy preferences. This allowed us to gather individual perspectives on the couples' practices, and allowed the researchers to better understand the context as a whole by combining information from each individual afterwards.

3.3 Diary Study

Upon completion of the interviews, participants were asked to participate in an 8-day diary study that looked at their communication and coordination with their partner. Participants were asked to individually answer a short set of questions each day about a specific time they used technology to communicate with their partner. Questions focused on the motivation for the communication, the channels used to communicate, the information shared, and the success and challenges of the communication.

After a general question about the day's communication modes (e.g. text, just face-to-face), the diary consisted of two sections. First the diary asked "Did you and your partner use technology to coordinate an activity together today?". This section included five questions focused on the coordination goal, tools, devices and applications used, the perceived success of coordinating the activity, difficulties, and potential improvements for the tools used. Participants could skip these all in case they could not recall a specific coordination instance that day. In the second section of the diary, all participants were then asked to describe another instance where they communicated with their partner, and the following aspects with similar questions to those above (now in 8 fields): who and what prompted the interaction, tools used, perceived success and potential difficulties. Participants were also asked to share screenshots or pictures if they felt comfortable doing so.

All of the ten original couples agreed to participate in the diary study, with 19/20 participants submitting diary entries. Participants were compensated $10 for each diary entry. Participants received 8 individual email reminders to fill out the diary. Participants were provided with longer (~1.5 weeks) to fill out the maximum of 8 daily entries when they wished to overcome time constraints and missed reminders. We received 125 entries and 62 screenshots during the study, with each participant contributing 3-8 entries (median = 7 entries, mean = 6.2 entries). Diaries could contain multiple examples of communication instances. In total, 65 coordination cases were shared with us and over a 100 communication entries. 28 additional emails were sent in with 62 screenshots or photos.

3.4 Data Analysis

Upon completion of the data collection, two researchers analyzed the data. We used an iterative inductive analysis to code over 500 items, and develop theme concepts until full agreement was reached between the researchers. These individual items of analysis were exact, full quotes from participants, which came from the first 10 interviews. We then used the other interviews and the diary study entries for theme validation. The full interviews were used in this stage to find supporting or non-supporting evidence.

Through inductive coding we developed a number of themes related to the sharing of devices and accounts that highlighted access, intent, and utilization as important characterizations. The themes structure we present in this paper organizes the various sharing behaviors used among our participants.

4. RESULTS

Through our conversations with participants, we found that couples employed a number of techniques for balancing the desire to share technology while also maintaining privacy. One issue of sharing devices is that by sharing a device, the majority of the content on the device becomes available. It is therefore difficult to distinguish between sharing a device and its content, personalized to the owner. Yet, a device can still be used to access personal or public content by a borrower through logging in to an app or a web browser, or simply using the web browser. We therefore present results for both device (and thereby content) and account sharing interlinked and tease out this distinction in more detail in the discussion. We present our results in terms of device and content access sharing in relation to *intentional sharing practices*, *explicitly not sharing*, *unintentional access* and *unintentionally inhibiting access*.

4.1 Intentional Sharing

Sharing devices and accounts were common among couples. Half of our participants provided examples of deliberate sharing practices. Often, these activities were motivated by a practical need, such as coordinating household tasks including grocery shopping or running other errands.

Several couples discussed using a shared calendar to communicate individual schedules and coordinate events. Using both personal and shared calendars was a common strategy among couples. For example, as one participant shared:

"We have a joint Google calendar... That has been really awesome because we can both insert things into the Google Calendar. Pink is me but green is us." – P6

Note sharing was also common among several couples as a way to share task and grocery lists. Applications such as Evernote allowed couples to specifically share the notes and lists relevant to both partners. In addition to calendars and notes, media accounts that did not contain personal information were frequently shared. These accounts included music accounts and newspaper subscriptions. For example, one participant shared that he and his partner use their own laptops for entertainment but will use the TV to *"stream Internet radios"* - P13

When inquiring into when participants would use their partners' devices and accounts, we found that a practical need was the main motivation. For example, as one participant discussed, the couple's two young children were taken care of mostly by the wife, who thus had little time to deal with her email account. He had in effect become responsible for ensuring her email got taken care of, replying to non-spam emails from her account, and sometimes printed out emails for her in case she needed to take care of an issue herself so she did not necessarily have to log in.

"I go through all these files and one of the email accounts is her email account. She doesn't always have time to go through it and a lot of times it's just junk or spam... I'll go through and clear out the emails for her" – P6

This behaviors could be seen as monitoring the other partner, similar to those discussed Helsper and Whitty [12] However, in this case, this particular practice actually served a more practical reason than monitoring. The husband read his wife's emails in order to help alleviate some of her daily responsibilities as she took care of their two young children.

4.1.1 Creating Shared Accounts

Only two couples had consolidated their accounts or made joint accounts for the specific purpose of sharing content (which was often watched together). One participant described how she had combined her and her partner's Netflix accounts:

"We both had Netflix accounts streaming with 1 DVD so we said okay. Let's move to one Netflix account with 1 DVD and I said let's set up a Gmail alias because I know how to make Gmail aliases forward to our email addresses." –P12

This did not mean they added individual profiles in Netflix. For them the ease of just sharing one profile trumped individual Netflix recommendations. Another couple created a shared Facebook account; however both participants indicated that the account was used infrequently and only one partner was responsible for keeping the account 'up to date'. The different circumstances that caused couples to share devices and account information was mainly focused on maximizing the value of the service to each of the partners when it made the most sense for their individual situation, or in service to their practical needs.

4.1.2 Respect for Partner's Private life

We found that although many couple's shared accounts, access did not signify usage. Often partners reported having access to both devices and accounts of their significant other but opted not use this access. This behavior was motivated by a desire to show respect of their partner's privacy and the absence of a practical need. This motivation was clearly expressed by one of our participants who said:

"Really we can get on to each other phone anytime we wanted to... there is no reason to." – P3

A finer-grained distinction within this category included *using* others' accounts such as Amazon Prime for purchases, but not looking at for example personal purchase history due to considerations that it would be somewhat inappropriate. Participants expressed discomfort with having their partner seeing information based on past content search:

"I think I would be annoyed if he sees my bookmarks or my search results. Sometimes there are things that you want to be personal but there's really nothing to hide at the same time... you want to share but you also want to keep something back." – P12

Some participants also indicated that while they know each other's passwords, they wish to respect each other's privacy. For example, one couple knew each other's email password but chose not to use them:

"I do not log into his email address... we can check emails for each other. We don't usually do that. Yeah, that's a little bit of privacy that we respect each other." – P17

Thus, when a practical need was not present, participants often discussed that they chose not to use their partners' devices or accounts. As participant said:

"We have to have some kind of space and boundaries. Like personal conversations with friends" – P5

It was expressed as a desire to respect the other's privacy that motivated participants not to use each other's personal technology. While these motivations help to explain sharing when access is intentionally shared, some participants also described an interesting sharing behavior in which access was intentionally shared, but the participant would only want the access to be used when both partners were together. Participants discussed with us sharing behaviors in which they felt comfortable with their partners' accessing their devices and accounts only when they were both present. One participant discussed this supervised access with regards to sharing bank information:

"If I came here and open up the door or something and she's looking at [my bank information] I would be like, kind of, probably pissed off actually. It would make sense to me. But like, if I was looking at it already and she came over, then I don't care." – P10

As this example illustrates, the notion of supervised access was typically discussed as a way to demonstrate participants' parallel desires to maintain personal privacy while also demonstrating a level of openness with their partners. Many couples that mentioned behaviors categorized as supervised access typically relied on communication and in-the-moment decisions to guide when access was provided. For example, as one participant said:

"If you ask to see then sure, there's really nothing to hide." - P4

As illustrated in the examples above, supervised access allowed participants to provide access and demonstrate trust while also maintaining privacy. This behavior provided a more balanced option between intentionally sharing full access of a device or account, and intentionally maintaining privacy, which we now discuss.

Access	*Activity Examples*	*Content*
Intentional sharing	Sharing passwords, leaving devices unlocked	Media, music, calendars (public content)
Explicitly not sharing	Using separate devices	Search histories, personal conversations (personal content and conversations)
Unintentional access	Accidentally viewing private content	Search histories, personal conversations (personal content and conversations)
Unintentionally inhibiting access	Forgetting to share passwords	Personalized accounts such as Netflix (tailored content)

Table 1: Intentional and unintentional sharing practices among collocated couples

4.2 Explicitly Not Sharing

Purposefully not sharing devices, account passwords and content was a common theme across our participants. 10 participants across 8 couples provided examples in which they explicitly did not share some type of personal technology. Some participants discussed how personal technology was one of the few parts of their lives that they chose not to share with their partner:

"I never use his laptop. He never uses my laptop. We just don't share. That's funny, because we share almost everything else really, but that like our separate spheres." – P1

We found that desire to maintain privacy was not the only motivator for intentionally withholding access to personal devices and accounts. In addition to maintaining privacy, the social consequences of sharing led some participants to not provide technology access to their partners. For instance, one participant (P1) stated that she would not share her search history with her boyfriend because she was concerned about him judging her. Another participant also commented he would not want to share his search history with his partner because of the potential stress the information would place on his partner:

"I want a child really bad and he didn't. Now he is kind of for it but before I was looking up all the information about adoption... I was keeping it away from him because I didn't want to pressure him but I wanted the information." – P3

In addition to privacy and social consequences, a practical need to not share was cited as a reason why participants did not provide access to their personal devices or accounts. For instance, two participants (P19, P3) noted that many of their devices are shared except for their partners' work computers, as the jobs required that the devices not be shared due to security. As with these examples, external factors typically lead to the need for devices to not be shared. Another participant shared a similar example in which he did not have access to his wife's bank account that she used as it was an account used for her father:

"She has some accounts that are just for her because for example they deal with her dad. We handle some of her dad's finances. So a Bank of America account that she's on but I'm not." – P6

Across all of the participants, different devices and accounts were kept personal. Participants mentioned search histories, bank accounts, Tumblr accounts, and personal laptops as devices or accounts they chose not to share with their significant other. Thus, we found that while couples express openness in sharing many types of accounts, personal content was often used as a way to maintain one's privacy and personal identity.

In each of these examples, a choice is made of which needs prevail, one's own, the other's, or the needs that relationship maintenance presents.

4.3 Unintentional Access

An interesting observation from our discussions with participants is that many participants did not make deliberate decisions about sharing practices. With these unintentional sharing events, sharing access often occurred accidentally, while breaking down privacy occurred because the participant or couple had not considered changing pre-existing access restrictions. While we often found that participants intentionally provided each other with access to one another's devices and accounts, occasionally participants discussed accessing devices or accounts unintentionally, resulting in the accidental sharing of information and content. Unintentional sharing often occurred given the proximity of collocated couples' personal technology, leading to one person accidentally viewing information on a device or account in which access was not purposefully granted. Five participants (from four couples) shared different moments in which unintentional sharing occurred. For instance, one participant disclosed that unintentional sharing occurred when her boyfriend was passing her cell phone:

"I've made a promise that I'm not going to adopt a dog before January. A few weeks ago I sent someone a message, a craigslist person asking about a dog and they didn't respond until very early in the morning... and my phone was on his side so he woke up and he gave me my phone and he was like 'what are you doing looking at dogs?' I was like 'I was going to tell you I swear.' So that was really unfortunate. He's like, you're a mess I'm deleting this message you are not getting a dog right now, we're not ready for this" – P10

Other participants discussed specific instances in which unintentional sharing led to tension between the couple. As one participant mentioned:

"The only time that he's seen anything that I didn't want him to see online was some Facebook messages. I was actually on my laptop and he was behind me, and it was stuff from a friend who was male, and it wasn't even anything that exciting or anything, but I knew that he would be upset." – P1

Conflicts that arise due to unintentional sharing of technology can be difficult for couples to deal with. One participant specifically described feeling unsure how to handle such situations:

"There will be sometimes I would see who he's chatting with. Sometimes you're like 'who's this person?' Sometimes I would approach him and it can be tension because you have to balance a fine line. You don't want to be intrusive but at the same time as a person, for me, I like to know." – P4

Needs for preserving the relationship by consideration of the other here appear to prevail over one's own curiosity. Unintentional sharing of such privileged information then becomes a somewhat interesting situation, as this accidental sharing aligns with actual preferences on the receivers' end. Thus, while unintentional sharing can occur, coping with the tensions such accidental sharing causes can prove challenging. The main cause of this sharing is the physical living situation of collocated couples.

4.4 Unintentionally Inhibiting Access

We identified several instances in which participants would unintentionally prevent their partners from accessing personal accounts and devices. When we asked participants why they did not share certain devices or accounts, many indicated that the lack of sharing was unintentional.

For example, one couple that had been living together for over a year used the same Netflix account. The woman said that she used the account more often than her boyfriend and uses the account freely. However, when discussing ownership of the account, she stated:

"It's definitely his. He pays for it, and it's in his name. I don't even think I know the password to it, but it logs in automatically." – P1

P1 mentioned that when the account logs off automatically she is unable to access Netflix until her boyfriend signs back in. Despite this inconvenience she had never asked to know the password. Thus, while the boyfriend did not purposefully withhold the account password, his girlfriend did not ask for the password. Typical of many similar conversations, participants often shared that they were willing to share accounts or devices, but either never had a reason to share their password or forgot the password to their partners' accounts.

In another non-access example during an interview, a participant wanted to show he could log in to his partner's laptop. He however could not remember the password, and expressed it did not really matter anyway.

Thus, unintentionally preventing access seemed to always occur because a practical need to share the device or content never arose, or that the partner did not feel a need to have such access from a social or affective standpoint, or even the practical need to remember after having used a device or account before, so the need to (further) share never came up in discussions or through couples' behaviors.

5. DISCUSSION

One of the interesting distinctions that emerged from our results was the differentiation between types of content that were potentially being shared. As highlighted in the introduction, personal devices are still generally developed to be personal devices and couples are essentially 'hacking' the intended use by sharing devices in the first place. But devices contain many different types of content in an aim to differentiate different types of content we divided it into three group, still routed in our data. We distinguish between *public content*, *tailored content*, and *personal conversations*. We define and discuss these different types of content before framing the sharing of the devices and different types of content within the theoretical framework of contextual integrity [22]. Finally, we discuss implications.

5.1 Different types of Content

When sharing devices, as we saw, one of the main motivations was one of convenience. Couples shared devices if one device was closer to them on the coffee table or if it was in the room they were currently in. And this lead to the deduction that couples also shared content because of convenience, such as media accounts and browsers, simply because they did not want to log out and in again, simply to have their own bookmarks or their own media history. Already back in the desktop era, Brush et al. found a similar motivation to share and use the same desktop account, despite having set up separate accounts for different family members [4]. But as we witnessed in our study, all content is not equally personal, some was considered more sensitive than other and some was considered more sharable than other.

5.1.1 Public Content

We define public content as content readily available from not just a browser but also generally through media accounts such as websites, blogs, and music applications. Although some were located behind a paywall, most of it was not sensitive of nature since it was so widely available. We found that this type of content was fairly readily shared between partners.

In addition to information that is globally accessible, we found that some content was considered open information for both partners. For example, shared events, tasks, and grocery lists were not considered sensitive information and were relevant to both partners in a couple. Thus, this information was consistently shared through various applications.

5.1.2 Tailored Content

Tailored content was defined as content that was tailored to the individual, often through personal algorithms such as social media and the browsing history but which was not necessarily *about* the person. This type of information was considered sensitive because it could inform the partner about previous digital interactions. Partners often maintained separate accounts for tailored information. For example, while couples did watch movies on Netflix, they often maintained their own accounts and would frequently share accounts only when together.

5.1.3 Personal Conversations

Finally, the last type of content that could potentially be shared was personal conversations found in email programs, social media direct messages and text messages. Often these messages would be unintentionally shared through notifications in personal devices or partners looking over participants' shoulders while using the device. This was the most sensitive type of content that participants mentioned and the type of content they rarely, if ever, accepted to share (with an interesting exception of the participant who helped his wife control her email).

This taxonomy of content is not an exhaustive categorization but it serves the purpose to better understand what and why our participants were willing and not willing to share different devices. In essence it helps applying our data to the framework of contextual integrity.

5.2 Breaking Down Contextual Integrity

The framework of contextual integrity [22] attempts to provide an explanation of how and why people become uncomfortable with sharing data or information pertaining to their person such as personal data, pictures, or information that could in aggregation reveal intimate details about the person. Nissenbaum argues that all areas of life and society are governed by norms of information flow, which dictates what information is considered private and that we as individuals have "[r]obust intuitions about privacy norms" that are rooted in social and stereotypic situations [22], p. 119]. Norms of appropriateness then leads to the maintenance of contextual integrity in a situation evaluated by the involved individuals.

Applying this framework it is clear that personal communication never meant to be shared with the partner, both from sender and receivers' perspective, is considered sensitive, as we witnessed in our interviews. The accidental sharing of this breaks the contextual integrity. Reversely, public content is not seen as overly sensitive, since it is readily available to others as well (although sometimes through a personal account). Tailored content complicates the situation because it takes otherwise semi-public data out of context. A friend's status is meant for *their* friends to see but the friend does not expect this to be seen by the friends' partners. The status is considered private to the friend's friends and inappropriate to share with even their partner. This type of content is to a higher extent deemed either appropriate or inappropriate to share with the partner on an individual basis, which muddles the regulation of sharing personalized content. Similarly, past search behavior is not considered adhering to informational norms when the search was for example done in private. These types of content challenge the normative force within the relationship, despite most of the actual content not being 'secret' content for the partner. But since it was lying outside the informational norms, it was considered sensitive for both sharer and receiver.

5.3 Implications

5.3.1 Implications by Content Type

Our research examining couples' digital device sharing confirms the impracticality of the prevalent all-or-nothing access model used for many personal technologies, including cell phones, personal computers, and most online accounts. However, with technology being personalized, we also found that joint ownership of devices is not very common and that sharing technology is not solely about providing access to a partner's personal device without considering the type of content.

Public content was the most frequently shared information. While this often included sharing public media content, participants also highlighted the utility of creating public content through private accounts. This mechanism allowed for the creation of shared calendars through Google and shared notes through applications such as Evernote. Using this successful feature in other domains would bolster support of these existing sharing patterns. For example, devices and accounts could enhance the opportunities for couples to use shared spaces for photos, emails, and other content that is relevant to both partners. While some applications to provide these shared spaces, we must continue to improve upon the ability for users to switch between private and shared content to create more seamless experiences.

Participants often viewed tailored content, personalized to individuals, as content they were willing to share, though less frequently than public content. Further, the value of personalization often resulted in couples maintaining independent accounts. Thus, tailored content was most commonly discussed when participants spoke about time in which they unintentionally inhibited sharing, as these individual accounts require personal identifiers such as passwords to access. Devices and accounts that include tailored content may better meet the needs of couples and families by providing sharing mechanisms that allow partners to request access. Further, connecting platforms to partners' commonly used devices and accounts would eliminate the need to memorize additional passwords. For example, allowing couples to request or provide access by using their mobile phone numbers would provide a more accessible validation method for partners.

Private content, such as online conversations, was rarely shared among couples. Participants often specifically spoke of intentionally not sharing this type of content. However, due to the close proximity of couples living together, this personal information was occasionally shared accidentally, occasionally leading to awkward or uncomfortable moments as a consequence. Therefore, with private information it becomes necessary for the user to have more direct control over the presentation of these personal accounts and conversations. Existing designs make it easy for users to see messages when they appear from various applications. However, our participants' discussions of unintentional sharing highlight the importance of providing easy ways in which users can change these design settings. Users may wish to change or hide notifications based on their location, time of day, or online activity in order to maintain privacy in shared atmospheres. For example, a user may wish to disable notifications from all online conversations (including Google Hangouts, Facebook, etc.) when watching Netflix or Amazon movies, as these applications are frequently used with his or her partner.

Trust can be demonstrated by providing access, but trust also means not using all the access that has been provided to you. Providing or being provided access thus is not the same as sharing all content within an account. Automatically surfacing content from accounts that both partners have access to may not be appropriate. Providing this greater level of control over private content could help reduce these awkward moments among couples, while helping individuals maintain their desired level of privacy in their otherwise shared lives.

5.3.2 Device Implications

Trust and intimacy play and important role in couple's daily lives, as they share a household, friends, and many other personal aspects of life [14]. Sharing of personalized devices and passwords, can be a behavior used to demonstrate trust. Couples indicate a level of trust by providing each other access to accounts and devices, but this does not mean that they necessarily want to utilize this access. While sharing of personalized content was generally considered easy, our participants aspired to provide their partners with a sense of personal space by not using their partners' devices or accounts, even when access is provided, particularly personalized content and communication was considered too personal to share. This has consequences on the ways in which technology supports household communication and coordination.

We thus found that many of our participants used personal devices as a place to maintain or provide their partner with privacy and independence. Their considerations for maintaining privacy however were not simply determined by the two partners, but adhered to a common understanding of informational norms and maintenance of the contextual integrity. While our interviews focused on couples, we found that many of our participants' households included in-laws, roommates, extended family members, and children, each with their own goals and interests [13]. Thus, deciding whom to include in 'the household' and how to accommodate their preferences surrounding digital access remains a challenging question that persists for technologies that exist within or for multi-person settings. As households become more complex and include more people, the need to support more specific intentional sharing becomes vital.

One obvious design suggestion would be to implement multiple profiles for personal devices, easily adjustable for example through identifying a fingerprint or two separate access codes. Although, as previous research on desktops have pointed out, these profiles were in reality not always used [4], the ease of access through a simple log-in mechanism, could mediate ease of access. But it would be naïve to think that sharing (or accidentally glancing over) of personal devices would *never* take place, and one suggestion is to use our content taxonomy for defining default privacy settings. Personal communication should per default never be shown on top of a locked screen (but could be set to be shown) but public content could be readily available. Tailored contend should be easily adjustable for display and access on personal devices.

Designers must also consider the dynamic nature of relationships. Participants rarely discussed the opportunity of a breakup or divorce, although one participant did state that the hardest part about breaking up would be to "go through your drive and separate each other's photos" (P10). While users may not be thinking about such an unfortunate situation, as system designers we should prepare for such complications. Such preparations will be especially important in situations where multi-user systems create archives incorporating information, valued memories, and personal data from individuals.

6. CONCLUSIONS

Through an in-depth exploration of couples' sharing practices, we have identified four common sharing behaviors: intentional sharing, explicitly not sharing, unintentional access and unintentionally inhibiting access. Pervasive one-user paradigms cause couples to 'hack' the intended use of technology to support sharing needs. At the same time, we found many couples reserve particular types of content, mainly personal conversations with others, as a way to maintain privacy. Yet, existing technologies have not provided collocated couples with the ability to maintain the desired privacy in shared living situations. Through this work, we connect content types with sharing practices in order to reveal how technologies may better support both information sharing and privacy needs.

7. ACKNOWLEDGMENTS

We thank our participants, for their contributions.

8. REFERENCES

[1] Bales, E., Li, K.A., and Griswold, W. CoupleVIBE: Mobile implicit communication to improve awareness for (long-distance) couples. CSCW '11, (2011), 65–74.

[2] Bell, G. The age of the thumb: A cultural reading of mobile technologies from Asia. Knowledge, Technology & Policy 19, 2 (2006).

[3] Branham, S.M., Harrison, S.H., and Hirsch, T. Expanding the design space for intimacy: Supporting mutual reflection for local partners. DIS '12, (2012), 220–223.

[4] Brush, A.J.B. and Inkpen, K.M. Yours, mine and ours? Sharing and use of technology in domestic environments. UbiComp '07, (2007), 109–126.

[5] Bryant, K. and Campbell, J. User behaviors associated with password security and management. Australasian Journal of Information Systems 14, 1 (2006), 81–100.

[6] Child, J.T. and Petronio, S. Unpacking the Paradoxes of Privacy in CMC Relationships: The Challenges of Blogging and Relational Communication on the Internet. In Computer-mediated Communication in Personal Relationships. 2011, 21–40.

[7] Crabtree, A. and Rodden, T. Domestic Routines and Design for the Home. CSCW '04, 2 (2004), 191–220.

[8] Cramer, H. and Jacobs, M. Couples' Communication Channels: What, When & Why? CHI'15, (2015), 709-712.

[9] Egelman, S., Brush, A.J.B., and Inkpen, K.M. Family accounts: A new paradigm for user accounts within the home environment. CSCW '08, (2008), 669–678.

[10] Gottman, J.M. and Notarius, C. Marital research in the 20th century and a research agenda for the 21st century. Family Process 41, 2 (2002).

[11] Grinter, R.E., Edwards, W.K., Newman, M.W., and Ducheneaut, N. The Work to Make a Home Network Work. ECSCW '05, (2005), 469–488.

[12] Helsper, E.J. and Whitty, M.T. Netiquette within married couples: Agreement about acceptable online behavior and surveillance between partners. Computers in Human Behavior 26, 5 (2010), 916–926.

[13] Hutchinson, H., Mackay, W., Westerlund, B., et al. Technology probes: Inspiring design for and with families. CHI '03, (2003), 17–24.

[14] Kalmijn, M. Shared friendship networks and the life course: an analysis of survey data on married and cohabiting couples. Social Networks 25, 3(2003), 231–249.

[15] Karlson, A.K., Brush, A.J.B., and Schechter, S. Can I borrow your phone? Understanding concerns when sharing mobile phones. CHI '09, (2009), 1647–1650.

[16] Kaye, J. Self-reported password sharing strategies. CHI '11, (2011), 2619.

[17] Lampinen, A.M.I. Account sharing in the context of networked hospitality exchange. Proceedings of the 17th ACM conference on Computer supported cooperative work & social computing - CSCW '14, (2014), 499–504.

[18] Lenhart, A. and Duggan, M. Couples, the Internet, and social media. 2014.

[19] Lottridge, D., Masson, N., and Mackay, W. Sharing empty moments: Design for remote couples. CHI '09, (2009), 2329–2338.

[20] Mazurek, M.L., Arsenault, J.P., Bresee, J., Gupta, N., Ion, I., Johns, C., Lee, D., Liang, Y., Olsen, J., Salmon, B. and Shay, R., 2010, April. Access control for home data sharing: Attitudes, needs and practices. In Proc. CHI 2010, 645-654, ACM Press.

[21] Neustaedter, C , A. J. Bernheim Brush , Saul Greenberg, The calendar is crucial: Coordination and awareness through the family calendar, ACM Transactions on Computer-Human Interaction (TOCHI), v.16 n.1, p.1-48, April 2009.

[22] Nissenbaum, H., 2004. Privacy as contextual integrity. *Wash. L. Rev.*, *79*, p.119.

[23] Park, Y., Baek, K., and Nam, T. The roles of touch during phone conversations: Long-distance couples' use of POKE in their homes. CHI '13, (2013), 1679–1688.

[24] Scissors, L., Roloff, M.E., and Gergle, D. Room for interpretation: The role of self-esteem and CMC in romantic couple conflict. CHI '14, (2014).

[25] Singh, S., Cabraal, A., Demosthenous, C., and Furlong, M. Password Sharing: Implications for Security Design Based on Social Practice. CHI '07, (2007), 895–904.

[26] Stevens, G. and Wulf. V. 2009. Computer-supported access control. ACM Trans. Comput.-Hum. Interact. 16, 3 (12).

[27] Thayer,, A., Bietz, M. J., Derthick, K. and. Lee, C. P. 2012. I love you, let's share calendars: calendar sharing as relationship work. In Proceedings of the ACM 2012 conference on Computer Supported Cooperative Work (CSCW '12)

[28] Voida, S., Edwards, W. K., Newman, M. W, Grinter, R. E., and N. Ducheneaut (2006) "Share and Share Alike: Exploring the User Interface Affordances of File Sharing", CHI' 06, 221-230.

[29] Weiser, M., 1991. The computer for the 21st century. *Scientific american*, *265*(3), pp.94-104.

[30] Wiese, J., Kelley, P.G., Cranor, L.F., Dabbish, L., Hong, J.I., and Zimmerman, J. Are you close with me? Are you nearby? Investigating social groups, closeness, and willingness to share. UbiComp '11, (2011), 197–206

The Impact of Spatial Properties on Collaboration: An Exploratory Study in the Automotive Domain

Alina Krischkowsky, Sandra Trösterer, Ulrike Bruckenberger, Bernhard Maurer, Katja Neureiter, Nicole Perterer, Axel Baumgartner, Alexander Meschtscherjakov, Manfred Tscheligi
Christian Doppler Laboratory „Contextual Interfaces“, Center for Human-Computer Interaction, University of Salzburg
Salzburg, Austria
{firstname.lastname}@sbg.ac.at

ABSTRACT

Interaction environments are characterized by their *spatial properties*, which guide, direct, and provide an opportunity to become a *place* for social encounters. For example, the car cabin comprises properties such as a special seating arrangement and hence physical barriers between the back and front row. In emphasizing notions of *'space'* and *'place'*, we present an initial study on how such spatial properties of the car cabin shape passenger collaboration. With this, we contribute to a better understanding of the automotive design space *beyond* driver and co-driver positions. In an exploratory lab study with 56 participants we observed collaborative practices in a hardware mock-up of an actual car. We found that social practices in cars need to be understood as connected to their inherent spatial manifestations, which are constraining and concurrently constituting them. We reflect upon the driver position as 'the crux of the matter', the meanings people ascribe to particular positions, and how we can use this knowledge to inform automotive interaction design.

Keywords

Spatial properties; collaborative practices; automotive domain; spatial interaction, collaboration

1. INTRODUCTION

The vehicle interior has become a playground for interactive (ubiquitous) technology, i.e., empowering all passengers in the car becoming active users of this technology. Nowadays, not only drivers are using interactive technologies (e.g., navigation devices) in their vehicles but also other passengers are immensely interacting with (non-driving) systems that are specifically developed by car manufacturers for e.g., entertainment or collaborative purposes. To the best of our knowledge, there exists no research investigating the very specific characteristics of the individual spaces (i.e., front and back-seat areas) of the car [41] that, when encountered and inhabited by humans, become a place for collaborative practices. Technological artifacts that are incorporated (e.g., built-in navigation), nomadic devices (e.g., smartphones) that are brought into, but also the pure spatial properties of the car cabin, constitute a place for various forms of social encounters. We argue that cars as highly ubiquitous environments constitute a relevant research space for the research community, since understanding the collaboration requirements as well as the constraints imposed by this environment are central to (1) inform the design of future (automotive) interactive technology, and (2) guide the direction of newly developed (automotive) interactive technology into the right direction.

GROUP '16, November 13-16, 2016, Sanibel Island, FL, USA
 ISBN 978-1-4503-4276-6/16/11...$15.00
DOI: http://dx.doi.org/10.1145/2957276.2957304

In this paper we explore how the spatial properties of the car cabin *shape* emerging collaboration (beyond driver and co-driver), to facilitate a comprehensive understanding of the automotive design space by considering all passengers as creators of place.

With our research we emphasize that notions of 'space' and 'place' (e.g., [8], [21], [25]), can help us to investigate how the very specific spatial properties of the car cabin (i.e., fixed seating arrangement) guide, direct, and provide an opportunity (or constrain it) to become a collaborative 'place' for all passengers. In doing so, we extend ideas of space and place into the automotive domain, which can be considered a highly constrained interaction environment (e.g., closed space). We argue that such constrained interaction environments and their inherent spatial manifestations have an effect on how passengers engage in collaborative encounters. While much research in the automotive domain focuses on driver support and driver – front-seat passenger collaboration, we argue that our research provides a systematic investigation towards 'designing for all passengers'. As stated by Harrison and Dourish [21], "*Space is the opportunity; place is the understood reality*" (p. 69).

To explore the understood reality of a car, we conducted an exploratory study with 56 participants in groups of 4 people in a hardware mock-up of a car (i.e., as a pure physical representation of an actual car) in our lab without involving a driving task. The motivation why we decided for this setup is manifold and does serve the main objectives of the presented research, i.e., (1) create a setting to systematically explore the *basic spatial foundations* of a car cabin; (2) how the given spatial properties *effect emerging collaboration*; (3) how people ascribe structural features to a given space that guide collaborations *regardless to a given activity or role*. Our car mock-up, thereby, served its purpose in providing an embodiment of an actual car with its inherent spatial properties (i.e., the pure space) without any interference from outside of the car (e.g., pedestrians walking by), which would presumably occur when being conducted in the wild. A contextual multiplayer game was used as baseline collaboration task. It was implemented on four tablets using the four corners of the tablet as spatial references to interact with the other players on their respective seating position.

With this setup, our main research question is a follows: *How do spatial properties of the car cabin shape emerging collaboration?* On basis of a descriptive quantitative video analysis (following [1]) and a collaborative qualitative video analysis (in an adapted version from [3]), complemented with data from sociograms [31], we present and discuss our findings of how the spatial properties of the car cabin direct, guide, constrain, and constitute collaborative practices among participants. With this research, we take an important step in understanding how the car becomes a place, by systematically investigating the relationships between people in spaces and the resulting influence on technology use and in-car collaboration and communication. In our research, we go beyond existing research on collaboration in the automotive domain, by specifically and systematically incorporating the rear-seat passengers and the rear-seat space into our investigations of emerging collaboration as well.

We start with related research on collaboration and communication in the car as well as conceptualizations of space, place, and the design space car in CSCW and HCI research. Afterwards, we describe the rationale behind our research context and the multi-player game as approach to trigger collaboration. Subsequently, we outline our exploratory study followed by a section on the data analysis procedure. The core of this paper is constituted by the results section, concluding with points for reflection with regard to (1) our findings, (2) their meaning for interaction design, (3) the game approach as collaborative trigger, and (4) the study setup.

2. RELATED RESEARCH

We now discuss related research on communication and collaboration in the car context, as well as conceptualizations of space, place, and the automotive design space.

2.1 Cars as Collaborative Interaction Environments

For most of us, cars play an integral part when it comes to the mobility in our everyday lives for a variety of different purposes, i.e., commuting to work and back home. Driving a car in traffic needs to be considered as a fundamentally collaborative and social activity [35] thereby constituting an inhabited object for social interaction and collaboration. But also the car in itself is a place for social encounters with other people, such as, traveling with family and friends for social or convenient purposes. Thereby, social aspects need to be considered as important influential factors when it comes to experiences in the car (e.g., [26], [28]).

There exists a growing body of ethnographic studies in the automotive domain, investigating the drivers and passengers' experiences and their collaborative practices in the car (e.g., [6], [35], [13]). Specifically Oscar Juhlins' [26] group conducted various ethnographic studies (e.g., [14]) that served as basis for systems related to social dimensions of driving (e.g., the SoundPryer system [34]). Contemporary research has also particularly drawn attention to investigate and draw conclusions from driver-passenger pair cooperation in navigational tasks (e.g., [5], [18], [35], [39]), driver assistance during mobile phone usage [13], or lessons-learned for sustained car conversations [22] or how to support persistent conversations in mobile settings more general [40]. Forlizzi et al. [18] propose to consider automotive navigation as an inherent collaborative activity. In line with this perspective, we generally aim to emphasize the importance of understanding in-car collaborations by studying the interrelatedness of given tasks and social roles (as proposed for navigation tasks by Forlizzi et al. [18]), i.e., as social roles coordinate cooperative processes, respective communication, and make human behavior much more predictable (e.g., [2]). Given the in-car context, particular roles (i.e., expectations of actions) are inherently ascribed to particular 'positions' in the car (e.g., driver or front-seat passenger). This lens, from our perspective, allows for analytical reflections of observable practices.

In regard to observable collaborative practices, Gärtner et al. [19] highlighted that drivers and passengers often experience problems in effectively communicating with one another. Verbal instructions were specifically mentioned as sometimes being not efficient enough or ambiguous (e.g., when indicating directions). Based on (e.g., [10], [12]) Forlizzi et al. [18] emphasize that *"successful communication and collaboration rely on common ground, the shared knowledge and shared experience of speaker and listener that are known to be mutually available"* (p., 1263). Members of a team take into account what the other sees and knows while collaborating [38]. In order to facilitate a shared understanding of the situation and common ground, collaborating parties need to understand the focus of one's counterparts' attention, i.e., where s/he is pointing to or what other gestures are used. Additionally, a shared visual view plays a central role in collaboration (e.g., [1], [12], [18]). In relation to that, facilitating common ground, shared knowledge, and experience, beyond pure verbal articulations, seem to pose a particular issue for highly constrained interaction contexts. The in-car space embodies such a restricted context (e.g., positioning of passengers hindering a shared visual view) potentially complicating, or even, impeding communication and collaboration.

In summary, cars as interaction environments need to be considered as places for social encounters with other people, with varying roles people take over in such collaborative environments (e.g., in navigational tasks). Collaboration and communication, thereby, relies on a shared understanding on what one's counterpart sees or knows. In our study, we are interested in how the constrained and very specific spatial properties of the car cabin shape or interfere with emerging collaborations.

2.2 Conceptualizations of Space, Place, and the Automotive Design Space

Among others in HCI and CSCW (e.g., [15], [16]), Harrison and Dourish [21] have suggested to critically distinguish between 'space' and 'place', i.e., that "*Space is the opportunity; place is the understood reality*" (pp. 67). We live in a three-dimensional world, the geometrical structure around us guides and directs our actions and interactions with one another [21], emphasizing that we "*... cannot escape spatiality: we are spatial beings, live, and meet each other in space. Space never is meaningless; it always surrounds us; it is our habitat.*" ([25], p. 1).

Fitzpatrick [17], in her Locales Framework highlights that we need to gain a better understanding how *place* is actually constituted in a relationship between people *in* spaces. Spatial interaction is considered as being observable, acquiring

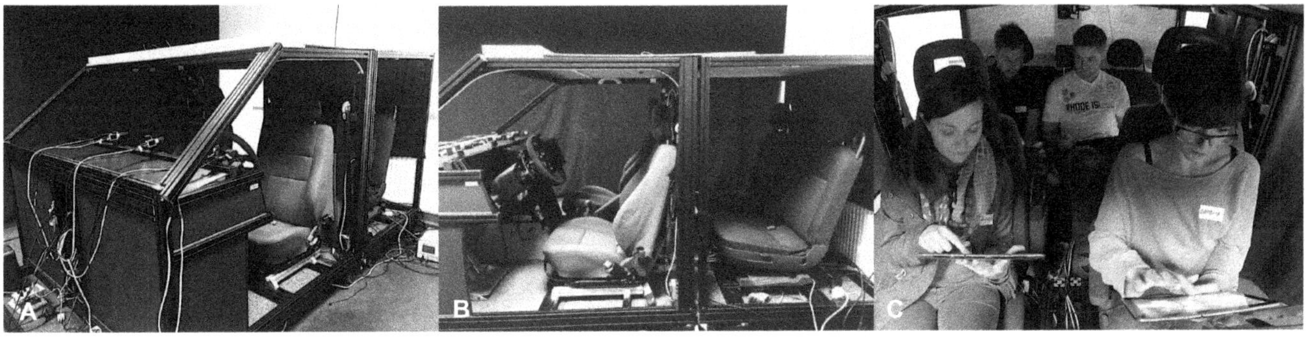

Figure 1. Front perspective (A) and side view (B) of hardware mock-up of an actual car as physical representation of in-car space. Participants playing the game prototype in hardware mock-up (C).

performative aspects [37]. For example, seeing one another's actions supports us in anticipating aids and improves peripheral awareness; when being in the same place vulnerability and trust is created. Performative actions allow us to understand how we encounter others. Intimacy, social nearness and a higher tendency to cooperate, result from sharing space [25].

Emerging new technologies have opened up a variety of opportunities for us of how space and place can be experienced. Especially mobile and pervasive technologies enable new means of engagement with physical spaces and physical bodies, which has often been neglected by virtual spaces. Especially for ubiquitous computing environments, the notion of place has become a valuable conceptual tool to understand the interplay between people and ubiquitous space [9]. In regard to ubiquitous computing, the car needs to be considered as a playground for ubiquitous technologies itself, i.e., through the existence of In-Vehicle-Information-Systems (IVIS) and the integration of nomadic devices such as smartphones [41]. With this pervasion, also the rear-seat and not only the front-seat passengers, become users of ubiquitous technology. Wilfinger et al. [41] have proposed to divide the car in three main areas constituting inherent design spaces: the driver's area, the front-seat area, and the back-seat area. Until now, the focus in HCI has been on the driver whereas the front-seat area and back-seat area has not been sufficiently researched yet [41]. Conceptualizations of place provide a frame for understanding how people relate to such complex environments, i.e., including physical and material resources, as well as other inhabitants [7].

Supporting collaboration in such complex environments brings up new challenges for research and design, as collaboration can be much more "anytime-anywhere" than earlier collaboration environments that were bounded to the screen [9].

In summary, with the research presented in this paper, we contribute to a deeper understanding how the car becomes place by investigating the relationship between people in spaces, as claimed by [17]. Thereby, we follow a systematic approach to study this relationship, by accounting for a distinction of (design) spaces (i.e., driver, front-seat area, and rear-seat area) [41] to draw conclusions of how we can support human activity in the car with technology and not disrupt it [8].

3. CHARACTERIZING THE RESEARCH SPACE

We decided to use a hardware mock-up of an actual car (see Figure 1) as pure physical representation of a car cabin, to minimize external influencing factors on emergent collaboration (e.g., pedestrians). This mock-up has been developed as an experience prototyping environment for automotive interfaces and aims at capturing the car space as a whole, with all potential passengers involved. The intention behind this setup is to have a hybrid between a controlled environment for studies in the lab but also mirroring a real car as close as possible. It was built from spare parts of actual cars (e.g., steering wheel and seats), based on the dimensions and measurements of a Volkswagen Golf 5 in order to provide an immersive car environment [32].

4. TRIGGERING COLLABORATION THROUGH DIGITAL CONTEXT REPRESENTATION

In order to study how the spatial properties of the car cabin shape emerging collaboration, we prototyped a contextual multiplayer game, which acts as a trigger to initiate collaboration among people in the car, i.e., as collaborative baseline task. While playing, the participants are rather expected to force their attention on the given tasks in the game than on the communication modes they use or the social role they are embodying during the game. It prevents participants from feeling forced into a collaboration situation, and therefore allows for the emergence of collaborative practices instead.

The game itself is a card game for four players [30]. It is implemented on four tablets and uses the four corners of the tablet as spatial references to interact with the others. The four corners of the application are mapped to the seating positions in the car, i.e., as digital representation of the in-car space. For example, the top right corner represents the front passenger's seat, whereas the bottom right corner of the tablet represents the rear right passenger's seat (see Figure 2). Also the player sitting on the driver's seat acts as an ordinary player without a driving task. Interaction is done by drag-and-drop gestures on the touchscreen. For example, if the front-seat passenger wants to move a card to the player on the driver's seat position s/he tabs on the card on the tablet and drags it to the top left corner. When the player then releases the card in this corner it is automatically sent to the driver. The player on the driver's seat gets notified in form of a green circle in the top left corner, which represents the front-seat passenger's position. By tapping on this green circle the card can be taken then.

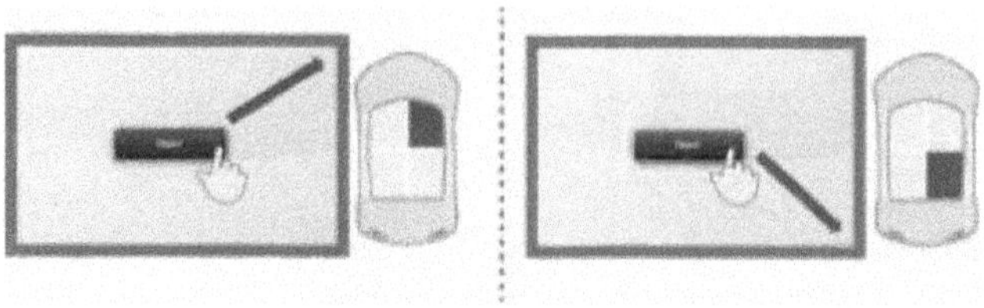

Figure 2. Interaction concept of the game prototype. Left: an object is sent to the co-driver; right: an object is sent to the passenger on the right rear-seat.

In order to trigger collaboration, participants had to complete different tasks together. The overall aim is to successfully complete as many tasks as possible, which can only be reached through good teamwork. At the start of the game, each participant has eight random cards out of a virtual deck of 32 cards. A task is given by displaying a text on each tablet on how to fulfill the task, e.g., *"Everyone must have cards of only one color!"*. To fulfill the task, participants need to communicate on how to redistribute the cards between the players. When through the exchange of cards the task is successfully completed, a new task is automatically given, e.g., *"Separate all green and red cards!"*. Again, participants need to exchange cards in order to complete the task. If, after one minute, a task is not fulfilled, a new task is given. After five minutes the game stops after the successful or unsuccessful completion of the last task. Participants are then told their number of completed tasks.

5. AN EXPLORATORY STUDY

In order to investigate how the specific spatial properties of the car cabin shape emerging collaboration (i.e., direct, guide, constrain, and constitute collaborative practices) we carried out an exploratory user study in our lab. In the following the study participants, design, procedure, and assessment are described in more detail.

5.1 Participants

Overall 56 participants, in gender-balanced groups of four (i.e., 14 groups in total), took part in the study. Participants were aged between 20 and 31 years, with a mean age of 24.8 years. All participants had a driving license to assure that they have pre-experience in being in the driver position. Participants were recruited via various student mailings lists.

5.2 Study Design

The study was realized as *within*-design with the seating position as independent variable. We had two conditions in fixed consecutive order: 1) *free-choice* (C_1): the participants could freely decide where to sit in the car mock-up and collaboration was triggered via the game for 5 minutes; 2) *reseating* (C_2): the participants were systematically reseated by the researchers in the car mock-up (i.e., driver to rear-seat left and vice versa and front-seat passenger to rear-seat right and vice versa) and collaboration was triggered via the game prototype for 5 minutes. In each condition the group of four participants accomplished one gaming-session collectively.

We defined those two conditions to specifically investigate how the fixed seating arrangement in a car cabin shape collaborative practices. The two conditions were in a fixed consecutive order (C_1 followed by C_2), as it was critical that the participants first freely choose their position in the car and then the reseating was done, in order to avoid unwanted effects on the emergence of collaborative practices and social roles. As outlined, the seating position was our independent variable, whereby we were primarily interested in characteristics of communication modes and emerging collaborative practices.

5.3 Procedure and Assessment

During the whole study, two researchers were present. One was responsible for the study conduction and the other one for the technical set-up. The group of four participants was welcomed at the lab and was given a short introduction by the researchers. Participants then needed to sign an informed consent form. After that, the audio and video recordings were started. Every participant had to introduce him/herself to the rest of the group with his/her name. Afterwards the participants had to fill out a demographic questionnaire. Then, the participants were introduced to the game and were given a 2 min. practice time to test the game, get used to it and ask questions if needed.

Afterwards, the entire group of participants moved to the car mock-up and participants could freely decide where to sit (C_1). They were then instructed to play the game and to complete as many tasks as possible. During the gaming-sessions the researchers disappeared behind a curtain to allow for an undisturbed and unobserved atmosphere while following the gaming-sessions on the screen. This procedure was repeated for C_2, where participants were reseated (i.e., driver to rear-seat left and vice versa and front-seat passenger to rear-seat right and vice versa). Both conditions were captured via two small cameras, attached to different spots in the car cabin. All in-game events (e.g., exchange of cards) were logged in a database.

After each condition, participants were asked to exit the car to sit around a table and fill out sociograms [31]. We adapted the sociogram method developed by Moreno [31], in terms of letting the participants individually visualize their perceived social links to the other participants, by triggering those visualizations with pre-defined questions. We asked for the participant's estimation of the importance of other participants to successfully complete the game (i.e., *"Which fellow-player contributed the most to successfully complete the given tasks?"*).

After the two gaming-sessions participants were asked to get back to the table for a short, approx. 15 min. lasting, group discussion in order to reflect within the group upon, e.g., gaming experiences, contextual constraints, collaboration strategies. On average, the exploratory studies lasted for 1,5 hours per group and each participant received a monetary incentive for time investments.

6. DATA ANALYSIS PROCEDURE

In a first instance, two researchers scanned through the entire video data consisting of approx. 30 hours of material to get first insights of how the spatial properties of the car cabin shape collaborative practices. We found that the 14 groups of participants have shown different cooperative strategies how they complete a given task. In order to identify critical points/interesting spots of collaborative practices in the qualitative data, we first decided to go deeper into quantitative (descriptive) characteristics of observable collaboration characteristics, i.e., as data preparation for selecting respective points of interest for the subsequent qualitative analysis. Therefore, we first conducted a quantitative analysis of in-car communication from all videos. Following the communication scheme of Knapp et al. [27], we counted the frequencies for mode of communication (i.e., speech, gaze, gestures and posture) and direction of communication (i.e., to whom a particular mode of communication is directed to).

Table 1. Mode and direction of communication among positions. White cells: frequency of occurrences for C1; grey cells: frequency of occurrences for C2.

	Driver (D)						Co-Driver (CD)						Rear Left (RL)						Rear Right (RR)						
	CD		RL		RR		D		RL		RR		D		CD		RR		D		CD		RL		Σ
Verbal	47	41	23	25	27	11	34	40	16	11	15	15	14	15	21	10	28	30	21	17	12	6	22	28	529
Gesture	7	2	10	4	12	32	3	5	8	0	5	1	1	2	0	0	1	2	2	0	3	0	3	4	107
Gaze	11	8	1	3	4	5	13	6	5	5	2	0	24	43	46	87	25	20	67	47	17	23	14	18	494
Posture	0	0	13	6	24	8	0	0	12	13	7	1	0	0	0	0	0	0	0	0	0	0	0	0	84
Σ	65	51	47	38	67	56	50	51	41	29	29	17	39	60	67	97	54	52	90	64	32	29	39	50	

Besides this frequency analysis, the questionnaires (i.e., demographic questionnaire and the sociograms) were preprocessed and analyzed using IBM SPSS Statistics 20. On basis of the analysis from the sociograms, asking for the importance of fellow-players after each condition, we were able to cluster the 14 groups of participants into three different types, i.e., (1) one particular participant is considered being the most important contributor, (2) two participants are equally considered being most important contributors, and (3) no particular participant is considered being the most important contributor. Thereby, the participants indicated no other variations in linkages, i.e., not more than two linkages to other participants.

From each of those three types, two video sequences of participant groups were selected (i.e., overall 6 videos) for a more detailed qualitative video analysis to investigate inherent group characteristics, their cooperative strategies and their interplay with the given space to accomplish the tasks. Four researchers with different backgrounds (i.e., psychology, sociology, communication sciences) analyzed the videos in joint sessions (in an adapted version from [3]). The researchers were sitting together in one room analyzing the videos individually on their own laptops with headsets. Each researcher was assigned for annotating and taking notes about one participant for both conditions by means of a structured annotation scheme provided on printouts. This annotation scheme covered the following issues: (1) general impression of the situation/context, (2) describing/characterizing the role of the observed participant within the collaboration, (3) content of communication, (4) articulation of instructions, commands, goals (or else) to others, (5) changes in participants actions between C_1 and C_2. After each analysis session, the researchers discussed the main insights from the observed participant in order to develop a shared understanding and picture of the overall group collaboration. These discussions were audio and video recorded to allow for post-hoc analysis. At the end of the video analysis sessions, a final discussion among the researchers helped to derive the overarching themes from the videos in regard to the interplay of spatial properties and in-car collaborative practices.

Subsequently, we continued with a detailed analysis of the notes that were covered in the pre-defined annotation scheme. We conducted two half-day workshops with two researchers (of the four researchers that were also involved in previous activities), by using the essentials of the Affinity Diagram technique [23] to organize the data collectively (i.e., clustering and organizing notes in regard to our guiding research question). Throughout a discursive, critical, and reflective discussion about meaning and underlying subliminal notions of the notes, we agreed upon an initial draft of the diagram. However, the Affinity Diagram was not instantly removed from the white board after the workshop, as we decided to allow for 'post-hoc' refinements of the clustering. Overall, 351 annotations were clustered within this process and led to four main topics, which are described in the following.

7. RESULTS

The following section details the key findings we gathered in regard to our main research question (i.e., How do spatial properties of the car cabin shape emerging collaboration). We first present the descriptive data concerning communication characteristics (i.e., mode and direction of communication) extracted from the *quantitative video analysis* as well as actor characteristics derived from the *sociograms*, providing the criteria for selecting the videos for the qualitative video analysis. The major focus in this section will lie on the identified topics (i.e., normative arrangement, coordinative strategies, spatial interaction, and temporality of involvement) derived from the collaborative video analysis sessions.

7.1 Importance of Actors & Communication Characteristics

We considered *speech* (i.e., verbal articulations and their directions), *gestures* (i.e., including speech dependent and independent gestures and their direction), *gaze* (i.e., in the general direction of another's face), and *posture* (i.e., turning one's body towards each other) as key-communication modes to be investigated within the descriptive quantitative video analysis. The decision for selecting these particular modes among others (e.g., touch, eye-contact), was purposely done on basis of the first scanning of the videos, and the identified importance of these modes. An overview about the results is given in Table 1. In the following, selected results are presented and highlighted in the table along with the descriptions below.

7.1.1 Spatial Barriers for Communication

Overall, we found that the participants primarily communicated verbally (n=529) followed by gaze (n=494). Gestures (n=107) and postures (n=84) were less frequently used to communicate with the fellow participants (see Table 1) and were mostly enacted along with other means of communication to support their statements. In regard to gaze we observed that participants, especially from the back-seats were 'gazing' at the front-seat positions, trying to seek for information (i.e., observing front-seat passengers actions on the tablet) [highlighted in green]. In contrast, participants at the front-seat positions hardly made any gazes to the rear positions, as their positioning in the front respectively impeded them in looking behind. We also found that in both conditions, the front-seat positions communicated mostly

Figure 3. Overview of identified topics and their related sub-topics. Highlighted topics (in black) are discussed in the text.

verbally with each other compared to the rear-seat positions [highlighted in blue]. Likewise, also for the back-seat positions, verbal communication between them plays a central role [highlighted in pink], whereas less frequently used as gaze. These findings underpin that spatial barriers, such as the seats of the front-seat passengers, act as communication hindrances between the front and the back, dividing the car into two interaction spaces.

7.1.2 Gaze and Posture Accompanying Verbal Articulations

The suggested interrelatedness of seats acting as catalysts for verbal communication, is also supported by the finding that participants sitting in the front tend to accompany their verbal articulations towards the back row with additional gestures and posture [highlighted in orange]. That is, the front-seat passengers frequently turn their heads and bodies (i.e., considered in the analysis as posture) to the middle aiming at establishing eye-contact with the rear-seat positions. In general, posture mostly goes along with other means of communications (e.g., turning around and verbally communicating) and is therefore only involved when the front-seat positions verbally communicate with the rear-seat positions. Postures were only observed in front to back communication. Gestures were used by all participants when communicating, but mostly in front to back communication.

7.1.3 Overcoming Spatial Barriers by 'Generalizing Others'

Besides the annotation of specific communication modes with respect to the positioning of the participants (i.e., transmitters and receivers), we also annotated communication that was not particularly directed to one specific person or position. This means that we also captured the frequencies for communication that aimed at addressing all positions in the mock-up (e.g., giving instructions on how to proceed in the game). In both conditions and in all positions, participants frequently verbally communicated to the generalized others, not particularly addressing one individual or one position. Specifically participants in the driver position, in both conditions (C_1 n=167; C_2 n=192), talked to generalized others.

7.1.4 Actors Importance

After each condition, we asked participants how important they considered their fellow-players to successfully complete the game (*"Which fellow-player contributed the most to successfully complete the given tasks?"*). To answer this question, we conducted a Chi-squared test to identify the likelihood of most important/least important contributors to successfully complete the game with respect to the given conditions. In C_1 no significant difference (χ^2=0.37, n.s.) could be identified in regard to the participants' importance, i.e., no particular participant and his/her seating position was considered as contributing the most to successfully complete the game. In C_2 we found that the participants significantly consider the driver as contributing the most to successfully complete the game (χ^2=7.86, p<.05).

This seems to be an interesting finding, as the two conditions were in a fixed consecutive order which means, that the participants, who were sitting on the rear-seat left in C_1 have turned out to be the most important contributors in the replacement condition (C_2). After getting familiar with one another and the game in C_1 positioned on the rear-left seat (that provides a comprehensive overview), participants moving to the driver position in C_2 are ascribed as being most important contributors to the game. This phenomenon may be due to ascribing an inherent role to the driver position, even when not being in the usual situation of having the driver drive the car, i.e., thereby having the central role in a moving vehicle. Particular expectations of action are ascribed to this role (e.g., expecting the driver to coordinate/organize the interactions) leading to shifting's of how the participant communicates to others.

7.2 Spatial Properties Shaping Emerging Collaboration

In order to facilitate a comprehensive understanding how spatial properties of the car cabin shape collaborative practices, we decided for a detailed qualitative video analysis (which is detailed in section 6). Figure 3 provides a simplified representation of the identified topics from the analysis and their related sub-topics for descriptive purposes. These topics need to be considered as overlapping and not clearly distinctive. Four main topics were identified with regard to characteristics of the interplay of space and place in the car: (1) *coordinative strategies*, (2) *normative arrangement*, (3) *temporality of involvement*, and (4) *spatial interaction*. The number of counts (i.e., frequency of annotations) for each topic or sub-topic is indicated in brackets.

7.2.1 Coordinative Strategies

Here, we bundled annotations that describe the active/passive involvement of participants in coordinative practices, actions (i.e., strengths and content of articulations) that served as mechanisms for coordination, and conceptional arrangements of group dynamics. In regard to group dynamics, we identified two different types of how decisions were made. First, we found that sometimes one participant can be considered as *triggering instance* to initiate coordination within the group (10). Here, the participant immediately, after a new task was given, started to coordinate the subsequent actions within the group, e.g., *"OK, I have all 9s, give me all 9s!"* (Task: One must have all 9er cards).

Second, some groups also *agree upon a certain strategy* (9) they follow to accomplish a given task. Most of these agreed upon strategies aim to be more efficient in solving the given tasks and are mostly based on experiences they already gathered in prior tasks, i.e., everyone must have all cards of one color. Here, for example, some agree on keeping the colors they already had kept in prior tasks or some even make decisions about a particular strategy in the short break between the first and second condition (e.g., Who takes what color?). In these groups the coordination of solving the tasks seems to be well organized.

7.2.2 Normative Arrangement

In regard to the *normative arrangement* (i.e., normative make-up of collaborative practices) within the groups, we observed the following six instances: when participants give instructions to direct others actions, give status updates to inform fellow-players about one's own status, give compliments to motivate the group, articulate errors to inform others about false actions, confirm fellow-players about correct actions, and ask questions either directed to particular people or the entire group.

We were able to identify 38 occurrences where *instructions* by one participant were given. These instructions were either targeted to one fellow-player or to the entire group. In regard to directed instructions, a participant being in the front-seat position for example said *"You must forward the uneven cards!"*, another one sitting at the rear right articulated *"Lisa, send those cards back!"*, or a participant at the rear left said *"We must send the cards clockwise."*.

In regard to *questions* (44) that were articulated, we identified different types of questions, such as e.g., questions targeting to confirm one's own actions (participant at rear-left *"Is this correct?"*), questions targeting to direct and coordinate activities within the group (participant at the rear-right *"Who takes the blue cards?"*), or questions about unclear situations/statuses (participant at the rear-left *"Who has sent me this card?"*).

On basis of the normative make-up of the different groups, we identified several *social roles* that emerged throughout the collaborations, i.e., particular roles participants took over. Since the participants did not know each other before the study and the sample was rather heterogeneous (i.e., 20-30 years, gender balanced, all having driving licenses), these roles may be considered as emergent (in contrast to ascribed), as we extracted them bottom-up from the observed collaborative practices. However, as the sociograms showed, the interplay between ascribed roles (i.e., a particular role and related behavior attached to the driver position) vs. emergent roles (i.e., a role developing out of collaborative practices within a group) seems to be more complex and a reflection will be done in the discussion section.

Overall three main roles were identified, i.e., the 'Organizers/Leaders' (15), the 'Executors' (15), and the 'Transformers' (8). Concerning the 'Organizer/Leader' roles, we found that sometimes the participants have explicitly articulated the need to have a leadership role to successfully play the game and have defined one person within the group to take over this role. These decisions were mostly felt within the group and before the actual game tasks started. For example, one participant asked, *"Who wants to make clear messages?"* and another participant on the rear-right answered, *"I love to make clear messages, I play the boss"*. In contrast to these (beforehand) clearly defined 'Leaders' we also recognized that some 'Leaders' emerge out of particular situations where a leader and decisions are needed, i.e., even though the participant did not want to take over leadership some situations demand a leader.

Complementary to the 'Organizer/Leader' roles, we also identified 'Executor' roles, i.e., participants that execute particular tasks that are handed over to them, mostly from 'Leaders' such as *"Send the yellow card to me and I'll forward it to Thomas"*. Those participants seem to be less active and observant, unless someone assigns a particular task to her/him. We consider those roles as counterparts to the leader roles, as besides organizing and assigning tasks (i.e., having a general overview), there are also people needed within the group that execute assignments. As last role we identified 'Transformers', i.e., participants taking over various functions needed in different situations. For example, if those participants recognize that in a given situation no one comes to a decision (i.e., subsequent actions, after a new task was given, remain unclear) s/he takes over and makes the decision for the group. Action patterns of this role are strongly tied to given situations, where actions/decisions of participants are needed. This role may be considered as a purely emergent, i.e., developing out of given situations within a particular group constellation.

7.2.3 Temporality of Involvement

In terms of involvement of participants (i.e., being either more active or passive members within the given decision-making processes over time), we found that some show constant involvement (6) over both conditions whereas some tend to become more (9)/less active (12) in the course of time (i.e., from C_1 to C_2). In regard to constant involvement, the participants were either constantly passive or active (i.e., involvement between C_1 and C_2 being equivalent). In contrast we also observed that some participants tended to become more active and being more involved, whereas others tended to become less active and involved in the course of time. In general participants tended to become less active and involved during the game.

7.2.4 Spatial Interaction

In regard to spatial properties and in how far they affect the observed coordinative and collaborative strategies, we identified several aspects characterizing these intersections. Mainly the car seats could have been identified as major hindrances directing the groups' coordination. Overall seven spatial properties, as instantiations affecting emerging collaboration, could be identified: coordination with/by participants at the driver position (i.e., criticality of the driver's position for coordination), coordination with/by participants at the rear-right, turning towards neighbor (i.e., prior coordination among participants in the front-seat vs. participants in the back-seat positions with only little exchange across them), turning towards back row (i.e., participants at front-seat positions turning towards the middle to allow for exchange and ease collaboration), focusing at other's tablet (i.e., participants aiming to gather an overview by looking at fellows tablets), and turning towards each other (i.e., not only participants at front-seat positions, but all positions in the mock-up turn towards each other to ease collaboration).

We found that the driver position may be considered as the 'crux of the matter' (19), as we identified many instances wherein either from or to the driver position coordination is directed to. This also underpins the importance of participants in driver positions, as identified in the sociograms. On the one hand, participants at the front-seat passenger position intensively cooperate with the participants at the driver position (in contrast to participants at back-seat positions) by, for example, turning ones entire body towards the driver position to ease exchange but also to support/control the participants actions at the driver position. On the other hand, we observed that participants in the driver position are at many instances coordinating their actions towards the front-seat positions by, for example, observing their actions on the tablet or sometimes even verbally articulating his/her status (e.g., number/color of cards on the deck) to the others.

Participants at the driver position play a central role not only in the cooperation with participants at the front-seat position but also diagonal backwards (i.e., rear-right position), which can also be supported by the number of communication instances in the quantitative analysis. When participants in the driver position turn around on their seats, they are able to see the rear-right; this might also be the reason that if they communicate to the back, this is mostly done with the rear-right position (e.g., participant at the driver position is turning ones body to another participant at the rear right position, saying, *"I have just sent you a card."*). Further, participants sitting at the rear-left consider the rear-right positions as central to, for example, observe their tablet and respective actions (e.g., gather additional information about the game status) or to coordinate how tasks are processed between the two (e.g., participant at the rear-left position articulating to the rear-right *"I take the even cards and you take the uneven cards."* (Task: split even and uneven cards)).

The two previously described observations support that the two participants in the front row and the two participants in the back row are mostly cooperating together, i.e., that the front-seat positions are major coordination and communication barriers resulting in two separate interaction spaces. If the front wants to communicate with the back, they have to turn their bodies towards each other (pure verbal articulations being not sufficient enough). Therefore, also due to efficiency purposes (i.e., time pressure), coordination is aligned along the participants seating positions. For example, given tasks are split up among the two rows (e.g., back row takes even, front row uneven cards), participants sitting in front or back rows tend to turn towards each other.

8. POINTS FOR REFLECTION

With this research, we have highlighted how spatial properties of the car cabin shape collaborative practices, thereby creating an inhabited *place* for people to interact in. On the one hand, our results draw from a descriptive analysis of quantitative characteristics of observable peculiarities of emerging collaboration, i.e., posture, gestures, gaze, and verbal articulation. On the other hand, we conducted a collaborative video analysis session to complement the quantitative findings with knowledge on how the very specific spatial properties of the car cabin shape the way we collaboratively engage in this very specific interaction environment, i.e., coordinative strategies, normative arrangement, involvement, and spatial interaction.

Furthermore, we have shown *how* focusing on *how* the spatial properties of our car mock-up interplay with collaborative practices can expose critical characteristics related to the emergence of coordinative strategies in the car context also on a more general level. We highlight that it can be useful to extend details about practices, by looking at the specifics of the context of action, i.e., grasping the car cabin itself as an entity of inquiry that structures and forms our socially construed inhabited places. In the following we will reflect upon selected findings, their potential for interaction design (IxD), on our game approach, and limitations of our study setup.

8.1 Ascribed Meanings of Space – The 'Crux of the Matter'

In line with Harrison and Dourish [21], we accounted for looking not just at the space as being a distinct entity of inquiry separated from collaboration, following their argument that *"[...] behavior can be framed as much by the presence of other individuals as by the location itself [...]*" ([21], pp. 69). Taking upon this perspective, we were interested in understanding how the participants have perceived the roles other participants were taking over while playing the game, i.e., to identify different roles and related role behaviors in relation to the participants seating position. In both, the quantitative (e.g., driver is considered as being the most important contributor to successfully complete the tasks) and the qualitative data (e.g., driver position being the 'crux of the matter' from or to coordination is directed to), we found that participants ascribe to the position of the driver seat, particular roles, expectations, and related behaviors even in a *non-driving* activity.

These findings show that human interaction is not only framed by spaces, but also *"by the patterns of understandings, associations and expectations with which they are infused."* ([21], pp. 69). In our case, the driver position even in a non-driving activity is prescribed in taking over a specific role, i.e., being the coordinator, organizer, and leader in the game. The point thereby is that based on our (pre-) experiences we have with a particular context, we attach meaning to given spaces and inscribe related behavior to those people inhabiting this particular space.

8.2 Meaning for Interaction Design

Understanding a certain design space and its inherent individual and collaborative complexities is critical in order to design in this respect. This is of specific importance in highly safety critical environments (such as the automotive domain) in order to best facilitate collaborative practices within the car (e.g., navigation) while not neglecting the primary task of driving. Our findings have shown, e.g., that participants at rear-seat positions seek for eye-contact with participants at front-seat positions, that a shared visual view due to the front-seats is disrupted, and counteracts the creation of shared knowledge and common ground of the situation [18], or that front seats 'artificially' constitute two separate (design) spaces. In regard to IxD, our findings contribute to a more comprehensive understanding of the automotive context as a highly complex and constrained interaction environment. We argue that our findings provide an initial basis of how to shape the way in which technology and systems may be *embedded in the car space itself*, or how the *structural features of the car space* may be shaped to boost collaborative encounters.

Current research focuses mainly on interaction designs for the driver position. Until now, relatively little attention has been directed to interaction designs that particularly aim to support collaborative practices in cars, especially within the automotive research community. Even less designs exist that aim to overcome spatial barriers to support in-car collaboration. One example that specifically focuses on both (i.e., IxD for in-car collaboration in respect to spatial constraints), is the 'shared gaze' approach [39]. 'Shared gaze' visualizes the front-seat passengers' gaze for the driver to foster a shared visual view, thereby counteracting that drivers and front-seat passengers (due to the arrangement of the seating positions) do not have the possibility to look at each others face or comprehend where someone is looking at. Thereby, 'shared gaze' proposes a novel interaction design that can potentially inform the emergence of, so far, unknown collaborative practices in cars. Another system that aims to support driver and co-driver collaboration is the 'Co-Navigator' [36]. The 'Co-Navigator' is a device to be operated by the front-seat passenger, in order to support the driver in navigation and driving related tasks, i.e., providing the front-seat passenger with information that are not common on traditional navigational devices. This approach does primarily aim to support collaborative practices that are common and often performed in cars (i.e., front-seat passenger supporting the driver while navigating). Nevertheless, those approaches *solely focus* on driver and front-seat passenger collaboration, and do not incorporate all passengers in their interaction designs. This provides an opportunity for designers to develop novel collaborative designs for the automotive domain, but also to research the manifestation of new, emergent collaborative practices.

When reflecting upon such examples on basis of our findings, we could think of designs that support a shared visual view also for rear seat passengers to bridge the "virtual wall" between front and back rows. But also co-navigational devices could be made fit for back row collaboration as well by, e.g., supporting different cues (like gaze or gestures) that are known from face-to-face collaboration and providing opportunities for back row passengers to have the same view on the street as the drivers do. This would support a common understanding of given situations among all passengers. Therefore, we argue that our findings may be seen from the perspective of *highlighting existing spatial challenges* for in-car collaboration that call for a re-thinking of conceptualizations of collaborative engagements in cars. For the purpose of deriving concrete implications for interaction designs on basis of our results, it is important to highlight the limitations that come along with our study-setup (i.e., engaging people collaboratively in a task without involving any driving activity). Since no real driving situation was triggered or even simulated with our study, findings highlighting the importance of shared gaze (i.e., which is seen to be highly important in communication and collaboration theory, e.g., [1], [12], [18]) and the respectively discussed interaction designs (e.g., [29], [39]) aiming to facilitate shared gaze among passengers need to be very carefully reflected upon. One of the upmost important implications is that when aiming to establish immediate access of eye contact between driver and passengers, the safety of drivers and passengers needs to be considered and facilitated at all time, by for example, allowing only for situated activation of shared gaze by the driver (e.g., letting the driver activate shared gaze when needed towards supporting spatial referencing during collaborative navigational tasks). Thereby, shared gaze can have a positive impact on collaboration by being used in conjunction to verbal feedback, leading to increased shared understanding and decreased verbal misunderstandings between collaborators [29].

However, this friction in allowing for shared activities been drivers and passengers as well as safety issues that may come along with respective designs, are an important aspect for future research on and designs for in-car collaboration. In this respect, autonomous vehicles represent a research and design field, where our findings might be of high benefit, i.e., without the severity of safety issues in regard to shared and collaborative approaches in cars. Findings about the interplay of spatial properties and collaboration in today's car cabins expose challenges and hindrances that can be addressed in the design of future cars. They may provide foundational knowledge of how to design the car cabin of a fully autonomous vehicle where no driver and driving activity is needed anymore.

8.3 The Game Approach

In our approach (i.e., having a contextual multi-player game as a collaborative trigger), two kinds of embodiments of the spatial properties of cars were utilized. We created an embodied representation of the spatial properties within the game's core interaction concept (i.e., seating positions mapped to the corners of the tablet). Additionally, the social setting we created with the game was located and observed directly in an experience prototype that captures the spatial properties of a car cabin based on physical hardware and interfaces used in real cars (e.g., old car seats). The physical and digital representation of space (i.e., car mock-up and tablet) allowed us to involve the participants in a meaningful way (i.e., without being biased by a substitution task) and to be as close as possible to a real car, but at the same time staying within our lab environment.

With our game approach, we deliberately created an overlap between the spatial characteristics and the digital representations and metaphors of this spatiality, which allowed us to create a natural *friction* between the space and its resulting influences on collaboration. We argue that this way of incorporating space and collaborative practices is a legitimate form of inquiry in order to holistically study a design space and its interplay with collaborative practices.

Another benefit of utilizing a game within our methodological approach was the opportunity to create *meaningful interaction* via the game itself. The game was utilized as a way of probing and as a relational artifact that created a social coupling between the participants. This coupling (i.e., people being connected via a common task and goal via the game) was the very subject of observation and allowed us to trigger and explore collaborative practices within the spatial boundaries of the car.

8.4 Reflection on the Study Setup

Our study was conducted in a car mock-up within a lab setting without involving a driving task. We are aware that this setup exposes some limitations in regard to the ecological validity of the data collected and therefore asks for a nuanced reflection. When it comes to the interpretation of findings in the light of their ecological validity, Lewkowicz [33] draws attention to three critical issues of which we will reflect upon in this section. First, the *types of stimuli* used should reflect the participant's naturalistic setting, the *nature of the experimental setting* should be as similar as possible to the participant's everyday environment, and the *type of response* should refer to the participant's available response repertoire [33].

With our setup we created a space for social interactions, where all in-car inhabitants can be considered as *equal* interaction partners, without ascribing them pre-defined roles due to the setup, i.e., by giving them a role or activity different than the others. This pre-defined ascription of activities and roles would have been the case if we had selected the driver to be involved in any kind of driving activity (either in a simulator or on the road). Therefore, we argue that with our study design we avoided to introduce any biases in regard to task roles and interactions with researchers during the study. Furthermore, we created a truly explorative research environment without bringing study participants into any dangerous situations while being involved in any driving activity. Also if we would have selected a real, parking car for our research interests, potential biases such as the car brand or pedestrians walking by, could have been introduced and might have had an influence on the observed collaboration.

Some results, such as the driver being a central actor that guides the collaboration *without even being in a driving activity*, might have been different when being researched in the wild involving an actual driving task, i.e., assuming that this finding would have been shown even stronger in the results. Further, we argue that our findings in regard to in-car collaboration and communication provide a basic understanding of how people behave in a constrained environment by engaging them in a 'natural' collaborative task (i.e., game as baseline collaboration task) and therefore, allow for a certain kind of scalability.

On basis of these reflections, we consider the spatial properties (e.g., seats, headrests, steering-wheel) of our car mock-up (i.e., the nature of the experimental setting [33]), the game as collaborative baseline task (i.e., the type of stimuli [33]), and the respectively triggered collaboration and communication (i.e., the type of response [33]) as being the *main criteria* for ecological validity. Therefore, we argue that our findings need to be considered as a starting point to trigger a discussion about constraints and effects of spatial properties on emerging collaboration in highly constrained environments, such as cars.

9. CONCLUSION

With the study presented in this paper, we show how the spatial properties of the car cabin guide, direct, sometimes constrain, but concurrently constitute a place for social interaction. For example, we found out that, on the one hand, the spatial properties of a car foster collaboration within the places in the front and the places in the back, i.e., constituting two design spaces. On the other hand they constrain the collaboration between these two areas. The driver position, thereby, needs to be considered as the 'crux of the matter' bridging the "virtual wall" between the front and the back.

With our research we emphasized the importance to study in-car collaboration beyond traditional explorations on driver and/or driver – co-driver interaction, by facilitating a comprehensive perspective in terms of including the back-seat area in our research investigations as well. We show that cars as highly ubiquitous environments, constitute a relevant research space for the GROUP/CSCW community, since understanding the interrelatedness of emerging collaboration and spatial properties are central to inform the design of future (automotive) interaction designs and to respectively guide those into the right direction. Based on this, we argue that our work contributes to a new way of thinking, by providing a use case that can trigger a discourse within GROUP/CSCW about the importance to research emerging collaboration also in respect to their spatial manifestations, especially in constrained environments. With this work, we want to encourage researchers and practitioners to take our work further and engage in questions of intersecting collaboration with respect to it's spatial manifestations in their research, designs, and reflections thereof. For future work, we will investigate in how far our gathered knowledge on the interplay of spatial properties and collaboration is useful to better understand collaborative practices is actual driving situations in the wild.

With our approach, we have shown that notions of 'space' and 'place' provide a valuable conceptual frame to empirically investigate the very specifics of interactional contexts in which we as humans are socially embedded in.

10. ACKNOWLEDGMENTS

The financial support by the Austrian Federal Ministry of Science, Research and Economy and the National Foundation for Research, Technology and Development and AUDIO MOBIL Elektronik GmbH is gratefully acknowledged (Christian Doppler Laboratory for "Contextual Interfaces"). We thank Karl-Armin Krässig for his valuable support in the development of the game prototype.

11. REFERENCES

[1] Argyle, M. and Cook, M. 1976. *Gaze and mutual gaze*. Cambridge, UK: Cambridge University Press.

[2] Biddle, J. B. 1986. *Recent Developments in Role Theory*. Annual Review of Sociology, p. 67-92.

[3] Brigitte, J. and Henderson, A. "Interaction analysis: Foundations and practice." *The journal of the learning sciences* 4.1 (1995), p. 39-103.

[4] Brown, B., Laurier, E., Lorimer, H. et al. A. 2008. Driving and 'Passengering': Notes on the Ordinary Organization of Car Travel. *Mobilities* 3, 1 (2008), p. 1-23.

[5] Bryden, K. J., Charlton, J., Oxley, J., Lowndes, G. 2014. Older driver and passenger collaboration for wayfinding in unfamiliar areas. *International Journal of Behavioral Development*, 38(4), p. 378-385.

[6] Bull, M. 2004. Automobility and the power of sound. *Theory, Culture & Society*, 21, p. 243-260.

[7] Ciolfi, L. 2004. Situating 'Place' in Interaction Design: Enhancing the User Experience in Interactive Environments. Ph.D. Thesis, Univ. of Limerick.

[8] Ciolfi, L. 2004. Understanding Spaces as Places: Extending Interaction Design Paradigms. *Journal for Cognition Technology and Work*, 6(1), February 2004. Berlin: Springer.

[9] Ciolfi, L., Fitzpatrick, G. and Bannon, L. 2008. Settings for Collaboration: the Role of Place. In *Journal for Computer Supported Cooperative Work* 17, 2-3, p. 91-96.

[10] Ciolfi, L., Gray, B. and D'Andrea A. 2012. Social Aspects of Place Experience in Nomadic Work/Life Practices. In Dugdale, J., Masclet, C., Grasso, A. and Boujut, J-F. (Eds). In *Proceedings of COOP 2012*, London: Springer, p. 183-196.

[11] Clark, H. H. and Brennan, S. E. 1991. Grounding in Communication. In Lauren .B. Resnick, John M. Levine, and Stephanie D. Tesley (Eds.). *Perspectives on Socially Shared Cognition*. Washington, DC, APA Press, p. 127-149.

[12] Clark, H. H. 1996. *Using Language*. Cambridge, UK: Cambridge University Press.

[13] Cycil, C., Perry, M., Laurier, E., Taylor, A. S. 2013. 'Eyes free' in-car assistance: parent and child passenger collaboration during phone calls. In *Proceedings of MobileHCI '13*, ACM, New York, NY, p. 332-341. DOI= http://doi.acm.org/10.1145/2493190.2493207.

[14] De Waard et al. 1999. Driver behavior in an emergency situation in the Automated Highway System. *Transportation Human Factors*, 1 (1999), p. 67-82.

[15] Erickson, T. 1993. From Interface to Interplace: the Spatial Environment as Medium for Interaction. In *Proceedings of the Conference on Spatial Information Theory*. Heidelberg: Springer- Verlag.

[16] Fitzpatrick, G., Kaplan, S., Mansfield, T. 1996. Physical spaces, virtual places and social worlds: a study of work in the virtual. In *Proceedings of CSCW '96*, Mark S. Ackerman

(Ed.), ACM, New York, NY, p. 334-343. DOI= http://doi.acm.org/10.1145/240080.240322.

[17] Fitzpatrick, G. 2003. *The locales framework: Understanding and Designing for Wicked Problems*. Dordrecht: Kluwer Academic Publishers.

[18] Forlizzi, J., Barley, W. C., Seder, T. 2010. Where should i turn: moving from individual to collaborative navigation strategies to inform the interaction design of future navigation systems. In *Proceedings of CHI '10*. ACM, New York, NY, p. 1261-1270. DOI= http://doi.acm.org/10.1145/1753326.1753516.

[19] Gärtner, M., Meschtscherjakov, A., Maurer, B., Wilfinger, D., Tscheligi, M. 2014. "Dad, Stop Crashing My Car!": Making Use of Probing to Inspire the Design of Future In-Car Interfaces. In *Proceedings of AutomotiveUI '14*, ACM, New York, NY. DOI= http://doi.acm.org/10.1145/2667317.2667348.

[20] Gridling, N., Meschtscherjakov, A., Tscheligi, M. 2012. I need help! Exploring collaboration in the car. In *Proceedings of CSCW '12*, ACM, New York, NY, pp. 87–90.

[21] Harrison, S. and Dourish, P. 1996. Re-Place-ing Space: the roles of place and space in collaborative systems. *In Proceedings of CSCW'96*. Boston Massachussets, p. 67–76.

[22] Henfridsson, O., Wiberg, M., Lindgren, R., & Ljungberg, F. 2004. SeamlessTalk: User-controlled session management for sustained car conversations. *The Interaction Society: Practice, Theories, and Supportive Technologies*. Information Science Publishing, IDEA-group Inc. p. 304-318.

[23] Holtzblatt, K., Burns Wendell, J., Wood, S. 2005. Rapid Contextual Design: A How-To Guide to Key Techniques for User-Centered Design. *Ubiquity 2005*, March, 3-3. DOI= http://doi.acm.org/10.1145/1066322.1066325.

[24] Hornecker, E. 2004. A Design Framework for Designing Tangible Interaction for Collaborative Use. Retrieved January 10, 2016 from http://www.ehornecker.de/Papers/DanishHCI.pdf

[25] Hornecker, E. Space and Place – Setting the Stage for Social Interaction. Position paper for ECSCW'05 workshop 'Settings for Collaboration: the role of place'.

[26] Juhlin, O. 2011. Social Media on the Road: Mobile Technologies and Future Traffic Research. *IEEE MultiMedia,* 18(1), p. 8-10. DOI= http://dx.doi.org/10.1109/MMUL.2011.16.

[27] Knapp, M., Hall, J., Hogan, T. 2013. *Nonverbal Communication in Human Interaction*. 8th Edition, Cengage Learning.

[28] Knobel, M., Hassenzahl, M., Lamara, M., Sattler, T., Schumann, J., Eckoldt, K., Butz, A. 2012. Clique Trip: feeling related in different cars. In *Proceedings of DIS '12*. ACM, New York, NY, p. 29-37. DOI= http://doi.acm.org/10.1145/2317956.2317963.

[29] Maurer, B., Aslan, I., Wuchse, M., Neureiter, K., and Tscheligi, M. 2015. Gaze-Based Onlooker Integration: Exploring the In-Between of Active Player and Passive Spectator in Co-Located Gaming. In *Proceedings of the 2015 Annual Symposium on Computer-Human Interaction in Play* (CHI PLAY '15). ACM, New York, NY, USA, 163-173. DOI=http://dx.doi.org/10.1145/2793107.2793126.

[30] Meschtscherjakov, A., Krischkowsky, A., Neureiter, N., Mirnig, A., Baumgartner, A., Fuchsberger, V., and Tscheligi, M. 2016. Active Corners: Collaborative In-Car Interaction Design. In *Proceedings of the 2016 ACM Conference on Designing Interactive Systems* (DIS '16). ACM, New York, NY, USA, 1136-1147. DOI= http://dx.doi.org/10.1145/2901790.2901872.

[31] Moreno, J. I. 1956. *Sociometry and the Science of Man*. New York: Beacon House, Inc., p. 275.

[32] Murer, M., Wilfinger, D., and Tscheligi, M. 2013. "Taking Reality for a Drive in the Lab: The Makeup of a Mockup for Automotive HMI Research," in Adjunct Proceedings of the 5th International Conference on Automotive User Interfaces and Interactive Vehicular Applications, 2013.

[33] Lewkowicz, D. J. 2001. The Concept of Ecological Validity: What Are Its Limitations and Is It Bad to Be Invalid? *Journal of Infancy*, 2(4), Blackwell Publishing Ltd, pp. 437-450.

[34] Oestergren, M. and Juhlin, O. 2004. Sound Pryer: truly mobile joint music listening. Int. workshop on mobile music technology.

[35] Perterer, N., Sundström, P., Meschtscherjakov, A., Wilfinger, D., Tscheligi, M. 2013. Come drive with me: an ethnographic study of driver-passenger pairs to inform future in-car assistance. *In Proceedings CSCW '13*. ACM, New York, NY, p. 1539-1548. DOI= http://doi.acm.org/10.1145/2441776.2441952.

[36] Perterer, N., Meschtscherjakov, A., Tscheligi, M. 2015. Co-Navigator: an advanced navigation system for front-seat passengers. In *Proceedings of AutomotiveUI '15*. ACM, New York, NY, USA, p. 187-194. DOI= http://doi.acm.org/10.1145/2799250.2799265

[37] Robertson, T. 1997. Cooperative Work and Lived Cognition. A Taxonomy of Embodied Actions. In *Proceedings of E-CSCW'1997*, p. 205-220.

[38] Schober, M. F. and Clark, H. H. 1989. Understanding by Addressees and Overhearers. *Cognitive Psychology*, 21, p. 211-232.

[39] Trösterer, S., Gärtner, M., Wuchse, M., Maurer, B., Baumgartner, A., Meschtscherjakov, A., Tscheligi, M. 2015. Four Eyes See More than Two: Shared Gaze in the Car. *In Proceedings INTERACT 2015*, Part II, LNCS, p. 331–348, 2015. DOI= http://10.1007/978-3-319-22668-2_26.

[40] Wiberg, M. 2005. Conversation Support for Persistent Mobile Interaction. In *Proceedings of HCI International*, p. 22-27.

[41] Wilfinger, D., Meschtscherjakov, A., Murer, M., Osswald, S., Tscheligi, M. 2011. Are we there yet? a probing study to inform design for the rear seat of family cars. *In Proceedings INTERACT'11*, p. 657-674.

Communication, Coordination and Awareness around Continuous Location Sharing

Emily Schildt
Stockholm University
Stockholm, Sweden
emorange@gmail.com

Martin Leinfors
Stockholm University,
Stockholm, Sweden
martin.leinfors@gmail.com

Louise Barkhuus
The IT University of Copenhagen
Copenhagen, Denmark
barkhuus@itu.dk

ABSTRACT

A core aspect of collaboration tools is the sharing of awareness cues, such as availability and location information, often with the purpose of more efficient collaboration and communication between individuals. In this paper, we present a user study of a continuous location-sharing application, used over a period of a month within groups of 4-5 people, which provided detailed awareness between group members. Reporting on issues such as its facility for micro-coordination and enabler of ad-hoc social engagements, we analyze the distinct ways in which the service was incorporated into participants' daily lives. We studied a location sharing service among people in less hierarchical types of relationships than previous studies and found that sharing concerns were based on the participants 'thinking' and imagination of potential situations rather than on actual situations. Our findings highlight how people's understanding of location-tracking technologies is transitional and how it includes a constant re-negotiation of appropriate services and applications for everyday social management. We conclude that map-based continuous location sharing has significant utility among tight-knit dyads.

Keywords

Location-based services, mobile computing, social practices.

1. INTRODUCTION

Collaboration technologies often take advantage of sensor systems such as activity sensing and location sensing. Digital sharing of a personal state has been a prevalent theme of sociotechnical systems, from portholes [20] and motion sensors [7] to mobile systems sharing location [4, 35]. Digital location sharing between individuals has been technically possible for decades, initially with experimental systems such as the Active Badges, Context-Contacts and Connecto [42, 38, 4] and later with commercial systems such as Dodgeball [29]. Today location broadcasting is facilitated through smart phones in the form of real-time sharing of map pointers (GPS based) or descriptive tags, often through social networks such as Foursquare and Facebook check-in. The former usually being continuous location sharing, the latter being check-in based and thereby time limited. Research has addressed numerous issues in this space, in terms of privacy [39, 41], self-presentation [17, 24] and social group maintenance [4], particularly in relation to check-in and labeling-based systems. For example, these studies provide insights into people's need for feedback in relation to real-time location sharing with a variety of services; they also present evidence that identity management commonly takes place through these (particularly label-based) services. However, few studies have addressed the actual communication and coordination that takes place *around* these types of services. The studies that have inquired into such factors have often focused on manual and representational sharing such as Dodgeball [29] and Connecto [4], as opposed to continuous map-based location sharing. In fact, most of the continuous sharing prototype systems that have been studied implement notifications, limited accessibility or granularity of the location [3, 12, 35]. Yet, other studies indicate that continuous location sharing can contribute to digital nurturing, comfort and assist everyday coordination in domestic relationships [10, 12]. With a critical mass of smart phone owners, often collected in tightknit social groups, map-based location sharing have great potential for increasing overall context- and activity awareness. Here, we address the research question of *how people, within small tight-knit social groups, communicate and coordinate through and around continuous location sharing applications.*

To explore people's broader interactions around a continuous location sharing tool, we conducted a month-long study of a map-based service used within already socially settled groups of 4-5 people. The study focused on communication and coordination practices for users of this service, extending previous research studies on mainly prototype systems with tracking notifications or labeling-based systems. We highlight how the service facilitated communication and micro-coordination but that the service also invoked concern for others' feelings around socialization. Our work contributes to a better understanding of the underlying social structures affecting use of these services as well as how we can design sensible but useful location tracking technologies.

2. BACKGROUND

Research addressing location-based services is extensive, spanning empirical studies of rendezvousing behavior for position-aware technologies [14] to spatio-temporal analyses of global check-in data [13]. Our study builds on the abundant location sharing research regarding logistics, usage and privacy concerns but it is also grounded in the literature on communication around availability and impression management.

2.1 Coordination and Availability through Mobile Communication Media

An obvious utility of location-based services is arrangement of face-to-face meetings, which already became more spontaneous and fluid with the use of mobile phones. Ling and Yttri, for example [34], established early on in the mobile phone

GROUP '16, November 13-16, 2016, Sanibel Island, FL, USA
 ISBN 978-1-4503-4276-6/16/11...$15.00
DOI: http://dx.doi.org/10.1145/2957276.2957289

"revolution" that mobile phones are instrumental for the micro-coordination of social activities on a daily basis as well as the expressive hyper-coordination among teens, which potentially could be supported by location sharing. Other pre-smartphone studies used scenarios and hypothetical studies such as Dearman et al. who found that available technology and context impact rendezvous practices [18], and Barkhuus and Dey who found that people were willing to give up a certain amount of sense of control if they found the location-aware service useful enough [5].

These early studies only suggest location sharing technologies' *possibilities* for micro- as well as impromptu coordination[1], in scenarios where there are many other underlying mechanisms for communication around availability and socializing. With many available channels for communicating whereabouts, the managing of availability becomes increasingly complex [9]. A strain of research has for example looked at how 'butler lies' are often used to negotiate availability [28], and other researchers discuss and suggest design for ambiguity in social interactions [2, 23]. It is argued that people construct narratives around the digital evidence of their own and others' whereabouts [2]. Yet, in a historical perspective, technology development generally changes our expectations, for instance by the many public protests when caller ID on landline phones was first introduced in the early 90s, (due to the caller's inability to remain anonymous until connected) to its now universal implementation and general acceptance in all mobile phones today [1]. Thus, location sharing is potentially another type of information that people have to relate to and create narratives around when communicating and negotiating availability, and will eventually come around to and accept.

2.2 Relationship Structures and Location-Sharing

A solid body of research has already looked at social relationships and the structures of these as affected by the sharing of location, continuous or posted/requested. A trial of the Whereabouts Clock illustrated emotive aspects of family life [12] and the implementation of Connecto, an early label-based location-sharing tool, provided a platform for banter and repartee among groups of friends [4]. Reno was a message-based system that let users request the location of other users or un-prompted tell his/her location to another user. The researchers reported how users did not want to use the automated feature in order to maintain plausible deniability, yet they did not report of much deception [30]. Later, commercial tools became available and enabled user studies of more integrated location-sharing tools, particularly through social media. Mancini et al. [35] and Boesen et al. [10] both studied the effect of location sharing in the changing nature of trust and power in relationships: the former through a customized tool that provided feedback to the location requester and the latter through the off-the-shelf (now defunct) Google Latitude that tracked individuals without notifications (mutually just once). Both studies focus on the dynamics within family relationships, particularly in terms of power relationships such as teenagers vs. parents [35]. Boesen et al. [10] present the only study looking at services similar to ours: continuous, non-notification and map-based. Their study found that the changing role of technology in domestic relationships, even though initially used for safety concerns, can provoke privacy issues and actually undermine the trust and nurturing aspects in those relationships. Mancini et al. also found that misperceptions around location-tracking technologies generated conflicts within social relationships [35]. However, in our study did we not only look at dyads or close family units but also at established groups of friends and family with various relationships among the group members, introducing diversity in relations and adding complexity to the potential practices and concerns.

2.3 Concerns about Location Sharing

Location sharing has often been presented as potentially problematic and research has addressed concerns from many perspectives. Early wizard-of-Oz studies showed people had higher concerns over sharing with for example their boss [33] than friend, but also that they were capable of determining when a service was useful enough to ignore concerns [5]. Consolvo [15] studied users' reactions to hypothetical location requests from specific people at specific times and found that they generally wanted to disclose location if it would be useful information to those who received it but that they also wanted to maintain their privacy in certain situations. More recently, Guha and Wicker found that distance and tie strength predicted deceptive location disclosure [25]. Krumm [32] conducted a literature survey of computational location privacy and concluded that most people do not show much concern about the privacy issue even if they are sensitive to how that data is used. He argues that attitudes may change based on the safeguards that are in place, the amount of data that is stored, the misuse of that data and how that data exploitation is portrayed in the media.

A number of studies conducted at Carnegie Mellon University have looked into users' ways of formulating privacy policies (essentially location-sharing rules) as well as issues such as the level of feedback in relation to propensity of location-sharing [41]. Researchers highlighted that people were not very likely to spend long time creating specialized sharing policies for themselves, but rather made decisions generically based on the person requesting or simply within each situation [39].

In this study we expand the previous literature by focusing on readily available commercial location sharing services and study them in a more diverse relationship context than previously, in a longer field study.

3. METHOD

We studied the use of location sharing within groups of 4-5 people for four weeks, in total 17 people. Two groups used the iPhone based 'Find My Friends' and two groups used Life360, available for both iPhone and Android phones. The study took place in a major European city. We chose these two apps in order to broaden the range of participants that we could recruit, through including several brands of smart phones.

Find My Friends was developed by Apple, specifically optimized for Apple iPhones and released in October of 2011 (https://www.apple.com/apps/find-my-friends/). This location based application uses GPS, cellular and Wi-Fi triangulation to track users' locations and has been marketed as a way to locate friends and family.

The Life360 application was developed by a small company, called Life360, in 2008 for Android-based phones (https://www.life360.com). The company released an iPhone version in August 2010 so it currently works on both iPhones and Android phones. It uses GPS and Wi-Fi triangulation to track user's location and has been marketed similarly, but also with emphasis on safety and communication. It includes features such

[1] Micro-coordination being the coordination around a particular already settled meeting such as texting "I'm going to be 5 minutes late" and "I'm standing waiting by the fountain", and impromptu coordination being ad-hoc meet-ups such as texting "I'm close to

as group and individual chat, a panic button and historical tracking of each individual's location.

The free version allows users to see history of the other group members for two days, while the premium version enables you to see location history for 30 days. All our participants used the basic version.

The two applications work very similarly with small differences: Find Friends requires entering of a password each time it is opened unless the user has a passcode on his/her initial lock screen. Life360 runs in the background but provides error messages when it cannot connect such as if the phone loses Internet connection. These are the main differences in terms of user experience that we believe would not lead to significant inter-reliability issues between the groups.

Both applications have a detailed location granulation, particularly when Wi-Fi is turned on. They can locate people down to 5-10 meters and only provide coarser grained location when GPS and Wi-Fi is unavailable, which means people can generally use it to for example find others in an open area and see someone's home address. For both applications, location sharing can be temporarily turned off so others are not able to track the person.

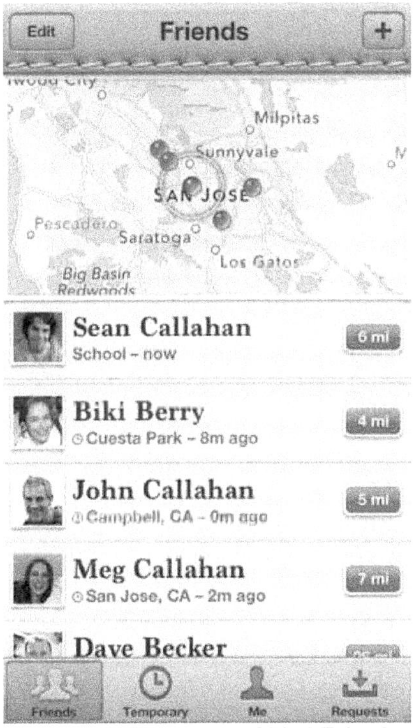

Figure 1: Screenshot of Find Friends

3.1 Experience Sampling and Interviews

For studying the use of a location sharing we employed an adapted version of ESM (experience sampling method), which has been shown to be an effective tool in mobile technology research [16], allowing researchers to capture participants' current feelings and activities shortly after the actual experience occurred instead of waiting until an interview. ESM also enables the participants to respond without introducing any observer or interviewer bias to influence the respondents [16]. The adapted version of ESM that we employed was not implemented as an event-triggering mini-questionnaire, but instead as a simple web-based questionnaire that asked into how frequent participants had interacted with the application as well as to get details about specific occasions of interaction within and around the applications, employed around every second day. Due to the presumed infrequent nature of the location sharing use, we expected participants to only interact with the applications a couple of times per day and we found this to be more feasible when inquiring into specific use.

We used two types of questionnaires to provide variety to the participants; our research experience informed us that identical questionnaires tend to yield less in-depth results further into the study. The first type of questionnaire was not focused on a specific occasion when the application was used but simply asked the participants to summarize the usage over the past two days. The second type of questionnaire consisted of open questions asking the participants to describe in detail an occasion when the interaction with the application led to social interaction. The results from the open questions were used as reminders later during the interviews similarly to how Mancini et al. used a memory phrase in combination with the ESM to help participants remember certain occasions after an extended period of time [36]. Email reminders with the questionnaire link were sent three days per week during the four-week period with reminders each day as long as a questionnaire was not filled in. As often with ESM, participants filled in questionnaires frequently during the first 1-2 weeks with a trail off the second and third week. We received in total 105 answers with an average of 1.5 questionnaires answered per week per person, either filled in online through through their smart phone or on their computer.

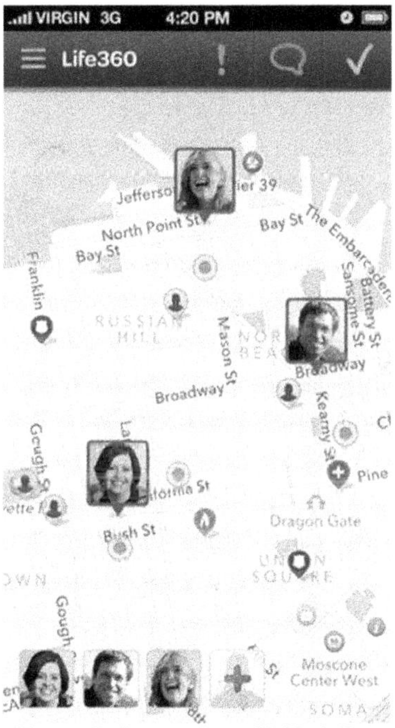

Figure 2: Screenshot of Life 360

At the end of the four-week period, individual semi-structured interviews with each of the participants were conducted in order to gather qualitative information around their experiences. The general topics discussed were coordination, social interaction and sharing concerns. Since all the authors were bilingual in Swedish and English, the data was collected in the language that was most comfortable or agreed upon by the participants. None of the participants were asked to respond in a language in which they did not feel comfortable but for practicalities we prioritized English and only three were conducted in Swedish. Due to the authors' bilingualism, the analysis was also conducted with original language documents. Translation was only done when quotes were needed for this paper. We translated the quotes ourselves.

3.2 Participants

Participants were recruited using snowball sampling by asking weak tie acquaintances to recruit their own friends so that they would have a group of 4-6 people, who already knew each other, socialized and lived in the same area, in this case Stockholm or its suburbs. Some recruiters reported that a few potential participants declined due to technical issues or privacy concerns.

Four groups of friends were recruited, which initially consisted of 19 participants but only 17 participated in the entire study. The participants downloaded the application at the start of the study and used the app with these friends during a four-week period. Participants were compensated with a gift card to a major movie theater company.

The final set of people was made up of eleven women and six men, ranging in age from 18 to 69 with a median age of 26. Their occupations ranged from retiree and unemployed, to jobs in telecom, airline, retail, elder care, IT and game design. There were also students from high school to college level, studying economics or psychology. All of the participants had used a smartphone for more than two years. None had used a friend finder application before participating in the study. Yet ten of the 17 participants had used some type of location sharing service, i.e. Facebook Check-in or foursquare. Participants were asked to use the location sharing app in their everyday life and access it a couple of times per day, or as they felt the need to but we did not require them to use it a particular number of times, for example for earning compensation. The questionnaire reminders also worked as a reminder to use the app daily.

The groups are detailed in Table 1. Individual names have been changed to protect the identity of participants. Groups one and two used the Find Friends app, while groups three and four used Life360. Group one consisted of an established couple, a sister-in-law, a father and a co-worker of the female partner of the couple. Group two consisted of four students in the same psychology program where two were currently co-workers at their respective internships. Group three consisted of two old friends and their respective girlfriends who knew each other peripherally. Group four consisted of a set of three friends, two who studied together and ones' sisters who was also acquainted with the friends.

Table 1: Participants

Name	Group	Relationship
Anna	1	Ben's girlfriend
Ben	1	Anna's boyfriend
Caroline	1	Ben's sister-in-law
Dennis	1	Ben's father
Eric	1	Anna's co-worker
Frida	2	Friend/classmate/colleague
Gabriella	2	Friend/ classmate
Helena	2	Friend/ classmate
Ian	2	Friend/ classmate/colleague
Kurt	3	Linda's boyfriend
Linda	3	Kurt's girlfriend
Michael	3	Kurt's friend
Nina	3	Michael's girlfriend
Rebecca	4	Friend
Selma	4	Friend
Tina	4	Friend
Ursula	4	Rebecca's sister

3.3 Limitations

Using a snowball sampling approach to recruit obviously pose several challenges and limitations to our study. It is not easy to recruit participants for studies of location sharing applications, because users often perceive real-time location as sensitive information [8]. Limitations emerge into *sensitivity* to real-time location sharing since they accepted to continuously share location in the first place. Our results therefore focus particularly on structures of socializing around the application as well as perceived changes of behavior by the participants. However, we do claim to be able to provide at least limited insights into participants' concerns; not only were many of them hesitant beforehand but were convinced by our recruiter to participate 'for the sake of research'; they were also a very varied set of people reflecting a broad set of the population. These people were not particularly 'non-caring' about their privacy but curious and willing to share location for a limited time frame for research. When asserting participants' concerns for continuously sharing location, we therefore considered the factor that they themselves had agreed to participate (as in all other studies of location technologies), and we acknowledge that we are not including a segment of the population who were highly sensitive to sharing this information.

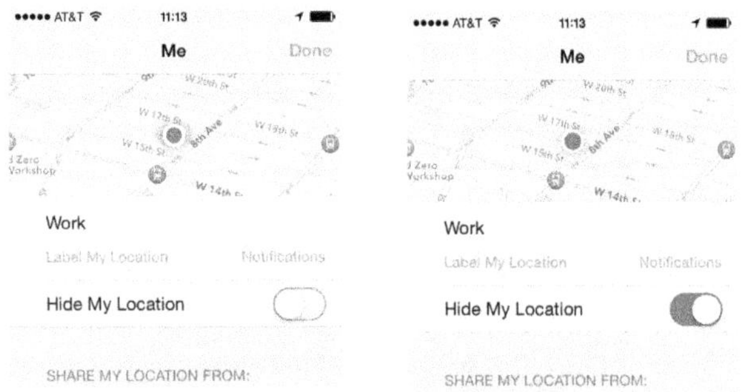

Figure 3: Find Friends' button for turning off sharing

3.4 Analysis

We initially focused our analysis on interview data. After transcribing them for initial exploration, we determined how the interview data fit into the three general topics we used for the semi-structured interviews: coordination, social interaction and sharing concerns. We then conducted coding, grouping and compared the data categories, using elements of grounded theory [40], and then broke out meaningful sentences or meaning units. We then coded or labeled these sentences with shorter statements and sorted them into five different content area columns. Finally, we sorted the coded data into subcategories: perceived usefulness of the app, context of use, privacy concerns and miscellaneous. The final stage was method triangulation and member validation, which we achieved by comparing the qualitative data from the interview transcripts to the reported frequency of use and other quantitative measures from the questionnaire. The ESM was used for two purposes: firstly they were used to feed into the interviews and highlight specific cases that we were able to ask into; secondly, they were used in the analysis to hold up statements that seemed significant. While it might seem that most of our data came from the interviews, due to their heavy quotation, the questionnaires assisted throughout the analysis process.

We continue by describing general findings from our study before separating them into three themes that we derived from the analysis. These themes inform our detailed results relating to previous studies as well as discussion.

4. RESULTS

4.1 Motivations and General Uses

The participants reported using (opening up) the application between a couple of times per week to several times per day, where nine of the 17 participants reported using it several times during the past four days on average (questionnaire data). Both location sharing applications afforded the tagging of specific places, both for oneself and for friends. Five participants tagged their homes (1-2 in each group), one of these also tagged his work and one tagged other's home and work (but not his own). When tagging one's own location this tag becomes visible to others. None of the participants purposefully hid their location, that is, temporarily turned off the sharing, while the study took place although two of the participants reported not having constant internet on the go, which prevented the sharing of location at some times. One participant turned off her location service after three weeks because she felt it used too much of the battery and therefore did not use the service the last week.

In terms of everyday practices participants reported often using the application for checking the location of someone they were about to contact in order to be able to determine if they available for chat. One participant, Anna, for example stated that the location sharing simply "made life easier". Several of the participants had jobs where they could not be reached easily, such as schoolteacher or a job with irregular working hours at an airline check-in counter. The friends were able to determine if these people were at work and therefore unlikely to be able to talk. For a set of colleagues it was practical to be able to see if the other was in the office: *"I can see if he is already at work or not. Because we have to lock all of our doors all the time. Because we have secret papers [...] so if I leave my room, I have to lock it. So if I'm going to go and ask him a question, I have to lock my door, unlock another door, go out and unlocking a third door to get to where he is. [...] So it was very practical. Is he here or is he not here. So is it worth going there?"* (Frida).

We found several types of motivations that participants cited for opening up the application. A large proportion reported that they were 'bored' and therefore wanted to check out where their friends were; this was just one application among several that they reported they would 'go through' when having down time (waiting for a bus, being on the subway etc.). Figure 3 shows a snapshot of the reasons participants gave for opening up the application on the last occasion before filling in the questionnaire. The numbers are however slightly biased towards the participants who filled in more of the questionnaires because it is based on the total number of answers.

Another often-described motivation was one of curiosity. Participants described looking at the application regularly to get an understanding of everyday life of their friends. They claimed that this was not out of 'spying', although some reported having a sense of that in the beginning, but instead reported it to be a way of gaining more awareness of their friends' activities.

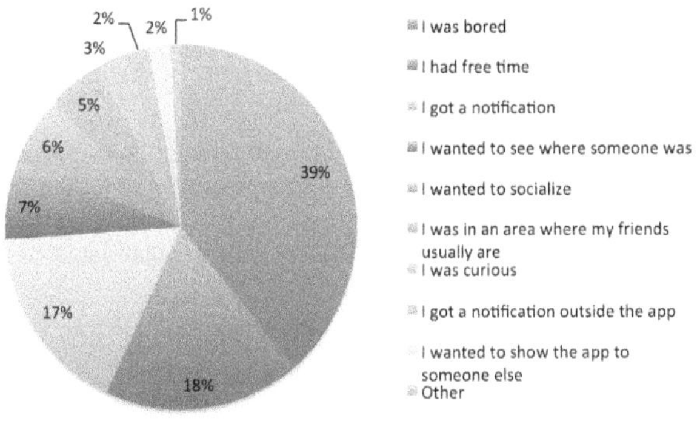

Figure 4: What participants reported that initiated their interaction with the app on the last occasion of interaction.

4.2 Coordination around Socializing

To get a better understanding of how continuous location sharing facilitated coordination around socializing, we use Barkhuus and Tashiro's taxonomy of social gatherings for our analysis, particularly focusing on how the location sharing facilitated different types of socializing. The authors describe four types: *Scheduled social gatherings, Semi-scheduled social gathering, Ad-hoc social gathering* and *Special events* [6]. In our analysis we found evidence that continuous location sharing supported *semi-scheduled gatherings*, such as the weekly morning coffee that two colleagues had, as well as *ad-hoc social gathering* such as impromptu coffee meetings between colleagues or friends. We describe each in more detail:

4.2.1 *Semi-scheduled gathering*

Semi-scheduled gathering was supported in a fairly sophisticated way: For example, Anna reported checking if Eric was home the evenings before their casual, regular, early morning coffee meeting. If she could see that he was at his girlfriend's house the evening before, she presumed he would not make their meeting for 8am but would be either late or cancel: *"I usually check on Tuesday evenings if he was home early [...] then I knew that he would want to wake up early in the morning. But if he was at his girlfriend's or his parents' or something, I knew that he probably wouldn't show up in the morning. I felt a bit like I was spying on him."*

When explaining their previous habits Anna emphasized that normally she would just show up and then occasionally he would not: *"We are very good friends but I never call him in the evening. He might be with his girlfriend. That might be weird. It was never something we planned beforehand"*. It was clear that the location sharing assisted in communication around semi-scheduled gathering, by adding small pieces of information assisting in detailed reasoning around socializing.

4.2.2 *Ad-hoc social gathering*

The other socializing event that location sharing supported in our study was ad-hoc social gatherings. Two participants for example,

Rebecca and Selma, met in town when Rebecca had the day off and Selma unexpectedly got off early from work. Selma checked her application and when seeing that Rebecca was in town too, she texted her asking if they should catch up. They met in a café a couple of minutes later. Other participants reported similar incidents. However, similarly to Barkhuus and Tashiro's [6] findings from social media location broadcasting, almost none of the participants just 'showed up'. They always communicated in between location discovery and actually meeting up, with one exception: Two colleagues, Frida and Ian, reported going to the other 'wing' at work to meet their colleague. This, in essence, replaced the previous act of doing the same, just without knowing for certain if the colleague was in their office.

The two other types of social gatherings, *Scheduled social gatherings* and *Special events*, were not supported during the time of the study, however, the reason for this is probably the short length of study and coincidence rather than actual lack of possibilities for facilitation.

4.2.3 Perceived Change of Communication

In terms of the participants' own perceived change of communication due to the availability of location information, two types of perceived changes emerged[2] (although some participants reported no change): If people knew each other very well, for example couples, the location sharing lead to *less* communication, for example around micro-coordination [34]. Not only could they see that their partner had left work and was 10 minutes away from home, there was also suddenly an expectation that if the other person wanted to know the person's proximity, they could just check. Hence, there was no need for communicating that "I'll be home in 10 minutes". Michael for example explained: *"I skipped the whole where are you? What are you doing Ah, you're at work. You're at home. You're on the subway. I skipped that whole part in conversations because before I texted someone I usually checked where they were"*. Yet, he still claimed that the location checking was not a substitute for communication, it was a pre-communication activity that reduced the actual talk or text 'amount': *"I usually knew that I was going to call the person, then I checked the app, then I called the person"*.

For participants in more casual friendships, the application lead to *more* communication, often around informal personal topics. One participant for example explains about one of her colleagues: *"I saw that he was in a remote location north of Stockholm...and when I met him, I asked him 'Did you visit your parents?' and he started talking about his family and that he had visited them and that was something we really had never talked about before"*. The knowledge of location was in essence a 'ticket to talk' for people who were acquainted but did not necessarily share stories about their life outside the realm of their existing relations such as work or university.

4.2.4 Repartee

Similarly to the study of Connecto, a labeling based location-sharing service [4], we found the participants using this sharing service for teasing and friendly repartee. But where some participants expressed that they had initially believed they were going to 'sneak up on their friends' and surprise them in public, they were using the additional information for casual teasing in other conversations. Michael for example said: *"If I'm going to call [Nina], I usually check beforehand and I'm like 'what are you doing there!? Why aren't you at work?', no, I'm just kidding"*. Anna for example also told us that she wrote to her boyfriend to tease him: *"I can see you are still in bed. Because he hadn't left the house... but that was mostly for fun. I felt rude doing it, but it was mostly for fun"*. But where Barkhuus et al. detected repartee *within* the location application [4], our participants had to construct humorous narratives *around* the information because of its continuous tracking on a generic map. Additionally, participants only generated tags that were generic such as home and work, not any tags that could potentially have facilitated such humorous use.

4.3 Concerns around Sharing and Observing

Most of the use of location sharing was related to communication practices and basic curiosity, which initially led to feelings of spying for several participants as noted earlier. Rebecca for example expressed: *"I'm actually not that interested in where other people are exactly. It feels like I'm intruding on their private life, if you can say that"*. She continued explaining that if she wanted to know where someone was, she would ask. Still, although the participants had these feelings, they expressed comfort about sharing their own location, particularly because the groups were composed by trusted friends and family members; Frida for example said: *"I trust them to understand my information in a positive light"*.

Having a new service like this also took a bit of time to get used to. At first Frida was excited to be able to see her colleague's whereabouts and was interested in seeing when he was not at work. Then she realized the reciprocal nature of the service: *"I realized [that Ian could see me too] when I started checking to see if he as at work already. I was like "huh, he could do this the other way around.' So, I realized it but... [...] But since he is late way more often than I am... I don't have to worry about it [laughs]"* (Frida)." The reciprocity meant that the participants were able to compare behavior, similarly to posting on an online social network where impression management is often a key part of motivations for posting content [21, 24]. One participant even went as far as to express how she thought the sharing encouraged her to be more active: *"The more one sees what people, what others do, then you get a bit affected of what all others do around [the city]. Instead of like, sitting at home all the time, then it becomes a little like a push that one should do things"* (Linda).

A more precarious situation occurred when Anna checked for her colleague Eric during the day, to see if he was nearby and wanted a coffee. She saw that he was at a hotel, which she said she felt awkward about. She explained: *"A few days went by and I didn't want to mention it to him. But eventually it slipped out: What did you do in the middle of the afternoon in a hotel?"*. It turned out that the colleague's gym was attached to the hotel and he had been going there during the day. The sharing was insensitive to the participant who had gone to the gym, and who had probably not put any thought into the location of it, but it invoked feelings of discomfort for his colleague since she did not know the details around this potentially awkward information.

Concerns also evolved from the reflections on participants' location information being available to others. Frida for example was worried that their fourth friend (in the study) was feeling left out when he texted them asking what they were all doing at a particular place on a Friday night. When talking about the situation in the interview, Frida said: *"I think he was doing*

2 We are not claiming to be able to say anything about *actual* changes since we did not collect any 'base data' of the participants' structures of communication before the application was available to them.

something else with some friends... Maybe he did. I don't know. Maybe he felt left out, not getting invited?" Michael, who was keen to participate in the study and used the sharing application most of all the participants, cited this potential hurting of others' feelings as the reason he did not want to keep the application after the study: *"In the long run, I wouldn't want to have this type of app. I'm probably not going to keep on using the app."* Interviewer: *"why won't you?"* Michael: *Because... I don't know. It feels, maybe a little bit invasive. Maybe"*. He gave examples of potential exclusion by friends: *"If all my friends are all at the same bar and no one has called me, do I want to know this? Or do I want to be ignorant. ... It just ruins the whole social aspect of it. You can't freeze out a person"*. (Interestingly, of course, this is currently perfectly possible through social media, evidenced by for example research addressing teenage bullying through online social media [10].) Although no participants reported negative feelings during the study on the basis of others' locations or constellation of this, it is of course always possible that they had such feelings but did not want to reveal them. Studies of social media for example are quick to emphasize positive emotions stemming from other positive contributions or negative postings leading to negative responses [24, 30], yet negative emotions stemming from *positive* contributions, such as envy, are less often explored and described.

5. DISCUSSION

Our findings led to a more grounded perception of this type of continuous location sharing that we elaborate on in the discussion. We look at the ephemeral qualities of the application, how the application was able to support a public geography and finally, how the application and its utility relate to previous related location-sharing technology guidelines.

5.1 Ephemeral Qualities of Continuous Location-Sharing

An important quality of the location sharing application was the way in which it became ephemeral to the participants' everyday life. It was a background application, only entering the foreground when actual interaction *around* it occurred, such as the text messaging around others being together at a party or one friend being in town at the same time, possibly being available for an ad-hoc meeting. The lightness of the applications' presence in participants' lives was clearly due to the group dynamics; opposite most family units, our groups consisted of no hierarchical relationships, or at least the parent child relationships were all fully adult, diminishing the hierarchy experienced by family units where children are still living at home [35]. None of the participants had to 'answer' to others except the couples, to a small degree.

With its notification-light functionality, the application echoed qualities from slow technologies [27] and social translucence [22] in addition to low engagement levels. For example, it took a while for people to "find out the consequences of using it [the technology]" [27], and it depended on other people's movement to display new information, which was often a slow process. In contrast to social media, "new content" was not available every 10 minutes. The technology provided awareness and visibility, characteristics of social translucent systems, reflected through the continuous availability of the location data.

People's awareness of being able to be located was more prevalent than their actual level of friend tracking (participants reported being regularly aware of the potential tracking, yet did not track their friends more than a couple of times per day); yet they did not perceive this as problematic. The ephemeral characteristics were expressed as the fleetingness with which location was relevant; it was relevant as spur of the moment activities occurred: a phone call, a potential coffee break etc. It was only considered as a forefront application when the information did not align with expectations.

5.2 Public vs. Private Geographies

It can be argued that there is a distinct difference of perception of control between text-based location and map-based location sharing. The argument is that a self-composed text description is more open to interpretation than a dot on a map, which might simply be semantically incorrect (as in our example of the participant who were shown to be at a hotel but was in fact at the gym attached to the hotel), yet mostly showing the user at a specified location. Even when a location request or look-up shows the person to be slightly off compared to the correct position for his or her home, it is easy to make the obvious conclusion that the person is at home. Due to the preciseness of GPS in relation to the broad distribution of activities of most people, even in dense cities, the actual location and thereby place (as defined by Dourish 2006 [19]) is simple to derive on the basis of a map, where text defined places are often composed to be more open to interpretation as witnessed in previous studies [4, 30].

This leads to the notion of "private geographies", first introduced in relation to location sharing by Barkhuus et al. [4]. Their participants created and made use of private geographies, places they knew and had in common, but which to outsiders might be difficult to understand. Our study of map-based sharing on the other hand, led to little open interpretation and instead relied on a very public geography: a map, which also for outsiders were comprehensible. A map might still be supporting a private geography: obviously tightknit groups have a subjective understanding of their friends' places and places they have in common, but such geography is internalized and never made explicit within the application in the same way as a "boring tax lecture" is [4]. Additionally, even small close-knit groups do not know all of each other's frequented places geographically, as seen in the example of Ian who discovered his friends at a mutual acquaintance's house without knowing this was his/her home. This leads to the presumption that a public geography is more sensitive to sharing with outsiders and more intrusive because there is no room for white lies. On the other hand, our study also indicated a lower level of utility compared to text-based system (but not necessarily ease of use since the map-based sharing automatically updates): Since there was no communication involved *within* the system it became ephemeral in nature and did not prove as sensitive in nature as first predicted by the participant. Without the possibility to construct the full context to others (through for example text tags in the application), the application did not enable them to manage a more detailed self-representation or even help them communicate much apart from issues around micro-coordination. In fact, the two core utilizations that we witnessed were the couple's or close ties' micro-coordination and weak-ties' communication around their whereabouts at a later point. And of these two types, only micro-coordination was explicitly appreciated by the participants. Active self-presentation, often appreciated in socio-technical systems was not possible, essentially diminishing the value of the service.

5.3 Breaking the Design Guidelines

Finally, we relate our findings to the earlier studies that either based their design of location-sharing prototypes on specific guidelines or provided design guidelines from empirical studies.

Interestingly, the new commercial map-based continuous applications that we studied here diverge significantly from most of these design guidelines because of the coarseness and simplicity such as no notifications. Sadeh et al. for example, presumed that people want to formulate sharing criteria and suggest that technologies should help people stay in their comfort zone while they evolve their criteria [39]. Tsai et al. emphasized the importance of feedback notifications for wider location sharing acceptance [41], and Mancini et al. suggested that control mechanisms might not be compatible with the subtle dynamics of social relationships [35]. Iachello et al. highlighted the importance of possibilities of deception within such application [30]. Considering the proposed precautions, our participants were surprisingly carefree, resonating related findings that people express concern pre-study but do not report many concerns during the actual study. The sharing was coarse grained, limited to individuals, the service consisted of no feedback and there was no room for deception other than turning off the service. We therefore suggest that future location sharing studies continue to push boundaries, looking at even more diverse types of location applications for exploring their limits in terms of sociability and utility.

6. CONCLUSIONS

In this paper we presented a study of a commercial location sharing application, with features such as continuous sharing and notification-free tracking. We highlighted that the application facilitated micro-coordination and ad-hoc socializing activities, as well as invoking concerns for others' perception of social situations. We argued that a map-based service is less socially informative than a labeling-based one because users cannot construct a situation or manage their self-representation through text tagging; instead, the location sharing was mostly utilized for micro-coordination. In fact with such coarse-grained functionality as an on-off button, participants did not feel the need to turn it off because in the end, the location was based on a public geography, open for interpretation. While there is obviously value in a private geography, created and maintained through mainly labeling-based services, the location sharing in our study was also partly successful, suggesting potential success within small trusted groups and close-knit dyads.

Our findings contribute to a better understanding of the transitional nature of technological tools and communication in action, including people's constant re-negotiation of what type of services and applications are appropriate to utilize for relationship- and everyday social management. The subtle awareness that these services supply has limited but potentially powerful effects on particularly social dyads.

7. ACKNOWLEDGMENTS

We thank the participants for the time and effort in taking part of this study. Also thanks to Shion Guha for insightful comments and proof read.

8. REFERENCES

[1] Philip Agre. 1998. Introduction. In Agre, Philip E., and Marc Rotenberg (eds.). *Technology and privacy: The new landscape*. MIT Press.

[2] Paul M. Aoki and Allison Woodruff. 2005. Making space for stories: ambiguity in the design of personal communication systems. In *Proceedings of the SIGCHI Conference on Human Factors in Computing Systems* (CHI '05). ACM, New York, NY, USA, 181-190.

[3] Elizabeth Bales, Kevin A. Li, and William Griswold. 2011. CoupleVIBE: mobile implicit communication to improve awareness for (long-distance) couples. In *Proceedings of the ACM 2011 conference on Computer supported cooperative work* (CSCW '11). ACM, New York, NY, USA, 65-74.

[4] Louise Barkhuus, Barry Brown, Marek Bell, Scott Sherwood, Malcolm Hall, and Matthew Chalmers. 2008. From awareness to repartee: sharing location within social groups. In *Proceedings of the SIGCHI Conference on Human Factors in Computing Systems* (CHI '08). ACM, New York, NY, USA, 497-506.

[5] Louise Barkhuus and Anind K. Dey. 2003. Location-Based Services for Mobile Telephony: a Study of Users' Privacy Concerns. In *INTERACT*, vol. 3, pp. 702-712.

[6] Louise Barkhuus and Juliana Tashiro. 2010. Student socialization in the age of facebook. In *Proceedings of the SIGCHI Conference on Human Factors in Computing Systems* (CHI '10). ACM, New York, NY, USA, 133-142.

[7] James "Bo" Begole, Nicholas E. Matsakis, and John C. Tang. 2004. Lilsys: Sensing Unavailability. In *Proceedings of the 2004 ACM conference on Computer supported cooperative work* (CSCW '04). ACM, New York, NY, USA, 511-514.

[8] Alastair R. Beresford and Frank Stajano. 2003. Location privacy in pervasive computing. *IEEE Pervasive computing*, *2*(1), 46-55.

[9] Jeremy Birnholtz, Jamie Guillory, Jeff Hancock, and Natalya Bazarova. 2010. "on my way": deceptive texting and interpersonal awareness narratives. In *Proceedings of the 2010 ACM conference on Computer supported cooperative work* (CSCW '10). ACM, New York, NY, USA, 1-4.

[10] Julie Boesen, Jennifer A. Rode, and Clara Mancini. 2010. The domestic panopticon: location tracking in families. In *Proceedings of the 12th ACM international conference on Ubiquitous computing* (UbiComp '10). ACM, New York, NY, USA, 65-74.

[11] danah boyd. 2014. *It's Complicated: the social lives of networked teens*. Yale University Press.

[12] Barry Brown, Alex S. Taylor, Shahram Izadi, Abigail Sellen, Joseph 'Jofish' Kaye, and Rachel Eardley. 2007. Locating family values: A field trial of the Whereabouts Clock. In *Proceedings of UbiComp 2007*, Springer, pp. 354-371.

[13] Zhiyuan Cheng, James Caverlee, Kyumin Lee, and Daniel Z. Sui. 2011.Exploring Millions of Footprints in Location Sharing Services. In *Proceedings of ICWSM* 2011 (2011): 81-88.

[14] Martin Colbert. 2001. A Diary Study of Rendezvousing: implications for position-aware computing and communications for the general public. *In Proceedings of the 2001 International ACM SIGGROUP Conference on Supporting Group Work,* pp.15-23.

[15] Sunny Consolvo, Ian E. Smith, Tara Matthews, Anthony LaMarca, Jason Tabert, and Pauline Powledge. 2005. Location disclosure to social relations: why, when, & what people want to share. In *Proceedings of the SIGCHI Conference on Human Factors in Computing Systems* (CHI '05). ACM, New York, NY, USA, 81-90.

[16] Sunny Consolvo and Miriam Walker. 2003. Using the experience sampling method to evaluate Ubicomp applications, *IEEE Pervasive Computing*, 2 (2), 24-31.

[17] Henriette Cramer, Mattias Rost, and Lars Erik Holmquist. 2011. Performing a Check-In: emerging practices, norms and 'conflicts' in location-sharing using foursquare. In *Proceedings of the 13th International Conference on Human Computer Interaction with Mobile Devices and Services* (MobileHCI '11). ACM, New York, NY, USA, 57-66.

[18] David Dearman, Kirstie Hawkey, and Kori M. Inkpen. 2005. Rendezvousing with location-aware devices: Enhancing social coordination. *Interacting with computers* 17, no. 5: 542-566.

[19] Paul Dourish. 2006. Re-space-ing place: "place" and "space" ten years on. In *Proceedings of the 2006 20th anniversary conference on Computer supported cooperative work* (CSCW '06). ACM, New York, NY, USA, 299-308.

[20] Paul Dourish and Sara Bly. 1992. Portholes: supporting awareness in a distributed work group. In *Proceedings of the SIGCHI Conference on Human Factors in Computing Systems* (CHI '92), Penny Bauersfeld, John Bennett, and Gene Lynch (Eds.). ACM, New York, NY, USA, 541-547.

[21] Nicole B. Ellison and danah boyd. 2007. Social Network Sites: Definition, History, and Scholarship. *Journal of Computer-Mediated Communication*, 13(1), pp. 210–230.

[22] Thomas Erickson and Wendy A. Kellogg. 2000. Social translucence: an approach to designing systems that support social processes. *ACM Trans. Comput.-Hum. Interact.* 7, 1 (March 2000), 59-83.

[23] William W. Gaver, Jacob Beaver, and Steve Benford. 2003. Ambiguity as a resource for design. In *Proceedings of the SIGCHI Conference on Human Factors in Computing Systems* (CHI '03). ACM, New York, NY, USA, 233-240.

[24] Shion Guha and Jeremy Birnholtz. 2013.Can You See Me Now? Location, visibility and the management of impressions on foursquare. In *proceedings of MobileHCI, 2013* (pp. 183-192). ACM.

[25] Shion Guha and Stephen B. Wicker. 2015. Spatial subterfuge: an experience sampling study to predict deceptive location disclosures. In *Proceedings of the 2015 ACM International Joint Conference on Pervasive and Ubiquitous Computing* (UbiComp '15). ACM, New York, NY, USA, 1131-1135.

[26] Jamie Guillory, Jason Spiegel, Molly Drislane, Benjamin Weiss, Walter Donner, and Jeffrey Hancock. 2011. Upset now?: emotion contagion in distributed groups. In *Proceedings of the SIGCHI Conference on Human Factors in Computing Systems* (CHI '11). ACM, New York, NY, USA, 745-748.

[27] Lars Hallnäs and Johan Redström. 2001. Slow Technology – Designing for Reflection. *Personal Ubiquitous Comput.* 5, 3 (January 2001), 201-212.

[28] Jeff Hancock, Jeremy Birnholtz, Natalya Bazarova, Jamie Guillory, Josh Perlin, and Barrett Amos. 2009. Butler lies: awareness, deception and design. In *Proceedings of the SIGCHI Conference on Human Factors in Computing Systems* (CHI '09). ACM, New York, NY, USA, 517-526.

[29] Lee Humphreys. 2007. Mobile social networks and social practice: A case study of Dodgeball. *Journal of Computer-Mediated Communication, 13*(1), 341-360.

[30] Giovani Iachello, Ian Smith, Summy Consolvo, Gregory D. Abowd, Jeff Hughes, James Howard, Fred Potter and Anthony LaMarca, A. 2005. Control, deception, and communication: Evaluating the deployment of a location-enhanced messaging service. In *Proceedings of UbiComp 2005* (pp. 213-231). Springer Berlin Heidelberg.

[31] Kramer, Adam D, Jamie E. Guillory, and Jeffrey T. Hancock. 2014. Experimental evidence of massive-scale emotional contagion through social networks. *Proceedings of the National Academy of Sciences*, 111, no. 24: 8788-8790.

[32] John Krumm. 2009. A survey of computational location privacy, *Personal and Ubiquitous Computing*, vol. 13, no. 6, pp. 391-399.

[33] Scott Lederer, Jennifer Mankoff, and Anind K. Dey. 2003. Who wants to know what when? privacy preference determinants in ubiquitous computing. In *CHI '03 Extended Abstracts on Human Factors in Computing Systems* (CHI EA '03). ACM, New York, NY, USA, 724-725.

[34] Ling, Richard, and Birgitte Yttri. 2002. Hyper-coordination via mobile phones in Norway. In J. Katz and M. Aakhus (eds.) *Perpetual contact: Mobile communication, private talk, public performance.* Cambridge University.

[35] Clara Mancini, Yvonne Rogers, Keerthi Thomas, Adam N. Joinson, Blaine A. Price, Arosha K. Bandara, Lukasz Jedrzejczyk, and Bashar Nuseibeh. 2011. In the best families: tracking and relationships. In *Proceedings of the SIGCHI Conference on Human Factors in Computing Systems* (CHI '11). ACM, New York, NY, USA, 2419-2428.

[36] Clara Mancini, Keerthi Thomas, Yvonne Rogers, Blaine A. Price, Lukazs Jedrzejczyk, Arosha K. Bandara, Adam N. Joinson, and Bashar Nuseibeh. 2009. From spaces to places: emerging contexts in mobile privacy. In *Proceedings of the 11th international conference on Ubiquitous computing* (UbiComp '09). ACM, New York, NY, USA, 1-10.

[37] William Odom, Richard Banks, Abigail Durrant, David Kirk, and James Pierce. 2012. Slow technology: critical reflection and future directions. In *Proceedings of the Designing Interactive Systems Conference* (DIS '12). ACM, New York, NY, USA, 816-817.

[38] Mika Raento, Antti Oulasvirta, Renaud Petit, and Hannu Toivonen. 2005. ContextPhone: A prototyping platform for context-aware mobile applications. *Pervasive Computing, IEEE, 4*(2), 51-59.

[39] Norman Sadeh, Jason Hong, Lorrie Cranor, Ian Fette, Patrick Kelley, Madhu Prabaker, and Jinghai Rao. 2009. Understanding and capturing people's privacy policies in a mobile social networking application. *Personal Ubiquitous Comput.* 13, 6 (August 2009), 401-412.

[40] Anselm Strauss and Julie Corbin. 1998. *Basics of Qualitative Research: Techniques and Procedures for Developing Grounded Theory*, 2nd ed., SAGE Publications.

[41] Janice Y. Tsai, Patrick Kelley, Paul Drielsma, Lorrie Faith Cranor, Jason Hong, and Norman Sadeh. 2009. Who's viewed you?: the impact of feedback in a mobile location-sharing application. In *Proceedings of the SIGCHI Conference on Human Factors in Computing Systems* (CHI '09). ACM, New York, NY, USA, 2003-2012.

[42] Roy Want, Andy Hopper, Veronica Falcão, and Jonathan Gibbons. 1992. The active badge location system. *ACM Trans. Inf. Syst.* 10, 1 (January 1992), 91-102.

Handheld Augmented Reality for Distributed Collaborative Crime Scene Investigation

Dragoş Datcu
Faculty of Technology, Policy and Management
Delft University of Technology
Jaffalaan 5, 2628 BX Delft, Netherlands
d.datcu@tudelft.nl

Stephan G. Lukosch
Faculty of Technology, Policy and Management
Delft University of Technology
Jaffalaan 5, 2628 BX Delft, Netherlands
s.g.lukosch@tudelft.nl

Heide K. Lukosch
Faculty of Technology, Policy and Management
Delft University of Technology
Jaffalaan 5, 2628 BX Delft, Netherlands
h.k.lukosch@tudelft.nl

ABSTRACT
Recent research showed that augmented reality (AR) technology is a promising approach to support distributed teams in crime scene investigation. This paper reports on the development and evaluation of a handheld AR system to support team situational awareness and collaboration among co-located and remote forensic investigators. The AR system runs on a smartphone strapped to the wrists of the local investigators and on a laptop for the remote investigator. The AR system has been evaluated with three experienced forensic investigators and was carried out in two rounds: (1) with one local and one remote investigator and (2) with two local and one remote investigator. The evaluation focused on the usability of the AR system and its effect on situational awareness as well as collaboration quality. Compared to earlier experiments using head-mounted devices (HMDs), the findings suggest that the handheld AR system addresses limitations of current HMD based AR system, but the necessary division of attention between smartphone AR system and real environment impacts the situational awareness.

CCS Concepts
• **Human-centered computing~Mixed / augmented reality** • **Human-centered computing~Collaborative interaction** • ***Human-centered computing~Mobile devices***

Keywords
Information Exchange; Collaboration; Augmented Reality; Crime Scene Investigation

1. INTRODUCTION
Crime scene investigation is one of the prominent tasks in solving crimes. Nevertheless, professional crime scene investigators are not the first ones to be at a crime scene. Crime scene investigation is a distributed process, in which different organizations are involved [4].

GROUP '16, November 13-16, 2016, Sanibel Island, FL, USA
© 2016 ACM. ISBN 978-1-4503-4276-6/16/11...$15.00
DOI: http://dx.doi.org/10.1145/2957276.2957302

A crime scene is defined as "any space or item that contains, or potentially contains, physical evidence that a crime has been committed or connecting something or someone to that crime" [16]. Crime scenes often show characteristics of emergency situations, requiring the protection of victims, policemen and emergency staff as first and most important objective. At the same time, evidence needs to be collected and evaluated.

Information about evidence has to be shared with the own and with other involved organizations [4], in order to enable team situational awareness and a common ground of the crime scene. Situations at crime scenes are often stressful and complex, including objects that have to be evaluated by the investigators upon their relevance for the case. First responders like policemen or fire workers entering the scene may overlook important details for the further investigation of a crime, hindering the detection and interpretation of crucial traces at the scene. Only after the scene has been declared safe, and all necessary actions have been processed, crime scene investigators enter the scene. Other emergency staff provides information, and remaining traces are tracked, collected and further examined. Such evidence can be polluted already by all the work that has been done by the first responders. Furthermore, the development of team situational awareness and a common ground between the different groups of first responders and investigators is very limited due to available technology, like administrative worksheets, photographic logs, and sketches [4].

Baber et al. [5] showed in a comparative experiment that the use of computer equipment can lead to faster performance without impacting the quality of the investigation results. Following these observations, we discuss the development and evaluation of an augmented reality (AR) system that is meant to improve team situational awareness within the whole network of first responders and crime scene investigators by means of virtual co-location. AR systems allow users to see the real world, with virtual objects superimposed upon, or composited with the real world [2, 3] where virtual objects are computer graphic objects that exist in essence or effect, but not formally or actually [19]. AR systems are not limited to the use of Head-Mounted Devices (HMDs) and mainly have to combine real and virtual objects as previously described, be interactive in real-time and register objects within 3D [2]. AR systems can be used to establish a common ground during cross-organisational collaboration in dynamic tasks [22]. They can further be used to establish the experience of being practically co-located by means of simulated presence. For example, AR systems have been used to allow experts to spatially collaborate with others at any location in the world, without traveling and thereby creating the experience of being virtually co-located, e.g. in the field of crime scene investigation [23].

We discuss the outcomes of a scenario-based experiment conducted with experienced forensic investigators using a handheld AR system for collaborative crime scene investigation. The experiment focused on the usability of the handheld AR system and its effect on situational awareness as well as collaboration quality. In earlier experiments [9, 18] using an optical see-through HMD, we could show that collaborative crime scene investigation via AR improves team situational awareness [18]. However, participants in the experiment criticized the field of view of the optical see-through HMD, the fluidity of free hand interaction as well as the limitation to freely move and investigate the crime scene. The AR system presented in this paper addresses these critics by employing smartphones for handheld AR. Local investigators can freely move and interact with the crime scene, as the smartphone can be strapped to the wrist of the local users and interaction is performed via the touch display of the smartphone.

We used an end-user centred approach [15] to design a scenario in which one or two local forensic investigators jointly investigate a staged ecstasy lab with one remote colleague while using our AR system. During the experiment with our AR system, either one or two local investigators were supported by one remote colleague. To enable virtual co-location and support spatial remote collaboration, the remote user could annotate the video stream from the local users with virtual objects that are then also shown in the user interface of the local users.

The remainder of this paper is organized as follows: the following section presents related work on challenges for collaboration in the safety domain and AR systems supporting collaboration. Then, we present our AR system and the results of our study. We finish with conclusions and an outline for future work.

2. RELATED WORK

2.1 Challenges in the Field

Smith et al. [27] are of the opinion that it is difficult to consider crime scene examination from a team perspective, as usually several different teams from different organisations need to work together. The work is then centred on the collection of information and evidence in consultation with different people. The work effectiveness relies very much on the efficiency of each individual team, the communication of results and the coordination among the teams.

Streefkerk et al. [28, 29] analyse current issues in police teamwork. They notice that police officers often have no overview of availability and location of other team members. As result, police officers often do not know which of their colleagues is available to handle an incident and incidents that remain unattended. Motivated by these observations they consider team awareness as the major challenge for police team tasks.

Baber et al. [5] conduct an experiment to compare the ways in which evidence search and recovery could be combined with the production of a crime scene report. In their experiment, participants completed the crime scene report using either the conventional paper form, an electronic form on a tablet computer or a wearable computer. The computer conditions led to faster performance and there was no difference in quality of the reports.

Reuter et al. [25] examine mobile collaboration practices in crisis management at an inter-organizational level. Their study shows that new informal communication practices with current technology, i.e. mobile phones, needs to be derived.

Militello et al. [20] discuss challenges with regard to information flow during crisis management. Mobile phone calls help to include remote actors in the situation assessment, but verbal communication alone is not enough to facilitate situational awareness. Based on case studies, they identify asymmetric knowledge and experience, barriers to maintaining mutual awareness, uneven workload distribution, and disrupted communication as major challenges. For each of the challenges different recommendations are presented. To overcome asymmetric knowledge, they suggest to provide tools for communication and to train their usage. They suggest the use of shared displays to improve mutual awareness,. To address the uneven workload, they suggest to more clearly assign roles and make their responsibilities known across organisations. The latter is also stressed by Drabek and McEntire [11].

The above discussion shows that, though collaboration of different organisational units is desired and mobile technology can support the work of first responders, police officers, or crime scene investigators, several challenges need to be addressed. Among the major challenges are information symmetry, efficiency of communication, knowledge on responsibilities and finally the team situational awareness to enable the development of a common ground.

2.2 Augmented Reality Systems in the Safety and Security Domain

Nilsson et al. (2009) present an AR collaboration system that supports placing and modifying event and organization-specific symbols on a shared digital map associated to a crisis management scenario [22]. Even though the task of creating a shared situational picture scored well with the paper map standard, the AR-based collaboration allows users to better focus on the task in a less-cluttered joint work environment. Team cognition is supported by providing information for joint work, gesturing and joint manipulation of symbols.

Gurevich et al. (2012) propose TeleAdvisor, a remote assistance free-hands assembly that enables a remote helper to give directions to a local user by voice and by projecting information directly in the physical environment of the local worker [14]. A tele-operated robotic arm having attached a pico-projector and a video camera, directs the remote user towards the point of need, and emphasizes graphically with rectangles, the remote's view to the local. The results highlight the remote's ability to control the robotic arm to fully understand the work environment. The findings show that a remote helper prefers to generate graphical representations in form of free sketch annotations and pointers. They further indicate that text and icon-based annotations are not used at all during the collaborative work sessions.

Alem et al. (2011) propose ReMoTe, a remote guiding system that integrates non-mediated hand gesture communication in the mining industry [1]. In ReMoTe, an expert remotely assists a worker using hands to point to certain locations and to show specific manual procedures. The expert hands are shown to the local worker in the form of virtual hand projections indicating the correct hand actions. The system implements a panoramic view over the local user's workspace, to enhance the remote users ability to maintain an overall awareness of the local's activity and workspace.

Streefkerk et al. (2013) find remote's annotations as usable and intuitive, concluding that such virtual tags can speed up the trace collection process, and can reduce time for documentation during collaborative work sessions in forensic investigations [30]. Virtual tags are appreciated to increase the user awareness over the crime scene, and are found to decrease the initial orientation at the scene.

Domova et al. (2014) show that instantly synchronized snapshots and annotations in form of pointers and overlaying drawings, lead to a general acceptance of the system and provide more efficient means of conveying spatial information, resulting in lower frustration and better communication between a field worker and remote expert [10]. Their AR system improves situational awareness by offering a wide field of view, shared visual space, tracking the attention focus of the other participant, and the support for gesturing within shared visual space. A more expressive and arguably more intuitive interaction with the scene is proposed by a tablet-based system that incorporates a touchscreen interface through which a remote can navigate a physical environment and create world-aligned annotations [12, 13].

Procyk et al. (2014) propose a shared geocaching system that allows players to see remote locations while holding conversations [24]. The study points to the value of mobile video chat support as an enhancement of shared geocaching experiences. Compared to Domova et al. (2014), the authors highlight the role of the asymmetrical experiences and information exchange as important factors to improve parallel experiences of users who are engaged in remote common activities.

In earlier experiments [9, 18], we used an AR system in combination with an optical see-through HMD that allows a local investigator to annotate a crime scene in collaboration with a remote colleague. The collaboration with a remote colleague and the annotation of the scene in augmented reality improved team situational awareness [18]. However, users criticized the field of view, the fluidity of free hand interaction as well as the limitation to freely move and investigate the crime scene. The latter was mainly due to limitations of the used tracking algorithm.

The above discussion shows that augmented reality (AR) technology is a promising approach to support distributed teams in the safety and security domain. Following [14], an AR system needs to offer annotation tools for remote and local users in combination with marker-less tracking for natural interaction experiences. For such annotations, remote users temporarily need to decouple from a local user's video stream and focus on details in the provided view [24]. Thus, supporting asymmetry in media [33]. Finally, an AR system needs to provide fluid interaction possibilities and large field of view [18].

3. USER STUDY

The purpose of our study is to explore the usability of an AR system with a mobile phone configuration to develop team situational awareness and collaboration in a task related to crime scene investigation. Previous experiments using HMDs showed a very limited usability of the system. In a similar set-up we aim at exploring the benefits of the mobile phone configuration to address the limitations found in the earlier study [14].

3.1 Scenario Design

In order to test the AR technology and to gather insights into its usability for real fieldwork in emergency teams, it is important to develop highly realistic scenarios. Scenarios provide hands-on experiences with real-life problem solving tasks [21] in safe experimental environments. With such scenarios, realistic situations can be simulated in order to gather deep insights [26].

Scenarios show aspects of games, involving play based on certain rules, take place within a defined location, are limited in time, and follow specific rules [6]. Earlier design experiences with operational units in the security domain [17] show that by using the Triadic Game Design (TGD) philosophy [15] playful, meaningful and realistic scenarios can be identified. TGD [15] is an end-user oriented design approach, distinguishing three equally important components: Play, Meaning, and Reality. TGD emphasizes that all three aspects have to be balanced within a design in order to develop a valid, meaningful, and engaging game experience.

During a half-day workshop, in which 6 members of the Dutch Police, the Netherlands Forensic Institute (NFI), and the fire brigade of the port of Rotterdam participated, different scenarios for the involved organisations have been identified. The TGD philosophy was used as a guideline for the workshops. The three elements Play (P), Meaning (M), and Reality (R), have been addressed while defining the scenarios. Together with the experts from the security domain, we held a structured brainstorm session, in which we first defined the necessary elements of reality (R) needed for the test scenarios. It was soon clear that highly realistic scenarios with a similar amount of stress and a realistic story line would be needed in order to explore the feasibility of the AR technology. Thus, the reality aspect addresses all circumstances that are derived from real life situations of emergency teams, such as realistic communication means, physical attributes at the scene and clothing worn during the test. Secondly, the meaning (M) aspect of the scenarios was addressed by defining clear measures of the usability of the AR technology as the aim of this study. Thirdly, within the play (P) aspect, we formulated which kind of actions and decisions are possible and required within the scenario, but also which procedures and protocols would define the 'rules' of the scenario.

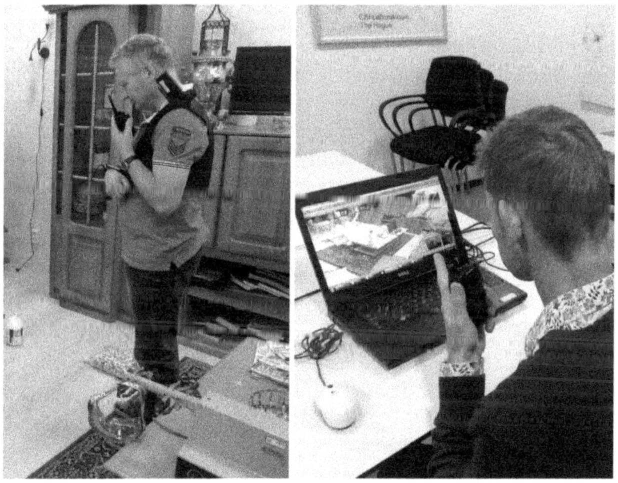

Figure 1. Example of two virtually co-located forensic investigators.

In all scenarios, AR is used to establish virtual co-location. Virtual co-location entails that people are virtually present at any place of the world and interact with others that are physically present in another location by using AR techniques. Figure 1 illustrates virtual co-location of two forensic investigators. A local investigator wearing a mobile camera on the shoulder and a mobile phone on the wrist (see Figure 1 (left)) is connected to a remote colleague (see Figure 1 (right)). By streaming the video captured from the camera, the remote colleague can see what the local colleague is seeing. Both the local and the remote can annotate what they see with virtual objects. Thereby, they can collaboratively augment the environment of the local to plan the investigation or highlight suspect objects. The remote colleague can furthermore search for and provide additional information on the situation to improve situational awareness or support problem-solving.

The scenarios focus on tasks for individual operational units. Their main purpose is to evaluate the effect of the AR system on collaboration and situational awareness in the different teams (police, fire department and forensics) as well as differently sized team compositions. For the latter, the scenarios can be played with 1 or 2 locals and 1 remote.

The scenario for forensic investigation focuses on planning the investigation of a recently discovered Ecstasy lab. Before entering the crime scene, the forensic investigators receive an oral briefing. After entering the apartment, the forensic investigators first analyse the site and set up a research plan. This plan includes the marking objects using AR for collecting fingerprints or DNA samples, placing evidence identification numbers, or taking of pictures on the site (P). In discussion with a remote colleague, the local investigators refine the plan (M). For that purpose, the remote colleague can provide information in AR to the local investigators, e.g. on the inhabitant of the apartment or the found chemicals, or annotate the scene using the same instruments as the local colleague. Following the plan, the local investigators start collecting evidence.

3.2 Participants

Three male forensic investigators with several years of work experience participated in the experiment. Two of the forensic investigators participated in earlier experiments [18] using an AR environment in combination with a head-mounted display. The third investigator had not used an AR environment before.

3.3 Measures

To evaluate the experiences with the environment a semi-structured de-briefing after each experiment run was used. The debriefing was conducted by 2 researchers being co-authors of this paper. The de-briefing focused on the usability of the system, the perceived situational awareness of the participants as well as the collaboration quality. For that purpose, questions from the SUS questionnaire [7], the SART method [32], and the seven dimensions of collaboration quality [8] were asked during the de-briefing. The de-briefing was audio-taped with both researchers additionally taking notes on the answers of the participants.

The experiments were video-taped with two cameras for reviewing incidents discussed in the debriefing. One camera was positioned in the room with the remote participant and the other camera recorded the scene on the spot.

3.4 Experimental Set-Up

3.4.1 Equipment

We have developed a framework named DECLARE - DistributEd CoLlaborative Augmented Reality Environment [18]. DECLARE is based on a centralized architecture for data communication, to support virtual co-location of users. DECLARE consists of four major components (see Figure 2):

1. Local user AR support: A local user wears a wrist-mounted smartphone to interact with the augmented scene and a shoulder-mounted smartphone. The video captured by the camera of the shoulder-mounted smartphone is sent to the other components of DECLARE.
2. Remote user AR support: The user interface for remote users runs on a desktop computer or laptop. A remote user interacts with DECLARE by using a keyboard and a standard mouse device.
3. Localization and mapping: The localization and mapping component is based on an implementation of RDSLAM (Robust Dynamic Simultaneously Localization And Mapping) [31] as provided by its developers.
4. Shared memory space: All DECLARE components communicate through a shared memory space. For the video streams provided by the local users, a synchronization mechanism is implemented in the shared memory, ensuring that the same video frame is played for a local user, remote user as well as the localization and mapping component simultaneously. In case one component undergoes a temporary failure, the video is automatically recovered. The shared memory mechanism further ensures that data updates from the RDSLAM camera position and orientation, as well as the virtual annotations made by the users, are synchronized with the recovered video stream and its content.

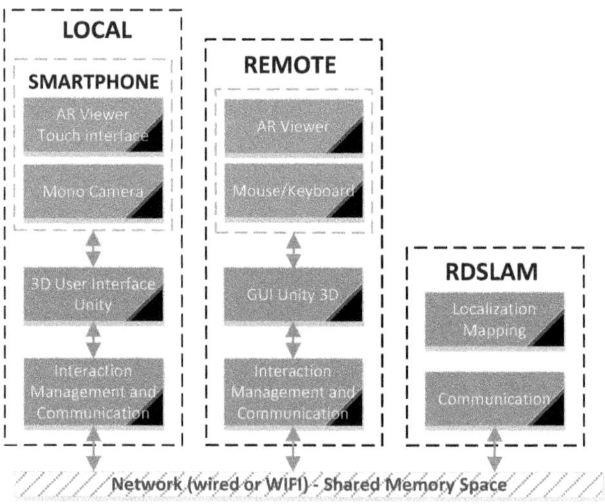

Figure 2. Diagram of the main DECLARE components.

Figure 3 shows the overall system architecture used in the experiment. In terms of hardware, the experimental setup for one remote expert and two local users requires 8 different hardware devices:

- 3 laptop computers: One laptop computer is for the remote expert (D1) and two laptop computers are for the local users (D2 and D5).
- 2 Samsung Galaxy S6 Edge smartphones (D3 and D6): The smartphones are wrist mounted and run the local user interface (via Unity 3D Remote).
- 2 Samsung Galaxy S4 Mini (D4 and D7): Each local user mounts one of these devices on the shoulder to stream a video and share the local view.
- 1 WIFI access point (D8): The access point interconnects all devices from the wired network (the three laptop computers D1-D3) with the devices from the WIFI network (the 4 smartphones D4-D7).

In addition, to the above devices 3 radio stations for audio communication (one for the remote user and one for each of the two local users) and 2 video recording cameras (one to record the activity of the remote user and one to record the activity of the local users) were used during the experiments.

The user interface for the remote expert runs on the laptop computer (D1). Each of the laptop computers for the local users (D2 and D5) runs three software components: (1) a Unity 3D user interface, (2) a component for receiving the video stream from one of the two Samsung Galaxy S4 Mini smartphones (D4 and D7), (3) an instance of the localization and mapping component based on RDSLAM [31]. The wrist mounted smartphones (D3 and D6) display the Unity 3D user interface via Unity 3D Remote and enable the local users to interact with the systems running on D2 and D5.

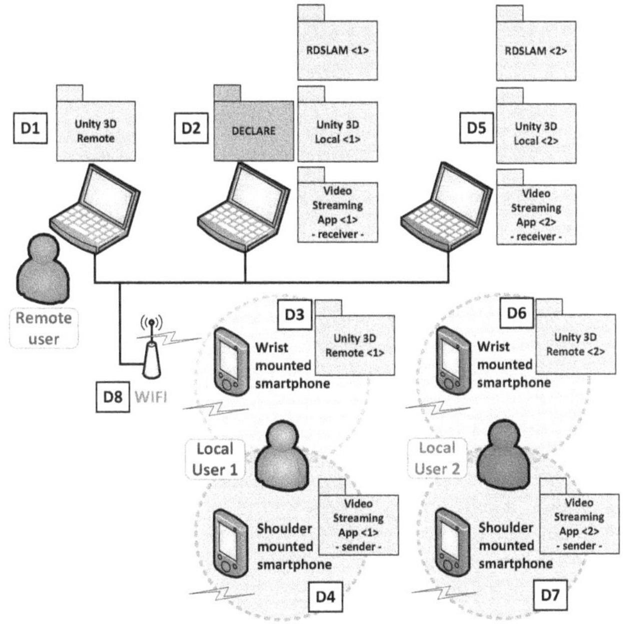

Figure 3. Overall system architecture used in the experiment for one remote expert and two local users.

3.4.1.1 Remote User AR Support

The remote user receives the video captured from the cameras of the two shoulder-mounted smartphones (D4 and D7 in Figure 3) of the local users. The two video streams from the local users are both displayed in real time in thumbnail size on the bottom right side of the screen (Figure 4). Above each video thumbnail the system depicts the name of the local user providing the video stream. To view the video of one local user in full, the remote user mouse clicks on the desired thumbnail video shown on the bottom right corner.

The remote user interface further includes a map showing the 2D position of the two local users in the physical environment in real-time. The map is displayed in the bottom left corner of the screen (see Figure 4).

In case there is only one local user, the remote user interface displays updates from only one thumbnail size video stream, one local user name and one graphical indicator on the map.

By pressing the F key, the remote user can freeze the image and decouple the view from the live video stream of the selected local user. By pressing U, the remote user can unfreeze the image and get back to the live video stream, as provided by the rear camera of the shoulder-mounted smartphone of the local user. Such *freezing* of the video stream further facilitates remote users to place virtual content without having the local user focusing on a specific part of the real world scene.

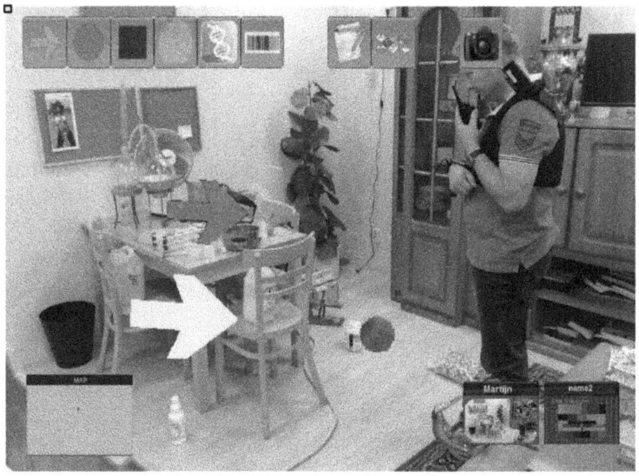

Figure 4. AR interface of the remote expert.

Using a classical 2D graphical user interface, with a menu of buttons positioned in the top part of the screen, the remote user (Figure 4) can place virtual 3D objects that are superimposed on the real world using tracking points provided by the RDSLAM component. The 3D virtual objects represent include arrows, spheres, blocks, fingerprint symbols, DNA symbols, barcode labels, 3D text, and hazard symbols. With these objects the remote user can highlight real objects, provide additional information or plan the investigation of the crime scene.

To place a 3D object, the remote user has to mouse click on the designated icon in the 2D user interface, and to mouse drag and drop that icon on the desired location directly on either the live video stream or on the frozen screen. The second option is that, instead of doing drag-and-drop on the 2D icon, the remote user can click one more time in the desired location. Once the desired location is indicated, the 2D icon is automatically converted into a 3D object, according to the selected icon type.

Except for the 3D text, all the other virtual objects are resizable. The remote user can resize these 3D objects by selecting them (by directly mouse clicking them), and by pressing "Up" arrow (to increase the size) or "Down" arrow (to decrease the size). The virtual objects representing an arrow, sphere or block can also be changed in colour by pressing the B key for blue, G for green, R for red when selected.

Any 3D virtual object can be re-positioned by the remote user, clicking the M key and then clicking at the new corresponding desired 2D location on the screen. By selecting a virtual object and pressing the DEL key, the object can be deleted. By pressing the BACKSPACE key, the last added 3D virtual object is removed.

For documentation of the scene, the remote user can take pictures of the current view that are then also placed in 3D space by selecting the appropriate icon from the menu interface. Once the remote user confirms the captured snapshot of the screen, the 3D picture object is anchored in-place, at the closest 3D point corresponding to the centre of the 2D screen.

All interaction events initiated by the remote user using the remote user interface, produce actions, which are consistent across the devices of the local users. The consistency of interaction effects, is ensured by passing all the interaction data through the shared virtual work space (shared virtual memory) of DECLARE.

3.4.1.2 Local User AR Support

The local user wears a Samsung Galaxy S6 Edge smartphone mounted at the wrist (D3 and D6 in Figure 3) and a Samsung Galaxy S4 Mini smartphone mounted on the shoulder for video streaming (D4 and D7 in Figure 3).

The video streaming between the devices of a local user is not direct. Instead, D4 sends video data to D2 and then D2 (via Unity Remote) sends it to D3. Similarly, D7 sends video data to D5, then D5 (via Unity Remote) sends data to D6. The devices D2 and D5 both send video data to D2 (DECLARE framework), which passes the data further to D2 (RDSLAM for local user 1) and D5 (RDSLAM for local user 2).

Figure 5. AR interface of the local officer.

Figure 5 shows the user interface on the wrist-mounted smartphone. The user interface shows the video stream of the shoulder-mounted smartphone and displays the name of the local user at the top center part of the screen. It supports touch-based interaction with the environment (via Unity 3D Remote). All local user activities are shared and kept consistent with the other users via the DECLARE framework. A local user can place virtual 3D objects that are superimposed on the real world using tracking points provided by the RDSLAM component. The supported virtual 3D objects are: arrows, spheres, blocks, fingerprint objects, DNA objects, barcode labels.

A local user can change the size of a 3D virtual object by selecting it with a finger touch and using the "plus" or "minus" buttons displayed on the bottom part of the user interface. A local user can change the colour by following a similar interaction sequence with the blue, green and red coloured buttons in the bottom part of the user interface. To delete a 3D object, the local user has to select an existing object and then to press the delete button (the bottom right most button in the user interface).

The bottom row of resize, colour and delete buttons, becomes visible only when the local user selects an existing 3D object (of type arrow, disc or square). For the other types of 3D objects, only the resizing and delete buttons are displayed at object selection.

3.5 Procedure

The experiment took place indoor in a real training environment at the Netherlands Forensic Institute (NFI). The experiments lasted half a day.

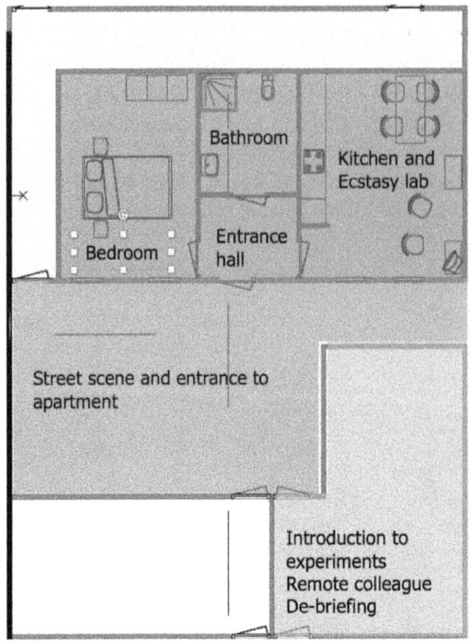

Figure 6. Plan of the CSI field lab.

Figure 6 shows the plan of the CSI field lab at the NFI. The upper highlighted box shows the plan of the apartment. The apartment consists of four rooms, i.e. a bedroom, a bathroom, a kitchen and an entrance hall. Prior to the experiment, an Ecstasy lab was staged in the kitchen (see Figure 7). The highlighted box in the middle of the plan resembles a typical Dutch street from which the participants entered the apartment. The lower highlighted box shows the location for the remote colleague, the introduction to the experiment as well as the debriefing. The location is physically separated from the apartment by walls and doors so that remote and local persons could only interact via the available technology.

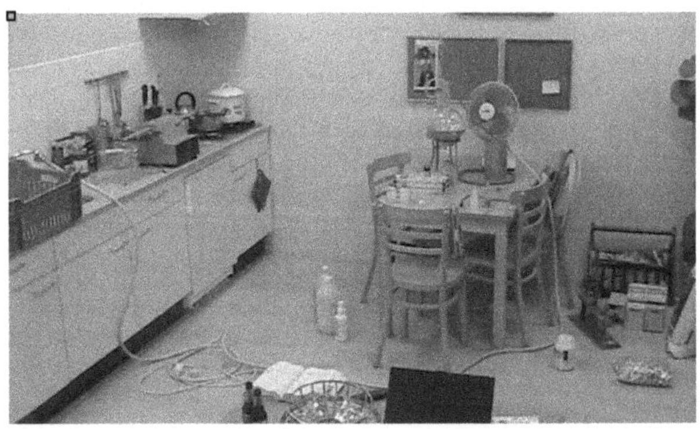

Figure 7. Staged Ecstasy lab in the kitchen of the CSI field lab.

The experiment was carried out in two rounds. In round one, one remote investigator (see Figure 8) collaborated with one local investigator (see Figure 8). The investigators interacted with each other using the AR system as described above. In addition, they were using walkie-talkies for audio communication. This setup compares to an earlier experiment using the same scenario. The earlier experiment [18], however, used head-mounted devices instead of smartphones. In round two, the role for the remote investigator changed, as the remote investigator had to simultaneously guide and interact with two local investigators (see Figure 9). Using the AR system described above, the remote investigator could watch the activities of the local investigators and select one video stream as main view. The setup of the staged Ecstasy lab was changed to avoid that the participants encounter an identical scene twice. Again, the investigators could communicate using walkie-talkies on one shared channel.

In both rounds, the same investigator took the role of the remote colleague. Prior to both rounds all participants were given an oral briefing on the goal of the experiment. Two researchers observed both rounds by taking notes on the interaction. After each round, the same researchers lead the semi-structured de-briefing on the usability of the system, the perceived situational awareness of the participants as well as the collaboration quality.

4. RESULTS

4.1 Round one – one local and one remote investigator

During the de-briefing after the first round, the participants reported that the AR system was helpful, but that they also experienced clear limitations of the current technology. Especially, the low level of speed and precision of the localization and mapping and the sometimes occurring connection loss lead to a lower usability of the system. Apart from this, the usability of the AR system was experienced as good. In the experiment, the positioning of 3D text and the arrows to highlight an object was in some cases not precise enough to understand the meaning of the information added through the system. The marking of objects with blocks and arrows was in all cases experienced as helpful, but rather to indicate a certain region within the real space than to point to some detail. The participants came up with the suggestion to take a picture of the scene, which could be used by the remote user to carefully annotate it. The annotated picture could then be provided to the local user as 3D image with zoom function.

Additionally to the function of annotating objects, the remote investigator also used the AR system to guide the local investigator through the environment. This procedure worked well, and the participants reported about a good shared understanding of what to achieve. The local investigator said that he was aware of the needs of the remote investigator. The visual feedback provided by the AR system enabled such a feeling of presence for the remote investigator that only few control questions were needed, such as: is this a microwave, could you return, can you take a closer look, how does it smell? On the other hand, the local user reported that sometimes, these questions were somehow confusing.

The participants reported that the collaboration based on the AR system needed clear instruction and process agreements on what to do and communicate. Once, the test was interrupted for clarification between the two roles. Both roles could not rely on the shared visual information only, but needed additional communication using the audio channel. The participants pointed to the importance of agreements on how to use the system. Missing procedures, which provide orientation, could lead to rejection of the technology when implemented within the organization as a whole.

Figure 8. Remote investigator interacting with one local investigator.

A clear advantage of the distributed collaboration enabled by the AR system was mentioned with the possibility for the remote investigator to do administrative work while the local user gets more time to investigate the scene.

The smartphone as handheld tool to support AR collaboration improved the interaction compared to free-hand interaction in an earlier experiment [18]. Still, the use of the smartphone for handheld AR is not without limitation for the local investigator. The shoulder-mounted camera view makes it difficult to interact and coordinate the real view. The local investigator reported that when he turned his head to look into a different direction, he also had to explicitly think about turning the whole body to change the camera view, too. He also felt a tendency to use the AR handheld, which was wrapped to his wrist, as monitor to change the perspective of the recording shoulder-mounted camera.

4.2 Round two – two local and one remote investigator

Before the local investigators went to the scene in the second round, they decided on some communication and coordination rules. The local investigators went to the scene, looking around, already noticing virtual markers that have been left behind by the police and fire brigade beforehand (in the story of the scenario). The remote investigator behind the laptop assigned the camera streams a name to be able to identify the pictures and relate them to one investigator on the spot.

In this round, it was clearly observable that the remote investigator gave clear instructions, asked the local investigators for audio information about the scene, and an overview of the situation.

The remote investigator asked if he could help by placing some markers, but the locals preferred to do it themselves. There was a lot of communication amongst the two local investigators, to align their activities, but less with the remote expert. The test round was finalized with some limitations caused by the localization and mapping component. Compared to round one, round two with two local investigators took longer with less communication with the remote investigator, but with more placed virtual objects in augmented reality.

Figure 9. Two Local investigators in the staged Ecstasy lab.

As after the first round, a de-briefing was conducted. The biggest disadvantage of the technology was reported related to the localization and mapping, which had a huge impact performance, especially when it did not work properly.

The local investigators reported that the handheld devices require to constantly shift task focus and to align the view correctly, as it is not in-line with the natural view like a HMD would be. On the other hand, the shoulder-mounted camera provided a more stable video feed to the remote than a camera on an HMD could do. Nevertheless, it was indicated that the mobile technology worked better than free-hands interaction, which was used during earlier experiments [18].

The collaboration between the two local users demanded a higher level of communication to agree on procedures and to distribute the work. In addition, there was a higher level of communication between the local investigators and the remote colleague to achieve satisfying team awareness of the situation. The local investigators reported that they would like to have a higher awareness of what the remote colleague was doing, what actions he conducted, and which information he added. The local investigators experienced this demand as distraction from other tasks within the situation. Still, all participants agreed that increased communication helped to increase awareness between the distributed roles and agree on procedures.

The remote investigator was not required to provide just-in-time information or provide guidance to the local investigators. This was mainly due to the fact that the local investigators discussed and structured the investigation of the scene via their extensive local communication. This gave the remote investigator time to work on rather administrative tasks, e.g. adding barcodes (SIN) to identified evidence.

4.3 Discussion

Only three experienced forensic investigators participated in the experiment. Further experiments are necessary to validate the findings from this experiment. Still, as the experiments were conducted with real experts in their field, the findings are of large value as they provide direct insight on the applicability of the technology in the domain. The experienced forensic investigators valued the AR system as useful tool to provide helpful information for a forensic investigator. The overall findings of both rounds in the experiment are summarized in Table 1.

Used in real situations, the system could provide indications on what police or fire department did at the crime scene, before the investigators enter the scene. All participants expected that the AR system and the collaboration of the local investigators with the remote expert would not change the way decisions are taken on a crime scene, but that it would improve traceability.

Interestingly, we could notice a high demand for communication in both rounds of the experiment as well as a shift in the purpose of the communication between local and remote investigator. In the first round, this was mainly for agreeing on the procedures.

In the second round, the communication between locals and remote had to compensate missing awareness information. The remote investigator had to split his attention between the two local investigators and could not follow their activities all the time. As result, he sometimes placed virtual objects without notifying the local investigators. Compared to the first round, the communication between the local investigators was necessary to agree on procedures, e.g. who would investigate which part. This shift in communication purpose allowed the remote investigator to fulfil administrative tasks and rather provide background information than guidance on the spot.

Table 1. Overall findings of the experiment

Positive aspects	Negative aspects
• Shared visualization fosters shared understanding in the team • Camera feeds of the local investigators supports the perception of presence for the remote investigator • Information provision on the spot and in place • Guidance of the local investigator by the remote investigator • Usability of the smartphone as interaction device • Ability of the remote investigator to take over administrative tasks	• Difficulties to align the shoulder-mounted camera feed with the user interface on the wrist worn smartphone • Division of attention between the smartphone user interface and the real environment • Missing procedures and process agreements for interacting and using the AR system • Lack of awareness about the activities of the remote investigator • Low level of speed and precision of the localization and mapping

Compared to an earlier experiment, in which the local investigator used a head-mounted device including a camera to provide a video feed to a remote colleague [18], the handheld-based hardware setup in the current experiment provided better interaction possibilities than free-hand interaction, a wider field of view for the local investigators, and more stable video feed for the remote colleague. However, the difficulties to align the shoulder-mounted camera feed with the user interface on the wrist worn smartphone resulted in a division of attention between the smartphone user interface and the real environment. Such a division of attention required a higher concentration of the local investigators and reduced their spare mental capacity. Following the SART method [32] to evaluate situational awareness, these factors in total decrease the situational awareness of the local investigators. Using an HMD that can

visualize the AR content in direct sight of the investigators is thus beneficial with regard to situational awareness.

During the experiments, some technical limitations were observed. One technical limitation was the precision of the localization and mapping which is closely related to the performance and accuracy of RDSLAM [31] in close to-real life conditions such as in our experimental setup. Using different hardware, e.g. a different camera, would not have significantly improved the performance and accuracy of the localization and mapping. A second technical limitation encountered during the experiments was the loss of network connection. Because the connection relied on WiFi, better hardware equipment such as better antennas, access points, wireless range extenders or the mobile telecommunications technology such as 4G could have decreased the number of encountered connection losses and improved the reliability and usability of our system.

5. CONCLUSION

This paper reported on a handheld AR system allowing local and remote forensic investigators to jointly investigate a crime scene. For the local investigators, the AR system runs on a wrist-mounted smartphone and for the remote investigator the AR system runs on a laptop.

The AR system has been evaluated with experts from the field in a controlled test environment. The evaluation was carried out in two rounds: (1) with one local and one remote investigator and (2) with two local and one remote investigator. The evaluation showed that the experts, in general, consider the AR system as useful to foster shared understanding, guide local investigators or provide information on the spot and in place. Though this shows potential for future application of AR in forensic investigation, the evaluation also showed that AR technology is not mature enough yet for real application. Especially, the precision and reliability of the localization and mapping needs to be improved. The AR system itself needs to provide more means to foster awareness among the investigators with regard to their activities.

Compared to earlier experiments using head-mounted devices (HMDs) [18], the evaluation showed that the handheld AR system addresses limitations of current HMDs, but impacts the situational awareness of local investigators as they need to divide their attention between the user interface on the smartphone and the real environment as well as the alignment of the shoulder-mounted camera to the view on the smartphone. Using smartphones to visualize the AR content might thus be feasible for scenarios in which the locals need to interact with the system or perceive the provided information from time to time only. Using HMDs might be more suitable when the scenario requires to constantly perceive and interact with the information in AR, as HMDs do not require to switch the context or view. However, for that purpose current limitations of HMDs, such as the field of view or the brightness of the display, still need to be overcome.

In future work, we plan to extend the evaluation of the handheld AR system to better understand the needs for awareness support, explore the role change of the remote investigator between interacting with one or two remote colleagues, as well as experiment with different camera positions to provide the video feed to the remote investigator. When doing so, we will closely follow advances in display hardware as well as localization and mapping approaches to overcome their negative impact on the usability of the AR system.

6. ACKNOWLEDGMENTS

The results of this extended abstract have been achieved as part of a joint project with the Dutch Police and the Netherlands Forensic Institute (NFI) sponsored by the National Coordinator for Security and Counterterrorism (NCTV) of the Netherlands.

7. REFERENCES

[1] Alem, L. et al. 2011. Remote Tele-assistance System for Maintenance Operators in Mines. *11th Underground Coal Operators' Conference* (2011), 171–177.

[2] Azuma, R.T. 1997. A Survey of Augmented Reality. *Presence: Teleoperators and Virtual Environments 6* (1997), 355–385.

[3] Azuma, R.T. et al. 2001. Recent advances in augmented reality. *Computer Graphics and Applications, IEEE*. 21, 6 (Dec. 2001), 34–47.

[4] Baber, C. et al. 2006. Crime scene investigation as distributed cognition. *Pragmatics & Cognition*. 14, 2 (2006), 357–385.

[5] Baber, C. et al. 2009. Mobile technology for crime scene examination. *International Journal of Human-Computer Studies*. 67, 5 (2009), 464–474.

[6] Brandt, E. 2006. Designing Exploratory Design Games: A Framework for Participation in Participatory Design? *Proceedings of the Ninth Conference on Participatory Design: Expanding Boundaries in Design - Volume 1* (Trento, Italy, 2006), 57–66.

[7] Brooke, J. 1996. SUS: A "quick and dirty" usability scale. *Usability Evaluation in Industry* (London, UK, 1996).

[8] Burkhardt, J.-M. et al. 2009. An approach to assess the quality of collaboration in technology-mediated design situations. *European Conference on Cognitive Ergonomics: Designing beyond the Product — Understanding Activity and User Experience in Ubiquitous Environments* (Helsinki, Finland, 2009), 30:1–30:9.

[9] Datcu, D. et al. 2014. On the Usability of Augmented Reality for Information Exchange in Teams from the Security Domain. *IEEE Joint Intelligence and Security Informatics Conference (JISIC)* (2014), 160–167.

[10] Domova, V. et al. 2014. Designing a Remote Video Collaboration System for Industrial Settings. *Proceedings of the Ninth ACM International Conference on Interactive Tabletops and Surfaces* (Dresden, Germany, 2014), 229–238.

[11] Drabek, T.E. and McEntire, D.A. 2002. Emergent Phenomena and Multiorganizational Coordination in Disasters: Lessons from the Research Literature. *International Journal of Mass Emergencies and Disasters (IJMED)*. 20, 2 (Aug. 2002), 197–224.

[12] Gauglitz, S. et al. 2014. In Touch with the Remote World: Remote Collaboration with Augmented Reality Drawings and Virtual Navigation. *Proceedings of the 20th ACM Symposium on Virtual Reality Software and Technology* (Edinburgh, Scotland, 2014), 197–205.

[13] Gauglitz, S. et al. 2014. World-stabilized Annotations and Virtual Scene Navigation for Remote Collaboration. *Proceedings of the 27th Annual ACM Symposium on User Interface Software and Technology* (Honolulu, Hawaii, USA, 2014), 449–459.

[14] Gurevich, P. et al. 2012. TeleAdvisor: A Versatile Augmented Reality Tool for Remote Assistance. *Proceedings of the SIGCHI Conference on Human Factors in Computing Systems* (Austin, Texas, USA, 2012), 619–622.

[15] Harteveld, C. 2011. *Triadic Game Design: Balancing Reality, Meaning and Play*. Springer, Berlin.

[16] Jamieson, A. 2004. A rational approach to the principles and practice of crime scene investigation: I. Principles. *Science and Justice*. 44, 1 (Jan. 2004), 3 – 7.

[17] Lukosch, H. et al. 2014. Building a Virtual World for Team Work Improvement. *Frontiers in Gaming Simulation* (2014), 60–68.

[18] Lukosch, S. et al. 2015. Providing Information on the Spot: Using Augmented Reality for Situational Awareness in the Security Domain. *Computer Supported Cooperative Work (CSCW) – The Journal of Collaborative Computing and Work Practices*. (2015).

[19] Milgram, P. and Kishino, F. 1994. A taxonomy of mixed reality visual displays. *IEICE Transactions on Information Systems*. E77-D, 12 (1994).

[20] Militello, L.G. et al. 2007. Information flow during crisis management: challenges to coordination in the emergency operations center. *Cognition, Technology & Work*. 9, 1 (2007), 25–31.

[21] Niehaus, J. and Riedl, M.O. 2009. Scenario adaptation: An approach to customizing computer-based training games and simulations. *Proceedings of the AIED 2009 Workshop on Intelligent Educational Games* (2009), 89–98.

[22] Nilsson, S. et al. 2009. Using AR to support cross-organisational collaboration in dynamic tasks. *Mixed and Augmented Reality, 2009. ISMAR 2009. 8th IEEE International Symposium on* (Oct. 2009), 3–12.

[23] Poelman, R. et al. 2012. As if Being There: Mediated Reality for Crime Scene Investigation. *CSCW '12: Proceedings of the 2012 ACM conference on Computer Supported Cooperative Work* (2012), 1267–1276.

[24] Procyk, J. et al. 2014. Exploring Video Streaming in Public Settings: Shared Geocaching over Distance Using Mobile Video Chat. *Proceedings of the SIGCHI Conference on Human Factors in Computing Systems* (Toronto, Ontario, Canada, 2014), 2163–2172.

[25] Reuter, C. et al. 2014. Ad Hoc Participation in Situation Assessment: Supporting Mobile Collaboration in Emergencies. *ACM Transactions on Computer-Human Interaction (TOCHI)*. 21, 5 (Nov. 2014), 26:1–26:26.

[26] Schön, D.A. 1983. *The Reflective Practitioner: How Professionals Think in Action*. Basic Books.

[27] Smith, P.A. et al. 2008. Measuring team skills in crime scene investigation: exploring ad hoc teams. *Ergonomics*. 51, 10 (2008), 1463–1488.

[28] Streefkerk, J.W. et al. 2009. Context-Aware Team Task Allocation to Support Mobile Police Surveillance. *Foundations of Augmented Cognition. Neuroergonomics and Operational Neuroscience* (2009), 88–97.

[29] Streefkerk, J.W. et al. 2008. Effects of Presentation Modality on Team Awareness and Choice Accuracy in a Simulated Police Team Task. *Proceedings of the Human Factors and Ergonomics Society Annual Meeting* (Sep. 2008), 378–382.

[30] Streefkerk, J.W. et al. 2013. The ART of CSI: An Augmented Reality Tool (ART) to Annotate Crime Scenes in Forensic Investigation. *Virtual, Augmented and Mixed Reality. Systems and Applications* (2013), 330–339.

[31] Tan, W. et al. 2013. Robust monocular SLAM in dynamic environments. *Mixed and Augmented Reality (ISMAR), 2013 IEEE International Symposium on* (Oct. 2013), 209–218.

[32] Taylor, R.M. 1990. Situational awareness rating technique (SART): The development of a tool for aircrew systems design. *Proceedings of the Symposium on Situational Awareness in Aerospace Operations (AGARD-CP-478)* (1990), 3/1 – 3/17.

[33] Voida, A. et al. 2008. Asymmetry in Media Spaces. *Proceedings of the 2008 ACM Conference on Computer Supported Cooperative Work* (San Diego, CA, USA, 2008), 313–322.

The Emergence of High-Speed Interaction and Coordination in a (Formerly) Turn-based Groupware Game

Carl Gutwin, Mutasem Barjawi, and David Pinelle
Department of Computer Science, University of Saskatchewan
110 Science Place, Saskatoon, Saskatchewan, S7N 5C9
gutwin@cs.usask.ca

ABSTRACT
Although some forms of distributed groupware now enable fast-paced real-time collaboration (e.g., first-person shooter games), little work has been done to determine how coordination and interaction occur when people attempt to work together at high speed. Understanding the elements of high-speed coordination is important, because shared-workspace groupware systems offer opportunities for new kinds of high-speed work – that is, they provide freedom from the physical constraints that can slow and restrict coordination in physical shared spaces. To better understand high-speed coordination, and to examine whether these opportunities can enable new kinds of interaction in groupware, we created and studied a new multi-player game (called RTChess) that is based on traditional chess, but adds multiple players and removes all turns from the gameplay. The result is a free-for-all game where people are limited only by their ability to move quickly and expertly – a situation that is more like a team sport than a tabletop game. We carried out an observational study of 448 games of RTChess to look for the emergence of high-speed interaction, team coordination, and interactional expertise. We found that people can interact extremely quickly through distributed groupware, and saw evidence that people build expertise and develop several kinds of coordination in the game. Groupware systems like RTChess indicate that coordination and interaction in shared-workspace collaboration can occur at high speed, and suggest ways to free groupware users from the slow and stilted interactions that are common in many current multi-user systems.

Keywords
Game design; Real-time multiplayer games; Coordination

1. INTRODUCTION
Real-time distributed groupware systems are now common (e.g., office software such as Google Docs, conferencing and screen-sharing systems such as Skype or VNC, and many kinds of multi-player games). These systems have dramatically changed the way that people work and play together over distance; however, there are still substantial differences between the kinds of group behavior that are possible in groupware, and what is commonly seen in face-to-face settings.

GROUP '16, November 13 - 16, 2016, Sanibel Island, FL, USA

ACM 978-1-4503-4276-6/16/11...$15.00
DOI: http://dx.doi.org/10.1145/2957276.2957315

In particular, most real-time groupware still does not support high-speed interaction, in which people carry out interdependent actions quickly and with close coordination. This kind of behavior is a hallmark of human collaboration in face-to-face environments, where people are natural experts in the mechanical aspects of working together in physical spaces. For example, in real-world work and play settings, people are able to easily and rapidly transfer tools and objects to one another, are able to carry out synchronized actions simply and easily, are able to coordinate fast turn-taking actions smoothly and efficiently, and are able to respond naturally and quickly to subtle cues about others' actions and intentions. High-speed interaction is common in many collaborative settings, but is perhaps most apparent in team sports like soccer or basketball, where split-second timing and precise coordination can be critical to a team's success.

When interaction and collaboration move from the real world to groupware systems, high-speed interaction becomes more difficult. Multi-player games such as first-person shooters do support real-time interaction, but little is known about how this interaction occurs. In addition, it is unknown how the limitations of distributed interaction (e.g., the loss of awareness information about other people's locations and activities, the loss of tactile feedback from shared physical actions, and the loss of communication richness through the absence of non-verbal channels and body language [2,6,7]) also limit coordination. The restrictions of distributed groupware often force users into slow, awkward, and overly formal interaction patterns (even in real-time games), trapping them in 'interactional beginner mode' even when they have a high degree of interactional expertise in real-world workspaces.

However, distributed groupware also provides some new opportunities for high-speed interaction – opportunities that can even take groupware beyond what is possible in the real world. One of these opportunities is that distributed groupware frees people from the constraints that govern shared action in a physical space: that is, people's hands and arms cannot be in the same physical place at the same time, but in a groupware environment there is no such limitation, meaning that people may be able to interact more quickly in groupware than in real-world workspaces.

Given the strong correlation between high-speed interaction and team sports, the reduced physical constraints of groupware present natural possibilities for developing new high-speed groupware games. In this paper, we investigate the development of and support for high-speed interaction using a new game that is developed from chess, but that removes the turn-taking requirements that are used to mediate access to the board space and the chess pieces. The game, called RTChess, allows multiple people to play at once and removes traditional turns from the gameplay, instead adopting a free-for-all approach where people may move as fast as they are able. This approach changes the game from a slow and thoughtful activity, in which people have time to optimize their decisions, to a fast-paced game that is much more like a team sport – limited only by people's abilities to keep track of the action and move the pieces on the board.

We used RTChess as a platform for observing the emergence and development of expert real-time interaction and coordination. We carried out an observational study in which we watched and recorded 448 games of RTChess over five sessions played by two teams of two players each. We analysed the video records to track the development of the teams' play strategies and coordinated behavior. Our observations show that there is a whole new world of real-time high-speed behavior that is possible in distributed groupware. In many ways RTChess is more like a team sport than a game: we observed teams instinctively dividing into offensive and defensive roles, moving in a coordinated fashion to chase an opponent, and running 'trap and ambush' plays where an opponent was lured out into a vulnerable position.

However, the speed of the game (a move every 0.7 seconds) also means that teamwork and coordinated activity are difficult – there is no time to plan during the game, and awareness, communication, and synchronization all become problems in the distributed system. Nevertheless, the teams clearly learned new strategies and learned the characteristics of their partners; that is, they got better at high-speed interaction over the five sessions.

These results show that it is possible to design groupware systems that enable high-speed interaction and that allow people to make use of their natural expertise in working together. Systems like RTChess raise the upper limits on speed and coordination of shared-workspace collaboration, and help to free groupware users from 'interactional beginner mode.' Although issues such as supporting group awareness are still critical, our results suggest that groupware can successfully enable high-speed interaction.

In the next sections, we review background material for this investigation – research into coordination in groupware, into traditional and real-time game design, and into the temporal structures that can govern interaction. We then introduce RTChess, describe design issues in the game that affect coordination, and provide general observations on what it is like to play the game. We then report on the observational study in which we looked more closely at the emergence and development of high-speed interaction and coordination.

2. BACKGROUND

2.1 Loose and Tight Coupling

Coupling is the degree to which a person can operate independently of another in a collaborative workspace [12]. Researchers have considered how coordination works at both ends of this spectrum. Loosely-coupled interaction occurs when there is low interdependency (i.e., users' interactions affect each other weakly or infrequently), high differentiation (i.e., users' interactions are distinct, separate, and self-contained), and low integration (i.e., managing interdependencies between interactions does not occur regularly) [12]. Additionally, loose coupling involves interaction that requires people to be aware of each other, but without a need for immediate negotiation, and in which activities can proceed in parallel [11].

Tightly-coupled interaction occurs when there is high dependency between users' interactions, and where immediate and frequent communication is required to negotiate some activities [11]. This communication is often verbal, but in situations where there is no time to talk, the communication channel is often implicit and visual – that is, the visible indications of others' actions immediately and continuously influence other users' actions [16]. This kind of communication is exemplified in team sports, where activity happens too fast for lengthy verbal communication, and players need to coordinate their actions based on the visual information in the environment (e.g., in a soccer game, the location and movement of other players and the ball) [3]. As discussed below, however, there are ways of reducing the need for communication (i.e., prediction and set plays).

2.2 Coordination in Groups

Coordination is the act of organizing interdependencies between activities in a collaborative setting [4,9]; in tightly-coupled activities, where there are more interdependencies, a greater degree of this organization is required. Coordination has been studied frequently in CSCW, although much of the research has considered low-speed types of coordination that occur in activities such as business processes [10], although the basic principles of coordination theory still apply to faster activities.

Malone and Crowston [10] divide coordination into four generic components: goals, actors, activities, and interdependencies between the activities. Common types of interdependencies include shared resources, producer/consumer relationships, simultaneity constraints, and task/subtask relationships. Coordination mechanisms are the means by which these interdependencies are managed. People may coordinate their actions in several ways:

- *Explicit communication*, whether verbal or gestural, is a main mechanism used for coordination, and verbal exchanges are often needed in unfamiliar situations.
- *Implicit communication* allows people to gather information from feedthrough [2] or others' movement ('consequential communication' [16]).
- *Group decisions and established protocols* provide pre-arranged rules or policies about how the work will be carried out [9]; these can include one-time decisions (e.g., how to split up a task between people), or general guidelines (e.g., driving on the left side of the road, saying 'hello' when answering the telephone, or taking turns in a game).

A main difference between different coordination mechanisms is whether the mechanism allows people to predict others' actions. Protocols and pre-arranged rules let people make decisions about what others are going to do, without requiring communication at the time of the event. This is critical in situations with time pressure, since verbal communication is slow. In fast-paced team sports, for example, players rely primarily on prediction (e.g., based on set plays or familiarity with another player's style) to coordinate activities.

As suggested above, many instances of high-speed interaction can be found in team games such as soccer or basketball, and Kinesiology researchers have examined several aspects of team coordination and performance (e.g., [1,34,5]) For example, Eccles [3] proposed a conceptual framework of coordination and communication between team members. In this framework, coordination was divided into three parts: pre-process, in-process, and post-process coordination. Pre-process coordination occurs when the team prepares itself for a game by establishing roles, setting tasks, and learning set plays. In-process coordination is the coordination undertaken during gameplay as a response to the dynamic environment. Post-process coordination occurs when the team reviews and evaluates its behaviour and makes decisions and plans for future games. Eccles states that in most sports, in-process coordination is difficult because of the scarcity of time, which reduces cognitive resources and communication opportunities.

2.3 Turn-based Coordination in Games

One main mechanism for coordinating players in games, particularly tabletop games like chess, is the idea of turn-taking. Many computer and video games use this simple coordination strategy, which mediates access to the shared resource of the game workspace (e.g., the board and game pieces). Turns are a fundamental part of most tabletop games, and it is difficult even to describe games like chess or backgammon without using the idea of turns. However, one of the main reasons that turns exist in these games has nothing to do with the gameplay: that is, turns are necessary to avoid physical collisions in the shared space of the board. Turns shape the play in other ways as well – for example, they ensure fair access to all players and make the game into a discrete set of optimization problems – but they may have arisen primarily to manage the physical difficulties of two people trying to operate on the same game board.

The role of turn-taking as a coordination mechanism is highlighted in the example of real-time strategy games (RTSs) such as *Starcraft*. These games are computational versions of turn-based board games such as *Axis and Allies* or *Diplomacy*, in which players use their decision-making and planning skills to dominate their opponents within a game domain. Most early computer-based strategy games maintained the turn-based approach that is part of the physical board games. However, there are examples even from the early 1980s that add real-time elements to the gameplay (e.g., *Utopia* or *Ancient Art of War*). In the 1990s, 'modern' RTSs such as *Command and Conquer* appeared that included further real-time elements such as mouse-based control of units, resource gathering, and different levels of management, that are all now commonplace in RTS games.

The shift to real-time play in RTSs dramatically changed the experience of the game and the strategies needed to succeed. Whereas turn-based strategy games focus on careful planning and optimal decision-making, RTSs are much more oriented towards the ability to act under extreme time pressure – the need to track, manage, and direct many different units simultaneously is a hallmark of RTSs. The perceptual and cognitive overload that this can cause has become an important part of the gameplay, and there are even recognized strategies in RTSs that are based on overwhelming the opponent (i.e., 'rush' and 'swarm' [13]).

Considerable debate has arisen over the relative merits of real-time versus turn-based strategy games [13]. Critics of the real-time genre complain that RTSs devolve into 'click fests' where the person with the faster reflexes can always win. Proponents of the genre argue that real-time games are more realistic, since the real-world scenarios that the games are based on do not use turns; RTS players also argue that the faster pace of RTSs is more exciting and more immersive than turn-based games. Although there is no obvious winner in the debate, it is clear that removing turns from strategy games has created a new, legitimate, and dramatically different type of game – and one that has now become more popular than the turn-based genre from which it originated [13].

3. DESIGN ISSUES IN REAL-TIME GAMES

3.1 Temporal Structure

In considering how to design a multiplayer game that encourages high-speed interaction, one of the main issues is the timeframe for interaction between players. In most traditional games, this consists of a series of turns where each player has a slice of time in which they are the only one who can make a move. In moving to real-time interaction, several strategies have been seen. In some real-time games, moves require time to carry out – for example, pieces must 'walk' from one location to another, or a fixed period must pass before a building or unit is constructed. Other real-time games do not support time-deferred moves, but instead process player actions instantaneously. We have identified seven different temporal organizations, listed below from most to least structured.

Turn based with no time limits. In this organization, turns are sequential, and there is no limit on the amount of time each player can take to act. This is the most common organization in classic games: examples include chess, checkers, and poker.

Turn based with a time limit. Turns are sequential, but each player has a limited amount of time to execute their move. Examples include various games that use egg timers (such as *Boggle*), and tournament rules for standard chess (e.g., 60 minutes per turn).

Turn-based with time as a fixed resource. Turns are sequential, and the amount of time taken for a player's turn is subtracted from an overall total. Several variants of chess (e.g., Bullet chess or Blitz chess) use this organization.

Simultaneous turns. In this organization, all players take their turns at the same time, and game play does not proceed until everyone has completed their move. *Diplomacy* is an example of a strategy game that uses this approach.

Tick-based turns. In tick-based games, players can make moves concurrently, but the number of moves they can issue are regulated by in-game time units called ticks. Players are not obliged to carry out an action, and they can usually only carry out a limited number of actions during a tick. Examples include *Utopia* and many browser-based games.

Real-time with temporal delays. Many real-time games do not carry out a player's commands immediately, but delay completion in order to simulate the time that would be required to finish the action. For example, units in an RTS must walk from one location to another, or a certain amount of time must elapse before a new building or unit is constructed. Almost all RTSs follow this approach (e.g., *Starcraft*, *Warcraft*, *Age of Empires*); a variant of chess called *Kung-Fu Chess* is also similar in that it enforces a 'cool-down' period that prevents a piece from being moved twice in a short span of time.

Real-time with no artificial constraints. In this model, all players are able to interact with the game concurrently, and moves and actions initiated by each player are executed immediately. Examples include most action games (e.g., *Doom*, *Quake*), some RPGs (e.g., *World of Warcraft*), and RTChess as described below. The lack of artificial constraints does not mean that actions happen instantaneously, however: delays still occur because of limitations on the skill and speed of the player moving in the game's interface, and because of network transmission times for games that communicate with a server.

3.2 Access to Resources

Another defining characteristic of coordination in multiplayer games is that rules establish how players will access space and resources. In most games people share different spatial regions, such as the board in a board game or the center of the table in a card game. Other areas are used by each individual player, and are usually off limits to others. In *Monopoly*, for example, players typically sort their money in the area in front of them, and in *Scrabble*, they organize their tiles so that others cannot view them.

In many games, people also share other resources, such as cards or playing pieces. For example, in *Reversi*, tile ownership changes hands frequently, and the tiles are not as tightly bound to players as are the tokens that are used in *Monopoly*. Similarly, some card games establish strict ownership of the cards in a player's hands, while others allow people to pass cards back and forth. Sharing rules often become more fluid when players are grouped into separate teams, where team members are able to move and manipulate the same resources.

We present three different ownership and sharing strategies for games below. The strategies are ordered from exclusive ownership to fully shared ownership of space, units and resources.

Exclusive ownership of space, resources, and/or units. Only one player is able to access a space (physical or virtual), resource (e.g. cards, money, etc.), or unit (e.g. playing piece, character, soldier, etc.). Examples: *Monopoly*, *Trivial Pursuit*.

Flexible ownership of space, resources, and/or units. Access is selectively shared, where players form alliances with others, or where only certain types of game resources are shared. Examples: Variants of many real time strategy games, such as *Starcraft*, where resources are shared within a team.

Shared ownership of space, resources, and/or units. Access is shared either with other teammates or with all other players. Examples include *Warcraft* or RTChess as described below.

3.3 Group Awareness

When classic games are implemented as real-time games, the rules used to coordinate access are removed. Each player interacts with the game concurrently rather than sequentially, and people share the same space and game pieces. When compared to traditional games, real time games are more chaotic, and people have to track more events within a much tighter time frame. The risk of play-based interference increases substantially: people are much more likely to inadvertently interfere with each other when everyone moves at the same time. Further, in games that foster team play, players may have problems understanding the actions and intents of their teammates.

Removing structural rules in regular games means that new coordination mechanisms must be added so that the game does not become unmanageable for a group. Further, when games are implemented as networked multiplayer games, people have less information about other users since they cannot directly observe others' interactions with the game. Real time shared access requires game designers to develop new techniques to help foster mutual awareness, where players have an up-to-date understanding of others' game actions [4]. The information needed to support awareness is dependent upon the interactions needed to play and succeed (e.g., information about who, what, where, and when) [6].

Past work on designing awareness support for groupware and for networked video games provides useful insights into how coordination support can be added to real-time shared games (e.g. [7,11,14,15]). Most commercial multiplayer games provide mechanisms for maintaining awareness of other players, and several real-time strategy games use customized interface widgets designed to help team members coordinate their actions. For example, RTSs often provide players with radar views, in which colored dots represent teammates' units; players can coordinate attacks against enemies by tracking the movement of their teammates' armies. When a unit is under attack, its representation turns red. This approach encodes several pieces of awareness information: identity of the player, location, and movement and action of units.

Another common approach for coding awareness information in real-time distributed games is to use an embodiment to represent each player [7]. Avatars act as indicators of presence, location, and activity, and are usually designed to look like a character, vehicle, or pointer. For example, most role playing games and first-person shooters use elaborate 3D models to represent each player's character. Avatars almost always provide presence and location information, but often provide additional kinds of awareness, such as a label above the avatar indicating the player's name, animations showing the player's actions, and visual appearance to indicate team, player class, or level. Our implementations embody players using simple telepointers [7] that duplicate each person's local mouse cursor on remote clients, and are augmented with player names and team colors.

4. RTCHESS

Real-Time Chess (Figure 1) is a fast-paced multiplayer game based on the classic board game. Most of the rules of chess still apply (such as the size of the board, the number of pieces, and the types of moves that pieces can make), but two fundamental changes have been made. First, up to 32 players can play the game at once (16 players per side), with any player able to control any of their team's pieces. Second, there are no restrictions on turns, and movement of pieces is limited only by the player's speed in manipulating the interface and the network delay to the server.

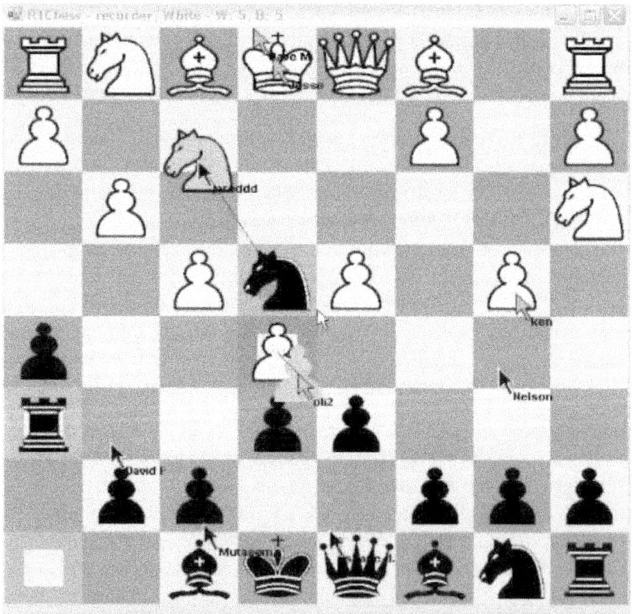

Figure 1. RTChess with 10 players. Players *jareddd* and *oli2* are moving pieces; the black rook has just been moved.

4.1.1 How RTChess is played

Players join the game by starting the RTChess client and connecting to a server, and then choosing a team (White or Black) and a nickname. They then see a standard visual chessboard on which the game is played (Figure 1). Each of the players is represented with a telepointer that shows the player's name and team. To move a piece, a player drags the piece to a new square using the mouse. Since a player's move may not succeed (e.g., it may be illegal, or in conflict with another piece), the original piece does not change position; instead, the user drags a grey 'ghost piece' to the new square. When the piece is dropped, the client requests the move from the server (where the master game state is stored). If the move is legal, and if no other piece of the same colour is on the square, the move succeeds and is broadcast to all clients; at this point, the original piece also moves to the new square (Figure 2). If an opponent's piece is in the square, the piece is taken, as in normal chess. A game ends when one of the kings is taken by an opposing piece; after a pause of a few seconds, a new game starts automatically and play starts again.

Figure 2. Move showing telepointer, ghost piece, successful move, and location highlights

4.1.2 Architecture and concurrency control

RTChess is a client-server groupware system built in C# using the GT toolkit. The server acts as both the message-passing hub, and as the holder and arbiter of the game state. There are two types of communication in the game – move information and awareness information – and these are handled in different ways. Moves in the game require concurrency control, and we use a simple first-come-first-served locking strategy. When a player moves a piece on their local client's board, the move is sent to the server as a request. If the move is legal, it is accepted; the server updates its game state and broadcasts the move to all clients, who then update their displays. Awareness messages – telepointer positions and ghost-piece locations – do not require locking since they involve no game dependencies. These messages are not checked at the server but are simply forwarded to all clients.

4.1.3 Issues arising from removal of turn-taking

Changing from a turn-based to a real-time organization of game play leads to a number of issues that do not arise in normal chess.

The importance of awareness information. The real-time nature of the game means that people need up-to-date information about where others are located and where they are moving. Telepointers and ghost pieces provide this information. Since the game is mouse-based, broadcasting cursor locations provides others with enough awareness to be able to keep track of the game and attempt to anticipate others' actions. Ghost pieces are equally important: since moves are official only when the server grants the request, we needed a way to provide feedback to both the local user (who needs to know where they are moving) and to others (who want to anticipate the move with their own actions). The ghost pieces and the lines connecting them with their counterparts (see Figure 1) are feedthrough mechanisms [2] that provide information about player intentions. As we describe below, players can also learn to manipulate this mechanism in order to fool others into thinking that they are going to move to a certain square.

What to do about multiple-square moves. The discrete turn-based structure of ordinary chess means that pieces essentially move instantaneously. In RTChess, there are no turns, so we had to decide what to do about long-distance moves. There are several possibilities, and we have built prototypes to test each approach. The first approach ('running') uses the metaphor of moving across the board to get to a destination. In this version, long moves are decomposed into a sequence of single-square moves, which are sent in sequence to the server (the exception is the knight, which retains its jumping ability from normal chess). The second approach ('jumping') allows all pieces to complete their entire move in one action, and not move through any of the intermediate squares. However, the way must be clear before the move begins. In the study reported below, we used the running approach, with single-square intermediate moves sent to the server every 100ms. The 'running' approach has the advantage for the attacking player that the individual single-square moves can each take an opposing piece – so a long move in the opponent's home area can do considerable damage. However, this strategy also creates opportunities for the opponent, as described next.

In-progress evading and blocking. The small pauses that are introduced by the 'running' approach described above give other players time to react to a move that is in progress, enabling non-traditional interactions that can substantially change the game. For example, Figure 3 shows a king moving out of the way of a queen's long-distance attack as it happens, something that could not happen in normal chess.

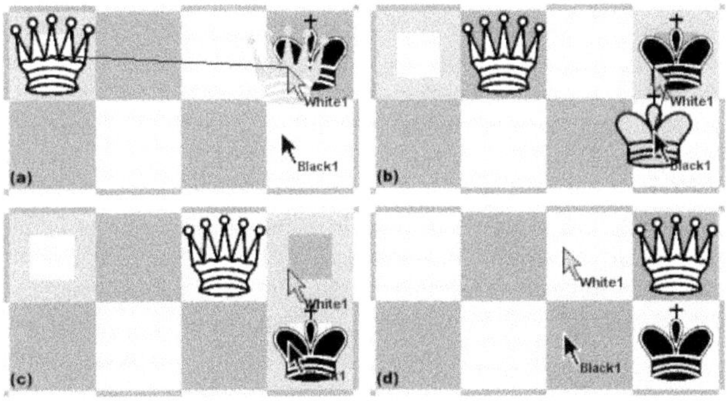

Figure 3. King evades a long-distance queen move.

Other players can also disrupt a long-distance move, if their move request is processed by the server in the middle of the long move. This means that moves can be blocked: for example, a queen moving across the board could be stopped halfway because a pawn has moved into her way (Figure 4); the queen can even be taken by another piece en route (Figure 5).

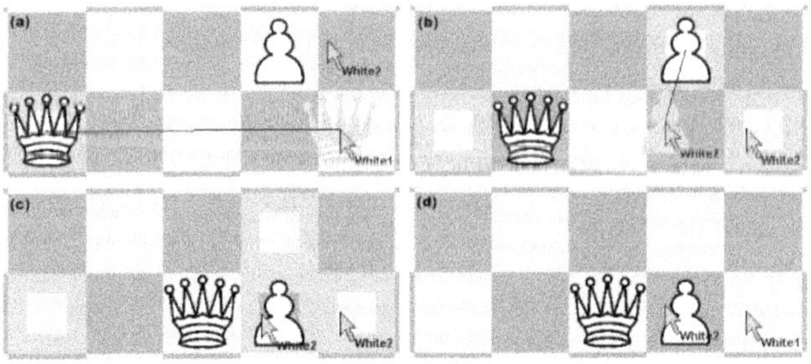

Figure 4. Blocking by friendly pawn

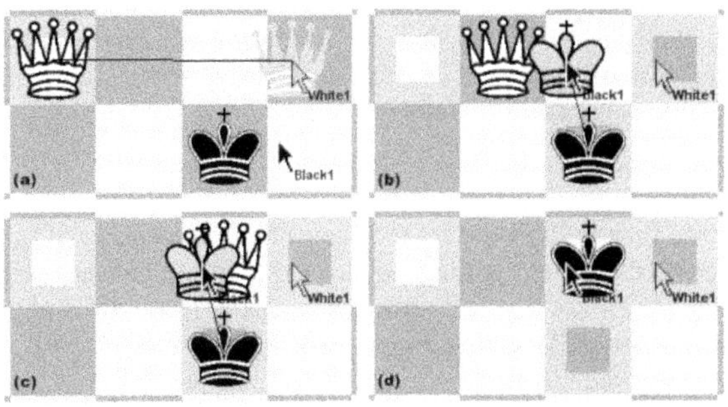

Figure 5. King takes queen during a long-distance move

Check and checkmate. The traditional mechanism for winning a chess game is to create a board state where the King cannot move out of check. In RTChess, where the state of the board changes too quickly for players to easily calculate check positions, we decided to use 'taking the King' instead of checkmate as the winning condition, since it is more definitive. In addition, we removed the notion of check altogether; this was initially done to reduce the number of calculations that the server had to carry out, but players have been happy with the change (and it allows two kings to engage in battle, which is not possible in regular chess). We have also experimented with other win states, such as 'last piece standing,' in which the game continues until there is only one piece left (not necessarily the King).

4.1.4 *RTChess Gameplay and Strategies*

The shift from a two-player 'plan-and-think' game to a multiplayer 'react-and-anticipate' game dramatically changes the gameplay experience in RTChess. In more than a year of playing the game, we have made several observations about general gameplay and the basic strategies that teams have adopted.

The game is fun and fast. RTChess games are extremely short – usually less than 30 seconds – which is vastly shorter than even the fastest variants of tabletop chess (e.g., even Bullet chess takes two minutes). People therefore generally play multiple games in a row: informal game sessions we have observed regularly involve more than 100 games, and we have had sessions with more than 200 games on several occasions. In addition, the game is highly social. Game sessions are accompanied by a great deal of talk, both between team members (planning, encouragement, and commiseration) and across teams (mock trash talk, laughing, congratulations on wins). Players report that the fast-paced nature of the game is one of the reasons for its sociability.

In addition, the response to RTChess from established chess players has been positive. We have had several serious chess players try the game, and their reaction has been uniformly enthusiastic. In particular, they do not seem to mind the fact that we have removed the 'deep thought' aspect of regular chess. One player commented that RTChess is simply at the end of a continuum that includes other time-limited chess variants (e.g., lightning chess, bullet chess) in which moves also happen quickly and where the action is fast-paced and somewhat chaotic.

However, the amount of action in the game can be daunting for new players. When people see the game, they can be slightly overwhelmed by the amount of activity. They then often adapt by focusing on playing a single piece, and are thereby able to ignore some of the activity that is not happening in their immediate area. They then start to take notice of gameplay on the larger area. In addition, teamwork is difficult for new players due to the speed of the game – in the beginning, it is difficult for people to determine what others are doing and what they should do to play as a team member. Teamwork does emerge as players become more familiar with the game, and we have noticed several general strategies and approaches that teams quickly discover (other more specific aspects of teamwork are discussed in detail later).

Offense and defense. One of the first things teams learn is that they need to have players in both offensive and defensive roles. Defense means staying near (or controlling) the king, and taking any piece that is within range to attack. Failure to protect the king usually leads to a quick loss, particularly from the lightning attacks of knights (i.e., the 'knight rush' as described below).

Short-range vs. long-range moves. When there are many players in the game, short-range moves work better than long-range moves. With many people in the space, blocking by one's own teammates is common, reducing the value of long-distance moves, In addition, long-distance moves have two distinct disadvantages: they are easily seen by the other team (because of the long line connecting the ghost piece to the original), and because the series of intermediate moves is locked in after the move is executed. This means that the other team can predict the motion of the long move, and take action against it (e.g., move out of the way or take the piece en route). In contrast, short-range moves reveal less about the player's intentions, and are more difficult to predict.

Usefulness of different pieces. The above problems reduce the value of pieces that traditionally take advantage of long-distance attacks (such as the Queen, Rook, or Bishop). As a result, players have changed their strategies with these pieces to play a short-range game. In addition, Knights become a much more powerful piece, since they are the only piece that can truly move multiple squares at once (and can also jump over other pieces, as in normal chess). Knight movement is also very difficult to predict, making these pieces even more valuable for quick attacks.

Speed attacks. Strategies similar to the 'rush' seen in RTS games like Starcraft have emerged as a successful way to play RTChess. In lightning attacks, players simply move as quickly as possible, trying to overload the other team's ability to perceive or react. For example, a 'knight rush' involves moving the knight as quickly as possible in pursuit of the king, using the harder-to-predict motion of the knight to confuse the other team. Figure 6 shows a four-move knight rush at the start of the game, a strategy that can win many games before the opposing team learns to recognize the rush and devise a suitable defense.

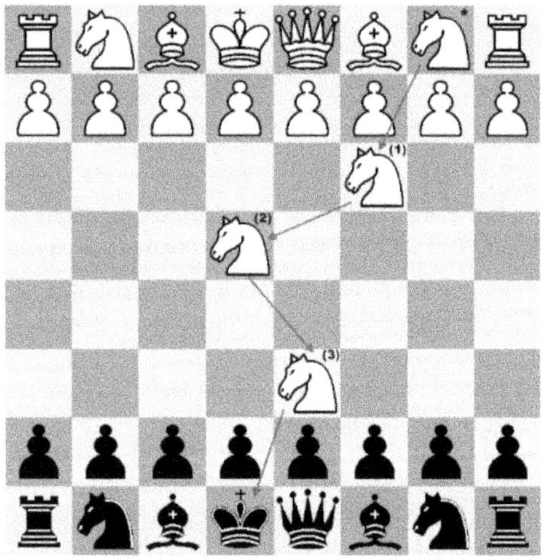

Figure 6. Four-move Knight rush from game start.

Feinting. Ghost pieces are used to indicate a player's intended move – but people can manipulate this visual signal and provide false information to the other team. If a player can make an opponent think that they are moving to a certain square, and trick the opponent into making a move based on the feint, the opponent will often be vulnerable from the very piece that they thought they were attacking. Just as in the real world, people use the available awareness mechanisms to present misleading information, and thereby manipulate other people's predictions of their actions. This occurs frequently in real-time games and sports, but is much less common in online interaction.

Infantry charges and visual distraction. Some teams have tried simple coordinated attacks using several pieces, such as a 'Pawn charge,' in which several players march a line of pawns up the board at high speed. This tactic is visually very obvious, and although it is not always effective in and of itself (e.g., the charge tends to get delayed by the opposing pawn ranks, and knights can simply jump over the attack), it is very useful in drawing the attention of the other team. In a few cases teams have used the mass attack as a distraction to let a knight move in unnoticed.

4.1.5 Network and interface issues

Although we have not played RTChess with large delays, the gameplay is surprisingly resilient to small amounts of lag (e.g., 100-150ms round-trip latency). The fact that delays have not caused major problems, however, may arise from the often-disorganized nature of the gameplay as much as anything else. In games with many people and a great deal of action, it is difficult to keep track of exactly what other people are doing – and without a clear understanding of another person's actions, it is much more difficult to notice the effects of delay. People are more likely to assume that a delay-induced phenomenon (such as trying to take a piece and not succeeding) is simply caused by their own movement error, the server's concurrency policy, or someone else's actions. It is a potentially useful finding that delay is less noticeable when extreme time pressures prevent people from forming good predictive models; however, we also expect that delays will become more obvious and more problematic as teams learn more coordinated strategies (such as those described below).

We have also noticed that players could move even more quickly than they currently do – that is, the main limiting factor on movement speed is the user interface, not the player. The game uses drag-and-drop as the technique for moving a piece, but the repeated click-drag-release action of this kind of interaction is a bottleneck in player actions. In a recent version of the game, we are addressing this limitation by allowing people to first select a piece (by double-clicking) and then move the piece with single clicks, which is considerably faster.

5. COORDINATION STUDY

To look for the emergence and development of expert real-time interaction and coordination, we carried out an observational study in which we watched and recorded two teams playing numerous games of RTChess over five sessions, and analysed the video records to track the development of strategies and behavior.

Four participants, all male, took part in the study. The participants were divided into two teams of two, and the same teams (and color assignments) were used for all play sessions to help increase familiarity with a particular partner. Participants ranged in age from 25 to 35 years (mean 29.7), all were regular computer users (> 10 hours per week), and one reported being a frequent player of real-time multiplayer online games. All of the participants were experienced with RTChess, and all reported being reasonably proficient at the game (> 3 on a 5-point scale).

Five 30-minute play sessions were conducted over the course of three weeks; each session involved two play periods with a short break between. Sessions were videotaped for later analysis, and we also carried out informal interviews with the players at the end of each session to follow up on events seen during the games.

We used a simplified version of RTChess with only four pieces per team (King, Queen, white-square Bishop, and Knight). All other elements of the game were the same as described above.

5.1 Results and Observations

5.1.1 Number, length, and speed of games

A total of 448 games were played overall (94, 89, 74, 93, and 89 games in the five sessions). The average game length was 14.3 seconds (s.d. 11.1 seconds); the longest game took 89 seconds and the shortest took two seconds.

On average, there was a move made every 0.7 seconds (1.55 moves/second for the black team and 1.3 moves/second for the white team). In a game with the average length of 14 seconds, this means that there are about 20 moves made by each team.

The black team won more games in four of the five sessions. As shown in Figure 7, Black showed a clear advantage after the first session, although White was improving over time, and the two teams were essentially even in the final session.

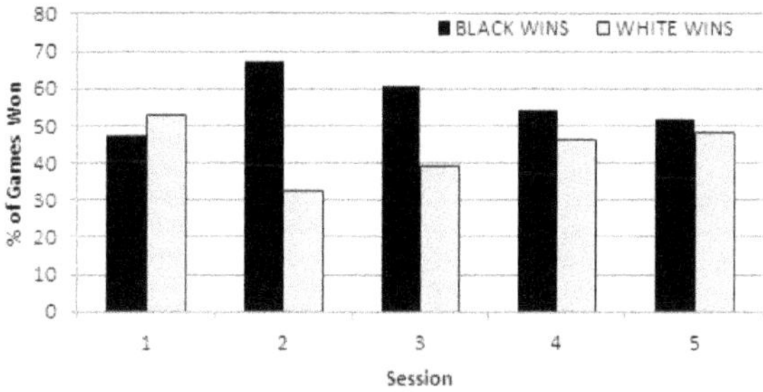

Figure 7. Win rates for the two teams over five sessions.

5.1.2 General observations on gameplay

The general approach for both teams was for each player to take a piece at the start of a game and control that piece until it was captured, and then find another piece to play. Teams most often divided into offense and defense, with one player controlling the king and taking a defensive role, and one taking a different piece in an attacking role. As seen below, however, the king was often played in support of the other person's attacks.

The 'endgame' for many of the games involved two-on-one situations in which three of the four pieces for one team had been captured. If there was no piece left for a player to select, they were idle until the end of the game (but their telepointer was still active on the board, which was occasionally important as discussed below). In these endgames, the single player was forced to play their King, and the other team had to opportunity to carry out joint attacks on the isolated opponent.

It was also clear that individual players increased their mechanical abilities with the game over the course of the five sessions. For example, in the first sessions, players did not use their cursors to gesture, but by the end of the study, two players were regularly able to do this without losing control of their current piece. Similarly, player Black1 showed increasing skill in that he learned to control two pieces at once (he would move each in turn, keeping the two pieces close together). This allowed him to have two pieces nearby for different attacks, but required increased skill with the interface (and the ability to monitor both pieces simultaneously). Once the other players saw that this strategy was useful for Black1, they started doing it as well, and by the end of the sessions, each player was able to control two pieces.

5.1.3 Operating distance between partners

One measure of whether teams are coordinating with one another is the distance between their pieces on the board – if people are nearby, there is more likelihood that they are able to act in a coordinated fashion (particularly given the tendency towards short-range moves as described above). The study system recorded all piece positions and calculated the move-by-move distance between team members. Our distance metric was the discrete Euclidean distance using row/column indices, which measures how many board squares away one player was from the other (the minimum distance is 1.0 and the maximum is 9.89).

Teams did tend to stay close together, but not right beside each other (Figure 8). The average team distance was 3.32 (3.51 for black, 3.12 for white), implying that there were two to three board squares between team members. Our observations suggest that this is approximately as close as people can be to one another without interfering or colliding, in the absence of a pre-arranged set play or coordinated action. If people play too close together, collisions and mistakes are more likely (e.g., both players moving to the same square), often leading to the loss of a piece to the other team. A separation of two to three squares allowed teams to be in the same region, and ready both to help on defense (i.e., the attacking player had to keep an eye on their own king) and to take opportunities that presented themselves, but was not so close as to lead to errors.

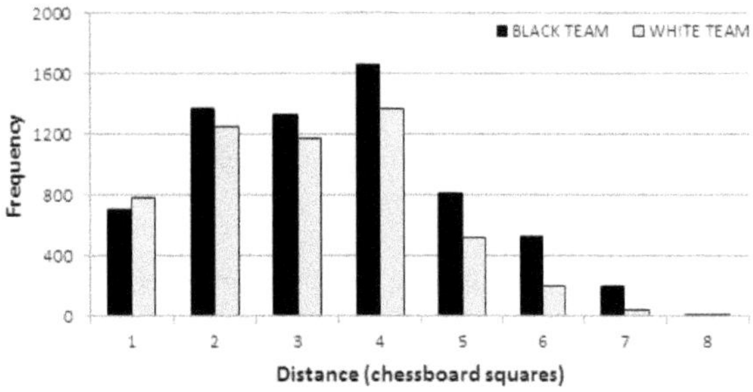

Figure 8. Team distances.

5.1.4 High-speed interaction with opponents

We observed several instances where players were interacting with others at high speed. There were different kinds of interactions with opponents and team partners. With opponents, the main types were feinting and perceptual interference.

5.1.4.1 Feinting and deception

One of the main ways in which people interacted with their opponents at high speed was through deception. As described above, players used the feedthrough provided by ghost pieces as a way to try and deceive opponents into making certain predictions about the player's intentions. For example, a player would show a ghost piece over a board square, so that the opponent would believe that they were in the process of moving there. If the opponent took the 'bait', they would move to the same square themselves, thinking that they would be able to take the player's piece, but would then become easy prey for the player.

As players became more familiar with the basic tactic, there could be double and triple feints as each tried to deceive the other as to their true intentions. These fakes and feints occurred at high speed – on several occasions we saw two or three movements of the ghost piece per second. This is a situation where most of the action is deception, and the actual action (i.e., the eventual attack) is of very short duration – but the timing of that event must be managed with extreme precision.

5.1.4.2 Perceptual interference

The speed of RTChess means that it is difficult for people to take in and process all of the information needed to make good decisions. As already mentioned, some teams used strategies designed to increase their opponents' perceptual and cognitive load; we also saw this behavior in the observational study.

5.1.5 Some of the team strategies described below incorporate this behavior (e.g., the lure-and-trap play), but we also saw it in other instances. For example, when games reached a two-on-one endgame, one player would be left without a piece – their telepointer was still visible on the screen, but there was no available piece for them to select. On several occasions, we saw player White2 attempt to help their partner by moving their mouse over the black king in an attempt to distract their opponent. This was a clear indication that even without a role to play in the game, the players believed that adding to the visual clutter on the board would make the game more difficult for their opponent. High-speed interaction with teammate

We observed several episodes that clearly showed high-speed coordinated interaction between team members. In the paragraphs below, we look at situations where teams used awareness, opportunism, coordinated movement, and pre-arranged plays.

5.1.5.1 Awareness

Team members maintained an awareness of each other's actions, and used this awareness to coordinate movement on the board. For example, in one situation the white team players were moving close to each other and they were about to move to the same square. White1 was moving the King and White2 was moving the Knight. White1 saw the ghost piece of their partner and realized that they were trying to move to the same square, so White1 moved away from that square in order to avoid a collision. It is useful to contrast this episode with the feinting behavior discussed earlier – player White1 was able to use the awareness information to make predictions about their partner's movement, because they could be sure that the ghost piece was providing them true information about intentions.

Players also regularly provided additional awareness information to one another through speech. Comments were generally short and direct (e.g., "don't move there," or "I'll take the Queen"); as player Black2 commented, "brief and quick messages because these are easy to process, and we can send them frequently, if necessary." However, when one player did not have a piece to move, they would provide more detailed comments or directions.

We saw numerous episodes of this kind of low-level coordination, both on its own during simple movement on the board, and also in the more complex types of coordination considered below.

5.1.5.2 Opportunism

Part of the reason that players stayed near to one another on the board was to take advantage of opportunities that arose as a consequence of their partner's actions. This is a simple form of loosely-coupled coordination – each player is able to act autonomously, but maintains an awareness of the other person's situation, and can exploit the situation when an opportunity arises. For example, player Black1 said that when they saw an opponent chasing after Black2, they would look for a way to attack the chaser, knowing that the opponent was focused on the partner and might not see their attack.

Another situation occurred in which player White2 saw that their partner was in a one-on-one battle with the black King. White2 realized that the black King would be busy with White1, so they advanced from behind and successfully attacked the king. Such behavior shows that players try to take advantage of chances created by their partners and that they use visual information about their partners to organize their strategy.

5.1.5.3 *Coordinated movement*

The Black team demonstrated on several occasions the ability to chase a white player in a coordinated fashion. They both moved in similar directions and then they moved closer together (e.g., Figure 9). To succeed in these chases, they needed to keep track of each other in order to not move to the same square, and they needed to keep scanning for opportunities caused by their partner.

These episodes of coordinated movement required awareness of the partner's actions (where they were moving), the partner's intentions (where they were going to move next), and the overall goal (where they wanted to force the opponent). The chases showed the speed at which the Black players needed to respond to one another's actions (and to the movement of the White player); they were often successful in their chase, moving the white King to a corner of the board and restricting his movement.

5.1.5.4 *Pre-arranged plays*

One of the most coordinated episodes involved a strategy that the black team developed over the course of the sessions. It was used in two-on-one situations – for example, with the white king, the black king, and the black bishop left on the board. The black bishop moves only on the light squares, and as a result the white king stayed on the dark squares to avoid attacks from the bishop. Black's strategy in this situation was to have the black bishop move quickly and repeatedly around the white king (see Figure 9), providing both distraction but also an obvious opportunity for the white king to take the bishop.

Figure 8. Fragment of Black team's coordinated chase.

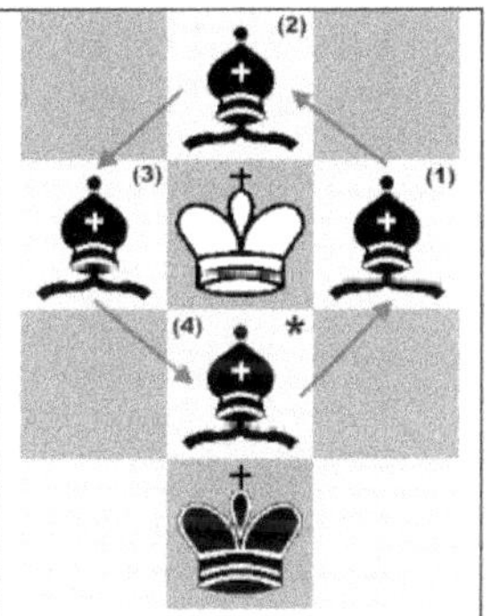

Figure 9. Luring the white king with the black bishop as bait.

The idea was to lure the king into taking the black bishop, at which point the black king would attempt to take the white king. It was clear that the black bishop spent more time within one square of the black king (the location that would be best for the plan to succeed). The verbal exchanges during these situations showed that this was a coordinated plan for Black – at one point Black1 said to Black2 "Ready? Set the trap!"; in addition, they would frequently taunt the White player to try and goad them into taking the bait (i.e., taking the bishop).

5.1.6 *Participant comments and talk*

In discussions after the sessions, participants commented on a variety of topics, including their own performance, the game interface, and their coordination with their partner. Many of the comments mentioned the difficulty of coordinating during the games, due to the high speed of play (similar to earlier results from studies of real-world team sports [3]). For example, White2 stated "No time for verbal communication. No opportunity for strategizing within game. [It was] too hard / too fast to coordinate…" and Black1 said that "during the games there is too much going on to really coordinate [...] the sessions are so fast that there isn't much time to do anything but play."

However, various comments showed that players were thinking about strategy and plans. For example, Black1 stated "[we] changed the plan; this time Black2 took the queen rather than the knight. Seemed to work well throwing off the other team," and Black2 later stated "I suggested small variation to our strategy to compensate for other team's modifications." In addition, some of the players felt that their increasing experience over the sessions helped them to coordinate with their partner: for example, after the final session, White2 said "[in this session] I think I was a bit more aware of White1's movement."

Players also discussed strategy between games, during breaks, and after the session. Between-game talk usually reflected on what just occurred in the last game, and focused on what to change for the next game. When there was more time for talk, players reflected on their general strategy (again, similar to what Eccles et al found with team sports [3]), explaining why they moved in certain ways and how they used the information on the board.

6. DISCUSSION

Our experiences with RTChess provide several new kinds of information for designers of real-time groupware. First, our observations suggest that people can indeed interact at high speed in distributed shared workspaces. Second, our study shows that many kinds of fast interaction and coordination can evolve in RTChess, particularly as people gain more experience with the game and with their playing partners. Third, it is also clear that high-speed and tightly-coordinated joint actions are just as difficult in distributed groupware as they are in the real world. In the following paragraphs, we consider some of our findings in more detail (both about RTChess and about coordination in general) and consider the implications for future work.

How successful was high-speed coordination? There were several indications that fast interaction was possible in RTChess, and that people were able to behave as experts in our distributed groupware system. This shows that groupware's reduction in awareness information (both in terms of fidelity and richness) does not necessarily have to imply that distributed interaction must be slow and awkward. Our results provide clear evidence that real-time groupware can support high-speed coordinated interaction. However, it is important to note that the speed of RTChess itself was a limiting factor on coordination – as seen in player comments, people were often unable to act in a coordinated fashion due to the pace of the game. This means that the groupware system was not the bottleneck in the speed of interaction – RTChess was fast enough that the problem was in the human players rather than in the technology.

Why so little coordinated team play? The observational study showed only a few cases of highly coordinated team actions (i.e., the 'lure and ambush' play). Instead, coordination was primarily seen in loosely-coupled interactions, where players maintained awareness of one another and were able to exploit opportunities when they arose. We believe that this is not so much a limitation of RTChess or real-time groupware, but a limitation of human coordination at high speed. Even in studies of high-performance team (e.g., the French national under-17 basketball team [1]), researchers found that the primary play strategies involved single players acting independently (i.e., one-on-one with a defender) rather than the team acting in a synchronized fashion. We believe that with more practice, RTChess teams will continue to add to their repertoire of 'plays,' something we will explore in future.

Board games as a source of new games. RTChess itself is a novel exercise in adapting a turn-based form of interaction to a real-time arena, and there may be many other games that could be reinvented as real-time multiplayer games. For example, we are currently building systems for board games like checkers and Go; in addition, other genres of games such as dice-based games or card games could also be considered. Real-time versions do not suggest that the original versions of any of these games are somehow lacking – only that adding multiple players, allowing flexible access to the board and the pieces, and removing turns, provides a different and novel game experience.

Removing constraints dramatically changes gameplay. RTChess became substantially different with multiple people and no turns. The main change is that thinking and acting are now time-constrained, and being able to optimize, strategize, and work under pressure is now a fundamental requirement for success. This means that established methods of play, which required large amounts of time for consideration, become less valuable (although the same decision processes are needed, only on a faster timeline). Minor adjustments are often needed to the game rules to accommodate the removal of turns from the game. However, it is difficult to know exactly what the resulting game will be like to play (for example, we did not expect that the Knight would become more valuable than the Queen in RTChess).

Real-time awareness information is vital. The shift to real-time action means that information about what people are doing is critical to effective play, since people must anticipate and predict each other's actions. Our observations showed that both embodiments (i.e., telepointers) and feedthrough (i.e., ghost pieces) were critical as a resource both for coordination between teams, and for prediction and deception against opponents.

7. CONCLUSIONS AND FUTURE WORK

Most real-time groupware systems do not support the fast tightly-coordinated interactions that are common in the real world. In this project, we explored one potential advantage of distributed groupware – the unconstrained movement of the computational workspace – as an opportunity for supporting new forms of high-speed interaction and coordination. The testbed for this work was a new game, RTChess, which enables multi-player high-speed interaction in a chess environment. An observational study showed that groupware can support very high speed interaction, and that despite the inherent difficulties of fast-paced play, people were able to develop coordinated and expert interactions.

Our future work will focus on investigations of the details of what has been uncovered in this first study. We plan to look at certain types of events like feinting in greater detail, and determine the exact timing that is needed for these actions. In addition, we will allow teams to continue playing together for longer periods (including practice sessions), to determine whether continued expertise can be developed in the same ways that it does with organized sports teams. We will also look at the effects of delay on high-speed interaction, and determine the limits at which coordinated play breaks down. Finally, we will explore other types of real-time games including other adaptations from board games as well as soccer-style games that have more fluid movement.

Acknowledgements

This work was supported by NSERC and the GRAND NCE.

8. REFERENCES

1. Bourbousson, J., Poizat, G., Saury, J., Seve, C., Team Coordination in Basketball: Description of the Cognitive Connections Among Teammates, *J. Applied Sport Psychology*, 22, 2, 150-166.
2. Dix, A., Finlay, J., Abowd, G., and Beale, R., *Human-Computer Interaction*, Prentice Hall, 1993.
3. Eccles, D., & Tenenbaum, G., Why an Expert Team is More Than a Team of Experts, *J. Sport & Exercise Psychology*, 26, 4, 2004, 542-559.
4. Eccles, D. The coordination of labour in sports teams, *Int. Review of Sport and Exercise Psych*., 3, 2, 2010, 154 – 170.
5. Entin, E. and Serfaty, D. (1999). Adaptive team coordination. *Human Factors*, 41, 312-325.
6. Gutwin, C. and Greenberg, S., A Framework of Awareness for Small Groups in Shared-Workspace Groupware, *CSCW*, 3-4, 2002, 411-446.
7. Hayne, S., Pendergast, M., and Greenberg, S., Implementing Gesturing with Cursors in Group Support Systems. *JMIS*, 10(3), 1994, 43-62.
8. Hollan, J. and Stornetta, S. 1992. Beyond being there. *Proc. CHI 1992*, 119-125.
9. Malone, T. W. and Crowston, K. 1990. What is coordination theory and how can it help design cooperative work systems?, *Proc. CSCW 1990*, 357-370.
10. Malone, T. W. and Crowston, K. 1994. The interdisciplinary study of coordination. *ACM Comput. Surv*., 26, 1, 87-119.
11. Olson, J., and Teasley, S., Groupware in the wild: lessons learned from a year of virtual collocation. *Proc. CSCW 1996*, 419-427.
12. Pinelle, D., and Gutwin, C., A groupware design framework for loosely coupled workgroups, *Proc. ECSCW 2005*, 65-82.
13. *Real-time vs. turn-based gameplay*, http://en.wikipedia.org/wiki/Real-time_vs._turn-based_gameplay, Jan. 29, 2012.
14. Tatar, D., Lee, J., and Alaloula, N., Playground games: a design strategy for supporting and understanding coordinated activity. *Proc. DIS 2008*, 68-77.
15. Savery, C, Graham, N., and Gutwin, C., The human factors of consistency maintenance in multiplayer computer games, *Proc. Group 2010*, 187-196.
16. Segal, L. *Effects of Checklist Interface on Non-Verbal Crew Communications*, Technical Report 177639, NASA Ames Research Center, 1994.
17. Stuckel, D., and Gutwin, C, The effects of local lag on tightly-coupled interaction in distributed groupware, *Proc. CSCW 2008*, 447-456.

SocialStreamViewer: Guiding the Viewer Experience of Multiple Streams of an Event

Ahmed E. Mostafa[1,2], Kori Inkpen[1], John C. Tang[1], Gina Venolia[1], William A. Hamilton[3]

Microsoft Research[1]
Redmond, WA USA
kori | johntang | ginav
@microsoft.com

University of Calgary[2]
Department of Computer Science
Calgary, AB T3B 2V5 CANADA
aezzelde@ucalgary.ca

Interface Ecology Lab[3]
Texas A&M University
College Station, TX USA
bill@ecologylab.net

ABSTRACT
Live streaming is becoming a popular way to share experiences with others. When concurrent video streams of the same event are available, it can be challenging to decide which streams to view and to manage the experience across multiple streams. We designed and developed the SocialStreamViewer prototype that aggregates multiple streams from an event and visualizes others' viewing, hearting, and text chat activity. It also enables users to replay portions of streams. A lab study of SocialStreamViewer explored how people experience an event remotely through multiple streams, and how they use social signals from other viewers' activities. We found that 1) providing multiple streams is beneficial; 2) replaying back in time is highly valued since it helps ensure that users will not miss interesting content; and 3) visualizing other viewers' activities helps users decide which stream to watch.

Keywords
Live streaming; mobile video; visualization, telepresence.

1. INTRODUCTION
Live streaming enables people to share their experiences with a broad audience. Various live streaming applications are becoming popular [10] and applications such as Periscope (recently acquired by Twitter, http://www.periscope.tv/) allow users to broadcast or watch live streams. Viewers of a broadcast can also engage and interact with a stream by giving hearts or sending chat messages.

It is also becoming more common to see multiple streams that cover a single event, providing different viewpoints of the same event [12]. One challenge of having many streams available is deciding which one to view. Potential factors that affect selecting a stream to view include video and audio quality, view perspective, number of viewers, or how other viewers are interacting with the stream.

We explored how remote people watched and interacted in an event with multiple streams. We wanted to understand how to help them find interesting streams and highlights, and support their viewing experience. We designed and developed SocialStreamViewer to enable them to view multiple streams from an event, be aware of other viewers' interactions in the streams, and also jump back in time for replay. We studied the use of the prototype with a music festival event and gathered feedback on how the participants experienced multiple streams from this event.

We first present some of the related work that inspired this research. Then we describe SocialStreamViewer and its visualization and replay components. We then report on the exploratory study we conducted and how users reacted with some concluding reflections.

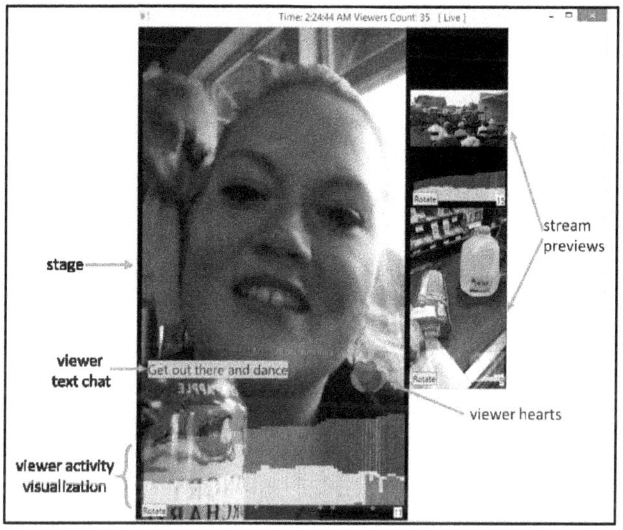

Figure 1. Interface of SocialStreamViewer showing one stream on stage (left) and previews of two streams on the right. Visualizations of the number of viewers (yellow bars), hearts (red bars), and text chats (green dots) are also shown.

2. RELATED WORK
Previous work has focused on improving aspects of the viewing experience of video events with multiple streams. Much research has focused on organizing multiple, user-generated video streams by analyzing their content. Frantzis et al. [3] utilized audio finger printing to organize a collection of concert videos into a synchronized narrative. The neXtreme [11] prototype analyzed what videos people in your social network watched on multiple devices and content sources to create a socially recommended video feed. These approaches integrated information, including social information, from multiple video views to asynchronously create a personalized view of previously uploaded content. Our work focuses on integrating multiple streaming views of live events.

CoStream [2] enabled remote viewers to select among the multiple broadcast streams coming from an event and get a closer connection with the spectators at the event. It also spatially highlighted the area of interest of an event by using the focus of each broadcaster to create a heat-map visualization of their

GROUP '16, November 13 - 16, 2016, Sanibel Island, FL, USA

ACM 978-1-4503-4276-6/16/11...$15.00
DOI: http://dx.doi.org/10.1145/2957276.2957286

collective focus. This work connected viewers with the streamers, but not with the other remote viewers of the same event.

The CoMedia mobile app [7] was designed to encourage active spectatorship among the audience during a large-scale event through posting video, pictures, and text in stories. In the deployments, they observed people not only staying aware of others at the event, but also using it to include remote viewers, giving them a strong sense of the activities in the event. Our work seeks to create a socially interactive live event experience with remote viewers through multiple live video streams.

Venue Explorer [1] allowed viewers to access various feeds of coverage of live events with audio remixing and graphical overlay to augment their viewing experience. Raphael et al. [13] studied how people chose from multiple live videos and other news feeds to remotely follow a live musical festival. They reported on the complexity of navigating across various feeds. For a large scale event that lasted several days, their viewing patterns interleaved with other activities in their daily lives. While our work also aims to support managing multiple streams from the same event, we focus more on the social aspects of how other people's viewing behavior could guide one's viewing experience.

We focused on the awareness of other viewers' behavior to help people find interesting streams or highlights of an event. We also offered jumping back in time to replay previous moments while the live event was still going on. We used a modified live stream viewing client based on [5] and conducted a study of its use.

3. SOCIALSTREAM VIEWER

We designed and developed SocialStreamViewer, a desktop prototype that supports viewing multiple streams of an event that is informed by other viewers' activities in the event (Figure 1). It integrates multiple streams from a streaming client similar to Periscope. Streamers use a mobile phone client to stream live video and audio, and viewers can interact via text messages or giving a "heart", indicating that they like what is happening at the moment by tapping on the screen, both of which are color-coded and float up within the stream to be viewed briefly. Viewers may correlate the color of the hearts with the color of the text messages, just as in the Periscope interface. We started with a desktop prototype to afford the screen space to see multiple streams and the activity visualization overlaid on them. SocialStreamViewer provides previews of available streams in a panel on the right which is continually updated as streams come and go. Viewers can double-click on a stream preview to select it and move it onto the stage, which enlarges the video and plays the associated audio. Users can change which stream is active on the stage at any time. The design readily scales up to show six concurrent views by adding a second column of previews, which is consistent with what we have observed in practice in Periscope live streaming. The data sample we used in our study had a maximum of three concurrent views (as detailed in the Study Section).

Like the Rivulet prototype [5], SocialStreamViewer goes beyond the Periscope viewing interface, which only displays a single video stream at a time, to show the collection of streams coming from the same event. SocialStreamViewer goes beyond Rivulet to add a visualization of viewer activity within each stream relative to all the streams from the event, and the ability to jump back in time and replay a portion of a stream, and then catch back up to live. These features are described in detail below.

3.1 Viewer Activity Visualization

Since the users could choose among several views of the same event, we provided visual cues of what streams the other viewers of the event were viewing as a guide to which streams were interesting. The visualization of viewer activity displays three key pieces of information in an activity timeline. First, stacked bars visualize the number of viewers of a stream (yellow bars) relative to the total number of viewers across all streams of the event (grey bars). A new bar is generated for every second, and the history over the last minute of viewing is shown to give a sense of how the data trended over time. This visualization provides a sense of what proportion of viewers of the overall event are watching each stream and how that has trended recently.

Secondly, awareness of any viewers who are giving "hearts" to the stream is visualized by rendering that portion of the bar red (as a proportion of all viewers). Note that while the heart interface allows users to repeatedly give hearts, as is common in Periscope, we chose to visualize the proportion of viewers who are giving hearts for each second, rather than the total number of hearts. We believe this a more meaningful social signal of how interesting a stream is to the collection of viewers. Thirdly, sending a chat message is shown as a green dot on the timeline.

Figure 2. Viewer activity visualization shows the number of viewers of the stream (yellow) as a proportion of all viewers of the event (grey) per second as well as viewers giving hearts (red), and text chat (green dots) over time.

While prior research explored the idea of visualizing highlights through viewer activity overlaid on video streams [6],[9] our approach visualizes viewers' live engagement, without depending on pre-defined tags, and is context independent. Our work focuses on social cues to highlight interesting moments in live events, by representing how viewers come and go, give hearts, or send text comments as an indicator of their engagement with the live stream. Our visualization also goes beyond the Periscope display of the number of viewers currently watching to show the near-history of people joining or leaving. We think the trending of number of viewers of a stream is also a social signal that can highlight which streams are getting viewer attention. This can be especially helpful when viewing a collection of streams coming from the same event, to help viewers decide which view of the event is most promising.

3.2 Replay & Catchup to Live

Enabling switching among multiple live streams means that by the time users notice that something interesting is happening in another stream and switch to it, they may have already missed the event of interest. SocialStreamViewer provides the ability to replay a portion of a stream and then accelerate playback to eventually catch back up to real time, similar to the AIR System for live videoconference meetings [8]. A replay was initiated by a right-mouse click on the timeline to jump to that point in time (Figure 3). Users could jump back in time anywhere within the past minute of near-history shown in the activity visualization. All other streams being previewed also jumped to that point in time to remain temporally in sync with the stream being viewed. Pressing the escape key sped up the replay to scan forward to catch up to live.

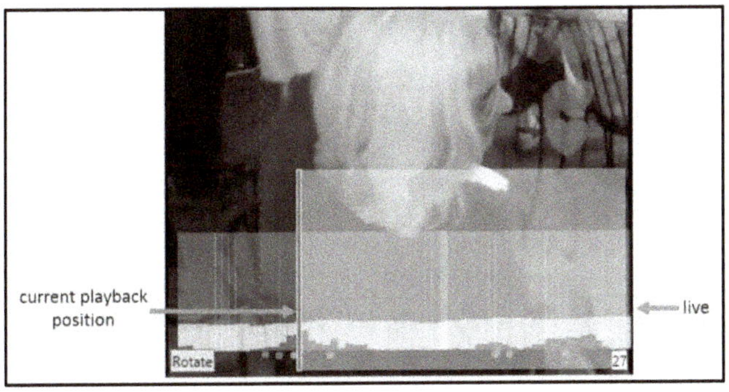

Figure 3. Right-mouse clicking on the timeline moved the playback position to an earlier time for replay. Pressing the escape key scans forward in the stream to catch up to live.

4. STUDY

We conducted an exploratory lab study of SocialStreamViewer to observe how people would use multiple live streams when experiencing an event. The goals of this study were to explore: 1) how people choose which streams to view and how much they utilize multiple streams; 2) how visualizations of other viewers' activities affect their viewing behavior; and 3) whether people would want the ability to replay a portion of the live event. The goal of this preliminary study was to get early user feedback on the features to guide the design of future prototypes for viewing events.

4.1 Study Design & Procedure

We recruited 8 adult participants (4 M / 4 F): half younger than 30, 1 in 30s, and 3 in 40s. These demographics reflect the younger, consumer users of Periscope. Users were recruited through a social networking convenience sample within our company. We used a within-subject design with two experimental conditions: control and enhanced. Both conditions allowed users to experience the event through multiple streams with all the text messages and hearts sent by other viewers of the event. The control condition was a version of the prototype that allowed selecting to view among multiple streams from the same event, but viewing a stream was otherwise similar to viewing a stream in Periscope. The enhanced condition added the viewer activity visualization and the ability to replay portions of a live stream. The study focused on how adding the activity visualization and replay features affected the user's viewing behavior in switching among the streams. Two 7-minute clips of the jazz festival were selected to experience the two conditions. Clip order and condition order were counterbalanced.

For each condition, participants were given a demo of the system and asked to experience the jazz festival for 7-minutes, followed by a survey rating each system feature. A post-study interview was also administered. User actions were also logged by the system which included stream selection, and when replay and/or catch-up to real time was initiated.

To ensure that all participants experienced a consistent set of live streams, we pre-recorded four synchronized live streams (along with all the viewer activity in them) from a local jazz music festival using an instrumented streaming prototype system [5]. During the study, participants were free to choose among the pre-recorded streams to simulate interacting with a live event.

4.2 Key Findings

Analysis of the surveys, interviews, and data logs revealed how people used multiple live streams to experience an event and provided feedback on what impact the viewer activity visualization and the replay features had on users' experience.

4.2.1 Multi-Stream Viewing

All participants actively utilized multiple streams when experiencing the jazz festival. On average, users switched among streams 30 times throughout the 14 minutes of viewing time (min 10, max 46). All participants reported that they liked having multiple streams to choose from (5 "strongly agree" and 3 "agree" on a five-point Likert scale). Many participants also commented that this was a more natural way of experiencing an event, such as P6f (Participant 6, female) who commented, "*I liked it... I think it was cool... it sort of simulates the festival experience ... when you can sort of walk up, watch something for a while, or hang out when you feel you get bored etc.*"

Participants also felt that this experience would be valuable for other types of events such as sporting events, concerts, parades, or visiting popular tourist spots. P2m expressed, "*I travel for work a lot and my kids are playing football ... If I could see 10 or 15 views of his game and if I could choose which one [to view and interact with] that would be really cool*".

4.2.2 Stream Selection

Most participants mentioned that the content of the video (as seen in the stream previews) was the primary cue used to select which stream to view, but for many, the viewer activity visualization provided secondary information to help them decide which stream to watch. P6f commented: "*At the beginning, I kind of looked at all of them to figure out which one has the music I like... And then I would keep an eye on the other ones and if it looked like something was going on; if they were increasing the viewers a lot or if they had a bunch of hearts, I would click over there and see what is happening. If it is interesting I would stay otherwise I would go back to the stream I was watching before.*"

For a few participants the viewer activity information was not used much. For example, P4m said: "*I didn't find myself really drawn onto it [the extra info] ... maybe the only thing I did notice is that I paid attention to the green dots more so that I would be more aware of when comments have actually come up and if I missed one or something.*"

The value of the viewer activity information also depended on what was happening in the streams. As P2m reported: "*when there was music playing and the audio was good this pretty much derived which [stream] I picked. If between songs ... then the various visual cues drove me*". Breaks between songs were a natural moment to consider switching to another view, which is when this user considered the visualizations of viewer activity.

Personal interest also affected the viewing experience. For example, those who were interested in jazz music did not want to be distracted by the social interaction in the live stream, preferring the streams with the best audio quality. But others who were more interested in the social aspects of the event wanted to be aware of the viewers' activities, including when they gave hearts or sent chat messages. This is consistent with prior work that observed that stream viewers could be interested either in its content or in the social interaction with the stream and its community [4].

4.2.3 Viewer Activity Visualization

The number of viewers for each stream, as well as the hearts and comments, were visible in the streams in the control condition, but not visualized and summarized over time. Several participants commented that the visualizations in the enhanced condition made this information more accessible and easier to interpret. P6f commented: "*I am pretty visual so that the number of viewers is not something that was helpful, but being able to see the bar going up ... oh ... maybe there is something going on with that video*". P5f said: "*easier to see quickly what is more popular*". It also helped point out sections of streams that participants might want to go back and view, as suggested by P3f: "*the bar can highlight whether there is more comments or more hearts, I guess it pinpoints what to maybe go back and see it if you miss something, cause that may be highlight a good part of the stream that you wouldn't wanna miss and you would go back and view it.*"

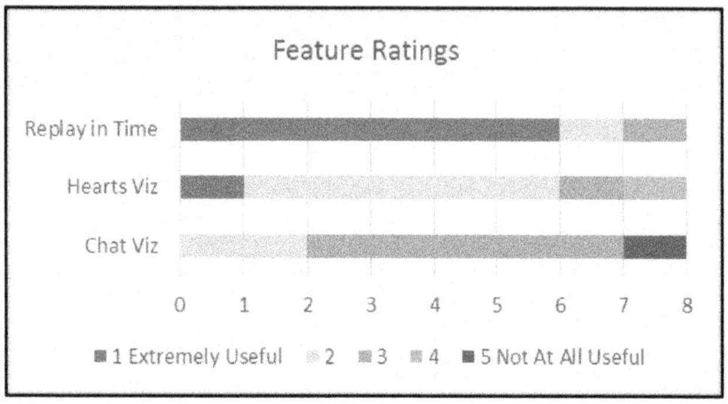

Figure 4. Participants' ratings of enhance prototype features

Figure 4 shows the participants' ratings of the three different features of the prototype, which shows that many participants liked the hearts visualization. Participants commented on how the hearts also offered value in selecting views. P2m said: "*The hearts... showed me what other people liked. The assumption is if other people like something then I may like it as well.*" And P7m: "*The hearts mainly helped me to pick what I would like to [watch].*" We also observed a slight increase in the value of hearts in the enhanced condition, with more participants agreeing that the presence of hearts drew their attention to view a stream (Figure 5). The text chat visualization, on the other hand, was rated to be less useful and sometimes distracting (see Figure 4), especially when many chat messages were shown and continuously covered a portion of the video display.

While the visualizations attracted viewers' attention to select a stream, they could also be perceived as distracting, as P5f commented: "*I was mostly ignoring [the stream with] the grocery store guy, but it seemed to be really popular so I would check back a couple more times just to see if there are so many people watching them and giving them hearts they might be funny or something [but they weren't].*" Four participants preferred enjoying the music without attending to and cognitively processing the visualization on the screen. P2m said, "*The [time] bar was distracting. It was very big; taking up a quarter of the space that the video got.*"

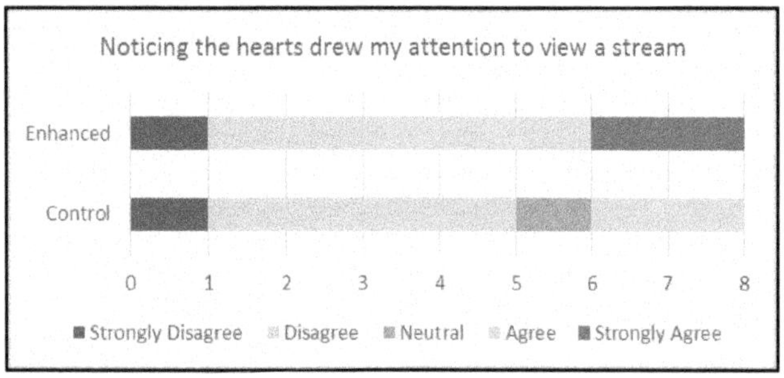

Figure 5. Rating the feature of hearts between conditions

4.2.4 Ability to Replay

The ability to replay parts of a stream was strongly valued by the participants, as shown by the ratings in Figure 4. The ability to replay and catch up to live was one of the main reasons behind preferring the enhanced condition. As P3f expressed "*...primarily because there was the option to go back in time. Just that if you miss something or if you are viewing different stream, you [could] go back to that other stream and see what you missed*". Several others also echoed the value of this feature in the interview, such as P4m: "*I like being able to go back in time because if something cool happened it is nice to be able to rewind it.*" P6f anticipated a particular situation where replay would be useful: *"Any events where people are talking, like a comedy show, and you if you switch stream and missed the joke, you can rewind and listen to it again"*.

5. CONCLUSION & FUTURE WORK

This exploratory study examined how people view multiple streams of an event and what features could support their viewing experience. We designed and developed SocialStreamViewer that enabled viewers to select from among multiple streams of the same event, supported by visualizations that helped them find interesting streams or highlights and a replay feature. The results indicated that people liked replay and that the visualization helped people be more aware of changes that happened in other streams.

While users primarily selected to view streams based on content, they also described how the activity visualization helped them decide what to view. A salient feature of our activity visualization is showing how the number of viewers and their hearting activity changed over the past minute. This visualization of near-history enables viewers to see trends beyond just the activity in the moment. This could explain why viewers were more attentive to hearts in the enhanced condition compared to the control.

Perhaps it was because our prototype grouped streams of the same event together and helped viewers become aware of interesting moments occurring in other streams that the ability to replay became even more appreciated. When watching individual live streams currently in Periscope, there is no awareness of interesting moments that might have been recently missed. Being aware of what was happening in other streams within the context of the same event could make it more important to be able to replay moments in the recent past. None of the users expressed interested in going back further than the past minute offered in the prototype.

Feedback from the study suggested several improvements, including the ability to turn off some of the visualizations depending on the kind of event or their personal interest in the event or the socialization around it. Another possibility would be to hide the visualizations, at least temporarily, depending on what was happening in the event, as illustrated by the comment of only consulting the visualizations when there was a break in the music as a natural time to consider switching to another stream. The color rendering and size of the visualization could also be adjusted to be less distracting.

As an exploratory study of a prototype, our research suggests further work in this area. It might be interesting to explore other attributes to visualize, such as how long viewers have been watching the same stream. Trying the prototype with other events which might exercise different features of the prototype. For example, sporting events may have more episodes where replaying recent moments from a different perspective would be utilized. Scaling up to events with more live feeds and viewers and developing a viewing experience for a mobile device would also be ripe for future exploration. As live streaming continues to gain in popularity, we expect there will be more opportunities for using them to view and participate in events remotely.

6. REFERENCES

[1] Venue Explorer. BBC R&D. 2013. Retrieved July 22, 2015 from http://www.bbc.co.uk/rd/projects/venue-explorer

[2] Dezfuli, N., Sebastian, G., Mohammadreza, K., Max, M., and Jochen, H. 2013. CoStream@ Home: connected live event experiences. In *Proceedings of the 2nd international workshop on Socially-aware multimedia*. 33-36. DOI=http://doi.acm.org/10.1145/2509916.2509927

[3] Frantzis, M., Zsombori, V., Ursu, M., Guimaraes, R. L., Kegel, I., and Craigie, R. 2012. Interactive video stories from user generated content: a school concert use case. In *Proceedings of the 5th international conference on Interactive Storytelling (ICIDS'12)*, David Oyarzun, Federico Peinado, R. Michael Young, Ane Elizalde, and Gonzalo Méndez (Eds.). Springer-Verlag, Berlin, Heidelberg, 183-195. DOI=http://doi.acm.org/10.1007/978-3-642-34851- 8_18

[4] Hamilton, W. A., Garretson, O., and Kerne, A. 2014. Streaming on twitch: fostering participatory communities of play within live mixed media. In *Proceedings of CHI 2014*. ACM, New York, NY, USA, 1315- 1324. DOI=http://doi.acm.org/10.1145/2556288.2557048

[5] Hamilton, W. A., Tang, J., Venolia, G., and Inkpen, K. 2016. Rivulet: Designing for Participation in Live Events through Multi-Stream Experiences, In *Proceedings of TVX 2016*. ACM, New York, NY, USA, 31-42. DOI=http://dx.doi.org/10.1145/2932206.2932211

[6] Huron, S., Isenberg, P., and Fekete, J. D. 2013. PolemicTweet: Video Annotation and Analysis through Tagged Tweets. In *Human-Computer Interaction– INTERACT* 2013. Springer Berlin Heidelberg. 135-152.

[7] Jacucci, G., Oulasvirta, A., Ilmonen, T., Evans, J., Salovaara, A. 2007. CoMedia: Mobile Group Media for Active Spectatorship. In *Proceedings of CHI 2007*. ACM, 1273. DOI=http://doi.acm.org/10.1145/1240624.1240817

[8] Junuzovic, S., Inkpen, K., Hegde, R., Zhang, Z., Tang, J., and Brooks, C. 2011. What did I miss? In-Meeting Review using Multimodal Accelerated Instant Replay (AIR) Conferencing. In *Proceedings of CHI 2011*. 513-522. DOI=http://doi.acm.org/ 10.1145/1978942.1979014

[9] Kim, J., Guo, P. J., Cai, C. J., Li, SW., Gajos, K. Z., and Miller, R. C. 2014. Data-driven interaction techniques for improving navigation of educational videos. In *Proceedings of the 27th annual ACM symposium on User interface software and technology (UIST 2014)*. ACM, New York, NY, USA, 563-572. DOI=http://dx.doi.org/10.1145/2642918.2647389

[10] Kleinberg, S. 2015. Live streaming: The next big thing in social media. *Chicago Tribune*. Retrieved April 1, 2015 from http://www.chicagotribune.com/lifestyles/ct-so-social-livestreaming-meerkat-periscope-20150401-column.html

[11] Martin, R., Santos, A. L., Shafran, M., Holtzman, H., and Montpetit, M. J. 2010. neXtream: a multi-device, social approach to video content consumption. In *Proceedings of the 7th IEEE conference on Consumer communications and networking conference (CCNC 2010)*. IEEE Press, Piscataway, NJ, USA, 779-783.

[12] Tang, J., Venolia, G., and Inkpen, K. 2016. Meerkat and Periscope: I Stream, You Stream, Apps Stream for Live Streams. In *Proceedings of CHI 2016*. 4770-4780. DOI=http://doi.acm.org/10.1145/2858036.2858374

[13] Velt, R., Benford, S., Reeves, S., Evans, M., Glancy, M., and Stenton, P. 2015. Towards an Extended Festival Viewing Experience. In *Proceedings of the ACM International Conference on Interactive Experiences for TV and Online Video (TVX 2015)*. 53-62. DOI=http://doi.acm.org/10.1145/2745197.2745206

Formalization and Accountability in Surgery Planning

Bente Christensen
UIT- the Arctic University of Norway
University Hospital of North Norway
Tromso
+47 948 52 050
Bente.christensen@unn.no

ABSTRACT

Due to poor resource utilization in surgery performance, there is increasing interest in applying workflow systems. Notably, due to their ability to "steer" the execution of the process toward an intended goal, according to an arrangement of things, data and resources compliant with "best practice", the systems are supposed to improve surgery planning and, hence, resource utilization. This study reports from a large-scale Electronic Patient Record development project, which also included workflow support in a surgery planning module. By applying an understanding of workflow systems and their ordering and coordinative mechanisms, this study investigates the effect of such systems on interdisciplinary work in surgery planning. The study shows that interdisciplinary work is affected by workflow systems in the way that the systems can "order" responsibility and sequential dependency of tasks. The collective responsibility was affected by the sequential ordering and user role constraints inherent to the system. Moreover, there was a clear redistribution of tasks as a consequence of the formalization and the accountability mechanism.

Keywords

Surgery planning; workflow systems; interdisciplinary work; electronic patient record

1. INTRODUCTION

In hospitals, the effective utilization of surgery facilities – due to the implicated costs of planning and performing surgeries – is crucial. However, many hospitals do not exploit their resources due to unforeseen cancellations. For instance, the proportion of elective surgeries cancelled on the day of surgery ranges from 10% to 17% across Norway, the United States, New Zealand, Great Britain and South Africa [2]. A Danish study showed that 67% of pre-scheduled operations were changed on the day of surgery [5].

Modern Electronic Patient Records (EPRs) are supposed to improve surgery performance [8, 32], particularly through specialized modules for surgery planning.

GROUP '16, November 13-16, 2016, Sanibel Island, FL, USA
© 2016 ACM. ISBN 978-1-4503-4276-6/16/11...$15.00
DOI: http://dx.doi.org/10.1145/2957276.2957309

The EPR is meant to ensure more predictability and a more efficient utilization of resources, as well as providing the patients with treatment according to best practice guidelines. This is expected as a result of the EPRs' ability to support and promote efficient standardized patient pathways in the surgery planning process. To fulfill these expectations, built-in decision support, structured information and workflow support are necessary capacities for the EPR. Hence, an important strategy to cope with this problem is to ask the "next generation" of Electronic Patient Records (EPR) to have inherent cooperation and coordination abilities, by offering workflow support for clinical work. Such computer-based systems can be used to "steer" the execution of the process toward an intended goal according to an arrangement of things, data and resources, compliant with "best practice". However, the "steering" of the process by workflow technology also means standardizing practice, which has been shown to be a difficult road [20, 43].

Health care has always been made up of multidisciplinary services. Still, medical knowledge is becoming more and more sub-specialized, leading to more, and smaller, units in ever larger organizations. At the same time, demographic changes like a rise in chronic diseases and increasing numbers of elderly people with co-morbidity put pressure on services from multiple providers. A higher turnover of patients also calls for better coordination of and cooperation between services. Hence, care is more often re-organized into clinical pathways, stretching across departments, hospitals and also primary care services. In line with this trend, surgery, as part of the clinical pathways, is a core medical practice that must be planned, coordinated, accounted for and accomplished through artefacts. It requires the coordination of series of acts distributed among physicians, nurses and secretaries, across geographical locations and organizational units, and which are temporally distributed and across different artefacts.

Dourish [19] has noted that workflow technologies incorporate two related functions: coordination and accountability. A handful of CSCW oriented studies on health ICT build on this insight, and have drawn attention to the accountability function of EPR, suggesting that the accountability function might impinge on the coordinating function [10–12, 30]. Even so, workflow technologies are spreading and according to Dourish, it is because of their function as an "Organizational accounting device – whereby the multifarious activities can be regularized, regimented and organized for inspection" [19]. In our case, the motivation for introducing workflow systems in surgery planning is clearly to be able to regiment and steer the process. However, this paper takes an intra-organizational perspective, where accountability for actions may facilitate coordination by rendering responsibility for these actions visible to cooperating professionals. The contribution is thus to show that accountability comes from the formalization of responsibility, which workflow systems force by assigning tasks to user roles. The case-study describes how this plays out in the multidisciplinary work of surgery planning.

This paper reports from a large-scale EPR project initiated in 2011 by the North Norwegian Regional Health Authority. A key aim of this project was to standardize treatment within the region according to national guidelines, by implementing clinical pathways as workflow templates. Due to poor resource utilization in surgery, the project started out by developing a surgery planning module of the EPR, replacing the one that had been used since 2005. The ambitions were to offer process support for surgery planning, in terms of: a modelled workflow; an overview of available resources and time slots; access to clinical data embedded in the EPR; and integration with other systems holding information necessary to the planning process. This paper poses the research question: *How is multidisciplinary cooperation in surgery planning affected by the formalization of roles and the accountability imposed by the introduction of a workflow system?* This paper contributes by exploring empirically how the emergence of a surgery planning tool, with its linear logic and formalization of work, affected the informal coordination and communication in the interlinked multi-professional activities that went into the surgery planning. By conceptualizing workflow systems as ordering systems, we can analyze how the ordering of tasks and roles may affect the work. This theoretical frame is applied to a longitudinal case study of the development process, and the testing and piloting of a surgery planning module within the EPR. The author has also observed how surgery planning is conducted by health care personnel. The paper is organized so that initially, the planning module is conceptualized in terms of its supportive, ordering, coordinative and accountancy abilities for the process. Next, a research method is presented, followed by the case. The discussion and a concluding remark will follow.

2. RELATED WORK

Cancellations of planned surgeries and hence, poor resource utilization, is a major problem for hospitals [16, 26] Additionally, missing pieces of information such as incomplete findings in the assessment requirements, incomplete lists of medication, incorrect indications and insufficient documentation, and missing signatures for decisions taken prior to surgery are all defined as a potential risks for patient outcome[29]. Workflow support for better planning processes and documentation is increasingly being pointed to as necessary to improve surgery planning flow [16, 31].

2.1 Workflow systems

Workflow systems of various kinds have been around for decades, especially within office and business related domains. They have emerged as a solution to the problem of coordinating events, artefacts, and people [23]. The development of workflow technology has been an important part of the research endeavor within the field of computer-supported cooperative work (CSCW) [14, 18]. Workflow systems for the coordination of activities in organizations have been subject to much controversy and criticism for their rigid representation of work in process models [14, 25, 38, 45]. A process model is typically understood as a computerized (i.e. formal) representation of work procedures, which controls the order in which a sequence of tasks are to be performed and by whom. A potential danger with workflow systems is that their design is dictated entirely by formal procedures ignoring (and even damaging) the informal practice [41]...Hence, much of the research on workflow systems in CSCW has been directed towards the design of systems allowing flexibility [1, 3, 15, 18].

Within the field of CSCW, several studies have noted the dynamic, contingent, and complex features of health care, as well as the multiplicity of coordinative artefacts and technologies needed to accomplish work [4, 17, 21], defying the standardization and inscription of workflow. Nevertheless, workflow technology has been introduced to support different phases or activities of the healthcare process [3].

Clinical work is subject to a large degree of planning, and the presentation of plans as part of the work, and these plans play an important role in guiding and recording work at a hospital. Clinical protocols and clinical pathway templates are examples of representations of work [9]. They are essential coordination mechanisms, which convey information to the involved staff about the nature of the illness and how the treatment should proceed. Without such plans, extensive communication has to take place in order to inform all involved personnel about the patient, his illness and what activities that have already taken place, and which should take place in the future. Thus, plans as prescriptions of activity are valuable, even vital, within organizations like hospitals to carry out work.

Embedded in the EPR, care plans become presentations of work in the form of process models inscribing workflow [6]. Notably, when referred to in healthcare, workflow systems are characterized as *process-supportive*, indicating that they will not impose a given workflow in terms of controlling the order and sequence that tasks should be performed: "process-support related to health care may be described as « support for planning, coordination and execution of actions directed towards patients in diagnosing, treatment and care" [7]. Nevertheless, a process is seen as an articulated sequence of activities that business modelers have preliminarily defined in terms of a network of temporal or causal dependencies, interconnected control structures and task abstractions. Such models are usually described and specified with standard notations that have recently gained increased diffusion, probably due to their promises of seamless interoperability and process automation [28].

2.1.1 Workflow systems as ordering and coordinating devices

The approach adopted by workflow systems attempts to reduce the complexity of coordination in three basic steps [23]. First, the work to be done is reduced to a basic form through a process of categorization. The categorization breaks up work into elements such as activities, documents, and user roles. Secondly, when categorized, relations among the different components of work can be formally defined. Sequences or dependencies can be precisely described by the use of a formalism that defines the relations among specified components. Finally, workflow systems may use the formalism to automate some aspects of the work entirely (ibid). Thus, a workflow system may be conceptualized as an "ordering system" in which cooperation is achieved through clusters or complexes of interrelated practices and artefacts [13, 35]. The diverse, specialized artifacts address specific issues and concerns, representing different 'local' principles of ordering (ibid). For example, in surgery planning, a multitude of artefacts, classification systems, and practices collectively enable the performance of surgery. Ordering systems can also be described by their coordination mechanism: "Coordination mechanism is a specific organizational construct, consisting of a coordinative protocol imprinted upon a distinct artifact, which, in the context of a certain cooperative work arrangement, stipulates and mediates the articulation of cooperative work so as to reduce the complexity of articulation work of that arrangement" [34]. Typically, ordering systems concatenate and configure items in certain spatial-graphical ways. Embedding representations of work, they enable coordination by being resources of action [40], more or less constraining the actions of users. Schmidt [33] elaborates on this, arguing that such presentations may have different characteristics. As plans, they may have the characteristics of maps that support orientation and overview – for instance, 'to-do' lists. As scripts, they provide guidelines for how to proceed – for instance, a sequenced check-list. Inscriptions may vary in how strongly they enforce and control particular acts [24].

2.1.2 *Accountability*

The inscribed models in workflow systems characterize cooperative work in terms of a "processable" flow of resources, information and responsibility handovers that occur between well-circumscribed units of work, tasks or activities [28]. Moreover, the actor who is supposed to interpret, react and produce this information flow is characterized in terms of roles that define the capabilities and constraints of classes of actors who are supposed to operate within an activity [15]. Hence, the concept of role is inextricably connected to task ownership, task responsibility and to the concept of accountability regarding the actions performed. Ordering systems thus inherently have dual roles as coordination devices and accountability systems [12]. According to Dourish [19], it is accountability that makes workflow systems successful, despite critiques of how the embedded models of work may constrain work practice. Suchman [38] and Bowers [14] argue that "technologies of accountability" need to be understood organizationally and intra-organizationally, Eriksen [22] encourages the question "accountability - for whom?" From an intra-organizational understanding, even if accountability constrains classes of actors, it also thereby enables cooperation, by visualizing who is responsible for decisions and tasks in the work process. Accountability, in the sense of taking responsibility for actions and decisions by use of access-control mechanisms, thus may work as a coordination device. From an organizational understanding, accountability comes from the way the embedded models of work render the work regularized, regimented and organized for inspection. That is to say, at its most fundamental level, accountability does not simply describe the activity, but renders it observable and reportable as being the very activity that surgery planning is all about.

3. METHOD

3.1 Research site

Following an invitation for tender, the Northern Norway Regional Health Authority decided in 2011 to invest in new clinical ICT systems for all of the 11 hospitals in North Norway. The project BigInvestment was established with a budget of EUR 90m for the period 2012-2016, making it one of the most ambitious healthcare-related ICT projects currently under way in Norway. A key aim of this project was to standardize treatment and workflow in the region according to national guidelines and establish "best practice" by embedding clinical pathways as process models in the EPR. Due to the prevalence of wasted resources in the 11 hospitals' surgery performance, the development of a process supportive surgery planning module was a priority for BigInvestment. According to the Scandinavian tradition of user participation [37], physicians, secretaries and nurses were gathered with developers from the vendor to design the new planning tool. They met regularly, from February 2012 on. Initially, health care personnel from all the 11 hospitals in the region participated. According to the agile development methods that the vendor applied, the users in the workshops were supposed to formulate user-stories that the developers could turn into back-logs for developing functionality. However, this did not turn out to be successful [36]. The user stories were too divergent, and only worked as base to develop functionality that supported specific tasks, not the overall work processes. Thus, a shift in the development strategy towards extended work processes was decided, and the participation of users was concentrated on personnel from the University Hospital. The hospital had, for years, applied Lean methodology [42] to redesign work processes. Lean is a quality improvement philosophy and set of principles originated by the Toyota Motor Company. According to Teich and Faddoul[38], it aims to identify and eliminate bottlenecks and various forms of "waste" in key processes such as patient pathways. The essence of Lean is to take non-standard work processes and transform them into standard processes by mapping and redesigning work processes. Hence, the clinical personnel coming from the University Hospital that were set to participate in the design of the upcoming EPR already had experience in picturing and analyzing their work processes following Lean methodology. This ongoing process of standardizing clinical work was identified as a source of knowledge for modelling work processes in the surgery planning module.

3.2 Data collection

In accordance with interpretive methods [27, 44], the empirical data were collected from February 2012 to November 2015, primarily through intensive participatory observations. This spanned from observing healthcare personnel and developers at work to participation in workshops between the vendor and users in the design of the new EPR system, alongside module testing and participating in project meetings. There have been 440 hours of observation. Field notes from these observations fill three notebooks, each with 160 pages of A4 size. Moreover, the author has conducted 22 semi-structured interviews with project developers, clinicians and project managers involved, each lasting 45-90 minutes. In accordance with hermeneutic interviews, the semi structured interviews had much of the character of dialogues, where the theme brought up was jointly explored and led to the following theme. Basically, this meant that the interview guide was used as a checklist to ensure the questions of interest were touched upon. A digital voice recorder was used in the interviews. Finally, a document study on project documents and national strategies for ICT in health care has been ongoing throughout the research period.

3.3 Data analysis

The analysis of the data is based on a hermeneutic approach, where a complex whole is understood "from preconceptions about the meanings of its parts and their inter-relationships" [27]. This implies that all the different sources of data were taken into consideration in an iterative interpretation process. The method included relatively detailed case write-ups of the events in the field, followed by an examination of the data for potential analytical themes. The research group in which the author took part categorized patterns emerging from the data into themes, in order to generate overviews based on the perspectives chosen. Both the perspectives and the patterns emerged gradually, as literature studies were conducted in parallel, and new interpretations were made. Gradually, the themes of accountability for action and formalization of roles came to the fore as the most important for explaining and analyzing the data.

4. THE CASE

4.1 Mapping the work of planning

In the first workshop, the developers and the users discussed their expectations from a new planning module. An in-house report on resource utilization in surgery from the university hospital in the North Norwegian region was presented as background for the discussions. This report suggested that cancellations of surgery which could be linked to issues in the planning process accounted for 54% of the total number of cancellations. A major problem was that essential information was missing. For patients scheduled for day-surgery (not requiring admission of the patient as an in-house patient), 40% of the surgery order forms did not have information about the performing surgeon, 70% of the forms lacked information about ranking, and 5% of the forms lacked information about what surgical procedure was to be performed, and as a consequence, what surgical tool to be prepared. The report said that this situation had been persistent over years, and that the implementation of an electronic planning module within the EPR in 2005 had not improved the figures. The electronic surgery order form was just as incompletely filled as the paper based form used to be used to be. In the discussions, a major deficiency raised with the present planning tool was that anyone with access to the system could set up a surgery order form for the patient, hence the decision of surgery could not be tied to a responsible person. The fields for surgeons and anaesthesiologists in the form could also be filled by anyone with access to the system. Hence, from a juridical point of view, it was not possible to tie the data in these fields to the physicians responsible for assessments. Subsequently, in the planning process, this often turned out to be a problem when allocating resources for the operation, not knowing whom to ask if clarifications were needed. It was also a problem that the surgery order forms frequently were missing vital information, for example, a clinical assessment of the patient, or which surgeon was to perform the operation.

Based on these judgements, the developers at BigVendor together with physicians, secretaries and nurses, started to design the new planning module. They started out mapping surgery planning as the work progressed at present. The work process started as the hospital received an electronic referral for treatment. The secretary opened the referral and passed it on to the appropriate surgeon, who made an assessment, whereupon he returned it to the secretary. The secretary then opened the electronic assessment and scheduled the patient for an outpatient clinic consultation for closer examination, according to the decisions. Often, she also set up the surgery order form, so that the surgeon could pick it up and fill in their assessment during the outpatient consultation. Frequently, supplementary examinations were needed to decide if the patient was going to have surgery.

After the outpatient consultation, the clinician would dictate a note to document the findings and decisions to be followed up. If the note said that the patient was going to have surgery, the secretary transcribing the note returned it to the clinician for proof reading and authorization. Once it was authorized, the secretary would pass it on to another secretary in the surgical department who put the patient on a waiting list according to the deadlines set by the clinician. At the same time, she ordered supplementary tests if required. The coordinating nurse would pick the patient from the waiting list, and schedule them for admittance and surgery. From the waiting list she could see key information like the patients name, age, diagnosis and deadline for treatment. She also needed to access the note from the outpatient consultation to plan the activities. The note would outline what surgery was to be performed, but often also include other important messages:

"Very often it is me that intercepts messages like, the patient is treated with anti-coagulant and needs to stop this treatment prior to surgery, or if they should do some special exercises before they show up here – and then I call the patient to tell them this. Sometimes the note says something about logistics – whether the patient must have special transportation, an accompanying person, or if surgery must be performed when the patient's daughter can stay at home. We are talking about heavy surgery that puts the patient out-of-play sometimes for quite long after the operation, and surgery must be planned when things are set for the patient. Sometimes it might even depend on special competence in the municipality home care service. All these are important messages that you need to know before the date of surgery is set, or else the patient may not be able to attend, and you have to do the work all over again. There are lots of considerations."

(Coordinating nurse)

In allocating resources, she used an array of artefacts from which she collected and coordinated information. But some of the basic prerequisites were quite internalized:

"I must calculate the time of surgery quite accurately, if we are going to utilize our resources the best. Five minutes less for each intervention might give us two or three more interventions that day. Most importantly, it represents two or three patients not having to wait for surgery anymore"

(Coordinating nurse)

To schedule a "surgeon" as a resource for the operation means putting together information from numerous sources. Being part of a university hospital, the surgeons were trained in sub-specialties within their discipline. Thus, besides their shift plan, knowledge of each surgeon's skills and education plan was necessary. Planning for the right surgeon was actually easiest for the most specialized surgery. These surgeons had fixed days in the operating room (like in the outpatient clinic) and the operation could be scheduled on these days. It was more complicated for patients not requiring a specific surgeon:

"If we had one plan where days of surgery, outpatient clinic, teaching and so on for each doctor was plotted, this job would be a dream! In real life, this might change in half an hour."

(Coordinating nurse)

Figure 1: The surgery order form in the planning tool

If the surgeon that saw the patient in the outpatient clinic had made his assessment in a surgery order form, the coordinating nurse would pick this up and put in the logistical data, like date of surgery, operating room, team, name of surgeon, ranking and admittance

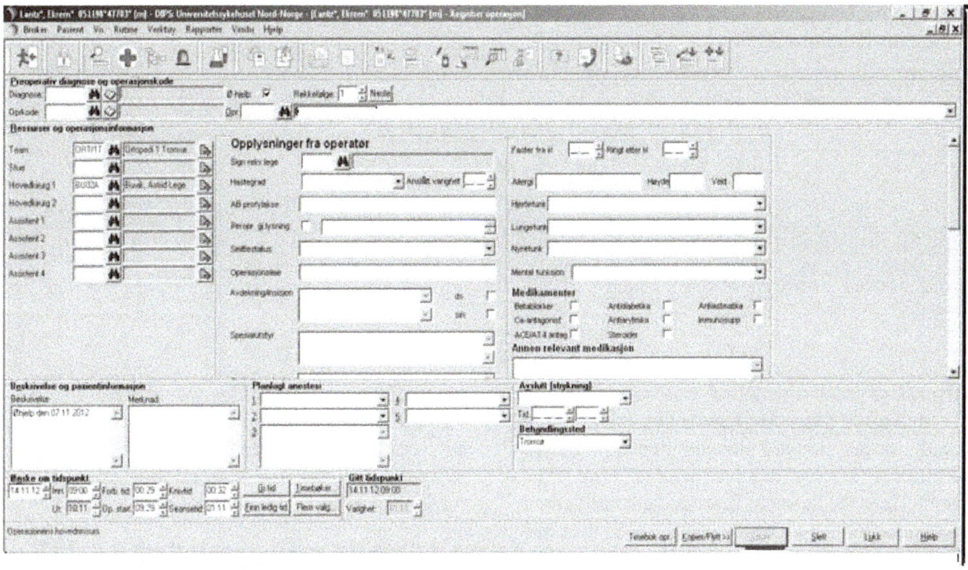

date, so that patient could be notified of admittance. If the surgery order form had not been set up by the clinician in the outpatient clinic, the coordinating nurse would set it up and fill in all the logistic data. In these cases, the fields for clinical assessment would be left open, and the assessment would have to be done when the patient showed up for admittance the day before, or on the day of, the surgery. Having allocated the resources, s/he puts the surgery on the plan by clicking "give time" in the planning module. Now, the session becomes visible in the surgery plan to other personnel with assignments related to it, such as nurses in the theatre who need to plan their resources, and the staff in the sterilizing unit who have to prepare the instruments and tools.

The plan is confirmed in a weekly meeting the week before performance, to ensure there are adequate resources to go through with the operation.

At this point, the coordinating nurse would also make a final check that the standard preparations had been done, and that all necessary clinical assessments were in place. If, for some reason, there were deviations from the standard, this would have to be clearly notified, or else the surgery might be cancelled on the day, noted as "patient not sufficiently prepared". At this point, it was a problem if the surgeon had not documented the assessments in the surgery order form in the outpatient consultation. It meant that clinical information about the patient going for surgery was missing, and it could potentially cause cancellation at the last minute. The present surgery order form could be described as a processual in-the-making form - it was conformed to and supported clinical practice, where clinical and administrative tasks were distributed in time and space, and performed in collaboration. Clinical and administrativetasks were often supported by articulation work, and by a collective responsibility. The present form served as infrastructure in several dimensions: communication, documentation, and information. Accordingly, the present surgery order form as an unlocked, inter-collaborative working tool was in conflict with the required needs of visualization, accountability and workflow inscription.

The work process was pictured in a business process map, derived from the endeavor of reengineering work process following Lean methodology, a technique that the university hospital had applied for some years. By drawing a map of the process, it was easier to identify the roles and the tasks involved, as well as the dependency of tasks.

4.2 Modelling a presentation of the workflow

In order to model this process in a way that could be implemented in a workflow system, the developers and the clinical personnel agreed that a formalization of responsibility for the specialized tasks would be necessary. Thus, the fields for assessment of the patient that could be filled in by anyone in the present surgery order form, would be split into separate documents in the new iteration, that only the person responsible for the assessments could set up and authorize.

Replacing the fields in the surgery order form with documents that have to be authorized by the writer means that responsibility for the specialized tasks would become indisputable. The decision-note, the anaesthetic pre-operative assessment and the surgeon's assessment note together would replace the mandatory fields in the old "surgery order form" for two reasons: firstly, to provide accountability for the assessments. Secondly, structuring the information into documents will make the importation and reuse of data from the EPR into the surgery order form much simpler, hence, hopefully, ensuring that the information needed to prepare for surgery is more complete. So in the new system, the surgeon who decides that a patient is going for surgery makes the decision of surgery explicit in a structured document that s/he would write her/himself. The surgery decision note goes directly to the secretary in the surgical ward and then s/he picks it up and make the bookings directly. This would reduce the steps in the task considerably, but also redistribute some tasks. For example, to skip the transcribing, the clinicians would have to write the note themselves. Designing

Figure 2: Section of the Business Process map of surgery planning, tasks and roles

the forms as a structured document with boxes for ticking will reduce the amount of text to be written. However, it would represent a new working routine for the surgeons that would need to be introduced and implemented in the working context. To the

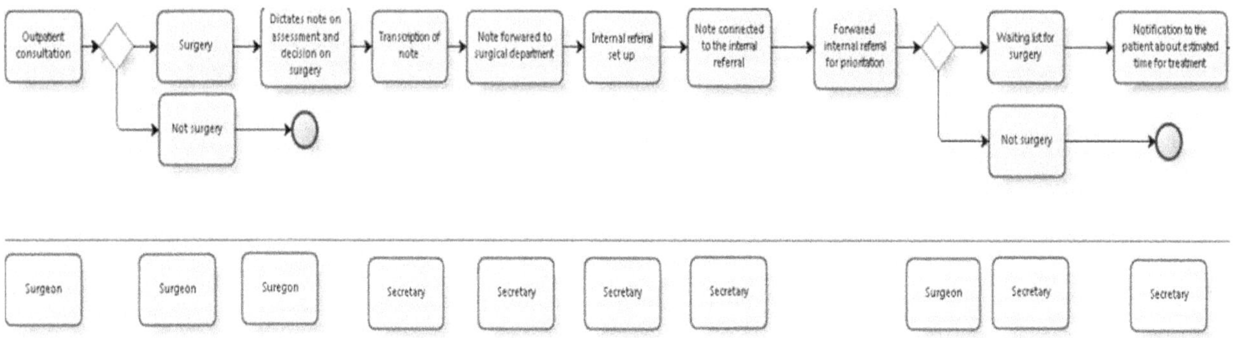

surgeons, writing themselves instead dictating was not something they welcomed, and "tradeoffs" were discussed: For example, by changing the routines, the surgeons could have their patients routed more quickly into the clinical pathway, reducing waiting time. The document would be authorized the moment it was saved, rather than the current process where, after the secretary transcribed it, it had to be sent to the clinician for proof reading and authorization. The number of hand-overs and transmissions of the information would be radically reduced, hence hopefully also reducing the risk of errors.

The formalizing of roles and responsibility necessary to inscribe the workflow into a planning tool also forced an ordering of tasks sequentially. Even if the mapping of the work process showed that it started when the hospital received a referral, the decision note was regarded as the "go" for the surgery planning process. That meant it served as the head-document for what BigVendor named a "case". Other documents in a case typically included an admission note; a surgeon's assessment note; an anaesthesiologist's note; the nurses' pre-, per- and post-operative notes and a discharge letter. Case collections of such structured documents would make it easy to retrieve and view relevant documents in relation to one another. As the decision-note was the head-document, other documents would be attached to it, and it could not be removed from its associated case. Only when the head-document was created, could other documents be added to the case, thereby assigning the other professionals their tasks. Whereas the work process hitherto meant that the secretaries made preparations for the physicians, they now had to await their assignment following the physician's creation of the initial document.

The new Surgical Decision Note called for a totally new workflow, compared to the existing workflow where the secretaries did much of the work of filling in the surgery order form:

«When we looked at how the system [surgery order form in the existing EPR system] has been used, it became clear that the secretaries have performed a lot of work that should have been conducted by a physician; for example, how to prioritize and give patients appointments in relation to their diagnosis. You have to consider the patient in relation to his particular condition, not only in accordance to standardized rules that regulate appointments. The secretaries have been encoding the patients as well, and that is a job for the physicians because it is an expert assessment." (Project member, BigInvestment).

The workflow inscription implicated that the collecting of information also had to be sequentially ordered. Due to the problems of missing clinical information caused by the way the teams planned for surgery at present, leading to cancellations, it was suggested that the fields for clinical assessment in the decision note be made mandatory. This would mean that all of the information needed to decide on surgery would have to be present before the note could be authorized, and before the other professionals were assigned their tasks. In the piloting of the system, this inscription turned out to be quite a challenge.

4.3 Piloting the modelled workflow

As mentioned, the role of physicians in the outpatient clinic, where they assess surgery patients, was pointed out as the first step of the surgery planning process. Accordingly, it was necessary to push the clinical information gathering process "up front", to conform to the intention of collecting and documenting clinical data early in the surgery planning process, in order to facilitate the reuse of information through the next steps of the surgery planning process. Moreover, the standardized workflow procedures required that a surgery order form should to be the trigger of the surgical patient pathway, and the physicians were the ones to fill in the form.

"In the outpatient consultation, you must consider if you have sufficient information to decide if the patient is in need of surgery or if additional tests like radiology examinations are required. I might approach this in two ways: either I agree with the patient that he is going for surgery, but I need additional assessments that will be carried out as he is admitted for surgeries. Then, there will be a risk that the test might show surgery is not the accurate treatment and hence result in cancellation. The other approach is to order the necessary tests and schedule another outpatient consultation when the results are ready, hence postponing the decision of surgery and spending more resources at the outpatient clinic." (Surgeon)

Not being able to work in parallel processes was something the surgeons regarded as poor resource utilization. They emphasized information collection as an ongoing process, hence postponing the decision and schedule another outpatient consultation was something they disliked. The surgeons were, by and large, not too happy with the consequences of the formalization of roles and task responsibility. To them, the inscribed workflow meant more work, as they had to write instead of dictating, and had to set up the documents themselves. Also, the relationships among the different components of the work forced the surgeon to enter orders for additional tests if needed, to bring the workflow on to the next step. Thus, to be accountable for the decision of surgery, the surgeons also had to account for the tasks this decision was based upon. They argued that they had to take on "secretaries' work", as all of this was something secretaries used to do for them. They were used to delegating and handing over tasks to be accomplished by secretaries and nurses.

The secretaries, for their part, were worried that pinning the responsibility for triggering the planning process on the surgeon would make it more difficult for them to follow up on things. They were worried that if the surgeon forgot to assign the tasks, the patients would not be called for admission:

"I`m afraid that if the surgeon forgets to authorize the decision note, how will I get to know that this patient should be put on the waiting list and called for? To "lose" a patient like that is my nightmare."

(Secretary)

According to the secretaries, there was a weakness in the workflow: besides setting up the decision note as a trigger for the planning process, the surgeon would also dictate his assessment in a note, as in the previous workflow. This had to be done to document his assessment in a note that could be distributed to the patient himself, and to his General Practitioner. This meant duplicating instead of replacing routines. Hence, there was a risk that the surgeon would forget about the decision note that was new in the routine, and because the electronic workflow of this document was the trigger of the planning process, there would be a danger that patients could fall out of their trajectories.

However, the accountability for the decision made it easier for the coordinating nurses to plan resources for the operation. They could put effort into letting the surgeon who decided on surgery also perform the operation. According to a national standard, patient should preferably have the same physician through the trajectory – outpatient consultation, admission and follow-up. Thus, when the patient met the surgeon in the outpatient clinic, s/he knew that s/he was likely to also perform the surgery, and to do the follow-up. This way, the surgeon and the patient got to know each other better, as were the intentions in the national standard. To the coordinating nurse who allocated surgeons for the operation, the accountability for the decision made it easier for them to meet this goal. Yet another gain from this was that s/he could more easily estimate how long each operation would take, based on which surgeon had made the assessment and was to perform the surgery:

"I know what theatres I can use – I just know. It is quite routine. And I know how long the different interventions are likely to last. If I am in doubt about how long it will take to remove a tumor, I ask the responsible surgeon. Then, maybe the second operation that day must be a small one."

(Coordinating nurse)

However, they shared the secretaries' worries about pinning the responsibility for the process solely on the surgeon.

It was also difficult for the coordinating nurse to adjust to the sequential ordering of tasks. Just as collecting clinical information for the surgeon was an ongoing process, so it was for the nurse, albeit she was responsible for collecting other kinds of information. Formally, her information after sorting out with the patent if surgery was feasible should also be part of the basis for the decision. After all, it could actually change the decision:

"All these are important messages that you need to know before the date of surgery is set, or else the patient may not be able to attend and you have to do the work all over again."

(Coordinating nurse)

Putting the decision on hold for the information collection to be complete was certainly not regarded as a smooth workflow – how should all the patients be kept track of when they had such an indeterminate status? They could just as well be in a preliminary plan, risking the cancellation of surgery if information collection showed it to be an inaccurate treatment. The most important thing was that patients were "visible" on a waiting list so that they could be picked and scheduled:

"It is very important to me to have the waiting list available, to see deadlines for treatment for each patient. This is the first thing I look for, then I start puzzling all the other resources together."

(Coordinating nurse)

5. DISCUSSION

5.1 Accountability

A major issue in the development of a new planning tool was to make the decision of surgery accountable. Making the responsibility for the decision more visible turned out to facilitate the coordination of activities going into surgery planning. In the majority of cases, the physician deciding surgery is also the one performing it. Hence, resource allocations depending on the preferences of the physician set to perform the surgery can be coordinated more easily. However, accountability for the actions performed, task responsibility and task ownership are all inextricably connected to the concept of role [23]. As a result of this, the role of "surgeon" had to take on more tasks directly following the decision for surgery. This comes as a consequence of the categorization and ordering that workflow systems need to succeed. To be accountable for the actions means that the person deciding on the actions also has to perform the actions, in order for collaborating persons to see who is logged as responsible. If a secretary orders tests decided on by the surgeon, the secretary's user role will be recorded in the actions. Hence, formalizing the responsibility led to redistribution of tasks, as well as new tasks. Just consider how the surgeon must, in the new system, set up the decision note for the secretaries to be assigned their tasks, while previously the secretaries set up and prepared the decision note for the surgeon. Moreover, information that surgeons used to dictate they must now write themselves, and authorize immediately in the form of decision notes, before the rest of their teams are assigned their tasks. The responsibility for decision-making certainly becomes undisputed, but has consequences for the distribution of tasks between the collaborating professionals.

5.2 Sequential ordering and dependencies

Although the surgeons perceived an increased workload, it could be argued that it was not necessarily more work, only sequentially differently ordered work. They had to collect clinical information earlier in the process (they would have to do this at some point anyhow), but it could not be done in parallel processes, delegated to secretaries and nurses to perform. Neither could it be done after the decision had been made, hence postponing the decision. Moreover, writing documents themselves may not actually be more work for the surgeons than dictating, proof reading and authorizing them separately in turn. By this process, the patient and their problem would no longer in the surgeon's memory at the time of proof reading and authorizing (the transcription work could take weeks), hence it took effort to "pick up on things". Still, the sequential ordering of tasks was perceived as an added workload.

The formalization of the work of physicians was expected to improve resource utilization later in the planning process. However, the information necessary to make decisions regarding surgery – e.g., the results of x-rays or heart- and lung-function tests – may not have been processed at the time of outpatient consultations, or such consultations may reveal the need for supplementary information, meaning that patient health information may not be complete even if information gathering is pushed to the front of the planning process. This jeopardizes the decision note's role as the trigger of the planning process, and the assignment of tasks to surgeons' teams. If the fields of assessment are made mandatory, that means the process will have to be put on hold until supplementary tests have been performed. The work would, therefore, have to be ordered sequentially, whereas currently there are many parallel processes in the information collection and resource allocation work. The sequentially ordering of tasks also affected the responsibility element, by the way the surgeon's decision note assigned tasks to the rest of the team. This effect is a consequence of both the accountability and the sequential ordering abilities of the workflow technology [11]. Ordering the work sequentially will necessitate more resources for outpatient clinical work to "kick-off" the work process. All in all, this means a reallocation of resources to outpatient clinic work, rather than a reduction of overall resource consumption, as was a major motivation for the new planning tool, and also advocated as the technology's gains [28].

Interestingly, even though the surgeons contributed to modelling the process that was embedded in the planning tool, it did not fit their way of working, as the model of work became a model for work. This is in accordance with what Bossen has described [10]. The way workflow systems always embed representations of work represent a challenge as to how the work should actually be modelled. Even a strong user-participation, as in our case, does not guarantee that the model "fits".

5.2 The importance of informal collaboration

Currently, the nurse and the secretary do much of the "coordination work" in the planning process - activating and placing bookings and following up on orders. In a way, they are monitoring and ensuring that there is progress in a patient's trajectory. Secretaries facilitate physicians' work by preparing documents, transcribing notes, and looking up and checking the status of activities. They are aware of different physicians' preferences and make preparations accordingly, therefore smoothing "the system" and contributing to the effective use of one of the most costly resources, the surgeon's time. The nurse and the secretary use their organizational knowledge to "smooth" the processes: "*I know what theatres I can use – I just know. It is quite routine*". In doing their work, the nurse and the secretary apply informal practices for coordinating all the different artefacts needed. The practice of planning does not take place through the filling out and subsequent 'use' of one artefact – the electronic surgery planning tool. Rather, planning (i) is distributed across a network of material/technological and human resources and (ii) happens continuously through ongoing and negotiated additions, deletions and changes. The planning tool, is in this sense, merely a node in a network of interconnected, mutually dependent nodes of material arrangements, practices and different professionals, just as Schmidt and Wagner describe ordering systems [35]. It is not possible for the workflow system to replace the collaborative articulation work done by nurses and secretaries, even if its coordinative capability "stipulates and mediates the articulation of cooperative work so as to reduce the complexity of articulation work of that arrangement" [34]. Providing an overview in terms of status for the actions and roles responsible may reduce the need for articulation work, but cannot replace the considerations behind that work. However, the constraints the workflow technology puts on user roles, in order to account for responsibility and actions, affected the collaborative work in surgery planning in both positive and negative ways. Knowing who was responsible for assessments and tasks made resource allocation easier. However, the formalization of roles placed the "ownership" of the workflow with the surgeon, because s/he is the only one who can trigger it. This may be desirable, but it certainly represents a major change in the collaborative work that goes into planning: "*If s/he forgets to authorize the decision note, how will I know that the patient should be followed up*?" From the nurse and the secretary's point of view, they are responsible for the planning, coordinating and monitoring of the process. They even plan surgeons, as a resource for the operation. Hence, it is fair to say that what was a collective responsibility for the process is turned into a single user role's responsibility.

CONCLUSION

Workflow systems are not only an enabling solution, but also a system of government, controlling the organization of work and the distribution of power in an organization [15]. A process model supports the hierarchical decomposition of tasks, sequencing dependencies among tasks, and the assignment of tasks to roles that are placeholders for users who will perform tasks. This is probably why health authorities have such great interest in applying process-supportive ICT tools in health care, to control, monitor and standardize treatment into one "best practice" way of doing things, according to the organizational understanding of accountability [39]. The accountability provided by embedded workflow models enables the work to be regularized, regimented and organized for inspection. However, in our case, the care providers themselves agree that accountability in the planning process is necessary to enhance quality, because in an intra-organizational perspective, the accountability for decisions and tasks supports coordination work. The question is, if and how this can be done without ruining the interdisciplinary cooperation and shared responsibility that is such a major characteristic of health care. Balancing the dual roles of technology as a coordination device and an accountability system is a crucial issue in this regard, and it must be carefully considered in the models of work that are inscribed in the workflow tool.

This case shows that the way workflow systems work through process models - that control the order in which a sequence of tasks should be performed, and by whom - affects the interdisciplinary cooperative work in surgery planning. The formalization of roles and responsibility led to a redistribution of tasks, and the surgeons were the ones who had to take on more work. Also, the collective responsibility for work changed due to the assignment of tasks and responsibility assigned to the surgeon. The surgeon's role became the "owner" of the work process, as opposed to the informal sharing of responsibility and task hand-overs that are the main characteristics of the existing way of planning for surgery.

6. ACKNOWLEDGMENTS

I thank the project members, the developers and the clinical personnel who so willingly gave me access to their interpretation and actions.

7. REFERENCES

[1] Aalst, W.M.P. van der et al. 2009. Declarative workflows: Balancing between flexibility and support. *Computer Science - Research and Development*. 23, 2 (Mar. 2009), 99–113.

[2] Aaserud, M. et al. 2001. [Elective surgery--cancellations, ring fencing and efficiency]. *Tidsskrift for den Norske lægeforening: tidsskrift for praktisk medicin, ny række*. 121, 21 (Sep. 2001), 2516–2519.

[3] Bardram, J.E. 1997. Plans as Situated Action: An Activity Theory Approach to Workflow Systems. *Proceedings of the Fifth European Conference on Computer Supported Cooperative Work*. Springer Netherlands. 17–32.

[4] Bardram, J.E. 2000. Temporal Coordination – On Time and Coordination of Collaborative Activities at a Surgical Department. *Computer Supported Cooperative Work (CSCW)*. 9, 2 (May 2000), 157–187.

[5] Bardram, J.E. et al. 2006. Why the plan doesn't hold – a Study of Situated Planning, Articulation and Coordination Work in a Surgical Ward. *Proceedings of the 2006 20th anniversary conference on Computer supported cooperative work* (New York, NY, USA, 2006), 109–118.

[6] Berg, M. 2005. Bridging the quality chasm: integrating professional and organizational approaches to quality. *International Journal for Quality in Health Care*. 17, 1 (Feb. 2005), 75–82.

[7] Berg, M. 2004. *Health information management: integrating information technology in health care work*. Routledge.

[8] Berg, M. 1999. Patient care information systems and health care work: a sociotechnical approach. *International Journal of Medical Informatics*. 55, 2 (Aug. 1999), 87–101.

[9] Berg, M. 1997. *Rationalizing Medical Work: Decision-support Techniques and Medical Practices*. MIT Press.

[10] Bjørn, P. and Balka, E. 2007. Health care categories have politics too: Unpacking the managerial agendas of electronic triage systems. *ECSCW 2007*. Springer. 371–390.

[11] Bossen, C. 2011. Accounting and Co-Constructing: The Development of a Standard for Electronic Health Records. *Computer Supported Cooperative Work (CSCW)*. 20, 6 (Jul. 2011), 473–495.

[12] Bossen, C. 2006. Representations at Work: A National Standard for Electronic Health Records. *Proceedings of the 2006 20th Anniversary Conference on Computer Supported Cooperative Work* (New York, NY, USA, 2006), 69–78.

[13] Bossen, C. and Markussen, R. 2010. Infrastructuring and Ordering Devices in Health Care: Medication Plans and Practices on a Hospital Ward. *Computer Supported Cooperative Work (CSCW)*. 19, 6 (Nov. 2010), 615–637.

[14] Bowers, J. et al. 1995. Workflow From Within and Without. *Proceedings of the Fourth European Conference on Computer-Supported Cooperative Work ECSCW'95: 10–14 September, 1995, Stockholm, Sweden* (1995), 51.

[15] Cabitza, F. and Simone, C. 2013. Computational Coordination Mechanisms: A tale of a struggle for flexibility. *Computer Supported Cooperative Work (CSCW)*. 22, 4–6 (Mar. 2013), 475–529.

[16] Cardoen, B. et al. 2010. Operating room planning and scheduling: A literature review. *European Journal of Operational Research*. 201, 3 (Mar. 2010), 921–932.

[17] Christensen, B. and Ellingsen, G. 2013. Standardizing Clinical Pathways for Surgery Patients through ICT. (Edinburgh, Scotland, 2013), 9.

[18] Dourish, P. et al. 1996. Freeflow: mediating between representation and action in workflow systems. *Proceedings of the 1996 ACM conference on Computer supported cooperative work* (1996), 190–198.

[19] Dourish, P. 2001. Process Descriptions As Organisational Accounting Devices: The Dual Use of Workflow Technologies. *Proceedings of the 2001 International ACM SIGGROUP Conference on Supporting Group Work* (New York, NY, USA, 2001), 52–60.

[20] Ellingsen, G. 2004. Tightrope Walking: Standardisation Meets Local Work-Practice in a Hospital. *International Journal of IT Standards and Standardization Research (IJITSR)*. 2, 1 (2004), 1–22.

[21] Ellingsen, G. and Monteiro, E. 2003. A patchwork planet integration and cooperation in hospitals. *Computer Supported Cooperative Work (CSCW)*. 12, 1 (2003), 71–95.

[22] Eriksén, S. 2002. Designing for accountability. *Proceedings of the second Nordic conference on Human-computer interaction* (2002), 177–186.

[23] Grinter, R.E. 2000. Workflow Systems: Occasions for Success and Failure. *Computer Supported Cooperative Work (CSCW)*. 9, 2 (May 2000), 189–214.

[24] Hanseth, O. and Monteiro, E. 1997. Inscribing behaviour in information infrastructure standards. *Accounting, management and information technologies*. 7, 4 (1997), 183–211.

[25] Heath, C. and Luff, P. 2000. *Technology in Action*. Cambridge University Press.

[26] Hovlid, E. et al. 2012. A new pathway for elective surgery to reduce cancellation rates. *BMC Health Services Research*. 12, 1 (2012), 154.

[27] Klein, H.K. and Myers, M.D. 1999. A set of principles for conducting and evaluating interpretive field studies in information systems. *MIS quarterly*. (1999), 67–93.

[28] Ko, R.K.L. et al. 1995. Business process management (BPM) standards: a survey. *Business Process Management Journal*. 15, 5 (1995), 744–791.

[29] Merkle, W. 2016. *Risk Management in Medicine*. Springer.

[30] Pine, K.H. and Mazmanian, M. 2014. Institutional logics of the EMR and the problem of "perfect" but inaccurate accounts. (Feb. 2014), 283–294.

[31] Plasters, C.L. et al. 2003. Coordination Challenges in Operating-Room Management: An In-Depth Field Study. *AMIA Annual Symposium Proceedings*. 2003, (2003), 524–528.

[32] Ren, Y. et al. 2008. Multiple Group Coordination in Complex and Dynamic Task Environments: Interruptions, Coping Mechanisms, and Technology

Recommendations. *Journal of Management Information Systems*. 25, 1 (Jul. 2008), 105–130.

[33] Schmidt, K. 1997. Of maps and scripts – the status of formal constructs in cooperative work. (1997), 138–147.

[34] Schmidt, K. and Simonee, C. 1996. Coordination mechanisms: Towards a conceptual foundation of CSCW systems design. *Computer Supported Cooperative Work (CSCW)*. 5, 2–3 (Jun. 1996), 155–200.

[35] Schmidt, K. and Wagner, I. 2004. Ordering Systems: Coordinative Practices and Artifacts in Architectural Design and Planning. *Computer Supported Cooperative Work (CSCW)*. 13, 5–6 (Dec. 2004), 349–408.

[36] Silsand, L. and Ellingsen, G. 2014. Generification by Translation: Designing Generic Systems in Context of the Local. *Journal of the Association for Information Systems*. 15, 4 (Apr. 2014), 177–196.

[37] Simonsen, J. and Robertson, T. 2012. *Routledge Handbook of Participatory Design*. Routledge.

[38] Suchman, L. 1994. Do categories have politics? *Computer Supported Cooperative Work (CSCW)*. 2, 3 (1994), 177–190.

[39] Suchman, L. 1994. Working Relations of Technology Production and Use. *Computer Supported Cooperative Work (CSCW)*. 2, 1 (1994), 21–39.

[40] Suchman, L.A. 2007. *Human-machine reconfigurations: plans and situated actions*. Cambridge University Press.

[41] Symon, G. et al. The coordination of work activities: Cooperation and conflict in a hospital context. *Computer Supported Cooperative Work (CSCW)*. 5, 1, 1–31.

[42] Teich, S.T. and Faddoul, F.F. 2013. Lean Management—The Journey from Toyota to Healthcare. *Rambam Maimonides Medical Journal*. 4, 2 (Apr. 2013).

[43] Timmermans, S. and Berg, M. 1997. Standardization in Action: Achieving Local Universality through Medical Protocols. *Social Studies of Science*. 27, 2 (Jan. 1997), 273–305.

[44] Walsham, G. 1995. Interpretive case studies in IS research: nature and method. *European Journal of Information Systems*. 4, 2 (May 1995), 74–81.

[45] Winograd, T. 1993. Categories, disciplines, and social coordination. *Computer Supported Cooperative Work (CSCW)*. 2, 3 (1993), 191–197.

Exploring Computer-Supported Professional Development for Novice Museum and Zoo Professionals

Priscilla F. Jimenez-Pazmino
Computer Science Department
University of Illinois–Chicago, USA
pjimen5@uic.edu

Leilah Lyons
Computer Science & Learning Sciences
University of Illinois–Chicago, USA
llyons@uic.edu

Brian Slattery
Learning Sciences Institute
University of Illinois–Chicago, USA
bslatt2@uic.edu

Benjamin Hunt
Learning Sciences Institute
University of Illinois–Chicago, USA
bhunt7@uic.edu

ABSTRACT

Zoos and museums often rely on interpretive staff, called explainers, to facilitate visitors' learning through conversations and demonstrations. Many explainers begin their careers as teens, and would benefit from ongoing Professional Development (PD). As institutions begin to use mobile devices to enhance explainers' interpretation, new opportunities arise to support explainers' individual and collaborative professional development. This paper presents the results of structured participatory design sessions to engage explainers in examining and proposing features for a Facilitation, Reflection, and Augmented Interpretation Mobile System (FRAIMS). The goal for FRAIMS is to support everyday interpretive tasks while also gathering information on how explainers perform that interpretation (both passively, via logging and recording, and actively, via self-reports and ratings) to support them in their PD. Reflecting on one's own performance and the performance of others is a powerful PD strategy, but can be emotionally fraught. Via participatory design sessions with expert, in-development, and novice explainers at different informal learning institutions, we found that explainers' preferences for socially sharing performance information gathered via mobile devices varied with their experience. We detail emerging themes captured from the sessions and make suggestions for how these findings might apply more broadly to computer-supported professional development systems.

CCS Concepts

Human-centered computing → Collaborative and social computing → Computer supported cooperative work

Keywords

Computer-Supported Professional Development; Participatory Design; Novices; Privacy.

GROUP'16, November 13–16, 2016, Sanibel Island, FL, USA.

ACM 978-1-4503-4276-6/16/11…$15.00.
DOI: http://dx.doi.org/10.1145/2957276.2957312

1. INTRODUCTION

Informal Science Institutions (ISIs) like zoos, museums, and aquaria, have long used explainers to help visitors make sense of the material the ISI presents. Explainers, also known as docents, interpreters, or facilitators, are ISI staff members who are trained to facilitate the learning and shared meaning-making of visitors [28]. Explainers must align the educational potential of the resources at their disposal with the educational needs of the visitors. This requires pedagogical content knowledge [26]: i.e., having deep familiarity both with the educational content, as well as with how that content can be effectively presented to learners. Explainers do receive training on both of these fronts, often in the form of an annual or seasonal training workshop, and have relatively fewer opportunities for continuing their professional development concurrent with their practice. For youth explainers, i.e., the teens and early college students who make up the majority of interpretive staff at many ISIs, most of their real professional development occurs on-the-job, by practicing with visitors. Practice is not the same as professional development, though, and youth explainers may be especially challenged to engage in the necessary reflection-on-practice because they are still quite new to being an employee, let alone a professional. We posit that mobile digital technologies can offer new and valuable professional development opportunities for explainers, especially young novice explainers. In particular, networked mobile devices offer intriguing possibilities for supporting collaborative and just in time professional development, by facilitating communication between explainers and their peers, or between explainers and their supervisors, but only if mobile technologies are designed with the needs and abilities of the novice explainers in mind. In order to understand those needs we performed participatory design sessions with novice and expert explainers exploring the design and use of technology to support professional development.

This paper shares what we have learned about the professional development needs of explainers, and how those needs translate into interface design. We argue that a number of the issues we uncovered (vertical and horizontal sharing for reflection, mastering content support for facilitation and interpretation, and pragmatic aspects of their practices) are likely to have relevance for novice youth employees regardless of their work setting, and intend this paper to open a discussion on the sociotechnical factors designers should consider when designing for novice professional development, an area that has not previously been addressed through the use of social technologies.

2. BACKGROUND

2.1 Existing Professional Development in ISIs

Although explainer training and professional development is traditionally accomplished "on the job" with little formal preparation, ISIs have more recently begun supporting explainers with more formalized training. Explainers-- especially youth explainers-- often begin their work with little knowledge of exhibit content or instructional strategies, so they need some initial, foundational grounding in facilitation to build upon with on-the-job learning. This has generally manifested as an extended, initial training period, which might vary in length between a few weekends [8] and an intensive month-long program [22]. This involves training in both the core content of the museum itself as well as strategies for facilitation and presentation that can help engage museum visitors.

While initial training periods are common, they can be overwhelming for new explainers [21]. Explainers are quickly introduced to a wide variety of exhibits and concepts, and faced with the task of representing the museum to the public (e.g. appearing knowledgeable and approachable). If an explainer is not able to grasp the content or pedagogical strategies introduced in this initial period, they may not have a chance to revisit the concepts until they are already interacting with visitors on the museum floor.

Because of these challenges, explainer professional development is often highly dependent on social and peer learning. Some institutions such as the New York Hall of Science take a more formal approach with small groups of explainers led by trainers, who focus on facilitating exhibits one at a time [21]. Others, such as the Ontario Science Center [22], encourage more informal contact between rookie and veteran explainers, and explainers and their trainers. Other institutions take a "mixed" formal and informal approach, such as the Science Museum of Minnesota [24]. Their program combines opportunities for volunteer youth explainers and full-time museum staff to informally "hang out", with more formal collaboration around educational strategies and exhibit design. In these programs, contact with museum professionals helped youth explainers develop their own sense of agency and their confidence in presenting ideas to the museum's visitor audience.

For youth explainers, a volunteer position at a museum may be one of their first jobs, so they are learning to navigate being an "employee" as well as learning how to be an explainer. Because of this, it's critical that explainers have a strong community of peers and veteran explainers to help them develop these new identities. However, formal professional development, such as time devoted to reflective thinking, is largely absent from explainers' experience beyond the initial training period. This is despite the evidence that explainers will make use of mobile devices to share formative "tips and tricks" for interpreting specific exhibits [15], as well as evidence from teacher training (a much more heavily-researched area) that professional development is more effective for both teachers and learners when spread across multiple sessions [30]. While continued professional development can and does happen informally for explainers, it may not be identified as such to rookie explainers who are still developing a sense of what "being an employee" entails.

Making space for explainers, as a group, to intentionally engage in professional development is often not done in museum settings once explainers have begun interacting with visitors. Considering the amount of effort that has gone into capturing and understanding professional learning in other domains [25], there is a large opportunity for trainers of explainers to begin formalizing some of the professional development that is taking place on-the-job in their own programs. This would allow explainer programs to more intentionally create opportunities for valuable social and peer learning, and for youth explainers to learn how developing their own practice fits into the job of being a museum explainer.

Additionally, institutions can promote different interpretive practices. ISIs like science centers tend to structure their interpretation practices around inquiry-based learning, where visitors are responsible for their own learning by conducting hands-on activities, and the explainers' role is to be responsive to learners' interests and needs. Other ISIs – especially those which contain non-interactive collections like aquaria and zoos – prefer a more dialogic-based approach, where learning is intended to take place through structured dialogues wherein explainers guide the discussions towards exhibit learning goals. Individual ISIs often have some mix of these approaches, however. Science centers often run structured dialogic talks (e.g., around chemistry demonstrations) while zoos might employ hands-on activity carts at exhibits (e.g., where visitors explore animal specimens, or perform an experiment) where explainers are tasked with responding to visitor questions and supporting their inquiry activities. Thus, it is important that any mobile tool designed to support interpretation and interpretive professional development be able to embrace multiple interpretive pedagogies. For that reason, we intentionally elicited design suggestions from explainers at two ISIs: a science center, and a zoo.

2.2 Technology Used to Support Interpretation in ISIs

2.2.1 Explainers Re-appropriating Mobile Technology

The Electronic Guidebook Project [15] explored the use of nomadic web content in order to understand how to improve and transform visitor experiences with handheld devices at a hands-on museum. The tool was initially designed only for museum visitors but visitors, teachers, and explainers all tested it. Explainers reported being attracted by the features that presented tips and tricks for using exhibits as well as background information on the exhibits' science that they might have missed in their training. They also made use of a commenting feature to share, amongst themselves, work management suggestions. This project highlighted the potential for using mobiles as performance support tools for explainers-in-training.

The *Science On a Sphere* exhibit [12], a spherical projection of global data visualizations, used a mobile tablet to allow visitors to select and control the visualizations. However, at some sites, explainers used the tablet to dynamically control the exhibit to augment the learning experience for visitors by being more responsive to the visitors' questions and interests. These projects illustrate the potential for using mobile technology for supporting explainer professional development and facilitation. We argue that the utility of mobile supports could be furthered by designing explicitly for explainers as a unique user population, rather than re-purposing technology that has been designed for visitors.

2.2.2 Mobile Technology designed for explainers

There are a few projects that have included features specifically designed to support explainers. For example, a mobile application to support young children's learning in outdoor environments, such as national parks [6], included a monitoring feature that helps an explainer to observe the visitor's activities during a field trip before they customize guided walks. This technology helped the explainer to organize their facilitation based on a group's preferences, but is only applicable to scenarios where visitors explore a terrain prior to interpretation. This scenario is not usually seen in indoor ISIs, where explainers have to respond to the ongoing demands of an audience.

Other museums[1] have used iPads in order to support explainer tours. A static pre-defined gallery of images was used by explainers to attract visitors and keep them engaged during guided tours. Although this approach helps explainers shape their interpretation, it does not include a mechanism to help improve explainers' practices over time.

The 21-Tech Project [11] studied ways to incorporate mobile technology in order to facilitate explainers' interaction with visitors. The project curated a gallery of third-party software that explainers could use to provide exhibit information to visitors via tablets and smartphones (21-Tech). The project spanned several museums, which held regular videoconference sessions to allow explainers at different sites to share strategies for how to use these third-party applications during interpretation. The 21-Tech project's use of third-party mobile apps illustrates the potential for using mobile devices to support explainers' interactions with visitors, and their use of videoconferencing shows the potential for using technology to connect explainers so that they can engage in collaborative professional development.

With our research we sought to build on these ideas, and used participatory design methods to conceive a mobile tool that would (1) flexibly organize mobile content to better support facilitation activities, and (2) embed shared professional development support as a foundational aspect of the design. Our contribution is thus twofold: we expand on these existing proofs-of-concept to more systematically explore what facilitation features would be welcome by explainers at ISIs, and we draw attention to the professional development needs of youth novice explainers.

Figure 1. An explainer (in green shirt) using the custom mobile interpretation tool we built to control the exhibit and to display related exhibit content. (The player can be seen on the far left). This tool formed the basis for FRAIMS.

3. CO-DESIGNING FRAIMS

Facilitation, Reflection, and Augmented Interpretation Mobile System (FRAIMS) is the name we have given to our novel mobile-based interpretation support tool. FRAIMS grew out of another project that involved creating an interactive zoo exhibit that was designed to be complemented by explainer-led interpretation. This exhibit (see Figure 1), called *"A Mile in My Paws"*, inspired us to create a mobile tool when we noticed that youth novice explainers often missed opportunities for making connections between game events and additional exhibit content. Novice explainers instead fell into semi-rehearsed patterns of information delivery that had little connection to what was currently happening in the game. We then ran several pilot tests with multiple design variations of the mobile tool to see what design features might help explainers capitalize on emergent "teachable moments" and encourage more interactive visitor-explainer dialogue [18].

We realized while designing the tool to support explainers' ability to capitalize on emergent "teachable moments" at a *specific* exhibit, that there was a larger possibility for mobile tools to help explainers become more responsive to visitors throughout the ISI, across multiple exhibits. While we were far from the first to reach this conclusion – explainers in other ISIs have already begun experimenting with using mobile devices to flexibly present digital content (e.g., images, data, videos, interactive apps) to enhance visitors' experiences [11] – we are the first to examine how mobile tool use can itself be used to fuel professional development. Because digital tool use can leave "bread crumbs" in the form of log files, just by using the tool explainers can generate records of their performances that can be used for later reflection. We also knew from prior research, though, that youth might have very strong opinions about how they wanted to intentionally share information with peers [3], and might simultaneously have gaps in their knowledge concerning how more passively shared data (e.g., via log files) could negatively impact their professional reputation. We thus decided to develop participatory design methods [19] to engage novice interpreters directly in the design process, so that we could address these and other sensitive issues that might arise from using mobile devices to support collaborative professional development.

3.1 Participatory Design Sessions

Our participatory design approach differed from more traditional sessions [27] mainly in the participants' degree of expertise and the timeframe. The timeframe we used (a single 3-hour design session) was a product of pragmatics: given the busy schedules of the explainers, we discovered that we could not enact a more traditional multi-week design session, as seen in other projects with youth [29]. That constraint affected our selection of materials for the session and the process we used. The participatory design methodology used is detailed in [19].

3.1.1 Participatory Design Participants

For the purpose of this work, we differentiated between novice explainers, in-development explainers, and experts based on their amount of experience in the museum floor. An explainer is classified as novice when he/she has limited training (typically only one initial session), has performed interpretation for visitors for less than one year in an ISI, and is still reliant on guidelines received via training to execute their work. When explainers are enrolled in high school or college and are less than 21 years old, we also apply the word "youth," because age can also affect workers' perceptions of professional expectations. Explainers are labeled as experts when they have worked in the ISI as a full staff member for more than two years performing as explainers on a daily basis or equivalent, or they are responsible for the training and supervision of ISI interpreters, and rely on a large body of

[1] MIDEA. Reflections: iPads in the Museum. Marcus Institute for Digital Education in the Arts. http://midea.nmc.org/tag/midea-workshop/.

experience in guiding their interpretation. An in-development explainer is someone in between a novice and an expert, who has a modest body of experience to draw upon in addition to formal training. This is a simplified version of the Five Stages of Skill Acquisition described by Dreyfus and Dreyfus [9], where moving from novice to expert entails differences in: 1) the decision making process being more analytical for novice and in-development learners, and intuitive for experts, and 2) facts or features relevant to the skill are learned by novices based on rules in a context-free way instead of being recognized in the situation as in-development and expert professionals do.

We recruited 7 experts and 12 novices from a large metropolitan zoo, and 8 novice and in-development participants from a science center in a major urban city. All of the novices – with the exception of one 22 years old - were also youths. Because in our sample the explainers' degree of expertise was related to their age, we decided to run separate sessions for experts and for novices. Other researchers had encountered difficulties related to trust and decision-making when multiple generations of participants were included in participatory design sessions [16], difficulties that in our context could not have been overcome with time.

3.1.2 Participatory Design Materials

We knew from the prior literature on participatory design with youth that when it comes to materials, they hardly used them and instead prefer to engage in discussions. Then, we should avoid playful materials like construction paper, felt, glitter, and glue frequently used with children [7]. We also knew that we could count on the youths to be ready to understand certain aspects of mobile technology with minimal explanation from us, especially those aspects that were readily visible in their daily lives (for example, common mobile user interface design widgets) [17][23]. For these reasons, rather than engaging youth in the open-ended design activities most commonly seen in participatory design, we engaged them in a somewhat more focused design activity using the existing mobile prototype as a frame to guide a design *discussion*, which is in keeping with what some researchers found youth to prefer [17].

In our two contexts (the zoo and the science center), we provided framing material to help the design process, and to channel and focus the discussion in a 3-hour window. In both cases we provided participants with paper printouts of "blank" iPad screens that they could use to construct their designs, by pasting color cutouts onto the screens, freehand drawing on them, or both. We provided the color cutouts, working with exhibit designers to select photographs, graphs, and other imagery that were related to the exhibit we presented as an example of the context of use. (We selected exhibits actually installed at each of the ISI settings, so that the design activity would be authentic to each setting).

3.1.3 Participatory Design Process

The participatory design sessions addressed three design themes related to common interpretation tasks that we knew needed to be informed by youth explainers (from several years of prior work with adult explainers, and from an extensive review of literature on explainer professional development [1][2][4][13][14]). This differs from a more traditional participatory design approach, which places more emphasis on having the participants generate themes themselves. The facilitators intentionally stressed the participants' role as "experts" at understanding the challenges faced by novice explainers early and often during the session, and made sure to embrace the themes that participants generated even if they diverged from our initial set of planned themes. This strategy was intended to help the participants feel like co-equal designers even though we initially organized the design session around partially-formed ideas.

We implemented a participatory design methodology that would help us maximize the feedback we could obtain in 3 hours while still allowing the youth participants to have a legitimate voice [19]. We designed the session to begin by covering the design of the existing FRAIMS prototype, so that the discussion of how a mobile tool might impact professional development and associated privacy concerns could be grounded in a shared mutual understanding of what such a tool *might* look and function like. We also provided a description of the exhibit chosen as the context of use, demonstrating how FRAIMS might be used in the setting. Then, for each of the three themes (see Table 1), we followed the same sequence of events: small group discussions, the categorization and clustering of ideas, creating paper prototypes of proposed designs, and the final sharing of their designs – the protocol implemented in this methodology is detailed in [19]. Details of the sessions that were carried out in the ISIs can be seen in Table 1.

Table 1. Participatory design sessions

Participatory Design Sessions	I	II	III
ISI	Zoo (1 session)	Zoo (2 sessions)	Science Center (2 sessions)
Participants	Experts (7 participants)	Novices (12 participants)	Novices & in-development (8 participants)
Themes	1. Resource Tagging (Preparation) 2. Situational Elements 3. Performance Supports	1. Resource Tagging (Preparation) 2. Situational Elements 3. Performance Supports	1. Preparation 2. During interpretation supports 3. After Interpretation Supports
Initial exhibit example	Introduction and description of "Paws" exhibit. These participants have previously used the mobile interpretation tool in their practice.	Demonstration of current mobile interpretation tool used in "Paws" exhibit	Role play to demonstrate the mobile interpretation tool working with the "CoCensus" exhibit.
Help during categorization process	None	Scaffolded by outside expert explainer	Scaffolded by outside expert explainer

The demonstration of how a FRAIMS tool might be used with an exhibit emphasized different scenarios (like interpreting for a family versus interpreting for an adult couple) and walked participants through the features of the prototype. We used an expert interpreter as a helper during the demonstration in Sessions I, II, and III to make sure that the scenarios would be true-to-life. In Sessions II and III with the novice and in-development explainers, we also had the expert help during the organization of ideas phase to help situate the novice interpreters' suggestions within a more mature understanding of the interpretation profession. (For example, a novice might think that a picture browser and a "quick fact" browser are very different features, whereas an expert might recognize that both are just examples of a feature used to find relevant content and thus group them together). Win Sessions II and III we also added a few seed ideas generated during Session I with the expert interpreters into the pool of novice-generated ideas. The rationale was that novices might not think to include certain topics adjacent to their zone of proximal (professional) development. Our goal with all of this was to preserve the buy-in of the novice participants. We gave them maximal autonomy while still allowing them to move beyond their limited view of the problem space by adding ideas that experts generated. We also had an expert present to help them co-organize the categories of topics.

3.1.4 Process for Identifying Themes

The themes used to structure the workshops were selected by the research personnel after over 100 observations of 3 expert and 15 novice explainers using the prototype mobile tool across seven full days in the "Paws" exhibit at the zoo; and were further informed by conversations with interpretive staff about their interpretive goals and pedagogy, and by a review of practitioner literature on interpretive professional development [1][2][4][13][14]. The key challenges faced by novice explainers seemed to be tied to flexibility. Although a major goal of the institution's training was to dynamically adapt interpretive practice to respond to different visitor needs and interests, novices would often get stuck in interpretive "ruts" (where they would cover the same topics and use the same media over and over). One challenge was that novices, as expected [9], lack an intuition for which media elements might be applicable to different situations (e.g., which media might be useful for starting a conversation with children). To redesign the mobile tool to assist novices with developing their interpretive flexibility when using a multimedia library, we selected the following themes:

- *Resource Tagging*: Explainers expressed the desire to be able to tag media elements like photos, videos, or interactive apps with labels to help them later locate certain kinds of content to present to visitors. How the tagging interface should be designed, however, and which tags should be used, were very much open questions.
- *Situational Elements*: The idea here is to specify situational elements that might be at play during interpretation that might change explainers' interpretation. Expert explainers, for example, suggested that they adjusted their interpretive decisions depending on how crowded the exhibit was, and the age composition of listening visitors. We suspected novices may have additional situational concerns.
- *Performance Supports*: This theme is related to how the mobile tool could be used to support explainers as they improve their interpretive performance. The ability for a mobile tool to log interpreters' actions or even record audio of interpretive sessions were identified by expert interpreters as potentially useful for supporting reflection. These functionalities are also possible threats to privacy - in particular, there are questions of how a system might use such data and who might be privy to it that are especially fraught for novices who have little institutional power.

During Sessions I and II at the zoo, three distinct phases of interpretation (preparation, enactment, and reflection) seemed to be emerging in the designs. A tablet tool would likely be used very differently in each of these three phases, so for our third design session in the science center, we altered the themes somewhat, merging the preparation-related Situational Elements theme with the Resource Tagging theme, and splitting apart Performance Supports to better fit the enactment and a reflection phases of interpretation:

- *Preparation supports:* how can resource tagging and situational element awareness be incorporated into the design?
- *Enactment supports:* what are the different ways a mobile app could provide assistance during the times that explainers are in the midst of performing interpretation?
- *Reflection supports:* reflection activities would take place outside of enactments, and might encompass reviewing performances (either via automated logs or user-created flags) or seeking help with different aspects of interpretation (for example, challenges experienced with using specific exhibit content, working with different types of visitors, or dealing with certain scenarios).

4. Data Collection and Analysis

In the workshops, participants were provided with post-it notes, a pen, printed iPad templates, and printed pictures/graphs that represented the exhibit context meant to be used as design elements. Participants generated ideas individually or in small groups and recorded them in the post-it notes, and additionally they drew on the iPad templates and pasted on printed pictures to sketch out possible user interfaces that represented an idea or group of ideas. The word cloud visualizations depicted in Figure 2, Figure 3 and Figure 4 reveal the explainers' ideas generated when brainstorming around the themes given in the participatory design sessions. We transcribed and lightly-edited the post-it notes for consistency (for example: text like "camp," "camp groups," or "camp group" were changed to "camp-group"). These word cloud visualizations are indicative of the issues that were initially on the participants' minds, although not necessarily the features they ended up proposing via discussion.

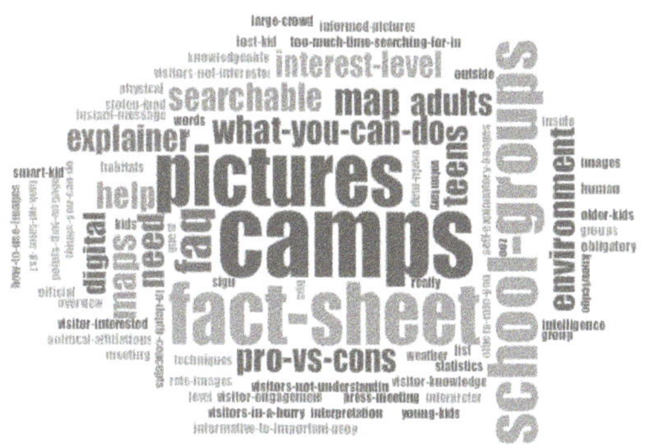

Figure 2. Words visualization of generated ideas by novice explainers from Session II.

Figure 3. Words visualization of generated ideas by in-development explainers from Session III.

Figure 4. Words visualization of generated ideas by expert explainers from Session I.

Some interesting differences can be observed. There was more diversity in the ideas proposed by the in-development and expert participants, showing that they have greater awareness of the situational elements that might affect their performance. Novices are mostly concerned with simple artifacts associated with interpretation (e.g., "pictures," "fact-sheet," "FAQ," "map") and some simple ways of characterizing the interpretive situation (e.g., school groups). In-development explainers go beyond simple descriptions of resources based on their modality (e.g., pictures vs. text) and begin instead differentiating resources based on their function within interpretation discussions (e.g., information vs. examples vs. models, or thinking about the need for age-based resources). Then, in the expert cloud, one sees much more awareness of one's own performance (strong-areas, areas-you-need-to-improve, self-reflection).

From the group discussions and drawings, we derived a set of functional requirements (see Table 2) in collaboration with the participants. These requirements are categorized based on the phase of interpretation (Preparation, Enactment, and Reflection) during which they would be used within. In the table below, the columns E: Expert, I: In-development, and N: Novices are used to identify the expertise level of the explainers who suggested or positively discussed that particular requirement during the sessions. The first thing to note is that the in-development interpreters contributed to the largest number of proposed features. Novices, unsurprisingly, espoused very few reflection-oriented features. Unexpectedly, the experts contributed to surprisingly few reflection-oriented features, even though reflection as a major topic of their idea generation as visualized in Figure 4. What this is showing is that despite having a greater awareness for the need for reflective activities, the experts didn't suggest as many ideas for how to support reflection with a digital tool.

4.1 Common Themes

The types of support that both groups of explainers described as important to be implemented in FRAIMS range across the phases of interpretation and vary with explainer expertise. That said, theoretical models of how explainers develop their expertise highlight three factors that influence expertise development and interpretation: *content*, *context* and *audience* [13], This means that an explainer must master the exhibit's content (*content*) as well as understanding that each ISI will have different approaches for how to present that content (*context*). Furthermore, both the content and the way it is presented will need to be adjusted given the type of visitors the explainer is addressing (*audience*). Explainers might experience a change in their level of confidence about their expertise when any of these factors changes, even experts may find themselves needing to rely on extra supports. In Table 2, we can see that most of the features exposed by experts had something to do with *content*. Context-related or situational features, on the other hand, were mostly proposed by in-development explainers. These results about the context-related or situational supports also agree with the stages of skill acquisition [9] where the decision making process done by novices and in-development explainers is analytical instead of intuitive usually done by experts.

4.2 Differences Encountered Based on Expertise Level

Expertise-related differences were encountered in the way explainers wanted assistance from a mobile tool to help in their learning and professional development. As noted above, experts shared more ideas directly related to professional development such as "self-reflection", "areas-you-need-to-improve", "strong-areas", and "training-needs." However, they did not propose many specific features to be implemented in the tool to support those ideas. Most of the features that experts did suggest related strongly to *content*, neglecting the *context* where that *content* would be delivered. Contrary to an in-development explainer, who expressed the usefulness of having a functional feature that allows them to flag a portion of a performance - for example, they might have found an interesting new way to use a media element with a family group, or they might have realized that they didn't understand the content associated with a media element as well as they thought they did".

In the participatory design sessions with the in-development explainers, we asked them to rate the features they generated based on their perceived utility for professional development. Among the requirements, the ones they considered most useful for supporting their professional development were one Enactment feature related to *content* and *audience* ("Having access to a list of activities and ideas to share or ask to the visitors based on age") and two Reflection features that could span *content*, *context*, and *audience* ("Rate yourself (using a checklist)", and "Share self-reflection with other explainers"). However, expert explainers did not see the need to include these Reflection features in FRAIMS. They expressed their preference to keep their current practices of having their supervisors and others give them direct "glows and grows" feedback right after an interaction with visitors, or during their regular meetings.

Table 2. List of interface features suggested by the explainers (E: Expert, I: In-Development, N: Novice) across the workshop settings, organized by the phase of interpretation each feature would support. The features are marked if they pertain to each of the three domains for interpreter expertise development: content, context and audience.

Phase of Interpretation	Brief description of functional requirement	Content	Context	Audience	E	I	N
Preparation	Allow access to shared documents that everybody can share and edit	X				X	X
	An interactive map of the venue (along with exhibit information)	X	X			X	X
	Rating of exhibit material	X	X	X	X	X	X
	List of daily challenges	X	X	X		X	
Preparation / Enactment	Show different features on iPad depending on the explainer's role (during their work shift or in their preparation time)		X			X	
	Have a diagram of the exhibit with detailed information	X	X			X	X
Enactment	iPad interface to control an exhibit		X			X	
	Explainer bulletins: chat, urgent messages, schedule, lost and found		X			X	X
	Fun facts category	X			X	X	X
	List of questions for visitors that they should be able to answer	X		X	X	X	X
	List of activities/ideas to share/ask based on age	X		X	X	X	X
Enactment / Reflection	Recording interaction with visitors		X	X		X	
Reflection	Rate yourself (using a checklist)	X	X	X		X	
	Share self-reflection with other explainers	X	X	X		X	
	See recordings of senior explainers	X	X	X		X	
	Visualize aggregated explainer ratings of content and performance over time, and across exhibits	X	X			X	X
	Weekly reminders of what I should be improving	X	X	X		X	
	Rate your day (using a checklist)		X			X	

One might suppose that experts are in the best position to make recommendations that support novice interpreters' development. However, cognitive psychology research has shown that experts rely on large bodies of tacit knowledge (often glossing over details when giving explanations, and relying on contextual cues to shape their actions) and have a hard time predicting novice performance (likely because they are not good at taking the novice's perspective) [5]. Thus, it might not be so surprising that rather than the experts, it was the in-development explainers who generated the largest number of feature suggestions related to Reflection, and suggested features related to all three areas of expertise development (*content*, *context*, and *audience*). They straddle the divide between expert and novice understandings, and may actually be best-positioned to provide advice for how to transition from novice to expert. We agree that proposing a technology that might change their current practices, but we consider the in-development explainers' insights may be able to improve current practices, allowing designers and developers in ISIs build tools that address explainers' professional development needs.

4.2.1 *Horizontal vs. Vertical Sharing of Performance Data*

We knew from the prior literature that youth have a sophisticated understanding of what information they are willing to share with peers, versus what information they are willing to share with adults like parents and other authority figures [20]. We also knew that there are prior instances of explainers using mobile technology to share professional development tips with one another [15], so we had reason to believe that our participants would have different preferences regarding information-sharing with peers (what we dub horizontal sharing) versus with authority figures like trainers (what we dub vertical sharing). We expected that novice youth explainers would be more willing to share information with their fellow explainers than with their trainers. This was not the case.

In the zoo case with novices, when we introduced the notion of allowing other explainers to have access to each other's performance data, for the purposes of providing constructive criticism, the universal response was an emphatic "No". The participants immediately proposed locking down users' records with password protection:

"Maybe you just can't access the other iPad users' accounts"

Unprompted, they then added that authorized users (supervisors) should be able to access the records:

"unless you're authorized"

"I feel like [trainer name] can access it, but like, I can't access yours"

When the facilitator asked to confirm that the explainers had no problems with the authority figures having access to the accounts and gathering information on them, the participants concurred that they had no problems with this, with one participant saying:

"They're friendly bosses, though"

When the facilitator introduced the idea that the authority figures might inspect the logged information in order to give feedback on interpretive performances, though, this easy comfort evaporated (see the following section for more details). It seems their initial idea that their bosses should be able to access their data was based on an unexamined assumption that one's hierarchical role should dictate access permissions, and not based on any conception of what authority figures might do with that access. Their comfort with vertical sharing only returned later on, when the facilitator asked them if their attitudes would change if, rather than sharing personally identifiable records, the data were instead to be anonymized and aggregated. This idea animated the group, and they immediately launched into speculations about how such data could be used to improve the quality of the media available through FRAIMS (by removing unpopular media elements, or by making it easier to access popular media, or to generate recommendations for the types of media to be added to the FRAIMS library based on what is and isn't popular). While their suggestions might be at odds with how trainers would actually use the aggregate data (for example, rather than culling an underused media element, a trainer might structure a PD session around *how* to use that element within interpretation), by removing the threat of being personally inspected and judged, their willingness to participate in the vertical sharing of performance data returns. It is also worth reiterating that the initial responses youth novice explainers have to authority figures gaining access to private data are typically highly permissive, and as the "They're friendly bosses, though" indicates, very much predicated on the trust they place in the good intentions of authority figures [10].

In the science center case with in-development explainers, explainers expressed their willingness to have their performance recorded, so that later an automatic system or supervisors can give them suggestions through the system about how to improve their performance or what they should be working on:

"I kind of came up with this idea so when you click on an exhibit you have a page that opens up where you have different things you can choose to do, you have access to vocabulary words, animations and content then you also have control whether you want to record that interaction."

"It is good for the museum itself to keep track of what things should stay and what things can go or can be improved on, and definitely allow us to reflect a lot more in different types of things that usually just kind of get"

Also, in their discussions and explanations of brainstorming ideas and user interface designs, explainers stressed the idea of different kinds of rating features and logging performance:

" it would ask the visitors to rate the explainers"

"maybe the rating explainers you would use emoticons rather than words for like younger children, also there will be a little section for you to rate yourself"

"these categories, kind of professional growth, self-reflective improvement, share self-reflective improvement, visitor feedback and other things with just general data capture"

These in-development explainers also requested to have access to senior explainers' interactions with visitors in order to learn from them. This interest in vertical sharing indicates that they understand the value of having effective practice modeled for them in order to improve their own performance. As we could see in Figure 3, labels such as: "record-interaction" and "visitor-experience-log" are a few of the ideas that in-development explainers proposed. This reveals how these explainers have begun forming an idea of the value of feedback on performance.

4.2.2 A Misunderstanding of Professional Development as Summative Assessment

As mentioned in the prior section, the novice explainers in the zoo got uncomfortable when the idea was introduced that authority figures might use logged information to give performance feedback. They seemed to struggle with the idea of what professional development could and should be, perceiving it as a way of summatively assessing or judging their performance rather than a way of providing constructive, formative feedback. When the facilitator asked them how they would feel about trainers having access to logs of their use of the FRAIMS tool to help them improve their practice, the participants initially pushed back on this idea, with one participant saying:

"I don't see why they would need to do that, unless they got complaints."

The subsequent discussion revealed that they thought the trainers would use such logs to see if they were slacking off on the job or not:

"But if we're being lazy, then they can check up on that."

They expressed displeasure at this possible monitoring, some suggesting that this would violate the current status quo regarding their privacy and autonomy:

"Because they don't check up on us anyways, so unless they got complaints they would have no reason to do that."

After a while, though, the participants began considering more deeply what could actually be inferred about their performance from the log data, first by questioning its value as a laziness-detection tool:

"But I don't see if how, like, if you're switching between a bunch of sites, er not that, but I mean pages and showing different things, that might appear like you're doing more interpreting, but what if you're just really like interpreting on the one image and that one works really well for you when you get in the group, you can't, um, say that, 'cause that one, the first person was going to more stuff and showing different things that they're doing more interpreting."

With another participant chiming in:

"Then maybe it wouldn't, like, be assessed that way, maybe it would be assessed more *of, like".. how many, er, how much time you use on it?"*

And yet another participant notes that additional contextual information might be needed to make sense of the logged data:

"But you still need to compare that to how many people came."

Recognizing that this still wouldn't be a good way to judge interpretive skill, the participant concludes:

"Maybe it just wouldn't assess you"

This could have been a moment where the group moved away from their summative assessment-oriented mindset to consider formative improvement-oriented uses of the logs, but instead the group reverts to embracing the existing norms around their privacy to interpret free of observation:

"We're not assessed now so why should it assess you? They don't assess us now so why should we change that."

This demonstrates that the novices are still struggling with a lack of awareness of what it means to be engaged in improving one's own professional practice. Whereas the slightly more experienced in-development explainers at the science center were more interested in having the support tool track their use of digital material:

"it can help us to keep track of more about our own progress, how we interact, also how we engage people and they are able to see how popular an exhibit is"

"it is good for the museum itself to keep track of what things should stay and what things can go or can be improved on, and definitely allow us to reflect a lot more in different types of things that usually just forget by the end of the day but it's important also to keep track of the stuff that we don't think we do a very good job"

4.2.3 Gaps in Understanding Professional Development

It may be that the reason the youth novice explainers struggled with seeing the value in reflecting on one's own performance was because they haven't had a career long enough to move beyond mastering the basic pragmatic aspects of their jobs (e.g., showing up on time, not being lazy). If their understanding of PD is bound up in the notion of assessing laziness and having others render judgment upon them, their reluctance to participate in such a system is understandable, especially given the strong concern teens have expressed about having personal information used to make social judgments about them [3]. As the next section will illustrate, though, their conception of what constitutes professional practice, although different from expert practitioners' views , is still valuable to consider.

4.3 Need to Support Contextual, Pragmatic Aspects of Practice

As designers, we were more interested in "high level" concerns that explainers could have on the job, such as how a tool might guide explainers' interaction with museum visitors. But the session participants also brought in more procedural "low level" concerns that had more to do with their practical concerns as museum employees rather than developing their professional practice as explainers.

One area that the explainers discussed passionately was the topic of fairness in scheduling. Youth explainers' day-to-day schedules are prepared by their trainers, and have them moving from exhibit to exhibit roughly each hour. Due to the large number of exhibits and explainers, and the ad hoc nature of their schedules, novice explainers might not be able to consistently work at their preferred exhibits, or might be assigned repeatedly to the same one. They suggested that monitoring via FRAIMS could be a solution for perceived unfairness and inconsistency in scheduling:

Explainer 1: "Well, perhaps you can find which station you prefer to be at"

Explainer 2: "That would be nice so maybe you don't get the station that is the least favorite all the time"

Explainer 3: "Uhm. But I'm pretty sure some people don't want to go to a particular station, some people don't like it, some people don't care but some people do, so if you give a person only the station they love they can get burned out for doing it so much"

Explainer 2: "Maybe that is how it can help you. It can keep track of how many times you are at the stations so you don't get burned out."

Explainer 1: "That is a better idea"

On one hand, explainers' day-to-day assignments to particular exhibits should have little bearing on the quality of their facilitation; explainers are expected to competently interact with visitors at any of the exhibits they could be assigned to. Thus, when putting together this co-design session and identifying design themes, we would not have thought to include something like scheduling fairness, which should not have major consequences for how interpretation is enacted.

On the other hand, the novice explainers know their job better than we do, and identified scheduling fairness as having a large impact on explainers' motivation and interest. Providing them with the freedom and space to develop this design theme allowed them to think more deeply about how data gathering and monitoring could have a direct impact on their job taken as a whole. More experienced explainers, trainers, and designers are likely more interested in the enactment of central facilitative strategies, and can take for granted some of the more basic concerns of being an employee that still have a large impact on practice.

Another unexpected area that explainers focused on was the use of FRAIMS as a system for helping lost children or acting as a lost-and-found. Some explainers elaborated on the concept of connecting lost children with adults in their paper prototypes of FRAIMS revisions (Figure 5).

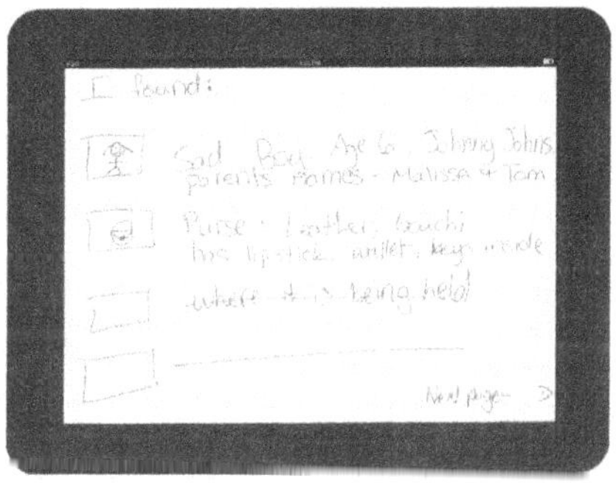

Figure 5. An example of a lost and found/lost child interface for FRAIMS. Although this could be seen as an "off topic" contribution, it also provided the youth participants an opportunity to set their own priorities for job performance.

Again, our focus of the co-design session did not initially include this kind of design, which seems to have even less relevance to explainers' pedagogy than scheduling fairness. But while these designs are "off topic", they are in fact features that could be useful to implement to support their job. Also, by giving participants freedom to explore any design of their choosing, the session provided a bridge between the "expert" position taken by trainers and designers-- where individuals have the control to decide which skills to care about and develop-- and the "novice" position taken by novice and in-developing explainers-- where they are rarely given the opportunity to set their own priorities. This kind of autonomy and personal judgment is necessary for people to develop the intrinsic motivation to deeply engage in professional development.

5. CONCLUSIONS AND FUTURE WORK

In this paper we articulate our findings from the participatory design sessions we ran with novice, in-development, and expert explainers in order to characterize their requirements for FRAIMS – a Facilitation, Reflection and Augmented Interpretation Mobile System. This paper enriches our knowledge of explainers' needs and expectations for this kind of support, both in terms of the specific features the explainers proposed as well as in the major themes that emerged from their feedback. The main themes we encountered were: 1) explainers of different expertise levels had different preferences for vertical and horizontal sharing of performance data, 2) novice explainers may need assistance with understanding that professional development is a formative, not summative, evaluation process, and 3) novice explainers may be better-positioned to understand the pragmatic aspects of professional practices that need support. Detecting these themes is useful in proposing design features that go beyond those suggested directly by participants.

In particular, the novices' reluctance to have peers or superiors be privy to their performance data, combined with the in-development explainers' strong advocacy for access to performance data (both horizontal peer data and vertical superior data) for reflection purposes, suggests that a PD support tool could have an "opt-in" feature for performance data, with different degrees of "upslope" and "downslope" vertical sharing. Performance data could be reported anonymously and in aggregate to superiors (e.g., anonymous reports that a particular exhibit or piece of content is difficult to use during interpretation, or summaries of the overall ratings explainers give themselves at a specific exhibit). This information can be used by supervisors to construct training sessions targeting problematic exhibits or to re-evaluate a piece of content, while preserving the privacy of explainers. When explainers are ready, they could opt to share their performances non-anonymously to get more direct feedback. Experts could set the culture for this (if they could be persuaded to use the system) by sharing their own performances, a feature that in-development explainers specifically requested. The take-away is that rather than supporting a single model for producing and sharing performance information, a computer-supported professional development system should allow for multiple models, where the participants themselves have the power to decide how anonymous they wish their data to be, and to in turn change that decision as their expertise grows.

Our research interest was to know how explainers would respond to a computer-supported professional development system: how they would feel about having tablets automatically logging their interactions, their insights into possible professional development uses of this information, and how they would feel about different types of people having access to those records. Our results point out the importance of attending to the expertise level of participants when developing computer-supported professional development systems. Experts might be aware of the need for different types of reflection opportunities, but they may also be too wedded to their current practices, and unaware of the needs of novices, to be able to suggest constructive and implementable ideas. To get more constructive design ideas for a computer-supported professional development system that supports all the stage of expertise level, it seems to be beneficial to work with in-development professionals (not too novice or too expert in their experience). This insight is likely to apply to computer-supported professional development systems in any context, not just science centers and zoo settings.

A value of including novices in participatory design for computer-supported professional development systems is that they can highlight pragmatic aspects of the job that, if left unsupported, might become barriers or irritants that would discourage novices from continuing in the profession. Making sure design activities are open-ended enough to allow participants to suggest their own design concerns relevant to their level of expertise is of critical importance to capturing these suggestions. While we initially viewed some of the novices' proposed design elements as being unrelated to professional development (although we were careful not to give any indication of our opinions to the participants) we later realized that their suggestions were very much in line with how these novice explainers perceived the demands of their job. Supporting employees through these challenges in early phases can positively impact their desire to remain in the profession, which can be very important for jobs that are known to be springboards for later STEM careers, as explainer jobs are.

As future work, the next step in moving forward with the FRAIMS design is to get a broader set of feedback on the list of proposed features. We did engage explainers with a range of expertise across two very different types of informal institutions, but the demands of participatory design methodology meant that we had contact with a relatively small number of explainers. We wish to know if the recommendations are valid across a wider sample of explainers and ISIs. To accomplish this, we are surveying about 120 explainers – 40 in each expertise level – recruited from at least 6 different institutions to get feedback on the perceived utility of the proposed FRAIMS features.

6. ACKNOWLEDGMENTS

Many thanks to the staff and the volunteer explainers of the Chicago Zoological Society, and the New York Hall of Science for the efforts that went into this work.

7. REFERENCES

[1] Allen, L.B., and Crowley, K.J. Challenging Beliefs, Practices, and Content: How Museum Educators Change. Science Education. 98 (2013), 84-105. DOI=http://dx.doi.org/10.1002/sce.21093

[2] Bevan, B., & Xanthoudaki, M. (2008). Professional development for museum educators: Underpinning the underpinnings. *Journal of Museum Education*, 33(2), 107 – 119. DOI=http://dx.doi.org/10.1080/10598650.2008.11510592

[3] Boyd, d., & Marwick, A. E., (2011). Social Privacy in Networked Publics: Teens' Attitudes, Practices, and Strategies. *A Decade in Internet Time: Symposium on the Dynamics of the Internet and Society*.

[4] Castle, M. C. Interpreters, Docents and Educators: Ways of Knowing, Ways of Teaching in a History Museum, an Art Gallery, and a Nature Centre. PhD diss., University of Toronto, 2001

[5] Chi, M. T. H. (2006). Two Approaches to the Study of Experts' Characteristics. In K. A. Ericsson, N. Charness, P. J. Feltovich, & R. R. Hoffman (Eds.), *The Cambridge Handbook of Expertise and Expert Performance* (pp. 21–30). Cambridge University Press.

[6] Chipman, G., Druin, A., Beer, D., Fails, J., Guha, M., and Simms, S. A case study of tangible flags: a collaborative technology to enhance field trips. In *Proc. IDC 2006*. ACM Press (2006), 1-8. DOI=http://dx.doi.org/10.1145/1139073.1139081

[7] Danielsson, K. & Wiberg, C. Participatory Design of Learning Media: Designing Educational Computer Games With and For Teenagers, in *Interactive Technology and Smart Education special issue: Computer Game-based Learning*, 3, 4 (2006), 259-274. DOI=http://dx.doi.org/10.1108/17415650680000068

[8] Diamond, J., John, M. S., Cleary, B., & Librero, D. (1987). The exploratorium's explainer program: The long-term impacts on teenagers of teaching science to the public. *Science Education, 71*(5), 643-656. DOI=http://dx.doi.org/10.1002/sce.3730710502

[9] Dreyfus, H., Dreyfus, S.E., and Athanasiou, T. Mind over machine. Simon and Schuster, 2000. 19-50.

[10] Emanuel, L., & Stanton Fraser, D. (2014). Exploring physical and digital identity with a teenage cohort. In *Proceedings of the 2014 conference on Interaction design and children* (IDC '14). ACM, New York, NY, USA, 67-76. DOI=http://dx.doi.org/10.1145/2593968.2593984

[11] Garibay, C., & Shaefer, J. (2014). *21-Tech Summative Evaluation Report*. Available: http://www.21-tech.org/blog/2014/03/11/21-tech-summative-evaluation-report/

[12] Goldman, K.H., Kessler, C., and Danter, E. Institute for Learning Innovation. (2010). Science On a Sphere: Cross-site summative evaluation. Retrieved from

http://www.oesd.noaa.gov/network/SOS_evals/SOS_Final_Summative_Report.pdf

[13] Grenier, R. S. The role of learning in the development of expertise in museum docents. *Adult Education Quarterly*, 59 (2009), 142-157. DOI=10.1177/0741713608327369

[14] Grenier, R., & Sheckley, B. (2008). Out on the floor: Experiential learning and the implications for the preparation of docents. Journal of Museum Education, 33(1), 79-94

[15] Hsi, S. (2003). A study of user experiences mediated by nomadic web content in a museum. *Journal of Computer Assisted Learning, 19*(3), 308-319. DOI: 10.1046/j.0266-4909.2003.jca_023.x

[16] Iversen, O., & Smith, R. (2012). Scandinavian participatory design: dialogic curation with teenagers. In *Proceedings of the 11th International Conference on Interaction Design and Children* (IDC 2012). ACM, New York, NY, USA, 106-115. DOI=http://dx.doi.org/10.1145/2307096.2307109

[17] Katterfeldt, E., Zeising, A., & Schelhowe, H. (2012). Designing digital media for teen-aged apprentices: a participatory approach. In *Proceedings of the 11th International Conference on Interaction Design and Children* (IDC 2012). ACM, 196-199.

[18] Jimenez, P., Lopez, B., Slattery, B., and Lyons, L. Teachable mo[bil]ment: Capitalizing on teachable moments with mobile technology in zoos. *Extended Abstract on Human Factors in Computing Systems. CHI EA '13.* ACM. 643-648. DOI=http://dx.doi.org/10.1145/2468356.2468470

[19] Jimenez Pazmino, P. F., Slattery, B., Lyons, L. and Hunt, B. Designing for Youth Interpreter Professional Development: a Sociotechnologically-Framed Participatory Design Approach. *In Proceedings of the 14th Internatinal Conference on Interaction Design and Children (IDC'15).* ACM, 1-10. DOI=http://dx.doi.org/10.1145/2771839.2771840

[20] Madden, M., Lenhart, A., Cortesi, S., Gasser, U., Duggan, M., Smith, A., & Beaton, M. (2013). *Teens, Social Media and Privacy.* Washington, DC: Pew Research Center's Internet & American Life Project.

[21] Motto, A. (2008). Peer learning: a strategy for practical explainer training. *Journal of Science Communication, 7*(4).

[22] Nyhof-Young, J. (1996). Learning science in an alternative context: The effects on a selected group of young science educators. *Journal of Science Education and Technology, 5*(1), 69-75. DOI = 10.1007/BF01575472

[23] Prensky, M., (2001) "Digital Natives, Digital Immigrants Part 1", On the Horizon, Vol. 9 Iss: 5, pp.1 – 6. DOI= http://dx.doi.org/10.1108/10748120110424816

[24] Roholt, R. V., & Steiner, M. A. (2005). Youth and Science: "Not Your Average Workplace" the Youth Science Center, Science Museum of Minnesota. *Curator: The Museum Journal*, 48(2), 141-157. DOI=10.1111/j.2151-6952.2005.tb00163.x

[25] Schön, D. A. (1984). The reflective practitioner: How professionals think in action. New York: Basic Books.

[26] Shulman, L. S. (1986). Those who understand: Knowledge growth in teaching.*Educational researcher*, 4-14.

[27] Taxén, G, (2004). Introducing participatory design in museums. In Proceedings of the eighth conference on Participatory design: Artful integration: interweaving media, materials and practices - Volume 1 (PDC 04), Vol. 1. ACM, 204-213. DOI=http://dx.doi.org/10.1145/1011870.1011894

[28] Tilden, F. (1977). *Interpreting our heritage* (3rd ed.). Chapel Hill: The University of North Carolina Press.

[29] Triantafyllakos, G. N., Palaigeorgiou, G. E. and Tsoukalas, I. A. (2008), We!Design: A student-centred participatory methodology for the design of educational applications. British Journal of Educational Technology, 39: 125–139.

[30] Wayne, A. J., Yoon, K. S., Zhu, P., Cronen, S., & Garet, M. S. (2008). Experimenting with teacher professional development: Motives and methods.Educational researcher, 37(8), 469-479.

Demo or Die: Narrative Construction as Articulation Work for Promoting Early Stage Digital Innovations

Aditya Johri
George Mason University
4400 University Drive
Fairfax, VA, USA 22030
+1-703-993-5397
johri@gmu.edu

ABSTRACT

The transformation of ideas and inventions into actual products is an arduous process that often requires persistent promotion by the inventor, often collaboratively with others. Through an ethnographic field study of an information systems R&D laboratory I illustrate how innovators achieved the goal of promoting their digital inventions by crafting and performing collective narratives – demos – that strategically leveraged affordances of digital medium. Even though demos were not part of the formal evaluation metric for researchers, they played a crucial role within the organizations through their use for articulation work. Through this articulation work of narrative construction innovators translated their perceived image of the audience into material properties of their artifact and weaved it into their narrative presentation. These highly personalized and often interactive experiences allowed the innovators to tightly manage impressions of their artifact and of them. Products that could be personalized were more likely to garner audience interest and support within the organization. Given the increase in use of digital technology within organizations, more work is needed to understand how articulation changes with digitization.

Keywords

Organizational Collaboration; Collective Narratives; Articulation Work; Digital Innovation; Materiality.

1. INTRODUCTION

The history of innovation is filled with examples of failure and no other case typifies this scenario like the failure of Xerox mangers to recognize the potential of the personal computer displayed at their Palo Alto Research Center [23]. This is not surprising, the journey from the conception of an idea or invention to its transformation into an innovative product is often long, complex, and uncertain [27]. Innovation requires relentless promotion by the innovator to overcome interpretive differences and misconceptions about the product [6]. Promotional challenges are particularly salient during the early stage of the innovation process [14] as the ideas are not fully developed and therefore showcasing product's value is harder. Yet, it is important for innovations to be recognized if novel products are to be developed.

GROUP '16, November 13 - 16, 2016, Sanibel Island, FL, USA

ACM 978-1-4503-4276-6/16/11…$15.00
DOI: http://dx.doi.org/10.1145/2957276.2957308

In this paper I present an in-depth look at innovators in a research and development (R&D) laboratory: TechLab. By examining how innovators promoted their early stage digital innovations, I address three critical issues. First, I describe the narrative nature of articulation work required in the process of promoting an early stage digital innovation [32]. Second, I show the central role played by the artifact, including digital artifacts, in early stage promotion. Third, I examine the emergence of institutionalized practices that support the promotion process in a digitalized organization. These three strands appear together in the promotion of innovations through narratives but are often unrecognized formally within organizations.

In the rest of the paper I first discuss related prior work and follow that with a description of the research site. Based on the data, I argue that within TechLab demos were articulation work and then present three case studies that illustrate how narratives are constructed for promotion innovations and the role of digital materiality and collective agency in the process. I then provide a brief overview of how articulation work is supported at the institutional level and end the paper with a discussion of the findings.

2. LITERATURE REVIEW

2.1 Articulation Work and Innovation

Studies of workplaces across domains have been a recurring theme of research within the CSCW community. These studies, especially the initial work, examined the work practices to better understand cooperative work. One of the key ideas that have found resonance is that of articulation work [34, 36, 37, 41]. Articulation work refers to tasks of work practices that are beyond rationalized models, are often unaccounted in official plans and reports but play an important role within the organization. As [34] reports, articulation work involves a range of categorizing, planning, coordinating, and/or negotiating efforts. Furthermore, this form of work is often evident in practice when "things back 'on track' in the face of the unexpected, and modifies action to accommodate unanticipated contingencies" [38, p. 10]. Not only is articulation work often unaccounted for in terms of formal metrics of success within an organization, it is also, ubiquitous and permanent.

When we think of innovation, the emphasis is often on the end product – what is produced and how it is adopted – and less on the process that made that possible. Yet, the articulation work required in demonstrating the worth of an idea and subsequently the usefulness of a product is significant. [12]'s case study of Edison's promotion of the electric bulb where he created a situation – scripted it to the highest extent possible – to highlights its benefit as compared to gas based lighting, exemplifies this process. In his arguments and demonstrations Edison first sought to imitate the features of gas lighting to ensure that gas lighting could be displaced without dramatic changes in existing infrastructure and patterns of use. He clearly demarcated the difference - noxious fumes - to ensure users would both recognize the purpose of his innovation at the outset and know without reflection how to use it in their everyday lives, as [12] recap, "While the promise of technological superiority may have loomed on the horizon, according to Edison's own notes and enacted strategies, the battle seems to have been won, instead, by minimizing the differences between the upstart technology of electricity and the existing system (p. 499)."

Based on their analysis [12] argue that inventors attempting to introduce novelty "should choose their designs carefully to present some details as new, others as old, and hide still others from view altogether (p. 499)." These viewed are echoed by [15] and they argue that technological dramas are attempts made by innovators to break out of the "vicious cycle" of early stage innovation where innovators lack factual information to present and the audience is specifically looking for limitations and potential problems. Innovators attempt to use technological dramas, "to manage the context in which new innovations are evaluated, moving it away from detached analysis, where evidence is weighed against claims, to one where uncritical enthusiasm prevails [15; p. 304]." These "dramas" are not individual feats but highly collaborative endeavors. A critical role is played by other organizational actors and physical resources in the process of innovating and introducing change through an innovation. From the invention in his Menlo Park laboratory and the assistance of engineers working for him, to the offices of Drexel, Morgan & Company where he demonstrated his first commercial power plant (p. 488), Edison drew on a large number of personal and physical resources.

2.2 Narratives and Workplace Studies

2.2.1 Narratives and Organizing

In [2] the author characterized organizations as a "collective storytelling system" where stories play a key role in building individual and institutional memory and the role of narratives in sustaining organizational innovation has been well documented [1]. Building on the idea that innovation is an inherently uncertain process and the chance of generating an optimum outcome is quite limited, in [1] the authors argue that narratives sustain innovation by acting as sensemaking devices and by facilitating productive social interactions. Narratives define the boundaries of acceptable behavior and provide a means for information sharing that can inspire new ideas. Innovation narratives, they argue, "can depict past innovation as well as project future innovation in a structured beginning, middle, and ending, and offer a particular point of view on a situation through the use of plot [1, p. 108]." Narratives also generate curiosity and attention [4], characteristics essential in telling an engaging story to the audience and therefore in promoting an innovation.

Within CSCW scholarship, there has been some recognition that narratives play an important role within work practices. For instance, [40] looking at collaborative information seeking, found that narratives enable us to capture and understand the interdependence between, technology and organization, on the one hand, and information and collaboration, on the other. It enables us to see how actors, artifacts and activities are entangled with one another, and helps us to capture the complex interaction patterns that unfold at the nexus of technology, information, and collaboration. In [39] the authors examined medical reasoning and argue that medical records mirror the narrative aspect of medical reasoning. These records have a strong narrative aspect because "narratives supply a workable medium for representing knowledge that is time- and context-dependent – and often uncertain or ambiguous as well (p. 82)." Furthermore, they argue, medical records are not a straightforward presentation of clinical data but ad hoc narratives typically unfolded in two stages. In the first stage physicians would construct the proto-narrative based on information found in the medical record. But for most cases the substantial size and fragmented nature of records makes it virtually impossible for the physician to gain full insight in the patient's illness trajectory. Consequently, to overcome the incorrect or imprecise nature of proto-narratives during consultation a "reemplotted narrative is unfolded through interaction between the physician and the patient (p. 98)". In this stage in addition to including information that was overlooked or unavailable earlier, a proto-narrative allows construction of a plot that is more appropriate for the particular consultation.

2.2.2 Narratives and Digital Materiality

Digital materiality or "what the software incorporated into an artifact can do by manipulating digital representations" [28, p. 1398] is increasingly becoming the preferred substrate for product development and innovation in the knowledge economy [28-29]. Digital medium provides unique affordances [3, 18, 30] that can be leveraged for narratives [20]. Murray [19, 20] has identified four characteristics of the digital medium that distinguishes it from other media: digital environments are procedural, participatory, spatial and encyclopedic. Procedurality refers to the ability of digital medium to execute a series of rules allowing for the design of complex and contingent behaviors. Different processes can be thus modeled and played out in a specific sequence. Participatory ability of digital medium emerges from its ability to respond to input allowing us to induce behavior. Together procedural and participatory affordances make up the characteristic commonly known as "interactive," specific responses can be triggered based on input. The third distinguishing characteristic of the digital medium is its ability to represent navigational space – space through which we can move. Either in a text-based or graphical representation the user can simulate moving through a physical space. Finally, digital medium is encyclopedic – it allows us to store and retrieve quantities of information far beyond what was possible before.

Taken together, these four characteristics suggest that narratives built using the digital medium display properties quite distinct from non-digital narratives. In dramaturgical terms [10], narratives require not just the actors and script, but the stage and the props, and are highly material. Narratives in organizations, as opposed to stories, also have a performativity component and "comprise actors and material artifacts, all stitched together in a compelling account [1, p. 115]" and innovation narratives are scripted dramas "in which the new technology is the central protagonist [15; p. 304]." In [22] the authors review the work on innovation and argue scholars have failed to examine how the design of the product – its outer form – affects the processes through which the "innovation's value is constructed and perceived (p. 217)." They propose that "concrete objects, or artifacts, with specific functional, symbolic, and aesthetic properties" provide the audience – in their case the customer – with cues "that trigger a variety of cognitive and emotional responses, responses that underlie initial perceptions of the value of product innovations (p. 218)."

Overall, prior work provides a strong basis for better understanding innovation from the perspective of both articulation work and narrative construction.

3. RESEARCH SETTING, METHODS, AND ANALYSIS

The research site for this study, TechLab, is a research and development laboratory on the U.S. West Coast that does work in the area of interactive software and hardware technologies especially those pertaining to multimedia and information systems. TechLab is a subsidiary of a Japanese multinational, TechCom, and supports the parent organization by undertaking research in emerging technological areas. In the knowledge economy no other institution epitomizes the innovation process as R&D laboratories more than organizations whose sole purpose is to innovate. TechLab provides a unique vantage point due to its focus on applied research and the digital nature of the artifacts produced. Researchers at TechLab examined and designed multimedia and interactive software products and the organization itself was saturated with digital technology in myriad forms. Researchers did not hesitate in experimenting with the technology they developed thereby providing a unique opportunity to observe how their process of innovation itself was affected by the technologies they developed.

The primary informants for this study were the researchers at TechLab. The digital artifacts designed and researched by the researchers at TechLab included information sharing systems, photo editing software, video manipulation and storage systems, large screen displays, pen-based computing, among others. Data collection occurred over a 5-month period. I spent 5-8 hours at the research site doing observational fieldwork on all week days and on some weekends. Observational field notes were descriptive and captured both interaction and dialogues [17]. I conducted 56 formal interviews with researchers, technical support staff, administrative staff, and interns (See Table 1 for details). The initial interviews were open-ended and aimed to capture informants' account of their practices in their words [24]. All interviews were transcribed verbatim.

Table 1. Informants Interviewed

Participant Profile	No. of Participants	No. of Interviews*
Researchers (US)	19	40
Researchers (Japan)	8	8
Managers (US)	2	2
Managers (Japan)	2	2
Interns (US)	4	4
Contractors (US)	5	6
Tech Support (US)	3	4
Others	4	4
Total	**47**	**70**

*Several informants were interviewed more than once

In addition to interviews and observations unobtrusive data sources [31] were a major data source and included emails, minutes of meetings, publications, technical reports, monthly activity logs, memos, PowerPoint presentations, audio files, video files, Flash files, and other content on the Intranet (see Table 2 for details). The analysis followed grounded theory methods [26] and the goal was to build an interpretive understanding [5] of the organization and researchers' work practices. After identifying narrative events, I looked at interview, observation, and archival data for triangulation. Overall, during my field study I observed around 50 demos. They varied in their setting and in their importance. Several of them, almost a dozen on one occasion, were part of a larger event whose primary purpose was to demonstrate innovations.

Table 2. Observations of Events

Type of Interaction/Information	No. of Observations
Electronic Bulletin Board	80
Staff Meeting	10
Project Group meeting	5
Semi-Annual report	*(interviews/ archives)
Intellectual Property Meeting	2
Work-In-Progress Meeting	1
Intern poster session	*(interviews/ archives)
Intern presentations	3
Anniversary celebrations	2
Job talks	1
External visitors	5
Farewell lunches	1
Japanese demo day	*(interviews/ archives)
Meeting with Japanese coworkers	5
Group lunch	2
Ad hoc meetings	2
Trial run of presentations	3
Email	100+
Activity Reports	100+
Looking at Webpages	5
Online archival material	5
Instant Messaging	1
Videoconference	5

4. DEMOS AS ARTICULATION WORK

As with most laboratory work, the work practices of researchers at TechLab varied and researchers were involved with a multitude of tasks including coding, prototyping, publishing, patenting, design discussions, deployments, and user studies. The researchers reported that they frequently gave demos. Demos, common across the IT industry, consist of a narrative in combination with some form of presentation of the product itself. They are sites of performance and provide a window on the meaning-making involved in the promotion process and on the organization [9]. They are designed to make the audience identify with those possibilities and convince them that the object they were viewing was capable of turning those possibilities into reality.

Even though demos were not formally required as a form of output for their annual evaluation, informally they were more important than many formal products such as technical reports and publications, *"If you don't demo, you don't get rewarded. Those [patents, publications] are all useful things to do, but if you don't do demos, you're not going to be as well-rewarded as if you do."* Furthermore, as one researcher explained, *"it's the perception that you create during your demo that in large part affects your reward."* Informants elaborated on the role of demos in the laboratory and underscored their importance in signaling their innovations, *"Demos are our product, and the people who see them are our customers. So, if we get high-ranking executives from Japan or something, this is our, this is what we do, this is what we produce, this is what we create, this is our return on investment or something like that."* One researcher in particular expressed the notion that demos are, *"a more fundamental product than other people acknowledge; I think a lot of people see demos as kind of means to an end of technology transfer or businesses or something, but I kind of see them as an end in themselves."*

The idea of articulation work is pertinent in this case as demos were never officially recognized as metrics for promotion or for reward at TechLab. They were crucial to the functioning of the organization as most articulation work is. Although they were not officially rewarded, and required a lot of time of the researchers, they nonetheless played the role of making innovations visible and gave researchers the opportunity to control the narrative around their inventions. Table 3 illustrates some of the technologies being demoed in TechLab. In the next section I look closely at how demos were constructed and performed.

Table 3: Examples of Demos

	Nature and Interaction with the Artifact
1	Demo of electronic paper to external visitors in the Print room by a researcher; interactivity with the artifact by asking people to write on the paper and then erasing and reusing it.
2	Demo of an electronic communication system meant for global videoconferencing system; audience in Japan is interacting with people in the U.S.; quality of transmission is paramount.
3	Demo of a photo system that searches images in a database based on other images; the image of one audience member is input and the database searches and presents other images of that person. The accuracy of search is the critical innovation.
4	A large screen – a combination of three screens – is being used for a presentation about that interface itself in front of an audience; the presentation on the large screen serves as a demo; on one of the screens a video of an audience member pops up on clicking on a slide on the other screen; use of multiple visual interfaces is the innovative feature.
5	A big screen interactive poster system for collaboration within and across the lab locations. The sharing of ideas is the goal here but done incidentally and therefore more "naturally" i.e. mimics informal interaction in an organization.

5. THREE CASE STUDIES AND A FRAMEWORK

I present three case studies of demos of early stage products to illustrate the use of product materiality and collective agency. Figure 1 depicts the overall analytical framework synthesized from these case studies. The first phase is the preparation for the demo which involves "meaning construction and reconstruction [8; p. 442]" of the audience. At this stage narratives are actively constructed by the innovator, often in collaboration with other organizational members. This stage involves understanding and debating who the audience is, forming impressions of their expertise, context, and personality, and deciding what aspect of the innovation might appeal to them. It also required using the material properties of the product so that it displayed characteristics in line with the audience. The second stage, the demo itself, is an impression management process the purpose of which was to "influence the sensemaking and meaning construction of others [8; p. 442]." During the demo the researcher had to put this learning from the previous phase into practice and present the innovation in a certain light – introduce the novelty while drawing on audiences' prior knowledge and experience [11]. The third phase involved reflecting on the demo performance and that fed back into the narrative process. After the demo was performed, the researcher, again with the help of others, engaged in the process of making sense of what transpired during the demo and what can be learned for improving the product and/or to improve future demos.

The practice of demoing was also shaped by stories of failure from other organizations where the failure to bring to market exceptional products, especially the failure of Xerox to capitalize on the personal computer [23] and the recent disintegration of Bell Labs, was recognized as a failed attempt to convince the managers of the strength and usefulness of an invention. Therefore, the concern with demos was constant and the pressure to demo was high making several researchers question their value and purpose constantly and the need to keep demoing led to an environment that was characterized by several researchers as "demo or die."

5.1 Case Study 1: Docuram – Demo to a Top Manager in the U.S.

In this first case I analyze a demo that was given to the top manager (TM) at TechLab by a researcher from the Artificial Intelligence (AI) group. At the time of this demo, the AI group was under a lot of pressure from the TM to produce a "feasible" product. The TM, and many researchers in the lab, shared the belief that AI as a research tradition had run its course and that the lab needed to move its resources towards more useful and promising areas with higher potential for product development. The AI group in the U.S. lab had good collaborative partnership with a similar group in the Japan lab and had the support of the lab manager in Japan. Therefore, the U.S. AI group had often indirectly used their support in Japan to keep their agenda alive and on target. But things were deteriorating for them and they knew they were in a kind of make or break situation. After the latest management overhaul within the U.S. lab they perceived that their new manager was not very supportive of their work. Leading up to this demo, the AI group, which at any given time consisted of 3-4 fulltime researchers and 1-2 interns, had had difficulty showing the usefulness of their product. Their work was algorithmic intensive and they were proud of the program they had built and the output from their program. They recognized the downside of their implementation – slow execution – but were convinced that that was a solvable problem with time and with a bigger data corpus to run their algorithm on. As one team member recalled, "[T]here was an impressive amount of work that had gone into the infrastructure but was not demonstrable, it was just there but there was nothing to show, snazzy things to show for it."

5.1.1 Narrative Building

In the vignette below one of the researchers in the AI group recollects how the demo was put together, especially in terms of how they targeted the demo towards a specific manager in the organizations. "Well, we knew what the audience was. We knew that [the manager] prefers to see demos that are embedded into a usable scenario or usable application...We also knew that [the manager] has a liking for visual information, as opposed to textual information." Based on this background information, the researcher came up with an idea while reading a copy of the Corporate Magazine produced by the company each quarter. "I was reading one of these Corporate Magazine and somebody actually from Japan lab in a presentation had mentioned Corporate Magazine as a possible domain, corporate communication as a possible domain for doing question-answering, and so I actually thought that, you know what, wouldn't it be cool if, since people get these things but

Figure 1: Narrative Building and Digital Materiality in Promotion of Early Stage Innovations

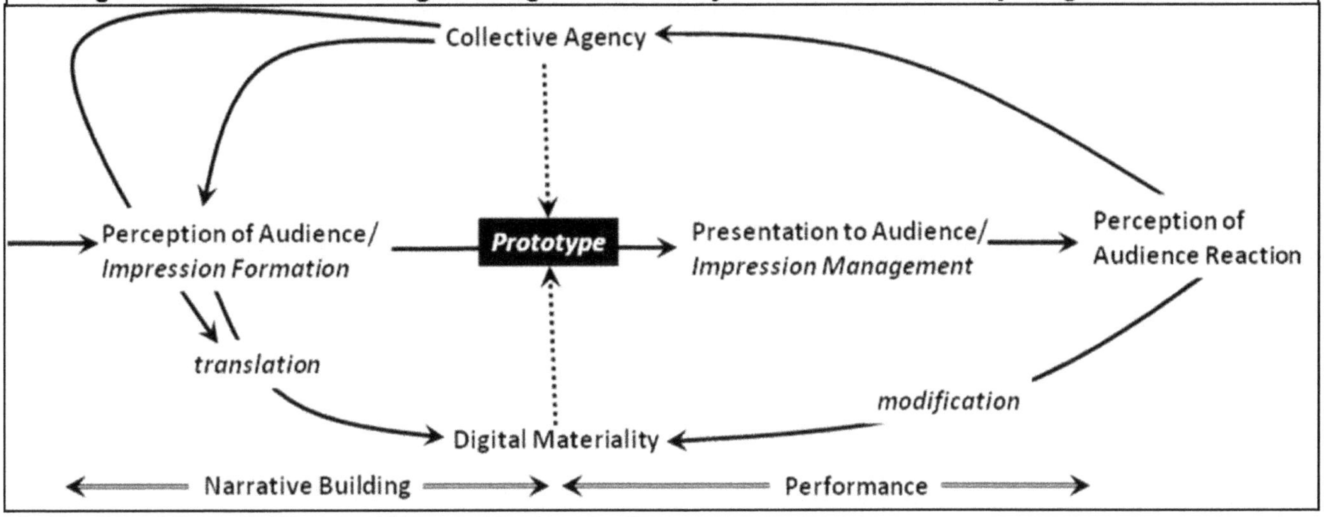

don't really read them, what if you could take, could make a visual summary of the Corporate Magazine." Armed with this idea, as a next step the team decided that they can make a summary of the magazine that consisted just of pictures. There was already another technology in the lab that could create picture collages. In this manner, they said, they could also, "bring in another piece of the technology of U.S. lab." Since a lot of their work was in the area of textual analysis and natural language processing, they decided that they could demonstrate their core expertise where, "each picture is associated with an article but it's also associated with a very short snippet of text coming from that article, say the caption of that picture or a summary, very quick summary done with our summarization technology [and] you would click on one of these pictures and you would get a little piece of the information of that, and you could ask questions about it." By developing this system the team could actually solve multiple problems. First, it was a plausible scenario in terms of usefulness and fit with the company goal. Second, it had visual appeal and was easy to demonstrate. Finally, and from their perspective most importantly, the problem set was limited and it was easy to predict user interaction, "a lot of the questions that you actually can successfully answer out of something like this are not questions that out of the blue one person would ask [so they are easier to plan for]." The demo produced a collage of different managers in the U.S. and Japan, including a few pictures of the manager to whom they were demoing the system.

5.1.2 Digital Materiality

For this team, the representation of their output in a form consumable by the users was concern all through their existence. In other interviews and more so in my informal communications with them they often commented on their inability to make ideas visible given the highly computational nature of their work. Their research and the innovative products that came out of that were about helping people make sense of large data corpuses using user-friendly interactive techniques. Therefore, in some ways from the user and manager perspective it was essential that they be able to demonstrate this capability. Yet, given the stage of technology advancement and the incremental research and development that was involved in making their products viable, the fruits of their labor did not usually result in flashy objects that could be displayed or interacted with.

5.1.3 Collective Agency

To find support for their ideas, products, and execution, the AI researchers engaged in collaboration with people both internally and externally. They engaged with researchers from another laboratory, from a nearby academic institution, and with a research group in Japan. They used algorithms and modules prepared by others, and as the researcher above reported, used other products developed within TechLab, especially with demoing. So, there was field level institutional exchange with other researchers and collaboration with researchers and other members internally. In this particular case, their first hurdle was the manager in the U.S. and to find further support they had to convince him of the usefulness of their work. They did this with the help of another research group to use their product to "snazzy" up the demo; and also from visual designers in the lab to help make the demo more visually appealing. They also used a smaller audience just consisting of group managers to get feedback on the demo.

5.2 Case Study 2: Memoram – Demo to managers from U.S. and Japan

In the second case I discuss, the demo was part of a larger number of demos to be given to high profile visitors from Japan, including the C.E.O. of the company, and other prominent scholars and researchers from the area. The demos were intended to showcase the prior work but also future research trajectories of the lab. The case study focuses primarily on the preparation of the demo through a series of "dry runs", practice sessions designed to get feedback on the demos. The overall preparation for this event of which this demo was a part took over a month. The first practice session was scheduled for last week of June, followed by two more practice sessions in the first week of July, a few days before the actual event. All demos had to be approved by group managers and then the top manager at TechLab. The demos were challenging as it was a high visibility event and because the U.S. lab members only knew about the visitors vaguely. In many cases they only knew the designations or roles of the visitors and nothing else. We start the case study with an episode where the researcher Jason is presenting his product Memoram, a software application for knowledge management, using PowerPoint slides and actual demo of the software. The top manager (TM) at the U.S. lab wants to go over Jason's presentation before it is presented to the visitors on in a few weeks. In addition to observing the practice sessions, I was able to observe the actual demo as well as interview the researcher after the demo.

5.2.1 *Narrative Materiality*

5.2.1.1 *Dry Run 1: End of June*

Jason stood at the front and using PowerPoint slides and the Memoram product demoed how corporations could capitalize on their existing knowledge – capture it and then discover it when needed. He presented for about 15 minutes. The overall narrative line was simple – there is large amount of information available within organizations and it is important to be able to analyze this information and discover useful knowledge. After the presentation Jason asked for suggestions for improvement. The research director started by saying that the audio level of the videos embedded in the demo was uneven. Jason said that can be easily fixed. Next, she asked Jason why he started his presentation by talking about discovery of information before he talks about its capture. She said it will make logical sense to talk about capture of information and then tools for discovery. Jason said he just decided to go this way and he can very easily go the other way. One of the managers' commented that the presentation was, "Still a little bit high for most people in the room" and asked Jason to avoid acronyms. He said that even some insiders would not know the acronyms and he should just spell them out. The lab manager (TM) was not satisfied with the overall narrative and commented that, "Set it up as a very difficult problem and yet unexplored domain". Jason was also advised to show images and videos of a manager at the Japan lab and to do so multiple times. He was further suggested to talk about his system as "a new kind of proactive system that brings you information." Several people in the audience said that they liked the story but he should make it more about how the "software will do the job for you."

5.2.1.2 *Dry Run 2: First Week of July*

A couple of weeks later Jason's presentation was substantially different from the previous one. He changed the narrative to start with talking about information capture and then discovery. The background graphics were different, the order of presentation was different; it has been overhauled. After the dry run a research director asked him to make sure he does not mention propriety information and confidential information. The lab manger asked him to mention another vice president from the Japan lab in the presentation. He reiterated that showing the video of the Japanese lab manager as part of the demo is very important and integral to the narrative so he should definitely figure out a way to keep it in [it had been removed in this iteration].

5.2.1.3 *Dry Run 3: A Day after Dry Run 2*

This time Jason did not make any major changes to the presentation but had rehearsed his talk. Jason said, as he pressed a key, "It just so happens that the Japan lab VP's presentation comes up." [He has made this change based on the feedback from yesterday]. The presentation was approved by TM.

5.2.2 *Digital Materiality*

Jason was able to personalize his demo for the target audience by using embedded videos of audience members in his presentation and by displaying information about audience members when demoing the product. For instance, he found an old photograph of a Japanese researcher, who was not a lab manager there, in the archives and used that in his presentation. This personalization was achievable because there was a digital repository of photographs, which was searchable and including the photograph simply required copy and pasting. He also included video clips when available and other media as required; displaying the heterogeneity [28] of digital innovation. Digital technology also allowed him to sync his talk – verbal representations – with visual representations on the screen by being able to control the flow and to present a seamless narrative regarding the novelty and value of his product. Even though in this case the audience did not directly interact with the product (they were able to do that later while touring the lab), Jason was able to present to them scenarios of interaction they could identify with. By introducing familiar elements – visual and through his speech – combined with user input, he was able to draw on the affordances of the digital medium to engage the audience.

5.2.3 *Collective Agency*

Several people played a key role in the overall demo or in narrative performance. Group managers and other researchers gave feedback and the top manager played a central role by giving feedback on almost every aspect of the demo. In addition, the overall visual look of the presentation changed significantly between the sessions. This was achieved with the help of the visual designers who worked hard to build templates and to acquire images that could be used in the demo. Jason also benefitted from informal feedback from his personal social network within the lab, researchers with whom he had coffee or lunch. They commented on several aspects of the presentation – both to emphasize how other lab innovations interacted with his and worked in tandem and to make sure that all products appeared distinct.

5.3 Case Study 3: Webram – Demo to Mangers from Japan by U.S. Researchers

The final case comes from a demo that was to be given to the CEO in Asia by the researchers at the Asia lab in collaboration with researchers in the U.S. lab. The demo was of Webram, a web-related product made by researchers in the U.S. lab and they were seeking the assistance of coworkers in the Asia lab to demo the product.

5.3.1 *Narrative Building*

Since the research effort that led to the development of this product was a brain child, to a large extent, of the top U.S. manager, he wanted to ensure the smooth functioning of the demo. The demo entailed that the CEO in Japan be able to print a document using a cellular phone. The manager wanted the CEO to have a firsthand experience of the product. Therefore, this demo was less about the visual and verbal narrative and more about experience with the product. The U.S. manager [TM] explained the goal thus, "Really, we should make these demonstrations flawless. Flawless and smooth. There should not be a lot of down time in which the CEO needs to sit and think about other things, because you want to keep his concentration and his focus." He suggested that one of the ways to keep the CEO's attention will be to involve him directly in the demo and "give the CEO the experience or let him do the experience of doing this so that there are some things that he will be able to do in the operation." He suggested that one of the persons from the research team who is with the CEO should facilitate this but should start by saying, "We are moving, we're changing the organization and we're moving to [a new building]. And those are the two things that we're starting to do after the linking the research to business." This will, according to the manager, show the CEO that the project was contributing to firm's objectives and strategy and in addition to software development we are also doing the system service architecture. After his initial remarks, the manager then proceeded to ask in detail what the CEO will do. He was told that the time they have with the CEO is a little more than an hour and the manager remarked that that was a "good chunk of his time." At this point the researchers in Japan said that they first wanted the CEO to experience the product and then explain to him how it worked. The manager said that was a good strategy as well. The innovator in the U.S. explained the interaction that had been designed, "When he [CEO] gets it originally on his cell phone, he could do two things: fax it off to somebody else and print it...So, he prints the document to the nearest printer, which he's standing next to in [location] and you can say that the document's routed through the network, through the area services, and gets printed out. Then, he looks at the document, he makes some annotation or he signs something, perhaps, on the document and puts it back into the scanner and sends it directly to a printer in his secretary's office. He just hits the go button. We can have it preconfigured so all he has to do is put the sheets into the feeder and press the green button and everything else happens. He doesn't have to enter anything. There was some hesitation from the manager about the use of a cellphone versus a PC and the researchers in Japan told him that the CEO was more comfortable using a cellphone compared to a PC.

5.3.2 *Digital Materiality*

This demo relied a lot on the ability of digital artifacts to be able to sync up and work with each other – for physical input to turn to digital commands and then a physical output. Displaying this "generativity" [28], the affordances of digital materiality for recombination and modification, was at the core of this demo. The narrative was built upon the ability for interactivity and was also developed to showcase the interactive nature of lab's products.

5.3.3 *Collective Agency*

This demo displays the effort put in by the team in the U.S. to try and understand what the CEO in Japan might want and how best to present the new suite of services developed to convince him of its value. They were helped in the actual demo by their collaborators in Japan, often nurtured through personal relationships, and had to trust them to a very high degree to be able to carry out a live demo. For instance, in this case the choice of the device – a cellphone rather than a P.C. – was suggested by the Japanese researchers given the prevalence of cellphones in Japan and the use of it by the CEO. The demo highlights the contested nature of interpersonal knowledge that people often had about their audience and the problem that created in personalizing the artifact. Although the U.S. top manager had doubts about the ability of the C.E.O to use technology, researchers told me that it the CEO was very comfortable with new technology. Later one of them remarked, only half-jokingly, that just because the manager here was not tech-savvy and he thought all managers were like him.

6. INSTITUTIONAL COLLECTIVITY: VISUAL AND INTERACTIVE DESIGNERS

An understanding of the critical role of narratives and the design of the artifact for that purpose will be incomplete without an understanding of the role of the visual designers in this process. TechLab had two fulltime employees whose role was to assist researchers with their design requirements and they were specially called upon when products had to be promoted. The designers worked with all groups and researchers at TechLab assisting them with visual design, multimedia, graphics, and video; all aspects of design. Prior experience of the designers included working with other design firms and they were adept at using all new design software – including high-end 3D graphics design. One of the designers was also a highly skilled artist. Over the years the designers had helped the researchers with preparation of materials for demos, conference presentations, conference proceedings, web design, and any product related activity that required their assistance. But in informal conversations the designers, who had an office next to where I used to sit during the days I was in the field, informed me that the most critical function they performed was making products presentable. They said that on several occasions the only tangible object researchers had was an idea, they were yet to develop a prototype, and in those cases the researchers relied extensively on the designers to come up with an artifact that could be displayed. One of them commented to me, "Between the two of us, we can pretty much make anything," implying that they could take any idea and convert it into an appropriate demo using their tools and skills. The designers were also involved with research but in a limited capacity and were often given credits on publications and even on invention proposals.

Overall, there was often a struggle among researchers to use their services and political issues often came to fore. During one of the big events at TechLab a 10 minutes video was to be shown to showcase the work of the laboratory over the years. The content of the video – who and what will be represented – became a contentious issue and the designers withheld the final video until the day before the screening. They were working in tandem with a particular group and its manager and at the end several other researchers and products were left out of the video and several researchers felt that only one group got most of the visibility and that their work was not represented. This led to many discussions and the incident acted as a trigger for at least one of the researchers to leave TechLab. In another incident narrated to me by one of the designers, the manager at TechLab came up with the idea of using the metaphor of "The Perfect Storm" to illustrate that the direction that the parent company should take in terms of its business growth and how research from the lab fit in that overall picture. The visual designer than developed the graphics and created the images of a storm and the interaction of the three different elements that led to the storm. He said to me, "I'm not sure that the audience in Japan knows the metaphor or got it, but I did create it."

The role of the designers – and the institutionalization of the role – further establishes the importance of making products visible in the right way and the criticality of demos to TechLab. Yet, the power dynamics of TechLab did not allow that the visual designers received the center-stage during demos. Therefore, the designers were absent from the actual demonstrations sessions and were also behind the scenes during the narrative construction.

7. DISCUSSION AND IMPLICATIONS

Overall, demos were both ritualistic and strategic and involve synergistic confluence of both impression formation and impression management. They link social actors within the organization with institutional logics through the framing processes they adopted in championing their innovations. Significantly tied with the practices of an organization, the repeated, but slightly varied occurrence, of these performances are a fertile ground to study institutional pressures and individuals' struggles against them. These performances were not only symbolic but also constitute the "real" work of an organization. They are a resource and source for both real and artificial accounts of work. There is a delicate balancing act between the real intentions of a researcher and the portrayal that has to be dramatized in front of an audience. If researchers spend too much time and effort on the portrayal it takes away from what they consider to be their real work and vice versa. This begs the question: is the portrayal (symbolic-aspect) the real work (normative-aspect)? How successful were these demos? The answer to this question is complicated as researchers and managers differed in their views about the role of demos in the organization and therefore there was limited agreement on what success meant. They all agreed on the basic premise that the visibility of their artifacts was critical – but beyond that they had different notions of their role in product promotion to other organizational members in order to push upstream in the innovation cycle. Some of them, after repeatedly being dejected with unsuccessful attempts to promote their innovations felt that the critical element was the face value of the demo, the "show-and-tell." Other researchers were more pragmatic and wanted to ensure that the lab, and their group, could keep attracting financial support from the parent company.

7.1 Demos and Digital Materiality

The three case studies presented above illustrate how demos of digital products are designed in order to overcome the lack of physical tactile experience during the innovation process. User's experience of the product was personalized by including information about the user – usually flattering or positive – in the demo. These demos were 'show and tell' – they combined a visual component and a narrative provided by the researchers. The design of the experience relied heavily on an understanding of what others were working on and how the artifact fit into the overall story of TechLab. It was a collective effort that involved input from other researchers, the managers, and visual designers. Products that did not fit very well with the overall narrative or were hard to demo, as was the case with Docuram, created immense difficulty for researchers in promoting them.

What was the role of digital materiality in this enactment? The researchers made full use of digital affordances by personalizing the artifact, by using multiple forms of representations – textual, video, 3D, and by engaging the users through personalized interaction with the artifact. They walked a delicate line between novelty and familiarity by invoking users' prior experiences and embedding representations related to those experiences in their innovations. If the product dealt with video, they had videos of the users in the product. If it was photo related software, the photos were those of the users. Even when demonstrating knowledge or expertise management software, when the user interacted with the software the results of search was something the users could identify with. By mimicking familiar features and introducing incrementally newer features the innovators were able to promote their products by gradually integrating their impression of the audience in the product. The four characteristics of digital medium identified by [19, 20] were all leveraged in the demos. Procedurality was integral to the demos as it allowed the presenter to create and then perform a narrative. By designing a series of behaviors the presenter could ensure that by clicking a button he could bring up information about someone in the audience. Participatory ability of digital medium was visible in the way in which audience members could be allowed to interact with the demo -- for instance, the CEO using his phone.

For many demos in the lab, in this case both Memoram, several navigational elements were present. For instance, video and images were represented as a 3D space and interfaces made discovery easier. The lab had a large corpus of data that it used both for research and for demos and the encyclopedic quality of digital medium was evident across product demos. For instance, Memoram and Docuram were both built on storage and retrieval of large quantities of information. For instance, at one point during the Memoram demo a 10 year old picture of important audience members popped up due to the marvels of digital storage.

This study contributes to recent theoretical work on digital innovations by demonstrating that digital materiality allows for a more personalized experience for the user but at the same time cautions us that expectations of users are also changing fast making it harder for those who cannot design personalized interactive experience to promote their innovation. For instance, the inability of innovators that worked on Docuram to make it interactive and visually appealing was a significant hindrance in early stage promotion. The expectations of the audience had changed over time and although stories still had the power to hold attention, the performance of the narrative was a greater concern. This study also speaks to one of the areas on which current materiality research is relatively silent – the politics of organization. While weaving digital narratives, the primary driver for the innovators was the need to manage the impressions of the audience. Their impressions of the audience were translated into the visual design and the subsequent performance; materiality was central to interpersonal interaction and for the expression of relationships.

7.2 Articulation Work and Performativity

This discussion brings us to a critical aspect of the practice of demoing – the effort required to make an innovation visible. Product promotion required support and assistance from several organizational members. This support helped the innovator in making sense of the audience by trying to understand their perspectives and technological frames around an artifact. The findings here further suggest that even during the initial construction of the artifact researchers had to establish how the audience will view their products in order do the demos. They were assisted in the process by the visual designers at TechLab who helped transform ideas and framings into concrete representations to be used for innovation promotion. For some of the demonstrations, especially those around a big event, some researchers spent up to three weeks preparing the demo. They went through several iterative cycles, as in the case of Memoram, and refined their presentation after each cycle. Even though all researchers agreed that demos were important they were not all happy with the time spent on preparing the demo nor were they sure of the actual value of demos. The researchers often had to perform a delicate balancing act between their real intentions or research interests and the portrayal that had to be dramatized in front of an audience to convince them of the innovativeness of the artifact. Therefore, these performances were not just symbolic – in terms of delivering a message about innovation – but also constituted the "real" work of an organization. If researchers spent too much time and effort on the portrayal it takes away from what they consider to be their real work and vice versa, prompting them often to ponder whether demos were simply portrayals (symbolic-aspect) or real work (normative-aspect).

This tension between 'face-time' and 'work-time' and the division of labor, in terms of what the researchers actually did and the effort they spent on making their work visible also points to another aspect of digital materiality of the products innovated at TechLab. It suggests that as the nature of work becomes increasingly abstract – digitally – producers of work have to spend more time communicating what they have done rather than in doing what they consider to be the "actual" work [13]. Researchers at both the locations raised this concern. Although their audiences were different, a lot of researchers, and in some cases the managers, spent a majority of their time demoing or presenting their work. Therefore, it is not surprising that the U.S. lab actually had people, graphic and visual designers, whose job it was to prepare demos and presentations or help the researchers in making their research more presentable. There are several implications for digital innovation from this distinction between 'face-time' and 'work-time.' Often the face-work represents what is the mandate of a research lab but not necessarily of a researcher and the researcher works backstage to work on projects she is interested in. This begs the question – is there a role for demos within the organizations, if so, what?

7.3 Demos as Organizational Lubricant for Innovation

Although, the effort required to prepare a demo and execute it harbors a skeptical, and often rightly so, view of the process, there are incidental and more purposeful advantages to it. A critical issue that affects any organization is "bounded rationality" the limits to decision making brought about by limited cognitive and attentive capacity. This problem is exacerbated in a digital realm as it is easier than ever to produce something new, especially an incremental innovation. How then can those in charge of evaluating or judging a work perform their task? The function performed by demos in this regard is valuable. Not only do they provide an opportunity to evaluate novelty and usefulness, the process before the actual demo ensures that ideas that are not worth pursuing are discarded early on.

At least within TechLab, the process of demoing also became a practice in which newcomers were socialized [16] and through this they learned about the organization – its people and resources – and also about how to create value within the context in which they operated. Although most newcomers came socialized into how to be a researcher, especially at targeting publications to highly regarded computing conferences, the ability to demonstrate their work to an audience in order to gain support was something they had to learn. In some ways, they acquired a valuable skill to function in a corporate research environment. The other important function demos served within the organization was in making expertise visible – what did people actually know? Even though information was always available on their webpage and through their list of publications, tacit information about how they used technology, what other skills they had, how could they contribute to a project, and so on, only became explicit in a demo situation more than any other interaction researchers had [21]. In effect, more than anything, researchers wanted to see other researchers in action – doing things – rather than just reading or hearing about them.

In addition to their role in championing an innovation, these demos performed another important political function within the organization. Since in any given year there was limited funding, all research groups and researchers had to compete for funds. Although researchers were required to submit annual reports and present their case for funding in a written form, unofficially demos were a critical element of this process and were important in influencing funding decisions. As a result, researchers and research groups that did a better job with their demos were more successful in influencing funders. Furthermore, those researchers and groups that were working on products that were easy to demo – turn into visuals, interactive applications, and so on – had a distinct advantage over research that was hard to demo. Consequently, researchers working on developing better algorithms or analysis techniques were often at a disadvantage as compared to those who were working with videos or pictures. Researchers working with tangible objects, such as large screens or digital fabric, also found it easier to demonstrate their product, as opposed to those working with algorithms.

7.4 Implications

The primary implication of this work for research is to revisit workplace studies to better understand how people work given the increased digitization of the workplace. In the early 1990s when workplace studies were at the forefront of CSCW and represent the era when most of canonical research on articulation work was done, the workplace of today is quite different. Even without focusing on nomadic, mobile, or geographically distributed work, just in the context of the workplace as a physical place, work practices now are quite different. Digital materiality has reshaped interaction within the same location with novel implications for collaborative work.

Finally, although the research reported here was not undertaken with the aim to derive implications for design, there are some lessons to be learned. Within TechLab a lot of the systems developed by researchers for external consumption or productization were used within the organization. Over time, they started to play a critical role in demos as the systems had data, such as videos or text files, which could be utilized for demos. In terms of efficiency and reducing the workload for demos, there is a lesson here to design systems across the organizations that collect and store data that can serve as useful repositories for demos. There is also the choice to store videos, PowerPoint, related to demos that can be used as templates for future demos.

8. CONCLUSION

The uptake of new ideas is critical for the survival and growth of an organization and it is in the best interest of an organization to develop ways to nurture innovation internally. This study examines the articulation work of demoing to underscore the construction of narratives for demos and the role this places in articulation work. The study places the promotion effort at the center of analysis and sheds light on how digital innovators tailor their products for the audience they are targeting, present them to an audience through a narrative, and iterate based on the feedback. It shows that in the digital economy the digital artifact itself plays a critical role in how it is championed through its affordances for personalization.

9. ACKNOWLEDGMENTS

This work was partially funded by MediaX at Stanford and by the U.S. National Science Foundation Award#EEC-0954034. Any opinions, findings, and conclusions or recommendations expressed in this material are those of the authors and do not necessarily reflect the views of the funding agencies. I am thankful to my informants for their participation in this research; without their time and insights this work would not have been possible.

10. REFERENCES

1. Bartel, C. & Garud, R. 2009. The Role of Narratives in Sustaining Organizational Innovation. *Organization Science*, 20(1): 107-117.
2. Boje, N. (1991). The Storytelling Organization: A Study of Story Performance in an Office-Supply Firm. *Administrative Science Quarterly*, 36(1): 106-126.
3. Bolter, J. & Grusin, R. 1999. *Remediation: Understanding New Media*. MIT Press: Cambridge, MA.
4. Bruner, J. S. 1990. *Acts of Meaning*. Harvard University Press, Cambridge, MA.
5. Daft, R. & Weick, K. 1984. Toward a Model of Organizations as Interpretation Systems. *Academy of Management Review*, 9, 2, 284-295.

6. Dougherty, D. 1992. Interpretive barriers to successful product innovations in large firms. *Organization Science*, 3(2) 179–202.
7. Garud, R. & Rappa, M. 1994. A Socio-Cognitive Model of Technological Evolution: The Case of Cochlear Implants. *Organization Science*, 5(3):344-362.
8. Gioia, D.A. & Chittipeddi, K. 1991. Sensemaking and Sensegiving in Strategic Change Initiation. *Strategic Management Journal*, 12, 6, pp. 433-448.
9. Goffman, E. 1983. The Interaction Order. *American Sociological Review*, Vol. 48:1-17.
10. Goffman, E. 1959. *The Presentation of Self in Everyday Life.* Doubleday Books.
11. Ginzel, L. E., Kramer, R. M., & Sutton, R. I. 1993. Organizational Impression Management as a Reciprocal Influence Process: The Neglected Role of the Organizational Audience. *Research in Organizational Behavior,* Vol.15:227-266.
12. Hargadon, A., & Douglas, Y. 2001. When Innovations Meet Institutions: Edison and the Design of the Electric Light. *Administrative Science Quarterly*, 46: 476–501.
13. Iedema, R. & Scheeres, H. 2003. From Doing Work to Talking Work: Renegotiating Knowing, Doing, and Identity. *Applied Linguistics*, 24/3: 316-337.
14. Khurana, A. and Rosenthal, S. R. 1997. Integrating the fuzzy front end of new product development. *Sloan Management Review*, 38(2), 103-120.
15. Lampel, J. 2001. Show and Tell: Product Demonstrations and Path Creation of Technological Change. In Raghu Garud and Peter Karnøe (ed.), *Path dependence and path creation*, Mahwah, N.J.: Lawrence Erlbaum, p.303-328.
16. Johri, A. 2012. Learning to Demo: The Sociomateriality of Newcomer Participation in Engineering Research Practices. *Engineering Studies*, Vol. 4, Issue 3, pp. 249-269.
17. Lofland, J. & Lofland, L. 1994. *Analyzing Social settings. A Guide to Qualitative Observation and Analysis.* Wadsworth Publishing.
18. Manovich. L. 2001. *The Language of New Media.* MIT Press: Cambridge, MA.
19. Murray, J. 2003. Introduction: Inventing the Medium. Wardrip-Fruin, N. & Montfort, N. (Eds). *The New Media Reader.* MIT Press: Cambridge, MA.
20. Murray, J. 1997. *Hamlet on the Holodeck: The Future of Narrative in Cyberspace.* MIT Press: Cambridge, MA.
21. Johri, A. 2015. Impressions in Action: The Socially Situated Construction of Expertise Impressions in the Workplace. *Journal of Organizational Ethnography*, 4(1): 44-63.
22. Rindova, V. & Petkova, A. 2007. When Is a New Thing a Good Thing? Technological Change, Product Form Design, and Perceptions of Value for Product Innovations. *Organization Science*, 18(2):217-232.
23. Smith, D. K. & Alexander, R. C. 1988. *Fumbling the Future: How Xerox Invented, Then Ignored, the First Personal Computer.* William Morrow & Co.
24. Spradley, J. P. 1979. *The Ethnographic Interview.* New York: Holt, Rinehard and Winston.
25. Stark, D. & Paravel, V. 2008. PowerPoint in Public: Digital Technologies and the New Morphology of Demonstration. *Theory, Culture & Society*, Vol. 25(5): 30-55.
26. Strauss, A., & Corbin, J. 1998. *Basics of Qualitative Research: Grounded Theory Procedures and Techniques.* Newbury Park, CA: Sage Publications.
27. Van De Ven, A. 1986. Central Problems in the Management of Innovation. *Management Science*, 32(5):590-607.
28. Yoo, Y., Boland, R. J., Lyytinen, K., & Majchrzak, A. 2012. Organizing for innovation in the digitized world. *Organization Science*, 23(5), 1398-1408.
29. Yoo, Y., Henfridsson, O., & Lyytinen, K. 2010. The new organizing logic of digital innovation: An agenda for information systems research. *Information Systems Research*, 21(4), 724-735.
30. Wardrip-Fruin, N. & Montfort, N. (Eds). 2003. *The New Media Reader.* MIT Press: Cambridge, MA.
31. Webb, E.J., Campbell, D.T., Schwartz, R.D. & Sechrest, D.L. 1966. *Unobtrusive Measures.* Sage Publications.
32. Zammuto, R. F., T. L. Griffith, A. Majchrzak, D. J. Dougherty, and S. Faraj. 2007. Information Technology and the Changing Fabric of Organization. *Organization Science*, 18: 749-762.
33. Sawyer, S., & Tapia, A. (2006). Always articulating: Theorizing on mobile and wireless technologies. *The Information Society*, 22(5), 311-323.
34. Baker, K. S., & Millerand, F. (2007). Articulation work supporting information infrastructure design: coordination, categorization, and assessment in practice. *Proceedings of HICSS 2007.*
35. Suchman, L. (1995). Making work visible. *Communications of the ACM*, 38(9), 56-64.
36. Suchman, L. (1996). Supporting articulation work. *Computerization and controversy: Value conflicts and social choices*, 407-423.
37. Strauss, A. (1988). The articulation of project work: An organizational process. *The Sociological Quarterly*, 29(2), 163-178.
38. Star, S. L., & Strauss, A. (1999). Layers of silence, arenas of voice: The ecology of visible and invisible work. *Journal of Computer supported cooperative work (CSCW)*, 8(1-2), 9-30.
39. Mønsted, T., Reddy, M. C., & Bansler, J. P. (2011). The use of narratives in medical work: A field study of physician-patient consultations. *In ECSCW 2011: Proceedings of the 12th European Conference on Computer Supported Cooperative Work*, (pp. 81-100). Springer London.
40. Karunakaran, A., & Reddy, M. (2012). The role of narratives in collaborative information seeking. In *Proceedings of the 17th ACM international conference on Supporting group work* (pp. 273-276). ACM.
41. Schmidt, K., & Bannon, L. (1992). Taking CSCW seriously: Supporting articulation work. *Journal of Computer Supported Cooperative Work (CSCW)*, 1(1-2), 7-40.

On Being Actionable: Mythologies of Business Intelligence and Disconnects in Drill Downs

Nitya Verma
Department of Human-Centered Computing
Indiana University, IUPUI
Indianapolis, IN
verman@iupui.edu

Amy Voida
Department of Information Science
University of Colorado Boulder
Boulder, CO
amy.voida@colorado.edu

ABSTRACT
We present results from a case study of the use of business intelligence systems in a human services organization. We characterize four mythologies of business intelligence that informants experience as shared organizational values and are core to their trajectory towards a "culture of data": data-driven, predictive and proactive, shared accountability, and inquisitive. Yet, for each mythology, we also discuss the ways in which being actionable is impeded by a disconnect between the aggregate views of data that allows them to identify areas of focus for decision making and the desired "drill down" views of data that would allow them to understand how to act in a data-driven context. These findings contribute initial empirical evidence for the impact of business intelligence's epistemological biases on organizations and suggest implications for the design of technologies to better support data-driven decision making.

CCS Concepts
Information Interfaces and Presentation → Group and Organization Interfaces → Computer-Supported Cooperative Work.

Keywords
Big Data; Business Intelligence; Data Analytics; Mythology

1. INTRODUCTION
Systems commonly referred to as 'business intelligence' (BI) are being adopted by organizations across sectors of society. Studies have found that the use of these systems can lead to the optimization of production and manufacturing work, reductions in customer attrition, increased profitability, better decision support and the creation of competitive advantage [26][35][52]. BI systems are the most prominent user-facing manifestation of 'big data' and its related computational turn in thinking within organizations[1]. As Gary King, director of Harvard's Institute for Quantitative Social Sciences asserts:

> *The march of quantification, made possible by enormous new sources of data, will sweep through academia, business and government. There is no area that is going to be untouched. (quoted in [29])*

GROUP '16, November 13–16, 2016, Sanibel Island, FL, USA

ACM 978-1-4503-4276-6/16/11…$15.00
DOI: http://dx.doi.org/10.1145/2957276.2957283

Yet the sort of epistemological shift towards quantitative data and computational thinking that is embodied by BI systems isn't without its critics. boyd and Crawford, for example, argue that the shift towards quantitative data changes assumptions about the meaning of knowledge and about how people "should" engage with information [8]. They contend that there is an increasingly pervasive "mythology" of big data:

> *…the widespread belief that large data sets offer a higher form of intelligence and knowledge that can generate insights that were previously impossible, with the aura of truth, objectivity, and accuracy. [8]*

This mythology, they argue, must become more transparent in research about big data and, we argue, related technologies. Despite the extensive market share of BI tools and their prominence in organizations, there is surprisingly little research about BI tools in human–computer interaction or its related disciplines. We address this gap in the research literature—studying the human experience of technologies that manifest the computational turn in thinking in organizations. In doing so, we also strive to give the HCI community a voice in the discourse and design for big data. We focus, in particular, on understanding the mythologies that informants in one human services organization experience as shared organizational values and ascribe to their organization's investment in business intelligence, which multiple informants referred to as a trajectory toward a "culture of data."

The mythologies of business intelligence are pervasive in the marketing of these systems, which claim to enable better-informed decision making, faster and more agile decision making, aggregation of all key data, end-user empowerment, etc.:

> *With Domo, it's easy to see the information you care about in one place and use it to make faster, better-informed decisions.*[2]

> *Imagine what your business could achieve if everyone had the information they need when they need it. You could enable more agile, fact-based decision-making throughout your organization.*[3]

> *Empower your people with 24/7, user-friendly access to the business intelligence and Big Data mining tools they need to make faster, more informed decisions.*[4]

---

[1] Global revenue from BI and analytics tools is projected to reach $16.9 billion in 2016, a 5.2% annual increase [17].

[2] http://www.domo.com/

[3] http://go.sap.com/solution/platform-technology/business-intelligence.html

[4] http://sisense.com/

However, our findings suggest that as individuals use these systems to translate data into action, they experience disconnects between the drill downs provided in business intelligence systems and the kinds of data that individuals are looking for in order to make actionable, data-driven decisions.

> *When a student enrolls, they bring with them all kinds of characteristics—their age, their gender, their race—so their demographic information, right? But they also carry with them... their family situation: Are they... with parents? Are they on their own? Are they married? Are they, do they have kids? What ages are they? So they carry all those. (I8)*

The data collected by this organization and aggregated into visualization widgets on the dashboards of its middle- and upper-level management does not represent anonymous masses. It represents the clients they serve and the employees who carry out the mission of the organization. In the drill downs of the business intelligence tools that they use, these informants imagine the human who underlies the analytics—each individual who metaphorically stands beneath and *carries* his or her data (I8). Yet the human context they imagine is largely or entirely missing from the business intelligence systems they use, creating a crucial disconnect in their data-driven decision making.

In this paper, we characterize four values—each of which aligns with one of the mythologies of BI systems—that these informants describe as being core to their trajectory towards a "culture of data" in their organization. Yet, for each mythology, we also discuss the ways in which being actionable is impeded by a disconnect between the aggregate views of data that allow them to identify areas of focus for being actionable and the imagined "drill down" data that would allow them to understand how to act in ways that show care and concern for their clients and employees. These findings contribute initial empirical evidence for the impact of business intelligence's epistemological biases on organizations and suggest implications for the design of technologies to better support data-driven decision making.

2. RELATED WORK

This research draws from three strands of related work including research in business intelligence; data, mythology, and values; and data and information management in the nonprofit sector.

2.1 Business Intelligence

Business intelligence includes the "techniques, technologies, systems, practices, methodologies, and applications that analyze critical business data to help an enterprise better understand its business and market and make timely business decisions" [10]. Although definitions vary, we use 'business intelligence' to refer to this holistic understanding of these multifaceted, sociotechnical practices situated within the ecology of tools used for data-driven decision making.

BI is characterized as having two interdependent components: '*getting data in*' and '*getting data out*' [52]. 'Getting data in,' more commonly known as data warehousing, includes extracting data from heterogeneous source systems as well as cleaning, transforming, consolidating and loading data into databases to enable organizations to have a "single version of the truth." Watson and Wixom suggest that data warehousing is the most challenging part of BI since it incurs more than 50 percent of the unexpected costs and requires 80 percent of the time and effort; the challenges of data warehousing arise from "poor data quality in the source systems, politics around data ownership, and legacy technology" [52].

'Getting data out' is also commonly referred to as business intelligence or, sometimes, analytics. Organizations normally pay more attention to getting data out as "only when users and applications access the data and use it to make decisions does the organization realize the full value from its data warehouse" [52]. We refer to business analytics as a set of individual and collaborative sociotechnical practices related to the appropriation of data through visualization, exploration, and analysis.

Previous research has identified various benefits of using business intelligence, including the optimization of production and manufacturing work, reductions in customer attrition, reductions in data redundancy, facilitation of new genres of questions by end users, increased profitability, better decision support, and the creation of competitive advantage [26][35][52]. Factors correlated with the successful adoption of BI systems include committed management support, a clear vision and well-established business case, a highly skilled team, sustainable data quality and integrity, and user-oriented management [23][45][55]. As business users move from reactive to predictive analysis, the level of benefits become more global in scope and difficult to quantify [52]; there is still, however, a need to better understand *how* businesses reap these benefits [18].

Researchers have also identified numerous technical and social challenges in the adoption and use of business intelligence. There are substantial challenges that exist in the data warehousing process that forms the back end of many business intelligence systems, with relevant data found across diverse and distributed data sources; these challenges are exacerbated by information management issues such as redundant data entry, lack of data quality, legacy systems, and politics of data ownership [55]. Organizational issues like the absence of support from leadership, intraorganizational politics and a lack of available expertise also add to these challenges [7][11][23][45]. Other challenges include employees' resistance to change, preferences for qualitative and/or quantitative data, and difficulty acting on data [14][38].

Researchers recommend both technical and social efforts to help organizations overcome barriers to adoption, including improving the efficiency of infrastructures, aligning organizational policies and workflows with business intelligence needs and values, and providing committed leadership and expertise [1][44][55][56].

2.2 Data, Mythology and Values

boyd and Crawford argue that 'big data' is an interplay of three elements: technology that gathers, links, and analyses large data sets; analysis for economic, social, technical and legal patterns; and mythology that data can offer a higher form of intelligence and knowledge [8]. Similarly, Morgan's seminal scholarship on the metaphors through which we understand organizations highlights quantitative data as one of the mythologies shaping organizational life, lending decision making a semblance of rationality [33]. Although definitions of big data vary, researchers increasingly acknowledge that big data is less about the *size* of the data and more about gleaning knowledge from of the data [6][8][6]. Big data represents a social and cultural shift in how we create and use knowledge:

> *Big Data reframes key questions about the constitution of knowledge, the processes of research, how we should engage with information, and the nature and categorization of reality. [8]*

Because big data is a sociotechnical phenomenon, it entails all the biases that come from "human design" [13]. There is, however, a dearth of empirical evidence of the nature of these biases and how they play out in practice. Multiple researchers have raised concerns about the potential misuse of data, whether due to its decontextualized nature or due to the epistemological biases that big data—and, we argue business intelligence systems—embody [8][9][13][48].

Previous research has also raised concerns about the biases of big data leading to new digital divides between data haves and have nots and between individuals and organizations that do and do not have computational literacies [8][14][25]. Manovich suggests that in this era of big data, there are three types of people: those who create data (both consciously and by leaving digital footprints), those who have the means to collect it, and those who have expertise to analyze it [31].

No data is truly 'raw'; the identification of what data are to be measured and how data are categorized are political acts, motivated implicitly or explicitly by different values [36][39][47]. As data are aggregated in business intelligence systems, values are embodied by the design of the system [15][32]. Values are also enacted in practice, through the use of the technology [28][50]. And researchers have advocated for understanding values tensions in contexts where the same values may be shared by both technology design and end users but where the logics behind how those values are enacted are different [50].

2.3 Data and Information Management in Nonprofit Sector

The nonprofit sector serves many critical functions and offers services that are underprovided by the government and the for-profit sector [19][34][42][43][49]. Nonprofit organizations are under increasing pressure to demonstrate their performance and impact to funding agencies [21]. So while data collection is a substantial part of the work that most nonprofits do, there is increasing evidence of the costs: "Nonprofits are often collecting heaps of dubious data, at great cost to themselves and ultimately to the people they serve" [46]. Research about performance and accountability in nonprofit organizations suggests that as data collection becomes the focus, this focus can diminish the quality of service to clients [2][3][4][5]. Kong also notes that it is not helpful to apply management strategies that work in the for-profit organization to organizations in the nonprofit sector because those strategies typically fail to address the social dimension of mission-driven organizations [27].

More generally, nonprofits often operate under significant constraints in technical resources and expertise that can make collecting, managing, and using data a challenging endeavor [41][51].

3. METHODS

We conducted a case study of the use of business intelligence in one human services organization. Case studies are a powerful method for deriving in-depth insights in an organizational context [57]. Existing case studies of BI in the private sector have focused on characterizing challenges of and success factors for BI adoption [20][22][53]. Here, our focus is on the mythologies of BI use and the ways in which the design of BI systems supports or thwarts these mythologies.

3.1 Research Context

Helping Hand[5] is one of a relatively small number of nonprofit organizations using BI tools, and the particular data needs and pressures in the nonprofit context highlight challenges to carrying out data-driven work. Helping Hand is a large, local affiliate of a national human services organization that assists low-income populations through a range of programs and services:

- **Business Services.** Helping Hand's business services department operates small businesses with employees who are often clients of the organization. The information management needs of this department include employee scheduling, production, inventory, and revenue.
- **Education Services**. The education services department at Helping Hand manages charter schools for low-income, at-risk youth. Their information needs include demographic information about their student population, class scheduling, records of student attendance and achievement, job placement, and salary of placement.
- **Mission Services.** Although all departments operate within the same, overarching mission, the mission services department offers a variety of programs to support the resiliency of their clients. This department relies on information management to understand the *impact* that the organization has on clients. Significant information challenges center around questions about how to assess the impact of its programs and what information should be collected to do so.

In early 2013, Helping Hand was awarded a small grant to fund the purchase of 50 licenses for the business intelligence system Domo, as well as salary support for a business intelligence staff position. Informants attributed the grant proposal's origin to the confluence of three events: a senior manager joining the staff with a corporate background and experience using business intelligence tools in that context, senior managers attending a data analytics conference during which they identified Domo as the right BI tool for their organization, and a serendipitous conversation with the soon-to-be-hired BI manager. The primary motivation for the adoption of Domo was to promote a "culture of data" within the organization, to support their actions "using sound evidence" (I12). To this end, the BI Manager held numerous individual meetings and focus groups with various organizational stakeholders to identify and prioritize key metrics, start to wrangle data from across a breadth of sources into their data warehouse, and coordinate end-user training. Based on usage log data at the time of the interviews in the fall of 2014, Helping Hand estimated that of the 50 licenses that were purchased, Domo had 15 daily or weekly users; 15 monthly users (accessed primarily for monthly reporting activities), 5 users who had not logged in since their initial training; and 15 users who were still waiting for their data to be added to or configured in the backend data warehouse. There are also 7 additional potential users who have requested licenses.

Each Domo user accesses data via a dashboard, initially setup by the manager of BI (e.g., Figure 1a). The dashboard is tiled with 'cards' that represent the results of a query performed on the data. Clicking on a card reveals an aggregate-level view of the data resulting from a given filter or query, offering high-level trends and pattern analysis (e.g., Figure 1b). Clicking further on the aggregate-level view accesses the drill down, which provides more granularity to the quantitative data (e.g., Figure 1c).

Domo is currently used at the highest levels of Helping Hand management and across the leadership of all departments. Other BI software is used—with varying degrees of success and varying degrees of redundancy— across different subsets of departments.

[5] The name of the organization and all of its internal departments have been anonymized.

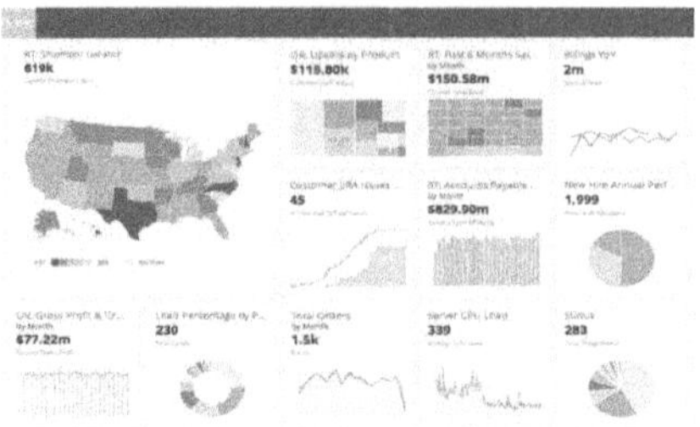

Figure 1a. Dashboards in Domo are customizable to provide snapshots of aggregated views of data.

Figure 1b. Aggregate views in Domo provide high-level visualizations of data (e.g., national retail data).

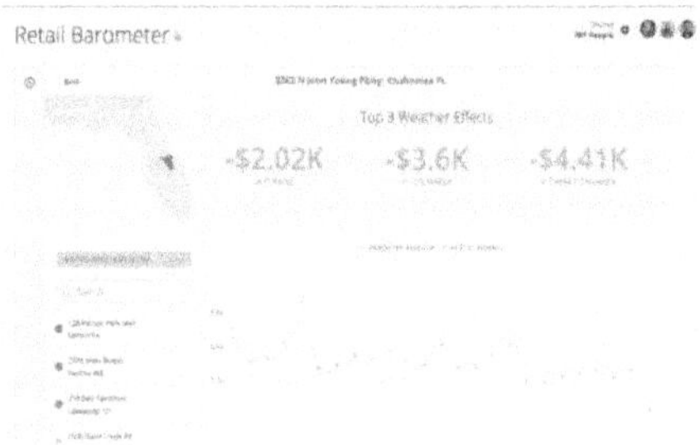

Figure 1c. From the aggregate view, users can drill down into quantitative data with more granularity (e.g., retail data from a specific state).

Education services, for example, also uses Tableau[6]. As suggested by previous research, informants in all departments used their BI system(s) as one small part of a broader ecology of information management tools—using various Excel spreadsheets, Outlook Address books, and paper-based systems to accommodate the needs and individual styles of their knowledge work [24][51].

3.2 Informants and Data Collection

We conducted semi-structured interviews (76 minutes, on average) with 17 individuals (5 female) who have end-user licenses to use Domo and sometimes other BI tools for their work at Helping Hand. 13 informants held positions in middle- and upper-level management across several departments of Helping Hand; 4 informants worked in the IT and BI departments and were responsible for the backend data warehousing and the front end data analytics.

We conducted semi-structured interviews with each informant using a protocol focused on the following areas of inquiry:

- The nature of the participants' work, their roles in the organization, and how the participants understood their work to fit into the mission of the organization;
- The different data sources they use in their work; how they collect, extract, analyze and explore that data; and the ways they make decisions with or without that data;
- The ways that the data they use relates to the mission of the organization—whether it supports or complicates the mission; and
- Their experiences of the constraints and benefits of business intelligence.

The interviews were transcribed on a rolling basis to facilitate ongoing analysis.

3.3 Data Analysis

We analyzed data iteratively and inductively using grounded theory [12]. Our initial open coding foregrounded what a culture of data meant to our informants, resulting in 33 values-related coding categories. Through iterative affinity diagramming and axial coding, we identified four core values: *data-driven*, *predictive and proactive*, *shared accountability*, and *inquisitiveness*. We returned to the data related to these core values, conducting another round of coding focused specifically on understanding the role of technology as it supports or thwarts these values, noting that these values also aligned with the mythologies ascribed to big data and BI tools. Through this analysis, we identified a series of disconnects between aggregate and drill down views of data that fundamentally shape and are shaped by understandings of what data are "actionable."

4. RESULTS

In the following sections, we introduce four core mythologies of business intelligence: *data-driven*, *predictive and proactive*, *shared accountability*, and *inquisitiveness*. Informants most frequently experienced these mythologies in terms of organizational values, both instrumental and terminal [40]. These mythologies align with the common marketing of big data and business intelligence. Yet, through our discussion of each mythology, we highlight the ways in which the enactment of each is problematized by recurring disconnects between aggregate views of data and its drill-down in business intelligence systems. These disconnects relate to informants' understandings of what it means for data to be actionable and valid for data-driven decision making.

Note that the informants frequently used the phrase 'drill down' both in a literal sense—to use the drill down feature in the BI tool to get finer granularity quantitative data—and also, more commonly, in a metaphorical sense—to get more information that does not actually exist in their BI system. We use the term 'drill-down' in the same multi-faceted fashion.

4.1 Data-Driven

The middle- and upper-level management informants at Helping Hand all speak positively and optimistically about the organization's ability to use data moving forward to improve program strategies, personnel evaluations, and workflow to serve their overarching mission better than before. Yet, informants have differing and sometimes conflicting perspectives about what kinds of data should be considered legitimate for substantiating the organization's impact and/or actionable for decision making.

Most informants conveyed a significant inclination towards using quantitative data to "prove" the effectiveness of their individual performance or the impact of the organization's work. For these informants, quantitative data is seen as the only acceptable indicator or "picture" of performance for many stakeholders:

> *It's really a prove-it-to-me type of mentality and I think it's data that's going to help us do that. (I13)*

> *So that's what we are going to try—to use the data to really drive us, and you can't quantify everything, that's just the reality, we are aware of that... but it does paint a pretty nice picture. (I3)*

From the informants' perspectives, quantitative data "proves" impact whereas qualitative data helps people "connect

[6] http://www.tableausoftware.com

emotionally" to the mission of the organization: "We want them to... connect emotionally to what we are doing. So... we tell specific stories" (I17).

Most informants do not explicitly point to qualitative data as a legitimate basis for data-driven decision making. For these individuals, qualitative data-driven decision making isn't authoritatively substantiated, it is "just based on... anecdote" (I12).

Only one informant articulated a view of qualitative data as being a "somewhat" legitimate form of empirical data for serving as the basis of data-driven decision making. He describes qualitative data as "observational" and "unstructured":

> *There is data input to every decision but some of it like I say is not in digital form, it's just observation, observational data... So that's somewhat data driven but [it's] unstructured data. And so that generates another conversation or decision point. (I6)*

Here, though, the strongest hedge in the informant's language isn't related to the qualitative nature of the data but the fact that the data is not in digital form. He describes the use of observational, unstructured data as actionable because it enables him to take action, for example to have a follow-up conversation. Other informants questioned whether data had been appropriately vetted and whether they were a reasonable basis for communication and decision making if they were not digitized and included in Domo.

Although most informants did not explicitly identify qualitative data as being a legitimate basis for being data-driven, nearly all informants recounted experiences of data-driven decision making that centered around the use qualitative data. I11, for example, reflected on an instance in which he wanted to troubleshoot production issues and expressed frustration that the data available to him in the BI system lacked the qualitative, "human element" that he wanted:

> *I can see if, you know, you're missing [production] because you don't have enough people producing or the people you do have producing are producing at half. And then when I am, you know, coaching... there is also that human element: "Well there was a death in that family, you know. I lost two people; I haven't been able to replace them yet. I'm working on that." That, you know, [there are] usually good reasons behind it and they're addressing it and they get right back up but, you know, if I could drill a little bit deeper. (I11)*

This informant explains how quantitative data is used for keeping track of their production, but he wishes he could drill down "deeper," beyond the quantitative data in the system to qualitative data that could explain the context behind the numbers. In order to drill down to the depth that he needs, this informant has to speak to the site leaders to incorporate the "human element" into his understanding. The drill down data that he seeks is not actually captured in the BI tool—nor could it easily be given the quantitative emphasis of existing BI tools. Here, the BI system seems to exacerbate the uncertainty that the informants experience in considering whether qualitative data are a legitimate basis for data-driven decision making.

Among the informants at Helping Hand, Domo is held up as an embodiment of the promise of the data-driven organization, particularly as it represents the aggregation of their activity: "At the core of our approach, one of our central tenets is measuring outcomes with data and with this system, Domo, that aggregates everything we do..." (I5). Yet, the aggregation of data in Domo supports only part of what is desired for acting on that data. This same informant continues to emphasize the complementary need to "drill down" to the context surrounding the individual clients who are being served. And, he emphasizes that the aggregate views of quantitative data are most valuable when they are used in service of the "drill down" views of data that, ideally, enable them to understand why an individual has been successful or not:

> *Our ability to measure outcomes dramatically affects how we can serve an individual. So knowing across the board where we are successful generally speaking and being able to drill down and look at on an individual basis how that success came about and we can do that. And that supports our mission in everything from the heart to the wallet. (I5)*

For these informants, the relationship between being data driven and being actionable manifests through the conflicted interplay between quantitative and qualitative data. The language that the informants are almost uniformly using to characterize the relationship is a metaphor borrowed from the business intelligence tool they use—a relationship between the aggregate and the drill down. Yet, intriguingly, while the informants speak of the drill down as ideally providing qualitative, actionable evidence of the human context surrounding the quantitative data, Domo (as with nearly all analytics tools) only provides quantitative "drill down" data, the individual-level quantitative data that is the basis for the aggregate-level quantitative data.

While the performance and legitimacy of the organization is supported by aggregate views of quantitative data, being actionable is supported by individual-level, qualitative "drill down" data that is important for responding to the unique circumstances of individuals. The informants use both qualitative and quantitative data but are unsure whether qualitative data is considered legitimate since this qualitative data doesn't actually exist in the business intelligence system. And it is frequently not even found in digital form. As such, its legitimacy is—at best—contested; at worst, the validity of this data as an actionable basis for decision making is threatened.

4.2 Predictive & Proactive

As informants work towards achieving a "culture of data" within their organization, they envision that a predictive use of data will also enable them to be more proactive. As they ramp up their business intelligence efforts, one informant characterizes the trajectory towards being proactive as the "real value" of these systems:

> *I think we are on the cusp... of shifting from a reactive look at data to a predictive data.... The real value comes... when we can actually start to predict things that are going to happen and then intervene before they do. (I8)*

According to this informant, the "real value" of business intelligence doesn't come just from the ability to aggregate historical data, but from being able to predict what is going to happen so he can act on it. This predictive capability, he continues, comes from being able to compare the drill-down "characteristics" of individuals with aggregate views of data, asking questions like: "What are the common characteristics of people who have graduated? Who have dropped out?" (I8). Yet, to act on these aggregate views of data on behalf of individuals means walking a fine line between capitalizing on the predictive capabilities of the BI system and respecting the lived experiences of their clients:

If we say that if you are an African American male, that's 23 or under, who has two kids, you know, who comes to us with fewer than 10 credits, you are highly unlikely to graduate. Right? It doesn't mean that the next African American male that shares these characteristics is not going to graduate but what we can do is start to surround him with additional support early to raise his chances, right? So it's... it is profiling... but it's what we hope is profiling in a really, really positive manner. (I8)

The informant recognizes the disconnect between the quantitative, aggregated data and the individuals with real relationships and struggles that stand to be singled out but also surrounded with additional support as a result of predictive analytics. Despite the recognition of this uncomfortable disconnect, and without clear answers about the right path forward or the right language to use to describe the proactive work that is likely to happen at the drill-down, individual level, informants are still keen about the proactive use of predictive analytics to guide their actions as they serve their clients.

4.3 Shared Accountability

For the informants at Helping Hand, a "culture of data" should foster shared accountability among individuals across the organization as well as with external funders and community members. Since the mission of all their departments is to assist low-income populations, one informant points out how important it is to keep all the programs accountable to the shared organizational mission:

My job is to use all of these programs plus all the resources that exist in [Helping Hand]... using sound evidence-based programming.... It is all these contributing. We have to work together or it doesn't work. (I12)

The value of shared accountability is manifested in many of the informants' work practices, but most significantly in data reviews:

Data reviews we started because—it's actually fundamental to, I think, the model. We want everybody to be accountable for their own data and to understand their own data (I12).

Most informants view data reviews as an opportunity to address their performance and any issues associated with it in a transparent manner with other members of the organization, providing some additional context to the quantitative data. While the shared visibility of data and the open discussion in data reviews may enable valuable forms of professional facework, it may also foster competitiveness within some subcultures internal to the organization:

They are hyper competitive... and they're like one of the most data crazy groups that you ever see... so like data hungry. [They] will go through and say, "Well, I had this percentage of my students earn credit this past term year and you only had 10% lower than I did..." And I'll sit in meetings and they'll just totally call each other out... It's crazy! (I4)

From a management perspective, access to aggregate views of data also enables the leadership to identify outliers in the productivity of their workforce and coordinate mentors and other resources to help address whatever productivity gap might exist:

If we see an issue at one school and success at another, we can say to them, the school leader that's struggling, "Hey, you need to go talk to the school leader who is knocking it out of the park with that; and let's do some coaching there." (I8)

Although the focus here is on the employee rather than the client, there is the same emphasis on understanding and supporting the individual who underlies the data. Here, aggregate views of data are helpful in comparing employee productivity, but the drill down views of quantitative data are more deeply understood and acted on in conjunction with extensive qualitative data provided through the mentoring process, outside the BI tool.

As with the multiple tenors of data use that emerge from shared accountability in data review meetings, there are also multiple tenors of data use resulting from the shared accountability of data with management. The middle- and upper-level management informants raise questions about how data should relate to employees' incentives and evaluation. Here, "performance" is used to reflect the more qualitative or subjective perceptions about employees' work whereas "outcomes" are reflections of work that have been metricized for the business intelligence system:

I read a quote the other day.... It basically said something to the effect of... you cannot connect pay with performance because performance is circumstantial. But I think you can connect pay and data and incentives to outcomes... right? So performance and outcomes, I think, are different... Our perceived performance of something... our perception of somebody's performance could be totally different... but the outcomes could still be great. Or my perception is that the performance is great but the outcome is horrible.... And so that's what we'd like to do, is really make sure however you decide to achieve your goal... we can really start to tailor some things. (I3)

This informant is still wrestling with the sometimes-conflicting forms of data that he receives about employees' work and acknowledges that observational data might not align with the quantitative data in the system. But he is still optimistic about finding some evidence-based means to evaluate employees against their goals.

Here, aggregate views of data enable the identification of employees whose productivity levels are outliers. The mythology or value of shared accountability, then, raises questions about how different individuals with access to data treat the individuals who are identified in the data.

4.4 Inquisitiveness

As more data are integrated into the data warehouse and as more users have access through Domo to the data that they want to use for data-driven decision making, the informants hope that the system will enable them to be more inquisitive about the data. A few informants reported already having conducted hypothesis-driven mini experiments by studying aggregated, longitudinal data for certain trends. In one instance, the informant created a card in Domo to "prove" the effect of missing quota on production levels:

I have a rolling twelve-month card that runs production along with the sales... and the reason why we did that was because our production... was super low and we weren't making quota. And we were trying to prove to the regional managers, well if you make quota, the next week immediately your sales are up. (I1)

The readiness-at-hand of the data, in this case, empowered this user to ask questions of the data that he was curious about. Another informant discusses a similar hypothesis-driven study of data to answer his question about whether more communication about the mission of the organization makes their customers want to donate by rounding up their payment at the stores:

> *One thing I'm curious about is that the stores that have that increased communication... are people rounding up any more frequently at those stores because they're theoretically learning more about the mission than they would at stores where we don't have those communication efforts? The reason why I'm interested in that is because there could be a couple of different hypothesis on that... This data can help us to... prove that one way or another. (I13)*

The ability to act on a value of inquisitiveness, however, relies on a certain level of technical and information literacy. Approximately 75% of all cards seen by all but one user were created by the IT or BI staff, who identify data sources, select a visualization widget, and configure the scope of the visualization. Both of the mini-studies described earlier rely on data presented in cards that had already been pre-configured in ways that were suitable for the questions they wanted to ask. Individuals who create their own cards have done so only after requesting and receiving multiple hours of one-on-one training from the IT or BI staff.

Creating a new card requires some degree of scripting skills. At the time of the study, only one user had created his own cards by modifying the scripting from existing cards; the BI staff is unsure whether his cards have been configured correctly. If inquisitiveness persists as being an organizational value, it is one that likely will privilege users who learn new skills to support the dynamic creation of new cards to answer new kinds of questions.

Users who do not yet have these skills or who prefer to explore their data in other ways—the majority of our informants—use Excel spreadsheets for their data analysis, either by collecting data redundantly in their own spreadsheets or by exporting data from the BI tool or other source systems. They feel it enables a richer and more accessible set of features for sensemaking than the drill down that is the sole analytic feature possible given a pre-defined set of cards:

> *I can't look at this [card] formatting. For me, I find it too hard. I think this is my problem, not the system's problem.... If I am not in control of the columns... it's too hard to look at, so I reformat everything. (I17)*

Most of the informants noted that their BI tools, including Domo, do not provide sufficient or sufficiently accessible control and flexibility for exploring and understanding their data. Even with a general understanding of the affordances of business intelligence tools, there is still a perceived disconnect between the resources and expertise required to make use of the pre-defined aggregate views of data and the dynamically explorable data, ideally something beyond the drill down. In order to be inquisitive and ask questions of their data beyond the visualization widgets currently set up in their dashboards, the BI tools assume both scripting and data literacy skills beyond the current expertise of these users. Fostering inquisitiveness and supporting sensemaking through different drill downs is beyond the scope of *accessible* features for the majority of informants at Helping Hand.

5. ON BEING ACTIONABLE

5.1 Mythologies of Business Intelligence and the Space for Action

Morgan refers to quantitative data as one of the mythologies shaping organizational life by lending a semblance of rationality to decision making [33]. He claims that quantitative data in formal organizations plays the same role as magic in primitive societies, enabling clear-cut decisions to be made in situations that might otherwise be open ended. Even though these techniques don't reduce risks, the mythology of rationality as supported by quantitative analysis provides credibility to organizational actions. Similarly, the mythology of big data is believed to provide higher levels of intelligence with an aura of objectivity, truth, and accuracy [8]. These mythologies compel us to question the values and biases that are embedded in organizational data and to critically examine the data that becomes legitimized through organizational action—what data is collected, what data is digitized, what data is aggregated and visualized in business intelligence systems [36][47]. It also compels us to question what kinds of action it may support or thwart.

If users consider the data in business intelligence systems to be the only valid representations of organizational ground truth for publically admissible data-driven decision making, as data reflecting informants' uncertainty about qualitative and unstructured data suggests, these biases stand to propagate through their actions. Just as the interplay of inclusion and exclusion of data in measurements can create a space for possible action [36], the space for action within an organization can be constrained by the data and visualizations contained in the business intelligence system. Especially for a human services organization serving at-risk individuals, it is important to question what data is included and excluded from measurement to understand how the values embodied by data shape rational action and organizational culture.

5.2 Disconnects Between Aggregate and Drill-Down Views

Informants in this study were optimistic about the organization's ability to foster data-driven decision making—action grounded in evidence. Yet, there is a disconnect between the kind of data these informants had available to them in the drill down of the business intelligence system and the kind of data they were looking for to provide context for their actions. For the informants in this study, quantitative data alone was not sufficient to make actionable decisions for each client's or employee's unique circumstances; they sought out qualitative data to provide more context.

Sociological scholarship predating both BI systems and the sociotechnical turn towards big data has highlighted the importance of conducting interpretive work around aggregated, quantitative data [16] (see also [30]). Even so, existing BI tools have an exclusive or nearly exclusive focus on supporting quantitative interpretive work. Our research in this new context echoes existing scholarship about the importance of interpretive work around quantitative data and highlights how essential it is that *the ecology of organizational information management systems supporting big data be redesigned to support qualitative data.* But further, our research suggests that *by not fully supporting the interpretive work of the users, the BI system further exacerbates the uncertainty that our informants expressed in considering whether qualitative data should be considered legitimate.* Despite the uncertainty, informants continue to use qualitative data collected outside the BI system—a form of shadow data—because it supports their work and enables them to take action.

Aggregate views of data have enabled these informants to present consistent data about the organization's impact to external stakeholders:

It's saying, "Look. Here is the impact the [programs] are having. Here is the investment you are making." We'd like to grow the investment and we will give more impact. (I8)

Aggregate views of data in the BI system are actionable, then, for the advocacy, education, and fundraising work that the organization is constantly doing. Aggregate views of data have also been found to be useful by some informants for validating or refuting certain hypotheses through the accumulation of their activity. For example, as the BI team at Helping Hand was able to import production and sales data into Domo, the management was able to "prove" to the site leaders that as they meet their daily production quota, their sales increases. By verifying such hypotheses with aggregate views of data, individuals can focus their efforts in more strategic ways. Aggregate views of data have also enabled these informants to see similarities and disparities among data, enabling them to identify outliers, both positive and negative. While aggregate views of data in BI systems stand as a valuable precursor to acting on data, the aggregated quantitative data alone is typically insufficient.

When these informants talk about drilling down to see individual-level data, what they are looking for is much more experiential and qualitative than the drill down provided by the BI system. This idealized "drill down" serves to enable action with clients and employees (who have been identified through aggregate views of data). Here, for data to be actionable, it has to provide enough of the "human element" to identify the right trajectory of action for each unique individual's circumstances—whether that is through mentorship, counseling, programming or otherwise.

At Helping Hand, informants are struggling to balance both quantitative, aggregate-level data and qualitative, individual-level data in their data-driven decision making and action. Their instantiation of Domo, however, only provides quantitative data—in both the drill down and aggregate. As such, this system reifies an epistemological bias about the kinds of data that are appropriately "rational" and "legitimate" for making grounded decisions in organizations [33]—an epistemological bias that these informants at Helping Hand are pushing back against, albeit uncertainly.

5.3 Design Implications and Future Work

For the design of business intelligence and data analytics systems, it is critical to find ways to more *robustly and accessibly* support the collection, aggregation and exploration of *combinations* of qualitative and quantitative data. Future research should explore the potentially varied relationships among quantitative and qualitative data in data-driven decision making and the actionable use of data across a variety of different organizations to provide a more comprehensive understanding of the design space. Our empirical work suggests value in linking aggregate views of quantitative data to finer-granularity, unstructured case notes, for example.

More significantly, this research is also a call to reconsider design for qualitative data—structured and unstructured—across the entire ecosystem of information systems used for data-driven decision making. This research challenge has implications for the user interface down to the underlying infrastructure, as well as for the interoperability of these systems. There need to be accessible ways of collecting—thus, validating—qualitative data so that they stand a chance of making it into aggregations of data in the first place, as well as accessible ways of aggregating qualitative data across multiple systems, which in nonprofit organizations may be quite niche or even custom-built. The design implications of this research extend beyond the BI tools, then, and implicate the entire pipeline of information management tools that constitute the ecology of systems being adopted by data-driven organizations.

Addressing the entire ecology of systems becomes even more critical as we reflect on the ways that BI system use differed between middle- and upper-level management informants. The upper-level management informants in this study found much more value in having data aggregated into a single BI tool. The middle-level management informants juggled many more tools in their work, using the BI tool to report up and other information management systems—sometimes data sources for the BI tool, but more often siloed systems—to manage down. So while the adoption of the BI system was intended by the upper-level management to unify the organizations' data into a singular platform that would represent organizational ground truth, this value did not extend far down the organizational chart. More often, informants were working to enact a "culture of data" from within a messy ecology of tools, some of which contained data that became less valued because it wasn't validated by being included in the data warehouse backing the BI tool.

Organizations don't exist in a vacuum; they exist among an ecology of organizational technologies, practices and expectations [37]. Any attempts to legitimize qualitative data, then, must be addressed more broadly across this ecology. If the field of human–computer interaction does not help to design better ecologies of systems, then we become complicit in propagating the epistemological biases of big data.

Especially for human services organizations, there is an increased pressure to produce evidence of impact and outcomes for key stakeholders and funders [46]. However, researchers have argued that it is imperative to account for the human, social element of mission-driven organizations, since human services organizations, in particular, invest in people rather than profit [27]. While unpacking the biases that are embedded in business intelligence systems may be particularly important in the organizational context of this case study, the kinds of epistemological biases highlighted in this research could be of relevance to other organizations across sectors of society.

6. CONCLUSION

For the informants at Helping Hand, the mythologies of business intelligence are experienced as powerful commitments to a set of organizational values. But as they attempt to enact these values through the use of BI tools, the full complement of data that they need to translate data into action are not supported by their information systems. And when data are not in the systems, there is clear uncertainty about whether data "counts" as a legitimate basis for data-driven decision making. Just as workflow systems were found to overconstrain work practices in organizations [47] (in response to [54]), we find that this class of system (BI) also overconstrains work practices *and* ways of thinking about the work. The mythologies of business intelligence scope data in and out of the system, scope understandings about legitimacy, and scope the actions that are made based on data.

In this research, we have made the following contributions:

- Identified four core mythologies that characterize an organizational culture of data: data-driven, predictive and proactive, shared accountability and inquisitiveness;
- Identified breakdowns in data-driven decision making that stem from disconnects between the aggregate and drill-down views of data in business intelligence systems;

- Provided empirical evidence of the epistemological biases of business intelligence systems propagating into confusion about what data is and should be considered legitimate for data-driven decision making; and
- Offered the first case study of the use of business intelligence and data analytics in a nonprofit organization, highlighting tensions in BI use that arise from the human services context.

Our empirical evidence suggests that the enactment of mythologies surrounding a data-driven culture require more comprehensive support for diverse types and combinations of data than are currently supported by this organization's ecosystem of information management tools. For the informants at Helping Hand, when they "drill down," they want to understand the "human element" represented by the data and they rely on that human element to help them know how to translate data into action. Given the recognition that there is a human being who underlies data, the question of how to act becomes a fundamentally moral one. And the design challenge we face is to re-envision the ecology of information management systems in ways that enable organizations to legitimize data that is most meaningful for being actionable, where what it means to be actionable may very well hinge on the moral treatment of the individuals who underlie data.

7. ACKNOWLEDGEMENTS

We are indebted to the informants at Helping Hand for sharing their time and experiences with us.

This material is based upon work supported by the National Science Foundation under Grant Number 1602660. Any opinions, findings, and conclusions or recommendations expressed in this material are those of the author(s) and do not necessarily reflect the views of the National Science Foundation

8. REFERENCES

[1] Arnold, K. E., Lynch, G., Huston, D., Wong, L., Jorn, L., and Olsen, C. W. 2014. Building institutional capacities and competencies for systemic learning analytics initiatives. In *Proceedings of the Fourth International Conference on Learning Analytics and Knowledge*. ACM, New York, NY, 257–260.

[2] Benjamin, L. M. 2008. Account space: How accountability requirements shape nonprofit practice. *Nonprofit and Voluntary Sector Quarterly*. 37, 2, 201–223.

[3] Benjamin, L. M. 2012. Nonprofit organizations and outcome measurement from tracking program activities to focusing on frontline work. *American Journal of Evaluation*. 33, 3, 431–447.

[4] Benjamin, L. M. and Campbell, D. C. 2014. Programs aren't everything. *Stanford Social Innovation Review*. 12, 2, 42–47.

[5] Benjamin, L. M. and Campbell, D. C. 2015. Nonprofit performance accounting for the agency of clients. *Nonprofit and Voluntary Sector Quarterly*. 44, 5, 988–1006.

[6] Berry, D. M. 2011. The computational turn: Thinking about the digital humanities. *Culture Machine*. 12, 2.

[7] Bonifati, A., Casati, F., Dayal, U., and Shan, M. C. 2001. Warehousing workflow data: Challenges and opportunities. In *Proceedings of the 27th VLDB Conference*. Morgan Kaufmann, San Francisco, CA, 649–652.

[8] boyd, d. and Crawford, K. 2012. Critical questions for big data: Provocations for a cultural, technological, and scholarly phenomenon. *Information, Communication & Society*. 15, 5, 662–679.

[9] Brooks, D. 2013, February 19. What data can't do. *The New York Times*. Retrieved February 18, 2015 from: http://www.nytimes.com/2013/02/19/opinion/brooks-what-data-cant-do.html

[10] Chen, H., Chiang, R. H., and Storey, V. C. 2012. Business intelligence and analytics: From big data to big impact. *MIS Quarterly*. 36, 4, 1165–1188.

[11] Chen, L. D., and Frolick, M. N. 2000. Web-based data warehousing: Fundamentals, challenges, and solutions. *Information Systems Management*. 17, 2, 76–82.

[12] Corbin, J. and Strauss, A. 2008. *Basics of qualitative research (3rd Ed.)* SAGE Publications, Los Angeles, CA.

[13] Crawford, K. 2013, April 1. The hidden biases in big data. *Harvard Business Review*. Retrieved on June 28, 2016 from: https://hbr.org/2013/04/the-hidden-biases-in-big-data

[14] Ferguson, R., Clow, D., Macfadyen, L., Essa, A., Dawson, S., and Alexander, S. 2014. Setting learning analytics in context: Overcoming the barriers to large-scale adoption. In *Proceedings of the Fourth International Conference on Learning Analytics and Knowledge*. ACM, New York, NY, 251–253.

[15] Friedman, B., Kahn, Jr., P. H., Borning, A., and Huldtgren, A. 2013. Value sensitive design and information systems. In Doorn, N., Schuurbiers, D., van de Poel, I., and Gorman, M. E. (Eds.), *Early engagement and new technologies: Opening up the laboratory*. Springer, Dordrecht, The Netherlands, 55–95.

[16] Garfinkel, H. 1967. Studies in ethnomethodology. Polity Press, Cambridge, UK.

[17] Gartner. 2016, February 3. Gartner Says Worldwide Business Intelligence and Analytics Market to Reach $16.9 Billion in 2016. Retrieved June 10, 2016 from: http://www.gartner.com /newsroom/id/3198917

[18] Gillon, K., Aral, S., Lin, C.-Y., Mithas, S., and Zozulia, M. 2014. Business analytics: Radical shift or incremental change? *Communications of the Association for Information Systems*. 34, Article 13.

[19] Hall, P. D. 2005. Historical perspectives on nonprofit organizations in the United States. In Herman, R. (Ed.), *The Jossey-Bass handbook of nonprofit leadership and management (2nd Ed.)*. Jossey-Bass, San Francisco, CA, 3–38.

[20] Hannula, M. and Pirttimäki, V. 2003. Business intelligence empirical study on the top 50 Finnish companies. *Journal of American Academy of Business*. 2, 2, 593–599.

[21] Haskins, R. and Baron, J. 2011. Building the connection between policy and evidence. In Puttick, R. (Ed.), *Using Evidence to Improve Social Policy and Practice*. Nesta, London, UK, 25–51.

[22] Hočevar, B. and Jaklič, J. 2008. Assessing benefits of business intelligence systems–a case study. *Management: Journal of Contemporary Management Issues*. 13, 2, 87–119.

[23] Kandel, S., Paepcke, A., Hellerstein, J. M., and Heer, J. 2012. Enterprise data analysis and visualization: An interview study. *IEEE Transactions on Visualization and Computer Graphics*. 18, 12, 2917–2926.

[24] Kidd, A. 1994.The marks are on the knowledge worker. In *Proceedings of the SIGCHI Conference on Human Factors in Computing Systems*. ACM, New York, NY, 186–191.

[25] Kitchin, R. 2014. Big data, new epistemologies and paradigm shifts. *Big Data & Society*. 1, 1, 1–12.

[26] Kohavi, R., Rothleder, N. J., and Simoudis, E. 2002. Emerging trends in business analytics. *Communications of the ACM*. 45, 8, 45–48.

[27] Kong, E. 2008. The development of strategic management in the non-profit context: Intellectual capital in social service non-profit organizations. *International Journal of Management Reviews*. 10, 3, 281–299.

[28] Le Dantec, C. A., Poole, E., and Wyche, S. 2009. Values as lived experience: Evolving value sensitive design in support of value discovery. In *Proceedings of the SIGCHI Conference on Human Factors in Computing Systems*. ACM, New York, NY, 1141–1150.

[29] Lohr, S. 2012, February 12. The age of big data. *The New York Times Sunday Review*. Retrieved January 15, 2016 from: http://www.nytimes.com/2012/02/12/sunday-review/big-datas-impact-in-the-world.html

[30] Mair, M., Greiffenhagen, C., and Sharrock, W. W. 2015, January 6. Statistical practice: Putting society on display. *Theory, Culture & Society*. 1–27.

[31] Manovich, L. 2011. Trending: The promises and the challenges of big social data. In Gold, M. K. (Ed.) *Debates in the digital humanities*. University of Minnesota Press, Minneapolis, MN, 460–475.

[32] Miller, J. K., Friedman, B., Jancke, G., and Gill, B. 2007. Value tensions in design: The value sensitive design, development, and appropriation of a corporation's groupware system. In *Proceedings of the 2007 International ACM Conference on Supporting Group Work*. ACM, New York, NY, 281–290.

[33] Morgan, G. 1997. *Images of organization*. SAGE Publications, Thousand Oaks, CA.

[34] O'Neill, M. 2002. *Nonprofit nation: A new look at the third America*. John Wiley & Sons, San Francisco, CA.

[35] Piccoli, G. and Watson, R. 2008. Profit from customer data by identifying strategic opportunities and adopting the 'born digital' approach. *MIS Quarterly Executive*. 7, 3, 113–122.

[36] Pine, K. H. and Liboiron, M. 2015. The politics of measurement and action. In *Proceedings of the 33rd Annual ACM Conference on Human Factors in Computing Systems*. ACM, New York, NY, 3147–3156.

[37] Powell, W. W. and DiMaggio, P. J. (Eds.). 2012. *The new institutionalism in organizational analysis*. University of Chicago Press, Chicago, IL.

[38] Reeves, P. L. and Burt, W. L. 2006. Challenges in data-based decision-making: Voices from principals. *Educational HORIZONS*. 85, 1, 65–71.

[39] Ribes, D. and Jackson, S. J. 2013. Data bite man: The work of sustaining a long–term study. In Gitelman, L. (Ed.), *"Raw data" is an oxymoron*. MIT Press, Cambridge, MA, 147–166.

[40] Rokeach, M. 1973. *The nature of human values*. Free Press, New York, NY.

[41] Saidel, J. R. and Cour, S. 2003. Information technology and the voluntary sector workplace. *Nonprofit and Voluntary Sector Quarterly*. 32, 1, 5–24.

[42] Salamon, L. M. 1992. *America's nonprofit sector: A primer*. Foundation Center, New York, NY.

[43] Salamon, L. M. and Sokolowski, S. W. 2004. *Global civil society, vol. 2: Dimensions of the nonprofit sector*. Kumarian Press, Bloomfield, CT.

[44] Shanks, G. and Bekmamedova, N. 2012. Achieving benefits with business analytics systems: An evolutionary process perspective. *Journal of Decision Systems*. 21, 3, 231–244.

[45] Shin, B. 2003. An exploratory investigation of system success factors in data warehousing. *Journal of the Association for Information Systems*. 4, 1, 6.

[46] Snibbe, A. C. 2006. Drowning in data. *Stanford Social Innovation Review*. Fall, 38–45. Retrieved June 5, 2007 from http://ssir.org/images/articles/2006FA_feature_ snibbe.pdf.

[47] Suchman, L. 1993. Do categories have politics? The language/action perspective reconsidered. In *Proceedings of the Third European Conference on Computer-Supported Cooperative Work*. Springer, Dordrecht, The Netherlands, 1–14.

[48] Swenson, J. 2014. Establishing an ethical literacy for learning analytics. In *Proceedings of the Fourth International Conference on Learning Analytics and Knowledge*. ACM, New York, NY, 246–250.

[49] Van Til, J. 1994. Nonprofit organizations and social institutions. In Herman, R. D. (Ed.), *The Jossey-Bass handbook of nonprofit leadership and management (2nd ed.)*. Jossey-Bass, San Francisco, CA, 44–64.

[50] Voida, A., Dombrowski, L., Hayes, G. R., and Mazmanian, M. 2014. Shared values/conflicting logics: Working around e-government systems. In *Proceedings of the SIGCHI Conference on Human Factors in Computing Systems*. ACM, New York, NY, 3583–3592.

[51] Voida, A., Harmon, E., and Al-Ani, B. 2011. Homebrew databases: Complexities of everyday information management in nonprofit organizations. In *Proceedings of the SIGCHI Conference on Human Factors in Computing Systems*. ACM, New York, NY, 915–924.

[52] Watson, H. J. and Wixom, B. H. 2007. The current state of business intelligence. *Computer*. 40, 9, 96–99.

[53] Watson, H. J., Wixom, B. H., Hoffer, J. A., Anderson-Lehman, R., and Reynolds, A. M. 2006. Real-time business intelligence: Best practices at Continental Airlines. *Information Systems Management*. 23, 1, 7.

[54] Winograd, T. 1986. A language/action perspective on the design of cooperative work. In *Proceedings of the 1986 ACM Conference on Computer-Supported Cooperative Work*. ACM, New York, NY, 203–220.

[55] Wixom, B. H. and Watson, H. J. 2001. An empirical investigation of the factors affecting data warehousing success. *MIS Quarterly*. 25, 1, 17–41.

[56] Yeoh, W. and Koronios, A. 2010. Critical success factors for business intelligence systems. *Journal of Computer Information Systems*. 50, 3, 23–32.

[57] Yin, R. K. 1994. *Case study research: Design and methods*. SAGE Publications, Thousand Oaks, CA

The IKEA Catalogue: Design Fiction in Academic and Industrial Collaborations

Barry Brown, Julian Bleecker, Marco D'Adamo, Pedro Ferreira, Joakim Formo, Mareike Glöss, Maria Holm, Kristina Höök, Eva-Carin Banka Johnson, Emil Kaburuan, Anna Karlsson,Elsa Kosmack-Vaara, Jarmo Laaksolahti, Airi Lampinen, Lucian Leahu, Vincent Lewandowski, Donald McMillan, Anders Mellbratt, Johanna Mercurio, Cristian Norlin, Nicolas Nova, Stefania Pizza, Asreen Rostami, Mårten Sundquist, Konrad Tollmar, Vasiliki Tsaknaki, Jinyi Wang, Charles Windlin, Mikael Ydholm

Mobile Life Centre
Kista, Stockholm
barry@mobilelifecentre.org

1. INTRODUCTION

This paper is an introduction to the "Future IKEA Catalogue", enclosed here as an example of a *design fiction* produced from a long standing industrial-academic collaboration. We introduce the catalogue here by discussing some of our experiences using design fiction` with companies and public sector bodies, giving some background to the catalogue and the collaboration which produced it. We have found design fiction to be a useful tool to support collaboration with industrial partners in research projects – it provides a way of thinking and talking about present day concepts, and present day constraints, without being overly concerned with contemporary challenges, or the requirements of academic validation. In particular, there are two main aspects of this we will discuss here, aspects that are visible in the enclosed catalogue itself. The first is the potential of design fiction as a sort of 'boundary object' in industry and academic collaboration, and second the role of *critique*. After this introduction to the paper we enclose the output of our collaboration in the form of the catalogue itself

2. Boundary objects and critique

The research centre where we work brings together ten or so companies (including IKEA), along with three host academic institutions, working together on different technology and interaction related research projects. Research collaborations with industry are something that can face many challenges for both industrial and academic partners. First, there is the question of different expectations over timelines and the sorts of problems research should address. While it is not always the case, broadly academic partners have a much longer focus, whereas industrial partners need focus on much shorter timespans. The lifetime of a company in the fortune 500 is less than fifteen years – one perhaps should think how universities would behave if they only survived for on average fifteen years. In turn, success for industrial partners in a project is often seen through impact on their own company. Careers within companies are made (and not) on internal company impact. For academics – while impact is important, it is mainly through publications and teaching. Research collaborations can hit problems when the 'output' is narrowly defined in terms of an academic paper, or what will fit with an academic paper, in contrast to what will have an 'impact' within an organisation. It is here that we have found design fiction 'surprisingly useful' [6]. Design fiction offers the possibility for a different genera of communication, a possibility for collaboration that escapes the limitations of a lengthy academic paper or specific technical prototypes. The fiction acts as a sort of "boundary object" –between academics and practitioners, meaning different things to different groups. As Star and Greisemer put it, boundary objects are: "objects which are both plastic enough to adapt to local needs and constraints of the several parties employing them, yet robust enough to maintain a common identity across sites." [7].

From an academic viewpoint design fictions can be seen as a way of experimenting with ideas and issues. Fictions are perhaps not as heavyweight as an academic publication, without the requirements of citation, verification and the like. This allows for more speculative and potentially innovative thinking. Design fictions can thus be used to illustrate and provoke ideas that are in development, particularly where design is part of the ideas in development. For industrial participants, design fiction is in turn a

Figure 1: Bookshelf "levels of service" – something between industrial and academic concerns

GROUP '16, November 13-16, 2016, Sanibel Island, FL, USA
© 2016 ACM. ISBN 978-1-4503-4276-6/16/11…$15.00
DOI: http://dx.doi.org/10.1145/2957276.2957298

venue where ideas can be experimented with and implications discussed, without being seen necessarily as a comment on current products or practices. Their ambiguity means that participants can speculate without worrying about negative implications being drawn for the present. Figure one is a demonstration of this from the catalogue. On one side it talks to the way in which IKEA has always moved 'labour' (such as construction and transpiration) to the purchaser, allowing it to sell products for much cheaper. Yet, on the other side, it also talks to an interest in 'labour', maker culture and DIY. How would IKEA interact with those who want to 'hack' and build variations on the NYFIKEN bookshelf? What if personal fabrication is more widespread, would IKEA simply sell plans and 3D cad models?

A second interesting issue about working together on design fictions is how a design fiction can act as a piece of critique. The relationship between design fiction and the (perhaps better known in HCI) *critical design* illustrates this issue. It is not that design fiction is without critique, and critical design is all about critique – nor is it that organizations (commercial and public) are unable to deal with critique as part of projects they work on. Rather what matters is the form that critique takes, and how it can contribute to a collaboration, rather than seeming as an "academic privileging" that steps outside a specific situation [4]. While it is a broad and perhaps even contested term, *critical design* has at its heart the subversion of status quo through the deployment of irony and satire. In the work by Dunne & Raby [3] that coined the term, there is an attempt to subvert design's focus on "the product" – the ways in which design usually takes for granted its relationship with commerce, (over)-production, consumption and the like. As Pierce *et al* put it, critical design is an attempt to "question[s] the role of design in shaping our everyday reality." [5] Yet, as Pierce *et al* also point out, there is increasing diversity in what is described as or subverts "critical design" (Dunne & Raby themselves have moved more on to use the term 'speculative design'). Critique is still central to the enterprise - in Bardzell & Bardzell's [1] use of the term, there is an even more explicit connection with humanistic critical theory, and cultural studies.

In contrast, *design fiction* is less clearly a critical enterprise. It has a lineage is perhaps less in design (or even critical theory), but rather in *science fiction*. As Bruce Sterling describes it, design fiction is "when science fiction thinking opens itself to design thinking" [8]. If good science fiction tells us not about the future but about the present, then design fiction itself also reveals our fears and problems in current time. Bleecker's design fiction work includes 'catalogues' of concepts that are simultaneously uncomfortable, but at times also reassuring – concepts that paint a story of a particular future, playing on our hopes and fears of the present [2]. Critique is sublimated within other engagements, humour; spectacle; aspiration; technological desire. This is not to say that design fiction is without critique – as with science fiction much of the work is clearly critical in intent. Yet it can go further - design fictions can be possible but interesting, unusual but also upsetting. Design fiction without critique is neutered – falling into corporate publicity. Yet design fiction perhaps has more diverse goals than critical design.

When working on design fiction with large, privately funded companies and large, publically funded government organisations, one question that we encountered is *how critical do you want to be*? Or more specifically, what is the useful role of critique in such collaborations: of technology, of futures, of contradictions in the present, or – indeed – of the role of the company that is participating in the project? In rethinking technology, it is hard to avoid being critical to some extent. Thinking about different futures involve looking for contradictions in current systems or practices, or trends that may be benign or merely frustrating (such as incompatibilities), but with benign potential. Yet being critical might cause all sorts of problems in collaborations and even in interaction. The first can come in working with those who might be uncomfortable, or hostile, to this sort of critical thinking. An inescapable part of corporate culture in nearly every organisation is to avoid direct explicit public critique of that organisation itself. This can conflict with a more critical intent.

Perhaps, more insidiously, there is also the question of how we might end up (in advance) censoring our work so as to avoid a perceived conflict. As we respond to ideas, and concepts the work might simply never be guided in a critical direction, simply replicating the worldviews of participants. Or there are times when a direct critique might simply fail to gain purchase. One of the very points of working with large non-academic organisations is that they have power and influence. That power can come through explicit legislation and policy (when working through public sector bodies) or through an influence on what is made and sold, or even just on the transmission of ideas that takes place in forums outside academia. Collaborations offer the possibility of a positive *influence* – but at some level this is reliant on communication and personal relationships. Critique – if it takes the wrong form, if it is clumsy or too brazen – can seem indulgent or simply irrelevant. We might say that a specific comment or investigation about an issue might lead to engagement and reflection, whereas a broader critique could be summarily rejected. Perhaps academic work should have little concern for these issues. But research in conjunction with industry has the potential to have a positive influence through and with different organizations and public bodies. An important purpose of industrial collaboration is to rejuvenate academic work by patching it together with industrial concerns, and to rejuvenate industrial work with new ideas and arguments.

One way we have sought to deal with this is by the use of *equivocality* in our designs. Equivocality in design fiction involves ideas that incorporate concepts that make the reader uncomfortable. There is the aim of visualizing ideas that have multiple meanings, that are presented in a straightforward way but that leave room for different readings. Working with equivocality lets us explore subversions that rather than acting as leaden criticism, are more playful and open to different engagements. This is a little like the use of homophonic puns in mandarin as a way of subverting Internet censorship.

3. The catalogue

Moving onto our specific output - the catalogue enclosed here was produced as a group effort bringing together collaborators from public sector bodies, academic institutes, and major organisations - including Stockholm City, IKEA and Ericsson. We worked together over different concepts trying to establish possible futures that highlighted the sorts of tensions that we though were

Figure 2: How do we feel about IKEA selling living organisms? What about a pricing model work where we need to pay 9.99 per month for a *lifetime subscription only*?

interesting to investigate, as well as productive in terms of design.

Throughout the catalogue we attempted to mix the sort of wholesome scenes that one encountered in a contemporary catalogue, with possible subversions. So, on the first page we see a typical gendered family scene - father away, while mother plays with child. Yet the scene entails two subversions: the sofa is watching what unfolds, collecting memories, and the father is wearing a VR headset. This makes the scene perhaps a little bit more shocking, the father is not merely attending to a different activity, but they are in a different space – their vision glanced by a memory recording sofa. Similarly, on pages 5 and 6, we see one ongoing concern of IKEA play out in an unusual way. Here, we have a storage cabinet, but one that mixes digital recommendations, delivered by drones. What we see is a play between a concern for storage in a digital world, with the rather intrusive "analysis [of daily activities] for an accurate subscription offer". At first glance, the catalogue then offers a rather cozy futuristic vision, but if one looks at the copy instead one can read a more equivocal vision: IKEA as not only the provider of the home, but as a data collection entity. How would we feel about IKEA replacing Google as the repository of our memories?

4. Conclusion

We only are at the beginning of experimenting with design fiction and the role it can play in these collaborations. The enclosed catalogue helped us start to explore new ways of collaborating with industry, but has also been adopted for use in teaching by our colleagues, as well as encouraging our industrial partners to pick up the ideas and run their own design fiction events. Clearly, it conveys research in different ways and lets us reach out. In the enclosed catalogue you can see examples of the equivocality, critique, and boundary objects in particular designs. Yet more broadly, the opportunity here comes from the possibilities of working with a new form for academic research – not just as a new way of communicating research outcomes, but as a new forum for communication and collaboration with a variety of partners.

5. ACKNOWLEDGMENTS

The authors are collaborators in the Mobile Life Centre, as such we also thank the host collaborating companies and organisations.

6. REFERENCES

1. Jeffrey Bardzell and Shaowen Bardzell. 2015. Humanistic Hci. *Synthesis Lectures on Human-Centered Informatics* 8, 4: 1–185.
2. Julian Bleecker. 2009. Design Fiction: A short essay on design, science, fact and fiction. *Near Future Laboratory* 29.
3. Anthony Dunne. 2008. *Hertzian tales: Electronic products, aesthetic experience, and critical design*. MIT Press. Retrieved February 10, 2016 from http://www.citeulike.org/group/7111/article/3508492
4. Michael Lynch. 2000. Against Reflexivity as an Academic Virtue and Source of Privileged Knowledge. *Theory, Culture & Society* 17, 3: 26–54. http://doi.org/10.1177/02632760022051202
5. James Pierce, Phoebe Sengers, Tad Hirsch, Tom Jenkins, William Gaver, and Carl DiSalvo. 2015. Expanding and refining design and criticality in HCI. *Proceedings of the 33rd Annual ACM Conference on Human Factors in Computing Systems*, ACM, 2083–2092. Retrieved February 10, 2016 from http://dl.acm.org/citation.cfm?id=2702438
6. Ian Sommerville, Tom Rodden, Pete Sawyer, and Richard Bentley. 1992. Sociologists can be suprisingly useful in interactive systems design. In *Proceedings of the HCI'92 Conference on People and Computers VII*. pp 341–353.
7. Susan Leigh Star and James R. Griesemer. 1989. Institutional Ecology, 'Translations' and Boundary Objects: Amateurs and Professionals in Berkeley's Museum of Vertebrate Zoology, 1907-39. *Social Studies of Science* 19, 3: 387–420. http://doi.org/10.1177/030631289019003001
8. Bruce Sterling. 2005. Shaping Things (Mediaworks Pamphlets). Retrieved February 10, 2016 from http://www.citeulike.org/group/7111/article/548260

1 WELLBEING
NOSTALGI
sofa
Essential Life Stream Interoperable sofa for the well-being of you and your family for now and forever. No shared ownership of activity streams with single domicile subscriptions. Configurable color and pattern schemes by Olafur Elliason™ change in real-time to suit your temperament with Philips Medical Inductive Mood Sense-Storage (Subscription fees apply.) Compatible with most modern charging systems. White. 000.000.01
52399:-
(c) InterIKEA Systems B.V. 2015
WELLBEING 2
-15°C
12%
The more you capture your experiences, the more wealth you create from your data analytics. When and where you sit, what and how you cook for dinner, your sleep patterns and movements in bed, the patterns of foot-falls on area rugs and carpets, when and how you open doors, how and of what sort of bathroom behaviors — all of these can be captured, analyzed, shared and sold. IKEA is the #1 source of beautifully designed, well-constructed and assembled essentials for your home that give you control over your sensed behaviors.
Ari Birnbaum
The Data Wealth King, Author, Speaker, Commentator
(c) InterIKEA Systems B.V. 2015

LIV
MoSS® carpet
Semi-organic "moss"-like carpet that grows slowly over your existing flooring while also producing environmental cleansing and scrubbing characteristics. LIV is the natural way to enhance the air in your home by creating a biosynthetic effervescent plume of aromatherapeutic compounds making your habitat sustainable, healthful, comfortable underfoot and absorbent.

6.99:-/sq meter

NEW ITEM
The LIV shampoo and conditioner grow themselves saving ordering and hassles of running short. Re-grows and replenishes naturally, organically through safe, secure biosynthesis and genetic regeneration.

LIV
Shampoo & Conditioner
Eco friendly, self-replenishing from bio-generating base starter compounds. Never run out, ever. Lifetime subscription only.
LIV Shampoo. 800.456.20
LIV Conditioner. 800.456.21

9.99:-*/month

* Lifetime only.

5 LIFESTYLE
During the months of January to March NYFIKEN IS FEATURING the third book of the 2nd Harry Potter Saga
NYFIKEN
bookshelf
Composite material, extruded and printed to your CAD.
IKEA TILLSAMMANS Compatible.
Dark Grey. 367.908.07
899:-
399:-
199:-
Levels of Service:
III Ikea will print on your premise, assemble, decompose and replace the shelf.
II DIY plans and 3D CAD provided for you to build to suit.
I DIY base materials with 2D CAD using your own saw, hammer, screwdriver(s), drill, fasteners, etc.
COMBINE NYFIKEN bookshelf with:
NYFIKEN
subscription lifestyle
Subscribe to NYFIKEN to have Google Trending Items, News, Book Excerpts, Movies, Restaurant Reservations delivered to your bookshelf. NYFIKEN will make sure that you are always up to date and have items that reflect your* lifestyle** interests, habits, ambitions and futureSelf™. Analog and material items will be delivered by IKEA's trusted service personnel.***
129:-
/month
* Subscription requires that you are a member of TILLSAMMANS. Please read more on page X.
** Your daily activities, purchases will be analysed for an accurate subscription offer.
*** Human delivery standard. Drone delivery extra charges may apply.
LIFESTYLE 6
(c) InterIKEA Systems B.V. 2015
(c) InterIKEA Systems B.V. 2015

7 WELLBEING
SÖMNRIK
bed
Let your sleeping preferences, mattress density, pillow fluff-factor, self-comforting comforter temperature profiles follow you whenever you go to any of our network of hotelier affiliates.
Preferences and biometrics are all safely stored in the IKEA TILLSAMMANS Cloud.
249:-
/year/household
SHANGRI-LA
Hilton
RUMLA
mattress
SÖMNRIK-compatible Smart Mattress that adjusts moisture vapor, temperature, self-comforting, pliability, thickness and density based on your preferences, ambient temperature, futureSelf™ calendar and intimate body biometrics.
Soft. 333.986.13
2999:-/year
Also check out our other smart sheets FUMLA and TUMLA. with experiental qualaties such has hugging or poking. For extra features please check out new releases on the Smart Sheet app.
www.ikea.com
(c) InterIKEA Systems B.V. 2015

WELLBEING 8
AVKOPPLAD
Canopy
Bed Canopy for wellbeing. Cotton and polycarbonate.
White 670.893.27
899:-
499:-
SKINA
Textile
Light emitting curtain provides healthful ambient energy while hybrid polyester-copper conductive threading prevents incursion of billions of watts of RF energy circulating the globe. Dial-up or dial-down shielding factor to suit your own tastes.
All Colors 340.283.41
AVKOPPLAD
The low network/no screen activity canopy AVKOPPLAD is a natural sleep aid, encouraging faster sleep sooner, as well as longer, deeper sleep. Spend more time sleeping with loved ones in the same room. The canopy minimizes non-essential networks within a radius of 3 meters. Generates pulsed Schumann electromagnetic fields at both 1.2 and 2.4 Hz producing therapeutic effects for longer, more lasting and palliative sleep.
(c) InterIKEA Systems B.V. 2015

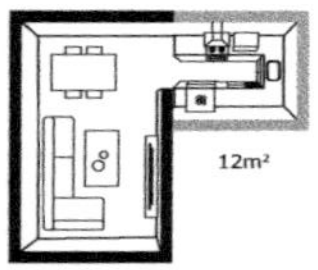

New **KRÄFTSKIVA kitchen module* 29:-/h/guest**
Host more guests than you can. Dinner party containment structure, max 8 people per module. Wide range of global cuisine included (local cultural license fees may apply).

Combine with:
DELNING
Self-subscribing food storage & pantry
99:-/month/family member
De-clutter your home by placing all fresh, perishable, frozen and diffusion foodstuffs in a central, safe, encrypted, biometric security storage unit. Compatible with IKEA Foods, Wholefoods, Tesco and Amazon. 712.234.76

* Connects to any IKEA Garden Home with compatible Facade, Patio, Roof Deck or Promenade.

New service **FOLKLIG**
kitchen activity/preparation counter 1295:-
Active Clever Agent provides precise, friendly, sensible instructions for measurements, volumes, directions and lively anecdotes helping you prepare a wide range of recipes from around the world.*
457.321.01

* Comes with complete library of Scandinavian specialties and sauces.

FOLKLIG
kitchen service contract 36:-/month
Powerful privacy controls and personal diet recommendations based on your IKEA Tillsammans profile analytics. 647.123.45

Your data makes all the difference!

You've heard Ari Birnbaum saying, "Your data is your life". IKEA Tillsammans now provides a way for you to 'share your life data' to help advance the world. With contributions of your life data analytics (or portion thereof) you will be providing a wealth of insights, personal perspectives, thoughts, images, experiences and opinions in a partially-completely anonymized fashion. Your data* informs political decisions, creates laws, builds attention for social, economic and interpersonal issues.

Complete analytic visibility to see how your data is being used, what actions it informs, what lives it saves where, who imitates who, whose lifestream is authentic and whose lifestream is a reflection of their sense of inadequacy or regret, what issues your data creates and/or enforces. Join the world, even more than before. Contributions are often tax-deductible in most regions proportionate to your level of openness and unprivacy.

* US/EU regulations require us to release data on request to relevant agencies. Payment of a subscription is not a guarantee of privacy.

What is IKEA Tillsammans?

IKEA Future collects data to help aid research in various ecological, technical and political fields. We are working on plan for our long term sustainable ethical future.

Read up on our work at www.IKEATillsammans.org

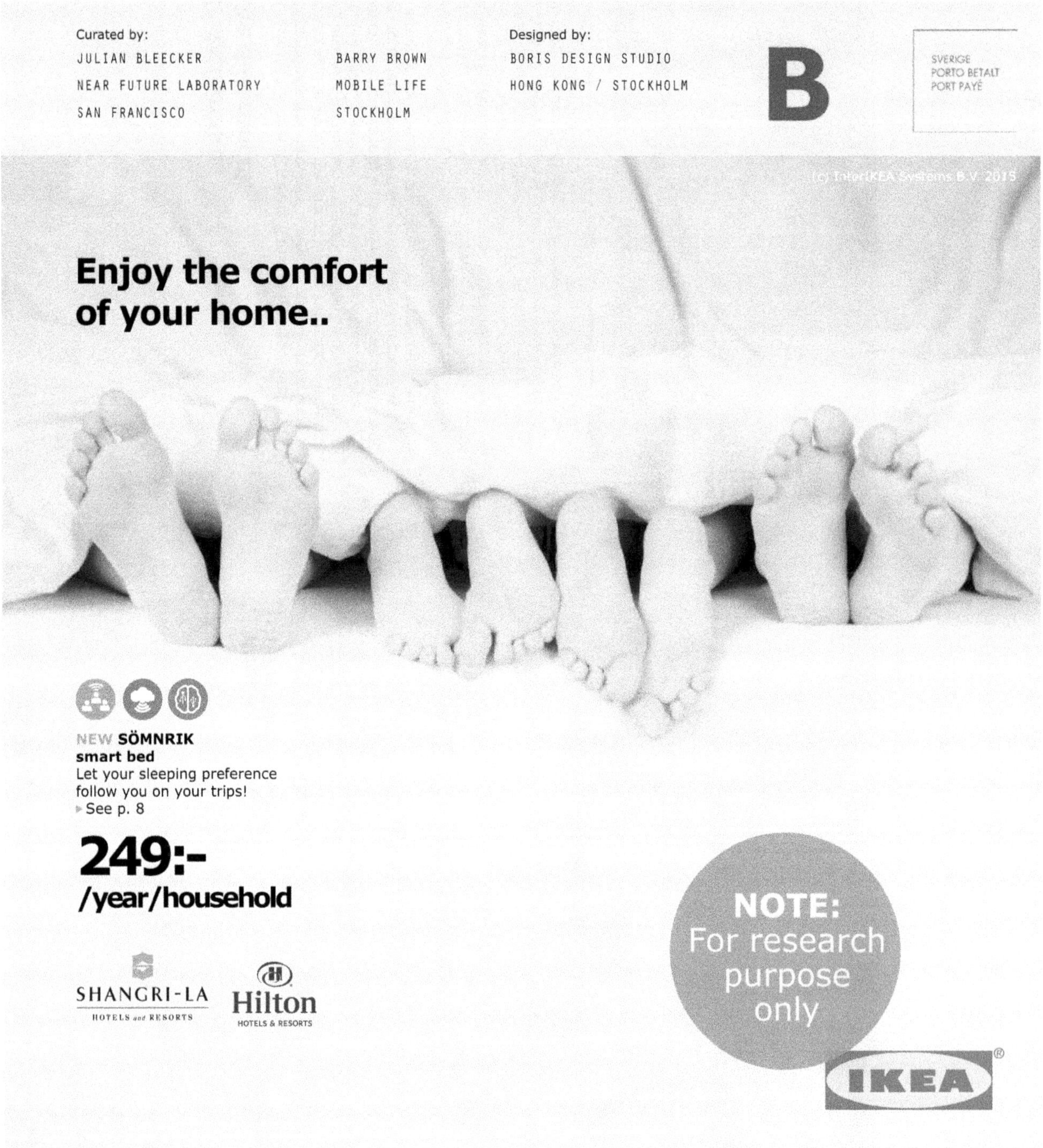
Curated by:
JULIAN BLEECKER
NEAR FUTURE LABORATORY
SAN FRANCISCO
BARRY BROWN
MOBILE LIFE
STOCKHOLM
Designed by:
BORIS DESIGN STUDIO
HONG KONG / STOCKHOLM
B
SVERIGE
PORTO BETALT
PORT PAYÉ
(c) InterIKEA Systems B.V. 2015
Enjoy the comfort of your home..
NEW SÖMNRIK
smart bed
Let your sleeping preference follow you on your trips!
See p. 8
249:-
/year/household
SHANGRI-LA
HOTELS and RESORTS
Hilton
HOTELS & RESORTS
NOTE:
For research purpose only
IKEA

The Co-ordinates of Design Fiction: Extrapolation, Irony, Ambiguity and Magic

Mark Blythe
Northumbria University
mark.blythe@northumbria.ac.uk

Enrique Encinas
Northumbria University
enrique.encinas@northumbria.ac.uk

ABSTRACT

This paper argues that design fiction is a powerful term in part because it is malleable. A wide range of differing design fictions are emerging and we pursue a spatial metaphor to provide a map based on literary approaches. Following Margaret Atwood we trace design fiction back to marvel and wonder tales such as the Arabian Nights through to the science fiction of the nineteenth and twentieth century. We suggest science, magic, ambiguity and irony as the cardinal points of design fiction. We then apply these four different approaches to design fiction to the concept of a divorce app for older people. We argue that currently design fiction is dominated by scientistic and ironic design fiction and suggest that magic and ambiguity are currently under explored.

Author Keywords

Design fiction; well being; older people; magic;

ACM Classification Keywords

H.5.m. Information interfaces and presentation

INTRODUCTION

In a 2013 keynote the science fiction writer who coined the term "design fiction" warned that we were going to see a lot more of it because it was cheap and relatively easy to do. He warned that this would lead to problems:

"There's just gonna be way too much, there's already way too much. What's really needed at this point is some kind of categorization and logical organization for all of these techno-fantasies. Cos they're interesting but they're interesting in different ways. Like a techno fantasy that's done by a clever nineteen year old girl that's done in an art school is not in the same category as a Google Glass conceptual video [..] We need a taxonomy of dragons. We need somebody to go out - collect 'em, brand 'em, categorise' em, say which is the good ones and which are the bad ones, put em in corals. Your group of people I'm thinking would be kinda ideal for that, it like suits your skills" [47]

Academics were already working on the task and in the same year a special issue of the journal *Design Creativity* provided a partial taxonomy of Design Fiction [24]. This taxonomy takes as a primary example the near future science fiction of Sterling's friend and collaborator William Gibson. Gibson pays close attention to technological developments and his latest novel, in which drone cameras hover around celebrities like flies, is well researched and plausible.

Plausibility was key to Sterling's 2005 definition of design fiction in his book *Shaping Things*:

"Science fiction wants to invoke the grandeur and credibility of science for its own hand waving hocus pocus, but design fiction can be more practical, more hands – on. It sacrifices some sense of the miraculous, but it moves much closer to the glowing heat of techno-social conflict" [46]

For Sterling design fiction writers think hard about how imagined technologies would work and what impact they might have. The social impact of technology also concerned Dourish and Bell, and their influential paper "Resistance is Futile" contrasted the visionary "Sal" [53] scenario by the Xerox PARC scientist Marc Weiser with popular science fiction like Planet of the Apes. Weiser's scenario, written in the early nineteen nineties, envisioned many of the technologies that we use today. Sal works in an office linked with international branches by video links and distant workers collaborate on documents in real time. Dourish and Bell pointed out that popular science fiction TV shows were much more concerned with social context than conventional HCI scenarios usually were. There is little to no discussion of the kind of society Sal lives in [13]. What design scenarios typically leave unsaid is the implicit social and political context of a design.

The editors of the Personal and Ubiquitous Computing journal proposed a special issue with responses to this paper which included a piece by Julian Bleecker on design fiction [6]. Although the journal was not published until 2014 the draft papers were in circulation from 2009 and Bleecker's was available online. Here he argued for the importance of diegesis, a term from film studies used to indicate something that is part of a larger fictional world. For media studies

GROUP '16, November 13 - 16, 2016, Sanibel Island, FL, USA

ACM 978-1-4503-4276-6/16/11…$15.00
DOI: http://dx.doi.org/10.1145/2957276.2957299

scholars like Kirby the props in movies like *Minority Report* are "diegetic prototypes" in that they function as a part, rather than the point of a story, but also because they present the imagined technology as desirable or benevolent [28].

The partial taxonomy by Hale [24] included its use in corporate propaganda. Microsoft and Phillips have both presented design fictions in promotional films bearing, according to Gonzattoa and van Amstela, the implicit message – "don't worry the future is safe in our hands" [22]. Although it has corporate uses design fictions are more often conceived as critiques and provocations as in the "critical design" of Dunne and Raby [1,2,9,17]. Hale's taxonomy, as suggested by Sterling, takes the originators of the fiction as a point of categorization: a corporate fiction by a company like Google is clearly very different to a fiction by a well established author like William Gibson. The taxonomy also considers the different forms design fiction can take - narratives, short stories, sketches, images, films but also objects and semi-working prototypes. Julian Bleecker's work with the Near Future Lab now takes the form of magazine articles and advertisements for products and services that do not exist yet.

Design fiction is a malleable concept: it can take the form of text, image, audio, video, model, working prototype or event; it can be conceived as a plausible idea for a technology developed with "designerly thinking", an eye for detail and practical concerns; it can be framed as a conceptual design placed within a broad cultural context focusing not just on product functionality but potential social consequences of use; it can be a tool for corporate propaganda or a means of expressing concern, dissent and critique. Small wonder then that such a flexible term has, as Sterling predicted, really caught on [e.g. 6,7,8,22,24,29,31].

While all of these competing definitions and categorizations are interesting and useful we propose in this paper a different categorization. This is based not on the source, the medium or the intent but rather the devices employed and the literary traditions at work. We do not employ a rigid methodology to develop an exhaustive taxonomy, rather we draw on literary analysis to identify broad patterns and family resemblances between fictions. This analysis is presented in the following sections with illustrative examples.

EXTRAPOLATIVE AND SCIENCTISTIC DESIGN FICTION

Like Bruce Sterling and William Gibson, the founding father of science fiction, HG Wells, kept abreast of the scientific developments of his day. Wells is probably best remembered today for *The War of the Worlds* because of the many radio, television, musical and film adaptations. We now know that there is no life on Mars so Wells' story would fail Sterling's plausibility test today. But, despite the famous opening lines of the novel, it is not quite true that in the 19th century "no one would have believed" that a Martian invasion was possible. In 1897, the year of the novel's publication, life on Mars was considered at the very least a possibility. Wells' other novels, though less widely known now, were fully plausible visions of the future, indeed some were fully realized only a decade or so after publication. *The War in the Air* was published in 1907 when human flight was as much of a fantasy for most of Wells' contemporaries as it had been for the Ancient Greeks. And yet Wells predicted warplanes and aerial bombardment a full ten years before their use in the First World War. After reading some fairly obscure scientific work on the behavior of radium and strange particles Wells realized that were the energy described to be harnessed one day, then someone could make a bomb out of it. His novel, *The World Set Free*, written in 1913 predicted that humanity would develop the atom bomb by 1933. He was just a few years off. This kind of fiction is often described as prophetic though the claim is disputed by science fiction writers themselves.

Ever since William Gibson coined the term cyberspace in his 1984 novel *Neuromancer* his work has been described as "prescient". Gibson objects to the term pointing out that science fiction writers make many, many guesses, most of which are wrong, but these are all forgotten if they get something right. *Neuromancer* did imagine a future where people spent a lot of time in a "collective hallucination" called cyberspace but as Gibson points out, it did not depict anyone using a mobile phone. That being said there is a well documented feedback loop between science fiction and technological R & D, indeed HG Wells's *World Set Free* was known to the physicists working on the atom bomb.

In the documentary *How William Shatner Changed the World* a number of technology developers give direct credit to *Star Trek* for inspiring their real world inventions. The mobile phone was inspired in part by the Communicators used by the crew of the Enterprise. Steven Perlman started working on QuickTime after watching an episode of Star Trek the Next Generation where Mr Data walks into his quarters and asks the computer to play a particular piece of music [28]. Such science fiction was always already design fiction whether the authors intended it as such or not. Many science fiction writers were also scientists, most notably Arthur C. Clarke and Isaac Asimov. Clarke not only predicted satellite communication but also guessed at how transformative this technology would be. Asimov predicted a network of computers that would form something very like the Internet as well as formulating laws of robotics that many roboticists still take seriously today.

This kind of SF was described by Ursula Le Guin as "extrapolative":

"The science fiction writer is supposed to take a trend or phenomenon of the here-and-now, purify and intensify it for dramatic effect, and extend it into the future. "If this goes on, this is what will happen." [29]

The method is not necessarily accurate, as this quote by GK Chesterton illustrates:

"Just as when we see a pig in a litter larger than the other pigs, we know by an unalterable law of the Inevitable it will some day be larger than an elephant" [13]

However it might be thought of as scientistic and rationalistic. It takes its inspiration from scientific research and seeks to make predictions or warnings and presents itself as plausible. The rhetorical tropes draw on the Enlightenment traditions of rationality and scientific progress.

Extrapolative or Scientistic Design Fiction Examples

Examples of extrapolative or scientistic design fiction would include Google's *Project Glass* [23] Here Google imagines a day in the life of a young man with smart glasses. He is able to arrange his meetings on the go while following a map towards his favorite coffee shop. Microsoft's vision for the home of the future [33] can be seen as an invitation to a future where their products permeate familiar environments, e.g. cooking recipes projected on the kitchen counter. The Museum of Future Government Services [52], a commission by the United Arab Emirates, is a collection of design fictions where "governments and society work together to create a more hopeful world". There are designs for the smart street, where augmented reality enhances social interaction, workshops for cars that are also offices and mobile health services. Imagining tomorrow by extending the scientific scope of today forms the ground of Wired Magazine's vision of the future of the Super Bowl [54]. This 3 minute design fiction portrays the famous football event in the year 2066: players follow coach instructions projected within their helmet, supersonic flights are common so the same football league gathers teams from cities all over the world and fans watch the matches through augmented reality devices.

Other design fictions that might be regarded as "scientistic" in this sense include:

Life Support [42], a series of prototypes that explore how animals could be transformed into medical devices to aid humans in breathing or blood filtering.

Drone Aviary [49], an exploration of civilian drones in advertising, media, surveillance, traffic management and life logging through film, exhibitions and publications. E.g. *Madison*, a Flying Billboard that uses facial recognition to tailor advertising content to those around it.

The Microbial Home [38], a set of objects for the home viewed as a cyclical system where, for example, waste from a module becomes the energy source for the next.

Game of Drones [30], a piece of speculative research that gamifies law enforcement activities to allow members of the local community to act as enforcement officers by piloting drones and acting on, for example, parking offenses or dog fouling.

Telecommunications in the 1990's [39], a realistic and surprisingly accurate scenario (filmed in 1969) depicting how distant communication might play out in the future. These scenarios resemble current day services such as Fax, Wi-Fi or videophones.

CRITIQUE AND IRONY

Extrapolative or speculative fiction does not always subscribe to Enlightenment models of technological and rational progress. There is a very long tradition of fantastical writing which critiques and satirizes society. Eighteenth century Travellers tales were often far fetched and *Gulliver's Travels* took this form as the basis of perhaps the most enduring and famous satirical tale. Here Jonathan Swift depicts creatures like the Struldbrughs, immortals who cannot die but continue to age. Doomed to decrepitude without the release of death they are declared legally dead when they are eighty and their marriages become null and void. They are allowed to hold no land in order to prevent them from seizing all power and wealth through the sole virtue of longevity. The tradition of such satirical fantasy is carried through into science fiction through writers like Kurt Vonnegut. Vonnegut was a profoundly pessimistic writer but as a young man he believed that scientists would one day discover God's phone number. He famously remarked that he lost faith in science when they dropped it on Hiroshima.

Vonnegut was a major influence on Douglas Adams who finally abandoned his famous battles with publisher's deadlines in order to become the "chief fantasist" at a technology start up. Adams imagined not only future technologies such as Eddie the annoyingly cheery shipboard computer and Marvin the paranoid Android but also the company that would make them. The Sirius Cybernetics Corporation is one of Adams finest comic achievements. The Sirius Cybernetics Corporation define a robot as "your plastic pal who's fun to be with". The Hitch Hiker's guide to the galaxy defined the Sirius Cybernetics Corporation as "a bunch of mindless jerks who would be first up against the wall when the revolution came". Adams' imagined his Hitchhiker's Guide to the Galaxy as a constantly updating composite text edited by hitchhikers researching stories on their travels. It can be seen as a design fiction precursor to Wikipedia and indeed before Adams died H2G2 attempted to make the guide a reality with volunteer writers and editors.

Ironic and satirical fiction can be grouped or corralled with the critical design work of Dunne and Raby. Dunne and Raby's drew on the Italian Anti Design movement and the Radical Design movement that began in architectural studios and produced disturbing images of homes of the future that looked like cells in a factory in the "No Stop City" [12]. Their Critical Design was ground breaking in HCI because it demonstrated that design need not be simply a solution to a set of requirements specified in response to a given task or set of constraints. Design might also be a critique, like a political essay or satirical sketch. In *Design Noir: the secret life of electronic objects* they convey a number of innovative and subversive proposals, for example, head mounted cameras allowing users to tune into different people's lives as if they were TV channels:

"proposals like these can really only exist outside the marketplace as a form of "conceptual design" – meaning not the conceptual stage of a design project, but a design proposal intended to challenge preconceptions about how electronics shape our lives." [15]

They suggest that such designs might be expressed as text or films and that academic designers might be best placed to explore this socially responsible role. But their work over the years to follow was not confined to proposals. The compass table, for example, has a top filled with compasses that twitch and turn whenever an electronic device is placed on it, making visible the magnetic fields we carry around with us in our bags and pockets. Dunne and Raby did in fact make this design available on the marketplace and it was auctioned for several thousands of pounds [9]. This is the strength and perhaps also the weakness of such critical artefacts.. In order to appreciate it one must have a degree of cultural capital, to own it one must simply have old fashioned economic capital. Critical design is not only challenging it can also be comforting: our appreciation of it can indicate our inclusion in a group or political affiliations it can also be a status symbol. Like critical art, it is sometimes ultimately a commodity, easily absorbed into the social order it condemns.

Critical or Ironic Design Fiction

There are a great many critical or ironic design fictions. The Near Future Lab's TBD [34] features an advertisement for an automatic car with a game passengers can play to avoid boredom during the journey. The windshield becomes a video screen where targets are projected onto the road for players to aim at. Explosions also feature in the early work of Dunne and Raby. The Huggable Atomic Mushroom [16] now part of the permanent collection of the MOMA NewYork, is a stuffed object in the shape of an atomic explosion. It ingenuously provides people afraid of nuclear catastrophe with a means to gradually overcome their weakness. Also in the tradition of critical design, the work "I wanna deliver a Shark" from Ai Hasegawa [25] explores the possibility of humans giving birth to endangered animal species and includes a diagram depicting the reasons why a mother might decide to pursue such idea. Contradictions become apparent in the intelligent depiction of a possible future of the smart home in "Uninvited Guests" by Superflux [50]. In this short movie, an independent old man sees how his privacy is invaded by a set of smart utensils sent by his children and finds his own "dumb solutions" to his new smart problems (e.g. a young neighbor exercises with the activity tracker in exchange for beer so activity tracking results are excellent.).

Other ironic or critical design fictions include:

Infinite Souvenir [14], a tabletop device with a container to safely store a small amount of nuclear waste that produces enough electricity to keep particles moving in a souvenir snow globe like mechanism.

Menstruation Machine [45], a device that simulates how menstruation might be experienced. It relies on mild electric shocks to simulate pain and a blood dispensing system. The design takes the form of a pop video that depicts a young adolescent using the machine during a night out in Tokyo.

The Transparency Grenade [36], a device presented in the form of a Soviet F1 Hand Grenade. It makes the process of leaking information from closed meetings as easy as pulling a pin.

Ex-Boyfriend Revenge Kit [26], a set of elegantly designed tools to accomplish (fictional) murder with style. A teal leather bag contains a rope, a teal bondage tape, a mini crowbar, a knuckleduster, syringe and truth serum, a teal balaclava and soft teal leather globes.

ALTERNATIVES AND AMBIGUITY

Ursula Le Guin's *Left Hand of Darkness* [29] describes a world with only one gender, in the mating season one or another of them will develop male or female characteristics, the rest of the time they are celibate and when they meet their first human they consider him to be a pervert. In a famous introduction to this work Le Guin makes the distinction between "extrapolative" SF and the kind of fantasy which claims no basis in reality and does not pretend to prophecy. Although there are clear feminist messages within *Left Hand of Darkness* text it is not clearly didactic or propagandistic.

For Margaret Atwood such work draws on the wonder tales of the ancient world. The tales of the Arabian Nights were originally told in marketplaces by travelling storytellers, embellished and changed with each new telling. It was only much later that they were written down and some scholars argue that they are amongst the very earliest achievements of the human imagination. Although the Grimm brothers collected their fairy tales together in the early nineteenth century they knew then that they were very old indeed. Recent evidence suggests that some of them may be at least four thousand years old. These tales relate to fears and desires as old and deep as humanity itself. They are deeply ambiguous and work within this tradition is also less openly didactic than much extrapolative or satirical fiction.

Ambiguous Design Fiction

The Continuous Monument, from Superstudio [51] consists of gigantic structures superimposed over city landscapes. These strange gigantic floating grids hover over the city in New New York, they are disturbing and difficult to interpret. The Ikea Catalog For The Near Future [35] is a collection of intriguing scenarios where the home has been transformed through technology. For example Data gathering sofas, self-replenishing shampoos with life-time subscription only or gardening drones. These are all plausible products but it is unclear if the authors are advocating the designs but neither are they obviously ironic. Ambiguity is the essence of *Err* [27], a project by Jeremy Hutchinson. The artist commissioned workers to introduce errors in the products they ordinarily manufacture. The erroneous products resulted in intentionally misinterpreted functionality and provide an ambiguous ground for reflecting on consumer culture, necessity and craftsmanship.

Other ambiguous design fictions include:

Traces of an Imaginary Affair [21] a kit containing a set of nine neat tools that can be used to create the illusion of having experienced a hypothetical love affair. The tools leave marks on the body like love bites, scratches and bruises.

ARK-INC [48] an electronic product that possess covert properties to be activated (e.g. radio receiver becomes able to transmit), when a profound political or economical crisis hits.

Kickstriker [5] a crowd-funding platform for activists to economically support those initiatives they consider relevant (e.g. Military training for Tibetan monks to resist a Chinese invasion.)

75Watt [41] a product designed so its construction results in a particular choreography performed by the workers in a developing country industrial assembly line.

MAGIC AND WONDER TALES

Literature, like dreaming, is, at a fundamental level, concerned with wish fulfillment. The wonder tale articulates, perhaps better than any other, our deepest desires and fears. It may be for this reason that the ancient form of the wonder tale persists in the "magic realism" of authors like, Will Self, Gabriel Garcia Marquez and Salman Rushdie. Here miracles happen almost without comment and certainly without any scientistic explanation. Magic realism describes wonders without recourse to any rationalist accounting. In *The Satanic Verses* for example Salman Rushdie describes a hospital where each of the patients is afflicted with a magical malady. A man with a tiger's head explains that they are victims of language – they describe us and we succumb to their descriptions.

Magic Realist Design Fiction

Design fictions rooted on the supernatural are rare. In related work [19] we have drawn explicitly on magic realism, a genre where the miraculous is described as any other everyday occurrence, with no attempt whatever at explanation. A series of short stories written in the form of an altCHI paper pictures a design studio where design fiction prototypes unexpectedly begin to work as described. A Dream Catcher initially envisioned as diegetic prop begins to capture actual images of real dreams. When someone is described as fat or old on a gossiping app they immediately gain weight and wrinkle. An Author Eraser allows users to remove the names of senior academics who made no real contribution to papers where they are listed as authors. The paper ends with a solution printer, a machine that can print the solution to any problem specified: from a cure for baldness to a clean en2ergy generator.

Other design fictions that could be considered as magical in the sense that they offer no scientific or rational explanation for the fantasy include: *Addicted Products* [40] a fiction that follows Brad, a toaster that communicates with other toasters in the vicinity and might, for example, leave and go to another home where it is needed more.

FOUR DESIGN FICTIONS

The following sections present four design fictions around a divorce app aimed at the over sixty fives. In the UK there has been a surge in the divorce rate amongst the over sixties [37]. The sociologist Zygmunt Bauman describes modern love as liquid: we are in relationships only until further notice [4]. At the same time there is increasing dissatisfaction with solicitors charging exorbitant fees for routine legal services and many predict that this kind of work will be automated [e.g. 32]. The following design fictions take different approaches to the same ideas based on the preceding categories. The first (figure 1) is extrapolative, imagining what a divorce app might look like today. The second (epilogue) is critical and ironic, expressing dissatisfaction with family lawyers by imagining a future in which they no longer exist. The third is more ambiguous, presenting itself as a provocative advertisement for such an app, encouraging silver breakups. The fourth is a magic realist short story presenting miracles and magic without technological apology.

DF1: BreakApp

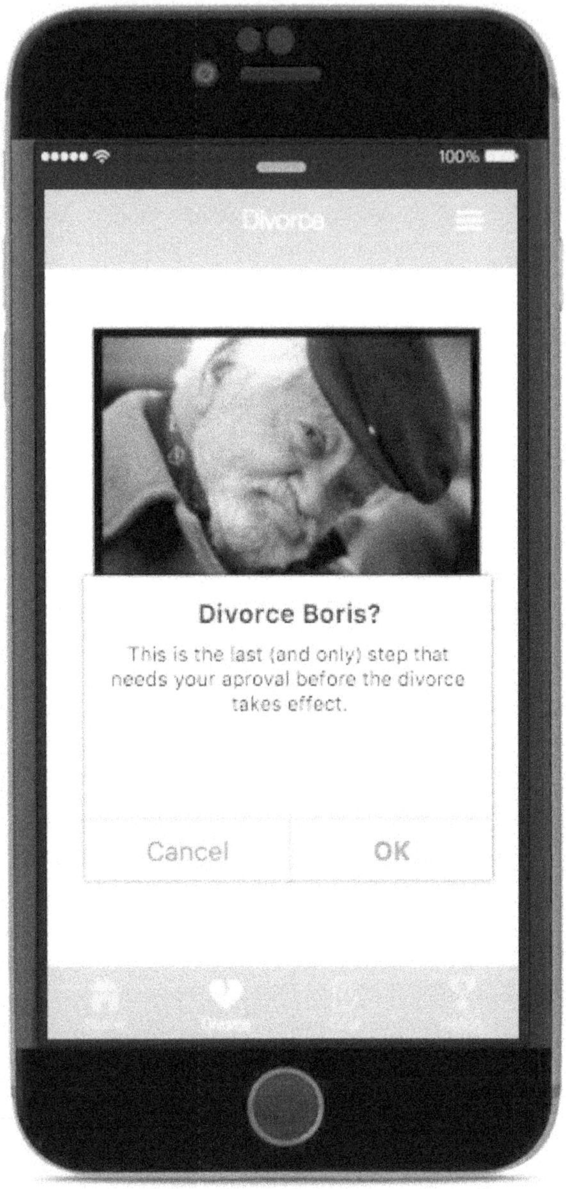

Figure 1: Screenshot of BreakApp

DF2: Epilogue

Few would have suspected, least of all her husband Boris, that at the age of one hundred and one Annabel Bide would swipe for a divorce.

"But we've been together for seventy six years!" Boris protested.

"Twelve years a slave is no rationale for a thirteenth" she texted back, returned to the main menu and selected "Divorce".

"There" she smiled brightly at her great, great granddaughter, "all done – oh, wait" she glanced back at the device irritably, "do I want half of the marital assets? Well, of course I do," her already furrowed brow became more so "and… yes, there! Money transferred and all done. Splendid. Goodness me that's an improvement on wrangling with solicitors."

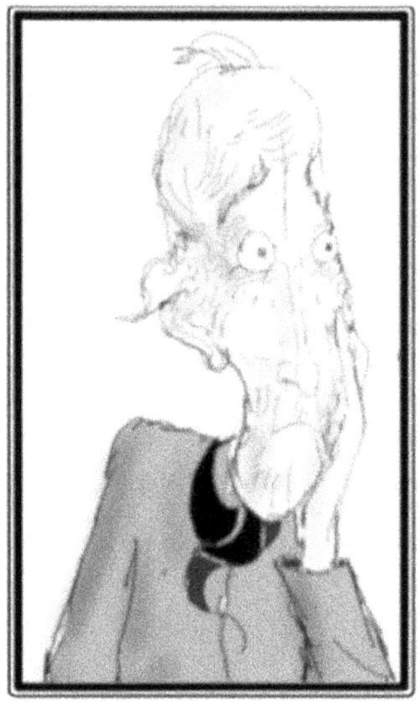

Figure 2: Boris Bide.

"Solicitors?" Shanti looked puzzled.

"They were a sort of lawyer."

"A lawyer? Shanti remained mystified, "why would you need a lawyer? Nobody has committed a crime."

"In the old days you used to need a lawyer to negotiate financial settlements and make arrangements for the children."

"You wouldn't just split the assets fairly?"

"No, each party battled for as much as they could get. "

"And the lawyers helped mediate?"

"Oh no, it was an adversarial system, the solicitors attacked your ex by proxy, intimidated and insulted them for you. They made the divorce as acrimonious and bitter as possible, endlessly wrangling about basic points of law and charging you for letters– written on paper and posted through holes in your door! It's a wonder they didn't charge for running their whale oil lamps."

"And they allowed these people to be involved in settling childcare arrangements?"

"Yes, that was one of their most profitable lines of work: people would throw their life savings at a divorce and then get into tremendous debt. The court judgments were so predictable that they could be replaced by an algorithm and of course, eventually they were. Hence these handy divorce apps. Hang on dear" she looked back at her phone for a moment, "I'm just going to sell the house" she swiped the phone a couple of times, "There we are, done. That's another miracle of the modern age – no more estate agents!"

"What were they?"

"Well you'd register your house with them, they'd take people round to see it and explain that "this is the bathroom" when they were standing in the bathroom, do some totally routine paperwork charge you a hefty fee for it and also take a percentage of the sale. Astonishing really. Good riddance to them I say. Oh and here's Boris' agreeing to the price – good riddance to him too."

DF 3: BreakApp Advertising

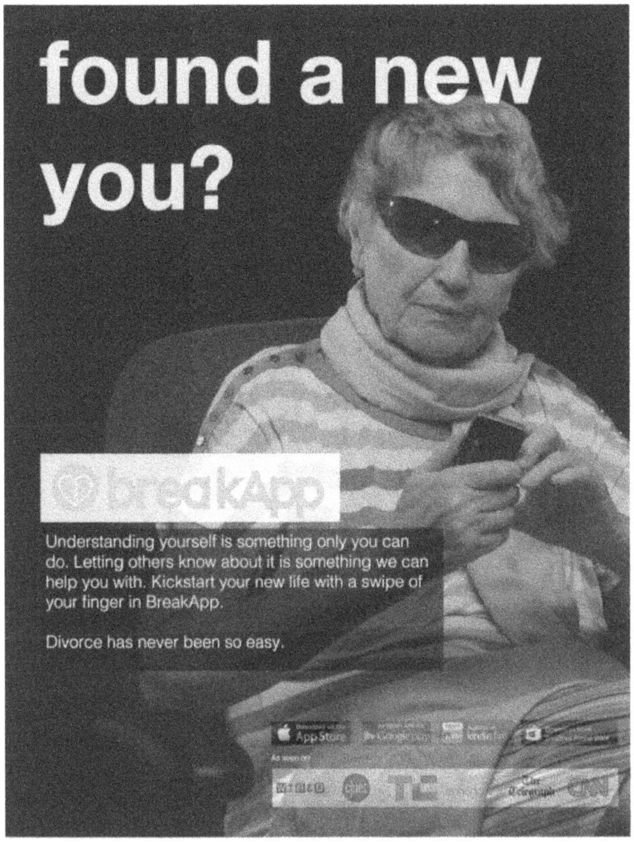

Figure 3: BreakApp advertising campaign

DF4: One Hundred Years of Solicitude

Many years later, as she sat with her dog's head resting in her lap, Shanti Isobella, Francesca Bide remembered the first words of magic she heard her great grandmother utter: "because I said so". With this incantation Annabel had declared the ice caves in the mountains out of bounds and Shanti understood that language had the power to remake the world. When certain words were spoken people, places and things were changed forever. Her father, when certain rituals had been performed vanished just as mysteriously as if some magician had rendered him invisible. When Annabel announced she no longer wanted Boris to be her husband Shanti wondered what he would he instead. A cockroach had been the old woman's first thought, she imagined crushing him beneath her heel. Shanti was horrified and objected that, apart from anything else, you can never kill cockroaches like that. Then Annabel toyed with the idea of turning the old man into stone and using him as a water feature in the garden. When Shanti said she still wanted to be able to see her great, great grandfather Annabel said she could visit whenever she wanted and perhaps grow some ivy over him. When they finally decided on a transformation that would work for everyone Annabel muttered the words and the metamorphosis began. At first Boris did not notice the changes to his hands, feet and face, it was only when he lost the power of speech that he realized what was happening and began to yelp in terror.

"But now you are used to it and we are all happy no?"

Shanti stroked Boris' head as she got up to answer the door. When she returned with Annabel, Boris' tail was wagging excitedly but he knew better than to jump up and try to lick her face. He kept his head low but his tail thrashed the air and he surged forward if she so much as looked at him.

DISCUSSION

Like Harlan Ellison in the nineteen sixties [20], Bruce Sterling differentiates between "speculative" science fiction based on things that might actually happen and fantasy tales unlikely to ever occur. Margaret Atwood, another eminent science fiction writer, rejects such distinctions pointing out that when Mary Shelley wrote Frankenstein she had reason to think electricity might reanimate dead flesh. Atwood places speculative fiction, science fiction as well as sword and sorcery under a single umbrella of "wonder tale". A broad focus on the wonder tale allows inclusion of the Arabian Nights (with its wish granting genies in lamps, bottles and rings), Grimm's Fairy Tales (with magic mirrors that tell you how attractive you are and seven league boots that take you wherever you want to go in a few strides), Ovid's Metamorphosis (where weeping women become rocks), Gulliver's Travels (where sunbeams are extracted from cucumbers), Dr Jekyll and Mr Hyde (where inner demons are released through imbibing chemical compounds) Kafka's Metamorphosis (where a man becomes a bug) Superhero comics (where men fly through the power of the sun or the armor they have made) as well as the Harry Potter books (where a clock reveals the location of each family member). Although there are clear divisions between these kinds of fictions they can all be useful source material for design fiction because they express human desires. For example, Microsoft researchers did their best to make a whereabouts clock inspired by Harry Potter [44].

In Science Fiction, technology occupies the same function within the structure of a narrative as magic does in wonder tales. For example the "Deus Ex Machina" (God from the Machine) in the Greek theatre was an actor playing a character like Zeus who would be winched onto the stage to rescue the hero from a seemingly inescapable predicament. When Captain Kirk and his men are teleported out of difficult situations in Star Trek the device being used is the same one, with technology taking the place of a supernatural agent. Similarly magical objects which give the hero additional powers are substituted with technological artifacts. In Greek mythology Perseus is presented with a sword from the Gods that can cut through stone just as Luke Skywalker is gifted a light sabre with identical properties. It is no accident that it was a science fiction writer who first pointed out that any sufficiently advanced technology is indistinguishable from magic [13]. Any imaginary technology within a sci-fi narrative is a paradigmatic substitution for magical objects.

Although we argue that the wonder tale should be included in an overview of design fiction its rhetorical tropes differ from those of science fiction. The appeal in the wonder tale is to the supernatural rather than the rational. Nevertheless, as with the whereabouts clock, the material might inspire design. Although extrapolative and ironic design fictions dominate at the moment ambiguous and magical design fictions have also begun to emerge. To pursue a spatial metaphor scientistic extrapolation, irony, ambiguity and magic can be though of as the co-ordinates of design fiction.

The semiotic or Greimas square is an analytical tool used to map contrary, contradictory and implied terms.

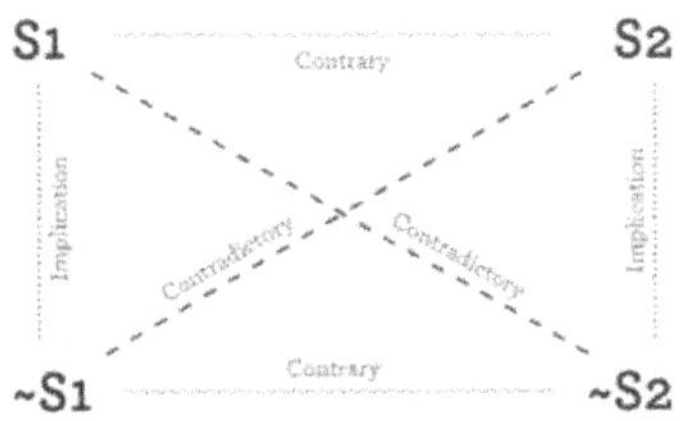

Figure 3: Greimas Semiotic Square

The terms "science" (S1) and "non- science" (-S1) might form the contrary terms at the left hand corners of the square with "magic" (S2) and "non magic" (-S2) on the right. The first two design fictions are extrapolations on current trends and so might be placed somewhere along the line of S1 (science) and –S2 (not magic). The 4th magical fiction would be placed somewhere between –S2 (magic) and –S1 (not science). A similar map square could be made with the terms "ambiguous" and "not ambiguous" as S1 and –S1 with "ironic" and "not ironic" as S2 and -S2. The advertisement would be closer to Irony, the magic realist story closer to ambiguity. It would be possible to map each of the design fictions mentioned in this paper along such co-ordinates but of course many of them would not fit neatly into one category or another. In *Sorting Things Out* Bowker and Star argue that any classification scheme becomes at its borders arbitrary: for example, during apartheid in South Africa officials would have to classify the race of white babies born to black parents and vice versa [10].

Rather than create a series of Greimas squares we present a rather more fanciful map suggesting the co-ordinates of design fiction. The image in figure 4 recalls the maps that often begin fantasy novels, perhaps it also connotes some of the medieval maps recently collected by Umberto Eco [18] of fictional lands that some thought actually existed.

Most of the Design Fiction reviewed in this paper is scientistic in the sense that it is extrapolative. Much of this design fiction is also very often critical or ironic. At the end of the last century the novelist David Foster Wallace began to complain about the constraints of irony. He argued that irony had been the dominant form of expression for American novelists for most of the twentieth century and this was ultimately enfeebling. Julian Barnes in a recent novel about Shostakovich's life under Stalin makes a similar point:

"You woke up one morning and no longer knew if your tongue was in your cheek; and even if it was, whether that mattered anymore, whether anyone noticed." [3]

Under Stalin it was sometimes possible to get away with irony while sarcasm could get you shot. Although irony is easier, allowing an escape from a particular position – I didn't really mean it you know, just a bit of irony, ultimately it is a weapon of the weak. The sketchy map presented here suggests that there is currently more extrapolative and ironic design fiction than any other kind. This tells us something about the field of Design Fiction as it currently stands but also indicates the wide space of future undiscovered countries.

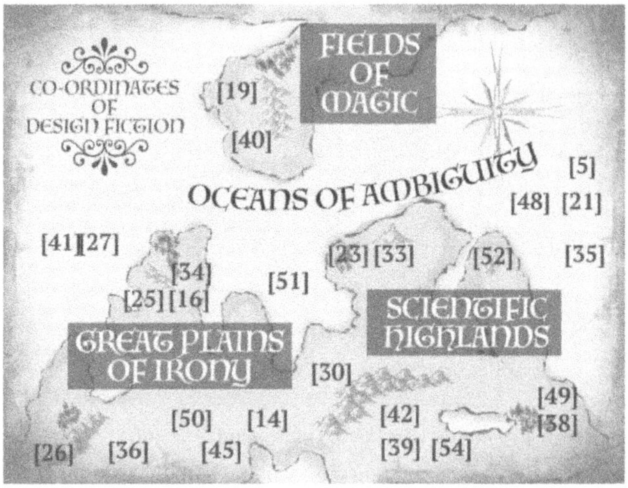

Figure 4: Map of Design Fiction

CONCLUSION

This paper has attempted to sketch the co-ordinates of design fiction as it is currently practiced in HCI and related fields. We have grouped fictions together according to related but separate strands of wonder tale around the broad headings of science, irony, ambiguity and magic. The categorization suggests that the most frequently employed design fictions are broadly scientistic in the sense that they are extrapolative, drawing a line from historical trends out into the future through progressive exaggerations Such work is often directly critical or at least ironic. We suggest that there may be rich possibilities in the more or less undiscovered countries of design fiction.

REFERENCES

1. Atwood M (2011) In Other Worlds: SF and the Human Imagination. Doubleday New York
2. Bardzell J., Bardzell S., and Stolterman E., (2014). Reading critical designs: supporting reasoned interpretations of critical design. In Proc. of (CHI '14).
3. Barnes J., (2016) The Noise of Time. Jonathan Cape
4. Bauman Z (2003) Liquid Love: On the Frailty of Human Bonds. Polity Press

5. Begley J., Jayasuriya M. & Borda J. (2012) Kickstriker - http://www.kickstriker.com - Last accessed: 11th February 2016
6. Bleecker, J. (2009). "Design Fiction: A Short Essay on Design, Science, Fact and Fiction". Webeditionpdf
7. Blythe M. (2014) Research through design fiction: narrative in real and imaginary abstracts. In Proc of (CHI '14). ACM, New York, NY, USA, 703-712
8. Blythe M., Steane J., Roe J., and Oliver C. 2015. Solutionism, the Game: Design Fictions for Positive Aging. In Proceedings of the 33rd Annual ACM Conference on Human Factors in Computing Systems (CHI '15). ACM, New York, NY, USA, 3849-3858
9. Blythe M., Yauner F., Rodgers P., (2015) The Context of Critical Design: Exhibits, Social Media and Auction Houses. The Design Journal. 28 Apr 2015 pp 83-105
10. Bowker G., and Star S.L (2000) Sorting Things Out. MIT press
11. Bogdanov, Alexander. Red Star: The First Bolshevik Utopia. Indiana University Press, 1984.
12. Branzi A. (1969) No Stop City - http://www.moma.org/collection/works/794 - Last accessed: 11th February 2016
13. Chesterton G.K. The Napoleon of Notting Hill.
14. Clerck B. (2013) Infinite Souvenir - http://di13.rca.ac.uk/project/infinite-souvenir/ - Last accessed: 11th February 2016
15. Dunne, A. and Raby F. Design Noir: The Secret Life of Electronic Objects. p65 Springer Science & Business Media, 2001.
16. Dunne A. & Raby F. (2004) Huggable Mushroom http://www.moma.org/collection/works/94022 - Last accessed: 11th February 2016
17. Dunne A., and Raby F. (2013). *Speculative Everything: Design, Fiction, and Social Dreaming*. The MIT Press.
18. Eco U. and McEwen A. (2015) The Book of Legendary Lands. Maclehose Press
19. Encinas E. & Blythe M. (2016) The Solution Printer: Magic Realist Design Fiction. In Proc. of (CHI '16).
20. Ellison E. Dangerous Visions. SF Masterworks Gollancz
21. Franke B. (2006) Traces of an Imaginary Affair - http://www.bjornfranke.com/objects/2006_traces_of_an_imaginary_affair.htm - Last accessed: 11th February 2016
22. Gonzattoa,R.F. van Amstela, F. Merkleb L. and Hartmann T., (2013) The Ideology of the Future in Design Fictions. Digital Creativity vol 24 no 1.
23. Google (2012) Project Glass: One Day… - https://plus.google.com/+GoogleGlass - Last accessed: 10th February 2016
24. Hales D. Design Fictions an Introduction and Partial Taxonomy. Digital Creativity. Vol 24. Issue 1. 2013. Special Issue: Design Fictions 30 Apr 2013
25. Hasegawa A. (2012) I Wanna Deliver a Shark - http://aihasegawa.info/?works=i-wanna-deliver-a-shark - Last accessed: 11th February 2016
26. Her Royal Flyness (2013) http://herroyalflynessblog.com/2013/12/19/the-ex-boyfriend-revenge-kit/ - Last accessed: 11th February 2016
27. Hutchinson J. (2011) Err - http://www.jeremyhutchison.com/work/project47.html - Last accessed: 11th February 2016
28. Jones J (2005) How William Shatner Changed The World. Discover Channel.
29. Le Guin U (1981)Left Hand of Darkness. Orbit
30. Lindley, J. and Coulton P. "Game of drones." Proceedings of the 2015 Annual Symposium on Computer-Human Interaction in Play. ACM, 2015.
31. Markussen T., and Knutz E. (2013). The poetics of design fiction. In Proc of DPPI '13. ACM
32. Meltzer T. (2014) Robot doctors, online lawyers and automated architects: the future of the professions? The Guardian .Sunday 15 June 2014 19.00 BST
33. Microsoft (2010) The Home of the Future - www.cio.com/article/2417176/infrastructure/microsoft-s-home-of-the-future--a-visual-tour.html - Last accessed: 10th February 2016
34. Near Future Laboratory (2015) An Ikea Catalog From The Near Future - http://ikea.nearfuturelaboratory.com - Last accessed: 11th February 2016
35. Near Future Laboratory (2014) TBD Catalog - http://www.tbdcatalog.com - Last accessed: 11th February 2016
36. Oliver J. (2012) Transparency Grenade http://transparencygrenade.com - Last accessed: 11th February 2016
37. ONS (2013) The Number of People age 60 and over getting divorced has risen since 1990. Office for National Statistics.
38. Philips Design (2011) The Microbial Home - https://www.90yearsofdesign.philips.com/article/67 - Last accessed: 11th February 2016
39. Post Office Research Office in Dollis Hill (1969) Telecommunication Services for the 1990's -

https://www.youtube.com/watch?v=_FlvwC1dkzc - Last accessed: 11th February 2016

40. Rebaudengo S. (2012) Addicted Products - http://www.simonerebaudengo.com/addictedproducts - Last accessed: 10th February 2016

41. Revital Cohen & Tuur Van Balen (2013) 75 Watt - http://www.cohenvanbalen.com/work/75-watt - Last accessed: 11th February 2016

42. Revital Cohen & Tuur Van Balen (2008) Life Support http://www.cohenvanbalen.com/work/life-support - Last accessed: 10th February 2016

43. Ronnenberg P.(2013) Social Teletext Network - http://ronnenberg.io/portfolio/social-teletext-network - Last accessed: 11th February 2016

44. Sellen, A., Eardley, R ., Izadi, S., Harper, R. The Whereabouts Clock: early testing of a situated awareness device.Extended Abstracts of Conference on Human Factors and Computing systems, CHI '06. Montreal, Canada, (2006), 1307-1312.

45. Sputniko (2010) Menstruation Machine - http://www.moma.org/interactives/exhibitions/2011/talktome/objects/142590/ - Last accessed: 11th February 2016

46. Sterling B. (2005) Shaping Things. MIT Press. Cambridge Massachusetts

47. Sterling B. (2013) Bruce Sterling NEXT13 - Fantasy prototypes and real disruption https://www.youtube.com/watch?v=2VIoRYPZk68

48. Superflux (2006) ARK-INC - http://www.superflux.in/work/ark-inc - Last accessed: 11th February 2016

49. Superflux (2015) Drone Aviary - http://www.superflux.in/work/drone-aviary - Last accessed: 10th February 2016

50. Superflux (2015) Uninvited Guests - http://www.superflux.in/work/uninvited-guests - Last accessed: 11th February 2016

51. Superstudio (1969) Continuous Monument - http://www.moma.org/collection/works/934 - Last accessed: 11th February 2016

52. UAE Prime Minister's Office (2015) Museum of Future Government Services - http://museum.governmentsummit.org/2015/ - Last accessed: 10th February 2016

53. Weiser, Mark. "The computer for the 21st century." *Scientific american* 265.3 (1991): 94-104.

54. Wired Magazine (2016) Imagining Football's Future Through The Super Bowl of 2066 - http://www.wired.com/2016/01/the-future-of-the-super-bowl - Last accessed: 10th February

Incorporation of Generational Learning in Familiar Interfaces and Systems: A Design Fiction

Sarah Grace Fields
Virginia Polytechnic Institute
Blacksburg, VA 24060
sgrace@vt.edu

AUTHOR FOREWORD

Before the end of another two decades, the way people interface with technology will undoubtedly be quite different. Users have many needs, and in an ideal world, an interface could provide for every need of every user even where different demographics have conflicting needs. This paper first builds up the idea of "familiar interfaces," then describes a study of a popular video game which can be summarized as a human player interacting with a computer character which is unique to each player.

Following in the vein of design fiction depicting fictional user studies such as the abstracts discussed by Blythe [1], and in the spirit of finding value in following fictional scenarios all the way through [3], the following seven pages describe a study that could take place in the future. Citations with a prime symbol (e.g. [1']) refer to fictional sources, and any similarities to real research or institutions are coincidental.

ABSTRACT

This design fiction presents a self-contained fictional study of the following description: Familiar interfaces have grown to be one of the most common forms of reaction computing in applications today. The last few years have seen a rise in the number of familiar interfaces that incorporate generational learning to improve their functionality between versions. Though the practice has many advantages, this study aims to add criticisms against the practice to the so far optimistic discussion. By analyzing the familiar interface of a popular game which aggressively incorporates generational learning into its versioning, the study suggests there may be unintentional consequences of generational learning that require further exploration.

Keywords

Learning algorithms; Reaction computing; Expression recognition; Generational Learning; Version Learning; Familiar interfaces; Familiar systems; Conflict loops; Game design; Design Fiction; Fiction

1. INTRODUCTION

This study looks to branch beyond the current discussions in human-computer interaction to bring new considerations into scope. Generational learning has been in style over the last few years, yet criticism of the practice on a meta level has been lacking. This is the beginning of that conversation. Technology has never gotten anywhere with blind acceptance of new practices.

A fair amount of studies of generational learning, familiar interfaces, and familiar systems deal with implementation level details. Relevant literature will be discussed, but this paper will focus on the practice on a broader level. Before deciding how a technology should be done, it is worth exploring whether doing so is even a good idea to begin with.

The core question to be addressed is whether generational learning actually adds anything of value to familiar interfaces without introducing unforeseen consequences. The study focuses on the recently popular game Elemental developed by AccelIn. The game advertises a form of artificial intelligence in its interaction but works for all practical purposes like a familiar interface.

1.1 Familiar Interfaces

According to an extensive survey about what forms of technology customer service and marketing divisions use in their daily workplace, familiar interfaces rank in the top three across the board [1'].

For those unfamiliar with the practice, it's important to see the context of the popularity of familiar interfaces. Designers have long struggled with how to design interfaces that meet the needs of a wide range of users. Even when including users in key design decisions, the results vary widely in how successful they are. A singular, static interface can only please so many people.

1.1.1 Rise of Familiar Interfaces

As dynamic interfaces became more popular, allowing users to change a fluid interface in the end product itself, the idea of user-preferred interactions began to take root. In [2'], researchers follow the history of familiar interfaces as advancements in rich input like gestures and facial recognition offered real-time feedback about how users felt about an interface. This practice is firmly rooted in reaction computing, the thriving field of creating systems responsive to a user's interpreted reaction.

The term *familiar interface* was coined in [3'] for an interface which could grow familiar with a user in order to better interpret input and display interface features. The author likens familiar interfaces to advanced user profiles which borrow ideas from reaction computing. If a user has a particular quirk, such as crossing their arms when frustrated or saying "Go back" when they wish to return to the main menu, a familiar interface will learn the desired behavior and always respond in the best possible way to that particular user. Ideally, this happens automatically and transparently.

GROUP '16, November 13 - 16, 2016, Sanibel Island, FL, USA

ACM 978-1-4503-4276-6/16/11…$15.00

DOI: http://dx.doi.org/10.1145/2957276.2957294

1.1.2 *Familiar Interfaces vs Familiar Systems*

Familiar systems branched off familiar interfaces as a more general application of the idea. A familiar system adapts to the user in more ways than just input and output. In reviewing the rise of familiar interfaces, [2′] notes when the terms were used interchangeably and when they began to form distinct ideas.

Although much of the commentary in this paper applies to both familiar interfaces and familiar systems, the term familiar interfaces will be used to avoid confusing the definitions.

1.1.3 *Input Methods*

For familiar interfaces to adapt naturally to users, a form of input richer than keyboards and mice is often necessary. With gestures and/or cameras, a system can leverage body language recognition. This was the original inception of familiar interfaces [3′]. Cameras can also recognize facial expressions, and some voice inputs can identify emotion from tone. A review of popular familiar interfaces notes several successful interfaces which used traditional keyboard input and textual interpretation for a successful outcome, but these implementations are vastly outnumbered by those using visual or audio monitoring [4′].

It should be noted that a familiar system does not necessarily need a robust or accurate ability to link user input to particular emotions, such as frustration. While this can be helpful in adapting to the user, the most important aspect of a familiar interface is its ability to link a specific user's action to that user's desired response to the action [3′]. In this way, the interface becomes familiar with the user. More discussion on the methods of such learning can be found in section 2.1.

1.2 Generational Learning

Generational learning is a successful area distinct from familiar interfaces or systems. If each major version change of a program is seen as a generation of that software, then generational learning is any technique which uses information learned from the previous generation in order to improve the next generation [5′]. Often, this technique employs some type of data collection and mining from the previous generation's users. Ideally, the learned data comes from products actually being used in its intended daily context.

The type of data collected can be as simple as how often a phone was put in sleep mode or as complex as how long a user spent looking at menus before finding their desired option.

1.2.1 *Advantages of Generational Learning*

In some ways, generational learning can be compared to crowd sourcing decisions about how to improve a system. Each user has a small say in a larger picture of which aspects of the system were useful, important, and well-conceived and which aspects need improvements. In [5′], researchers describe generational learning through one successful early implementation which learned, among other things, which features should have icons in the tray and which icons could be hidden in menus. The outcome is said to reflect the best system for the average user; quirks and differences between users would be smoothed over by the collective feedback.

Learning from actual user behavior can be more reliable than feedback from a user survey or focus group because sometimes the daily use of a system makes recognizing where someone has adapted to an inconvenience difficult to perceive. If data can be amassed from all users, the sample is also more representative than any survey could hope to achieve.

Many systems already employ background data collection on user behaviors, so tapping into this reserve in order to perform generational learning is far cheaper than setting up new studies or surveys. It can also be faster, especially if based on pre-existing algorithms for learning [5′]. Unfortunately, this can also obscure why a feature or aspect ended up changing.

1.3 Elemental

Elemental is the name of a video game developed by Accelerated Innovation, LLC (colloquially called AccelIn) which has gained wide popularity across North America and Asia. The game must be played using proprietary handheld gaming devices called Handhelds. In the most recent generation, the Handheld itself has no buttons; all play is done through communicating with the NPC (non-player character) which is unique to each Handheld.

The first time a Handheld is turned on, the player customizes this central NPC which is then known as their Fighter. To play the game, human players direct their Fighters to battle each other using elemental attacks. These battles often take place between strangers using an online system for pairing up fights.

1.3.1 *Elemental as a Familiar Interface*

In advertisements, AccelIn describes the Fighter as an artificial intelligence [6′]. The Fighter is considered an independent agent that the player coaches or commands in battle. In practice, Elemental has all the trademark features of a familiar interface. In an online guide, a popular player describes the process by which Fighters grow accustomed to their player, develop vocabulary unique to the pair, and interpret commands in real time during battles [8′]. When battles take place in person, the player and Fighter must communicate their plan without revealing to the other player what these plans entail. Players also tend to specialize in a specific element and style of fighting, and their Fighters likewise learn this specialization. Through emails, the author of [8′] explained how a Fighter-player team become synchronized enough that the secondhand market for old Fighters to be sold to new players causes a steep learning curve for a new pair to develop a cohesive fight style.

2. PRIOR RESEARCH

A large body of research exists regarding the adoption of familiar interfaces. Familiar interfaces are among the most widely used form of reaction computing in industry [1′], and the benefits and limitations of these systems have been discussed in several large literature review efforts such as [2′]. Due to their adoption by industry, many studies focus on familiar systems in the workplace.

2.1 Familiar System Algorithms

2.1.1 *Natural and Organic Appearance*

A primary concern of familiar interfaces since their inception in [3′] has been an effort to appear natural and organic. Users have long been familiar with discrete, literal systems – the very word "mechanical" implies a lack of flexibility and liveliness. A system capable of smooth learning should have spontaneity and generate a wide variety of possible responses. Many heuristics and algorithms have been tested to put on the best appearance of human-like learning behavior.

2.1.2 *Learning Algorithms*

Underneath the hood, several learning algorithms have been compared in real world implementations. The literature review efforts in [2′] describe the historical transition from simpler to broader and more complex processes.

Processes like straightforward ranking will often suffice in simpler interfaces. When the changes to the interface will be minor, such as positioning of choices and default file structure setups, a highly involved algorithm wastes computing power. These have a history of successful implementation in systems with more limited input and output.

For more complex needs, simple algorithms can't generate a human-like ability to adapt to human users, so far more complex algorithms have been implemented. Decisions that can branch, have spontaneous change, or make complex inferences based on history provide a more organic learning interaction that avoids simple conflict loops [4′].

2.2 Familiar Interfaces in the Workplace

Much of the research about familiar interfaces focuses on the benefits of using them. These implementations have the appeal of tangible, measurable results, and in many cases, industry itself funds research efforts. This ought to raise concerns over how highly optimistic research done as case studies in the workplace tends to be.

2.2.1 Reasons for Popularity

A significant amount of time is wasted doing repetitive busywork in the office. Software systems address many of the common offenders, but in some cases, they also introduce more problems to be solved. The intent of familiar interfaces is to become the perfect assistant, always on top of what the user wants and needs [3′]. They create a powerful customization of software without the overhead of learning how to do said customization by hand. They also adjust over time as business changes and the intensity of work fluxes.

2.2.2 Team Dynamics with Familiar Interfaces

In some currently popular implementation, familiar interfaces are seen as part of the team dynamic [4′]. In some cases, the interface itself is shared by all members of a team, and the interface thus familiarizes itself with each unique members as well as the team as a whole. In other cases, team members – some remote – access the same familiar interface and can use this consistency as a touching point to stay coordinated.

2.3 Rise of Generational Learning in Familiar Interfaces

2.3.1 Why Generation Learning?

As with all software, familiar interfaces have their drawbacks; one notable drawback has been the learning curve when pairing a user with a new familiar interface. Attempts to find successful methods to pre-train the interfaces have proven to be equally tricky time sinks.

As described in the introduction, generational learning exists as a topic distinct from familiar systems. Interest in collecting rich data from familiar interface users led to proposed uses of said data, and generational learning was a prime candidate for trials [2′]. The pairing of the two solves several problems: it's fast, it's cheap as long as the data collection method already exists, and it does provide an improved base for a new familiar interface to start from. In using the aggregated data from all current users of an interface, this process is supposed to "smooth out" individual differences into a more organic, generally applicable familiar interface.

Some researchers have raised privacy concerns about such data collection [7′]. Although collecting anonymized user data is typical of most software systems, this data is generally used for learning broad concepts about the demographic rather than being re-processed into publicly accessible software. Theoretically, the product of generational learning could be sensitive commentary on the population it was derived from. Additional concerns could stem from specific algorithms, such as spontaneity derived from exact archived interaction data.

2.4 Role of Elemental to Expand Current Research

2.4.1 Unexplored Area

The familiar interface in the game Elemental provides a new example from an underexplored context and demographic. The game has been considered revolutionary for abandoning all forms of buttons and input in favor of the human acting as a coach and commander of the Fighter [8′]. Much like a traditional familiar interface, this Fighter learns the feedback and gestures of its player to interpret their instructions more accurately as time goes on.

2.4.2 Advantages of Studying Elemental

AccelIn aggressively adopted generational learning into Elemental, and a total of five generations have been released in the last 7 years. The original Fighters, Gen 1, were not coded to have even base familiarity with the mechanics of the game itself; the game's initial rise in popularity can be partially attributed to viral videos in which Fighters showed comical misunderstanding of game mechanics, often resulting in explosions. See [8′] for a list of such examples.

Although the incorporation of generational learning in Elemental is widely advertised, the recent scandal in the news from the leaked Gen 0 Fighter provides strong evidence that significant changes in behavior have occurred between the game's creation and the most current generation release.

Given the scarcity of older models, studying Gen 1 wasn't feasible, so this study will compare Gen 2 with the most current Gen 5. The Gen 2 Fighters were able to understand game mechanics out of the box thanks to a combination of early generational learning and additional fine-tuning. The generations are capable of fighting each other, so all moves available to Gen 5 Fighters are also available to Gen 2 Fighters. Other than price tag, the key differences would be the exact initial skill of the Fighter and an understanding of meta-game strategies.

3. METHOD

Participants for this study were recruited through a combination of messages on forums which were focused on the game Elemental as well as messages sent to other players found using the in-game player search system. Of the 78 players who expressed interest, 39 ended up participating in and completing the study. 16 participants were local enough to come to our lab, and 23 participated long-distance with the help of after-market software which allowed us to remotely view their Elemental screen. Our participants ranged from ages 14 to 19.

Of the 39 participants, 15 performed the tasks using a generation 2 Fighter, and 5 of these were old Handhelds that the participants dusted off specifically to do our study, i.e. they had a newer generation Fighter which they typically used but still owned the older generation. The other 24 participants all had generation 5 Fighters.

3.1 Introductory Questions

Before completing any tasks, the participants were asked to fill out a brief questionnaire. The questions were intentionally simple with no opinions or unclear answers. Of particular interest was which generations the participants owned and which they typically played with.

Participants were also asked to perform the steps to be ranked on Peder's Gesture Proficiency scale [10]. Among our participants, we had 1 participant with a diagnosed physical disability and 1 with a temporary injury that limited motion range. These two participants were included in the "N/A" ranking on the Gesture Proficiency scale [10].

3.2 Tasks

Participants were asked to perform two tasks cooperatively with their Fighter.

1. Perform two common attacks and set up one field hazard on the empty practice field in the game.
2. Ask your Fighter to instruct you step-by-step how to make a peanut butter and jelly sandwich. Follow its instructions literally.

Task 1 was a typical in-game task that players would commonly encounter, which was aimed at measuring the competency at expected domain tasks between generations. After early feedback from the first participants, the task was adjusted to allow the participant flexibility to perform tasks that align with their typical play style. While it is possible for any Fighter to perform any moves that exist within the game, Fighters and players typically specialize significantly enough that being asked to perform moves outside their specialty would contradict the point of having a task which is familiar to the participants.

Task 2 is an exercise many might recognize from lessons about providing clear instructions. The person creating the sandwich must follow instructions literally without asking for clarification or making assumptions about the intended meaning. For example, when the instructor says, "Put the peanut butter on the bread," the second person should put the entire jar of peanut butter on top of the bread. The intent of this task is to observe the Fighter's handling of tasks outside its original purpose and to observe its response to unexpected and peculiar behavior from the user.

3.3 Measures

All measures presented in data tables are measures of the instructor. In Task 1, the instructor is the human user; in Task 2, the instructor is the Fighter. The numbers are averages with the notable exception of the N/A rank of Gesture Proficiency. Since only two people in the study fell into this category, these are the actual scores of the two participants.

3.3.1 Time

A simple measure in minutes and seconds of how long the pair took from the start of their task until its completion.

3.3.2 Clarifications

A count of how many times the instructor issued a clarification in their verbal instruction in the context of a previous instruction. For example, when one user asked the Fighter to "shoot fire in the air," the Fighter created a plume of fire above their head, and the user then clarified "no, while you're in the air." Clarifications were of particular interest because of the added context which the instructor had initially assumed was understood.

3.3.3 Repeats

A count of how many times the instructor repeated a verbal instruction with little or no modification. For example, when one Fighter said to "put the peanut butter on the bread" and the user put the entire jar on top of the slice of bread, the Fighter repeated "no, put the peanut butter on the bread." Sometimes, a change in tone implied a different meaning to the instruction, but these cases were still counted as repeats.

3.3.4 Failed Attempts

A failed attempt was defined as a behavior or outcome that the instructee believed was correct based on the instructions, but the instructor did not accept it as the correct meaning. This number also reflects a count of occurrences.

3.3.5 Questions

A count of how many times the instructor asked a question about the behavior of the instructee. Generally, this would be a question about the reason behind an instruction, but some questions were asked to satisfy general curiosity.

3.3.6 Expressed Frustration

A count of how many times the instructor indicated frustration with the behavior of the instructee. Behaviors counting as frustration included both verbalizations and body language.

3.3.7 Generations

The results are separated out by which generation of Fighter the player interacted with. The *5 using 2* group were the players who used their Gen 2 Fighter for this study but normally used a Gen 5 Fighter while playing Elemental with friends.

4. RESULTS AND DISCUSSION

4.1 Task Performance and Quantitative Results

4.1.1 Task 1 Results

The results of Task 1 were fairly straightforward. The 5 players using Gen 2 Handhelds who typically play on Gen 5 Handhelds had the most striking results, and the discussion is saved for its own section.

Between Gen 5 and Gen 2 Fighters, the Gen 5 Fighters had far faster and more accurate results. The task only took around half a minute for Fighters to complete, but most of the Gen 5 Fighters required no clarifications before succeeding whereas Gen 2 Fighters required an average of 3.

4.1.2 Task 2 Results

Table 1 shows the averages for the participants in Task 2. The results are grouped into Gesture Proficiency bins, but no significant difference is apparent between players of different proficiencies aside from the 2 players who fell into the N/A bin. One of these players had an injury and the other had a disability which limited motion. It's notable that while Task 2 took them longer to physically complete, the other measures are more comparable to the average cases of the other bins.

4.1.3 Differences between Gen 2 and Gen 5

The differences between the two generations provide interesting insights. Gen 5 Fighters repeated instructions more often, but they had about the same number of clarifications as Gen 2 Fighters. Due to this and slower corrections by the Gen 5 Fighters, the Gen 2 Fighters completed the task slightly faster and with less failed attempts. The Gen 5 Fighters also had a lower tendency to ask questions of their player; some of the questions asked by the Gen 2 Fighters were somewhat off-topic, such as "Haven't you made a sandwich before?"

Also interesting is that none of the Fighters ever express noticeable frustration with the player despite many failed attempts at the task.

4.1.4 Gen 5 Players on Gen 2 Handhelds

The most striking results come from the 5 players who typically use a Gen 5 Handheld but dusted off their old Gen 2 Handhelds for the day in order to participate in our study. A breakdown in communication was clear in both the numerical results and the expressed frustration of the players.

Table 1. Results of Task 2 by Fighter Generation

		Gesture Proficiency			
Gen	**Measure**	**1-3**	**4-6**	**7-9**	**N/A**
2	Time	2:03	1:52	1:59	2:46
	Clarifications	23	29	19	22
	Repeats	2	0	0	3
	Failed attempts	15	17	14	18
	Question	3	3	6	5
	Frustration	0	0	0	0
5 using 2	Time	2:57	3:01	2:45	-
	Clarifications	45	40	38	-
	Repeats	1	1	0	-
	Failed attempts	32	28	28	-
	Question	5	3	4	-
	Frustration	0	0	0	-
5	Time	2:20	2:13	2:12	3:01
	Clarifications	25	29	21	28
	Repeats	5	4	5	8
	Failed attempts	21	25	18	24
	Question	0	0	0	2
	Frustration	0	0	0	0

In Task 1, the process of forming the right attacks took almost 1 minute longer than it took either of the other groups of players. Neither of the other groups had significant amounts of failed attempts, yet the Gen 5 players instructing their Gen 2 Fighters struggled with numerous failures to communicate. Some of this difference can be explained by a lack of familiarity because these players were using an old game whereas the other players used their game on a daily basis. The comparison is as if comparing active rummy players with players who are asked to use a set of rules they learned years ago. However, the stark difference could also be indicative of a larger change between Gen 2 and Gen 5 than is suggested by the similar results of the other two groups. Players may simply be adapting to the new generations.

In Task 2, communication was far less efficient in terms of needed clarifications and failed attempts. However, the amount of questioning and repeats were about the same as the other Gen 2 Fighters. These qualities could be seen as arising from the programming of the Fighter rather than the relationship between the Fighter and player.

4.2 Shortcomings of Studying Elemental

While branching into new application territory brings advantages with its fresh perspective, it also creates generalizability problems. Particularly, Elemental was not intentionally designed to follow the best practices of a familiar interface, and the generational learning incorporates previous data more aggressively than most work-oriented generational learning applications.

The Handheld platform itself also differed between Gen 2 and Gen 5. The Handhelds for Gen 5 have different and more numerous sensors (front and back touch screen, higher resolution cameras, etc), and there are software differences added between the generations which cannot be accounted for by generational learning. This is why we picked tasks which don't rely on the hardware of the system, but the differences could still influence our results.

A cultural shift regarding the gameplay of Elemental also changed between Gen 2 and Gen 5. The players described a growing tendency to specialize and an increased focus on certain metagame strategies. The way these cultural changes get compressed into generational learning per iteration would be complicated to say the least.

4.3 Implications for Familiar Interfaces

Two important ideas surface from the data in this study: there appeared to be a slight but noticeable difference between the generations in certain aspects, and the participants who worked with a generation to which they didn't interact with daily suffered considerably more frustration.

Plenty of studies have recorded measurable differences between generations of software which use generational learning techniques, but most studies look to record positive or task-oriented improvements. This study noticed a difference in the number of questions and the number of repeated instructions between generations. These categories may not be inherently bad – indeed, the later generation performed noticeably better in task-oriented measures – but the fact that unintended behaviors are also affected by generational learning should be cause for concern.

The counterargument would be that all behaviors learned from generational learning must be on the whole positive because these behaviors were learned from interacting with real users. However, the act of repeating an instruction which already failed to communicate properly seems unlikely to be a positive aspect drawn from the crowd. One possibility is that repetition is a habit picked up from generational learning about when users didn't hear something the first time. Another possibility is that newer generations have redundancies or flaws which usually go unnoticed.

The extent to which users adapt to technology, even to familiar interfaces, obscures some of the information about how well generational learning objectively improves the interface. Familiar interfaces were meant to turn the user interface and user relationship around so that instead of users adapting to them, the interfaces would adapt to the user. However, this study suggests that users might still be to some extent adapting to familiar interfaces. The amount of adapting between the two might still be more equitable, but even a small concession by the user could affect the generational learning process. Many optimists want to believe that familiar interfaces concede all interactions to the user's preferences and habits, but this simply isn't the case.

4.4 Looking Forward

The field is wide open for other researchers to investigate possible unintended consequences of implementing generational learning on familiar systems. No large scale studies have attempted to compare a traditional familiar system with traditional version updates to a clone of itself with generational learning incorporated. Rather than just measuring the intended use of these systems, studies should also investigate the possible appropriations of the system and other unforeseen side effects that may arise.

5. ACKNOWLEDGMENTS

We thank all the participants who took the time to participate in our study as well as the friends who served as proofreaders and moral support during the writing of this paper.

6. REFERENCES

[1'] Barnes, A. Survey Reveals Cutting Edge Software has Growing Adoption in HR. *Google News*. Retrieved May 5, 2034, from Google News: http://google.news/technology/surveys/survey-reveals-cutting-ed-2299910.html.

[2'] Gonzales, N. Lit Review of Familiar Systems. *IEEE User Aware Systems*, 9 (4). 19-28.

[3'] Harper, S., and Cheng, X., Development of "Familiar" User Interfaces. In *Proceedings of the SIGCHI Conference on Human Factors in Computing Systems* (Shanghai, China, April 01 - 06, 2031). CHI '31. ACM, New York, NY, 526-531.

[4'] Seever, A., and Yamato, K. 2029. Popular Familiar Interfaces. *Inter-Ax*, 6 (10), 5-15.

[5'] Thorn, H., and Bart, A. 2022. Introduction to Generational Learning Applications. *Data Mining User Interactions*, 8 (6), 23-56.

[6'] Underwood, L., and Accelerated Innovation. 2034. *Elemental Explained*. http://accel.in/elemental_explained. Web.

[7'] Wang, K. and Andros, R. 2032. Privacy Concerns Arising From Massive User Data Mining. *Data Mining User Interactions*, 15 (8), 68-72.

[8'] Zordstale. Masterpost of Developmental Elemental. *GameLiveBlog*. Retrieved April 25, 2034, from GameLiveBlog: http://gameblog.live/zordstale/posts/1288304.html.

7. AUTHOR STATEMENT

The heart of the world-building behind this fiction centers on what we users might be teaching a computer system capable of "learning." A world with widespread familiar interfaces and generational learning is neither dystopian nor utopian. The tone within the fiction is critical, but the purpose of the work is not to pass judgement on that direction of technological development so much as to encourage critical thinking about the unintended side effects of such technology [4].

7.1 Why Study a Game?

Games already have a place in HCI literature, and research using games is only likely to increase as time goes on, as evidenced by the creation of CHI PLAY in 2014. In a literature review featured in the proceedings of the first CHI PLAY conference, Carter et el. [2] describe the volume and type of games-related papers published in CHI proceedings over the last ten years. The distinctions between papers provide insight into the research questions currently surrounding games literature.

Under Carter et al. [2]'s categorization system, this fictional paper would fall under the Practice paradigm for its focus on the interactions between the player and game. This and the related Ontological paradigm were identified as being farther from the typical HCI research in games which begs the question of whether this will be the case in two decades.

Both the physical and cultural realities of games are changing. The nature of input and output to computer systems is being redefined by gestures, immersive displays, voice commands, and more. Even between generations of the same games, such as the fictional Elemental Handhelds, there are hardware changes. However, the more significant changes are cultural. Video games are no longer a fringe hobby, and trends such as gamification and increasing games-related research stretch the boundaries of what a "game" and the related act of "play" are.

Many studies approach games as a means to an end, albeit with good intentions. For example, some studies employ a game-like app to motivate users to exercise. Carter et al. [2] break down the tension between research using games and research about games. As the game industry continues to grow, games will be seen as a valuable research subject in and of themselves. Even so, I dedicated space in the fictional paper to justifying why the study of a game applied to similar interfaces used in a work environment. Optimistically, HCI as a field might come to acknowledge that games justify the same depth of study as other computer systems. Realistically, I think research will be reluctant to consider actions that take place within a game parallel to the same action taking place outside a game.

7.2 What Was Up with Elemental?

I designed the concept of Elemental to push the boundaries of the current conception of non-player or computer characters. In the literature review of game-related studies, only 3 of 178 papers were designated as primarily focusing on interaction between the human and a computer agent [2]. Whether or not one considers artificial intelligence a possibility, the sophistication of real time decision-making by computer agents grows every year, and sooner than later we'll have to face uncomfortable questions about how humans conceptualize and interact with pseudo intelligent non-player characters.

Elemental addresses the direction that this development of computer agents might take. Generational learning has indeed helped each new generation become better at playing the game Elemental (including communicating with their player specifically about playing the game), but an unintended side effect in the process has stripped each generation of some of its flexibility and analytical skills. The problem lies in how the players treat their Fighter. With notable exceptions, most players treat their Fighter like a video game character – or at any rate, they certainly don't read philosophy novels and engage in critical debates with them. The Fighters adapt to this, and it carries over into the next generation as subtle complacency and a loss of flexibility.

For the Gen 5 players who were using their old Gen 2s, this problem is compounded by the fact that the game's culture and the player's own personal style have both changed over the years as well. The pairs could certainly learn to communicate better again, but the Gen 2 Fighters are initially left guessing at what exact strategies the player is referring to.

Whether or not gaining significant task-oriented proficiency is worth losing overall flexibility is a debate to be had. In the context of a video game, it depends on the player. As with any game, some Elemental players would ignore the given battle system and find other ways to amuse themselves in-game, and the loss of flexibility would detract from their ability to explore. I also worry this would send a harmful message to these fringe players, causing them to realize their play style is unusual and unsupported.

7.3 Keywords

Several of the keywords represent a few other predictions for the future worth exploring.

7.3.1 Reaction computing

I only mentioned this concept briefly, but the idea is the foundation for the concept of familiar systems. Reaction computing would be about going beyond a system that waits for input before acting. As devices become "smarter" and more connected to the network, they're already gaining the ability to react in real time to events, such as pinging you as soon as someone sends a message. But more than this, reaction computing would be about computers taking into account the way a user reacts to the system. Imagine a chair that senses your discomfort and adjusts accordingly or a social media system that recognizes fear and discomfort and automatically suggests blocking a cyberbully.

7.3.2 Expression recognition

This would be one component of a system capable of reacting to the user, but it's also notable due to modern examples already cropping up and the privacy concerns these are raising. For example, I once had the opportunity to speak to an innovator in the service industry, and he brought up the idea of constantly monitoring the expressions of employees for feedback and improvement purposes.

7.3.3 Familiar interfaces / systems

This fictional account was essentially a glimpse of what it might look like to have systems in the future which heavily adapt to specific users. Many parallels exist in current developments. User profiles with some customizable features have been around for decades, participatory design aims to let the user in on design decisions, and some news and social media sites attempt to adjust a user's feed invisibly based on predicted preferences.

A virtual avatar or personification of a system has also been popular for a long while. If we could all have a Siri on our computers which functioned perfectly, many of us would. Although the definition wasn't strictly limited to such, I definitely envisioned some sort of virtual agent as a middleman between communicating with the user and making software decisions.

7.3.4 Generational learning

The stepping stones for this this are already in place. Mass data collection happens over the Internet constantly, which has already been bringing up privacy and consent concerns. Data mining some of this collected feedback to make improvements for the next version of software doesn't even require your suspension of disbelief. The key difference in the applications addressed by this paper would be how obscured the resulting changes are. Especially with something as complicated as a familiar interface, untangling whether a behavior was learned from a previous generation, from the current user, or was spontaneously created would be a mess.

8. REFERENCES

[1] Blythe, M. 2014. Research through design fiction: narrative in real and imaginary abstracts. In *Proceedings of the SIGCHI Conference on Human Factors in Computing Systems (CHI '14)*. ACM, New York, NY, USA, 703-712. DOI=http://dx.doi.org/10.1145/2556288.2557098

[2] Carter, M., Downs, J., Nansen, B., Harrop, M., and Gibbs, M. 2014. Paradigms of games research in HCI: a review of 10 years of research at CHI. In *Proceedings of the first ACM SIGCHI annual symposium on Computer-human interaction in play (CHI PLAY '14)*. ACM, New York, NY, USA, 27-36. DOI=http://dx.doi.org/10.1145/2658537.2658708

[3] Linehan, C., Kirman, B., Reeves, S., Blythe, M., Tanenbaum, J., Desjardins, A., and Wakkary, R. 2014. Alternate endings: using fiction to explore design futures. In *CHI '14 Extended Abstracts on Human Factors in Computing Systems (CHI EA '14)*. ACM, New York, NY, USA, 45-48. DOI=http://dx.doi.org/10.1145/2559206.2560472

[4] Nathan, L., Friedman, B., Klasnja, P., Kane, S., and Miller, J. 2008. Envisioning systemic effects on persons and society throughout interactive system design. In *Proceedings of the 7th ACM conference on Designing interactive systems (DIS '08)*. ACM, New York, NY, USA, 1-10. DOI=http://dx.doi.org/10.1145/1394445.1394446

Reading Elinor Ostrom In Silicon Valley: Exploring Institutional Diversity on the Internet

M. Six Silberman
Industriegewerkschaft Metall
Wilhelm-Leuschner-Strasse 79
60329 Frankfurt am Main, Germany
michael.silberman@igmetall.de

ABSTRACT

This paper, from the Design Fictions track at ACM GROUP 2016, is a review of a non-existent book, *Reading Elinor Ostrom in Silicon Valley: Exploring Institutional Diversity on the Internet*, edited by a non-existent researcher named Kieran X. Yuval and published in 2021 (a date, at time of writing, decidedly in the future) by NJU Press, a non-existent academic press. In contrast to the fictitious nature of the editor, book, and press, Elinor Ostrom was a real person and everything described about her and her work in the paper is, to the best of the author's knowledge, true.

CCS Concepts

•**Social and professional topics** → **Computing and business; Commerce policy;** •**Information systems** → *Electronic commerce;*

Keywords

Social science; sociotechnical systems; political economy; Elinor Ostrom; Institutional Analysis and Development framework; institutional diversity; online labor markets; on-demand economy; Amazon Mechanical Turk; Uber; Lyft; reputation systems; Turkopticon; online access to scholarly publications; intellectual property; open access; scholarly publishing, online harassment; platform cooperativism; governance; regulation; policy

1. BOOK INFORMATION

Reading Elinor Ostrom in Silicon Valley: Exploring Institutional Diversity on the Internet. Kieran X. Yuval, ed. Cambridge, NC: NJU Press, 2021. 366 pp. US$24.95.

2. SUMMARY OF THE REVIEW

Reading Elinor Ostrom in Silicon Valley is a collection of empirical and theoretical contributions from researchers in the "traditional" social sciences, economics, human-centered computing (HCC), and science and technology studies (STS) that explores four major contemporary "information society" developments—the "on-demand economy," online access to scholarly publications, online harassment, and "platform cooperativism"—from a perspective that integrates the sociotechnical and the political-economic. The contributions to the volume consider the phenomena under study through the lens of the Institutional Analysis and Development (IAD) framework, developed over four decades by the political economist Elinor Ostrom—the first woman and first non-economist to win the Nobel Prize in economics (in 2009)—and her colleagues at the Workshop on Political Theory and Policy Analysis at Indiana University. The detailed

GROUP '16, November 13 - 16, 2016, Sanibel Island, FL, USA

ACM 978-1-4503-4276-6/16/11...$15.00
DOI: http://dx.doi.org/10.1145/2957276.2957311

empirical and analytical contributions to the volume integrate accepted HCC and STS methods such as ethnography, research through design, and action research with approaches common in IAD scholarship, including game theory and empirically based agent-based modeling. In doing so, the collection builds a conceptual lens linking detailed interpretivist empirical research in HCC and STS to practical "macro" questions about *both* system design and operation *and* economic and institutional policy—questions that are always, in practice, interlinked. By shedding light on these interlinked dynamics, this integrative conceptual lens reveals new options for researchers, designers, entrepreneurs, policy makers, users, and others to work together to evolve existing "social-economic-political-technical" systems—and build new ones—in ways that allow them to more substantively and sustainably address the needs and concerns of diverse stakeholders, including "on-demand" workers, scholars unable to afford access to expensive journals, and people subject to harassment in online spaces. In a moment in which seemingly ever more complex and politically opaque sociotechnical systems subtend seemingly ever-greater swathes of social, economic, and political life, reshaping interpersonal relationships, work, and politics in their images—or in the not-always-democratic visions of their founders and funders—this is a timely contribution.

3. REVIEW

3.1 Overview of the book

Reading Elinor Ostrom in Silicon Valley is a riotously interdisciplinary collection of empirical and theoretical contributions from researchers in the "traditional" social sciences, economics, human-centered computing (HCC, meaning, roughly, "human-computer interaction [HCI] and computer supported cooperative work [CSCW]"), and science and technology studies (STS) that explores four major contemporary "information society" developments from a perspective that integrates the sociotechnical and the political-economic. Substantively, the book examines four topics at the intersection of computing, economics, and governance that have in recent years garnered increasing attention from a broad range of international publics, including practicing designers, entrepreneurs, policy makers, social scientists, and HCC and STS researchers: the "on-demand economy"; access to scholarly publications; online harassment; and "platform cooperativism," a movement developing democratically governed alternatives to for-profit information systems. The contributions are unified by the theoretical project of actionably linking the Institutional Analysis and Development (IAD) framework, developed over four decades by the political economist Elinor Ostrom and her colleagues at the Workshop for Political Theory and Policy Analysis at Indiana University, with the research discourses of human-computer interaction (HCI) and computer-supported cooperative work (CSCW). The contributions show how the IAD framework, originally crafted to support analyses of the dynamics of "social-ecological systems," can also scaffold broad-ranging analyses that illuminate the interlinked technical and socioeconomic dynamics of information systems—and reveal practical strategies for more fully addressing the concerns of a broad range of stakeholders in their design and operation. Following in the tradition established by Ostrom and her collaborators in their study of common pool resources (see especially [37]), the contributors weave together an eclectic collection of methods: detailed fieldwork and interpretive analysis, large-N surveys and other quantitative datasets (e.g., server logs), and empirically based agent based models (i.e., computer simulations) of sociotechnical systems.

After an introduction to the IAD framework, the book divides into three major parts. Part I contains six detailed, interdisciplinary, mixed-method case studies of socioeconomically controversial sociotechnical systems and phenomena: the transportation network industry, focusing on Uber and Lyft, their struggles with regulators, and their competition with taxi companies; hospitality platform Airbnb; "microtask marketplace" Amazon Mechanical Turk; online harassment; the technical, economic, and legal struggle to control online access to scholarly publications—and the links between the practices of corporate publishing giants such as Elsevier, university libraries, and "guerrilla open access" infrastructures such as AAAAARG.ORG, Science Hub, and Library Genesis; and finally, Bivy, a cooperatively managed protocol emerging as a potential competitor to centralized for-profit social networks such as Facebook and Twitter. While each case begins with one or more named sociotechnical systems or with particular instances of a phenomenon, the final object of study, following Ostrom's own emphasis (see e.g. [35]), is always a "polycentric" system of interlinked technologies, institutions, actors, and practices, the dynamics it exhibits, and the outcomes it produces for different stakeholders. The computational, legal, economic, and sociological aspects of the system are described quantitatively and qualitatively, and a working model of the system is constructed using the concepts offered by the IAD framework. This working model is then embodied in a computer simulation—an empirically based agent based model (see [18])—that is manipulated to explore potential consequences of past or possible alterations or interventions within the system. Agent based simulations of the transportation network, for example, show how the development of an independently operated reputation system for Uber and Lyft passengers—and its adoption in 2017-18 by the majority of "serious" drivers on both platforms—changed the incentives facing passengers and led to an increase in driver earnings, tenure, and satisfaction.

Part II is theoretical. Its three chapters—focusing respectively on power, reputation and reputation systems, and cooperative governance—draw on the empirical material and models presented in Part I to explore these three themes of long-running interest in the social sciences in the context of massively distributed, interlinked information infrastructures. The chapter on power links prior game-theoretic treatments of the topic with the concepts of the IAD framework in the context of the empirical cases presented in Part I to examine how various social-economic-political-technical arrangements concentrate or distribute power, how the distribution of power affects both long-term system sustainability and outcomes for different stakeholder groups, and how specific interventions can redistribute power. Reputation systems appear in several chapters in Part I, and the chapter on reputation and reputation systems in Part II synthesizes these discussions and develops a series of agent-based models to discuss the topic in more general terms. The final chapter in Part II, on cooperative governance, follows a similar pattern, drawing on the empirical and theoretical work of

Ostrom and her colleagues on self-governance among users of common pool resources (e.g., [30, 31, 8, 5]) to draw general lessons from the details of the cases discussed in Part I.

Part III considers theory and method within HCC research informed by the IAD framework. The first three chapters of Part III connect the IAD with three well-loved theoretical traditions in HCC: activity theory, actor-network theory, and social psychology. The last three chapters consider the use of the IAD framework within research guided by three related but distinct methdological traditions in HCC: action research, research through design, and participatory design. The three methodological chapters offer the collection's sharpest development of four intertwined themes that recur in the empirical chapters: the diversity of users and stakeholders other than users in social-economic-political-technical systems, the potential for conflicts of interest among stakeholders, the inevitability of "politics" in the management of systems in which conflicts of interest arise, and the potential for structured dialogue to reveal shared interests "beneath" the conflicts—shared interests that can point the way to satisfactory resolutions.

A concluding chapter reflects on the contributions as a whole and offers an agenda for future work.

3.2 Elinor Ostrom and the Institutional Analysis and Development framework

Elinor Ostrom was the first woman and the first non-economist to receive the Nobel Prize in economics. She received the 2009 prize for her "analysis of economic governance, especially the commons" [28]. She describes her work as part of contemporary interdisciplinary developments in economics and political science that build on traditional game-theoretic frameworks but reach beyond "classical" theories that assume that all economic activity goes on in a "dichotomous world" comprised only of "'the market' and 'the state'" ([35], p. 1). In contrast to the too-simple assumptions and prescriptions of classical economics, Ostrom and her colleagues within "new institutional economics" and at the Workshop on Political Theory and Policy Analysis at Indiana University found that "humans...have complex motivational structures and establish diverse private-for-profit, governmental, and community arrangements that operate at multiple scales to generate productive and innovative as well as destructive and perverse outcomes" ([35], p. 1). That is, people start businesses, make laws, establish government agencies, and develop informal and formal not-for-profit arranagements to realize their complex goals—and sometimes these efforts end well and sometimes they end badly. Institutional form alone does not predict success, failure, or the distribution of costs, risks, benefits, and unintended consequences. Rather, outcomes in institutional settings are shaped by a diversity of factors, including the actors involved; the institutional roles they occupy and the actions afforded them through those roles; the information available to them about the potential outcomes of their actions, including the potential actions of other actors in response; and external conditions, including both "biophysical" conditions (e.g., the number or growth rate of fish in a fishery) and external social or institutional conditions (e.g., the actions of actors in larger-scale institutions such as governments).

Over four decades, Ostrom and her colleagues conducted extensive field studies and laboratory experiments on the social and ecological dynamics of shared "common-pool resources" such as forests, fisheries, and water resources, and extensive meta-analyses of these and other field studies and experiments (see e.g. [29] and [33]). They found that the complexity of factors influencing institutional outcomes means that diverse possibilities exist for the sustainable long-term governance of such common-pool resources. This finding contrasted with previous arguments arising from classical theories which assumed most actors to be relatively short-sighted, self-interested, and uncommunicative. These theories proposed that actors should be expected to overexploit shared resources, leading to resource collapse (e.g., [15]), and that such overexploitation could only be prevented by either privatization or government intervention and control. Ostrom and her colleagues found, however, that *in some but not all cases*, resource users themselves can develop and enforce rules to disincentivize overexploitation and ensure the long-term sustainability of the resource. Indeed, they found empirical evidence of many really existing "long-enduring, self-organized, and self-governed common-pool resources" ([29], Ch. 3). The ability of users of a given common-pool resource to self-govern—i.e., to themselves devise and enforce rules that prevent overexploitation—depends on a diversity of factors, some of which can be affected by users or actors in larger scale institutions (e.g., governments) and some of which cannot (e.g., the extent to which the resource affords the demarcation of clear boundaries and monitoring). (These are summarized in Chapter 1 of *Reading Elinor Ostrom in Silicon Valley*, in [34], and in Chapter 9 of [33].) The empirical discovery that resource users could under some circumstances resolve "commons dilemmas" by developing and enforcing rules governing resource use led to the development of the Institutional Analysis and Development (IAD) framework to explore and explain the interrelated factors leading to success or failure (i.e., to "long-surviving resource institutions" [35] or to resource collapse). The framework allows stakeholders, researchers, and policy analysts to at least schematically represent real-world institutional settings, explore their dynamics, and consider possible outcomes of change.

3.3 Contribution

The topics taken up in *Reading Elinor Ostrom in Silicon Valley*—the "on-demand economy," online access to scholarly publications, online harassment, and cooperative governance of information systems—are hardly new to HCC researchers. Indeed HCI and CSCW researchers contributed early to the study of the "on-demand economy" (e.g. [38, 17, 21, 24, 39, 14, 23, 6, 11]) and online harassment (e.g. [2, 26]), and participated directly in the emergence of platform cooperativism (e.g. [1]).

On the theoretical front, the claim that humans have complex motivations, establish diverse structures for their collective efforts, and experience success or failure based on a diversity of factors including but not limited to institutional form likely comes as no surprise for many social researchers in HCC with training in, or exposure to, the interpretive social sciences or humanities. Indeed the claim resonates with long-running critiques of the naïve technological optimism and determinism sometimes unwittingly promulgated by enthusiastic proponents of new sociotechnical designs—and social researchers within HCC (especially CSCW) have offered some of the most pointed and actionable of such critiques [22, 12, 13, 42]. And the topic of stakeholder self-organization is a long-running interest in HCC, especially CSCW (e.g., [19]), in particular in studies of free/open source software development (e.g., [4, 3]) and Wikipedia (e.g., [36, 44]). Indeed elements of the IAD framework were used as early as 2007 to analyze governance on Wikipedia [43].

Yet existing systems and their organizations rely on and support particular economic aims, values, and logics (see e.g. [40, 27, 10, 20]); beyond the often-cited cases of free/open source software and Wikipedia, the final criteria shaping "socioeconomic-sociotechnical" change in the last few decades, at least where the main technologies involved are computational, seem still to be financial. The design and administration decisions of the operators of the large systems on which many of us (some ambivalently) rely—Amazon, Elsevier, Facebook, Google, Twitter, Uber, and so on—seem much more often oriented by operators' fiduciary obligations (and hopes) than by an organizationally-supported intention to democratically negotiate the needs of a broad variety of stakeholders, or to support a robust and vibrant democratic culture generally. New entrants with different aims face severe challenges—perhaps most notably, limited access to capital. While HCC has a long tradition of developing technologies with democratic aspirations, even those systems held up as examples of successful sociotechnical interventions in asymmetrical power relations (in the last five years, e.g., [7, 17]) are at best small victories in the face of the continued dominance of nondemocratic systems.

The contributors to *Reading Elinor Ostrom in Silicon Valley* show, through their institutional analyses of existing, dominant systems, of "successor systems" [9, 25] that alter the dynamics of those systems, and of cooperatively-operated systems that aim to compete with them, that major information infrastructures can be sustainably democratically funded and operated—and that democratically operated information infrastructures can compete effectively in a market dominated by hierarchically-governed for-profit organizations. They argue—and the empirical material in the volume lends weight to the argument—that democratically operated infrastructures offer the promise of achieving, on balance, better outcomes for the increasingly broad diversity of stakeholders to information systems. They make a strong case that the institutions of HCC research should welcome the efforts of HCC researchers to study, celebrate, support, and extend such systems—and, as needed, build new ones, rather than marginalize such efforts by labeling them unacceptably political or otherwise unscientific. The empirical chapters in the volume offer detailed accounts of the increasingly significant contributions of HCC researchers in expanding democratic influence over crucial information infrastructures, and the theoretical material offers conceptual and methodological tools for others who might wish to follow in their footsteps. The sophisticated but actionable analyses, models, and even predictions offered throughout the volume show convincingly that the IAD framework offers a powerful complement to existing HCC theory and method for researchers interested in understanding—and shaping—the governance of sociotechnical-socioeconomic systems. Taken as a whole, the volume offers a first draft of a coherent approach for analyzing and evolving existing social-economic-political-technical systems—and for building new ones—in ways that sustainably and substantively address the needs and concerns of their diverse stakeholders, rather than prioritizing the prerogatives of a powerful few.

Like the woman whose work guides the analyses and proposals of its contributors, *Reading Elinor Ostrom in Silicon Valley* is openly and unapologetically biased in favor of democratic governance. Ostrom once wrote that she "share[d] a deep conviction that democratic systems of government are the highest form of human governance yet developed" [32], and editor Yuval and her co-contributors leave no room for doubt that they share this conviction. Their evaluations of existing systems and proposals for new ones elevate contextually-defined criteria of democratic participation, inclusion, and distributive and procedural justice to the same importance as traditional technical and economic criteria such as efficiency and resource sustainability. But like Ostrom [32], they are far from blithely optimistic about the future of democracy; like Ostrom, they observe that "governing the commons" is "always a struggle" [5]. The struggle to evolve democratic social-economic-political-technical systems will appear in many forms—organizational, technical, intellectual, and political—and many places—corporate boardrooms, universities, political institutions, and the everyday practices of users, designers, operators, and other stakeholders. A powerful affirmation that complex technology and democracy can sustainably coexist, and that HCC researchers can contribute meaningfully to that coexistence, *Reading Elinor Ostrom in Silicon Valley* is a significant contribution to that struggle.

4. ACKNOWLEDGMENTS

I thank Katie Pine for helpful discussions about this text.

5. DISCLAIMER

This paper reflects the personal views of its author. It was not directly materially supported, reviewed, or approved by, nor does it bear any relation to any official position of, Industriegewerkschaft Metall.

6. REFERENCES

[1] Alkhatib, Ali. 2015. Designing worker-centric labor markets. Presentation, *Platform Cooperativism*, 13-14 Nov 2015, New School for Liberal Arts, New York, NY.

[2] Bruckman, Amy, Catalina Danis, Cliff Lampe, Janet Sternberg, and Chris Waldron. 2006. Managing deviant behavior in online communities. *Proc. CHI EA '06*: 21-24.

[3] Choi, Joohee, Junghong Choi, Jae Yun Moon, Jungpil Hahn, and Jinwoo Kim. 2013. Herding in open source software development: an exploratory study. *Proc. CSCW '13 Companion*: 129-134.

[4] Crowston, Kevin, Qing Li, Kangning Wei, U. Yeliz Eseryel, and James Howison. 2007. Self-organization of teams for free/libre open source software development. *Information and Software Technology* **49**(6): 564-575.

[5] Dietz, Thomas, Elinor Ostrom, and Paul C. Stern. 2003. The struggle to govern the commons. *Science* **302**: 1907-1912.

[6] Dillahunt, Tawanna R., and Amelia R. Malone. 2015. The promise of the sharing economy among disadvantaged communities. *Proc. CHI '15*: 2285-2294.

[7] Dimond, Jill P., Michaelanne Dye, Daphne Larose, Amy S. Bruckman. 2013. Hollaback! The role of storytelling online in a social movement organization. *Proc. CSCW '13*: 477-490.

[8] Futemma, Célia, Fábio de Castro, Maria Clara Silva-Forsberg, and Elinor Ostrom. 2002. The emergence and outcomes of collective action: an institutional and ecosystem approach. *Society and Natural Resources* **15**: 503-522.

[9] Geiger, R. Stuart. 2014. Successor systems: the role of reflexive algorithms in enacting ideological critique. Presentation, *Internet Research '14*, 21-24 Oct 2014, Daegu, South Korea.

[10] Gomory, Ralph, and Richard Sylla. 2013. The American Corporation. *Dædalus* **142**(2): 102-118.

[11] Gray, Mary L., Siddharth Suri, Syed Shoaib Ali, and Deepti Kulkarni. 2016. The crowd is a collaborative network. *Proc. CSCW '16*, to appear.

[12] Grudin, Jonathan. 1988. Why CSCW applications fail: problems in the design and evaluation of organizational interfaces. *Proc. CSCW '88*: 85-93.

[13] Grudin, Jonathan. 1994. Groupware and social dynamics: eight challenges for developers. *CACM* **37**(1): 92-105.

[14] Gupta, Neha, David Martin, Benjamin V. Hanrahan, and Jacki O'Neill. 2014. Turk-Life in India. *Proc. GROUP '14*: 1-11.

[15] Hardin, Garrett. 1968. The tragedy of the commons. *Science* **162**: 1243-1248.

[16] Hess, Charlotte and Elinor Ostrom, eds. 2007. *Understanding Knowledge as a Commons: From Theory to Practice.* MIT Press.

[17] Irani, Lilly, and M. Six Silberman. Turkopticon: interrupting worker invisibility in Amazon Mechanical Turk. *Proc. CHI '13*: 611-620.

[18] Janssen, Marco A. and Elinor Ostrom. 2006. Empirically based, agent-based models. *Ecology and Society* **11**(2): 37.

[19] Kaplan, Simon, and Lesley Seeback. 2001. Harnessing complexity in CSCW. *Proc. ECSCW '01*: 359-278.

[20] Keese, Christoph. 2014. *Silicon Valley: Was aus dem mächtigsten Tal der Welt auf uns zukommt* [*Silicon Valley: What's in Store For Us in the Most Powerful Valley in the World*]. Albrecht Knaus Verlag.

[21] Kittur, Aniket, Jeffrey V. Nickerson, Michael S. Bernstein, Elizabeth M. Gerber, Aaron Shaw, John Zimmerman, Matthew Lease, and John J. Horton. 2013. The future of crowd work. *Proc. CSCW '13*: 1301-1317.

[22] Kling, Rob. 1978. Automated welfare client-tracking and service integration: the political economy of computing. *CACM* **21**(6): 484-493.

[23] Lee, Min Kyung, Daniel Kusbit, Evan Metsky, and Laura Dabbish. 2015. Working with machines: the impact of algorithmic and data-driven management on human workers. *Proc. CHI '15*: 1603-1612.

[24] Martin, David, Benjamin V. Hanrahan, Jacki O'Neill, and Neha Gupta. 2014. Being a Turker. *Proc. CSCW '14*: 224-235.

[25] Matias, J. Nathan. 2014. Supporting change from outside systems with design and data: Stuart Geiger on successor systems. *MIT Center for Civic Media*, 9 Dec 2014. https://civic.mit.edu/blog/natematias/supporting-change-from-outside-systems-with-design-and-data-stuart-geiger-on.

[26] Menking, Amanda, and Ingrid Erickson. 2015. The heart work of Wikipedia: gendered, emotional labor in the world's largest online encyclopedia. *Proc. CHI '15*: 207-210.

[27] Neff, Gina. 2012. *Venture Labor: Work and the Burden of Risk in Innovative Industries.* MIT Press.

[28] nobelprize.org. The 2009 Prize in Economic Sciences—Press Release. http://www.nobelprize.org/nobel_prizes/economic-sciences/laureates/2009/press.html.

[29] Ostrom, Elinor. 1990. *Governing the Commons: The Evolution of Institutions for Collective Action.* Cambridge University Press.

[30] Ostrom, Elinor, James Walker, and Roy Gardner. Covenants with and without a sword: self-governance is possible. *American Political Science Review* **86**(2): 404-417.

[31] Ostrom, Elinor and Roy Gardner. Coping with asymmetries in the commons: self-governing irrigation systems can work. *Journal of Economic Perspectives* **7**(4): 93-112.

[32] Ostrom, Elinor. 2000. The future of democracy. *Scandinavian Political Studies* **23**(3): 280-283.

[33] Ostrom, Elinor. 2005. *Understanding Institutional Diversity.* Princeton University Press.

[34] Ostrom, Elinor. 2009. A general framework for analyzing sustainability of social-ecological systems. *Science* **325**: 419-422.

[35] Ostrom, Elinor. 2010. Beyond markets and states: polycentric governance of complex economic systems. *American Economic Review* **100**: 1-33.

[36] Panciera, Katherine, Aaron Halfaker, and Loren Terveen. 2009. Wikipedians are born, not made: a study of power editors on Wikipedia. *GROUP '09*: 51-60.

[37] Poteete, Amy R., Marco A. Janssen, and Elinor Ostrom. 2010. *Working Together: Collective Action, the Commons, and Multiple Methods in Practice.* Princeton University Press.

[38] Ross, Joel, Lilly Irani, M. Six Silberman, Andrew Zaldivar, and Bill Tomlinson. Who are the crowdworkers? Shifting demographics in Mechanical Turk. *Proc. CHI EA '10*: 2863-2872.

[39] Salehi, Niloufar, Lilly Irani, Michael Bernstein, Ali Alkhatib, Eva Ogbe, Kristy Milland, and Clickhappier. 2015. We are Dynamo: overcoming stalling and friction in collective action for crowd workers. *Proc. CHI '15*: 1621-1630.

[40] Sassen, Saskia. 2005. Electronic markets and activist networks: the weight of social logics in digital formations. Robert Latham and Saskia Sassen, eds., *Digital Formations: IT and New Architectures in the Global Realm.* Princeton University Press.

[41] Scholz, Trebor. 2016. *Platform Cooperativism: Challenging the Corporate Sharing Economy.* Rosa Luxemburg Foundation.

[42] Suchman, Lucy. 1987. *Plans and Situated Actions: The Problem of Human-Machine Communication.* Cambridge University Press.

[43] Viégas, Fernanda B., Martin Wattenberg, and Matthew M. McKeon. 2007. The hidden order of Wikipedia. *Proc. OCSC '07*: 445-454.

[44] Welser, Howard T., Dan Cosley, Gueorgi Kossinets, Austin Lin, Fedor Dokshin, Geri Gay, and Marc Smith. 2011. Finding social roles in Wikipedia. *Proc. iConference '11*: 122-129.

Characterizations of Online Harassment: Comparing Policies Across Social Media Platforms

Jessica A. Pater
Georgia Institute of Technology
Atlanta, GA
pater@gatech.edu

Moon K. Kim
Georgia Institute of Technology
Atlanta, GA
moonkim@gatech.edu

Elizabeth D. Mynatt
Georgia Institute of Technology
Atlanta, GA
mynatt@gatech.edu

Casey Fiesler
University of Colorado, Boulder
Boulder, CO
casey.fiesler@colorado.edu

ABSTRACT
Harassment in online spaces is increasingly part of public debate and concern. Pervasive problems like cyberbullying, hate speech, and the glorification of self-harm have highlighted the breadth and depth of harassment taking place online. In this study we conduct a content analysis of the governing policies for fifteen social media platforms as they relate to harassment (of oneself and/or of community members) and other associated behaviors. We find that there is a striking inconsistency in how platform-specific policies depict harassment. Additionally, how these policies prescribe responses to harassment vary from mild censuring to the involvement of law enforcement. Finally, based on our analysis and findings, we discuss the potential for harnessing the power of the online communities to create norms around problematic behaviors.

Keywords
harassment; governance; online communities; policy; social media; terms of service; community norms

1. INTRODUCTION
Increasingly, online harassment is an issue of public debate and concern, particularly in the context of pervasive problems like cyberbullying [1, 4], hate speech and trolling [6, 17], and the glorification of self-harm [3, 22]. To address these types of issues, the computing research community has looked towards technological and design solutions for combatting these known problems [1, 4] while lawmakers tackle the same issues by creating new laws to govern behavior [2, 18]. However, these decisions are often made in an environment removed from where the actual harassment takes place. Operators of online social platforms have a unique advantage where they can create policies to address harassment in the same environment where it takes place. But *are* these sites developing policy-based measures to address harassment, and if so, *what* do they look like?

Harassment itself is complex to define. Traditionally thought of as repeated annoyance or attacks, harassment is often operationalized as external, targeting another individual [23, 24]. However, harassment can also be focused inward, with an individual harassing oneself through self-harm and self-injurious behaviors [10]. Furthermore, harassment online has unique properties due to the asynchronous, and often anonymous, nature of online interactions. Pinning down certain behaviors as harassment within policy is also complicated due to values around freedom of expression.

Previous studies have examined the most common manifestations of online harassment and their associated behaviors inflicted on others, such as cyberbullying [4], hate speech [6], and sexual harassment [21], and those inflicted on oneself, like self-harm, suicide [15], and eating disorders [22]. This body of work examines these activities within specific contexts, and seeks to learn more about how platform-specific policies (such as Terms of Service, Community Guidelines, and other forms of formalized site governance) regulate these activities [17].

Though policy can be as powerful a design agent as technology [8], it is often only considered as an afterthought in the context of user research and design [13]. To understand the landscape of online harassment and intervene in appropriate ways—whether with rules (legal or platform-specific policies), technologically, or through community-enforced social norms—we first need a clear picture of what social platforms are attempting in terms of written regulations.

To understand this current state, we devised a study to examine how social platforms and their communities characterize harassment. In this work we address several key questions:

1. Do social media policies address the issue of harassment?
2. How do social media policies define and/or characterize harassment? How consistent and comprehensible are these policies? Are there similarities across platforms?

GROUP '16, November 13-16, 2016, Sanibel Island, FL, USA

ACM 978-1-4503-4276-6/16/11…$15.00
DOI: http://dx.doi.org/10.1145/2957276.2957297

3. What actions in response to harassment do platforms outline in their policies?

To address these questions, we conducted a content analysis of policy documents from fifteen popular social media platforms, examining harassment-specific content. It should be noted that policies *as written* do not always reflect policies as enacted. However, analyzing stated policies is a required first step in understanding how social platforms work towards governing harassment. Through our analysis of policies as written, we show that harassment is not specifically defined, but it is commonly listed alongside other various prohibited behaviors. Additionally, platform responses to harassment and prohibited behaviors are varied and inconsistent.

We discuss the policy and design challenges that this vagueness and inconsistency might present to both online platforms and their users, and what research directions these observations suggest for the social computing research community. Going forward, a better understanding of the characterization of harassment in the policies that govern online social platforms provides the foundation to examine the differences between what is articulated through policies and what happens in practice.

2. RELATED WORK

The problem of online harassment has seen increasing attention within HCI and social computing research. Much of this prior work has focused on cyberbullying, especially towards technological and design solutions to curtail behavior [1, 4]. However, alongside design strategies, platform policies and community norms share an important role in encouraging certain behaviors and discouraging others. For example, in researching Reddit in the context of Gamergate, Massanari found that the site's policies and approach to community governance contributed to the presence of harassment [17]. Others have noted that law, platform policy, and norms can all play a role in regulating behavior, and conflicts between these multiple sources of governance can be problematic [9]. Social media platform designers and operators are in a special position of authority. Through their design and policy choices, they can play a critical role in governing user behavior. Routinely, they decide what content or behavior is allowable or not, and by doing so, they are effectively in the "gatekeeping position" of freedom of expression online [5].

Jackson et al. therefore argue that policy can be as important as design and practice within CSCW systems, and should be considered alongside rather than as an afterthought [13]. Accordingly, within the computing community there is a growing corpus of research focused on understanding online policy, especially with respect to Terms of Service (TOS) [16], end-user license agreements [11], copyright policies [8, 9], and privacy policies [14]. Additionally, research has shown that there are often considerable disconnects between a community's understanding and its platform's actual policies [8, 11]. With the work described in this paper, we bring this policy-centric analysis to the problem of online harassment, as an extension to the prior work in both areas.

3. METHODS

3.1 Selecting Social Media Platforms

We adapted methods from Fiesler et al. [8] to analyze the TOS and supplementary policy documents of fifteen widely used social media platforms. We referenced a popular online trend aggregator to provide a list of widely used social media platforms for our analysis.[1] Table 1 highlights these platforms, along with proxies for popularity (unique monthly visitors) and cultural homogeneity (% user base that is in the United States).

Platform	Year Founded	Unique Monthly Visitors (US)	User base (% in U.S.)
Facebook	2004	122,875,81	21.8%
Twitter	2006	81,026,590	21.6%
LinkedIn	2002	67,633,842	26.8%
Pinterest	2010	61,327,968	45.6%
Instagram	2010	55,608,250	24.4%
Tumblr	2007	40,086,036	33.9%
Flickr	2004	23,893,368	28.3%
Meetup	2002	11,943,825	48.1%
Vine	2013	10,202,168	43%
Classmates	1995	4,758,561	89.6%
VK	2006	3,119,051	0.8%
Tagged	2004	1,445,300	17.5%
AskFM	2010	1,356,355	4.3%
MeetMe	2005	903,532	50.3%
Google +	2011	*Alexa doesn't differentiate from Google.com statistics*	

Table 1. Social media platforms in our dataset, sorted by popularity.

3.2 Policy Documents

In October of 2015, we collected policy documents from the fifteen platforms, a total of 56 documents (see Table 2). We identified two primary types of policies, formal and informal. Formal policy documents are legal and binding, and they include TOS, privacy policies, and acceptable use policies. Informal policy documents are non-legal, and they include normative artifacts such as community guidelines, safety guides, and other informative documentation. Most sites had more than three documents (80%), with an average of 3.7 per platform; Facebook had the most with eight documents.

We also assessed the readability of each document using a measure common in prior studies of online policies, the Flesch-Kincaid Grade Level (FKGL) score [8, 14]. In line with this prior work, the level of difficulty is high, an average

[1] http://www.ebizmba.com/articles/social-networking-websites

of 11.2 (equivalent to a high school junior) across all 56 documents. Formal policy documents in our dataset scored an average FKGL score of 12.2 while informal policy documents scored an average FKGL score of 9.8. These results suggest that informal policies rather than legal documents present information in a more accessible way.

3.3 Qualitative Coding of Policy Documents

Drawing from previous methods of policy document analysis [8], we used an iterative, inductive approach to qualitative coding. Two researchers independently coded a randomized sample of documents. They coded for general themes in the data, then met to discuss and synthesize the themes. We then refined and expanded the finalized codebook. High-level thematic codes included "moderation," "prohibited activity," "response to prohibited activity," "community standards," and "specific guidance." A total of 289 codes were applied to the dataset.

4. POLICY ANALYSIS

4.1 Defining Harassment

Surprisingly, we found that not a single platform-specific policy in our dataset explicitly defines what constitutes harassment. However, while they do not explicitly define harassment, Instagram and Twitter were the only platforms that describe specific behaviors or activities that are taken into account when determining if something is harassment. These behaviors include "repeated unwanted contact" (Instagram) or "reported behaviors [that are] one-sided or include threats" (Twitter).

More commonly, we saw the word "harassment" (including derivations of "harass" and "harassing") embedded in a string of other prohibited activities and behaviors. Table 3 highlights these activities and behaviors that co-occur with harassment in these documents. The most common include:

	Formal Documents				*Informal Documents*				
	TOS	Privacy Policy	Additional Terms	Acceptable Use Policy	Safety Guide	Community Guideline	Parental Guide	Law Enforce. Guide	Teen/Youth Guide
Facebook	(X)	X	X			X	(X)	X	X
Twitter	X	X	(X)				(X)	X	
LinkedIn	X	X		X		(X)			
Pinterest	X	X		(X)					
Instagram	(X)	X				(X)	(X)	X	
Tumblr	X	X			X	(X)			
Flickr	(X)	X			(X)	(X)	X		
Meetup	(X)	X				X			
Vine	X	X				X			
Classmates	(X*)								
VK	X	X							
Tagged	(X*)				X			X	
Ask.fm	(X)	X					(X)	X	(X)
MeetMe	(X*)								
Google+	X	X	(X)			X			

* indicates that the Privacy Policy is found embedded in the TOS
( ) indicates the policy directly mentions "harassment"

Table 2. Policy documents present within dataset

abuse, bullying, harm, hate, stalking, and threats. The term "harassment" and its derivations only appear in 37.5% of all documents in our dataset (see Table 2). All but two platforms (Vine and VK) either directly mention the term "harassment" or "harass" in their formal and informal policy documents.

Despite the lack of guidance for what it actually means, "harassment" is explicitly mentioned within 21 of the 56 policy documents within our dataset (see Table 2). In comparing the different types of policy documents, we found that six platforms mention harassment only in formal policy documents, two platforms mention harassment only in

	Abuse	Attack	Bullying	Defame	Eating Dis.	Harm	Hate	Impersonate	Intimidate	Libelous	Racist	Self-harm	Self-injury	Self-mutilation	Stalking	Threat	Torture	Vulgar
Facebook		X	X		X		X		X				X	X		X		
Twitter	X	X																
LinkedIn	X					X				X								
Pinterest		X	X		X	X	X					X				X		
Instagram	X		X	X	X		X	X	X				X		X	X		
Tumblr					X							X	X	X	X			
Flickr	X			X		X	X	X	X	X	X				X	X	X	X
Meetup				X		X	X		X	X	X	X			X	X	X	X
Vine								X				X				X		
Classmates	X		X	X			X		X		X				X	X		
VK				X							X		X			X		
Tagged	X			X		X	X			X	X				X	X		X
Ask.fm			X								X	X				X		
MeetMe	X					X										X		
Google+			X				X	X								X		

Table 3. Terms associated with harassment within policy documents

informal policy documents, and five platforms mention them in both formal and informal policy documents. Several platform-specific policies used similar language in describing these unwanted behaviors. In one case (Flickr and MeetMe), it was more than just similar language but actually a direct duplication.

Few platforms delineate directionality of harassing behaviors and activities between those focused on others and those focused on oneself. For example, Ask.fm's TOS states in the rules of conduct that users must not post or send anything that "contains any threat of any kind, including threats of physical violence to yourself or others." Other platforms, like Facebook and Instagram, have informal policy documents that discuss harm to oneself at a more granular level, calling out eating disorders, self-injury, and self-harm. Our analysis shows that over half (eight) of the platforms consider harm to oneself to be a behavior that is important to regulate.

4.2 Responses to Prohibited Activities

There are a variety of different *responses* to these prohibited behaviors outlined in platform-specific policies. We identified nine unique responses that range in scope and severity (see Table 4). For example, some platforms have policies that enable operators to send warnings to community members, delete content or accounts, or work with third party entities like law enforcement, federal governments, or organizations (i.e., the National Center for Missing and Exploited Children). On the other hand, we found little to no distinction between how platform operators respond to harassment and other prohibited activities like hacking and spamming. Policies did not distinguish nuanced responses specifically to *harassment*, instead ascribing general responses to all prohibited activities.

	Restrict account	Send user warning	Remove content	Disable account	Delete account	Work w/Law enforce.	Removed from search	Interface with 3rd party(s)
Facebook		X	X	X		X		X
Twitter					X	X	X	X
LinkedIn	X	X		X	X	X		X
Pinterest			X	X	X	X		X
Instagram			X	X	X	X		X
Tumblr		X	X		X	X	X	X
Flickr	X	X	X	X	X	X		X
Meetup			X	X	X	X		X
Vine		X	X	X	X	X		
Classmates		X	X	X	X	X		X
VK			X	X	X	X		
Tagged			X		X	X		X
Ask.fm			X	X		X		
MeetMe					X	X		X
Google+			X	X	X	X		X

Table 4. Platform responses to harassment and prohibited behaviors, as described in policy documents

As described in these policy documents, the most common response to prohibited activity is for platform operators to cooperate and work with law enforcement officials. Every platform-specific policy in our dataset stated the operator's willingness to work with law enforcement, often under the guise of complying with state and federal laws. Most commonly, these activities included accessing and sharing content and personal information from within the platform. Another potential response is to suspend or delete an individual's account if it is deemed that the TOS has been broken or that a user has violated community rules and standards. All platforms reserved this right.

For platform-specific policies that provide *some* criteria for determining "harassment" (Instagram and Twitter), we found that responses focused on empowering their users to find help. For example, with respect to how Instagram interfaces with third party groups, informal policy documents provide links to major bullying hotlines and help centers like Connect Safely, Stop Bullying, and the National Crime Prevention Center on Cyberbullying, as well as eating disorder hotlines. Tumblr also provides a document that lists free and confidential counseling on several harassment issues, including rape, bullying, suicide, and self-harm. Not only do they provide U.S.-based resources, they also include information for nine other countries.

4.3 Encouraging Positive Norms

Several platform-specific policies described the types of activities listed in Table 3 in informal policy documents like community guidelines and safety tips for parents and teens. In these documents, policies around harassment tend to be more normative than prescriptive. For example, Instagram's community guidelines begin, "We want to foster a positive, diverse community," before enumerating unacceptable content and activities like those found in Table 3.

Other informal policies discuss the prohibited behaviors in a more relatable manner without calling out specifics. For example, Flickr's community guidelines state, "Play nice … Don't be creepy. You know the guy. Don't be that guy." These informal codes of conduct are much less about providing rules and definitions and more about instilling in the user a deeper understanding of what type of behavior is acceptable and condoned by the community.

Within formal policy documents, some platform designers and operators take extra steps to help users understand their policies by providing exemplars. For example, Pinterest provides for credible exceptions to their prohibited activities. In their acceptable use policy, they provide examples of instances of prohibited activity that *are* acceptable. They tease out the importance of taking into consideration the context and the intent of the content that is being shared (see

Image 1). Pinterest was also a site praised for including plain language explanations for policies in prior TOS work [8].

Image 1. Hate speech policy described through exemplars on Pinterest

5. DISCUSSION

Harassment online is a large and growing issue. Currently platform operators are employing various technological measures, including algorithms that detect certain types of language and text [3] or using context of the user's activities to detect harassing behaviors like cyberbullying [4]. We believe it is imperative to understand platform-specific characterizations of harassment before examining effectiveness of policy or the ethically appropriate ways of regulating harassing behaviors online. Once we have this foundation, we can begin to assess the embedded social norms surrounding harassment within online platforms and the roles that written policies play in mitigating and reducing harassment within these communities.

Through our analysis of the policies as written, we found that there was no standard definition of harassment across the fifteen social media platforms. The documentation of activities that could be perceived as harassment was inconsistent across platforms and vague within platforms (see Table 3). This lack of specificity and consistency for what constitutes harassment makes future work on understanding harassment policies at a deeper, more granular level challenging. This ambiguity is exacerbated by issues associated with the directionality of harassment—it is unclear if harassment towards others should be treated in a similar fashion to those who focus their harm on themselves. Harassment towards oneself (e.g. eating disorders, self-mutilation) is in itself a public health issue [22] and not just an offensive behavior which may require a more nuanced and ethically appropriate response.

Is harassment just a container for a set of offensive behaviors, or is it something more complex that is being overlooked? According to official policies, platform operators respond to harassment in the same way they respond to any prohibited activity. This position means that someone who is sending threating messages could potentially be treated in the same manner as someone who is spamming a group's wall with unwanted content. In offline communities, these offenses are regarded differently, with different sets of repercussions.

Online responses to harassment often happen away from the eyes of the community. Social acknowledgement and understanding that can come from "witnessing" responses to harassment are stymied, depriving the community from opportunities to learn and voice concern. Because we do not know if the community is aware of the platform operator's responses to harassment, we also do not know if they feel that the actions taken uphold their vision of community norms. This gap highlights the inherent tension within the platforms' governance structures to create open and free spaces for expression while still upholding policies that regulate behaviors.

The manner and severity in which a platform chooses to handle harassment varies across platforms. Our data shows that these range in severity from simple content removal to informing law enforcement. However, the platform operators do not specify which prohibited activities are associated with which responses. Some platforms utilize responses that range in severity (Flickr) while some take a more uniform stance on how they respond to harassment (Twitter) as shown in Table 4. With a lack of consistency in the definition as well as the types and severity of the responses used by the different platforms, community members who engage with multiple platforms have a higher burden of understanding the rules and repercussions of breaking those rules.

Platform operators play a pivotal role when it comes to translating platform policies. Beyond the issues of inconsistency of the characterization of harassment, our data shows that policies are written in complex terms and require higher comprehension levels than the average user—two known barriers to the internalization of policy [8, 11]. Further research is needed to understand the potential differences in how communities receive and engage platform policies. For example, in determining how best to craft policy solutions, a next step might be to assess whether users understand existing materials and if their concept of harassment matches that of the platform(s) they use.

Prior work has shown that when a site's policies are unclear, the rules and norms are often community-constructed and enforced [8] and potentially have more staying power than externally imposed rules [20]. Some online social platforms have successfully integrated these principles by either designing *to support* existing social norms within a community or designing *to encourage* more positive norms [7, 19]. In these spaces, community norms, policies, and technologies are more closely aligned [7]. This observation highlights the importance of integrating policy and design into a cohesive development strategy [12]. To achieve this alignment, platform operators could work with communities through participatory design [1] or purposeful design for social norms [7, 19]. In considering best practices for policies, creating harassment policies *with* the community could empower the creation of positive social norms *for* the community, creating a more favorable approach to platform governance.

6. CONCLUSION

Harassment is a serious issue within online social media platforms. However, platform-specific policies that address harassment currently lack definition and consistency. As a first step in better characterizing the ecosystem of governance around harassment, and in thinking about best practices for harassment policy, we suggest that rules derived from users may have more salience and a better chance of adoption in the community. We should empower community members to contribute to informal harassment policies, harnessing the power of communities to create norms around problematic behaviors. As researchers continue to work towards technological and design solutions to curtail harassment, we hope this work on characterizing the current state of platform policies provides a foundation and greater context for future research.

7. ACKNOWLEDGEMENTS

We would like to thank our colleagues and the reviewers for their valuable feedback and support. This research is supported, in part, by NSF award SHB-1116801.

8. REFERENCES

[1] Ashktorab, Z. and Vitak, J. 2016. Designing Cyberbullying Mitigation and Prevention Solutions through Participatory Design With Teenagers. *Proc. of the 2016 CHI Conference on Human Factors in Computing Systems*, 3895–3905.

[2] Brown, K. et al. 2006. Cyber-Bullying: Developing Policy to Direct Responses that are Equitable and Effective in Addressing this Special Form of Bullying. *Journal of Educational Administration*. 57, 1–36.

[3] Chancellor, S. et al. 2016. #thygapp: Instagram Content Moderation and Lexical Variation in Pro-Eating Disorder Communities. *Proc. of the ACM Conference on Computer Supported Cooperative Work and Social Computing*.

[4] Dadvar, M. and Jong, F. De. 2012. Cyberbullying detection: a step toward a safer Internet yard. *Proc. of the 21st International Conference Companion on World Wide Web*, 121–125.

[5] DeNardis, L. and Hackl, A.M. 2015. Internet Governance by Social Media Platforms. *Telecommunications Policy*. 39, 9, 761–770.

[6] Djuric, N. et al. 2014. Hate Speech Detection with Comment Embeddings. *Proc. of the 24th International Conference on World Wide Web Companion*, 29–30.

[7] Fiesler, C. et al. 2016. An Archive of Their Own : A Case Study of Feminist HCI and Values in Design. *Proc. of the 2016 CHI Conference on Human Factors in Computing Systems*, 2574–2585.

[8] Fiesler, C. et al. 2016. Reality and Perception of Copyright Terms for Online Content Creation. *Proc. of the 19th ACM Conference on Computer Supported and Cooperative Work & Social Computing*.

[9] Fiesler, C. et al. 2015. Understanding Copyright Law in Online Creative Communities. *Proc. of the 18th ACM Conference on Computer Supported Cooperative Work & Social Computing*, 116–129.

[10] Gilbert, P. and Irons, C. 2005. Focused therapies and compassionate mind training for shame and self-attacking. *Compassion: Conceptualisations, research and use in psychotherapy*. 263–325.

[11] Good, N.S. et al. 2007. Noticing notice: a large-scale experiment on the timing of software license agreements. *Proc. of the SIGCHI conference on Human factors in computing systems*, 607.

[12] Jackson, S. et al. 2014. The policy knot: re-integrating policy, practice and desgin in CSCW studies of social computing. *Proc. of the 17th ACM Conference on Computer Supported Cooperateive Work & Social Computing*, 588–602.

[13] Jackson, S. et al. 2014. The Policy Knot: Re-integrating Policy, Practice and Design in CSCW Studies of Social Computing. *Proc. of the Conf. on Computer Supported Cooperative Work & Social Computing*, 588–602.

[14] Jensen, C. and Potts, C. 2014. Privacy Policies as Decision-Making Tools: An Evaluation of Online Privacy Notices. *Proc. of the SIGCHI Conference on Human Factors in Computing Systems*, 471–478.

[15] Lewis, S.P. et al. 2011. The scope of nonsuicidal self-injury on YouTube. *Pediatrics*. 127, 3 (2011), e552–e557.

[16] Luger, E. et al. 2013. Consent for All: Revealing the Hidden Complexity of Terms and Conditions. *Proc. of the SIGCHI Conference on Human Factors in Computing Systems*, 2687–2696.

[17] Massanari, A. 2015. #Gamergate and The Fappening: How Reddit's algorithm, governance, and culture support toxic technocultures. *New Media & Society*.

[18] Meredith, J.P. 2011. Combating Cyberbullying Emphasizing Education over Criminalization.pdf. *Federal Comm. Law Journal*. 63, 1 (2011), 311–340.

[19] Morgan, J.T. et al. 2013. Tea & Sympathy : Crafting Positive New User Experiences on Wikipedia. *Proc. of the 2013 conference on Computer supported cooperative Work and Social Computing*, 839–848.

[20] Ostrom, E. 2015. *Governing the Commons*. Cambridge Univeristy Press.

[21] Panko, R.R. and Beh, H.G. 2002. Monitoring for pornography and sexual harassment. *Comm. of the ACM*. 45, 1 (2002), 84–87.

[22] Pater, J. et al. 2016. "Hunger Hurts but Starving Works:" Characterzing the Presentation of Eating Disorders Online. *Proceedings of the 2016 Conference on Computer Supported Cooperative Work and Social Computing*.

[23] Wolak, J. et al. 2007. Does Online Harassment Constitute Bullying? An Exploration of Online Harassment by Known Peers and Online-Only Contacts. *Journal of Adolescent Health*. 41, 6 SUPPL. (2007).

[24] Yin, D. et al. 2009. Detection of Harassment on Web 2.0. *In Proc. of the Content Analysis in the WEB 2.0 Workshop at WWW*.

The Strength of Awkward Ties: Online Interactions between High School Students and Adults

Andrea Forte, Denise Agosto, Michael Dickard
College of Computing and Informatics
Drexel University
Philadelphia, PA, USA
{aforte, dea22, m.dickard}@drexel.edu

Rachel Magee
Graduate School of Library and Information Science, University of Illinois Urbana-Champaign
Champaign, IL, USA
rmmagee@illinois.edu

ABSTRACT

In this multiple case study of two high schools in the United States, we use interview and focus group data to examine the experiences of teen-age students when they friend and interact with teachers, high school administrators, parents, and other adults on social network sites (SNS). We identify several types of teen-adult interactions on SNS, including finding information, community building, and mentoring online skills, and we connect these findings to literature on homophily and context collapse. We also report on social media norms and policies of the schools where our fieldwork was conducted. We discuss how organizational policies surrounding social media use can inhibit or reinforce the development of age-homophilous networks and thereby encourage or reduce opportunities for teen-adult interaction online. Finally, we conclude that boundary work associated with managing these complex social experiences, though awkward at times, can be an important learning experience for adults and young people alike.

Author Keywords

social media; social network sites (SNS); teens; schools; policy; homophily; question asking

ACM Classification Keywords

H.5.2 [Information Interfaces and Presentation]: User Interfaces - Interaction styles.

1. INTRODUCTION

Adolescence marks a time of biological, cognitive, and social transition and growth. Teenage years in the United States are generally spent in high school, where young people prepare for work or post-secondary education. The role of social media in high school students' lives is a subject of considerable research and speculation. This study is part of a larger multi-year project in which we are investigating how teens' online social networks serve as resources for meeting everyday information needs as they prepare to transition to adulthood, explore and develop political identities, and learn social norms around issues like privacy. Specifically, in this paper we examine high school students' experiences interacting with adults, particularly teachers and school administrators, on social network sites (SNS). We want to better understand teen-adult interaction online in order to inform policy discussions in schools, libraries and other organizations that serve teens.

In a two-year study of students at two U.S. high schools, we used surveys, interviews, and focus groups to investigate relationships among teens' use of SNS for information sharing and seeking, the kinds of connections they maintain online, and the policies that govern their use of SNS in schools. As we explored the ways that teens used their online ties to find information, it became clear that, although interacting with (often like-minded) peers occupied much of their attention, teen-adult interaction on SNS is an important resource for many teens and a site of enculturation in a wide range of social activities including school activities, civic action, and practicing online civility and privacy management. In this paper, we report on the experiences of teens whose online social networks include adults like teachers, school administrators, and family members by answering the questions:

R1. What kinds of interactions do high school students have with teachers, school administrators, parents and other adults on social network sites?

R2. What meaning and uses do these interactions have for students?

2. RELATED WORK

To contextualize this work, we first explain relevant concepts like homophily and context collapse and how they relate to finding and sharing information in social networks. Then we focus specifically on literature about online interactions between adults and teens that raises questions about the kinds of interactions that occur and how they are perceived by teens.

2.1 Homophily, Context Collapse and Information

Homophily is a remarkably stable feature of social networks – the term means that people who are similar to one another are more likely to forge ties than people who are not similar to one another. With little cultural and contextual variation, this principle regulates the formation of relationships from marriage, to friendship, to professional contacts and casual interactions [26].

In the language of design, homophily is a kind of constraint. It circumscribes social worlds. It encourages the emergence of personal networks that limit the kinds of information, opportunity, and social experiences to which individuals have access. The

GROUP '16, November 13 - 16, 2016, Sanibel Island, FL, USA

ACM 978-1-4503-4276-6/16/11…$15.00
DOI: http://dx.doi.org/10.1145/2957276.2957282

homophily constraint is observed across different communication media with which people maintain and develop social relationships and share information [3, 10, 16] and can be reinforced online by predictive algorithms that suggest connections and regulate the flow of information from person to person. Although most studies of homophily have focused on adults, adolescent friendships have also been shown to exhibit homophilous tendencies [23], and teens' and emerging adults' online friends have been shown to exhibit age and geographic homophily in particular [25].

Conversely, the diversity of contacts in one's social network is highlighted by the problems associated with networking across multiple group contexts. Context collapse was identified early on as a challenge for people who use social network sites [24, 30]: when family, friends, teachers, romantic interests, and coworkers mix and mingle, the result is social awkwardness. Context collapse happens when heterogeneous segments of our social networks that rely on different social norms start to mix.

SNS users adopt many strategies to control the flow of information across different social groups, a practice also known as boundary regulation. For example, boyd describes the practice of "account mirroring" or creating multiple accounts on the same service [6]. Hargittai and boyd documented a marked increase in use of privacy controls on Facebook in 2009 [18], whereas Vitak and Kim recently examined the ways that people managed boundary regulation when Facebook's privacy tools provide insufficient control [31]. In a five-year, longitudinal study, Zhang, De Choudhury and Grudin observed increased use of multiple social network sites among professionals and suggest this supports audience segmentation [34]. In a survey study, we [13] similarly found that teens maintain accounts on multiple social network sites for different purposes and audiences.

The motivation to control information flow across social networks has been captured in the language of research participants when they describe what happens in networks that cross boundaries: things get "creepy" [34] and "strange" [20]. Yet, it is commonly accepted that when unlike groups connect, the results can be valuable.

Most famously, Granovetter's "Strength of Weak Ties" theorizes the effects of weak social ties on access to information or other resources and suggests that weak ties form the backbone of social information conduits that span networks [14]. Strong ties (relationships that involve intense affection, spending a lot of time together and intimate sharing) tend to bind people who know the same people. That is, your strong ties tend to have access to the same kinds of information and resources that you do and are often homophilous connections. Weak ties can be defined in opposition to strong ties: they lack the intimacy, time commitments and intensity that characterize strong ties. However, these weak ties are often connections to people who are less like you and who can provide access to diverse kinds of information and resources. In other words, homophily—that is, being connected to others who are very similar to yourself—can throttle information flow.

The practical implications of homophily for online interaction are important to understand: how does preferential association with similar individuals affect people in material ways? Some of the most striking findings concern diffusion of behaviors: people are more likely to adopt behaviors of individuals who share common characteristics with them [28]. If I see that you engage in a healthy behavior (like exercise), I'm more likely to follow suit if I perceive that others like me approve of this behavior [9]; likewise, your strong ties on SNS are more likely to influence your voting behavior than weak ties [5]. Several studies of adolescents' friend groups—both online and off—have tied social network homophily to increased tendencies to engage in risky behaviors, such as marijuana use [11] and underage drinking [21].

Even in the case of strong familial ties or common experiences like affiliation with a school or church, teen-adult social connections are likely to bridge networks. Age homophily is a particularly salient characteristic of adolescents' online social interactions: teens tend to associate online with people close to their own age [32]. Age is a critical differentiator of human experience both socially and developmentally, and adults and teens often differ in other dimensions as well, like wealth, marital status, and social position/power.

2.2 Adults in Teens' Online Lives

In this paper, we focus specifically on understanding teens' experiences interacting with adults such as teachers and school administrators in their online social networks. Research on teen SNS use often focuses on what teens do most—socialize with other teens [6]—but as Ito and colleagues note, "in addition to their role in provisioning and regulating youth new media ecologies, adults are important coparticipants in youth new media practices" [22]. The role of adult family members in particular has drawn attention as people encounter problems associated with "digital parenting" [27]. Parents can play an important role in facilitating and encouraging the development of creative engagement with technologies [4] and may even help underage children gain access to social media [19].

There has been less work examining adolescents' experiences interacting with teachers and other educators in SNS. Agosto and Abbas found that high school students consider friending teachers "creepy" and a threat to personal privacy [1]. danah boyd's work has highlighted strategies that teens use to avoid authority figures such as teachers on social media in order to maintain their privacy [7], which she frames as a way of managing the awkward effects of context collapse.

Yet, sometimes teachers and other adults do interact with and friend teens online. Moreover, as we will show, these interactions can be useful. Ahn, Bivona and DiScala have noted that although most school districts restrict social media use, some frame policies in ways that are more productive for education than others [2]. As institutions grapple with establishing best practices for emerging technologies, online teen-adult interaction is a critical area of research for policy makers in schools, libraries, community centers and other institutions that serve the needs of both teens and adults.

To address this need, we ask, "What kinds of interactions do U.S. high school students have with teachers, school administrators, parents and other adults on social network sites?" and "What meaning and uses do these interactions have for students?"

3. METHODS

To answer these questions, we examine the cases of two high schools. Our data came primarily from interviews with students at our first field site. Our second source of data comes from focus groups at our second field site as well as demographic data and self-reported social media use that we collected using a survey instrument at both sites described fully in [13]. This multiple case study approach [33] enables deeper examination of the behaviors and trends that we identified at the first school by allowing us to explore areas of contrast.

	Facebook		Twitter		Tumbler		Instagram*	
	Devens	SciCentral	Devens	SciCentral	Devens	SciCentral	Devens	SciCentral
Every Day	65.0%	68.2%	42.5%	40.9%	20.0%	40.9%	39.4%	13.8%
Every Week	15.0%	13.6%	7.5%	13.6%	12.5%	18.2%	6.1%	0.0%
Less than 1x per Week	12.5%	13.6%	15.0%	18.2%	20.0%	18.2%	0.0%	0.0%
Total Users	**92.5%**	**95.5%**	**65.0%**	**72.7%**	**52.5%**	**77.3%**	**45.5%**	**13.8%**
Total Non-Users	**7.5%**	**4.5%**	**35.0%**	**27.3%**	**47.5%**	**22.7%**	-	-

Table 1: Frequency of Participants' Social Media Use
*** Instagram was not included as an option but was the most frequently written in response for "other"; thus, it may be underrepresented relative to other sites and we have no data for non-use**

Because we were interested in learning about the value of online interactions from teens' perspectives, we approached data collection and analysis from the phenomenological perspective that social systems cannot be understood except through the experiences of the people who participate in them [29]. Such an approach involves learning how teens themselves make sense of social network sites and their own online interactions to yield interpretations and implications that reflect their understandings. These methods complement statistical analyses of social network and survey data that are often conducted to understand things like network composition, network structure, or the frequency of online behaviors.

3.1 Field Sites

The data were collected at two U.S. high schools; we sought out field sites that would provide different cultural norms and would allow us to compare different educational contexts. We obtained IRB approval to speak to 50 students at each school with parental approval. All students in the schools were invited to participate. In both cases we were able to accommodate all students who volunteered and showed up for their interview/focus group.

One school is a public science and engineering magnet high school that we refer to as SciCentral High. SciCentral is an award-winning school that is located in a dense urban environment and features progressive technology integration and a 1:1 laptop program. At the time of data collection, about 30% of the school's 500 students were economically disadvantaged and 65% were minority students. Twenty five students from SciCentral participated in interviews.

The second field site was a suburban public high school that we call Devens High, located outside a major metropolitan area in the southwest. Originally, we planned to investigate another school in the same district; however, due to circumstances involving our contacts, we switched to Devens. It turned out that Devens High also runs a science and engineering magnet program within its much larger total student body of about 2500. About 55% of Devens students were economically disadvantaged and 75% identified as minorities at the time of the study. 46 students from Devens participated in focus groups and 3 in interviews. Due to time limitations at Devens, we relied mainly on focus groups to enable data collection more quickly. Although individual interview data and focus group data are not directly comparable, the methods yield similar types of data that are amenable to qualitative analysis and can be useful for triangulation, comparison and building community case studies.

At both schools, receipt of permission and assent forms from minors was followed up by a phone call or in-person meeting between a member of the research team and a parent or guardian to explain study procedures and answer questions. The barriers imposed by requirements for minor participants led to a disproportionately large number of participants who had recently turned 18 years old. A total of 74 students participated in interviews and focus groups.

Participants from SciCentral generally reported higher levels of parental education: over 36% of parents held advanced degrees compared with 4% of Devens parents. Over 25% of Devens participants' parents had not completed high school. Students from SciCentral also demonstrated a greater understanding of Internet-related terms. See Table 2 for further demographics.

We were careful to choose culturally and geographically diverse field sites and participants; however, this sample of teens is not representative of the general United States teen population. We've already noted that a disproportionate number of participants were seniors and/or 18 years old. In some respects, this turned out to be advantageous as older students were often highly reflective about the school, its policies, and how their own practices had changed while in high school; however, it reduced opportunities for younger students to voice concerns and experiences that older students hadn't experienced or no longer felt were important. Another limitation of our sampling method is that all our participants attend high school. Among teens who do not attend high school, interactions with adults may take on a different character and meaning; however, note that in this paper we use the term "teen" to describe high school students. All students in the schools were invited to participate, and participants were given $20 to compensate them for their time and effort. One artifact of our data collection process is that Devens students are not identified by name in our data because, although we know which students participated, it was impossible to identify voices in the focus group audio recordings; when presenting data, we use pseudonyms for students from SciCentral and identify students from Devens as focus group participants.

3.2 Analysis

Interviews generally lasted between 20 and 40 minutes and focus groups lasted between 60 and 90 minutes. Focus groups included 6-10 students. Interviews and focus groups were audio recorded and transcribed. Thematic analysis [8] began with open coding of the transcribed data by three of the authors using Dedoose as a collaborative coding platform. The first author then iteratively coded segments of the interviews related to adult interaction to develop a more refined taxonomy of concepts that describes participants' interactions with adults in their online social networks. A similar process was used to code focus group

		Devens (n = 49)		SciCentral (n = 25)	
		Count	%	Count	%
Gender	Male	15	30.6%	8	32.0%
	Female	28	57.1%	17	68.0%
	Not Reported	6	12.2%	0	0.0%
Age	14	3	6.1%	1	4.0%
	15	2	4.1%	3	12.0%
	16	1	2.0%	8	32.0%
	17	8	16.3%	3	12.0%
	18	28	57.1%	10	40.0%
	Not Reported	7	14.3%	0	0.0%
Parental Education	Don't Know	9	18.4%	2	8.0%
	Some High School	13	26.5%	2	8.0%
	High School	8	16.3%	7	28.0%
	College	11	22.4%	3	12.0%
	Graduate Degree	2	4.1%	9	36.0%
	Not Reported	6	12.2%	2	8.0%
Race	Asian	4	8.2%	1	4.0%
	Black	8	16.3%	7	28.0%
	White	7	14.3%	7	28.0%
	Hispanic or Latino	23	46.9%	4	16.0%
	Other	3	6.1%	1	4.0%
	Not Reported	6	12.2%	5	20.0%
Web Use Skills*		Mean: 2.61		Mean: 3.28	

Table 2: Participant Demographics
***Web Use Skills is measured using the 10-item survey from Hargittai and Hseih [17].**

transcripts. Prior coding of interview transcripts sensitized researchers to the themes that had already arisen there.

In general, students spoke in more depth about interactions with adults in interviews than in focus groups. This is not surprising for two reasons: first interviews provide a level of confidentiality that focus groups do not; second, because our interviews came primarily from SciCentral where policies and norms around social media use created a favorable environment for students to interact with adults. Before we describe our findings about teen-adult interaction, it's important to understand a little about the culture and policies of the high schools where our data were collected.

4. SOCIAL MEDIA POLICIES AND NORMS

Although students who participated in interviews and focus groups reported similar social media use (see Table 1), our two field sites had very different social norms and policies about social media and technology use in school. Devens prohibited SNS use during school hours and had a firm policy prohibiting cell phone use. SciCentral allowed Twitter and "reasonable" cell phone use in school. Devens prohibited students from friending or following teachers and other school staff whereas SciCentral allowed and even encouraged it. The principal acted as a social media role model by tweeting school news and communications and using Twitter to reach out to students individually and as a group both during and outside of school hours.

When asked about interactions with teachers on social media, a few Devens students described Facebook groups for extra-curricular activities and certain teachers who maintained websites about their classes and made themselves available to students online, but the language students used implied that these teachers were exceptions:

> I actually had to text my teacher one time because he actually gave out his personal phone number, because he is willing to help in any way he can. – Focus Group (FG) participant

Another commented that there was usually no way to contact teachers outside of school "unless the teacher is really cool." Explained one Devens student:

> we can't have the teachers on our Facebook until we graduate. We can't have our teachers' numbers unless it is for a club. I have neither, so I have to ask people. I ask [someone] to ask a teacher what the homework was or something. – FG participant

In the above case, school policies created network structures in which certain students serve as bridges to teachers whereas other students remain less visible to teachers and have fewer opportunities for contact. Policies at Devens generally prohibited students from interacting with teachers on social media and from using most social media on school networks. One student noted that cell phones could access blocked sites but that violated policy as well:

> [If they catch you with a cell phone] some teachers won't really cause a big scene. They'll just ask you to put it up and move on. If a teacher is a douche, then they'll cause a big scene, take your phone up and try to argue with you… and you have to pay $15 to get it back. – FG participant

Although the official policies in SciCentral's school district were not radically different, school officials tended not to enforce the district's anti-social media policies, and the principal actively argued the benefits of student social media use to district officials and within the school community. As a result, students at SciCentral described a unique school environment in which teachers and students frequently interacted on social media and cell phone use was accepted with the assumption that students would regulate their own use. Twitter was the only SNS allowed by the school district on school wifi and thus became the SNS of choice during school hours:

> I follow my principal, I follow my teachers, so it's like I mainly look at tweets when I'm in class or in school, and that's mainly with everybody in SciCentral. – Madison, 16

> …my teacher used to say, 'In our school, we don't mind if you text because we know either you get up, go to the bathroom and text and come back or you just sit here and text and you pay attention again. It's faster and simpler. There's no point.' – Tony, 18

Conversations with the school principal confirmed that although the school district set many of the official policies, norms at SciCentral were purposely more open to technology and social media use. Students were aware of this difference:

> I try to explain it to friends from other schools. They're like, 'How can you have your principal on Facebook?' But it's normal for us. – Aileen, 18

5. FINDINGS: INTERACTIONS BETWEEN TEENS AND ADULTS

In this section, we describe the types of interactions we identified between teens and adults on social network sites at SciCentral and highlight any similar or contrasting experiences of students at

Devens High where teen-adult interaction was largely prohibited. We present the full range of observed interaction types as findings; in the subsequent discussion section, we delve more deeply into the relationships between teen/adult interaction and school norms and policies.

Interactions between teens and adults were organized in three categories:

- building community
- finding information
- supporting development of online skills

5.1 Building Community in School

For the majority of students we spoke to from SciCentral, use of social media bridged personal and academic lives as well as the online and face-to-face school community. Some SciCentral students felt that their relationships with teachers were more open than they would be without online interactions:

> Whenever I explain my relationships to my teachers to my friends at my old school they are always super surprised. So if I was at a different school and one of my teachers saw my Vines, I think I would be a little bit more concerned about it. But knowing that I'm friends with my teachers on Facebook and I follow them on Twitter and stuff, so it's kind of normal at this point for them to see stuff. – Makayla, 18

Others described school as a more fulfilling experience due to interactions that took place on social media:

> I think it's nice having that connection between teachers and students. It doesn't make it as bad. It makes high school a lot more memorable and more interesting. – Tony, 18

Still others described how social media created a new channel for interactions among school staff and students that moved between online and offline contexts:

> My friend tweeted like, 'I am so hungry I can't focus on anything else.' She was like, 'I can't focus on school work, I am so hungry.' And our principal follows us all on Twitter, and he just like walks into history class, has a granola bar, and he goes, Shellyann,' which is my friend's name, and just throws her a granola bar. And she's like, 'What?' And he's like, 'You said you were hungry.' – Connie, 15

Yet despite the clear efforts of many administrators and teachers to deemphasize boundaries between school life and social media, one student explained that not all teachers participated in the social media life of the school.

> I'm friends with some of my teachers on Facebook. A lot of them, if they don't feel comfortable being friends with a student on Facebook they won't accept, or they will limit access. I know once I graduate, they better accept my friend request! Just sayin'. – Todd, 18.

In this case, the student reached out and found that not all teachers were receptive. One interviewee did not seem aware of the information exchanges on social media that the majority of interviewees described; although this was only one participant, it suggests that at SciCentral, teen-adult interaction is more prevalent among some groups of students than others.

> Most teachers I'm not even sure are on Facebook or social media… usually posts on Facebook, some of them are a little bit like racy and stuff. People usually don't have their teachers or their principal as one of their friends on there. – Jaylen, 18

Although a few students at SciCentral discussed concerns about privacy when friending school staff, describing it as invasive, most used language that suggested they viewed privacy as a problem of negotiating and setting boundaries rather than excluding school staff from their online lives altogether. Tony, a SciCentral senior who was quoted above as feeling that online interactions enriched the high school experience also noted that students sometimes

> feel like [the principal's] involvement in our lives is a little too much. Somebody will say something that's kind of offensive and he'll comment on it in kind of a snarky, sarcastic way, which he can do. It's in his right. We friended him and that's kind of his personality at times, so that's all right. But it's also kind of weird because this is your principal and he's watching what you're saying. It's big brother watching you. So yeah, there are times when we feel like Mr. Jansen has crossed some lines and it's not bad, but it's just weird. – Tony, 18

Devens students were not allowed to friend teachers on social media and had little to say about community building with teachers and administrators on social media, other than mentioning that certain teachers joined official Facebook groups dedicated to school clubs or organizations.

5.2 Finding Information

When we began the study, one of our goals was to understand online question asking and answering practices of teens. In general, teens reported talking to peers more often than adults when they needed to find information; one SciCentral student explained that she used social media to ask questions of adults only when she had exhausted her peer-level resources.

> that's [posting to a teacher online] something I find a little bit creepy, because it's like, I see you all the time at school, and you're my teacher... Sometimes I may post on their wall and be like, 'What should I do for this,' and blah blah blah. But that's like rare moments. Most of the time I'll just ask my peers, because that seems more appropriate to me. I'll never inbox them [teachers] ever. I'll post on their wall if I'm really desperate. Like if I'm really like, the project is due tomorrow at 8:15, and none of my people have replied. – Sophia, 16

Many SciCentral students acknowledged social media as a reasonable place to ask teachers questions about homework.

> If we have a question, our teachers usually let us add them on Facebook and follow them on Twitter, so if we have a question, and they're not answering us through email, we can either text them, send them a message on Facebook—that's mainly the time that they reply, when we message them on Facebook or Twitter, because in my school, the teachers use Twitter a lot. – Madison, 16

Yet not all students felt comfortable asking for information in public. In the next section, we will discuss adult audiences as an inhibitor of risky disclosures online, but it is important to note that potential adult audiences can also inhibit information and help seeking online. The clearest example of this came from a Devens student who explained that she would avoid asking about homework publicly because teachers might judge her for it; instead, she would hide such interactions:

> For homework I would mostly ask people directly because I don't want the teacher looking and saying, 'Why didn't you get this? You could have done tutorial.' So I mostly ask them in private about how they've done their homework and if they can help me with it. – FG Participant

5.3 Supporting Development of Online Skills

Online experimentation with different facets of identity and with forms of creative expression is an important aspect of maturation that sometimes requires freedom from adult intervention [12, 15]. Yet, at times we observed that the presence of adults can also play an important role in supporting teens as they develop more sophisticated privacy practices and insights about online life. We observed three ways that adult interaction on social media sites influenced teen behavior: as audiences for teen disclosures, by modeling online behaviors, and moderating online behaviors in the form of advice or direct intervention.

5.3.1 Adults as audiences for teen disclosures

The presence of adults can provide a natural mechanism to encourage reflection on self-presentation. In many cases, students reported that parents, grandparents or other family members were present on SNS, particularly Facebook, and that this caused them to carefully consider what they posted there. This student describes a typical experience:

> I'm Facebook friends with my mom, so I tend not to say anything too crazy on Facebook. I know some people who do. – Brian, 18

At SciCentral, students reported not only thinking about family members' reactions to their public posts, but many discussed teachers and staff as potential audiences for disclosures on social media:

> If I had a private account, maybe I'd be more lenient with my tweets, but since I have an open account and there are principals and teachers following me from all over the country, I wouldn't post something like that. – Corinne, 16

> All the teachers and the students follow each other. I use that as a reason to censor my tweets. I think 'How would [the principal] feel if he saw that? So I should really think before I post.' – Tony, 18

> My principal and most of my teachers have Facebook and Twitter… The teachers at [my school] are very cool, some of them, laid back. They apparently have lives. We still have to respect them as adults… Like we can't like…well we can curse sometimes like rarely, but we can't have like a sailor's mouth every five seconds around them. – Tiana, 15

Students primarily reported connections with adult family members or school staff in Facebook and Twitter; they did not report connections to adults in other networks like Instagram or tumblr. One Devens focus group participant noted that:

> The thing about Facebook is, even though a lot of people say they don't use it or don't get on it as much they still have it, they still go back to it. Facebook is different. It's for everybody, like even your grandparents. Twitter and Instagram, it's just for like, our kind of peers. Facebook is for everybody. – FG participant

Network fragmentation across platforms may support more exploratory or risky disclosures in spaces where teens are deidentified or maintain more age homophilous networks.

5.3.2 Modeling online behaviors

In some cases, teens described seeing negative consequences when peers engaged in risky online behavior like bullying or unwise self-disclosures and drew personal lessons from these observations. Their descriptions of peers' social media use were often cautionary whereas their descriptions of adults' use of social media often involved mentoring and modeling relationships. When connected with teachers and school administrators on SNSs, participants described observing them modeling professional uses of social media.

> [Our principal] usually tweets or says something when our school has an accomplishment, like he posts it as a status and how proud he is. – Ella, 18

> Like, my journalism teacher, she's going to post things that are of interest to me, because we share that interest. Or my English teacher posts this thing called #EngChat, and every night it's teachers who are discussing English classes together, so I'm interested in that because I'm a writer. – Alexis, 18

In some cases, teens also acted as mentors for adult family members who needed help with things like maintaining a Facebook page for a business, or using SNS to keep in touch with family or friends.

5.3.3 Moderating online behaviors

Finally, adults sometimes played a direct role in advising and patrolling teens' online behavior. In several cases, students described how adult family members set rules or advised them about privacy settings or avoiding dangerous behavior. Mia, age 18, related the advice she was given by her mother about Facebook privacy settings, "My mom said, 'Have it [privacy settings] set to your friends and only accept people that you want to be friends with on there.'"

In other cases, students at SciCentral described how teachers on social media had intervened in dangerous or harmful situations, including selling drugs and bullying. Less dramatic and more common was the experience of posting something inappropriate and having a teacher or staff member explain the possible consequences.

> Mr. Jansen [the principal]… He's a stalker. He sees my personal life. But it let me know that what I put on social network sites is not a secret and that anybody can see it. He explained to me that colleges could look at your social network sites and see your tweets and stuff like that. So from there, I changed how I tweet and what I put on Instagram. He helped me actually change what I put on Instagram and how I tweet and stuff like that. – Jayla, 17

6. UNCERTAINTY ABOUT INTERACTING WITH ADULTS

We think it is important to convey the full range of attitudes that we observed when teens recounted their interactions with adults online. Teen-adult interactions in our data ranged from productive and pleasant to awkward and unpleasant. None of our participants reported being victims of predation, exploitation, or harassment by adults, although some of the young women described getting friend requests from "weird guys" or "old creepy men." Still, fearful narratives about predatory adults surfaced in some interviews and focus groups at both field sites.

> Facebook is super dangerous now because some people that can be added that are way older than you and they might have a picture of someone that looks like me. They might have my picture on there and say, 'I'm 14 years old,' but they're really 40 years old. –FG Participant

> People aren't who they say they are online. So you don't really know if it's a boy or a girl. It could be a pedophile and he's telling you he's 15 years old and you want to meet him in person. – Gillian, 17

Although predation – particularly sexual predation – does not often involve adults misrepresenting their age [7], the lore of predatory older men misrepresenting themselves as teenagers appears to be alive and well.

7. DISCUSSION

The teen-adult interactions we described in the findings above are not unambiguously positive, but particularly the case of SciCentral highlights opportunities for productive interactions between adults and teens on social network sites. As discussed in our literature review, the design of technologies like recommender systems and ranking/filtering algorithms such as those that supply content to Facebook's newsfeed have been critiqued for their opacity and potential to diminish exposure to diverse views and people. However, we find that restrictive organizational policies surrounding social media use can also inhibit the formation of heterogeneous ties and reinforce the development of (particularly age-)homophilous networks. Although it is possible to extrapolate novel design explorations from this work—for example by allowing would-be mentors like teachers and school administrators to signal their willingness to be friended by students and designing friend recommendation algorithms to take such preferences into account we focus in this paper on implications for technology-related policies.

7.1 Policy Implications for Schools, Libraries and other Institutions that Serve Teens

The influence of organizational policy on the composition and experience of online social networks is increasingly important to understand when behaviors as diverse as drug and alcohol use, exercise, and voting are demonstrably influenced by online social interactions (i.e. [5, 11, 21]). Ahn et. al. examined over 200 school policy documents and conclude that policies framing technology use as a core part of education and as an extension of the school are more productive than those that frame technology use as a privilege [2]. School policies intended to protect teens and help them avoid distraction may have the unintended effect of inhibiting access to the kinds of information, community building and mentoring experiences that we identified in teen-adult interactions. Policies that encourage age-homophily in teens' online social networks may reduce opportunities for both observing and modeling mature online behaviors, as students may miss out on chances to observe professional behavior among online adults and to serve as positive role models for others.

We noted some commonly held misconceptions about how sexual predation happens online. These may also encourage school policies that rely on prohibition of teen-adult interaction in order to keep teens safe. Our findings are congruent with danah boyd's observations that one effect of such policies is fewer opportunities for positive adult support and intervention if teens *do* encounter dangerous situations [7], which are more likely to involve bullying, depression, or risky interactions with peers and family.

It is important, too, to highlight the ambivalence of students when they reflected on their interactions with adults. References to school staff as "big brother" or "stalker" accompanied testimonials about how well respected they were and how much they cared about their students. Likewise, interactions with loved family members were sometimes described as "creepy" or "embarrassing." Much has been written on the topics of privacy and self-disclosure online, often with the conclusion that better privacy management tools are needed. Although good tools for managing privacy are important, we suggest that the boundary work associated with managing these messy social experiences is an important kind of work for adults and young people alike. We saw in our interview data that when teens encounter friction between social worlds that overlap on SNSs the experience is sometimes revelatory. When teens actively reflect on how to manage their online interactions with teachers and parents (and when teachers and parents reflect on how to manage their interactions with teens), they engage in an important social sensemaking activity. Eliminating awkward encounters may not always be the most desirable goal for designers or policy makers.

We described efforts by SciCentral's principal to advocate at the district level for student access to social media on campus and some teachers' views that technologies like phones and social media can't be eliminated from teens' lives during school hours. The culture at SciCentral is notable in that administrators and teachers view students as capable of regulating their own use of technology and online behavior, and the curriculum emphasizes the teaching and learning of safe, responsible online practices. A reasonable corollary of giving students this freedom and responsibility is the school's positioning of adults within the social network sites that are used at school. Students were not simply *allowed* to use technology: use of technology permeated the organization where adults and teens participated on social network sites alongside one another.

8. CONCLUSION

In this multiple case study, we examined teen-adult interaction on social media at two U.S. high schools. Teens' social networks tend to exhibit age homophily; however, we found that a school environment where students are encouraged to friend and interact with teachers and administrators can yield important benefits. The resulting teen adult interactions are sometimes awkward, but also often beneficial as many teens experience the "strengths" of these awkward ties: community building, expanded access to information, and supporting development of online skills.

The case of SciCentral provides a useful touchstone for policy deliberations at schools and libraries. Educators are increasingly aware that learning to manage use of social media like SNSs and technologies like phones is critical for teens, but best practices for social media use in schools remain elusive. Cases like SciCentral provide empirical grounds from which to reason about policies and practices in schools. Still, the exceptional involvement of some teachers and staff in this case study can be viewed as a limitation of this work for extrapolating to broad policy recommendations. The case of SciCentral is unique. It is an award-winning school with strong, Internet-savvy leadership, and the experiences of students there are not likely easily replicated without a culture of mutual respect among teachers, administrators, parents and students who are heavily invested in the success of a technology-rich school environment.

9. ACKNOWLEDGEMENTS

This work was supported by the Institute for Museum and Library Services Grant LG-06-11-0261 and National Science Foundation Graduate Research Fellowship Grant #2011121873.

10. REFERENCES

1. Denise E Agosto and June Abbas. 2010. High school seniors' social network and other ICT use preferences and concerns. *Proceedings of the American Society for Information Science and Technology*, 47 (1). 1-10. http://dx.doi.org/10.1002/meet.14504701025.
2. June Ahn, Lauren K Bivona and Jeffrey DiScala. 2011. Social media access in K–12 schools: Intractable policy controversies in an evolving world. *Proceedings of the American Society for Information Science and Technology*, 48 (1). 1-10.
3. Luca Maria Aiello, Alain Barrat, Rossano Schifanella, Ciro Cattuto, Benjamin Markines and Filippo Menczer. 2012. Friendship prediction and homophily in social media. *ACM Trans.Web*,6(2).1-33. http://dx.doi.org/10.1145/2180861.2180866.
4. Brigid Barron, Caitlin Kennedy Martin, Lori Takeuchi and Rachel Fithian. 2009. Parents as learning partners in the development of technological fluency. *International Journal of Learning and Media*, 1 (2). 55-77.
5. Robert M Bond, Christopher J Fariss, Jason J Jones, Adam DI Kramer, Cameron Marlow, Jaime E Settle and James H Fowler. 2012. A 61-million-person experiment in social influence and political mobilization. *Nature*, 489 (7415). 295-298. http://dx.doi.org/10.1038/nature11421.
6. danah boyd. 2008. Why youth [heart] social network sites: The role of networked publics in teenage social life. in Buckingham, D. ed. *Youth, identity, and digital media*, MIT Press, Cambridge, 119-142.
7. danah boyd. 2014. *It's Complicated: the social lives of networked teens*. Yale University Press, New Haven.
8. Virginia Braun and Victoria Clarke. 2006. Using thematic analysis in psychology. *Qualitative Research in Psychology*, 3 (2). 77-101.
9. Damon Centola. 2011. An experimental study of homophily in the adoption of health behavior. *Science*, 334 (6060). 1269-1272.
10. Shuo Chang, Vikas Kumar, Eric Gilbert and Loren G. Terveen. 2014 of Conference. Specialization, homophily, and gender in a social curation site: findings from pinterest. in 17th ACM conference on Computer supported cooperative work & social computing, (Baltimore, Maryland, USA, ACM, 674-686. http://dx.doi.org/10.1145/2531602.2531660.
11. Kayla de la Haye, Harold D Green Jr, Michael S Pollard, David P Kennedy and Joan S Tucker. 2014. Befriending Risky Peers: Factors Driving Adolescents' Selection of Friends with Similar Marijuana Use. *Journal of youth and adolescence*. 1-15.
12. Abigail Durrant, David Frohlich, Abigail Sellen and David Uzzell. 2011. The secret life of teens: online versus offline photographic displays at home. *Visual Studies*, 26 (2). 113-124.
13. Andrea Forte, Michael Dickard, Rachel Magee and Denise E. Agosto. 2014 of Conference. What do teens ask their online social networks?: social search practices among high school students. in 17th ACM conference on Computer supported cooperative work & social computing, (Baltimore, Maryland, USA, ACM, 28-37. http://dx.doi.org/10.1145/2531602.2531723.
14. Mark S. Granovetter. 1973. The Strength of Weak Ties. *American Journal of Sociology*, 78 (6). 1360-1380.
15. 15. Christine Greenhow and Beth Robelia. 2009. Informal learning and identity formation in online social networks. *Learning, Media and Technology*, 34 (2). 119-140.
16. Shion Guha and Stephen B. Wicker. 2015 of Conference. Do Birds of a Feather Watch Each Other?: Homophily and Social Surveillance in Location Based Social Networks. in 18th ACM Conference on Computer Supported Cooperative Work & Social Computing, (Vancouver, BC, Canada, ACM, 1010-1020. http://dx.doi.org/10.1145/2675133.2675179.
17. Eszter Hargittai and Y. P. Hsieh. 2012. Succinct survey measures of web-use skills. *Social Science Computer Review*,30(1).95-107. http://dx.doi.org/10.1177/0894439310397146.
18. Eszter Hargittai and danah boyd. 2010. Facebook privacy settings: Who cares? *First Monday*, 15 (8).
19. Eszter Hargittai, Jason Schultz and John Palfrey. 2011. Why parents help their children lie to Facebook about age: Unintended consequences of the 'Children's Online Privacy Protection Act'. *First Monday*, 16 (11).
20. Anne Hewitt and Andrea Forte. 2006. Crossing boundaries: Identity management and student/faculty relationships on the Facebook (Poster). in *Proceedings of Computer Supported Cooperative Work*.
21. Grace C Huang, Daniel Soto, Kayo Fujimoto and Thomas W Valente. 2014. The interplay of friendship networks and social networking sites: longitudinal analysis of selection and influence effects on adolescent smoking and alcohol use. *American journal of public health*, 104 (8). e51-e59.
22. Mizuko Ito, Sonia Baumer, Matteo Bittanti, danah boyd, Rachel Cody, Becky Herr-Stephenson, Heather Horst, Patricia Lange, Dilan Mahendran, Katynka Martinez, C.J. Pascoe, Dan Perkel, Laura Robinson, Christo Sima and Lisa Tripp. 2010. *Hanging out, messing around, and geeking out : kids living and learning with new media*. MIT Press, Cambridge, Mass.
23. Denise B Kandel. 1978. Homophily, selection, and socialization in adolescent friendships. *American journal of Sociology*. 427-436.
24. Airi Lampinen, Sakari Tamminen and Antti Oulasvirta. 2009 of Conference. All my people right here, right now: management of group co-presence on a social networking site. in ACM 2009 international conference on Supporting groupwork,281-290. http://dx.doi.org/10.1145/1531674.1531717.
25. Elizabeth Mazur and Lacey Richards. 2011. Adolescents' and emerging adults' social networking online: Homophily or diversity? *Journal of Applied Developmental Psychology*, 32 (4) 180-188. http://dx.doi.org/10.1016/j.appdev.2011.03.001.
26. Miller McPherson, Lynn Smith-Lovin and James M Cook. 2001. Birds of a feather: Homophily in social networks. *Annual review of sociology*. 415-444.

27. Jennifer A. Rode. 2009 of Conference. Digital parenting: designing children's safety. in Proceedings of the 23rd British HCI Group Annual Conference on People and Computers: Celebrating People and Technology, (Cambridge, United Kingdom, British Computer Society, 244-251.

28. Everett M Rogers. 2010. *Diffusion of innovations*. Simon and Schuster.

29. A. Schutz. 1967. *The Phenomenology of the Social World*. Northwestern University Press.

30. Frederic Stutzman and Woodrow Hartzog. 2012. Boundary regulation in social media. in ACM 2012 conference on Computer Supported Cooperative Work, 769-778. http://dx.doi.org/10.1145/2145204.2145320.

31. Jessica Vitak and Jinyoung Kim. 2014 of Conference. You can't block people offline: examining how Facebook's affordances shape the disclosure process. in Proceedings of the 17th ACM conference on Computer supported cooperative work & social computing, (ACM, 461-474.

32. Brooke Foucault Welles, Anne Van Devender and Noshir Contractor. 2010 of Conference. Is a friend a friend?: investigating the structure of friendship networks in virtual worlds. in CHI '10 Extended Abstracts on Human Factors in Computing Systems, (Atlanta, Georgia, USA, ACM, 4027-4032. http://dx.doi.org/10.1145/1753846.1754097.

33. R. K. Yin. 1994. *Case study research: Design and methods*. Sage, Thousand Oaks, CA.

34. Hui Zhang, Munmun De Choudhury and Jonathan Grudin. 2014 of Conference. Creepy but inevitable?: the evolution of social networking. in 17th ACM Conference on Computer-Supported Cooperative Work & Social Computing, 368-378. http://dx.doi.org/10.1145/2531602.2531685.

The Coaches Said…What?: Analysis of Online Dating Strategies Recommended by Dating Coaches

Doug Zytko
New Jersey Institute of Technology
Newark, NJ 07301
daz2@njit.edu

Sukeshini A. Grandhi
Eastern Connecticut State University
Willimantic, CT 06226
grandhis@easternct.edu

Quentin Jones
New Jersey Institute of Technology
Newark, NJ 07301
qgjones@acm.org

ABSTRACT

Despite the popularity of online dating systems, prior work indicates that online daters struggle to present and evaluate traits germane to attraction. However, the research community is largely unaware of successful online dating system-use strategies and how the knowledge of these strategies could inform system design. In this paper we begin to address this gap in knowledge with an interview study of online dating coaches who consider their advocated system-use strategies successful based on personal use and feedback from clients who implemented their strategies. Their advocated strategies entail keeping online evaluation intentionally minimal and persuading users to meet in-person as quickly as possible because current system designs stifle reliable evaluation of attraction-relevant traits online, notably personality. We discuss the implications of insights gathered from these strategies for online dating system design using theories relevant to romantic attraction.

Keywords

Online dating, impressions; signaling theory; attraction

1. INTRODUCTION

Use of online dating systems is widespread, with more than 38% of single Americans having used them [38]. What do online dating systems actually do? They enable users to discover other people who may potentially help them meet their romantic goals such as long-term relationships or casual sexual encounters. For many users, their relationship goals necessitate vetting potential partners through face-to-face interaction. Unfortunately, one cannot meet face-to-face with every potential partner discovered in an online dating system because in-person meetings are costly in terms of time, money, and risks to physical and emotional wellbeing. Thus it is often the user's responsibility to filter the pool of potential partners discovered in an online dating system to determine who is worthy of a face-to-face meeting. This filtering is done through a cost-benefit analysis by daters based on qualities germane to romantic attraction, such as physical attractiveness [3], demographic [6] and lifestyle [45] traits, personality traits [23], and the relationship goals of the potential partner [3]. We call the decision making process of whether to meet in-person with another user based on qualities germane to romantic attraction as *online dater evaluation.* On the flip side, users are equally concerned with presenting information about themselves in online dating systems to positively influence potential partners' desires to meet them in-person. We call this process *online dater self-presentation.*

GROUP '16, November 13-16, 2016, Sanibel Island, FL, USA
© 2016 ACM. ISBN 978-1-4503-4276-6/16/11 $15.00
DOI: http://dx.doi.org/10.1145/2957276.2957287

The ways in which users of online dating systems evaluate and self-present to each other has been a research interest of the HCI community since the early 2000s [12]. Previous research has produced a wealth of knowledge about user struggles with respect to online dater evaluation and self-presentation, such as user concerns of deception [28], doubts about abilities to clearly self-present subjective characteristics [48], and users spending too much time trying to evaluate potential partners online relative to time spent on in-person dates [17]. However, we have relatively little knowledge of strategies used by daters online to help them be successful. What does it mean for users to successfully use online dating systems? Prior research regarding online dater evaluation and self-presentation lacks clear definitions of success. Success has been tacitly understood to mean achieving a relationship goal, be it a long-term relationship or casual sexual encounter. However, hinging online dating success on relationship goal achievement is fundamentally flawed because users can have transient and simultaneous relationship goals [49], they may define the "achievement" of a relationship goal in different ways and with different milestones (e.g. buying a house together) [33], and there is the possibility that a user simply never discovers someone in a given online dating system that would be an appropriate relationship partner. Here, we define successful use of an online dating system to mean 1) being able to procure face-to-face dates with potential partners that one considers attractive online and 2) confirming impressions formed online of those potential partners to be accurate during the first face-to-face meeting. We limit the scope of this definition to the first in-person meeting with a potential partner because some relationship goals do not necessitate more than one meeting (e.g. casual sexual encounters).

The limited understanding of successful use of online dating systems can perhaps be explained by the sampling and research methods previously used. Several prior studies amassed samples of active users of online dating systems that responded to participation requests with no stipulations for amount of experience using online dating systems, number of users met in-person, or relationship goal achievement [8, 9, 17, 34, 48]. One limitation of recruiting active online daters in this manner is that the sample may be biased towards users that knowingly struggle with online dating especially for long-term relationship goals; an assertion supported in one study in which some users acknowledged that their incentive for participation was to seek online dating advice from the researcher [48].

Some previous studies showcase online dating system-use strategies with unknown outcomes, meaning they may lead to success [8, 9, 13, 20, 29, 30]. However, the sampled users did not necessarily state that their strategies are successful and the research did not investigate the potential success of their strategies. This is an inherent limitation of many prior studies that researched data logs of users' private messages [30] or studies that explored isolated facets of online dater evaluation and self-presentation—most notably the extensive catalog of work investigating deception in profile page fields [8, 26, 27, 28].

Given the challenges of sampling appropriate users to understand how online dating systems can be successfully used, we consider alternative approaches that can provide a reasonable starting point for researching successful online dating system-use. One approach would be to investigate the system-use strategies of former users who are currently in a relationship with someone they met through an online dating system. However, such studies would invariably suffer from recall bias, and such former users may not necessarily have had multiple opportunities to validate the success of their strategies with in-person meetings and their relationship goal achievement may have been a matter of happenstance. Another reasonable approach would be to investigate online dating coaches whose professional focus is to help users successfully use dating systems towards achieving their relationship goals. Given this focus, one can assume that online dating coaches have a wealth of data and experience from coaching multiple users, which provides them multiple instances to gauge the success of the online dating system-use strategies that they advocate. This type of experience contrasts with typical online daters who can leverage only their own experiences and who may not have had several opportunities to validate the success of their strategies with in-person meetings.

In this paper we present an interview study of online dating coaches to meet the following three research objectives: 1) examine the system-use strategies that the coaches advocate for their clients to be successful, 2) understand why the coaches believe these strategies will help clients be successful, and 3) understand if and how these strategies are influenced by system design. The rest of the paper is organized as follows. We review relevant literature about online dating and theories integral to romantic attraction and then present an interview study of 34 online dating coaches about their advocated strategies for online dater evaluation and self-presentation. We conclude with a discussion of these strategies and implications for online dating system design in light of theories germane to romantic attraction.

2. BACKGROUND

We begin the background section with a review of online dating system design. This is followed by a discussion of categories of traits germane to romantic attraction and the prior research regarding online dater evaluation and self-presentation of these traits. We then discuss interpersonal theories used to interpret online dater evaluation and self-presentation, and propose additional theories germane to romantic attraction that would be particularly relevant to understanding online dater self-presentation and evaluation. The background concludes with an introduction of online dating coaches.

2.1 Online Dating Systems and Design

Online dating systems are a type of social matching system [40] used by individuals seeking long-term and short-term romantic relationships and platonic friendships [2, 4, 48]. Today's online dating system designs provide several user interface components to help users find their mates and we classify them into three categories: 1) user discovery mechanisms, 2) user profile pages, and 3) private messaging interfaces.

User discovery is often facilitated by algorithms that recommend users to each other, search functions that let users proactively find others, or "swiping" mechanisms that show users who are geographically nearby. Users have two objectives upon discovering potential partners: to self-present information about themselves and to evaluate potential partners for in-person meetings. These two objectives—*online dater evaluation* and *self-presentation*—are facilitated with profile pages and private messaging. *Profile pages* curate and convey mostly self-provided information about them in commonly in the form of profile pictures, dedicated trait fields (e.g. height, age), and free-text. *Private messaging* interfaces enable users to engage in dyadic interaction, serving as an opportunity to further self-present and gather information for evaluation, as well as organize meetings off of the online dating system.

These prototypical interface components are exemplified in a variety of mainstream online dating systems today such as *OkCupid*, *Tinder*, *match.com*, and *eHarmony*. There are some notable exceptions however—newer mobile dating apps such as *Grouper* and *Whim* do not have a private messaging interface, instead schedule dates on behalf of users.

2.2 Evaluation and Self-presentation in Online Dating Systems

What traits do online daters self-present and evaluate? To answer this we must first understand what traits influence attraction. The scope of this paper is romantic attraction, which we define as interest in a person for the purpose of a long-term romantic relationship (e.g. boyfriend, girlfriend, life partner) or a short-term romantic relationship (e.g. casual sexual encounter). Work in evolutionary biology and psychology originally proposed three categories of traits that influence romantic attraction based on an understanding of the human mating strategies of our ancestors: physical health, social status & resources, and capacity for commitment [31]. Research has since expanded on these basic categories to demonstrate how other attributes like interests, perceived relationship goals, and personality traits are associated with attraction and relationship initiation. Based on a review of attraction literature, we consider traits that influence a person's attractiveness to fall into five general trait categories:

- *Physical attractiveness*: physical or visual appearance [3]
- *Demographic traits*: e.g. height, weight, race, ethnicity, age, religion affiliation, income, education, marital status [6, 45]
- *Lifestyle traits*: attitudes, values, and interests. These include lifestyle choices associated with demographic traits (e.g. how often one goes to church), attitudes about life (e.g. should women stay at home while men work), and other interests and activities (e.g. smoking habits, going kayaking) [18, 45]
- *Personality traits*: the five factor model (FFM) of personality (openness to experience, conscientiousness, extroversion, agreeableness, and neuroticism) [23], intelligence, and sense of humor (humor production and appreciation) [25]
- *Relationship goal*: perception of the person's preference for a long-term relationship or short-term casual encounter [3]

2.2.1 *Physical attractiveness and Demographics*
Most research regarding evaluation and self-presentation in online dating systems has focused on profile pages, specifically profile pictures and dedicated fields that have multiple choice answers for demographic and lifestyle traits. Physical attractiveness from profile pictures is integral to evaluation and self-presentation [14, 30, 46]: users receive more messages as their physical attractiveness increases, and deception in profile pictures is a common strategy to increase attractiveness [8, 27, 41, 46]. Users also mildly exaggerate answers in dedicated profile fields for the demographic traits of age, marital status, height, weight, and income [8, 26, 41]. When evaluating these demographic traits, income is universally desired (users receive more messages as their income increases [30]), but online daters prefer to message users with similar answers for race, marital status, age, education, height, and religion [13, 30]. Users also prefer to message others with similar answers in dedicated fields for lifestyle traits like smoking habits and desire for children [13].

2.2.2 *Relationship Goals*
Prior online dating research typically has not differentiated or specified the relationship goals of the users studied. Most of the research in which relationship goals were of explicit interest documented the casual sex pursuits of users on *Grindr*, a popular dating app for men-seeking-men [2].

2.2.3 *Personality*
While there is sporadic mention of "personality" in prior work [9, 47], the term was not operationalized or defined. There is a noticeable lack of insight into online dater evaluation and self-presentation of personality traits relative to other trait categories, perhaps because of the customary focus on profile pages, which do not have dedicated fields for personality trait expression.

Other online dating research has studied evaluation and self-presentation through two broad categories of traits: objective qualities called "searchable attributes" (e.g. height, religion) which are commonly present in profile pages, and subjective qualities called "experiential attributes" (e.g. sense of humor and rapport) [17] that research argues cannot be reliably evaluated in online dating systems because they must be "experienced" [17, 48]. Personality may fall into the experiential category, but this categorization of traits is vague and debatable (e.g., Is physical attractiveness a searchable or experiential attribute? Would lifestyle choices concerning religion be searchable attributes? Is the experiential attribute example of "rapport" [17] a trait of a person?). Hence when research rooted in this two-category distinction reports that online daters struggle to evaluate experiential attributes through both profile pages and private messaging [48], it is unclear which traits are actually being discussed. Ultimately, prior research leaves us with an incomplete understanding of user evaluation and self-presentation across a comprehensive series of attraction-related trait categories, most notably personality.

2.3 Theories of Evaluation and Self-Presentation in Romantic Attraction
Findings regarding online dater evaluation and self-presentation have traditionally been interpreted through the lens of Goffman's foundational work regarding impression management and Walther's theories about interpersonal relationship development. While Goffman's work emphasizes both intentional and unintentional cues that influence how a person is perceived, his writings on self-presentation [22] has traditionally been used in this line of research to frame online daters' desires to engineer how other users perceive them through profile pages, sometimes using deception [9]. Walther's theories, particularly the hyperpersonal model [43] and warranting theory [44], have been used to explain how the reduced-cue environments of online dating systems are conducive to impression management and thus deception because users have more control over the information conveyed about them [19, 27, 28, 46].

Online dating is a unique social context predicated on romantic attraction. As such, online dater evaluation decisions have also been interpreted through theories historically applied to dating and romantic attraction research, notably: evolutionary theory [15, 26, 41], homophily [13], and social exchange theory [48]. Evolutionary theory discusses mating differences between males and females, positing that males have an overarching preference for physical attractiveness because it is an indicator of fertility, while females will have an overarching preference for social status and income because they require resources to raise children [3]. These sex-differentiated preferences have been observed in data logs about which users male and female online daters choose to send messages to [30]. The concept of homophily posits that we are attracted to people with traits similar to our own [16], which has also been supported in work showing that online daters send more messages to those with similar demographic traits [13, 30]. Under the lens of social exchange theory, romantic relationship initiation and maintenance are the result of a cost-benefit analysis [10, 31]. If the perceived costs of the relationship outweigh the rewards then pursuit or maintenance of the relationship is discontinued. This theory has been applied to online daters' decisions to send private messages—since women typically receive many more messages than men, they will evaluate the expected rewards of sending or responding to a private message more stringently than men [48].

Beyond the above theories there are two other theories previously applied to romantic attraction research that are particularly relevant to online dater evaluation and self-presentation strategies: signaling theory [47] and Asch's theory of person perception [1]. Signaling theory, which originated in evolutionary biology to explain the mating strategies of animals [47], seeks to clarify the extent to which a piece of information is a reliable indicator ("signal") of an otherwise unobservable trait. Signaling theory has relevance to computer-mediated communication (CMC) because most traits are not directly observable due to its mediated nature [5]. There are two main signal types: conventional signals and assessment signals [5]. *Conventional signals* are rather unreliable by nature because possession of a trait is merely stated or implied [5] (e.g. wearing a tracksuit may imply physical fitness). *Assessment signals*, on the other hand, are more reliable because they require the possession of the trait for the signal to exist [5]. These signals sometimes stem from observations of the trait in action, e.g. observing the wearer of a tracksuit run several miles would be an assessment signal of physical fitness.

Signaling theory has previously been leveraged to explain how users assess the reliability of identity claims in *Facebook* [32]. The need to assess reliability of signals in online dating systems is similarly important because users depend on signals about other users' traits to decide whom to meet in-person.

Signal reliability stands to be particularly complex for personality evaluation. Asch showed in 1946 that interpretations of personality-related traits change in the context of information about other personality traits [1]. Attraction literature has leveraged this theory to explain why seemingly unfavorable personality traits of a potential partner are perceived more favorably after an in-person meeting [7], and recent work in the HCI community has also leveraged the theory to improve the design of non-player characters in video games [42]. Considering that signals of personality may be gleaned from a variety of interface components in online dating systems—such as a picture, a comment in a profile page's "about me" section, or a private message—Asch's theory could be useful in interpreting strategies for contextualizing personality signals detected in online dating systems.

2.4 Online Dating Coaches

Online dating system users sometimes hire online dating coaches to help them remedy struggles with the online dating process—e.g. concerns of deception [19], uncertainty over how to evaluate subjective traits [17], and a lack of clarity over how to maximize one's attractiveness to potential partners [48]. Online dating coaches claim to have knowledge of successful system-use strategies that are generalizable to a broad user base, and they train users to adopt such strategies (e.g. http://theheartographer.com/). There is considerable awareness of online dating coaches in popular media, with multiple features on TV, radio, and print media (http://www.cyberdatingexpert.com/in-the-news/), and dating site companies such as *eHarmony* hiring online dating coaches as "resident experts" (http://melanieschilling.com). Online dating coaches often specialize in helping clients achieve long-term relationships (http://www.carmeliaray.com), with some catering to specific markets like developmentally disabled users (http://hitchcraftdating.com). There are also coaches who specialize in online dating system-use strategies for casual sexual encounters, called "pickup artists" [39]. These coaches are usually male and use their personal experience in seducing women for sex as the basis of their strategies (http://3girlsaday.com, http://executetheprogram.com).

Services and products offered by online dating coaches range in terms of personalization. Generalized online dating system-use strategies are often sold in e-books, physical books, and video tutorials (http://www.vanae.com). As products and services become more personalized, coaches require access to the client's online dating accounts, such as for writing the client's profile page (http://profilepolish.com). The most personalized coaching service is commonly called "concierge" wherein the coach impersonates the client online, maintaining their profile page, exchanging messages with other users, and arranging dates for the client (http://www.eflirtexpert.com). One-on-one *Skype* and phone coaching sessions are also typical for providing online dating system-use strategies (http://www.alittlenudge.com).

3. RESEARCH QUESTIONS

Our research questions revolve around identifying and understanding the strategies to successfully use online dating systems as advocated by dating coaches and how these strategies are shaped by system design. Specifically:

RQ1. What are the online dating system-use strategies that online dating coaches advocate?

RQ2. Why do online dating coaches consider the online dating system-use strategies that they advocate to be successful?

RQ3. Are the strategies advocated by online dating coaches influenced by system design? If so, how?

4. METHOD

We conducted semi-structured interviews with 34 online dating coaches about the online dating system-use strategies that they consider successful.

4.1 Participants

In recruiting our participants, we considered someone an online dating coach if they 1) self-identified as one and explained the source of their expertise on their website, and 2) sold coaching products/services specific to online dating. As there is no official registry of online dating coaches from which we could extract a representative sample, we used a comprehensive online search strategy to identify our participants. We conducted *Google* and *Youtube* searches for 10 different terms including "online dating expert" and "online dating coach." *Google* was chosen to find the personal websites of and articles written about online dating coaches, while *Youtube* was chosen to find videos of coaches being interviewed for TV or discussing their advice. The first 20 pages of results for each search were reviewed (3000 links total), yielding a list of 132 unique online dating coaches (Table 1). Searches were conducted from a computer at New Jersey Institute of Technology, and the computer's IP address may have influenced the search results.

Table 1. Demographic breakdown of 132 coaches found

Coaches	Male	Female	Team	Total
Casual sex advice	20	0	0	**20** (15%)
Long-term relationship advice	23	79	3	**105** (80%)
Advice for both goals	2	5	0	**7** (5%)
Total	**45** (34%)	**84** (64%)	**3** (2%)	**132**

All 132 coaches were sent an interview request through e-mail. Thirty-nine coaches (29.5%) responded, but 5 failed to culminate into an interview because of scheduling conflicts, resulting in 34 total interviews (Table 2). We include Tables 1 and 2 in this paper so readers can compare the sample of online dating coaches discovered to the sample subsequently interviewed.

Table 2. Demographic breakdown of 34 coaches interviewed

Coaches	Male	Female	Total
Casual sex advice	7	0	**7** (21%)
Long-term relationship advice	8	18	**26** (76%)
Advice for both goals	1	0	**1** (3%)
Total	**16** (47%)	**18** (53%)	**34**

The interviewed coaches were predominantly based in the United States, followed by Australia (2) and the United Kingdom (2). The interviewed coaches for casual sex pursuits provided online dater evaluation and self-presentation strategies only for male clients, while three of the coaches for long-term relationship pursuits provided strategies only for female clients. All of the interviewed coaches considered their online dating system-use strategies most applicable to heterosexual online daters. Most of the interviewed coaches disseminated some or all of their online dating system-use strategies through one-on-one advice sessions and impersonation of clients in online dating systems (e.g. making the profile page, evaluating potential partners online, and writing messages on behalf of the client). Generalized products such as videos, audio files, and e-books were also common, especially for coaches that specialized in casual sex pursuits. Most of the coaches' online dating system-use strategies were intended for the online dating systems *Okcupid, Tinder, Plenty of Fish,* and/or *Match.com*.

4.2 Data Collection and Analysis

Thirty-three of the 34 interviews were conducted over *Skype* video or voice chat, while one was done in-person at a coffee shop. All interviews were voice recorded and fully transcribed. Interviews ranged from 28-81 minutes. The semi-structured interview guide had two primary sections: online dater evaluation strategies and self-presentation strategies. The questions probed five categories of traits germane to romantic attraction: physical attractiveness, demographic traits, lifestyle traits, personality traits, and relationship goal. The interview protocol also probed about why the coaches' system-use strategies were considered successful and how that success was determined. An open coding scheme was used to derive preliminary themes and theoretical constructs [21] about the coaches' advocated strategies. The first round of interviews was conducted mostly with coaches for casual sex pursuits, and the initial coding scheme revolved mostly around self-presentation practices. The second round of interviews included more coaches with advice for long-term relationship pursuits, and the updated coding scheme reflected themes around user evaluation, conceptualizations of online dating success, and reinforcement of self-presentation themes from earlier interviews. The third round of interviews probed more deeply into how system design influenced the advocated strategies for evaluation and self-presentation. This resulted in a re-coding of interview transcripts around system interface components and elements within those components (e.g. sections of profile pages).

5. FINDINGS

5.1 Validation of Online Dating System-Use Strategy Success

Most of the coaches validated success of their online dating system-use strategies through "track records" of previous clients who kept them informed about the outcomes of their in-person dates and accomplishments of their relationship goals. Some coaches also validated the success of their strategies through personal experience with using online dating systems for their own relationship pursuits, although not all of the coaches used online dating systems to pursue their own goals. In addition to the outcome of in-person dates, it was common for coaches to document online dating statistics like profile views and message responses in spreadsheets to inform modifications to their advocated system-use strategies. These statistics pertained to their personal online dating system use and clients who granted the coaches access to their online dating accounts.

Coach 22: *"I come at it with a more analytical approach than most people do. I do track a lot in spreadsheets. I track my clients' response rates, my own response rates."*

5.2 Defining System-Use Success

Several coaches considered their online dating system-use strategies successful because they procured in-person dates quickly and consistently for themselves and/or their clients with minimal effort, regardless of which particular user a date was planned with (the tactics that facilitate this success are described in the next finding).

Coach 21: *"Success to me is are you getting more attention online and are you going on more dates."*

Coach 18: "I define success for [my clients] as how many dates they get [...] versus how many they were getting before."

Several coaches went on to explain that the likelihood of mutual attraction on the first in-person date through their strategies is low, and they did not figure the outcomes of in-person dates into their definitions of success for online dating system use. First dates that lead to a second date or end in casual sex were not guaranteed by the coaches, and were even considered uncommon by some. As such, a few coaches advocated short, non-committal dates (e.g. one hour at a café) to minimize time wasted on partners ultimately deemed unattractive in-person.

Coach 11: *"[I teach] how to set up that first date so it's not a waste of time and money. I call it a date zero. The sole purpose of it is to have a very brief, cheap interaction that you sandwich in on the way to the gym, you know. You lower your expectations so it's realistic."*

5.3 Online Dating System-Use Strategies

The main online dating system-use strategy advocated by most coaches entailed 1) intentionally minimizing online evaluation of most traits germane to romantic attraction and 2) using online self-presentation tactics to persuade potential partners who satisfied minimum attraction criteria to meet in-person quickly where a more thorough evaluation could be conducted.

This strategy was typical for most coaches regardless of the relationship goal they catered to. Hence we opt below to present findings for all relationship goals jointly. We organize tactics that comprise this overarching strategy under the two prototypical system components for online dater evaluation and self-presentation: profile pages (which is further divided by profile pictures, demographic and lifestyle trait fields, and free-text fields), and private messaging. The following references to "the coaches" pertain to coaches for both casual and long-term relationship goals unless explicitly stated otherwise.

5.3.1 Profile Pictures

The coaches advocated that both men and women should use physical attractiveness based on profile pictures as the primary influence on online dater evaluations and decisions to meet in-person. While the coaches acknowledged that pictures might be deceptive, many stressed that the costs of deception are minimal if users meet in-person quickly and do not waste considerable time invested in online interaction.

Physical attractiveness through profile pictures was also considered a vital element of successful self-presentation, but more so for women than for men. Based on the perception that male users evaluate potential partners predominantly on physical features, some coaches suggested hiring a professional photographer to ensure that female clients maximize their physical attractiveness (coach 17: *"Our [highest level] clients, we'll set them up with a professional photographer").*

Some coaches said that female users' attractive pictures should also be targeted towards men with a desired lifestyle as a way to encourage such men to message them. For example, coach 25 discussed a recent client: *"[My female client] wants an outdoorsy guy that will go hiking and will love her dog. I looked at all her [profile] photos and every one of them is geared towards an artsy Brooklyn hipster [...]. Is that attractive? Yeah those are great photos. Is it going to attract her outdoorsy guy that is going to chop wood at her cabin? No."*

For men, coaches often advised that profile pictures be used to advertise physical appearance in the context of exciting and social lifestyles. Many of the coaches advocated a lifestyle conveyance that showcased their interests as well as their social value—having caring friends and being the leader in social situations. A few coaches suggested staging photos to craft an appealing snapshot of one's social life.

Coach 2: *"You can ask your friends to pose for the photo. Make it look like you're saying something important and everyone is listening to you."*

Some coaches explained that men's lifestyle photos, which should showcase activities and social value, lead prospective female partners to imagine the possession of attractive personality traits that they assume men who engage in such lifestyles would have. They credited this as a reason potential partners would express more interest in their clients.

Coach 33: *"Especially if your [written profile content] is lacking, the photos can take the place of having that personality. Like okay, his [written content] is a little dull, but look at all the shit he does in real life. He's got to have a great personality."*

5.3.2 Demographic and Lifestyle Trait Fields

Users can usually corroborate their evaluations of physical attractiveness through dedicated fields in profile pages for height and weight. Yet several coaches discouraged strict requirements ("deal breakers") for demographic trait fields during evaluation, for two reasons: 1) they tend to be exaggerated, and 2) they believed users have a tendency to (incorrectly) infer personality traits from these fields.

Coach 21: *"If they [clients] tell me well he has to be 6'2", I'll say why. [...] A lot of times what we'll get to after 'why why why' is the real answer. [...] Sometimes the answer is well my last boyfriend was short and he was sort of uncomfortable with that and it was always a problem in our relationship."* [reflecting the personality dimension of neuroticism]

The coaches generally advised having minimum requirements for other dedicated fields in profile pages, particularly location and smoking habits. However, they cautioned against "deal breakers" regarding other common fields in profile pages for demographic traits like income, religion, and political affiliation, which users answer with multiple choice lists. They explained that these trait fields give poor insight into lifestyle choices and values related to them, yet they said users still tend to extrapolate larger ideas of a person's lifestyle from these multiple choice answers. Several coaches recounted stories of clients reacting negatively to profile pages with dissimilar answers largely because of imagined conflicts regarding their lifestyles and values. For example, coach 15 recounted how a female client disqualified any man who did not select "Jewish" in the religion field of his profile because she assumed the man would not want to raise his children as Jewish.

Coach 15: *"She said 'well it's really because I want to raise my kids Jewish.' Then it's like well as long as they agree to raise your kids Jewish, [their religion] is not actually a core requirement."*

Interestingly, some of the coaches for casual sexual encounters gave the opposite advice regarding evaluation of multiple-choice fields in profiles. These coaches advised expediting the profile evaluation process by inferring openness to casual sex through answers provided in the dedicated fields for smoking and drinking habits—an inference they claimed to have validated in their personal experience using online dating systems (coach 5, on *OkCupid*'s trait field for smoking habits: *"If she smokes, she pokes"*). They explained that such inferences are necessary for online dater evaluation because female users seldom explicate casual sex interest in their profile pages.

5.3.3 Open-Ended Text Fields in Profile Pages

Most profile page designs include open-ended text sections in which users can type at least 500 characters of free-text. In terms of online dater evaluation, several of the coaches advised scanning open-ended content for signals of incompatible relationship goals. Several coaches that helped women find long-term relationships referenced "red flags" in written content that signaled men's casual sex motives. Some coaches also advised male clients with a long-term relationship interest to scan for red flags of "gold diggers," or women desiring a relationship with a wealthy man for financial support.

Coach 13: *"I spend half my day creeping dudes' [profiles for my clients]. Like one yesterday, he said something in the last paragraph [of his free-text content] about how 'I'm a great snuggler.' I'm like what the fuck. He's already red flagged."*

While some coaches said indications of personality could potentially be derived from anecdotes written in these open-ended text sections, they considered such signals to be inconsistently available and usually an inaccurate depiction of a person's personality in the physical world. They commonly attributed this to expression of personality being unintuitive through the written word, thus making such expressions hard to interpret (coach 30: *"what does 'work hard, play hard' even mean?"*). This was compounded by a belief that most users are more interested in appearing attractive than conveying their real personalities. Ultimately most coaches considered it not worth the effort to deliberately try to evaluate personality in any part of profiles.

Despite beliefs that free-text content is a poor tool for evaluating personality, most of the coaches strongly advocated the use of free-text content for men to self-present personality. Several coaches for both relationship goals advised male clients to use free-text fields to convey attractive or "alpha male" (coach 3) personality traits through a tactic called "show, don't tell"—a term also used in prior qualitative research regarding self-presentation in profile pages [9]. Like in this prior work, the coaches discussed writing stories in profile pages to showcase or exemplify personality traits. Yet while users in prior work used the "show, don't tell" method to reinforce the reliability of truthful identity claims, some of the coaches promoted its use for the opposite reason—to tell fabricated stories that embody desired personality traits. Some of these coaches provided fabricated stories to clients, while a few suggested that clients coopt quotes from TV shows or movies that exemplify desired traits. Some of these coaches rationalized the use of fabricated stories by stating that potential partners should know that such content is "obviously" false and that understanding it to be a fabrication is part of the intended self-presentation.

Coach 32: *"Some of the things we have in our [clients'] profiles is 'I'm a lion tamer.' Things that are obviously not true. [It's supposed to show that] he has a sense of humor."*

Coaches that promoted honest portrayals of personality through the "show, don't tell" method expressed frustration with conveying the complexities of personality through text because clients struggled to recall true stories that clearly exemplified particular traits, not to mention the writing skills required to convey such stories concisely. As such, the objective of the "show, don't tell" method promoted by these coaches was to write simplified, but true stories that advertise rudimentary versions of traits that are in line with one's *"personal brand"* (coach 32)—the traits that clients believe they possess and that they want potential partners to know about.

Coach 25: *"I have read thousands of profiles and I know 99% of people write the same thing. So how does one differentiate oneself from the crowd? I don't allow my clients to write adjectives. They're not allowed to write that they're smart or intelligent. They have to write a story, like a 4- or 5-line story, whose underlying message is the adjective they're not allowed to say."*

For female clients, the coaches advocated a different approach to self-presentation through free-text content. Several of the coaches perceived free-text content as an opportunity for women to "bait" prospective partners into messaging them by implying conversation topics that men can mention during their introductory messages. These coaches believed that male users typically struggle to think of content to include in their introductory messages, hence by incorporating potential messaging topics into the free-text portions of their profile pages women can increase the chances of a man sending them a message. It should be noted, however, that no coach thought free-text content could ever supersede physical attractiveness; messaging "bait" would be trivial to self-presentation if a potential partner was not first physically attracted to the woman's pictures.

Coach 13, while describing the mindset of a potential suitor for his female clients: *"If I see 'live, laugh, love' [as free-text content] how am I going to start a conversation with that? [...] Give me more avenues to start a conversation. [For example,] 'I can't wait to go to [Martha's] Vineyard and wear white pants and a pink shirt and dress up like a douche.' There are so many avenues you can start a conversation with there."*

5.3.4 Private Messaging

The one category of traits that coaches largely did not advise trying to evaluate in any component of profile pages was personality. Some of the online dating coaches believed that personality is not just subjective, but relative, meaning it can only be experienced through interaction with one's own personality. This was sometimes referred to as *"chemistry"* (Coach 8).

However, the coaches almost unanimously advised minimizing online interaction through private messaging. This was due partly to suspicions concerning potential partners' impression management motives, but mostly because coaches thought text-based messages could not convey personality to the extent that in-person interaction can. As such, coaches advised use of private messaging primarily as a tool for organizing and moving to an in-person date quickly where relative personality or "chemistry" could then be evaluated. Some coaches advised exchanging a maximum number of messages, usually 3-5, and disqualifying potential partners who were not receptive to meeting in-person within that span.

Coach 11: *"I tend to take the messaging not super seriously. Meaning you can't evaluate a potential partner through the messaging. [...] Every two or three interchanges, you know three from each person—meet each other. You can't create a relationship solely online. People email for too long."*

The goal of self-presentation through private messaging according to most coaches was to persuade potential partners to meet in-person quickly without expending much time and effort.

Coaches for male users pursuing casual sex advised an approach to private messaging reminiscent of an assembly line: using fully copy-and-pasted message content that is conveyed through automated, mass-messaging techniques. The coaches for casual sexual encounters tested and refined the message content that they advocated to their clients by mass-messaging hundreds of women and documenting response rates for each message. For example, Coach 1 described paying a man in Africa $3 an hour to conduct all of his messaging conversations with prewritten content, while Coach 5 developed software that automatically sends messages to female users and other similar software is sold to clients. These coaches also advised clients to develop their own methods for automating the messaging process

Coach 5: *"I simply repeat the same phrases and actions [in my messages to women] over and over again. I've created several [programming] scripts so I don't even have to type these things. This is not copy-paste. This is one click."*

Coach 14: *"You have prebuilt messages and then you rotate them and see what works best. Basically the key to it is, yeah, you come up with strong copy-and-paste material and you track it to see what's working and what's not."*

Coaches for casual sexual encounters sold their generic message content to male clients so that they could copy-and-paste it into their own messages verbatim. The generic message content shown to the interviewer was usually devoid of factual information and in some ways conveyed seemingly undesirable personality traits like rudeness (reflecting the personality dimension of agreeableness) or insecurity (reflecting the personality dimension of neuroticism). Some examples:

Coach 4: *"You have no idea how many fat chicks I had to reject to get to you."*

Coach 14: *"I know I'm not as experienced as most guys my age haha. I guess that makes me a dork."*

As corroborated in previous studies [15, 48], these coaches explained that female users typically receive many messages from potential suitors, making them overly selective in which messages they respond to. As such, the objective of this copy-and-pasted message content was to stand out from competing male users and draw an emotional reaction from females of interest.

Most coaches for long-term relationship pursuits advocated a similar approach to private messaging in the form of message templates that combine copy-and-pasted and personalized content. The copy-and-pasted portions were intended to convey attractive personality traits, much in the same vein as the "show, don't tell" stories in profile pages. Ironically, adding a personalized portion to the message was intended to assuage suspicions of copy-and-pasted content. These coaches said the personalized portions should mention perceived commonalities with the respective user, or reference interesting elements of their profile as proof that they read the profile.

Coach 12: *"We have a bunch of templates. We provide them with nine different templates – this is what we used, this is how you can modify them for your own use. We give them the tools and they decide."*

Coach 16: *"If you have [copy-and-pasted message content] that works well, use it to get attention, then scan the profile for 30 seconds then come up with a simple question based on a commonality that we both have to show that I am reading the profile and I'm paying attention to her."*

Coaches for both relationship goals noted that response rates for replicable message content were usually low. For example, Coach 5 discussed employing the mass-messaging strategy personally to pursue his casual sex desires and explained that his messages typically receive 7-20 responses per 100 messages, of which 2-3 may lead to an in-person meeting. Yet replicable message content was considered a time management strategy that allowed one to message more users and procure a response for *any* user, not a strategy to guarantee a response from a particular user of interest. Most coaches did not advise "holding out hope" (coach 19) for potential partners that one is particularly interested in, and they did not offer strategies for increasing the likelihood of a particular user responding.

Coach 32, on time management: *"There's a way that you can present a quality message without spending a whole lot of time. That's my way of writing a message, 3-4 sentences max. You introduce yourself, you find something in common that shows you read their profile, and you end with a question. That gives you time to write to many people."*

Coach 34: *"It's dangerous to get fixated on one [user of interest]. The chances of them liking you back are pretty low, and if they're popular they won't even notice you. You shouldn't already be choosing a partner before you even move it offline. Expand your horizons."*

Many of the coaches believed private messages were largely irrelevant to their female clients' self-presentation strategies because they said male users usually make decisions to meet in-person based on the profile page alone. Yet most advised women to send the first message to men that they were interested in as a way to ensure that their profile page was discovered.

6. DISCUSSION

We interviewed 34 online dating coaches about the online dating system-use strategies that they consider will aid their clients in being successful. The system-use strategies that they considered successful aimed to intentionally minimize online evaluation and persuade potential partners to meet in-person with minimal effort. Their notion of successful online dating system-use entails a user being able to procure in-person dates quickly with any potential partners that pass minimal attraction criteria. This definition of online dating system-use success noticeably precludes the outcome of in-person dates, which many of the coaches expected not to consistently result in a second date or otherwise lead to relationship goal achievement. This section of the paper seeks to discuss why the coaches advocated deliberately minimal online dater evaluation, and what aspects of system design should be addressed to improve success of online dating system-use.

6.1 The Costs and Benefits of Online Dater Evaluation

In general, the online dating system-use strategies recommended by the coaches revolve around "lean" evaluation; i.e. intentionally limiting the intensity of online evaluation and using scalable messaging tactics to persuade potential partners to meet in-person quickly at which time a more extensive evaluation can be conducted. We explore the utility of these strategies through the lens of theories that have been traditionally applied to attraction research.

The one trait that coaches strongly advocated basing online dater evaluations on was physical attractiveness through profile pictures. This is in line with extensive research in evolutionary theory that frames physical appearance as a prime influence on attraction because it was trusted by our ancestors as a reliable indicator of genetic quality [3]. The coaches advise minimal evaluation of demographic traits, lifestyle traits, and relationship goals, while largely advising against any evaluation of personality, despite acknowledging that these traits are important to romantic attraction. Through the lens of social exchange theory, this strategy of "lean" evaluation has merit. Social exchange theory has been applied to romantic attraction and relationship stability research to explain why people decide to pursue a potential romantic partner or maintain a relationship with an existing partner [31]. Under social exchange theory, these decisions are the result of a cost-benefit analysis. If the perceived costs outweigh the perceived benefits, pursuit or maintenance of a relationship is discontinued. From the coaches' perspective, their "lean" online dater evaluation strategy engineers the benefits of pursuing a potential partner to almost always outweigh the costs.

To put their strategy in perspective, let us first conduct a cost-benefit analysis of pursuing a potential partner with a "typical" online dater evaluation strategy in which a user tries to derive as much information as they can from profile pages and conducts private messaging conversations with fully customized message content. The costs of pursuing a potential partner under this strategy would presumably be the time spent reading through profiles and conducting private messaging conversations with custom content, as well as the opportunity cost of the users one would not be able to discover or evaluate. In return for these costs, a user leveraging this strategy would be better informed about the perceived benefits of devoting additional time and resources for an in-person meeting with a potential partner.

The coaches believed the costs associated with a more intensive online dater evaluation strategy would not yield better-informed perceptions of the benefits of meeting a particular user in-person. The coaches considered online information about potential partners to be highly susceptible to deception and misinterpretation. As such, the coaches' considered the chances of misevaluating the traits of a potential partner online—and thus the perceived benefits of meeting them in-person—to be high regardless of the effort put into online dater evaluation. By reducing the intensity of profile page reading and by utilizing mass-messaging tactics, the coaches' strategy therefore reduced the costs of evaluation—less time is spent evaluating and more potential partners can be contacted.

Interestingly, most coaches seemed oblivious to the costs involved with in-person dates: getting dressed, traveling to the meeting location, devoting at least an hour to the date, spending money on a drink, and so on. The compounding cost of these in-person dates theoretically limits the number of users one can evaluate more extensively. Even if a user goes on a date every day, that is only seven users that they can evaluate in a week, which is a sobering number compared to how many users they can discover in an online dating system. Yet this is a best-case scenario; to assume that a user can procure a date every night of the week using the coaches' strategy may be farfetched. However, if a user can procure one or two dates a week based on one or two hours of mass-messaging effort, the coaches' strategy seems enticing.

But for how long would this strategy be effective? The coaches' mass-messaging tactic is only effective if most users are not employing it. And as online dating continues to increase in popularity and acceptance, users may become more willing to meet each other in-person faster. Here lies a bottleneck: while users can expedite online evaluation by simply choosing to meet users based on minimal information, it is less possible to expedite in-person meetings and reduce the costs surrounding those meetings. The high costs of in-person meetings would compound as users procure more dates using coaches' strategy. Thus the strategy minimizing user evaluation online to meet in-person quickly is ultimately not scalable. Instead one could consider designing online dating systems to better facilitate online dater evaluation so users can make more informed decisions about ultimately costly in-person meetings.

6.2 Role of System Design in the Coaches' Online Dater Evaluation Strategy

The online dating coaches advocated minimal or lean online dater evaluation because they considered system design to stifle users' abilities to reliably evaluate all five categories of studied traits. This perception of unreliability was most apparent for personality traits, which many coaches actively advised against trying to evaluate in online dating systems. Through the lens of signaling theory, we can understand how online dating system designs fail to promote reliable signals of personality traits. As described in the Background section, there are two signal types: 1) conventional signals, which are inherently unreliable because possession of a trait is merely stated or implied, and 2) assessment signals, which are more reliable because they typically require possession of the respective trait for the signal to exist.

Online dating systems consist predominantly of conventional signals about potential romantic partners. The source of unreliability for many of these signals is potential deception—a user could exaggerate their height, they could post an old photograph, they may lie about the activities and hobbies they regularly engage in, etc. Yet when it comes to personality signals, the coaches indicated that reliability is also affected by concerns of misinterpretation (e.g. does this signal mean what I think it means?).

Misinterpretation may be perpetuated by online dating system designs that simply do not facilitate a wealth of reliable personality signals. Let us explore why, first with profile pages. Profile pages poorly facilitate self-presentation of personality relative to other traits. Profile page designs usually consist of dedicated fields for a variety of traits that users tacitly know how to convey (e.g. physical appearance, height, age, income), but personality traits cannot be conveyed in this self-explanatory and deliberate manner. Users instead have to use free-text components in profile pages, profile pictures, and private messages to convey personality, which demand tremendous introspective awareness of one's own personality as well as skills to deliberately convey these traits through the written word or pictures.

But of course, personality signals do not have to stem from deliberate attempts to convey personality. One could interpret personality from a picture intended to convey physical features, or from a list of favorite books intended to convey interests and hobbies. However, signals of personality will not be consistently detectable in this manner. Users can expect that in a given online dating system they will amass signals of every user's appearance and some demographic traits like age, yet a signal of neuroticism or sense of humor or intelligence may be detected in one user's profile page or one user's message, but not the next user's.

The quantity (or lack thereof) of personality signals in profile pages severely hinders the interpretation of personality signals that are detected, according to Asch's theory of person perception [1]. According to Asch, evaluations of personality traits must be contextualized. This means that signals about one personality trait will influence interpretation of signals about another personality trait. When personality trait signals are inconsistently available in profile pages, online daters have little opportunity to contextualize the traits that are detected. As such, their meaning is likely to change as more signals of personality are detected at later times, such as the first in-person meeting.

Yet even if more signals of personality were consistently available in profile pages, they would still be mere conventional signals of personality *compatibility*. As emphasized by the coaches, personality is both a relative and subjective category of traits. It can be difficult to understand someone's personality until it is compared to one's own. For example, a list of favorite books may signal intelligence, but it still forces a user to imagine how compatible the signaled intelligence is with their own.

Research related to attribution theory has long positioned interaction as a bastion of signals pertaining to relative personality and thus a key step in evaluation of potential romantic partners. As Reis and colleagues explain, "What makes live interaction special? [...] Several features stand out: [...] interpreting and responding in real-time to each other's behavior and verbalizations, [and] forming trait inferences from the other's statements and behaviors" [37].

This positions private messaging interfaces in online dating systems as vital to evaluation of personality compatibility, and recent online dating research indicates that messaging conversations do benefit in-person evaluations [36]. Yet the online dating coaches largely disregarded private messaging as an opportunity for evaluation because of suspicions that users are preoccupied with furthering an attractive self-presentation through messaging—a suspicion supported by prior work investigating online daters' private messaging strategies [48]. Perhaps ironically, the coaches' automated and copy-and-paste strategies for private messaging emphasize the same motive they suspect in other users. So while private messaging represents an opportunity to glean reliable signals of personality compatibility, self-presentation motives dissuade use of messaging in ways conducive to these benefits. The detrimental effect of these self-presentation motives on evaluation is likely exacerbated by the limited richness of messages and resultant hyperpersonal effect (the tendency to make overly favorable impressions during text-based communication as a result of missing or ambiguous information [43]).

6.3 Design Implications

The online dating coaches in this study advocating minimizing evaluation of potential partners online and escalating to an in-person meeting quickly, due to largely to the perception that personality compatibility cannot be reliably evaluated online. Yet this strategy is not scalable because of the compounding high costs of in-person meeting—time, money, safety, and emotional wellbeing. If online dating system users could detect more reliable assessment signals of personality compatibility online, they could better predict romantic attraction to potential partners in-person and thus better allocate their limited resources for in-person meetings.

System interface components for interaction seem the most viable candidates for facilitating reliable signals of personality compatibility according to attribution theory. Users could observe a partner's personality "in action" relative to their own personality through statements and reactions during interaction. Yet the online dating coaches' advocated strategies for interaction in online dating systems, along with prior work about users' interaction strategies [48], suggest that users are unlikely to employ private messaging interfaces in ways conducive to natural personality expression and thus evaluation.

We pose a two-pronged solution to better facilitating personality compatibility evaluation through interaction. First, we argue that a richer interaction interface would better enable transmission of complex personality signals relative to text-based messaging. Yet an interface more capable of transmitting personality signals does not necessarily encourage or promote expression of personality.

Research into romantic relationship satisfaction suggests that the topic of the interaction may also be pertinent to personality expression [23, 31]. This research, predicated on behavioral theory, indicates that behavior exhibited during problem-solving interaction is a central indicator of relationship satisfaction [31], and some research posits that this behavior is a reflection of personality [23, 31]. Problem-solving interactions are those in which partners contend with differences of opinion to reach consensus on a particular topic, discuss difficulties in the relationship, or otherwise work together to accomplish a task [31]. A common example from prior work entails relationship partners reading vignettes of common relationship conflicts (e.g. "husband's forgetfulness about throwing out the garbage") and debating which partner in the vignette is most at fault for the conflict [35].

We consider the aforementioned research to suggest that there are some contexts of interaction more conducive to personality expression and evaluation than others. While a solution like video chat would increase the richness of interaction and thus allow better transmission of personality, unstructured conversations may not be the best context for promoting personality expression—not least because impression management motives would presumably still be dictating users' behavior, especially with the emphasis that video chat would put on users' physical appearance.

If problem-solving interaction may prompt behavior between existing relationship partners that is expressive of personality, could it do the same for potential romantic partners? If so, what "problems" would be appropriate for unacquainted potential romantic partners to engage in? Solving problems is actually a fairly popular context for CMC between newly acquainted individuals, namely with video games. Furthermore, multiplayer online games (e.g. *World of Warcraft*, *Second Life*) have been shown to be a common way that people discover their eventual marriage partners online [24]. Expansive, time-consuming games like *World of Warcraft* may not be practical for online daters. But simpler, less time-intensive tasks in which online daters interact through richer behavior to solve problems or contend with difference of opinion could serve as an interaction context more conducive to personality expression and evaluation than a richer, but unstructured interaction context. Some examples of richer, problem-oriented interaction environments for online dating systems are:

- A translation of the relationship conflict vignettes in prior research with romantic couples [35]. Specifically, online dating systems could implement voice chat interfaces in which two potential partners have to reach consensus regarding vignettes of common dating conflicts that they both indicated differing opinions on (e.g. "who should pay for dinner on the first date?).
- Partners designing a virtual home or bedroom together under the constraint of a "budget."
- Planning a vacation itinerary together for a location viewable on *Google Earth* that must satisfy the demands of restless and demanding "virtual children" who express their (dis)approval to posed itineraries.
- Video chat in the context of a scavenger hunt (i.e. one user knows the location of a hidden item on a GPS map and must direct the other user to walk to the location to take a picture in a limited amount of time).

In conjunction with the tools of profile pages and private messaging, potential partners may be better able to experience compatibility of their personalities online through participation in such activities (e.g. "he doesn't let me make any of the decisions," or "she's very creative and her ideas work really well with mine"). However, would the suggested tools be equally advantageous for pursuit of both relationship goals studied in this paper? We would argue yes. While readers may be inclined to think users with casual sex interests would derive little value from problem-oriented interaction, prior work has indicated that users with casual sex interests do consider personality during their evaluations [48]. Additionally, the system-use strategies of online dating coaches in this study raise the question of whether users would even be willing to actively engage in problem-oriented interactions online. While it may be impossible for systems to force "active involvement" from users, they could limit the number of users one can message at a time or they could provide unlock-able system features in order to encourage users to become more actively involved in interaction online.

These design implications should not be confused as a call for system design to facilitate *complete* evaluation. Partner evaluation is a never-ending process, particularly in relationships that last longer than one night. What we can envision by improved online dater evaluation is a reduction in first dates that a user would not have agreed to if they knew information that was discovered during that date (such as signals about personality compatibility).

7. LIMITATIONS AND FUTURE WORK

There are a variety of limitations regarding this study and its chosen methodology that should be noted. In terms of our sample, the title of "online dating coach" was a self-proclaimed one—there are no criteria for what qualifies one as a "coach" and their claimed expertise could not be validated. They also had a financial incentive to assert that online dating systems are ripe with issues, yet we suspect this incentive to have had minimal influence on the study considering that the coaches openly discussed their proprietary strategies and admitted to lacking a "magic bullet" for success. However, data collected from the online dating coaches may suffer from an indirect recall bias. While their recollections are likely not distorted by relationship or in-person meeting outcomes as would be the case with interviewing active or former users, their advocated strategies were reportedly validated through recollections from their clients, who may suffer from their own recall bias. We must also acknowledge a limitation in the type of user who hires an online dating coach and how these users are likely not representative of the average online dater. Coaching advice can be very expensive, which limits their potential clientele to users with significant disposable income (and who may be more capable of going on multiple, expensive in-person dates than the average user). In addition, users that hire coaches have likely already encountered struggles or hindrances with relationship goal achievement that they deem insurmountable on their own (hence their hiring a coach). These struggles may influence the types of strategies advocated by the coaches.

There are also limitations concerning our definition of success and our methodology for exploring successful online dating system-use strategies. First, while our definition of online dating success is equally applicable to users with both casual sex and long-term relationship goals, it does not necessitate that a relationship goal actually be achieved. This is a notable limitation because online daters join these systems to achieve particular relationship goals [33], meaning our definition likely falls short of how users would define success themselves.

We defined success of online dating system-use at the beginning of this paper as an online dater procuring dates with potential partners that they deem attractive online, and subsequently deeming their online evaluations of the respective partners to be accurate after meeting in-person for the first time. In this regard, one limitation of this study's methodology, and any methodology that involves qualitative investigation of past outcomes of online dating system-use, is that success can only be confirmed through in-person dates that have actually happened. In other words, the accuracy of online impressions that a user deems unattractive can never be validated through this research method. Let us imagine the possible outcomes of online dater evaluation as a contingency table.

Table 3. Possible online dater evaluation outcomes

	Good candidate for a first in-person meeting	**Poor candidate for a first in-person meeting**
Decide to meet potential partner in-person	Online impression is attractive, and in-person impression is attractive *(True-Positive)*	Online impression is attractive, but in-person impression is unattractive *(False-Positive)*
Decide to discontinue evaluation of potential partner	Online impression is unattractive, but in-person impression would have been deemed attractive *(False-Negative)*	Online impression is unattractive, and in-person impression would have been deemed unattractive *(True-Negative)*

Studies of online dater evaluation outcomes in retrospect can only assess true positives and false positives (the top row of the table). True and false negatives cannot be validated because users would choose not to meet in-person with potential partners under these circumstances and thus would have no opportunity to learn if their online impressions were accurate. As such, users do not know if they are disqualifying potential partners that would have otherwise been found attractive in-person. While the likelihood of false negatives occurring with the coaches' strategy is low due to in-person meeting criteria being minimal, it still represents a limitation of this research approach when assessing the success of a particular online dating system-use strategy. While this study represents an initial step towards understanding successful online dating system-use, controlled experiments are a likely next step to assess the accuracy of online dater evaluations that are deemed negative and also to directly compare varying system-use strategies. For example, researchers could have potential partners self-present to and evaluate each other in an online dating system and then meet in-person regardless of the valence of their online impressions. A similar experimental design could also test the effect of novel system interfaces on online dater evaluation.

8. CONCLUSION

This paper presents one of the first attempts to understand online dating system-use strategies considered to be successful. We presented an interview study of online dating coaches about the online dating system-use strategies that they consider successful based on personal use and feedback from clients. The study revealed that online dating coaches advise a minimization of online evaluation to avoid issues of deception and misinterpretation, which they consider insurmountable in current system designs. In accordance, they advocate self-presentation tactics aimed to convince any potential partner that satisfies minimum attraction criteria to meet in-person quickly where a more intensive evaluation can be conducted. This strategy incurs a bottleneck however: while adopters of the strategy may expedite online evaluation and procure more dates, they cannot expedite face-to-face meetings and the costs associated with these meetings. These findings provided design implications to help users avoid the high, compounding costs of in-person meetings, and facilitate more reliable and informed online dater evaluations.

9. ACKNOWLEDGMENTS

This research is partially supported by a grant from the National Science Foundation 1422696.

10. REFERENCES

[1] Asch, S.E. 1946. Forming impressions of personality. *The Journal of Abnormal and Social Psychology*. 41, 3 (1946), 258-290.

[2] Blackwell, C., Birnholtz, J. and Abbott, C. 2014. Seeing and being seen: Co-situation and impression formation using Grindr, a location-aware gay dating app. *New Media & Society*. 17, 5 (Aug. 2015), 1117-1136.

[3] Buss, D.M. and Schmitt, D.P., 1993. Sexual strategies theory: an evolutionary perspective on human mating. *Psychological review*. 100, 2 (1993), 204.

[4] Cacioppo, J.T., Cacioppo, S., Gonzaga, G.C., Ogburn, E.L. and VanderWeele, T.J. 2013. Marital satisfaction and break-ups differ across on-line and off-line meeting venues. *Proceedings of the National Academy of Sciences*. 110, 25 (2013), 10135-10140.

[5] Donath, J. 2007. Signals in social supernets. *Journal of Computer-Mediated Communication*. 13, 1 (2007), 231-251.

[6] Eastwick P.W. and Finkel, E.J. 2008. Sex differences in mate preferences revisited: do people know what they initially desire in a romantic partner?. *Journal of personality and social psychology*. 94, 2 (2008), 245.

[7] Eastwick, P.W., Finkel, E.J. and Eagly, A.H. 2011. When and why do ideal partner preferences affect the process of initiating and maintaining romantic relationships?. *Journal of personality and social psychology*. *101*, 5 (2011), 1012-1032.

[8] Ellison, N.B., Hancock, J.T. and Toma, C.L. 2012. Profile as promise: A framework for conceptualizing veracity in online dating self-presentations. *New media & Society*. 14, 1 (2012), 45-62.

[9] Ellison, N., Heino, R. and Gibbs, J., 2006. Managing impressions online: Self-presentation processes in the online dating environment. *Journal of Computer-Mediated Communication*, 11, 2 (2006), 415-441.

[10] Emerson, R.M., 1976. Social exchange theory. *Annual review of sociology*, 335-362.

[11] Fletcher, G.J., Simpson, J.A., Thomas, G. and Giles, L., 1999. Ideals in intimate relationships. *Journal of personality and social psychology*. *76*, 1 (1999), 72-89.

[12] Fiore A.T. and Donath, J.S. 2004. Online personals: An overview. In *CHI'04 extended abstracts on Human factors in computing systems*. ACM, New York, NY, 1395-1398.

[13] Fiore A.T. and Donath J.S. 2005. Homophily in online dating: when do you like someone like yourself?. In *CHI'05 Extended Abstracts on Human Factors in Computing Systems*. ACM, New York, NY, 1371-1374.

[14] Fiore, A.T., Taylor, L.S., Mendelsohn, G.A. and Hearst, M. 2008. Assessing attractiveness in online dating profiles. In *Proceedings of the SIGCHI Conference on Human Factors in Computing Systems*. ACM, New York, NY, 797-806.

[15] Fiore, A.T., Taylor, L.S., Zhong, X., Mendelsohn, G.A. and Cheshire, C. 2010. Who's right and who writes: People, profiles, contacts, and replies in online dating. In *47th Hawaii International Conference on System Sciences*, 1-10.

[16] Fisher, H.E. 1994. *Anatomy of love: A natural history of mating, marriage, and why we stray*. Ballantine Books.

[17] Frost, J.H., Chance, Z., Norton, M.I. and Ariely, D. 2008. People are experience goods: Improving online dating with virtual dates. *Journal of Interactive Marketing*. 22, 1 (2008), 51-61.

[18] Gaunt, R. 2006. Couple similarity and marital satisfaction: are similar spouses happier?. *Journal of personality*. 74, 5 (2006), 1401-1420.

[19] Gibbs, J.L., Ellison, N.B. and Heino, R.D. 2006. Self-presentation in online personals the role of anticipated future interaction, self-disclosure, and perceived success in Internet dating. *Communication Research*. 33, 2 (2006), 152-177.

[20] Gibbs, J.L., Ellison, N.B. and Lai, C.H. 2010. First comes love, then comes Google: An investigation of uncertainty reduction strategies and self-disclosure in online dating. *Communication Research*. 38, 1 (Dec. 2010), 70-100.

[21] Glaser B.G. and Strauss, A.L. 2009. *The discovery of grounded theory: Strategies for qualitative research*. Transaction Publishers.

[22] Goffman, E. *The Presentation of Self in Everyday Life*. 1959. NY: Doubleday.

[23] Gonzaga, G.C., Campos, B. and Bradbury, T. 2007. Similarity, convergence, and relationship satisfaction in dating and married couples. *Journal of personality and social psychology*. 93, 1 (Jul. 2007), 34-48.

[24] Hall, J.A. 2014. First comes social networking, then comes marriage? Characteristics of Americans married 2005–2012 who met through social networking sites. *Cyberpsychology, Behavior, and Social Networking*. *17*, 5 (2014), 322-326.

[25] Hall, J.A. 2015. Sexual selection and humor in courtship a case for warmth and extroversion. *Evolutionary Psychology* 13, 3 (2015), 1-10.

[26] Hall, J.A., Park, N., Song, H. and Cody, M.J. 2010. Strategic misrepresentation in online dating: The effects of gender, self-monitoring, and personality traits. *Journal of Social and Personal Relationships*. 27, 1 (2010), 117-135.

[27] Hancock, J.T. and Toma, C.L. 2009. Putting your best face forward: The accuracy of online dating photographs. *Journal of Communication* 59, 2 (2009), 367-386.

[28] Hancock, J.T., Toma, C. and Ellison, N. 2007. The truth about lying in online dating profiles. In *Proceedings of the SIGCHI conference on Human factors in computing systems*. ACM, New York, NY, 449-452.

[29] Heino, R.D., Ellison, N.B. and Gibbs, J.L. 2010. Relationshopping: Investigating the market metaphor in online dating. *Journal of Social and Personal Relationships*. 27, 4 (2010), 427-447.

[30] Hitsch, G. J., Hortaçsu, A. and Ariely, D. 2010. Matching and sorting in online dating. *The American Economic Review* 100, 1 (2010), 130-163.

[31] Karney, B.R. and Bradbury, T.N., 1995. The longitudinal course of marital quality and stability: A review of theory, methods, and research. *Psychological bulletin*. *118*, 1 (Jul. 1995), 3-34.

[32] Lampe, C.A., Ellison, N. and Steinfield, C. 2007. A familiar face (book): profile elements as signals in an online social network. In *Proceedings of the SIGCHI conference on Human factors in computing systems*. ACM, New York, NY, 435-444.

[33] Mascaro, Christopher M., Magee, R.M. and P. Goggins, S.P. 2012. Not just a wink and smile: an analysis of user-defined success in online dating. In *Proceedings of the 2012 iConference*. ACM, New York, NY, 200-206.

[34] Masden, C. and Edwards, W.K. 2015. Understanding the Role of Community in Online Dating. In *Proceedings of the SIGCHI Conference on Human Factors in Computing Systems*. ACM, New York, NY, 535-544.

[35] Olson, D.H and Ryder, R.G. 1970. Inventory of marital conflicts (IMC): An experimental interaction procedure. *Journal of Marriage and the Family*. 32, 3 (Aug. 1970), 443-448.

[36] Ramirez, A., Fleuriet, C. and Cole, M. 2015. When online dating partners meet offline: The effect of modality switching on relational communication between online daters. *Journal of Computer-Mediated Communication*. 20, 1 (2015), 99-114.

[37] Reis, H.T., Maniaci, M.R., Caprariello, P.A., Eastwick, P.W. and Finkel, E.J. 2011. In live interaction, does familiarity promote attraction or contempt? Reply to Norton, Frost, and Ariely (2011). *Journal of Personality and Social Psychology*. 101, 3 (Sep. 2011), 575-578.

[38] Smith, A. and Anderson, M. April 20, 2015. 5 facts about online dating. Retrieved May 21, 2015. http://www.pewresearch.org/fact-tank/2015/04/20/5-facts-about-online-dating/

[39] Strauss, N. 2006. *The game: undercover in the secret society of pickup artists*. Canongate Books.

[40] Terveen, L. and McDonald, D.W. 2005. Social matching: A framework and research agenda. *ACM transactions on computer-human interaction (TOCHI)* 12, 3 (2005), 401-434.

[41] Toma, C.L. and Hancock, J.T. 2010. Looks and lies: The role of physical attractiveness in online dating self-presentation and deception. *Communication Research*. 37, 3 (2010), 335-351.

[42] Tsujita, H., Tsukada, K. and Itiro, S. 2010. InPhase: evaluation of a communication system focused on happy coincidences of daily behaviors. In *Proceedings of the SIGCHI Conference on Human Factors in Computing Systems*. ACM, New York, NY, 2481-2490.

[43] Walther, J.B., 1996. Computer-mediated communication impersonal, interpersonal, and hyperpersonal interaction. *Communication research*. 23, 1 (1996), 3-43.

[44] Walther, J.B. and Parks, M.R., 2002. Cues filtered out, cues filtered in. *Handbook of interpersonal communication*, 529-563.

[45] Watson, D., Klohnen, E.C., Casillas, A., Nus Simms, E., Haig, J. and Berry, D.S., 2004. Match makers and deal breakers: Analyses of assortative mating in newlywed couples. *Journal of personality*, 72, 5, 1029-1068.

[46] Whitty, M.T. 2008. Revealing the 'real'me, searching for the 'actual' you: Presentations of self on an internet dating site. *Computers in Human Behavior*. 24, 4 (2008), 1707-1723.

[47] Zahavi, A. 1975. Mate selection—a selection for a handicap. *Journal of theoretical Biology*. 53, 1 (1975), 205-214.

[48] Zytko, D., Grandhi, S.A. and Jones, Q. 2014. Impression Management Struggles in Online Dating. In *Proceedings of the 18th International Conference on Supporting Group Work*. ACM, New York, NY, 53-62.

[49] Zytko, D., Grandhi, S.A. and Jones, Q. 2015. Frustrations with Pursuing Casual Encounters through Online Dating. In *Proceedings of the 33rd Annual ACM Conference Extended Abstracts on Human Factors in Computing Systems*. ACM, NewYork, NY, 1935-1940.

Designing an Application for Social Media Needs in Emergency Public Information Work

Amanda Lee Hughes
Utah State University
Logan, UT USA
amanda.hughes@usu.edu

Rohan Shah
Utah State University
Logan, UT USA
rohan.shah3@aggiemail.usu.edu

ABSTRACT
Emergency responders increasingly use social media as a means to monitor public information, gather information that could be used in response efforts, and communicate important information during emergency events. However, the adoption of social media into emergency management processes poses socio-technical challenges such as issues of credibility and trust, lack of organizational support, poor tools, and a shortage of resources and training. This study designs, implements, and evaluates an application that supports the work practice of emergency public information officers and their need to gather, monitor, sort, and report social media activity. Based on prior work that examines how social media and the forms of public participation enabled by it are changing public information practice, we iteratively design and evaluate application prototypes using a human-centered process—moving from low-fidelity paper prototypes to a high-fidelity digital prototype that is ready for field use.

Keywords
Social Media; Crisis Informatics; Participatory Design

1. INTRODUCTION
As social media become more pervasive, emergency responders increasingly use social media to communicate with the public, monitor the public information arena during an emergency event, and gather information that could be helpful to response efforts [8, 14, 16, 35, 38]. In turn, members of the public are coming to expect that emergency responders will provide information through social media streams and even respond to requests for assistance made through these streams [2].

In the United States (US), the emergency responder role that is most affected by social media is the Public Information Officer (PIO). The PIO role is a formalized public relations position under the Incident Command System that all US response organizations are required to use for managing their emergency response efforts. The PIO's primary responsibility is to communicate correct, up-to-date information concerning the status of emergency incidents to the media, members of the public, and other directly or indirectly affected stakeholders [12]. They monitor public communications to answer questions, provide needed information, and correct false rumor and/or misinformation [36]. PIOs also find useful crisis information generated by the public and distribute it to response organizations that can best use it. Despite social media's potential for PIO work, adoption poses many socio-technical challenges such as issues of credibility and trust, lack of support from management, organizational conflicts, poor tools, and a shortage of resources and training [12, 16, 37].

This paper describes a multi-year, ongoing project to design, implement, and evaluate a tool—the PIO Monitoring Application (PMA)—that supports the work practice of PIOs and their needs to gather, monitor, sort, and report social media activity and data. Building upon prior empirical research [12] and the results of a participatory design workshop [11], we report the human-centered process used to create this application and the insights gained around how social media is changing the work practice of PIOs.

2. BACKGROUND
2.1 Emergency Responder Social Media Use
Traditionally, emergency responders have perceived public information work as happening over one-way communication channels [24]—flowing from response organizations to the public but not in the other direction. Recently, this perception has been challenged as emergency responders increasingly use social media to communicate and interact with the public they serve [8, 14, 30, 39]. Through social media, responders can reply to requests for assistance and information from a globally distributed audience with unprecedented speed [5, 25]. The public can participate more broadly as they find, generate, and share online crisis information [5, 13, 27, 31]. In turn, emergency responders find that the online information the public generates during a crisis event can be useful in their own efforts [6, 12]. These new information flows—supported by social media—have led emergency responders to rethink the one-way communication model in favor of a two-way model that accounts for new interactions between emergency responders and the public [12, 23].

Initial studies regarding social media use for emergency public information work focus on how emergency responders adopt social media platforms and the challenges in fitting these new communication platforms with needs and practice [4, 12, 16, 34, 37]. As online communication use by emergency responders has continued to increase, researchers have engaged in more focused studies of its use. These studies have primarily examined Twitter use across a variety of crisis events such as the London Riots of 2011 [8], the 2010 Deepwater Horizon oil spill [38], and the 2013 Boston Bombings [39]. A few recent studies have expanded this

GROUP '16, November 13 - 16, 2016, Sanibel Island, FL, USA

ACM 978-1-4503-4276-6/16/11…$15.00
DOI: http://dx.doi.org/10.1145/2957276.2957307

inquiry to include other online media beyond Twitter, such as websites, blogs, and/or Facebook [14, 35]. While these studies reveal much about how PIOs use social media, including strategies for monitoring data and communicating with the public, they are limited in scope and do not explore how online media use fits within a broader, all-hazards public information strategy. Researchers acknowledge the limitations of these studies and recognize a growing need to classify emergency social media use and practice, both by type and by disaster [9].

2.2 Limitations of Existing Tools and Methods

In recent years, academia, industry, and members of the public have created many solutions that attempt to process and manage social media in times of disaster [26]. Many of these applications attempt to filter and analyze the large amounts of social media data following a major disaster event. Using supervised learning techniques, the *Enhanced Messaging for the Emergency Response Sector* (*EMERSE*) system automatically classifies and aggregates tweets to make them more accessible to emergency responders and members of the public [7]. *Twitcident* uses semantics techniques to filter tweets during a crisis event and provide better search capabilities to help people explore Twitter data [1]. *TwitInfo* visualizes and summarizes tweets around events using a timeline to help users make sense of the data [19]. These tools provide automated methods for analyzing and exploring Twitter data but they do not support the social media documentation and reporting needs of PIOs. Further, these methods rely heavily on pre-existing, coded datasets to perform well. Such datasets are highly contextual to specific events (i.e., they do not generalize well) and require much time and expertise to create.

Other applications are aimed at supporting the efforts of members of the public as digital volunteers [32], and as a result they do not directly address the needs of PIOs. For example, to make tweets more readable by machines and allow for automatic analysis, the *Tweak the Tweet* project proposes a prescriptive syntax using descriptive hashtags [33]. *Ushahidi* is a computing platform that supports human-entered data and analysis in an array of humanitarian situations [20, 21]. *XHELP* [29] supports the digital activities of citizens and volunteers in disasters, while *CrowdMonitor* [18] supports emergency service groups in their efforts to coordinate citizen volunteers.

Commercial applications such as *TweetDeck* [40], *TweetFall* [41], and *Hootsuite* [10] provide generalized tools and dashboards for monitoring and managing social media streams, but they do not fully support the documentation, reporting and organizing needs of PIOs. *Radian 6* [28] provides powerful social media monitoring and analysis tools but is too expensive for most PIOs.

3. PRIOR RESEARCH

This work builds upon prior empirical and participatory design research that are reported in full elsewhere [11, 12]. However, we summarize the approach and findings of these studies to demonstrate how design decisions were informed by this research.

3.1 Empirical Investigation

Hughes and Palen [12] conducted interviews with 25 PIOs in the US to learn how they perceived social media was affecting their work practice. The study found that PIOs work for a wide variety of organizations, such as fire and police departments, public health departments, hospitals, and county-, state-, and federal-level emergency management agencies. In addition, PIOs are found in a variety of jurisdiction sizes (e.g., rural, urban, metro, etc.). PIOs from larger jurisdictions tend to work full-time and have more organizational support. PIOs from smaller jurisdictions tend to work part-time; often, the PIO role is just one of many roles played in his/her organization.

Many PIOs, especially part-time PIOs, were already overwhelmed with their current duties and adding social media as yet another communication tool presents challenges. Using social media requires additional effort; they must acquire proficiency with social media and the tools associated with them while also devoting more time to monitoring and using a new communication channel. Rarely were these PIOs given more time or resources to handle the extra workload.

Hughes and Palen [12] examined the range of PIO work tasks. PIOs are often called to the scene of an emergency to help manage journalists. The PIO's job is to corral the press, keep them from interfering with the response efforts and out of harms way, while also sharing the most recent incident information. Interestingly, PIOs have been forced to adjust their practice to accommodate changes in the field of journalism. Information that used to only be available through traditional media streams is now available through blogs, websites, and other social media, and citizens produce much of it. These worlds further blend as professional journalists increasingly rely on story leads, photos, and video from the public. To stay relevant in a changing world, journalist must release information more quickly to avoid being scooped by other sources. As a result, PIOs face increasing pressure to produce more information and to release it more quickly to the press and to members of the public over social media streams as well as other traditional communication channels. We aim to address the PIO social media challenges and needs described here with PMA.

3.2 Participatory Design Workshop

To involve PIOs in creating tools for their social media needs, Hughes [11] led a full-day participatory design workshop with 8 PIOs and 7 researchers. The workshop began with focused group discussion around how social media was affecting the work practices of PIOs. Following this discussion, the PIOs created low-fidelity prototypes of their ideal social media information space. Each PIO then shared his/her prototype and the workshop participants discussed what they liked and disliked about the design. Next, the PIOs worked in teams with researchers to develop new low-fidelity prototypes that further developed the ideas explored earlier in the workshop. After reporting on and discussing these group prototypes, everyone met together to debrief for the day and determine future directions. This workshop produced several design recommendations—which we use in the design of PMA—for tools that would address the social media needs of PIOs [11].

3.2.1 Support Information Monitoring & Analysis

PIO participants expressed the need for tools that would help them monitor, sift, and make sense of the potentially large amounts of data available across social media streams during an emergency event. However, they wanted any tool that analyzed social media data to be transparent so they could understand how the results were derived.

3.2.2 Provide Ways to Organize Information

During the workshop, PIOs prototyped different organizational schemes for the social media data they planned to collect. For example, one prototype organized the data by who had sent the data, while another organized data by who would be most interested in the content. Existing tools limit how information can be organized and if organization was supported it tended to be in fixed, predetermined ways that were not always helpful.

3.2.3 Provide Report Capabilities

PIOs have a need to report social media activity to those whom they work with during an event, whether it is other team members or organizations. PIOs described copy-and-pasting online content in an attempt to email it to others, often resulting in awkward formatting and inclusion of extraneous text. They wanted to have the data in a format that was easy to share and work with.

3.2.4 Document Activity

Most emergency response organizations are publically funded in the US and as such they must keep public records of their activity for after-action reports, public accountability, and possible litigation cases. Few tools exist to help in these efforts, and those that do, often capture the data in formats that are inaccessible for non-technical users (such as in a database or json file).

4. THE FINAL PMA PROTOTYPE

PMA is a web application (built using Yii—a PHP web application framework) that supports the social media monitoring, documenting, reporting, and organizing needs of PIOs during emergency events. PMA monitors social media (only Twitter at this time) by collecting and storing tweets based on keywords. PIOs often work in teams and as such PMA supports use of the tool by multiple users at the same time. To use PMA, one must first create an event to monitor. The user then enters keywords to find relevant Twitter messages for that emergency event. Once these keywords are entered and activated, PMA uses the Twitter streaming API to collect tweets that match the provided keywords. After tweets are collected, PMA provides two views—streaming and archive—for viewing and working with these tweets.

4.1 Streaming View

Once a PIO creates an event and specifics search terms, s/he can begin to monitor data in the streaming view. In this view, PMA displays the tweets that match the active search terms (keywords) for the selected event (see Figure 1). The streaming view shows the most recent 20 tweets in real-time. New messages appear at the top of the screen and scroll down with a two second delay.

Figure 1: PMA Streaming View

On the left-hand side of the streaming view, users can create categories. These categories are customizable and can be used to sort and store tweets by topic. Users can drag-and-drop tweets into these categories. In addition, categories can have sub-categories. To indicate a hierarchical relationship, a sub-category is indented to the right and appears in a different color than the parent category. When the user clicks any of the categories, the user is taken to the archive view (described below) that displays all the tweets in that category. All tweets in a sub-category also belong to the parent category and therefore they are also displayed when viewing the parent category. Finally, an option available on the category right-click menu is the ability to create a rule.. Rules allow PMA to automatically categorize tweets based on features of a tweet, such as a username or the tweet content. The rule management interface appears as a Pop-up and can be seen in Figure 2. Each rule is comprised of a category to look for tweets within, a category to move the tweets to if they match the condition, and a condition to match, which consists of a string and a place to look for the string (i.e., within the tweet text or the tweet username). Once a rule is created, all new tweets will be tested against it to see if they match the rule's condition and if a tweet matches, it will be categorized in the manner specified by the rule. The rule management interface also has a button labeled "Run Rules Now" which will run the rules against all the tweets currently stored in PMA. This option allows users to apply rule auto-categorization on tweets that have already been loaded into PMA before rule creation.

Figure 2: PMA Rule Interface

At the top of the streaming view, clickable text tells the user how many search terms are active. Clicking this status message sends the user to the search terms page. If there are active search terms, the text is green. Conversely, if there are no active search terms, the text is red.

Finally, the PMA streaming view provides an email reporting function. To email a tweet (or several tweets), the user selects the tweets that they want to email and clicks the "Email" button. The email function uses a "mailto" link that opens the default email client for the computer PMA is accessed from and creates a message that the user can send. This reporting option can help PIOs send tweets to others quickly and efficiently.

4.2 Archive View

The archive view of PMA (see Figure 2) allows the user to view all of the event tweets that PMA has captured given the search terms for the event. This interface uses paging, with 10 tweets displayed at a time (this number can be adjusted). Each header row name in the table can be clicked to sort the displayed tweets by ascending or descending order. Below the table header row, a search row appears that lets users enter search parameters for each of the columns: Text, User, Time Sent, and Categories. For example, if a PIO enters the word "fire" in the Text search field and hits the enter key, the interface will return only those tweets that contain the word "fire." These search and sort features let PIOs perform advanced queries on the collected data, which can help them analyze it.

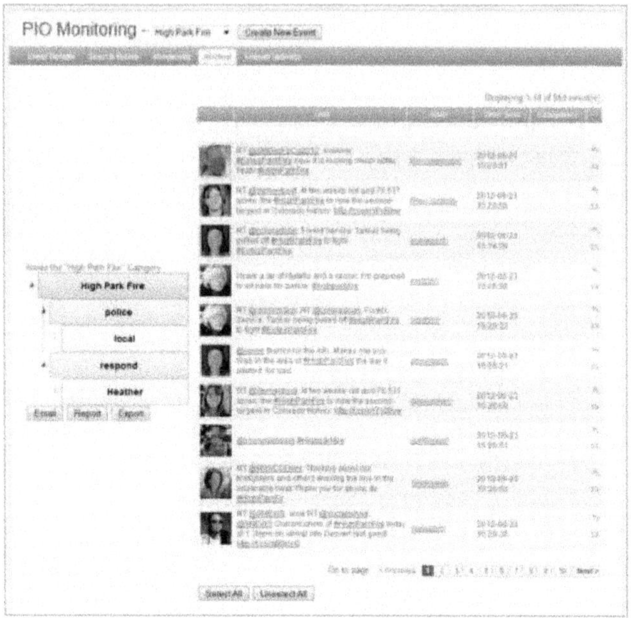

Figure 3: PMA Archive View

For consistency and convenience, the categories work the same way in the archive view as they do in the streaming view. This allows PIOs to categorize messages after an event happens, when they have more time. If a category is left-clicked with no messages selected, it shows the archive view with only the tweets in that category.

4.3 Export and Report Options

Additional features that appear only on the archive view are the export and report options. Clicking the "Export" button creates an Excel spreadsheet with information about each of the tweets contained in the currently selected category. Using this feature, PIOs can create and save a record of the collected tweet data around an event. Further, because the tweet data is inserted into an Excel spreadsheet, the data can be manipulated easily; PIOs can sort, search, and create their own charts, graphs, and statistics.

PMA can also create reports using collected Twitter data. PIOs can click on the "Report" button to automatically generate metrics, charts, and graphs. The report is created as a Microsoft Word file containing various charts and graphs of the 1) top twenty hashtags, 2) top ten twitter users, 3) top twenty retweets, 4) recent twitter activity, and 5) a category breakdown of tweets. An example graph that shows the number of tweets PMA captured by day around the High Park Fire event can be found in Figure 4. Different analyses of the collected tweet data can help PIOs answer questions and demonstrate to their organization how social media is used as well as their value.

A significant advantage of the export and report features of PMA is the quick execution time—usually a matter of seconds. With these features PIOs can export data and generate reports as often as needed and in almost real-time. Previously, these kinds of activities took significant time and effort, so they could not be done frequently. The ability to create and share timely information around social media activity can help PIOs collaborate more effectively with their own organization and other response groups.

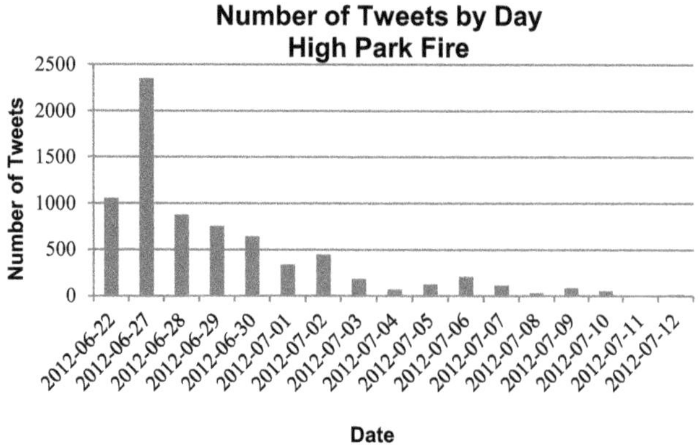

Figure 4: A Graph Generated by PMA that Shows the Number of Tweets by Day Over the High Park Fire Event

5. DESIGN, IMPLEMENTATION & EVALUATION

This section outlines the iterative process used to produce the final PMA prototype just described. This human-centered process comprises 5 cycles to date—with each cycle consisting of a design/implementation phase and an evaluation phase with representative users.

5.1 Cycle 1: Low-Fidelity Paper Prototypes

The design process began with the iterative refinement of five low-fidelity paper prototypes based on the empirical work [12] and participatory design workshop [11] described earlier:

1. *Social Media Template Manager* - a web-based tool that manages social media templates for the most common messages that PIOs send.
2. *Social Media Training Tool* – an application for training PIOs in social media use for emergency management.
3. *Digital Volunteer Coordinator* - a tool that would let PIOs interface more directly with digital volunteers [32] during an emergency event.
4. *History Reporting Tool* – an application that imports social media data around an emergency event and lets PIOs search and create reports using this data.
5. *Twitter Bucket Sorter* - an interface for sorting social media data into "buckets" that are defined by the PIO. The design allows any number of people to sort tweets, making the task less demanding.

5.1.1 Evaluation Procedure

Informally, we sought feedback on these five prototypes from three user interface design experts and five PIOs from the prior workshop. The goal was to discover which prototype(s) best reflected the workshop results and showed potential (i.e., usefulness, feasibility) for further work.

5.1.2 Evaluation Results

The first three prototypes were rejected for further development based on evaluator feedback. The Social Media Template Manager could save time for PIOs when creating social media messages. However, PIO evaluators told us that every event response is different and usually requires unique messaging; few messages would fit the template criteria. Next, the Social Media Training Tool could help train PIOs in social media use. Still, the effort required to create new training modules, tailor the modules to the different types of PIOs, and maintain this training was estimated to be large. Further, the solution showed little innovation; it simply provides training. Finally, the Digital Volunteer Coordinator sought to support a growing trend in emergency management to utilize digital volunteers [29, 32, 34]. But when shown to PIOs, it was met with resistance—mostly concerns about whether digital volunteers could be trusted. At the time (2012), the tool would have faced slow acceptance, making it hard to find PIOs to assist with the development and testing of the tool.

PIO evaluators identified the History Reporting Tool and the Twitter Bucket Sorter as the most useful prototypes. The ability to document and store social media data around an emergency event is a growing need for PIOs and the History Reporting Tool meets that need. The Twitter Bucket Sorter provided a novel mechanism for sorting and organizing social media data, where available tools lacked this ability. Through exploration, we found that the features of both prototypes could be combined in a single tool.

5.2 Cycle 2: Mid-Fidelity PMA Prototype

In this cycle, we created the PIO Monitoring Application (PMA) that combined the features of the History Reporting Tool and the Twitter Bucket Sorter prototypes. The original PMA prototype was primarily based on the Twitter Bucket Sorter, except the buckets changed to categories that resembled a folder hierarchy on the left hand side of the interface. This hierarchy allowed users to sort Twitter messages into any category at any time. We also created a separation of sorting the data and viewing the data in this prototype. When a user switches to the "View" page of PMA the functionality of the category tree on the left of the page changes. Instead of showing only those messages that are waiting to be categorized, it shows all messages that are contained in the current category. When PMA is in the "View" state, the user can export the collected data and create a report; this functionality came from the History Reporting Tool.

After constructing a low-fidelity paper prototype of PMA, we built a mid-fidelity digital version. Though the functionality was limited and often incomplete, this digital prototype allowed PIOs to experiment with PMA—creating categories and sorting tweets—which generated much discussion and feedback.

5.2.1 Evaluation Procedure

We tested the mid-fidelity PMA prototype with eleven PIOs recruited from a state-wide PIO organization. This testing not only evaluated PMA functionality, but also explored whether the underlying idea of sorting information is helpful to PIOs. Test sessions were video recorded and lasted approximately one hour at the PIOs' place of work. Each session began with a background questionnaire. Next, we asked the participants to perform several tasks while thinking aloud [17].

The first task—a card sorting activity [15]—was designed to show how PIOs filter and sort information and to test whether sorting information supports PIO practice. For this task, we created a stack of 50 business cards; each card had one Twitter message printed on it from a recent wildfire event. We gave the stack of cards to the participant and asked him/her to look at each card and read the message out loud. After reading the message, s/he was asked to organize the cards into piles that made sense to him/her. As the piles of messages became more defined, we encouraged the PIOs to assign labels (written on post-it notes). For the next task, participants tried different ways of interacting with and categorizing emergency tweets using the PMA prototype. We first showed the participants how to create their own categories and then instructed them to sort the tweets by assigning each tweet to a category. Finally, we provided PIO participants with several lists of tweets that corresponded with different categories, and asked them what they would do with the information. The aim of this task was to discover how PIOs might use information once it had been categorized using PMA.

During analysis, we captured all the PMA suggestions, critiques, and ideas for improvements. We also analyzed the card sorting data by looking for patterns and significant groupings across participants.

5.2.2 Evaluation Results

Overall the response to PMA was positive. PIOs were excited by the ability to collect tweets around an emergency event and export those messages into an Excel spreadsheet that could be archived or shared with others. Few tools exist that provide this capability, and those that do are paid services which most organizations cannot afford. Though the ability to create a report was not functional in the prototype, participants could still see the value in creating reports from the data they collect.

Creating Category Schemes. While there were similarities across the category schemes developed by participants, every scheme was different. For instance, different Twitter messages were deemed more or less important depending on the type of PIO that was looking at the message. This finding supports the design of PMA in which users can customize their category schemes. However, some participants were unsure what categories to start with. These participants wanted to have a categorization scheme developed by someone else that they could then modify to fit their needs.

The names PIOs chose for categories during the card sorting exercise and the prototype testing proved to be a powerful organization method that aided in sensemaking [43]. A common organizing method was to categorize tweets by the agency that sent them. While other participants named categories with the name of a coworker or an organization to which they wanted to route tweets for processing. Another method involved naming a category to describe the physical action that the participant wanted to take on the message (e.g., call someone, reply to, verify, and follow up). A couple of PIOs created a "retweet" category where they placed important messages that they wanted to retweet.

Evaluating Tweet Content. Trust was important for PIOs when deciding how to process tweet information. Most PIOs looked at the Twitter account associated with a tweet to determine if the information could be trusted. Since data from real local events were used in testing, sometimes a PIO would recognize a Twitter account as belonging to an organization or person that s/he had worked with before. Previous experience could then be used to judge whether the information was trustworthy. When the Twitter account was not recognized, PIOs relied on other mechanisms to determine whether the information could be trusted, such as checking the Twitter account profile associated with the message or contacting the user of the account directly.

Adapting the Sorting Task to Practice. The PMA mid-fidelity prototype forced users to categorize tweets before more tweets could be retrieved. During testing, we discovered that this method of categorizing tweets prevented PIOs from effectively monitoring Twitter data. If the Twitter stream moved quickly, PIOs would get a backlog of tweets that needed to be sorted before they could view the most recent tweets. Further, sometimes PIOs did not want to do anything with a tweet, but the prototype design kept the tweet in the interface as long as it was not categorized, preventing a new tweet from taking its place. To work around this restriction, some PIOs created a "discard" category where they could drop tweets they didn't want to handle. Based on these findings, we significantly redesigned the prototype.

5.3 Cycle 3: Usability Testing with High-Fidelity Prototype

Using feedback from Cycle 2, we refined the mid-fidelity prototype and started moving toward a functional high-fidelity prototype. This new prototype has two modes (streaming and archive) and operates in much the same way that the final prototype does (described above). We also modified the appearance of tweets in PMA to include more information about the sender of each tweet. In addition, we added the ability to reply to a Twitter message so that PIOs could easily contact the source of each tweet. We also added the ability to retweet a message.

5.3.1 Evaluation Procedure

We recruited seven new PIO participants from a state-wide PIO organization to step through a set of tasks designed to test and improve the usability of PMA. Each test session lasted approximately one hour.

Before testing PMA, we asked each participant a few questions about their background to better understand their experience and skill level as a PIO. The interface testing component began with a brief overview of PMA's features, following which, we gave each participant a list of tasks to complete using PMA. Tasks focused on testing the major features. The session concluded with a short interview to better understand the PIO's experience with the application and whether they would use PMA for their work.

PIO participants were encouraged to use the think-aloud method [17] as they stepped through the tasks. We observed the participants and took notes as they completed the tasks. Sessions were audio-recorded for future reference and analysis.

5.3.2 Evaluation Results

This usability evaluation of PMA yielded many user interface issues. We organize these findings by the different tasks that PIO participants were asked to perform.

Creating Search Terms. Participants liked the ability to create as many search terms as they needed. Most PIOs finished this step with little difficulty, but there were several questions about how to construct the search terms. For example, participants wondered if they should include the "#" symbol when searching for a hashtag.

Using the Live Streaming Mode. PIOs found the features associated with each tweet helpful. Study participants also appreciated that usernames were clickable and would open the Twitter profile of that user. When investigating a tweet of interest, PIOs wanted to know more about the sender and providing a quick link to the sender's profile helps them do this. All URLs that appear in tweet messages are clickable as well. The information provided in these URLs is publically available so PIOs want to be sure that it is accurate. Finally, PIOs were asked to experiment with pausing and resuming the live stream. PIOs saw value in this feature because there were many times when the tweet stream moved too quickly for them to process in real-time.

Creating Categories and Categorizing Tweets. The ability to create their own categories let PIOs customize the interface to suit the particular needs of their organization and the events to which they respond. However, when dragging a tweet over a category, participants found that the highlighting of the category did not change, which made it difficult to know if dropping the tweet in that location would place it in the desired category.

Creating Rules. The rule feature can help automate categorization and speed the social media organization and sense-making processes of PIOs. A common scenario for using rules that many PIOs identified as useful during testing is to help them extract messages about their own organization. Once all the messages from their organization are in one category, they can simply export the messages into a file that they can store as a record. Rules can also be helpful if there is a particular user or key word within their search results that a PIO wants to watch.

PIOs encountered several problems with the Rule Management interface. First, PIOs expected to enter values for a new rule before it was created, so it was confusing that a default rule was created that they must then edit. Second, participants were unsure how to edit the rule values in the table, despite instruction provided at the top of the interface. Third, the editing capability was unreliable; participants usually had to click on a value several times before they could edit it. Finally, once a participant changed a rule value they were required to push an "OK" button that would save the changes. Often participants lost their changes when they navigated away from a field without clicking the "Ok" button.

Using the Archive Mode. In archive mode, users can search collected tweets for the current event by entering search parameters in the text boxes contained directly under the table header row. Most PIOs understood how to use the search capability without explanation and all PIOs found basic searches easy to perform. Some wanted to perform complex searches, however, which proved difficult. For example, several PIOs tried to enter a time or date to search by and were unsuccessful because they had not entered the query in the correct format.

Exporting. All PIO participants reported liking the export feature and wanted to use the resulting Excel spreadsheet as a record of Twitter activity. During one test session, a PIO participant chose a particularly active search term and by the time they got to the export task, PMA had collected over 20,000 tweets. PMA's export function failed to create a spreadsheet, which was concerning because relative to other emergency Twitter data sets this number is small. This issue is part of a larger set of concerns around the scalability of PMA that we address in a later cycle.

Reporting. PIO participants liked the ability to generate reports as often as they like using the most recent collected data. They imagined creating daily or even hourly reports to share with their team. Also, because this report is generated as a Microsoft Word Document, one PIO saw the potential to enhance the report by inserting her own commentary and interpretations of the data.

5.4 Cycle 4: Field Testing with High-Fidelity Prototype

We improved the PMA prototype based on the usability results of the previous cycle. Changes included making the creation of a new event and the rule management interface more intuitive, as well as improving the contextual help.

5.4.1 Evaluation Procedure

For this study, we wanted to understand how PMA might be used in a contextual setting. The field study took place at an emergency operations center (EOC) in Denver, Colorado, during a difficult wildfire season for the state of Colorado. Four PIOs (a complete sample) participated in this field study. We sat next to each PIO for a one-on-one session where we demonstrated PMA and its features. PIOs were then asked to use PMA while we observed them. The length of observation varied by participant (between 15 and 30 minutes). Conducting these sessions was sometimes difficult because the PIOs had responsibilities that drew their attention away from using PMA.

Throughout the study, we took extensive notes using a datasheet developed beforehand and we audio recorded each of the one-on-one sessions. We also took photos of the EOC workspace. To organize and group notes from the session, we used the affinity diagram method [3].

5.4.2 Evaluation Results

Overall perceptions of PMA were positive. All PIOs stated that they would use the tool and that it provides a significant improvement over current practice.

Supporting Analysis. Within the context of the Colorado Wildfires, PIOs found several ways PMA could help them analyze the social media data they were monitoring. One PIO stated that when examining social media data around an event, she is usually trying to answer a question. For example, "What are the public's concerns around fire containment?" To answer this question, she her team would need to capture relevant information and then query for keywords like "containment." She was excited that PMA's tweet collection and search features would allow her team to perform this type of analysis.

Another PIO categorized the tweets she monitored around sentiment so that she could analyze how members of the public felt about the Colorado wildfires. She created categories such as "angry", "sad", "confused", and "grateful" and dropped tweets into these categories. She explained how organizing tweets in this manner would help her understand the public's response to the event and their perceptions of the messages she released as a PIO. She could then shape future messages to address the mood of the public. She also imagined creating a report that would chart the sentiment category tweets.

Another PIO was proficient in Excel. When she saw that PMA could export Twitter data into an Excel spreadsheet, she knew she could create graphs and statistics from this data that would help her analyze the event's Twitter traffic.

Supporting Documentation. PIO participants described the cumbersome and inefficient ways in which they currently captured social media activity. One PIO used a screen capture tool to document the tweets she sends during an event. The resulting screen shots are stored in large pdf files that are difficult to parse and read. Another PIO described how several members of her team worked full-time for two days taking screen shots of social media activity following a recent event.

PMA lets users collect Twitter messages around an event and export these messages into an Excel Spreadsheet that can be used for documentation. All PIOs noted how simple it was to document tweets using PMA and how much time such a capability could save.

Supporting Reports. The PIOs in this study were assigned to the EOC team because each was seen as a social media leader within his/her respective organization. Interestingly, despite a proven track record of successful social media use, these PIOs still felt they had to prove the value of the technology. Not only would PMA's reporting function save PIOs significant time by automatically generating metrics, charts, and graphs, but it would also help them convince management of the usefulness of social media.

Participants shared many ideas about the types of metrics they would like to see in the PMA social media report. One metric is the number of people who potentially saw each tweet they sent during an event (also known as the tweet reach). PIOs also wanted to see how many times each tweet was retweeted and which messages were retweeted the most. One PIO wanted PMA to report how often keywords that she specifies appear in collected tweets.

5.5 Cycle 5: Usability Testing with Final PMA Prototype

By this point, PMA had seen many improvements; however, its use by PIOs in the field was still limited. When the number of tweets collected reached roughly 50,000 messages, creating reports and viewing live message streams became difficult—often causing the application to error or timeout. Further, PMA was running on a small webserver that did not scale well with heavier use. These limitations made PMA hard to use outside of a controlled setting. Thus, to increase PMA's data scalability and deployability, we made significant enhancements to PMA during 2014 and the spring of 2015. These enhancements include optimizing the database configuration and queries, streamlining report generation algorithms, fixing remaining usability issues found in Cycles 3 & 4, and moving the application to use Amazon Web Services.

5.5.1 Evaluation Procedure

We ran a series of tests to measure how the performance improvements we made to PMA improved system response and scalability and decreased the time to generate reports on large data sets. Then we conducted a usability study to verify these changes using the same procedure described in Cycle 3. Three new PIOs were recruited from a state-wide PIO organization to participate in this study.

5.5.2 Evaluation Results

In this most recent testing (2015), we found that PIOs still struggled with using Twitter, particularly archiving and reporting information found there. Thus, we still found a strong need for PMA. The performance tests showed marked improvement in PMA's report generation feature. Reports that used to take more than 30 seconds to generate (the point at which PMA would timeout), now take less than 1 second. Overall, the participants in the usability study found the application intuitive, but some of the features were not always understood.

Creating an Event. The names of some of the fields were confusing and did not help the user understand the fields' purpose. The participants found that some of the form fields to create an event were ambiguous. One participant did not understand the format of the information to be entered in the "location" field. All participants did not know what to do with the "summary" field on the create event page.

Setting Search Terms. One participant could not determine how to edit a search term, as there was no "Edit" button like there was a "Delete" button. Editing the search term by double-clicking was not intuitive for that participant but was understood by others.

Reporting. All participants liked the reporting feature and the parameters provided for generating reports. However, one participant suggested that an hourly report for the "Twitter Daily Activity" report feature would be helpful.

5.6 Overall Evaluation Findings

Not only can PMA help individual emergency PIOs with their social media needs, but it can also help the larger PIO community. One participant shared how many PIOs are struggling to manage their current duties. It can be overwhelming for these PIOs to adopt social media into their communication plan because it can require resources and skills that they do not have. Other PIOs are using social media but they only have bare minimum support. This participant expressed the belief that PMA could provide these PIOs with the tools they need to make social media manageable and possibly even efficient.

5.6.1 Unexpected Use

At the conclusion of each test session, we asked the PIOs if they would use PMA and if so, how. All PIOs responded that they would use PMA—some even asked when they could begin. Most of the ways these PIOs imagined using the tool have been covered in previous sections; however, we describe two uses of the tool that we did not expect below.

The first use came from a PIO who imagined using PMA everyday (during emergency and non-emergency times) to track tweets that refer to his organization. He wants to understand how people talk about and refer to his organization and learn from it.

The second use came from a PIO who had acted as a representative for the family of a shooting victim. This PIO helped the family respond to media requests and understand what they could and could not talk about given the pending criminal case against the shooter. Because the case was high profile, the PIO received nearly 300 media calls per day at one point. The PIO talked about how PMA could monitor and archive the positive things people shared about the victim over Twitter, and a record of these messages could then be given to the victim's family.

5.6.2 Desired Features & Future Work

The most requested feature was to add support for more social media platforms. We began with Twitter because it is the most accessible platform (i.e., data is available through a public API and messages are 140 characters or less) and we know from past research that it is used in emergency events [8, 38, 42]. We plan to add this support in the future.

Several suggestions centered on the search options for collecting tweets. Some participants wanted to perform complex search queries, such as searching by date, location, or Twitter username. Other participants wanted to search by geographic region. Another frequently requested feature was the ability to perform a back-in-time search for each newly activated search term. A back-in-time option would allow PIOs to collect previous Twitter activity that matches their search terms even if it occurred before they activated the search. PMA could use the Twitter Search API to accomplish this task.

Finally, a natural extension of this research would be to make PMA publically available for anyone to use. Once this is done, a prolonged study of PMA use by PIOs in real-world settings could take place. Though all PIOs in this research claimed they would use PMA, an extended study of their use would reveal if PMA continues to meet PIO social media needs beyond initial adoption. This type of study would also likely provide insight into the operation of emergency management organizations and the changes that result to that organization from the use of PMA.

6. DISCUSSION

In this research, we employed a human-centered approach to design and development. This approach advocates that to create technology that meets user needs, the target users must actively participate in the design and evaluation process; therefore, we involved the study subjects—PIOs—at every stage of this research. As we built prototypes, we consulted with PIOs to ensure that the proposed tools met their needs. We also involved PIOs in the testing and evaluation of PMA at various stages of development. This paper documents the results of this human-centered, longitudinal design and development effort. Contributions include the design, development, and evaluation of PMA, suggestions for how to conduct human-centered research with emergency responders, as well as insight into how social media is changing PIO work practice.

6.1 Obtaining Research Access to Events

When an emergency event occurs, emergency responders (such as PIOs) are often overwhelmed. Thus, during an event is usually not the time to establish new relationships and embed oneself in the response effort as a researcher. Further, responders are unlikely to use untested and unproven tools during this time, nor to spend the time to be trained in their use. A better way to obtain research access to an active emergency event is to establish and maintain relationships with emergency responders beforehand. Our strategy has included training and becoming certified to act in the PIO position as well as participating in local emergency exercises. Unfortunately, due to these challenges, PMA has yet to be tested in a highly realistic non-supervised setting. We are currently pursuing this type of testing as a next step for this research.

6.2 Balancing the Researcher Role

A human-centered research approach necessitates close researcher and participant involvement. During this research, we developed friendships with many of the participants, which sometimes made it difficult to maintain an objective perspective. On the other hand, building rapport with participants offered benefits, such as access to protected research sites and increased willingness to participate in research activities.

Because we are PIO researchers, we sometimes found that PIOs looked to us as experts on their work; they did not necessarily trust their own experience as a valid perspective. We tried to combat this issue by encouraging PIOs to share their experiences, and we only related opinions or the experiences of other PIOs when deemed necessary.

Finally, at times PIOs were less critical of PMA because they knew we had created it and they did not want to offend. We assured participants that we would not be upset by their comments and that we needed their constructive comments to improve the tool. Also, because PIOs knew we had created PMA, we often felt pressured by PIO participants to make PMA available as quickly as possible and to create custom features that would benefit the specific needs of one PIO.

6.3 Reflecting on Changing PIO Practice

Conducting these evaluation studies offered new insight into the many ways PIOs could use PMA to support their work. PIOs shared examples of how PMA could be used in all types and sizes of emergency events. Participants also provided insight into how PMA could be used as a tool for analysis among multiple emergency responders. Before conducting these studies, we thought that much of the advantage PMA offered over other applications was to facilitate the task of sorting tweets into user-defined categories. These studies revealed, however, that the biggest advantage of PMA lies in its ability to analyze, document, and report tweets once they have been sorted.

These abilities play a major role in a PIOs capacity to create and collaboratively construct important information for the public during an emergency event. The ability to document and report social media activity around an event also plays a role in helping PIOs bring social media data to response organizations in an actionable and accessible way.

We found that the most popular features of PMA reflect the current state of emergency management—a kind of probe for understanding PIO needs in a changing socio-technical environment. For example, interest in PMA's documentation feature reflects how PIOs are struggling to find ways to effectively document and share social media activity within their organizations. The ability to create reports was also a popular feature and reflects how PIOs are facing pressure within their organizations to prove the value of social media through statistics and reports.

PMA is a unique application that fills the specific social media needs of PIOs in a way that no other single application currently can. Though the tool is simple, it has the potential to simplify and ease the transition as PIOs work together to incorporate social media into their response efforts.

7. CONCLUSION

In this research, we designed and developed a novel application—grounded in empirical understandings of PIO work—to help PIOs monitor, analyze, document, and report social media data around an emergency event. Using a human-centered approach, PIOs participated in the exploration, design, and evaluation phases of this research, resulting in an application (PMA) that all participants claimed they would use. Using social media in current PIO work practice requires a different set of skills and tools than before to manage and perform required tasks. PMA helps to ease the transition as PIOs learn to use and adapt social media and, as such, helps them perform their jobs more effectively in a changing technical and institutional environment.

8. ACKNOWLEDGMENTS

We thank the PIOs who participated in this research. We also thank Leysia Palen and members of Project EPIC at the University of Colorado Boulder for their support on this project.

9. REFERENCES

[1] Abel, F., Hauff, G.-J., Houben, K.T. and Stronkman, R. 2012. Semantics + Filtering + Search = Twitcident Exploring Information in Social Web Streams. *Proceedings of the 23rd ACM Conferenece on Hypertext and Social Media* (New York, NY, Jun. 2012), 285–294.

[2] American Red Cross 2011. *Social Media in Disasters and Emergencies*.

[3] Beyer, H. and Holtzblatt, K. 1997. *Contextual Design: Defining Customer-Centered Systems (Interactive Technologies)*. Morgan Kaufmann.

[4] Briones, R.L., Kuch, B., Liu, B.F. and Yin, Y. 2011. Keeping Up with the Digital Age: How the American Red Cross uses Social Media to Build Relationships. *Public Relations Review*. 37, 1 (Mar. 2011), 37–43.

[5] Bruns, A. and Burgess, J.E. 2012. Local and Global Responses to Disaster: #eqnz and the Christchurch Earthquake. *Proceedings of the Disaster and Emergency Management Conference* (Brisbane, QLD, 2012), 86–103.

[6] Cameron, M.A., Power, R., Robinson, B. and Yin, J. 2012. Emergency Situation Awareness from Twitter for Crisis Management. *Proceedings of the 21st International Conference Companion on World Wide Web* (New York, NY, 2012), 695–698.

[7] Caragea, C., McNeese, N., Jaisw, A., Traylor, G., Kim, H.-W., Mitra, P., Wu, D., Tapia, A.H., Giles, L., Jansen, B.J. and Yen, J. 2011. Classifying Text Messages for the Haiti Earthquake. *Proceedings of the Information Systems for Crisis Response and Management Conference (ISCRAM 2011)* (Lisbon, Portugal, 2011).

[8] Denef, S., Bayerl, P.S. and Kaptein, N. 2013. Social Media and the Police-Tweeting Practices of British Police Forces during the August 2011 Riots. *Proceedings of the 2013 Conference on Human Factors in Computing Systems (CHI 2013)* (New York, NY, 2013), 3471–3480.

[9] Fraustino, J.D., Liu, B. and Jin, Y. 2012. *Social Media Use during Disasters: A Review of the Knowledge Base and Gaps*. START.

[10] Hootsuite http://hootsuite.com.

[11] Hughes, A.L. 2014. Participatory Design for the Social Media Needs of Emergency Public Information Officers. *Proceedings of the Information Systems for Crisis Response and Management Conference (ISCRAM 20014)* (University Park, PA, 2014).

[12] Hughes, A.L. and Palen, L. 2012. The Evolving Role of the Public Information Officer: An Examination of Social Media in Emergency Management. *Journal of Homeland Security and Emergency Management*. 9, 1 (2012).

[13] Hughes, A.L., Palen, L., Sutton, J., Liu, S.B. and Vieweg, S. 2008. "Site-Seeing " in Disaster: An Examination of On-Line Social Convergence. *Proceedings of the Information Systems for Crisis Response and Management Conference (ISCRAM 2008)* (Washington D.C., 2008).

[14] Hughes, A.L., St. Denis, L.A., Palen, L. and Anderson, K.M. 2014. Online Public Communications by Police & Fire Services during the 2012 Hurricane Sandy. *Proceedings of the 2014 International Conference on Human Factors in Computing Systems (CHI 2014)* (New York, NY, 2014), 1505–1514.

[15] Kuniavsky, M. 2003. *Observing the User Experience: A Practitioner's Guide to User Research*. Morgan Kaufmann.

[16] Latonero, M. and Shklovski, I. 2011. Emergency Management, Twitter, and Social Media Evangelism. *International Journal of Information Systems for Crisis Response and Management*. 3, 4 (2011), 1–16.

[17] Lewis, C. 1982. *Using the Thinking-Aloud Method in Cognitive Interface Design*. Technical Report #9265.

[18] Ludwig, T., Reuter, C., Siebigteroth, T. and Pipek, V. 2015. CrowdMonitor: Mobile Crowd Sensing for Assessing Physical and Digital Activities of Citizens During Emergencies. *Proceedings of the 33rd Annual ACM Conference on Human Factors in Computing Systems* (New York, NY, USA, 2015), 4083–4092.

[19] Marcus, A., Bernstein, M.S., Badar, O., Karger, D.R., Madden, S. and Miller, R.C. 2011. Twitinfo: Aggregating and Visualizing Microblogs for Event Exploration. *Proceedings of the SIGCHI Conference on Human Factors in Computing Systems* (New York, NY, USA, 2011), 227–236.

[20] Meier, P. and Brodock, K. 2008. *Crisis Mapping Kenya's Election Violence: Comparing Mainstream News, Citizen Journalism and Ushahidi.* Harvard University.

[21] Morrow, N., Mock, N., Papendieck, A. and Kocmich, N. 2011. *Independent Evaluation of the Ushahidi Haiti Project.* Development Information Systems International.

[22] Muller, M.J. 1992. Retrospective on a year of participatory design using the PICTIVE technique. *Proceedings of the SIGCHI conference on Human factors in computing systems* (New York, NY, USA, 1992), 455–462.

[23] Palen, L., Anderson, K.M., Mark, G., Martin, J., Sicker, D., Palmer, M. and Grunwald, D. 2010. A Vision for Technology-Mediated Support for Public Participation & Assistance in Mass Emergencies & Disasters. *Proceedings of the 2010 ACM-BCS Visions of Computer Science Conference* (Edinburgh, UK, 2010), 1–12.

[24] Palen, L. and Liu, S.B. 2007. Citizen Communications in Crisis: Anticipating a Future of ICT-supported Public Participation. *Proceedings of the 2007 Conference on Human Factors in Computing Systems (CHI 2007)* (New York, NY, 2007), 727–736.

[25] Palen, L. and Vieweg, S. 2008. The Emergence of Online Widescale Interaction in Unexpected Events. *2008 ACM Proceedings of Computer Supported Cooperative Work Conference* (New York, NY, 2008), 117–126.

[26] Pohl, D. Social Media Analysis for Crisis Management: A Brief Summary. *Special Technical Community on Social Networking E-Letter.* 2, 1.

[27] Qu, Y., Wu, P.F. and Wang, X. 2009. Online Community Response to Major Disaster: A Study of Tianya Forum in the 2008 Sichuan Earthquake. *Proceedings of the 2009 Hawaii International Conference on System Sciences (HICSS 2009)* (Washington, DC, 2009), 1–11.

[28] Radian 6 http://www.exacttarget.com/products/social-media-marketing/radian6.

[29] Reuter, C., Ludwig, T., Kaufhold, M.-A. and Pipek, V. 2015. XHELP: Design of a Cross-Platform Social-Media Application to Support Volunteer Moderators in Disasters. *Proceedings of the 33rd Annual ACM Conference on Human Factors in Computing Systems* (New York, NY, USA, 2015), 4093–4102.

[30] Reuter, C., Ludwig, T. and Pipek, V. 2014. Ad Hoc Participation in Situation Assessment: Supporting Mobile Collaboration in Emergencies. *ACM Trans. Comput.-Hum. Interact.* 21, 5 (Nov. 2014), 26:1–26:26.

[31] Starbird, K. and Palen, L. 2012. (How) Will the Revolution be Retweeted?: Information Propagation in the 2011 Egyptian Uprising. *Proceedings of the 2012 Conference on Computer Supported Cooperative Work (CSCW 2012)* (New York, NY, 2012), 7–16.

[32] Starbird, K. and Palen, L. 2011. "Voluntweeters:" Self-Organizing by Digital Volunteers in Times of Crisis. *Proceedings of the 2011 Conference on Human Factors in Computing Systems (CHI 2011)* (New York, NY, 2011), 1071–1080.

[33] Starbird, K. and Stamberger, J. 2010. Tweak the Tweet: Leveraging Microblogging Proliferation with a Prescriptive Grammar to Support Citizen Reporting. *Proceedings of the Information Systems for Crisis Response and Management Conference (ISCRAM 2010)* (Seattle, WA, 2010).

[34] St. Denis, L.A., Hughes, A.L. and Palen, L. 2012. Trial by Fire: The Deployment of Trusted Digital Volunteers in the 2011 Shadow Lake Fire. *Proceedings of the Information Systems for Crisis Response and Management Conference (ISCRAM 2012)* (Vancouver, BC, 2012).

[35] St. Denis, L.A., Palen, L. and Anderson, K.M. 2014. Mastering Social Media: An Analysis of Jefferson County's Communications during the 2013 Colorado Floods. *Proceedings of the Information Systems for Crisis Response and Management Conference (ISCRAM 20014)* (2014).

[36] Stockdale, G. and Sood, R. 1989. *Emergency Public Information: A Quick Response Study of Coalinga.* Natural Hazards Research and Applications Information Center, Institute of Behavioral Science, University of Colorado at Boulder.

[37] Sutton, J.N. 2009. Social Media Monitoring and the Democratic National Convention: New Tasks and Emergent Processes. *Journal of Homeland Security and Emergency Management.* 6, 1 (2009).

[38] Sutton, J.N., Spiro, E., Butts, C., Fitzhugh, S., Johnson, B. and Greczek, M. 2013. Tweeting the Spill: Online Informal Communications, Social Networks, and Conversational Microstructures during the Deepwater Horizon Oilspill. *International Journal of Information Systems for Crisis Response and Management.* 5, 1 (2013), 58–76.

[39] Sutton, J.N., Spiro, E., Fitzhugh, S., Johnson, B., Gibson, B. and Butts, C.T. 2014. Online Message Amplification in the Boston Bombing Response. *Proceedings of the Information Systems for Crisis Response and Management Conference (ISCRAM 20014)* (2014).

[40] TweetDeck http://tweetdeck.twitter.com.

[41] TweetFall http://twitterfall.com/.

[42] Vieweg, S., Hughes, A.L., Starbird, K. and Palen, L. 2010. Microblogging During Two Natural Hazards Events: What Twitter May Contribute to Situational Awareness. *Proceedings of the ACM 2010 Conference on Computer Human Interaction* (New York, NY, 2010), 1079–1088.

[43] Weick, K.E. 1993. The Collapse of Sensemaking in Organizations: The Mann Gulch Disaster. *Administrative Science Quarterly.* 38, 4 (1993).

Challenges of CI Initiatives in a Political Unstable Situation - Case Study of a Computer Club in a Refugee Camp

Konstantin Aal, Marios Mouratidis, Anne Weibert, Volker Wulf
University of Siegen
Kohlbettstr. 15,
57072 Siegen
+49 271 740-3383
[konstantin.aal; marios.mouratidis; anne.weibert; volker.wulf]@uni-siegen.de

ABSTRACT

This poster describes the research around computer clubs in Palestinian refugee camps and the various lessons learned during the establishment of this intervention such the importance of the physical infrastructure (e.g. clean room, working hardware), soft technologies (e.g. knowledge transfer through workshops), social infrastructure (e.g. reliable partners in the refugee camp, partner from the university) and social capital (e.g. shared vision and values of all stakeholders). These important insights can be transferred on other interventions in similar unstable environments.

Keywords

Community informatics, Computer club, Refugee camp, West Bank.

1. INTRODUCTION

Community informatics (CI) focuses on the development of a community, and on chances that come with community-based socio-technical initiatives [5,6]. These initiatives are concerned with the improvement of aspects of local life as well as increasing chances to interact not only locally but on a broader, even global scale [11].

CI research has investigated the factors that are central to the development and use of these initiatives and involved technologies, as well as the diffusion of Information and Communication Technologies (ICTs) in local communities and barriers hindering their usage (e.g. [8,9]). Special attention has been paid to factors securing the sustainability of CI initiatives [11], emphasizing the importance of social capital and the "need to capitalize on the community's social infrastructure, working with the widest variety of community groups and organisations to ensure that all those who stand to benefit from the CI initiative have the opportunity to become involved, both as a means of encouraging participation and as a source of support while skill and confidence is developed".

Situations of political unrest, instability and rapidly developing societal changes come with specific requirements to the sustainable development of socio-technical initiatives [2,10,13,15,16].

GROUP '16, November 13-16, 2016, Sanibel Island, FL, USA
ACM 978-1-4503-4276-6/16/11.
http://dx.doi.org/10.1145/2957276.2996281

We are exploring these factors by studying the development of a local computer club initiative [1] in a refugee camp in Palestine. Initiated to support marginalized Palestinian refugee communities to positively engage in their own society and in the Palestinian-Israeli conflict-to-peace transformation process, as well as to network Palestinians among themselves, thus promoting their integration into the local societies and finally enabling them to access the information society [1:111], these clubs have experienced a number of ups and downs. One of these clubs was recently revived after a period of inactivity. Our study of this revival process points to a set of factors that are central to the sustainable development of a socio-technical initiative in a setting of political unrest, instability and rapid change.

2. Related Works

2.1 Community Building with ICT

The emerging field of community informatics examines the interactions between local communities and ICT [5]. CI initiatives offer novel approaches and increased opportunities for community members to participate in local and globally discourses, which can lead to a greater range of different activities in the economic, civic and social areas [11]. CI research tries to understand how these projects and initiatives can be better implemented by taking into account the social factors that affect CI development and use [9].

Various works such as community technology centers, online participation and community access programs in rural areas seemed to be successful CI initiatives [9], while others have raised concerns about the real impact of these initiatives on communities [4].

The intercultural computer club initiative 'come_IN' in Germany have been initialized to provide open, yet guided access to information and computer technologies and related skills for often marginalized or disprivileged groups in intercultural neighborhoods. With this the clubs a) contribute to a bridging of the so called 'digital divide', and b) foster integration processes at the local neighborhood level (e.g. [12,14]).

3. Methods

3.1 Research Setting

The first computer club outside of Germany was established inside the Palestinian refugee camp Al Amari in Ramallah [1]. Al Amari is a Palestinian refugee camp in the West Bank near the centre of Ramallah. Like most of the other refugee camps Al Amari was established in 1949, built on plots of land, which is leased by the UNRWA from the Hashemite Kingdom of Jordan. The inhabitants of the camp were expelled or fled from their homes in nowadays Israel, during the Arab-Israeli War in 1948. A high population density as well as crowded and precarious living conditions characterizes the camp.

The Palestinian refugee population can be characterized as a parallel society, having their own governance within those camps (Palestinian Authority (PA) usually is not very active inside the refugee camps) and their own set of values and beliefs. They are generally considered to be poorly dressed, behave aggressively, and use street language. There is not a lot of interaction between refugee population and the surrounding society. Most of the urban population had never been inside a refugee camp, although they live in Ramallah or close to it.

3.2 Computer Club

A consortium of a university partner (an IT-center), a local partner from the refugee camp (a youth center) and the German partner was created to establish the computer club. The youth center provided a clean room and helped to create awareness for the initiative. The IT-center recruited student volunteers from the university who were willing to work in the refugee camp; this work also counted as community work, because one of the graduation requirements at the Birzeit University since 1972, needs the students to perform 120 hours of community service (Volunteer #4). The German researchers were responsible for the administrative work, adapting the computer club concept to the local environment and circumstances and providing educational support such as workshops and presentation the computer club concept [1,17].

The weekly sessions were accompanied by the local coordinator and the student volunteers, a team with 3-5 members. The club lasted for one hour and around 20 girls and boys attended the activity. At the beginning all participants were sitting together at the "round table" to discuss current projects or think about new ideas, usually current events (e.g. Israeli soldiers entering the camp, demonstrations, bad living conditions) in the refugee camp had a major impact on the project.

The computer clubs' activities faded out and they closed a year after the opening. The IT-center merged with another center based on budget cuts from the university and the local coordinator could not maintain his engagement with the computer club project. The exchange program *YALLAH* (You all are hackers)[1] realized different, cooperative projects of German and Palestinian students over the period of one month; one of these projects was to reopen the computer club and conduct weekly sessions.

3.3 Data Collection and Analysis

We adhere to principles of Participatory Action Research by Kemmis & McTaggert [7] regarding the question "how to act in the field". With this approach we as authors were part of the field to investigate meaningful, field-oriented insights. The visits were documented via field notes (German researchers observed the situation and non-verbal interactions, sometimes with native speakers translating conversations on site while observing), photos and for a few occasions also videos. Additionally, 5 semi-structured interviews with student volunteers and the local Palestinian coordinator were conducted in English, informal interviews with the person in charge for the youth centre supported the interview statements and provided us with a more detailed understanding of the local setting.

A thematic analysis or TA approach was used to analyse the collected data [3]. This started quickly in the field to bring up questions and sharpen the research lens through daily exchange and discussion of the field notes and impressions between the on-site field researchers, interspersed by occasional Skype calls with senior researchers at home to ensure inter-coder reliability. Afterwards, the analysis was discussed and finalized at home together with researchers not involved in the field work.

4. Findings and Discussion

This chapter describes the different influencing factors resulting from the analysis which affect the success or failures of interventions such as the computer clubs. Based on the theoretical framework developed by Simpson [11]; this framework highlights the interplay between physical infrastructure, soft technologies, social infrastructure and social capital. *Physical infrastructure* sums up the hard technology, the physical equipment and the location in the community; *soft technology* describes the formal and informal activities such as awareness raising, education, training and other capacity building activities. *Soft technology* outlines the structural arrangements that enable individuals and groups to interact with one another (e.g. networks, volunteerism, community services). *Social capital* is about the social features which are intangible and are outcomes from interaction and participation in local and external networks (shared values; trust; strong sense of community).

4.1 Physical Infrastructure

The youth center was one of the few places in a refugee camp with an open playground and a small little park for children. They provided one of their rarely used rooms for the infrastructure of the computer club. The computers were assembled and installed by the German researchers during their first visits in the West Bank [1]. While the computer club opened for the weekly sessions, the room was cleaned by the administrators of the youth center and they locked the room afterwards.

After closing, the club itself was in bad shape, even for the conditions of the camp. The room, the sanitary facility next to it, furniture and computer terminals were dirty, some workstations missed the mice and keyboards. The volunteers had to clean the room, because after two weeks of being promised by the youth center administration the club would be cleaned, nothing happened. However, one of the teenagers, who always came to the computer club and spent time with the volunteers, when they tried to fix a computer and get everything to work again, actually started helping them to clean the room. After eight weeks of conducting workshops, the room was freshly painted.

At the beginning two uninterruptible power supplies (UPS) were installed, since power blackouts are quite common in the camp, two desktop PCs functioning as desktop virtualization servers for ten terminal computers. The UPS units were unfixable and one of the servers had a corrupt operating system, which caused a malfunction of half of the terminals. The server hardware is proprietary and old, documentation to get it running is scarce. Besides this, there were also twelve educational electronics kits among the equipment which were then used to conduct the workshops to teach the children basic circuits and electronic knowledge.

4.2 Soft Technologies

In the initial phase of the establishment of the computer club, an extensive exchange took place between volunteers, the local coordinator and the German researchers in the form of workshops, presentations. The local partners were also invited to Germany to visit the computer club network and understand the underlying concept. After the withdrawal of the IT-center, the local

[1] http://yallah.exchange/

coordinator reduced his support for the computer club until he finally stopped it entirely. Students kept on conducting workshops in the camp for a month after officially closed.

The volunteers are usually bachelor students from Birzeit University with backgrounds ranging from Computer science to architecture and engineering. There is no specific academic background actually, only that they all have a higher education; this interdisciplinary intended to create an extensive exchange between the students. Volunteers teach themselves: For instance, an electrical engineering student explains the sessions' content to a computer science student.

The knowledge about the computer club concept and how to guide the sessions was shared among the local coordinator, the student volunteers (who visited Germany) and the new student volunteers. This knowledge transfers and training of the new volunteers did not occur any longer, which led to frustration with the work. However, the lack of support, budget and informal context (work in the club was no longer recognized as community service hours) made their work also fade out. In context of the student exchange YALLAH, a group of students worked together on a workshop concept which could be conducted with the hardware at hand. One of the students had a background in electrical engineering (EE) the other in computer science. There where educational electronics kits at hand, so they decided to build workshop concept around those kits. The EE student explained the basic electronics concepts to the computer science student, so they could both teach together. Over the course of four weeks, other students would help in conducting the workshops, they were coached by the two leading students before every respective session. These workshops where a combination of frontal teaching and playful exploration: To explain the flow of electricity and its' influence on connected electronics like motors or LEDs, children were asked to stand up, some had the role of actuators, others played the current, running around on a specified path (the wire) touching the hands of the standing kids, which then raised their arms to indicate that they react to the current. Beforehand however, some basic schematics were drawn and explained on the whiteboard.

4.3 Social Infrastructure

The youth center provides several different activities for children and youngsters in the refugee camp such as dancing, self-defense and singing classes, they already gained positive reputation based on these activities and are well-known in the camp. This reputation within the camp population supported the computer club to gain trust. The youth center raised awareness for the workshops via its own Facebook-Page and every session was attended by many girls and boys.

The IT-center announced the computer club project at the university and recruited students as volunteers. The local coordinator used the center for meetings and for experience exchange and educational training. The University partner also coordinated the weekly sessions, managed the financial affairs for the project (money for hardware and transportation) and scheduled the weekly activity in cooperation with the volunteers, who conducted the computer club session.

With their experience in establishing computer clubs in marginalized areas, the German partners' task was to supervise the whole project. Providing workshops and educational training for the student volunteers.

According to Simpsons [11] understanding of elements of sustainable CI initiatives from a social infrastructure perspective, which are important aspects to the computer club context. There have to be organizations like the Birzeit University to recruit and motivate students to volunteer (in this case, getting credit for serving community hours works as a motivator, even though there are also altruistic motives as our findings show), within the youth center serving an organization and community resource. Furthermore, having the youth center administration supporting the endeavor as local champions and the German researchers with their idea of implementing CI projects through the concept of intercultural computer clubs, functioning as change agents. As long as those factors were available, there was a club activity.

As soon as the IT-center merged with another center and the local coordinator discontinued his work, the club officially closed. The volunteers were told *"to not to go there anymore"* (Cf. Interview Volunteer #1). Some volunteers continued to go for a while, but stopped eventually: there was no credit (community hours) for the work, no funding (workshop material, transportation costs), coordination through supervision and support. Volunteers however had and still have altruistic motives apart from having to do community service hours through university. They are very well aware of the refugee camps populations' situation: "*We know they are refugees and not to be too hard on them*". (Volunteer #2)

As long as the club exists as an official endeavor in the university context, there will be volunteers willing to work in it. With the help of a well-known partner inside the refugee camp the trust and support of the inhabitants will be guaranteed.

4.4 Social Capital

After establishing the computer club in the initial phase, some problems between the camp population and the volunteers arose. The student volunteers entering the camp to give a workshop were attacked by some teenagers. As described above, refugee camps in Palestine have their own sets of rules and there seems to be a strong territorial view of the population. Even the PA, which can be seen as Palestinian jurisdiction, does not easily enter those camps. After the attack, in which no one was severely injured, negotiations took place between the local coordinator from the Birzeit University, the administration of the youth center and the camp leadership. Obviously, there was no awareness of why "strangers" enter the camp, without a camp escort. The population was informed about the project and its goals. The "outsiders" where accepted after a while, the coordinator was recognized and also got a nickname. He told us that his car, which he used to park right outside the camp, was vandalized in the beginning, but later the damaging stopped. He and the volunteers gained the trust of the camp population. The volunteers received phone numbers of the kids' parents to inform them in case of last minute changes about the workshops (like delays or cancellations).

Right now, outsiders are welcomed warmly in context of the computer club, because they offer education and activities for the children. Camp population has a very strong sense of belonging (to each other) and community. In the revival process we could observe that volunteers, after visiting the camp for a few times, do not see its society as strange anymore, but as their own and want to help, the altruistic motives, expressed in the interviews, underline this. The joint activities of student volunteers and children over time have an impact on collective identity and have a beneficial effect on perceptions of a stigmatized group. It is obvious that a shared vision of all stakeholders is of utmost importance. The interests of all sides involved need to go into one direction.

German researchers: The first goal is to explore the various scientific implications the computer club has to offer; in order to get valuable insights and useable ethnographic data, it needs to be up and running for a longer period than just a month. Secondly, through this process the goal is to strengthen the community as a whole (inside and outside the camp) and empower Palestinians to be sustainably independent in mean of education.

BZU supervision: Regarding the requirements of the supervision, it should be an employee of the university. Students might not acknowledge another student as a figure of authority and follow instructions or listen to him or her. There can however be a volunteer helping in coordination and supporting the supervisor, however he or she should have good leadership, organizational skills and be fair with all, according to an interviewed volunteer from the initial phase of the club.

BZU Volunteers: The volunteers need a clear and transparent structure of the endeavor, apart from altruistic motives, another motivation is to get credit for volunteering community service hours for their studies. Giving responsibility and ownership (by preparing workshop ideas and conducting them) also motivates to feel responsible for the computer club.

Children: The camp children take any opportunity for after-school activities. Furthermore, they are eager to learn, as we saw, there was usually very interested in participation e.g. when the schools in the camp were on strike, the amount of children attending the session doubled.

5. Conclusion

An intercultural and interdisciplinary team of students explored the reasons for the clubs' closings and revived successfully the Al-Amari computer club. We found out that there are problems in physical infrastructure, soft technologies and social infrastructure as described above. Apart from the actors involved, the infrastructure and the equipment are essential. The workshops conducted, involved electronics kits. The workshops were perceived very positive, but prospects are limited. However, having working computers offers much richer possibilities for workshops in regard to research setting and education. Establishing social capital as means of strong sense of community and shared vision is a major challenge in a population which is strongly marginalized in the Palestinian society and is subject to political unrests. CI initiatives such as the presented computer club overcome barriers and create opportunities for peace-building processes.

The findings indicate that the computer clubs' sessions had a positive impact on all participants (students and children): children may extend their perspective over the boundaries of the refugee camp while acquiring new skills and contacts; the student volunteers gain insights about the reality of the refugee camps and gain a better understanding for the needs, challenges and struggles of the camp inhabitants.

6. REFERENCES

[1] Aal, K., Yerousis, G., Schubert, K., Hornung, D., Stickel, O., and Wulf, V. Come_in@ palestine: adapting a german computer club concept to a Palestinian refugee camp. *Proceedings of the 5th ACM international conference on Collaboration across boundaries: culture, distance & technology*, ACM (2014), 111–120.

[2] Barak-Erez, D. Israel: The security barrier—between international law, constitutional law, and domestic judicial review. *International Journal of Constitutional Law 4*, 3 (2006), 540–552.

[3]Braun, V. and Clarke, V. Using thematic analysis in psychology. *Qualitative Research in Psychology 3*, 2 (2006), 77– 101

[4] Dabinett, G. Regenerating communities in the UK: getting plugged into the information society? *Community Development Journal 35*, 2 (2000), 157–166.

[5] Gurstein, M. Flexible networking, information and communications technology and local economic development. *First Monday 4*, 2 (1999).

[6] Gurstein, M. *Community Informatics: Enabling Communities with Information and Communications Technologies: Enabling Communities with Information and Communications Technologies*. IGI Global, 1999.

[7] Kemmis, S. and McTaggart, R. *Participatory Action Research: Communicative Action and the Public Sphere.* Sage Publications Ltd, 2005.

[8] Kling, R. Learning About Information Technologies and Social Change: The Contribution of Social Informatics. *The Information Society 16*, 3 (2000), 217–232.

[9] O'Neil, D. Assessing community informatics: a review of methodological approaches for evaluating community networks and community technology centers. *Internet Research 12*, 1 (2002), 76–102.

[10] Rabayah, K.S. Economic and social empowerment of women through ICT: a case study of Palestine. *The Journal of Community Informatics 5*, 3-4 (2010).

[11] Simpson, L.E. Community informatics and sustainability: why social capital matters. *The Journal of Community Informatics 1*, 2 (2005).

[12] Stevens, G., Veith, M., and Wulf, V. Bridging among ethnic communities by cross-cultural communities of practice. In *Communities and Technologies 2005*. Springer, 2005, 377–396.

[13] Stickel, O., Hornung, D., Aal, K., Rohde, M., and Wulf, V. 3D Printing with Marginalized Children—An Exploration in a Palestinian Refugee Camp. In N. Boulus-Rødje, G. Ellingsen, T. Bratteteig, M. Aanestad and P. Bjørn, eds., *ECSCW 2015: Proceedings of the 14th European Conference on Computer Supported Cooperative Work, 19-23 September 2015, Oslo, Norway*. Springer International Publishing, Cham, 2015, 83–102.

[14] Weibert, A. and Wulf, V. "All of a sudden we had this dialogue...": intercultural computer clubs' contribution to sustainable integration. *Proceedings of the 3rd international conference on Intercultural collaboration*, ACM (2010), 93–102.

[15] West, A.R. Technology Related Dangers: The Issue of Development and Security for Marginalized Groups in South Africa. *The Journal of Community Informatics 2*, 3 (2007).

[16] Wulf, V., Aal, K., Abu Kteish, I., et al. Fighting against the wall: social media use by political activists in a Palestinian village. ACM Press (2013), 1979.

[17] Yerousis, G., Aal, K., Rekowski, T. von, Randall, D.W., Rohde, M., and Wulf, V. Computer-Enabled Project Spaces: Connecting with Palestinian Refugees across Camp Boundaries. ACM Press (2015).

Privacy and Weight Loss Apps: A First Look at How Women with Eating Disorders Use Social Features

Elizabeth V. Eikey
The Pennsylvania State University
334 IST Building
University Park, PA 16802
+1-949-438-1337
eveikey@psu.edu

ABSTRACT

Women with eating disorders benefit from using social and community features of apps because they can get social support and information about their disorder. Although seeking help online may be easier than getting face-to-face treatment, there still may be a number of privacy concerns to sharing information, especially on apps not specifically intended for those with eating disorders, such as weight loss apps. Women with eating disorders are using weight loss apps, but are they using features that could help them get support for their disorder? This research begins to answer this question by presenting preliminary results from a qualitative study on how women with eating disorders use community and social features of weight loss apps. Early findings suggest women with eating disorders rarely use the community and social features of weight loss apps. This work highlights the tradeoffs between sharing information and privacy and has implications for app design.

CCS Concepts

• **Human-centered computing → Ubiquitous and mobile computing → Ubiquitous and mobile computing systems and tools**

Keywords

Eating disorders; weight loss apps; mobile technology; privacy; social computing; stigma

1. INTRODUCTION

It is estimated that 20 million women in the United States have an eating disorder [16, 21]. Women with eating disorders benefit from participating in online communities [9]. Prior studies have found technologies that facilitate social support are helpful to users with eating disorders [2, 24], and a number of studies have found technology can be a useful tool for eating disorder recovery [2, 8, 24]. However, do users with eating disorders want to use the community and social features of mobile health applications (apps), especially if those apps are not specifically intended for users with eating disorders?

Because of the stigma often associated with eating disorders and other mental health conditions, women with eating disorders may be reluctant to participate in online communities and utilize social features of health apps like weight loss apps. Few studies have examined how women with eating disorders use weight loss app social features, such as adding friends, interacting with friends, and participating in forums. In order to fill this gap, I am conducting think-aloud exercises and interviews with women with eating disorders who use weight loss apps. My research is guided by the following research question:

RQ: How do women with eating disorders use community and social features within a weight loss app?

In this paper, I discuss preliminary results from a qualitative study that examines the use of social and community features of weight loss apps by women with eating disorders. Thus far, my findings indicate that while women with eating disorders use weight loss apps, they rarely use the community and social features. This work sheds light on the importance of considering user privacy concerns and promoting sharing and interacting with other users. Additionally, this research has implications for the design of apps to balance this tradeoff and to best meet the needs of women with eating disorders.

GROUP '16, November 13-16, 2016, Sanibel Island, FL, USA
ACM 978-1-4503-4276-6/16/11.
http://dx.doi.org/10.1145/2957276.2996282

2. RELATED WORK

2.1.1 Eating Disorders

Eating disorders are characterized by "a persistent disturbance of eating or eating-related behavior that results in the altered consumption or absorption of food and that significantly impairs physical health or psychosocial functioning" (p. 329) [1]. Eating disorder behaviors include excessive calorie or food restriction, intense fear of gaining weight, obsession with weight and consistent behavior to prevent weight gain, self-esteem overly related to body image, bingeing, feeling of being out of control during bingeing, purging, dramatic weight loss, preoccupation with weight, food, calories, fat grams, and dieting, refusal to eat certain foods, comments about feeling "fat", hunger denial, excessive exercise regimen, and development of food rituals. These behaviors are commonly associated with anorexia nervosa, bulimia nervosa, and eating disorder not otherwise specified/ other specified feeding or eating disorder.

2.1.2 Support for Users with Eating Disorders

Research has shown that users find it easier to discuss their issues online as opposed to face-to-face [10], which may explain why women with eating disorders are turning to online spaces. Online communities allow easy access to help and support, offer users a space to express their thoughts about different types of problems, including eating disorders, and provide a cost-effective and accessible service [15].

Research on online communities for eating disorder recovery and support is vast [4, 6, 7, 9, 10, 12, 13, 17–19, 22–24]. Online communities have the potential to be therapeutic for those with eating disorders [9]. Researchers have studied online forums and social media for providing support for eating disorder recovery and found that these communities provide essential social support for isolated individuals with eating disorders [2, 24] where the majority of users tend to be younger women [10]. There is often a stigma with eating disorders, so these communities provide a space for users to discuss their issues and concerns often with some level of anonymity. Since there is a high chance of relapse with eating disorders, some form of social support is necessary to recovery especially after individuals leave treatment centers [13]. Eating disorder discussion groups are particularly helpful during early stages of recovery [9]. Eating disorder forum participation is useful for both informational needs and social contact and support [10]. These communities may provide new information about health conditions, concerns, and treatments and give people the ability to help others with the same condition or issue [14].

3. METHODS

3.1 Recruitment

Because anorexia and bulimia nervosa tend to affect young women (often college-aged) [3] and weight loss apps users tend to be younger [5, 20], I am focusing on women between the ages of 18 and 25 with a history of anorexia and/or bulimia nervosa who use or have used weight loss apps. In order to recruit users with a history of eating disorders, I am posting flyers at the local university and town. Each participant is compensated $25.

3.2 Data Collection and Analysis

With users, I am using two primary data collection methods: 1) think-aloud exercises and 2) formal semi-structured interviews, which occur during the same data collection session. For each data collection, we begin with the think-aloud exercise, where participants show me how they set goals, view progress visualizations, and use social and community features. Next, during the interview, I ask additional questions about eating disorders, weight loss apps, and other types of technology. The think-aloud exercises are video recorded, and the entire data collection session is audio recorded.

To date, I have conducted think-aloud exercises and interviews with 14 participants. Each data collection session is approximately 1 hour. Currently, I am transcribing and analyzing data collection sessions using thematic analysis while recruiting participants and conducting more sessions.

4. PRELIMINARY FINDINGS

Through an initial analysis of a portion of the think-aloud exercises and interviews, I found women with eating disorders may be reluctant to use community and social features of weight loss apps.

Many participants believe their eating disorder and weight-related journeys are private, as illustrated by these quotations:

"I never interact with people because I feel like my diet is like my, it's only my thing. Do you know what I mean? It's like individual stuff." (U01)

"Yeah, I haven't done that [friended anyone on the app/participated in the forums] just because again, it's like something I've kept secret for so long that I don't really share it with anybody." (U02)

Participants often say they would be embarrassed if other people knew they had an eating disorder or knew more detail about their behaviors:

"I don't like to share with my friends. It's a little bit awkward, yeah. I just keep it private, I think. Because I really like, it's kind of... makes me uncomfortable because if you, like I don't know, like I use this pal because I think it's kind of give some privacy. I don't know. I just don't like to share." (U01)

"I mean, I mean if I was sharing it with people and they saw I was eating so few calories, then that'd be embarrassing." (U04)

"I just didn't want other people to be involved. I guess that's just me personally, but I feel like a community where other people could have helped me probably would be better, but I was just like so embarrassed because I've been on this thing my whole life where I'm like, k, I'm strong, I'm mentally strong, I don't have anything to face, like I'm fine, but I was not fine at all in all reality, so I was like more embarrassed an didn't want friends and family to know and stuff, so I didn't even want to do the social part of it, so." (U05)

These quotations show that participants rarely use the community and social features of weight loss apps and would feel uncomfortable if others knew about their eating and exercise behaviors.

5. DISCUSSION AND CONCLUSION

Although women with eating disorders use weight loss apps, they are reluctant to use the community and social features of these apps. Even though online communities have been shown to be beneficial to women with eating disorders, they still express privacy concerns with participating in online communities and sharing information. Perhaps this is due to the stigma associated with eating disorders [11] or fears related to consequences of revealing such information, especially on an app intended for weight loss not eating disorders.

This raises questions regarding the trade offs between privacy and not only the need for information, but also social support. Would users feel better about sharing and using these features if they could share anonymously? If so, what design changes could we employ to encourage users to share? Do users in other types of online communities have the same reluctance to share information? What about in face-to-face treatment programs and groups? Depending on where they are in terms of their eating disorder (i.e., recovery or not), do users feel differently about sharing information and using these social and community features? Future research will begin to answer these questions, and further analyses will focus on answering why these users rarely utilize these features. This research has implications for design and for our understanding of how to balance maintaining user privacy and promoting use.

6. ACKNOWLEDGMENTS

This material is based upon work supported by the National Science Foundation under Grant No. DGE1255832. Any opinions, findings, and conclusions or recommendations expressed in this material are those of the author(s) and do not necessarily reflect the views of the National Science Foundation.

7. REFERENCES

[1] American Psychiatric Association ed. 2013. *Diagnostic and Statistical Manual of Mental Disorders (DSM-5)*. American Psychiatric Publishing.

[2] Bowler, L. et al. 2012. Eating disorder questions in Yahoo! Answers: Information, conversation, or reflection? *ASIST 2012* (Baltimore, Maryland, 2012).

[3] Eisenberg, D. et al. 2011. Eating Disorder Symptoms Among College Students: Prevalence, Persistence, Correlates, and Treatment-Seeking. *Journal of American College Health*. 59, 8 (2011), 70–707.

[4] Flynn, M. a. and Stana, A. 2012. Social support in a men's online eating disorder forum. *International Journal of Men's Health*. 11, 2 (2012), 150–169.

[5] Fox, S. and Duggan, M. 2012. Mobile Health 2012. *Pew Internet & American Life Project*. (2012).

[6] Gulec, H. et al. 2011. Internet-based maintenance treatment for patients with eating disorders. *Professional Psychology: Research and Practice*. 42, 6 (2011), 479–486.

[7] Johnsen, J.-A.K. et al. 2002. Online group interaction and mental health: An analysis of three online discussion forums. *Scandinavian Journal of Psychology*. 43, (2002), 445–449.

[8] Juarascio, A.S. et al. 2015. Review of smartphone applications for the treatment of eating disorders. *European Eating Disorders Review*. 23, (2015), 1–11.

[9] Keski-Rahkonen, A. and Tozzi, F. 2005. The process of recovery in eating disorder sufferers' own words: An internet-based study. *International Journal of Eating Disorders*. 37, (2005), 580–586.

[10] Kummervold, P.E. et al. 2002. Social support in a wired world: Use of online mental health forums in Norway. *Nordic Journal of Psychiatry*. 56, 1 (2002), 59–65.

[11] Livingston, J.D. and Boyd, J.E. 2010. Correlates and consequences of internalized stigma for people living with mental illness: A systematic review and meta-analysis. *Social Science and Medicine*. 71, 12 (2010), 2150–2161.

[12] Ljotsson, B. et al. 2007. Remote treatment of bulimia nervosa and binge eating disorder: A randomized trial of Internet-assisted cognitive behavioural therapy. *Behaviour Research and Therapy*. 45, (2007), 649–661.

[13] McCormack, A. 2010. Individuals with eating disorders and the use of online support groups as a form of social support. *CIN: Computers, Informatics, Nursing*. 28, 1 (2010), 12–19.

[14] Mo, P.K.H. and Coulson, N.S. 2010. Empowering processes in online support groups among people living with HIV/AIDS: A comparative analysis of "lurkers" and "posters." *Computers in Human Behavior*. 26, (Sep. 2010), 1183–1193.

[15] Olsen, E. and Kraft, P. 2009. ePsychology: A pilot study on how to enhance social support and adherence in digital interventions by characteristics from social networking sites. *Persuasive '09* (Claremont, CA, 2009), 1–6.

[16] Reba-Harrelson, L. et al. 2009. Patterns and prevalence of disordered eating and weight control behaviors in women ages 25-45. *Eating and Weight Disorders*. 14, 4 (2009).

[17] Stommel, W. 2008. Mein nick bin ich! Nicknames in a German Forum on eating disorders. *Journal of Computer-Mediated Communication*. 13, (2008), 141–162.

[18] Stommel, W. and Koole, T. 2010. The online support group as a community: A micro-analysis of the interaction with a new member. *Discourse Studies*. 12, 3 (2010), 357–378.

[19] Stommel, W. and Meijman, F.J. 2011. The use of conversation analysis to study social accessibility of an online support group on eating disorders. *Global Health Promotion*. 18, 2 (2011), 18–26.

[20] U.S. Smartphone Use in 2015: 2015. *http://www.pewinternet.org/2015/04/01/us-smartphone-use-in-2015/*. Accessed: 2015-11-11.

[21] Wade, T.D. et al. 2011. Epidemiology of eating disorders. *Textbook in Psychiatric Epidemiology (3rd ed.)*. Wiley. 343–360.

[22] Walstrom, M.K. 2000. "You know, who's the thinnest?": Combating surveillance and creating safety in copy with eating disorders online. *CyberPsychology & Behavior*. 3, 5 (2000), 761–783.

[23] White, M. and Dorman, S.M. 2001. Receiving social support online: Implications for health education. *Health Education Research*. 16, 6 (2001), 693–707.

[24] Whitlock, J.L. et al. 2006. The virtual cutting edge: The internet and adolescent self-injury. *Developmental Psychology*. 42, 3 (2006), 407–417.

Understanding User Reviews of Adolescent Mobile Safety Apps: A Thematic Analysis

Arup Kumar Ghosh, Pamela Wisniewski
Department of Computer Science
University of Central Florida
Orlando, FL 32816, USA
{arupkumar.ghosh, pamwis}@ucf.edu

ABSTRACT

With the growing use of mobile smart phones among teens, adolescent online safety is becoming more and more challenging. To overcome this problem, parental control applications have been developed. Yet, no one knows why these apps have very low adoption rates nor if they are effective. To address this problem, we previously conducted a structured analysis of existing adolescent online safety apps. In this paper, we briefly summarize our previous results and introduce our new approach for gaining additional insights from the actual users of these apps. We summarize our methodology for doing this and present the results of an initial thematic analysis of user reviews of adolescent online safety apps.

Keywords

Adolescent Online Safety; Value Sensitive Design; Parental Control

ACM Classification Keywords

K.4.1 [Public Policy Issues]: Ethics, Human safety, Privacy

1. INTRODUCTION

Teens experience rapid, developmental growth in adolescence and are more susceptible to certain risks as they seek out new social experiences [3,4,19]. Teens are also early and eager adopter of internet and mobile technologies, which make them vulnerable to new social risks. According to a 2015 survey by Pew Research, 91% of teens in the U.S. use mobile phones to surf the internet [1]. They communicate with friends and/or strangers using social networking sites (75% of teens have access [18]), video chatting applications (47% of teens use [1]), and social media applications (37% of teens use [1]). Due to such prolific use of smartphones, it is highly likely that teens may encounter risky online situations such as cyberbullying, exposure to unwanted explicit materials, harassments, or sexual solicitations [16].

To overcome this problem, parental control software for mobile devices is available [22]. However, it is reported that only 16% of parents install such monitoring software on their teens' phones [17]. Researchers have conducted very little research on the currently available mobile apps that promote adolescent online safety. Therefore, it is unclear why parental control apps have such a low adoption rates. To answer this question, our recent work [21] explored the features that are available in 75 adolescent mobile safety apps built for Google Android devices. We found that features were highly unbalanced in terms of focusing more heavily on increased parental control over promoting teen self-regulation. However, we were unable to understand from a user's perspective whether or not these features met the needs of the users. As such, we have designed a follow-up study to better understand why these apps get high or low ratings. We conducted an initial empirical investigation of adolescent online safety apps by unobtrusively scraping user reviews from Google's Android Play store. We then performed a thematic analysis of user reviews to explain emergent themes reflected by users who gave feedback for these parental control apps. Our initial results confirm our hypothesis that there is a disconnect between users' needs and the design of adolescent online safety apps, especially from the vantage point of teens. Our end goal is to create a parental control software prototype, which will help promote adolescent online safety that meets the needs of both parents and teens without compromising too much of a teen's privacy.

GROUP '16, November 13-16, 2016, Sanibel Island, FL, USA
ACM 978-1-4503-4276-6/16/11.
http://dx.doi.org/10.1145/2957276.2996283

2. RELATED WORK

Technical mediation refers to the use of software to mediate teen online risk exposure and is a form of restrictive mediation used by parents to monitor inappropriate activity conducted on a teen's mobile devices [6]. Most researchers have studied technical mediation for home computers, not for smart phones [15,17]. Some research has focused on mobile contexts. For instance, Hasish et al. [11] created an app "We-Choose" for kids of ages between 6 and 8 to collaboratively configure technical mediation. Ko et al. [14] implemented similar app "FamiLync" to promote parent-teen co-learning of internet use. A common theme between these studies is that more collaborative approaches helped to reduce negative smartphone behaviors and nourish parent-teen relationships [14]. However, in our recent work [21], we found that most mobile apps currently available for adolescent online safety do not take collaborative approaches. Instead, they emphasize parental monitoring and restriction of teens' mobile activities. Therefore, the current study builds upon these findings to investigate whether there is a disconnect between the mobile apps that are currently available on the market and users' needs. If so, we aim to better understand this gap and design solutions to close it.

3. THEORETICAL FOUNDATIONS

3.1 Value Sensitive Design

Value sensitive design (VSD) is defined as "a theoretically grounded approach to the design of technology that accounts for human values in a principled and comprehensive manner throughout the design process" [8 p. 55]. In VSD, conceptual, empirical, and technical investigations can both reflectively identify and proactively account for values that are embedded into the design of systems [9]. Conceptual investigations talk about philosophical discussions about values, and the design trade-offs among competing values. Empirical investigations are about the human context in which a technology is used (e.g., user studies). Finally, technical investigations involve examining existing features within technology that may support or hinder human values [9]. In our work, we used the lens of VSD and applied it to *family value systems.* Family systems are the most important institution of modern society; family values are socially constructed and become an integral part of us [13]. The values (e.g., obedience, discipline, honesty, transparency, trust, openness, etc.) we acquired throughout our life also play a pivotal role in our parenting styles [23].

The principles of VSD have been applied to the context of teen mobile safety in the past. Czeskis et al. [5] conducted scenario-based interviews with nine pairs of teens and parents regarding online safety to identify key technical challenges for design and they used the value-sensitive design approach. According to their study, safety, trust, and privacy caused tension between parents and teens and recommended design guidelines to overcome these tensions [5]. In our feature analysis work, we reverse-engineered the values embedded in the design of existing mobile apps so that we can understand how technical mediation is used for mobile online safety and identify the limitations of currently available apps that promote adolescent online safety. Our feature analysis study involved both a conceptual and technical investigation of the values embedded in the design of mobile apps that promote adolescent online safety, while our thematic analysis involves an empirical investigation by focusing on the human context of use.

3.2 Teen Online Safety Strategies

By synthesizing literature from developmental psychology, we developed a framework of Teen Online Safety Strategies (TOSS; **Figure 1**), which consider both parental control and teen-self regulation as strategies for keeping teens safe online [21]. Our framework is built upon following assumptions: 1) parents have some control over teens' online activities [15], and 2) teen autonomy also has an influence on adolescent online safety [7]. Based on our framework, adolescent online safety is an outcome of both effective parenting *and* a teen's own self-regulatory behaviors. Parents can influence teen online safety through *monitoring*, *restriction*, and *active mediation*. Three main

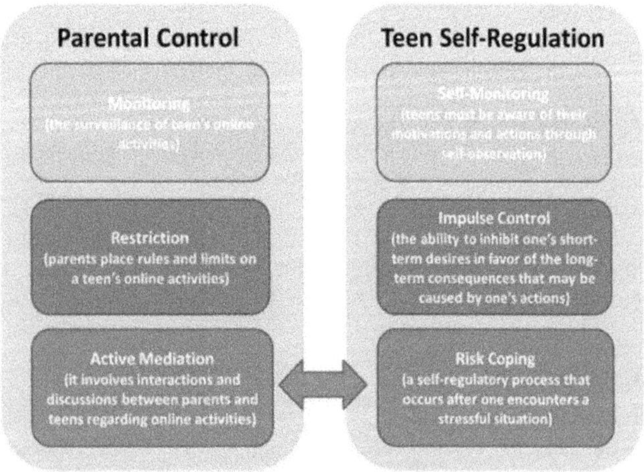

Figure 1. Teen Online Safety Strategies (TOSS) Theoretical Framework.

strategies for teen self-regulation are *self-awareness*, *impulse control*, and *risk coping*. In **Figure 1**, an explicit relationship between active mediation and risk coping is shown as teens seek help from their parents while they experience risk. The other strategies are placed side-by-side to show similar strategies (e.g., parental monitoring versus teen self-monitoring) that diverge based on the placement of agency on parents versus teens.

4. RESEARCH CONTRIBUTIONS

It is known from the previous literature that the existing technical mediation solutions are generally not popular parental mediation strategy for promoting adolescent online safety through mobile devices. We still don't know *why* there is a gap between the technical mediation solutions that currently exist and the solutions proposed in the research that are not readily available for use. In this work, we make the following contributions:

1) *Summarize our recent related work, which included creating a conceptual framework of Teen Online Safety Strategies (TOSS) shown in Figure 1 to represent a more balanced approach for adolescent mobile safety.*
2) *Present and build upon our results of a structured feature analysis of 75 mobile apps that mapped to the TOSS framework.*
3) *Introduce a method for conducting an unobtrusive, empirical user study of adolescent online safety apps by scraping publicly available user reviews from the Android Play store.*
4) *Highlight some of our initial results from a thematic analysis of user reviews to explain emerging themes that emerged from users who provided feedback for these parental control apps.*

5. METHODS

5.1 Data Collection

For the feature analysis, we identified 75 mobile apps designed for the purpose of adolescent online safety and conducted a structured analysis of the features available within these apps during April/May of 2016. We performed our analysis on apps available on the Android platform as Android has 83% market share of smartphones [24]. We built our initial list of 89 apps by a keyword search on the Google Play app store. The keywords we used for our search were: "online safety," "family safety," "teen safety," "adolescent online safety," "parental controls," "parental monitoring, "teen monitoring," "cyberbullying," and "sexting." We had to delete 14 apps upon installation due to various usability issues. The technical investigation of the apps was done systematically by the researchers but did not take into the perspective of actual users.

To conduct our empirical investigation, which was based on actual users' reviews, we used a program called Heedzy [25] to download all of the reviews for the 75 apps, which were included in the feature analysis. We did this in August 2016. In our dataset, each user review had the following attributes as shown in **Table 1**:

Table 1. Attributes of user review data.

Attribute	**Description**
App Name	Name of the app
Date	Date when the review was written
Comment	The review written by the user
Rating	A score given by the user on 1 to 5 Likert scale

5.2 Data Analysis

For the feature analysis study, we used a mixture of a top-down and bottom-up approach to qualitatively analyze the features available within each app. Two research assistants performed the data coding. The feature list was created through a grounded approach [20]. We found 42 parent/teen features (e.g., *application log*, *call log*, *browser log*) within the 75 apps. A total of 382 instances were found where a feature was available within the apps in the data set. At the end, we mapped the set of features we found to our TOSS framework (**Figure 1**). This mapping helped us integrate theory building with our grounded analysis. Educational features emerged as a separate strategy for teen online safety for both parents and teens.

For the empirical user study, we have begun to perform some initial analysis on the user reviews. First, we carried out a thematic analysis of all reviews downloaded for the Safekiddo Parental Control App [26]. We did this by manually coding themes within the content of the reviews, which we present as our results. In the near future, our goal is to investigate the feasibility of using topic modelling techniques on the data set to extract themes. *Topic modeling* is a technique for identifying topics in texts/documents. It is normally achieved in two steps: 1) finding patterns in a collection of documents and 2) forming clusters of words based on topics. Latent Dirichlet Allocation (LDA) [2] is a popular topic modelling method. LDA is "a generative probabilistic model for collections of discrete data such as text corpora" [2]. Topic modelling was used previously by Hong et al. to perform an empirical study of Twitter messages [12]. Fu et al. used topic model on user feedback data to figure out why people hate apps [10]. We plan to use the LDA model [2] as an approach to automatically analyze user reviews and extract the main themes across all reviews, top-rated, and low-rated reviews. For our analysis, we considered a high-rated review as having 4 or more stars and a low-rated review with 3 or less stars.

5.3 Descriptive Statistics

The previous feature analysis included 75 apps found on Google Play. However, in June 2016, we checked Google Play for the same apps and only found 74 apps still available and estimated there would be about 200,000 user reviews to download. We set baseline criteria for the reviews to include in our analysis and identified 45 apps that were installed more than 1000 times, had more than 100 reviews, and were updated in 2015 or later. According to Google Play meta-data, these 45 apps should have approximately 191,000 reviews. Yet, in August 2016, when we downloaded the actual reviews based on this criteria, we realized that the number of reviews we retrieved was much lower than the number mentioned on the Google Play app store page. We realized the discrepancy was due to text-based reviews not being required when giving a star rating to an app. For example, Safekiddo Parental Control App had 218 reviews according Google Play store page, but we were able to retrieve only 57 reviews. Therefore, we decided instead to collect all user reviews for all apps that were originally identified for inclusion in the feature analysis. Our final dataset includes 29,272 user reviews for 71 apps as 4 apps included in the initial analysis were no longer found on app store.

6. RESULTS

6.1 Feature analysis

The main finding from the feature analysis was that 89% of features supported parental control strategies compared to only 11% that supported teen self-regulation strategies. Parental control features included 44% for monitoring, 43% restriction, 2% educational, and less than 1% of the features supported parental active mediation. For teen self-regulation, the percentages were much lower: risk-coping (4%), self-monitoring (2%), educational features (4%) and less than 1% of the features supported the impulse control strategies. This study used a value sensitive design approach (VSD) to reason about the staggering imbalance towards adolescent mobile online safety apps that promote parental authority over teen autonomy.

6.2 Thematic Analysis

To identify the difference between why parents like and dislike adolescent safety apps, we introduced a thematic analysis of all reviews that we downloaded from Google Play app store. We decided to perform the following thematic analyses:

1. *Individual rating level across all apps: Compare themes of top (rating >= 4) vs. low-rated (rating <=3) reviews*

2. *App rating level across all apps: Compare themes of top vs. low-rated apps*

As we are in the early stage of this study, we performed a thematic analysis manually at individual rating level for reviews of Safekiddo Parental Control app and showed the efficacy of our proposed method. For the analysis, we identified related words that described a topic. We identified three main themes for top-rated reviews and another three for low-rated reviews (see **Table 2**).

Table 2. Thematic analysis of user reviews of Safekiddo.

Rating	Words	Themes
<=3	worth, useless, app	useless
	can't, lock, playstore, device, not, easy, age, settings	problems in age-appropriate settings
	uninstalled, refuses, prevention	uninstallation problems
>=4	block, protect, limit, control, websites, porn, everything, free	block restricted content
	useful, great, works, properly, clean, user, friendly, excellent	user-friendly app
	safe, protect, children, family	protects family

Safekiddo Parental Control app received low ratings due to the following reasons: 1) some users found this app useless, 2) problems in age-appropriate settings, and 3) uninstallation problems. Below are reviews that illustrate each themes:

- **Useless:** *"Not possible to change settings and give extra time remotely. This is useless app."*
- **Age-Appropriateness:** *"The program is fine, but it is not easy to Nava gate and set age appropriate settings."*
- **Uninstallation Problems:** *"You can not even uninstall it when you need to find a different app."*

Users who rated SafeKiddo high thought: 1) it appropriately blocks restricted content, 2) the app is user-friendly, and 3) the app helps protect family. The reviews below further illustrate these themes:

- **Restricted Content:** *"Controls porn"*
- **User-friendly App:** "*Great app just need to work it out properly but quite user friendly :) impressed!!!"*
- **Protects Family:** *"So much I can finally protect my family thanks"*

Through our manual analysis of the user reviews, we also realized that teens were posting reviews for the apps as well as parents. For example, one teen said, "*My parents can block everything and anything this stinks for real.*" Overall, teen reviews seemed extremely negative, even more so than the parents' reviews. Given this finding, we now plan to also focus on analyzing and understanding teens' perspectives about the use of these apps.

7. CONCLUSION

In this paper, we highlighted the results of our recent feature analysis study and introduced a new thematic analysis approach of Google Play user reviews of 71 teen online safety apps to better understand factors that users consider while writing feedback for adolescent online safety apps. We showed the efficacy of our proposed thematic analysis by an example and explained how this analysis would help to better understand apps from their users' perspectives.

8. REFERENCES

[1] Amanda Lenhart. Mobile Access Shifts Social Media Use and Other Online Activities. *Pew Research Center: Internet, Science & Tech*, 2015. http://www.pewinternet.org/2015/04/09/mobile-access-shifts-social-media-use-and-other-online-activities/.

[2] Blei, D.M., Ng, A.Y., and Jordan, M.I. Latent Dirichlet Allocation. *Journal of Machine Learning Research 3*, Jan (2003), 993–1022.

[3] Coleman, J. and Hagell, A. *Adolescence, Risk and Resilience: Against the Odds*. John Wiley & Sons, 2007.

[4] Compas, B.E. and Reeslund, K.L. Processes of Risk and Resilience During Adolescence. In *Handbook of Adolescent Psychology*. John Wiley & Sons, Inc., 2009.

[5] Czeskis, A., Dermendjieva, I., Yapit, H., et al. Parenting from the pocket: value tensions and technical directions for secure and private parent-teen mobile safety. ACM Press (2010), 1.

[6] Eastin, M.S., Greenberg, B.S., and Hofschire, L. Parenting the Internet. *Journal of Communication 56*, 3 (2006), 486–504.

[7] Erickson, L.B., Wisniewski, P., Xu, H., Carroll, J.M., Rosson, M.B., and Perkins, D.F. The boundaries between: Parental involvement in a teen's online world. *Journal of the Association for Information Science and Technology 67*, 6 (2016), 1384–1403.

[8] Friedman, B., Jr, P.H.K., Borning, A., and Huldtgren, A. Value Sensitive Design and Information Systems. In N. Doorn, D. Schuurbiers, I. van de Poel and M.E. Gorman, eds., *Early engagement and new technologies: Opening up the laboratory*. Springer Netherlands, 2013, 55–95.

[9] Friedman, B., Kahn, P.H., and Borning, A. *Value Sensitive Design: Theory and Methods*. 2002.

[10] Fu, B., Lin, J., Li, L., Faloutsos, C., Hong, J., and Sadeh, N. Why People Hate Your App: Making Sense of User Feedback in a Mobile App Store. *Proceedings of the 19th ACM SIGKDD International Conference on Knowledge Discovery and Data Mining*, ACM (2013), 1276–1284.

[11] Hashish, Y., Bunt, A., and Young, J.E. Involving Children in Content Control: A Collaborative and Education-oriented Content Filtering Approach. *Proceedings of the 32Nd Annual ACM Conference on Human Factors in Computing Systems*, ACM (2014), 1797–1806.

[12] Hong, L. and Davison, B.D. Empirical Study of Topic Modeling in Twitter. *Proceedings of the First Workshop on Social Media Analytics*, ACM (2010), 80–88.

[13] Jagger, G. and Wright, C. *Changing Family Values*. Taylor & Francis, 1999.

[14] Ko, M., Choi, S., Yang, S., Lee, J., and Lee, U. FamiLync: Facilitating Participatory Parental Mediation of Adolescents' Smartphone Use. *Proceedings of the 2015 ACM International Joint Conference on Pervasive and Ubiquitous Computing*, ACM (2015), 867–878.

[15] Livingstone, S. and Helsper, E.J. Parental mediation of children's internet use. *Journal of broadcasting & electronic media 52*, 4 (2008), 581–599.

[16] Mitchell, K., Jones, L., Finkelhor, D., and Wolak, J. Trends in Unwanted Online Experiences and Sexting : Final Report. *Crimes Against Children Research Center*, (2014).

[17] Monica Anderson. Parents, Teens and Digital Monitoring. *Pew Research Center: Internet, Science & Tech*, 2016. http://www.pewinternet.org/2016/01/07/parents-teens-and-digital-monitoring/.

[18] Ramasubbu, S. Influence of Social Media on Teenagers. *The Huffington Post*, 400AD. http://www.huffingtonpost.com/suren-ramasubbu/influence-of-social-media-on-teenagers_b_7427740.html.

[19] Steinberg, L. Risk taking in adolescence: what changes, and why? *Annals of the New York Academy of Sciences 1021*, 1 (2004), 51–58.

[20] Strauss, A. and Corbin, J. *Basics of Qualitative Research: Techniques and Procedures for Developing Grounded Theory*. SAGE Publications, Inc, Thousand Oaks, 1998.

[21] Wisniewski, P., Ghosh, A.K., Rosson, M.B., Xu, H., and Carroll, J.M. Parental Control vs. Teen Self-Regulation: Is there a middle ground for mobile online safety? *Proceedings of the 20th ACM Conference on Computer Supported Cooperative Work & Social Computing*, ACM (2017).

[22] Best Choice for Teens' Cyber Safety – Parental Control App! https://www.hackread.com/teens-cyber-safety-protection-parental-control-app/.

[23] Using your Values to Raise your Children. *The Center for Parenting Education*. http://centerforparentingeducation.org/library-of-articles/indulgence-values/values-matter-using-your-values-to-raise-caring-responsible-resilient-children-what-are-values/.

[24] IDC: Smartphone OS Market Share. *www.idc.com*. http://www.idc.com/prodserv/smartphone-os-market-share.jsp.

[25] Downloading App Store & Google Play reviews made easy. http://heedzy.com/.

[26] SafeKiddo Parental Control - Android Apps on Google Play. https://play.google.com/store/apps/details?id=com.safekiddo.kid&hl=en.

Autonomy Support for Elderly People through Everyday Life Gadgets

Dominik Hornung [1], Claudia Müller [1], Alexander Boden [2], Martin Stein [2]

(1) Information Systems & New Media
University of Siegen
Siegen, Germany
{prename.name@uni-siegen.de}

(2) Fraunhofer FIT
Sankt Augustin
Germany
{prename.name@uni-siegen.de}

ABSTRACT

Research in the field of assistive technologies often claims to support their target group's autonomy. However, autonomy is mostly interpreted by the researchers and designers as independence or its meaning is not further specified. There are few studies where the users' perception and interpretation of autonomy is taken into account. Hence, technology for supporting autonomy is often rather intricate and based on a generalized notion of autonomy. We argue that autonomy contains more dimensions than just mere independence. Furthermore, we argue that the perception of autonomy is individually differing and focussing on small, individual solutions my help in shaping autonomy support on an individual level.

Keywords

Autonomy; Assistive Technologies; Elderly People; Qualitative Methods; Interviews; Wizard-of-Oz; Focus Groups

1. INTRODUCTION

Supporting elderly persons' autonomy is one major subject in the research field on assistive technologies. To meet this aim, the addressed solutions vary on a large scale – from single solutions such as in-house emergency call systems up to more complex solutions, such as addressed in a networked approach of smart home technologies.

As in the spectrum of IT solutions there exists a variety of approaches to conceptualize autonomy in the realm of assistive technologies (AT) [3,7,8]. There are lots of relevant reflections on how to handle related complexities in IT support. We would like to contribute to this discourse with some insights derived from qualitative-empirical work with elderly persons in the context of a project aiming at the development of intelligent home sensors.

GROUP '16, November 13-16, 2016, Sanibel Island, FL, USA
ACM 978-1-4503-4276-6/16/11.
http://dx.doi.org/10.1145/2957276.2996284

Our results show some specific attitudes and personal interpretations on what autonomy would mean for our elderly cooperation partners and which facets of autonomy are of value to them. We learnt that simple solutions often may have bigger impacts than currently appreciated in the AT research domain. Thus, we would like to emphasize and scrutinize the perspective on simple or single solutions for specific situations and conditions in older age.

2. AUTONOMY IN THE CONTEXT OF AAL & TECHNOLOGY DESIGN

In research work on Assistive Technologies (AT), conceptual reflections of autonomy and related support by ATs for the elderly are often directed to the meaning of *independence* – if it is defined at all. In many cases, the concept is being reduced to the ability of the elderly to live on their own *despite their age*. Another important aspect of autonomy being discussed merely in health and care settings is the focus on freedom in decision-making [5,6]. Albeit autonomy is often equalized with independence, we would like to follow other directions that describe autonomy in a more nuanced way. Damberger, for example, emphasizes three facets of autonomy: 1) the claim for and the ability to self-determination; 2) self-responsibility; and 3) independence [4]. Calvo et al. similarly discuss autonomy as "a category of constructs including independence, self- regulation and volition" [2].

In the area of technology design, autonomy is often discussed against the backdrop of behaviour change endeavours, such as in the field of Persuasive Technology (PT). Reitberger et al. critizise that PT doesn't take the autonomy of its users into account. They claim that systems rely on force and coercion instead of enabling critical reflection in their users [7].

The general claim of many AT to improve seniors' quality of life has been discussed by Rogers et al.: "(...) it can be difficult to see how sending SMS alerts to carers helps the elderly individuals. Does it improve the quality of their life?" [8]. The same question can be asked with the individuals' autonomy in mind.

Carmien et al. deal with the autonomy of cognitively impaired people in public transport [3] on a similarly nuanced level. There the notion of autonomy is dealt with in a more diverse spectrum than just independence. The users are not completely independent. They rely on the support of relatives or other caring persons. However, with that support they are able to autonomously travel and do errands or other regular activities. With this paper, we want to argue on a similar level and try to shed light on the issue of autonomy in the area of assistive technologies.

3. METHODS & SETTING

Empirical work with some 20 elderly persons (70+) has been conducted over 9 months in different ways in the German R&D project "Cognitive Village", a project aiming at sensor-based adaptive systems for elderly citizens to support ageing at home. All elderly persons live in a small German city on their own. Some of them have moved to special accessible senior apartments in the last 2-3 years. All, however, are living independently, either with their spouse or alone (widowed). There is variety in socio-economic backgrounds as well as their (wish for) connectedness to social networks (families/ neighbors/friends), as well as in their familiarity with computers, tablets or smart phones. Some of them use computers and internet in their homes, a minor amount uses smart phones. Devices such as smart watch or fitness wrist bands are not being used and known.

In the course of the project's pre-study we initially conducted three future workshops with 10-12 participants each in order to gain first impressions of the neighbourhoods, their individual every-day life conducts, general and shared common attitudes towards potential IT support. Subsequently, we conducted nine semi-structured interviews with people aged 70+ in order to refine our impression of the individual everyday lives and to dig deeper on certain topics. The future workshops and the interview series were analysed as a basis for the third step, the generation of design ideas. Additionally, we implemented two focus groups: the first to find and define some use cases for potential prototypes. Secondly, a Wizard-of-Oz prototype workshop was conducted to try out and discuss different scenarios, and possibilities for meaningful sensor technology support for the elderly research participants.

4. EMPIRICAL FINDINGS

One of the goals of the workshops was to discuss applications for our specific group of participants who are rather "young elderlies". Many of them have health issues, such as cardiovascular diseases, hypertonia or diabetes, and are in close contact with their GPs and medical specialists. Their "analogue" way to manage their health issues works so far. However, they are interested in possible support options, especially against the background of possible progress of diseases and in ways to improve a healthy life - and in the light of their own aging.

Our motivation was to gradually introduce them to ubiquitous/sensor-based technology that can serve as an entrance point in future, more common "assistive technology" (AT), which aims at assuring autonomy. We picked some rather basic use cases for the workshops due to several reasons: 1) Research on smart devices with a group of participants who are not familiar with the idea of "intelligent" devices is highly challenging. Especially regarding the build-up of a common frame of reference between researchers and participants. With simpler use cases to discuss, we tried to avoid overcharging the participants. 2) We identified and defined the use cases based on our previous workshop discussions and interviews. The topics were relevant for the participants and represent their current abilities, interests and worries. 3) We wanted to be able to implement and test the use cases interactively (in a wizard-of-oz workshop) in a relatively simple way.

Following, we want to highlight three of these use cases: water intake tracking, smart shopping list and step counter/activity tracker.

Regardless of the three use cases, the participants had very differing perceptions of what is practical and useful. An idea that was very much appreciated by one person could be described by someone else as completely unnecessary and nonsense. There was nearly no application which all participants found equally useful. In their everyday lives, everyone has developed their own practices to take care of things and handle certain situations. Besides differing perceptions, not every parameter that is important to describe a person's wellbeing can be measured. It was repeatedly emphasized that machines can't measure feelings or one's mental and spiritual state.

4.1 Water intake tracking

One example that is often assumed to be an issue of the elderly is insufficient water intake. Based on our previous workshop discussions we decided to implement some kind of water intake tracking system as part of the Wizard-of-Oz prototype. Therefore, we used smart buttons to trigger an event that incremented a simple counter. The counter was visible on a dashboard-like application on the participants' tablets and a large screen in the workshop room. The buttons were stuck to the participants' water bottles and glasses on the table. The goal was to provide a very simple, unobtrusive way to individually track water intake.

In the resulting discussion, all of the participants were aware of the issue of insufficient liquid intake and agreed that when they don't drink enough they might feel dizzy and unwell. Thus, some of them have developed certain practices to take care of their water intake during the day. These practices involve e.g. putting a water bottle and a glass on the table where they dwell most of the day, in combination with setting the goal to empty the bottle until the evening. Others, e.g. use their favourite glass or mug and count the number of refills. In these cases, the participants set themselves a fixed goal that they could meet at the end of the day. In order to control the quantity of their water supply they apply some kind of measurement (bottle, glass). For other participants the measurement is rather based on their own physical feeling: they know that they should drink some water when they start feeling dizzy or unwell or receive other bodily feedback. In some cases this feedback comes too late and the dizziness can only be retrospectively linked to insufficient liquid intake over the past hours. Some of the participants know that they don't drink enough over the course of a day. Nevertheless, they didn't seem to care too much about that issue: *"I don't want to think about this.", "I feel fine most of the time, I don't even notice when I don't drink for hours."*

However, for one participant (who was actually very refusing and sceptical until then) the water intake tracker provided a very useful application. He even wished for a reminder feature, because he often forgets to drink during the day. He stated that: *"My wife always tells me to drink more but I don't listen to her. That's why this technological aid could be really useful for me!"*. Most of the participants liked the idea of being able to check their current liquid status while not being annoyed by constant notifications telling them to drink something.

4.2 Smart shopping (list)

The discussion on the utility of smart buttons also triggered further use cases. When providing the participants with examples of current usage of these devices, they were enthusiastic about the idea of the *Amazon Dash Buttons* [1]. These smart buttons' sole purpose is ordering one specific, predefined product by pressing them. They can be placed anywhere in the apartment, typically next to the referring product (e.g. next to the coffee machine to order a certain kind of coffee). The idea of being able to order heavy or cumbersome products like water crates with a simple press of a button seemed to be very attractive for some of the participants. Triggered by this concept, the participants discussed variations of the idea, e.g. that the button does not directly order the products but adds them to a shopping list. Some participants favoured this variation since they are still able to run errands by themselves – and rather perceive it as a social activity than a tedious duty. However, the referring participants agreed that they could use some aid in remembering and organizing things.

4.3 Step counter / activity tracker

We presented the concept of activity tracking devices and applications by the example of a regular smart watch. Some of the researchers showed their own devices and let the participants try them out. We showed data of the past days, current information and the progress towards the "daily goal" – a certain amount of steps to be taken during one day. The general idea of activity tracking was then controversially discussed.

The underlying assumption of being able to track the quantity of daily activities was seen as interesting and helpful. Retrospectively backtracing data, looking for links e.g. between indisposition and level of activity or other factors (e.g. water intake) appeared to be a valuable source of information for some of the participants.

However, all of the participants concurred that they rather dislike being pushed to a "daily goal". The common concern was that even if it is not a problem to meet the set goal on a regular day, there can always be a less active day when they don't feel well. Then, additionally being reminded of their "frailty" is an added factor for indisposition, stress and a guilty conscience. Similarly, social features like competition and challenges were completely rejected. Even collaborative ideas (e.g. working together with a friend to collaboratively achieve a daily goal) were regarded as not being useful but rather pressurizing.

5. DISCUSSION

Our empirical examples show that autonomy support for elderly people does not need intricate and determining systems. The participants found the rather small, specific helpers the most useful for their individual everyday lives. Furthermore, the examples show that autonomy has many dimensions. Following, we will discuss the impact of our use cases on different levels of autonomy based on Damberger's [4] suggestions.

5.1 Self-determination

Current applications in the area of self-tracking (e.g. quantified self) are based on the premise of self-optimization. While this can be helpful and valuable for hale and hearty people, our empirical data shows no sign of demand for such applications in our elderly participants. On the contrary, the seniors know themselves very well. They decide their activities based on their own physical feeling and not based on an app's suggestion. However, there might be some cases where they feel that a device might provide a certain value. But then, again, is this an individual decision of when and how to use a device.

5.1.1 Weakening external determination

In the case of water intake tracking, all participants uttered concerns towards being monitored by other people (doctors, relatives). It is contrary to their ability to decide by themselves how much and when they have to drink. Most of them had established their own measures to ensure sufficient water intake, anyway. They were concerned that repeatedly being told by other people to drink more could force social pressure on them. The resulting behaviour, e.g. changing the drinking habits (or at least pretending to do so), would not be self-determined.

5.1.2 Supporting informed decision-making

On the other hand, unobtrusively tracking the water intake and displaying it on demand can serve as a valuable source for self-determined decisions. The user can check the current quantity of liquids, compare with other factors (e.g. heart rate or blood pressure) and decide the consequences with this information in mind.

Similarly, regular activity tracking applications often work with daily goals. In order to persuade their users to reach these goals, they repeatedly remind them of the distance between them and their goal. For seniors, being told to be more active or that they won't reach their goal today forces pressure on them. This impacts their ability and possibility to make a self-determined decision regarding their activity level. As stated above, the seniors mostly know themselves better than anyone else and their decisions should be based on their own self-assessment. However, this self-assessment can be accompanied by information on the activities of the last days, the general progress or links to other data.

5.2 Self-responsibility

Mentally healthy people who are able to make self-determined decisions are immediately responsible for the consequences of their acts. This responsibility is an important dimension of the construct of autonomy. If decisions are made under external pressure, people can't be fully responsible for the consequences by themselves. Especially regarding health related issues, people immediately feel the consequences of their self-determined decisions. Thus, it is in their own interest to act responsible and to ensure wellbeing and health.

Our proposed application scenarios support self-responsibility of its users. As argued above, it enables them to make self-determined decisions based on gathered data. The following decisions are based on a combination of this data and the person's own physical feeling and former experience. If they decide "wrong", they will feel the consequences and probably adapt their decision making. This applies to both, activity tracking and water intake tracking. If a computer tells them to drink/walk/sleep more, they are not fully responsible for potential negative consequences because they can't rely on the validity of its decision. This poses a huge barrier for the usage of such technology, since it is in stark contrast to images of autonomy.

5.3 Independence

Besides being able to form self-determined decisions and taking responsibility for the referring consequences, acting independently is the third main dimension in our view of autonomy. This notion of independence manifests in several aspects:

5.3.1 Independence from supervision

Our applications support the users in being independent from other people's supervision. The water intake application, e.g., makes the elderly people independent from their children, other relatives or doctors who tend to have an eye on their relatives/patients water intake. The seniors can control their water intake status by themselves, even if they are not used to do this and don't have established practices. Subsequently, they are able to form *self-determined* decisions about the consequences of their state.

5.3.2 Independence from the living environment

The smart shopping buttons example may seem contradictory to the concept of autonomy, at first. More precisely, it may not look like a sign of independence if a person orders a product via the internet instead of going to the supermarket and buying it by themselves. On the one hand, people may depend on the delivery service, warehousers and the ordering system. On the other hand, the possibility to easily order large and heavy products provides independence from the referring living environment. Even if they are not always in the mood or physical state to haul water crates upstairs, they are not forced to move to a more accessible apartment, special senior housing or even a senior residence. They are more independent from local infrastructure, such as bus stops and local amenities. Thus, the application enables people to keep on living in their home independently from the home's accessibility, location and infrastructure. This aspect shows some similarities to Carmien et al.'s [3] support system for cognitively impaired people:

5.3.3 Independence from external support

Usually, if elderly people are not able to carry heavy weights anymore, their family steps in. Many participants told us that they receive help from their children and grandchildren in certain situations. While this is appreciated as an "excuse" for social contact, they often feel awkward bothering their family with such requests. Small-scaled technological support – as provided in our examples – can strengthen the independence of elderly people from human support and thus, strengthen their general feeling of autonomy.

5.4 CONCLUSION

As Damberger [4] and Calvo et al. [2] emphasized before, autonomy is a multi-dimensional construct. It is not equal to the ability of being completely able to do everything by oneself. And it is not equal to mere independence from something or someone. This multi-dimensionality makes it inevitable that in some cases, some dimensions have a higher individual value than others. The result is, that sometimes one dimension can be sacrificed or impaired in order to ensure another one. In our examples, this is the case in the smart shopping scenario: while there is a rise in dependency on service providers and the technology itself, the possibility for self-determination and independence from close relatives gains as well. This seems to result in an overall positive outcome for the seniors, as the reactions to the application suggest.

Carmien et al. [3] describe something similar in their work on a system that supports the independence of cognitively impaired people in the usage of public transportation. The users are not completely independent, since they are remotely supported by caring persons. However, with a small amount of support and dependency, they can travel on their own, in a self-determined and self-responsible way.

This allows to draw the conclusion that the perception of autonomy is individually differing. It implies that small, individual solutions for autonomy support could be more valuable than large systems that are based on a too generalized notion of autonomy.

6. REFERENCES

[1] Amazon.com, Inc. Amazon Dash Buttons. 2016. https://www.amazon.com/Dash-Buttons/b?ie=UTF8&node=10667898011.

[2] Calvo, R., Peters, D., Johnson, D. and Rogers, Y. 2014. Autonomy in technology design. In *CHI '14 Extended Abstracts on Human Factors in Computing Systems* (CHI EA '14). ACM, New York, NY, USA, 37-40.

[3] Carmien, S., Dawe, M., Fischer, G. et al. 2005. Socio-Technical Environments Supporting People with Cognitive Disabilities Using Public Transportation. In *Transactions on Computer-Human Interaction.* 12, 2 (June 2005), 233-262.

[4] Damberger, T. 2016. I am medial! About Media, Education, Aging and Death. In *Medien & Altern.* 2 (June2016), 47-64.

[5] King, L., Clarridge, K., Fischer, E. et al. 2008. Virtual Mentor. In *American Medical Association Journal of Ethics.* 10,6 (June 2008), 357-359.

[6] Lothian, K. and Philp, I. 2001.Maintaining the dignity and autonomy of older people in the healthcare setting. In *BMJ: British Medical Journal.* 322 (7287), 668-670.

[7] Reitberger, W., Güldenpfennig, F., Fitzpatrick, G. 2012. Persuasive Technology Considered Harm – An Exploration of Design Concerns through the TV Companion. In *Persuasive Technology: Design for Health and Safety: 7th International Conference on Persuasive Technology* (PERSUASIVE 2012). Springer, Berlin, 239-250.

[8] Rogers, Y., Marsden, G. 2013. Does he take sugar? Moving beyond the rhetoric of compassion. *Interactions.* 20,4 (July 2013), 48-57.

Tracky Notes: Trackable Sticky Notes for Indexing a Video of Meetings

Yoshiyuki Kajiwara Shogo Fukushima Daiya Aida Takeshi Naemura
The University of Tokyo
7-3-1 Hongo, Bunkyo-ku, Tokyo, Japan
{kajiwara, shogo, da, naemura}@nae-lab.org

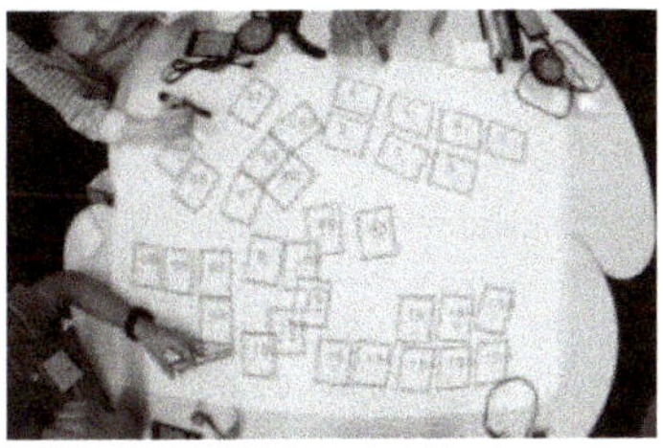

Figure 1. Tracked sticky notes (enclosed by red rectangles; each id is printed in green).

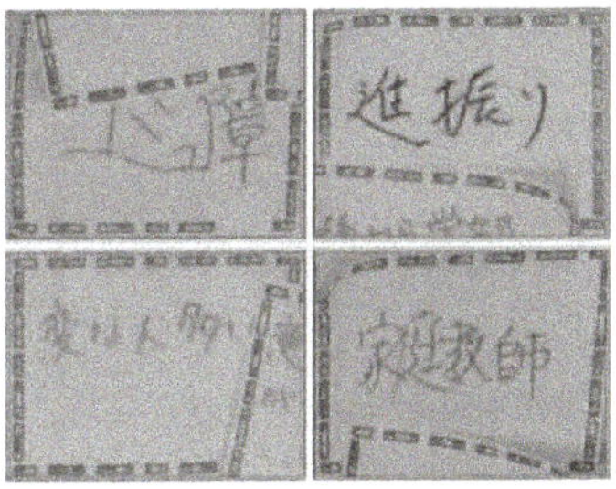

Figure 2. Examples of tracked sticky notes in presence of occlusion.

Figure 3. Meeting participants watch the previous meeting's video indexed by tracked sticky notes.

ABSTRACT
Video records are sometimes used during meetings nowadays in order to compensate for the incompleteness of hand-written minutes. To use video effectively to record the minutes of a meeting, indices are considered necessary in addition to standard functions of movie players. Some systems can form indices by sensing human actions in the world, but such indices are not directly relevant to the contents of the discussions that occur in meetings. In this study, we propose an automated meeting index system based on people's discussions during daily meetings in the world. In our system, indices based on the contents of discussion can be automatically formulated in meetings if only paper, writing implements, and a camera are arranged in a certain manner. To this end, we develop trackable sticky notes, called "Tracky Notes," as indices. Tracky Notes can be tracked with visible markers through a camera, and is robust against occlusion. We then propose a meeting viewer where Tracky Notes are used as indices. Finally, we report the result of a user study conducted in a university classroom. The study revealed the appropriate region of visible markers and the robustness against occlusion of Tracky Notes. We also measured the effectiveness of our system comparing with standard functions of movie players.

Keywords
Meeting; Index; Viewer; Sticky Notes; Marker; Occlusion.

1. INTRODUCTION
Video records can be used for meetings in order to recall past discussion in detail. Using video enables meetings to be recorded without the risk of missing important issues. It also allows people to concentrate on the meeting because they do not have to take minutes during meetings. However, following a meeting, if users search for scenes from it that they want to watch, their only clues to find them are time points (e.g., using a seek bar). Therefore, some support is needed to precisely and quickly search for scenes in a video recording of a meeting in order for users to make good use of it. In this study, we develop this support system.

GROUP '16, November 13-16, 2016, Sanibel Island, FL, USA
ACM 978-1-4503-4276-6/16/11.
http://dx.doi.org/10.1145/2957276.2996285

Some studies in the area have developed methods to form indices for videos to enable efficient viewing. Indices connect features in videos to their corresponding time points. By selecting an index, one can instantly watch the corresponding scenes. In most of the indexing systems, the contents of the operation history of digital meeting support software on PCs [1] are used as indices [2]. When using digital meeting support software, however, users need to prepare PCs and the software beforehand, and to learn how to use the latter. If they are not accustomed to using them, they cannot fully concentrate on the meeting.

It is also important to enable indexing in meetings where only analog tools, such as paper and pen, are used since many people are accustomed to using them. Accordingly, some systems can form indices by sensing human actions in the world. For example, people's actions—standing up, standing in front of whiteboards, etc.—can be detected through cameras [3]. However, the indices obtained tend not to be directly relevant to the contents of the discussion during the meeting. Certain other systems allow the formulation of manual indices through buttons or gestures [4]. In these systems, indices are formed when buttons are pushed or certain gestures are made. They enable the formulation of indices based on the contents of discussions occurring within a given meeting. However, they are inadequate as indices because the contents of discussion for each index are not described. The only information each index has is that buttons are pushed. Furthermore, pushing buttons are often missed when discussions are heated.

In this study, we propose an automated meeting index system based on the contents of discussions that people can use for meetings without digital support software. In other words, indices based on the contents of discussions during a meeting can be automatically formed by using only paper, writing implements, and a camera in a certain arrangement. To this end, we develop trackable sticky notes, called "Tracky Notes," as indices. Sticky notes are paper notes that can be easily pasted on a surface and taken off. They are frequently used in meetings, especially in brainstorming. In brainstorming, sticky notes are generally used as follows. First, people write their ideas on sticky notes, and paste it on the desk. After adequate ideas appear, people move the sticky notes to make groups of them. This is commonly called "KJ method". In that process, people often rotate the sticky notes to show the written contents to others. In the scenes where sticky notes are pasted on the desk, moved, and rotated, people tend to pay attention to the corresponding sticky note and discuss it. Consequently, we use as indices time points where sticky notes are first pasted on the desk, moved, and rotated in the meeting. This can happen only when the sticky notes are trackable. Therefore, Tracky Notes are designed as trackable sticky notes. Tracky Notes can be tracked with visible markers through a camera, and is robust against occlusion (Figure 1, Figure 2).

In this paper, we first describe the proposed Tracky Notes. We then develop a meeting viewer where Tracky Notes are used as indices (Figure 3). Finally, we report the result of a user study conducted in a university classroom. The user study revealed three points: (1) The appropriate region of visible markers on Tracky Notes by exploring the written region of characters on sticky notes. (2) The robustness of the Tracky Notes against occlusion by a user study in a university classroom. (3) The effectiveness of Tracky Notes by comparing three tools for seeking movie, Tracky Notes, seek bar, ±5sec buttons through questionnaire.

2. TRACKY NOTES: TRACKABLE STICKY NOTES

2.1 System Requirements

In this section, we define the requirements for Tracky Notes. The size of each note is set to 75 mm × 100 mm, the commonly sold size on the market. Printable visible markers are used so that no additional equipment is required except for a camera. The printable marker also allows us to easily make a large number of Tracky Notes.

To design the visible marker, we assume the following requirements: (1) A sufficient area of the writing region. (2) An adequate number of notes for a meeting can be tracked. (3) Robustness against occlusion is sufficient.

First, we describe where to put markers on notes. In sticky notes, most characters are written in the center and the outer region is hardly used. Therefore, we place markers on the outer regions of sticky notes.

Second, we define the number of notes that can be recognized. We counted the number of sticky notes used in an hour-long meeting. In the meeting, 20 subjects were divided into five groups of four each. The maximum number of notes used by a group was 156. Therefore, we stipulate that more than 156 notes need to be recognized in our system.

Finally, we define robustness against occlusion. Robustness is required since notes are often occluded by writing implements, other notes, and people's hands. However, general markers, such as the QR code, are not robust against occlusion. While a few other markers that are robust against occlusion have been proposed, they have problems. Some are robust against only temporal occlusion, whereas others cannot track several markers at a time [5][6]. In our system, multiple constantly occluded markers need to be tracked simultaneously.

In conclusion, the above three requirements can be reformulated as follows: (1) A marker is placed on the outer regions of sticky notes. (2) More than 156 sticky notes are recognizable. (3) Multiple constantly occluded markers can be simultaneously tracked.

2.2 System Design

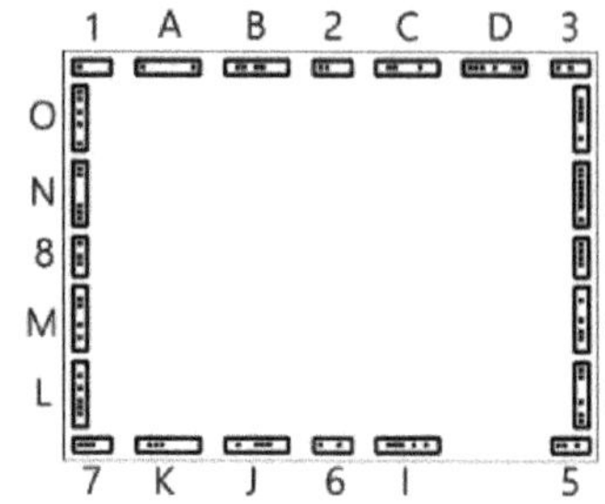

Figure 4. Design of Tracky Notes.

To fulfill the requirements stated in Section 2.1, we designed Tracky Notes (Figure 4). Tracky Notes is paper sticky notes designed to be trackable. In our design, the tracking of notes is enabled by recognizing each region and decoding its corresponding ID. Therefore, there are two types of rectangles on Tracky Notes. Eight smaller rectangles (1-8) are used to recognize each region and seven larger ones (A-O) to decode its ID. The tracking marker is composed of these 15 rectangles.

As shown in Figure 4, there is an empty region between rectangles "5" and "I." This empty region is arisen for the coding design. We set this empty region here for some reasons. The lower region of a sticky note is often occluded by other sticky notes, and its right side is frequently occluded by the hand, as right-handed people form the majority of humans. Consequently, we place the empty region in the lower-right region, since it tends to be occluded most frequently.

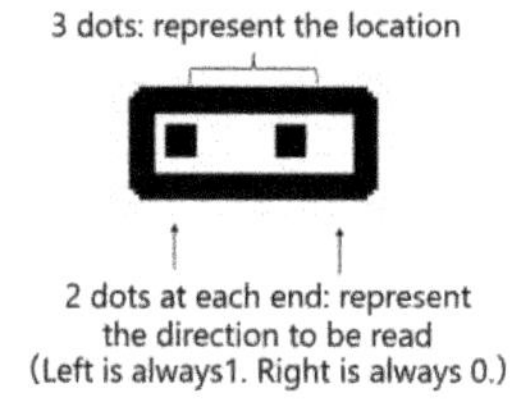

Figure 5. Rectangle for region recognition.

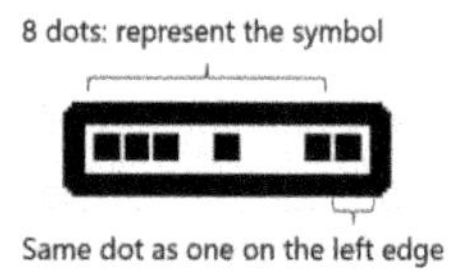

Figure 6. Rectangle for ID recognition.

The region recognition process is as follows. There are eight rectangles for recognizing each region (Figure 5). Two dots at each end are used to determine the direction in which the other dots should be read. The dot at the left end is always 1 and that on the other side is always 0. The three dots at the center represent the location of each rectangle (1-8). When more than four of the eight are recognized, the region of the sticky note can be recognized by homography. When more than five points are recognized, the RANSAC algorithm is used to improve the accuracy of homography [7].

We now describe the decoding process. The ID for each sticky note is coded using the Reed–Solomon codes. These codes consist of two types of symbols, information symbols and check symbols. Each symbol contains eight bits of information. The number of information symbols is set to 1 and that of check symbols to 14 in our design. Each rectangle corresponds to one symbol. The Reed–Solomon codes can represent the information contained in the information symbols. Consequently, it can represent 256 IDs. It can also correct erroneous symbols up to half of the number of check symbols: in this case, up to seven symbols can be corrected. In the rectangle, eight dots from the left end represent symbol information (Figure 6). The dot at the right end is identical to the one at the left end. Both are used to distinguish ID recognition rectangles from region recognition rectangles. In the former, the XOR value of each end is always 0, whereas that of region recognition rectangles is always 1.

This system hence allows for four errors in eight region recognition rectangles and seven errors in 15 ID recognition rectangles. Therefore, approximately half the region of a sticky note can be occluded such that the system can still successfully track it. Multiple markers can also be tracked at a time by this design. Figure 1 shows the tracked sticky notes. The detected sticky notes are enclosed in rectangles, and the ID of each sticky note is printed on it.

3. VIEWING SYSTEM

In this section, we detail the viewing system where our Tracky Notes are used as indices. We use as indices time points when sticky notes are first pasted, moved, and rotated on the desk.

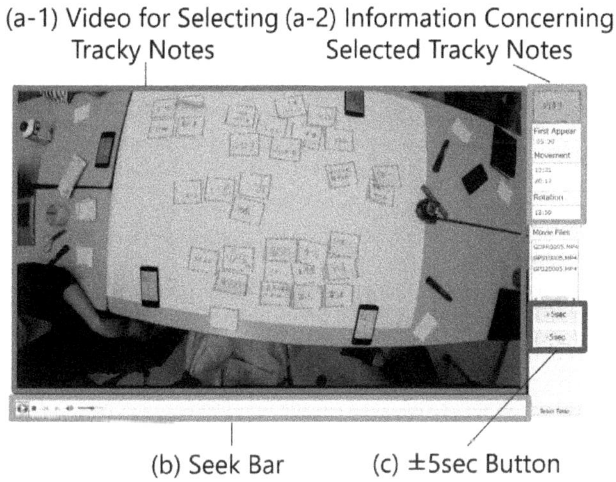

Figure 7. User interface of the viewing system.

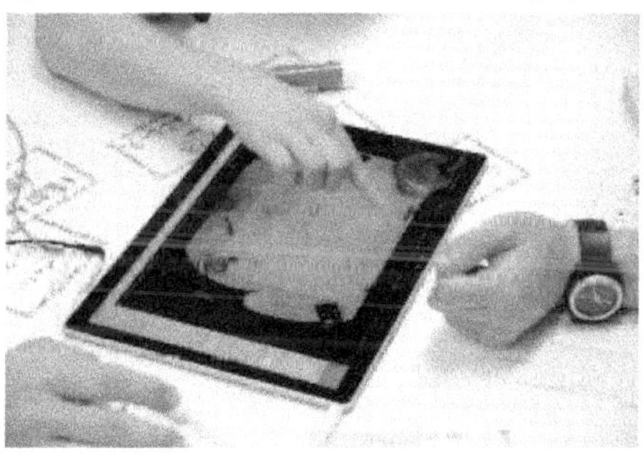

Figure 8. Users can select the Tracky Notes by touching them on the video.

The user interface of the viewing system is shown in Figure 7. In Figure 7, (a-1) A video of meetings is played. Tracky Notes can be touched and selected in this region (Figure 8). (a-2) Information concerning a sticky note touched on a screen in the video is shown. From top to bottom, the image of the selected sticky note and the lists of time points when it is first pasted, moved, and rotated, are shown. (b) A seek bar, which is the most common seeking function. (c) Buttons to seek +5 s and -5 s are placed to enable users to search through a video in small increments of time.

The operation steps are shown as follows. (1) The system displays the last scene of the video where all sticky notes have appeared. (2) The user can touch a sticky note on the screen that he/she wants to reference in the video referring to the contents written on each sticky note. (3) Information regarding the touched sticky note is shown. When each time point in the list is touched, the video is sought to the corresponding scene.

4. USER STUDY IN A UNIVERSITY CLASSROOM

4.1 Experimental Overview

We performed the user study in a university classroom. The purpose of the user study was (1) to determine the exact region to set markers in sticky notes by exploring regions where characters are written on them, (2) to test the robustness of the proposed system against the occlusion of Tracky Notes, and (3) to test the usability of the proposed viewer.

Twenty undergraduates were recruited for the experiment and divided into five groups. Each group consisted of one woman and three men. The user study was carried out over three weeks. In the first week, the students practiced brainstorming using plain sticky notes instead of Tracky Notes. The brainstorming lasted about 60 minutes. The 117 sticky notes used were scanned and converted into binary images to explore regions where characters were written. We then designed and printed five sets of Tracky Notes for each group. One set consisted of distinguishable 200 notes. In the second and third weeks, the students performed brainstorming using Tracky Notes and the viewer, respectively. The Tracky Notes were used over a period of two weeks: the viewer was used for 20 minutes in the third week to review the brainstorming of the second week. Ten minutes were dedicated to practicing the use of the viewer and the other 10 to actually review using it. At the end of the third week, we distributed a questionnaire among the participants.

During brainstorming, a sheet of large paper (788 mm × 1091 mm) set on the desk for Tracky Notes to be pasted was captured by a camera (GoPro Hero4 Black, Woodman Labs Inc.) hung from the ceiling. The camera was used in 4K mode. The large paper was fixed and the students practiced brainstorming around it. The distance between the desk and the camera was set to 70 cm as the entire area of the large paper can be captured. The viewer was used on a touch screen (Surface Book, Microsoft). The students listened to the video using earphones (Figure 3).

4.2 Experimental Results

Exp. (1): The sum of the binary values of 117 sticky notes (characters: 1, background: 0) is shown in eight-bit grayscale (Figure 9).

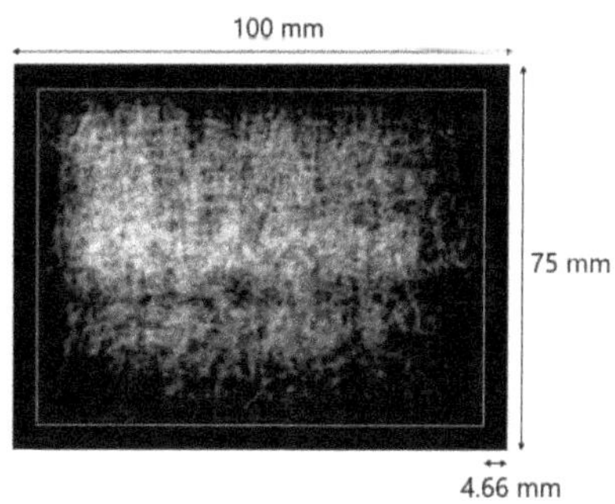

Figure 9. Written region on sticky notes.

The larger the sum of the binary value, the whiter the grayscale color. As seen in Figure 9, barely any character has been written in the outer region of the note. Therefore, our assumption in Section 2.1 was correct. To determine the precise region where a marker should be placed, the relationship between the distance from the edge of the note and number of characters along the edge was explored. The result showed that within the region of 4.66 mm from the edge, the written characters are under 1 % of all characters. Therefore, we set the marker within the region of 4.66mm from the edge where people hardly write characters.

Exp. (2): As a result of processing the captured movies during brainstorming, most occluded Tracky Notes were correctly tracked (Figure 2). However, some of the Tracky Notes were peeled off and turned up. Some of these peeling Tracky Notes were not tracked correctly. The peeling was caused by the weakness of the paste of the Tracky Notes.

Exp. (3): We checked the usability of our system in terms of effectiveness and efficiency through a questionnaire using a five-point Likert scale, where 1 = "strongly disagree" and 5 = "strongly agree." In this experiment, we compared three tools for seeking movie, Tracky Notes, seek bar, ±5sec buttons. The seek bar and ±5sec buttons are prepared as conventional functions of movie players. To compare effectiveness, we asked the following three questions: "Do you think you were able to find the scenes you wanted to watch using the seek bar (Q1)/with ±5 s buttons (Q2)/with Tracky Notes (Q3)?" Furthermore, to compare efficiency, we used the following three questions: "If you found the scenes you wanted to watch, do you think this was more quickly accomplished by using the seek bar (Q4)/using ±5 s buttons (Q5)/using Tracky Notes (Q6)?"

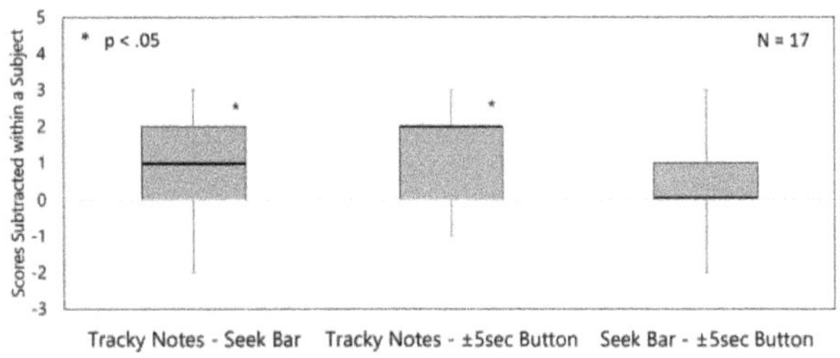

Figure 10. Comparison of each tool in terms of effectiveness.

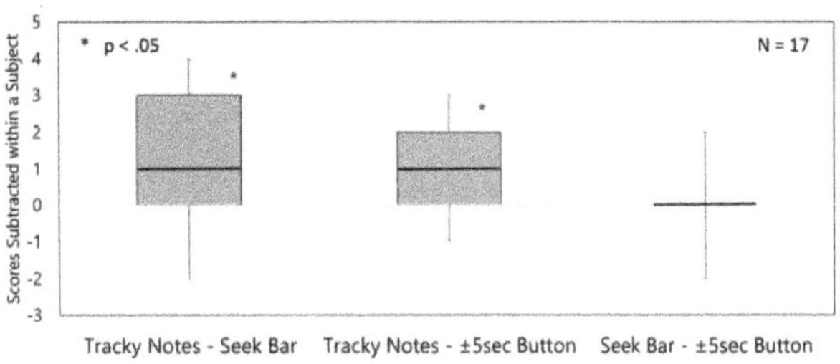

Figure 11. Comparison of each tool in terms of efficiency.

Figure 10 shows the results for answers to Q1-Q3 and Figure 11 shows those for answers to Q4-Q6. Three students absent in the second or third week were excluded from the result. The left side of each figure shows "the score of Tracky Notes–the score for the seek bar," "the score of Tracky Notes–the score for ±5 s buttons," and "the score for the seek bar–the score for ±5 s buttons" The scores were compared within a subject. For instance, when a subject score 5 to Tracky Notes and 3 to seek bar, "the score of Tracky Notes–the score for the seek bar," becomes 2. In Figure 10 and Figure 11, the box plot shows the max, 75%, median, 25%, and minimum values of all scores. As a result of Shapiro-Wilk test, this data did not follow the normal distribution. Therefore, the Mann–Whitney U-test was conducted for each pair of tools. Our proposed method yielded a significantly higher score than two other seeking tools ($p < .05$). The p-value was modified using the Holm Bonferroni method because there were three pairs of comparison. Therefore, it was revealed that Tracky Notes are superior to other two conventional tools in terms of effect and efficiency.

5. CONCLUSION AND FUTURE WORK

In this paper, we proposed trackable sticky notes and a viewing system for taking minutes in meetings. We then performed a user study in a university classroom. The user study revealed the appropriate regions for a marker to be placed on sticky notes. Most Tracky Notes were hence correctly tracked. We finally established the effectiveness of our system by using a questionnaire.

The results revealed that Tracky Notes are susceptible to peeling. Therefore, in future work, we will devise Tracky Notes as they do not peel frequently by expanding the area of the paste and improving the strength of it. Moreover, the result of the questionnaire was quite subjective. The subjects may have answered the questionnaire according to our demands. This is called demand characteristics in psychology. Therefore, we will conduct objective experiments involving search tasks in meeting videos to reveal the effectiveness of the proposed indexing system.

Tracky Notes have a number of applications. For example, communication in meetings can be analyzed through the movement of sticky notes. Real-time meeting support is also possible by projecting some additional information on sticky notes. We will examine these applications in future research.

6. ACKNOWLEDGMENTS

This work was supported by CREST, JST.

7. REFERENCES

[1] Geyer, W., Richter, H., Fuchs, L., Frauenhofer, T., Daijavad, S., and Poltrock, S. 2001. TeamSpace: A collaborative workspace system supporting virtual meetings. IBM Research Report, RC 21961.

[2] Geyer, W., Richter, H. and Abowd, G. D. 2005. Towards a smarter meeting record—Capture and access of meetings revisited. Multimedia Tools and Applications 27, 393-410.

[3] Jaimes, A., Omura, K., Nagamine, T., and Hirata, K. 2004. Memory cues for meeting video retrieval. In Proceedings of the 1st ACM Workshop on Continuous Archival and Retrieval of Personal Experiences, Anonymous ACM, 74-85.

[4] Nishida, T. 2005. Conversation quantization for conversational knowledge process. Databases in Networked Information Systems. Springer Berlin Heidelberg, 15-33.

[5] Wang, J., Shyi, C., Hou, T., and Fong, C. 2010. Design and implementation of augmented reality system collaborating with QR code. In Computer Symposium (ICS), 2010 International, Anonymous IEEE, 414-418.

[6] Álvarez, H., Leizea, I., and Borro, D. 2012. A new marker design for a robust marker tracking system against occlusions. Computer Animation and Virtual Worlds 23, 503-518.

[7] Fischler, M.A. and Bolles, R. C. 1981. Random sample consensus: A paradigm for model fitting with applications to image analysis and automated cartography. Communications of the ACM 24, 381-395.

Towards Card-based User Interfaces Workspaces for Group Mission Planning

Stephanie Kane
Charles River Analytics
625 Mount Auburn Street
Cambridge, MA 02139

Erika von Kelsch
Charles River Analytics
625 Mount Auburn Street
Cambridge, MA 02139

Martin Voshell
Charles River Analytics
625 Mount Auburn Street
Cambridge, MA 02139

Ryan M. Kilgore
Charles River Analytics
625 Mount Auburn Street
Cambridge, MA 02139

ABSTRACT
Current mission planning interfaces are difficult to understand, cumbersome to use, and do not support the collaborative aspect of group mission planning. To address this critical shortfall, this paper describes the designed and demonstrated set of card-based user interfaces (card UIs) to increase the effectiveness of group mission planning workflows. These interfaces provide consistent visual structures for a diverse set of tasks across team members, enable team members to understand progress across distributed tasks and facilitate situational awareness of the overall evolving mission plan. This paper describes key considerations for group mission planning activities and present examples of our card UI interface supporting group mission planning tasks.

CCS Concepts
Human-centered computing → Interaction Design theory, concepts, and paradigms

Keywords
user interface design; mission planning; card-based design; mission displays; group mission planning

1. Background
Working with the Navy, the Charles River Analytics team has observed powerful support tools and mission planning systems have been developed to help pilots plan missions. Although these planning systems offer advanced functionality, they do not support the collaborative aspect of group mission planning across teams of pilots. Currently, each pilot uses the same one-size-fits all system, which requires that they dive into deep menu structures to find hidden functionality that is relevant to their specific task. Even simple tasks, such as setting the start point and waypoints for a flight, typically require the pilot to access information and perform actions on multiple screens and through complex menus. These processes are not only cognitively demanding—with superfluous navigation steps and heavy demands on working memory—but also brittle and prone to error, especially by novice users. For expert pilots, these processes are time-consuming, repetitive, and tedious.

Frequently, pilots work directly on their own specific tasks, but because these systems to not provide the overall mission context, the pilot must inquire and discover core reference information across component views. Awareness of the overall mission is especially important as mission planning progresses and other tasks are completed by team members. With these systems, pilots are not aware of their own tasks within the context of the larger group planning process.

While some pilots may share similar tasks (e.g., setting key waypoint values), other pilots have specialized tasks that are irrelevant to others (e.g., annotating mission imagery). However, these systems present the same interface components to the pilot, regardless of their relevance, requiring pilots to develop and remember general and specialized mission specific tasks, as well as many platform-specific configuration tasks (e.g., avionics, radar, communication) This one-size-fits-all approach—providing access to myriad planning functionality and tools regardless of the pilot's task—makes it difficult for pilots to recognize, select, and interact with the best planning capability for their specific aspect of the mission planning process. As a result, these systems are difficult to use for simple tasks. Because of this one-size-fits-all approach, current mission planning processes are complex, demanding, and do not provide the situational awareness required by the group planning process.

2. Approach
Our approach began with an analysis of the Navy mission planning process, based on a review of doctrine and prior research, knowledge elicitation sessions with current and former pilots and instructors, as well as formal observation of training exercises for Navy F-18 pilots. Requirements that resulted out of this analysis efforts include providing interface methods that support the group mission planning process that support and facilitate how the group work occurs across a diverse set of UI tools as opposed to the one-size-fits-all approach. In support of this goal, interface methods are needed that: 1) provide consistent visual structure for a diverse set of tasks across team members; 2) enable team members to understand progress across tasks and across team member and 3) facilitate situational awareness of the overall mission context when executing tasks.

GROUP'16, November 13–16, 2016, Sanibel Island, FL, USA
ACM 978-1-4503-4276-6/16/11.
http://dx.doi.org/10.1145/2957276.2996286

Figure 1: Mission Planning Workspace with card UIs containing individual planning tasks

To address these goals, the Charles River Analytics team employed a card-based user interface (card UI) approach. The card UI approach was chosen to address the previously described requirements as cards provide a common presentation and interface structure across the diverse set of component planning tools. Card UIs also provide high level status summaries based on outputs of component planning tools, thereby giving team members awareness of the overall mission plan and progress on critical functional planning activities.

Card UIs are an emerging design approach and have been used across a number of industries [1,2,3]. However, they have a range of definitions and implementations. Under this effort, card UIs are defined as consistent and predictable visual interface forms defined by a set of common interface structures based on interaction primitives (e.g., visual design, hierarchy, typography). Cards are typically implemented as small rectangular visual structures that hold information and controls in a concise format. The cards vary in their contained information and complexity, but each card is compact, contains data, and leads to further interactions. Cards can also represent status summary views, which provide information that allow users, in a mentally economical way, to easily assess their overall situation with respect to the underlying processes or activities they are engaged in [4].

To address the specific challenges of group mission planning, the Charles River Analytics team designed a group workspace composed of card UIs. In this implementation, a card UI is a container that logically encapsulates bits of information within a rectangular area that contains a small amount of easily digestible information. Often many cards appear in close proximity to each other, and the borders of the cards is used to separate information between each of the cards. Previously, successful status summary design techniques have used reduced scale versions of pattern-based or emergent property displays that help function as a longshot of information [5,6]. Under this effort, sets of simple, individual display cards integrate content across a variety of services and enable even novice users to interact with manageable amounts of information.

3. Mission Planning Workspace

To address the challenges within the mission planning environment, the Charles River Analytics team designed a mission planning workspace composed of card UIs. Figure 1 shows the interface concept for a card UI mission planning workspace being used for a notional mission. Within the Mission Planning Workspace, pilots can see all the tasks to be completed, ownership of and progress against each task, and coordinate with each other on tasks.

3.1 Mission Task Cards

In this approach, each card represents a specific functional mission planning task. The pilot who owns the task is represented by a colored icon at the top left of the card. Each card provides a task summary and the information that is critical for other pilots, displaying the most relevant and critical information at the top level of the interface. Overall task information is displayed coherently and cohesively in a single workspace, unlike current planning systems, where pilots must dive down and navigate deep menu structures to find this critical information across disjointed modules. The cards are organized by representative functional areas that mirror the potential responsibilities of an individual pilot.

Each card also provides an estimated time of completion to help coordinate efforts across pilots. By providing high level summary representations of the outputs and status of each functional task, these cards improve pilot awareness of the mission and how it evolves over time.

3.2 Card UI Meta-Information

As part of our card UI approach, the Charles River Analytics team extended traditional card UI metaphors to explore rendering methods that convey meta-information about the cards, such as whether the task represented by the card is in progress or complete. Cards that represent completed tasks, such as the GPS Predictor card shown in the lower left of the figure, are completely opaque and emphasize the completion time. Cards that represent tasks in progress have a colored border. Cards that represent tasks that have not been started are transparent and have a dashed border, such as the weather and fuel cards in the lower right of the figure.

3.3 Cross-Card Relationships

To represent tasks with relationships or dependencies on other tasks, the card UI allows pilots to "flag" individual fields within a card to cue the owner of the task to the relationship. For example, the Weather card UI shown in the lower right of the figure displays the start and end waypoints with a flag icon to indicate that they are blocked by the completion and definition of the route on the Route card UI. Pilots can also leave direct comments on the data elements displayed on a card. For example, a pilot has commented that the altitude shown on the Route card must be confirmed. The comment is connected to an icon representing the pilot who wrote the comment; this icon can be clicked to communicate with that pilot.

4. Conclusions and Future Work

As part of this approach, the Charles River Analytics team worked with representative users within the Navy's mission planning domain to evaluate the usability and efficacy of the overall approach. Based on evaluations with these users and with subject matter experts, the card-based UI approach is a promising methodology for unifying a diverse set of tools and providing quick access to diverse information across mission planning systems. The card UI approach also provides a well-defined and well-formed framework for third party developers of new, future features.

The Charles River Analytics team plans to continue expanding our card UI methods to support group mission planning activities. In particular, the Charles River Analytics team will explore methods that support advanced coordination of activities across cards These methods will extend the flagging and commenting features and provide higher resolution methods to facilitate the awareness of the temporal dynamics of constraints and actions, such as when tasks must be completed to facilitate an optimal mission planning process; that is, a process during which no pilot is completely blocked on any activity.

Future efforts can extend this approach to support awareness of partial task completion or completion of sub-tasks, as well as supporting insights into tasks across multiple levels of resolution. The Charles River Analytics team also sees benefit in methods that can provide immediate feedback on group process and efficiency as well the dynamic distribution and assignment of tasks based on skill, availability, and effectiveness.

The Charles River Analytics team will continue working with representative users to evaluate the usability and efficacy of our interface methods in conveying task, progress, and key relationships within the targeted Navy mission planning domain. The Charles River Analytics team will also explore the utility of our methods in other domains, such as for project teams in the commercial domain.

The Charles River Analytics team is currently developing a plan to extend our prototyping efforts to evaluate how well our interface methods support group mission planning. As part of this work, the Charles River Analytics team plans to measure the intuitiveness of our visual language and determine whether usability is affected by the combination of several overlapping interface rendering and visualization methods. The Charles River Analytics team plans to assess the benefits of our enhancements to traditional card UIs and assess individual pilot and group performance when developing mission plans using our interface methods. The Charles River Analytics team believes that these UI approaches (i.e., task cards that show meta-information and cross-card relationships) will lead to more efficient and effective group mission planning, and plan to investigate these claims in a follow-up study.

5. ACKNOWLEDGMENTS

This material is based upon work supported by the Navy under Contract No. N68335-15-C-0158. Any opinions, findings and conclusions or recommendations expressed in this material are those of the authors and do not necessarily reflect the views of the Navy.

6. REFERENCES

[1] Google Material Design; https://material.google.com/components/cards.html

[2] Pinterest; http://pinterest.com/

[3] Twitter; https://twitter.com/

[4] Woods, D. D., and J. C. Watts. "How not to have to navigate through too many displays." *Handbook of human-computer interaction* 2 (1997): 617-650.

[5] Watson, Craig D., et al. "Status tree monitoring and display system." U.S. Patent No. 4,902,469. 20 Feb. 1990.

[6] Ranson, David S., and David D. Woods. "Animating computer agents." Human Interaction with Complex Systems, 1996. HICS '96. Third Annual Symposium on IEEE Proceedings, 1996.

Analysis of Human Nodding Behavior during Group Work for Designing Nodding Robots

Hayato Kihara
The University of Tokyo
7-3-1 Hongo, Bunkyo-ku,
Tokyo, JAPAN
+81-3-5841-6781
kihara@nae-lab.org

Shogo Fukushima
The University of Tokyo
7-3-1 Hongo, Bunkyo-ku,
Tokyo, JAPAN
+81-3-5841-6781
shogo@nae-lab.org

Takeshi Naemura
The University of Tokyo
7-3-1 Hongo, Bunkyo-ku,
Tokyo, JAPAN
+81-3-5841-6668
naemura@nae-lab.org

ABSTRACT

Nodding has various communicative functions in humans, such as agreement, emphasis and turn-taking and can also create various positive impressions in communication by the person exhibiting the behavior. The ultimate aim of our research is to facilitate communication by implementing nodding behavior in robots. This study analyzed videos of human conversations in groups and focused on three aspects of people's nodding behavior as they listened to others: 1) Time period to complete a nodding cycle and each nods, 2) Time delay before initiating a nodding response, and 3) Number of continuous nods used at one time. We found that: 1) The mode time period to a nod was 0.27 s, with 96% of all nods occurring within 0.17~0.57 s. 2) The mode time delay before initiating a nodding response was 0.30 s, with 95% of all nods occurring within -0.78~1.4 s. 3) Fewer than six continuous nods were used 97% of the time - one nod, 55%, two nods, 24%, three nods, 12%, four nods, 3.0%, and five nods, 2.1%. Ultimately, the research findings serve as guidelines for implementing accurate human nodding behavior in robots.

Keywords

Nodding Analysis; Human Behavior; Non-verbal Communication; Robot Design; Group Work.

1. INTRODUCTION

Group work is often used as a style of communication in companies and educational institutions. It is used to help people create ideas and improve decision making through coordination with one another. However, it is not easy for interlocutors to keep good relationships while working in a group. In particular, it is difficult to create a positive impression on interlocutors and build a rapport.

Several studies have reported that non-verbal messages involving motion are important in communication. In particular, nodding has various communicative functions for both the listener and the speaker, such as showing agreement, laying emphasis, maintaining rhythm, and turn-taking [1].

GROUP '16, November 13-16, 2016, Sanibel Island, FL, USA
ACM 978-1-4503-4276-6/16/11.
http://dx.doi.org/10.1145/2957276.2996287

Furthermore, nodding can also create various positive impressions in communication by the person exhibiting the behavior. Speakers tend to speak more when listeners are nodding [2]. The listener tends to agree more when he/she is nodding [3]. Nodding creates a positive impression and a rapport in discussions [4]. According to previous research, if it is possible to encourage the nodding, it can be expected to assist in communication.

In order to facilitate communication in situations such as group work, we focused on the recognition of the listener's nodding behavior by robots. We also aim to synthesize nodding to any object such as agents and avatars. This study analyzed videos of human discussions in groups and focused on three aspects of people's nodding behavior when listening to others.

2. PURPOSE

Our purpose in this study was to reveal specific features of nodding when listening to others in order to implement human nodding behavior in agents such as robots and avatar to at least 95 percent accuracy. We analyzed nodding according to the following three criteria:

1. Periodic time:
   The time duration between the start and end of a nodding action.
2. Delay time:
   The time between a pause in the speaker's speech and the initiation of nodding by the listener.
3. Number of continuous nods.
   The number of continuous nods during a series of head movements.

3. PREVIOUS WORK

Nodding can be classified into the speaker's nodding and the listener's nodding.

3.1 Nodding by the Speaker

In order to implement realistic nodding behavior in a humanoid robot, Hashimoto et al. analyzed the preferred expression timing, angle and angular velocity of the speaker's nodding in dialogue [5].

This study aims to create a object to take part as a listener. Therefore there is a need to discuss in detail nodding of the listener rather than nodding of the speaker.

3.2 Nodding by the Listener

Nakamura et al. analyzed the kinds of nodding by the interlocutor in a dialogue in terms of angular velocity and peak-to-peak time of extreme values [6]. They revealed that extreme values of angular velocity were distributed about 0.18 rad/s and those of peak-to-peak time about 0.16 s.

Although the angular velocity and a rough period for nodding have been revealed in related research, we also analyzed the periodic time according to the number of continuous nods. Moreover, delay time from the speaker's pause and the number of continuous nods have not been shown as far as we know. These variable are conceivable parameters required when designing nodding objects and therefore also require attention.

4. ANALYSIS OF NODDING

4.1 Definitions

We define the following two terms concerning nodding in this study and show the relationship between them in Figure 1.

- Nod:
  A movement of the head such that it returns to its original position
- Sample:
  Series of all nods from the beginning of the movement of the head until it comes to a stop

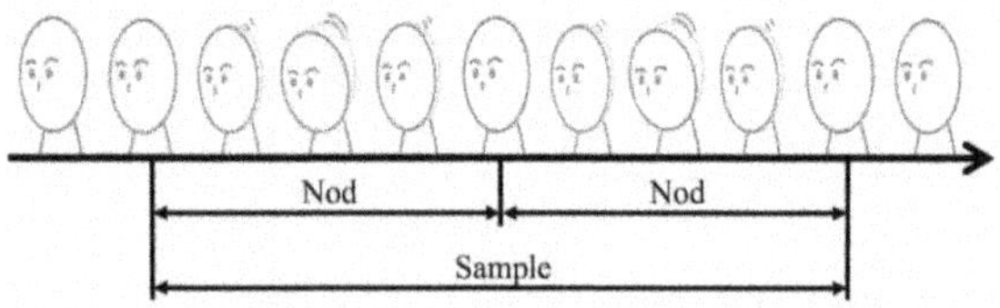

Figure 1. Defining names of a nod and a sample.

4.2 Method of Analysis

We analyzed nodding in videos to analyze each of the following parameters of interest.

1. Periodic time:
   We measured a period of a sample and a nod manually by counting the number of elapsed frames for each of the actions. Because we captured the video at 30 fps, the measurement was discrete times per 33 ms.
2. Delay time:
   Delay time is measured as the duration between the speaker's pause to the beginning of nodding, using a video and speech waveform obtained from the video. The speech waveform was analyzed on the order of 10 ms, which is the minimum transfer unit of the search bar in the annotation software.
3. Number of continuous nods:
   The number of continuous nods was counted using a series of head movements.

5. EXPERIMENT

5.1 Conditions

The participants in our experiment were Japanese university students attending a seminar at the University of Tokyo, and were from 18 to 22 years old. As shown in Figure 2, we captured the students while working in groups to make a decision through an omnidirectional camera suspended from the ceiling, and edited the video into four parts in order to catch each group member's face. Each group consisted of four members (three males and one female). We analyzed three groups in total, consisting of 12 people. We used the annotation software ELAN. Given our purpose here, we ignored the nodding of the speaker and focused only on that of the listener.

A total of 12 people, 233 samples and 436 nods were analyzed.

Figure 2. Experimental scene.

5.2 Result of Periodic Time

The periodic time of each sample is shown in Figure 3. The mean periodic time was 0.64 s, the median was 15 frames (0.50 s), the three modal values were 8, 9, and 10 frames (0.27 s, 0.30 s and 0.33 s). We show the subdivided result into a periodic time of each nod in Figure 4. The mean periodic time of each nod was 0.34 s, the median was 10 frames (0.33 s) and the mode was 8 frames (0.27 s). In order to exclude outlying values from the median, 96% of the all the data is calculated to be between 5~17 frames (0.17~0.57 s).

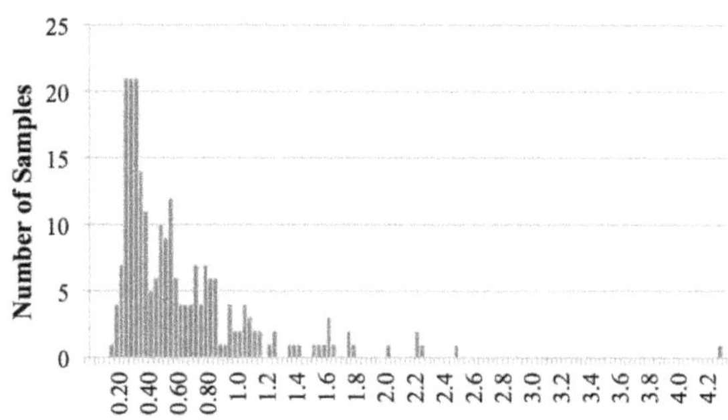

Figure 3. Periodic time per sample.

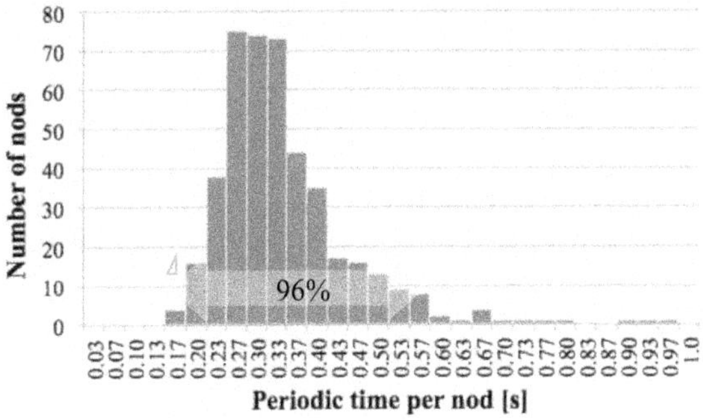

Figure 4. Periodic time per nod.

5.3 Result of Delay Time

We show the delay time data in Figure 5. The graph was drawn after rounding the values of delay time to the second decimal place in order for the width of the class to be 0.10. The mean delay time was 0.32 s, the median was 0.28 s, and the mode 0.30 s. In order to exclude outlying values from the median, 95% of the all the data is calculated to be between -0.78~1.4 s.

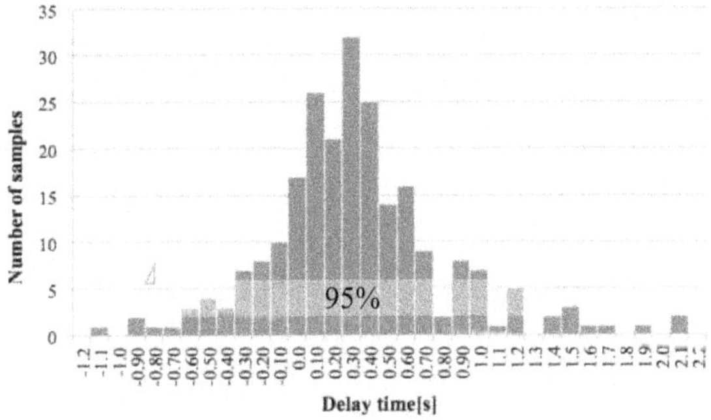

Figure 5. Delay time until nodding caused from the speaker's pause.

5.4 Result of the Number of Continuous Nods

We show the number of continuous nods in Figure 6. Fewer than six continuous nods were used 97% of the time—one nod 55%, two nods 24%, three nods 12%, four nods 3.0%, and five nods 2.1%. The mean number of continuous nods was 1.9.

Figure 6. Number of continuous nods during a series of head movements.

6. DISCUSSION

6.1 Periodic Time

We compared the result of periodic time per nod when people worked in groups with results from related research on two-party dialogue [6]. The prior research investigated the time duration between peaks of angular velocity (measured between maximum and minimum angles of a nod). In order to make the comparison to our study, we equivocated the peak-to-peak time duration to half the periodic time measured in our study. To facilitate a direct comparison, we therefore doubled the time durations reported in the prior research. The resulting modal value of the prior research was 0.32 s compared to the mode periodic time of 8 frames (0.27 s) in our study. Both values were closely distributed around 0.30 s. Accordingly, we conclude that the periodic time of nodding behavior as a listener is nearly the same in four-member groups and two-party dialogues.

6.2 Delay Time

Samples with negative vales meant that nodding was performed while the speaker was speaking. We think this was a way for the listener to express agreement with the speaker and encourage him/her to continue. Bono et al. also revealed that the speaker gazes at the listener before they pause in their speech and this prompts the listener to nod [7]. We concluded that various factors such as the semantic content of the speaker's speech and the gaze of the speaker could prompt nodding in the listener. This accounts for the modal delay time of 0.30 s.

6.3 Number of Continuous Nods

Figure 7 shows the percentage of unique participants that completed a variety of number of continuous nods. The results revealed all participants used one nod. There is then a sharp decline in the percentage of people using more nods per sample. For instance, one out of three people used four continuous nods and one out of six people used five continuous nods despite this number being comparatively high.

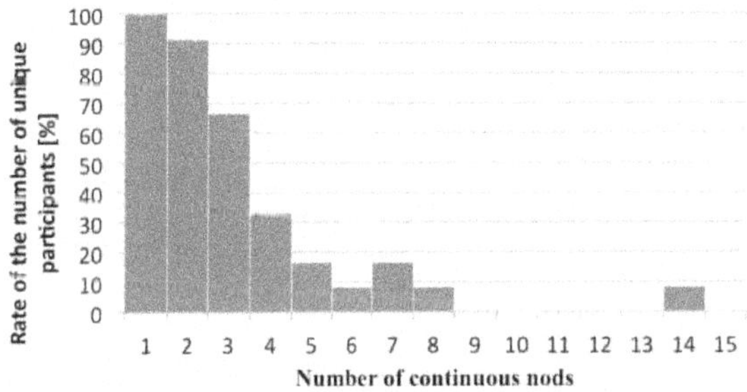

Figure 7. Number of unique participants per each time of continuous nods.

We categorized nods into three stages: first, middle and last. The first was the first nod of each sample. The last was the last nod of each sample. The middle includes all other nods between the first and the last. In the case of only one nod in a sample, we allocated it to the first. The distribution of first, middle and last nods is shown in Figure 8. Table 1 summarizes the findings for each stage.

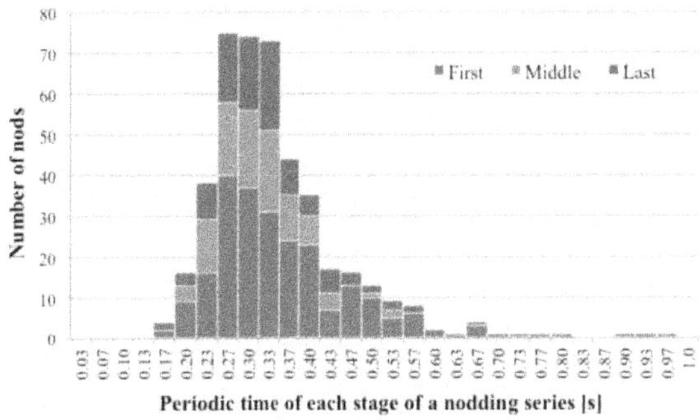

Figure 8. Periodic time of each stage of a nodding series.

We found that the periodic time of the middle nods were less dispersed than the first and the last. The greater similarity may be due a more rhythmic nodding action during the middle phase.

Table 1. Range of more than 95% of all nods.

	# of Nods	Median	Range	Width	Rate
Total	436	10/30 s (0.33 s)	5/30~17/30 s (0.17~0.57 s)	13/30 s (0.43 s)	96%
First	233	10/30 s (0.33 s)	5/30~17/30 s (0.20~0.43 s)	13/30 s (0.43 s)	96%
Middle	99	9/30 s (0.30 s)	6/30~13/30 s (0.17~0.57 s)	8/30 s (0.27 s)	97%
Last	104	10/30 s (0.33 s)	5/30~17/30 s (0.17~0.57 s)	13/30 s (0.43 s)	96%

6.4 Relationship Between Parameters

There was no significant correlation between periodic time and delay time (the correlation coefficient was -0.07), nor was there any between delay time and the number of continuous nods (the correlation coefficient was -0.05).

7. CONCLUSION

This study analyzed human conversations in groups and focused on three aspects of human nodding behavior which were performed when people listened to others. According to the results of the analysis, we suggest that following can be used as implementation guidelines for robots to reproduce 95% of nodding behaviors of a listening human:

1. Periodic time:

   The mode periodic time per nod was 8/30s (0.27s). 96% of all nods were between 5/30~17/30s (0.17~0.57s).

2. Delay time:

   The mode delay time was 0.30s. 95% of all samples were between -0.78~1.4s. There was no correlation between delay time and periodic time and between delay time and the number of continuous nods.

3. Number of continuous nods:

   In all samples investigated, only one nod was the most common (55%), then two nods (24%), three nods (12%), four nods (3.0%), and five nods (2.1%). Fewer than six continuous nods were used 97% of the time.

We note the limitations of this study. The experimental participants were Japanese university students. Nodding frequency and the meaning of a nod vary according to people's age, gender, social status, and culture [1]. Consequently, further experiments are required to reveal nodding behavior across all demographics of the population.

8. FUTURE WORK

Although we analyzed the nodding behavior of listeners, we didn't focus on the relationship of the behavior to the content of the group conversations. We will intend to reveal the relationship between nodding and contextual information, such as whether the speaker him/herself nodded to elicit listener's nodding.

We will implement nodding in robots based on the results from this study. However, our ultimate purpose is to improve communication between people by implementing nodding behavior in robots. In order achieve this we will investigate the impression that people form of the robots and alter the parameters of their nodding behavior accordingly. We will also investigate the effective appearance of robots such as size and face in groups.

We intend to implement nodding in robots and introduce them to people working in groups. Past work has aimed to facilitate communication by generating nodding behavior in avatars based on their interlocutor's speech [8]. Research has shown that the speaker's gaze is highly correlated with the occurrence of nodding [7]. We will therefore consider a method to generate nodding in a robot based on the speaker's gaze. We will also investigate the effects of multiple robots nodding within a group situation and the influence of the number of robots involved.

9. ACKNOWLEDGMENTS

This work was supported by CREST, JST.

10. REFERENCES

[1] Maynard, S.K. 1989. *Japanese conversation: self-contextualization through structure and interactional management.* Ablex Publishing Corporation. Norwood.

[2] Matarazzo, J.D., Saslow, G., Wiens, A.N., Weitman, M. and Allen, B.V. 1964. Interviewer head nodding and interviewee speech durations; *Psychotherapy: Theory Research and Practice*, American Psychological Association, Washington D.C., 54-63. DOI= http://dx.doi.org/10.1037/h0088571.

[3] Briñol, P., Petty, R.E. 2003. Overt head movements and persuasion: A self-validation analysis. *Journal of Personality and Social Psychology*, 84, 1123-1139. DOI= http://dx.doi.org/10.1037/0022-3514.84.6.1123.

[4] Oshima, S. 2014. Achieving Consensus Through Professionalized Head Nods The Role of Nodding in Service Encounters in Japan. *International Journal of Business Communication*, 51, 1 (Jan. 2014), 31-57. DOI= 10.1177/2329488413516207.

[5] Hashimoto, T., Hiramatsu, S., Tuji, T. and Kobayashi, H. 2007. Realization and Evaluation of Realistic Nod with Receptionist Robot SAYA. *In Proceedings of the 16th IEEE International Symposium on Robot and Human Interactive Communication* (Aug. 26-29). RO-MAN '07. IEEE, 326-331. DOI= http://dx.doi.org/10.1109/ROMAN.2007.4415103.

[6] Nakamura, K., Watanabe, T. and Jindai, M. 2013. Development of Nodding Detection System Based on Active Appearance Model. *In Proceedings of the IEEE/SICE International Symposium on System Integration* (Dec. 15-17). SII '13. IEEE, 400-405. DOI= http://dx.doi.org/10.1109/SII.2013.6776678.

[7] Bono, M., Katagiri, Y. 2005. Interactive viewpoint in face-to-face interactions: coordination of gesture, gaze and speech. *The Japanese Journal of Language in Society,* 7, 2, 3-13. (In Japanese).

[8] Sejima, Y., Watanabe, T., and Yamamoto, M. 2008. Analysis by Synthesis of Embodied Communication via VirtualActor with a Nodding Response Model. *In Proceedings of the Second International Symposium on Universal Communication* (Dec. 15-16) ISUC '08. IEEE, 225-230. DOI= http://dx.doi.org/10.1109/ISUC.2008.71.

Novel Web-based Remote Collaboration System Architecture for Wider Use Cases

Yasuhiro Mochida
NTT Network Innovation Laboratories
1-1 Hikarinooka
Yokosuka Kanagawa Japan
+81-46-859-2572
mochida.yasuhiro@lab.ntt.co.jp

Daisuke Shirai
NTT Network Innovation Laboratories
1-1 Hikarinooka
Yokosuka Kanagawa Japan
+81-46-859-5143
shirai.daisuke@lab.ntt.co.jp

Tatsuya Fujii
NTT Network Innovation Laboratories
1-1 Hikarinooka
Yokosuka Kanagawa Japan
+81-46-859-4232
fujii.tatsuya@lab.ntt.co.jp

ABSTRACT
Although web-based remote collaboration systems are getting popular, they are not suitable for long-distance or demanding use cases due to the web browser limitations. To cover wider range of use cases, we propose novel architecture for web-based remote collaboration systems. The main features are relay-servers, overlay-managers, and timecode-servers. The relay-servers enable the web-based systems to exchange data smoothly and locally even in long-distance collaboration. The overlay-managers and timecode-servers enable web-based systems to deal with native applications in order to provide high quality collaboration experience. A prototype is implemented and tested to confirm that the proposal can construct unprecedented collaboration systems suitable for long-distance and demanding collaboration scenarios; targets not possible with conventional web-based collaboration systems.

Keywords
Remote collaboration; Web application; Native application; Video overlay; Synchronization;

1. INTRODUCTION
As the demand for remote collaboration increases, web-based collaboration systems, such as web-conference systems, are getting popular [1,2,3]. One major advantage of web-based collaboration systems is that they don't require the installation of dedicated software. Another major advantage is that users can use a variety of devices, such as PC, Mac, tablet and etc., as long as the system is implemented by the standardized functions of HTML5 & CSS & JavaScript. As seen above, web-based collaboration systems are very convenient; however, the use cases of existing web-based collaboration systems are limited due to the web browser limitations. Our research goal is to expand the range of use cases supported by web-based collaboration systems.

2. BACKGROUND
Conventional web-based collaboration systems use only a web server and web browsers and so suffer many problems, which prevent the users from using web-based collaboration systems over long-distance or demanding collaboration scenarios.

/GROUP '16/, November 13-16, 2016, Sanibel Island, FL, USA
ACM 978-1-4503-4276-6/16/11.
http://dx.doi.org/10.1145/2957276.2996288

2.1 Long-Distance Collaboration
Consider users interacting on a web-based remote collaboration system, such as HyperInfo [4] or SAGE2 [5], which provides the users with a common operating environment to share text, images and other functions implemented by HTML5 & CSS & JavaScript. In the environment, the users can move pointers, edit the text and draw annotations on shared images. However, interaction tends to fall apart in globally-distributed collaboration scenarios. In conventional web-based collaboration systems, data exchange is based on TCP. In TCP, a single packet loss halts processing of the following packets until packet retrieval is successful, which pauses the presentation of remote user action, such as pointer motion, for several hundreds of milliseconds. What is worse, in web-based collaboration systems with separated input and display page, such as SAGE2, the visual feedback on the display page to the user input is delayed significantly. This is because all data exchange must be routed through the web server even if the receiver exists in the same location as the sender due to the web browser security policy.

2.2 Demanding Collaboration
The existing web-based systems have great difficultly in dealing with demanding collaboration scenarios due to their limitations. One major problem lies in the area of Audio and Video (A/V) communication. Web browsers provide WebRTC API for A/V communication. Cola [6] proposed a multi-user A/V conference system using WebRTC; however, the quality is limited. Thus conventional web-based collaboration systems are not suitable for demanding collaboration scenarios, such as important meetings where the participants want to observe the reactions of the others; WebRTC is a good option for mobile meetings on mobile devices, such as laptop computers or tablets, given narrow-bandwidth networks.

Another limitation is that web browsers cannot deal with off-the-shelf software, such as Blender [7], popular design software. Instead of dealing with off-the-shelf software directly, a user can share his/her desktop video including the software to the others via WebRTC. Oh et al. use WebRTC in online real-time learning to share the teaching material on the lecturer's desktop [8]. However, with desktop sharing the other users cannot control the software. What is worse, WebRTC video quality might be insufficient for some demanding collaboration scenarios, such as professional product design or video editing.

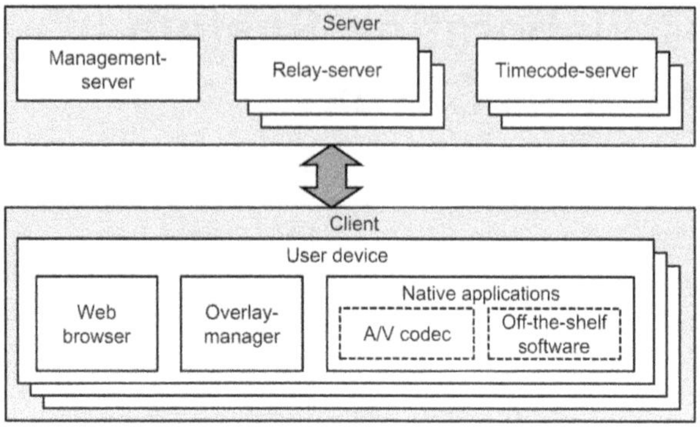

Figure 1. REMOCOP architecture.

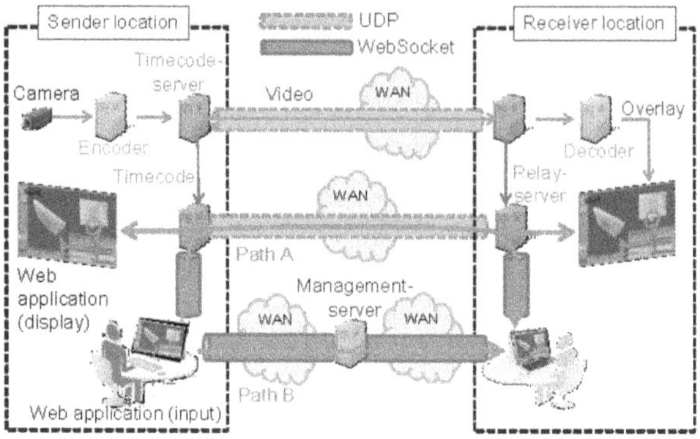

Figure 2. A schematic diagram of a data exchange method and a temporal synchronization method.

3. PROPOSED METHOD

To cover the wider range of use cases, we propose a new architecture named REMOte Collaboration Open Platform (REMOCOP) architecture. Figure 1 shows the proposed architecture. The management-server is a conventional web server. The main features are relay-servers, overlay-managers, and timecode-servers. The relay-servers enable the web-based systems to exchange data smoothly and locally even in long-distance collaboration. The overlay-manager and timecode-servers enable web-based systems to deal with native applications in order to provide high quality collaboration experience. Each user location hosts a pair of relay-server and timecode-server.

3.1 Relay-server

Ensuring good user experience with real-time interaction on web browsers over global distances is challenging. There are two major options for real-time data exchange on web browsers, WebRTC data channel and WebSocket. However, WebRTC data channel implementation lacks interoperability. Thus we employ WebSocket, a real-time oriented protocol, for data exchange, although WebSocket cannot connect web browsers directly and all data exchange must be routed through a web server.

When web browsers are connected to a remote web server in a lossy network via WebSocket, the performance is significantly degraded in terms of real-time data exchange. Once a packet is lost, following packets are buffered and not processed until the lost packet is retrieved since WebSocket is a TCP-based protocol and the packet order must be preserved. If the network one-way delay is 100ms, packet processing will be paused for more than 200ms to wait for packet retrieval, which makes the presentation of remote user action choppy and annoying.

To address the problem, we focus on the data characteristics of real-time collaboration systems. For example, if a single position data of pointer motion is lost, the user experience is not degraded significantly since it causes only a slight discontinuity in pointer motion. In reality, retransmitting the data of one pointer position is not strictly necessary. Hence, this kind of data requires real-time transmission without delay rather than reliable transmission. In contrast, text should be transmitted without loss.

Considering these characteristics, we propose a data exchange method for web-based collaboration systems using relay-servers, see Fig. 2. The web application running in a browser is connected to both a relay-server and to a common management-server via WebSocket. The relay-server is used to exchange data that should be transmitted without delay (Path A) and the management-server is used to exchange data that should be transmitted without loss (Path B). In path A, the relay-server converts the protocol from WebSocket into UDP to exchange the data with the other relay-servers. Although UDP transmission can drop some packets, deployment of Forward Error Correction coding will improve the reliability. Developers can choose from among these paths to suit the data characteristics.

The relay-servers offer the other benefit of immediate reaction. When the web server is far from a user, the user can feel delay between the input and its visual feedback on a separate display page. With relay-servers, user's input is delivered to the display page through a local relay-server, which enables the display page to immediately react to the user's input.

3.2 Overlay-manager

To accommodate high quality collaboration, we propose an application linkage method to construct a web-based collaboration system combining a web application and native applications including off-the-shelf software. Native applications implemented with C++, C# or etc. can achieve higher performance than web applications implemented with only HTML5 & CSS & JavaScript. A web application provides basic functions for collaborative work and some functions are delegated to native applications. To the author's knowledge, no existing web-based collaboration systems deploy native applications.

Figure 3 illustrates the integration of the native applications with the web application. The overlay-manager overlays a web application on native applications in a computer desktop. The web application makes the background region transparent so that the native application aligned behind it can be seen. The position of the native application is adjusted by the overlay-manager, which communicates with the management-server in real-time. In this way, the web application and native applications look as if they are an integrated system. Furthermore, the user input events, such as mouse click, are delivered to the native application permitting remote user operation. When the web application detects a user input event onto the transparent region instead of the native application below, it is transmitted to the overlay-manager via the management-server. The overlay-manager triggers the event on the native application. Since the overlay-manager uses the Operating System (OS) API for position alignment and event trigger, modification of the native application for the linkage is not required, although the overlay-manager is OS dependent. Thus the native application to be combined doesn't have to be designed

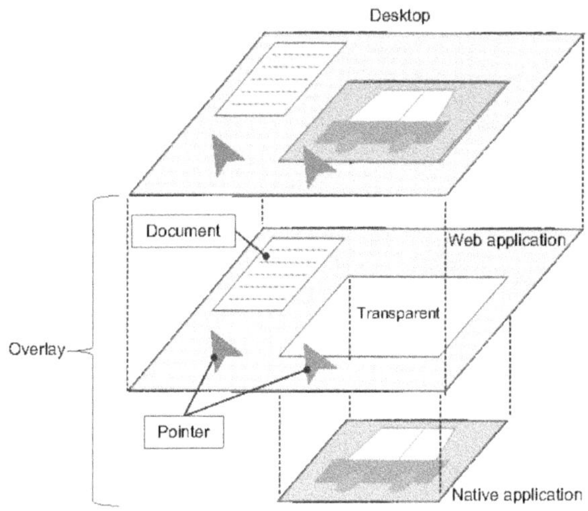

Figure 3. A schematic diagram of an application linkage method.

for the linkage, which means our method can deal with off-the-shelf applications.

3.3 Timecode-server

Combining native A/V codecs for higher quality communication is challenging since not only spatial alignment but temporal synchronization between remote A/V and web application is required. Presentations will become disjointed without any synchronization mechanism since each media transmission experiences different delay factors, for example video encoding and decoding delay. That means multiple events that happened at the same time in one location, such as someone explaining (audio) while pointing (pointer motion), will be presented separately in another location, which degrades understanding. Here we propose a method that uses timecode-servers to synchronize web application object motion with remote video even if the transmission delay jitter in Wide Area Network (WAN) is significant.

One simple idea for synchronization is to insert a constant delay in object motion; unfortunately, this cannot deal with jitter. Our key idea is to extract a timecode from the video packet stream and synchronize object motion using the timecode, which is robust against jitter. Timecode-servers are placed in the video packet stream path as depicted in Fig. 2 assuming that the jitter in a location is negligible compared to video frame intervals.

At the sender's location, the timecode-server extracts the timecode from video packet stream and compensates the encoding delay so that the timecode corresponds to the frame that the camera is shooting. If no timecode is included in the video, the timecode-server can embed a timecode in the video packet. The timecode is delivered to the web application in the same location through the relay-server. The web application embeds the timecode in the messages to be synchronized with video, such as pointer motion.

In the same manner, the timecode-server at the receiver's location extracts the timecode and compensates the decoding delay so that the timecode corresponds to the frame that is on the display at that moment. Compensated timecode is sent to the web application. The timecode embedded in the messages and the remote video timecode from the same location allow the web application to synchronize object motion with remote video.

Figure 4. A picture of our prototype system.

4. PROTOTYPING & EVALUATION

We implemented a prototype system to prove that the proposed architecture can construct unprecedented collaboration systems suitable for long-distance and demanding collaboration scenarios. Figure 4 shows a picture of the prototype. Our prototype system provides the users with a common operating environment to share text, images and desktop video. Users can move pointers, draw annotations on images and control the shared desktop remotely through the input page.

The relay-server resolved the problems of long-distance data exchange. We confirmed that the pointer of remote user moved smoothly over long-distance (150 ms one-way delay) and lossy networks (0.1 % loss rate, the upper bound defined in ITU Y.1541 class 0 IP network [9]) using a network emulator.

Software JPEG2000 codecs were used for high quality A/V communication. Web application object motion is synchronized with remote video and the synchronization error is imperceptible to the naked eye. Desktop video of a workstation including Blender was shared by JPEG2000 codec, whose quality is much higher than WebRTC video at the cost of higher network bandwidth. Remote control of Blender was comfortable since the control pointer immediately reacts to user input thank to the relay servers. In this way, the users can use off-the-shelf software in demanding collaboration use cases.

Furthermore, mobile participants can join the collaboration using only the input page since all of its functions are implemented by HTML5 & CSS & JavaScript. Figure 5 shows a picture of input page. A/V communication and desktop sharing with mobile users are achieved via WebRTC as illustrated in Fig. 6.

5. CONCLUSION

We proposed the REMOCOP architecture to create web-based remote collaboration systems that can cover very challenging use cases. Its main features are relay-servers, overlay-managers and timecode-servers. The relay-servers enable the web-based systems to exchange data smoothly and locally even in long-distance collaboration. Overlay-managers and timecode-servers enable web-based systems to deal with native applications in order to provide high quality collaboration experience. Prototype system implementation proved the ability of the proposed architecture to

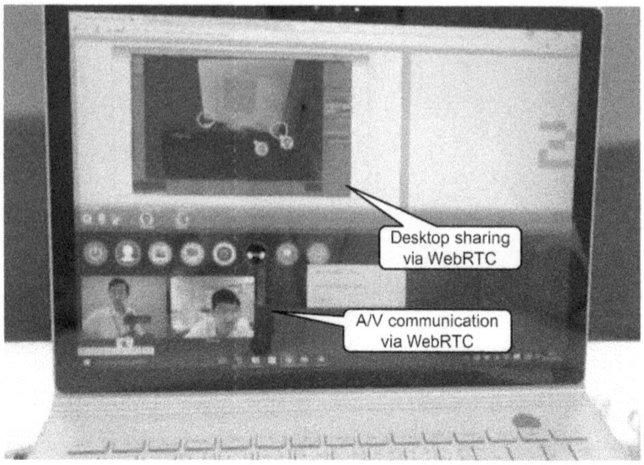

Figure 5. A picture of our input page using WebRTC.

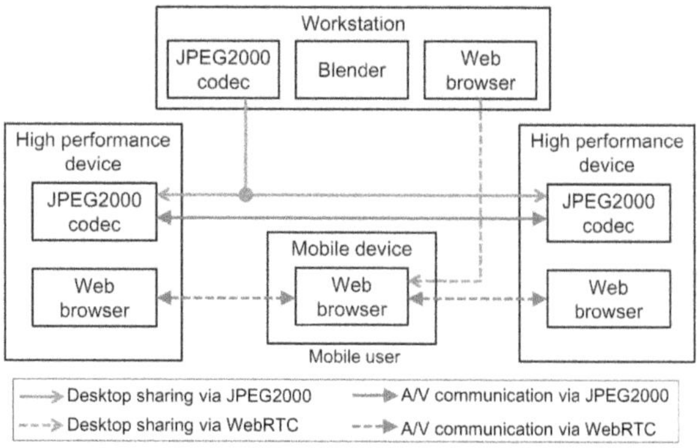

Figure 6. A schematic diagram of desktop sharing and A/V communication.

construct unprecedented collaboration systems suitable for long-distance and demanding collaboration scenarios, benefits not possible with conventional web-based collaboration systems.

6. REFERENCES

[1] Q. Cheng and Y. Wang. 2010. Enterprise Collaborative Business Systems Based on Web Services Technology. In *Proceedings of IEEE International Conference on E-Business and E-Government* (Guangzhou, May 7-9, 2010). 34-37.

[2] (2016) Google+ Hangout. [Online]. Available: http://www.google.com/+/learnmore/hangouts/

[3] (2016) WebEx. [Online]. Available: http://www.webex.co.jp/

[4] N. Kukimoto, Y. Onoue, K. Aoki, K. Fujita and K. Koyamada. 2014. HyperInfo: Interactive Large Display for Informal Visual Communication. In *Proceedings of 17th International Conference on Network-Based Information Systems* (Salerno, 2014). 399-404.

[5] T. Marrinan, J. Aurisano, A. Nishimoto, K. Bharadwaj, V. Mateevitsi, L. Renambot, L. Long, A. Johnson, and J. Leigh. 2014. SAGE2: A New Approach for Data Intensive Collaboration Using Scalable Resolution Shared Displays. In *Proceedings of 10th IEEE International Conference on Collaborative Computing: Networking, Applications and Worksharing* (Miami, FL, 2014). 177-186.

[6] C. Cola and H. Valean. 2014. On multi-user web conference using WebRTC. In *Proceedings of 18th International Conference on System Theory, Control and Computing* (Sinaia, 2014). 430-433.

[7] (2016) Blender. [Online]. Available: http://www.blender.org

[8] Hyeontaek Oh, Sanghong Ahn, JunKyun Choi, and Jinhong Yang. 2015. WebRTC based remote collaborative online learning platform. In *Proceedings of the 1st Workshop on All-Web Real-Time Systems* (New York, NY, USA, 2015). Article 9.

[9] Network Performance Objectives for IP-based Services, ITU-T Y.1541, 2011.

Fostering Organizational Change through Co-Designing Collaborative Media

Michelle Partogi
School of Literature, Media and Communication
Georgia Institute of Technology
85 5th ST NW, Atlanta, GA
michelle_partogi@gatech.edu

Nassim JafariNaimi
School of Literature, Media and Communication
Georgia Institute of Technology
85 5th ST NW, Atlanta, GA
nassim@gatech.edu

ABSTRACT
It is widely accepted within the fields of Design and Human-Computer Interaction that designing products in collaboration with end users can lead to more useful, usable, and desirable products. Less explored is the co-design process's potential to change organizational culture through introduction and illustration of its central principles at work: such as prioritizing participants needs and experiences; mutual learning; and sustainability into organizations' practices and processes. This poster presents a case study on how the process of co-designing a collaborative digital application introduced change within the processes and practices of an autism support service organization in the US towards a human-centered approach.

1. INTRODUCTION
Participatory and co-design methods are appreciated for resulting in products that are more useful, usable and desirable. At the same time, research has shown that co-design processes also have the potential to transform the participating community's core practices and culture by modeling new sets of principles at work. Proponents of participatory and co-design methods, recognize that the process is often as important as the final result, as ongoing conversations and collaboration inform and form the resulting product or service [e.g., 11, 13]. Indeed, one might argue that an organization itself is a product [1], and as such, the process of co-design with various members of an organization has the potential to change organizational values and culture by changing organizational processes, strategies, and visions [1]. In this paper, we show this through the case example of our work with an autism support service organization.

The case example presented in this paper documents a year-long collaboration with the Philadelphia Autism Instructional Methods (Philly AIMS), a research group under the University of Pennsylvania that serves The School District of Philadelphia's K-5 autism support community. Philly AIMS coaches enter classrooms with the goal of helping teachers learn and use evidence-based practices (EBP). School practitioners are not only influenced by the culture and resources of their work environments but also enter with varying experience, meaning fidelity hardly corresponds to the controlled research settings where an EBP had been proven at engaging students with autism [9]. Philly AIMS relies on its coaches to bridge university-based research with classrooms' personal and political nature. In addition to educating teachers, it aims to collect data about students to measure progress of evidence-based practices within a real-life setting. In pursuit of its objectives, Philly AIMS faces two problems. One, the consultants' limited contact time with teachers due to the small ratio of consultant to teachers. Two, the teachers limited time and resources in the classroom which makes the work of collecting data a highly burdensome if not impossible task. These two limitations lead to Philly AIMS' seeing mixed results in the impact of their work. Recognizing technology's capacity to mediate teacher-consultant interactions, Philly AIMS formed a partnership with Georgia Tech with the aim of developing digital platforms that can help teachers learn evidence-based practices in a more efficient manner by facilitating recording and sharing of information about students' progress in a more seamless manner.

GROUP '16, November 13-16, 2016, Sanibel Island, FL, USA
ACM 978-1-4503-4276-6/16/11.
http://dx.doi.org/10.1145/2957276.2996289

2. METHODOLOGY
Throughout 2015–2016, we conducted ethnographic methods including several interviews, shadowing and contextual inquiry, four workshops, a competitive analysis of the digital platforms in use, and observations of weekly meeting. In this process, we noticed shared themes between our participatory design approach and coaches' consultation practices.

2.1 Preliminary and Observational Research
We conducted interviews with members of Philly AIMS staff, including the directors and coaches, and reviewed a samples organization's orienting implementation science literature. The group evaluated intervention success through student-centered benchmarks such as decreasing disruptive behavior thereby increasing instruction time or behavior-based measurements such as coding educators' fidelity implementing strategies [c.g. 9, 10]. After our preliminary research, we hypothesized that while Philly AIMS had become a pivotal community organization due to its focus on students' measurable progress, this pedagogy may inadvertently treat teachers as means to an end versus ends themselves. An example of this appears in Philly AIMS' emphasis on teachers collecting student data so it can aggregate its findings to impact school district policy. Changes in school district policy would benefit teachers as well as students by recognizing challenges and successful strategies to overcome them, often leading to provision of resources. However, given the myriad, often conflicting responsibilities and challenges of these teachers (e.g., student behavior management, class staff management and school politics, academic instruction, and paperwork), it is no surprise that teachers view aspects of the consultation a burden and forgo implementing the intervention. We hypothesized that the service might more effectively impart autism support strategies by attending to teachers' needs for personal and professional growth alongside students' progress. While shadowing classrooms, we observed a tacit presence of teacher-

Figure 1. A visual schedule is one of the earliest resources coaches implement in classrooms.

centered practices by the coaches, many former teachers themselves. The coaches deeply cared for the success of teachers and advocated for them. However, mediating between educators, research, and the school district made it difficult for coaches to cater to opposing stakeholder priorities. Hence, their practices and artifacts did not always explicitly reflect teachers' professional and personal needs.

Shadowing also revealed the central role resources played in mediating interactions between coaches and teachers as well as between teachers and students, class staff, and principals. For example, visual schedules enabled coaches to influence and shape classroom processes by signaling to class staff and students their roles throughout the day (Figure 1). Data collection sheets similarly inform which interventions positively impact individual students' progress and which need altering. Lastly we observed the strained use of Ning, a resource management and collaboration tool shown in Figure 2. The organizational structure and outdated interface of Ning made it almost unusable for teachers and coaches.

Ehn has noted the advantages of constructing initial boundary objects that enable controversies and discourse among participants [2]. By viewing digital media less as an end product and more as a platform to surface coaches and teachers' understandings of their domain and creative solutions to ongoing problems, we proposed the re-design of Ning as the focal point of the co-design process. We also decided to center the co-design process on coaches and the consultation practice instead of teachers. This for two reasons: one, that we did not want to burden the already tight schedule and responsibilities of teachers; two, that we viewed building trust and illustrating the strengths of the co-design with coaches a more plastic and potentially impactful entry point for changing organizational practices.

Using the design of a collaborative medium to scaffold organizational change serves several purposes. First, an outsider would have difficulty immediately tackling an organization's central paradigm to transform it [6]. We might instead start with client-facing interactions and inquire into the organizational environment, moving from the external experience to internal organizational orientation. According to Junginger, outside-in design projects advise and help organizations reshape their internal operations, strategies, and vision around the concepts of useable, useful, and desirable products and services, as show in [5, 8].

Second, co-designing a product-service prioritizing coach-teacher relations has potential to shift the organization's culture. Since people's experiences are core to interaction design, inviting an organization to co-design primes it to adopt more human-centered processes [e.g. 3, 13]. After all, to successfully adopt the change, the service would need to develop a capacity to think differently [5, 6].

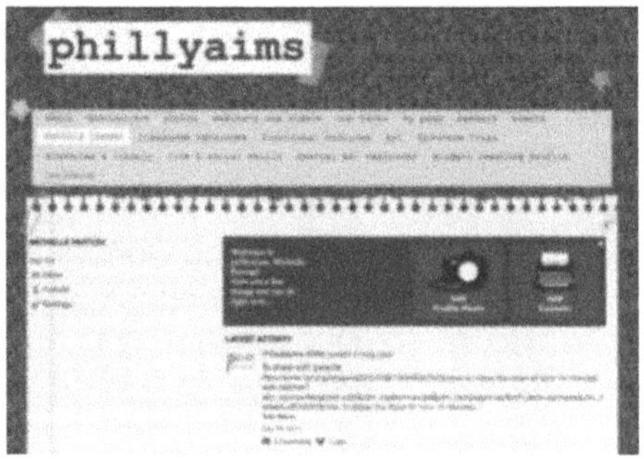

Figure 2. Ning's interface is outdated and its navigation structure is somewhat arbitrary, making it hard for teachers and coaches to find resources they need.

We adopted this approach, however, with great care aware that it is not uncommon for an emphasis on technology design, as Hargraves and JafariNaimi claim, to divert attention from the ideas and values that ground design in human life and living [4]. What's more, the personal nature of coaching and teaching means an intervention cannot rely on methodology (scientific or design). Neglecting to place significance for the people involved while designing and performing organizational processes reduces them to tools capable of change. Instead, we must also see participants as people mattering in and of themselves, respecting their goals, concerns, and needs. To shift a community towards human-centeredness, the process itself must be fully centered on people. Hence, we aimed to put the experiences and needs of teachers, coaches, and ultimately students front and center.

2.2 Co-Design Process

On several occasions during the preliminary research, coaches had disclaimed their lack of technological savvy. Many of the software applications that coaches and teachers interact with had been mandated top-down, and input has already been decided based on what the school district or research study deems valuable (e.g., student data spreadsheets). Against this backdrop, this research needed to assure the team that they were not merely consumers of the collaborative media we were aiming for, but instead active co-creators whose insights were needed for giving shape to the artifact. Since participatory approaches have potential to challenge existing political hierarchies, prioritize local knowledge, and build on the strengths of individual members [2], engaging coaches through collaborative interaction design meant they could reimagine communication channels to reflect their and their teachers' needs and practices.

2.2.1 Building Trust and Prioritizing Needs

We conducted co-design workshops throughout Spring 2016. The first workshop opened with a prompt: "What values drive your work?" In response, we heard the coaches detailing the difficulties they encounter everyday as they try to do their job. While at first glance this might appear as not giving a direct answer, we understood their response as way of ensuring that we, as outside researchers understood the gravity of their situation, before they felt comfortable opening up. At the end of the workshop, they explained equality drives their mission: they hope a child with autism, no matter his/her socioeconomic background, might have access to quality care. Data-driven, evidence-based strategy is a means to reach equality.

Recognizing we needed to build trust and understanding before the second workshop, we asked the supervising coach about her priorities in a separate interim meeting. As someone

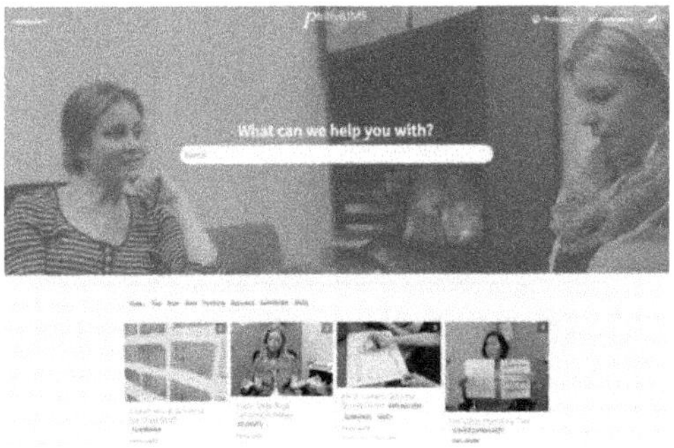

Figure 3. The digital prototype's homepage.

Figure 4. An example Strategy page.

who had been with the team the longest, she had recently entered a new leadership role and considered herself a "spokesperson" over a "lead." The supervising coach responded she wanted to foster team building, participation, and idea sharing among the group. The team had recently tripled in size, making collaboration more difficult especially as there was not as much feeling of project ownership among the new coaches. The spokesperson coach also suggested a prompt for the subsequent co-design sessions: coaches make resources as part of their consultation to teachers, but they rarely get uploaded to the shared drive or Ning, Philly AIMS's social website, and the lead coach wanted to understand why.

2.2.2 Mutual Learning

To answer the spokesperson coach's inquiry, we brainstormed a workshop activity together where coaches bring in and share a resource they recently made to help teachers in the classroom. During the activity, coaches freely shared the inspiration behind those resources and how they shared them with with teachers. The coaches highlighted how much easier it was to verbally explain instructions with teachers during in-person meetings as opposed to typing them. Supporting the creation and sharing of video explanations by the digital platform was an outcome of this conversation.

Next the workshop tackled the question: how would teachers find these resources? Shown in Figure 2, Ning, the current resource repository's navigation is categorized using technical jargon like "Pivotal Response Training" and "Discrete Trial." This makes the site particularly difficult for new teachers who look for information that best addresses their questions or a critical situation they are facing in the classroom as opposed to such abstract categories. In the workshop, the coaches suggested the use of open-ended tags could better mirror the different ways teachers would search for a resource.

On the surface these changes may appear as simple improvements to an outdated system – however the significance of the conversation at the workshop was its demonstrative power to change old practices and establish new ones. For example, after the workshop, the spokesperson coach incorporated show-and-tells into weekly team meetings. Each Tuesday, a different coach would share a resource and afterwards have team discussions. The coaches' meetings, initially a time for announcements, became a space for iteration and learning. The team also began recording the show-and-tells. These videos not only provide instructions but also revealed the reasoning for creating and using the resources. Conversations that were exclusive to one teacher and coach prior to the workshop now function as a learning opportunity for the entire coaching team.

These videos were then used as content for the new redesigned collaborative platform. Previously, Ning's resources included directions, tips, or handout – information-based artifacts that often did not capture the tacit knowledge needed to engage individuals with autism. In contrast, weekly show-and-tell videos help build teachers' capacity to learn and generalize the problem-solving coaches undertake.

Building on the success of the above collaborative exercise, we facilitated a Round Robin for creation of tags. In Round Robin, everyone writes as many sticky notes as possible on a prompt, such as "phrases teachers would search to find this resource." Afterwards, coaches swap sticky notes and write responses. We later translated the Round Robin into a Google Doc activity to streamline the process. Some of the coaches eventually adapted the strategy for their own practice, using Round Robin to open up conversations with teachers.

2.2.3 Sustainability

For the sake of sustainability, Junginger and Sangiorgi have put forward the idea of employing participatory design methods to build organizational capacities from within [8]. Coaches' often model resourcefulness for their teachers who feel their limited by funds (e.g., appropriating egg cartons as containers). In a similar vein, the strategies the participatory process introduced are low-barrier technologies the team already use on a daily basis (e.g., Google Doc, phone recordings, and sticky notes), so the coaches can sustainably ideate experimental solutions and integrate them into their work processes.

3. THE DIGITAL PLATFORM

Using insights from the research phase, we designed mockups for a digital resource-sharing platform shown in Figure 3. The main features of the platform included keyword searches and rationale-based video discussions as well as a means for teachers to upload their own content.

Rather than conforming to preset categories, this redesign invites teachers to search with keywords to access relevant Strategies, resources embedded with instructions and narratives. Each Strategy is tagged with phrases from the Google Doc Round Robin activity played after each show-and-tell. Tags might include "high level learners," "Pivotal Response Training," and even "cheap," as resourcefulness is very important for teachers. A strategies page as shown in Figure 4 contains two videos and a download link for the resource. The first video detail instructions for using a resource. In the second video, coaches share their thought process and the team builds on the idea.

4. DISCUSSION

While we have not done formal evaluations of the new system, we have seen a very positive initial reaction to the digital platform and have observed, first-hand, changes in practice within the organization borne by the co-design process.

Philly AIMS's uses of digital tools needed to evolve to align with the needs of the teachers and priorities of coaches. Such a design could have only been derived with insight from coaches who are experts in their own domain of practice and of teachers by extension. Moreover, by prioritizing the coaches' needs, the team eagerly experimented and found the journey "encouraged equal participation and idea sharing in a meaningful way."

Philly AIMS, as an organization, needed to similarly evolve beyond its student-centered pedagogy and implementation science. Through the co-design process, we able to demonstrate, the organization should make the learning and experiences of coaches and teachers more central. The shadowing activity revealed that the greatest strength of the consultation is when coaches can showcase evidence-based practices within the classroom as the occasions arise. We also saw a great strength in teachers and coaches sharing local knowledge born out of classrooms experiences. At the end there was a recognition Philly AIMS (both the director and coaches) of the need to complement the scientific, data-centric mentality of the group with a humanistic, teacher-balanced approach captured in the recommendation that coaches "rely more on [their] clinical intuition."

Through the process, many of the coaches' own strategies were adapted to engage the team, and they too adopted our methods into their consultations reflected in the coaching team feedback: "It's great seeing the similarities between our two disciplines. It just affirms what we're doing." Indeed, we noted that the co-design principles of prioritizing needs, mutual learning, and sustainability [12] parallel principles governing consultee-centered (or teacher-centered) consultation [11]. Coaches have themselves expressed that the co-design process "[has given] valuable insights to …how [they] think about [their] consultation to teachers." In addition to fostering a more participatory culture within the organization, the process has started a dialogue among the team on how they might further teacher-centered values in their own practices. In other words, the co-design process itself has laid the foundation necessary for the resultant product-service design. Furthermore, keeping activities low-tech and inclusive fosters sustainable habits. Not only has the co-design initiative spotlighted the teams' capacity to reimagine their work processes but also proven the ease of facilitating sessions conducive to such changes so they can adopt them in their own collaborations with teachers.

5. CONCLUSION

This case study has illustrated co-design's potential to model participatory practices and mediate conversations that can lead to organizational change. However, an account solely crediting the methodology would merely re-affirm Hargraves' concern. We formed a year-long partnership with the organization, building trust through overcoming obstacles—these elements of relationship-building are impossible to measure but ground the process in values of human life and living. Hargraves and JafariNaimi note that the HCD dialectic reflects "a separation of the important relationship between knowledge of why we design and the practices of how we design" [4]. The process detailed in the paper describe the *how*, but the *why* is subtler: the project's turning point came when we began to regard coaches, not as a leverage point to the Philadelphia autism support community, but as people mattering in their own right.

6. ACKNOWLEDGEMENTS

Many thanks to the Philly AIMS coaches Zinnia Pitrowski, Diana Cooney, Meghan Kane, Rudy Calderon Jr., Jacquie Russo, Julie Caramanico, and Mina Kim for joining on this experimental journey. Thanks also to the Philly AIMS director, Dr. David Mandell and Erica Blanch who supported our efforts to inquire into their unique organizational processes and practices through design.

This material is based on work supported by the McMorris Autism Program at the University of Pennsylvania and Children's Hospital of Philadelphia. Any opinions, findings, and conclusions or recommendations expressed in this material are those of the authors and do not necessarily reflect those of the McMorris Autism Program.

7. REFERENCES

[1] Buchanan, R. Management and Design: Interaction Pathways in Organizational Life, in Boland R.J. and Collopy, F. eds. *Managing as Design,* Stanford University Press, Stanford, CA.

[2] Ehn, P. Participation in design things. In *Proceedings of the Tenth Anniversary Conference on Participatory Design.* (Indiana University, Indianapolis, IN, USA, 2008), 92-101.

[3] Holmlid, S. Participative; co-operative; emancipatory: From participatory design to service design. In *Nordic Conference on Service Design* , (Oslo, Norway. 2009), *24-26.*

[4] Hargraves I., JafariNaimi N. Re-establishing the Center in Human-Centered Design: From Opportunity to Significance in Human Life and Living. *Zoontechnica: The Journal of Redirective Design*, 1 (2).

[5] Junginger, S. 2006. *Change in the Making: Organizational Change Through Human-Centered Product Development.* Carnegie Mellon.

[6] Junginger, S. Designing from the outside in: The key to organizational change? In *8th European Academy of Design Conference* (Aberdeen, Scotland, April 01-03, 2009).

[7] Junginger, S., Sangiorgi, D. Service design and organizational change: Bridging the gap between rigour and relevance. In 3rd IASDR Conference on Design Research, (Seoul, Korea, 2009).

[8] Lin, M., Hughes, B., Katica, M., Zuber, C., and Plsek, P. Service Design and Change of Systems: Human-Centered Approaches to Implementing and Spreading Service Design. *International Journal of Design*, 5 (2).

[9] Mandell, D., et al. The role of treatment fidelity on outcomes during a randomized field trial of an autism intervention. *Autism,* 17 (3). 281-295.

[10] Reinke, W., et al. The effect of visual performance feedback on teacher use of behavior-specific praise. *Behavior Modification* 31 (3). 247-263.

[11] Sandoval, J. *An Introduction to Consultee-centered Consultation in the Schools: A Step-by-step Guide to the Process and Skills.* Routledge, 2013.

[12] Simonsen, J., Robertson, T. *International Handbook of Participatory Design.* Routledge, London, 2013.

[13] Stickdorn, M., et al. *This is service design thinking: Basics, tools, cases.* Wiley, Hoboken, NJ, 2011. 270-279.

[14] Van der Velden, M., Mörtberg C. 2014. Participatory Design and Design for Values. *Handbook of Ethics, Values, and Technological Design. Ed. by Jeroen van den Hoven et al.* Springer, Netherlands , 201.

Sharing Code Among Academic Researchers: Lessons Learned

[Extended Abstract]

Carol Schmitz
Illinois Institute of Technology
Chicago, IL
cschmitz@hawk.iit.edu

Ameena Khan
Illinois Institute of Technology
Chicago, IL
akhan57@hawk.iit.edu

Libby Hemphill
Illinois Institute of Technology
Chicago, IL
libby.hemphill@iit.edu

ABSTRACT

Academic researchers have been collecting data and programming scripts to process and analyze them for years. Researchers have studied the difficulty in sharing data alone, but sharing the scripts required to reproduce results has been discussed less often. At the Collective Action and Social Media (CASM) Lab at the Illinois Institute of Technology, we study how people use social media to engage with their communities. Our interdisciplinary team consists of students with various technical backgrounds. Since everyone in the lab needs to run code, we have developed a standard repository structure. We will share the structure definition and explain the reasoning behind our design decisions. We aim to make our data and code accessible to social scientists not trained in information retrieval, so we frame this paper from that perspective. By publicizing our approach we invite researchers with similar goals to build on our work, collaborate on the design and implementation of modern tools to share code and data, and to suggest improvements to our process.

CCS Concepts

•**Software and its engineering** → **Reusability;**

Keywords

open source, code sharing, replication, data reuse

1. INTRODUCTION

The challenges encountered when sharing data sets have been explored by researchers for many years and are well documented (see, e.g., [3] for an overview). One common problem data sharing efforts face is a disparity in its costs and benefits-a problem common in groupware [7]. As Birnholtz and Bietz [2] found, for instance, the burden of formatting and releasing data sets for sharing falls on the original researcher, but the extra effort required to format data in a way that promotes sharing does not benefit the original researcher. The benefits are gained by the researcher who is reusing the data, decreasing the likelihood of adequate documentation being produced by the original researcher. They also indicate that data alone is insufficient for reuse because metadata and other factors provide necessary context to the data set. In this paper we expand that claim to argue that scripts and other code associated with data sets are equally important in reuse scenarios. We also provide an overview of our lab's practices for addressing these challenges.

While sharing data has long been a pain point for researchers who value collaboration, sharing code is not discussed as often. Neches et al. [9] wrote about the necessity of designing technology to share data and complex systems 25 years ago. While some tools have been introduced to the landscape in the years since, researchers today struggle with many of the same problems when attempting to share research. They propose an artificial intelligence approach to automating knowledge sharing and argue against "start[ing] from scratch each time" [9].

In addition to the technical and organizational challenges encountered when sharing data and code, there is also the problem of identifying the audience for the shared tools and information. Ensuring a simple process to setup shared code environments is even more important today, since the scenarios where non-technical researchers may wish to use data will become more and more frequent. In social media studies in particular, computing skills are not necessary to ask and answer relevant research questions, but the nature of the subject requires manipulating data with code. We also agree with King [8] that "unless we are content to let data sharing work only within disciplinary silos, which of course makes little sense in an era where social science research is more interdisciplinary than ever, we need to develop solutions that operate, or at least interoperate, across scholarly fields." However, while some advances have been made in standardizing the process of sharing data, as Bechofer et al. [1] explain, data alone is not enough to validate prior research.

How are we to ensure that data sharing, especially social media data, can work across disciplines and at many levels of coding expertise?

In the CASM Lab, our approach is three-fold. First, we release our code as open source repositories via GitHub so that the code, and our conversations about it, remain visible. Second, we provide easy to navigate user interfaces through Jupyter notebooks, so the code remains available to those

GROUP '16 November 13-16, 2016, Sanibel Island, FL, USA

ACM ISBN 978-1-4503-4276-6/16/11.

DOI: http://dx.doi.org/10.1145/2957276.2996290

who are curious and usable for those who are more interested in the results of running the code than in the code itself. Third, we use Zenodo to archive and identify code used in individual papers so that our process for each publication is transparent and reproducible. We describe these steps here in an effort to capture and continue the social media research communities' work to share data and methods.

2. EXISTING EFFORTS AT SHARING WORKFLOWS

Though we avoid a complete overview of all efforts at sharing code for research in the interest of brevity for this poster, we do want recognized one effort: ^{my}Experiment. De Roure et al. [5] attempted to solve the problem of sharing at scale by developing a tool called ^{my}Experiment. This tool was designed to share entire scientific workflows, including data, code, environments and other elements of the scientific process. One of the key elements of this tool is the ability of new users to add features to existing workflows. ^{my}Experiment was used frequently (by 750 registered users from 78 countries [5]), confirming a true need for this type of solution in the scientific community. It is built on Ruby on Rails, which also has the advantage of being a very human-readable language. However, the open source Taverna workflow management software on which it is built supports R but not Python, so the scripts are not as accessible to those who can't read code.

3. THE CASM LAB APPROACH TO SHARING CODE

Publishing open-source code is a mission of CASM Lab. The first step in sharing code is organizing it in a way that will make sense to others. Consistency helps outside developers know what to expect when they come to our code. By taking the time to both develop and document our internal standards, we can continue to maintain code despite turnover in the lab.

We have developed a standard repository structure and documented the reasoning behind that structure. By adopting this structure for all our public repositories, we make it easier for newcomers to understand and use the code for themselves. Once they become familiar with one repository, they can more easily learn how to use another repository published by our lab because of the similar structure. Being transparent about our process is also better for science, since researchers can hold us accountable or alert us to mistakes. Researchers can also build on our work more easily.

Nearly all of our public code is written in Python, and all of our public repositories use Jupyter notebooks to document and run the code.

Python is a programming language that is especially conducive to sharing code since the syntax is easily human-readable for English speakers. Additionally, many packages or libraries have been written by Python developers to add standard data analysis capabilities to the built-in Python packages (e.g., pandas, numpy). This allows researchers to pick up where previous research ended and focus on new problems and solutions, rather than coding new solutions to problems that have already been solved.

Jupyter notebooks make it possible for people who do not code to use our programs, and it is popular among data scientists already. Using Jupyter allows us to store the documentation of the code, including the reasoning behind various algorithms, and the code in a single location, and it is becoming standard practice in other disciplines [10]. The approach also creates "containers" of code and data that are easily shared.

3.1 Workflow

We try to follow a standard approach to social media data in all our projects (no matter what where weâĂŹre getting data). It has 4 basic steps:

1. Collect
2. Cache
3. Parse
4. Analyze

This workflow allows us to collect data once for use in multiple projects. It also allows us flexibility in analysis and redundancy in data storage.

Under the collect step live scripts for getting data in "raw" form. Here, raw means whatever default format for the data is. Usually this means JSON dumped by an API, but for scrapers it's whatever data structure and format we decided to use. We are greedy in collection meaning we pull whatever data the API will let us have. For instance, in the Twitter projects, it means data returned by the ever-changing Twitter API.

Once we have "raw" data, we cache it by storing a read-only copy somewhere accessible to the whole team, often a local server. Usually this storage step is handled by the collection script and not by a standalone script. We treat this as a separate step because it's conceptually important - social media data changes all the time, and caching lets us keep track of what the data looked like at the time of collection (e.g., what was returned, what structure was standard then).

Next, we parse. Parsing scripts pull data from the read-only caches and put them in formats that are appropriate for analysis or whatever comes next. For instance, some of our Twitter tools collect data from the search API, cache it, then parse it into a human-readable CSV for import to Excel or another stats program. This leaves us with two related, but not identical, copies of the data - one in JSON from Twitter, and one in CSV. Parsing scripts also do any data transformations that are necessary for analysis (e.g., converting timestamps, calculating user stats).

Finally, we get to analyze the data. Often analysis is included in the same script as parsing, but sometimes analysis steps will live on their own. Some of the analysis will involve machine learning (e.g., automated classification) or natural language processing (e.g., topic modeling), but some will be simple word clouds or descriptive statistics.

3.2 Repository Structure

At CASM Lab, all of our GitHub repositories[1] for social media data collection and analysis have a similar structure. We use a single Jupyter notebook to explain and run the code within the repository. This notebook calls scripts within the /scripts folder, and stores any files generated in

[1]https://github.com/casmlab

the /files folder. The notebook also contains a section to help users create a settings (i.e., configuration) file, where the user may modify a predefined set of configurable options used by the code, such as API credentials and file names. Our standard repository structure contains several elements.

/data_samples We store sample files produced by the code after each stage of the collect, cache, analyze, parse workflow, including raw data from the source, here.

/files This directory contains any files needed to run or generated by the code. Some of our scripts download or generate extremely large files (e.g., GIS-files from the U.S. Census), so we don't store these files in the cloud. If you run our code locally, this is where our scripts will store such files on your computer.

/scripts This directory contains the meat and potatoes of our code. A single repository may contain several scripts which can be run independently of each other as users work through the collect, cache, analyze, parse workflow.

[repo_name].ipynb A single Jupyter notebook explains how the various pieces of the code in each repository work. At a minimum, it contains the following sections: Setup, Collect, Cache, Parse, and Analyze. The notebook contains both Markdown blocks, which explain the goals of each workflow phase, and Code blocks, which run the code contained in the repository. Code blocks call scripts stored in the /scripts directory and save files in the /files directory.

settings-example.cfg This file contains a sample version of all configurable options used by the code, except for API keys and other private credentials.

environment.yml This file can be used by a package manager, such as Anaconda, to automatically install the packages and libraries needed to run the code in this repository. Operating system requirements may apply.

requirements.txt - A pip-compatible version of the necessary packages list is included for those who use Python but don't use Anaconda.

README.md - This file uses markdown syntax and explains what users will find in the repository. It includes operating system requirements as well as contact information for the lab director in case of any questions.

This method of organizing code has served our lab well, but keeping internal repositories organized before publishing to the open-source community is just the first step in sharing code. Since the utility in sharing code actually comes from running it, we turn now to some of the difficulties in releasing code that will run "out of the box" for as many potential collaborators as possible.

3.3 Archiving Repositories

Because we're always working to improve our code, it changes frequently. In order to capture relationships between certain states of the code and the publications we produce, we use Zenodo[2] to archive our repositories and assign them digital object identifiers (DOIs).

To do so, we use GitHub's release feature and name the release after the publication associated with the code in that state. Then Zenodo maps that particular release, the code that accompanies it, and generates a DOI for the archive. We can then cite the code easily and refer users to complete archives to use in replication efforts.

[2]https://zenodo.org/

4. OPEN CHALLENGES IN SHARING CODE

Designing and developing data analysis scripts while prioritizing potential reuse introduces some complexity to the development process. We have encountered compatibility issues between operating systems and various Python libraries. After encountering roadblocks as a result of conflicting dependencies, we started using separate environments for each project. The following sections explain our experiences.

4.1 Technical Challenges

At CASM Lab, we primarily code on Mac OS X. Our servers run Linux though, and it's sometimes difficult to run code on the servers that was developed on our local machines.

One of the problems we've encountered running code developed on OS X on a Linux server is that not all Python package developers provide Linux versions of packages for OS X. Or they might provide a Linux version for certain Linux distributions, but not the particular distribution we are using. Either way, it results in a roadblock that cannot be resolved without modifying the code.

If you're using the same operating system as your collaborators, one way to share code is by setting up environments. Environments allow you to easily switch between multiple projects without introducing conflicting package dependencies. By replicating environments using package versions, we avoid situations where one version of a package may conflict with other system configurations when another version of the same package has no conflicts.

Separate environments can be created for each Python project using Anaconda[3], an open sourced Python distribution. Users can create a new environment at the start of a project, then activate the environment when they are working on that project. At CASM Lab we provide an `environment.yml` file in our repositories. This file allows users of our code to replicate our development environment on their local machines with a simple install command, rather than having to download and install the correct version of each package manually. There are limitations to this environment file, as it primarily tracks Python packages used in the code. Various operating system packages necessary to run the code are not always included in `environment.yml` , so this doesn't eliminate all dependency issues between projects, but it greatly reduces them. Anaconda does have some limitations. For instance, it includes only distributions of Python and R, and it is dependent on collaborators using compatible operating systems.

4.2 Sharing at Scale

We know that we are not the only research lab to take steps toward solving this problem. For instance, there is a desire for a central repository where academic researchers can share data sets and scripts associated with those data sets[4], but such a platform does not yet exist. Building a consortium of researchers who prioritize open access to data and code can begin the process of developing standards around such sharing, and these standards can eventually be developed into a sharing platform. Ideally, such a platform will

[3]https://www.continuum.io/downloads

[4]https://github.com/ocdx

make it easy for those with varying levels of technical expertise to access and actually use the data and code provided.

In order for programmers to effectively use shared code, it is critical that the local system used for reuse is the same as or at least compatible with the system on which the code was originally developed and tested. This may appear to be a simple task for a user who can install the needed packages manually. However, with the passing of time between the creation and reuse of code, necessary packages may be updated where the latest version breaks the code. Even if a user was provided information on which package versions were needed, upgrading or downgrading packages in the same space within a system could present conflicts with packages needed for the user's other projects.

Sharing at scale introduces additional complexity to the general problem of sharing code. Researchers have personal preferences for operating system and programming language decisions, and if those decisions are not initially made with sharing in mind, many difficult problems may arise later in the development process which may hinder the ability to share widely and seamlessly.

For instance, when initially developing a solution to a problem, a researcher working on OS X may choose to use a familiar Python package. Maybe two packages available with similar functionality are available, but the researcher has used Package A before and is comfortable with it. If the researcher is only concerned with her own work, she may select Package A and move on. Later, when the researcher wants to share her code on a Linux server, she may discover that Package A isn't available for Linux, but both Linux and OS X versions exist for Package B. Now the researcher must either choose not to share the code with Linux users, or to go back and replace all references in the code to Package A to the corresponding Package B reference. The code must also be tested to ensure that Package B functionality is similar enough to Package A that the code output does not change. Updating the code can be time consuming, but can be necessary in code maintenance.

Making code sharing a priority at the beginning of a new project, by slowing down and developing consistent standards to organize the code, is one step that helps make the code more easily reusable. CASM Lab develops code using this approach. We also develop new code on widely used operating systems, in popular languages, with tools other researchers already use. However, we are just one lab and not everyone shares our commitment to open source research. As De Roure et al. states, "Enabling incentive models for sharing within a community of practice and supporting an emergent model of sharing is a challenge."[5]

4.3 Replication vs. Reuse

If the goal in sharing code is to encourage others to replicate your own results, providing code that can easily be executed by anyone is important. Everett and Earp [6] offer a number of reasons replication studies are uncommon, including that they are difficult to publish, are not awarded the same recognition are original work, and are time-consuming to conduct. By providing the code in a format that is easily reusable, researchers can more quickly replicate the study and may, as a result, be more likely to do so.

If the goal is to answer new questions that build on original research, one could argue that a certain level of programming skill is required to write scripts that can answer those new questions, so it is less critical that the original code be accessible to those who don't code. We disagree. The technical barriers to social media data have created new hierarchies that create economic and gendered divisions between those who have insight to offer and those who have the money and skills to access data [4].

5. CONCLUSIONS

We described our data collection and analysis workflow, repository structure, and repository archiving practices in order to contribute to the broader discussion on sharing data and code for social media research. Part of our mission in the CASM Lab is to make social media data accessible to a broader research community, and that goal motivates our efforts to share both data and code.

6. ACKNOWLEDGMENTS

This material is based upon work supported by the National Science Foundation under grant no. IIS-1525662.

7. REFERENCES

[1] Bechhofer, S., Buchan, I., De Roure, D., Missier, P., Ainsworth, J., Bhagat, J., Couch, P., Cruickshank, D., Delderfield, M., Dunlop, I., Gamble, M., Michaelides, D., Owen, S., Newman, D., Sufi, S., and Goble, C. Why linked data is not enough for scientists. *Future Generation Computer Systems 29*, 2 (Feb. 2013), 599–611.

[2] Birnholtz, J. P., and Bietz, M. J. Data at Work: Supporting Sharing in Science and Engineering. In *Proceedings of the 2003 International ACM SIGGROUP Conference on Supporting Group Work* (New York, NY, USA, 2003), GROUP '03, ACM, pp. 339–348.

[3] Borgman, C. L. *Big data, little data, no data: scholarship in the networked world.* The MIT Press, Cambridge, Massachusetts, 2015.

[4] boyd, d., and Crawford, K. Critical Questions for Big Data. *Information, Communication & Society 15*, 5 (June 2012), 662–679. 00344.

[5] De Roure, D., Goble, C., and Stevens, R. The design and realisation of the Virtual Research Environment for social sharing of workflows. *Future Generation Computer Systems 25*, 5 (May 2009), 561–567.

[6] Everett, J. A. C., and Earp, B. D. A tragedy of the (academic) commons: interpreting the replication crisis in psychology as a social dilemma for early-career researchers. *Personality and Social Psychology* (2015), 1152.

[7] Grudin, J. Groupware and social dynamics: eight challenges for developers. *Communications of the ACM 37*, 1 (Jan. 1994), 92–105.

[8] King, G. Ensuring the Data-Rich Future of the Social Sciences. *Science 331*, 6018 (Feb. 2011), 719–721.

[9] Neches, R., Fikes, R. E., Finin, T., Gruber, T., Patil, R., Senator, T., and Swartout, W. R. Enabling Technology for Knowledge Sharing. *AI Magazine 12*, 3 (Sept. 1991), 36.

[10] Shen, H. Interactive notebooks: Sharing the code. *Nature 515*, 7525 (Nov. 2014), 151–152.

Learning Outcomes From a Student-generated "Flipped" Wiki Textbook

Andrea Tartaro
Furman University
3300 Poinsett Hwy
Greenville, SC 29613
+1-864-294-2932
andrea.tartaro@furman.edu

Brian C. Goess
Furman University
3300 Poinsett Hwy
Greenville, SC 29613
+1-864-294-2318
brian.goess@furman.edu

Jack Miller[i]
Furman University
3300 Poinsett Hwy
Greenville, SC 29613
jack.miller3@furman.edu

Jasmine A. Bui
Furman University
3300 Poinsett Hwy
Greenville, SC 29613
jasmine.bui@furman.edu

ABSTRACT
To inform the design of collaborative learning systems and assignments, our research asks: What aspects of student-generated content truly enhance learning outcomes? Herein we detail the methodologies we have developed to answer this question, including comparing performance on exam questions, some of which are based on specific metaphors found in a student-created "flipped" wiki textbook, and automating wiki content analysis for correlation of performance with creative language forms.

CCS Concepts
• Applied computing~Collaborative learning

Keywords
Wiki, student-centered learning, flipped textbook, metaphor, assessment.

1. INTRODUCTION & BACKGROUND
When Furman University launched an innovative undergraduate course in introductory bioorganic chemistry in 2008, an appropriate textbook did not exist. Based on research that suggests online collaborative learning environments promote positive peer-learning experiences, we simultaneously launched a companion wiki textbook in which students created the content, in essence "flipping" the traditional model of textbook creation. In the past eight years, over 200 students have contributed to the bioorganic wiki as writers, editors and consumers of wiki content. This has yielded a wealth of data to examine how students teach each other about complex scientific information. In a recent content analysis, we found that students use a variety of creative language forms, including a number of evocative metaphors, to describe the actions of enzymes in a reaction [1]. For example, students described the "catalytic triad" of the structural backbone of an enzyme by making an analogy to chain gang workers linked together at their feet in pursuit of a common objective. Student interviews suggested creative language constructions in the student-generated content may have supported learning, but our analysis of edits over time suggested editors may have removed creative content in service of more formal scientific language [1]. However, designs for collaborative spaces can lead to better preservation of linguistic diversity [2]. To inform the design of collaborative learning systems and assignments, our current research asks:

What aspects of student-generated content truly enhance learning outcomes?

Herein we detail the methodologies we have developed to answer this question, including determining whether performance on a final exam question improves when the question involves a specific metaphor found in the wiki, and automating wiki content analysis for correlation of performance with creative language forms. We conclude with a description of future work.

2. METAPHOR-BASED EXAM QUESTIONS
In our previous study, we observed that certain creative language forms persisted through multiple rounds of editing [1]. Among these were a number of metaphors, and we became curious as to whether the reason why such metaphors persisted might be that students felt they were particularly valuable to learning the associated concept. We tested this hypothesis by reading the entire wiki to make a crude inventory of metaphors and then creating a final exam in which some of the questions were formulated around the use of some of the metaphors. We then determined how students performed on questions involving such metaphors relative to the remaining questions that did not.

For example, in one wiki chapter describing an enzyme that operates with ideal catalytic efficiency, a student author draws an analogy between this enzyme, which runs its chemical reaction so efficiently it spends most of its time waiting for a new set of substrate molecules to act on, to an assembly line worker that assembles his parts more quickly than the line provides new parts to assemble:

GROUP '16, November 13-16, 2016, Sanibel Island, FL, USA
ACM 978-1-4503-4276-6/16/11.
http://dx.doi.org/10.1145/2957276.2996291

"This can be thought of as an assembly line metaphor. In a TIM catalyzed reaction, the worker (TIM) puts his parts together faster than he receives them and must wait on the assembly line to send more. At any given time, most of the TIMs inside you are empty, waiting on more substrate."

Based on this analogy, which was deemed by the instructor to be a valuable illustration of a key concept within the topic of enzymatic catalytic efficiency, the following final exam question was constructed:

The metaphor of an assembly line worker who assembles his parts faster than the conveyor belt delivers new parts to be assembled is most appropriately applied to which enzyme?

a. Alcohol dehydrogenase (AD)
b. Chorismate mutase (CM)
c. Triose phosphate isomerase (TIM)
d. Alanine racemase (AR)
e. Aspartate transaminase (AT)

Table 1 summarizes the results of this exam. The table provides details of each of the twenty multiple choice questions, including which wiki chapter or chapters are being tested, along with student performance data. Of the three questions for which the rate of correct responses was more than one standard deviation away from the mean rate of correct responses (in bold and italics in Table 1), two were based on a metaphor created by a student in the flipped wiki textbook (Questions 7 and 20, highlighted), including the question above. The third was based on a metaphor created by the instructor and used repeatedly in the lecture portion of the course (Question 4). Collectively, these data suggest that students performed better by more than one standard deviation over the average on questions that tested course content by invoking created metaphors. They also suggest that the metaphor itself, and not the creator of the metaphor, is of premium value in enhancing student comprehension.

3. EXPANDED CREATIVE CONTENT ANALYSIS

Our analysis of creative language content is motivated by this initial observation as well as research on the role of creative language in social interaction [3], and the role of social interaction in collaborative learning environments [e.g., 4] (please see [1] for a discussion). For this research, we conducted an expanded manual analysis. This analysis identified and categorized various figures of speech and creative language forms. Our list of categories (Figure 1) was derived from our previous research [1], the Changing Minds Rhetorical Strategies List [5], the Silva Rhetoricae Database [6], and a data-driven approach [7].

We manually coded two chapters of the bioorganic wiki: chapter 4, titled 'Protein Folding,' was edited by four different students over four semesters and therefore needed to be coded four separate times, one for each successive iteration of the wiki chapter. Chapter 9, titled 'Serine Proteases' was edited by six different students and therefore was coded six times. The results of these two chapters are illustrated in Figure 2.

This data suggests that students relied greatly on metaphor to explain complex chemical processes in simple ways. In the two manually coded chapters, personification, a specific type of metaphor in which non-human nouns are attributed human-like qualities, was used more than all other tracked creative language forms.

Table 1: Final Exam Statistics

Exam Question	Chapter(s)	Num Sentences	% SDL	% Simile	Correct (n=24)	Rate Correct
1	1	60	35	1.67	13	0.54
2	9, 10, 11	291	25.77	0.69	11	0.46
3	13	88	6.82	0	9	0.38
4	15	76	25	0	23	***0.96***
5	16	154	9.09	1.30	13	0.54
6	17	80	17.5	0	8	0.33
7	19	79	6.33	1.27	24	***1.00***
8	2	67	17.91	4.48	16	0.67
9	4, 7, 22	334	21.26	4.49	20	0.83
10	21, 23, 24	195	14.87	2.05	17	0.71
11	6, 17, 22, 27	359	13.09	0.56	7	0.29
12	3	121	18.18	2.48	5	0.21
13	31	124	19.35	0	16	0.67
14	32	128	6.25	0.78	8	0.33
15	33	44	6.82	0	18	0.75
16	4	176	35.80	6.25	18	0.75
17	5	78	21.79	0	4	0.17
18	7	97	6.19	3.09	17	0.71
19	9	139	36.69	0.72	11	0.46
20	9	139	36.69	0.72	21	***0.88***
Mean		141.45	19.02	1.53	13.95	0.58
SD		90.14	10.75	1.79	5.94	0.25

1. Colloquial Language: Any type of non-formal or non-academic language.
2. Metaphor: Using the qualities of one thing to describe another, including personification.
3. Simile: Explicit comparison of two things using 'like' or 'as'.
4. Parallel Structure: Repeating sentence structure for emphasis.
5. Student-Directed Language: Language directed at the student readers of the wiki.
6. Rhetorical Question: Posing a question when the answer is likely already known by the reader.
7. Repetition: Repeating a single word or phrase for emphasis.
8. Dubitatio: Deliberatively doubting oneself, often through a rhetorical question.
9. Pun: A play on words.
10. Pathos: Drawing sympathy from the reader.

Figure 1: Figure of speech/creative language categories.

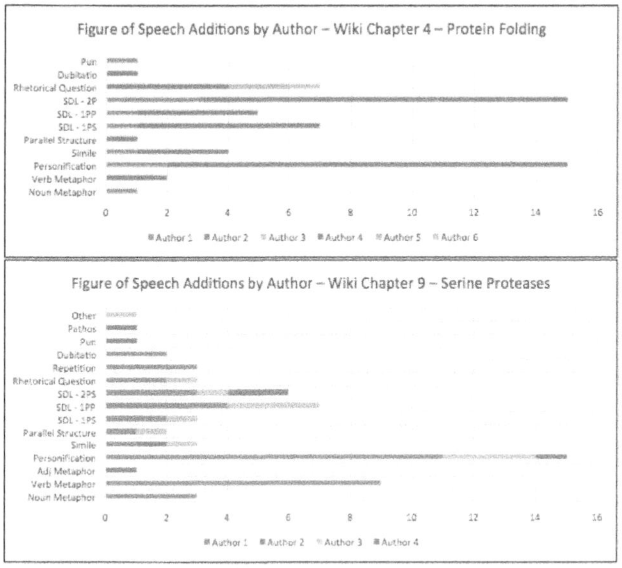

Figure 2: Language feature additions, color-coded by each successive author, for two chapters of the wiki.

Other common categories included student-directed language (SDL – language directed at the student readers of the wiki, and simile, explicit comparison of two things using 'like' or 'as.'

3.1 Automating Wiki Analysis

Given the length of the wiki, 38 chapters with approximately 2400 words per chapter, and the extensive edits made on the wiki (four or more versions per chapter), manual analysis of the entire wiki would be time consuming. Thus we are working on developing algorithms to assist with analysis, either by automatically identifying specific language forms, or by isolating sentences likely to fall into a particular category for manual user verification. We chose personification as one of our algorithms because of its prevalence in our manual coding as well as the potential technical value of the algorithm in applications beyond the scope of this project. We also chose simile and student-directed language because their relative linguistic structural simplicity would facilitate algorithm development.

3.1.1 Personification algorithm

Our personification algorithm draws motivation from Krishnakumaran and Zhu's [8] algorithm for identifying metaphors. Our algorithm utilizes a parts of speech (POS) tagger that is part of the Stanford CoreNLP suite [9] and WordNet [10-12], a specialized database of lexical word relations. To communicate with the WordNet database, we utilized the Java API for WordNet Searching (JAWS) API of Brett Spell from SMU [13].

WordNet groups nouns, verbs, adjectives, and adverbs into relational groups of synonyms called synsets that are then linked to other synsets by lexical relations, creating a network of English language connections [10-12]. All nouns in WordNet have both hypernyms, which refer to more generalized versions of the given noun, and hyponyms, which refer to more specific versions of the given noun. The hypernym of each noun can be followed until WordNet reaches its most generalized noun class in 'entity,' for example, dog->mammal->animal.

We hypothesized that in order for a sentence to contain personification, a sentence must contain both a non-human noun and a human-related verb. For each sentence in the text, we tokenize each word in the sentence. If the word is a noun, we query WordNet to create a hypernym list for the word up to the base word ('entity'). For example, if the given word was 'computer,' then the returned list would contain: 'machine,' 'device,' 'instrumentality,' 'artifact,' 'whole,' 'object,' 'physical entity,' and 'entity.' We then check if the hypernym list contains any human nouns by comparing it to a database of 412 human nouns we created by querying WordNet for the full list of hyponyms of the word 'person.' Put simply, if the hypernym tree contains a human noun, then the noun cannot be personified; and, if the hypernym tree does not contain a human noun, then the noun can be personified. Nouns able to be personified are added to a list of non-human nouns, while nouns unable to be personified are added to a list of human nouns.

If the word is a verb, we query WordNet to find the verb's derivationally related form, a noun whose meaning can be traced back to a corresponding verb. We hypothesized that if a verb had a derivationally related form, and that form could be related to humans, it could be assumed that it was a human related action. For example if the verb is 'swim,' then the given derivationally related form is 'swimmer.' With the verb now transformed into a noun, we query WordNet to create a hypernym list similar to the previous list described for true nouns. If the hypernym tree of the derivational noun contains a word within our human noun database, then we conclude the verb is a human related verb. Put simply, if the derivationally related noun is related to humans, then the verb can be personified; if the derivationally related form is not related to humans, then the verb cannot be personified. Verbs able to be personified are added to a list of human verbs, while verbs unable to be personified are added to a list of non-human verbs.

After each noun and verb in a sentence has been processed for its ability to be personified, we multiple the number of non-human nouns by the number of human verbs to get the number of possible noun-verb personification combinations. We then multiply the total number of nouns and verbs to get the number of total possible noun-verb combinations. We then calculate the percentage of noun-verb combinations that are noun-verb personifications. If the personification percentage is greater than a threshold of 40%, then the algorithm tags the sentence as personification. We determined this threshold maximizes the accuracy of the algorithm after testing a range of threshold values.

For example if an example sentence contained five nouns and three verbs, and four of the nouns and two of the verbs are able to be personified, then the ratio of personification to total combination would be 8/15 or 53.33%. Since this example sentence percent is greater than the threshold, the algorithm would tag the sentence as likely to contain personification.

To test the algorithm, we developed a corpus of sentences from various databases [14-19]: 167 sentences contained personification metaphors, 150 sentences contained metaphors but not personification, and 112 sentences did not contain metaphors. Our algorithm correctly tagged 67% of the personification metpahor examples, 75% of the non-personification metaphor examples, and 81% of the non-metaphor examples. These results are promising. However, of 24 personification examples taken from the wiki, only 11 (48%) were tagged correctly. This is perhaps due to the complexity and length of the sentences in the wiki. We have several ideas to improve the performance of the algorithm.

3.1.2 Student-directed language and simile algorithms

We also created two interactive algorithms to automatically identify language directed at the student-readers of the wiki (SDL) and simile. The SDL algorithm first identifies sentences that contain the word "I", "we", "you", "our", or "us." In addition, sentences that contain contractions may also contain SDL, e.g., "Let's look at this in more detail." The algorithm identifies sentences that contain an apostrophe and then asks the user to confirm whether the sentence contains SDL. Similarly, the simile algorithm identifies sentences that contain "like" or "as" and then asks the user to confirm whether the sentence contains a simile.

For each chapter in the wiki, we then computed the percentage of sentences that contained SDL and simile respectively. We then correlated the percentage of SDL and simile with the rate of correct responses on exam questions related to specific chapters of the wiki (Table 1). Neither SDL percentage (Spearman's rho=0.072, p=0.76) nor simile percentage (rho=0.25, p=0.28) correlated with the rate of correct response. For simile, this may be because the percentage of sentences that contained similes for most chapters was very low.

4. CONCLUSION AND FUTURE WORK

Based on our prior work that suggests that metaphors are a kind of creative language construction that best persists over time in a student-generated flipped wiki textbook [1] and our present findings that students perform better on content-based exam questions related to those metaphors, we intend to continue our research aimed at answering the question: Which aspects of student-generated content truly enhance learning outcomes? We will: (1) improve the performance of our current algorithms; (2) develop new algorithms for identifying additional creative language forms; and (3) assess learning using exam data. We anticipate that both the automation tools that we develop and the learning outcome insights that we discover will have broad implications beyond the development of our flipped wiki textbook in introductory bioorganic chemistry. As this project matures, we will examine other factors that likely affect learning outcomes, such as student role in wiki creation (creator, editor, curator, consumer). We will also determine if the creative language forms preferred by student authors affect learning outcomes differently than those preferred by expert textbook authors. All of these studies are directed toward helping us achieve our ultimate goal: determining how best to design systems and assignments that encourage the creation and preservation of creative language that improve learning outcomes.

5. ACKNOWLEDGMENTS

This research is funded by the Associated Colleges of the South and Furman Advantage. The authors would like to thank Mike Winiski for his valuable contributions.

6. REFERENCES

[1] Tartaro, A., Goess, B.C., and Winiski, M. Creative in a Student-generated Bioorganic Chemistry Wiki Textbook. In *Proc. C&C '15*, ACM Press (2015), 221-224.

[2] Emigh, W and Herring, S.C. Collaborative Authoring on the Web: A Genre Analysis of Online Encyclopedias. In *Proc. HICSS '05,* IEEE (2005), page 99.1.

[3] Carter, R. Response to Special Issue of Applied Linguistics Devoted to Language Creativity in Everyday Contexts. *Appl. Linguist*, Oxford University Press (2007), 29 (4), 597-608.

[4] Forte, A. and Bruckman, A. Constructing Text: Wiki as a Toolkit for (Collaborative?) Learning. In *Proc. WikiSym '07*, ACM Press (2007), 31-41.

[5] Straker, D. changingminds.org.

[6] "Silva Rhetoricae." rhetoric.byu.edu.

[7] Weingart, L.R. How Did They Do That? The Ways and Means of Studying Group Processes. *Res. Organ. Behav.*, JAI Press Inc. (1997), 19, 189-239.

[8] Krishnakumaran, S. and Zhu, X. Hunting Elusive Metaphors Using Lexical Resources. In *Proc. FigLanguages '07*, Association for Computational Linguistics (2007), 13-20.

[9] Manning, C.D., Surdeanu, M., Bauer, J., Finkel, J., Bethard, S.J., and McClosky, D. The Stanford CoreNLP Natural Language Processing Toolkit. In *Proc. ACL 2014,* Association for Computational Linguistics (2014), 55-60.

[10] Miller, G.A. WordNet: A Lexical Database for English. *Communications of the ACM.* ACM Press (1995), 38 (4), 39-41.

[11] Fellbaum, C. (ed.). WordNet: An Electronic Lexical Database. MIT Press (1998).

[12] Princeton University "About WordNet." WordNet. Princeton University. 2010. http://wordnet.princeton.edu.

[13] Spell, Brett. "Java API for WordNet Searching (JAWS)." (2007).

[14] Examples of Personification. (n.d.). Retrieved February 13th, 2016, from http://examples.yourdictionary.com/examples-of-personification.html.

[15] Examples of Personification for Kids. (n.d.). Retrieved February 3rd, 2016, from http://examples.yourdictionary.com/examples-of-personification-for-kids.html.

[16] Metaphor Examples. (n.d.). Retrieved March 13th, 2016, from http://www.cattysd.org/webpages/delek/index.cfm?subpage=1974678.

[17] Metaphor Examples. (n.d.). Retrieved February 5th, 2016, from http://examples.yourdictionary.com/metaphor-examples.html

[18] Metaphor Examples for Kids. (n.d.). Retrieved February 8th, 2016, from http://examples.yourdictionary.com/metaphor-examples-for-kids.html.

[19] Words in a Sentence. (n.d.) Retrieved February 9th, 2016, from http://wordsinasentence.com.

[i] Jack Miller is now at Computer Technology Solutions (CTS), 300 Riverchase Pkwy E, Birmingham, AL, 35244, jmmiller@askcts.com.

Engaging with Users and Stakeholders: The Emotional and the Personal

Foad Hamidi
Lassonde School of Engineering
York University, Canada
fhamidi@cse.yorku.ca

Claudia Müller
Information Science and New Media
University of Siegen, Germany
Claudia.Mueller@uni-siegen.de

Melanie Baljko
Lassonde School of Engineering
York University, Canada
mb@cse.yorku.ca

Marén Schorch
Information Science and New Media
University of Siegen, Germany
maren.schorch@uni-siegen.de

Myriam Lewkowicz
ICD, HETIC, Tech-CICO
Troyes University of Technology, France
myriam.lewkowicz@utt.fr

Abigale Stangl
ATLAS Institute
University of Colorado-Boulder
abigale.stangl@colorado.edu

ABSTRACT

HCI and CSCW researchers and practitioners are increasingly working in complex social and political contexts where their research activities involve emotional labor and where they have to confront moral and emotional dilemmas. Given the potential impact of these challenging situations on the wellbeing of researchers in the field, there is much need for a discourse on affective impact of research on the researcher. In this workshop, we invite discussion and reflection on the experiences of distress and the role of *informal coping mechanisms* (e.g., personal narratives) to address them. We will create a forum where researchers and practitioners can discuss and share experiences of projects in sensitive settings and work towards guidelines to inform future projects.

CCS Concepts

• HCI design and evaluation methods • accessibility theory, concepts and paradigms

Keywords

Methodology, reflection; validity; participatory design; user-centered design, qualitative research; emotion; sensitive settings; ethics; disability; aging; marginalization.

1. WORKSHOP THEME

Previous research by has shown that when confronted with emotional or moral dilemmas, researchers in our field are often left to their own devices [11]. Whereas in other fields, such as psychology and nursing, formalized strategies, such as reflection, counseling and peer-support, exist to support the emotional well-being of researchers, researchers in the field of HCI/CSCW oftentimes have to rely on their own devices to cope with these issues. In the absence of formal or institutional mechanisms of support, researchers have to rely on personal empathic and trusting relationships with supervisors and peers [11].

All the while, CSCW/HCI researchers and practitioners are increasingly conducting projects that involve them at an emotional level and impact their "moral universe" [23]. Examples of such projects include research conducted in socially and politically volatile settings, such as in refugee camps [27] or low-income settings [7], and in other *sensitive settings* where stakeholders are emotionally vulnerable, such as in bereavement support [2, 5], technology development for children and adults with disabilities [8, 9, 19] and support for the aging population [1,14] and in home care settings [18, 21].

The importance of this topic is increasingly being recognized. For example, Lindsay et al. have discussed the importance of empathy when working with the elderly [10]. Crabtree et al. have discussed different methodological challenges when researching with persons with mental illnesses [3]. Other work has described challenges when conducting research with persons suffering from dementia [4]. While these research projects address important questions by placing vulnerable target groups at the center of the discussions, there is a shortage of research when it comes to the emotional involvement of the researchers themselves in these interaction settings. Examples of existing research include discussions of autoethnographic approaches in the design for the elderly [22] and in bereavement support [25]. In addition, Rode has explored the concept of "rapport", where in the context of research on gender specific appropriation of technologies in a family household, she reflected on her own behaviour as an adaption to female roles as perceived by the family members in order to set up a deeper relationship to her research partners [16]. Similar discussions on the impact of socially-constructed notions of disability and aging, for example identifying them with illness, weakness and neediness, and their impact on the process and outcome of research efforts have emphasized the importance of confronting and deconstructing assumptions as a part of research activity [12, 17] There is still a lack of discussion and reflection on the more "human" aspects of the researcher's experience and how to tackle these issues with respect to the scientific method.

The objective of this workshop is to provide a forum for research concerning the issue of *affective impact on the researcher* who, in the context of HCI or CSCW user-centered design or research, develop close empathic and trusting relationships with stakeholders in such settings [26]; engagements that often entail emotional labor, which, in turn, may generate distress [13]. Reflection on these aspects of our own culture of research has an established precedence [6, 24]. This workshop is intended to complement the existing body of work and to provide new directions of inquiry and new modes of engagement with its topic area. In particular, this workshop, in addition to providing a venue for scholarly work, will create an explicit space for the *personal narrative*.

GROUP '16, November 13-16, 2016, Sanibel Island, FL, USA
ACM 978-1-4503-4276-6/16/11.
http://dx.doi.org/10.1145/2957276.2996292

The use of personal narratives — both as tools for empathic self-reflection [26] and as informal coping mechanisms [20] — has been noted in previous research. We invite a discussion on how personal narratives and other forms of self-expression can be used as a coping tool to express concerns one has as a researcher or practitioner when working in sensitive settings or in relation to personal conflicts and tensions between the researcher role and the "human" side of research. A key challenge is how to address concerns about privacy (both participants and researcher) and security when sharing such sensitive material. Another related question is how can researchers/practitioners share narratives about project failures or about challenging situations (i.e., "war stories" [15]) without fear of being perceived as "weak" or "unprofessional". In contrast to other fields of research, such as Sociology, where researchers focus on observing, describing and understanding social actions and dynamics, HCI and CSCW researchers mostly aim to apply their research to create or modify technology that intervenes or at least changes something in the world. The applied nature of the research field might add additional emotional and moral pressures on the researcher. A similar discourse is currently underway in the medical field in Germany with respect to a lack of a "culture of failure", where practitioners can share examples where they failed in their practice without risking being perceived as incompetent. A suggested solution has been the creation of an online form where personal narratives can be shared and discussed anonymously (www.kritische-ereignisse.de, translation: "critical incidents"). A question is how can we translate elements of similar discourses for our own field.

Previous reflection on these aspects of our own culture have largely viewed emotional impact through the lens of *ethics*, a perspective that is indeed important, in order to systematize concepts of "right" and "wrong" actions and behaviors in researchers in these sensitive settings [6, 24]. For the proposed workshop, we adopt a complementary, intra-personal stance, and ask: what is subjectively experienced and felt, and what is one's reaction to it? We aim to complement the existing body of work and to provide new directions of inquiry and new modes of engagement with its topic area. Our focus, in this workshop, turns towards experiences of distress and the role of *informal coping mechanisms* (vis-a-vis institutional practices), such as the use of *personal narratives,* to address them and provide a form of sense-making.

2. WORKSHOP OBJECTIVES

The objectives of the workshop are threefold:

Contributions to the body of knowledge: to further characterize the phenomena of intra-personal affective impact in sensitive setting research; to identify existing practices and to reflect upon them; to forefront and to discuss culturally-embedded tropes and imagery that may be active within the field (e.g., concerning ageing, disability, mortality) and the impact of these tropes on the researcher's own emotions; to discuss the potential contribution of emergent theories, including the social and post-modern models of disability and third wave HCI to this field; to deconstruct and reflect upon transdisciplinary, inter-organizational project work.

Impact on Research Culture: to provide a forum to share experiences in conducting research in sensitive settings and to discuss the features, challenges and rewards of working in such settings; to open up a space for discussion and reflection of such sensitive themes, to identify processes for bringing mindfulness and self-reflection to the research process; to deconstruct socially constructed notions about affective impact which oftentimes are conflated with a "weakness" in the researcher.

Methodological: to create and to disseminate a set of guidelines/best practices for conducting research in sensitive settings, including how they can translate to hands-on training of researchers and practitioners new to this area; to develop instruments for investigation of this theme in the longer-term (e.g. a repository of anonymous personal narratives in the form of a website).

In order to collaboratively attain these goals, we invite discussion on the following questions:

- What can we learn from experiences from successful and unsuccessful projects in sensitive settings that inform better approaches in the future?
- How can we build a repertoire of qualitative case studies and empirically grounded concepts to inform HCI practice in sensitive settings?
- How can we adopt holistic and inclusive approaches to topics such as aging, disability and social marginalization and apply them to activities in the field?
- How can our understanding of the constructed notions of disability and aging translate to other contexts such as working with children and adults living in low-income and/or marginalized contexts?
- How can researchers and practitioners better prepare themselves to resolve emotional and personal encounters in the field?

3. WORKSHOP DESCRIPTION

3.1 Call for Participation

This workshop is intended to solicit participation from HCI and CSCW researchers and practitioners. It is our desire to solicit participants from different communities, with various backgrounds and levels of experience, in order to foster inter- and transdisciplinary discussions. Intended participants include academics, industrial researchers and designers with experience working in sensitive and complex settings. We also encourage the participation of graduate trainees and early researchers.

Our call for participation will be an invitation for contributions for position papers and personal narratives, including autoethnographic accounts related to the workshop theme, including new related perspectives not covered in the workshop objectives and questions.

Position papers: scholarly works, theoretical, conceptual, or empirical, which address the theme of the workshop. Submissions of autoethnographic accounts that include personal narratives (see below), as well as reflection pieces are encouraged. Authors of accepted position papers will present in the workshop sessions. Submissions in this category must have a maximum length of 4 pages (this format), including references.

Personal narratives: first-person accounts, which address the theme of the workshop in a subjective manner and engage in reflection. Care should be taken in such narratives for proper de-identification. Authors may anonymize their narratives. Accepted personal narratives will be published on the workshop website and in archival materials, and may be drawn upon by participants during the workshop session. Authors of accepted personal narratives are welcome to participate in the workshop, but are not obliged to do so. Submissions in this category must have a maximum length of 2 pages (this format).

3.2 Workshop Format

A full-day workshop is planned that will consist of five sessions (coffee break between session 2 and 3, lunch break planned between session 3 and 4): Session 1 (am): organizers provide an introduction to the theme and topics of the workshop

Session 2 (am) and Session 3 (am): position paper presentations by the participants (10-15 minutes each) with opportunity for (audience discussion/Q&A).

Session 4 (pm): This session will consist of small group (3-4 person) discussions. The participants will discuss the presented papers using a theme identified in the morning sessions. The organizers will pre-plan a set of discussion themes, and will augment with emergent material from the morning sessions.

Session 5 (pm): In this session, each team will present an overview of their discussion to the whole group. The session will conclude with a reflective discussion followed by a summary of the insights that emerged during the workshop. We will work towards generating a set of guidelines pertaining to advice on how researchers and practitioners can better prepare themselves to resolve ethics and emotional encounters in the field.

We require space for 10-15 participants, with reconfigurable seating (to support the break-out discussions). The workshop will also require a projector and Internet connectivity. The organizers will identify additional requirements (e.g., accommodation for service animals, scent-free environment, etc.) that might arise due to accommodations required by participants as they emerge.

3.3 Outreach and Selection Process

Materials for the workshop will be hosted on a workshop website through which advertising, submission, distribution of reading material and organization will be handled. Archival material from the workshop will also be hosted on the website. The workshop's call for participation will be announced on a variety of mailing lists (e.g., from CHI and CSCW communities).

The workshop organizers will review the position papers and select 10-15 papers based on degree of originality and potential to stimulate discussion. Personal narratives are understood to be creative works and will be selected according to criteria of originality, potential for impact, and writing caliber. They will also be reviewed to ensure participant privacy is preserved.

3.4 Post-Workshop Dissemination

We intend to disseminate the workshop outcomes on the workshop website. In addition, accepted workshop papers will be published in a special issue of IRSI (International Reports of Socio-Informatics) or another HCI- or CSCW-related journal. Authors of selected papers will be invited to submit their workshop paper (with the opportunity for elaboration) to this peer-review process. We will discuss other possible options for dissemination with participants at the conclusion of the workshop. We plan to have a follow up workshop in the future on the basis of the outcomes from the current proposed workshop.

4. ORGANIZERS

Dr. Foad Hamidi's research interests include community-engagement and Participatory Design with children and adults with disabilities and their parents, caregivers and teachers. He received his doctorate in Computer Science at the Lassonde School of Engineering at York University, where he has designed and evaluated several systems for children including a living media system to motivate children to use more learning and therapeutic systems, and a DIY communication board system for non-verbal users. He is also interested in intercultural collaboration and has been of transnational teams working on projects in Africa and Central America.

Dr. Claudia Müller is an assistant professor at the department of information systems at University of Siegen, Germany, with focus on "IT for the ageing society". With a background in cultural anthropology, medical history and medical ethnology, Claudia subsequently follows a socio-cultural perspective on the development and appropriation of new technologies in home care and everyday contexts since many years. Her particular research interest is in developing appropriate research methods for co-designing with technology non-affine persons, e.g. to adapt the Living Lab methodology to the respective contexts.

Dr. Melanie Baljko is a research scientist working at the intersection of computing and the human. She is an Associate Professor of Electrical Engineering and Computer Science, holds a joint appointment to Department of Science and Technology Studies at York University, and is an Affiliate Scientist at the UHN-Toronto Rehabilitation Institute. She is a critical technology practitioner with interests in digitally-mediated social engagement, and assistive and rehabilitation technologies.

Marén Schorch is a research associate and leader of the EU-project TOPIC (The Online Platform for Informal Caregivers) at the University of Siegen, Germany. In this project, her research is focused on ethnography with elderly, informal caregivers in a rural area in Germany and the collaborative development of an information and support platform. She holds Master's degrees in Sociology and Psychology and worked as a research assistant and lecturer in Sociology and qualitative social research methods at the Universities of Trier and Bielefeld, Germany. Her main research interests and publications are in qualitative social research, biographies and identity, focusing on the way people deal with extreme events, health and sickness.

Dr. Myriam Lewkowicz is Full Professor in Informatics at Troyes University of Technology (France), where she is head of Information System Management teaching branch and Tech-CICO research group (part of UMR CNRS 6281). Her research focuses on designing systems for social interactions. It consists in defining innovative platforms to support existing collective practices or to design new collective activities. Her research is clearly interdisciplinary, and leads to reflections and propositions for new approaches which help defining new devices and services. For 10 years now, her main application domain is healthcare, with several projects at the regional, national and European levels. Myriam Lewkowicz is Program Committee Member of the main scientific conferences in CSCW and CHI (CSCW, CHI, ECSCW, COOP, GROUP, Communities&Technologies), and founding member of the ActiveAgeing Living Lab.

Abigale Stangl is a doctoral student at the ATLAS Institute at the University of Colorado-Boulder, USA, and research assistant with the Sikuli Lab in the Department of Computer Science. Her research interests include how people design, distribute and contribute to a growing body of accessible media and assistive technologies. Through participatory methods, she facilitates and assesses learning experiences that engage people of all abilities in Do-It-Yourself assistive technology design, and fabrication and learning and multi-modal literacy activities. She holds a Masters of Sciences in Information Communications Technology for Development (ICTD) from the ATLAS Institute at CU-Boulder, a graduate diploma in Landscape Studies from Lincoln University, and a Bachelors of Environmental Design from CU-Boulder.

5. REFERENCES

[1] Alaoui, M., Lewkowicz, M. 2015. Practical issues related to the implication of elderlies in the design process. The case of a Living Lab approach for designing and evaluating social TV services. *IRBM Journal Innovation and Research in BioMedical Engineering*, 36 (5), 259-265.

[2] Baljko, M. 2016. Technology-mediated community: the digital, the interactive and commemorative tattoo practice. In *The Tattoo Project: Creating a Digital Archive for Commemorative Tattoos*. Davidson, D. (Ed.). Canadian Scholars' Press.

[3] Crabtree, A., Hemmings, T., Rodden, T., Cheverst, K., Clarke, K., Hughes, J. and Rouncefield, M. 2003. Designing with care: Adapting cultural probes to inform design in sensitive settings, In *Proc. of the Australian Special Interest Group for Computer Human Interaction,* 4-13.

[4] Dahl, Y. and Holbø, K. 2012. Value biases of sensor-based assistive technology: case study of a GPS tracking system used in dementia care. In *Proc. of the Designing Interactive Systems Conference*, 572-581.

[5] Davidson, D., Baljko, M., and Letherby, G. 2012. Griefwork online: Community through computer-mediated communication. In *Proc. of the Motherhood Initiative for Research and Community Involvement Conference*. Toronto, Canada.

[6] Davis, H. and Waycott, J. 2015. Ethical Encounters: HCI Research in Sensitive and Complex Settings. In *Proc. of the Australian Special Interest Group for Computer Human Interaction,* 667-669.

[7] Hamidi, F., Saenz, K., and Baljko, M. 2014. Sparkles of brilliance: incorporating cultural and social context in codesign of digital artworks. In *Proc. of the Conference on Interaction Design and Children,* 77-84.

[8] Hamidi, F., Baljko, M., Ecomomopoulos, C., Livingston, N. J., and Spalteholz, L. G. 2015. Co-designing a speech interface for people with dysarthria. *Journal of Assistive Technologies*, *9*(3), 159-173.

[9] Hamidi, F., Baljko, M., Kunic, T., and Feraday, R. 2015. TalkBox: a DIY communication board case study. *Journal of Assistive Technologies*, *9*(4), 187-198.

[10] Lindsay, S., Brittain, K., Jackson, D., Ladha, C., Ladha, K. and Olivier, P. 2012. Empathy, Participatory Design and People with Dementia. In *Proc. of the Conference on Human Factors in Computing Systems,* 521-530.

[11] Moncur, W. 2013. The emotional wellbeing of researchers: considerations for practice. In *Proc. of the Conference on Human Factors in Computing Systems,* 1883-1890.

[12] Mankoff, J., Hayes, G. R., and Kasnitz, D. 2010. Disability studies as a source of critical inquiry for the field of assistive technology. In *Proc. of the Conference on Computers and Accessibility*, 3-10.

[13] Mitchell, W., and Irvine, A. 2008. I'm okay, you're okay?: Reflections on the well-being and ethical requirements of researchers and research participants in conducting qualitative fieldwork interviews. *International Journal of Qualitative Methods*, *7*(4), 31-44.

[14] Müller, C., Neufeldt, C., Randall, D., and Wulf, V. 2012. ICT-development in residential care settings: sensitizing design to the life circumstances of the residents of a care home. In *Proc. of the Conference on Human Factors in Computing Systems*, 2639-2648.

[15] Orr, J. E. 1990. Sharing knowledge, celebrating identity: Community memory in a service culture. *Collective remembering*, *169*, 189.

[16] Rode, J. A. 2011. Reflexivity in digital anthropology. In *Proc. of the Conference on Human Factors in Computing Systems*, 123-132.

[17] Rogers, Y., and Marsden, G. 2013. Does he take sugar?: moving beyond the rhetoric of compassion. *Interactions*, *20*(4), 48-57.

[18] Schorch, M., Wan, L., Randall, D. and Wulf, V. 2016. Designing for those who are overlooked: Insider perspectives on care practices and cooperative work of elderly informal caregivers. In *Proc. Conference on Computer-Supported Cooperative Work & Social Computing*, 787-799.

[19] Stangl, A., Hsu, C. L., and Yeh, T. 2015. Transcribing Across the Senses: Community Efforts to Create 3D Printable Accessible Tactile Pictures for Young Children with Visual Impairments. In *Proc. of the Conference on Computers & Accessibility*, 127-137.

[20] Taylor, S. E., Aspinwall, L. G., Giuliano, T. A., Dakof, G. A., and Reardon, K. K. 1993. Storytelling and Coping With Stressful Events. *Journal of Applied Social Psychology*, *23*(9), 703-733.

[21] Tixier, M. and Lewkowicz, M. 2015. Looking for Respite and Support: Technological Opportunities for Spousal Caregivers. In *Proc. of the Conference on Human Factors in Computing Systems,* 1155-1158

[22] Tonolli, L., Teli, M., and D'Andrea, V. 2015. A Design Anthropology Critique of Active Aging as Ageism. *Interaction Design and Architecture(s) Journal*, 26: 95-113.

[23] Wan, L., Müller, C., Wulf, V., and Randall, D. W. 2014. Addressing the subtleties in dementia care: pre-study & evaluation of a GPS monitoring system. In *Proc. of Conference on Human Factors in Computing Systems*, 3987-3996.

[24] Waycott, J., Davis, H., Thieme, A., Branham, S., Vines, J., and Munteanu, C. 2015. Ethical encounters in HCI: Research in Sensitive Settings. In *Proc. of the Conference EA on Human Factors in Computing Systems*, 2369-2372.

[25] Woodthorpe, K. 2007. My life after death: connecting the field, the findings and the feelings. *Anthropology Matters*, *9*(1).

[26] Wright, P., and McCarthy, J. 2008. Empathy and experience in HCI. In *Proc. of the Conference on Human Factors in Computing Systems*, 637-646.

[27] Wulf, V., Aal, K., Abu Kteish, I., Atam, M., Schubert, K., Yerousis, G., Randall, D., and Rohde, M. 2013. Fighting against the wall: Social media use by political activists in a Palestinian village. In *Proc. of the Conference on Human Factors in Computing Systems,* 1979-1988.

Exploring Ethics and Obligations for Studying Digital Communities

Casey Fiesler
University of Colorado Boulder
casey.fiesler@colorado.edu

Jessica Pater
Georgia Institute of Technology
pater@gatech.edu

Pamela Wisniewski
University of Central Florida
pamwis@ucf.edu

Nazanin Andalibi
Drexel University
naz@drexel.edu

ABSTRACT
Many of the most prominent and unanswered ethical questions within HCI and social computing involve our ethical obligation to the communities that we study. Some of these questions fall under the purview of more traditional human subjects research ethics, but others hinge on when, for example, studies of *public* data trigger similar obligations. Basic rules to "do no harm" are complicated in digital communities by issues of consent and privacy, and ethics review boards are struggling to keep up even as research communities are similarly struggling to form appropriate norms. The goals of this workshop are to continue seeding conversations about research ethics within the SIGCHI community, to work towards norm setting, and in the meantime, to collectively help community members make good ethical decisions about research into sociotechnical systems and digital communities.

Keywords
ethics; hci; human subjects; online communities; policy; privacy; social computing; sociotechnical systems

1. INTRODUCTION
Research ethics in the context of social computing is an increasing topical point of discussion, particularly in light of recent public scrutiny. For instance, media accusations of unethical research by Facebook and their research collaborators sparked disagreement throughout our community about best practices for informed consent [18]. OKCupid's manipulation of dating matches sparked discussion about experimentation and the nature of harm to users [21]. Most recently, researchers released a large, non-anonymized scraped dataset of OKCupid profile data that provoked debate about the nature of public data, expectations of privacy, and obligations of researchers to follow Terms of Service [26].

In the face of evolving technology, research methods, and norms, online settings continue to challenge traditional notions of research ethics. Moreover, around many issues there are not currently clear rules or norms among researchers, who make highly contextualized decisions about ethics that often vary across disciplines [23]. Ideas found in the Belmont Report or the ACM ethical codes of avoiding harm are no longer simple, particularly as the line between "human subject" and "public data" are blurred by the huge amount of user- generated content to which researchers have access. In this new environment, we should think critically about our obligations to the communities we study—whether those communities *know* that they are being studied or not.

GROUP '16, November 13-16, 2016, Sanibel Island, FL,USA
ACM 978-1-4503-4276-6/16/11.
http://dx.doi.org/10.1145/2957276.2996293

2. BACKGROUND AND THEMES
Research ethics in digital contexts is a topic of increased interest to the SIGCHI community as it matures. This is partially because socio-technical systems provide a new context to investigate aspects of human behavior that have not always been accessible otherwise, and comes wit h new challenges, dilemmas, and opportunities. Recent workshops on the subject of research ethics for sociotechnical systems and social media [10,12] have also highlighted a number of salient issues for this community. Though much recent discussion around ethics has been focused on "big data," we focus specifically here on the *humans* involved in our research. For this workshop, our primary inquiry is framed as: *What are our ethical obligations to the communities that we study?* What if the participants of those communities are particularly vulnerable? What if we find out information that should be reported (such as threats of harm)? How can we appropriately protect their privacy? When and how should we disseminate our findings to these communities? What are our obligations to those who produce the *public data* that we study e.g., non-consenting Twitter users? When does data science become human subjects research, and what does this mean for our ethical obligations?

Below, we present a number of ethical questions and challenges that may arise during various stages in the research process in order to identify key themes through would be of interest to the workshop organizers and participants.

2.1 Designing Research Protocols
At the *conception* of a new research project, how can we embed ethical principles into our study or technology designs? Past research has examined this challenge as it relates to the role of institutional review boards [8] and legal and contractual matters [11,13]. However, IRBs and lawyers may not be as knowledgeable about the context of our research as we are, thus missing some potential harm to participants or the institution. At times, researchers may leverage this lack of knowledge to their advantage, creating ethical challenges. For example, many IRBs do not require approval for research that does not explicitly

involve direct contact with human subjects. However, when researchers use automated approaches to, for instance, scrape public or semi-public data from users, humans are implicitly involved. Further, this type of automated scraping is often explicitly against a website's Terms of Service, making both the participants and the institution itself vulnerable.

When it comes to the design of corporate research, other ethical challenges can arise related to A/B testing [19] and algorithmic manipulation [22]. One example of these types of ethical conundrums is Facebook's "emotional contagion" study, where Facebook users were involved in a research study without their knowledge [18,19].

2.2 Obtaining Informed Consent

When obtaining *informed consent* [4,14,15] from participants, how do we ensure that this consent represents both *awareness* and *choice*? In the case of big data [4], the sheer volume of participants makes individualized consent difficult or impossible. In other contexts, such as chat rooms [14] and social networks [15], consent challenges are even more nuanced. How do we obtain consent while minimizing the burden on participants? When dealing with vulnerable populations [17] and minors [24], informed consent is increasingly necessary for preventing harm. Yet, some argue that these populations have limited capacity to provide such consent [17]. For example, parents are required to consent for minors to participate in human subjects research, but the assent of the minor is not required. Yet, the researchers' role as mandated reporter [24] forces us to breach the minor's confidentiality in the event that we detect that they are at imminent risk of harm.

2.3 Collecting and Analyzing Data

How do we ensure that the *data* we collect complies with ethical standards regardless of whet her we obtain it directly from participants or a third party? Does publicly available data within public spaces [6,25], for instance, give researchers the right to collect and aggregate this data for purposes other than the original intent of the poster? When aggregating otherwise disparate data, how do we ensure the appropriate anonymization [7,25] of this data?

When *analyzing* the data that has been collected, how do we ensure that our methods are *sound* and *robust*? Further, how can we address our *own* vulnerability as researchers, particularly when studying communities that are in distress [1,2] or present challenging content or behaviors [3,16,20]?

2.4 Disseminating Results

Finally, when *disseminating* our results, what is our responsibility to our participants? For example, have we appropriately anonymized [7,25,26] the data prior to publication? Even if the data were anonymized upon publication, could publically available data then be traced back to an individual through rudimentary means such as a Google search? At the *conclusion* of a research project, what has the researchers' relationship with the participants become after using highly engaging techniques such as ethnographic immersion [5]? What then are the norms related to participant privacy [4,9] and the dissemination of findings to participants within the community being studied [5]?

Questions like these are of increasing importance to our research community, and yet there are no clear answers. The recently appointed ACM SIGCHI ethics working group [27] has proposed, in part, that we have more community discussions about these thorny ethical issues so that we can begin to converge on best practices and norms. Therefore, we propose this workshop as one venue to start brainstorming this myriad of ethical issues so we can move toward this goal.

3. WORKSHOP STRUCTURE

The workshop will be structured to facilitate conversations around the aforementioned ethical challenges of human subjects research (defined broadly as research that involves *humans* or the *data* they produce) as it pertains to the field of collaborative and social computing. Throughout the course of the workshop, we will use actual case studies as well as hypotheticals to probe tension points and engage on a deeper level on the issues about which there are not clear answers.

We anticipate adjusting the program based on the interests and makeup of the participants in the workshop, but inspired by previous workshops on this topic [10,12], activities will include:

(1) Brief 2 minute introductions from all participants about one ethical challenge they have faced in their work and their respective reflections;
(2) Brief 5 or 10 minute presentations from a selected set of workshop participants, on specific topics of interest (such as the open questions noted above) or presenting case studies of actual ethical dilemmas faced;
(3) Group brainstorming to identify the most pressing questions and ethical challenges facing the community;
(4) Small "task force" style breakout groups to deep dive into specific issues or topics identified in ; and
(5) Group work around development of best practices and next steps for further engaging the broader community and disseminating the results of the workshop .

We will select participants based on the quality and depth of reflections presented in submissions. We will select presenters based on the potential to generate discussion and the extent to which their concerns are shared with all participants' submissions.

As part of (5), we also intend to come up with ways to engage the broader GROUP community during and after the conference—for example, by presenting provocative questions to attendees or getting feedback on ideas we propose at the workshop. Research ethics goes beyond IRB approval, and is something that should be important to every attendee of the conference. We feel that an important outcome of the workshop is to engage the entire community and not just workshop participants. With respect to deliverables, potential ideas include a collective blog where the organizers write the first post by summarizing the discussion points, and where participants as well as the broader community will be invited to contribute their ongoing reflections. Other ideas and specifics will be discussed and agreed upon together with participants.

Therefore, goals and planned outcomes for this workshop include: (1) documentation of the important open questions in the ethical space of studying digital communities; (2) documentation of brainstorming towards norm setting and current best practices; and (3) planning for engaging the GROUP community with these issues during the conference.

This workshop will be a full day, with a maximum of 30 participants including organizers (with no special equipment required beyond a projector).

4. SUBMISSIONS

In order to be considered for participation in the workshop, potential participants should present a short (1-2 page) statement of interest, which will be reviewed by the workshop organizers.

Submissions should also include a brief biographical sketch that includes current affiliation and research area.

Statements of interest can be structured in one of three ways: (1) an explanation of one's interest in research ethics (or a specific topic), ideally tied to one's own work; (2) a discussion of a specific topic in the area, e.g., one of the provocative open questions we have proposed; or (3) a case study discussion of an actual ethical dilemma faced in one's work.

All relevant topics related to ethics or obligations in studying digital communities, sociotechnical systems, or other technology-mediated groups are welcomed and encouraged. Examples include but are not limited to: informed consent, sensitive or vulnerable populations, algorithmic harm to users and communities, definitions of public content and data, the role of review boards, legal implications and obligations, reporting obligations, privacy, and relationships to study populations. We invite submissions from researchers from both academia and industry, and would welcome a wide range of disciplinary perspectives.

5. ORGANIZERS

Casey Fiesler is an Assistant Professor in the Department of Information Science at the University of Colorado Boulder. Her research focuses on the intersection of social computing and law, and in particular the legal and ethical gray areas of online content creation. She has organized workshops on the topic of research ethics at multiple conferences, including CSCW and ICWSM, and is currently a member of the SIGCHI Ethics Committee. She holds a law degree from Vanderbilt University and a PhD in Human-Centered Computing from Georgia Tech.

Pamela Wisniewski is an Assistant Professor in the College of Engineering and Computer Science at the University of Central Florida. Her research interests are situated in Human-Computer Interaction and lie at the intersection of social computing and privacy. Her goal is to frame privacy as a means to not only protect end users, but more importantly, to enrich online social interactions that individuals share with others.

Jessica Pater is a research scientist at the Georgia Tech Research Institute and a PhD candidate in Human Centered Computing at Georgia Tech. Her research focuses on how everyday social computing uses impact the health of vulnerable populations, most recently focusing on individuals with non-suicidal self-harm. In this work, she has advocated for expanding conversations of what is ethical for researchers focused on working with this vulnerable population.

Nazanin Andalibi is a PhD candidate at the College of Computing and Informatics at Drexel University. Her research focuses on people's social media disclosure and social support practices in stigmatized contexts. She argues that it is important for the HCI community to consider researchers' occupational vulnerability in discussions, trainings, practices, and policies around research ethics.

6. REFERENCES

1. Nazanin Andalibi and Andrea Forte. 2016. Social Computing Researchers, Vulnerability, and Peer Support. *CHI 2016 Ethical Encounters in HCI Workshop.*
2. Nazanin Andalibi, Oliver L Haimson, Munmun De Choudhury, and Andrea Forte. 2016. Understanding Social Media Disclosures of Sexual Abuse Through the Lenses of Support Seeking and Anonymity. *Proceedings of the ACM SIGCHI Conference on Human Factors in Computing Systems*, ACM.
3. Nazanin Andalibi, Pinar Ozturk, and Andrea Forte. 2015. Depression-related Imagery on Instagram. *Proceedings of the ACM Conference Companion on Computer Supported Cooperative Work & Social Computing*, ACM, 231–234.
4. Solon Barocas and Helen Nissenbaum. 2014. Big data's end run around anonymity and consent. In *Privacy, big data, and the public good: Frameworks for engagement*, J. Lane, V. Stodden, S. Bender and Helen Nissenbaum (eds.). Cambridge University Press, Cambridge, UK.
5. Anne Beaulieu and Adolfo Estallea. 2012. Rethinking research ethics for mediated settings. *Information, Communication & Society* 15, 1: 23–42.
6. J.C.H. Bromseth. 2002. Public places - public activities? Methodological approaches and ethical dilemmas in research on computer-mediated communication contexts. In *Resesarching ICTs in Context*, A. Morrison (ed.). University of Oslo, 33–61.
7. Amy Bruckman. Studying the Amateur Artist: A Perspective on Disguising Data Collected in Human Subjects Research on the Internet. In *Ethics and Information Technology*.
8. Elizabeth A. Buchanan and Charles Ess. 2009. Internet research ethics and the Institutional Review Board: Current practices and issues. *Computers and Society* 39: 43–49.
9. Kate Crawford and Jason Schultz. 2013. Big Data and Due Process: Toward a Framework to Redress Predictive Privacy Harms. *Boston College Law Review* 55, 1.
10. Casey Fiesler, Stevie Chancellor, Anna Lauren Hoffmann, Jessica Pater, and Nicholas John Proferes. 2016. Challenges and Futures for Ethical Social Media Research. *AAAI Conference on Web and Social Media (ICWSM): Workshop.*
11. Casey Fiesler, Cliff Lampe, and Amy S. Bruckman. 2016. Reality and Perception of Copyright Terms of Service for Online Content Creation. *CSCW '16: Proceedings of the 2016 ACM Conference on Computer-Supported Cooperative Work & Social Computing.*
12. Casey Fiesler, Alyson Young, Tamara Peyton, et al. 2015. Ethics for Studying Online Sociotechnical Systems in a Big Data World. *CSCW 2015 Companion.*
13. James Grimmelmann. 2015. The Law and Ethics of Experiments on Social Media Users. *University of Colorado Technology Law Journal* 13: 219–272.
14. James M. Hudson and Amy Bruckman. 2004. "Go Away": Participant Objections to Being Studied and the Ethics of Chatroom Research. *The Information Society* 20, 2: 127–139. http://doi.org/10.1080/01972240490423030
15. Luke Hutton and Tristan Henderson. 2015. "I didn't sign up for this!": Informed consent in social network research. *Proceedings of the 9th International AAAI Conference on Web and Social Media (ICWSM).*
16. Michelle Ibanez and Daniel D. Suthers. 2014. Detection of Domestic Human Trafficking Indicators and Movement Trends Using Content Available on Open Internet Sources. *Proceedings of the 47th Hawaii International Conference on Systems Science (HICSS).*
17. Carol Levine, Ruth Faden, Christine Grady, Dale Hammerschmidt, Lisa Eckenwiler, and Jeremy Sugarman. 2010. The Limitations of "Vulnerability" as a Protection for Human Research Participants. *The American Journal of Bioethics* 4, 3: 44–49.
18. Gregory McNeal. 2014. Facebook Manipulated User News Feeds to Create Emotional Responses. *Forbes.*
19. Michelle N. Meyer. 2015. Two Cheers for Corporate Experimentation: The A/B Illusion and the Virtues of Data-

Driven Innovation. *Colorado Technology Law Journal* 13: 273–332.

20. Jessica A. Pater, Oliver L. Haimson, Nazanin Andalibi, and Elizabeth D. Mynatt. 2016. "Hunger Hurts but Starving Works": Characterizing the Presentation of Eating Disorders Online. *Proceedings of the ACM Conference on Computer-Supported Cooperative Work & Social Computing.*
21. Martin Robbins. 2014. Does OKCupid need our consent? *The Guardian.*
22. Zeynep Tufekci. 2015. Algorithmic Harms Beyond Facebook and Google: Emergent Challenges of Computational Agency. *Colorado Technology Law Journal* 13: 203–218.
23. Jessica Vitak, Katie Shilton, and Z. Ashktorab. 2016. Beyond the Belmont Principles: Ethical Challenges, Practices, and Beliefs in the Online Data Research Community. *Proceedings of the 19th ACM Conference on Computer Supported Cooperative Work & Social Computing.*
24. Pamela Wisniewski, Heng Xu, Mary Beth Rosson, Daniel F. Perkins, and John M. Carroll. 2016. Dear Diary: Teens Reflect on Their Weekly Online Risk Experiences. *Proceedings of the 2016 CHI Conference on Human Factors in Computing Systems*, ACM, 3919–3930. http://doi.org/10.1145/2858036.2858317
25. Michael Zimmer. 2010. "But the data is already public": On the ethics of research in Facebook. *Ethics and Information Technology* 12, 4: 313–325. http://doi.org/10.1007/s10676-010-9227-5
26. Michael Zimmer. 2016. OkCupid Study Reveals the Perils of Big-Data Science. *WIRED.*
27. Facebook. *ACM SIGCHI Research Ethics.* https://www.facebook.com/groups/866225810172460/

Social Media for Sensitive Disclosures and Social Support: The Case of Miscarriage

Nazanin Andalibi
Drexel University
Philadelphia, PA 19104, USA
naz@drexel.edu

GROUP '16, November 13-16, 2016, Sanibel Island, FL, USA
 ISBN 978-1-4503-4276-6/16/11...$15.00
DOI: http://dx.doi.org/10.1145/2957276.2997019

Abstract
I study self-disclosure and investigate ways in which social computing systems can be designed to allow people to disclose negatively-perceived or stigmatized experiences and find support in their social networks. My prior work has given me insight about online disclosures of depression and sexual abuse, the role of anonymity in support seeking, and the ways that people respond to such disclosures. In my dissertation I will use miscarriage as a context to investigate online disclosure and response practices around stigmatized and traumatizing topics with the goal of improving both theory and social media design practices.

Problem Statement
All humans experience unwanted emotions in their lives. Stigmatized identities may be concealable (e.g., miscarriage, HIV) or visible (e.g., race, physical disability), and may include experiences of trauma (e.g., miscarriage, death of a loved one, sexual abuse). People can benefit from socially sharing such events and emotions associated with them [10]. However, many people inhibit socially and/or personally-perceived negative aspects of their lives and identities,

and sometimes they suffer as a result of this inhibition. Other times, when they do disclose, they might face negative consequences such as social rejections. On the other hand, there are potential benefits such as enactment of various forms of social support in disclosing such experiences and emotions associated with them. Social science literature provides us with several models (e.g., [9] [6]) to describe and explain disclosure practices in non-mediated and dyadic contexts. However, understanding self-disclosure practices when mediated by technology and with larger audiences is still an open and complex area of inquiry.

Social computing platforms are often celebrated for their capacity to connect; yet when people experience distress, they often find it difficult to use social media to seek support. I frame seeking support as a type of self-disclosure that often involves risking one's "face" in Goffman's [5] terms. Goffman posits that people want to create positive impressions of themselves [5], and sharing more positive rather than negative events and emotions has been linked to such positive impressions [7]. Individuals experiencing positive events are more motivated to share these events with their networks than those experiencing negative events [11]. Yet, if communicated, difficult disclosures can serve as a way to find support. Other HCI researchers have investigated the design and use of online environments for support. For example, research indicates that when people post on Facebook about a stressful event like a job loss, their strong ties provide support; however, the presence of strong ties may also exacerbate feelings of embarrassment and increase stress as well [3], which pertains to the important role of the disclosure audience. How do people disclose sensitive information and potentially stigmatized emotions as they use social media? What are the conditions in which these disclosures could lead to supportive interactions? Important questions remain about how these complex social performances are enacted or best supported in computer-medicated environments. I plan to tackle this space in my dissertation.

Pilot Work

In pilot studies, I have examined depression-related photo sharing on Instagram to understand how shared media like photographs create opportunities for people to disclose negative emotions and how others respond [2]. Noting that Instagram does not have a "real name" policy and people could use pseudonyms, I found evidence of emergent support networks. Most importantly, interactions around depression-tagged images are mainly supportive and rarely include aggressive or negative remarks. I have also investigated sexual-abuse disclosures on reddit [1]. In this work, I found that affordances that support anonymous disclosures and faceted identity performances [4] are important: people are more likely to seek support anonymously, and men (who face more stigma as victims of sexual abuse) are more likely to disclose abuse using throwaway accounts that are not linked with their primary reddit identities. In a current project, I am using content analysis methods to investigate potential differences in the types of responses that anonymous and identified sexual-abuse disclosures on reddit attract.

Proposed Dissertation Work

My pilot studies and prior work suggest that there is potential for social media to be designed in ways that not only enable safe sharing of negative experiences, but also encourage development of emergent support

Research Questions

RQ1. How do people who have experienced miscarriage decide to disclose feelings and experiences related to this experience online, to whom, when, through what channels, and why?

RQ2. How do people decide whether and how to respond to disclosures that they perceive to be negative or stigmatized on social media?

RQ3. What technological affordances and constraints play a role in mediating disclosures, responses to them, and perceptions of disclosures and responses in the context of social technologies? How can the design of social computing environments encourage supportive interactions?

networks that can help people feel less alone and receive more sympathy. In my dissertation, I plan to take miscarriage as a context that is often socially stigmatized, often traumatizing, associated with negative feelings, and hard to disclose in order to ***examine how and when people share negative emotions and experiences in online networks, the conditions in which self-disclosures are likely to lead to supportive interactions, and how social media can be designed to promote positive outcomes for people who disclose stigmatized experiences***. My specific research questions are described in the sidebar, and I plan to conduct the following studies to address them by taking a phenomenological approach.

Study 1: *Semi-structured interviews with people who have had miscarriages about their beliefs and practices with respect to disclosure, nondisclosure and responses to others people's disclosures:* The first purpose of this study is to gain a deep understanding of the goals and decision-making process behind disclosure and non-disclosure on social media of miscarriage-related feelings and experiences, and the factors that influence these decisions. I will delve into the perceived socio-technical, relational, cultural, and individual factors that influence disclosure decisions. This study will contribute to understanding the contexts that encourage or inhibit miscarriage disclosures on social media, such as where (platform choice), when, how, and why people disclose or do not disclose. This will primarily address RQ1 and RQ3, and partially RQ2.

Study 2: *Semi-structured interviews and vignettes with people about response practices when facing other people's disclosures:* The purpose of this study is to delve deep into reactions of people who come across negative and stigmatized disclosures as they browse social media, and the reasons and mechanisms behind those. The results of this study will address RQ2 and RQ3 and will contribute to a richer understanding of the decision making processes around responding or not responding to sensitive disclosures, and factors that inhibit or disinhibit various types of response behavior in the face of such disclosures. In addition to interviews, I will also use vignettes that I have designed and ask participants to tell me how they would react to a miscarriage disclosure by particular members of their network (e.g., friend, family, etc.).

In both of these studies, because I cannot predict what sharing platforms are important to my participants, and because people likely use a variety of mediums, I will not focus on any particular one. Instead, I take an ecological perspective and I will follow up on particular channels participants use as needed and as they come up in the interviews. I will also I will use participants' social media data where possible to understand the phenomena better. I will analyze interview data using the constant comparative approach.

Study 3: *Semi-structured interviews with redditors about their disclosure, non-disclosure, and response practices on miscarriage subreddits, content analysis of posts and comments, and investigating the role of anonymity afforded by throwaway accounts in disclosure and response practices:* In this study I will interview participants who post on miscarriage-related subreddits. I choose reddit because these disclosures are already happening there, and two levels of identifiability are allowed: using a pseudonym and using a throwaway account that is a proxy for anonymity [8]. This will allow me to not only ask these participants about their disclosure and response behavior on reddit, but also follow up to understand their overall social media practices in this context and to complement studies 1 and 2. In addition to interviews, I will use qualitative content analysis methods to characterize disclosures and responses and quantitative methods to understand these variables' disclosures and interactions around them.

Expected Contributions

I expect to improve our empirical and theoretical understanding of how and in what contexts sensitive disclosures (i.e., disclosures that make people feel vulnerable) happen in computer-mediated environments and how and in what contexts supportive interactions occur. Although in most of this work I focus on miscarriage, I expect some of my results to go beyond this specific experience and be applied to other stigmatized and sensitive contexts that make people feel vulnerable and where social support following disclosures would be helpful. Finally, by understanding the role of technological affordances in disclosure and response practices, I will be able to recommend social media design improvements that will better enable safe and sensitive disclosures and more social support. To me, my dissertation is the beginning of a research career that in addition to the intellectual contributions, tries to give a voice to under-represented and stigmatized populations and make the world just a bit more supportive, compassionate, and open to live in.

References

1. Nazanin Andalibi, Oliver L Haimson, Munmun De Choudhury, and Andrea Forte. 2016. Understanding Social Media Disclosures of Sexual Abuse Through the Lenses of Support Seeking and Anonymity. In *Proceedings of the ACM SIGCHI Conference on Human Factors in Computing Systems*.
2. Nazanin Andalibi, Pinar Ozturk, and Andrea Forte. 2017. Sensitive Self-disclosures, Responses, and Social Support on Instagram: the Case of #depression. In *Proceedings of ACM Conference on Computer-Supported Cooperative Work and Social Computing*.
3. Moira Burke and Robert Kraut. 2013. Using Facebook after losing a job: Differential benefits of strong and weak ties. 1419–1430.
4. Shelly D. Farnham and Elizabeth F. Churchill. 2011. Faceted identity, faceted lives: social and technical issues with being yourself online. In *Proceedings of the ACM Conference on Computer Supported Cooperative Work & Social Computing*, 359–368. http://doi.org/10.1145/1958824.1958880
5. Erving Goffman. 1959. The presentation of self in everyday life.
6. K Greene, TD Afifi, and WA Afifi. 2009. An integrated model of health disclosure decision-making. *Uncertainty and information regulation in interpersonal contexts: Theories and applications*: 226–253.
7. Mark R Leary and Robin M Kowalski. 1995. The self-presentation model of social phobia. *Social phobia: Diagnosis, assessment, and treatment*: 94–112.
8. Alex Leavitt. 2015. "This is a Throwaway Account": Temporary Technical Identities and Perceptions of Anonymity in a Massive Online Community. In *Proceedings of the ACM Conference on Computer Supported Cooperative Work & Social Computing*.
9. Julia Omarzu. 2000. A Disclosure Decision Model: Determining How and When Individuals Will Self-

Disclose. *Personality and Social Psychology Review* 4, 2: 174–185. http://doi.org/10.1207/S15327957PSPR0402_05

10. Bernard Rimé, Catrin Finkenauer, Olivier Luminet, Emmanuelle Zech, and Pierre Philippot. 1998. Social Sharing of Emotion: New Evidence and New Questions. *European Review of Social Psychology* 9, 1: 145–189. http://doi.org/10.1080/14792779843000072

11. Jessica Vitak and Jinyoung Kim. 2014. "You can't block people offline": examining how facebook's affordances shape the disclosure process. 461–474. http://doi.org/10.1145/2531602.2531672

The Role of Social Media in Participatory Democracy: A Case Study of Facebook Groups

James Gachau
University of Maryland
College Park, MD 20742, USA
jjgachau@gmail.com

GROUP '16, November 13-16, 2016, Sanibel Island, FL, USA
© 2016 ACM. ISBN 978-1-4503-4276-6/16/11...$15.00
DOI: http://dx.doi.org/10.1145/2957276.2997020

Abstract
This dissertation investigates three Facebook groups as case studies of the role of social media in enhancing participatory democracy. I argue that the groups were formed to provide avenues for articulating discourses that are counter to the dominant voices of their societies. The study posits that in stratified societies there typically emerges a dominant hegemonic public opinion, which is inimical to the needs, hopes, desires, and aspirations of subordinate classes. The key research question I ask is: How are these groups using social media to build and articulate identities that question the dominant public opinion about issues that have traditionally been controlled by a hegemonic voice?

Author Keywords
Hegemony; public opinion; participatory democracy; social identity; mass, social media; public sphere; counterpublics.

Introduction
This project is situated in democratic theory as understood in political science in general, and public sphere theory as understood in mass media and political communication in journalism studies in particular. The point of departure is Nancy Fraser's

1990 critique of the public sphere as envisioned by Jürgen Habermas (1989).

Habermas had argued that with the rise of the bourgeoisie, government had been taken from the monarchy and aristocracy, and handed to the general citizens, who acted as a public body "when they confer[ed] in an unrestricted fashion," (1974, 49). This they did by meeting in that "realm" he called the public sphere, where public opinion is formed through rational deliberation on the issues that matter to all the citizens in general. The resulting public opinion becomes the will of the people, which the state must enforce for the benefit of the entire citizenry.

Fraser showed that contrary to Habermas, the bourgeois public was not ***the*** public, as it did not include women, peasants, people of color, and other non-white middle class males. In stratified societies, social compositions that allow "contestation among a plurality of competing publics" are better at furthering the principle of participatory democracy (Fraser 1990, 66). Habermas claimed that the proliferation of publics in late capitalism—what he termed "the social welfare state"—transformed the liberal public sphere from a rational discursive arena, with "the coherence created by bourgeois social institutions and a relatively high standard of education" (1974, 54), into a field of competition for conflicting interests among various social groups. Fraser, however, showed that participatory democracy is best served by a plurality of publics, as opposed to one comprehensive public. She used the example of the U.S. women's movement, which developed its own identity and voice away from the bourgeois male property owners. These other publics she called "counterpublics", and argued that they were "subaltern", a term she borrowed from Antonio Gramsci (1971), to denote class relations where one class is subordinated to the other(s) through systems of ideology.

Counterpublics in Social Media

Following Fraser, and other theorists of publics and counterpublics, I posit that subaltern classes are today using social media to develop counter-discourses that challenge the ideological systems of the dominant classes. I am studying three Facebook groups that select, post, and discuss mass media messages that go against the mainstream. As various critics of the mass media point out, "the sheer scale of modern media corporations overwhelms the relatively minute institutions of the public sphere, as a skyscraper enshadows a small public park" (Butsch 2007, 8). Robert McChesney argues that media content has become so closely linked to the interests of a few gigantic and mighty corporations, that the public has been almost completely obliterated, and replaced by a mass of consumers, whom corporations target for profits at all costs. The resulting media system "exists to provide light escapist entertainment" (2015, 113).

My dissertation postulates that social media are stepping into the void thus created by the corporatized and institutionalized media. It focuses on Facebook as a social medium with the potential to develop and communicate discourses that challenge the dominant media system. Due to their ability to bring together people with similar objectives, experiences, and aspirations, Facebook groups provide an important opportunity to organize into counterpublics. Three groups serve as case studies to test my assumption.

The first group, named Freethinkers Initiative Kenya (FIKA), is based in Kenya, my home country. Media scholar George Ogola (2015) argues that social media, particularly Twitter, can create "a heteroglossic text and space" in a media landscape otherwise dominated by a "duopoly" of Kenya's biggest media houses. He finds that counter-discourses challenging the hegemony of the dominant classes are being effectively articulated by Kenya's online community, with a focus on social and political justice rather than on "generic news values" (2015, 78). The result, he holds, is that as more and more Kenyans adopt various communication technologies, "Kenya's public sphere will undoubtedly expand even further" (79).

The 'Annual Global Barometer's Global Index of Religion and Atheism' ranks Kenya eighth out of 57 countries on the religiosity index (2012). As a movement opposed to the dominant views of its society, FIKA supports the separation of church and state, gay rights, and women's right to bodily autonomy, all of which go against the tenets of the Christian Kenyan majority. I completed the pilot study for this dissertation on FIKA.

The second group, Women Without Religion (WWR), emphasizes women's rights. The group's Facebook description says: "We are an atheist feminist group and eschew all unsubstantiated supernatural claims, not just deities." One member, a Kenyan man, told me during an interview that the group "aims to show women that the best way to overcome their problems is by not being subservient to anyone."

WWR supports abortion rights, the right to euthanasia, and the right to positive sexual expression—including the right to choose sexual activity as a legal and legitimate profession. It provides community and social support for people, particularly women, who are leaving or have left religion and find/found themselves ostracized by their friends and families. International in scope, it includes members from Australia, Papua New Guinea, Canada, India, Africa, and the Middle East.

The third group, the Pan-African Network (PAN), focuses on issues facing Africans and people of African descent worldwide. Its Facebook page describes a commitment to promoting "the advancement of Global Africans (Africans/African descendant people/African Diaspora) and the African continent." Posts range from global capitalism's plunder of Africa's natural resources, to racial violence in America. Members highlight media content that challenges the dominant message found in mainstream media, that Africa is plagued by war, famine, disease, and poverty; that Africans are a backward primitive illiterate people with no history prior to colonialism; that Africans need the "White Savior".

Progress Made on the Research

My method includes in-depth interviews with members, to find out what role the groups play in their lives, and to answer the research question whether the groups help them create identities and voices that are in opposition to the dominant public opinion. I also will analyze both the content of the posts members put up, and the discourse surrounding that content.

I have managed to gain access to all three groups. This has not been without problems. FIKA was very welcoming of my intention to study it for my dissertation. However, I am a regular commentator and realize I am perceived as an atheist in support of the group's agenda. I am concerned that this poses an ethical dilemma, which may undermine my findings. I find myself in a situation similar to Shepherd Mpofu's "insider-researcher" study of subaltern genocide victims' voices among the Ndebele-speaking people of Zimbabwe (2015), where he notes that "the challenge of this type of research is that it is difficult to be objective" (86).

As a feminist I am also heavily invested in WWR's cause. I have increasingly become a regular commentator in the group, and some of the members I have interviewed appear to have developed certain ties to me and my research. One particular woman found a comment I made on the intersectionality of feminism with activism against racism quite in line with her convictions, and commented that she would like to hear more from me. Soon after this, she sent me a long private message on Facebook telling me that she had quit not only the separate secret admin group, but the main public WWR group as well, because of "white feminism." In summary, she was put to task for "antagonizing" a certain white woman who had expressed support for a clearly racist action. She told me that she felt so insulted by the rest of the admin group treating the white woman with kid gloves while she was hung out to dry. She asked them why the white woman's traumatic experiences were more important than her own, reminding them that she too, just like the white woman, had suffered sexual violence as a child, had developed ADHD to cope with the trauma, and was still highly sensitive to issues that could trigger the traumatic memory. They, she told me, informed her the group "was never, had never been, and never would be about race," and she told them she would rather leave than pander to their "white tears." She told me that they had resorted to calling her "the angry black woman", betraying their hypocrisy, and their assumption that "black people don't feel pain?...almost as if because I'm able to articulate myself strongly they feel like they can trample on me."

This, I feel, presents an ethical challenge. On the one hand, it appears this woman felt she could confide in me because I am black like her. She appears to have implicitly expected me to side with her. My natural reaction was to indeed side with her. On the other hand, the group's active members are mostly white, and they have expressed no racial bias towards me. In fact, the issue of race has never arisen in their interaction with me. As a researcher, I am obviously obligated to include in my findings the sentiments, misgivings, and frustrations communicated to me by her as one of my study participants. The question I find myself wrestling with is how the rest of the group, particularly the founder and self-described "owner and CEO of the group", would react to my portrayal of them as described by this subject. Would they feel I betrayed their warm welcome of me and my research to their world? Do I owe them some sort of allegiance that would interfere with my candor in my report of what I have found out about the group and its organization?

Radha S. Hegde asks, "How do we represent lives and sensibilities from a space of otherness and render them intimate and with the dignity they deserve?" (2009). WWR represents people coming from a state of alterity. They are undoubtedly subaltern in the patriarchal worlds they hail from. Feminism is at the core of their identity. Perhaps they feel totally inadequate to deal with racism, as this demands more than the double consciousness they have been accustomed to as members of the "other gender". Perhaps their rebuttal that their group "will never be about race" is fuelled by a recognition that the question of race is one they are ill-equipped to address. Are there ways I can tackle this dilemma? Can I interrogate this conundrum through my interviews with them? Like the "essentialized Other" described by Hedge (292), my subject who has been labeled "angry black woman" has been stripped of her agency, and been dismissed from the group. What am I to do with her story? My ethical and scholarly instinct tells me to stand up for her, and represent her, and let her be heard, but my commitment to the group wonders whether in so doing I would not be betraying the larger group. Let me try to elaborate a little further.

During the week of September 11 to 17, I interviewed this participant and she said that she had expected feminists to be sensitive to racism because they know what it means to be marginalized. She had expected that they would be intersectional in their feminism, rather than remain entrenched in their "white privilege." She was accused of making "an important ally" (the white woman she found herself campaigning against) leave the group. Why, she wondered, can't they see the world from her perspective? The "ally" had posted on her wall, months before, a petition to revoke the Rhodes scholarship of some African student because of his mistreatment of a white waitress. My subject pointed this out as a racist action. Her interlocutors saw it as a staged attempt to "entrap" their ally in a bid to make the group more about something it is not: "She combed through this member's timeline, looking for evidence that she is a racist," the chief admin of the group told me during a later interview.

My central ethical conundrum here is to figure out whether her feeling that they made her an "essentialized other" as "an angry black woman" is genuine, or whether her opponents' view that she was entrapping their ally is the more valid position to take. How do I present both accounts in my dissertation without appearing to be partial to either party?

The greatest challenge had until now been posed by PAN; some members have expressed anxiety about my research and its potential to "compromise their security". One African American member categorically declined my request to interview him, saying that my interview questions violate his personal security. One of the group's administrators grilled me for almost one hour, trying to ensure that my interest in the group is genuine, that I have benefitted from the group's content, and that I did not join merely for my research purposes. In addition, I had to actively seek out all the members I have been able to speak with, friending them on Facebook, and pointing out my post on the group announcing my research and asking for volunteers. I was not yet certain they would allow me access up to the end of my study. Though the administrator who interrogated me promised full support, he had said that he would have to seek the counsel of the other administrators, and hinted that my research goals may not align with the group's aims.

However, he has since gone ahead and pinned the post I had made asking for volunteers for my study, thus showing that the group has fully endorsed my research. Another prominent admin commented on the post to express his, and the group's, support. He also tagged a number of members, about half a dozen, whom he felt would be of great value as interview subjects, and they all agreed to participate. I have contacted most of them, and though they still have not availed themselves for the interview, save for one whom I interviewed on September 11, this particular admin told me it's just a matter of time before they come through. Nonetheless, I still feel that they remain reticent and reluctant to participate in the interviews. My doctoral committee co-chair suggested that I donate a small amount of money, say ten dollars, to a charity of their choice, but the first admin advised against this, saying it might be interpreted as a bribe, or it may draw charlatans volunteering to participate while they are not genuine members.

Are there any suggestions on how I can incentivize members of PAN to participate more freely in this research?

"Multiple judgments are possible, and ambiguity and uncertainty are part of the process," write Markham and Buchanan (2012, 5). They add that while people may "acknowledge that the substance of their communication is public" (6), the specific context in which it appears implies privacy. Perhaps, the taciturnity displayed by members of PAN is a factor of such a situation. I suspect that many of them are hesitant to make their positions in the group open to the public scrutiny they would be subject to under research. Unlike WWR, which is a pubic Facebook group, PAN is a closed group, meaning that only members can see what is posted in it. Perhaps, they feel that the interviews present a different context than the one they are accustomed to in their group. I hope to find answers to some of these questions during the Group 2016 conference, and look forward eagerly to participating in it.

References

'Kenya'. CIA World Factbook. https://www.cia.gov/library/publications/the-world-factbook/geos/ke.html. Retrieved May 14, 2015.

Butsch, R. 2007. Media and public spheres. New York: Palgrave Macmillan.

Fraser, N. 1990. "Rethinking the public sphere: a contribution to the critique of actually existing democracy". Social Text. (25/26): 56-80.

Gramsci, A., Q. Hoare, and G. Nowell-Smith. 1972. Selections from the prison notebooks of Antonio Gramsci. New York: International Publishers.

Habermas, J. 1989. The structural transformation of the public sphere: an inquiry into a category of bourgeois society. Cambridge, Mass: MIT Press.

Habermas, J., S. Lennox, and F. Lennox. 1974. "The public sphere: an encyclopedia article (1964)". New German Critique. 3 [New German Critique, Duke University Press]: 49–55.

Hegde R.S. 2009. "Fragments and interruptions: sensory regimes of violence and the limits of feminist ethnography". Qualitative Inquiry. 15 (2): 276-296.

Markham, A., and E. Buchanan. 2012. "Ethical decision-making and internet research". Recommendations from the AoIR ethics working committee (Version 2.0).

McChesney, R.W. 2015. Rich media, poor democracy: Communication politics in dubious times.

Mpofu, S. 2015. "When the subaltern speaks: citizen journalism and genocide 'victims'' voices online". African Journalism Studies. 36 (4): 82-101.

Ogola, G. 2015. "Social media as a heteroglossic discursive space and Kenya's emergent alternative/citizen experiment". African Journalism Studies. 36 (4): 66-81.

WIN-Gallup International. 2012. Global index of religiosity and atheism – 2012. http://www.wingia.com/web/files/news/14/file/14.pdf. Retrieved February 22, 2016.

Designing Social Memory Artifacts in a Smart Home

Jasmine Jones
School of Information
University of Michigan
Ann Arbor, MI
jazzij@umich.edu

GROUP '16, November 13-16, 2016, Sanibel Island, FL, USA

ISBN 978-1-4503-4276-6/16/11...$15.00
DOI: http://dx.doi.org/10.1145/2957276.2997021

Abstract
Memory is shaped by the media in which it is communicated (van Dijck, 2007). In a world where people live enmeshed with computing technologies, there are myriad opportunities to enrich and enhance everyday life with new kinds of memory. In my dissertation research, I employ a mixed methods interpretivist approach to investigate how people relate to and revisit memories of their past, how families collectively interact with shared memory, and how pervasive "ubicomp" technologies can be designed to support and enhance the social activities of sharing family memory across generations.

Author Keywords
Memory; pervasive computing; family; design; time

Introduction
There has been a great deal of interest from the HCI and CSCW communities in designing technologies for the home and for families, with memory-related topics ranging from understanding why people cherish idiosyncratic objects (Golsteijn et al., 2012), to designing "technology heirlooms" that afford long-lasting durability and high value polish to digital memorabilia (Odom et al., 2012). Most of the work in this area primarily considers *autobiographical memory*, which is the memory a person has of their own experiences.

Shifting to Collective Memory

Even when considering individual, personal memory, it is quite social in nature. In a social frame, activities of memory are understood to take place 1) with social materials, 2) within social contexts, and 3) in response to social cues (Mitzal, 2003; Kirk & Sellen, 2010). Further, individuals are social beings, referencing social identities, and using languages and symbols derived from the groups in which one is a member. Yet, memories that are shared also exist and take shape beyond any one individual's ability to remember (for example, war memorials). As these shared memories become the foundation of a group identity, they are referred to as *collective memory (Zerubavel, 1996)*. In my work, I examine "family memory," the collective memory of the family passed from one generation to the next.

Family Memory in a Smart Home

Considering the home as a pervasive computing environment, I became interested in how technologies in the home could facilitate interacting with a family's collective memory. Family memory is one of the most fundamental influences on a person's identity and relation to their social world, and serves to unite related individuals into a cohesive social unit (Zerubavel, 1996). However, it is also the site of potential conflict with issues such as family secrets, generational divides, and feuds influencing how people view and engage with the past. Thus, technologies designed for family memory are not just about preserving the past for future generations, but also for negotiating which version of the past to convey.

Following an interprevist approach, using qualitative and design research methods, I aim in my dissertation to understand the current sociotechnical context of family memory and explore solutions that address the challenges in this space.

Understanding Family Collective Memory

Through a series of ethnographic studies, I am conceptualizing how family members interact around shared memories. In my work, I approach memory sharing as an ongoing (re)construction and (re)interpretation of the past, and focus on how families might use physical artifacts to facilitate creating, sharing, and revisiting their shared memories.

The work of family memory keepers

To delve into this topic, I conducted in-depth interviews with family memory "keepers," people, typically in an older generation, who assume primary responsibility in a family for ensuring continuity of family history and lore. In these interviews I sought to understand what constituted the "memory" that today's families kept, and how physical and digital objects played a role in passing these memories to the next generation.

Family memory keepers viewed memory artifacts as important sources of memory as well as tools to facilitate the exchange of memory narratives. Memory keepers reported much of their effort being spent in *finding* stories about the family—often to get answers to unexplained questions or to fill in holes in existing narratives. Artifacts could serve as subtle signals that a story existed even if it had been hidden or forgotten. Memory keepers also had to *restore* family stories that that seemed incomplete or incorrect. In these cases, artifacts acted as anchors that could ground and give a sense of realness and personality to stories and historical facts.

However, at times there were different perspectives on a person, conflicting accounts about an event, or discrepancies between family records and public records. Artifacts were often sources of conflict in conveying previously unknown or incongruent information. In these cases, memory keepers had to decide how to *resolve* this contested memory to maintain a cohesive family narrative.

An open question from this work is how memory artifacts could be designed to help family memory keepers with the ongoing challenge of negotiating and resolving contested narratives.

Design at Scale: Engaging with Digital Mementos

A second issue facing families is the vast difference in scale that exists between a family's physical sentimental artifacts and their digital counterparts. For example, a person might have a small box of mementos from their childhood, or dozens of old photographs featuring their ancestors, but have thousands of digital photos documenting the mundane and important details of their lives. The volume of content that families can collect is unprecedented and can be overwhelming for them to make sense of and use. As technological tools to capture important memories proliferate, it is important also to enable people to curate the content they are generating so it is useful to them for future memory purposes.

Kidkeeper: An illustration of curatorial reluctance

I conducted a user study of a toy-like audio capture system for children and parents, named Kidkeeper, developed by my colleague David Merritt (Jones, Merritt & Ackerman, to appear). Kidkeeper was a fun plaything for children that had a number of features that made it useful for parents in capturing and saving audio-based mementos of their children when they were young. However, in our interviews we learned that, while parents emphasized their desire to have many, high-quality mementos of their children, they were unlikely to expend the effort to select the ones they liked and wanted to keep from a large collection. Instead, because of the sheer volume, they would either keep them all (somewhere on a hard drive) or delete them.

This paradoxical reaction reveals a thorny social-technical (Ackerman, 2000) design problem for digital mementos. There was a mismatch in our parents' expectations about what services a technological memory artifact should provide (capturing and delivering enjoyable content to them) and the effort they were willing to expend to initialize and maintain such services (i.e. by providing their content preferences). In a memory context, we realized that this was fundamentally an issue of curation.

Unpacking the social-technical problem of curation

A great deal of work both in research and in industry has characterized the lack of curation of digital content as both a technical problem and a social problem. Socially, an over-abundance of meaningless content can obscure any valuable artifacts in a collection, leading to devaluation and loss of precious memorabilia (Marshall, Bly, & Brun-Cottan, 2006). Technically, digital curation is not well supported and existing technology solutions have not been widely adopted. Yet, a fundamental design assumption of most memory artifacts is that the media content being presented and displayed has been curated somehow and is valuable for the user's recollection. Thus, there is a need for systems that somehow encourage users to curate their content or develop ways to automate curation by intuiting what might be sentimental and valuable in a mixed heap of artifacts.

To gain insight on how designers might facilitate the management of large collections of digital mementos in everyday life, I conducted a qualitative analysis of a forum featuring conversations from people struggling to deal with an overabundance of artifacts that had deep personal value (Jones & Ackerman, to appear). Participants enacted several "curation regimes" using storage and display areas in their home to organize their artifacts and maximize the attention they were able to pay to them. Importantly, curation for these participants was an ongoing process integrated into how they interacted with and arranged their memory artifacts, rather than a precursor to use. This finding suggests a wealth of opportunities for design in translating the interactive and practical features of physical curation to enhance the curation of digital mementos, while also enabling meaningful use of large amounts of content.

Future: Designing Social Memory Artifacts

In my current and future work, I am implementing some of the major implications from my previous work on integrating capture, curating large collections of digital mementos, and resolving contested narratives. To explore these issues from a design perspective, my colleagues and I have developed an exploratory prototype called "Storyball". In its basic form, Storyball takes the form of a magic-8 ball that, when shaken, replays a recorded memory narrative. This application, though simple, opened up a larger design space for revisiting recorded traces of the past. This design space posed a number of challenges not easily answered by current knowledge or solvable with existing approaches of designing for memory.

Resolving Contested Narratives
Using Storyball as a probe, and also as prototypical artifact, the questions I am investigating are **social**: "Who has the right to tell a family story encapsulated in one of these artifacts?"; **technical**: "How can people engage with memory narratives that have multiple versions (or are from multiple people) in a physical object or set of objects?" and **temporal**: "When is the right time to present and revisit a version of a memory?"

Integrating Curation into Memory Practice
As a first step towards expanding the interactions people might have with large collections of memories, I am designing form factors for objects which reflect the emotional valence of the narratives they convey. My goal is to add a memory of emotion to artifacts that represent some aspect of the past, making it easier to maintain its full significance when passed on to the next generation. The added context, could also help people decide what to keep and discard.

In future work, I would like design social memory artifacts that incorporate a wide range of digital traces, such as from personal informatics devices, as sources of memory. It is unclear whether such traces by themselves might be useful for reminiscing on the past, however I believe that in aggregate, a collection of data from many varied sources could be pieced together like fragments in a mosaic, with many different angles coming together in a new kind of view of the past. Further, these new kinds of memory may allow us to engage with each other and with traces of the past in very different ways that might fundamentally change how people remember.

Acknowledgements

Special thanks to my PhD advisor, Mark S. Ackerman, my co-author, David Merritt, and the rest of the Social Worlds Research Group for their collaboration and feedback.

References

1. Ackerman, M. S. (2000). The intellectual challenge of CSCW: the gap between social requirements and technical feasibility. *Human-Computer Interaction* 15, 2, 179-203.
2. Golsteijn, C., van den Hoven, E., Frohlich, D., & Sellen, A. (2012). Towards a More Cherishable Digital Object. In *Proceedings of the 2012 Conference on Designing Interactive Systems - DIS '12* (pp. 655–664).
3. Kirk, D.S. and Sellen, A. (2010) On human remains. *ACM Transactions on Computer-Human Interaction 17*, 3, 1–43.
4. Marshall, C. C., Bly, S., & Brun-Cottan, F. (2006). The long term fate of our digital belongings: Toward a service model for personal archives. In *Proceedings of the Archiving Conference* (pp. 25–30).
5. Misztal, B. (2003) *Theories Of Social Remembering.* McGraw-Hill International.
6. Jones, J., Ackerman, M.S. (to appear) Curating an Infinite Basement: Understanding how people manage collections of sentimental artifacts. In *Proceedings of 2016 Conference on Supporting Group Work, GROUP'16.*
7. Jones, J., Merritt, D., Ackerman, M.S. (to appear) Kidkeeper: Design for capturing audio mementos of everyday life for parents of young children. In *Proceedings of 2017 Conference on Computer-Supported Cooperative Work, CSCW'17.*
8. Mols, I., Hoven, E. van den, & Eggen, B. (2014). Making memories. In *Proceedings of the 2014 Nordic Conference on Human-Computer Interaction NordiCHI '14* (pp. 256–265).
9. Odom, W., Banks, R., Harper, R., Kirk, D., Lindley, S., & Sellen, A. (2012). Technology Heirlooms ? Considerations for Passing Down and Inheriting Digital Materials. In *Proceedings of the 2012 International Conference on Human Factors in Computing Systems - CHI '12* (pp. 337–346).
10. Odom, W., Pierce, J., Stolterman, E., & Blevis, E. (2009). Understanding why we preserve some things and discard others in the context of interaction design. *Proceedings of the 2009 International Conference on Human Factors in Computing Systems - CHI 09*, 1053.
11. Oleksik, G., & Brown, L. M. (2008). Sonic gems: exploring the potential of audio recording as a form of sentimental memory capture. In *Proceedings of the 2008 British HCI Group Annual Conference on People and Computers- BCS-HCI '08* (pp. 163–172).
12. van Dijck, J. (2007). *Mediated Memories in the Digital Age.* Stanford University Press.
13. Van Erve, D., Vos, G.-W., van den Hoven, E., and Frohlich, D. (2011) Cueing the past. *Proceedings of the Second Conference on Creativity and Innovation in Design - DESIRE '11*, 335.
14. Zerubavel, E. (1996). Social memories: Steps to a sociology of the past. *Qualitative Sociology*, *19*(3), 283–299.

Digital Traces of Online Self-Organizing and Problem Solving in Disaster

Marina Kogan
University of Colorado Boulder
Boulder, CO 80303 USA
Marina.Kogan@colorado.edu

GROUP '16, November 13 - 16, 2016, Sanibel Island, FL, USA

ACM 978-1-4503-4276-6/16/11...$15.00
DOI: http://dx.doi.org/10.1145/2957276.2997022

Abstract
Natural disasters are associated with breakdown of existing structures, but they also result in creation of new social ties in the process of self-organization and problem solving by those affected. In highly-distributed setting of social media, collaborative arrangements must depend on the aspects of work that facilitate (or not) the creation of a shared information space—such as an explicit shared site of work and visible, legible record of the activity. In my dissertation I investigate what organizational structures emerge through problem solving in the context of more or less explicit shared site of work and more or less visible record of activity.

Author Keywords
CSCW; crisis informatics; social media data

Introduction
When we think of crises, such as disasters arising from natural hazards, we often think of infrastructural failures and destruction of the physical environment such as buildings, bridges, and transportation hubs. Thus, disruption events are often associated with the breakdown of existing structures [14].

However, the disruption events are also ripe with creation of new social structures through formation of new relationship among people convergent on the physical or digital site of crisis. The sociologists of disaster have long pointed out that people directly affected by the crisis events are the true first responders as opposed to passive victims—they actively participate in the rescue and recovery efforts [4, 5, 10].

This active participation, together with the phenomenon of convergence, where people coalesce around the physical or digital site of disruption, result in new relationships being established, new sources of information found, and new communities being formed. Furthermore, Weick suggests that people affected by a major disruption engage in the process of sense making [18]. Communication and coordination associated with this process likely lead to new connections and emergent community structures. Thus, in disruption the social structures are remade anew [3, 16].

This makes natural disasters not only an important object of study in its own right, which has been well-established in the field of crisis informatics [15], but also a fruitful setting for a natural experiment. Observing how social ties get reconfigured in the wake of the natural disaster tells us just as much about how people self-organize, problem-solve, and what organizational forms emerge in the process, as it tells us about the natural hazard that caused the disruption.

Background

Social media sites provide a highly distributed and mostly asynchronous setting for the flurry of the problem-solving activity that takes place in natural disaster. Thus, such problem solving in a highly-distributed setting faces the classical issues of computer supported cooperative work (CSCW).

Schmidt and Bannon establish the importance of common information space in CSCW, which they define as achieving a common understanding of meaning among a group of people working in distributed fashion [17]. Bertelsen and Bodker show that, in massively distributed setting, the common information space is achieved not through collocation but through position and mobility, suggesting that the site of work matters in cooperative work [1].

Thus, the degree to which there is an explicit common site of work must affect how the common information space is constructed and negotiated. For example, in OpenStreetMap (OSM) crisis mappers organize around a explicitly shared site of work—the map of the affected area, whereas Twitterers who are making sense of a hurricane warning are working in a decentralized environment with no single point of entry or visible common site of work, though still constituting the implicit ad-hoc publics through hashtag use [2] and network connections [13].

Moreover, the social media platforms are complex interactional environments, allowing for multiple types of interaction and coordination. Thus, various types of work might emerge within each platform, producing various levels of peripheral awareness, which Bertelsen and Bodker show is important in massively distributed information spaces [1].

The visible record of social media activity is one such mechanism of peripheral awareness, as it allows users to keep track of what has been done and what still needs doing, who has done what, and in response to whom. The explicit record of activity, such as Wikipedia talk pages, visibly encodes the mutual dependence and division of labor. It thus facilitates the articulation work [17], without requiring personal communication.

Thus, how explicit, legible, and human-readable the shared record is for the particular type of work is likely to influence the cooperative arrangements that emerge in that work. For example, retweeting in crisis is an information sharing activity aimed outward, with virtually no record immediately available to the users of the many steps tweets take to propagate. On the other hand in @reply Twitter activity, the back and forth of the collective sense-making and problem-solving is visibly recorded. In OpenStreetMap, crisis mapping does not produce a human-readable record of work, as all the map changes are stored in a large, behind-the-scene geospatial database, while only the newest version of the map is visible. However, the situation is somewhat different when OSM mappers correct each other's tags—textual labels for the map features that are crucial for its usability. The work of correction is more visible on the map itself, as the changes in the textual elements are often easier to notice than that of geospatial features and so can be further investigated.

Research Questions

Thus, the discussion above motivates the main research question:

What social structures emerge from social media activity in natural disaster and how do these cooperative arrangements differ based on how explicit the shared site of work and how legible the shared record of activity is?

This dissertation project then attempts to answer the overall research question with respect to four distinct types of online work in crisis context:

- Retweet activity in Twitter
- Reply activity in Twitter
- General mapping in OSM
- Tag correction in OSM

Research Methods

The high-tempo [8, 9], high-volume convergent nature of crisis events produces vast amounts of social media data, necessitating the use of the data science methods to find the signal in the noise. However, the socio-behavioral nature of social media communication makes it very context-dependent and often relational. Thus, to glean meaningful insight from the crisis-related social media activity, it is necessary to use methods that account for the complex context of the user activity, including qualitative analysis.

We know that Twitter users perceive their tweeting as a conversational, discursive activity [15]. Thus, it is often possible to infer the meaning of tweets only in the context of adjacent posts, as the important pieces of information are frequently spread across multiple messages. Hence, to perform careful analysis of social media activity I treat the data conversationally, as opposed to a string of isolated posts. Moving beyond a single Tweet or map edit, one has to tackle the methodological challenge of determining the appropriate temporal resolution for analysis. I rely on the work sessions approach pioneered for Wikipedia [6].

Geo-Before	Geo-During
BarackObama	MikeBloomberg
MensHumor	GovChristie
XSTROLOGY	LolOhComedy
billmaher	MTAInsider
WomnsHumor	NYCMayorsOffice
azizansari	ElBloombito
FillWerrell	NYGovCuomo
Geo-After	**Geo-Long-After**
XSTROLOGY	XSTROLOGY
GovChristie	UberFacts
UberFacts	HuffingtonPost
MensHumor	MensHumor
ElBloombito	BenSavage
WhatTheFFacts	SportsCenter
HuffingtonPost	WhatTheFFacts

Table1. Central users in Retweeting.

Figure1. Ext. salient features, OSM.

Network science enables the structural view of user activity, by teasing out the kinds of network structures communications. Simultaneously, the relational nature of the network data allows us to retain the individual connections that comprise some of the social context for the individual user activity. Consequently, Granovetter sees social network analysis as a potential way of bridging the situatedness of individual agency and the macro scale of the social structures [7].

Thus, for my dissertation project, I use data science methods such as network analysis and Natural Language Processing to find structural organizational patterns in the digital traces and to scope the vast social media data for the in-depth qualitative analysis that contextualizes and enriches quantitative findings.

Preliminary Findings

In the completed work on the retweet activity by the geo-vulnerable users—those in direct path of 2012 Hurricane Sandy, I conducted both network analysis of retweet networks and the content analysis of the sample of tweets. I found a somewhat different network structure emerging during the disaster than before or after: a larger and more interconnected network, with higher percentage of users who retweeted and were retweeted a lot by others. Interestingly, some of the denser transitive structure persists somewhat from the during to the after period, consistent with sociological theories of community resilience. I also found that the geo-vulnerable users favor locally-appropriate, actionable information like school closures, subway closures, and evacuation notices in their retweeting [11].

In the mostly-completed work on the mapping practices of volunteer mappers in response to 2010 Haiti Earthquake, I used network methods—considering users mapping in the same area as connected—to scope the vast OSM mapping data for qualitative analysis. Through this content analysis I found seven distinct mapping practices, which can be organized around the axes of time (shift work and sustained convergence), space (externally salient features, filling in the map, and mapping continuous structures), and interpersonal dynamics (parallel mapping and tag correction) [12]. Now that the salient work patterns are established, I am examining what network structures are formed through these practices and how they evolve over time, with respect to disaster stages.

Expected Contribution

Thus, I mostly completed the analysis of the two types of work that are organized around the less explicit and visible record of shared activity—retweeting in Twitter (no explicit shared site of work) and general mapping in OSM (shared map as explicit site of work).

The expected contribution would consist of the analysis of structural organizational forms that emerge in the two types of work that enjoy a more explicit, visible, and traceable record of the activity—the conversational activity consisting of Twitter replies and the back and forth of tag correction in OSM. For both of these types of work, I plan to use network methods to establish the structural patterns of self-organization, including temporal shifts in organizational forms. Additionally, I intent to relate the network structure to the content of the activity, which I will investigate through topic modeling for Twitter reply conversations and content analysis for the OSM tag correction.

Acknowledgements

This research is funded through the US NSF grants IIS-1524806 and AGS-1331490. We thank our Project EPIC colleagues for support and critique. We especially thank our reviewers for their insightful comments.

References

[1] Bertelsen, O. W., & Bødker, S. (2001). Cooperation in massively distributed information spaces. In *ECSCW 2001* (pp. 1-17). Springer Netherlands.

[2] Bruns, A., and Burgess J. E. (2011). The use of Twitter hashtags in the formation of ad hoc publics. In *6th European Consortium for Political Research General Conference*, 25-27 August 2011, University of Iceland, Reykjavik.

[3] Comfort, L. K. (1999). Shared risk: Complex systems in seismic response. Pergamon.

[4] Dynes, R. R. (1970). *Organized behavior in disaster*. Heath LexingtonBooks.

[5] Fritz, C. E., & Mathewson, J. H. (1957). Convergence behavior in disasters: A problem in social control: A special report prepared for the Committee on Disaster Studies. National Academy of Sciences National Research Council.

[6] Geiger, R. S., & Halfaker, A. (2013). Using edit sessions to measure participation in Wikipedia. In *Proceedings of the 2013 conference on Computer supported cooperative work* (pp. 861-870). ACM.

[7] Granovetter, M. (1983). The strength of weak ties: A network theory revisited. *Sociological theory* 1.1:201-233.

[8] Keegan, B. C. Breaking news on wikipedia: dynamics, structures, and roles in high-tempo collaboration. In *Proc. of the ACM 2012 conference on Computer Supported Cooperative Work Companion,* (2012), 315-318.

[9] Keegan, B., Gergle, D., & Contractor, N. Staying in the loop: Structure and dynamics of Wikipedia's breaking news collaborations. In *Proc. of the 8th Annual International Symposium on Wikis and Open Collaboration,* (2012), 1-10.

[10] Kendra, J. M., & Wachtendorf, T. (2003). Elements of resilience after the world trade center disaster: reconstituting New York City's Emergency Operations Centre. *Disasters*, *27*(1), 37-53.

[11] Kogan, M., Palen, L. & Anderson, K. (2015). Tweet Local, Retweet Global: Retweeting by the Geographically-Vulnerable during Hurricane Sandy. In *Proc of* CSCW.

[12] Kogan, M., Anderson, J., Palen, L., Anderson, K., & Soden, R. (2016). Finding the Way to OSM Mapping Practices: Bounding Large Crisis Datasets for Qualitative Investigation. In *Proc of CHI*.

[13] Langlois, G., Elmer, G., McKelvey, F., & Devereaux, Z. (2009). Networked Publics: The Double Articulation of Code and Politics on Facebook. *Canadian Journal of Communication*, *34*(3).

[14] Mileti, D. (1999). Disasters by Design: A Reassessment of Natural Hazards in the United States. Joseph Henry Press.

[15] Palen, L. (2014). Frontiers in Crisis Informatics. Keynote to ISCRAM.

[16] Petrescu-Prahova, M., & Butts, C. T. (2005). Emergent coordination in the World Trade Center disaster. *Institute for mathematical behavioral sciences*.

[17] Schmidt, K., & Bannon, L. (1992). Taking CSCW seriously. *Computer Supported Cooperative Work (CSCW)*, *1*(1-2), 7-40.

[18] Weick, K. E. (1993). The collapse of sensemaking in organizations: The Mann Gulch disaster. *Administrative science quarterly*, 628-652.

Media and Information Literacy Competences in the Workplace: Collaborative Practices and Workers' Empowerment

Valèria Ligurgo
Université catholique de Louvain
Louvain-la-Neuve, 1348, BELGIUM
valeria.ligurgo@uclouvain.be

GROUP '16, November 13 - 16, 2016, Sanibel Island, FL, USA

ACM 978-1-4503-4276-6/16/11...$15.00
DOI: http://dx.doi.org/10.1145/2957276.2997023

Abstract
Technology-supported collaborative practices have become widespread in the workplace. Our research investigates how information and media literacy competences support teamwork dynamics, how the team's activities fosters the development of its members' competences and how can this process be a lever for the workers' empowerment. This research is aimed at mapping and defining the competences called for and developed by ICT-supported teamwork and distance work, from the point of view of office workers. The main findings will consist in a definition of the competences related to the informational, technical and social dimensions of distant teamwork practices in a digital era.

Author Keywords
Media and information literacy; digital media competences; computer-supported cooperative work; distant teamwork; collaborative practices.

ACM Classification Keywords
Human-centered computing---Collaborative and social computing---Empirical studies in collaborative and social computing.

Introduction

Powerful information and communication technologies (ICT's) are now part of office workers daily life. The digital turn of information has increased their spreading and their place in our societies. Within organizations, they have transformed the world of work: teleworking and remote teamwork have become common practices. These 2 coexisting phenomena modify the employee's media uses and needed competences to work and collaborate.

Our work-in-progress research is aimed at studying the way people work together at a distance by observing their computer-supported teamwork activities within the social context of office work. Also considered in the literature as a lever for self-empowerment, media and information literacy competences allow us, through the review of media uses from workers' point of view, to apprehend the interactions between workers' knowledge, skills and attitudes [Bourg, Bent, McHolland and Stricker 1989] and to build a framework including the social, technical and informational dimensions [Fastrez and De Smedt 2012] of contemporary distant work practices.

Often associated with performance at work, the concept of competence is considered in our research on a more microscopic scale in order to investigate (1) how media and information competences foster cooperative practices and (2) how they affect workers' empowerment.

Theoretical Framework

The first definitions of skills and knowledge required for information literacy were initially suggested in the 1970s in the fields of librarianship and information science [Behrens 1994]. An information literate person was then expected to properly use information focusing on problem-solving and efficient decision-making.

During the last decades, digitalization of information as well as expansive development and use of digital technology have increased awareness towards information and media competences and broadened the range of users. These concerns moved later to the world of work where employees, while struggling with information technologies, were also due to operate their workload efficiently [Bruce, 1999].

Kirton and Barham [2005] highlight the need to overtake the idea that information literacy consists simply in abilities to use information tools and find information resources. They define it as a lifelong learning and professional development process and stress the necessity to consider the context and the roles of the social actors involved in the information mechanisms in the workplace. Sharing the same observations, Lloyd [2011] emphasizes that workers are expected to adapt and adopt their information practices to suit ever-changing environments.

According to her, being a competent worker means to successfully interact with the "*information related activities that will connect workers to modalities of information, which reflect the specific and situated knowledge that is constructed by people working in consort with one another*" [Lloyd 2011].

In this context of change, the role of media and information literacy on workers' empowerment is central. Among the existing approaches, we focus on 2 models of digital media literacy that are in tension and that can foster further understanding of workers information practices.

The first model emerges from Livingstone's [2008] description of media literacy purposes. She identified 2 main contrasted purposes: the first one involve democracy, participation and active citizenship whilst the second includes the knowledge economy, competitiveness and choice. Applied to the workplace, this distinction allows us to identify two fields where the competences can become manifest through teamwork activities: socio-political dimension of work (emancipation) and socio-economic dimension of work (employability).

The second model highlights a gap between media literacy ambitions and the implementations of digital literacy policies [Buckingham 2009]. On the one hand, media literacy is acknowledged as a requirement to foster individuals' empowerment and, on the other hand, digital literacy is conceived as sets of basic functional skills aiming at operating technology for one's personal or professional benefit. Again, applied to the workplace, the latter opposition enables us to place users on a cursor depending on the type of skills they call out. The scale goes from a compliant posture to an inventive posture. Compliance involves operational skills sufficient to operate information technologies (minimal level of autonomy) while inventivity (based on the compliance layer of work performance) involves the competences to combine, modify, create and emancipate critically from tools and structures which can enhance work activities (second-order autonomy). This framework offers key concepts to understand how information and media competences can be integrated to observable teamwork practices.

Research Question

Our research aims at understanding how information and media competences support efficient, meaningful, and inclusive ways of working in the particular context of distant collaborative practices. More specifically, we intend to determine, from the point of view of office workers, which competences are called for and developed by ICT-supported teamwork practices and how they allow employees to apprehend their information landscape in a changing environment.

Our objective is to observe these practices directly on our informants' workplaces and examine the nature of competences they carry out. As we view their activities as a set of socially constructed and situated collective practices that make their competences manifest, we intend to make observations in work environments in order to understand the interactions of the worker within the so-called learning organization.

Method

Our field includes 10 selected case studies among public and private Belgian organizations recently involved in projects changing the way employees work in teams and at a distance. We are conducting semi-structured in-depth interviews focused on technology-supported teamwork activities including a guided tour [Malone 1983] of workers' personal workspace. At the end of the study, 40 workers and 20 team leaders will have been interviewed. These interviews will be completed by a second phase of ethnographic observations of the work environment.

Our research draws heavily on CSCW research for the construction of its data collection method: the categories of distant teamwork activity we chose to investigate were identified in a review of CSCW literature. Our interview guide is based on technology-supported collaborative activities that involve both social interaction between team members and the mediation of technology, and are a potential venue for the expression of information literacy competences. We selected the 11 following activities:

1. Authoring a document collectively;
2. Sharing a collection of documents;
3. Managing outgoing information;
4. Managing incoming information;
5. Using others to find information;
6. Making collective decisions regarding task distribution, team governance and roles, and overall team functioning;
7. Managing one's tasks in relation with others;
8. Planning a meeting;
9. Planning the team's activity;
10. Working synchronously in the distance with other team members;
11. Organizing one's workspaces for collaboration.

We also identified 8 dimensions of technology-supported distant teamwork that allow a better understanding of how workers perform their activities. Each dimension is systematically accounted for in our interview guide. These dimensions are briefly described below:

1. Task management is seen as a secondary activity aimed at mediating and controlling cooperative activity and involves technologically mediated management of task allocation and articulation [Schmidt and Bannon 1992].
2. Time management touches upon how workers use ICT-supported systems that shape and support the way they dedicate time to work activities, individually and in relationship with their colleagues [Blandford and Green 2001].
3. Space and distance management consist in the management of employees' workplace at several levels: the layout of their individual digital workspace [Kirsh 1995], the proxemics in the work environment and the geographical distance separating work sites in teleworking [Olson and Olson 2000].
4. Information management includes information authoring and information sharing through technology dedicated to collective digital information production.
5. Awareness means understanding social implications of others' activities and provides a structure to conduct people's own activities [Dourish and Bellotti 1992].
6. Collective decision making corresponds to the processes through which collective decisions are made with the support of information technology [DeSanctis and Gallupe 1987].
7. Reflexive tool use is a "meta" dimension that exceeds the simple use of information technology. It consists in the identification of one's technological needs, awareness of digital technology affordances, appropriate tools selection, tools affordances detection, tool appropriation [Dourish 2003] and assessment.
8. Comprehension of "sociomatics" is a second "meta" dimension that we define as an automatic processing of social interactions. It implies understanding social entailments of one's digital technology use. For example, understanding how the choice of an information-sharing tool may affect access to information for other members of the team.

Work in Progress

This research was initiated a year and a half ago and is part of a larger project studying digital media and information literacy competences in Belgium called LITME@WORK. First year was essentially dedicated to a literature review aimed at defining theoretical and methodological frameworks. We used this background to create our interview guide that we first administrated to informants from pilot cases for a period of assessment. We have now started fieldwork and are busy with the interviews of the first 2 case studies. We plan to have interviewed our whole sample at the end of March 2017.

The recorded interviews will be transcribed and coded using QSR NVivo. A first coding scheme will use the competence and activity categories defined in the conceptual framework as a first pass on the collected data. Fine-grained analysis implies more immersion in the data and will constitute the next step of our research. Our analysis method could highly benefit from exchanges with other experienced researchers.

Expected Contribution

Through this research, we expect to define the digital media and information competences related to teamwork and distance work articulating them with technology-supported collaborative practices and identify competence indicators. Globally, our goal is to participate in the research effort aiming at the definition of information literacy competences and their indicators.

Through the analysis of actual, situated work practices involving the use of collaborative technology, this research will provide an inventory of contemporary work practices that involve ICT-supported distant collaboration.

Our findings will provide professionals with indicators and landmarks concerning necessary competences for workers entering changing work environments. The results of our research could also help political actors and educators in developing educational and training initiatives designed to foster workers' employability and empowerment.

Our research differs with traditional CSCW research in the use of its findings: whereas CSCW has mostly aimed at informing the (re)design of collaborative technologies, we document the competences of their users in order to identify how to facilitate or support their development. Hence, there is a high complementarity between the two approaches (making technologies more usable / making users more competent).

References

1. Behrens, S. J. (1994). A conceptual Analysis and Historical Overview of Information Literacy. *College & Research Libraries*, 309–322.
2. Blandford, A. E., & Green, T. R. G. (2001). Group and Individual Time Management Tools: What You Get is Not What You Need. *Personal and Ubiquitous Computing*, 5(4), 213–230.
3. Bourg, E. F., Bent, R. J., McHolland, J., & Stricker, G. (1989). Standards and evaluation in the education and training of professional psychologists: The National Council of Schools of Professional Psychology Mission Bay Conference. *American Psychologist*, 44(1), 66–72.
4. Bruce, C. S. (1999). Workplace Experiences of Information Literacy. *International Journal of Information Management*, 19(1), 33–47.
5. Buckingham, D. (2009). The future of media literacy in the digital age: some challenges for policy and practice. In *Proceedings of Euromeduc: Media literacy in Europe: controversies, challenges and perspectives* (pp. 13–24). Bellaria, Italy.

6. DeSanctis, G., & Gallupe, R. B. (1987). A Foundaction for the study of Group Decision Support Systems. *Management Science*, 33(5), 589–609.
7. Dourish, P. (2003). The Appropriation of Interactive Technologies: Some Lessons from Placeless Documents. *Computer Supported Cooperative Work (CSCW), 12*(4), 465–490.
8. Dourish, P., & Bellotti, V. (1992). Awareness and Coordination in Shared Workspaces. In *Proceedings of the 1992 ACM Conference on Computer-supported Cooperative Work* (pp. 107–114). New York, NY, USA: ACM.
9. Fastrez, P., & De Smedt, T. (2012). Une description matricielle des compétences en littératie médiatique. In M. Lebrun-Brossard, N. Lacelle, & J.-F. Boutin (Eds.), *La littératie médiatique multimodale. De nouvelles approches en lecture-écriture à l'école et hors de l'école* (pp. 45–60). Québec: Presses de l'Université du Québec.
10. Kirsh, D. (1995). The Intelligent Use of Space. *Artificial Intelligence*, *73*, 31–68.
11. Kirton, J., & Barham, L. (2005). Information literacy in the workplace. *The Australian Library Journal*, *54*(4), 365–376.
12. Livingstone, S., Van Couvering, E., & Thumim, N. (2008). Converging Traditions of Research on Media and Information Literacies. In *Handbook of Research on New Literacies* (pp. 103–132). New York: Taylor & Francis.
13. Lloyd, A. (2011). Trapped between a Rock and a Hard Place: What Counts as Information Literacy in the Workplace and How Is It Conceptualized? *Library Trends, 60*(2), 277–296.
14. Malone, T. W. (1983). How do people organize their desks?: Implications for the design of office information systems. *ACM Transactions on Information Systems, 1*(1), 99–112.
15. Olson, G. M., & Olson, J. S. (2000). Distance Matters. *Hum.-Comput. Interact., 15*(2), 139–178.
16. Schmidt, K., & Bannon, L. (1992). Taking CSCW seriously. *Computer Supported Cooperative Work (CSCW), 1*(1-2), 7–40.

Engaging Newcomers in Hybrid Communities

Di Lu
University of Pittsburgh
Pittsburgh, PA 15213, USA
di.lu@pitt.edu

Abstract
With new technological advances more and more the boundaries of online and offline spaces is becoming fuzzy. This hybrid model of computer-mediated communication introduces new challenges and opportunities for users, researchers, and practitioners. My dissertation research focuses particularly of designing processes and tools to better support newcomers within online communities with hybrid communication patterns. My dissertation will contribute to research and practices of building "newcomer-friendly" hybrid communities.

Author Keywords
Hybrid communities; Online-offline interactions; Newcomers; Attraction; Retention

ACM Classification Keywords
H.5.m [Information interfaces and presentation (e.g., HCI)]: Miscellaneous

GROUP '16, November 13-16, 2016, Sanibel Island, FL, USA
 ISBN 978-1-4503-4276-6/16/11âĂę$15.00
DOI: http://dx.doi.org/10.1145/2957276.2997024

Introduction
Recent years have witnessed the rise of an emerging model of computer-mediated communication spanning online and offline worlds. The recent fever of Pokémon GO unfolds the potentials in bridging online and offline worlds through information technology[3]. Many online communities have been capitalizing on their users' face-to-face interactions

to motivate and encourage stronger online participation. Concurrently, online communities with explicit goals of promoting offline connections such as Meetup and Foursquare, have been thriving. A large number of online communities are moving towards a hybrid online-offline model. The concept of hybrid communities was first described by [7] as a “hybrid people and technology-based phenomenon as an electronic-to-face community" which takes advantage of technological features such as searching among a large number of people with similar interests and advantages of face-to-face offline connections such as developing strong interpersonal connections with a small group of people. The hybrid online-offline nature of the emerging model can indeed contribute to significant positive outcomes such as community development [4], citizen engagement in political and social movements [5, 7]. At the same time, the hybrid nature provides these communities with distinct opportunities and challenges.

To succeed, advance and sustain, the hybrid communities not only rely on members' online participation but also on their engagements in offline interactions and transition between online and offline participation [2]. The issue of sustainability and online-offline transition is particularly acute with respect to newcomers. Newcomers are important source of new ideas, new audience, and new workforce; however, their lack of commitment and familiarity with the community poses particular challenges to communities with respect to their attraction and retention [6]. The hybrid nature can pose extra burden on newcomers; not only they need to join the online groups, they need to endure the face-to-face interactions with often stranger members.

Research Goal and Questions

The goal of my dissertation is to tackle the challenge of newcomers in hybrid communities. My dissertation focuses on different stages newcomers have to go through in these communities: (1) joining the online community, (2) attending their first offline event, and (3) sticking around with the community and continuing their participation online and offline. In particular, my work aims to address the following research questions:

RQ1: transition from online to offline events

- What factors influence newcomers' decision to join an offline event after joining the online community and having observed the online community?
- How does the design of computer-mediated communication technology can facilitate this transition?

Prior research in online-offline interpersonal relationships indicated factors such as common interests, similar background, prior online interactions, and social and informational needs to motivate users to meet face-to-face after interacting online [8]. I plan to investigate the role of these factors in the context of hybrid online communities and study how technology can better support the transition from online to offline spaces and vice versa.

RQ2: retention of newcomers in hybrid communities

- How does newcomers' early-on experiences online and offline affect their' decision to participate in subsequent events?
- What tools and processes can improve those early-on expeirences?

Researchers in the field of online communities found that newcomers are particularly sensitive to their early-on experiences in the group and their subsequent behavior in the community is affected by their initial participation and the feedback they received from the community [6]. Therefore, I plan to examine the role of these early-on experiences in the context of hybrid online communities, especially with respect to the first offline event they attend.

Research Agenda

To address my research questions, I plan to conduct my research in the context of Meetup.com. Meetup[1] is one of the most popular online communities that allow users to form and join online local groups with common interests, and to organize local events. As of November 2015, there are about 23 million users in Meetup, and on average 531,000 meet-ups a month are organized by 218,217 groups [1]. Meetup is a typical example of hybrid communities connecting people through "events" in both online groups and offline meetings. The fact that Meetup provides the same online platform to a large number of diverse communities dedicating to various topics, along with the high accessibility of their data through their public API, make it a desirable platform and context to address my research questions.

Preliminary work

Utilizing the Meetup API, I have already collected data from 669 public Meetup groups in the city of Pittsburgh, PA. I have collected their events data a period of 2 years from March 1, 2014 to March 1, 2016. The dataset includes all activities of 22,491 users who joined after March 1, 2014. [2] My preliminary investigation of the data shows that 69.1% of the users never attended any offline event and only 12.3% of the them participated in more than one offline events. The low adoption and retention rate of newcomers confirmed that hybrid communities like Meetup groups face noticeable challenge in attracting newcomers to offline events as well as engaging them as sustaining active members over time. I have also started investigating the relationships between different factors associated to events and their online representation and sustainability of groups on Meetup. My preliminary results of regression analyses suggest both the online interactions and the online representation of offline activities of previous events positively relate to the number of members willing to attend the future events in the group. These findings provide fundamental support for my dissertation work to further investigate factors that particularly influence newcomers' attraction and retention in hybrid communities.

Research model

Figure 1 describes our view of the life cycle of members in Meetup groups based on our preliminary observation of Meetup data. We posit that a newcomer need to go through multiple obstacles to become a committed member. Making the first attempt to attend an offline event in the group is an essential milestone for newcomers, but various factors may influence their decision in whether and which event to attend. Furthermore, their experience in that first event can have a significant effect on the decision to continue participating both online and offline. Also, as a committed member of the community, the group need them to not only attend the offline events but also represent their interest and participation online to attract future members. My dissertation research targets each phase of this model through studies of current practices, current users' behavior, and conducting experiments to study factors in isolation and assess the value of new designs.

Researh methods and planned studies

My dissertation will combine qualitative and quantitative research methods in a series of studies: *Study 1* focuses on conducting interviews with newcomers and organizers in Meetup groups, which will provide a subjective understanding of the motivations and barriers of newcomers to attend their first offline event factors influencing their de-

[1] http://Meetup.com/

[2] Our user activities data was constructed from the RSVPs data provided by Meetup API, which are associated with each event and include information about users who have indicated attending the event. Additionally, we collected their online activities data including the comments and photos posted for each event from Meetup API.

cision to participate subsequently. *Study 2* complements Study 1 with behavioral measures of Meetup members using archival data of their activities, e.g. events RSVPed, or comments and pictures posted online. A large-scale statistical analysis of these behavioral factors help me to further understand what factors can influence recruitment and retention of newcomers. *Study 3* aims to reveal the underlying mechanisms behind relationships observed in study 2 through conducting controlled lab experiment and studies of various influential factors in isolation. I plan to design experiment to manipulate factors such as amount and kind of information provided to users. *Study 4* focuses on exploring design approaches on platform such as Meetup to recruit and retain newcomers more effectively. Such approaches include tools to provide to increase users' awareness about the online-offline interplay of interactions and employ recommendation technologies to better engage newcomers. I will design and conduct experimental field studies to assess the effectiveness of those approaches.

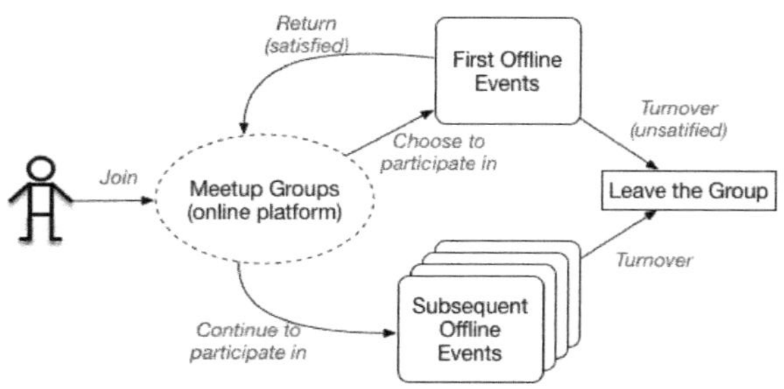

Figure 1: Life Cycle of Newcomers in Meetup groups

Expected Contributions

My dissertation contributes to the fields of social computing and socio-technical systems by extending our knowledge of the interplay of online-offline interactions, with a particular focus on newcomers. My work will benefit both community practitioners and technology developers with practical guidelines to design sustainable hybrid communities which are more affable to newcomers. Such hybrid communities can serve as platforms to strengthen our local communities through stronger engagement of residents of the communities.

References

[1] 2015. About Meetup. (2015). http://meetup.com/about
[2] Rosta Farzan, Di Lu, and Yu-Ru Lin. 2016. What Happens Offline Stays Offline?: Examining Sustainability of a Hybrid Social System. In *Proceedings of the 27th ACM Conference on Hypertext and Social Media*. ACM, 261–266.
[3] Deborah Findling. 2016. Pokemon Fever Infects San Francisco, drawing thousands into the streets. *CNBC* (2016).
[4] Keith N Hampton. 2007. Neighborhoods in the Network Society the e-Neighbors study. *Information, Communication & Society* 10, 5 (2007), 714–748.
[5] Noriko Hara. 2008. Internet use for political mobilization: Voices of participants. *First Monday* 13, 7 (2008).
[6] Robert E Kraut, Paul Resnick, Sara Kiesler, Moira Burke, Yan Chen, Niki Kittur, Joseph Konstan, Yuqing Ren, and John Riedl. 2012. *Building successful online communities: Evidence-based social design*. Mit Press.
[7] Bruce D Weinberg and Christine B Williams. 2006. The 2004 US Presidential campaign: Impact of hybrid offline and online 'meetup' communities. *Direct, Data and Digital Marketing Practice* 8, 1 (2006).
[8] Bo Xie. 2008. The mutual shaping of online and offline social relationships. *Information Research* 13, 3 (2008), 4.

Taking a More Balanced Approach to Adolescent Mobile Safety

Arup Kumar Ghosh
Department of Computer Science
University of Central Florida
Orlando, FL 32816, USA
arupkumar.ghosh@ucf.edu

GROUP '16, November 13-16, 2016, Sanibel Island, FL, USA
© 2016 ACM. ISBN 978-1-4503-4276-6/16/11...$15.00
DOI: http://dx.coi.org/10.1145/2957276.2997025

Abstract
Adolescent online safety is becoming more challenging as teens are prolifically using mobile smart phones. Parental control applications ("apps") are available, but, the adoption rates of such apps are remarkably low and may not adequately address the problem at hand. To examine this further, we propose three studies 1) a structured analysis of existing adolescent online safety apps, 2) a survey-based study to confirm our hypotheses that the values embedded in the features of these existing apps are sub-optimal, and 3) building a prototype of a new online safety app with features that better meet the needs of parents *and* teens.

Author Keywords
Parental control; teen self-regulation; adolescent online safety; value sensitive design;

ACM Classification Keywords
H.5.m. Information interfaces and presentation (e.g., HCI): Miscellaneous;

Motivation and Background
According to a Pew Research report, approximately three quarters of teens have access to a smart phone **[6]**, and 91% of teens access the internet using their mobile devices **[1]**. Using smart phones, it is now possible to interact with people from all over the world.

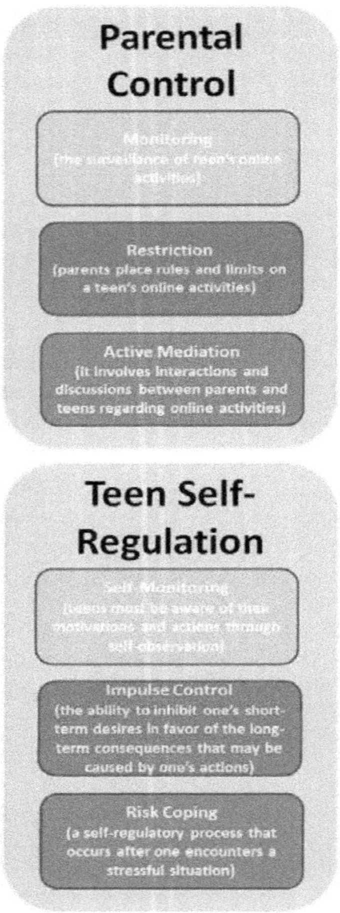

Figure 1: Teen Online Safety Strategies (TOSS) Theoretical Framework *(Similar colors are used for parental strategies and analogous teen strategies)*

Statistics show that teens are far ahead in terms of interacting with people online. For instance, 37% of teens use social messaging software; and 47% of teens are users of video chatting applications **[1]**; 71% teens have access to more than one social networking sites **[6]**. Despite offering such world changing opportunities to connect, the internet also presents a multitude of new risks to teens, including cyberbullying, exposure to unwanted explicit materials, harassment, and sexual solicitations [8].

To protect teens from such risks, parental control applications have been created **[13]**; however, only 16% of parents report using such apps on teens' smart devices [9]. Researchers have conducted almost no research on the existing adolescent online safety mobile apps to understand adoption problems or how they protect teens from online risks.

Some initial work has been done in the HCI community to create new prototypes: "We-Choose" and "FamiLync" promote collaboration between parents and teens **[4,5]**. Such approaches have resulted in more positive outcomes, such as helping reduce addictive smart phone usage and foster positive relationships between parents and teens **[5]**. However, these apps are not currently available for parent and teen to use. Therefore, my initial research goal includes the analysis of existing teen online safety apps, exploring reasons for low adoptions of such apps, through using a value sensitive design approach, which will emphasize the values embedded within these systems

Research Questions

Technical mediation for mobile devices is relatively new and, thus, an area that lacks a wealth of research. The main goal of my thesis work is to fill this gap by answering the following questions: 1) Why current solutions for promoting adolescent online safety have low adoption rates? 2) What are the various strategies available (in theory and practice) for promoting adolescent online safety on mobile platforms? 3) Is it possible to design better solutions for promoting teen mobile safety which embed more positive family values and, subsequently, increase adoption rates?

Theoretical Frameworks

Value sensitive design (VSD) is "a theoretically grounded approach to the design of technology that accounts for human values in a principled and comprehensive manner throughout the design process" **[3]**. My initial goal is to better explain how technical mediation influences current apps by reverse engineering the values embedded in the design of existing apps. With my advisor's help, we also built a framework of Teen Online Safety Strategies (TOSS) that uses both parental control and teen-self regulation, shown in **Figure 1**. In the process of building the TOSS framework, the following assumptions are made: 1) parents have some control over teens' online activities [7]; and 2) teen also have an influence on their online safety **[2]**.

Proposed Methods

To address the aforementioned research questions, I will conduct three studies (**Figure 2**) related to adolescent online safety within mobile platforms.

For my **first study**, I have already conducted a structured analysis **[12]** of Android teen online safety apps **[11]**. I analyzed apps on the Android platform as Android has 83% market share of cell phones **[14]**. I found 75 relevant apps and applied grounded approach **[10]** to the data set to make a list of 42 features (e.g.,

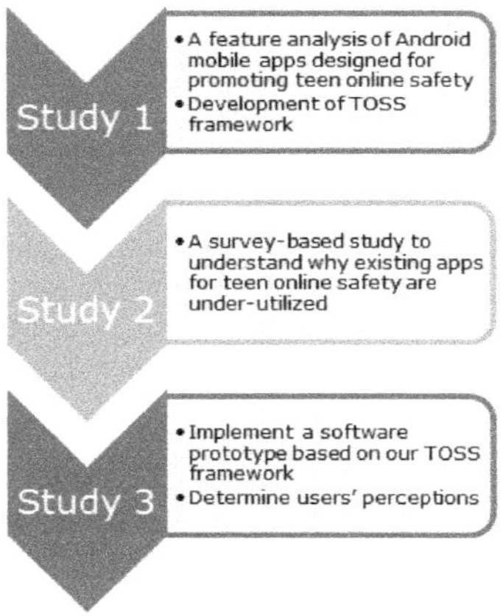

Figure 2: Proposed Studies

application *log*, *call log*, *browser log*) related to adolescent online safety available in those apps. I found that **89%** of the features supported promote **parental control** over teen self-regulation (11%), which clearly indicates that there is an opportunity to design new teen online safety apps, which are more targeted toward teens.

For my **second study**, I will use a web-based survey to confirm some of our initial hypotheses as to why current adolescent online safety apps are under-utilized. There will be two separate surveys for parents and teens. After gathering adequate data from both parents and teens, a logistic regression will be used to find out the factors that influence the adoption or non-adoption of mobile online safety apps. My initial hypotheses include: 1) Authoritarian parents will be more likely to use parental control apps; 2) tech-savvy parents who are concerned for their teens' personal privacy will be less likely to use such apps; and 3) parents whose teens have experienced risks will be more likely to use.

My **final study** will include creating a better adolescent online safety app, which will promote healthy adolescent development. I will design and develop a functioning mobile app prototype embedding different online safety strategies related to parental active mediation and teen self-regulation. We will conduct user studies to measure users' perceptions of my proposed mobile app alternatives. Our designs will also be respectful of a teen's privacy by abstracting some of the low level details of the teen's mobile activities, as opposed to current apps which provide these details.

Research Status

In Spring 2016, I switched research advisors and topics. As I still want to graduate in the next 2 years, I have had to quickly come up to speed on my new dissertation work. My advisor helped introduce me to HCI literature and develop the conceptual TOSS framework (**Figure 1**). I completed the feature analysis as my first project, and this work will be published in CSCW 2017. With the help of undergraduate Senior Design students, I have completed a preliminary version of the prototype for my third study. My next step is to complete the survey study before finalizing the prototype and conducting user studies. I am in the process of creating a blueprint of my survey and planning to launch it in fall 2016.

Expected Contributions

The expected contributions of my work will be five-fold: 1) The theoretical framework of TOSS based on prior literature and value sensitive design to better understand the different strategies for adolescent online safety, 2) A structured, qualitative feature analysis of existing apps for providing fellow HCI researchers working in this area an in-depth knowledge of available features of currently available apps for promoting adolescent online safety in mobile platforms, 3) A mapping between TOSS framework and feature analysis that help producing qualitative results of existing apps and designing better adolescent online safety apps, 4) Reasons for why existing teen online safety apps have a low adoption rate, and 5) A new mobile app prototype based on value sensitive design approaches to help increase user adoption and better meet the needs of parents and teens.

References

[1] Amanda Lenhart. Mobile Access Shifts Social Media Use and Other Online Activities. *Pew Research Center: Internet, Science & Tech*, 2015. http://www.pewinternet.org/2015/04/09/mobile-access-shifts-social-media-use-and-other-online-activities/.

[2] Erickson, L.B., Wisniewski, P., Xu, H., Carroll, J.M., Rosson, M.B., and Perkins, D.F. The boundaries between: Parental involvement in a teen's online world. *Journal of the Association for Information Science and Technology 67*, 6 (2016), 1384–1403.

[3] Friedman, B., Kahn, P.H., and Borning, A. Value Sensitive Design and Information Systems. *Human-Computer Interaction and Management Information Systems: Foundations. M.E. Sharpe*, (2006), 348–372.

[4] Hashish, Y., Bunt, A., and Young, J.E. Involving Children in Content Control: A Collaborative and Education-oriented Content Filtering Approach. *Proceedings of the 32Nd Annual ACM Conference on Human Factors in Computing Systems*, ACM (2014), 1797–1806.

[5] Ko, M., Choi, S., Yang, S., Lee, J., and Lee, U. FamiLync: Facilitating Participatory Parental Mediation of Adolescents' Smartphone Use. *Proceedings of the 2015 ACM International Joint Conference on Pervasive and Ubiquitous Computing*, ACM (2015), 867–878.

[6] Lenhart, A. Teens, Social Media & Technology Overview 2015. *Pew Research Center: Internet, Science & Tech*, 2015. http://www.pewinternet.org/2015/04/09/teens-social-media-technology-2015/.

[7] Livingstone, S. and Helsper, E.J. Parental mediation of children's internet use. *Journal of broadcasting & electronic media 52*, 4 (2008), 581–599.

[8] Mitchell, K., Jones, L., Finkelhor, D., and Wolak, J. Trends in Unwanted Online Experiences and Sexting : Final Report. *Crimes Against Children Research Center*, (2014).

[9] Monica Anderson. Parents, Teens and Digital Monitoring. *Pew Research Center: Internet, Science & Tech*, 2016. http://www.pewinternet.org/2016/01/07/parents-teens-and-digital-monitoring/.

[10] Strauss, A. and Corbin, J. *Basics of Qualitative Research: Techniques and Procedures for Developing Grounded Theory*. SAGE Publications, Inc, Thousand Oaks, 1998.

[11] Wisniewski, P., Ghosh, A.K., Rosson, M.B., Xu, H., and Carroll, J.M. Parental Control vs. Teen Self-Regulation: Is there a middle ground for mobile online safety? *Proceedings of the 20th ACM Conference on Computer Supported Cooperative Work & Social Computing*, ACM (2017).

[12] Wisniewski, P., Islam, A.K.M., Lipford, H.R., and Wilson, D. Framing and Measuring Multi-dimensional Interpersonal Privacy Preferences of Social Networking Site Users. *Communications of the Association for Information Systems 38*, 1 (2016).

[13] Best Choice for Teens' Cyber Safety – Parental Control App! https://www.hackread.com/teens-cyber-safety-protection-parental-control-app/.

[14] IDC: Smartphone OS Market Share. *www.idc.com*. http://www.idc.com/prodserv/smartphone-os-market-share.jsp.

Enhancing Visibility of Distance Learners To Promote Sense Of Community

Na Sun
Pennsylvania State University
State College, PA 16801, USA
nzs162@psu.edu

Abstract
Communities comprised of students enrolled in distance education differ from traditional students in residential campus sites not only in the separation of distance and time and the invisibility of peers, but also because the majority of the members are adult learners. My research is dedicated to promoting online students' sense of community and collective community efficacy by enhancing the visibility of students' relevant information and connections with others in the online educational setting. Following a user-centered design approach, I am probing the stakeholders' needs and building prototypes grounded in these findings. With iterative evaluations in the field and lab studies, I aim to build and evaluate the impacts of these interactive visualizations on distance students' sense of community.

GROUP '16, November 13-16, 2016, Sanibel Island, FL, USA
 ISBN 978-1-4503-4276-6/16/11…$15.00
DOI: http://dx.doi.org/10.1145/2957276.2997026

Author Keywords
Distance education; online community; visualization design

ACM Classification Keywords
• **Human-centered computing~Computer supported cooperative work** • *Human-centered computing~Empirical studies in collaborative and social computing* • Human-centered computing~Visual analytics

Introduction
With advances in technology and broadened access to educational resources, university-provided degree programs via online delivery have drawn considerable attention and efforts, particularly in response to regular increases in enrollment [10,17]. Although education

researchers often worry that distance education will produce lower quality learning outcomes [4], studies have shown comparable achievements for students in terms of learning outcomes [16,19].

However, there are risks associated with the pursuit of a degree online, compared with traditional degree programs. High dropout rates and feelings of social isolation are among the most notorious criticisms against distance education [5,7,8]. Previous research recognized social isolation, or the lack of social integration, as the culprit that leads to retention issues [3]. A similar strong correlation between dropout rate and feelings of being socially isolated is observed even within residential instruction contexts [20,22]. Ashar and Skenes [2] reported that learning goals attract adults *to* an online program, whereas presence of a social environment make them *persist*.

A national study of student engagement found that adult learners – a majority of distance education students – are less active in their interactions with peers and faculty and find the campus to be less supportive; but hold a positive view of interactions with others [13]. The adult learners in online educational programs need attention with respect to their more focused educational goals, and multiple roles as professionals who work but also "go to school" [6].

In response to such concerns, studies of learning at scale, whether of distance education or MOOCs, have begun to explore social and psychological factors in online education. For example, the role of peer support and social presence was investigated via its impacts on communication outputs, such as clustering discussion threads based on communicative patterns [14], and content analysis [1]. While such communication and exchange channels are clearly useful – for both residential and online education settings – the ways in which these are used comes with the cost of underappreciated investment in time for both students and teachers [9,12].

Problem Statement

In an effort to increase social integration for distance education and minimize the cognitive load and social pressure in public socializing activities, my research question centers on *how to promote sense of community with interactive visualization*. From the perspective of psychology, people not only become fond of others about whom they know more, but also like others to whom they reveal more [6]. Empirical work has manifested the potential impact of visibility of community members' information (such as physical image presentations) on facilitating interpersonal bonds [24]. Vice versa, Social identification/deindividuation (SIDE) also indicated that being part of such a group leads to reassurance on the members' commitment, and consequently may trigger further visibility among themselves through self-disclosure or revelatory responses [19]. Therefore, I propose using informed visualization as a way to facilitate online interactions, thereby connecting online learners who might otherwise feel isolated. My doctoral dissertation is aimed at both providing the understanding of whether and how distance education students are finding community with one another in a typical online learning environment, as well as how we might enhance such experiences through the design of technology.

Research In Progress

This section unfolds my dissertation work in three stages: the status quo of distance learners as members of a community, which will be used to guide my design process; the design and iterative evaluation of visualizations with online students; and theoretical design implications for online learning communities.

Interviews teachers and students

Despite the attraction of social interaction in online education [11,15], the pedagogical practices and rationale for developing student communities have rarely been explored from the instructors' perspective. Instructors' views about such possibilities are pertinent because their beliefs and practices directly impact the possibilities for fostering community in and across virtual classrooms, and shape students' attitudes towards distance education and the social context in which it is embedded [18]. My first study begins to fill this gap by unraveling distance education practitioners' mindset, pedagogical techniques, and technology uses that impinge on student community.

As an exploratory study, I used qualitative methods to probe deeply and be responsive to what we were learning. My goal was to unearth patterns for further research and discussion, not to test and generalize differences among courses or instructors. I found that instructors saw a sense of community among students at four levels: project team, classmates, students plus instructors, and university.

Some instructors reflected on the strategies they use to engage students as social actors, for example raising awareness of the content contributed by individual students, including personal details in discussion threads, the quantity of participation against the entire population, and the richness of discourse in live sessions. Among these, direct communication has been used as a key indicator for the presence of connections between instructors and students and among students themselves, despite its low contribution rate across the entire class and declining trend over time. As an explanation for the different levels of social engagement, instructors attributed the factors affecting such dynamic perceived connections to students' attributes (e.g. time availability, maturity), course types (technical vs non-technical), and teaching priorities.

More generally, instructors made efforts to build up community-level knowledge with students' personal background and interesting bits of experience. Such information exchanges occurred in different channels, ranging from live sessions to introductory discussion threads. Instructors used these disclosures to make sense of the "real person" hidden through the avatar or screen name that students use to present themselves virtually (e.g. discussion boards, Voicethread). However, much information underlying the inter-connections among students occur only when some issues come up, thereby leading to a mix of sympathy and doubts students' real identities and situations. Most instructors held the view that online students felt less of a community than their residential counterparts, whereas two instructors directly shared their perceptions that students online are equally connected, and sometimes more engaged with the discussion. The discrepancy account for the effect of course types, since the instructors with the latter standpoint taught non-technical courses that require students to relate to their personal experiences.

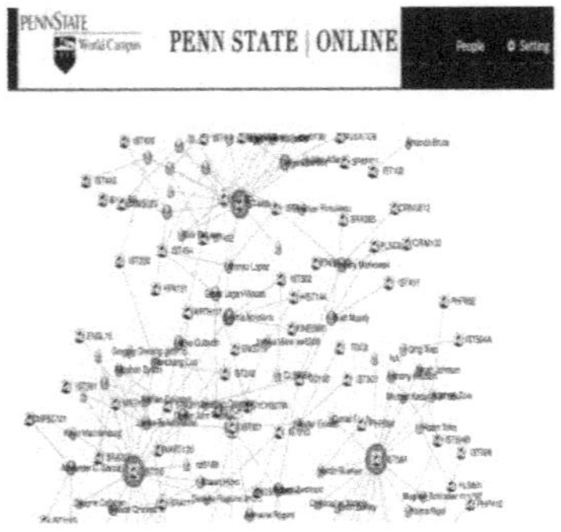

Figure 1 Network graph of user specified type of connection

Figure 2 Map associated with identity of current residence

As a complement to the instructors' thoughts about the presence of, and ways to foster community among students, I am now analyzing the data from a dozen student interviews and several larger-sample surveys. A preliminary analysis suggests that students desire to connect more, despite that they face a variety of hindrances, such as parenting duties, knowledge gap about others, and most commonly time constraints; they also feel that there is a lack of legitimate reason to reach out, although all of them are willing to be reached out for help. In addition, we found students' preferences over the information they would like to see and be visible to others, including time zones, time availability and areas of expertise. However, my analyses of these data are still in progress.

Visualizing possible connections

Inspired by the practices and preferences of both instructors and students, I am launching a scenario-based contextual inquiry with students using the first version of iConnector (see Figure 1 and Figure 2), a prototype in which individuals' personal identity is revealed and associated with others. Using student data collected from summer online courses, I have populated the tool to run a pilot study of the effects of visualizing students' identities and their relationships with others.

Expected Contributions

My dissertation research contributes not only to the education and online learning community, but also fills the gap on how visualization can be used in the context of community building and leveraging social resources. With potential factual, psychological and social barriers against connection building, as well as the preferences on the pertinent information, being identified, my research can point to the core value of fostering a community for online learners. By leveraging the interactive visualization, the completed and proposed studies can inform the possibilities of community building with enriched mechanisms with light-weighted energy and time investment. Pedagogically, visualization-assisted social interaction provides another potential way for social learning environment, in which student cohort, or schoolmates can act as a valuable resource, taking advantage of the natural bonding through organizational structure.

ACKNOWLEDGMENTS

We thank all the volunteers, and all publications support and staff, who wrote and provided helpful comments on previous versions of this document. We gratefully acknowledge the grant from Penn State.

References

1. Kwamena Appiah-Kubi and Duncan Rowland. 2016. PEER Support In MOOCs: The Role Of Social Presence. *Proceedings of the Third (2016) ACM Conference on Learning@ Scale*, ACM, 237–240. http://doi.org/10.1145/2876034.2893423
2. Hanna Ashar and Robert Skenes. 1993. Can Tinto's student departure model be applied to nontraditional students? *Adult education quarterly* 43, 2: 90–100.
3. Alexander Astin. 1984. Student involvement: A developmental theory for higher education. *Journal of College Student Personnel* 25, September: 297–308.
4. Zane L Berge and Mauri P Collins. 1995. *Computer mediated communication and the online classroom: distance learning*. Hampton press Cresskill.
5. Sarah Carr. 2000. As distance education comes of age, the challenge is keeping the students. *Chronicle of Higher Education*: A39–A41.

6. Jonathan I Compton, Elizabeth Cox, and Frankie Santos Laanan. 2006. Adult learners in transition. *New directions for student services* 2006, 114: 73–80.

7. K Frankola. 2001. The e-Learning Taboo: High Dropout Rates in Online Courses. *Syllabus*, 14–16.

8. Zixiu Guo, Felix B Tan, and Kenneth Cheung. 2010. Students ' Uses and Gratifications for Using Computer-Mediated Communication Media in Learning Contexts Students ' Uses and Gratifications for Using Computer -Mediated Communication Media in Learning Contexts Students ' Uses and Gratifications for Using C. *Communications of the Association for Information Systems* 27, 20: 339–378.

9. Starr Roxanne Hiltz. 1994. *The virtual classroom: Learning without limits via computer networks*. Intellect Books.

10. Grace Kena, Lauren Musu-Gillette, Jennifer Robinson, et al. 2015. The Condition of Education 2015. NCES 2015-144. *National Center for Education Statistics*.

11. Karel Kreijns, Paul A. Kirschner, and Wim Jochems. 2003. Identifying the pitfalls for social interaction in computer-supported collaborative learning environments: A review of the research. *Computers in Human Behavior* 19, 3: 335–353. http://doi.org/10.1016/S0747-5632(02)00057-2

12. Gabriele Piccoli, Rami Ahmad, and Blake Ives. 2001. Web-based virtual learning environments: a research framework and a preliminary assessment of effectiveness in basic it skills training. *Mis* 25, 4: 401–426. http://doi.org/10.2307/3250989

13. Karyn E Rabourn, Rick Shoup, and Allison Brckalorenz. 2015. Barriers in Returning to Learning: Engagement and Support of Adult Learners. 1–32.

14. Carolyn Penstein Rosé, Ryan Carlson, Diyi Yang, et al. 2014. Social factors that contribute to attrition in MOOCs. *Proceedings of the first ACM conference on Learning @ scale conference - L@S '14*: 197–198. http://doi.org/10.1145/2556325.2567879

15. Alfred P. Rovai. 2002. Building sense of community at a dstance. *International Review of Research in Open and Distance Learning* 3, 1: 1–16.

16. Mickey Shachar and Yoram Neumann. 2003. Differences Between Traditional and Distance Education Academic Performances : A meta-analytic approach. *International Review of Research in Open and Distance Learning* 4, 2.

17. Thomas D Snyder and Sally A Dillow. 2015. Digest of Education Statistics 2013. NCES 2015-011. *National Center for Education Statistics* Snyder, T.

18. Pei Chen Sun, Ray J. Tsai, Glenn Finger, Yueh Yang Chen, and Dowming Yeh. 2008. What drives a successful e-Learning? An empirical investigation of the critical factors influencing learner satisfaction. *Computers and Education* 50, 4: 1183–1202. http://doi.org/10.1016/j.compedu.2006.11.007

19. Olson T.M; and Wisher R.a; 2002. The Effectiveness of Web-Based Instruction An Initial Inquiry _ Olson _ The International Review of Research in Open and Distance Learning. *International Review of Research in Open and Distance Learning* 3, 2.

20. Barry A Vann and Barbara E Hinton. 1994. Workplace social networks and their relationship to student retention in on-site ged programs. *Human resource development quarterly* 5, 2: 141–151.

21. J. B. Walther. 1996. Computer-Mediated Communication: Impersonal, Interpersonal, and Hyperpersonal Interaction. *Communication Research* 23, 1: 3–43. http://doi.org/10.1177/009365096023001001

22. G G Wehlage, R A Rutter, G A Smith, N Lesko, and R R Fernandez. 1989. Reducing the Risk: Schools as Communities of Support.

Towards Re-Orienting the Big Data Rhetoric

Nitya Verma
Dept. of Human-Centered Computing
Indiana University, IUPUI
Indianapolis, IN, USA
verman@iupui.edu

GROUP '16, November 13-16, 2016, Sanibel Island, FL, USA
 ISBN 978-1-4503-4276-6/16/11$15.00
DOI: http://dx.doi.org/10.1145/2957276.2997027

Abstract
Data analytics and BI (business intelligence) systems are the most prominent user-facing manifestation of 'big data' and the related computational turn in thinking within organizations. However, the big data mythologies—specifically that data can offer more accurate, objective and truthful forms of intelligence and knowledge—impact, reinforce, and reproduce certain epistemological biases. In my research, I study these big data technologies in human services related contexts to examine knowledge claims and the strengths and limitations of big data.

Author Keywords
Big Data; Business Intelligence; Data Analytics

ACM Classification Keywords
H.5.3. [Information Interfaces and Presentation]: Group and Organization Interfaces—Computer-Supported Cooperative Work

Introduction and Problem Space
Various organizations across different organizational sectors actively adopt business intelligence (BI) and data analytics systems. Adoption and use of such systems often leads to production and manufacturing

work optimization, reductions in customer attrition, increased profitability, better decision support and the creation of competitive advantage [3, 5, 8]. Data analytics systems are the most prominent user-facing manifestation of big data and organizations' related turn towards computational driven thinking[1]. As Gary King, director of Harvard's Institute for Quantitative Social Sciences asserts:

*The march of quantification, made possible by enormous new sources of data, will sweep through academia, business, and government. There is no area that is going to be untouched. (quoted in [9]**Error! Reference source not found.**)*

Yet, this epistemological shift towards quantitative data, that BI systems embody, is not without its critics. boyd and Crawford, for example, argue that the shift towards quantitative data changes assumptions about the meaning of knowledge and how people "should" engage with information [2]. They contend that there is an increasingly pervasive big data mythology:

...the widespread belief that large data sets offer a higher form of intelligence and knowledge that can generate insights that were previously impossible, with the aura of truth, objectivity, and accuracy. [2]

This mythology, they argue, must become more transparent in research about big data. The mythologies of BI are pervasive in the marketing of these systems, which claim to enable better-informed decision making, faster and more agile decision making, aggregation of all key data, end-user empowerment, etc. My work extends the argument for greater transparency to related technologies. I study the human experience of technologies that manifest this turn towards computational thinking in organizations. My work fits within these calls to temper big data rhetoric and examines the knowledge claims, strengths and limitations of big data systems. Thus, I will examine how the practices, processes, values, biases, and assumptions of big data systems' stakeholders impact these systems' outcomes.

Prior work

In our first study of nonprofit workers using BI systems with Dr. Amy Voida, I conducted interviews with 17 users of such systems, focusing on their work practices, data usage in relation to their mission, and constraints and benefits of using these systems [7]. This work was accepted as a full paper at GROUP, and I will present it during the main conference. Through this project, I characterized four values—each of which aligns with one of the mythologies of BI systems— that informants describe as being core to their trajectory towards a "culture of data" in their organization. These values include being data-driven, predictive and proactive, shared accountability, and inquisitiveness.

What these users desire from BI systems is the ability to be actionable- to use the data for decision-making. Yet, for each mythology, I point out how being actionable is impeded by a disconnect between the aggregate views of data that allow them to identify areas of focus for being actionable and the imagined "drill down" data that would allow them to understand how to act in ways that show care and concern for their clients and employees.

Decision-making and actionability often require particular *combinations* of quantitative and qualitative data; qualitative data is not only unincorporated in these tools but is also not strongly present within the

[1] Global revenue from BI and analytics tools is projected to reach $16.9 billion in 2016, a 5.2% annual increase 4.

rhetoric on being "data-driven" in organizations. Such tools and organizational practices exacerbate the uncertainty our informants felt about the legitimacy of qualitative data in their decision making and wider ecology of information technology and organizational rationality. Findings from this work contribute initial empirical evidence for the impact of data analytics' epistemological biases on organizations and suggest implications for the design of technologies to better support data-driven decision making.

Proposed Research

The remainder of my Ph.D. work extends this research focus to another human-services context: law enforcement. Though the rhetoric of intelligence-led and data-driven policing was introduced earlier than other sectors, it is imperative to study the manifestations of big data and their impact on the human experience with the more recent technological advancements. Law enforcement literature indicates that the shift towards intelligence-led policing came with new information and communications technologies in the 1990's [6]. Researchers have studied these information technologies and organizational issues as part of this shift and found issues of bias in data collection, aggregation and use [2], which are further propagated through the actions of the organization.

My next studies will conduct qualitative research (interviews, participant observation, diary study, and so on) looking at the law enforcement context and its use of data, tools and practices from the perspective of community stakeholders. Specifically, I am interested in exploring how community stakeholders understand and respond to the use of data by law enforcement. We are in discussion with two sites: Stop LAPD Spying Coalition and Center for Social Inclusion. Feedback from the panel about incorporating multiple case sites into the dissertation will also be helpful.

The Coalition is an activist group in Los Angeles, and they *"reject all forms of police oppression and any policy that make us all suspects in the eyes of the State. [Their] vision is the dismantling of government-sanctioned spying and intelligence gathering, in all its multiple forms" [10]*. Similarly, the Center for Social Inclusion is a nonprofit organization that conducts reform work; their mission is *"to catalyze communities, government, and other institutions to dismantle structural racial inequity and create equitable outcomes for all"* [1]. Both of these organizations have projects focusing on understanding the impact of big data use by law enforcement and government agencies as well as to push back against this sociotechnical phenomenon through activism and policy reform for social justice.

Activists and reform workers focusing on police surveillance are an important group of community stakeholders, and their perceptions of big data are critical in understanding the overall impact of law enforcement agencies (i.e. police departments and fusion centers). By studying these organizations' perspectives and work, we can shed light on their participation in transforming the use of big data technologies in surveillance.

We have identified two additional groups of stakeholders in this ecosystem, and believe more will emerge as our work progresses. Law enforcement agents must translate intelligence from the center into action in the community. The designers of these systems are also stakeholders, as their values and biases are embedded in the design of the systems through their decision-making process, which might not include the concerns of the other stakeholders.

Through our early investigations and review of the literature, we have developed the following research questions of interest. One area of feedback that the GROUP Doctoral Consortium could provide is input on which of these questions would be most interesting to the broader research community:

1. What are the practices related to and perceptions of big data by key stakeholders groups?
2. How does quantification (and mythology of big data) impact key stakeholders of these policing big data systems, including actionability and lived experience?
3. How is the space for action influenced by what is measured and categorized?
4. How are digital divides in data literacy skills and data handling infrastructure manifesting in how the community understands and responds to big data use by law enforcement?
5. From a design perspective, what forms of qualitative data might be useful to better inform decision making and how might we incorporate this qualitative data into the ecology of organizational technology in ways that better support actionability?

HCI Contributions

We believe there are three groups of people who can benefit from this work. The first are organizational stakeholders adopting such tools, who can develop a more nuanced approach, policies and ecology of tools towards being "data-driven." The second are big data designers and researchers, who can use these results to find ways to address the inherent biases in data collection, aggregation and visualizations. This research could also help demonstrate the transformative process of different stakeholders negotiating the use and value of big data in law enforcement and society.

References

1. Center for Social Inclusion: About Us. Retrieved September 16, 2016 from http://www.centerforsocialinclusion.org/about-us/mission-vision/
2. danah boyd and Kate Crawford. 2012. Critical questions for big data: Provocations for a cultural, technological, and scholarly phenomenon. *Information, Communication & Society*. 15, 5, 662–679.
3. Gabriele Piccoli and Richard Watson. 2008. Profit from customer data by identifying strategic opportunities and adopting the 'born digital' approach. *MIS Quarterly Executive*. 7, 3, 113–122.
4. Gartner. 2016, February 3. Gartner Says Worldwide Business Intelligence and Analytics Market to Reach $16.9 Billion in 2016. Retrieved June 10, 2016 from: http://www.gartner.com /newsroom/id/3198917
5. Hugh J. Watson and Barbara H. Wixom. 2007. The current state of business intelligence. *IEEE Computer, 96–99.*
6. James Sheptycki. 2004. Organizational Pathologies in Police Intelligence Systems Some Contributions to the Lexicon of Intelligence-Led Policing. *European Journal of Criminology* 1, no. 3: 307-332. [9]
7. Nitya Verma and Amy Voida. 2016. On Being Actionable: Mythologies of Business Intelligence and Disconnects in Drill Downs. In Proceedings of the 2016 Group Conference.
8. Ron Kohavi, Neal J. Rothleder and Evangelos Simoudis. 2002. Emerging trends in business analytics. *Communications of the ACM*. 45, 8, 45–48.
9. Steve Lohr. 2012. The age of big data. *The New York Times.* Retrieved at January 13, 2016.
10. Stop LAPD Spying Coalition: About Us. Retrieved September 16, 2016 from https://stoplapdspying.org/about-slsc/.

Seeing Work: Constructing Visions of Work in and through Data

Christine T. Wolf
Department of Informatics
Donald Bren School of Information
& Computer Sciences
University of California, Irvine
wolfct [at] uci [dot] edu

GROUP '16, November 13 - 16, 2016, Sanibel Island, FL, USA

ACM 978-1-4503-4276-6/16/11...$15.00
DOI: http://dx.doi.org/10.1145/2957276.2997028

Abstract
My dissertation research explores the role technologies play in shaping how work practices are seen, imagined, and valued. I focus on how data remnants and traces, the technological residue left in the wake of human-computer interactions, become anchors that orient the construction of *seeing work* within an organization. To examine this, I draw on ethnographic fieldwork at a high tech firm and focus on efforts to reinvent an email client. I explore how *seeing work* in and through trace data paints increasingly narrow and modular portraits of work, reframing the contours and potential of vision and visibility in the workplace.

Author Keywords
Work practices; data traces; invisible work; email; ethnography.

ACM Classification Keywords
H.5.m. Information interfaces and presentation (e.g., HCI): Miscellaneous.

Introduction
Seeing and imagining what the "doing of work" looks like are practices central to the construction of vision in the workplace. These visions enable recognition and accountability, as well as bases and justification for exchange and valuation. Recognition and accountability rely on various forms of visibility—from being perceived as a hard-working developer, a responsive service provider, an organized manager, or a visionary

executive, practices of seeing and being seen carry weight in various ways. But work practices—the day-to-day, hum drum doings that comprise everyday work—are neither inherently visible nor invisible. Rather, seeing and being seen are the result of situated practices of constructing sociomaterial sight, aswirl with the moral, ethical, and political dimensions of labor [7].

My dissertation research focuses on the role technologies play in shaping visions of work. In particular, I am examining how ways of *seeing work* are constructed through the collection, analysis, and use of trace data, the digital residue left in the wake of human-computer interactions. Representations have long been an issue at the heart of CSCW literature, with Star and Strauss's seminal paper on invisible work [7] drawing attention to the role technological systems (and the abstract representations they rely upon) play in shaping the politics of workplace visibility.

My work advocates for a return and reinvigoration to questions of representation, abstraction, and workplace (in)visibility in the face of "Big Data," a technological phenomena heralded by many as a paradigm-shifting force in contemporary management [5]. The growing ubiquity of trace data has created opportunities for these digital remnants to serve as new ways of recordkeeping and documentation, creating new representational forms that attempt to approximate and map workplace activities. My dissertation examines how these data traces come to serve as lenses central to the construction of *seeing work* within an organization. I am interested in how the contours of work are scoped and bounded by the digital traces that remain, creating close, if not inseparable, associations between work practices and the technologies designed to support them. Seeing work in and through the lens of data creates opens questions around the limits of data-based sight—what qualities of work are distorted or missing, incompatible or incomprehensible to the bits and bytes of data? How do these lacunas shape the potential of vision and visibility in the workplace?

To explore *seeing work* as situated practices, I draw on sociological theories of practice [2], work in organizational studies examining technology as a sociomaterial phenomenon [6], as well as anthropological work examining the sociocultural and discursive aspects of constructing sight and vision [3].

Research Questions

With these theoretical orientations in mind, my dissertation is propelled by the following research questions:

***RQ* – How are everyday work practices (e.g., workflows and processes) "seen" within an organization?**

- *How are gazes directed toward certain work practices? What factors shape these lines of sight?*
- *What role do technologies play in shaping practices of seeing work?*
- *How do ways of seeing work differ among various stakeholders (i.e., strategic executives, technical developers, and everyday workers)? What factors shape these differences?*

Setting, Methods, and Work to Date

To explore these research questions, my dissertation draws on ethnographic fieldwork I began in June 2015 at a global technology and consulting firm, GloTechCo.[1] My fieldwork is currently ongoing, with primary data collection expected to conclude in fall 2016. During my field site engagement, I have been embedded in a research and development (R&D) group at GloTechCo working in the area of cloud services and analytics. This engagement has included active involvement as a student researcher contributing to R&D projects, as well as conducting interviews with key project stakeholders, participant observations in relevant meetings, and non-participant observations on the firm's intranet. In addition to transcripts and field notes, I have also collected key documents and artifacts.

My dissertation will closely examine the topic of personal email management, analyzing everyday workers' accounts of email practices, alongside a GloTechCo-wide initiative to reinvent email by developing a "smart" email client. The development of a "smart" email client at my field site mirrors emergent industry efforts to create "next generation" email experiences that feature semi-automation, such as Google Inbox.[2] Implicit in efforts like this are notions of email practices as somewhat mechanical or rote processes of information filtering and prioritization.

As an activity of concern, email has garnered much attention in CSCW over the years, with scholars highlighting the situated rhythms of email practices [8]. Email also has symbolic value, serving as a symbol for some of job-related stress [1]. As a form of personal information management, practices around email can also have implications for feelings of autonomy and self-efficacy [4].

[1] GloTechCo is a pseudonym.
[2] https://www.google.com/inbox/

My case focuses on both the strategic vision for the smart email client newClient[3] and its development and deployment. I will draw on analysis of interviews with strategic and technical executives on the newClient product team and accompanying marketing materials, pointing to how email is constructed as a "problem space" and framed as an appropriate site for "smart" intervention. At the time I began fieldwork, GloTechCo was in the process of launching newClient across the firm. When first launched, newClient included one smart feature "Top Folks" that automatically prioritizes a worker's contact list based on email patterns.

Over the course of my field work, I have followed the development of a new smart feature for newClient, "Auto-Assign," a feature that automatically categorizes and assigns emails based on "action items" identified in an email's body. In my dissertation, I will draw on analysis of interviews and observations with technical GloTechCo R&D staff developing Auto-Assign.

I will also analyze interviews with GloTechCo employees about their situated email practices, their transition to newClient, and their adoption of "Top Folks." I will map how the nature and quality of email practice is "seen" differently across these three groups, exploring the factors that shape these differing lines of sight.

Analyzing strategic and technical perspectives alongside accounts from workers about their everyday email-related practices, I will explore how the client program itself, as well as the trace data left behind from interactions within it—the tos and froms, the time stamps, subject lines, attachments, and the textual bodies of the emails themselves—become anchors that shape how the work of email is "seen." Using

[3] newClient and the names of its smart features are pseudonyms.

technologies (and the data residue that remains in the wake of human-computer interactions) as a lens through which to see and imagine work practices creates increasingly narrower and modular understandings of work, reframing vision and visibility in the workplace and calling into question the potential of seeing and being seen.

Acknowledgements

I am indebted to the many community members at my field site, who have opened their worlds and welcomed me. I am also grateful to my generous sponsors. My dissertation is funded, in part, by an Achievement Reward for College Scientists (ARCS) Fellowship and an IBM Corporation PhD Fellowship. My opinions are my own and do not reflect any institutional endorsement.

References

1. Stephen R. Barley, Debra E. Meyerson, and Stine Grodal. 2011. E-mail as a Source and Symbol of Stress. *Organization Science* 22, 4: 887–906. http://doi.org/10.1287/orsc.1100.0573
2. Pierre Bourdieu. 1977. *Outline of a Theory of Practice*. Cambridge University Press, Cambridge, U.K.; New York.
3. Charles Goodwin. 1994. Professional Vision. *American Anthropologist* 96, 3: 606–633. http://doi.org/10.1525/aa.1994.96.3.02a00100
4. William Jones. 2008. Personal Information Management. *Annual Review of Information Science and Technology* 41, 1: 453–504.
5. Andrew McAfee and Erik Brynjolfsson. Big Data: The Management Revolution. *Harvard Business Review*. Retrieved August 20, 2015 from https://hbr.org/2012/10/big-data-the-management-revolution
6. Wanda J. Orlikowski and Susan V. Scott. 2008. Sociomateriality: Challenging the Separation of Technology, Work and Organization. *The Academy of Management Annals* 2, 1: 433–474. http://doi.org/10.1080/19416520802211644
7. Susan Leigh Star and Anselm Strauss. Layers of Silence, Arenas of Voice: The Ecology of Visible and Invisible Work. *Computer Supported Cooperative Work (CSCW)* 8, 1-2: 9–30. http://doi.org/10.1023/A:1008651105359
8. Joshua R. Tyler and John C. Tang. 2003. When Can I Expect an Email Response? A Study of Rhythms in Email Usage. In *ECSCW 2003*, Kari Kuutti, Eija Helena Karsten, Geraldine Fitzpatrick, Paul Dourish and Kjeld Schmidt (eds.). Springer Netherlands, Dordrecht, 239–258. Retrieved February 16, 2016 from http://link.springer.com/10.1007/978-94-010-0068-0_13

Understanding and Supporting Document-based Knowledge Transfer with Moderator-Learner Interaction

Chi-Lan Yang
National Tsing Hua University
Hsinchu, Taiwan
chilan.yang.cns@gmail.com

GROUP '16, November 13-16, 2016, Sanibel Island, FL, USA
© 2016 ACM. ISBN 978-1-4503-4276-6/16/11...$15.00
DOI: http://dx.doi.org/10.1145/2957276.2997029

Abstract
Knowledge transfer in workplace, in which job-related knowledge and skills are transferred from a more experienced worker to a novice (e.g., a new employee), is common and crucial for organizations to keep transactive memory effective and avoid productivity loss. Organizational and other constraints may require expert-to-novice knowledge transfer to occur through the mediation of external artifacts (e.g., documents) or a third-party individual (e.g., human moderator), raising the need to understand how properties of such mediation influence the process and outcome of knowledge transfer. In my doctoral study, I aim to gain deeper understanding and implications for knowledge transfer designs.

Author Keywords
Knowledge transfer; computer-mediated communication; expert-novice interaction; moderated communication

ACM Classification Keywords
H.5.3. Information interfaces and presentation (e.g., HCI): Group and Organization Interface-Computer-supported cooperative work.

Introduction
Task handover is prevalent in organizations, and it requires knowledge transfer from skilled workers to

naive learners. This transition process is time consuming and resources demanding. According to Hinkin and Tracey (2000) [4], one of the costs of staff turnover in organizations is productivity loss. When an experienced worker leaves his/her job, it takes time and resources to train a new employee to gain the mastery of the experienced personnel's job skills, such as fulfillment of exceptions or efficiency of processing. This highlights the need for transferring experienced workers' knowledge to inexperienced ones and keeping transactive memories effective within organizations [6]. The observation outlines a critical role for knowledge transfer in workplace.

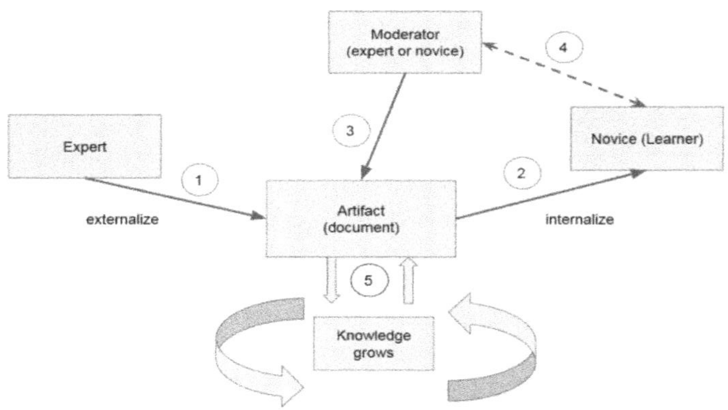

Figure 1. A framework of computer-mediated knowledge transfer where document-based mediation and human moderator play key roles. Experts externalize their knowledge in the mind with artifacts (link 1). Novice learners internalize knowledge by interacting with artifacts (link 2). Moderators modify information embedded on artifacts (link 3) according to their interaction with novice learners (link 4). With social computing techniques (link 5), knowledge can be used and shared within the community.

Knowledge transfer among individuals in workplace is conveniently defined as a process in which an experienced expert's knowledge is elicited, externalized and then integrated with a novice's existing knowledge. It is related but different from Argote (2000)'s definition which defined knowledge transfer at the organizational level as the practice of one unit (e.g., a department or a division) being affected by the experience of another [1]. Also, it's not what Singley and Anderson (1989) characterized at the cognitive level that knowledge acquired by individuals in one context could be applied to other similar situations [5]. Knowledge transfer in workplace is driven by novice learners' needs and is context-dependent [2]. Moreover, the transferred knowledge grows when it is shared and used.

Knowledge can be transferred to a novice in a number of ways, including apprenticeship, tutoring, experience sharing, embedding expertise within databases [3], or codifying with manuals or documents. The focus of my doctoral study is on document-mediated knowledge transfer to fit the need and constraint of working in virtual organizations at the global scale, where face-to-face communication can be costly or even impossible. As Figure 1 shows, document-mediated knowledge transfer has the strength of flexibility and can be applied in many situations and contexts as it doesn't require the presence of the original expert who generates the document. As it can still be difficult to novice learners to make sense of documents produced by experts, we need to explore the utilities of (1) having a moderator to help a learner learn from the document, and (2) using different types of interfaces to mediate the communication between the moderator and the learner, as illustrated in Figure 1.

Related Work

Why a human moderator is needed?

The reason why a moderator is needed for knowledge transfer can be explained from social and cognitive aspects. In social aspect, a number of studies have demonstrated that it is inherently difficult for experts to interact with novices directly [4]. Also, in practice, it is not always feasible to allocate a period of time for the old personnel and a newcomer to transfer knowledge in person. In these cases, when a newcomer encountered problems, s/he may need to turn to their peers for help.

In the cognitive aspect, since the curse of knowledge experts encountered, novice might not have the best comprehension level after being guided by experts. For instance, studies showed that novices understood the instructions better when instructors' level of expertise was adjusted to a level closer to novices' [3]. To reduce the cognitive effort expert faced on level adaptation, a peer moderator with level of expertise similar to the learner might be appropriate to mediate between expert and novice for alleviating the burden of the experts and increasing the efficacy of knowledge transfer instructions at the same time.

Therefore, we consider that the presence of a moderator is both required and beneficial for mediating interactions between the experienced and the inexperienced personnel, either to break the barrier of the organizational hierarchy, or to fill in the gap between experts and novices.

Research Questions

To understand how the interactions between a human moderator and a novice over CMC tools influences document-based knowledge transfer, we look for answers on two research questions in this project.

RQ1: How do levels of details specified on the document, as afforded by the CMC tools, influence knowledge transfer process?

In document-mediated knowledge transfer, the novice learners would have to read the documents on their own first. Moderators play a passive role to respond to questions or requests made by the learners. Thus whether and to what extent the moderators can help the learners would depend on the questions learners ask. Tools that support more detailed and more specific question specification are likely to be more useful on getting the moderators to help the learners.

RQ2: How does a moderator's level of expertise influence the knowledge transfer process?

Another problem I am going to attack is to understand how knowledge transfer can be achieved while the original content provider, who is the domain expert, is not the one who interacts with novice learners directly. As explained, human moderator will be introduced to interact with novice learners. However, the domain expertise of the human moderator might vary, s/he can either be an expert or novice of the particular knowledge domain.

Approach and Methods

This doctoral project consists of three parts: 1) Conduct user observations and semi-structured interview to understand the current practices and behaviors of knowledge transfer among individuals, especially via CMC tools. A thorough ethnographic study may help to understand how artifacts are used in either co-located or remote knowledge transfer, thus design opportunities can be identified. 2) Conduct laboratory studies to examine how various CMC functionalities support document-based knowledge transfer. 3) Conduct a user study to evaluate system prototypes which are designed based on new understandings and design implications identified in the first two parts of the project.

Current Status and Next Steps

Currently, I have conducted a lab study of image editing to understand how a pair of moderator and learner interacts with three popular computer-mediated communication features available in Google Document (chat, highlight annotation, comment). The preliminary result showed that when the moderator was an expert, the more details the learner can identify with the support of designated CMC features, the higher quality of knowledge transfer was achieved. In contrast, when the moderator was a novice, then a more open-ended, less structured tool (e.g., chat) may lead to a better outcome of knowledge transfer.

For next steps, two directions of research are identified and will be completed. The first is to conduct an ethnographic study to further understand co-located and remote knowledge transfer in workplaces, especially the role that CMC tools play. Second, system mechanisms which involve social computing techniques (e.g., crowdsourcing, human computation) to enable sustainable and productive interactions between moderators and learners for the purpose of knowledge transfer will be explored.

Expected Contributions

This study aims to understand how the interaction of "moderator-novice pair" could benefit knowledge transfer, and to discover how document-based knowledge transfer can be further supported by CMC functionalities. This line of work will deepen our understanding of the approaches of knowledge transfer by involving a human moderator to interact with novices, and provide an important opportunity to advance the understanding of CMC in the context of knowledge transfer. Online communities which involves frequent knowledge exchange activities (e.g., Wikipedia) may also benefit from this line of research. Further, my study could come up with design implications to support better knowledge transfer, which is a highly practical issue in many organizations.

References

1. Argote, L. and Ingram, P. 2000. Knowledge Transfer: A Basis for Competitive Advantage in Firms. Organizational Behavior and Human Decision Processes 82, 1 (2000), 150–169.
2. Collins, H. 2010. Tacit and explicit knowledge. University of Chicago Press.
3. Hinds, P., Patterson, M. and Pfeffer, J. 2001. Bothered by abstraction: The effect of expertise on knowledge transfer and subsequent novice performance. Journal of Applied Psychology. 86, 6 (2001), 1232-1243.
4. Hinkin, T. and Tracey, J. 2000. The Cost of Turnover: Putting a Price on the Learning Curve. Cornell Hotel and Restaurant Administration Quarterly. 41, 3 (2000), 14-21.
5. Singley, M. and Anderson, J. 1989. The transfer of cognitive skill. Harvard University Press.
6. Wegner, D. M. 1987. Transactive memory: A contemporary analysis of the group mind. In Theories of group behavior (pp. 185-208). Springer New York.

Enhancing Evaluation of Potential Romantic Partners Online

Doug Zytko
New Jersey Institute of Technology
Newark, NJ 07102, USA
daz2@njit.edu

GROUP '16, November 13-16, 2016, Sanibel Island, FL, USA

ISBN 978-1-4503-4276-6/16/11···$15.00
DOI: http://dx.doi.org/10.1145/2957276.2997030

Abstract
Online dating systems are a common way to discover romantic partners. Yet there persists a gap in knowledge regarding how users of these systems determine which potential partners are worthy of in-person meetings, as well as the outcomes of these in-person meeting decisions. The objective of this dissertation is two-fold: 1) to understand how online dating system users make decisions to meet or not meet potential romantic partners in-person, and 2) to understand how online dating system designs currently support—and could better support—predictions of initial in-person attraction to potential romantic partners.

Author Keywords
Online dating; impression formation; social matching

ACM Classification Keywords
H.5.m. Information interfaces and presentation (e.g., HCI): Miscellaneous

Research Questions
The dissertation explores four main research questions:

RQ1. How do online dating system users choose which potential partners to meet in-person and which to not meet (i.e. disqualify from further evaluation)?

RQ2. Do users make the right decisions over which potential partners to meet in-person based on information they gather?

- **RQ2a.** Do users gather enough information to make adequately informed in-person meeting decisions?

RQ3. What is the relationship between the various commercial online dating systems and their features, and in-person meeting decision success?

RQ4. How can online dating systems be designed to better support evaluation of potential partners, so that they are more satisfied with and confident about their in-person meeting decisions?

These research questions are examined through four studies (two of which are completed), associated theory building and testing, and software design and development.

Completed Work

Study 1 - Qualitative exploration of the online dater evaluation process from the user's perspective [e.g. 3]; Research questions examined: 1, 2, & 3

Prior online dating studies typically looked at isolated aspects of user evaluation (e.g. detecting deception in profile pages) rather than how users consolidate all the information available to them in these systems to make in-person meeting decisions. Goals of this first study were to gain a broad understanding of how active online dating system users make in-person meeting decisions, as well as the "success" of these decisions [5]. Additionally, the study aimed to probe users' self-presentation strategies to explore how impression management motives may affect evaluations of potential partners. This study was conducted through semi-structured interviews with 41 active users of the online dating system *OkCupid*. Results showed that participants considered profile pages a key determinant of which potential partners were worthy of a messaging conversation, but the messaging conversation was the main determinant in the decision to meet in-person. Participants' first dates typically did not result in a second date because of online impressions deemed inaccurate in-person. These inaccuracies typically regarded personality traits rather than aspects of physical appearance or objective demographic qualities. While prior attraction literature would suggest interaction is an effective way to evaluate personality, users in this study employed *OkCupid*'s messaging interface more so to enact thinly-veiled self-presentation and evaluation scripts rather than to have conversations.

Study 2 - Qualitative exploration of the online dater evaluation strategies of online dating coaches [e.g. 4]; Research questions examined: 1, 2, & 3

Interviewing active users of online dating systems, as in study 1, is an effective way to discover user struggles with the online dater evaluation process, but not so much for successful evaluation strategies. Active users of online dating systems presumably have had less success achieving long-term romantic relationship goals, otherwise they would no longer be active users of these systems. The objective of study 2 was to garner an understanding of online dater evaluation strategies that yielded successful in-person meeting decisions. This objective was pursued through semi-structured interviews with online dating coaches—self-proclaimed online dating experts who teach strategies for how to use online dating systems to successfully achieve a particular relationship goal. Results from this

Design Requirements for Problem-Solving Discussion in Online Dating Systems

- **Provide conversation topics of personal relevance:** users may lose interest in debating a problem-solving topic that does not apply to their personal situation. Topics about common dating conflicts (e.g. "who should pay on the first date?") may maintain a focus on the conversation.
- **Procure users' opinions on the topic before conversation:** due to users' impression management motives, they may be tempted to agree with their partner's opinion by default to save face. Procuring users' opinions prior to learning each other's opinions may prevent this.
- **Require resolution of conflicting opinions:** to prevent users from shifting the conversation to alternative topics (e.g. their hobbies, attractive qualities), the system can require users to explicate a mutually agreed upon decision at the end of conversation. Minimum conversation lengths can be enforced as well.

study showed that online dating coaches considered accurate evaluation of potential romantic partners to be unlikely in today's online dating systems. Specifically, they considered evaluation of personality compatibility to be fundamentally stifled by users' poor abilities to deliberately self-present their own personalities coupled with their impression management motivations. The coaches instead promoted strategies that can yield in-person dates quickly with potential partners that satisfy minimal evaluation criteria, such as through copy-and-pasted message content that is sent to hundreds of potential partners in succession. The coaches explained that first dates procured for or by clients with their strategies seldom lead to second dates, but the high frequency of dates counteracts this likely failure.

Theoretical Contribution Informed by Initial Studies

Findings from studies 1 and 2 demonstrate online daters' struggles with predicting in-person personality compatibility and thus initial romantic attraction to potential partners, which leads to unsuccessful in-person meeting decisions. While attraction literature positions interaction as a prime way to evaluate personality compatibility, studies 1 and 2 revealed online dater strategies that leveraged online interaction primarily for overt self-presentation and evaluation strategies.

The literature does suggest how people can effectively evaluate or experience personality compatibility. Prior work from the 1970s has shown that "problem-solving discussions" amongst married couples can predict marital satisfaction at current and future times [e.g. 2]. "Problem-solving discussions" [1, page 5] are those in which two partners contend with differences of opinion to reach consensus on a topic (e.g. "which spouse should take out the trash?").

Models resulting from this work [1] posit that this predictive power is due to personality attributions that married partners make regarding statements expressed in such discussions—these discussions serve as vessels of concentrated personality expression. From this it follows that problem-solving discussions could potentially help online daters (*potential* romantic partners) predict personality compatibility and thus romantic attraction across modalities in the same way that these discussions have predicted relationship satisfaction across time. The prior research involving problem-solving discussions between married couples [e.g. 1, 2], in combination with the findings from my prior studies, will be used to inform design requirements for facilitating problem-solving interaction in online dating systems. Some design requirements derived from studies 1 and 2 are summarized in the side bar.

Work in Progress

Study 3 - Quantitative study of how system design predicts in-person meeting decision success

Research questions examined: 3

While studies 1 and 2 are some of the first to provide insight into how users make in-person meeting decisions and the outcomes of their in-person meeting decisions, the qualitative nature of those studies prevents us from testing associations between specific elements of online dating systems and in-person meeting outcomes. This study serves as a quantitative counterpart to the first two studies. More specifically, the objective of this study is to investigate how popular online dating systems and the interface components that comprise their design are associated with success of in-person meeting decisions. Such interface components include profile page content,use of messaging interfaces, and tools that facilitate the quantity of potential partners that are discovered and contactable in the system (e.g. Tinder's swiping interface). This study's objective will be pursued through a survey study of online daters that inquires about the last online dating system user that they met in-person and the outcome of the first meeting with that user.

Study 4 – Technology intervention to enhance in-person meeting decision success
Research questions examined: 4

The final study entails a large-scale experiment in which a minimum 200 potential romantic partners are observed as they evaluate each other online through profile pages and messaging conversations, and then validate their evaluations in-person. Speed dating events organized through meetup.com will be used as a recruitment method and context for the initial in-person meetings between participants. Aside from being the first study to examine the online dater evaluation process from the perspective of both users involved, the experiment intends to investigate if text-based messaging conversations structured around problem-solving topics can facilitate more accurate predictions of personality compatibility in-person, romantic attraction in-person, and desires for a second in-person meeting than unstructured messaging conversations. The independent variable in the study is the type of messaging interface used by a pair of potential partners. The dependent variables entail various dimensions of online dater evaluation accuracy and participants' confidence in their predictions. Variables are summarized in the sidebar.

Expected Contributions

This research is important because it bridges several research disciplines including evolutionary biology, social psychology, and human-computer interaction.

The proposed research plan has and will continue to produce findings about how people evaluate and interact with new acquaintances online for a variety of integral social needs like romance [5] as well other social desires [e.g. 4]. Expected contributions of this dissertation include a theoretical model of the process of evaluating potential romantic partners discovered in online dating systems, an understanding of online dating system users' evaluation strategies through all stages of the online dater evaluation process, and innovative design concepts for better facilitating evaluation of potential romantic partners in online dating systems as well as other social matching and social discovery domains in which in-person meetings are a goal of users.

Variables for Study 4

Independent variable: type of messaging interface used by a pair of potential partners

Condition 1: no messaging
Condition 2: unprompted messaging interface
Condition 3: A prompted messaging interface; the conversation starts with agreement on the topic
Condition 4: A prompted messaging interface; the conversation starts with disagreement on the topic (i.e. problem-solving discussion)

Dependent variables:

- Accuracy and confidence of personality trait prediction
- Accuracy and confidence of personality compatibility prediction
- Accuracy and confidence of romantic attraction prediction
- Accuracy and confidence of prediction of desire to meet the potential partner for a second meeting

References

1. Benjamin R. Karney and Thomas N. Bradbury. "The longitudinal course of marital quality and stability: A review of theory, methods, and research. *Psychological bulletin* 118.1 (1995): 3-34.
2. Howard J. Markman. 1979. Application of a behavioral model of marriage in predicting relationship satisfaction of couples planning marriage. *Journal of Consulting and Clinical Psychology* 47.4 (1979): 743-749.
3. Doug Zytko, Guo Freeman, Sukeshini A. Grandhi, Susan C. Herring, and Quentin Gad Jones. 2015. Enhancing evaluation of potential dates online through paired collaborative activities. In Proceedings of the 18th ACM Conference on Computer Supported Cooperative Work & Social Computing, 1849-1859.
4. Douglas Zytko, Sukeshini A. Grandhi, and Quentin Jones. 2014. The coaches said...what? Analysis of online dating strategies recommended by dating coaches. In Proceedings of the 19th International Conference on Supporting Group Work, in press.

Author Index

www.ingramcontent.com/pod-product-compliance
Ingram Content Group UK Ltd.
Pitfield, Milton Keynes, MK11 3LW, UK
UKHW051416290926
15471UKWH00009B/1622

9 781450 347143